Microsoft® Office 2010

ILLUSTRATED

First Course

Introductory

Microsoft® Office 2010

ILLUSTRATED

First Course

Introductory

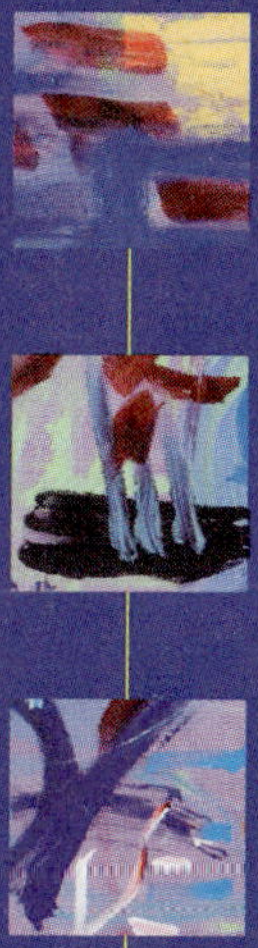

Beskeen • Cram • Duffy
Friedrichsen • Reding

COURSE TECHNOLOGY
CENGAGE Learning™

Australia • Brazil • Japan • Korea • Mexico • Singapore • Spain • United Kingdom • United States

COURSE TECHNOLOGY
CENGAGE Learning™

Microsoft® Office 2010—Illustrated Introductory, First Course, International Edition

Beskeen/Cram/Duffy/Friedrichsen/Reding

Vice President, Publisher: Nicole Jones Pinard

Executive Editor: Marjorie Hunt

Associate Acquisitions Editor: Brandi Shailer

Senior Product Manager: Christina Kling Garrett

Associate Product Manager: Michelle Camisa

Editorial Assistant: Kim Klasner

Director of Marketing: Cheryl Costantini

Senior Marketing Manager: Ryan DeGrote

Marketing Coordinator: Kristen Panciocco

Contributing Authors: Rachel Biheller Bunin, Barbara Clemens, Katherine T. Pinard

Developmental Editors: Rachel Biheller Bunin, Barbara Clemens, Pamela Conrad, Kim Crowley, Jeanne Herring, Lisa Ruffolo

Content Project Managers: Danielle Chouhan, Heather Hopkins, Melissa Panagos, Lisa Weidenfeld

Copy Editor: John Bosco and Mark Goodin

Proofreader: Harold Johnson and Vicki Zimmer

Indexer: BIM Indexing and Proofreading Services

QA Manuscript Reviewers: John Bosco, John Frietas, Serge Palladino, Susan Pedicini, Jeff Schwartz, Danielle Shaw, Marianne Snow, Susan Whalen

Print Buyer: Fola Orekoya

Cover Designer: GEX Publishing Services

Cover Artist: Mark Hunt

Composition: GEX Publishing Services

For product information and technology assistance, contact us at
Cengage Learning Customer & Sales Support, 1-800-354-9706

For permission to use material from this text or product, submit all requests online at **www.cengage.com/permissions**
Further permissions questions can be emailed to
permissionrequest@cengage.com

Library of Congress Control Number: 2010931058

International Edition:

ISBN-13: 978-1-111-52797-6

ISBN-10: 1-111-52797-0

Cengage Learning International Offices

Asia
www.cengageasia.com
tel: (65) 6410 1200

Australia/New Zealand
www.cengage.com.au
tel: (61) 3 9685 4111

Brazil
www.cengage.com.br
tel: (55) 11 3665 9900

India
www.cengage.co.in
tel: (91) 11 4364 1111

Latin America
www.cengage.com.mx
tel: (52) 55 1500 6000

UK/Europe/Middle East/Africa
www.cengage.co.uk
tel: (44) 0 1264 332 424

Represented in Canada by
Nelson Education, Ltd.
tel: (416) 752 9100 / (800) 668 0671
www.nelson.com

Cengage Learning is a leading provider of customized learning solutions with office locations around the globe, including Singapore, the United Kingdom, Australia, Mexico, Brazil, and Japan. Locate your local office at: **www.cengage.com/global**

For product information: **www.cengage.com/international**
Visit your local office: **www.cengage.com/global**
Visit our corporate website: **www.cengage.com**

Printed in the United States of America
3 4 5 6 7 8 9 18 17 16 15 14 13 12 11

"AVAILABILITY OF RESOURCES MAY DIFFER BY REGION. Check with your local Cengage Learning representative for details."

Brief Contents

Contents

Concepts 2010

Internet 2010

Integration 2010

Access 2010

Preface

Welcome to *Microsoft Office 2010—Illustrated Introductory, First Course*. If this is your first experience with the Illustrated series, you'll see that this book has a unique design: each skill is presented on two facing pages, with steps on the left and screens on the right. The layout makes it easy to learn a skill without having to read a lot of text and flip pages to see an illustration.

This book is an ideal learning tool for a wide range of learners—the "rookies" will find the clean design easy to follow and focused with only essential information presented, and the "hotshots" will appreciate being able to move quickly through the lessons to find the information they need without reading a lot of text. The design also makes this a great reference after the course is over! See the illustration on the right to learn more about the pedagogical and design elements of a typical lesson.

About This Edition

- **Fully Updated.** Updated examples and exercises throughout highlight the new features of Microsoft Office 2010. New Appendix covers cloud computing concepts and using Microsoft Office Web Apps.
- **Maps to SAM 2010.** This book is designed to work with SAM (Skills Assessment Manager) 2010. **SAM Assessment** contains performance-based, hands-on SAM exams for each unit of this book, and **SAM Training** provides hands-on training for skills covered in the book. Each Independent Challenge 1 exercise is available in **SAM Projects**, which is auto-grading software that provides both students and instructors with immediate, detailed feedback (SAM sold separately.) See page xii for more information on SAM.

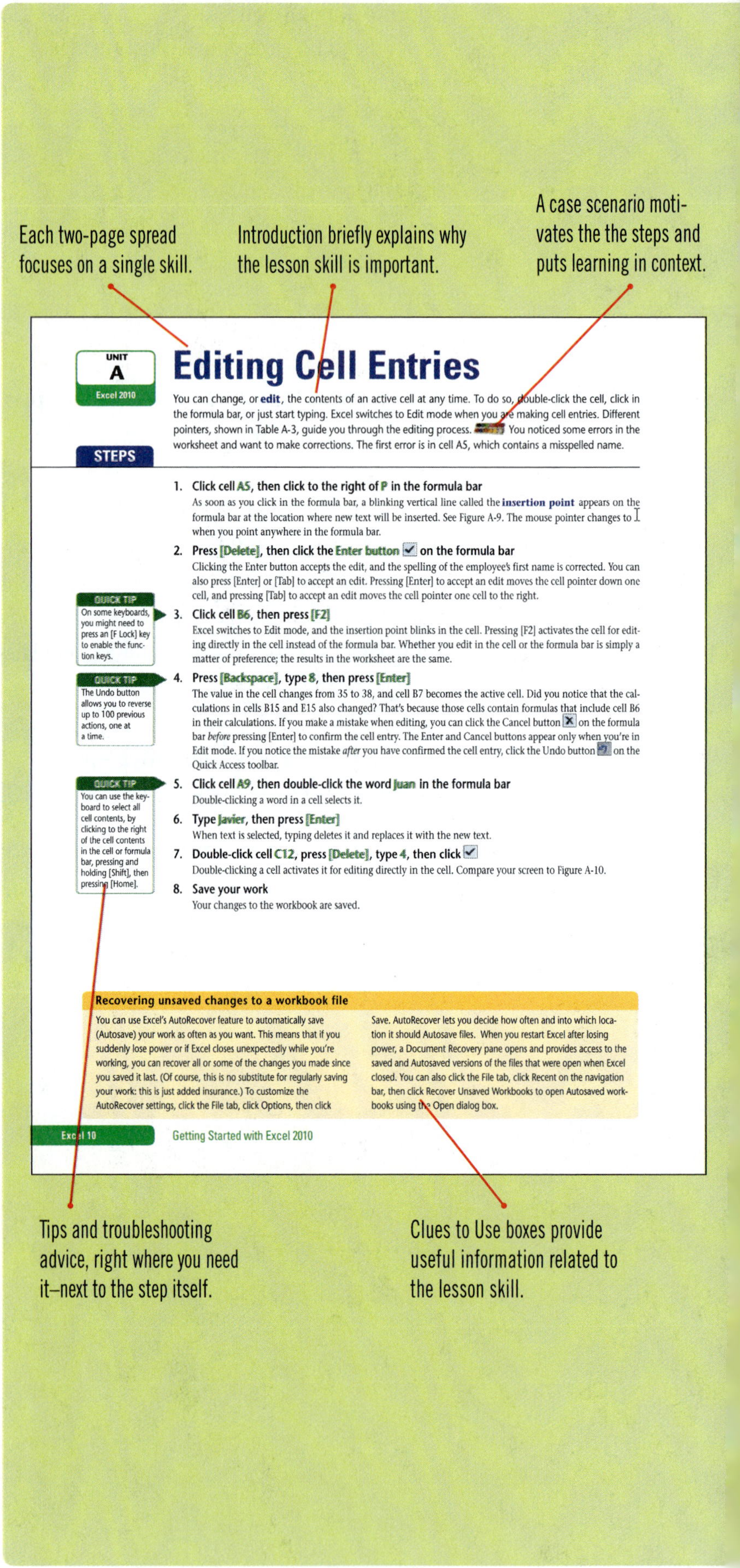

Large screen shots keep students on track as they complete steps

Brightly colored tabs indicate which section of the book you are in.

FIGURE A-9: Worksheet in Edit mode

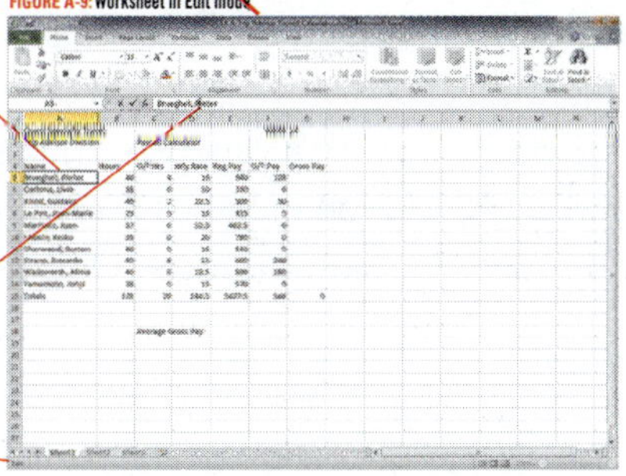

Excel 2010

FIGURE A-10: Edited worksheet

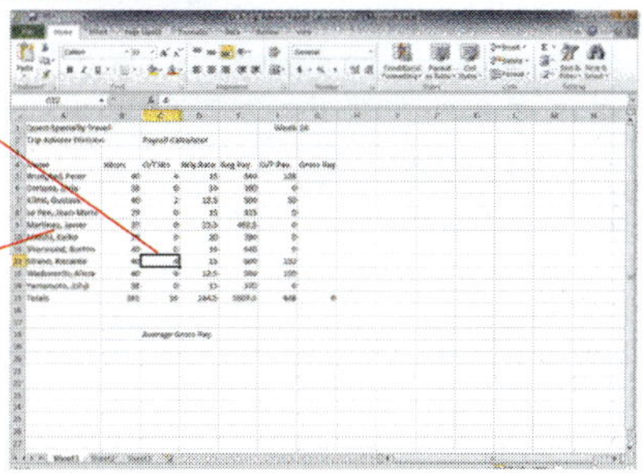

TABLE A-3: Common pointers in Excel

name	pointer	use to	visible over the
Normal		Select a cell or range; indicates Ready mode	Active worksheet
Fill handle	+	Copy cell contents to adjacent cells	Lower-right corner of the active cell or range
I-beam	I	Edit cell contents in active cell or formula bar	Active cell in Edit mode or over the formula bar
Move		Change the location of the selected cell(s)	Perimeter of the active cell(s)
Copy		Create a duplicate of the selected cell(s)	Perimeter of the active cell(s) when [Ctrl] is pressed
Column resize		Change the width of a column	Border between column heading indicators

Getting Started with Excel 2010 Excel 11

Tables provide helpful summaries of key terms, buttons, or keyboard shortcuts.

Assignments

The lessons use Quest Specialty Travel, a fictional adventure travel company, as the case study. The assignments on the light yellow pages at the end of each unit increase in difficulty. Assignments include:

- **Concepts Review** consist of multiple choice, matching, and screen identification questions.
- **Skills Reviews** are hands-on, step-by-step exercises that review the skills covered in each lesson in the unit.
- **Independent Challenges** are case projects requiring critical thinking and application of the unit skills. The Independent Challenges increase in difficulty, with the first one in each unit being the easiest. Independent Challenges 2 and 3 become increasingly open-ended, requiring more independent problem solving.
- **SAM Projects** is live-in-the-application autograding software that provides immediate and detailed feedback reports to students and instructors. Each Independent Challenge 1 exercise in this book is available in SAM Projects. (Purchase of a SAM Projects pincode is required.)
- **Real Life Independent Challenges** are practical exercises in which students create documents to help them with their every day lives.
- **Advanced Challenge Exercises** set within the Independent Challenges provide optional steps for more advanced students.
- **Visual Workshops** are practical, self-graded capstone projects that require independent problem solving.

About SAM

SAM is the premier proficiency-based assessment and training environment for Microsoft Office. Web-based software along with an inviting user interface provide maximum teaching and learning flexibility. SAM builds students' skills and confidence with a variety of real-life simulations, and SAM Projects' assignments prepare students for today's workplace.

The SAM system includes Assessment, Training, and Projects, featuring page references and remediation for this book as well as Course Technology's Microsoft Office textbooks. With SAM, instructors can enjoy the flexibility of creating assignments based on content from their favorite Microsoft Office books or based on specific course objectives. Instructors appreciate the scheduling and reporting options that have made SAM the market-leading online testing and training software for over a decade. Over 2,000 performance-based questions and matching Training simulations, as well as tens of thousands of objective-based questions from many Course Technology texts, provide instructors with a variety of choices across multiple applications from the introductory level through the comprehensive level. The inclusion of hands-on Projects guarantee that student knowledge will skyrocket from the practice of solving real-world situations using Microsoft Office software.

SAM Assessment

- Content for these hands-on, performance-based tasks includes Word, Excel, Access, PowerPoint, Internet Explorer, Outlook, and Windows. Includes tens of thousands of objective-based questions from many Course Technology texts.

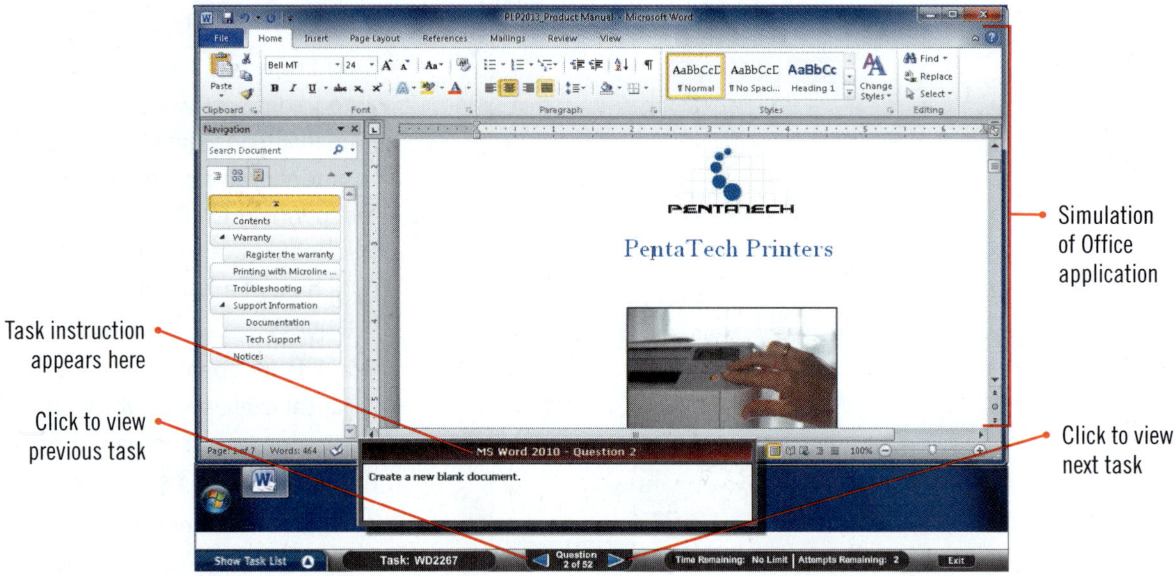

SAM Training

- Observe mode allows the student to watch and listen to a task as it is being completed.
- Practice mode allows the student to follow guided arrows and hear audio prompts to help visual learners know how to complete a task.
- Apply mode allows the student to prove what they've learned by completing a task using helpful instructions.

SAM Projects

- Live-in-the-application assignments in Word, Excel, Access and PowerPoint that help students be sure they know how to effectively communicate, solve a problem or make a decision.
- Students receive detailed feedback on their project within minutes.
- Additionally, teaches proper file management techniques.
- Ensures that academic integrity is not compromised, with unique anti-cheating detection encrypted into the data files.

Instructor Resources

The Instructor Resources CD is Course Technology's way of putting the resources and information needed to teach and learn effectively into your hands. With an integrated array of teaching and learning tools that offer you and your students a broad range of technology-based instructional options, we believe this CD represents the highest quality and most cutting edge resources available to instructors today. The resources available with this book are:

- **Instructor's Manual**—Available as an electronic file, the Instructor's Manual includes detailed lecture topics with teaching tips for each unit.

- **Sample Syllabus**—Prepare and customize your course easily using this sample course outline.

- **PowerPoint Presentations**—Each unit has a corresponding PowerPoint presentation that you can use in lecture, distribute to your students, or customize to suit your course.

- **Figure Files**—The figures in the text are provided on the Instructor Resources CD to help you illustrate key topics or concepts. You can create traditional overhead transparencies by printing the figure files. Or you can create electronic slide shows by using the figures in a presentation program such as PowerPoint.

- **Solutions to Exercises**—Solutions to Exercises contains every file students are asked to create or modify in the lessons and end-of-unit material. Also provided in this section, there is a document outlining the solutions for the end-of-unit Concepts Review, Skills Review, and Independent Challenges. An Annotated Solution File and Grading Rubric accompany each file and can be used together for quick and easy grading.

- **Data Files for Students**—To complete most of the units in this book, your students will need Data Files. You can post the Data Files on a file server for students to copy. The Data Files are available on the Instructor Resources CD-ROM, the Review Pack, and can also be downloaded from cengagebrain.com. For more information on how to download the Data Files, see the inside back cover.

Instruct students to use the Data Files List included on the Review Pack and the Instructor Resources CD. This list gives instructions on copying and organizing files.

- **ExamView**—ExamView is a powerful testing software package that allows you to create and administer printed, computer (LAN-based), and Internet exams. ExamView includes hundreds of questions that correspond to the topics covered in this text, enabling students to generate detailed study guides that include page references for further review. The computer-based and Internet testing components allow students to take exams at their computers, and also saves you time by grading each exam automatically.

Content for Online Learning.

Course Technology has partnered with the leading distance learning solution providers and class-management platforms today. To access this material, visit www.cengage.com/webtutor and search for your title. Instructor resources include the following: additional case projects, sample syllabi, PowerPoint presentations, and more. For additional information, please contact your sales representative. For students to access this material, they must have purchased a WebTutor PIN-code specific to this title and your campus platform. The resources for students might include (based on instructor preferences): topic reviews, review questions, practice tests, and more.

Acknowledgements

Instructor Advisory Board

We thank our Instructor Advisory Board who gave us their opinions and guided our decisions as we developed this new edition. They are as follows:

Terri Helfand, Chaffey Community College

Barbara Comfort, J. Sargeant Reynolds Community College

Brenda Nielsen, Mesa Community College

Sharon Cotman, Thomas Nelson Community College

Marian Meyer, Central New Mexico Community College

Audrey Styer, Morton College

Richard Alexander, Heald College

Xiaodong Qiao, Heald College

Student Advisory Board

We also thank our Student Advisory Board members, who shared their experiences using the book and offered suggestions to make it better: **Latasha Jefferson**, Thomas Nelson Community College, **Gary Williams**, Thomas Nelson Community College, **Stephanie Miller**, J. Sargeant Reynolds Community College, **Sarah Styer**, Morton Community College, **Missy Marino**, Chaffey College

Author Acknowledgements

David W. Beskeen Being a part of the extremely talented and experienced Office Illustrated team makes working on this book that much more enjoyable—many thanks to RBB, CKG, the production group, the testers, and the rest of the Cengage team! I also want to acknowledge my family, especially my parents Don and Darlene, for all they have done for me...I am forever grateful.

Carol Cram A big thank you to my development editor Barbara Clemens for her patience, good humor, and insight! And, as always, everything I do is made possible by Gregg and Julia. They make everything worthwhile.

Jennifer Duffy Many talented people at Course Technology worked tirelessly to shape this book—thank you all. I am especially grateful to Pam Conrad, editor extraordinaire, whose dedication, wisdom, and precision are evident on every page.

Lisa Friedrichsen The Access portion is dedicated to my students, and all who are using this book to teach and learn about Access. Thank you. Also, thank you to all of the professionals who helped me create this book.

Elizabeth Eisner Reding Creating a book of this magnitude is a team effort. I would like to thank my husband, Michael, as well as Christina Kling Garrett, the project manager, and my development editor, Jeanne Herring, for her suggestions and corrections. I would also like to thank the production and editorial staff for all their hard work that made this project a reality.

Credits

Essential Computer Concepts:

Figures 1, 14 & 25: © iStockphoto.com

Figure 2: PRNewsFoto/Verizon Wireless

Figure 3: Courtesy of NASA

Figure 4: Courtesy of Intel Corporation

Figure 5: Courtesy of AMD

Figure 10: Courtesy of Kingston Digital Inc.

Figures 11a & 12b: Courtesy of Logitech

Figures 11b, 12a & 21-24: Courtesy of © 2010 Microsoft Corporation. All rights reserved. Microsoft product screenshot(s) reprinted with permission from Microsoft Corporation

Figures 13a & 13b: Courtesy of IBM Corporation

Figures 15a, 15b, & 16: Courtesy of Hewlett-Packard Company

Figure 17: Courtesy of Belkin

Figure 18: Courtesy of D-Link Systems, Inc.

Figure 20: Courtesy of Trend Micro Inc.

PowerPoint 2010 Units:

C-5 Photo courtesy of Janet Moffat

C-18 Photo courtesy of Jennifer Beskeen

C-21, C-22 Photos courtesy of Barbara Clemens

D-3 Photo courtesy of Donna Goudy

D-4, D-5 Photos courtesy of Janet Moffat

Read This Before You Begin

Frequently Asked Questions

What are Data Files?

A Data File is a partially completed Word document, Excel workbook, Access database, PowerPoint Presentation, or another type of file that you use to complete the steps in the units and exercises to create the final document that you submit to your instructor. Each unit opener page lists the Data Files that you need for that unit.

Where are the Data Files?

Your instructor will provide the Data Files to you or direct you to a location on a network drive from which you can download them. For information on how to download the Data Files from cengagebrain.com, see the inside back cover.

What software was used to write and test this book?

This book was written and tested using a typical installation of Microsoft Office 2010 Professional Plus on a computer with a typical installation of Microsoft Windows 7 Ultimate.

The browser used for any Web-dependent steps is Internet Explorer 8.

Do I need to be connected to the Internet to complete the steps and exercises in this book?

Some of the exercises in this book require that your computer be connected to the Internet. If you are not connected to the Internet, see your instructor for information on how to complete the exercises.

What do I do if my screen is different from the figures shown in this book?

This book was written and tested on computers with monitors set at a resolution of 1024 × 768. If your screen shows more or less information than the figures in the book, your monitor is probably set at a higher or lower resolution. If you don't see something on your screen, you might have to scroll down or up to see the object identified in the figures.

The Ribbon—the blue area at the top of the screen—in Microsoft Office 2010 adapts to different resolutions. If your monitor is set at a lower resolution than 1024 × 768, you might not see all of the buttons shown in the figures. The groups of buttons will always appear, but the entire group might be condensed into a single button that you need to click to access the buttons described in the instructions.

UNIT
A
Windows 7

Getting Started with Windows 7

Files You Will Need:
No files needed.

The Windows 7 operating system lets you use your computer. Windows 7 shares many features with other Windows programs, so once you learn how to work with Windows 7, you will find it easier to use the programs that run on your computer. In this unit, you learn to start Windows 7 and work with windows and other screen objects. You work with icons that represent programs and files, and you move and resize windows. As you use your computer, you will often have more than one window on your screen, so it's important that you learn how to manage them. As you complete this unit, you create a simple drawing in a program called Paint to help you learn how to use buttons, menus, and dialog boxes. After finding assistance in the Windows 7 Help and Support system, you end your Windows 7 session. As a new Oceania tour manager for Quest Specialty Travel (QST), you need to develop basic Windows skills to keep track of tour bookings.

OBJECTIVES

- Start Windows 7
- Learn the Windows 7 desktop
- Point and click
- Start a Windows 7 program
- Work with windows
- Work with multiple windows
- Use command buttons, menus, and dialog boxes
- Get help
- Exit Windows 7

UNIT
A
Windows 7

Starting Windows 7

Windows 7 is an **operating system**, which is a program that lets you run your computer. A **program** is a set of instructions written for a computer. When you turn on your computer, the Windows 7 operating system starts automatically. If your computer did not have an operating system, you wouldn't see anything on the screen when you turn it on. For each user, the operating system can reserve a special area called a **user account** where each user can keep his or her own files. If your computer is set up for more than one user, you might need to **log in**, or select your user account name when the computer starts. If you are the only user on your computer, you won't have to select an account. You might also need to enter a **password**, a special sequence of numbers and letters each user can create. A password allows you to enter and use the files in your user account area. Users cannot see each others' account areas without their passwords, so passwords help keep your computer information secure. After you log in, you see a welcome message, and then the Windows 7 desktop. You will learn about the desktop in the next lesson. Your supervisor, Evelyn Swazey, asks you to start learning about the Windows 7 operating system.

STEPS

1. **Push your computer's power button, which might look like or , then if the monitor is not turned on, press its power button to turn it on**

   On a desktop computer, the power button is probably on the front panel. On a laptop computer it's most likely at the top of the keys on your keyboard. After a few moments, a Starting Windows message appears. Then you might see a screen that lets you choose a user account, as shown in Figure A-1.

TROUBLE
If you do not see a screen that lets you choose a user account, go to Step 3.

2. **Click a user name if necessary**

   The name you click represents your user account that lets you use the computer. The user account may have your name assigned to it, or it might have a general name, like Student, or Lab User. A password screen may appear. If necessary, ask your instructor or technical support person which user account and password you should use.

TROUBLE
If you clicked the wrong user in Step 2, change to the correct user by clicking the Switch user button on the password screen.

3. **Type your password if necessary, using uppercase and lowercase letters as necessary, as shown in Figure A-2**

   Passwords are **case sensitive**, which means that if you type any letter using capital letters when lowercase letters are needed, Windows will not allow you to access your account. For example, if your password is "book", typing "Book" or "BOOK" will not let you enter your account. As you type your password, its characters appear as a series of dots on the screen. This makes it more difficult for anyone watching you to see your password, giving you additional security.

TROUBLE
If you type your password incorrectly, you see "The user name or password is incorrect." Click OK to try again. To help you remember, Windows shows the Password Hint that you entered when you created your password.

4. **Click the Go button**

   You see a welcome message, and then the Windows 7 desktop, shown in Figure A-3.

FIGURE A-1: Selecting a user name

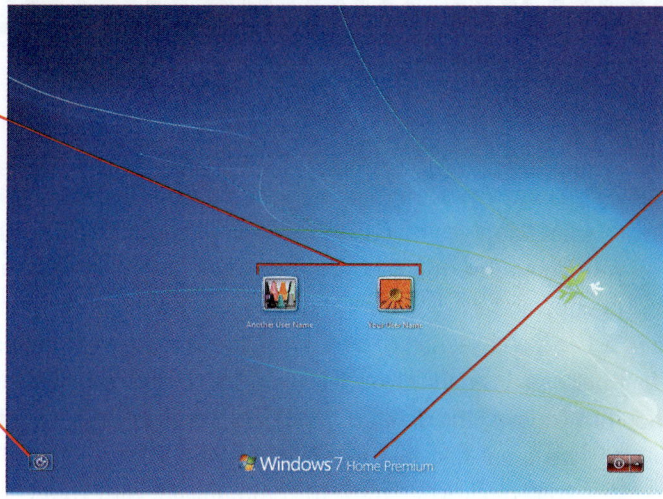

FIGURE A-2: Password screen

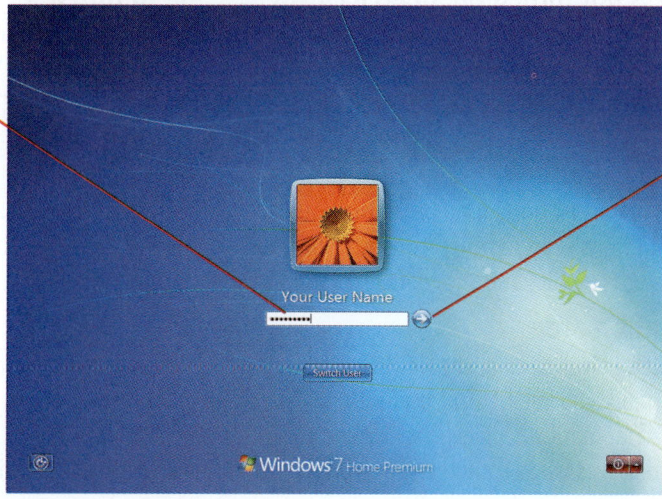

FIGURE A-3: Windows 7 desktop

UNIT
A
Windows 7

Learning the Windows 7 Desktop

After Windows 7 starts up, you see the Windows 7 desktop. The **desktop** consists of a shaded or picture background with small graphics called icons. **Icons** are small images that represent items such as the Recycle Bin on your computer. You can rearrange, add, and delete desktop icons. Like an actual desktop, the Windows 7 desktop acts as your work area. You can use the desktop to manage the files and folders on your computer. A **file** is a collection of stored information, such as a letter, video, or program. A **folder** is a container that helps you organize your files, just like a cardboard folder on your desk. If you're using a new installation of Windows, the desktop might show only a Recycle Bin icon in the upper-left corner and the **taskbar**, the horizontal bar at the bottom of your screen. Evelyn asks you to explore the Windows 7 desktop to begin learning how to communicate with your computer.

DETAILS

Windows 7 computers show these desktop elements. Refer to Figure A-4.

- **Start button**
  The **Start button** is your launching point when you want to communicate with your computer. You can use the Start button to start programs, to open windows that show you the contents of your computer, and to end your Windows session and turn off your computer.

> **QUICK TIP**
> If your taskbar is a different color than the one in Figure A-4, your computer might have different settings. This won't affect your work in this chapter.

- **Taskbar**
  The **taskbar** is the horizontal bar at the bottom of the desktop. The taskbar contains the Start button as well as other buttons representing programs, folders, and files. You can use these buttons to immediately open programs or view files and programs that are on your computer.
- **Notification area**
  The **notification area** at the right side of the taskbar contains icons that represent informational messages and programs you might find useful. It also contains information about the current date and time. Some programs automatically place icons here so they are easily available to you. The notification area also displays pop-up messages when something on your computer needs your attention.
- **Recycle Bin**
  Like the wastepaper basket in your office, the **Recycle Bin** is where you place the files and folders that you don't need anymore and want to delete. All objects you place in the Recycle Bin stay there until you empty it. If you put an object there by mistake, you can easily retrieve it, as long as you haven't emptied the bin.
- **Desktop background**
  The **desktop background** is the shaded area behind your desktop objects. You can change the desktop background to show different colors or even pictures.

You might see the following on your desktop:

- **Icons and shortcuts**
  On the desktop background, you can place icons called **shortcuts**, which you can double-click to access programs, files, folders, and devices that you use frequently. That way, they are immediately available to you.
- **Gadgets**
  Gadgets are optional programs that present helpful or entertaining information on your desktop. They include items such as clocks, current news headlines, calendars, picture albums, and weather reports. Some gadgets come with Windows 7 and you can easily place them on your desktop. You can download additional gadgets from the Internet. Figure A-5 shows a desktop that has a desktop background picture and shortcuts to programs, folders, and devices, as well as four gadgets.

FIGURE A-4: Windows 7 desktop after a new Windows installation

FIGURE A-5: Windows 7 desktop with shortcuts, gadgets, and a picture background

What if my desktop looks different from these figures?

If you are using a computer that has been used by others, a different version of Windows 7, or a computer in a school lab, your desktop might be a different color, it might have a different design on it, or it might have different shortcuts and gadgets. Your Recycle Bin might be in a different desktop location. Don't be concerned with these differences. They will not interfere with your work in these units.

Pointing and Clicking

After you start Windows 7 and see the desktop, you can communicate with Windows using a pointing device. A **pointing device** controls the movement of the mouse pointer on your computer screen. The **mouse pointer** is a small arrow or other symbol that moves on the screen. The mouse pointer's shape changes depending on where you point and on the options available to you when you point. Your pointing device could be a mouse, trackball, touchpad, pointing stick, on-screen touch pointer, or a tablet. Figure A-6 shows some common pointing devices. A pointing device might be attached to your computer with a wire, connect wirelessly using an electronic signal, or it might be built into your computer. There are five basic **pointing device actions** you use to communicate with your computer: pointing, clicking, double-clicking, dragging, and right-clicking. Table A-1 describes each action. As you prepare to work on your tour schedule, you communicate with your computer using the basic pointing device actions.

STEPS

1. **Locate the mouse pointer on the desktop, then move your pointing device left, right, up, and down**
   The mouse pointer moves in the same direction as your pointing device.
2. **Move your pointing device so the mouse pointer is over the Recycle Bin**
   You are pointing to the Recycle Bin. The pointer shape is the **Select pointer**. The Recycle Bin icon becomes **highlighted**, looking as though it is framed in a box with a lighter color background and a border.
3. **While pointing to the Recycle Bin, press and quickly release the left mouse button once, then move the pointer away from the Recycle Bin**
   Click a desktop icon once to **select** it, and then the interior of the border around it changes color. When you select an icon, you signal Windows 7 that you want to perform an action. You can also use pointing to identify screen items.
4. **Point to (but do not click) the Internet Explorer button on the taskbar**
   The button border appears and an informational message called a **ScreenTip** identifies the program the button represents.
5. **Move the mouse pointer over the time and date in the notification area in the lower-right corner of the screen, read the ScreenTip, then click once**
   A pop-up window appears, containing a calendar and a clock displaying the current date and time.
6. **Place the tip of the mouse pointer over the Recycle Bin, then quickly click twice**
   You **double-clicked** the Recycle Bin. A window opens, showing the contents of the Recycle Bin, shown in Figure A-7. The area near the top of the screen is the **Address bar**, which shows the name of the item you have opened. If your Recycle Bin contains any discarded items, they appear in the white area below the Address bar. You can use single clicking to close a window.
7. **Place the tip of the mouse pointer over the Close button in the upper-right corner of the Recycle Bin window, notice the Close ScreenTip, then click once**
   The Recycle Bin window closes. You can use dragging to move icons on the desktop.
8. **Point to the Recycle Bin icon, press and hold down the left mouse button, move the pointing device (or drag your finger over the touchpad) so the object moves right about an inch, as shown in Figure A-8, then release the mouse button**
   You dragged the Recycle Bin icon to a new location.
9. **Repeat Step 8 to drag the Recycle Bin back to its original location**

QUICK TIP
Use the tip of the pointer when pointing to an object.

TROUBLE
You need to double-click quickly, with a fast click-click, without moving the mouse. If a window didn't open, try again with a faster click-click.

QUICK TIP
You'll use dragging in other Windows 7 programs to move folders, files, and other objects to new locations.

FIGURE A-6: Pointing devices

FIGURE A-7: Recycle Bin window

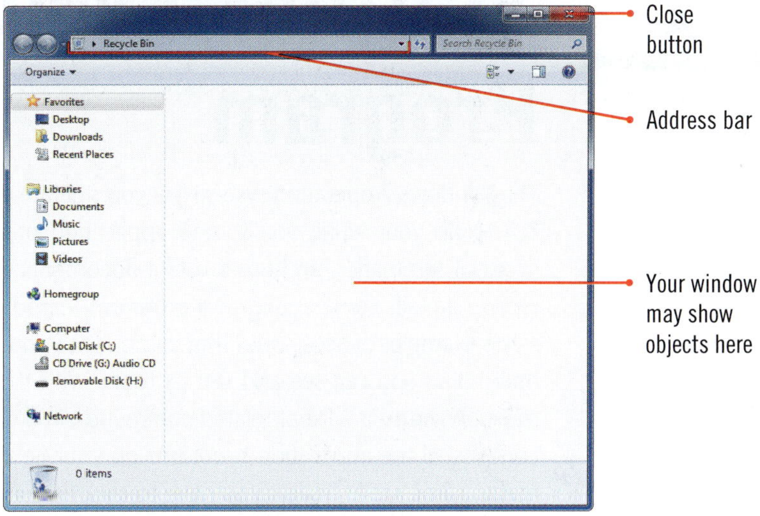

FIGURE A-8: Dragging the Recycle Bin icon

TABLE A-1: Five pointing device actions

action	how to	use for
Pointing	Move the pointing device to position the tip of the pointer over an object, option, or item	Highlighting objects or options, or displaying informational boxes called ScreenTips
Clicking	Quickly press and release the left mouse button once	Selecting objects or commands, opening menus or items on the taskbar
Double-clicking	Quickly press and release the left mouse button twice	Opening programs, folders, or files represented by desktop icons
Dragging	Point to an object, press and hold down the left mouse button, move the object to a new location, then release the mouse button	Moving objects, such as icons on the desktop
Right-clicking	Point to an object, then press and release the right mouse button	Displaying a shortcut menu containing options specific to the object

Using right-clicking

For some actions, you click items using the right mouse button, known as right-clicking. You can **right-click** almost any icon on your desktop to open a shortcut menu. A **shortcut menu** lists common commands for an object. A **command** is an instruction to perform a task, such as emptying the Recycle Bin. The shortcut menu commands depend on the object you right-click. Figure A-9 shows the shortcut menu that appears if you right-click the Recycle Bin. Then you click (with the left mouse button) a shortcut menu command to issue that command.

FIGURE A-9: Right-click to show shortcut menu

UNIT
A
Windows 7

Starting a Windows 7 Program

The Windows 7 operating system lets you operate your computer and see the programs and files it contains. But to do your work, you'll need application programs. **Application programs** let you create letters, financial summaries, and other useful documents as well as view Web pages on the Internet and send and receive e-mail. Some application programs, called **accessories**, come with Windows 7. (See Table A-2 for some examples of accessories that come with Windows 7.) To use an application program, you must start (or open) it so you can see and use its tools. With Windows 7 you start application programs using the Start menu. A **menu** is a list of related commands. You use the Start menu to open the All Programs menu, which contains all the application programs on your computer. You can see some programs on the All Programs menu; some are in folders you have to click first. To start a program, you click its name on the All Programs menu. Evelyn asks you to explore the Paint accessory program for creating brochure graphics.

STEPS

1. **Click the Start button on the taskbar in the lower-left corner of screen**
   The Start menu opens, showing frequently used programs on the left side. The gray area on the right contains links to folders and other locations you are likely to use frequently. It also lets you get help and shut down your computer. See Figure A-10. Not all the programs available on your computer are shown.
2. **Point to All Programs**
   This menu shows programs installed on your computer. Your program list will differ, depending on what you (or your lab) have installed on your machine. Some program names are immediately available, and others are inside folders.
3. **Click the Accessories folder**
   A list of Windows accessory programs appears, as shown in Figure A-11. The program names are indented to the right from the Accessories folder, meaning that they are inside that folder.
4. **Move the pointer over Paint and click once**
   The Paint program window opens on your screen, as shown in Figure A-12. When Windows opens an application program, it starts the program from your computer's hard disk, where it's permanently stored. Then it places the program in your computer's memory so you can use it.
5. **If your Paint window fills the screen completely, click the Restore Down button in the upper-right corner of the window**
   If your Paint window doesn't look like Figure A-12, point to the lower-right corner of the window until the pointer becomes , then drag until it matches the figure.

Searching for programs and files using the Start menu

If you need to find a program, folder, or file on your computer quickly, the Search programs and files box on the Start menu can help. Click the Start button, then type the name of the item you want to find in the Search programs and files box. As you type, Windows 7 lists all programs, documents, e-mail messages, and files that contain the text you typed in a box above the Search box. The items appear as links, which means you only have to click the hand pointer on the item you want, and Windows 7 opens it.

FIGURE A-10: Start menu

FIGURE A-11: Accessories folder on All Programs menu

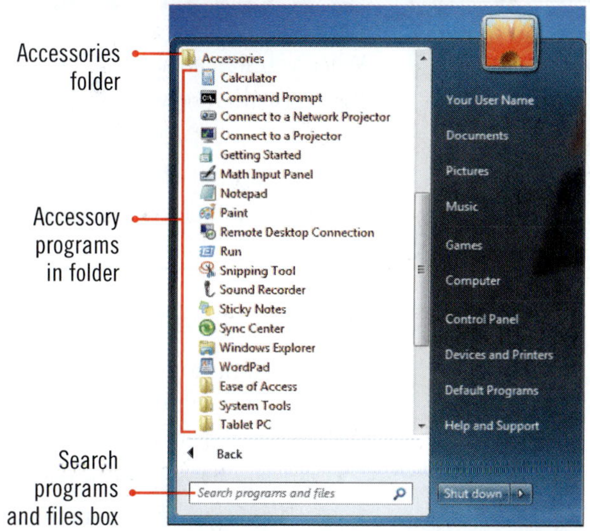

FIGURE A-12: Paint program window

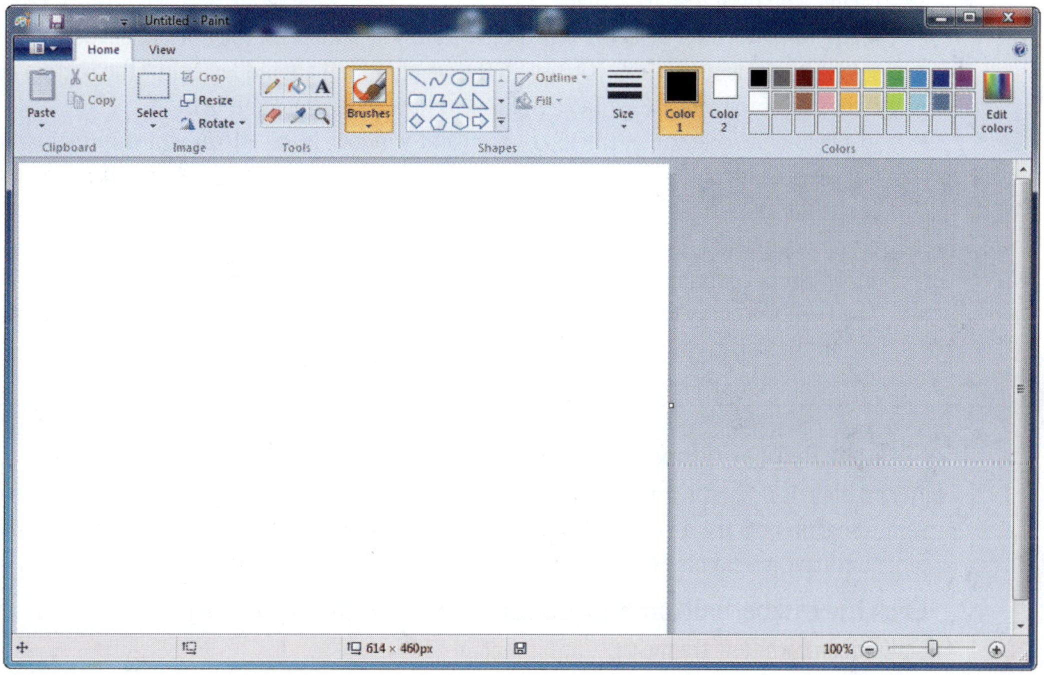

TABLE A-2: Some Windows 7 Accessory programs

accessory program name	use to
Math Input Panel	Interpret math expressions handwritten on a tablet and create a formula suitable for printing or inserting in another program
Notepad	Create text files with basic text formatting
Paint	Create and edit drawings using lines, shapes, and colors
Snipping Tool	Capture an image of any screen area that you can save to use in a document
Sticky Notes	Create short text notes that you can use to set reminders or create to-do lists for yourself
Windows Explorer	View and organize the files and folders on your computer
WordPad	Type letters or other text documents with formatting

UNIT
A
Windows 7

Working with Windows

When you start an application program, its **program window** opens, showing you the tools you need to use the program. A new, blank file also opens. In the Paint program, you create a drawing that you can save as a file and print. All windows in the Windows 7 operating system have similar window elements. Once you can use a window in one program, you can then work with windows in many other programs. As you develop your tour marketing plans, you work with the open Paint window using Windows 7 elements.

DETAILS

Many windows have the following common elements. Refer to Figure A-13:

- At the top of every open window, you see a **title bar**, a transparent or solid-colored strip that contains the name of the program and document you opened. This document has not been saved, so it has the temporary name "Untitled." On the right side of the title bar, you see three icons.

  The **Minimize button** temporarily hides the window, making it a button on the taskbar. The program is still running, but its window is hidden until you click its taskbar button to display it again. The **Maximize button** enlarges the window to fill the entire computer screen. If a window is already maximized, the Maximize button changes to the **Restore Down button**. Restoring a window reduces it to the last nonmaximized size. The **Close button** closes the program. To use it later, you need to start it again.
- Many windows have a **scroll bar** on the right side and/or on the bottom of the window. You click the scroll bar elements to show parts of your document that are hidden below the bottom edge or off to the right side of the screen. See Table A-3 to learn the parts of a scroll bar.
- Just below the title bar, at the top of the Paint window, is the **Ribbon**, a strip that contains tabs. **Tabs** are pages that contain buttons that you click to perform actions. The Paint window has two tabs, the Home tab and the View tab. Tabs are divided into **groups** of command buttons. The Home tab has five groups: Clipboard, Image, Tools, Shapes, and Colors. Some programs have **menus**, words you click to show lists of commands, and **toolbars**, containing program buttons.
- The **Quick Access toolbar**, in the upper-left corner of the window, lets you quickly perform common actions such as saving a file.

QUICK TIP
If your Ribbon looks different from Figure A-13, your window is a little narrower. A narrow window collapses some buttons so you can only see group names. In that case, you might need to click a group name to see buttons.

STEPS

1. **Click the Paint window Minimize button**
   The program is now represented only by its button on the taskbar. See Figure A-14. The taskbar button for the Paint program now has a gradient background with blue and white shading. Taskbar buttons for closed programs have a solid blue background.
2. **Click the taskbar button representing the Paint program**
   The program window reappears.
3. **Drag the Paint scroll box down, notice the lower edge of the Paint canvas that appears, then click the Paint Up scroll arrow until you see the top edge of the canvas**
   In the Ribbon, the Home tab is in front of the View tab.
4. **Point to the View tab with the tip of the mouse pointer, then click the View tab once**
   The View tab moves in front of the Home tab and shows commands for viewing your drawings. The View tab has three groups: Zoom, Show or hide, and Display.
5. **Click the Home tab**
6. **Click the Paint window Maximize button**
   The window fills the screen and the Maximize button becomes the Restore Down button.
7. **Click the Paint window's Restore Down button**
   The Paint window returns to its previous size on the screen.

TROUBLE
If your screen resolution is set higher than 1024 × 768, you might not see a scroll box. You can continue with the lesson.

QUICK TIP
To quickly restore down the selected window, press and hold down the Windows key and then press the down arrow key.

FIGURE A-13: Paint program window elements

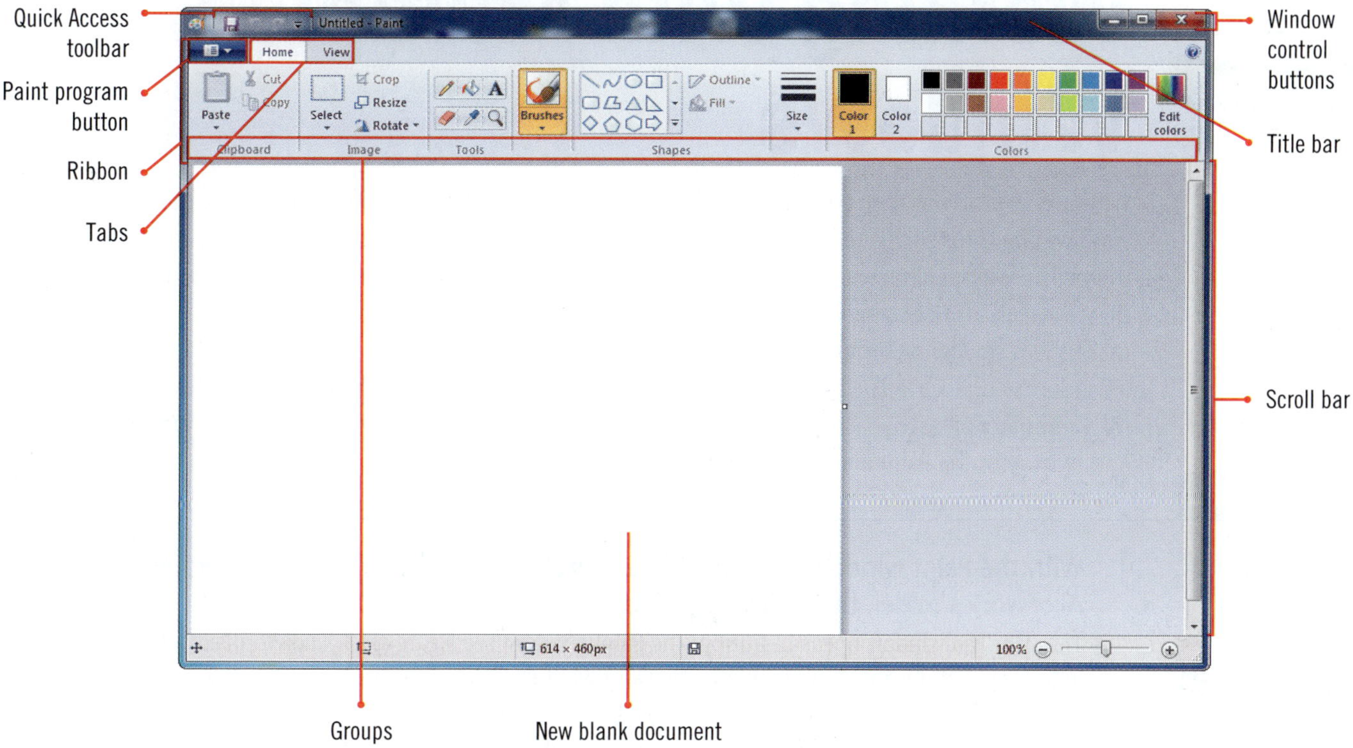

FIGURE A-14: Taskbar showing Paint program button

TABLE A-3: Parts of a scroll bar

name	looks like	use for
Scroll box	(Size may vary)	Drag to scroll quickly through a long document
Scroll arrows		Click to scroll up or down in small amounts
Shaded area	(Above and below scroll box)	Click to move up or down by one screen

Using the Quick Access toolbar

On the left side of the title bar, the Quick Access toolbar lets you perform common tasks with just one click. The Save button saves the changes you have made to a document. The Undo button lets you reverse (undo) the last action you performed. The Redo button reinstates the change you just undid. Use the Customize Quick Access Toolbar button to add other frequently used buttons to the toolbar, move the toolbar below the Ribbon, or hide the Ribbon.

UNIT
A
Windows 7

Working with Multiple Windows

Windows 7 lets you work with more than one program at a time. If you open two or more programs, a window opens for each one. You can work with each open program window, going back and forth between them. The window in front is called the **active window**. Any other open window behind the active window is called an **inactive window**. For ease in working with multiple windows, you can move, arrange, make them smaller or larger, minimize, or restore them so they're not in the way. To resize a window, drag a window's edge, called its **border**. You can also use the taskbar to switch between windows. See Table A-4 for a summary of taskbar actions. Keeping the Paint program open, you open the WordPad program and work with the Paint and WordPad program windows.

STEPS

1. **With the Paint window open, click the Start button, point to All Programs, click the Accessories folder, then click WordPad**

   The WordPad window opens in front of the Paint window. See Figure A-15. The WordPad window is in front, indicating that it is the active window. The Paint window is the inactive window. On the taskbar, the gradient backgrounds on the WordPad and Paint program buttons on the taskbar tell you that both programs are open. You want to move the WordPad window out of the way so you can see both windows at once.

2. **Point to a blank part of the WordPad window title bar, then drag the WordPad window so you can see more of the Paint window**

3. **Click once on the Paint window's title bar**

   The Paint window is now the active window and appears in front of the WordPad window. You can make any window active by clicking it. You can use the taskbar to do the same thing. You can also move among open program windows by pressing and holding down the [Alt] key on your keyboard and pressing the [Tab] key. A small window opens in the middle of the screen, showing miniature versions of each open program window. Each time you press [Tab], you select the next open program window. When you release [Tab] and [Alt], the selected program window becomes active.

4. **On the taskbar, click the WordPad window button**

   The WordPad window is now active. When you open multiple windows on the desktop, you may need to resize windows so they don't get in the way of other open windows. You can use dragging to resize a window.

5. **Point to the lower-right corner of the WordPad window until the pointer becomes ↘, then drag up and to the left about an inch to make the window smaller**

   Windows 7 has a special feature that lets you automatically resize a window so it fills half the screen.

6. **Point to the WordPad window title bar, drag the window to the left side of the screen until the mouse pointer reaches the screen edge and the left half of the screen turns a transparent blue color, then release the mouse button**

   The WordPad window "snaps" to fill the left side of the screen.

7. **Point to the Paint window title bar, then drag the window to the right side of the screen until it snaps to fill the right half of the screen**

   The Paint window fills the right side of the screen. The Snap feature makes it easy to arrange windows side by side to view the contents of both at the same time.

8. **Click the WordPad window Close button then click the Maximize button in the Paint window's title bar**

   The WordPad program closes, so you can no longer use its tools unless you open it again. The Paint program window remains open and fills the screen.

QUICK TIP
To click an inactive window to make it active, click its title bar, window edge, or a blank area. To move a window, you must drag its title bar.

QUICK TIP
To instantly minimize all inactive windows, point to the active window's title bar, and quickly "shake" the window back and forth. This feature is called Aero Shake.

TROUBLE
Point to any edge of a window until you see the ⇔ or ⇕ pointer and drag to make it larger or smaller in one direction only.

FIGURE A-15: WordPad window in front of Paint window

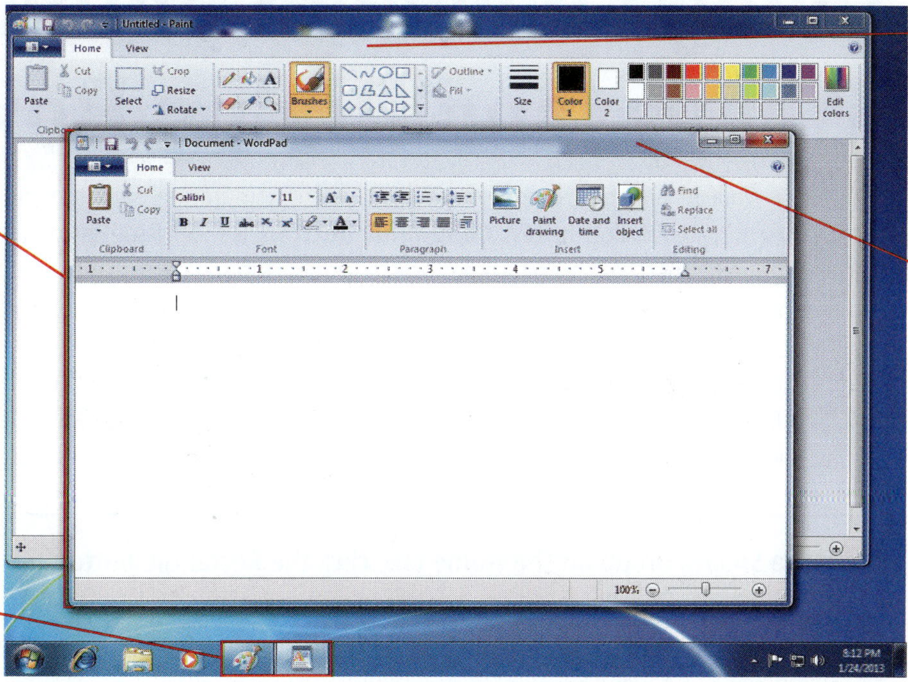

TABLE A-4: Using the Windows taskbar

to	do this
Add buttons to taskbar	Drag a program name from the Start menu over the taskbar, until a ScreenTip reads Pin to Taskbar
Change order of taskbar buttons	Drag any icon to a new taskbar location
See a list of recent documents opened in a taskbar program	Right-click taskbar program button
Close a document using the taskbar	Point to taskbar button, point to document name in jump list, then click Close button
Minimize all open windows	Click Show desktop button to the right of taskbar date and time
Redisplay all minimized windows	Click Show desktop button to the right of taskbar date and time
Make all windows transparent (Aero only)	Point to Show desktop button to the right of taskbar date and time
See preview of documents in taskbar (Aero only)	Point to taskbar button for open program

Switching windows with Windows Aero

Windows Aero is a set of special effects for Windows 7. If your windows have transparent "glass" backgrounds like those shown in the figures in this book, your Aero feature is turned on. Your windows show subtle animations when you minimize, maximize, and move windows. When you arrange windows using Aero, your windows can appear in a three-dimensional stack that you can quickly view without having to click the taskbar. To achieve this effect, called **Aero Flip 3D**, press and hold [Ctrl][Windows logo key], then press [Tab]. Press [Tab] repeatedly to move through the stack, then press [Enter] to enlarge the document in the front of the stack. In addition, when you point to a taskbar button, Aero shows you small previews of the document, photo, or video—a feature called **Aero Peek**. Aero is turned on automatically when you start Windows, if you have an appropriate video card and enough computer memory to run Aero. If it is not on, to turn on the Aero feature, right-click the desktop, left-click Personalize, then select one of the Aero Themes.

Using Command Buttons, Menus, and Dialog Boxes

When you work in an open program window, you communicate with the program using command buttons, menus, and dialog boxes. **Command buttons** let you issue instructions to modify program objects. Command buttons are sometimes organized on a Ribbon into tabs, and then into groups like those in the Paint window. Some command buttons have text on them, and others only have icons that represent what they do. Other command buttons reveal **menus**, lists of commands you can choose. And some command buttons open up a **dialog box**, a window with controls that lets you tell Windows what you want. Table A-5 lists the common types of controls you find in dialog boxes. You use command buttons, menus, and dialog boxes to communicate with the Paint program.

STEPS

1. **In the Shapes group on the Home tab, click the Rectangle button**
2. **In the Colors group, click the Gold button, move the pointer over the white drawing area, called the canvas, then drag to draw a rectangle a similar size to the one in Figure A-16**

> **QUICK TIP**
> If you need to move the oval, use the keyboard arrow keys to move it left, right, up, or down.

3. **In the Shapes group, click the Oval button, click the Green color button in the Colors group, then drag a small oval above the rectangle, using Figure A-16 as a guide**

> **TROUBLE**
> Don't be concerned if your object isn't exactly like the one in the figure.

4. **Click the Fill with color icon in the Tools group, click the Light turquoise color button in the Colors group, click inside the oval, click the Purple color button, then click inside the rectangle, and compare your drawing to Figure A-16**
5. **In the Image group, click the Select list arrow, then click Select all, as shown in Figure A-17**

   The Select menu has several menu commands. The Select all command selects the entire drawing, as indicated by the dotted line surrounding the white drawing area.
6. **In the Image group, click the Rotate or flip button, then click Rotate right 90°**
7. **Click the Paint menu button just below the title bar, then click Print**

   The Print dialog box opens, as shown in Figure A-18. This dialog box lets you choose a printer, specify which part of your document or drawing you want to print, and choose how many copies you want to print. The **default**, or automatically selected, number of copies is 1, which is what you want.

> **TROUBLE**
> If you prefer not to print your document, click Cancel.

8. **Click Print**

   The drawing prints on your printer. You decide to close the program without saving your drawing.
9. **Click, click Exit, then click Don't Save**

TABLE A-5: Common dialog box controls

element	example	description
Text box	132	A box in which you type text or numbers
Spin box	1	A box with up and down arrows; click arrows or type to increase or decrease value
Option button		A small circle you click to select the option
Check box		Turns an option on when checked or off when unchecked
List box	Select Printer Add Printer Dell Laser Printer 3000cn PCL6 Fax	A box that lets you select an option from a list of options
Command button	Save	A button that completes or cancels the selected settings

FIGURE A-16: Rectangle and oval shapes with fill

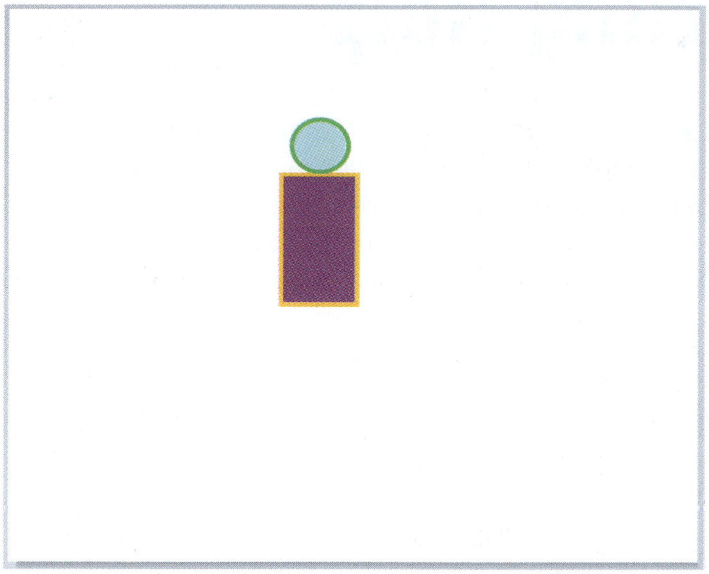

FIGURE A-17: Select list arrow

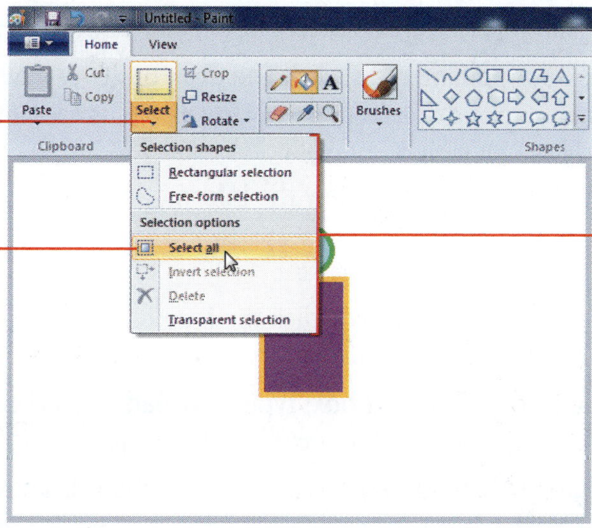

FIGURE A-18: Print dialog box

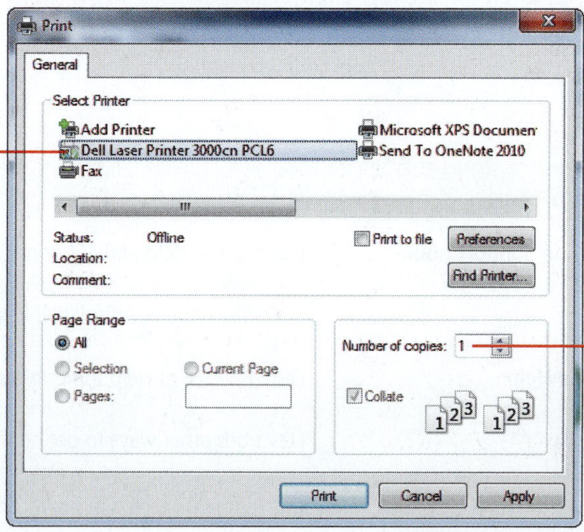

Getting Help

As you use Windows 7, you might feel ready to learn more about it, or you might have a problem and need some advice. You can open the Windows 7 Help and Support to find information you need. You can browse Help and Support topics by clicking a category, such as "Learn about Windows Basics." Within this category, you see more specific categories. Each category has topics in blue or purple text called **links** that you can click to learn more. You can also search Help and Support by typing one or more descriptive words called **keywords**, such as "taskbar," to ask Windows to find topics related to your keywords. The Help toolbar contains icons that give you more Help options. Table A-6 describes the Help toolbar icons. You use Windows 7 help to learn more about Windows and the WordPad accessory.

STEPS

TROUBLE

If your computer is not connected to the Internet, you will see an alert at the top of the Help window. You can continue with the steps in this lesson.

QUICK TIP

If you are using a mouse with a scroll wheel, you can use the scroll wheel to scroll up and down. If you are using a touchpad, the right side of your touchpad might let you scroll.

QUICK TIP

Search text is not case sensitive. Typing wordpad, Wordpad, or WordPad finds the same results.

1. **Click the Start button, then on the right side of the Start menu, click Help and Support**

   The Windows Help and Support window opens, as shown in Figure A-19. A search box appears near the top of the window. Three topics appear as blue or purple text, meaning that they are links. Below them, you see descriptive text and a link to a Web site that contains more information about Windows.

2. **Under Not sure where to start?, position the hand pointer over Learn about Windows Basics, then click once**

   Several categories of Windows Basics topics appear, with links under each one.

3. **Under Desktop fundamentals, click The desktop (overview)**

   Help and Support information about the desktop appears, divided into several categories. Some of the text appears as a blue or purple link.

4. **Drag the scroll box down to view the information, then drag the scroll box back to the top of the scroll bar**

   You decide to learn more about the taskbar.

5. **Under The desktop (overview), click the blue or purple text The taskbar (overview), then scroll down and read the information about the taskbar**

6. **Click in the Search Help text box, type wordpad, then click the Search Help button**

   A list of links related to the WordPad accessory program appears. See Figure A-20.

7. **Click Using WordPad, scroll down if necessary, then click Create, open, and save documents**

8. **Scroll down and view the information, clicking any other links that interest you**

9. **Click the Close button in the upper-right corner of the Windows Help and Support window**

   The Windows Help and Support window closes.

TABLE A-6: Help toolbar icons

help toolbar icon	name	action
	Help and Support home	Displays the Help and Support Home page
	Print	Prints the currently-displayed help topic
	Browse Help	Displays a list of Help topics organized by subject
Ask	Ask	Describes other ways to get help
Options	Options	Lets you print, browse, search, set Help text size, and adjust settings

FIGURE A-19: Windows Help and Support window

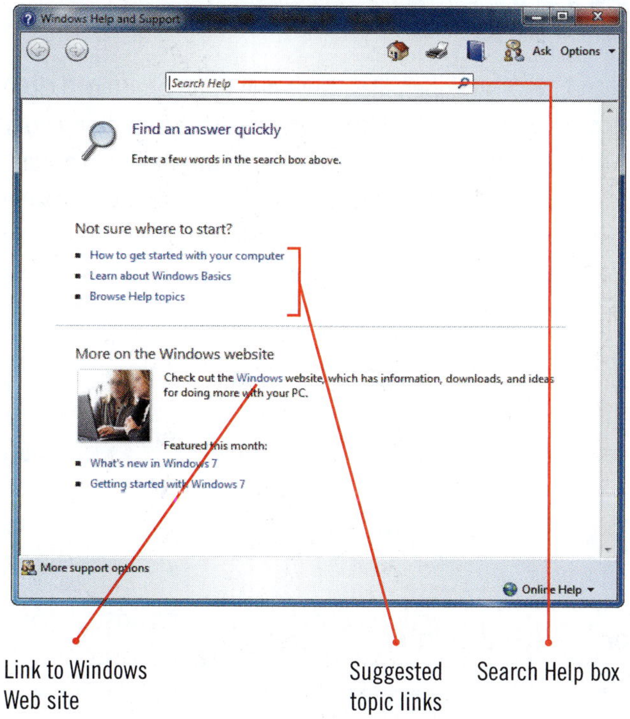

FIGURE A-20: Results of a search on WordPad

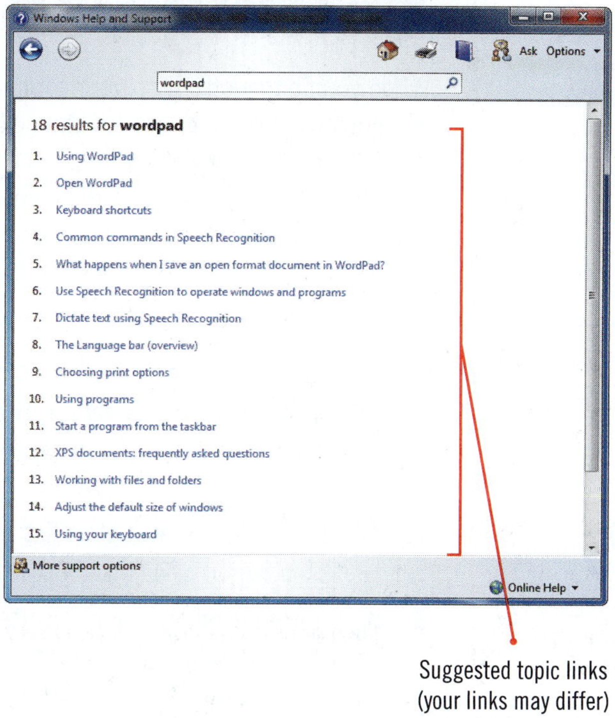

Finding other ways to get help

As you use Windows 7, you might want more help than you can find by clicking links or searching. You will find many other methods in the Windows Help and Support Home window. Click the Windows website link to locate blogs (Web logs, which are personal commentaries), downloads, Windows 7 video tours, and other current Windows 7 resources. Click the Ask button in the Help and Support window toolbar to learn about **Windows Remote Assistance**, which lets you connect with another computer, perhaps that of a trusted friend or instructor, so they can operate your computer using an Internet connection. The same window lets you open Microsoft Answers. **Microsoft Answers** is a website the lets you search **forums** (electronic gathering places where anyone can add questions and answers on computer issues), Microsoft help files, and even on-screen video demonstrations about selected topics.

UNIT A

Windows 7

Exiting Windows 7

When you finish working on your computer, save and close any open files, close any open programs, close any open windows, and exit (or **shut down**) Windows 7. Table A-7 shows several options for ending your Windows 7 sessions. Whichever option you choose, it's important to shut down your computer in an orderly way. If you turn off or unplug the computer while Windows 7 is running, you could lose data or damage Windows 7 and your computer. If you are working in a computer lab, follow your instructor's directions and your lab's policies for ending your Windows 7 session. You have examined the basic ways you can use Windows 7, so you are ready to end your Windows 7 session.

STEPS

1. **Click the Start button on the taskbar**

   The lower-right corner of the Start menu lets you shut down your computer. It also displays a menu with other options for ending a Windows 7 session.

2. **Point to the Power button list arrow, as shown in Figure A-21**

   The Power button menu lists other shutdown options.

3. **If you are working in a computer lab, follow the instructions provided by your instructor or technical support person for ending your Windows 7 session. If you are working on your own computer, click Shut down or the option you prefer for ending your Windows 7 session**

4. **After you shut down your computer, you may also need to turn off your monitor and other hardware devices, such as a printer, to conserve energy**

TROUBLE

If a previous user has customized your computer, your button and menu commands might be in different locations. For example, the Power button may show "Restart," and "Shut down" may appear on the menu.

Installing updates when you exit Windows

Sometimes, after you shut down your machine, you might find that your machine does not shut down immediately. Instead, Windows might install software updates. If your power button shows this yellow icon, that means that Windows will install updates on your next shutdown. If you see a window indicating that updates are being installed, do not unplug or press the power switch to turn off your machine. Allow the updates to install completely. After the updates are installed, your computer will shut down, as you originally requested.

FIGURE A-21: Shutting down your computer

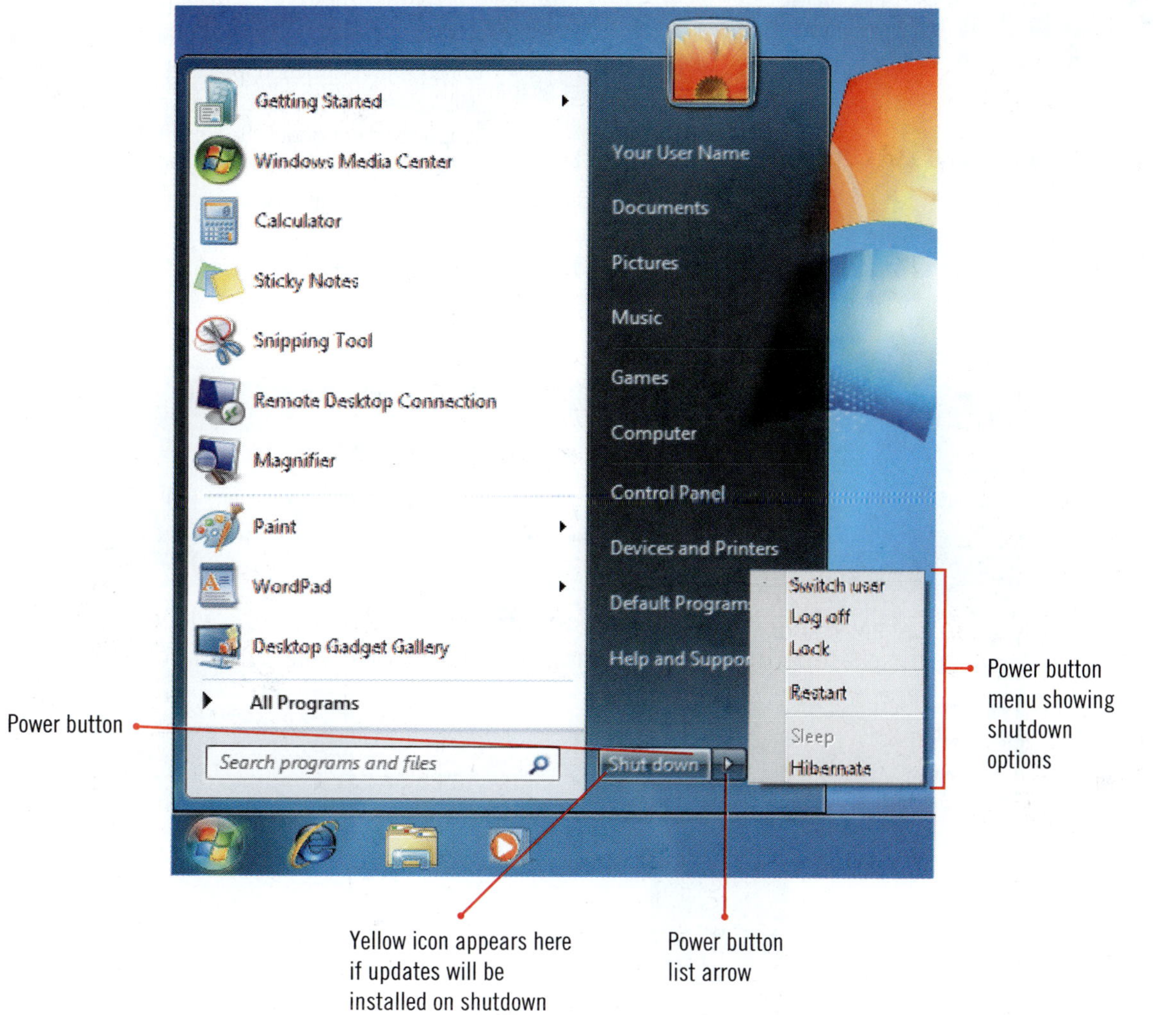

TABLE A-7: Options for ending a Windows 7 session

option	description	click
Shut down	Completely turns off your computer	Start button, Shut down
Switch user	Locks your user account and displays the Welcome screen so another user can log on	Start button, Power button list arrow, Switch user
Log off	Closes all windows, programs, and documents, then displays the Log in screen	Start button, Power button list arrow, Log off
Lock	Locks computer so only current user (or administrator) can use it	Start button, Power button list arrow, Lock
Restart	Shuts down your computer, then restarts it	Start button, Power button list arrow, Restart
Sleep	Puts computer in a low-power state while preserving your session in the computer's memory	Start button, Power button list arrow, Sleep
Hibernate	Turns off computer drives and screens but saves image of your work; when you turn machine on, it starts where you left off	Start button, Power button list arrow, Hibernate

Practice

Concepts Review

For current SAM information, including versions and content details, visit SAM Central (http://samcentral.course.com). If you have a SAM user profile, you may have access to hands-on instruction, practice, and assessment of the skills covered in this unit. Since various versions of SAM are supported throughout the life of this text, check with your instructor for the correct instructions and URL/Web site for accessing assignments.

Label the elements of the Windows 7 window shown in Figure A-22.

FIGURE A-22

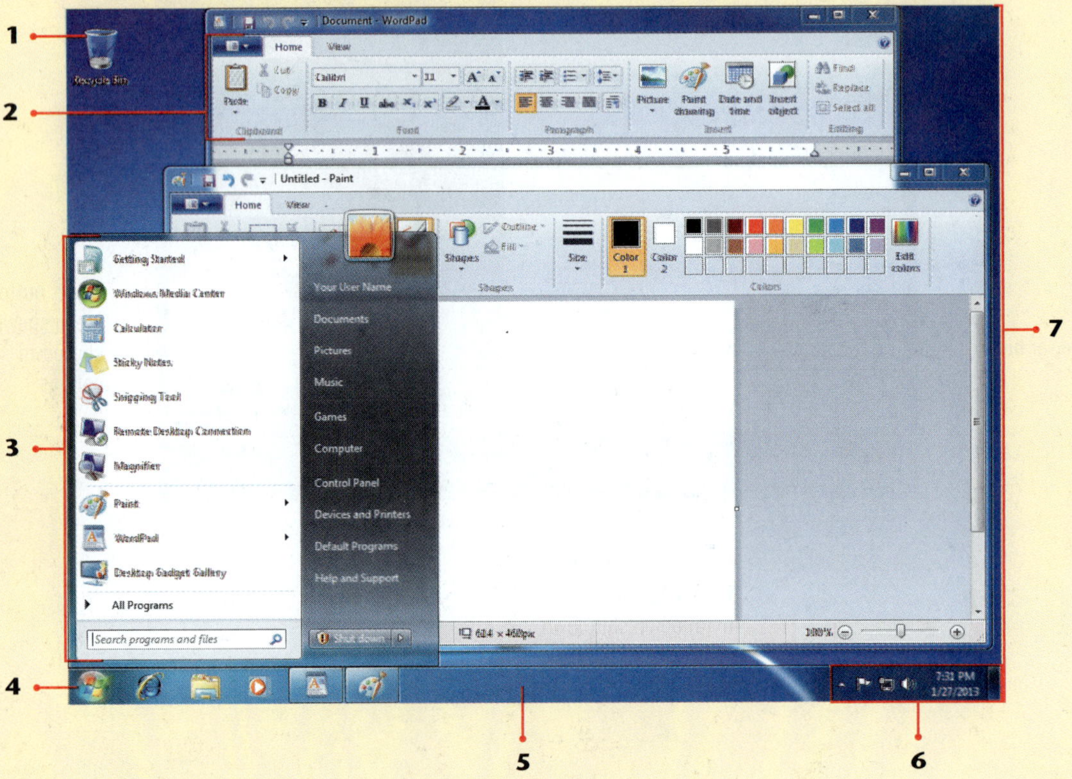

Match each term with the statement that best describes it.

8. Accessory	**a.** A sequence of numbers and letters users create to keep information secure
9. Keyword	**b.** The window in front of other windows
10. Trackball	**c.** Horizontal strip at bottom of screen that contains buttons
11. Active window	**d.** A pointing device
12. Password	**e.** Application program that comes with Windows 7
13. Operating system	**f.** Descriptive word you use to search Windows Help and Support
14. Taskbar	**g.** A program necessary to run your computer

Select the best answer from the list of choices.

15. What part of a window shows the name of the program you opened?

a. Title bar
b. Scroll bar
c. Ribbon
d. Quick Access toolbar

16. You use the Maximize button to:
- **a.** Restore a window to a previous size.
- **b.** Expand a window to fill the entire screen.
- **c.** Temporarily hide a window.
- **d.** Scroll down a window.

17. Which of the following is not an accessory program?
- **a.** Snipping Tool
- **b.** Paint
- **c.** WordPad
- **d.** Windows 7

18. Which button do you click to reduce an open window to a button on the taskbar?
- **a.** Maximize button
- **b.** Restore Down button
- **c.** Minimize button
- **d.** Close button

19. Right-clicking is an action that:
- **a.** Starts a program.
- **b.** Requires a password.
- **c.** Displays a shortcut menu.
- **d.** Opens the taskbar.

20. The Windows 7 feature that shows windows with transparent "glass" backgrounds is:
- **a.** Paint.
- **b.** Aero.
- **c.** Taskbar.
- **d.** Sticky Notes.

21. Windows 7 is a(n):
- **a.** Accessory program.
- **b.** Application program.
- **c.** Operating system.
- **d.** Gadget.

Skills Review

1. Start Windows 7.
- **a.** If your computer and monitor are not running, press your computer's and your monitor's power buttons.
- **b.** If necessary, click the user name that represents your user account.
- **c.** Enter a password if necessary, using correct uppercase and lowercase letters.

2. Learn the Windows 7 desktop.
- **a.** Examine the Windows 7 desktop to identify the Start button, the taskbar, the notification area, the Recycle Bin, the desktop background, desktop icons, and gadgets, if any.

3. Point and click.
- **a.** On the Windows desktop, select the Recycle Bin.
- **b.** Open the Start menu, then close it.
- **c.** Open the clock and calendar on the right side of the taskbar.
- **d.** Click the desktop to close the calendar.
- **e.** Open the Recycle Bin window, then close it.

4. Start a Windows 7 program.
- **a.** Use the Start button to open the Start menu.
- **b.** Open the All Programs menu.
- **c.** On the All Programs menu, open the Accessories folder.
- **d.** Open the WordPad accessory.

5. Work with Windows.
- **a.** Minimize the WordPad window.
- **b.** Redisplay it using a taskbar button.
- **c.** In the WordPad window, click the WordPad button in the Ribbon, then click the About WordPad command. (*Hint*: The WordPad button is next to the Home tab.)
- **d.** Close the About WordPad window.
- **e.** Maximize the WordPad window, then restore it down.
- **f.** Display the View tab in the WordPad window.

Skills Review (continued)

6. **Work with multiple windows.**
   a. Leaving WordPad open, open Paint.
   b. Make the WordPad window the active window.
   c. Make the Paint window the active window.
   d. Minimize the Paint window.
   e. Drag the WordPad window so it automatically fills the left side of the screen.
   f. Redisplay the Paint window.
   g. Drag the Paint window so it automatically fills the right side of the screen.
   h. Close the WordPad window, maximize the Paint window, then restore down the Paint window.
7. **Use command buttons, menus, and dialog boxes.**
   a. In the Paint window, draw a red triangle, similar to Figure A-23.
   b. Use the Fill with color button to fill the triangle with a gold color.
   c. Draw a green rectangle just below the triangle.
   d. Use the Fill with color button to fill the green triangle with a light turquoise color.
   e. Fill the drawing background with purple and compare your drawing with Figure A-23.
   f. Use the Select list arrow and menu to select the entire drawing, then use the Rotate or flip command to rotate the drawing left 90°.
   g. Close the Paint program without saving the drawing.

FIGURE A-23

8. **Get help.**
   a. Open the Windows Help and Support window.
   b. Open the "How to get started with your computer" topic.
   c. Open the "First week tasks" topic, click a link called "Create a user account", then read the topic information.
   d. In the Search Help text box, search for help about user accounts.
   e. Find the link that describes what a user account is and click it.
   f. Read the topic, then close the Windows Help and Support window.
9. **Exit Windows 7.**
   a. Shut down your computer using the Shut down command or the command for your work or school setting.
   b. Turn off your monitor.

Independent Challenge 1

You work for Will's Percussion, an Oregon manufacturer of drums and drumsticks. The company ships percussion instruments and supplies to music stores and musicians in the United States and Canada. The owner, Will, gives seminars at drummer conventions on how to avoid repetitive stress injuries to the hands and arms. He knows this can also be a big problem for computer users as well, so he asks you to research the topic and write some guidelines for the company's employees.

a. Start your computer, log on to Windows 7 if necessary, then open Windows Help and Support.
b. Click the Learn about Windows Basics link.
c. In the Learn about your computer section, read the topic about using your mouse.
d. At the bottom of the topic, read the Tips for using your mouse safely.
e. Using pencil and paper, write a short memo to Will listing, in your own words, the most important tips for avoiding soreness or injury when using a mouse. Close the Windows Help and Support window, then exit Windows.

Independent Challenge 2

You are the new manager for Katharine Anne's Designs, a business that supplies floral arrangements to New York businesses. The company maintains four delivery vans that supply flowers to various locations. Katharine asks you to investigate how the Windows 7 Calculator accessory can help her company be a responsible energy consumer.

Independent Challenge 2 (continued)

a. Start your computer, log on to Windows 7 if necessary, then open the Windows 7 accessory called Calculator.
b. Drag the Calculator window to place it in the lower-left corner of the desktop just above the taskbar.
c. Minimize the Calculator window, then redisplay it.
d. Click to enter the number 87 on the Calculator.
e. Click the division sign (/) button.
f. Click the number 2.
g. Click the equals sign button (=), and write the result shown in the Calculator window on a piece of paper. See Figure A-24.
h. Click the Help menu in the Calculator window, then click View Help. In the Using Calculator window, determine the three ways of entering calculations in the Calculator. Write the three methods on your handwritten list.
i. Close the Help window.

FIGURE A-24

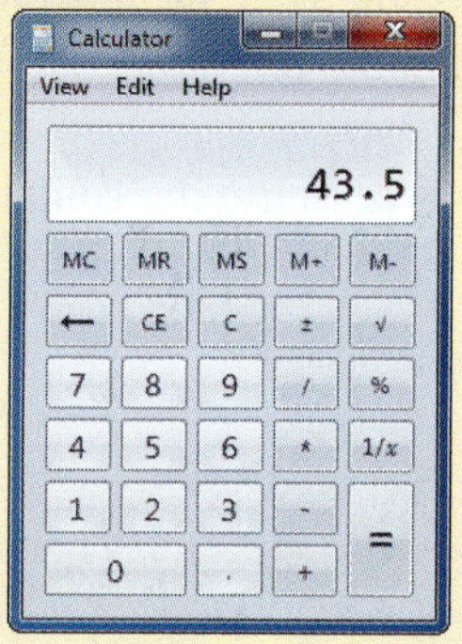

Advanced Challenge Exercise

- Open the View menu on the Calculator window, and click Date calculation.
- Click the list arrow under Select the date calculation you want, then click Calculate the difference between two dates.
- Write how Katharine's business might use this to calculate the length of time it takes a customer to pay an invoice.
- Click the View menu, point to Worksheets, then click Fuel economy (mpg).
- Click in the Distance (miles) text box and enter 100; click in the Fuel used (gallons) text box and type 5, then use the Calculate button to calculate the mileage.
- Write a short paragraph on how Katharine can use this feature to help calculate her van mileage.
- Click the View menu and return to the Basic view.
- Try to click the Calculator window's Maximize button. Note the result and add this fact to your document.

j. Close the Calculator, then exit Windows.

Independent Challenge 3

You are the office manager for Peter's Pet Shipping, a service business in Vancouver, BC that specializes in air shipping of cats and dogs to Canada and the northern United States. It's important to know the temperature in the destination city, so that the animals won't be in danger from extreme temperatures when they are unloaded from the aircraft. Peter has asked you to find a way to easily monitor temperatures in destination cities. You decide to use a Windows gadget so you can see current temperatures in Celsius on your desktop.

To complete this Independent Challenge, you need an Internet connection. You also need permission to add gadgets to the Windows Desktop. If you are working in a computer lab, check with your instructor or technical support person.

a. Start your computer, log on to Windows 7 if necessary, then click the Start button, open the All Programs menu, then click Desktop Gadget Gallery.
b. Double-click the Weather gadget, then close the Gallery window.
c. Move the pointer over the Weather gadget on the desktop, then notice the small buttons that appear on its right side.
d. Click the Larger size button (the middle button).
e. Click the Options button (the third button down) to open the weather options window.
f. In the Select current location text box, type Juneau, Alaska, then click the Search button.
g. Verify that the window shows the current location as "Juneau, Alaska."
h. Click the Celsius option button, then click OK.
i. To close the gadget, point to the gadget, then click the Close button (the top button).
j. Write Peter a memo outlining how you can use the Windows Weather gadget to help keep pets safe, then exit Windows.

Real Life Independent Challenge

As a professional photographer, you often evaluate pictures. You decide to explore a Windows Desktop gadget that will let you display a slide show on your desktop using photos you choose.

To complete this Independent Challenge, you need an Internet connection. You also need permission to add gadgets to the Windows Desktop. If you are working in a computer lab, check with your instructor or technical support person.

a. Start your computer, log on to Windows 7 if necessary, click the Start button, open the All Programs menu, then click Desktop Gadget Gallery.
b. Double-click the Slide Show gadget, then close the Gallery window.
c. Move the pointer over the Slide Show gadget on the desktop, then notice the small buttons that appear on its right side.
d. Click the Larger size button (the second button down).
e. Click the Options button (the third button down) to open the Slide Show options window.
f. Click the Folder list arrow and click the My Pictures folder. If you do not have pictures on your computer, click the Sample Pictures folder.
g. Click the Show each picture list arrow and select a duration.
h. Click the Transition between pictures list arrow and select a transition.
i. If you want the pictures to be in random order, click the Shuffle pictures check box.
j. Click OK.

Advanced Challenge Exercise

ACE

- Place the mouse pointer over the Slide Show window, then right-click.
- Point to Opacity and left-click an opacity level, then move the mouse pointer over the desktop. Adjust the opacity to the level you prefer.
- Drag the gadget to the desktop location you choose.

k. View your slide show, click the Slide Show window's Close button, then exit Windows.

Visual Workshop

As owner of Icons Plus, an icon design business, you decide to customize your desktop and resize your Help window to better suit your needs as you work with Paint. Organize your screen as shown in Figure A-25. Note the position of the Recycle Bin, the location of the Paint window, and the size and location of the Help and Support window. Write a paragraph summarizing how you used clicking and dragging to make your screen look like Figure A-25. Then exit Windows.

FIGURE A-25

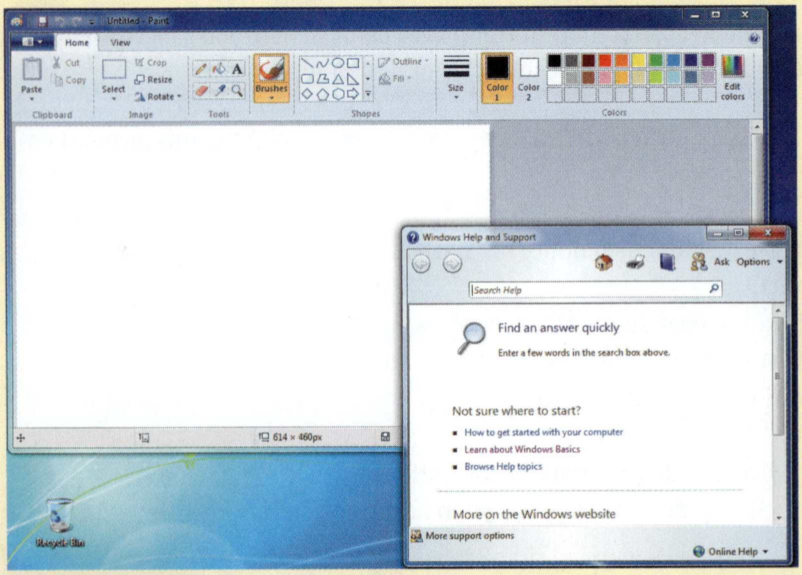

UNIT
B
Windows 7

Understanding File Management

Files You Will Need:
No files needed.

To work with the folders and files on your computer, you need to understand how your computer stores them. You should also know how to organize them so you can always find the information you need. These skills are called **file management** skills. When you create a document and save it as a file, it is important that you save the file in a place where you can find it later. To keep your computer files organized, you will need to copy, move, and rename them. When you have files you don't need any more, it's a good idea to move or delete them so your computer has only current files. Your supervisor, Evelyn Swazey, asks you to learn how to manage your computer files so you can begin creating and organizing documents for the upcoming Oceania tours.

OBJECTIVES

- Understand folders and files
- Create and save a file
- Explore the files and folders on your computer
- Change file and folder views
- Open, edit, and save files
- Copy files
- Move and rename files
- Search for files, folders, and programs
- Delete and restore files

UNIT B

Windows 7

Understanding Folders and Files

As you work with your computer programs, you create and save files, such as letters, drawings, or budgets. When you save files, you usually save them inside folders, which are storage areas on your computer. You use folders to group related files, as with paper folders in a file cabinet. The files and folders on your computer are organized in a **file hierarchy**, a system that arranges files and folders in different levels, like the branches of a tree. Figure B-1 shows a sample file hierarchy. Evelyn asks you to look at some important facts about files and folders to help you store your Oceania tour files.

DETAILS

Use the following guidelines as you organize files using your computer's file hierarchy:

- **Use folders and subfolders to organize files**

  As you work with your computer, you can add folders to your hierarchy and rename them to help you organize your work. You should give folders unique names that help you easily identify them. You can also create **subfolders**, which are folders that are inside of other folders. Windows comes with several existing folders, such as My Documents, My Music, and My Pictures, that you can use as a starting point.

QUICK TIP

You can also start Windows Explorer by clicking the Windows Explorer button on the taskbar.

- **View files in windows**

  You view your computer contents by opening a **window**, like the one in Figure B-2. A window is divided into sections. The **Navigation pane** on the left side of the window shows the folder structure on your computer. When you click a folder in the Navigation pane, you see its contents in the **File list** on the right side. The **Details pane** at the bottom of the window provides information about selected files in the File list. A window actually opens in an accessory program called **Windows Explorer**, although the program name does not appear on the window. You can open this program from the Start menu, or just double-click a folder to open its window and view its contents.

- **Understand file addresses**

  A window also contains an **Address bar**, an area just below the title bar that shows the location, or address, of the files that appear in the File list. An **address** is a sequence of folder names separated by the ▸ symbol that describes a file's location in the file hierarchy. An address shows the folder with the highest hierarchy level on the left and steps through each hierarchy level toward the right, sometimes called a **path**. For example, the My Documents folder might contain a subfolder named Notes. In this case, the Address bar would show My Documents ▸ Notes. Each location between the ▸ symbols represents a level in the file hierarchy.

QUICK TIP

Remember that you single-click a folder or subfolder in the Address bar to show its contents. But in the File list, you double-click a subfolder to open it.

- **Navigate upward and downward using the Address bar and File list**

  You can use the Address bar and the File list to move up or down in the hierarchy one or more levels at a time. To **navigate upward** in your computer's hierarchy, you can click a folder or subfolder name in the Address bar. For example, in Figure B-2, you would move up in the hierarchy by clicking once on Users in the Address bar. Then the File list would show the subfolders and files inside the Users folder. To **navigate downward** in the hierarchy, double-click a subfolder in the File list. The path in the Address bar then shows the path to that subfolder.

- **Navigate upward and downward using the Navigation pane**

  You can also use the Navigation pane to navigate among folders. Move the mouse pointer over the Navigation pane, then click the small triangles or to the left of a folder name to show ▷ or hide ◢ the folder's contents under the folder name. Subfolders appear indented under the folders that contain them, showing that they are inside that folder. Figure B-2 shows a folder named Users in the Navigation pane. The subfolders Katharine, Public, and Your User Name are inside the Users folder.

FIGURE B-1: Sample folder and file hierarchy

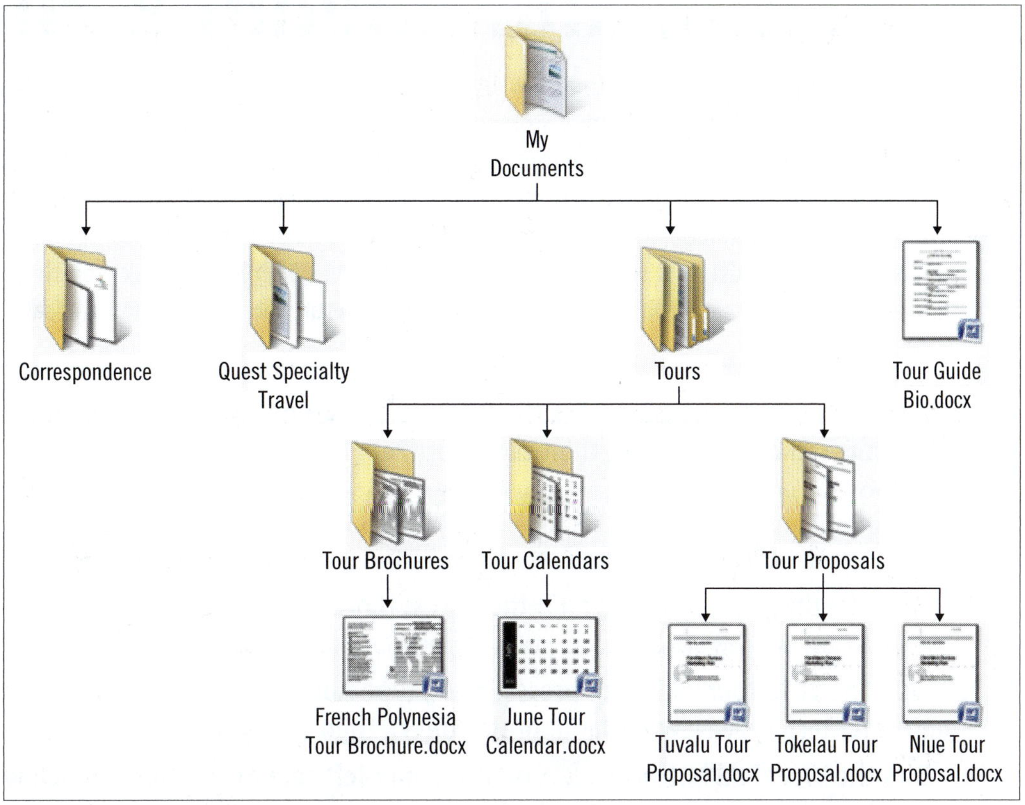

FIGURE B-2: Windows Explorer window

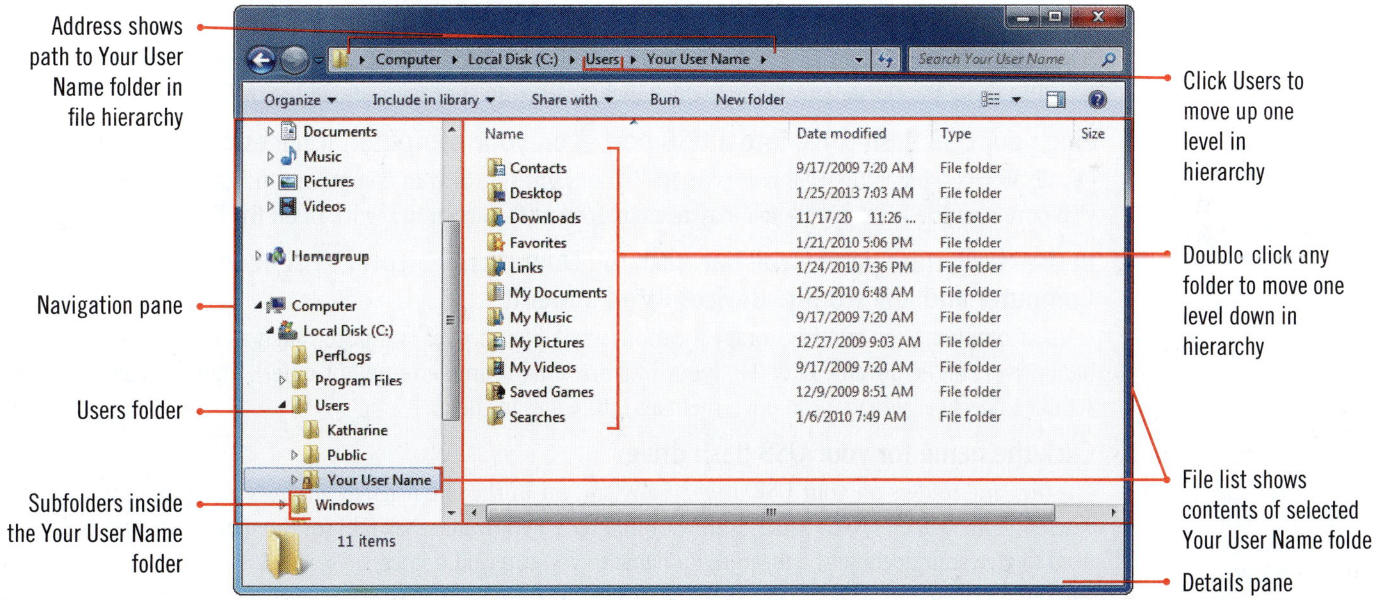

Plan your file organization

As you manage your files, you should plan how you want to organize them. First, identify the types of files you work with, such as images, music, and reports. Think about the content, such as personal, business, clients, or projects. Then think of a folder organization that will help you find them later. For example, use subfolders in the My Pictures folder to separate family photos from business photos or to group them by year. In the My Documents folder, you might group personal files in one subfolder and business files in another subfolder. Then create additional subfolders to further separate sets of files. You can always move files among folders and rename folders. You should periodically reevaluate your folder structure to make sure that it continues to meet your needs.

UNIT
B
Windows 7

Creating and Saving a File

After you start a program and create a new file, the file exists only in your computer's **random access memory (RAM)**, which is a temporary storage location. RAM only contains information when your computer is on. When you turn off your computer, it automatically clears the contents of RAM. So you need to save a new file onto a storage device that permanently stores the file so that you can open, change, and use it later. One important storage device is your computer's hard disk built into your computer. Another popular option is a **USB flash drive**, a small, portable storage device. Evelyn asks you to use the WordPad accessory program to create a short summary of an Oceania tour planning meeting and save it.

STEPS

1. **Start Windows if necessary, click the Start button on the taskbar, point to All Programs, click Accessories, then click WordPad**
   The WordPad program opens. Near the top of the screen you see the Ribbon containing command buttons, similar to those you used in Paint in Unit A. The Home tab appears in front. A new, blank document appears in the document window. The blinking insertion point shows you where the next character you type will appear.
2. **Type Meeting Notes, October 11, then press [Enter]**
   WordPad inserts a new blank line and places the insertion point at the beginning of the next line.

> **TROUBLE**
> If you make a typing mistake, press [Backspace] to delete the character to the left of the insertion point.

3. **Type The 2013 tour will visit:, press [Enter], type Australia, press [Enter], type Micronesia, press [Enter], type New Zealand, press [Enter], then type your name; see Figure B-3**
4. **Click the WordPad button on the upper-left side of the window below the title bar, then click Save on the WordPad menu**
   The first time you save a file using the Save button, the Save As dialog box opens. Use this dialog box to name the document file and choose a storage location for it. The Save As dialog box has many of the same elements as a Windows Explorer window, including an Address bar, a Navigation pane, and a File list. Below the Address bar, the **toolbar** contains command buttons you can click to perform actions. In the Address bar, you can see that WordPad chose the Documents library (which includes the My Documents folder) as the storage location.

> **TROUBLE**
> If you don't have a USB flash drive, save the document in the My Documents folder instead.

5. **Plug your USB flash drive into a USB port on your computer, if necessary**
   On a laptop computer, the USB port is on the left or right side of your computer. On a desktop computer, the USB port is on the front panel (you may need to open a small door to see it), or on the back panel.
6. **In the Navigation pane scroll bar, click the Down scroll arrow as needed to see Computer and any storage devices listed under it**
   Under Computer, you see the storage locations available on your computer, such as Local Disk (C:) (your hard drive) and Removable Disk (H:) (your USB drive name and letter might differ). These storage locations act like folders because you can open them and store files in them.
7. **Click the name for your USB flash drive**
   The files and folders on your USB drive, if any, appear in the File list. The Address bar shows the location where the file will be saved, which is now Computer > Removable Disk (H:) (or the name of your drive). You need to give your document a meaningful name so you can find it later.

> **TROUBLE**
> If your Save As dialog box or title bar does not show the .rtf file extension, open any Windows Explorer window, click Organize in the toolbar, click Folder and search options, click the View tab, then under Files and Folders, click to remove the check mark from Hide extensions for known file types.

8. **Click in the Filename text box to select the default name Document, type Oceania Meeting, compare your screen to Figure B-4, then click Save**
   The document is saved as a file on your USB flash drive. The filename Oceania Meeting.rtf appears in the title bar at the top of the window. The ".rtf" at the end of the filename is the file extension. A **file extension** is a three- or four-letter sequence, preceded by a period, that identifies the file as a particular type of document, in this case Rich Text Format, to your computer. The WordPad program creates files using the RTF format. Windows adds the .rtf file extension automatically after you click Save.
9. **Click the Close button on the WordPad window**
   The WordPad program closes. Your meeting minutes are now saved on your USB flash drive.

FIGURE B-3: Saving a document

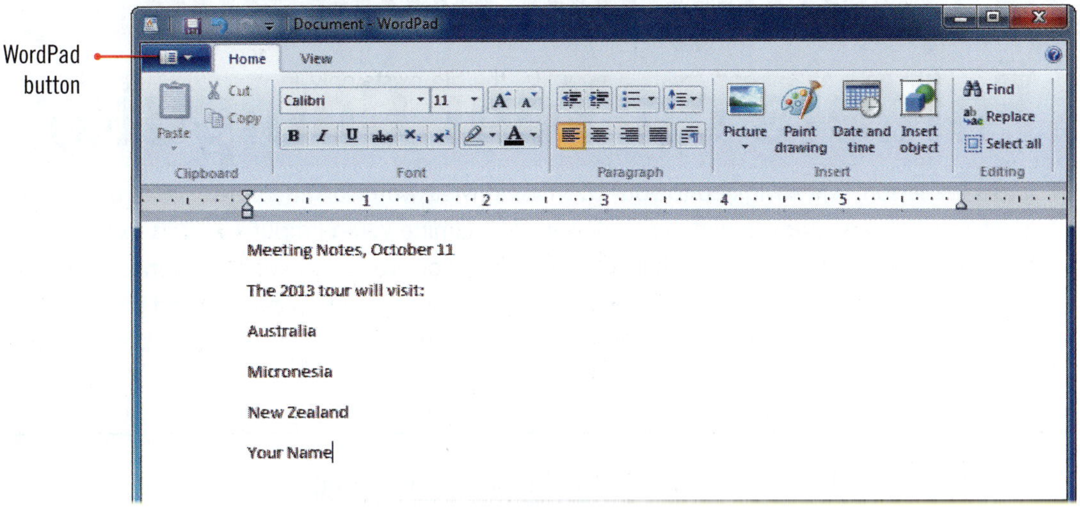

FIGURE B-4: Save As dialog box

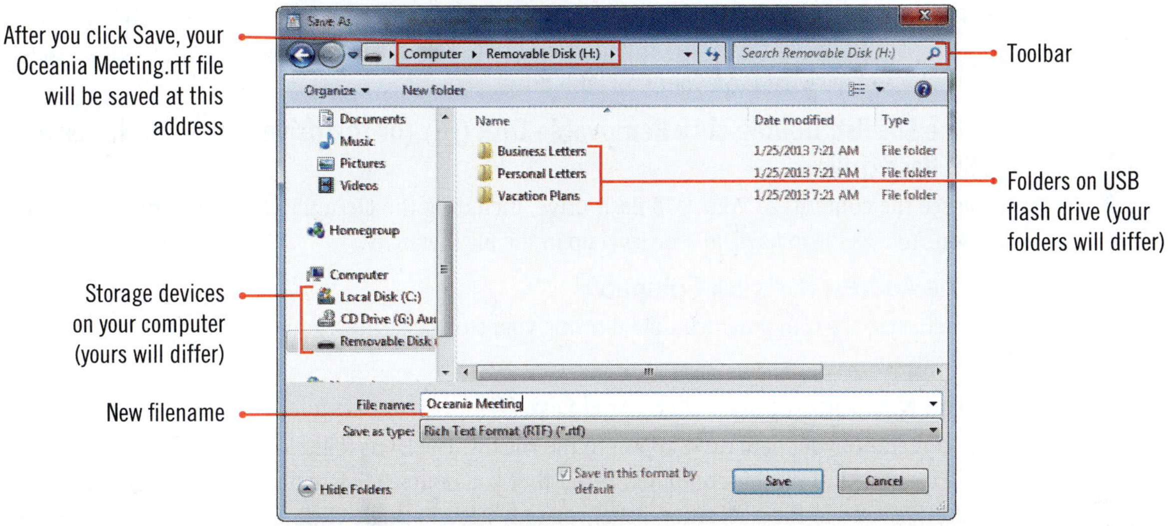

Using Windows 7 libraries

The Navigation pane contains not only files and folders, but also Libraries. A **library** gathers files and folders from different locations on your computer and displays them in one location. For example, you might have pictures in several different folders on your storage devices. You can add these folder locations to your Pictures library. Then when you want to see all your pictures, you open your Pictures library, instead of several different folders. The picture files stay in their original locations, but their names appear in the Pictures library. A library is not a folder that stores files, but rather a way of viewing similar types of documents that you have stored in multiple locations on your computer. Figure B-5 shows the four libraries that come with Windows 7: Documents, Music, Pictures, and Videos. To help you distinguish between library locations and actual folder locations, library names differ from actual folder names. For example, the My Documents folder is on your hard drive, but the library name is Documents. To add a location to a library, click the blue locations link (at the top of the File list) in the library you want to add to, click the Add button, navigate to the folder location you want to add, then click Include folder. If you delete a file or folder from a library, you delete them from their source locations. If you delete a library, you do not delete the files in it. The Documents Library that comes with Windows already has the My Documents folder listed as a save location. So if you save a document to the Documents library, it is automatically saved to your My Documents folder.

FIGURE B-5: Libraries

UNIT
B
Windows 7

Exploring the Files and Folders on Your Computer

In the last lesson, you navigated to your USB flash drive as you worked in the Save As dialog box. But even if you're not saving a document, you will want to examine your computer and its existing folder and file structure. That way, you'll know where to save files as you work with Windows application programs. In a Windows Explorer window, you can navigate through your computer contents using the File list, the Address bar, and the Navigation pane. As you prepare for the Oceania tours, you look at the files and folders on your computer.

STEPS

TROUBLE
If you don't see the colored bar, click the More Options list arrow on the menu bar, then click Tiles.

TROUBLE
If you do not have a USB flash drive, click the Documents library in the Navigation pane instead.

QUICK TIP
Click the Back button, to the left of the Address bar, to return to the window you last viewed. In the Address bar, click ▸ to the right of a folder name to see a list of the subfolders. If the folder is open, its name appears in bold.

1. **Click the Start button on the taskbar, then click Computer**
   Your computer's storage devices appear in a window, as shown in Figure B-6, including hard drives; devices with removable storage, such as CD and DVD drives or USB flash drives; and portable devices such as personal digital assistants (PDAs). Table B-1 lists examples of different drive types. A colored bar shows you how much space has been taken up on your hard drive. You decide to move down a level in your computer's hierarchy and see what is on your USB flash drive.
2. **In the File list, double-click Removable Disk (H:) (or the drive name and letter for your USB flash drive)**
   You see the contents of your USB flash drive, including the Oceania Meeting.rtf file you saved in the last lesson. You decide to navigate one level up in the file hierarchy.
3. **In the Address bar, click Computer**
   You return to the Computer window showing your storage devices. You decide to look at the contents of your hard drive.
4. **In the Navigation pane, click Local Disk (C:)**
   The contents of your hard drive appear in the File list. The Users folder contains a subfolder for each user who has a user account on this computer. Recall that you double-click items in the File list to open them. In the Address bar and in the Navigation pane, you only need to single-click.
5. **In the File list, double-click the Users folder**
   You see folders for each user registered on your computer. You might see a folder with your user account name on it. Each user's folder contains that person's documents. User folder names are the log-in names that were entered when your computer was set up. When a user logs in, the computer allows that user access to the folder with the same user name. If you are using a computer with more than one user, you might not have permission to view other users' folders. There is also a Public folder that any user can open.
6. **Double-click the folder with your user name on it**
   Depending on how your computer is set up, this folder might be labeled with your name; however, if you are using a computer in a lab or a public location, your folder might be called Student or Computer User or something similar. You see a list of folders, such as My Documents, My Music, and others. See Figure B-7.
7. **Double-click My Documents**
   You see the folders and documents you can open and work with. In the Address bar, the path to the My Documents folder is Computer ▸ Local Disk (C:) ▸ Users ▸ Your User Name ▸ My Documents. You decide to return to the Computer window.
8. **In the Navigation pane, click Computer**
   You moved up three levels in your hierarchy. You can also move one level up at a time in your file hierarchy by pressing the [Backspace] key on your keyboard. You once again see your computer's storage devices.

FIGURE B-6: Computer window showing storage devices

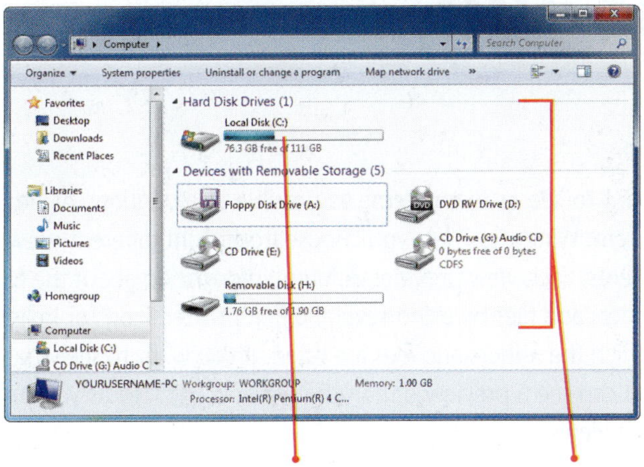

FIGURE B-7: Your User Name folder

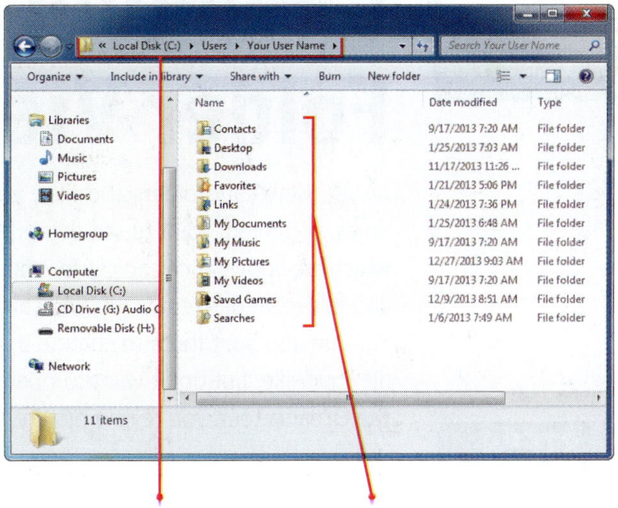

TABLE B-1: Drive names and icons

drive type	drive icon	drive name
hard drive		C:
CD drive		Next available drive letter, such as D:
DVD drive		Next available drive letter, such as E:
USB flash drive		Next available drive letter, such as F, G:, or H:

Sharing information with homegroups and libraries

Windows 7 lets you create a **homegroup**, a named set of computers that can share information. If your computer is in a homegroup with other Windows 7 computers, you can share libraries and printers with those computers. Click Start, then click Control Panel. Under Network and Internet, click Choose homegroup and sharing options. Click to place a check mark next to the libraries and printers you want to share, then click Save changes. To share libraries that you have created on your computer with others in your homegroup, click Start, click your user name, then in the Navigation pane, click the library you want to share, click Share with on the toolbar, then click the sharing option you want, as shown in Figure B-8.

FIGURE B-8: Sharing a library

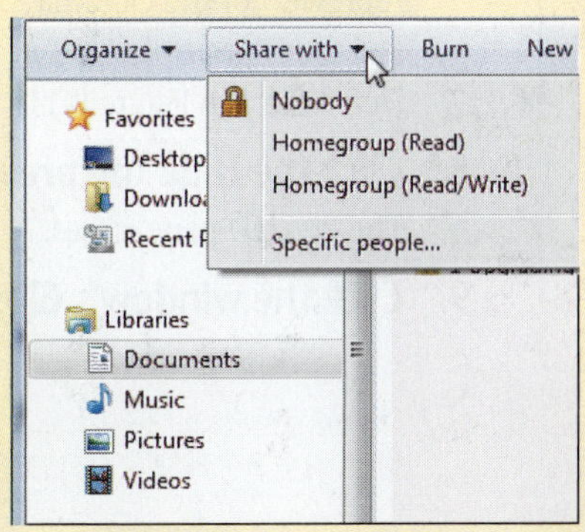

UNIT B
Windows 7

Changing File and Folder Views

As you view your folders and files, you might want to see as many items as possible in a window. At other times, you might want to see details about each item. Windows 7 lets you choose from eight different **views**, which are appearance choices for your folder contents. Each view provides different information about the files and folders in different ways. You can list your folders and files by using several different-sized icons or in lists. You can also **sort** them to change the order in which the folders and files are listed. If you want to see what a file looks like, but don't want to open the file, you can see a preview of it in the window. As you plan the Oceania tour, you review picture files in various views.

STEPS

1. **In the Navigation pane, under Libraries, click Pictures, then in the File list, double-click the Sample Pictures folder**
   You opened the Sample Pictures folder, which is inside your Pictures library.
2. **In the toolbar, click the More options list arrow next to the Change your view icon**
   The list of available views appears in a shortcut menu. See Figure B-9.
3. **Click Large Icons**
   In this view, the pictures appear as large-sized icons in the File list, as shown in Figure B-10. For image files, this view is very helpful. You can click any view name or you can drag a slider control to move through each of the available views.
4. **Click the Change your view More options list arrow again, point to the slider, then drag it so it's next to Details**
   As you drag, Live Preview shows you how each view looks in your folder. In Details view, you can see filenames, the date that files were created or modified, and other information. In Details view, you can also control the order in which the folders and files appear. In the Name column heading, you see a small triangle Name . This indicates that the sample pictures are in alphabetical order (A, B, C,...).
5. **Click the Name column heading**
   The items now appear in descending (Z, Y, X,...) order. The icon in the column header changes to Name .
6. **Click the Show the preview pane button in the toolbar**
   The Preview pane opens on the right side of the screen. The **Preview pane** is an area on the right side of a window that shows you what a selected file looks like without opening it. It is especially useful for document files so you can see the first few paragraphs of a large document.
7. **Click the name of your USB flash drive in the Navigation pane, then click the Oceania Meeting.rtf filename in the File list**
   A preview of the Oceania Meeting file you created earlier in this unit appears in the Preview pane. The WordPad file is not open, but you can still see its contents. The Details pane gives you information about the selected file. See Figure B-11.
8. **Click the Hide the preview pane button**
   The Preview pane closes.
9. **Click the window's Close button**

QUICK TIP
You can also click the Change your view button (not its list arrow) repeatedly to cycle through five of the eight views.

QUICK TIP
Click a column heading a second time to reverse the order.

QUICK TIP
The Navigation pane also contains Favorites, which are links to folders you use frequently. To add a folder to your Favorites list, open the folder in the File list. Right-click the Favorites link in the Navigation pane, then left-click Add current location to Favorites.

FIGURE B-9: More options shortcut menu showing views

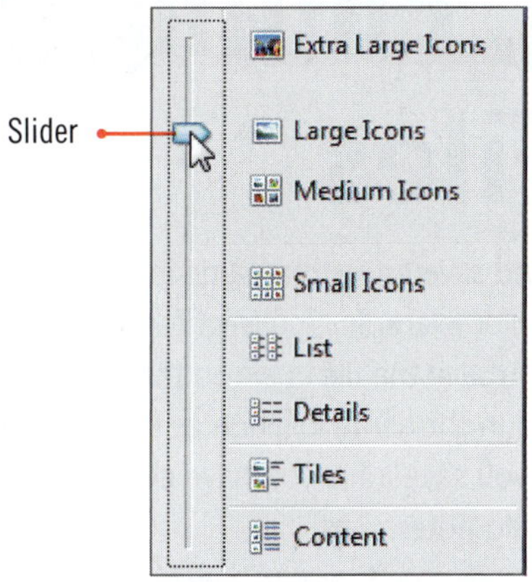

FIGURE B-10: Sample pictures library as large icons

FIGURE B-11: Preview of selected Oceania Meeting.rtf file

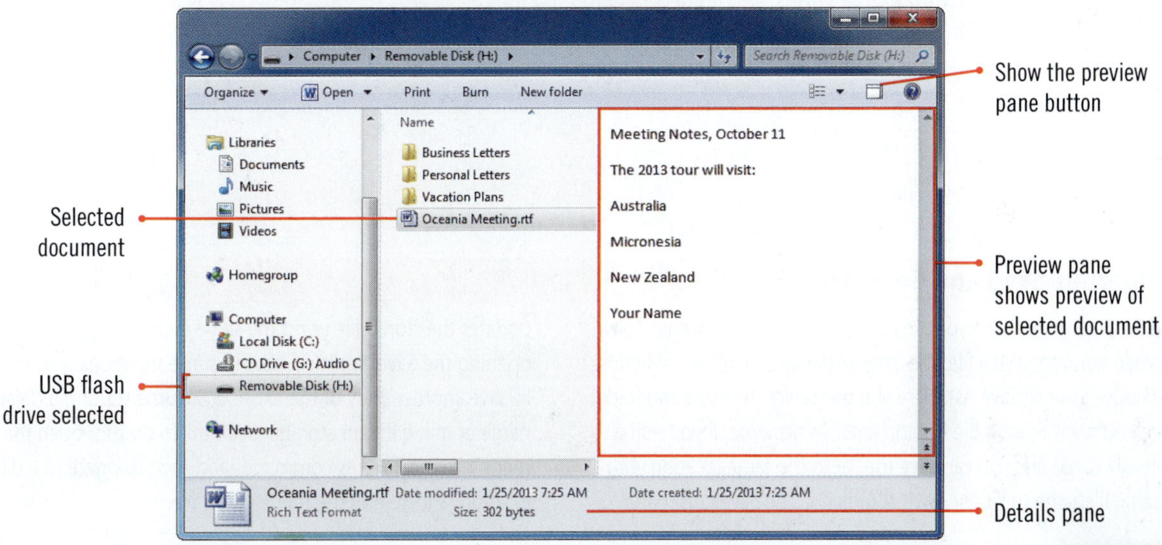

UNIT
B
Windows 7

Opening, Editing, and Saving Files

Once you have created a file and saved it with a name in a folder on a storage device, you can easily open it and **edit** (make changes to) it. For example, you might want to add or delete text to a document, or change the color in a drawing. Then you save the file again so that it contains your latest changes. Usually you save a file with the same filename and in the same location as the original, which replaces the existing file with the latest, updated version. When you save a file you have changed, you use the Save command. Evelyn asks you to complete the meeting notes.

STEPS

1. **Click the Start button on the taskbar, point to All Programs, click the Accessories folder, then click WordPad**

   If you use WordPad frequently, it's name might appear on the left side of the Start menu. If it does, you can click it there to open it.

2. **Click the WordPad button, then click Open**

   The Open dialog box opens. It has the same sections as the Save As dialog box and the Windows Explorer windows you used earlier in this unit. You decide to navigate to the location where you saved your Oceania Meeting.rtf file so you can open it.

TROUBLE

If you are not using a USB flash drive, click an appropriate storage location in the Navigation pane.

3. **Scroll down in the Navigation pane if necessary until you see Computer, then click Removable Disk (H:) (or the drive name and letter for your USB flash drive)**

   The contents of your USB flash drive appear in the File list, as shown in Figure B-12.

QUICK TIP

You can also double-click the filename in the File list to open the file.

4. **Click Oceania Meeting.rtf in the File list, then click Open**

   The document you created earlier opens.

5. **Click to the right of the "d" in New Zealand, press [Enter], then type Evelyn Swazey closed the meeting.**

   The edited document includes the text you just typed. See Figure B-13.

QUICK TIP

Instead of using the WordPad menu and Save command to save a document, you can also click the Save button in the Quick Access toolbar at the top of the WordPad window.

6. **Click the WordPad button, then click Save, as shown in Figure B-14**

   WordPad saves the document with your most recent changes, using the filename and location you specified when you saved it for the first time. When you save an existing file, the Save As dialog box does not open.

7. **Click , then click Exit**

Comparing Save and Save As

The WordPad menu has two save command options—Save and Save As. When you first save a file, the Save As dialog box opens (whether you choose Save or Save As). Here you can select the drive and folder where you want to save the file and enter its filename. If you edit a previously saved file, you can save the file to the same location with the same filename using the Save command. The Save command updates the stored file using the same location and filename without opening the Save As dialog box. In some situations, you might want to save another copy of the existing document using a different filename or in a different storage location. To do this, open the document, use the Save As command, and then navigate to a different location, and/or edit the name of the file.

FIGURE B-12: Navigating in the Open dialog box

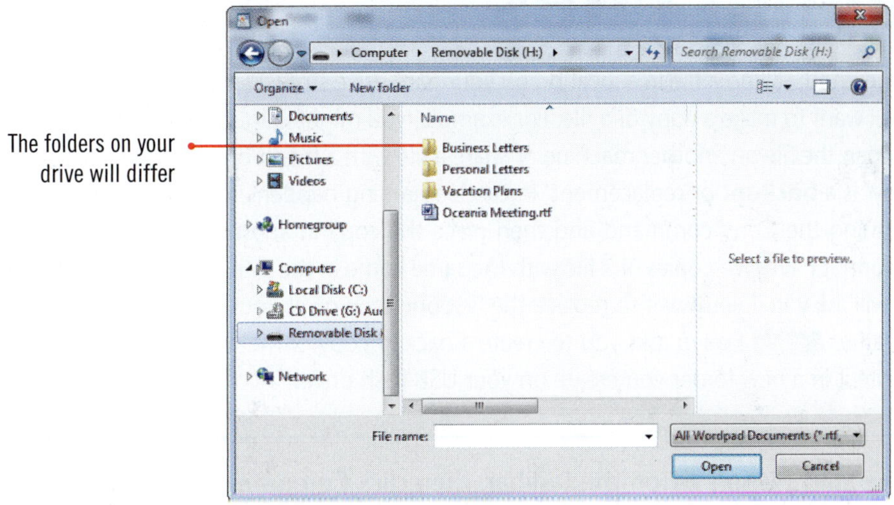

FIGURE B-13: Edited document

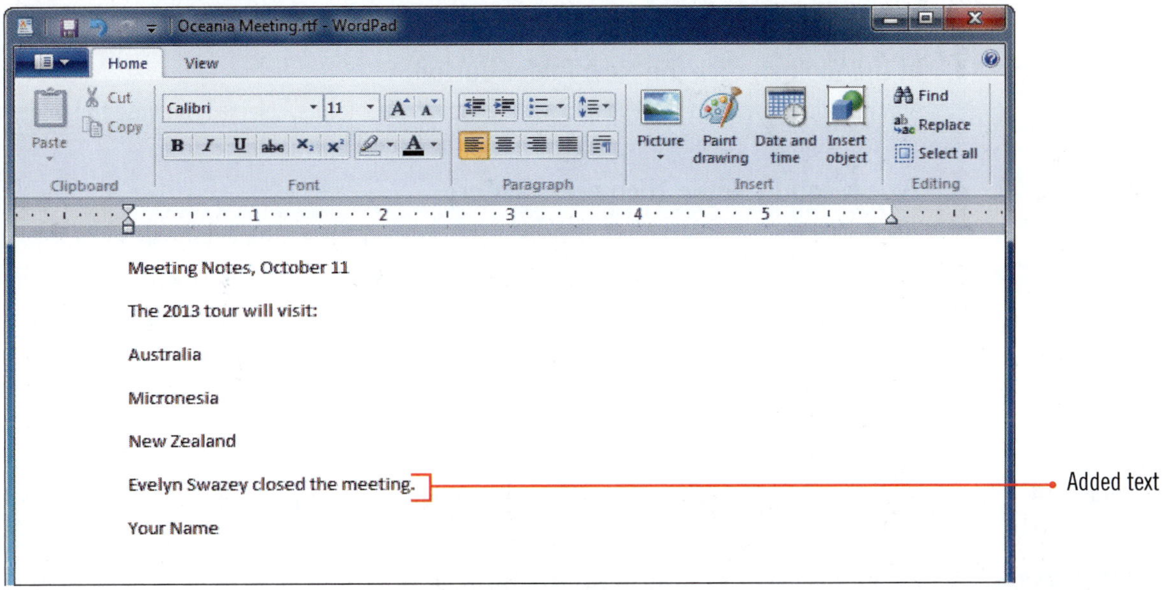

FIGURE B-14: Saving a revised document

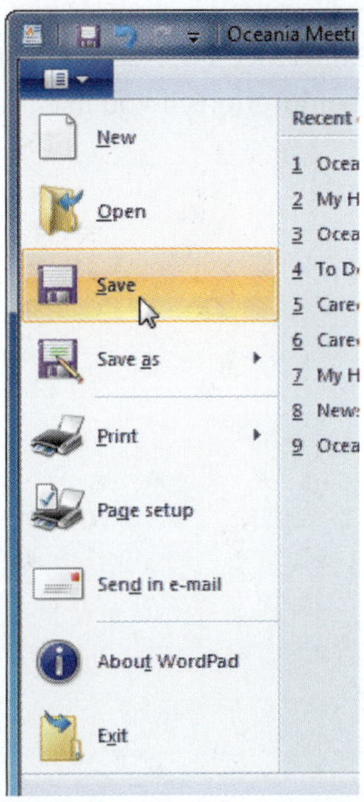

UNIT
B
Windows 7

Copying Files

As you have learned, saving a file in a location on your hard drive stores it so you can open it later. But sometimes you will want to make a copy of a file. For example, you might want to put a copy on a USB flash drive so you can open the file on another machine or share a file with a friend or colleague. Or you might want to create a copy as a **backup**, or replacement, in case something happens to your original file. You copy files and folders using the Copy command and then place the copy in another location using the Paste command. You cannot have two copies of a file with the same name in the same folder. If you attempt to do this, Windows 7 will ask you if you want to replace the first one then gives you a chance to give the second copy a different name. Evelyn asks you to create a backup copy of the meeting notes document you created and paste it in a new folder you create on your USB flash drive.

STEPS

1. **Click the Start button on the taskbar, then click Computer**
2. **In the File list, double-click Removable Disk (H:) (or the drive name and letter for your USB flash drive)**

   First you create the new folder Evelyn needs.
3. **In the toolbar, click the New folder button**

   A new folder appears in the File list, with its name, New folder, selected. Because the folder name is selected, any text you type replaces the selected text as the folder name.
4. **Type Meeting Notes, then press [Enter]**

   You named the new folder Meeting Notes. Next, you copy your original Oceania Meeting.rtf file.
5. **In the File list, click the Oceania Meeting.rtf document you saved earlier, click the Organize button on the toolbar, then click Copy, as shown in Figure B-15**

   When you use the Copy command, Windows 7 places a duplicate copy of the file in an area of your computer's random access memory called the **clipboard**, ready to paste, or place, in a new location. Copying and pasting a file leaves the file in its original location. The copied file remains on the clipboard until you copy something else or end your Windows 7 session.
6. **In the File list, double-click the Meeting Notes folder**

   The folder opens.
7. **Click the Organize button on the toolbar, then click Paste**

   A copy of your Oceania Meeting.rtf file is pasted into your new Meeting Notes folder. See Figure B-16. You now have two copies of the Oceania Meeting.rtf file: one on your USB flash drive in the main folder, and a copy of the file in a folder called Meeting Notes on your USB flash drive. The file remains on the clipboard so you can paste it again to other locations if you like.

QUICK TIP
You can also copy a file by right-clicking the file in the File list and then clicking Copy. To use the keyboard, press and hold [Ctrl] and press [C], then release both keys.

QUICK TIP
To paste using the keyboard, press and hold [Ctrl] and press [V], then release both keys.

FIGURE B-15: Copying a file

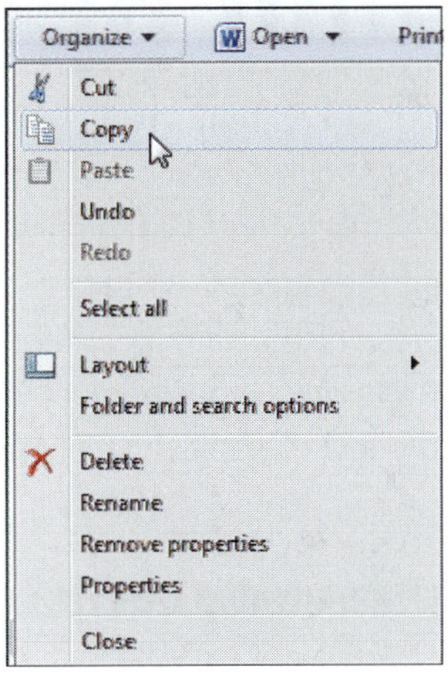

FIGURE B-16: Duplicate file pasted into Meeting Notes folder

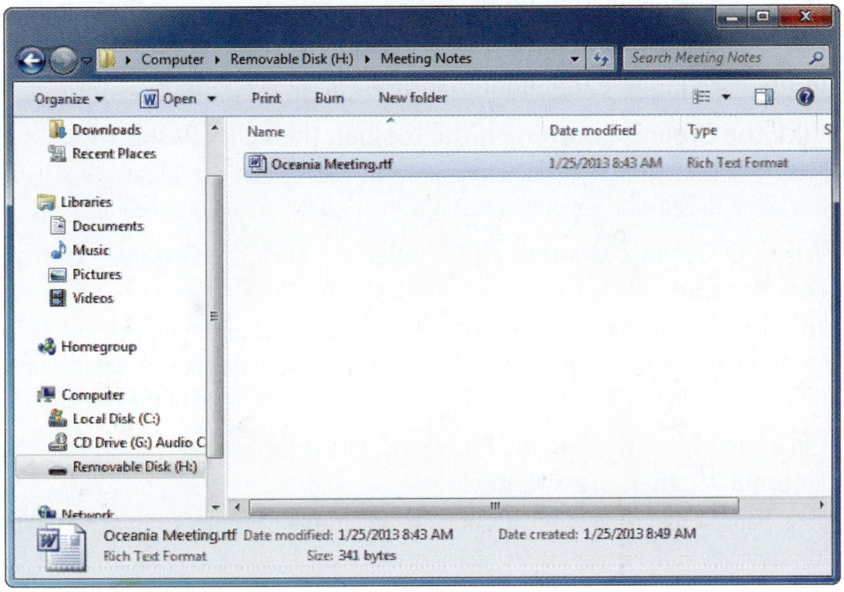

Copying files using Send to

You can also copy and paste a file to an external storage device using the Send to command. In a window, right-click the file you want to copy, point to Send to, then in the shortcut menu, click the name of the device where you want to send a copy of the file. This leaves the original file on your hard drive and creates a copy on the external device, all with just one command. See Table B-2 for a short summary of other shortcut menu commands.

TABLE B-2: Selected Send to menu commands

menu option	use to	menu option	use to
Compressed (zipped) folder	Create a new compressed (smaller) file with a .zip file extension	Documents	Copy the file to the Documents library
Desktop (create shortcut)	Create a shortcut (link) for the file on the desktop	DVD RW Drive (D:)	Copy the file to your computer's DVD drive
Mail recipient	Create an e-mail with the file attached to it (only if you have an e-mail program on your computer)	Removable Disk (H:)	Copy the file to your removable disk (H:)

UNIT
B
Windows 7

Moving and Renaming Files

As you work with files, you might need to move files or folders to another location. You can move one or more files or folders. You might move them to a different folder on the same drive or a different drive. When you **move** a file, the file is transferred to the new location and no longer exists in its original location. You can move a file using the Cut and Paste commands. After you create a file, you might find that the original name you gave the file isn't clear anymore, so you can rename it to make it more descriptive or accurate. You decide to move your original Oceania Meeting.rtf document to your Documents library. After you move it, you decide to edit the filename so it better describes the file contents.

STEPS

QUICK TIP
You can also cut a file by right-clicking the file in the File list and then clicking Cut. To use the keyboard, press and hold [Ctrl] and press [X], then release both keys.

QUICK TIP
You can also paste a file by right-clicking an empty area in the File list and then clicking Paste. To use the keyboard, press and hold [Ctrl] and press [V], then release both keys.

1. **In the Address bar, click Removable Disk (H:) (or the drive name and letter for your USB flash drive)**
2. **Click the Oceania Meeting.rtf document to select it**
3. **Click the Organize button on the toolbar, then click Cut**
   The icon representing the cut file becomes lighter in color, indicating you have cut it, as shown in Figure B-17. You navigate to your Documents library, in preparation for pasting the cut document there.
4. **In the Navigation Pane, under Libraries, click Documents**
5. **Click the Organize button on the toolbar, then click Paste**
   The Oceania Meeting.rtf document appears in your Documents library. See Figure B-18. The filename could be clearer, to help you remember that it contains notes from your meeting.
6. **With the Oceania Meeting.rtf file selected, click the Organize button on the toolbar, then click Rename**
   The filename is highlighted. In a window, the file extension cannot change because it identifies the file to WordPad. If you delete the file extension, the file cannot be opened. You could type a new name to replace the old one, but you decide to add the word "Notes" to the end of the filename instead.
7. **Click the I after the "g" in "Meeting", press [Spacebar], then type Notes, as shown in Figure B-19, then press [Enter]**
   You changed the name of the document copy in the Documents library. The filename now reads Oceania Meeting Notes.rtf.
8. **Close the window**

FIGURE B-17: Cutting a file

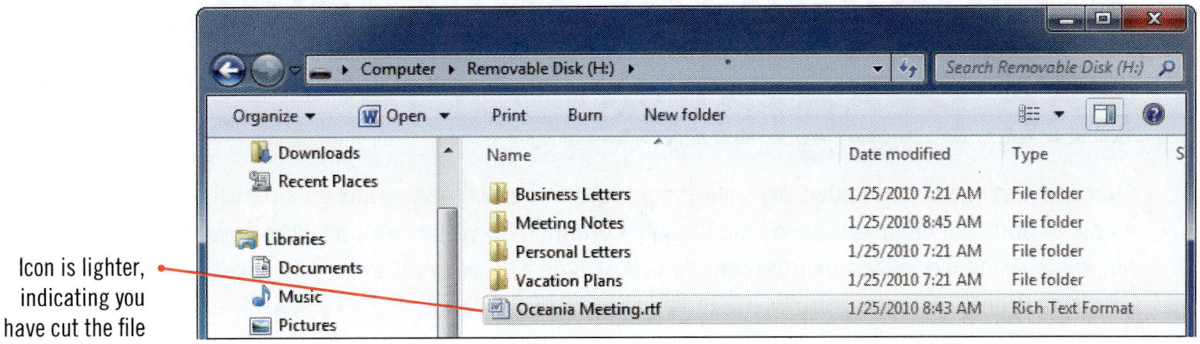

FIGURE B-18: Pasted file in Documents library

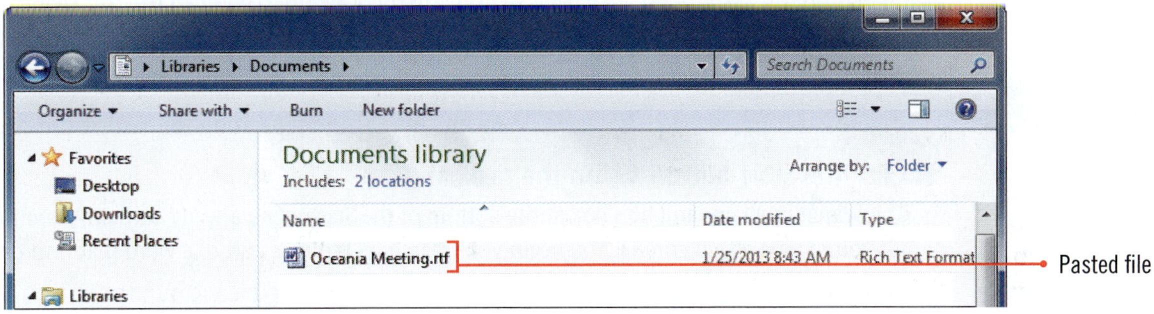

FIGURE B-19: Renaming a file

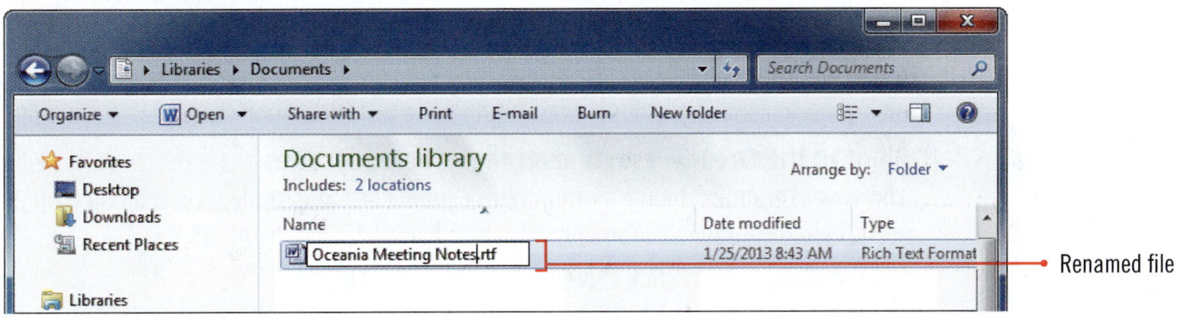

Using drag and drop to copy or move files to new locations

You can also use the mouse to copy a file and place the copy in a new location. **Drag and drop** is a technique in which you use your pointing device to drag a file or folder into a different folder and then drop it, or let go of the mouse button, to place it in that folder. Using drag and drop does not copy your file to the clipboard. If you drag and drop a file to a folder on another drive, Windows *copies* the file. See Figure B-20. However, if you drag and drop a file to a folder on the same drive, Windows 7 *moves* the file into that folder instead. If you want to move a file to another drive, hold down [Shift] while you drag and drop. If you want to copy a file to another folder on the same drive, hold down [Ctrl] while you drag and drop.

FIGURE B-20: Copying a file using drag and drop

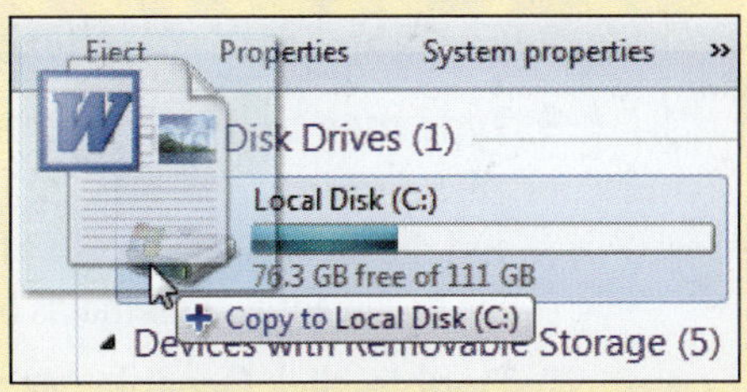

UNIT B
Windows 7

Searching for Files, Folders, and Programs

After copying or moving folders and files, you might forget where you stored a particular folder or file, its name, or both. Or you might need help finding a program on your computer. **Windows Search** helps you quickly find any file, folder, or program. You must type one or more letter sequences or words that help Windows 7 identify the item you want. The search text you type is called your **search criteria**. Your search criteria can be a filename, part of a filename, or any other characters you choose. Windows 7 will find files with that information in its name or with that information inside the file. For example, if you type "word," Windows 7 will find the program Microsoft Word, any documents with "word" in its title, or any document with "word" inside the file. To search your entire computer, including its attached drives, you can use the Search box on the Start menu. To search within a particular folder, you can use the Search box in a Windows Explorer window. You want to locate the copy of the Oceania Meeting Notes.rtf document so you can print it for a colleague.

STEPS

QUICK TIP
Search text is not case sensitive. Typing lowercase "mee", you will still find items that start with "Mee" or "mee".

TROUBLE
Your file might open in another program on your computer that reads RTF files. You can continue with the lesson.

TROUBLE
If you do not have a USB flash drive, click another storage location in the Navigation pane.

1. **Click the Start button on the taskbar**
   The Search programs and files box at the bottom of the Start menu already contains the insertion point, ready for you to type search criteria. You begin your search by typing a part of a word that is in the filename.
2. **Type me**
   Even before you finish typing the word "meeting", the Start menu lists all programs, files, and Control Panel items that have the letters "me" in their title or somewhere inside the file or the file properties. See Figure B-21. Your search results will differ, depending on the programs and files on your computer. **File properties** are details that Windows stores about a file. Windows arranges the search results into categories.
3. **Type e**
   The search results narrow to only the files that contain "mee". The search results become more specific every time you add more text to your criteria finding the two versions of your meeting notes file. See Figure B-22.
4. **Point to the Oceania Meeting.rtf filename under Files**
   The ScreenTip shows the file location. This Oceania Meeting.rtf file is on the USB flash drive. The filenames are links to the document. You only need to single-click a file to open it.
5. **Under Documents, click Oceania Meeting Notes.rtf**
   The file opens in WordPad.
6. **Click the Close button in the program window's title bar**
   You can search in a folder or on a drive using the search box in any Windows Explorer window.
7. **Click , click Computer, in the Navigation pane click Removable Disk (H:) (or the drive name and letter for your USB flash drive)**
8. **Click the Search Removable Disk (H:) text box, to the right of the Address bar**
9. **Type mee to list all files and folders on your USB flash drive that contain "mee"**
   The search criterion, mee, is highlighted in the filenames. The results include the folder called Meeting Notes and the file named Oceania Meeting.rtf. Because you navigated to your USB flash drive, Windows only lists the document version that is on that drive. See Figure B-23.
10. **Double-click Oceania Meeting.rtf in the File list to open the document file in WordPad, view the file, close WordPad, then close the Windows Explorer window**

FIGURE B-21: Searching on criterion "me"

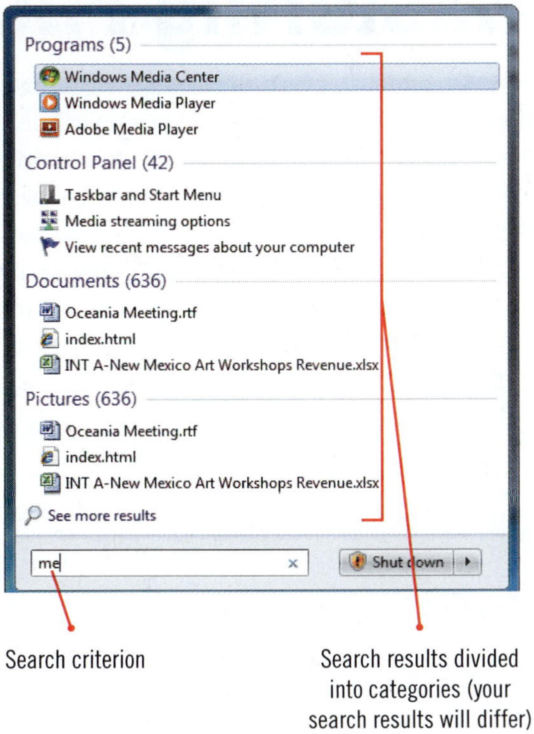

FIGURE B-22: Searching on criterion "mee"

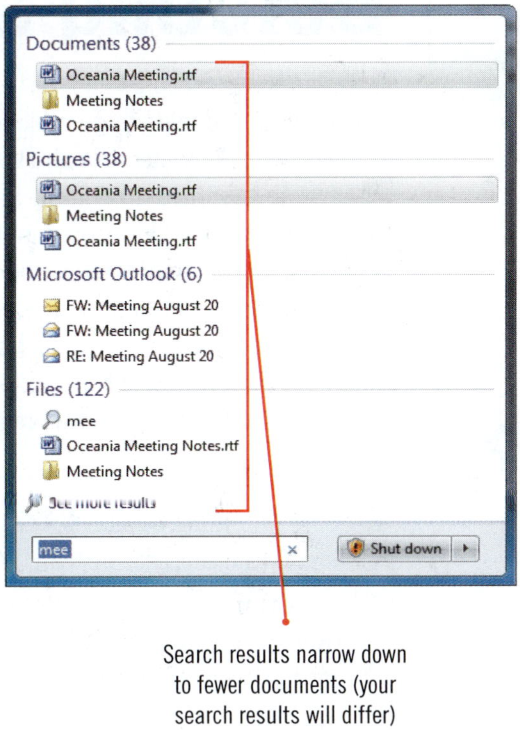

FIGURE B-23: Searching using the Search Computer text box in folder window

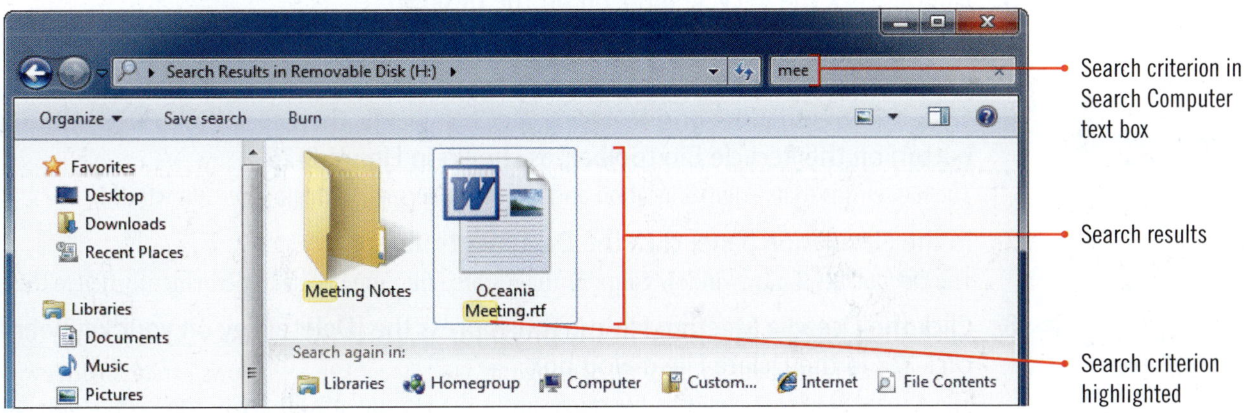

Performing more advanced searches

To locate all files that have the same file extension (such as .rtf), type the file extension as your search criterion. If you want to locate files created by a certain person, use the first name, last name, or first and last name as your search criteria. If you want to locate files created on a certain date, type the date (for example, 7/9/2012) as your search criterion. If you remember the title in a document, type the title as your search criterion. If you have created e-mail contacts in your Contacts folder, you can type the person's name to find his or her e-mail address.

UNIT B
Windows 7

Deleting and Restoring Files

If you no longer need a folder or file, you can delete (or remove) it from the storage device. By regularly deleting files and folders you no longer need and emptying the Recycle Bin, you free up valuable storage space on your computer. This also keeps your computer uncluttered. Windows 7 places folders and files you delete from your hard drive in the Recycle Bin. If you delete a folder, Windows 7 removes the folder as well as all files and subfolders stored in it. If you later discover that you need a deleted file or folder, you can restore it to its original location, but only if you have not yet emptied the Recycle Bin. Emptying the Recycle Bin permanently removes the deleted folders and files from your computer. However, files and folders you delete from a removable drive, such as a USB flash drive, do not go to the Recycle Bin. They are immediately and permanently deleted and cannot be restored. You delete the meeting notes copy saved in the Documents library and then restore it.

STEPS

1. **Click the Start button on the taskbar, then click Documents**
   Your Documents library opens.
2. **Click Oceania Meeting Notes.rtf to select it, click the Organize button on the toolbar, then click Delete**
   The Delete File dialog box opens so you can confirm the deletion, as shown in Figure B-24.
3. **Click Yes**
   You deleted the file from the Documents library. Windows moved it into the Recycle Bin.
4. **Click the Minimize button on the window's title bar and examine the Recycle Bin icon**
   The Recycle Bin icon appears to contain crumpled paper. This tells you that the Recycle Bin contains deleted folders and files.
5. **Double-click the Recycle Bin icon on the desktop**
   The Recycle Bin window opens and displays any previously deleted folders and files, including the Oceania Meeting Notes.rtf file.
6. **Click the Oceania Meeting Notes.rtf file to select it, then click the Restore this item button on the Recycle Bin toolbar, as shown in Figure B-25**
   The file returns to its original location and no longer appears in the Recycle Bin window.
7. **In the Navigation pane, click the Documents library**
   The Documents library window contains the restored file. You decide to permanently delete this file.
8. **Click the Oceania Meeting Notes.rtf file, press the [Delete] key on your keyboard, then click Yes in the Delete File dialog box**
   The Oceania Meeting Notes.rtf file moves from the Documents library to the Recycle Bin. You decide to permanently delete all documents in the Recycle Bin.
   NOTE: If you are using a computer that belongs to someone else, or that is in a computer lab, make sure you have permission to empty the Recycle Bin before proceeding with the next step.
9. **Minimize the window, double-click the Recycle Bin, click the Empty the Recycle Bin button on the toolbar, click Yes in the dialog box, then close all open windows**

QUICK TIP
If the Recycle Bin icon does not contain crumpled paper, then it is empty.

QUICK TIP
To delete a file completely in one action, click the file to select it, press and hold [Shift], then press [Delete]. A message will ask if you want to permanently delete the file. If you click Yes, Windows deletes the file without sending it to the Recycle Bin. Use caution, however, because you cannot restore the file.

FIGURE B-24: Delete File dialog box

FIGURE B-25: Restoring a file from the Recycle Bin

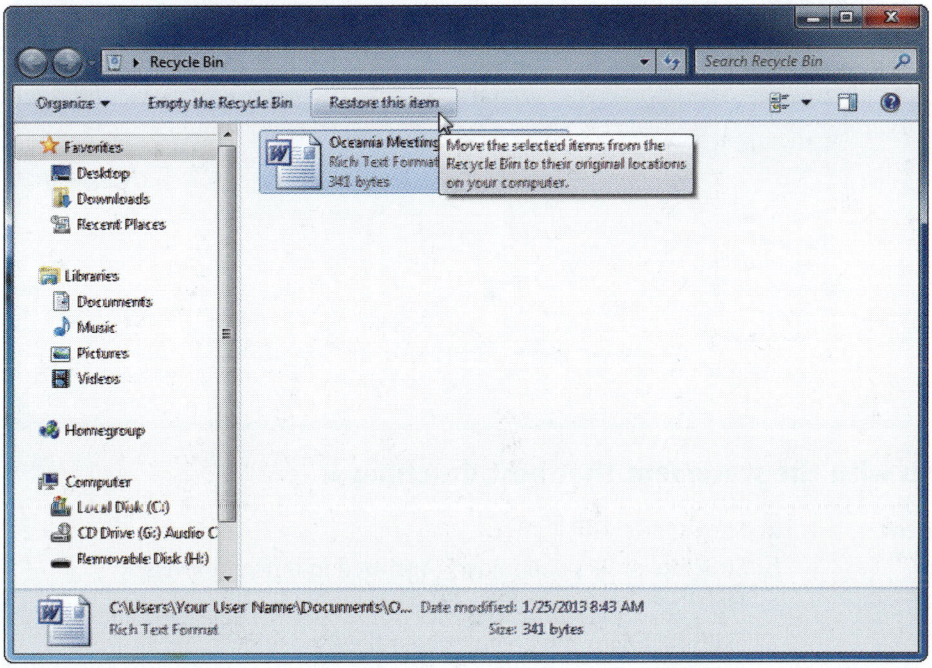

Selecting more than one file

You might want to select a group of files or folders in order to cut, copy, or delete them all at once. To select a group of items that are next to each other in a window, click the first item in the group, press and hold [Shift], then click the last item in the group. Both items you click and all the items between them become selected. To select files that are not next to each other, click the first file, press and hold [Ctrl], then click the other items you want to select as a group. Then you can copy, cut, or delete the group of files or folders you selected.

Practice

Concepts Review

For current SAM information, including versions and content details, visit SAM Central (http://samcentral.course.com). If you have a SAM user profile, you may have access to hands-on instruction, practice, and assessment of the skills covered in this unit. Since various versions of SAM are supported throughout the life of this text, check with your instructor for the correct instructions and URL/Web site for accessing assignments.

Label the elements of the Windows 7 window shown in Figure B-26.

FIGURE B-26

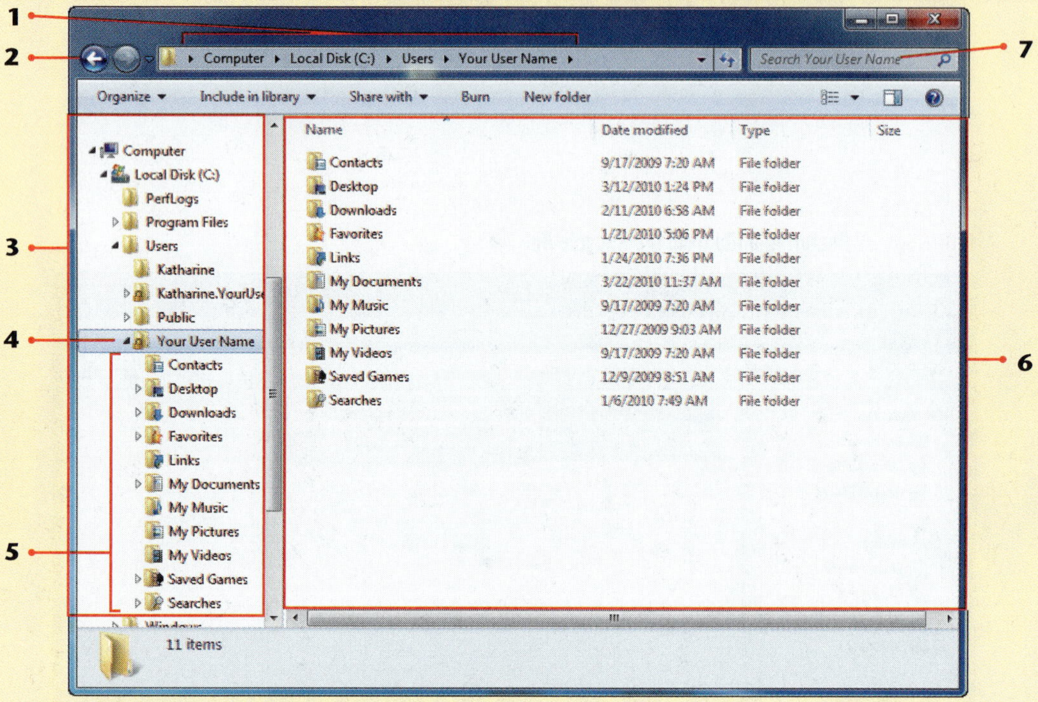

Match each term with the statement that best describes it.

8. File management	**a.** Shows file's path
9. File extension	**b.** Structure of files and folders organized in different levels
10. Address bar	**c.** Describes a file's location in the file hierarchy
11. Path	**d.** Skills that help you organize your files and folders
12. Library	**e.** Contains buttons in a Windows Explorer window
13. Toolbar	**f.** A three- or four-letter sequence, preceded by a period, that identifies the type of file
14. File hierarchy	**g.** Gathers files and folders from different computer locations

Select the best answer from the list of choices.

15. The way your files appear in the Details window is determined by the:

a. Path.
b. View.
c. Subfolder.
d. Criterion.

16. When you move a file:

a. It remains in its original location.
b. It is no longer in its original location.
c. It is copied to another location.
d. It is no longer in your file hierarchy.

17. The text you type in the Search programs and files box on the Start menu is called:

a. Search criteria.
b. RAM.
c. Sorting.
d. Clipboard.

18. Which of the following is not a window section?

a. Address bar
b. File list
c. Navigation pane
d. Clipboard

19. Which part of a window lets you see a file's contents without opening the file?

a. File list
b. Preview pane
c. Navigation pane
d. Address bar

20. In a file hierarchy, a folder inside another folder is called a:

a. Subfolder.
b. Internal hard disk.
c. Clipboard.
d. Path.

21. After you delete a file from your hard disk, it is automatically placed in the:

a. USB flash drive.
b. Clipboard.
c. Recycle bin.
d. Search box.

22. When you copy a file, it is automatically placed on the:

a. Preview pane.
b. My Documents folder.
c. Hierarchy.
d. Clipboard.

Skills Review

1. Understand folders and files.

a. Assume that you sell books as a home business. How would you organize your folders and files using a file hierarchy? How would you use folders and subfolders? Draw a diagram and write a short paragraph explaining your answer.

2. Create and save a file.

a. Connect your USB flash drive to a USB port on your computer, then open WordPad from the All Programs menu.
b. Type **Marketing Plan: Oceania Tours** as the title, then start a new line.
c. Type your name, then press [Enter] twice.
d. Create the following list:

Brochures
Direct e-mail
Web ads
Travel conventions

e. Save the WordPad file with the filename **Oceania Marketing Plan.rtf** on your USB flash drive.
f. View the filename in the WordPad title bar, then close WordPad.

3. Explore the files and folders on your computer.

a. Open a Windows Explorer window that shows the contents of your computer.
b. Use the File list to navigate to your USB flash drive. (If you do not have a USB flash drive, navigate to your Documents library using the Navigation pane.)
c. Use the Address bar to navigate to Computer again.
d. Use the Navigation pane to navigate to your hard drive.
e. Use the File list to open the Users folder, and then open the folder that represents your user name.
f. Open the My Documents folder. (*Hint*: The path is Local Disk (C:) ▸ Users ▸ [Your User Name] ▸ My Documents.)
g. Use the Navigation pane to navigate back to your computer contents.

4. Change file and folder views.

a. Navigate to your USB flash drive using the method of your choice.
b. View its contents as large icons.
c. Use the View slider to view the drive contents in all the other seven views.
d. Use the Change your view button to cycle through the five available views.
e. Open the Preview pane, then click a file and view its preview. Repeat with two more files.
f. Close the Preview pane.

Skills Review (continued)

5. **Open, edit, and save files.**
   a. Open WordPad.
   b. Use the Open dialog box to open the Oceania Marketing Plan.rtf document you created.
   c. After the text "Travel conventions," add a line with the text **Canadian magazines**.
   d. Save the document and close WordPad.
6. **Copy files.**
   a. In the Windows Explorer window, navigate to your USB flash drive if necessary.
   b. Copy the Oceania Marketing Plan.rtf document.
   c. Create a new folder named **Marketing** on your USB flash drive, then open the folder. (If you don't have a USB flash drive, create the folder in your Documents library.)
   d. Paste the document copy in the new folder.
7. **Move and rename files.**
   a. Navigate to your USB flash drive.
   b. Select the original Oceania Marketing Plan.rtf document, then cut it.
   c. Navigate to your Documents library and paste the file there.
   d. Rename the file **Oceania Marketing Plan - Backup.rtf**.
8. **Search for files, folders, and programs.**
   a. Use the Search programs and files box on the Start menu to enter the search criterion **ma**.
   b. Change your search criterion so it reads **mar**.
   c. Open the backup copy of your Oceania Marketing Plan document from the Start menu, then close WordPad.
   d. In Windows Explorer, navigate to your Documents library, then use the criterion **mar** in the Search Documents box.
   e. Open the backup copy of the Oceania Marketing Plan document from the File list, then close WordPad.
9. **Delete and restore files.**
   a. Navigate to your Documents library if necessary.
   b. Delete the Oceania Marketing Plan - Backup.rtf file.
   c. Open the Recycle Bin, and restore the document to its original location, navigate to your Documents library, then move the Oceania Marketing Plan - Backup file to your USB flash drive.

Independent Challenge 1

To meet the needs of pet owners in your town, you have opened a pet-sitting business named PetCare. Customers hire you to care for their pets in their own homes when the pet owners go on vacation. To promote your new business, you want to develop a newspaper ad and a flyer.

a. Connect your USB flash drive to your computer, if necessary.
b. Create a new folder named **PetCare** on your USB flash drive.
c. In the PetCare folder, create two subfolders named **Advertising** and **Flyers**.
d. Use WordPad to create a short ad for your local newspaper that describes your business:
   - Use the name of the business as the title for your document.
   - Write a short paragraph about the business. Include a fictitious location, street address, and phone number.
   - After the paragraph, type your name.
e. Save the WordPad document with the filename **Newspaper Ad** in the Advertising folder, then close the document and exit WordPad.
f. Open a Windows Explorer window, and navigate to the Advertising folder.
g. View the contents in at least three different views, then choose the view option that you prefer.
h. Copy the Newspaper Ad.rtf file, and paste a copy in the Flyers folder.
i. Rename the copy **Newspaper Ad Backup.rtf**.
j. Close the folder.

Independent Challenge 2

As a freelance editor for several national publishers, you depend on your computer to meet critical deadlines. Whenever you encounter a computer problem, you contact a computer consultant who helps you resolve the problem. This consultant asked you to document, or keep records of, your computer's current settings.

a. Connect your USB flash drive to your computer, if necessary.
b. Open the Computer window so that you can view information on your drives and other installed hardware.
c. View the window contents using three different views, then choose the one you prefer.
d. Open WordPad and create a document with the title **My Hardware Documentation** and your name on separate lines.
e. List the names of the hard drive (or drives), devices with removable storage, and any other hardware devices, installed on the computer you are using. Also include the total size and amount of free space on your hard drive(s) and removable storage drive(s). (*Hint*: If you need to check the Computer window for this information, use the taskbar button for the Computer window to view your drives, then use the WordPad taskbar button to return to WordPad.)

Advanced Challenge Exercise

- Navigate your computer's file hierarchy, and determine its various levels.
- On paper, draw a diagram showing your file hierarchy, starting with Computer at the top, and going down at least four levels if available.

f. Save the WordPad document with the filename **My Hardware Documentation** on your USB flash drive.
g. Preview your document, print your WordPad document, then close WordPad.

Independent Challenge 3

You are an attorney at Lopez, Rickland, and Willgor, a large law firm. You participate in your firm's community outreach program by speaking at career days in area high schools. You teach students about career opportunities available in the field of law. You want to create a folder structure on your USB flash drive to store the files for each session.

a. Connect your USB flash drive to your computer, then open the window for your USB flash drive.
b. Create a folder named **Career Days**.
c. In the Career Days folder, create a subfolder named **Mather High**.

Advanced Challenge Exercise

- In the Mather High folder, create subfolders named **Class Outline** and **Visual Aids**.
- Rename the Visual Aids folder **Class Handouts**.
- Create a new folder named **Interactive Presentations** in the Class Handouts subfolder.

d. Close the Mather High window.
e. Use WordPad to create a document with the title **Career Areas** and your name on separate lines, and the following list of items:

Current Opportunities:
Attorney
Corrections Officer
Forensic Scientist
Paralegal
Judge

f. Save the WordPad document with the filename **Careers Listing.rtf** in the Mather High folder. (*Hint:* After you switch to your USB flash drive in the Save As dialog box, open the Career Days folder, then open the Mather High folder before saving the file.)
g. Close WordPad.

Independent Challenge 3 (continued)

h. Open WordPad and the Careers Listing document again, then add **Court Reporter** to the bottom of the list, then save the file and close WordPad.
i. Using pencil and paper, draw a diagram of your new folder structure.
j. Use the Start menu to search your computer using the search criterion **car**. Locate the Careers Listing.rtf document in the list, and use the link to open the file.
k. Close the file.

Real Life Independent Challenge

Think of a hobby or volunteer activity that you do now, or one that you would like to do. You will use your computer to help you manage your plans or ideas for this activity.

a. Using paper and a pencil, sketch a folder structure using at least two subfolders that you could create on your USB flash drive to contain your documents for this activity.
b. Connect your USB flash drive to your computer, then open the window for your USB flash drive.
c. Create the folder structure for your activity, using your sketch as a reference.
d. Think of at least three tasks that you can do to further your work in your chosen activity.
e. Open WordPad and create a document with the title **Next Steps** at the top of the page and your name on the next line.
f. List the three tasks, then save the file in one of the folders you created on your USB flash drive, using the title **To Do.rtf**.
g. Close WordPad, then open a Windows Explorer window for the folder where you stored the document.
h. Create a copy of the file, give the copy a new name, then place a copy of the document in your Documents library.
i. Delete the document copy from your Documents library.
j. Open the Recycle Bin window, and restore the document to the Documents library.

Visual Workshop

You are a technical support specialist at Emergency Services. The company supplies medical staff members to hospital emergency rooms in Los Angeles. You need to respond to your company's employee questions quickly and thoroughly. You decide that it is time to evaluate and reorganize the folder structure on your computer. That way, you'll be able to respond more quickly to staff requests. Create the folder structure shown in Figure B-27 on your USB flash drive. As you work, use WordPad to prepare a simple outline of the steps you follow to create the folder structure. Add your name to the document, and store it in an appropriate location.

FIGURE B-27

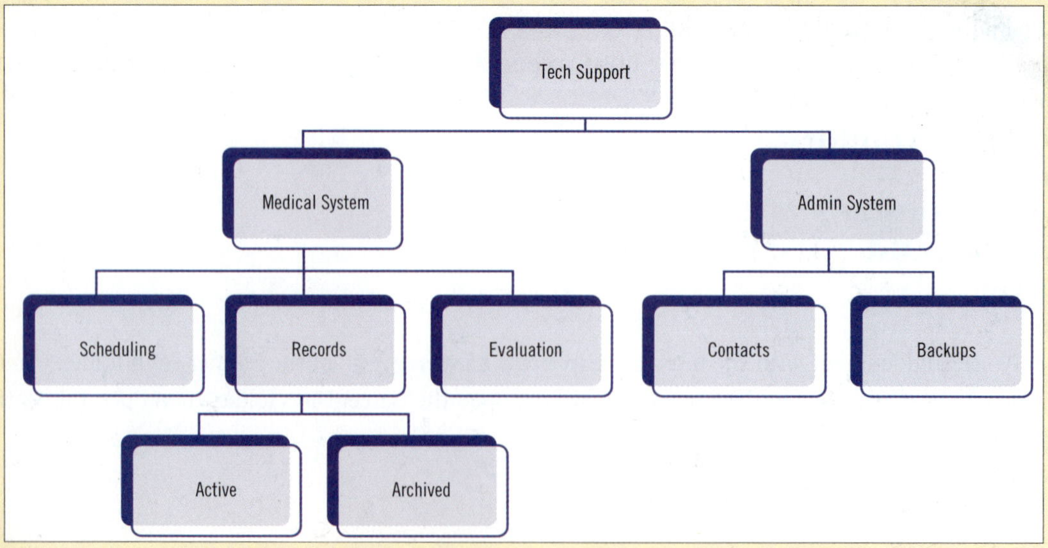

UNIT
A
Concepts 2010

Understanding Essential Computer Concepts

Files You Will Need:
No files needed.

Computers are essential tools in almost all kinds of activity in virtually every type of business. In this unit, you will learn about computers and their components. You will learn about input and output, how a computer processes data and stores information, how information is transmitted, and ways to secure that information. Quest Specialty Travel is expanding its North American offices and just purchased Sheehan Tours, an established travel agency in Boston, Massachusetts. Sheehan Tours has been in business for over 40 years and has a large customer base. Unfortunately, its computer system is outdated. Its office contains a hodgepodge of computer equipment, most of which was purchased used, and only one computer is connected to the Internet. Kevin O'Brien, the manager of the New York office, has been sent to the new Boston office to help them switch to Quest's business practices. He has already ordered and installed new computer equipment. His next task is to teach the staff how to use the new equipment.

OBJECTIVES

- Investigate types of computers
- Examine computer systems
- Investigate data representation
- Understand memory
- Understand storage media
- Examine input devices
- Examine output devices
- Explore data communications
- Learn about networks
- Learn about security threats
- Understand system software
- Understand application software

UNIT A

Concepts 2010

Investigating Types of Computers

A **computer** is an electronic device that accepts information and instructions from a user, manipulates the information according to the instructions, displays the information in some way, and stores the information for retrieval later. Computers are classified by their size, speed, and capabilities. Most of the staff at Sheehan Tours do not know anything about computers except for the ones that sit on their desks, so Kevin decides to start with a basic explanation of the types of computers available.

DETAILS

The following list describes various types of computers:

- **Personal computers (PCs)** are computers typically used by a single user, for use in the home or office. Personal computers are used for general computing tasks such as word processing, manipulating numbers, working with photographs or graphics, exchanging email, and accessing the Internet. In common usage, the term "PC" refers to personal computers that use Microsoft Windows. Personal computers that are sold only by Apple, Inc. are referred to as Macs (short for Macintosh).

QUICK TIP
Desktop PCs and notebook computers range in price from as low as $300 to as much as several thousands of dollars for high-end machines.

- The following are types of personal computers:
  - **Desktop computers** are designed to sit compactly on a desk.
  - **Notebook computers** (also referred to as **laptop computers**), similar to the one shown in Figure A-1, are small, lightweight, and designed for portability.
  - **Tablet PCs** are notebook computers that have a screen on which the user can write with a stylus.
  - **Subnotebook computers**, sometimes called **ultraportable computers** or **mini notebooks** are notebook computers that are smaller and lighter than ordinary notebooks. **Netbooks**, a type of subnotebook computers, are notebooks that are primarily designed to allow users to access the Internet and check email.
  - **Slate computers** are thin computers that do not have an external keyboard or a mouse. Users touch the screen or use a stylus to accomplish tasks. Slate computers are primarily used to read electronic books, view video, and access the Internet.

QUICK TIP
Machines dedicated primarily to playing games, such as the Xbox and PlayStation, are also computers.

- **Hand-held computers** are small computers that fit in the palm of your hand. Hand-held computers have more limited capabilities than personal computers.
  - **Smartphones**, like the one shown in Figure A-2, are used to make and receive phone calls, maintain an address book, electronic appointment book, calculator, and notepad, send email, connect to the Internet, play music, take photos or video, and even perform some of the same functions as a PC, such as word processing.
  - **MP3 players** are hand-held computers that are primarily used to store and play music, although some models can also be used to play digital movies or television shows.
- **Mainframe computers** are used by larger businesses and government agencies to provide centralized storage, processing, and management for large amounts of data. The price of a mainframe computer varies widely, from several hundred thousand dollars to close to one million dollars.
- The largest and fastest computers, called **supercomputers**, are used by large corporations and government agencies when the tremendous volume of data would seriously delay processing on a mainframe computer. A supercomputer, like the one shown in Figure A-3, can cost millions of dollars.

Converging technologies

Every year, the lines between the types of computers are growing more and more blurry. Handheld devices like smartphones are more powerful than the first notebook computers were, and today's desktop PCs are far more powerful than the mainframe computers of a few decades ago. As new technologies are developed, consumers will need fewer and fewer devices to accomplish their tasks.

FIGURE A-1: Notebook computer

FIGURE A-2: Smartphone

FIGURE A-3: Supercomputer

Concepts 2010

Examining Computer Systems

A **computer system** includes computer hardware and software. **Hardware** refers to the physical components of a computer. **Software** refers to the intangible components of a computer system, particularly the **programs**, or lists of instructions, that the computer needs to perform a specific task. The **operating system** is special software that controls basic input and output, allocates system resources, manages storage space, maintains security, and detects equipment failure.  Kevin explains how computers work and points out the main components of a computer system.

DETAILS

The following list provides an overview of computer system components and how they work:

- The design and construction of a computer is referred to as its **architecture** or **configuration**. The technical details about each hardware component are called **specifications**. For example, a computer system might be configured to include a printer; a specification for that printer might be a print speed of eight pages per minute or the capacity to print in color.
- The hardware and the software of a computer system work together to process data. **Data** refers to the words, numbers, figures, sounds, and graphics that describe people, events, things, and ideas. Modifying data is referred to as **processing**.
- In a computer, processing tasks occur on the **motherboard**, which is located inside the computer and is the main electronic component of the computer. See Figure A-4. The motherboard is a **circuit board**, which is a rigid piece of insulating material with **circuits**—electrical paths—on it that control specific functions. The motherboard contains the following processing hardware:
    - The **microprocessor**, also called the **processor** or the **central processing unit (CPU)**, consists of transistors and electronic circuits on a silicon chip (an integrated circuit embedded in semiconductor material). See Figure A-5. The processor is mounted on the motherboard and is responsible for executing instructions to process information.
    - **Cards** are removable circuit boards that are inserted into slots in the motherboard to expand the capabilities of the motherboard. For example, a sound card translates the digital audio information from the computer into analog sounds that the human ear can hear.
- The data or instructions you type into the computer are called **input**. The result of the computer processing input is referred to as **output**. The computer itself takes care of the processing functions, but it needs additional components, called **peripheral devices**, to accomplish the input, output, and storage functions.
    - You use an **input device**, such as a keyboard or a mouse, to enter data and issue commands. **Commands** are input instructions that tell the computer how to process data. For example, you might want to center the title and double-space the text of a report. You use the appropriate commands in the word processing program that instruct the computer to modify the data you have input so the report text is double-spaced and the report title is centered.
    - Output can be in many different forms, including reports, documents, graphs, sounds, and pictures. Computers produce output using **output devices**, such as a monitor or printer.
    - The output you create using a computer can be stored either inside the computer itself or on an external storage device, such as a DVD. You will learn more about storage devices later in this unit.

FIGURE A-4: Motherboard

FIGURE A-5: Microprocessor (front and back views)

Comparing microprocessor speeds

How fast a computer can process instructions depends partially on the speed of the microprocessor. Among other factors, the speed of the microprocessor is determined by its clock speed, word size, and whether it is single or dual core. **Clock speed** is measured in **megahertz (MHz)**, millions of cycles per second, or in **gigahertz (GHz)**, billions of cycles per second. **Word size** refers to the number of bits—the smallest unit of information in a computer—that are processed at one time; for example, a 32-bit processor processes 32 bits at a time. A computer with a large word size can process faster than a computer with a small word size. PCs come with 32-bit or 64-bit processors. Finally, a **dual-core processor**, one that has two processors on a single chip, can process information up to twice as fast as a **single-core processor**, one with one processor on the chip. Likewise, a **quad-core processor**, with four processors on a chip, processes information up to four times as fast as a single-core processor.

Investigating Data Representation

In order to understand how data is processed in a computer, you first need to learn how the computer represents and stores data. To a computer, the characters used in human language, such as the characters in a word processed document, are meaningless because it is an electronic device. Kevin gives a basic description of how information is represented inside a computer.

DETAILS

The following information will help you understand data processing:

- Like a light bulb, the computer must interpret every signal as either "on" or "off." To do this, a computer represents data as distinct or separate numbers. Specifically, it represents "on" with a 1 and "off" with a 0. These numbers are referred to as **binary digits**, or **bits**.
- A series of eight bits is called a **byte**. As Figure A-6 shows, the byte that represents the integer value 0 is 00000000, with all eight bits "off" or set to 0. The byte that represents the integer value 1 is 00000001, and the byte that represents 255 is 11111111.
- A **kilobyte (KB** or simply **K)** is 1024 bytes, or approximately one thousand bytes. A **megabyte (MB)** is 1,048,576 bytes, or about one million bytes. A **gigabyte (GB)** is 1,073,741,824 bytes, or about one billion bytes. A **terabyte (TB)** is 1,024 GB, or approximately one trillion bytes.
- Personal computers commonly use the ASCII system to represent character data. **ASCII** (pronounced "ASK-ee") stands for **American Standard Code for Information Interchange**. Each ASCII number represents an English character. Computers translate ASCII into binary data so that they can process it.
    - The original ASCII system used 7 bits to represent the numbers 0 (0000000) through 127 (1111111) to stand for 128 common characters and nonprinting control characters. Because bits are usually arranged in bytes, the eighth bit is reserved for error checking.
    - Extended ASCII uses eight bits and includes the numbers 128 (10000000) through 255 (11111111) to represent additional characters and symbols. Extended ASCII was developed to add codes for punctuation marks, symbols, such as $ and ©, and additional characters, such as é and ü, that were not included in the original 128 codes.
    - Most computers use the original ASCII definitions, but not all computers use the same definitions for Extended ASCII. Computers that run the Windows operating system use the set of Extended ASCII definitions defined by the American National Standards Institute (ANSI). Figure A-7 shows sample ASCII code with ANSI standard Extended ASCII characters.

FIGURE A-6: Binary representation of numbers

Number	Binary representation
0	00000000
1	00000001
2	00000010
3	00000011
4	00000100
5	00000101
6	00000110
7	00000111
8	00001000
⋮	⋮
253	11111101
254	11111110
255	11111111

FIGURE A-7: Sample ASCII code representing letters and symbols

Character	ASCII Code	Binary Number
(space)	32	00100000
$	36	00100100
A	65	01000001
B	66	01000010
a	97	01100001
b	98	01100010
?	129	10000001
£	163	10100011
®	217	11011001
é	233	11101001

UNIT A

Concepts 2010

Understanding Memory

In addition to the microprocessor, another important component of personal computer hardware is the **memory**, which stores instructions and data. Your computer has five types of memory: random access memory, cache memory, virtual memory, read-only memory, and complementary metal oxide semiconductor memory. Kevin realizes that most of the Sheehan Tours staff don't understand the difference between memory types, so he explains the different types of memory.

DETAILS

QUICK TIP
When the computer is off, RAM is empty.

QUICK TIP
You can often add more RAM to a computer by installing additional memory cards on the motherboard. You cannot add ROM; it is permanently installed on the motherboard.

QUICK TIP
The act of turning on the computer is sometimes called **booting up**.

Types of memory include the following:

- **Random access memory (RAM)** temporarily holds programs and data while the computer is on and allows the computer to access that information randomly; in other words, RAM doesn't need to access data in the same sequence in which it was stored. For example, if you are writing a report, the microprocessor temporarily copies the word processing program you are using into RAM so the microprocessor can quickly access the instructions that you will need as you type and format your report. The characters you type are also stored in RAM, along with the character formats, graphics, and other objects that you might use. RAM consists of chips on cards that plug into the motherboard.
  - Most personal computers use **synchronous dynamic random access memory (SDRAM)**, which is synchronized with the processor to allow faster access to its contents.
  - RAM is sometimes referred to as **volatile memory** or **temporary memory** because it is constantly changing as long as the computer is on and is cleared when the computer is turned off.
  - **Memory capacity**, sometimes referred to as **storage capacity**, is the amount of data that the computer can handle at any given time and is measured in megabytes or gigabytes. For example, a computer that has 2 GB of RAM has the capacity to temporarily store more than two billion bits of data at one time.
- **Cache memory**, sometimes called **RAM cache** or **CPU cache**, is a special, high-speed memory chip on the motherboard or CPU itself that stores frequently accessed and recently accessed data and commands instead of in RAM.
- **Virtual memory** is space on the computer's storage devices that simulates additional RAM. It enables programs to run as if your computer had more RAM by moving data and commands from RAM to the computer's permanent storage device and swapping in the new data and commands. See Figure A-8. Virtual memory, however, is much slower than RAM.
- **Read-only memory (ROM)** is a chip on the motherboard that has been prerecorded with data. ROM permanently stores the set of instructions that the computer uses to check the computer system's components to make sure they are working and to activate the essential software that controls the processing function when you turn the computer on.
  - ROM contains a set of instructions called the **BIOS (basic input/output system)**, which tells the computer to initialize the motherboard, how to recognize devices connected to the computer, and to start the boot process. The **boot process** is the set of events that occurs between the moment you turn on the computer and the moment you can begin to use the computer. The set of instructions for executing the boot process is stored in ROM.
  - ROM never changes and it remains intact when the computer is turned off; therefore, it is called **nonvolatile memory** or **permanent memory**.
- **Complementary metal oxide semiconductor (CMOS**, pronounced "SEE-moss") **memory** is a chip installed on the motherboard that is activated during the boot process and identifies where essential software is stored.
  - A small rechargeable battery powers CMOS so its contents are saved when the computer is turned off. CMOS changes every time you add or remove hardware on your computer system.
  - CMOS, often referred to as **semipermanent memory**, changes when hardware is added or removed, but doesn't empty when the computer is shut off.
  - Because CMOS retains its contents when the computer is turned off, the date and time are stored there.

FIGURE A-8: How virtual memory works

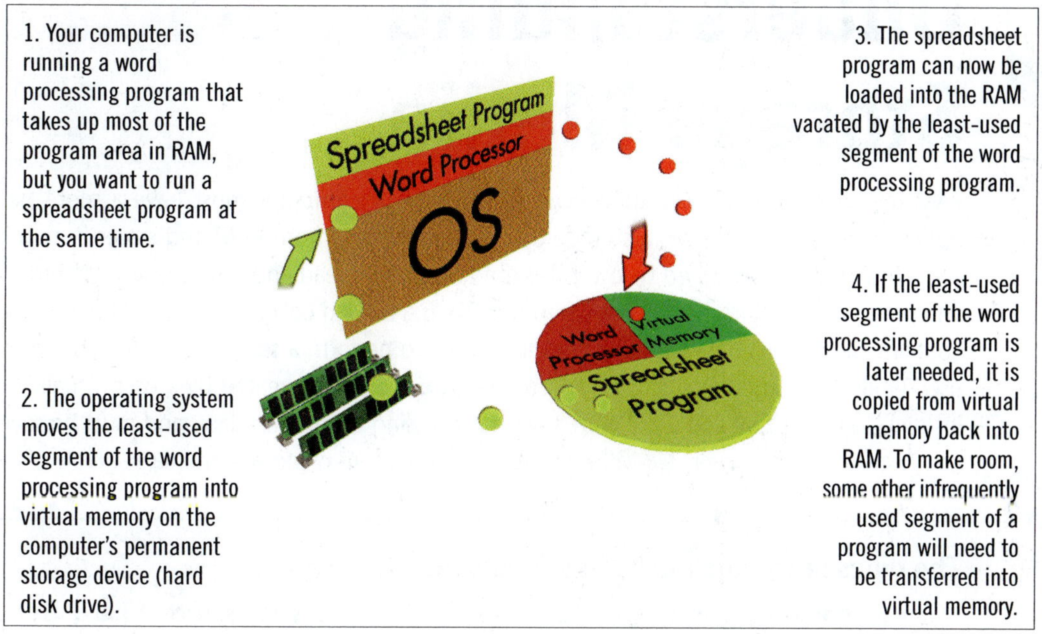

Upgrading RAM

One of the easiest ways to make your computer run faster is to add more RAM. The more RAM a computer has, the more instructions and data can be stored there. You can often add more RAM to a computer by installing additional memory cards on the motherboard. Currently, you can buy from 512 MB to 16 GB RAM cards, and usually, you can add more than one card. Check your computer's specifications to see what size RAM cards the slots on your motherboard will accept. Note that if your computer has a 32-bit processor, it can't use more than 4 GB of RAM, even if the computer has places to plug in more cards.

UNIT A

Concepts 2010

Understanding Storage Media

RAM retains data only while the power is on, so your computer must have a more permanent storage option. As Figure A-9 shows, a storage device receives data from RAM and stores it on a storage medium, some of which are described below. Later the data can be read and sent back to RAM to use again. All data and programs are stored as files. A computer **file** is a named collection of stored data. An **executable file** contains the instructions that tell a computer how to perform a specific task; for instance, the files that are used while the computer starts are executable. A **data file** is created by a user, usually with software. For instance, a report that you write with a word processing program is data, and must be saved as a data file if you want to access it later. Kevin explains the types of storage media available.

DETAILS

The types of storage media are discussed below:

- **Magnetic storage media** store data as magnetized particles on a surface. A **hard disk**, also called a hard disk drive, is the most common type of magnetic storage media. It contains several magnetic oxide-covered metal platters that are usually sealed in a case inside the computer. You can also purchase external hard drives for extra or backup storage.

QUICK TIP

Optical storage devices, such as CDs and DVDs, are much more durable than magnetic storage media.

- **Optical storage devices** are polycarbonate discs coated with a reflective metal on which data is stored using laser technology as a trail of tiny pits or dark spots in the surface of the disc. The data that these pits or spots represent can then be "read" with a beam of laser light.
  - The first standard optical storage device available for personal computers was the **CD (compact disc)**. One CD can store 700 MB of data.
  - A **DVD**, though the same size as a CD, can store between 4.7 and 15.9 GB of data, depending on whether data is stored on one or two sides of the disc, and how many layers of data each side contains. The term *DVD* is no longer an acronym, although it was originally an acronym for *digital video disc* and later was sometimes updated to *digital versatile disc*.
  - **Blu-ray** discs store 25 GB of data per layer. They are used for storing high-definition video.
- **Flash memory** (also called **solid state storage**) is similar to ROM except that it can be written to more than once. **Flash memory cards** are small, portable cards encased in hard plastic to which data can be written and rewritten. They are used in digital cameras, handheld computers, video game controllers, and other devices.
- A popular type of flash memory is a **USB flash storage device**, also called a **USB drive** or a **flash drive**. See Figure A-10.
  - USB drives for personal computers are available in a wide range of sizes from one to 64 GB of data. They are becoming more popular for use as a secondary or backup storage device for data typically stored on a hard disk drive.
  - USB drives plug directly into the USB port of a personal computer; the computer recognizes the device as another disk drive. The location and letter designation of USB ports varies with the brand and model of computer you are using, but the physical port may be on the front, back, or side of a computer.
  - USB flash storage devices are about the size of a pack of gum and often have a ring that you can attach to a key chain.

QUICK TIP

There is only one way to insert a flash drive, so if you're having problems inserting the drive into the slot, turn the drive over and try again.

FIGURE A-9: Storage devices and RAM

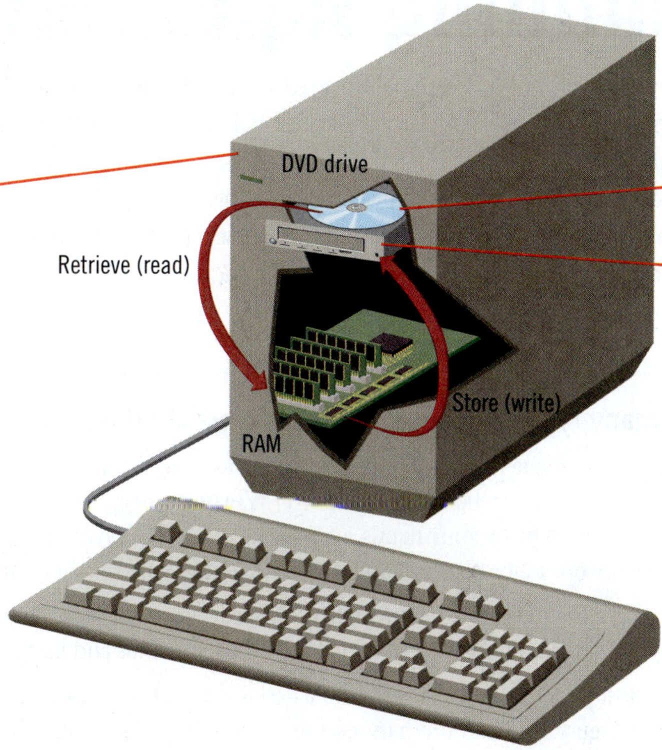

FIGURE A-10: USB flash storage device

Rewriting on optical storage

To store data on a CD, you need to record it on a **CD-R (compact disc recordable)** or **CD-RW (compact disc rewritable)** drive and a CD-R or CD-RW disc. CDs that you buy with software or music already on them are CD-ROMs (compact disc read-only memory)—you can read from them, but you cannot record additional data onto them. On a CD-R, after the data is recorded, you cannot erase or modify it, but you can add new data to the disc, as long as the disc has not been finalized. In contrast, you can re-record a CD-RW. Recordable DVD drives are also available. As with CDs, you can buy a DVD to which you can record only once, or a rewritable DVD to which you can record and then re-record data. Recordable DVDs come in two formats, **DVD-R** and **DVD+R**, and likewise re-recordable DVDs come in two formats, **DVD-RW** and **DVD+RW**. DVD drives on new computers are capable of reading from and writing to both -RW and +RW DVDs and CDs, as well as DVDs with two layers. **BD-R** are Blu-ray discs that you can record to once, and **BD-RE** are Blu-ray discs that you can record to multiple times. You need a Blu-ray drive to use Blu-ray discs.

UNIT A

Concepts 2010

Examining Input Devices

Before a computer can produce useful information, people must get data into the computer. This is accomplished by using input devices. In a typical personal computer system, you input data and commands by using an **input device** such as a keyboard or a mouse. Computers can also receive input from a storage device. You will learn about storage devices later in this unit. As Kevin explains peripheral devices to the Sheehan Tours staff, they ask several questions about input devices. For example, one person doesn't understand the difference between a mouse and a trackball. Kevin continues his explanation with a discussion of various input devices.

DETAILS

There are many types of input devices, as described below:

- One of the most frequently used input devices is a **keyboard**. The top keyboard in Figure A-11 is a standard keyboard. The bottom keyboard in Figure A-11 is **ergonomic**, which means that it has been designed to fit the natural placement of your hands and should reduce the risk of repetitive-motion injuries. Many keyboards, like the ones shown, have additional keys programmed as shortcut keys to commonly used functions.
- Another common input device is a **pointing device**, which controls the **pointer**, a small arrow or other symbol on the screen. Pointing devices are used to select commands and manipulate text or graphics on the screen.
    - The most popular pointing device for a desktop computer is a **mouse**, such as the one shown on the left side in Figure A-12. An ordinary mouse has a rolling ball on its underside, and an optical mouse has a tiny camera on its underside that takes pictures as the mouse is moved. You control the pointer by moving the entire mouse. A mouse usually has two or more buttons for clicking commands. A mouse might also have a **scroll wheel** that you roll to scroll the page on the screen and that may function as one of the buttons.
    - The **trackball**, such as the one shown on the right side in Figure A-12, is similar to a mouse except that the rolling ball is on the top side and you control the movement of the pointer by moving only the ball.
    - Notebook computers are usually equipped with a touch pad or a pointing stick. See Figure A-13. A **touch pad** is a touch-sensitive device that you drag your finger over to control the pointer. The buttons are located at the bottom of the touch pad. A **pointing stick** is a small device that looks like a pencil eraser embedded among the typing keys that you push up, left, right, or down to move the pointer. Two buttons equivalent to mouse buttons are located in front of the spacebar on the keyboard.
- A **touchscreen** is a display that while showing you the output, allows you to touch it with your finger or a stylus to input commands. Touchscreens are found on some ATMs, smartphones, and MP3 players. Tablet PCs and slate computers use touchscreen technology, and the newest operating system from Microsoft, Windows 7, supports touchscreens.
- A **scanner** is a device that transfers the content on a piece of paper into memory. To do this, you place a piece of paper on the glass, a beam of light moves across the glass similar to a photocopier, and stores the image or words on the paper as digital information. You can scan a document or a photo and save it as an image file, or you can scan a document and have the text "read" by the scanner and saved in a document file for editing later.
- Microphones are another type of input device. You can use them to record sound for certain types of files, or, if you have the voice-recognition software, you can use them to input data and commands.
- Input devices can be connected to the computer with cables or wirelessly. Wireless input devices connect to the computer using infrared or radio frequency technology, similar to a remote control for a television.

QUICK TIP

Another way to avoid repetitive motion injuries is to take frequent breaks when working at a computer and stretch your hands and wrists.

Understanding assistive devices

People with physical impairments or disabilities can use computers because of advances in making computers accessible to everyone. For example, people who cannot use their arms or hands instead can use foot, head, or eye movements to control the pointer. People with poor vision can use keyboards with large keys for input, screen enlargers to enlarge the type and images on the monitor, or screen readers to read the content of the screen aloud. Computers have even been developed that can be controlled by a person's thoughts, that is, the brain's electromagnetic waves.

FIGURE A-11: Keyboards

FIGURE A-12: Personal computer pointing devices

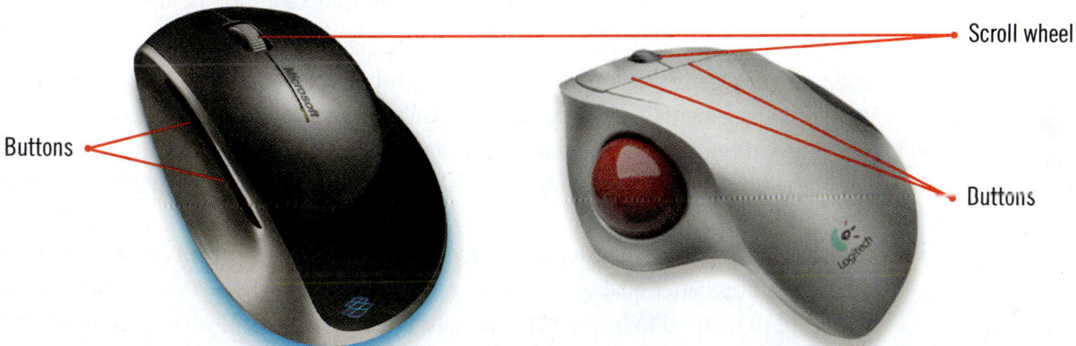

FIGURE A-13: Notebook pointing devices

Touch pad

Pointing stick

Examining Output Devices

As stated earlier, output is the result of processing data; **output devices** show you those results. The most commonly used output devices are monitors and printers. Kevin continues his discussion of peripheral devices with an explanation of output devices.

DETAILS

Output devices are described below:

> **QUICK TIP**
> One problem with LCD monitors is that when you view the monitor from an angle, it can be hard to see the images on it. LED backlighting helps solve this problem.

- The **monitor** displays the output from a computer.
    - The monitor shown in Figure A-14 is a **flat panel monitor**, a lightweight monitor that takes up very little room on the desktop. Most flat panel monitors use **LCD (liquid crystal display)** technology, which creates the image you see on the screen by manipulating light within a layer of liquid crystal. LCD monitors require a backlight. Flat-panel monitors labeled as **LED (light emitting diode)** monitors use LEDs to provide the backlight. LED backlighting is more energy efficient than ordinary backlighting.
    - Monitor **screen size** is the diagonal measurement from one corner of the screen to the other. In general, monitors on desktop computers range in size from 15" to 30", whereas monitors on notebook computers range in size from 12" to 20".
    - Most monitors have a **graphics display**, which divides the screen into a matrix of small dots called **pixels**. **Resolution** is the number of pixels the monitor displays. Standard resolutions range from 640 × 480 to 1920 × 1200. If your screen is small, a 1600 × 1200 resolution will make the objects on the screen too small to see clearly. **Dot pitch (dp)** measures the distance between pixels, so a smaller dot pitch means a sharper image. A .28 or .26 dot pitch is typical for today's monitors.
    - To display graphics, a computer must have a **graphics card**, also called a **video display adapter** or **video card**, or a built-in **graphics processor** (sometimes called a **built-in graphics card**). The graphics card or processor controls the signals the computer sends to the monitor.

> **QUICK TIP**
> The speed of laser and inkjet printers is measured in **pages per minute (ppm)**. The speed of dot matrix printers is measured in **characters per second (cps)**.

- A **printer** produces a paper copy, often called **hard copy**, of the text or graphics processed by the computer. There are three popular categories of printers: laser printers, inkjet printers, and dot matrix printers.
    - **Laser printers**, like the one shown on the left in Figure A-15, are popular for business use because they produce high-quality output quickly and efficiently. In a laser printer, a temporary laser image is transferred onto paper with a powdery substance called **toner**.
    - **Inkjet printers**, such as the one shown on the right in Figure A-15, are popular printers for home use. These printers spray ink onto paper and produce output whose quality is comparable to that of a laser printer.
    - **Dot matrix printers** transfer ink to the paper by striking a ribbon with pins. A 24-pin dot matrix printer produces better quality print than a 9-pin. Dot matrix printers are most often used when a large number of pages need to be printed fairly quickly or when a business needs to print multi-page continuous forms.
- Speakers allow you to hear sounds from the computer. Speakers can be separate peripheral devices attached to the computer, or they can be built in to the monitor. For speakers to work, a sound card must be installed on the motherboard. The sound card converts sounds so that they can be broadcast through speakers.

FIGURE A-14: LCD monitor

FIGURE A-15: Printers

Laser printer

Inkjet printer

Exploring Data Communications

Data communications is the transmission of data from one computer to another or to a peripheral device. The computer that originates the message is the **sender**. The message is sent over some type of **channel**, such as a telephone or coaxial cable. The computer or device at the message's destination is the **receiver**. The rules that establish an orderly transfer of data between the sender and the receiver are called **protocols**. The transmission protocol between a computer and its peripheral devices is handled by a **device driver**, or simply **driver**, which is a computer program that can establish communication because it contains information about the characteristics of your computer and of the device. The Sheehan Tours staff will use their computers to connect to the computers at the Quest headquarters in California as well as to surf the Internet, so Kevin next explains how computers communicate.

DETAILS

The following describes some of the ways that computers communicate:

QUICK TIP
An internal peripheral device such as a hard disk drive may plug directly into the motherboard, or it may have an attached controller card.

QUICK TIP
USB ports can be on the front, back, or side of a computer.

- The data path between the microprocessor, RAM, and the peripherals along which communication travels is called the **data bus**.
- An external peripheral device must have a corresponding **expansion port** and **cable** that connect it to the computer. Inside the computer, each port connects to a **controller card**, sometimes called an **expansion card** or **interface card**. These cards plug into electrical connectors on the motherboard called **expansion slots** or **slots**. Personal computers can have several types of ports, including parallel, serial, SCSI, USB, MIDI, and Ethernet. Figure A-16 shows the ports on one desktop personal computer.
- A **USB (Universal Serial Bus) port** is a high-speed serial port which allows multiple connections at the same port. The device you install must have a **USB connector**, a small rectangular plug, as shown in Figure A-17. When you plug the USB connector into the USB port, the computer recognizes the device and allows you to use it immediately. USB flash storage devices plug into USB ports. For most USB devices, power is supplied via the port, so there is no need for extra power cables.
- Another standard for transferring information between digital devices similar to USB is FireWire. **FireWire** was developed by Apple Computer company and the Institute of Electrical and Electronics Engineers (IEEE) standardized the technology as the **IEEE 1394 interface**. Data transfers are significantly faster using this type of connection than using a USB connection.
- Monitors are connected to computers through HDMI, DVI, or VGA ports. **HDMI (high-definition multimedia interface)** transmits video and audio digitally, **DVI (digital video interface)** transmits video digitally, and **VGA (video graphics array)** allows analog video transmission.
- Speakers and a microphone connect to a computer via ports on the sound card.
- A keyboard and a mouse connect via **PS/2 ports** or USB ports. A wireless keyboard or mouse connects via a special connector that plugs into a USB port. Printers also connect via a USB port.
- You can connect to another computer, a LAN, a **modem** (a device that connects your computer to a standard telephone jack or to a cable connection), or sometimes directly to the Internet using an **Ethernet port**. Ethernet ports allow data to be transmitted at high speeds.

FIGURE A-16: Computer expansion ports

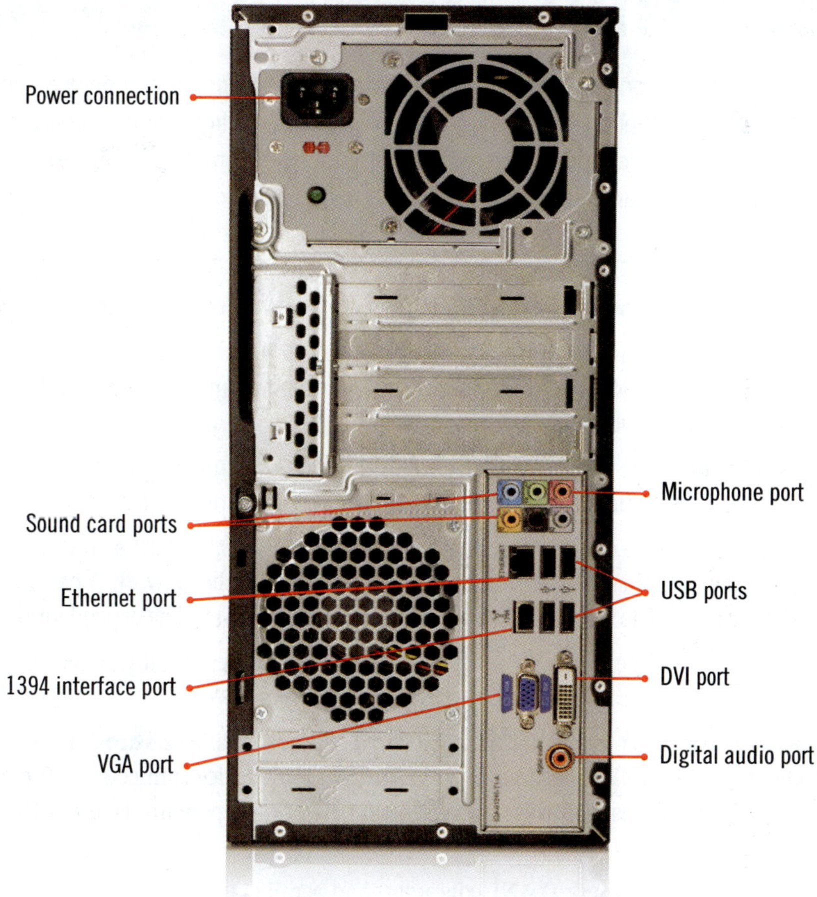

FIGURE A-17: USB connector

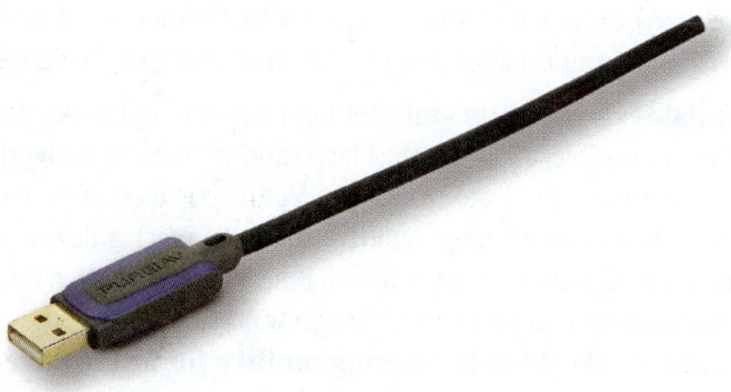

UNIT
A
Concepts 2010

Learning about Networks

A **network** connects one computer to other computers and peripheral devices, enabling you to share data and resources with others. There are a variety of network configurations; however, any type of network has some basic characteristics and requirements that you should know. Kevin continues his discussion of how computers communicate with an explanation of networking.

DETAILS

Components of networks and the types of networks are described below:

- Each computer that is part of the network must have a **network interface card (NIC)** installed. This card creates a communications channel between the computer and the network. A cable is used to connect the NIC port to the network.
- **Network software** is also essential, establishing the communications protocols that will be observed on the network and controlling the "traffic flow" as data travels throughout the network.
- Some networks have one or more computers, called **servers**, that act as the central storage location for programs and provide mass storage for most of the data used on the network. A network with a server and computers dependent on the server is called a **client/server network**. The dependent computers are the **clients**.
- When a network does not have a server, all the computers essentially are equal, and programs and data are distributed among them. This is called a **peer-to-peer network**.
- A personal computer that is not connected to a network is called a **standalone computer**. When it is connected to the network, it becomes a **workstation**. Any device connected to the network is called a **node**. A **router** is a device that controls traffic between network components. Figure A-18 illustrates a typical network configuration.
- In a **local area network (LAN)**, computers and peripheral devices are located relatively close to each other, generally in the same building.
- A **wide area network (WAN)** is more than one LAN connected together. The **Internet** is the largest example of a WAN.

QUICK TIP
The **World Wide Web** is subset of the Internet, and is a huge database of information stored on network servers.

- In a **wireless local area network (WLAN)**, computers and peripherals use high-frequency radio waves instead of wires to communicate and connect in a network. **Wi-Fi** (short for **wireless fidelity**) is the term created by the nonprofit Wi-Fi Alliance to describe networks connected using a standard radio frequency established by the Institute of Electrical and Electronics Engineers (IEEE). Wi-Fi is used over short distances to connect computers to a LAN.
- A **personal area network (PAN)** is a network that allows two or more devices located close to each other to communicate or to connect a device to the Internet. In a PAN, devices are connected with cables or wireless.
  - **Infrared technology** uses infrared light waves to beam data from one device to another. The devices must be compatible, and they must be positioned close to each other with their infrared ports pointed at each other to communicate. This is the technology used in TV remote controls.
  - **Bluetooth** uses short range radio waves to connect a device wirelessly to another device or to the Internet. The devices must each have a Bluetooth transmitter, but unlike infrared connections, they can communicate around corners or through walls.
- **WiMAX** (short for **Worldwide Interoperability for Microwave Access**), another standard defined by the IEEE, allows computer users to connect over many miles to a LAN. A WiMAX tower sends signals to a WiMAX receiver built or plugged into a computer. WiMAX towers can communicate with each other or with a company that provides connections to the Internet.

FIGURE A-18: Typical network configuration

Understanding telecommunications

Telecommunications means communicating over a comparatively long distance using a phone line or some other data conduit. To make this connection, you must use a modem. Modem stands for *mo*dulator-*dem*odulator. The modem converts the **digital**, or stop-start, **signals** your computer outputs into **analog**, or continuous wave, **signals** (sound waves) that can traverse ordinary phone lines. Figure A-19 shows the telecommunications process, in which a modem converts digital signals to analog signals at the sending site (modulates) and a second modem converts the analog signals back into digital signals at the receiving site (demodulates). Most computers today come with a built-in 56 K modem and NIC (network interface card). 56 K represents the modem's capability to send and receive about 56,000 **bits per second (bps)**. People who want to use a high-speed connection either over phone lines, such as a **DSL (digital subscriber line)**, or over a cable connection, usually need to purchase an external DSL or cable modem separately. High-speed connections are often called **broadband connections**.

FIGURE A-19: Using modems to send and receive data

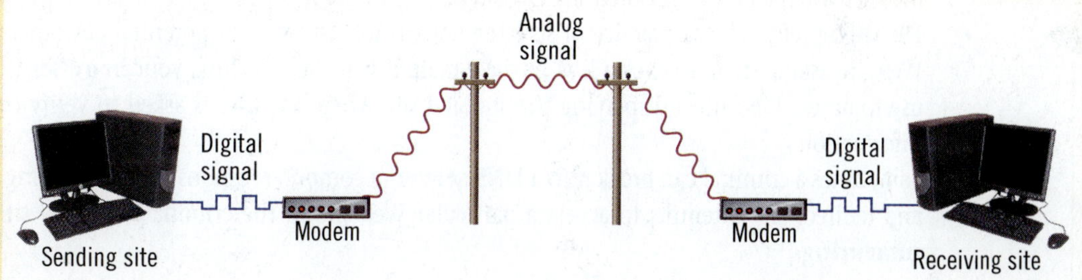

Concepts 2010

UNIT A
Concepts 2010

Learning about Security Threats

Security refers to the steps a computer owner takes to prevent unauthorized use of or damage to the computer. Once a computer is connected to a network, it is essential that the computer be protected against possible threats from people intent on stealing information or causing malicious damage. Kevin explains how important it is to be vigilant about keeping the office computers secure and reviews ways to do this.

DETAILS

Several types of security threats are discussed below:

- **Malware** is a broad term that describes any program that is intended to cause harm or convey information to others without the owner's permission.
    - Unscrupulous programmers deliberately construct harmful programs, called **viruses**, which instruct your computer to perform destructive activities, such as erasing a disk drive. Some viruses are more annoying than destructive, but some can be harmful, erasing data or causing your hard disk to require reformatting. **Antivirus software**, sometimes referred to as **virus protection software**, searches executable files for the sequences of characters that may cause harm and disinfects the files by erasing or disabling those commands. Figure A-20 shows the dialog box that appears when the Trend Micro antivirus program is scanning a computer for potential threats.
    - Some software programs contain other programs called **spyware** that track a computer user's Internet usage and send this data back to the company or person that created it. Most often, this is done without the computer user's permission or knowledge. **Anti-spyware software** can detect these programs and delete them.

QUICK TIP
Some specific types of viruses are called worms; another type is a Trojan horse. Antivirus software usually protects against both types.

QUICK TIP
Adware is software installed with another program usually with the user's permission that generates advertising revenue for the program's creator by displaying ads targeted to the program's user.

- A **firewall** is like a locked door on your computer. It prevents other computers on the Internet from accessing your computer and prevents programs on it from accessing the Internet without your permission. A firewall can be either hardware or software.
    - A hardware firewall provides strong protection against incoming threats. A router usually has a built-in firewall.
    - Software firewalls track all incoming and outgoing traffic. If a program that never accessed the Internet before attempts to do so, the user is notified and can choose to forbid access. There are several free software firewall packages available.
- Criminals are getting more aggressive as they try to figure out new ways to access computer users' personal information and passwords.
    - A Web site set up to look exactly like another Web site, such as a bank's Web site, but which does not actually belong to the organization portrayed in the site, is a **spoofed** site. The site developer creates a **URL** (address on the Web) that looks similar to a URL from the legitimate site. Usually, spoofed sites are set up to try to convince customers of the real site to enter personal information, such as credit card numbers, Social Security numbers, and passwords, so that the thief collecting the information can use it to steal the customer's money or identity. Figure A-21 shows the alert displayed in the Internet Explorer browser when a known spoofed site is visited.
    - **Phishing** refers to the practice of sending e-mails to customers or potential customers of a legitimate Web site asking them to click a link in the e-mail. If you click the link, your **browser** (the software you use to access Web sites) displaying the spoofed site where the user is asked to verify or enter personal information.
    - Sometimes a criminal can break into a **DNS server** (a computer responsible for directing Internet traffic) and redirect any attempts to access a particular Web site to the criminal's spoofed site. This is called **pharming**.

QUICK TIP
Never click a URL in a suspected phishing message. Open your browser and type the URL of the organization into the Address or Location bar instead.

FIGURE A-20: Antivirus scan in progress

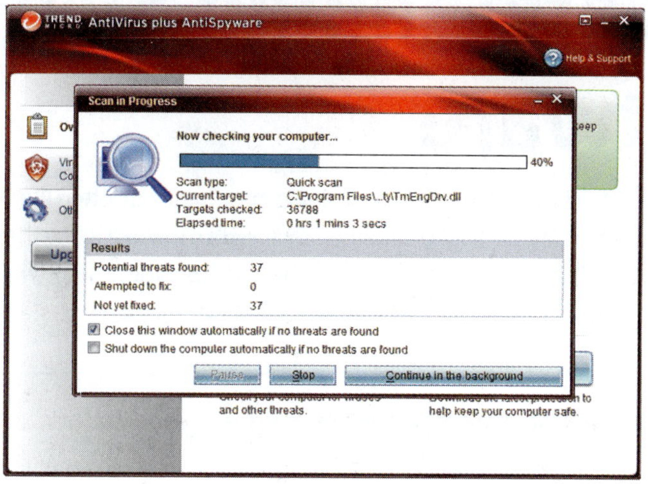

FIGURE A-21: The Internet Explorer browser when visiting a known spoofed site

Message warns you that the website has been reported as unsafe

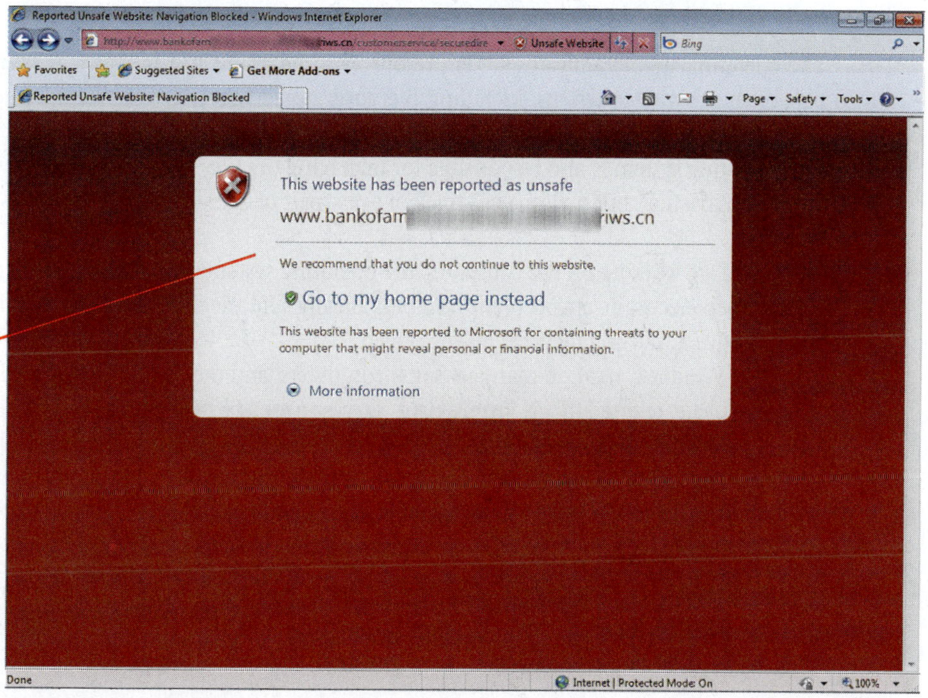

Protecting information with passwords

You can protect data on your computer by using passwords. You can set up accounts on your computer for multiple users and require that users sign in with a username and password before they can use the computer. This is known as **logging in** or **logging on**. You can also protect individual files on your computer so that people who try to open or alter a file need to type the password before they are allowed access to the file. Many Web sites require a username and password to access the information stored on it. To prevent anyone from guessing your passwords, you should always create and use strong passwords. A **strong password** consists of at least eight characters of upper- and lowercase letters and numbers. Avoid using common personal information, such as birthdays and addresses, in your password.

Understanding System Software

Sometimes the term software refers to a single program, but often the term refers to a collection of programs and data that are packaged together. **System software** helps the computer carry out its basic operating tasks. Before Kevin describes the various types of software that people use to accomplish things like writing memos, he needs to describe system software.

DETAILS

The components of system software are described below:

- System software manages the fundamental operations of your computer, such as loading programs and data into memory, executing programs, saving data to disks, displaying information on the monitor, and transmitting data through a port to a peripheral device. There are four types of system software: operating systems, utilities, device drivers, and programming languages.

QUICK TIP
The operating system's responsibility to maintain security may include requiring a username and password or checking the computer for virus infection.

- Recall that an **operating system** allocates system resources, manages storage space, maintains security, detects equipment failure, and controls basic input and output. **Input and output**, or **I/O**, is the flow of data from the microprocessor to memory to peripherals and back again.
    - The operating system allocates system resources so programs run properly. A **system resource** is any part of the computer system, including memory, storage devices, and the microprocessor, that can be used by a computer program.
    - The operating system is also responsible for managing the files on your storage devices. Not only does it open and save files, but it also keeps track of every part of every file for you and lets you know if any part is missing.
    - While you are working on the computer, the operating system is constantly guarding against equipment failure. Each electronic circuit is checked periodically, and the moment a problem is detected, the user is notified with a warning message on the screen.
    - Microsoft Windows, used on many personal computers, and the MAC OS, used exclusively on Macintosh computers, are referred to as **operating environments** because they provide a **graphical user interface** (**GUI**, pronounced "goo-ey") that acts as a liaison between the user and all of the computer's hardware and software. Figure A-22 shows the starting screen on a computer using Microsoft Windows 7.
- **Utilities** are another category of system software that augment the operating system by taking over some of its responsibility for allocating hardware resources.
- As you learned earlier in the discussion of ports, device drivers handle the transmission protocol between a computer and its peripherals. When you add a device to an existing computer, part of its installation includes adding its device driver to the computer's configuration.

QUICK TIP
Some examples of popular programming languages are BASIC, Visual Basic, C, C++, C#, Java, and Delphi.

- Computer **programming languages**, which a programmer uses to write computer instructions, are also part of the system software. The instructions are translated into electrical signals that the computer can manipulate and process.

FIGURE A-22: Windows 7 starting screen

Examining Windows 7 hardware requirements

Windows 7, the newest version of the Windows operating system, requires a computer with at least a 1 GHz processor, 1 GB of RAM for the 32-bit version or 2 GB of RAM for the 64-bit version, a DirectX 9 graphics processor, 128 MB of specialized graphics RAM, and 16 GB of available space for the 32-bit version or 20 GB for the 64-bit version. Keep in mind that these are the minimum recommendations. To prevent your computer from slowing to a crawl, you should consider upgrading the amount of RAM and the processor speed.

UNIT A

Concepts 2010

Understanding Application Software

Application software enables you to perform specific computer tasks. Many programs allow users to use data created in one application in a document created by another application. **Object linking and embedding (OLE)** refers to the ability to use data from another file, called the **source**. **Embedding** occurs when you copy and paste the source data in the new file. **Linking** allows you to create a connection between the source data and the copy in the new file. The link updates the copy every time a change is made to the source data. The seamless nature of OLE among some applications is referred to as **integration**. Now that the Sheehan Tours staff understands system software, Kevin describes some common application software.

DETAILS

Typical application software includes the following:

QUICK TIP
Most document production software allows you to perform **copy-and-paste** and **cut-and-paste operations**, to duplicate or move words around.

- **Document production software** includes word processing software, desktop publishing software, e-mail editors, and Web authoring software. All of these production tools have a variety of features that assist you in writing and formatting documents, including changing the **font** (the style of type) or adding color and design elements. Most offer **spell checking** to help you avoid typographical and spelling errors, as shown in Figure A-23.
- **Spreadsheet software** is a numerical analysis tool. Spreadsheet software creates a **worksheet**, composed of a grid of columns and rows. You can type data into the cells, and then enter mathematical formulas into other cells that reference the data. Figure A-24 shows a typical worksheet that includes a simple calculation and the data in the spreadsheet represented as a simple graph.
- **Database management software** lets you collect and manage data. A **database** is a collection of information stored on one or more computers organized in a uniform format of records and fields. A **record** is a collection of data items in a database. A **field** is one piece of information in the record. An example of a database is the online catalog of books at a library; the catalog contains one record for each book in the library, and each record contains fields that identify the title, the author, and the subjects under which the book can be classified.
- **Graphics** and **presentation software** allow you to create illustrations, diagrams, graphs, and charts that can be projected before a group, printed out for quick reference, or transmitted to remote computers. You can also use **clip art**, simple drawings that are included as collections with many software packages.
- **Photo editing software** allows you to manipulate digital photos. You can make the images brighter, add special effects, add other images, or crop the photo to include only relevant parts of the image. Examples of photo editing software are Adobe Photoshop and Picasa. **Video editing software**, such as Windows Live Movie Maker or Adobe Premier, allows you to edit video by clipping it, adding captions and a soundtrack, or rearranging clips.
- **Multimedia authoring software** allows you to record digital sound files, video files, and animations that can be included in presentations and other documents.

QUICK TIP
Some information management software allows you to synchronize information between a PDA and a desktop or notebook computer.

- **Information management software** keeps track of schedules, appointments, contacts, and "to-do" lists. Most e-mail software allows users to add all the information about contacts to the list of e-mail addresses. In addition, some software, such as Microsoft Outlook, combines a contact list with information management components, such as a calendar and to-do list.
- **Web site creation and management software** allows you to create and manage Web sites. They allow you to see what the Web pages will look like as you create them.

FIGURE A-23: Checking the spelling in a document

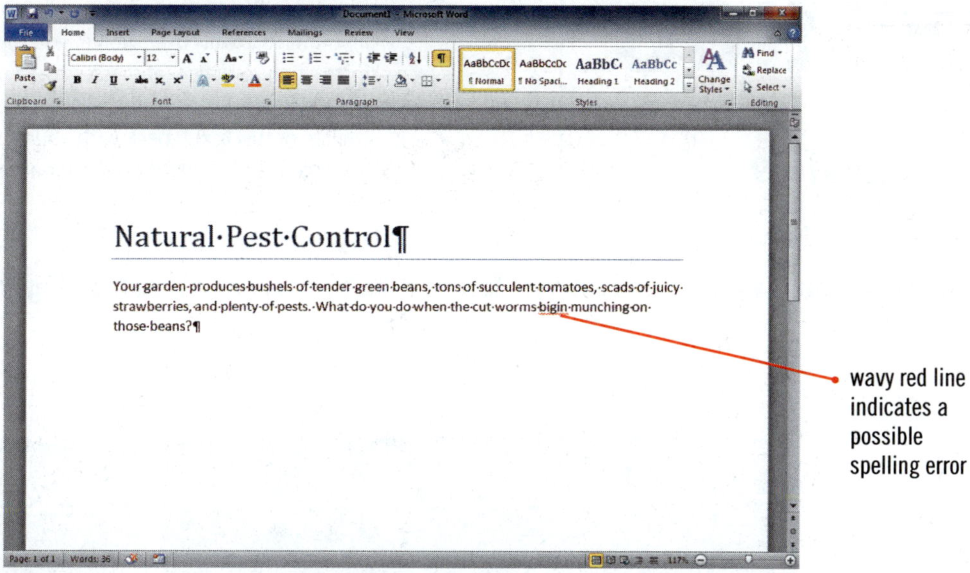

FIGURE A-24: Typical worksheet with numerical data and a graph

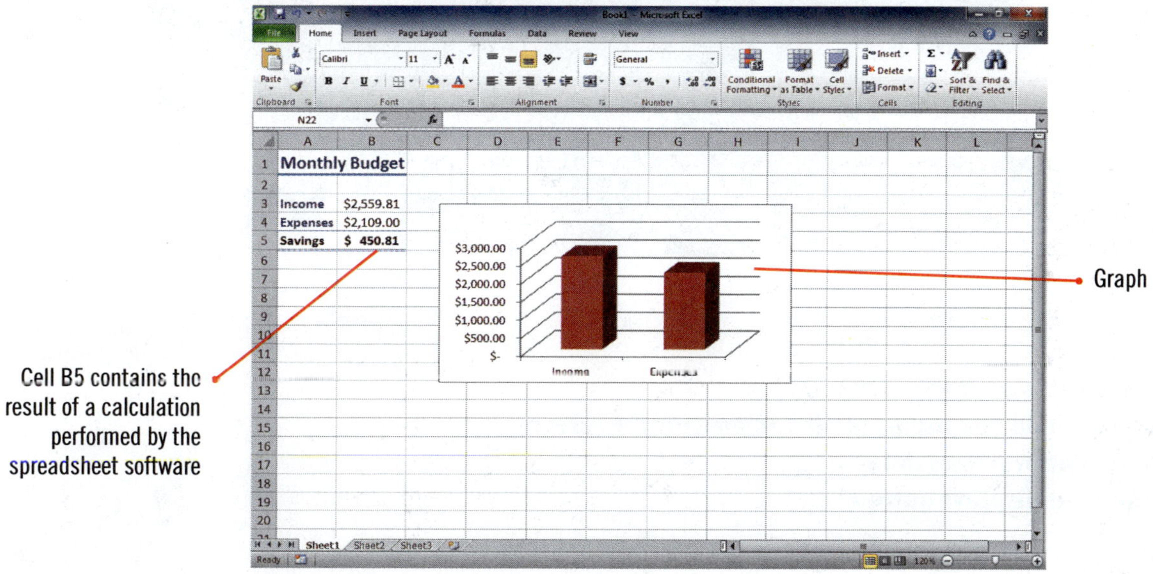

Computing in the cloud

Cloud computing means that data, applications, and even resources are stored on servers accessed over the Internet rather than on users' computers, and you access only what you need when you need it. Many individuals and companies are moving towards "the cloud" for at least some of their needs. For example, some companies provide space and computing power to developers for a fee. Individuals might subscribe to a backup service such as Carbonite or Mozy so that their data is automatically backed up on a computer at the physical location of those companies. Google Docs and Microsoft Web Apps provide both free and paid versions of various applications that you access by logging in to their Web sites. For now, these applications are not as robust as the applications you install on your own machine, but that is likely to change in the future.

Practice

Concepts Review

For current SAM information, including versions and content details, visit SAM Central (http://www.cengage.com/samcentral). If you have a SAM user profile, you may have access to hands-on instruction, practice, and assessment of the skills covered in this unit. Since various versions of SAM are supported throughout the life of this text, check with your instructor for the correct instructions and URL/Web site for accessing assignments.

Match the statements with the elements labeled in the screen shown in Figure A-25.

FIGURE A-25

1. **Which component is used to enter text?**
2. **Which component do you use to point to items on the screen?**
3. **Which component processes data?**
4. **Which component displays output?**

Match each term with the statement that best describes it.

5. **netbook**
6. **commands**
7. **byte**
8. **RAM**
9. **hard disk**
10. **expansion slot**
11. **server**
12. **spyware**
13. **operating system**
14. **database**

a. Temporarily holds data and programs while the computer is on
b. A type of subnotebook computer that is primarily designed to allow users to access the Internet and check e-mail
c. Magnetic storage media that is usually sealed in a case inside the computer
d. A collection of information stored on one or more computers organized in a uniform format of records and fields
e. Series of eight bits
f. A computer on a network that acts as the central storage location for programs and data used on the network
g. Software that allocates resources, manages storage space, maintains security, and controls I/O
h. A program that tracks a user's Internet usage without the user's permission
i. A slot on the motherboard into which a controller card for a peripheral device is inserted
j. Input instructions that tell the computer how to process data

Select the best answer from the list of choices.

15. **Which one of the following would not be considered a personal computer?**
 a. Desktop
 b. Mainframe
 c. Notebook
 d. Tablet PC

16. **The intangible components of a computer system, including the programs, are called:**
 a. peripherals
 b. hardware
 c. software
 d. price

17. **What part of the computer is responsible for executing instructions to process information?**
 a. Peripheral device
 b. Card
 c. Motherboard
 d. Processor

18. **What are the technical details about each hardware component called?**
 a. Configuration
 b. Specifications
 c. Circuits
 d. Cards

19. **Keyboards, monitors, and printers are all examples of which of the following?**
 a. Peripheral devices
 b. Input devices
 c. Output devices
 d. Software

20. **Which of the following is a pointing device that allows you to control the pointer by moving the entire device around on a desk?**
 a. Mouse
 b. Trackball
 c. Touch pad
 d. Pointing stick

21. **In order to display graphics, a computer needs a monitor and a(n):**
 a. expansion port
 b. graphics card or processor
 c. network card (NIC)
 d. sound card

22. **What do you call each 1 or 0 used in the representation of computer data?**
 a. An ASCII
 b. A pixel
 c. A bit
 d. A byte

23. What is a megabyte?

a. 10 kilobytes
b. About a million bytes
c. One-half a gigabyte
d. About a million bits

24. Which of the following permanently stores the set of instructions that the computer uses to activate the software that controls the processing function when you turn the computer on?

a. RAM
b. ROM
c. The hard disk
d. CPU cache

25. Which of the following is space on the computer's storage devices that simulates additional RAM?

a. Read-only memory
b. Cache memory
c. Volatile memory
d. Virtual memory

26. Which of the following temporarily stores data and programs while you are using them?

a. RAM
b. ROM
c. The hard disk
d. CPU cache

27. Which of the following is not a permanent storage medium?

a. Hard disk
b. Optical disk
c. DVD
d. RAM

28. The transmission protocol between a computer and its peripheral devices is handled by a:

a. driver
b. controller card
c. channel
d. data bus

29. Which of the following is the data path between the microprocessor, RAM, and the peripherals?

a. Cable
b. Data bus
c. Data channel
d. Data port

30. The computer that originates a message to send to another computer is called the:

a. channel
b. sender
c. receiver
d. driver

31. A personal computer that is connected to a network is called a:

a. netbook
b. desktop
c. workstation
d. channel

32. Which of the following acts as a locked door on a computer?

a. DNS server
b. Antivirus software
c. Spyware
d. Firewall

33. A ______________ consists of connected computers and peripheral devices that are located relatively close to each other.

a. PAN
b. LAN
c. WAN
d. WLAN

34. When data, applications, and resources are stored on servers rather than on users' computers, it is referred to as ______________.

a. sky computing
b. cloud computing
c. shared computing
d. leased computing

35. A Web site set up to look exactly like another Web site, such as a bank's Web site, but which does not actually belong to the organization portrayed in the site, is a ______________ site.

a. phished
b. spoofed
c. served
d. malware

Independent Challenge 1

This Independent Challenge requires an Internet connection.

In order to run the newest software, many people need to upgrade their existing computer system or buy a brand new one. What do you do with your old computer when you purchase a new one? Most municipalities have enacted laws regulating the disposal of electronics. Research these laws in your city and state and write a brief report describing them.

- **a.** Start your browser, go to your favorite search engine, and then search for information about laws regarding the disposal of electronics in your city and state. Try finding your city's Web site and searching it for the information, or use **electronics disposal laws** followed by your city name as a search term and then repeat that search with your state's name in place of your city's name.
- **b.** Open each Web site that you find in a separate tab or browser window.
- **c.** Read the information on each Web site. Can some components be thrown away? Are there laws that apply only to monitors? Are there different laws for individuals and businesses? Does the size of the business matter? Are manufacturers or resellers required to accept used components that they manufactured or sold?

Advanced Challenge Exercise

- Search for organizations to which you can donate your computer.
- How do these organizations promise to protect your privacy?
- Can you take a deduction on your federal income tax for your donation?

- **d.** Write a short report describing your findings. Include the URLs for all relevant Web sites. (*Hint*: If you are using a word processor to write your report, you can copy the URLs from your browser and paste them into the document. Drag to select the entire URL in the Address or Location bar in your browser. Right-click the selected text, then click Copy on the shortcut menu. Position the insertion point in the document where you want the URL to appear, then press [Ctrl][V].)

Independent Challenge 2

This Independent Challenge requires an Internet connection.

New viruses are discovered on an almost daily basis. If you surf the Internet or exchange e-mail, it is important to use updated anti-virus software. Research the most current virus threats and create a table listing the threats and details about them.

- **a.** Start your browser, go to Trend Micro's Web site at **www.trendmicro.com**, and then click the TrendWatch link under the Threat Meter. On the TrendWatch page, click the Current Threat Activity link, click the Malware & Vulnerability Information link, and then click the View the Malware Map link. (If you don't see that link, type **Malware Map** in the Search box on the page, then click the link to Malware Map in the list of search results.)
- **b.** Click links to the top five threats, and then read the description of each threat. The pages describing the threats might open in a new tab.
- **c.** Open a new word processing document and create a table listing each virus threat, a description of what each virus does, how widely each virus is distributed based on the number of infected computers, and how damaging each virus is (the Risk level).
- **d.** In your browser, go to the Security Advisor on CA's Web site at **www3.ca.com/securityadvisor**, and then click the Virus Information Center link. If any of the top five virus threats are different from the ones on the Trend Micro site, add them to your table. (*Hint*: After you click a virus name, check the "Also known as" list.)
- **e.** For any viruses that are already in your table because they were on the Trend Micro site, read the CA description to see if there is any additional information describing how the virus could damage your system. Add this information to your table.

Independent Challenge 3

This Independent Challenge requires an Internet connection.

One of the keyboards shown in this unit is an ergonomic keyboard. Ergonomics is the study of the design of a workspace so that the worker can work efficiently and avoid injury. The U.S. Occupational Safety and Health Administration (OSHA) has developed guidelines that describe a healthy computer work environment. Research these guidelines and evaluate your workspace.

- **a.** Start your browser, and then go to **www.osha.gov/SLTC/etools/computerworkstations**.
- **b.** Read the information on the main page. Follow links to descriptions of the best arrangement for equipment you use when working on a computer. (*Hint*: Look for the Workstation Components link, and point to it to open a submenu of links.)
- **c.** Locate and print the checklist for evaluating your workspace. (*Hint*: Click the Checklist link, then click the View/Print the Evaluation Checklist PDF link. A new tab or window opens and the checklist opens in Adobe Acrobat Reader, a program that displays PDF files. If a dialog box opens telling you that you need to install Acrobat Reader to continue, ask your instructor or technical support person for help.)
- **d.** Using the checklist, evaluate each of the conditions listed. If a condition does not apply to you, write N/A (not applicable) in the Yes column.

Advanced Challenge Exercise

ACE

- Use the OSHA Web site or a search engine to research repetitive motion injuries to which computer users are susceptible.
- Evaluate your risk for at least three common injuries.
- On the OSHA checklist, note what injury or injuries each applicable item or behavior will help prevent.

Real Life Independent Challenge

You are buying a new desktop computer. You want the computer to run Windows 7 and Microsoft Office 2010, and you want to make sure you are protected against security threats. You would like a large flat panel monitor and you need a printer. However, you have a limited budget, and can spend no more than $800 for everything (all hardware and software).

a. To help you organize your information, create the table shown in Figure A-26.

FIGURE A-26

	Your Requirements	Computer Retailer #1	Computer Retailer #2	Computer Retailer #3
Windows 7 (Edition)				
Office 2010 (Edition)				
Brand of computer				
Processor (brand and speed)				
RAM (amount)				
Video RAM (amount)				
Hard disk (size)				
Monitor (type and size)				
Printer (type and speed)				
Speakers				
Antivirus software				
Firewall (software or router with built-in firewall)				
System price				
Additional costs				
Total price				

b. Decide which edition of Windows 7 you want, and enter it in the Your Requirements column of the table. To read a description of the available editions, go to www.microsoft.com and search the Microsoft Web site for information about the Windows 7 Editions.

c. Research the hardware requirements for running the edition of Windows 7 you selected. Search the Microsoft Web site again for the minimum and recommended hardware requirements for running Windows 7.

d. Decide which edition of Office 2010 you want and enter it in the first column of the table. Search the Microsoft Web site to find a description of the software included with each edition of Office 2010, and then search for the hardware requirements for running the edition of Office 2010 that you chose. If necessary, change the hardware requirements in the table.

e. Research the cost of your new computer system. To begin, visit local stores, look at advertisements, or search the Web for computer system retailers. Most computer retailers sell complete systems that come with all the necessary hardware, an operating system, and additional software already installed. In the Computer Retailer #1 column of the table, fill in the specifications for the system you chose. If any item listed as a minimum requirement is not included with the system you chose, find the cost of adding that item and enter the price in the table. Repeat this process with systems from two other retailers, entering the specifications in the Computer Retailer #2 and Computer Retailer #3 columns.

f. If the system you chose does not come with a printer, search the Web for an inexpensive color inkjet printer.

g. If the system you chose does not come with antivirus software, search the Web for the cost, if any, of an antivirus software package. Make sure you look up reviews of the package you chose. Decide whether to purchase this software or download a free one, and enter this cost in the table.

h. If you decide you need a router with a built-in firewall, search the Web for the price of one. Enter this information in the table.

i. Total the costs you entered in the table for the various items. Is the total cost $800 or less? If not, revisit some of the items. Can you get a less expensive printer? Do you need to downgrade to a less expensive monitor? Likewise, if you are under budget, upgrade a part of your system; perhaps you can afford to upgrade the monitor to a larger, flat panel monitor. Reevaluate your choices if necessary and try to get your total cost close to $800.

UNIT
A
Internet 2010

Getting Started with Internet Explorer 8

Files You Will Need:
No files needed.

In this unit, you learn how to use the Internet Explorer 8 browser to find information on the World Wide Web (WWW or the Web). You will learn how to navigate to Web sites on the Web, how to navigate from one Web page to another, and how to search for information on the Web. You will also learn how to view Web pages while protecting your privacy, computer, and personal information. In addition, you learn how to get on-screen help as you use Internet Explorer. You need to connect to the Internet to complete this unit. Quest Specialty Travel (QST) management has decided to provide laptop computers with mobile Internet technology to all tour guides. Guides can then use the Internet to research the latest information on local weather, events, and news while traveling with the groups. Each computer will have Internet Explorer 8 installed as the browser. Your job is to train the guides to use Internet Explorer 8 and teach them how to find information on the Internet during their tours.

OBJECTIVES

- Understand Web browsers
- Explore the browser
- View and navigate Web pages
- Use tabbed browsing
- Save favorite Web pages
- Browse safely
- Search for information
- Get Help and exit Internet Explorer

UNIT
A
Internet 2010

Understanding Web Browsers

The **Web** (also called the **World Wide Web** or **WWW**) is the part of the Internet that contains interconnected Web pages. **Web pages** are electronic documents that can contain text, graphics, sound, and video. A **Web browser** (also called a **browser**) is a software program that lets you open and display Web pages. You must use a browser to view Web pages that are on the Web. Browsers, such as Microsoft Internet Explorer, Opera, FireFox, and Safari, make navigating the Web easy. When you view Web pages with a browser, you click words, phrases, or graphics called **hyperlinks**, or simply **links**, to connect to and view other Web pages. Links on a Web page can also open graphics or text files or play sound or video files. This unit features **Internet Explorer**, a popular browser that is part of the Microsoft Windows operating system. Figure A-1 shows a Web page from a U.S. government Web site. This site provides a wealth of information for citizens, tourists, businesses, and just about anybody looking for facts or figures about the United States. Your manager has asked you to prepare for your first training session with the tour guides. You review the features and benefits of using Internet Explorer.

DETAILS

- **Display Web sites**

  A **Web site** is a group of Web pages focused on a particular subject. Web sites originate all over the world. Web sites exist for individuals, businesses, museums, governments, organizations, and educational institutions. Web sites cover topics in the arts, music, politics, education, sports, and commerce. QST tour guides can use the Web to get up-to-date information about the places they are touring. They click the hyperlinks or "links" on Web pages to move from one Web page to another to get maps and directions, explore shopping areas, find out about special events, determine currency conversion rates, get weather forecasts, read news, and view photographs.

- **Play audio and video clips**

  A Web browser can play audio and video clips if your computer has the appropriate hardware, such as speakers. In their research, tour guides find Web pages that include video clips of historic buildings, shopping trips, local stories and customs, or other information about a region.

- **Search the Web for information and save a list of favorite Web pages**

  A **search engine** is a special Web site that quickly searches the Internet for Web sites based on words or phrases that you enter. QST tour guides use search engines to look for Web sites that focus on a particular country, government, or travel region or on a specific topic of interest. They can save a list of links to Web pages they might need to visit again, such as a page for a specific museum, city, or map, creating a list of favorite Web sites that they can quickly access to view later.

QUICK TIP

Be sure you understand the terms of use before you use any content, such as text or graphics, taken from a Web site.

- **Save, share, e-mail, or print Web page text and graphics**

  If you want to keep the information or an image you find on the Web, you can save it as a file on your computer, to use it later or to share with others. You can also copy the information temporarily to the Clipboard, where it is available for pasting into other programs. For example, just by clicking a few links on the www.usa.gov site, you can link to the National Park Service National Register of Historic Places National Register of Travel Itineraries shown in Figure A-2. Tour guides can save this page, copy and paste it into another program, or print maps or directions from the Web to hand out to their groups. They can e-mail the link or the page directly from the browser window to another person who is set up for e-mail. The person receives the page or link to the page as part of an e-mail message and can view the page on his or her computer.

FIGURE A-1: A Web page

FIGURE A-2: National Register of Historic Places Web site

Building an international community

The World Wide Web has become an integral component of corporate culture, educational institutions, and personal lives around the world. The Web was created in Switzerland in 1991 to allow links between documents on the Internet. The **Internet** is a network of connected computers and computer networks located around the world. A **computer network** is the hardware and software that makes it possible for two or more computers to share information and resources. The first graphical Web browser, Mosaic, was introduced at the University of Illinois in 1993 to allow people to use the Internet to view Web pages. Mosaic led to the development of browsers such as Netscape Navigator and Internet Explorer. By some estimates, more than 600 million computers worldwide now connect to the Internet through telephone lines, cables, satellites, and other telecommunications media. Through the Internet, these computers can share information, including text, graphics, sound, video, and computer programs. Today, Web pages exist from nearly every country in the world, creating an international community. Millions of people worldwide use the Web daily for commerce, education, and entertainment. Anyone with a computer and an Internet connection can use this rich information source that now contains more than 25 billion Web pages.

UNIT A
Internet 2010

Exploring the Browser

When you start the Internet Explorer browser, its program window opens. The easiest way to start the browser is by clicking the Internet Explorer icon. You can use the Internet Explorer window toolbar buttons and menus to navigate the Web to find the information you need. In the browser window, you can view one or more Web pages. Each page opens on a separate tab. The tab in front is the **active tab**. Before you show the tour guides how to view Web pages and navigate from one page to another, you review the components of the Internet Explorer browser window.

STEPS

QUICK TIP
You can click the Start button on the taskbar, click All Programs, then click Internet Explorer.

1. **Locate the Internet Explorer icon on your Windows taskbar**
The location of the Internet Explorer icon, shown in Figure A-3, might vary on different computers. Some computers have the Internet Explorer icon in more than one location. The icon might be "pinned" to the Start menu, so you can click the Start button on the taskbar, then click Internet Explorer. If the icon is on your desktop, double-click it to start the program.

QUICK TIP
The term 'load' is often used to describe opening a page in a browser.

2. **Click the Internet Explorer icon on the Windows taskbar, then if necessary, click the Maximize button on the Internet Explorer title bar**
Internet Explorer opens and displays your home page. A **home page** is the first Web page that opens every time you start Internet Explorer. "Home page" also applies to the main page that opens when you first go to a Web site. Figure A-4 shows the Quest Specialty Travel home page. Look at the home page on your screen, which will differ, and compare the elements, using Figure A-4 as a guide.

DETAILS

The elements of the Internet Explorer browser window include the following:

- The **title bar** contains the name of the Web page currently open in the Web browser's active tab window.
- The **Address bar** displays the address of the Web page currently opened in the active tab. The **Uniform Resource Locator (URL)**, or the Web page's address, appears in the Address box on the Address bar after you open the page. If you click the Address box list arrow, you see a list of addresses you have recently entered in the Address box. The Address bar also has buttons to refresh a page, to stop the loading of a Web page, and to move forward and back from one Web page to another.
- You use the **Search box** to help find Web sites about a particular topic. You can enter a keyword or words in the Search box, then click the Search button. Click the Search list arrow to choose the search engine to use. When the search is complete, a list of related Web sites opens in a search results Web page.
- The **menu bar** provides access to most of the browser's features through a series of menus.
- The **Favorites bar** is a convenient place to store links to Web pages that you use often. You can add a link to the Favorites bar by dragging the icon that precedes the URL in the Address bar to the Favorites bar. Web page addresses that you place in the Favorites bar are also available in the Favorites tab when you click the Favorites button to open the Favorites Center. The **Favorites Center** includes three tabs. Feeds keeps track of your subscriptions. History maintains an organized list of links to the Web sites you visited and sorts them by when you visited them.
- The **Command bar**, located to the right of the Web page tabs, provides buttons with list arrows that let you open menus. The menu commands let you set your home page, manage and print Web pages, apply safety and privacy settings, and customize the browser. Many commonly used commands available on menus are more quickly accomplished using the toolbar buttons. Depending on the programs installed on your computer, you might have additional buttons.
- The **browser window** is the area in the center of the window where the current Web page appears.
- The **tabs** identify the current Web page or pages open in the browser. **Tabbed browsing** allows you to open more than one Web page at a time in a browser window.
- The **vertical scroll bar** appears along the right side of a page if the page is longer than the window's viewable area. The **scroll box** indicates your relative position within the Web page.

QUICK TIP
Right-click any toolbar and then click Menu Bar to display the menu bar.

QUICK TIP
To display toolbars, such as the menu bar and status bar, click the Tools list arrow on the Command bar, point to Toolbars, and then click the name of the bar you want to display. Or, right-click the area to the right of the last open tab, then click a toolbar name.

FIGURE A-3: Starting Internet Explorer 8

FIGURE A-4: Elements of the Internet Explorer window

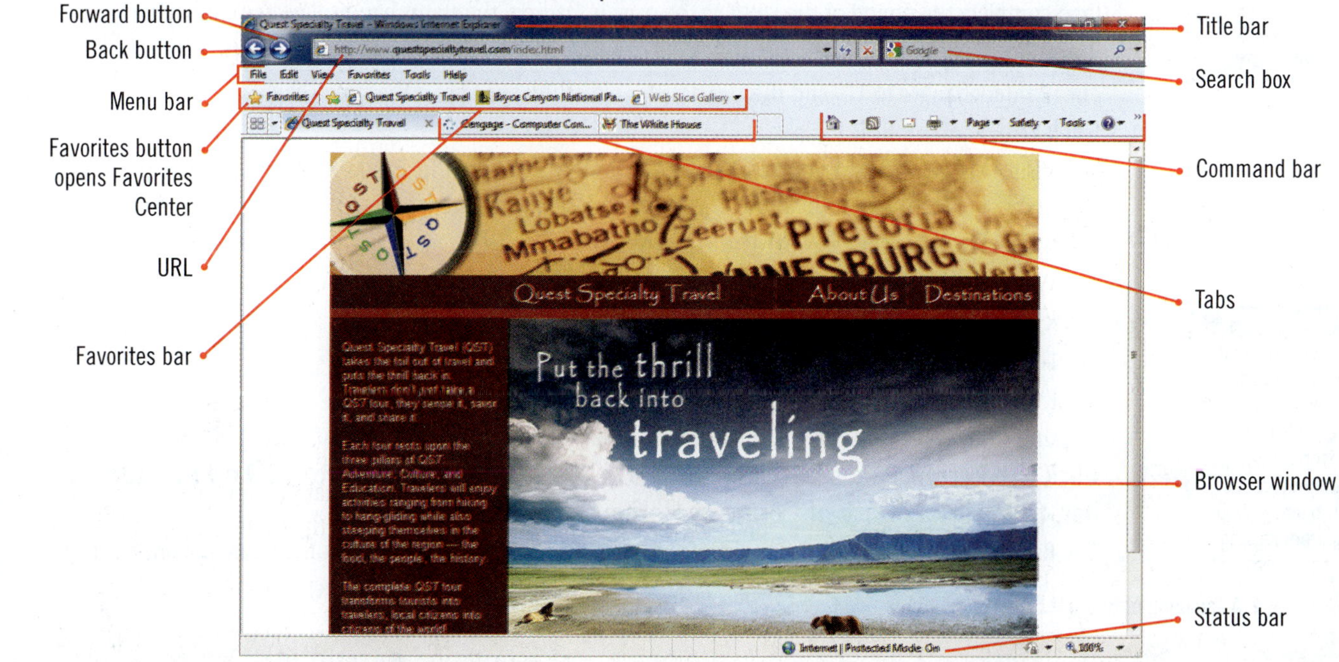

Understanding the status bar

The status bar can give you valuable information as you use Internet Explorer. It displays information about your connection progress whenever you open a new Web page. It notifies you when you connect to another Web site. As a page loads, a green progress bar shows the percentage of information transferred from the Web server to your browser. The status bar displays "Done" when the page is loaded. When you move your mouse pointer over links on the Web page, the status bar displays the Web addresses. It lets you know if pop-ups are blocked on the page. Information about your Internet Security appears on the status bar; you can change your security setting by double-clicking the Internet Security section. The Zoom Level button appears on the right side of the status bar. You can hide or display the status bar using the Toolbars command on the View menu, on the Tools menu in the Command bar, or on the IE8 shortcut menu.

UNIT A Internet 2010

Viewing and Navigating Web Pages

Moving between Web pages located at different addresses is simple with hyperlinks. **Hyperlinks** let you navigate to, or open, another location on the same Web page or jump to an entirely different Web page. You can follow these links to see more information about a topic by clicking a linked word or phrase. You can use the navigation tools in Internet Explorer to move around the Web. You can navigate from page to page using the Forward and Back buttons, as well as the Home button. Table A-1 describes additional buttons that are available on the Address bar and the Command bar. You look at the Library of Congress Web site for information for a tour traveling to Washington, D.C.

STEPS

TROUBLE
Because Web pages change frequently, the Web page you load might look different from that shown in the figure.

QUICK TIP
Move the pointer over the Back or Forward button to display a ScreenTip showing which page will appear when the button is clicked.

QUICK TIP
If you change your mind or if a page takes too long to load, you can click the Stop button on the Address bar to stop a new Web page from loading.

1. **Click anywhere in the Address box on the Address bar**
   The current address is highlighted; any text you type replaces it.
2. **Type www.loc.gov, then press [Enter]**
   After a few seconds, the home page for the Library of Congress opens in the browser window, as shown in Figure A-5, and the status bar displays "Done." If you typed a specific address in the Address bar previously, the AutoComplete feature recognizes the first few characters you type. A list opens below the Address box containing the addresses in which the typed letters appear; you can click the URL in the list to open the page rather than complete the typing of the URL. As the page is loading, the status bar displays the connection process.
3. **Place your mouse pointer on the Visitors link in the Resources for section**
   The pointer changes to and the URL for the hyperlink appears in the status bar.
4. **Click the Visitors link**
   The Visitors page opens in your Web browser window, as shown in Figure A-6. The name of the Web page appears on the front tab in the browser window. A Web page icon appears to the left of the Web page name.
5. **Click the Back button on the Address bar**
   The Web page that you viewed, the Library of Congress home page, opens in the browser window.
6. **Click the Forward button on the Address bar**
   The Forward button opens the Visitors page in the browser window again.
7. **Click the Home button on the Command bar**
   Clicking the Home button opens the home page set for your installation of Internet Explorer.
8. **Click the Recent Pages button to the right of the Forward button on the Address bar, then click Library of Congress Home**
   The Recent Pages button displays a list of the last pages that you visited. Click the name to view the page.

TABLE A-1: A sampling of Internet Explorer 8 buttons

name	button	description	name	button	description
Recent Pages		Lists recently viewed pages	Favorites		Opens Favorites Center
Compatibility		Shows pages made for old browsers	View Feeds		Adds current RSS Feed to Favorites Center
Refresh		Refreshes the contents of current page	Read Mail		Starts Microsoft Outlook (if installed)
Stop		Stops loading new page	Print		Prints current Web page
Search		Searches for Web sites	Help		Displays Help window
Home		Opens the home page	Add to Favorites Bar		Adds current site to Favorites bar

FIGURE A-5: Home page for the Library of Congress

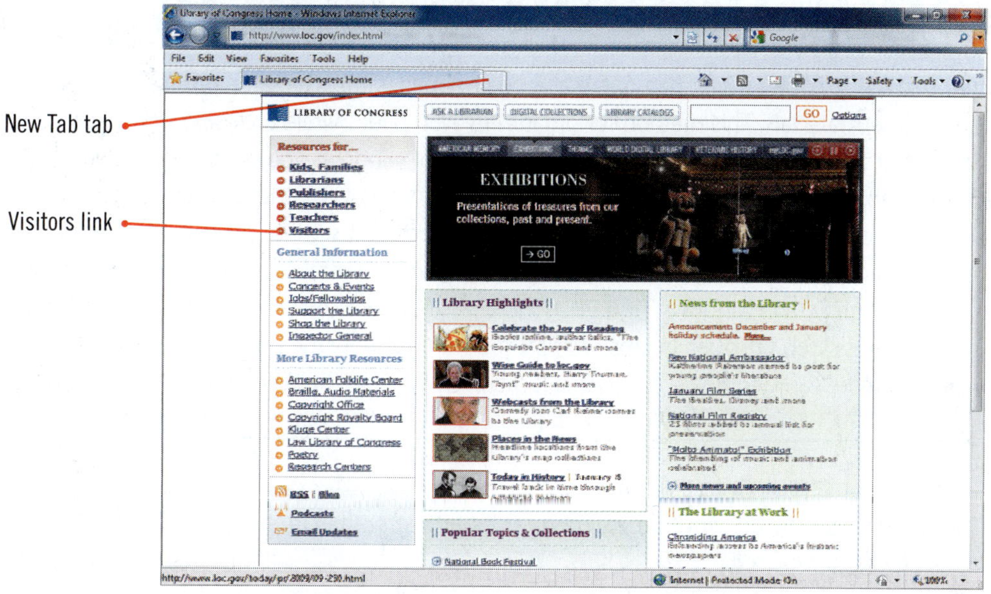

FIGURE A-6: Visitors Web page at the Library of Congress Web site

Setting the home page

When you click the Home button on the Command bar, the page that is specified as the home page opens in your Web browser window. Each time you start Internet Explorer, the first page that appears is your home page. You can easily select a different home page to open each time you start Internet Explorer. Go to the page that you want to be your home page, click the Home button list arrow on the Command bar, then click Add or Change Home Page to open the Add or Change Home Page dialog box. See Figure A-7. When the dialog box opens, select the option that identifies how you want to set the Web page as your home page. If you have more than one tab open, you will see all these options. You can also click Tools on the menu bar, then click Internet Options to open the Internet Options dialog box. Click the General tab if necessary, and click the Use current button in the Home page area to specify the current page as your home page.

FIGURE A-7: Add or Change Home Page dialog box

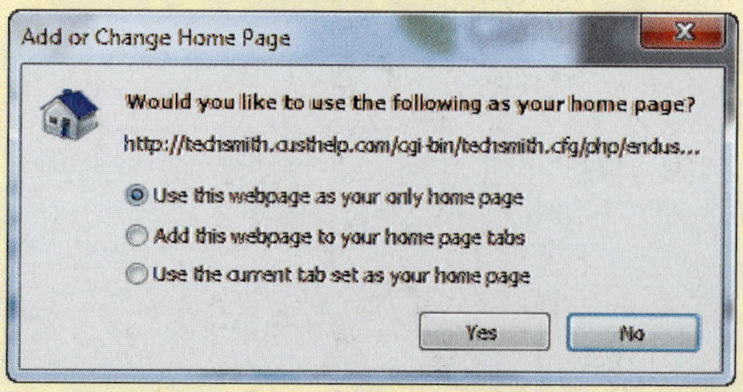

Internet 2010

UNIT A Internet 2010

Using Tabbed Browsing

Tabbed browsing allows more than one Web page to open within the same browser window. Each window appears on a separate tab. This method for organizing Web pages while browsing makes navigation between Web pages fast and simple. It also minimizes the number of windows you need open on your desktop as you browse the Web. You can also open several Internet Explorer windows at the same time, each with its own series of Web pages accessible by tabs. You can easily change the default settings for tabbed browsing. For example, you can have several pages open automatically for a Web site on several tabs, or you can bypass the tab settings to open pages in their own windows. Figure A-8 shows an Internet Explorer window with several pages from the Library of Congress Web site open in tabs. You want to show the tour guides how tabbed browsing will allow them to more easily compare events in a location by viewing the Web pages in one browsing session.

STEPS

1. **Type www.usa.gov in the Address bar, then press [Enter]**
   The Web page for the U.S. government opens. It is on the front tab in the browser window.
2. **Click the New Tab tab in the browser window**
   The about:Tabs Web page appears as a new tab in the browser window, as shown in Figure A-9.
3. **Click the Close Tab button in the New tab**
   The usa.gov Web page is now the only Web page open in the browser window.
4. **Scroll down the page, on the right side of the page, in the Government Agencies section, right-click the State Government link, click Open in New Tab on the shortcut menu, then click the State Government:USA.gov tab to display the Web page**
5. **Press and hold [Ctrl], click any state link, then click the state tab**
   There are many ways to open a Web page in a new tab. Using tabbed browsing, you now have three Web pages open in one browser window. These tabs are part of a **tab group**, a set of tabs that have the same color to indicate that they originated from the same Web page. Color coding helps organize tabs that originate from the same Web site.
6. **Position the mouse pointer over each tab to display the ScreenTip for each**
   Each ScreenTip tells you the name and URL of the Web page in the tab.
7. **Click the Quick Tabs button to the left of the first tab**
   Thumbnail images of open tabs appear in Quick Tabs view, as shown in Figure A-10.
8. **Click the Close Tab button for the second and third thumbnails in Quick Tabs view, then click the USA.gov tab**
   Quick Tabs view closes, and the USA.gov tab is open in the window.

QUICK TIP
If someone has clicked the Don't show this page again check box on the about:Tabs page, you will see a Web page rather than the about:Tabs Web page.

QUICK TIP
Click the tab for a Web page to display that Web page in front.

Understanding URLs

Every Web page has a unique address on the Web, also known as its URL. Browser software locates a Web page based on its address. All Web page addresses begin with "http," which stands for Hypertext Transfer Protocol, the set of rules for exchanging files on the Web. Web sites that begin "https" are secure sites. These letters are followed by a colon and two forward slashes. Most pages begin with "www" (which indicates that the page is on the World Wide Web), followed by a dot, or period, and then the Web site's name, known as the **domain name**. Following the domain name is another dot and the top-level domain, such as com (for commercial sites), edu (for educational institutions), or org (for organizations). The **top-level domain** tells you the type of site you are visiting. After the top-level domain, another slash and one or more folder names and a filename might appear.

FIGURE A-8: Tabbed browsing

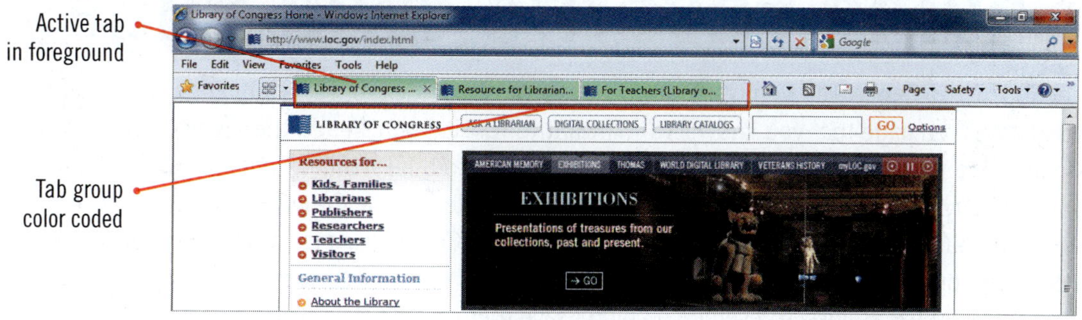

FIGURE A-9: The about:Tabs Web page in a second tab

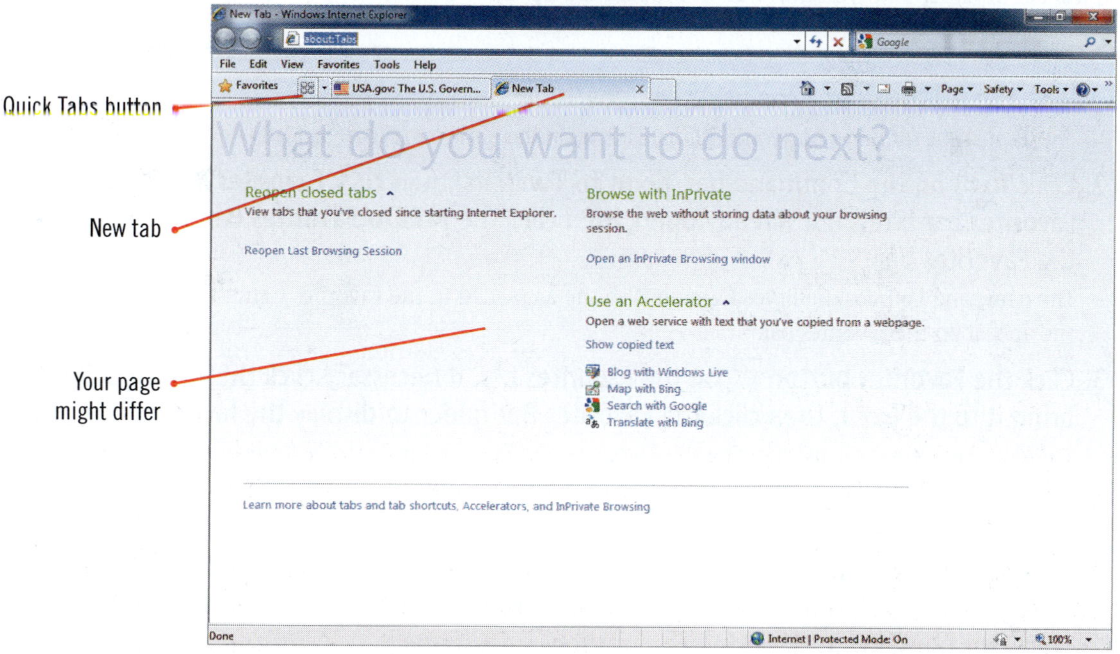

FIGURE A-10: Quick Tabs view

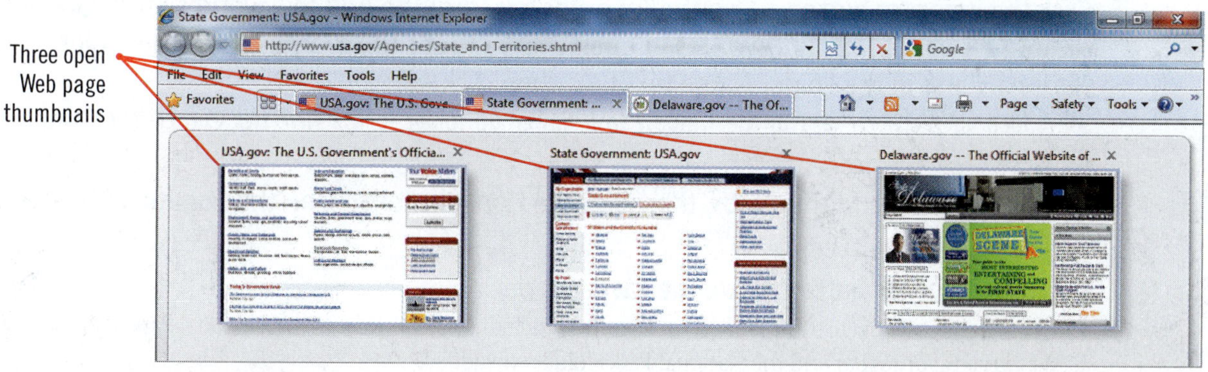

Closing pages when you have several open tabs

When you finish looking at Web pages using Internet Explorer, you might find that you have several tabs open. To exit the program and close all open tabs, you either click File on the menu bar and click Exit, or click the Close button on the title bar. A dialog box opens, asking if you want to close all the tabs or just the current tab. If you don't want to close the program, you can right-click any tab, close the tab group, close other tabs, ungroup a tab, re-open a closed tab, or see a list of recently closed tabs that you can reopen. Internet Explorer lets you re-open closed tabs when tabs are closed inadvertently during your current browsing session. If you have tabs open when you close your browser window, you can choose to re-open your last browsing session the next time you open Internet Explorer. Click the Tools button on the Command bar, then click Reopen Last Browsing Session.

Saving Favorite Web Pages

The **Favorites Center** lets you create your own list of Web pages you visit frequently, or **favorites**. When you find a Web page that you know you will want to revisit, you can add the site address to the Favorites Center or to the Favorites bar. After you add a Web page to the Favorites Center or Favorites bar, you can automatically access that page by clicking the Favorites button on the Command bar or by clicking Favorites on the menu bar and then clicking the link. The Favorites Center also includes the Feeds and History tabs. **Feeds** are your subscriptions to Web site updates and news. The History tab lists Web sites you have visited. These sites appear as links, so even if you didn't save them as favorites, you can click the link to revisit the site. Tour guides want to be able to revisit some travel Web sites without having to write the URLs on a sheet of paper and type the URLs in the Address bar each time.

STEPS

1. **Click the Address bar, type www.nps.gov/brca, then press [Enter]**
   The home page for Bryce Canyon National Park opens, as shown in Figure A-11.

2. **Click Tools on the Command bar, point to Toolbars, then click Favorites Bar to open the Favorites bar if it is not already open, then click the Add to Favorites Bar button on the Favorites bar**
   The name and URL for the Bryce Canyon Web site are added to the Favorites Center in the Favorites folder and appear on the Favorites bar.

QUICK TIP
To create a new folder, right-click any item and then click Create New Folder.

3. **Click the Favorites button on the Favorites bar, if necessary click the Favorites tab to bring it to the front, then click the Favorites Bar folder to display the favorites it contains**
   The Favorites Center opens, showing the Bryce Canyon favorite inside the Favorites Bar folder. The Favorites Center shows the folders in which you can place the URLs for your favorite Web pages. You can drag Web page addresses from the Address bar to place them in folders.

4. Click the Favorites button to close the Favorites Center, **click the New Tab tab, type www.nps.gov/yell in the Address bar, press [Enter], click the New Tab tab, type www.nps.gov/zion in the Address bar, then press [Enter]**
   You opened new tabs for Yellowstone National Park and Zion National Park.

5. **Click the Favorites button on the Favorites bar, click the Add to Favorites list arrow, click Add Current Tabs to Favorites to open the Add Tabs to Favorites dialog box, type National Parks in the Folder Name text box, then click Add**
   You added all the open tabs in the window to a tab group folder in the Favorites Center. The Favorites Center closes.

QUICK TIP
If you do not create a folder, the most recently added favorites appear at the bottom of the Favorites list.

6. **Close the second and third tabs, then click the Home button on the Command bar to return to your home page**

7. **Click the Favorites button on the Favorites bar**
   The Favorites Center opens. You see a list of Favorites, including the Bryce Canyon National Park favorite you added to the Favorites bar and the National Parks folder you added.

8. **Click the Bryce Canyon National Park link in the Favorites Center**
   The Bryce Canyon home page opens in your Web browser window.

QUICK TIP
To open the individual links in the folder, click the group folder, then click each favorite's arrow to open each link in its own tab.

9. **Click , point to the National Parks folder, then click the Open 'National Parks' in a tab group arrow to open the list of links in that Folder**
   Tab groups are color coded when you open them as a group. Refer to Figure A-12.

10. **Close all but one of the Web pages, leaving one tab open in the browser window**

FIGURE A-11: Home page for Bryce Canyon National Park

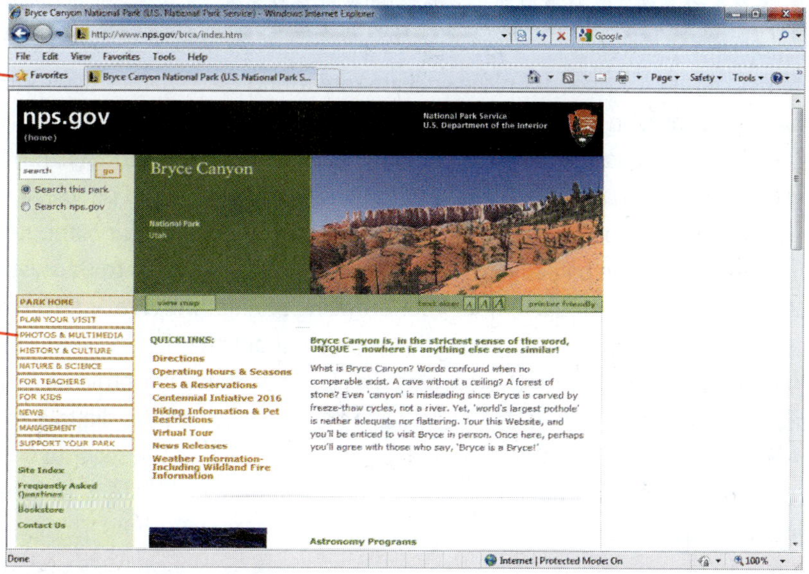

FIGURE A-12: Favorites Center

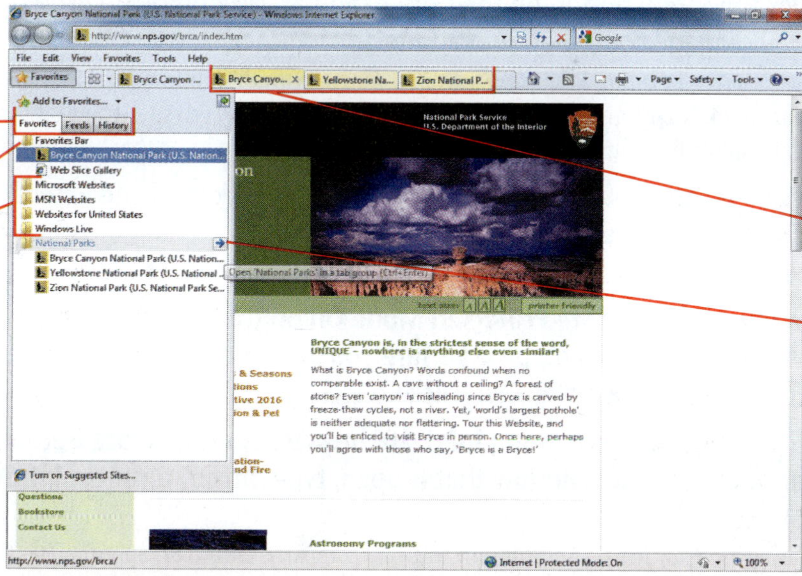

Creating and organizing favorites

To keep your Favorites Center list manageable, only add pages that you expect to visit again. You can organize your list of favorites by placing them into folders by category. For example, you might want to create folders according to your interests, such as sports, cooking, and travel. Favorites can be listed individually or placed in folders in the Favorites Center or on the Favorites bar. To add a folder to your Favorites Center, click the Add to Favorites list arrow in the Favorites Center, then click Organize Favorites. The Organize Favorites dialog box opens, as shown in Figure A-13. Click the New Folder button, then type the folder name and press [Enter] to add a new folder to the list of folders and favorites. You can move a favorite to a specific folder by clicking the favorite, clicking the Move button to open the Browse For Folder dialog box, and then selecting the folder or creating a new folder in which to add the favorite you want to move. You can also drag and drop a favorite into a folder, and you can rename favorites and folders. Information about a selected favorite appears below the list.

FIGURE A-13: Organize Favorites dialog box

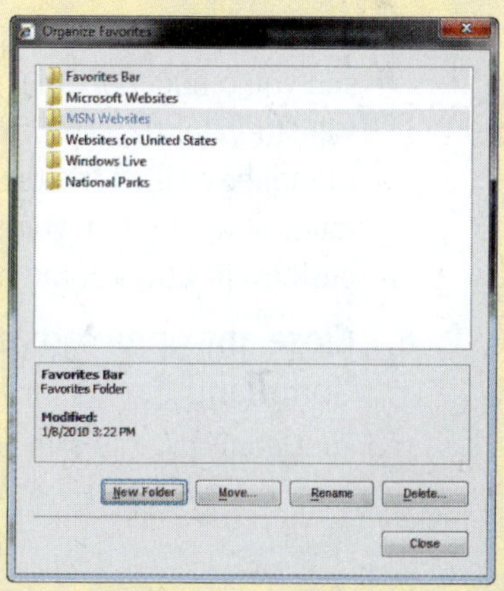

Internet 2010

Browsing Safely

The Internet can be a wonderful place to learn interesting facts, gather news, find directions, and acquire new skills. But it can also be a place where your privacy is at risk, where you can infect your computer with viruses, and where you can be subject to identity theft. Fortunately, browsers have built-in features that can help protect you from many of these harmful programs, situations, and people. If you exercise safe browsing habits, make sensible choices, and let your browser protect you and your computer from malicious software, browsing the Internet can be a fun and rewarding experience. **InPrivate Browsing** lets you view Web sites without the browser storing data about your browsing session. **InPrivate Filtering** helps prevent Web site or third-party developers from collecting information about the sites you visit. Internet Security properties let you set the security levels for trusted sites. The Security Status bar provides icons and color coding to let you know that your transactions are over a secure connection and the digital certificate is valid for the site. A **digital certificate** verifies the identity of a person or indicates the security of a Web site. Certificates are issued by trusted companies known as Certification Authorities. You learn about how to surf safely using Internet Explorer 8.

STEPS

TROUBLE

If you don't see a dialog box after clicking InPrivate Filtering, your filtering has already been activated. You can click InPrivate Filtering Settings instead.

TROUBLE

If your settings are different, ask your resource person before changing them.

1. **Click the Safety button on the Command bar, click InPrivate Browsing, type www.cengage.com, then press [Enter]**

   The Cengage Learning Web page opens in a new browser window with InPrivate Browsing turned on. See Figure A-14. No information from your visit to this or other Web sites you visit through this browser window will be stored on your computer.

2. **Click the Safety button on the Command bar, click InPrivate Filtering, read the information in the dialog box, then click Cancel**

   You want to be able to visit the site and have information transmitted to your computer.

3. **Double-click Internet | Protected Mode On on the status bar, review the settings in the Internet Security dialog box, be sure you are set for Internet and that Enable Protected Mode has a check mark, then click Cancel**

4. **Click the Cengage Learning InPrivate browser window Close button, click in the Address Bar of the browser window that is open, type http://turbotax.intuit.com/, then press [Enter]**

   The Web site for the tax preparation software company, TurboTax, appears. The URL begins with http:// and the Address bar is gray and black text on a light bluish-gray background. See Figure A-15.

5. **Click the Sign In button near the top of the Turbo Tax page, click Check e-File status, then move the mouse pointer over INTUIT INC in the Security Status bar on the right side of the Address bar to read the ScreenTip about the site**

   The URL in the Address bar is now green. See Figure A-16. This secure or encrypted site address begins with https rather than http, and you see a lock icon to the right of the URL. This Web site has a secure connection, and you can identify the Web site through the site's certificate. Security status bar colors tell you the levels of validation for the certificate. Red means the certificate is out of date. Yellow means the certification authority cannot be verified and there might be a problem. White means the certificate has normal validation and communication between your browser and the site is encrypted, but the authority makes no guarantees about the business practices of the site. Green is the most secure, indicating extended validation.

6. **Close any open tabs except the first tab, then click the Home button on the Command bar**

   Your home page appears in the browser window.

FIGURE A-14: InPrivate Browsing

FIGURE A-15: TurboTax Web site

FIGURE A-16: Secure Web site

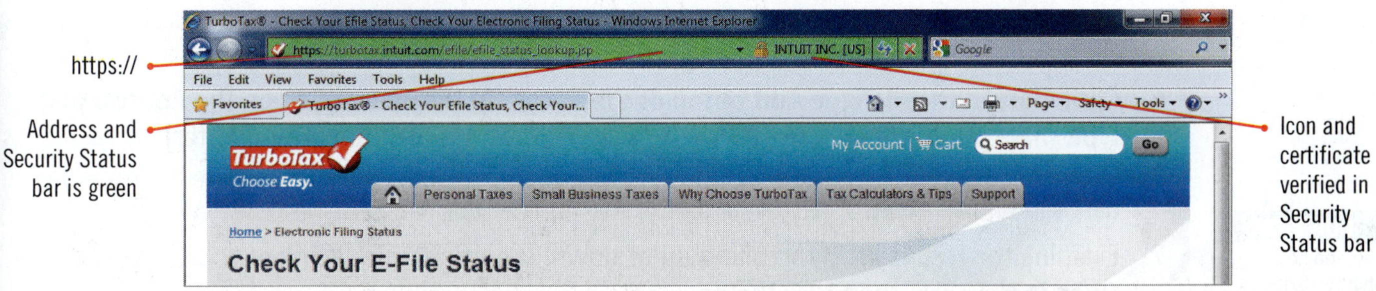

Phishing and the SmartScreen Filter

Phishing is an illicit activity used by hackers to trick computer users into revealing personal or financial information through an e-mail message or Web site. If you receive an e-mail message that looks like a notice from a trusted source, such as your bank or credit card company, be wary of its contents. Your bank will never ask you to click a link and provide personal information. In a phishing e-mail message, the link you click will take you to a fraudulent site where you are asked to provide personal information, such as an account number or password. This information is then typically used for identity theft. **SmartScreen Filter** is a feature in Internet Explorer 8 that helps detect phishing Web sites. SmartScreen Filter can also help protect you from installing malicious software on your computer. Click the Safety button on the Command bar, point to SmartScreen Filter, then click one of the options: Check This Website, Turn Off SmartScreen Filter, or Report Unsafe Website.

UNIT A

Internet 2010

Searching for Information

A search for information using the Internet Explorer **Search bar** is based on criteria called **keywords**, which are words related to the topic for which you are searching. To search using the Search bar, you can enter a keyword or words in the Search box. As you start typing, the default search provider will offer suggestions for Web sites. You can click a suggestion or you can complete your entry and then click the Search button to start the search. The **Search box** lets you search using the selected search provider. Some popular search providers are Bing (formerly Windows Live Search), MSN Search, Google, and Yahoo! Search. You can also go directly to the search provider Web site, such as www.google.com or www.yahoo.com, and do a Web search. The search provider locates information and shows you a list of links to Web sites related to your search topic. You can click one of the links in the list to go quickly to a site. Once at a site, you can use the Find feature to search keywords on the page. You decide to show the tour guides how to look for travel information for tourists with limited mobility by searching with the browser.

STEPS

QUICK TIP
Each search engine differs slightly in the way it formats search results, the way it records the number of Internet sites in the database, and how often it updates its database.

1. **Click the Address bar, type www.google.com, then press [Enter]**
   The Google home page opens in the browser window. Google is a commercial company that runs a search engine. Search providers such as Bing, Yahoo!, Google, Ask, and Lycos routinely use software programs to methodically catalog, or crawl, through the entire Internet and create huge databases with links to Web pages and their URLs. When you enter a keyword or phrase, the search engine examines its database index for relevant information and displays a list of Web sites.
2. **Type limited mobility in the Search box in the Internet Explorer Search Bar, notice how the drop-down list offers suggestions for your search, press [Spacebar], type vacations, then click Google Search**
   Your search results appear as a list of links to related Web sites with a description of each site.

QUICK TIP
Topic searches, which limit the search to a specific subject such as travel, science, or history, are available through Web sites such as Expedia.com, About.com, and Wikipedia.com.

3. **Click any link to view a Web page, click the Back button on the Address bar twice to return to the Google home page, then click the New Tab tab to open a new tab**
4. **Click the Search list arrow on the Search bar**
   The default search engine for Internet Explorer 8 is Bing. If another search engine, such as Google, is listed, you can use that as well.
5. **Click Manage Search Providers**
   You use the Manage Add-ons dialog box, shown in Figure A-17, to set another Web site as the default or to rank the listing order. You decide to investigate online photo sharing, since tour guests like to exchange photos.
6. **Click Close in the Manage Add-ons dialog box, click in the Search box on the Address bar, type share photos online, review the Search Suggestions list, then press [Enter]**
   As shown in Figure A-18, your search results appear as a list of related Web sites in the browser window. You can click any link to open a Web page or a list of Web pages relating to a specific category.

QUICK TIP
Press and hold [Shift][Ctrl], then click any hyperlink to open a Web page in a new tab in the foreground.

7. **Examine the results list by scrolling up or down, then right-click a link of your choice, click Open in New Tab, then click the new tab**
   The related page with information about sharing photographs opens. The tabs for each open Web page are color coded to help you organize your findings. Use the Find feature to find information about free offers on the Web site.

QUICK TIP
Press [Ctrl][F] to open the Find bar.

8. **Click Edit on the menu bar, click Find on this Page to open the Find bar, then type photo**
   The word "photo" is highlighted, and the number of matches is in the Find bar. See Figure A-19.
9. **Close the Find bar, close all open tabs except the first tab, then click the Home button on the Command bar**
   Your home page appears in the browser window.

FIGURE A-17: Manage Add-ons dialog box

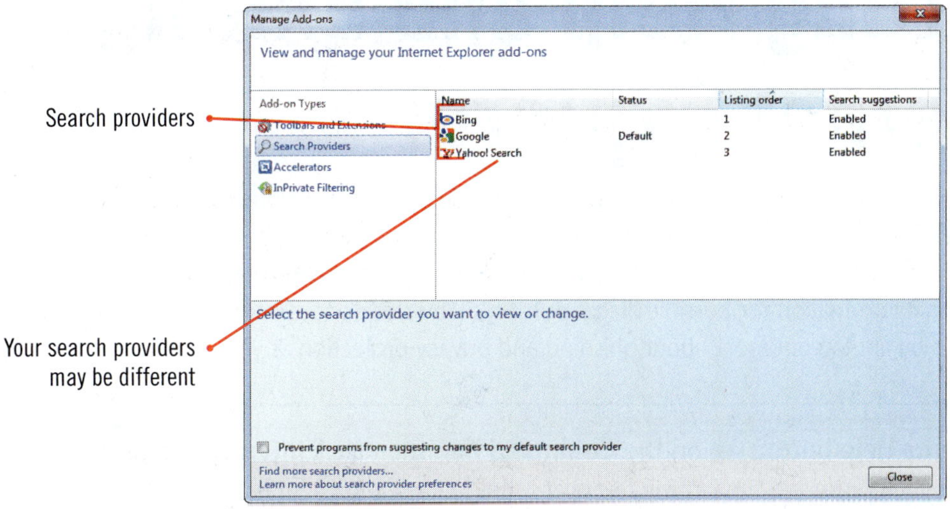

FIGURE A-18: Search results

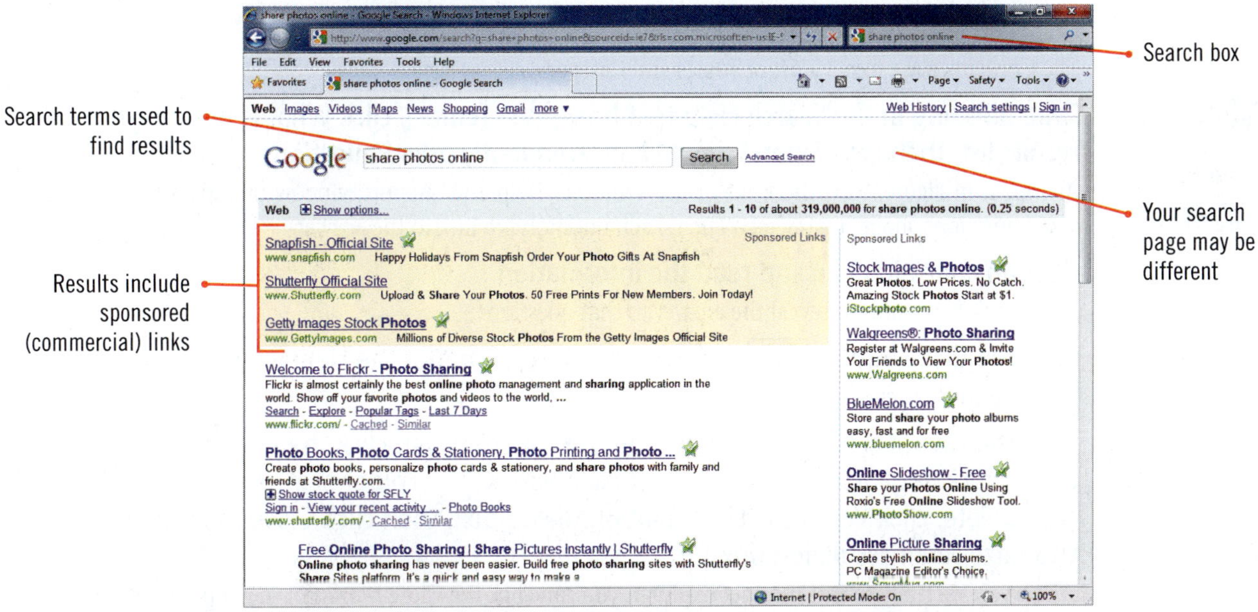

FIGURE A-19: Finding text on a page

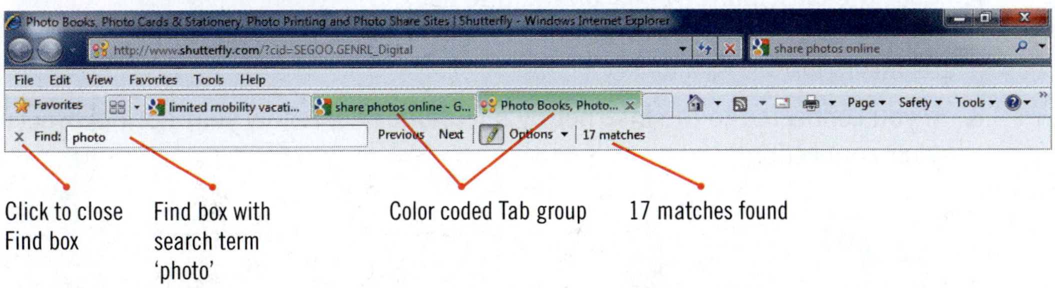

Blocking pop-ups

Pop-ups are windows that open on your screen as you visit Web sites, generally to advertise products you might or might not want. Often they are annoying, so you might choose to block them. Internet Explorer comes with a built-in Pop-up Blocker. Click Tools on the Command bar, point to Pop-up Blocker, then click Turn Off Pop-up Blocker to turn it off if you want pop-ups, or click Pop-up Blocker Settings to open the Pop-up Blocker Settings dialog box to permit pop-ups from specific Web sites. You can also control notifications and set the filter level. Notifications will play a sound or show the Information bar if a pop-up is blocked. Filter levels can be set to Low, Medium, or High.

UNIT
A
Internet 2010

Getting Help and Exiting Internet Explorer

Internet Explorer provides a Help system with information and instructions on various features and commands. While demonstrating Internet Explorer, you were asked about the purpose of the Phishing Filter on the status bar. **Phishing** is an illicit activity in which people send you fraudulent Web sites to gather your personal information for possible illegal purposes. You decide to demonstrate the Help system to the tour guides by finding out more about phishing and privacy protection as you use Internet Explorer.

STEPS

1. **Click the Help button on the Command bar, then click Internet Explorer Help**
   The Windows Help and Support window opens. You can type a keyword in the Search Help text box, or you can click links to access several Help features. The buttons at the top of the Window give you other ways to explore the Help System. Refer to Figure A-20.
2. **Click the Browse Help button on the Help toolbar**
   The Contents page shows a list of Topics and Categories of interest.
3. **Type phishing in the Search Help text box, press [Enter], click What is phishing? in the results list, then click SmartScreen Filter: frequently asked questions**
   As shown in Figure A-21, the links in the Windows Help and Support window provide a list of frequently asked questions about SmartScreen Filter. Each question is a link to the answer.
4. **Click any question link and read the information**
   The question expands to reveal the answer to that question.
5. **Click the Close button in the upper-right corner of the Help window**
   The Help window closes.
6. **Click the Favorites button Favorites on the Favorites bar, click the Add to Favorites list arrow, click Organize Favorites, select each Favorite or Folder that you added in this unit, click Delete, click Yes in the confirmation dialog box, then click Close to close the Organize Favorites dialog box**
   When you are ready to exit Internet Explorer, you can click the Close button in the upper-right corner of the title bar in the browser window or click Exit on the File menu. You do not need to save files before you exit.
7. **Click the Close button on the title bar**
   The Internet Explorer browser window closes. If you have more than one tab open, you will see a dialog box, confirming that you want to close all tabs.
8. **If you connected to the Internet by telephone line, follow your normal procedure to close your connection**

QUICK TIP
Click Show all to display all the answers at once, then scroll as needed to read all the text.

Expanding the power of IE8 using Accelerators

The Web offers such a host of services that sometimes it's hard to remember what is available at any given time. You can use the Internet Explorer **Accelerator** feature to enhance your Web experiences. While visiting a Web page, highlight a word or phrase to display the Accelerator button, and click the Accelerator button to link to services related to the selected text such as mapping, translation, or searching. You can also preview services before you click by resting your mouse pointer over the Accelerator.

FIGURE A-20: Windows Help and Support

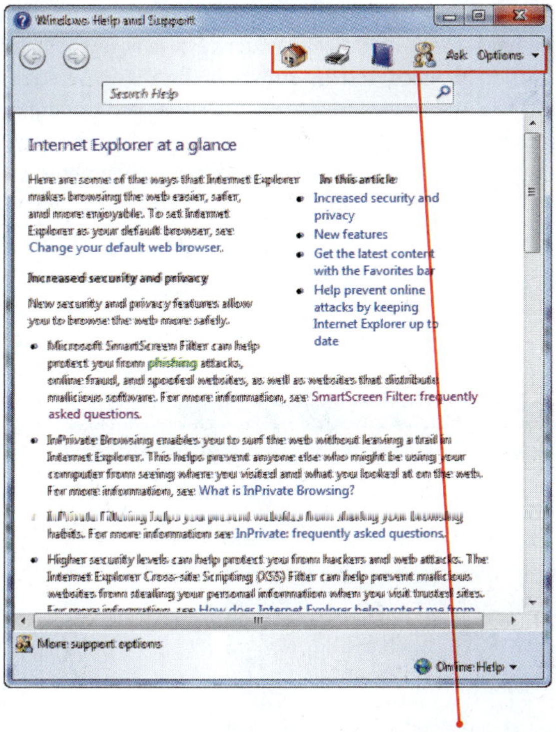

Help window buttons

FIGURE A-21: SmartScreen Filter FAQs

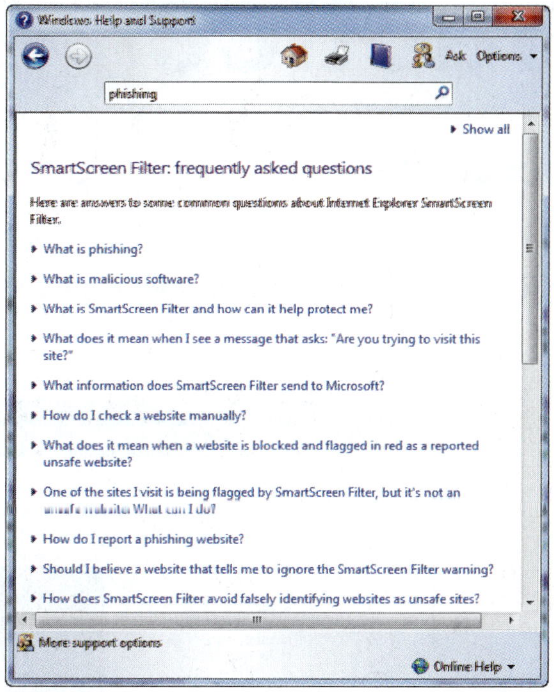

TABLE A-2: Print dialog box options

option group	tab	description
Select Printer	General	Displays information about the name, status, type, and location of the printer
Page Range	General	Choose to print current page, all pages, a range of pages, or a selection
Number of copies	General	Indicates the number of copies of each page to print and their sequence
Print frames	Options	In a Web page containing frames, allows you to print frames as laid out, only the selected frame, or all frames individually
Print all linked documents	Options	Opens and prints each document referenced by a link
Print table of links	Options	Prints links in a table at the end of the document
Orientation	(Depends on printer)	Allows you to specify landscape or portrait page orientation

Printing a Web page

When you print a Web page, its text and any graphics appear on the printed page. To print a Web page without previewing the page or changing any settings, click the Print button on the Command bar. However, Internet Explorer provides ways to customize your printouts using the Page Setup dialog box. Click the Print list arrow on the Command bar, then click Page Setup to adjust margins, change the page orientation, change headers and footers, adjust the print space to best meet your printing needs, and shrink text so that the contents of a Web page fit on one page. You can also edit the footers and headers. To have your name appear on the printed page, type your name in the Header or Footer text box. By default, the current URL and the date and time are printed on the page, so people can see the URL and visit the Web site if they want to. To open the Print dialog box, click the Print list arrow on the Command bar, then click Print. The options in the Print dialog box, shown in Table A-2, allow you to specify print options such as the number of copies and the page range. With Internet Explorer, you can preview a Web page before printing by using Print Preview, which is helpful because some Web pages are lengthy and you might only want to print the pages that have the information relevant to your task.

Practice

Concepts Review

For current SAM information, including versions and content details, visit SAM Central (http://www.cengage.com/samcentral). If you have a SAM user profile, you may have access to hands-on instruction, practice, and assessment of the skills covered in this unit. Since various versions of SAM are supported throughout the life of this text, check with your instructor for the correct instructions and URL/Web site for accessing assignments.

Label each element of the Internet Explorer browser window shown in Figure A-22.

FIGURE A-22

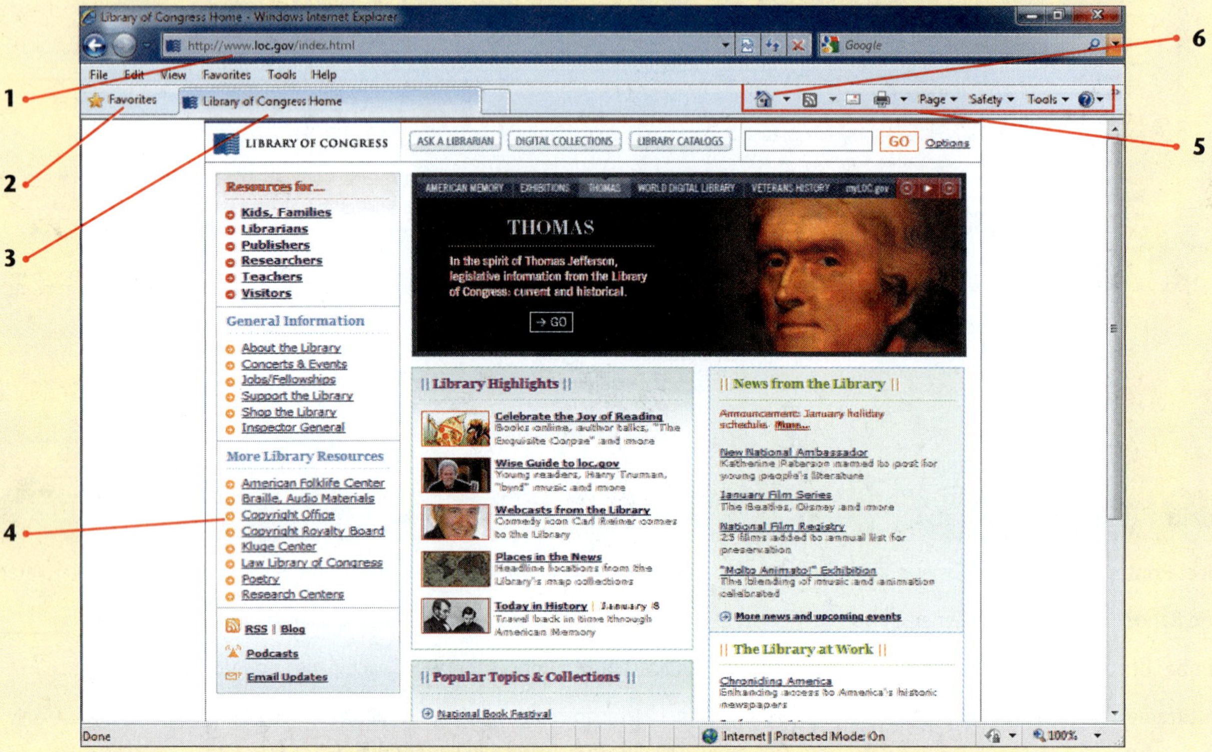

Match each term with the statement that best describes it.

7. Hyperlink	**a.** Displays a list of saved links to Web pages
8. Quick Tabs button	**b.** Can turn green and display a lock icon
9. Favorites Center	**c.** Use to display all open Web pages as thumbnails
10. Address box	**d.** Click to view a new Web page
11. Security Status bar	**e.** Displays the URL for the currently displayed page

Select the best answer from the list of choices.

12. Software programs such as Internet Explorer and Safari are ______________.

- **a.** Web companions
- **b.** Web browsers
- **c.** Web documents
- **d.** Web windows

13. Which of the following functions is NOT true about the status bar?

- **a.** Displays information about your connection progress
- **b.** Notifies you when you connect to another Web site
- **c.** Displays search results
- **d.** Displays "Done" when the page is loaded

14. You can tell when you open links from a Web page in new tabs because each new tab from the same Web site is ______________.

- **a.** color coded
- **b.** open
- **c.** numbered
- **d.** labelled

15. ______________ browsing allows you to open more than one Web page at a time in a browser window.

- **a.** Tabbed
- **b.** Web
- **c.** Linked
- **d.** InPrivate

16. You can search for Web sites by category by entering a keyword in the ______________ bar.

- **a.** Search
- **b.** Favorites
- **c.** Home
- **d.** Link

17. The letters following the dot after the domain name are called the ______________ domain and tell you the type of site you are visiting.

- **a.** top-level
- **b.** home-level
- **c.** dot-com
- **d.** main-level

18. Turn on the ______________ feature to prevent the browser from storing data about your browsing session.

- **a.** Protected Mode
- **b.** InPrivate
- **c.** Accelerator
- **d.** phishing

19. Words or graphics on a Web page that, when clicked, enable you to navigate to another Web page location are called ______________.

- **a.** tabs
- **b.** Web browsers
- **c.** hyperlinks
- **d.** buttons

20. Using the Internet to gather personal information without the knowledge or permission of the person whose information is being collected is called ______________.

- **a.** phishing
- **b.** linking
- **c.** popping
- **d.** spam

21. For easy access to maps, search engines, or other features, select text and then click the ______________ icon that appears.

- **a.** Lock
- **b.** Accelerator
- **c.** Certificate
- **d.** Filter

Skills Review

1. Start Internet Explorer.

- **a.** Make sure your computer is connected to the Internet.
- **b.** Start Internet Explorer.

2. Explore the browser window.

- **a.** Identify the Command bar, menu bar, Address bar, Search box, Favorites bar, status bar, URL, browser window, and scroll bar.
- **b.** Identify the buttons and sections for setting security, stopping a page from loading, searching, viewing favorites, and returning to the home page.
- **c.** Identify the complete URL of the current Web page.

Skills Review (continued)

3. View and navigate Web pages.

- **a.** Open the Web page **www.nps.gov** using the Address bar to open the Web page shown in Figure A-23.
- **b.** Click a link on the Web page to view a new Web page.
- **c.** Return to the default home page for your browser.
- **d.** Click the Back button.
- **e.** Follow another link to investigate the content.
- **f.** Return to the default home page for your browser.

FIGURE A-23

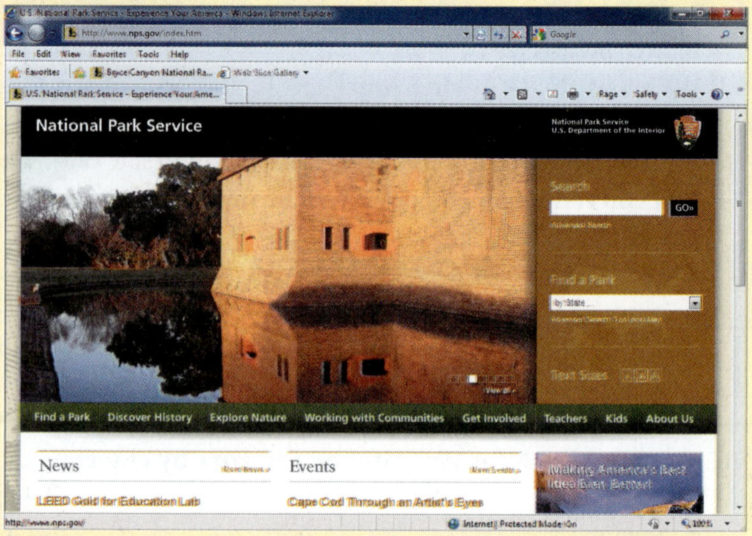

4. Use tabbed browsing.

- **a.** Open the Web page **www.nytimes.com** using the Address bar.
- **b.** Right-click a link on the Web page to open an article in a new tab.
- **c.** Click the New Tab tab to open a third tab in the browser window, then open **www.cnn.com** in the new tab using the Address bar.
- **d.** Press and hold [Ctrl], then click a link on the CNN home page to open a fourth tab.
- **e.** Click the Quick Tabs button to view all four Web pages as thumbnails.
- **f.** Click the first thumbnail to view the Web page.
- **g.** Close all tabs except for the New York Times tab.

5. Save favorite Web pages.

- **a.** Open the Web page **www.nps.gov** using the Address bar.
- **b.** Add the Web page to your Favorites bar and in the Favorites Bar folder in the Favorites Center.
- **c.** Return to the default home page for your browser.
- **d.** Using the Favorites Center, return to the National Park Service home page.
- **e.** Close all tabs, return to your home page.

6. Browse safely.

- **a.** Turn on InPrivate Browsing in a new browser window.
- **b.** Enter **www.microsoft.com** in the Address bar of the InPrivate browser window, noticing the InPrivate logo.
- **c.** Click the Safety button on the Command bar, point to SmartScreen Filter, click Check This Website, read the information, then click OK twice.
- **d.** Close the InPrivate Browser window and return to your home page.
- **e.** Double-click the Internet security area on the status bar to check the Internet Zone on your computer, review the settings, then click Cancel.
- **f.** Go to **www.pnc.com**. What does the Security Status bar tell you about this bank's Web site?
- **g.** Right-click a link on this Web page and open the page in a new tab. What does the Security Status bar tell you about this Web page? What does the color of the tab tell you about this page?
- **h.** Close all open tabs except the first one, return to your home page.

7. Search for information.

- **a.** Click the Search box.
- **b.** Enter any keyword or phrase for which you would like to find information, then execute the search and review the results.
- **c.** Click any link in the search results page and read the Web page.
- **d.** Enter the URL for a search engine in the Address bar (you can use **www.google.com**, **www.ask.com**, **www.bing.com**, or **www.yahoo.com**).

Skills Review (continued)

   e. Enter any keyword or phrase for which you would like to find information, then start the search using the search engine.
   f. View the resulting list of links, then click a link and review the Web page.
   g. Return to the search results page, then explore some of the other hyperlinks you found.

8. Get Help and exit Internet Explorer.
   a. Open Microsoft Internet Explorer Help, then search for a topic of interest to you.
   b. Click any link for any topic you want to learn more about.
   c. Read the results.
   d. Close the Windows Help and Support window.
   e. Delete any Favorites you created using the Organize Favorites dialog box.
   f. Exit Internet Explorer.

Independent Challenge 1

You are an aspiring journalist interested in understanding how different journalists approach the same story. You decide to use the Web to find some articles for comparison.

a. Start Internet Explorer.
b. Read and compare the coverage of a current international news story using two of the following sites:

• CNN	www.cnn.com
• MSNBC News	www.msnbc.com
• National Public Radio	www.npr.org
• ABC News	www.abcnews.com
• CBS News	www.cbsnews.com

c. Open each news story in its own tab in the browser window.
d. Use the Page Setup dialog box to add your name as a footer to the printed page, then print one page of the same story from both sites that you chose using the Shrink to Fit option.

Advanced Challenge Exercise

- You should be able to find many English language versions of non-U.S. papers. Use your favorite search engine to locate an online news media source from a country other than the United States. You can search on keywords such as **Asian newspapers** or **European newspapers**.
- See if you can find the news story you researched in Step b.
- Read the article.
- Use the Page Setup dialog box to add your name as a footer to the printed page, then print one page of the article from the site that you chose.

e. Close all but one of the tabs, then exit Internet Explorer.

Independent Challenge 2

You have been asked by your local community college to teach a short course on classic films from the 1960s and 1970s. The class will meet four times; each class will begin with a screening and will be followed by a discussion. You decide to use the Web to research the material.

a. Start Internet Explorer.
b. Go to your favorite search engine, then use a keyword search to find a Web site that contains information about films made in the 1960s.
c. Find two films from the 1960s that you want to show as part of the course. View the information about each film in a separate tab in the browser window.
d. Click several links on the film site and review the online resources.
e. Search the film site to find two films from the 1970s. View the information about each film in a separate tab in the browser window.
f. Select text on a Web page, use an Accelerator to find more information.
g. Add the film site as a favorite to the Favorites Center.
h. Use the Page Setup dialog box to add your name as a footer to the printed page, then print one page for each film from the site.

Advanced Challenge Exercise

- Find one page that includes a link for media such as audio or video.
- Click the link and listen to the audio or play the video.
- After listening to or viewing the media file, close the window.

i. Delete the film site from the Favorites Center, then exit Internet Explorer.

Independent Challenge 3

As a student of American political history, you want to learn about your representatives in the U.S. government. You decide to use the Web to get information about this topic.

a. Start Internet Explorer, then open the following government Web site: **www.thomas.gov**.
b. Explore the site to find information about members of Congress. Use the Page Setup dialog box to add your name as a footer to the printed page, then print one page from that site.
c. In a new tab, open the Web site **www.senate.gov**, the U.S. Senate home page.
d. Use the Find feature to find a word on the page. See Figure A-24. How many matches did you find? Did you notice how Find starts working immediately?
e. Click the Senators link, then find a link to a Web site for a senator who represents the state that you would most like to visit. Click the link, then print one page from that site.
f. Explore three links on the senator's Web site to learn more about those topics, opening each page in a new tab.
g. Use the Quick Tabs feature to navigate between the Web pages.
h. Use the Page Setup dialog box to add your name as a footer to the printed page, then print one page from one of the related sites.
i. Exit Internet Explorer.

FIGURE A-24

Real Life Independent Challenge

You would like to select a search engine to use consistently when you search the Web. You decide to compare several search engines to determine which one you like the most. The best way to compare is to have some prior knowledge of the information that you might expect to see in the search results list. In order to do this, you search on what you know best: your school, the town you live in, and even your own name!

a. Start Internet Explorer. Using two of the search sites listed Table A-3 below, type the name of the town where you live into the Search text box, and then search for the topic.

b. Click File on the menu bar, click Page Setup, add your name as a footer to the printed page, click OK, then print the first page of the results from each search. Circle the name of the search engine and the number of results it produced.

c. Using two of the search sites listed in Table A-3, or any other search site you know of or can find, type the name of your school into the Search text box, and then search for the topic. Use the Page Setup dialog box to add your name as a footer to the printed page, then print the first page of the results from each search. Circle the name of the search engine and the number of results it produced.

d. Click the Search List arrow, then click Find More Providers. In the Add-ons gallery, click the link for a new provider and add it to your installation of Internet Explorer. You want to use the new provider to find information on a topic of your choice.

e. Using two of the search sites listed in Table A-3, or any other search site you know of or can find, type your name into the Search text box, and then search for the topic. Use the Page Setup dialog box to add your name as a footer to the printed page, then print the first page of the results from each search. Circle the name of the search engine and the number of results it produced.

f. On a sheet of paper, write which search engine you think is better and include a few reasons for your preference.

TABLE A-3: Search providers

provider	address
Yahoo!	www.yahoo.com
Bing	www.bing.com
Google	www.google.com
Ask	www.ask.com

Advanced Challenge Exercise

- Create a folder in the Favorites Center called **Search Results**.
- Add the home page for your favorite search engine to the Favorites Center, in the Search Results folder.
- Return to your home page, then use the Favorites Center to go to the search engine home page.
- Delete the Search Results folder and search engine home page from the Favorites Center.

g. Click the Search Box list arrow, click Manage Search Providers to open the Manage Add-ons dialog box, select the provider you added, then click Remove. Remove any folders or Web sites you added to the Favorites Center, then click Close.

h. Exit Internet Explorer.

Visual Workshop

Graphics you find as you view pages on the Web can be static images, video, or animated graphics. Find a Web site that includes a video, as shown in Figure A-25. View at least one video on a news site and one video on a topic-specific Web site such as an organization, scientific, or tourism site. Write a brief summary of the videos you watched. Did you have to download a special program to watch the video? Identify the Web sites on which the videos were located.

FIGURE A-25

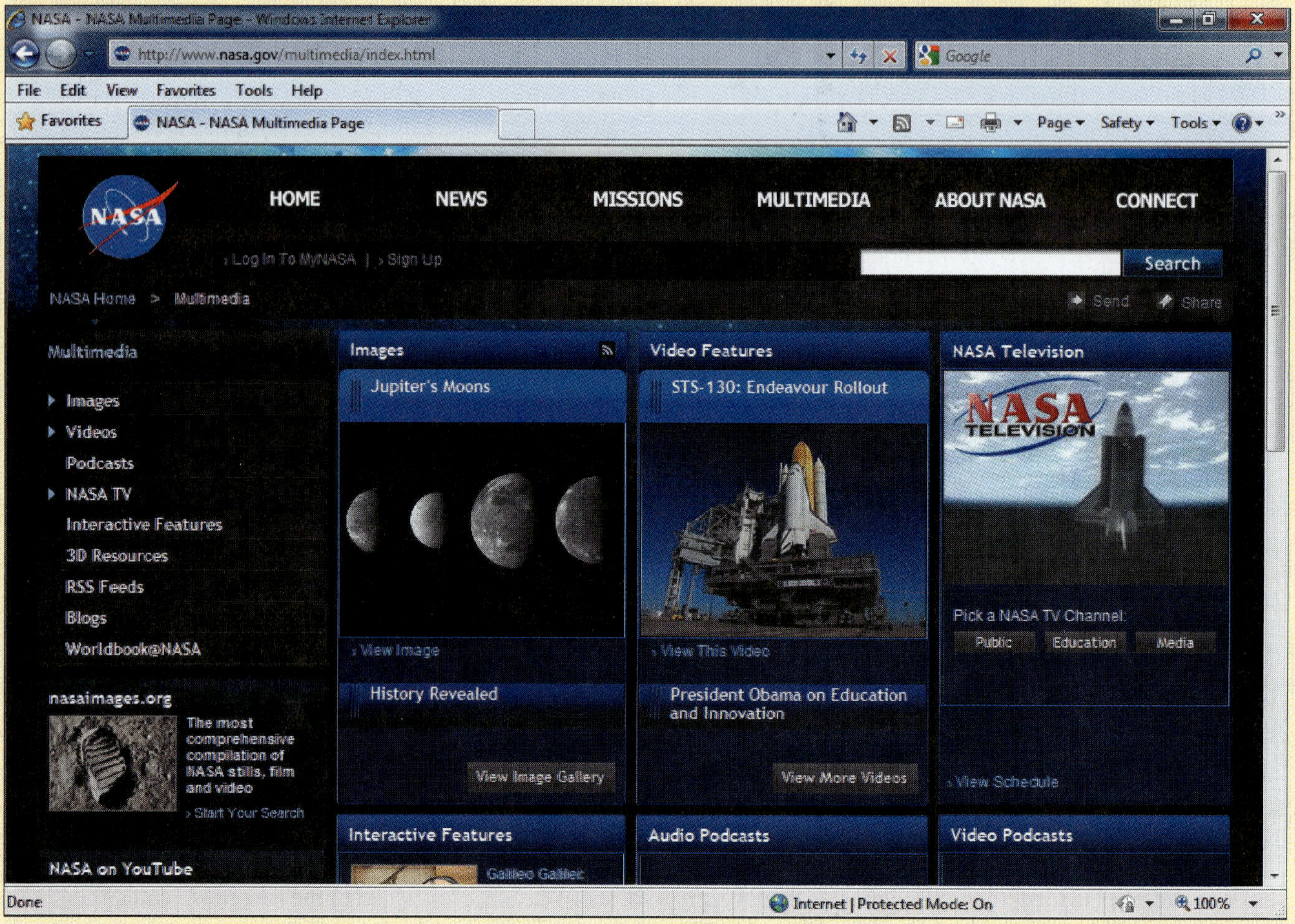

UNIT
A
Office 2010

Getting Started with Microsoft Office 2010

Files You Will Need:
OFFICE A-1.xlsx

Microsoft Office 2010 is a group of software programs designed to help you create documents, collaborate with coworkers, and track and analyze information. Each program is designed so you can work quickly and efficiently to create professional-looking results. You use different Office programs to accomplish specific tasks, such as writing a letter or producing a sales presentation, yet all the programs have a similar look and feel. Once you become familiar with one program, you'll find it easy to transfer your knowledge to the others. This unit introduces you to the most frequently used programs in Office, as well as common features they all share.

OBJECTIVES

- Understand the Office 2010 suite
- Start and exit an Office program
- View the Office 2010 user interface
- Create and save a file
- Open a file and save it with a new name
- View and print your work
- Get Help and close a file

UNIT
A
Office 2010

Understanding the Office 2010 Suite

Microsoft Office 2010 features an intuitive, context-sensitive user interface, so you can get up to speed faster and use advanced features with greater ease. The programs in Office are bundled together in a group called a **suite** (although you can also purchase them separately). The Office suite is available in several configurations, but all include Word, Excel, and PowerPoint. Other configurations include Access, Outlook, Publisher, and other programs. Each program in Office is best suited for completing specific types of tasks, though there is some overlap in capabilities.

DETAILS

The Office programs covered in this book include:

- **Microsoft Word 2010**
  When you need to create any kind of text-based document, such as a memo, newsletter, or multipage report, Word is the program to use. You can easily make your documents look great by inserting eye-catching graphics and using formatting tools such as themes, which are available in most Office programs. **Themes** are predesigned combinations of color and formatting attributes you can apply to a document. The Word document shown in Figure A-1 was formatted with the Solstice theme.
- **Microsoft Excel 2010**
  Excel is the perfect solution when you need to work with numeric values and make calculations. It puts the power of formulas, functions, charts, and other analytical tools into the hands of every user, so you can analyze sales projections, calculate loan payments, and present your findings in style. The Excel worksheet shown in Figure A-1 tracks personal expenses. Because Excel automatically recalculates results whenever a value changes, the information is always up to date. A chart illustrates how the monthly expenses are broken down.
- **Microsoft PowerPoint 2010**
  Using PowerPoint, it's easy to create powerful presentations complete with graphics, transitions, and even a soundtrack. Using professionally designed themes and clip art, you can quickly and easily create dynamic slide shows such as the one shown in Figure A-1.
- **Microsoft Access 2010**
  Access helps you keep track of large amounts of quantitative data, such as product inventories or employee records. The form shown in Figure A-1 was created for a grocery store inventory database. Employees use the form to enter data about each item. Using Access enables employees to quickly find specific information such as price and quantity without hunting through store shelves and stockrooms.

Microsoft Office has benefits beyond the power of each program, including:

- **Common user interface: Improving business processes**
  Because the Office suite programs have a similar **interface**, or look and feel, your experience using one program's tools makes it easy to learn those in the other programs. In addition, Office documents are **compatible** with one another, meaning that you can easily incorporate, or **integrate**, an Excel chart into a PowerPoint slide, or an Access table into a Word document.
- **Collaboration: Simplifying how people work together**
  Office recognizes the way people do business today, and supports the emphasis on communication and knowledge sharing within companies and across the globe. All Office programs include the capability to incorporate feedback—called **online collaboration**—across the Internet or a company network.

FIGURE A-1: Microsoft Office 2010 documents

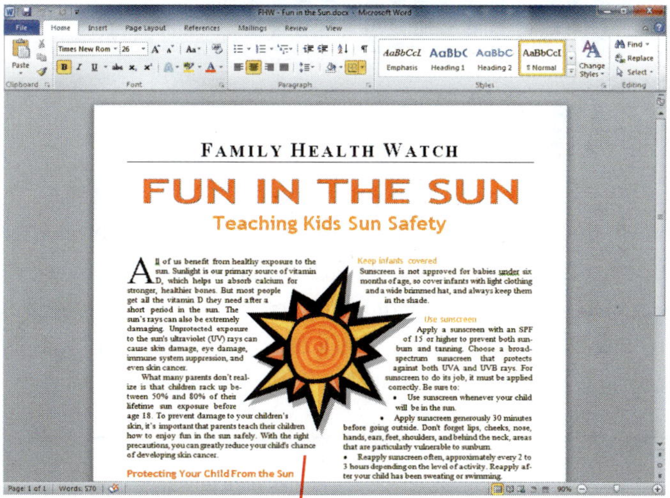

Newsletter created in Word

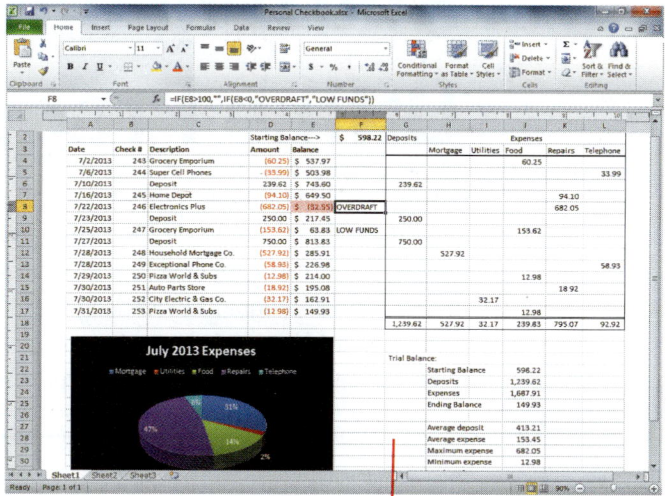

Checkbook register created in Excel

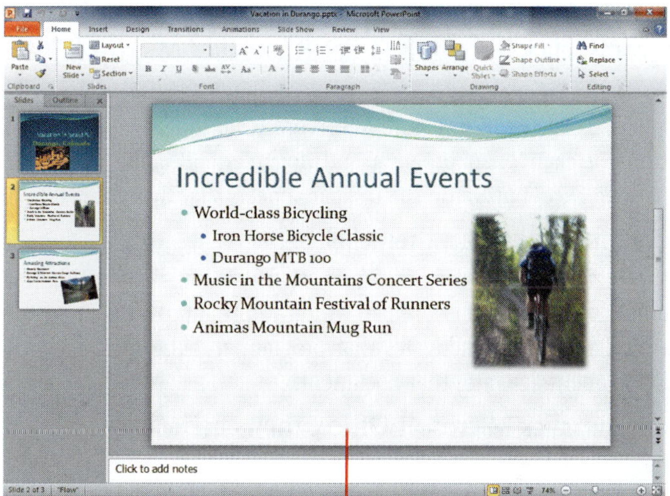

Tourism presentation created in PowerPoint

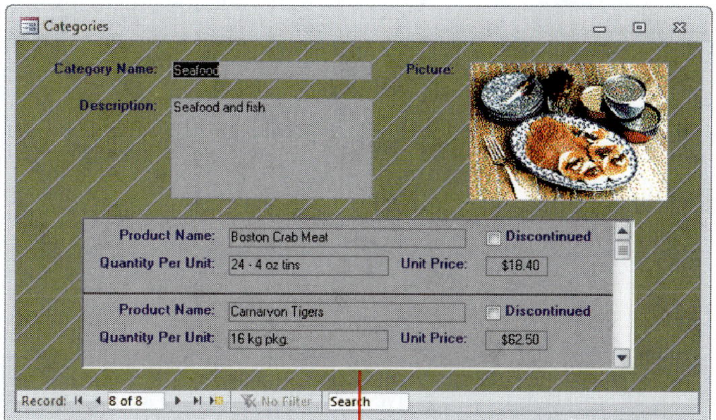

Store inventory form created in Access

Deciding which program to use

Every Office program includes tools that go far beyond what you might expect. For example, although Excel is primarily designed for making calculations, you can use it to create a database. So when you're planning a project, how do you decide which Office program to use? The general rule of thumb is to use the program best suited for your intended task, and make use of supporting tools in the program if you need them. Word is best for creating text-based documents, Excel is best for making mathematical calculations, PowerPoint is best for preparing presentations, and Access is best for managing quantitative data. Although the capabilities of Office are so vast that you *could* create an inventory in Excel or a budget in Word, you'll find greater flexibility and efficiency by using the program designed for the task. And remember, you can always create a file in one program, and then insert it in a document in another program when you need to, such as including sales projections (Excel) in a memo (Word).

UNIT
A
Office 2010

Starting and Exiting an Office Program

The first step in using an Office program is to open, or **launch**, it on your computer. The easiest ways to launch a program are to click the Start button on the Windows taskbar or to double-click an icon on your desktop. You can have multiple programs open on your computer simultaneously, and you can move between open programs by clicking the desired program or document button on the taskbar or by using the [Alt][Tab] keyboard shortcut combination. When working, you'll often want to open multiple programs in Office and switch among them as you work. Begin by launching a few Office programs now.

STEPS

QUICK TIP
You can also launch a program by double-clicking a desktop icon or clicking the program name on the Start menu.

QUICK TIP
It is not necessary to close one program before opening another.

QUICK TIP
As you work in Windows, your computer adapts to your activities. You may notice that after clicking the Start button, the name of the program you want to open appears in the Start menu above All Programs; if so, you can click it to start the program.

TROUBLE
If you don't have Access installed on your computer, proceed to the next lesson.

1. **Click the Start button on the taskbar**

   The Start menu opens. If the taskbar is hidden, you can display it by pointing to the bottom of the screen. Depending on your taskbar property settings, the taskbar may be displayed at all times, or only when you point to that area of the screen. For more information, or to change your taskbar properties, consult your instructor or technical support person.

2. **Click All Programs, scroll down if necessary in the All Programs menu, click Microsoft Office as shown in Figure A-2, then click Microsoft Word 2010**

   Word 2010 starts, and the program window opens on your screen.

3. **Click on the taskbar, click All Programs, click Microsoft Office, then click Microsoft Excel 2010**

   Excel 2010 starts, and the program window opens, as shown in Figure A-3. Word is no longer visible, but it remains open. The taskbar displays a button for each open program and document. Because this Excel document is **active**, or in front and available, the Excel button on the taskbar appears slightly lighter.

4. **Point to the Word program button on the taskbar, then click**

   The Word program window is now in front. When the Aero feature is turned on in Windows 7, pointing to a program button on the taskbar displays a thumbnail version of each open window in that program above the program button. Clicking a program button on the taskbar activates that program and the most recently active document. Clicking a thumbnail of a document activates that document.

5. **Click on the taskbar, click All Programs, click Microsoft Office, then click Microsoft PowerPoint 2010**

   PowerPoint 2010 starts and becomes the active program.

6. **Click the Excel program button on the taskbar**

   Excel is now the active program.

7. **Click on the taskbar, click All Programs, click Microsoft Office, then click Microsoft Access 2010**

   Access 2010 starts and becomes the active program. Now all four Office programs are open at the same time.

8. **Click Exit on the navigation bar in the Access program window, as shown in Figure A-4**

   Access closes, leaving Excel active and Word and PowerPoint open.

Using shortcut keys to move between Office programs

As an alternative to the Windows taskbar, you can use a keyboard shortcut to move among open Office programs. The [Alt][Tab] keyboard combination lets you either switch quickly to the next open program or file or choose one from a gallery. To switch immediately to the next open program or file, press [Alt][Tab]. To choose from all open programs and files, press and hold [Alt], then press and release [Tab] without releasing [Alt]. A gallery opens on screen, displaying the filename and a thumbnail image of each open program and file, as well as of the desktop. Each time you press [Tab] while holding [Alt], the selection cycles to the next open file or location. Release [Alt] when the program, file, or location you want to activate is selected.

FIGURE A-2: Start menu

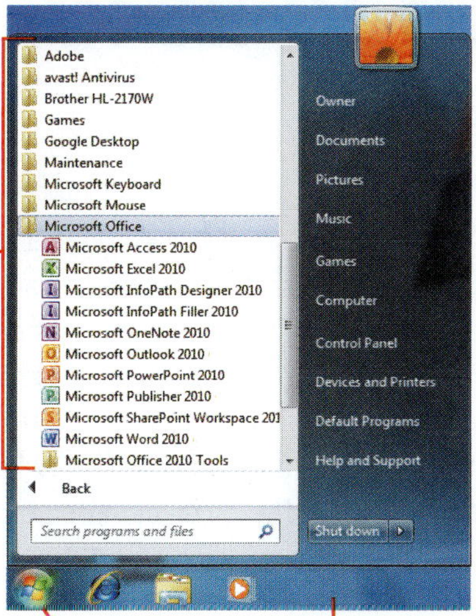

FIGURE A-3: Excel program window and Windows taskbar

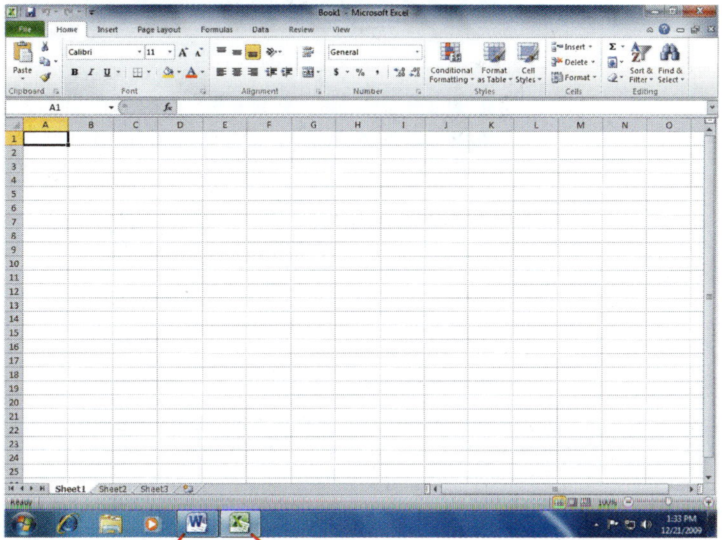

FIGURE A-4: Access program window

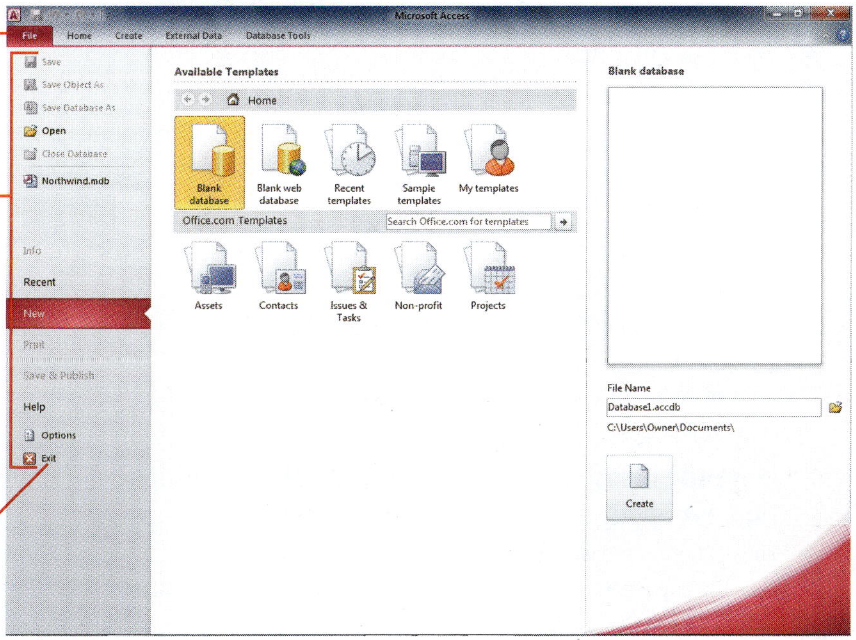

Windows Live and Microsoft Office Web Apps

All Office programs include the capability to incorporate feedback—called online collaboration—across the Internet or a company network. Using **cloud computing** (work done in a virtual environment), you can take advantage of Web programs called Microsoft Office Web Apps, which are simplified versions of the programs found in the Microsoft Office 2010 suite. Because these programs are online, they take up no computer disk space and are accessed using Windows Live SkyDrive, a free service from Microsoft. Using Windows Live SkyDrive, you and your colleagues can create and store documents in a "cloud" and make the documents available to whomever you grant access. To use Windows Live SkyDrive, you need a free Windows Live ID, which you obtain at the Windows Live Web site. You can find more information in the "Working with Windows Live and Office Web Apps" appendix.

UNIT A
Office 2010

Viewing the Office 2010 User Interface

One of the benefits of using Office is that the programs have much in common, making them easy to learn and making it simple to move from one to another. Individual Office programs have always shared many features, but the innovations in the Office 2010 user interface mean even greater similarity among them all. That means you can also use your knowledge of one program to get up to speed in another. A **user interface** is a collective term for all the ways you interact with a software program. The user interface in Office 2010 provides intuitive ways to choose commands, work with files, and navigate in the program window. Familiarize yourself with some of the common interface elements in Office by examining the PowerPoint program window.

STEPS

QUICK TIP
In addition to the standard tabs on the Ribbon, **contextual tabs** open when needed to complete a specific task; they appear in an accent color and close when no longer needed. To minimize the display of the buttons and commands on tabs, click the Minimize the Ribbon button on the right end of the Ribbon.

1. **Click the PowerPoint program button on the taskbar**

   PowerPoint becomes the active program. Refer to Figure A-5 to identify common elements of the Office user interface. The **document window** occupies most of the screen. In PowerPoint, a blank slide appears in the document window, so you can build your slide show. At the top of every Office program window is a **title bar** that displays the document name and program name. Below the title bar is the **Ribbon**, which displays commands you're likely to need for the current task. Commands are organized onto **tabs**. The tab names appear at the top of the Ribbon, and the active tab appears in front. The Ribbon in every Office program includes tabs specific to the program, but all Office programs include a File tab and Home tab on the left end of the Ribbon.

2. **Click the File tab**

   The File tab opens, displaying **Backstage view**. The navigation bar on the left side of Backstage view contains commands to perform actions common to most Office programs, such as opening a file, saving a file, and closing the current program. Just above the File tab is the **Quick Access toolbar**, which also includes buttons for common Office commands.

3. **Click the File tab again to close Backstage view and return to the document window, then click the Design tab on the Ribbon**

   To display a different tab, you click the tab on the Ribbon. Each tab contains related commands arranged into **groups** to make features easy to find. On the Design tab, the Themes group displays available design themes in a **gallery**, or visual collection of choices you can browse. Many groups contain a **dialog box launcher**, an icon you can click to open a dialog box or task pane from which to choose related commands.

QUICK TIP
Live Preview is available in many galleries and menus throughout Office.

4. **Move the mouse pointer over the Angles theme in the Themes group as shown in Figure A-6, but do not click the mouse button**

   The Angles theme is temporarily applied to the slide in the document window. However, because you did not click the theme, you did not permanently change the slide. With the **Live Preview** feature, you can point to a choice, see the results right in the document, and then decide if you want to make the change.

QUICK TIP
If you accidentally click a theme, click the Undo button on the Quick Access toolbar.

5. **Move away from the Ribbon and towards the slide**

   If you had clicked the Angles theme, it would be applied to this slide. Instead, the slide remains unchanged.

QUICK TIP
You can also use the Zoom button in the Zoom group on the View tab to enlarge or reduce a document's appearance.

6. **Point to the Zoom slider on the status bar, then drag to the right until the Zoom level reads 166%**

   The slide display is enlarged. Zoom tools are located on the status bar. You can drag the slider or click the Zoom In or Zoom Out buttons to zoom in or out on an area of interest. **Zooming in**, or choosing a higher percentage, makes a document appear bigger on screen, but less of it fits on the screen at once; **zooming out**, or choosing a lower percentage, lets you see more of the document but at a reduced size.

7. **Drag on the status bar to the left until the Zoom level reads 73%**

FIGURE A-5: PowerPoint program window

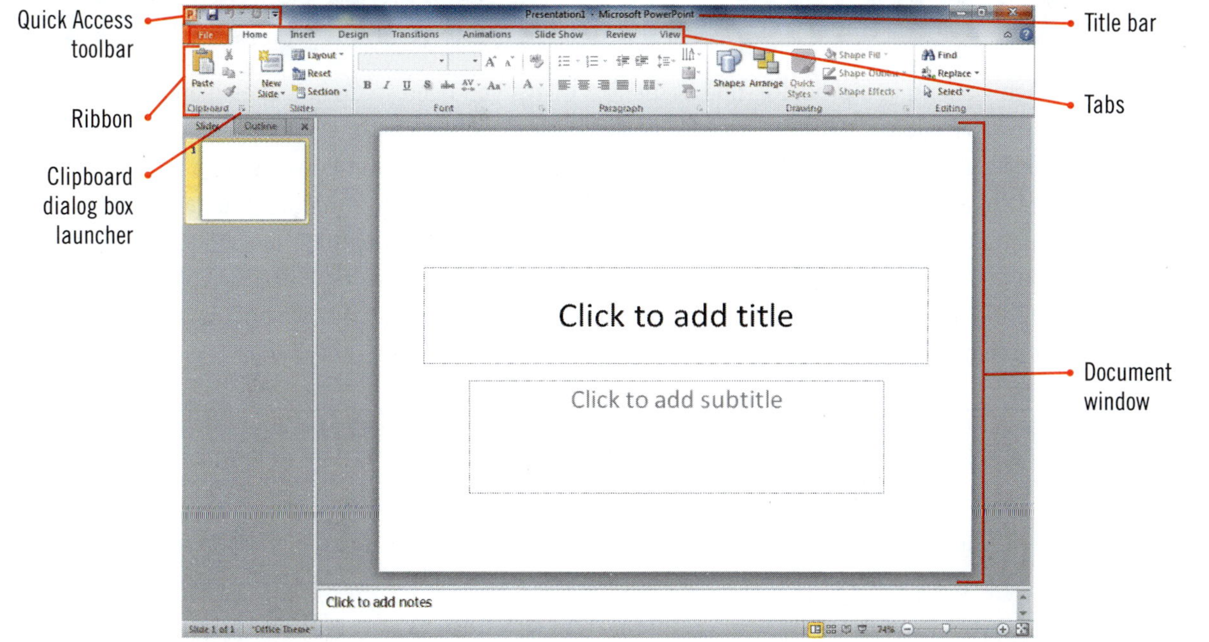

FIGURE A-6: Viewing a theme with Live Preview

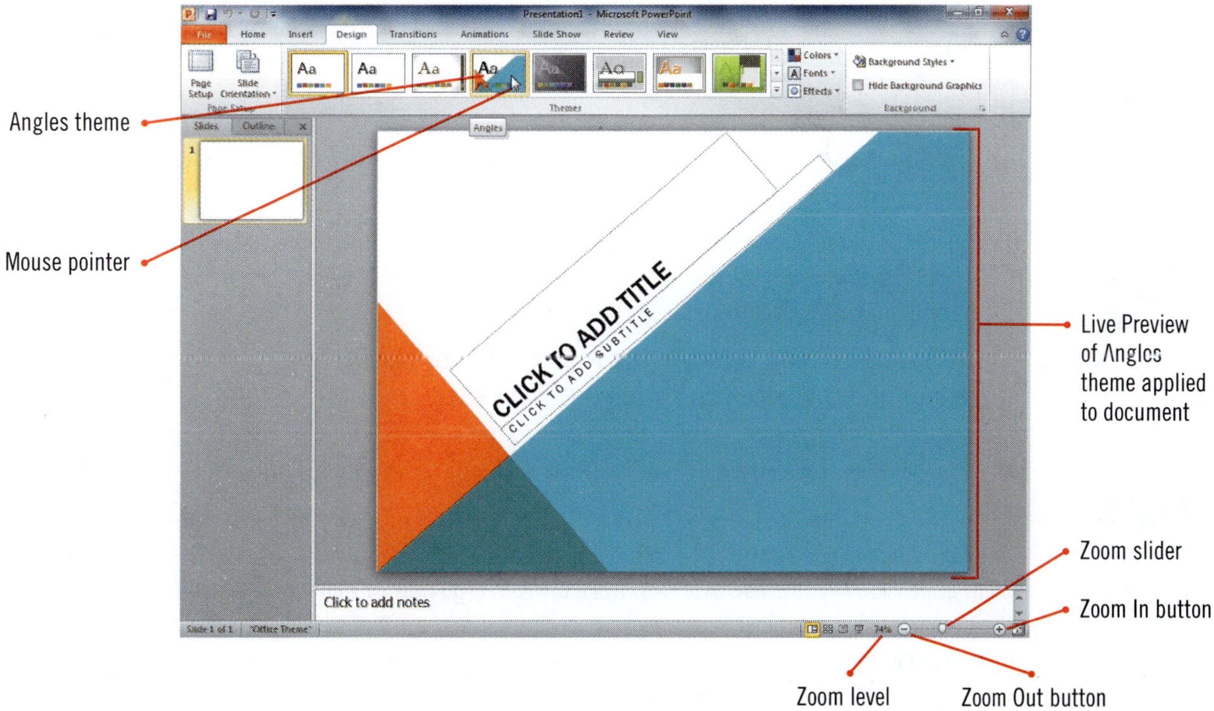

Office 2010

Using Backstage view

Backstage view in each Microsoft Office program offers "one stop shopping" for many commonly performed tasks, such as opening and saving a file, printing and previewing a document, defining document properties, sharing information, and exiting a program. Backstage view opens when you click the File tab in any Office program, and while features such as the Ribbon, Mini toolbar, and Live Preview all help you work *in* your documents, the File tab and Backstage view help you work *with* your documents.

UNIT
A
Office 2010

Creating and Saving a File

When working in a program, one of the first things you need to do is to create and save a file. A **file** is a stored collection of data. Saving a file enables you to work on a project now, then put it away and work on it again later. In some Office programs, including Word, Excel, and PowerPoint, a new file is automatically created when you start the program, so all you have to do is enter some data and save it. In Access, you must expressly create a file before you enter any data. You should give your files meaningful names and save them in an appropriate location so that they're easy to find. Use Word to familiarize yourself with the process of creating and saving a document. First you'll type some notes about a possible location for a corporate meeting, then you'll save the information for later use.

STEPS

1. **Click the Word program button on the taskbar**
2. **Type Locations for Corporate Meeting, then press [Enter] twice**

   The text appears in the document window, and the **insertion point** blinks on a new blank line. The insertion point indicates where the next typed text will appear.
3. **Type Las Vegas, NV, press [Enter], type Orlando, FL, press [Enter], type Boston, MA, press [Enter] twice, then type your name**

   Compare your document to Figure A-7.
4. **Click the Save button on the Quick Access toolbar**

   Because this is the first time you are saving this document, the Save As dialog box opens, as shown in Figure A-8. The Save As dialog box includes options for assigning a filename and storage location. Once you save a file for the first time, clicking saves any changes to the file *without* opening the Save As dialog box, because no additional information is needed. The Address bar in the Save As dialog box displays the default location for saving the file, but you can change it to any location. The File name field contains a suggested name for the document based on text in the file, but you can enter a different name.
5. **Type OF A-Potential Corporate Meeting Locations**

   The text you type replaces the highlighted text. (The "OF A-" in the filename indicates that the file is created in Office Unit A. You will see similar designations throughout this book when files are named. For example, a file named in Excel Unit B would begin with "EX B-" .)
6. **In the Save As dialog box, use the Address bar or Navigation Pane to navigate to the drive and folder where you store your Data Files**

   Many students store files on a flash drive, but you can also store files on your computer, a network drive, or any storage device indicated by your instructor or technical support person.
7. **Click Save**

   The Save As dialog box closes, the new file is saved to the location you specified, then the name of the document appears in the title bar, as shown in Figure A-9. (You may or may not see the file extension ".docx" after the filename.) See Table A-1 for a description of the different types of files you create in Office, and the file extensions associated with each.

QUICK TIP

A filename can be up to 255 characters, including a file extension, and can include upper- or lowercase characters and spaces, but not ?, ", /, \, <, >, *, |, or :.

QUICK TIP

Saving a file to the Desktop creates a desktop icon that you can double-click to both launch a program and open a document.

QUICK TIP

To create a new blank file when a file is open, click the File tab, click New on the navigation bar, then click Create near the bottom of the document preview pane.

TABLE A-1: Common filenames and default file extensions

file created in	is called a	and has the default extension
Word	document	.docx
Excel	workbook	.xlsx
PowerPoint	presentation	.pptx
Access	database	.accdb

FIGURE A-7: Document created in Word

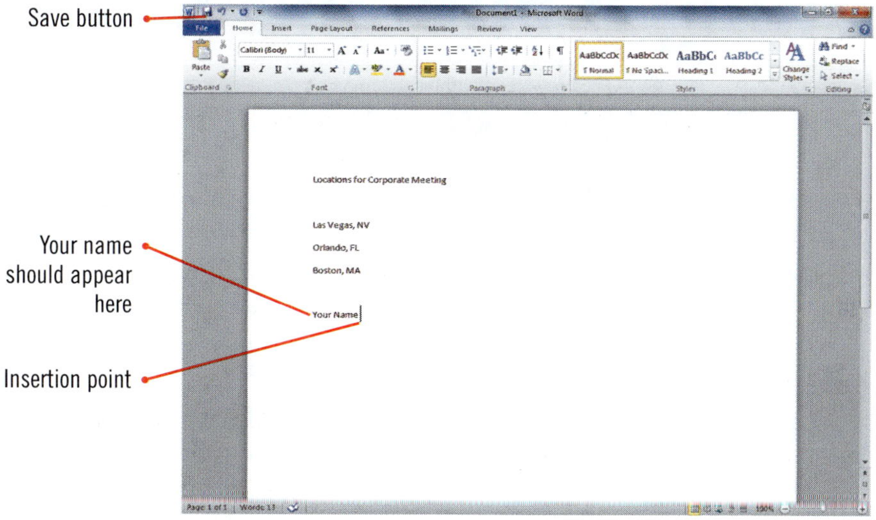

FIGURE A-8: Save As dialog box

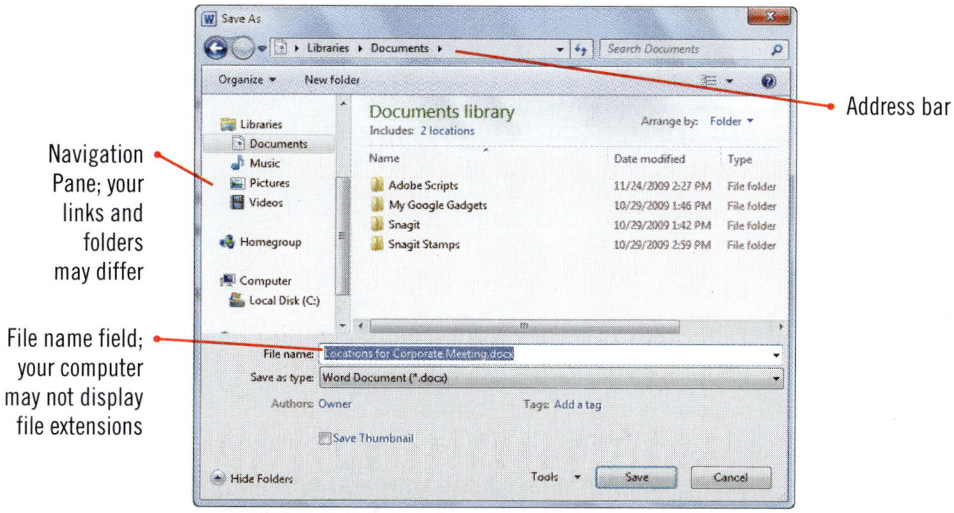

FIGURE A-9: Saved and named Word document

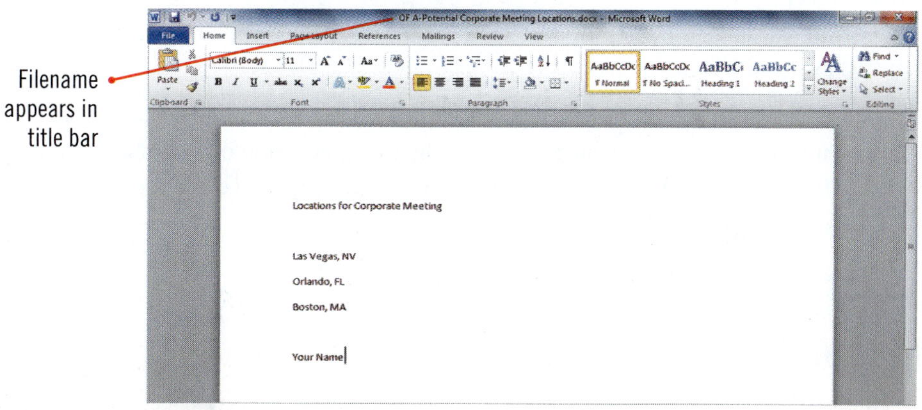

Using the Office Clipboard

You can use the Office Clipboard to cut and copy items from one Office program and paste them into others. The Office Clipboard can store a maximum of 24 items. To access it, open the Office Clipboard task pane by clicking the dialog box launcher in the Clipboard group on the Home tab. Each time you copy a selection, it is saved in the Office Clipboard. Each entry in the Office Clipboard includes an icon that tells you the program it was created in. To paste an entry, click in the document where you want it to appear, then click the item in the Office Clipboard. To delete an item from the Office Clipboard, right-click the item, then click Delete.

UNIT A
Office 2010

Opening a File and Saving It with a New Name

In many cases as you work in Office, you start with a blank document, but often you need to use an existing file. It might be a file you or a coworker created earlier as a work in progress, or it could be a complete document that you want to use as the basis for another. For example, you might want to create a budget for this year using the budget you created last year; you could type in all the categories and information from scratch, or you could open last year's budget, save it with a new name, and just make changes to update it for the current year. By opening the existing file and saving it with the Save As command, you create a duplicate that you can modify to your heart's content, while the original file remains intact. Use Excel to open an existing workbook file, and save it with a new name so the original remains unchanged.

STEPS

QUICK TIP
Click Recent on the navigation bar to display a list of recent workbooks; click a file in the list to open it.

1. **Click the Excel program button on the taskbar, click the File tab, then click Open on the navigation bar**
   The Open dialog box opens, where you can navigate to any drive or folder accessible to your computer to locate a file.

2. **In the Open dialog box, navigate to the drive and folder where you store your Data Files**
   The files available in the current folder are listed, as shown in Figure A-10. This folder contains one file.

TROUBLE
Click Enable Editing on the Protected View bar near the top of your document window if prompted.

3. **Click OFFICE A-1.xlsx, then click Open**
   The dialog box closes, and the file opens in Excel. An Excel file is an electronic spreadsheet, so it looks different from a Word document or a PowerPoint slide.

4. **Click the File tab, then click Save As on the navigation bar**
   The Save As dialog box opens, and the current filename is highlighted in the File name text box. Using the Save As command enables you to create a copy of the current, existing file with a new name. This action preserves the original file and creates a new file that you can modify.

QUICK TIP
The Save As command works identically in all Office programs, except Access; in Access, this command lets you save a copy of the current database object, such as a table or form, with a new name, but not a copy of the entire database.

5. **Navigate to the drive and folder where you store your Data Files if necessary, type OF A-Budget for Corporate Meeting in the File name text box, as shown in Figure A-11, then click Save**
   A copy of the existing workbook is created with the new name. The original file, Office A-1.xlsx, closes automatically.

6. **Click cell A19, type your name, then press [Enter], as shown in Figure A-12**
   In Excel, you enter data in cells, which are formed by the intersection of a row and a column. Cell A19 is at the intersection of column A and row 19. When you press [Enter], the cell pointer moves to cell A20.

7. **Click the Save button on the Quick Access toolbar**
   Your name appears in the workbook, and your changes to the file are saved.

Working in Compatibility Mode

Not everyone upgrades to the newest version of Office. As a general rule, new software versions are **backward compatible**, meaning that documents saved by an older version can be read by newer software. To open documents created in older Office versions, Office 2010 includes a feature called Compatibility Mode. When you use Office 2010 to open a file created in an earlier version of Office, "Compatibility Mode" appears in the title bar, letting you know the file was created in an earlier but usable version of the program. If you are working with someone who may not be using the newest version of the software, you can avoid possible incompatibility problems by saving your file in another, earlier format. To do this in an Office program, click the File tab, click Save As on the navigation bar, click the Save as type list arrow in the Save As dialog box, then click an option on the list. For example, if you're working in Excel, click Excel 97-2003 Workbook format in the Save as type list to save an Excel file so that it can be opened in Excel 97 or Excel 2003.

FIGURE A-10: Open dialog box

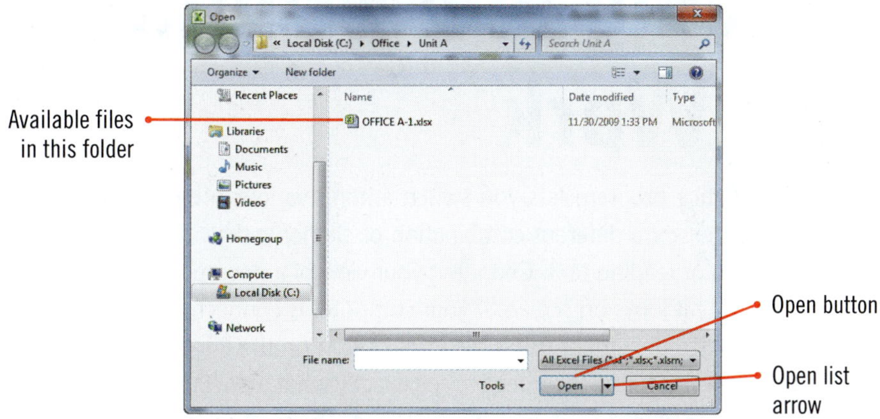

FIGURE A-11: Save As dialog box

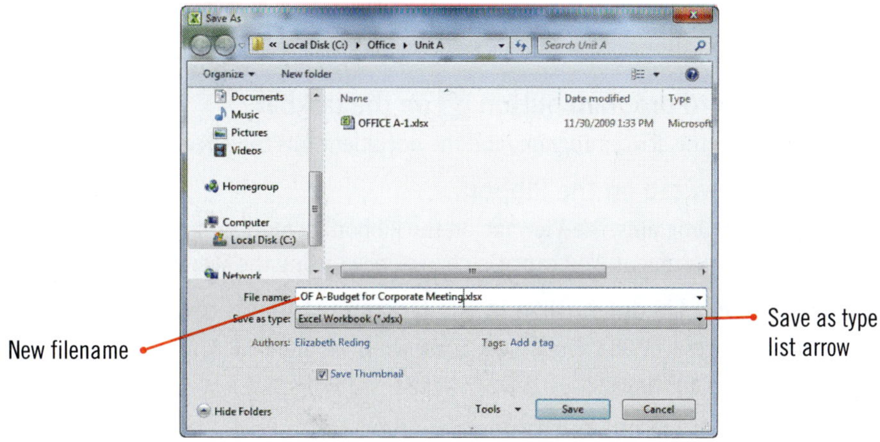

FIGURE A-12: Your name added to the workbook

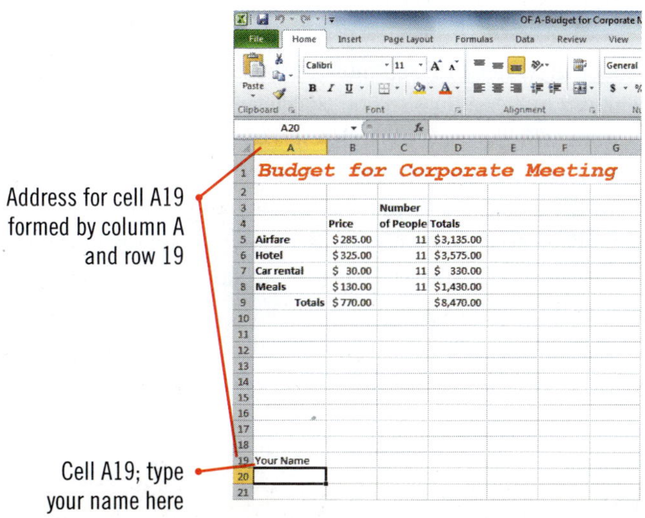

Exploring File Open options

You might have noticed that the Open button on the Open dialog box includes an arrow. In a dialog box, if a button includes an arrow you can click the button to invoke the command, or you can click the arrow to choose from a list of related commands. The Open list arrow includes several related commands, including Open Read-Only and Open as Copy. Clicking Open Read-Only opens a file that you can only save with a new name; you cannot save changes to the original file. Clicking Open as Copy creates a copy of the file already saved and named with the word "Copy" in the title. Like the Save As command, these commands provide additional ways to use copies of existing files while ensuring that original files do not get changed by mistake.

UNIT A
Office 2010

Viewing and Printing Your Work

Each Microsoft Office program lets you switch among various **views** of the document window to show more or fewer details or a different combination of elements that make it easier to complete certain tasks, such as formatting or reading text. Changing your view of a document does not affect the file in any way, it affects only the way it looks on screen. If your computer is connected to a printer or a print server, you can easily print any Office document using the Print button on the Print tab in Backstage view. Printing can be as simple as **previewing** the document to see exactly what a document will look like when it is printed and then clicking the Print button. Or, you can customize the print job by printing only selected pages or making other choices. Experiment with changing your view of a Word document, and then preview and print your work.

STEPS

1. **Click the Word program button on the taskbar**
   Word becomes the active program, and the document fills the screen.
2. **Click the View tab on the Ribbon**
   In most Office programs, the View tab on the Ribbon includes groups and commands for changing your view of the current document. You can also change views using the View buttons on the status bar.
3. **Click the Web Layout button in the Document Views group on the View tab**
   The view changes to Web Layout view, as shown in Figure A-13. This view shows how the document will look if you save it as a Web page.
4. **Click the Print Layout button on the View tab**
   You return to Print Layout view, the default view in Word.
5. **Click the File tab, then click Print on the navigation bar**
   The Print tab opens in Backstage view. The preview pane on the right side of the window automatically displays a preview of how your document will look when printed, showing the entire page on screen at once. Compare your screen to Figure A-14. Options in the Settings section enable you to change settings such as margins, orientation, and paper size before printing. To change a setting, click it, and then click the new setting you want. For instance, to change from Letter paper size to Legal, click Letter in the Settings section, then click Legal on the menu that opens. The document preview is updated as you change the settings. You also can use the Settings section to change which pages to print and even the number of pages you print on each sheet of printed paper. If you have multiple printers from which to choose, you can change from one installed printer to another by clicking the current printer in the Printer section, then clicking the name of the installed printer you want to use. The Print section contains the Print button and also enables you to select the number of copies of the document to print.
6. **Click the Print button in the Print section**
   A copy of the document prints, and Backstage view closes.

QUICK TIP
You can add the Quick Print button to the Quick Access toolbar by clicking the Customize Quick Access Toolbar button, then clicking Quick Print. The Quick Print button prints one copy of your document using the default settings.

Customizing the Quick Access toolbar

You can customize the Quick Access toolbar to display your favorite commands. To do so, click the Customize Quick Access Toolbar button in the title bar, then click the command you want to add. If you don't see the command in the list, click More Commands to open the Quick Access Toolbar tab of the current program's Options dialog box. In the Options dialog box, use the Choose commands from list to choose a category, click the desired command in the list on the left, click Add to add it to the Quick Access toolbar, then click OK. To remove a button from the toolbar, click the name in the list on the right in the Options dialog box, then click Remove. To add a command to the Quick Access toolbar on the fly, simply right-click the button on the Ribbon, then click Add to Quick Access Toolbar on the shortcut menu. To move the Quick Access toolbar below the Ribbon, click the Customize Quick Access Toolbar button, and then click Show Below the Ribbon.

FIGURE A-13: Web Layout view

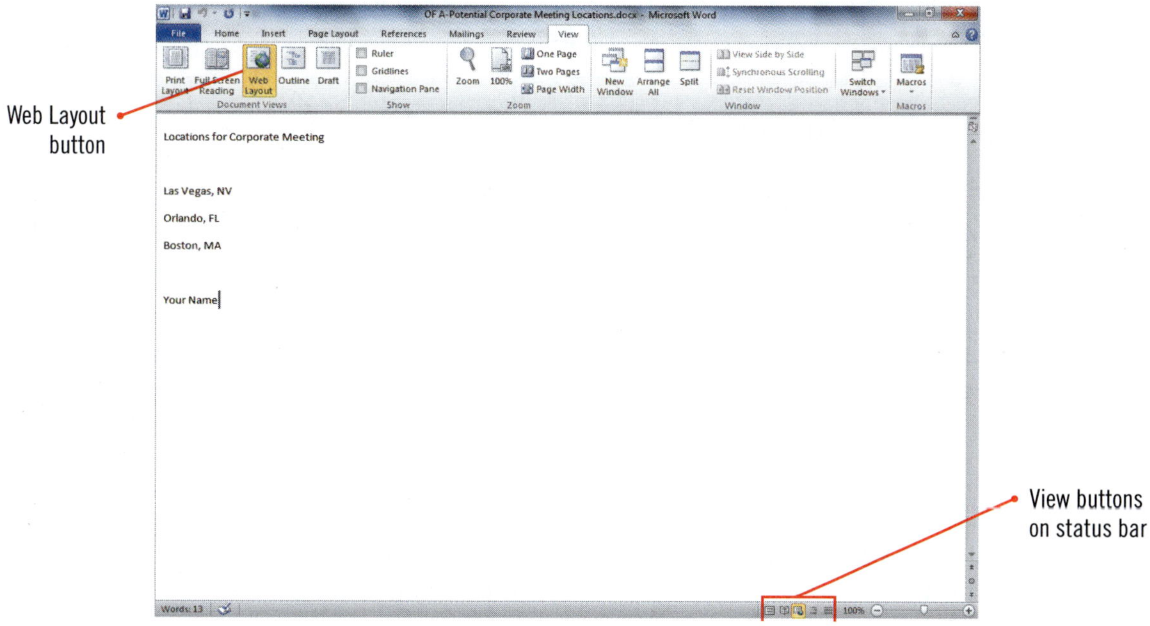

FIGURE A-14: Print tab in Backstage view

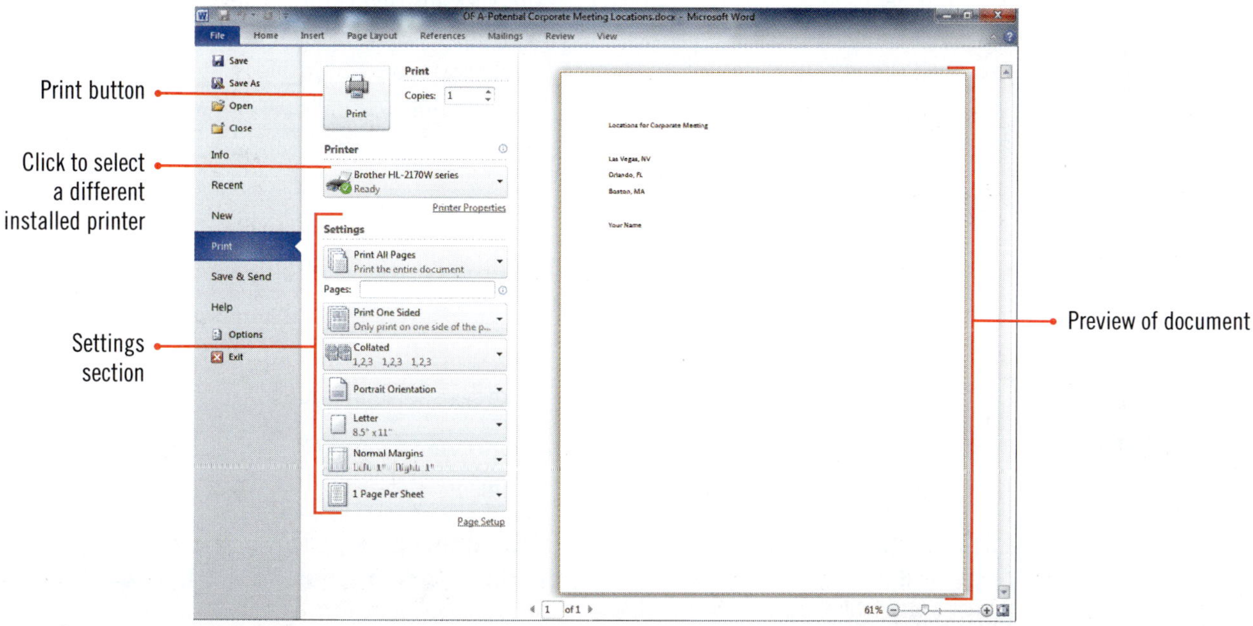

Creating a screen capture

A **screen capture** is a digital image of your screen, as if you took a picture of it with a camera. For instance, you might want to take a screen capture if an error message occurs and you want Technical Support to see exactly what's on the screen. You can create a screen capture using features found in Windows 7 or Office 2010. Windows 7 comes with the Snipping Tool, a separate program designed to capture whole screens or portions of screens. To open the Snipping Tool, click it on the Start menu or click All Programs, click Accessories, then click Snipping Tool. After opening the Snipping Tool, drag the pointer on the screen to select the area of the screen you want to capture. When you release the mouse button, the screen capture opens in the Snipping Tool window, and you can save, copy, or send it in an e-mail. In Word, Excel, and PowerPoint 2010, you can capture screens or portions of screens and insert them in the current document using the Screenshot button on the Insert tab. And finally, you can create a screen capture by pressing [PrtScn]. (Keyboards differ, but you may find the [PrtScn] button in or near your keyboard's function keys.) Pressing this key places a digital image of your screen in the Windows temporary storage area known as the **Clipboard**. Open the document where you want the screen capture to appear, click the Home tab on the Ribbon (if necessary), then click the Paste button on the Home tab. The screen capture is pasted into the document.

UNIT A
Office 2010

Getting Help and Closing a File

You can get comprehensive help at any time by pressing [F1] in an Office program. You can also get help in the form of a ScreenTip by pointing to almost any icon in the program window. When you're finished working in an Office document, you have a few choices regarding ending your work session. You can close a file or exit a program by using the File tab or by clicking a button on the title bar. Closing a file leaves a program running, while exiting a program closes all the open files in that program as well as the program itself. In all cases, Office reminds you if you try to close a file or exit a program and your document contains unsaved changes. Explore the Help system in Microsoft Office, and then close your documents and exit any open programs.

STEPS

TROUBLE
If the Table of Contents pane doesn't appear on the left in the Help window, click the Show Table of Contents button on the Help toolbar to show it.

QUICK TIP
You can also open the Help window by clicking the Microsoft Office Word Help button to the right of the tabs on the Ribbon.

QUICK TIP
You can print the entire current topic by clicking the Print button on the Help toolbar, then clicking Print in the Print dialog box.

1. **Point to the Zoom button on the View tab of the Ribbon**
   A ScreenTip appears that describes how the Zoom button works and explains where to find other zoom controls.
2. **Press [F1]**
   The Word Help window opens, as shown in Figure A-15, displaying the home page for help in Word on the right and the Table of Contents pane on the left. In both panes of the Help window, each entry is a hyperlink you can click to open a list of related topics. The Help window also includes a toolbar of useful Help commands and a Search field. The connection status at the bottom of the Help window indicates that the connection to Office.com is active. Office.com supplements the help content available on your computer with a wide variety of up-to-date topics, templates, and training. If you are not connected to the Internet, the Help window displays only the help content available on your computer.
3. **Click the Creating documents link in the Table of Contents pane**
   The icon next to Creating documents changes, and a list of subtopics expands beneath the topic.
4. **Click the Create a document link in the subtopics list in the Table of Contents pane**
   The topic opens in the right pane of the Help window, as shown in Figure A-16.
5. **Click Delete a document under "What do you want to do?" in the right pane**
   The link leads to information about deleting a document.
6. **Click the Accessibility link in the Table of Contents pane, click the Accessibility features in Word link, read the information in the right pane, then click the Help window Close button**
7. **Click the File tab, then click Close on the navigation bar; if a dialog box opens asking whether you want to save your changes, click Save**
   The Potential Corporate Meeting Locations document closes, leaving the Word program open.
8. **Click the File tab, then click Exit on the navigation bar**
   Word closes, and the Excel program window is active.
9. **Click the File tab, click Exit on the navigation bar to exit Excel, click the PowerPoint program button on the taskbar if necessary, click the File tab, then click Exit on the navigation bar to exit PowerPoint**
   Excel and PowerPoint both close.

FIGURE A-15: Word Help window

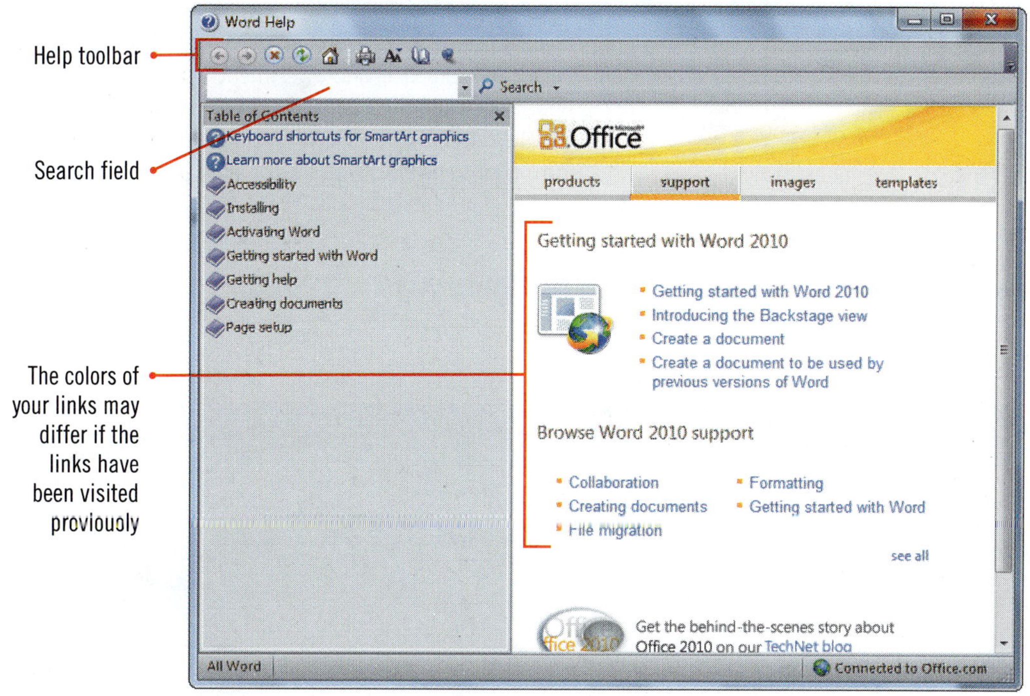

FIGURE A-16: Create a document Help topic

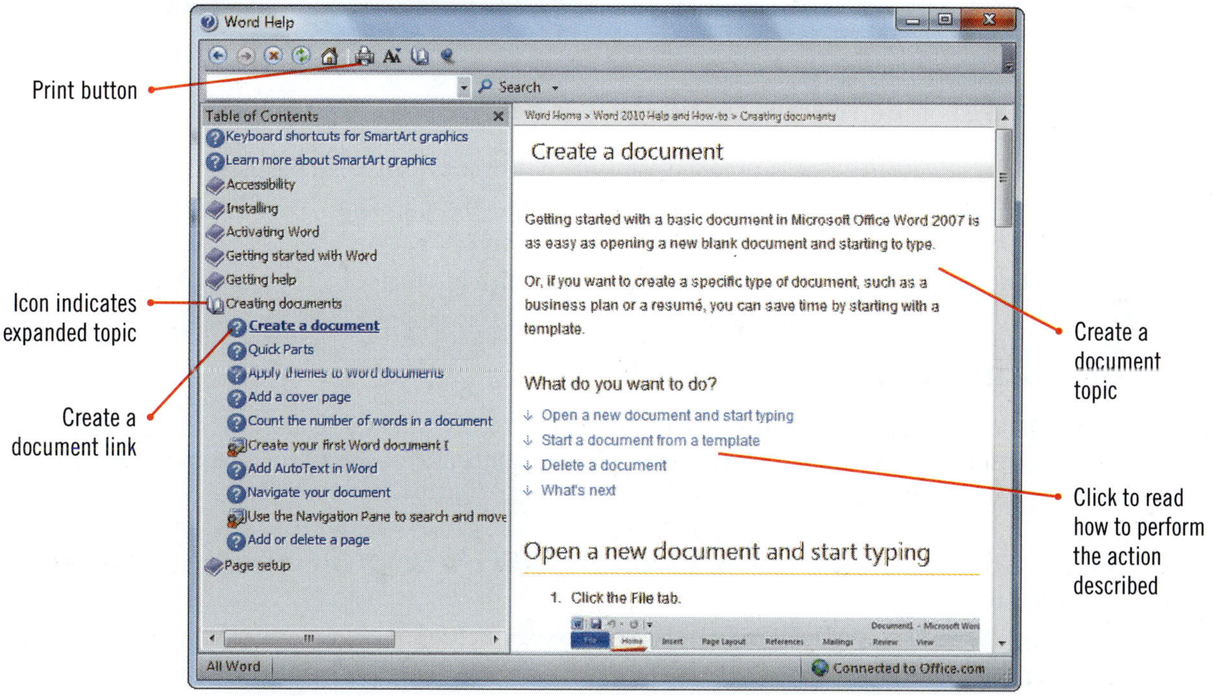

Recovering a document

Each Office program has a built-in recovery feature that allows you to open and save files that were open at the time of an interruption such as a power failure. When you restart the program(s) after an interruption, the Document Recovery task pane opens on the left side of your screen displaying both original and recovered versions of the files that were open. If you're not sure which file to open (original or recovered), it's usually better to open the recovered file because it will contain the latest information. You can, however, open and review all versions of the file that were recovered and save the best one. Each file listed in the Document Recovery task pane displays a list arrow with options that allow you to open the file, save it as is, delete it, or show repairs made to it during recovery.

Practice

For current SAM information, including versions and content details, visit SAM Central (http://www.cengage.com/samcentral). If you have a SAM user profile, you may have access to hands-on instruction, practice, and assessment of the skills covered in this unit. Since various versions of SAM are supported throughout the life of this text, check with your instructor for the correct instructions and URL/Web site for accessing assignments.

Concepts Review

Label the elements of the program window shown in Figure A-17.

FIGURE A-17

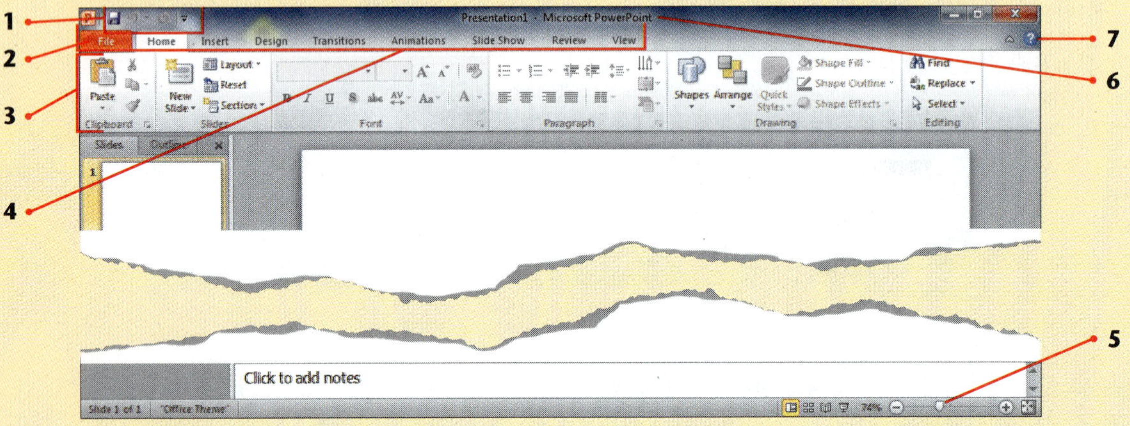

Match each project with the program for which it is best suited.

8. Microsoft Access	**a.** Corporate convention budget with expense projections
9. Microsoft Excel	**b.** Business cover letter for a job application
10. Microsoft Word	**c.** Department store inventory
11. Microsoft PowerPoint	**d.** Presentation for city council meeting

Independent Challenge 1

You just accepted an administrative position with a local independently owned produce vendor that has recently invested in computers and is now considering purchasing Microsoft Office for the company. You are asked to propose ways Office might help the business. You produce your document in Word.

a. Start Word, then save the document as **OF A-Microsoft Office Document** in the drive and folder where you store your Data Files.

b. Type **Microsoft Word**, press [Enter] twice, type **Microsoft Excel**, press [Enter] twice, type **Microsoft PowerPoint**, press [Enter] twice, type **Microsoft Access**, press [Enter] twice, then type your name.

c. Click the line beneath each program name, type at least two tasks suited to that program (each separated by a comma), then press [Enter].

Advanced Challenge Exercise

- Press the [PrtScn] button to create a screen capture.
- Click after your name, press [Enter] to move to a blank line below your name, then click the Paste button in the Clipboard group on the Home tab.

d. Save the document, then submit your work to your instructor as directed.

e. Exit Word.

UNIT A
Word 2010

Creating Documents with Word 2010

Files You Will Need:
WD A-1.docx

Microsoft Word 2010 is a word processing program that makes it easy to create a variety of professional-looking documents, from simple letters and memos to newsletters, research papers, blog posts, business cards, résumés, financial reports, and other documents that include multiple pages of text and sophisticated formatting. In this unit, you will explore the editing and formatting features available in Word and create two documents. You have been hired to work in the Marketing Department at Quest Specialty Travel (QST), a tour company that specializes in cultural tourism and adventure travel. Shortly after reporting to your new office, Ron Dawson, the vice president of marketing, asks you to use Word to create a memo to the marketing staff and a fax to one of the tour developers.

OBJECTIVES

- Understand word processing software
- Explore the Word program window
- Start a document
- Save a document
- Select text
- Format text using the Mini toolbar
- Create a document using a template
- View and navigate a document

UNIT
A
Word 2010

Understanding Word Processing Software

A **word processing program** is a software program that includes tools for entering, editing, and formatting text and graphics. Microsoft Word is a powerful word processing program that allows you to create and enhance a wide range of documents quickly and easily. Figure A-1 shows the first page of a report created using Word and illustrates some of the Word features you can use to enhance your documents. The electronic files you create using Word are called **documents**. One of the benefits of using Word is that document files can be stored on a hard disk, CD, flash drive, or other storage device, making them easy to transport, exchange, and revise. Before beginning your memo to the marketing staff, you explore the editing and formatting features available in Word.

DETAILS

You can use Word to accomplish the following tasks:

- **Type and edit text**
  The Word editing tools make it simple to insert and delete text in a document. You can add text to the middle of an existing paragraph, replace text with other text, undo an editing change, and correct typing, spelling, and grammatical errors with ease.

- **Copy and move text from one location to another**
  Using the more advanced editing features of Word, you can copy or move text from one location and insert it in a different location in a document. You also can copy and move text between documents. This means you don't have to retype text that is already entered in a document.

- **Format text and paragraphs with fonts, colors, and other elements**
  The sophisticated formatting tools in Word allow you to make the text in your documents come alive. You can change the size, style, and color of text, add lines and shading to paragraphs, and enhance lists with bullets and numbers. Creatively formatting text helps to highlight important ideas in your documents.

- **Format and design pages**
  The page-formatting features in Word give you power to design attractive newsletters, create powerful résumés, and produce documents such as research papers, business cards, CD labels, and books. You can change the paper size and orientation of your documents, organize text in columns, and control the layout of text and graphics on each page of a document. For quick results, Word includes preformatted cover pages, pull quotes, and headers and footers, as well as galleries of coordinated text, table, and graphic styles that you can rely on to give documents a polished look. If you are writing a research paper, Word makes it easy to manage reference sources and create footnotes, endnotes, and bibliographies.

- **Enhance documents with tables, charts, diagrams, and graphics**
  Using the powerful graphics tools in Word, you can spice up your documents with pictures, photographs, lines, shapes, and diagrams. You also can illustrate your documents with tables and charts to help convey your message in a visually interesting way.

- **Use Mail Merge to create form letters and mailing labels**
  The Word Mail Merge feature allows you to send personalized form letters to many different people. You can also use Mail Merge to create mailing labels, directories, e-mail messages, and other types of documents.

- **Share documents securely**
  The security features in Word make it quick and easy to remove comments, tracked changes, and unwanted personal information from your files before you share them with others. You can also add a password or a digital signature to a document and convert a file to a format suitable for publishing on the Web.

FIGURE A-1: A report created using Word

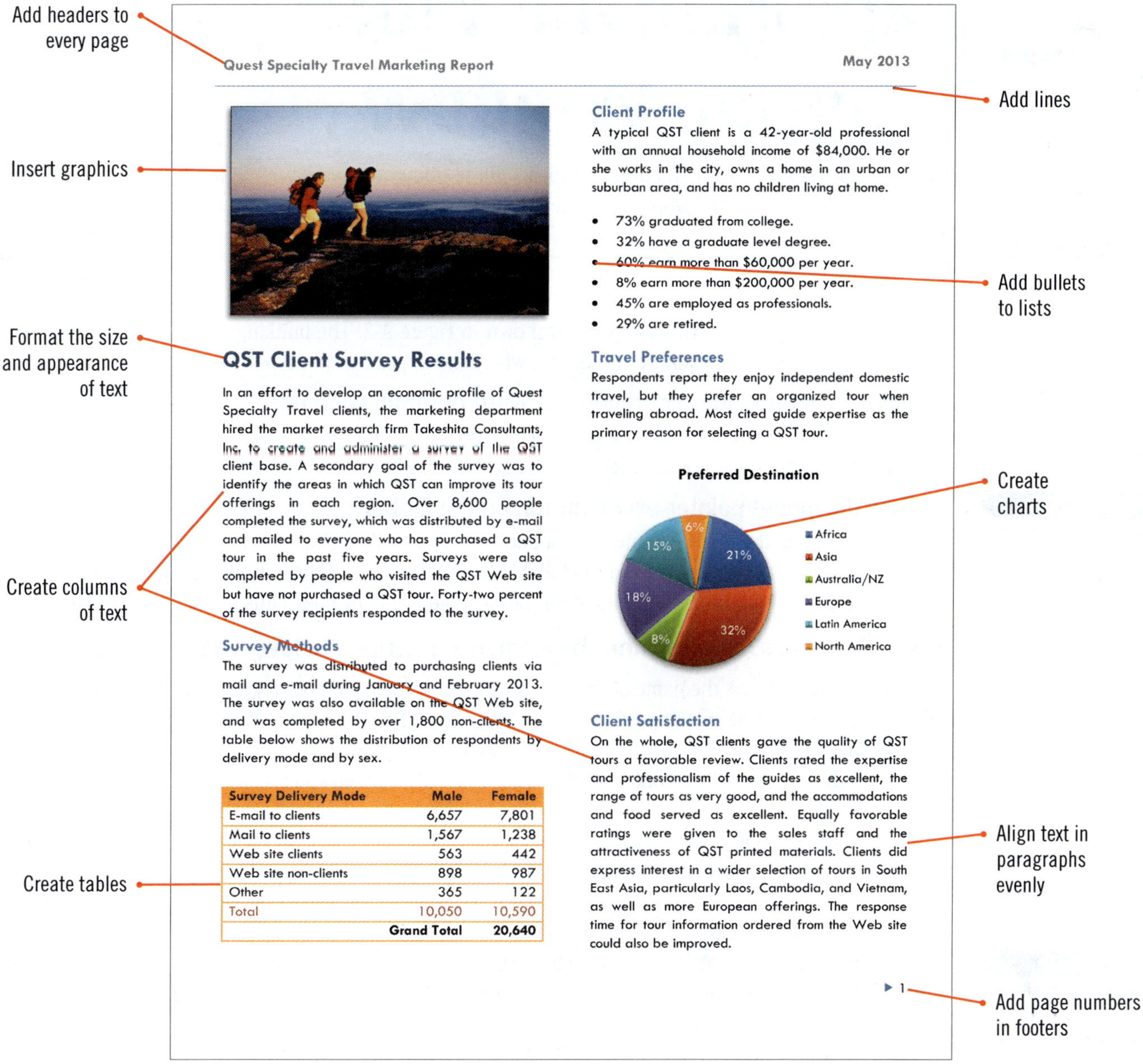

Quest Specialty Travel Marketing Report — May 2013

QST Client Survey Results

In an effort to develop an economic profile of Quest Specialty Travel clients, the marketing department hired the market research firm Takeshita Consultants, Inc. to create and administer a survey of the QST client base. A secondary goal of the survey was to identify the areas in which QST can improve its tour offerings in each region. Over 8,600 people completed the survey, which was distributed by e-mail and mailed to everyone who has purchased a QST tour in the past five years. Surveys were also completed by people who visited the QST Web site but have not purchased a QST tour. Forty-two percent of the survey recipients responded to the survey.

Survey Methods

The survey was distributed to purchasing clients via mail and e-mail during January and February 2013. The survey was also available on the QST Web site, and was completed by over 1,800 non-clients. The table below shows the distribution of respondents by delivery mode and by sex.

Survey Delivery Mode	Male	Female
E-mail to clients	6,657	7,801
Mail to clients	1,567	1,238
Web site clients	563	442
Web site non-clients	898	987
Other	365	122
Total	10,050	10,590
	Grand Total	**20,640**

Client Profile

A typical QST client is a 42-year-old professional with an annual household income of $84,000. He or she works in the city, owns a home in an urban or suburban area, and has no children living at home.

- 73% graduated from college.
- 32% have a graduate level degree.
- 60% earn more than $60,000 per year.
- 8% earn more than $200,000 per year.
- 45% are employed as professionals.
- 29% are retired.

Travel Preferences

Respondents report they enjoy independent domestic travel, but they prefer an organized tour when traveling abroad. Most cited guide expertise as the primary reason for selecting a QST tour.

Preferred Destination

Client Satisfaction

On the whole, QST clients gave the quality of QST tours a favorable review. Clients rated the expertise and professionalism of the guides as excellent, the range of tours as very good, and the accommodations and food served as excellent. Equally favorable ratings were given to the sales staff and the attractiveness of QST printed materials. Clients did express interest in a wider selection of tours in South East Asia, particularly Laos, Cambodia, and Vietnam, as well as more European offerings. The response time for tour information ordered from the Web site could also be improved.

▶ 1

Word 2010

Planning a document

Before you create a new document, it's a good idea to spend time planning it. Identify the message you want to convey, the audience for your document, and the elements, such as tables or charts, you want to include. You should also think about the tone and look of your document—are you writing a business letter, which should be written in a pleasant, but serious tone and have a formal appearance, or are you creating a flyer that must be colorful, eye-catching, and fun to read? The purpose and audience for your document determine the appropriate design. Planning the layout and design of a document involves deciding how to organize the text, selecting the fonts to use, identifying the graphics to include, and selecting the formatting elements that will enhance the message and appeal of the document. For longer documents, such as newsletters, it can be useful to sketch the layout and design of each page before you begin.

UNIT A
Word 2010

Exploring the Word Program Window

When you start Word, a blank document appears in the document window in Print Layout view. You examine the elements of the Word program window.

STEPS

1. **Start Word**

   The **Word program window** opens, as shown in Figure A-2. The blinking vertical line in the document window is the **insertion point**. It indicates where text appears as you type.

2. **Move the mouse pointer around the Word program window**

   The mouse pointer changes shape depending on where it is in the Word program window. You use pointers to move the insertion point or to select text to edit. Table A-1 describes common pointers in Word.

QUICK TIP
The buttons visible on your Ribbon may differ.

3. **Place the mouse pointer over a button on the Ribbon**

   When you place the mouse pointer over a button or some other elements of the Word program window, a ScreenTip appears. A **ScreenTip** is a label that identifies the name of the button or feature, briefly describes its function, conveys any keyboard shortcut for the command, and includes a link to associated help topics, if any.

Using Figure A-2 as a guide, find the elements described below in your program window:

- The **title bar** displays the name of the document and the name of the program. Until you give a new document a different name, its temporary name is Document1. The title bar also contains resizing buttons and the program Close button. These buttons are common to all Windows programs.
- The **Quick Access toolbar** contains buttons for saving a document and for undoing, redoing, and repeating a change. You can modify the Quick Access toolbar to include the commands you use frequently.
- The **File tab** provides access to **Backstage view**, where you manage files and the information about them. Backstage view includes commands related to working with documents, such as opening, printing, and saving a document. The File tab also provides access to resources for help using Word and to the Word Options dialog box, which is used to customize the way you use Word.
- The **Ribbon** contains the Word tabs. Each **tab** on the Ribbon includes buttons for commands related to editing and formatting documents. The commands are organized in **groups**. For example, the Home tab includes the Clipboard, Font, Paragraph, Styles, and Editing groups. The Ribbon also includes the **Microsoft Word Help button**, which you use to access the Word Help system.
- The **document window** displays the current document. You enter text and format your document in the document window.
- The rulers appear in the document window in Print Layout view. The **horizontal ruler** displays left and right document margins as well as the tab settings and paragraph indents, if any, for the paragraph in which the insertion point is located. The **vertical ruler** displays the top and bottom document margins.
- The **vertical scroll bar** and the **horizontal scroll bar** are used to display different parts of the document in the document window. The scroll bars include **scroll boxes** and **scroll arrows**, which you can use to scroll through a document.
- The **status bar** displays the page number of the current page, the total number of pages and words in the document, and the status of spelling and grammar checking. It also includes the view buttons, the Zoom level button, and the Zoom slider. You can customize the status bar to display other information.
- The **view buttons** on the status bar allow you to display the document in Print Layout, Full Screen Reading, Web Layout, Outline, or Draft view.
- The **Zoom level** button and the **Zoom slider** provide quick ways to enlarge and decrease the size of the document in the document window, making it easy to zoom in on a detail of a document or to view the layout of the document as a whole.

QUICK TIP
To display a different tab, you simply click its name on the Ribbon.

TROUBLE
Click the View Ruler button at the top of the vertical scroll bar to display the rulers if they are not already displayed.

FIGURE A-2: Elements of the Word program window

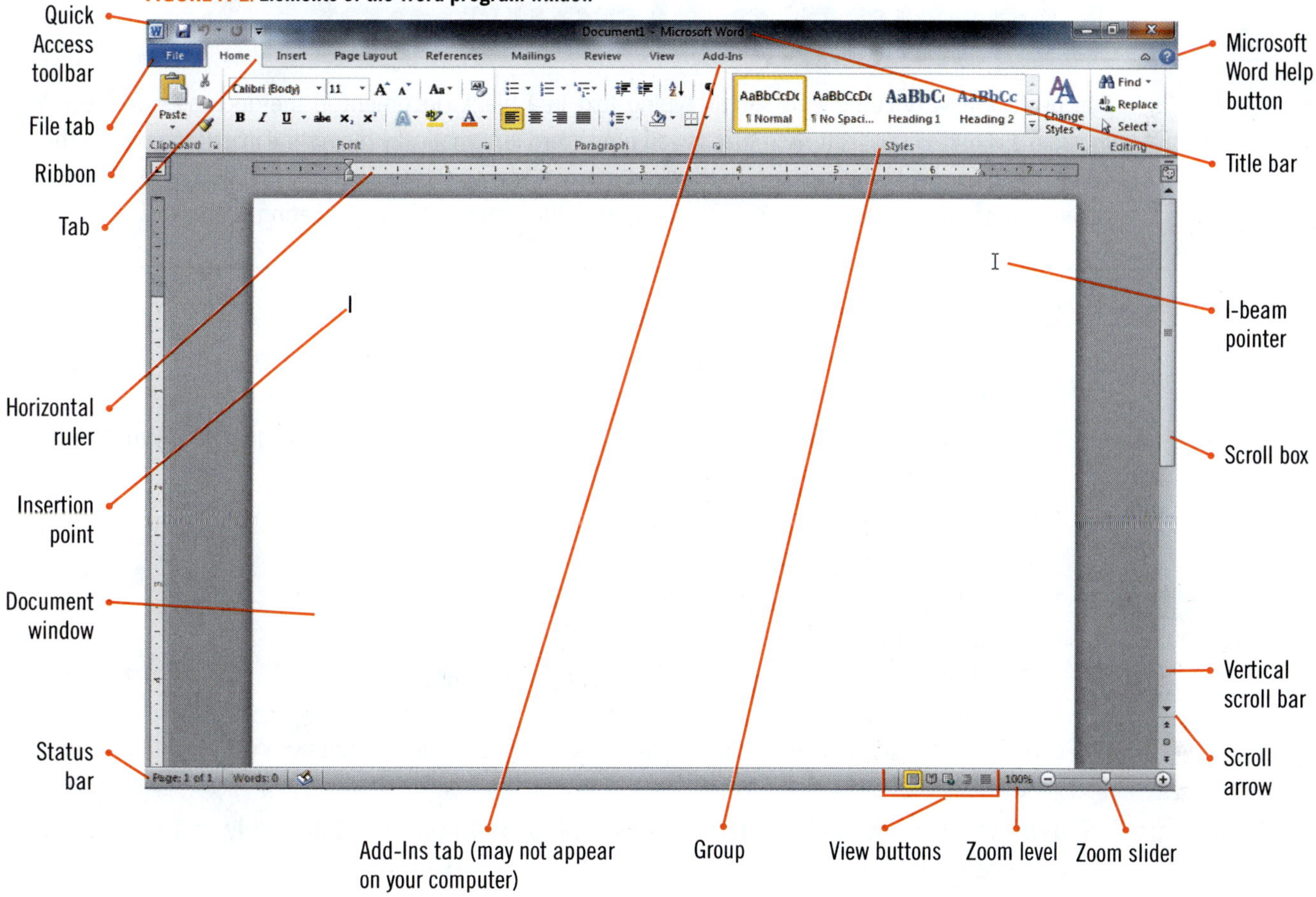

TABLE A-1: Common mouse pointers in Word

name	pointer	use to
I-beam pointer		Move the insertion point in a document or to select text
Click and Type pointers, including left-align and center-align	or	Move the insertion point to a blank area of a document in Print Layout or Web Layout view; double-clicking with a Click and Type pointer automatically applies the paragraph formatting (alignment and indentation) required to position text or a graphic at that location in the document
Selection pointer		Click a button or other element of the Word program window; appears when you point to elements of the Word program window
Right-pointing arrow pointer		Select a line or lines of text; appears when you point to the left edge of a line of text in the document window
Hand pointer		Open a hyperlink; appears when you point to a hyperlink in a task pane or when you press [Ctrl] and point to a hyperlink in a document
Hide white space pointer		Hide the white space in the top and bottom margins of a document in Print Layout view
Show white space pointer		Show the white space in the top and bottom margins of a document in Print Layout view

UNIT
A
Word 2010

Starting a Document

You begin a new document by simply typing text in a blank document in the document window. Word includes a **word-wrap** feature so that as you type Word automatically moves the insertion point to the next line of the document when you reach the right margin. You only press [Enter] when you want to start a new paragraph or insert a blank line. You type a quick memo to the marketing staff.

STEPS

TROUBLE
If you press the wrong key, press [Backspace] to erase the mistake, then try again.

QUICK TIP
Wavy lines and other automatic feature markers appear on screen but do not print.

TROUBLE
To reverse an AutoCorrect adjustment, immediately click the Undo button on the Quick Access toolbar.

QUICK TIP
If you want uniform spacing between lines and paragraphs, apply the No Spacing style to the document by clicking the No Spacing button in the Styles group on the Home tab before you begin to type. Alternatively, select the text and then click the No Spacing button.

1. **Type Memorandum, then press [Enter] twice**
   Each time you press [Enter] the insertion point moves to the start of the next line.
2. **Type TO:, then press [Tab] twice**
   Pressing [Tab] moves the insertion point several spaces to the right. You can use the [Tab] key to align the text in a memo header or to indent the first line of a paragraph.
3. **Type QST Managers, then press [Enter]**
   The insertion point moves to the start of the next line.
4. **Type: FROM: [Tab] [Tab] Ron Dawson [Enter]**
   DATE: [Tab] [Tab] July 7, 2013 [Enter]
   RE: [Tab] [Tab] Marketing Meeting [Enter] [Enter]
   Red or green wavy lines may appear under the words you typed, indicating a possible spelling or grammar error. Spelling and grammar checking is one of the many automatic features you will encounter as you type. Table A-2 describes several of these automatic features. You can correct any typing errors you make later.
5. **Type The next marketing staff meeting will be held on the 11th of July at 1 p.m. in the conference room on the ground floor., then press [Spacebar]**
   As you type, notice that the insertion point moves automatically to the next line of the document. You also might notice that Word automatically changed "11th" to "11th" in the memo. This feature is called **AutoCorrect**. AutoCorrect automatically makes typographical adjustments and detects and adjusts typing errors, certain misspelled words (such as "taht" for "that"), and incorrect capitalization as you type.
6. **Type Heading the agenda will be the launch of our new High Atlas Trek, a rigorous ten-day walking tour of the sunny valleys, remote Berber villages, and steep slopes of Morocco's High Atlas, scheduled for September 2015.**
   When you type the first few characters of "September," the Word AutoComplete feature displays the complete word in a ScreenTip. **AutoComplete** suggests text to insert quickly into your documents. You can ignore AutoComplete for now. Your memo should resemble Figure A-3.
7. **Press [Enter], then type Kai Haketa is in Marrakech hammering out the details. A preliminary draft of the tour brochure is attached. Bring your creative ideas for launching this exciting new tour to the meeting.**
   When you press [Enter] and type the new paragraph, notice that Word adds more space between the paragraphs than it does between the lines in each paragraph. This is part of the default style for paragraphs in Word, called the **Normal style**.
8. **Position the I pointer after for (but before the space) in the last line of the first paragraph, then click**
   Clicking moves the insertion point after "for."
9. **Press [Backspace] three times, then type to depart in**
   Pressing [Backspace] removes the character before the insertion point.
10. **Move the insertion point before staff in the first sentence, then press [Delete] six times to remove the word "staff" and the space after it**
    Pressing [Delete] removes the character after the insertion point. Figure A-4 shows the revised memo.

FIGURE A-3: Memo text in the document window

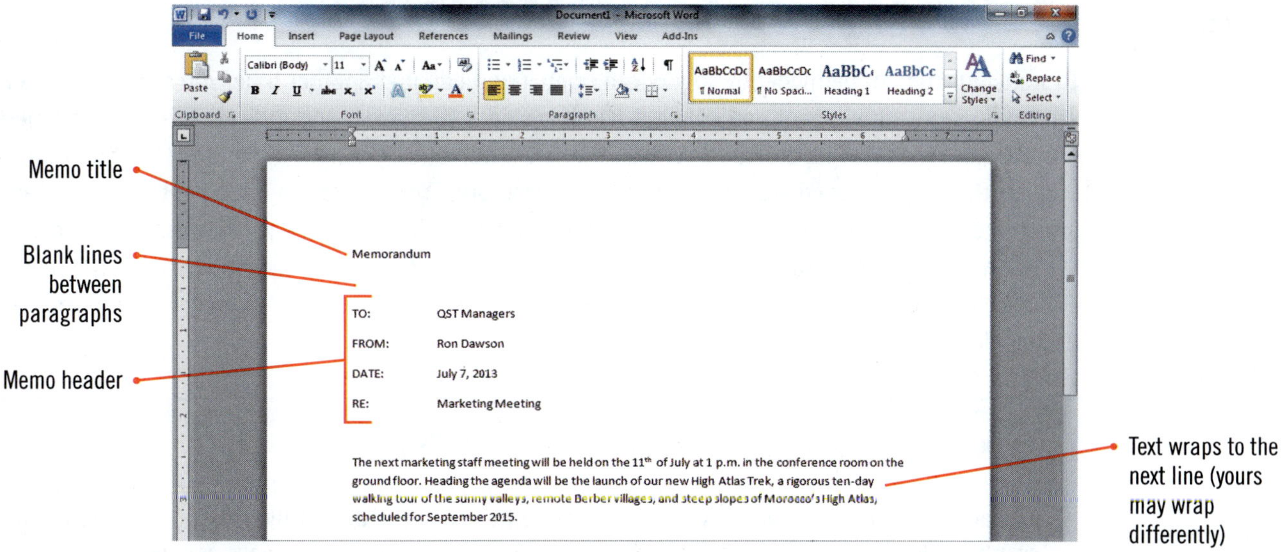

FIGURE A-4: Edited memo text

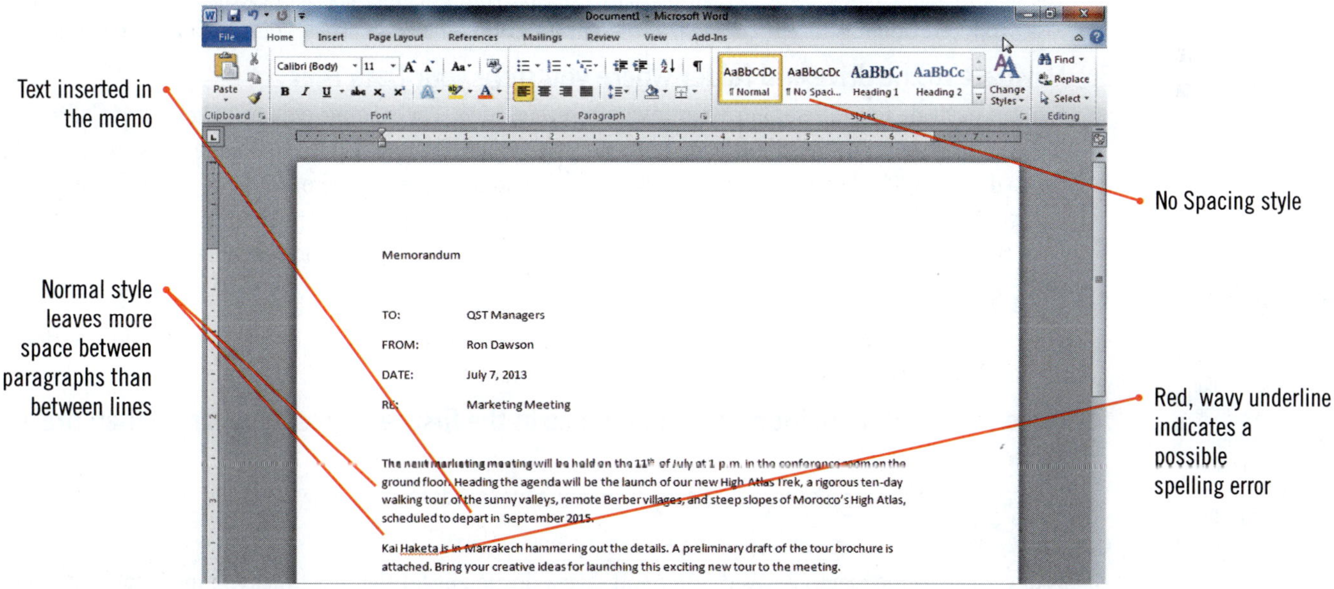

TABLE A-2: Automatic features that appear as you type in Word

feature	what appears	to use
AutoComplete	A ScreenTip suggesting text to insert appears as you type	Press [Enter] to insert the text suggested by the ScreenTip; continue typing to reject the suggestion
AutoCorrect	A small blue box appears when you place the pointer over text corrected by AutoCorrect; an AutoCorrect Options button appears when you point to the blue box	Word automatically corrects typos, minor spelling errors, and capitalization, and adds typographical symbols (such as © and ™) as you type; to reverse an AutoCorrect adjustment, click the AutoCorrect Options list arrow, then click the option that will undo the action
Spelling and Grammar	A red wavy line under a word indicates a possible misspelling; a green wavy line under text indicates a possible grammar error	Right-click red- or green-underlined text to display a shortcut menu of correction options; click a correction option to accept it and remove the wavy underline

UNIT
A
Word 2010

Saving a Document

To store a document permanently so you can open it and edit it at another time, you must save it as a **file**. When you **save** a document you give it a name, called a **filename**, and indicate the location where you want to store the file. Files created in Word 2010 are automatically assigned the .docx file extension to distinguish them from files created in other software programs. You can save a document using the Save button on the Quick Access toolbar or the Save command on the File tab. Once you have saved a document for the first time, you should save it again every few minutes and always before printing so that the saved file is updated to reflect your latest changes. You save your memo using a descriptive filename and the default file extension.

STEPS

TROUBLE
If you don't see the extension .docx as part of the filename, the setting in Windows to display file extensions is not active.

1. **Click the Save button on the Quick Access toolbar**

   The first time you save a document, the Save As dialog box opens, as shown in Figure A-5. The default filename, Memorandum, appears in the File name text box. The default filename is based on the first few words of the document. The default file extension, .docx, appears in the Save as type list box. Table A-3 describes the functions of some of the buttons in the Save As dialog box.

2. **Type WD A-Morocco Tour Memo in the File name text box**

   The new filename replaces the default filename. Giving your documents brief descriptive filenames makes it easier to locate and organize them later. You do not need to type .docx when you type a new filename.

3. **Navigate to the drive and folder where you store your Data Files**

   You can navigate to a different drive or folder in several ways. For example, you can click a drive or folder in the Address bar or the navigation pane to go directly to that location. Click the double arrow in the Address bar to display a list of drives and folders. You can also double-click a drive or folder in the folder window to change the active location. When you are finished navigating to the drive or folder where you store your Data Files, that location appears in the Address bar. Your Save As dialog box should resemble Figure A-6.

QUICK TIP
To save a document so it can be opened in an older version of Word, click the Save as type list arrow, then click Word 97-2003 Document (*.doc).

4. **Click Save**

   The document is saved to the drive and folder you specified in the Save As dialog box, and the title bar displays the new filename, WD A-Morocco Tour Memo.docx.

5. **Place the insertion point before conference in the first sentence, type large, then press [Spacebar]**

   You can continue to work on a document after you have saved it with a new filename.

6. **Click**

   Your change to the memo is saved. After you save a document for the first time, you must continue to save the changes you make to the document. You also can press [Ctrl][S] to save a document.

Windows Live and Microsoft Office Web Apps

All Office programs include the capability to incorporate feedback—called online collaboration—across the Internet or a company network. Using **cloud computing** (work done in a virtual environment), you can take advantage of Web programs called Microsoft Office Web Apps, which are simplified versions of the programs found in the Microsoft Office 2010 suite. Because these programs are online, they take up no computer disk space and are accessed using Windows Live SkyDrive, a free service from Microsoft. Using Windows Live SkyDrive, you and your colleagues can create and store documents in a "cloud" and make the documents available to whomever you grant access. To use Windows Live SkyDrive, you need a free Windows Live ID, which you obtain at the Windows Live Web site. You can find more information in the "Working with Windows Live and Office Web Apps" appendix.

FIGURE A-5: Save As dialog box

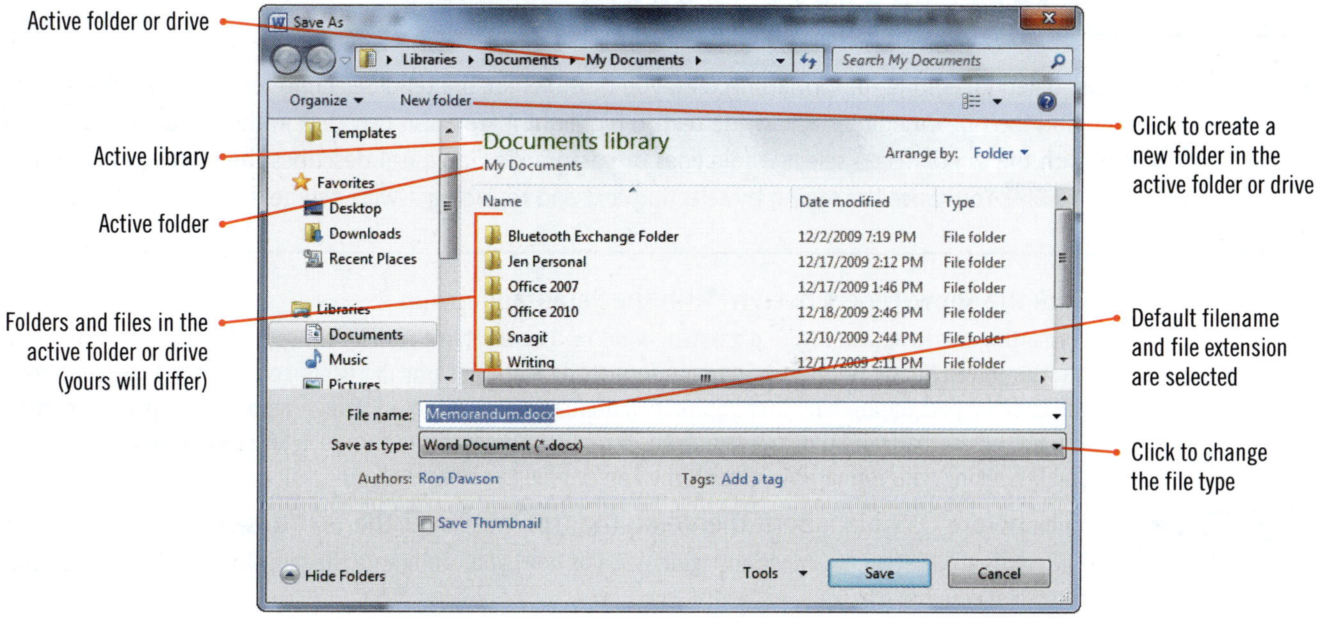

FIGURE A-6: File to be saved to the Unit A folder

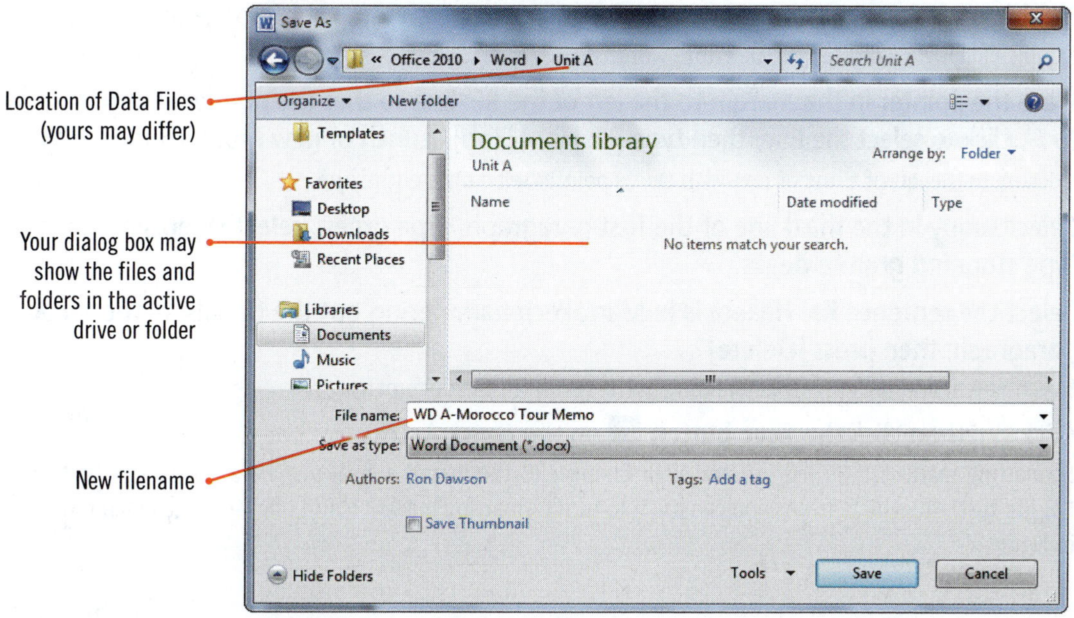

TABLE A-3: Save As dialog box buttons

button	use to
Back	Navigate back to the last location shown in the Address bar
Forward	Navigate to the location that was previously shown in the Address bar
Organize ▾ Organize	Open a menu of commands related to organizing the selected file or folder, including Cut, Copy, Delete, Rename, and Properties
New folder New folder	Create a new folder in the current folder or drive
Change your view	Change the way folder and file information is shown in the folder window in the Save As dialog box; click the Change your view button to toggle between views, or click the list arrow to open a menu of view options

UNIT
A
Word 2010

Selecting Text

Before deleting, editing, or formatting text, you must **select** the text. Selecting text involves clicking and dragging the I-beam pointer across the text to highlight it. You also can click in the margin to the left of text with the pointer to select whole lines or paragraphs. Table A-4 describes the many ways to select text. You revise the memo by selecting text and replacing it with new text.

STEPS

1. **Click the Show/Hide ¶ button ¶ in the Paragraph group**
   Formatting marks appear in the document window. **Formatting marks** are special characters that appear on your screen but do not print. Common formatting marks include the paragraph symbol (¶), which shows the end of a paragraph—wherever you press [Enter]; the dot symbol (·), which represents a space—wherever you press [Spacebar]; and the arrow symbol (→), which shows the location of a tab stop—wherever you press [Tab]. Working with formatting marks turned on can help you to select, edit, and format text with precision.

QUICK TIP
You deselect text by clicking anywhere in the document window.

2. **Click before QST Managers, then drag the I pointer over the text to select it**
   The words are selected, as shown in Figure A-7. For now, you can ignore the faint toolbar that appears over text when you first select it.
3. **Type Marketing Staff**
   The text you type replaces the selected text.
4. **Double-click Ron, type your first name, double-click Dawson, then type your last name**
   Double-clicking a word selects the entire word.

TROUBLE
If you delete text by mistake, immediately click the Undo button on the Quick Access toolbar to restore the deleted text to the document.

5. **Place the pointer in the margin to the left of the RE: line so that the pointer changes to , click to select the line, then type RE: [Tab] [Tab] Launch of new Morocco trekking tour**
   Clicking to the left of a line of text with the pointer selects the entire line.
6. **Select sunny in the third line of the first paragraph, type green, select steep slopes, then type stunning granite peaks**
7. **Select the sentence Kai Haketa is in Marrakech hammering out the details. in the second paragraph, then press [Delete]**
   Selecting text and pressing [Delete] removes the text from the document.

QUICK TIP
Always save before and after editing text.

8. **Click ¶, then click the Save button on the Quick Access toolbar**
   Formatting marks are turned off, and your changes to the memo are saved. The Show/Hide ¶ button is a **toggle button**, which means you can use it to turn formatting marks on and off. The edited memo is shown in Figure A-8.

FIGURE A-7: Text selected in the memo

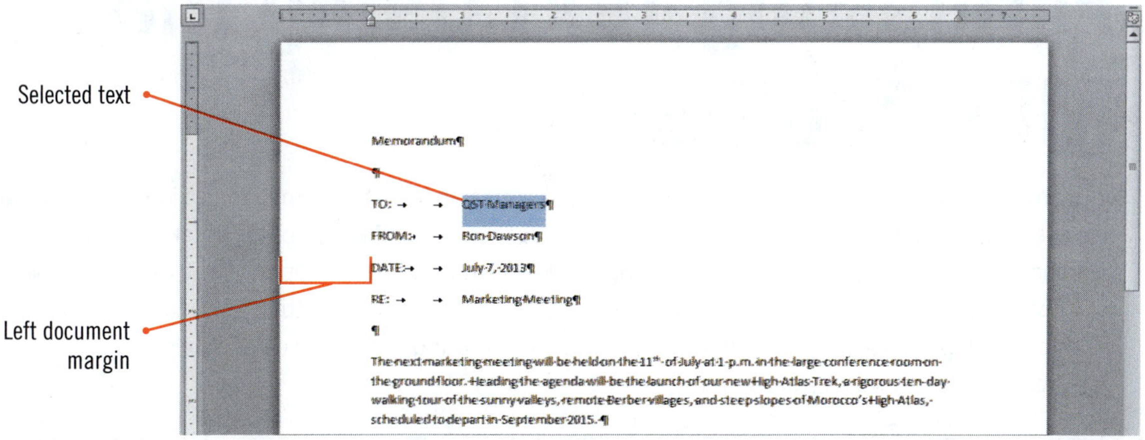

FIGURE A-8: Edited memo with replacement text

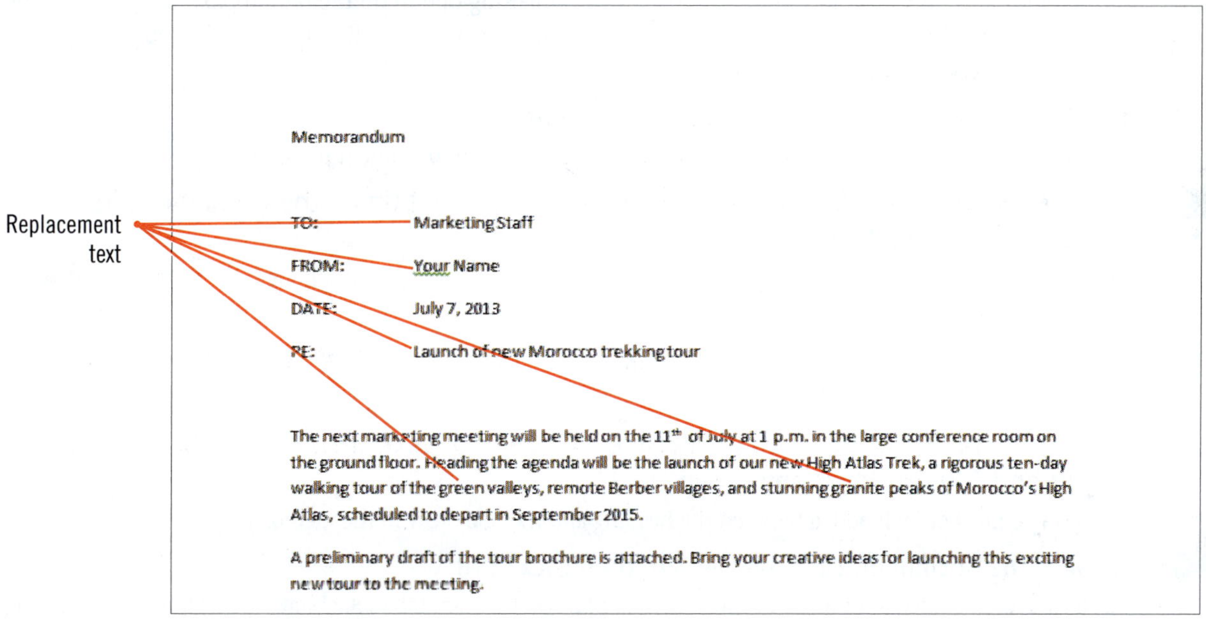

TABLE A-4: Methods for selecting text

to select	use the pointer to
Any amount of text	Drag over the text
A word	Double-click the word
A line of text	Click with the pointer to the left of the line
A sentence	Press and hold [Ctrl], then click the sentence
A paragraph	Triple-click the paragraph or double-click with the pointer to the left of the paragraph
A large block of text	Click at the beginning of the selection, press and hold [Shift], then click at the end of the selection
Multiple nonconsecutive selections	Select the first selection, then press and hold [Ctrl] as you select each additional selection
An entire document	Triple-click with the pointer to the left of any text; press [Ctrl][A]; or click the Select button in the Editing group on the Home tab, and then click Select All

UNIT A
Word 2010

Formatting Text Using the Mini Toolbar

Formatting text is a fast and fun way to spruce up the appearance of a document and highlight important information. You can easily change the font, color, size, style, and other attributes of text by selecting the text and clicking a command on the Home tab. The **Mini toolbar**, which appears faintly above text when you first select it, also includes commonly used text and paragraph formatting commands. You enhance the appearance of the memo by formatting the text using the Mini toolbar. When you are finished, you preview the memo for errors and then print it.

STEPS

TROUBLE
If the Mini toolbar disappears, right-click the selection to display it again.

1. **Double-click Memorandum**

   The Mini toolbar appears in ghosted fashion over the selected text. When you point to the Mini toolbar, it becomes solid, as shown in Figure A-9. You click a formatting option on the Mini toolbar to apply it to the selected text. Table A-5 describes the function of the buttons on the Mini toolbar. The buttons on the Mini toolbar are also available on the Ribbon.

2. **Click the Center button on the Mini toolbar**

   The word "Memorandum" is centered between the left and right document margins.

QUICK TIP
Click the Shrink Font button to decrease the font size.

3. **Click the Grow Font button on the Mini toolbar eight times, then click the Bold button on the Mini toolbar**

   Each time you click the Grow Font button the selected text is enlarged. Applying **bold** to the text makes it thicker and darker.

4. **Select TO:, click B, select FROM:, click B, select DATE:, click B, select RE:, then click B**

   Bold is applied to the heading text.

5. **Click the blank line between the RE: line and the body text, then click the Bottom Border button in the Paragraph group**

   A single-line border is added between the heading and the body text in the memo.

QUICK TIP
You can customize your Quick Access toolbar to include the Quick Print button, which prints a document using the default print settings.

6. **Save the document, click the File tab, then click Print**

   Information related to printing the document appears on the Print tab in Backstage view. Options for printing the document appear on the left side of the Print tab and a preview of the document as it will look when printed appears on the right side, as shown in Figure A-10. Before you print a document, it's a good habit to examine it closely so you can identify and correct any problems.

7. **Click the Zoom In button five times, then proofread your document carefully for errors**

   The document is enlarged in print preview. If you notice errors in your document, you need to correct them before you print. To do this, press [Esc] or click the Home tab to close Backstage view, correct any mistakes, save your changes, click the File tab, and then click the Print command again to be ready to print the document.

8. **Click the Print button on the Print tab**

   A copy of the memo prints using the default print settings. To change the current printer, change the number of copies to print, select what pages of a document to print, or modify another print setting, you simply change the appropriate setting on the Print tab before clicking the Print button.

9. **Click the File tab, then click Close**

   The document closes, but the Word program window remains open.

FIGURE A-9: Mini toolbar

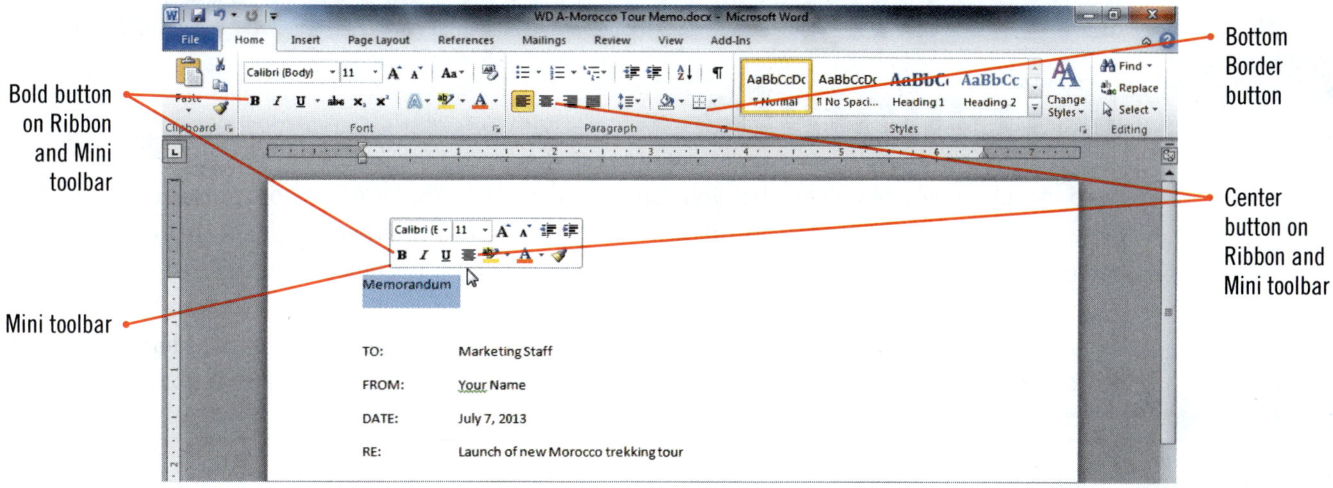

FIGURE A-10: Preview of the completed memo

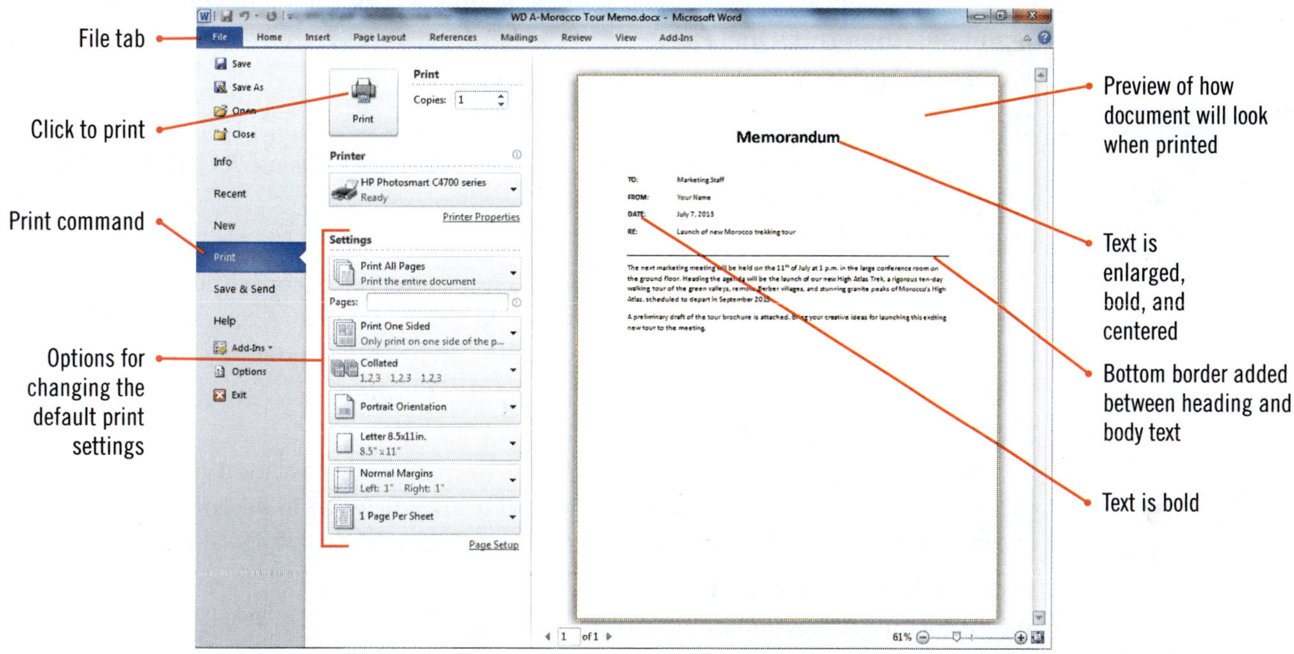

TABLE A-5: Buttons on the Mini toolbar

button	use to	button	use to
Calibri (E	Change the font of text	*I*	Italicize text
11	Change the font size of text	U	Underline text
A	Make text larger	≡	Center text between the margins
A	Make text smaller	ab	Apply colored highlighting to text
⇤	Decrease the indent level of a paragraph	A	Change the color of text
⇥	Increase the indent level of a paragraph	🖌	Copy the formats applied to text to other text
B	Apply bold to text		

UNIT
A
Word 2010

Creating a Document Using a Template

Word includes many templates that you can use to create faxes, letters, reports, brochures, and other professionally designed documents quickly. A **template** is a formatted document that contains placeholder text,which you replace with your own text. To create a document that is based on a template, you use the New command on the File tab, and then select a template to use. You can then customize the document and save it with a new filename. You want to fax a draft of the Morocco tour brochure to Kai Haketa, the tour developer for Africa. You use a template to create a fax cover sheet.

STEPS

QUICK TIP
To create a new blank document, click Create.

QUICK TIP
Double-clicking a template icon also opens a new document based on the template.

QUICK TIP
You can delete a content control by right-clicking it, and then clicking Remove Content Control on the menu that opens.

1. **Click the File tab, then click New**

   The New tab opens in Backstage view, as shown in Figure A-11.

2. **Click Sample templates in the Available Templates section, scroll down the list of Available Templates, then click Oriel Fax**

   A preview of the Oriel Fax template appears in the preview section.

3. **Click Create**

   The Oriel Fax template opens as a new document in the document window. It contains placeholder text, which you can replace with your own information.

4. **Click [Pick the date]**

   The placeholder text is selected and appears inside a content control. A **content control** is an interactive object that you use to customize a document with your own information. A content control might include placeholder text, a drop-down list of choices, or a calendar. To deselect a content control, you click a blank area of the document.

5. **Click the Pick the date list arrow**

   A calendar opens below the content control. You use the calendar to select the date you want to appear on your document—simply click a date on the calendar to enter that date in the document. You can use the arrows to the left and right of the month and year to scroll the calendar and display a different month.

6. **Click the Today button on the calendar**

   The current date replaces the placeholder text.

7. **Click [TYPE THE RECIPIENT NAME], type Kai Haketa, Guest, click [Type the recipient fax number], then type 1-212-44-555-1510**

   You do not need to drag to select the placeholder text in a content control, you can simply click it. The text you type replaces the placeholder text.

8. **Click [Type the recipient phone number], press [Delete] twice, press [Backspace] seven times, then type HOTEL MARRAKECH, ROOM 1275**

   The recipient phone number content control is removed from the document.

9. **If the text in the From line is not your name, drag to select the text, then type your name**

   When the document is created, Word automatically enters the user name identified in the Word Options dialog box in the From line. This text is not placeholder text, so you have to drag to select it.

10. **Replace the remaining heading placeholder text with the text shown in Figure A-12, delete the CC: content control, click the File tab, click Save As, then save the document as WD A-Kai Fax to the drive and folder where you store your Data Files**

    The document is saved with the filename WD A-Kai Fax.

FIGURE A-11: New tab in Backstage view

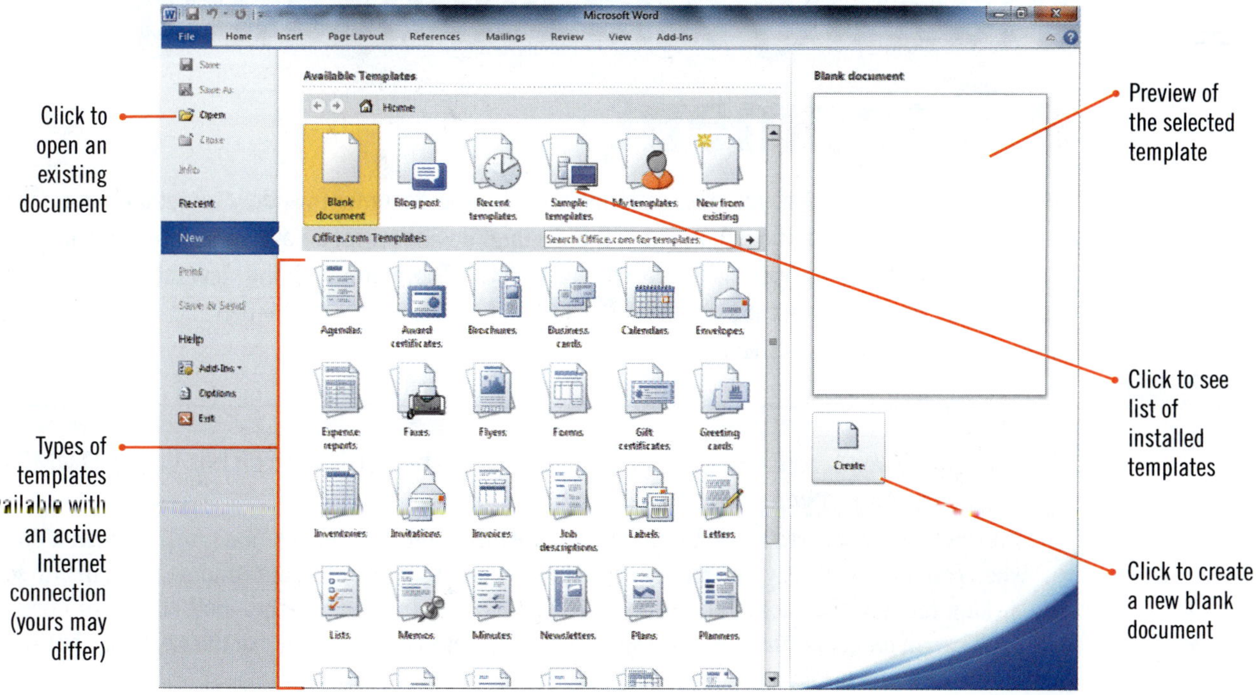

FIGURE A-12: Document created using the Oriel fax template

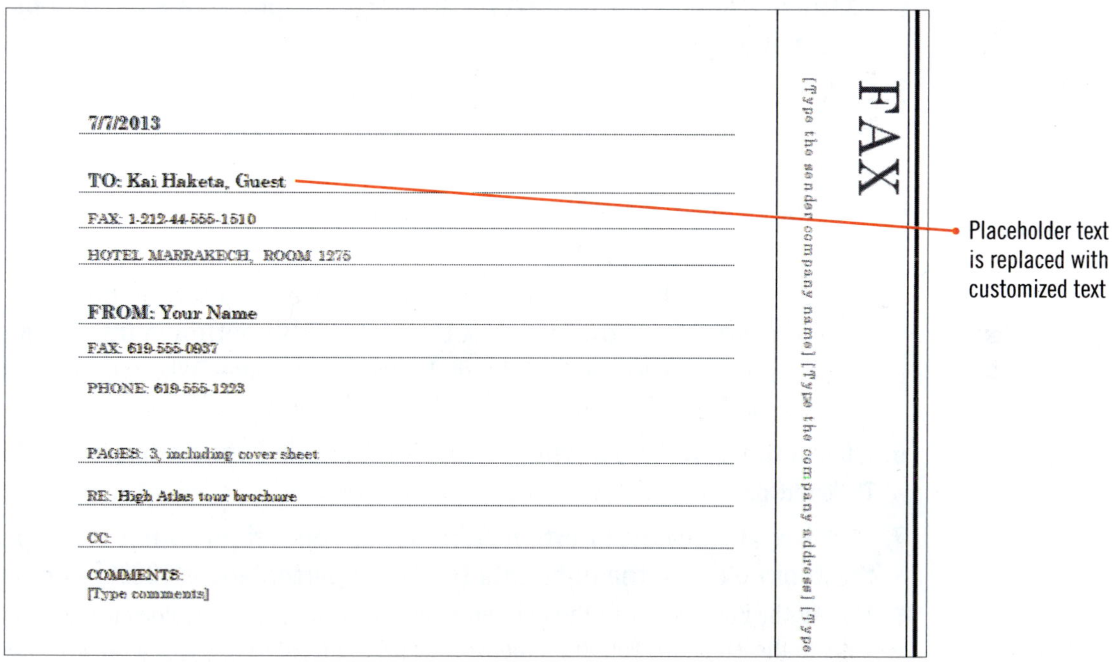

Using the Undo, Redo, and Repeat commands

Word remembers the editing and formatting changes you make so that you can easily reverse or repeat them. You can reverse the last action you took by clicking the Undo button on the Quick Access toolbar, or you can undo a series of actions by clicking the Undo list arrow and selecting the action you want to reverse. When you undo an action using the Undo list arrow, you also undo all the actions above it in the list—that is, all actions that were performed after the action you selected. Similarly, you can keep the change you just reversed by using the Redo button on the Quick Access toolbar. The Redo button appears only immediately after clicking the Undo button to undo a change.

If you want to repeat an action you just completed, you can use the Repeat button on the Quick Access toolbar. For example, if you just typed "thank you," clicking inserts "thank you" at the location of the insertion point. If you just applied bold, clicking applies bold to the currently selected text. You also can repeat the last action you took by pressing [F4].

UNIT
A
Word 2010

Viewing and Navigating a Document

The Word Zoom feature lets you enlarge a document in the document window to get a close-up view of a detail or reduce the size of the document in the document window for an overview of the layout as a whole. You zoom in and out on a document using the tools in the Zoom group on the View tab and the Zoom level buttons and Zoom slider on the status bar. You find it is helpful to zoom in and out on the document as you finalize the fax cover sheet.

STEPS

1. **Click the down scroll arrow at the bottom of the vertical scroll bar until COMMENTS: is near the top of your document window**
   The scroll arrows or scroll bars allow you to **scroll** through a document. You scroll through a document when you want to display different parts of the document in the document window. You can also scroll by clicking the scroll bar above and below the scroll box, or by dragging the scroll box up or down in the scroll bar. In longer documents, you can click the Previous Page button or the Next Page button on the scroll bar to display the document page by page.
2. **Click [Type comments], then type A draft copy of the High Atlas tour brochure is attached. Please revise the text for accuracy. The photos are for placement only. Have you hired a photographer yet?**
3. **Click the Zoom level button 100% on the status bar**
   The Zoom dialog box opens. You use the Zoom dialog box to select a zoom level for displaying the document in the document window.
4. **Click the Whole page option button, then click OK**
   The entire document is displayed in the document window.
5. **Click the text at the bottom of the page to move the insertion point to the bottom of the page, click the View tab, then click the Page Width button in the Zoom group**
   The document is enlarged to the width of the document window. When you enlarge a document, the area where the insertion point is located appears in the document window.
6. **Click in the Urgent box, type x, then click the One Page button in the Zoom group**
   The entire document is displayed in the document window.
7. **Click Fax to move the insertion point to the upper-right corner of the page, then move the Zoom slider to the right until the Zoom percentage is 100%, as shown in Figure A-13**
   Moving the Zoom slider to the right enlarges the document in the document window. Moving the zoom slider to the left allows you to see more of the page at a reduced size. You can also move the Zoom slider by clicking a point on the Zoom slide, or by clicking the Zoom Out and Zoom In buttons.
8. **Click the Zoom In button three times, right-click the vertical placeholder [Type the sender company name], click Remove Content Control, right-click [Type the company address], click Remove Content Control, click [Type the company phone number], then type Quest Specialty Travel, San Diego, CA**
   The text you type replaces the vertical placeholder text. You do not always need to replace the placeholder text with the type of information suggested in the content control.
9. **Click 130%, click the 100% option button, click OK, then save the document**
   The completed fax cover sheet is shown in Figure A-14.
10. **Submit the document to your instructor, close the file, then exit Word**

QUICK TIP
You can also click the Zoom button in the Zoom group on the View tab to open the Zoom dialog box.

TROUBLE
Your company name content control might include the name of a company, such as Microsoft. Right-click it and then click Remove Content Control, or select the text and press [Delete].

FIGURE A-13: Zoom slider

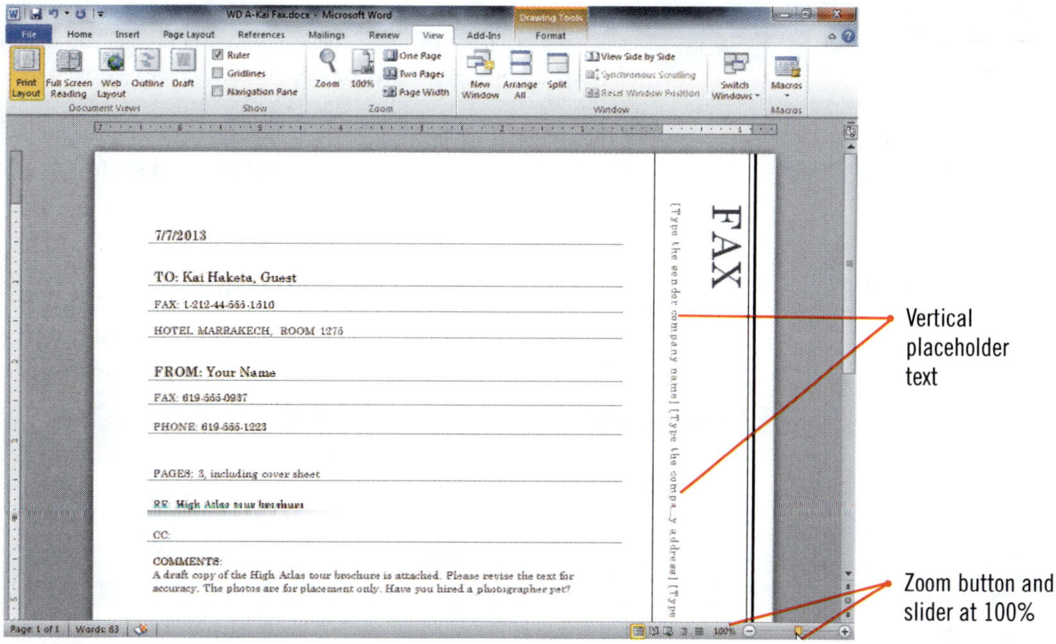

FIGURE A-14: Completed fax cover sheet

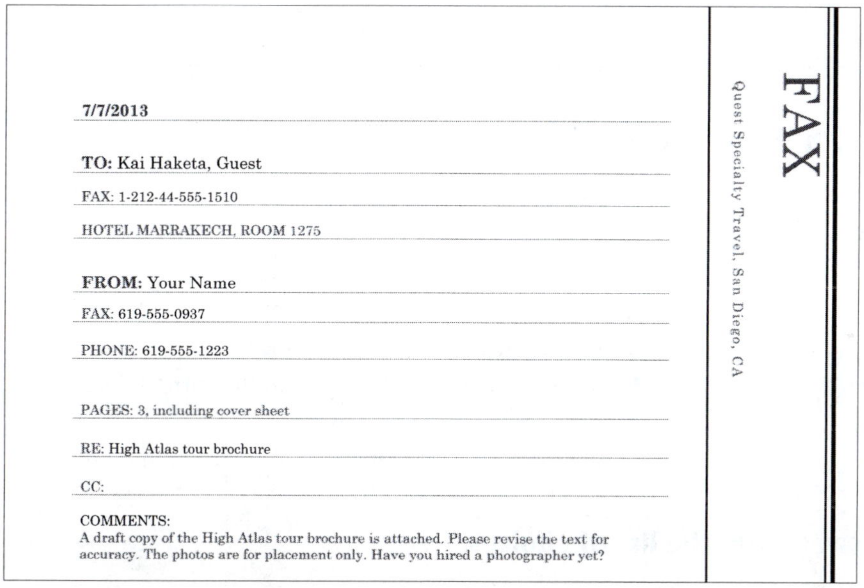
FAX

Quest Specialty Travel, San Diego, CA

7/7/2013

TO: Kai Haketa, Guest

FAX: 1-212-44-555-1510

HOTEL MARRAKECH, ROOM 1275

FROM: Your Name

FAX: 619-555-0937

PHONE: 619-555-1223

PAGES: 3, including cover sheet

RE: High Atlas tour brochure

CC:

COMMENTS:
A draft copy of the High Atlas tour brochure is attached. Please revise the text for accuracy. The photos are for placement only. Have you hired a photographer yet?

Using Word document views

Document **views** are different ways of displaying a document in the document window. Each Word view provides features that are useful for working on different types of documents. The default view, **Print Layout view**, displays a document as it will look on a printed page. Print Layout view is helpful for formatting text and pages, including adjusting document margins, creating columns of text, inserting graphics, and formatting headers and footers. Also useful is **Draft view**, which shows a simplified layout of a document, without margins, headers and footers, or graphics. When you want to quickly type, edit, and format text, it's often easiest to work in Draft view. Other Word views are helpful for performing specialized tasks. **Full Screen Reading view** displays document text so that it is easy to read and annotate. You can easily highlight content, add comments, and track and review changes in Full Screen Reading view. **Web Layout view** allows you to format Web pages or documents that will be viewed on a computer screen. In Web Layout view, a document appears just as it will when viewed with a Web browser. Finally, **Outline view** is useful for editing and formatting longer documents that include multiple headings. Outline view allows you to reorganize text by moving the headings. You switch between views by clicking the view buttons on the status bar or by using the commands on the View tab. Changing views does not affect how the printed document will appear. It simply changes the way you view the document in the document window.

Practice

For current SAM information, including versions and content details, visit SAM Central (http://www.cengage.com/samcentral). If you have a SAM user profile, you may have access to hands-on instruction, practice, and assessment of the skills covered in this unit. Since various versions of SAM are supported throughout the life of this text, check with your instructor for the correct instructions and URL/Web site for accessing assignments.

Concepts Review

Label the elements of the Word program window shown in Figure A-15.

FIGURE A-15

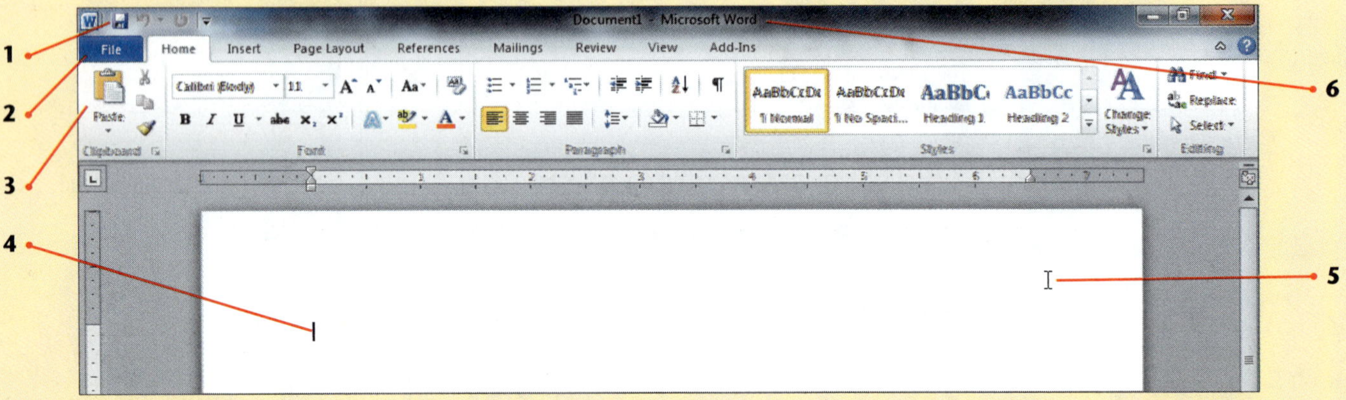

Match each term with the statement that best describes it.

7. Template	**a.** Provides access to Word commands
8. Formatting marks	**b.** A formatted document that contains placeholder text
9. Status bar	**c.** Displays tab settings and paragraph indents
10. Ribbon	**d.** Enlarges and reduces the document in the document window
11. AutoComplete	**e.** Suggests text to insert into a document
12. Horizontal ruler	**f.** Displays the number of pages in the current document
13. AutoCorrect	**g.** Fixes certain errors as you type
14. Zoom slider	**h.** Special characters that appear on screen but do not print

Select the best answer from the list of choices.

15. Which tab includes buttons for formatting text?

a. View
b. Page Layout
c. Insert
d. Home

16. Which of the following shows the number of words in the document?

a. The status bar
b. The Mini toolbar
c. The title bar
d. The Ribbon

17. Which element of the Word program window shows the settings for the top and bottom document margins?

a. Vertical scroll bar
b. View tab
c. Vertical ruler
d. Status bar

18. Which of the following is not included in a ScreenTip for a command?

a. Description of the function of the command
b. Link to a help topic on the command
c. Keyboard shortcut for the command
d. Alternative location of the command

19. Which view is best for annotating text with comments and highlighting?

- **a.** Full Screen Reading view
- **b.** Draft view
- **c.** Print Layout view
- **d.** Outline view

20. What is the default file extension for a document created in Word 2010?

- **a.** .dot
- **b.** .doc
- **c.** .dotx
- **d.** .docx

Skills Review

1. Explore the Word program window.

- **a.** Start Word.
- **b.** Identify as many elements of the Word program window as you can without referring to the unit material.
- **c.** Click the File tab, then click the Info, Recent, New, Print, Save & Send, and Help commands.
- **d.** Click each tab on the Ribbon, review the groups and buttons on each tab, then return to the Home tab.
- **e.** Point to each button on the Home tab and read the ScreenTips.
- **f.** Click the view buttons to view the blank document in each view, then return to Print Layout view.
- **g.** Use the Zoom slider to zoom all the way in and all the way out on the document, then return to 100%.

2. Start a document.

- **a.** In a new blank document, type **FAX** at the top of the page, then press [Enter] two times.
- **b.** Type the following, pressing [Tab] as indicated and pressing [Enter] at the end of each line:
  To: [Tab] [Tab] **Matthew Donner**
  From: [Tab] [Tab] **Your Name**
  Date: [Tab] [Tab] **Today's date**
  Re: [Tab] [Tab] **Reservation confirmation**
  Pages: [Tab] [Tab] **1**
  Fax: [Tab] [Tab] **(802) 555-5478**
- **c.** Press [Enter] again, then type **Thank you for your interest in our summer festival weekend package, which includes accommodations for three nights in downtown Toronto, continental breakfast, and a festival pass. Rooms are still available during the following festivals: International Jazz Festival, Comedy Festival, Toronto Fringe Festival, and the Festival of Arts. Please see the attached schedule for festival dates and details.**
- **d.** Press [Enter], then type **To make a reservation, please call me at (416) 555-7482. I will need payment in full by the 3rd of June to hold a room. No one knows how to celebrate summer like Torontonians!**
- **e.** Insert **Grand Prix Festival,** before International Jazz Festival.
- **f.** Using the [Backspace] key, delete **1** in the Pages: line, then type **2**.
- **g.** Using the [Delete] key, delete **festival** in the last sentence of the first paragraph.

3. Save a document.

- **a.** Click the Save button on the Quick Access toolbar.
- **b.** Save the document as **WD A-Donner Fax** with the default file extension to the drive and folder where you store your Data Files.
- **c.** After your name, type a comma, press [Spacebar], then type **Global Toronto**
- **d.** Save the document.

4. Select text.

- **a.** Turn on formatting marks.
- **b.** Select the **Re:** line, then type **Re:** [Tab] [Tab] **Summer Festival Weekend Package**
- **c.** Select **three** in the first sentence, then type **two**.
- **d.** Select **3rd of June** in the second sentence of the last paragraph, type **15th of May**, select **room**, then type **reservation**.
- **e.** Delete the sentence **No one knows how to celebrate summer like Torontonians!**
- **f.** Turn off the display of formatting marks, then save the document.

Skills Review (continued)

5. **Format text using the Mini toolbar.**
   a. Select **FAX**, then click the Grow Font button on the Mini toolbar 11 times.
   b. Apply bold to the word **FAX**, then center it on the page.
   c. Apply a bottom border under the word **FAX**.
   d. Apply bold to the following words in the fax heading: **To:**, **From:**, **Date:**, **Re:**, **Pages:**, and **Fax:**.
   e. Preview the document using the Print command.
   f. Zoom in on the document, then proofread the fax.
   g. Correct any typing errors in your document, then save the document. Compare your document to Figure A-16.
   h. Submit the fax to your instructor, then close the document.

FIGURE A-16

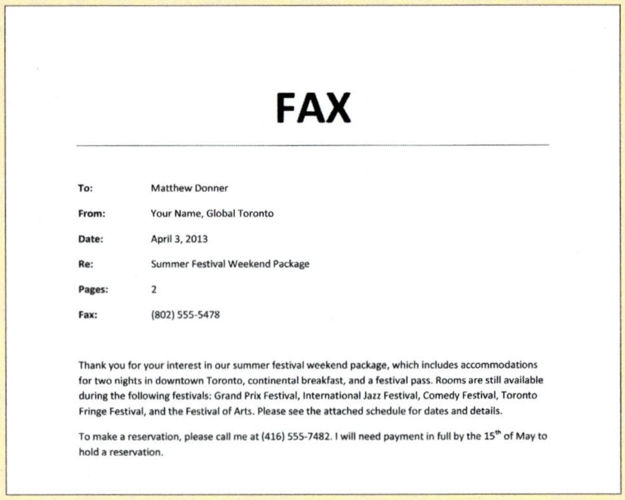
FAX

To: Matthew Donner
From: Your Name, Global Toronto
Date: April 3, 2013
Re: Summer Festival Weekend Package
Pages: 2
Fax: (802) 555-5478

Thank you for your interest in our summer festival weekend package, which includes accommodations for two nights in downtown Toronto, continental breakfast, and a festival pass. Rooms are still available during the following festivals: Grand Prix Festival, International Jazz Festival, Comedy Festival, Toronto Fringe Festival, and the Festival of Arts. Please see the attached schedule for dates and details.

To make a reservation, please call me at (416) 555-7482. I will need payment in full by the 15th of May to hold a reservation.

6. **Create a document using a template.**
   a. Click the File tab, click New, then click Sample templates.
   b. Create a new document using the Origin Fax template.
   c. Insert today's date using the date content control.
   d. If your name is not on the From line, select the text in the From content control, then type your name.
   e. Click the "Type the sender phone number" placeholder text, press [Delete]; click the "Type the sender fax number" placeholder text, type **555-5748**; click the "Type the sender company name" placeholder text, then type **Global Toronto**.
   f. Type **Janice Richard** to replace the "To:" placeholder text; select "Phone:", type **Re**; type **Sold out summer packages** to replace the "Type the recipient phone number" placeholder text; type **555-1176** to replace the "Type the recipient fax number" placeholder text; then type **Toronto Chamber of Commerce** to replace the "Type the recipient company name" placeholder text.
   g. Save the document with the filename **WD A-Sold Out Fax** to the drive and folder where you store your Data Files.
7. **View and navigate a document.**
   a. Scroll down until Comments is near the top of your document window.
   b. Replace the Comments placeholder text with the following text: **Packages for the following summer festivals are sold out: First Peoples' Festival, Chamber Music Festival, and Dragon Boat Race Festival. We had expected these packages to be less popular than those for the bigger festivals, but interest has been high. Next year, we will increase our bookings for these festivals by 30%.**
   c. Use the Zoom dialog box to view the Whole Page.
   d. Click **Comments** to move the insertion point to the middle of the page, then use the Zoom slider to set the Zoom percentage at approximately 100%.
   e. Scroll to the bottom of the page, click in the Please Recycle box, type **x** if one is not added automatically when you click the box, then save your changes.
   f. Preview the document, then correct any errors, saving changes if necessary. Compare your document to Figure A-17. Submit the document to your instructor, close the file, then exit Word.

FIGURE A-17

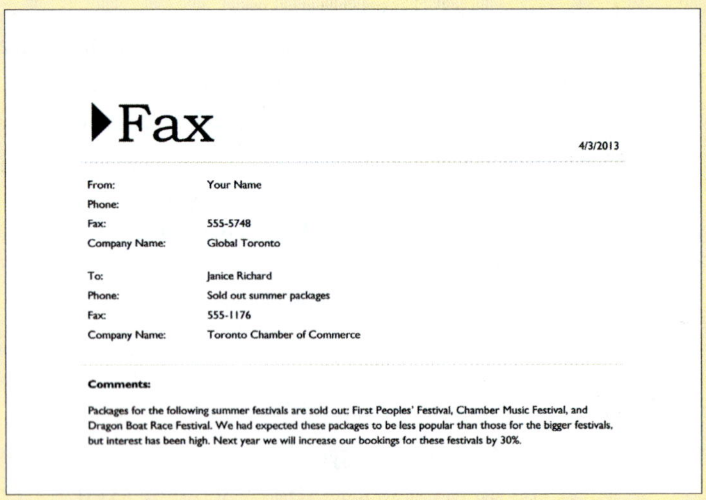
Fax

4/3/2013

From: Your Name
Phone:
Fax: 555-5748
Company Name: Global Toronto

To: Janice Richard
Phone: Sold out summer packages
Fax: 555-1176
Company Name: Toronto Chamber of Commerce

Comments:

Packages for the following summer festivals are sold out: First Peoples' Festival, Chamber Music Festival, and Dragon Boat Race Festival. We had expected these packages to be less popular than those for the bigger festivals, but interest has been high. Next year we will increase our bookings for these festivals by 30%.

Independent Challenge 1

If you have a SAM 2010 user profile, an autogradable SAM version of this assignment may be available at http://www.cengage.com/sam2010. Check with your instructor to confirm that this assignment is available in SAM. To use the SAM version of this assignment, log into the SAM 2010 Web site and download the instruction and start files.

Yesterday you interviewed for a job as marketing director at Chelsea Design Services. You spoke with several people at the company, including Rena Gupta, chief executive officer, whose business card is shown in Figure A-18. You need to write a follow-up letter to Ms. Gupta, thanking her for the interview and expressing your interest in the company and the position. She also asked you to send her some samples of your marketing work, which you will enclose with the letter.

FIGURE A-18

a. Start Word and save a new blank document as **WD A-Gupta Letter** to the drive and folder where you store your Data Files.

b. Begin the letter by clicking the No Spacing button in the Styles group. You use this button to apply the No Spacing style to the document so that your document does not include extra space between paragraphs.

c. Type a personal letterhead for the letter that includes your name, address, telephone number, and e-mail address. If Word formats your e-mail address as a hyperlink, right-click your e-mail address, then click Remove Hyperlink.
(*Note*: Format the letterhead after you finish typing the letter.)

d. Three lines below the bottom of the letterhead, type today's date.

e. Four lines below the date, type the inside address, referring to Figure A-18 for the address information. Be sure to include the recipient's title, company name, and full mailing address in the inside address.

f. Two lines below the inside address, type **Dear Ms. Gupta:** for the salutation.

g. Two lines below the salutation, type the body of the letter according to the following guidelines:
- In the first paragraph, thank her for the interview. Then restate your interest in the position and express your desire to work for the company. Add any specific details you think will enhance the power of your letter.
- In the second paragraph, note that you are enclosing three samples of your work, and explain something about the samples you are enclosing.
- Type a short final paragraph.

h. Two lines below the last body paragraph, type a closing, then four lines below the closing, type the signature block. Be sure to include your name in the signature block.

i. Two lines below the signature block, type an enclosure notation. (*Hint*: An enclosure notation usually includes the word "Enclosures" or the abbreviation "Enc." followed by the number of enclosures in parentheses.)

j. Format the letterhead with bold, centering, and a bottom border.

k. Save your changes.

l. Preview the letter, submit it to your instructor, then close the document and exit Word.

Independent Challenge 2

Your company has recently installed Word 2010 on its company network. As the training manager, it's your responsibility to teach employees how to use the new software productively. Now that they have begun working with Word 2010, several employees have asked you about sharing documents with colleagues using Windows Live SkyDrive. In response, you wrote a memo to all employees explaining Windows Live SkyDrive, some of its features, and how to register for a Windows Live ID. You now need to format the memo before distributing it.

a. Start Word, open the file **WD A-1.docx** from the drive and folder where you store your Data Files, then read the memo to get a feel for its contents.

b. Save the file as **WD A-SkyDrive Memo** to the drive and folder where you store your Data Files.

Independent Challenge 2 (continued)

c. Replace the information in the memo header with the information shown in Figure A-19. Make sure to include your name in the From line and the current date in the Date line.

d. Apply bold to **To:**, **From:**, **Date:**, and **Re:**.

e. Increase the size of **WORD TRAINING MEMORANDUM** to match Figure A-19, center the text on the page, add a border below it, then save your changes.

FIGURE A-19

WORD TRAINING MEMORANDUM

To:	All employees
From:	Your Name, Training Manager
Date:	Today's Date
Re:	Windows Live SkyDrive

Advanced Challenge Exercise

ACE

- Using the Font list on the Mini toolbar, apply a different font to **WORD TRAINING MEMORANDUM**. Make sure to select a font that is appropriate for a business memo.
- Using the Font Color button on the Mini toolbar, change the color of **WORD TRAINING MEMORANDUM** to an appropriate color.
- Save a copy of the memo in Word 97-2003 Document (*.doc) format as **WD A-SkyDrive Memo ACE** to the drive or folder where you store your Data Files. (*Hint*: Use the Save as type list arrow in the Save As dialog box.)

f. Preview the memo, submit it to your instructor, then close the document and exit Word.

Independent Challenge 3

You are an expert on global warming. The president of the National Park Association, Nathan Cummings, has asked you to be the keynote speaker at an upcoming conference on the impact of climate change on the national parks, to be held in Glacier National Park. You use one of the Word letter templates to write a letter to Mr. Cummings accepting the invitation and confirming the details. Your letter to Mr. Cummings should reference the following information:

- The conference will be held August 4–6, 2013, at the Many Glacier Hotel in the park.
- You have been asked to speak for an hour on Saturday, August 5, followed by one half hour for questions.
- Mr. Cummings suggested the lecture topic "Melting Glaciers, Changing Ecosystems."
- Your talk will include a 45-minute slide presentation.
- The National Park Association will make your travel arrangements.
- Your preference is to arrive at Glacier Park International Airport in Kalispell on the morning of Friday, August 4, and to depart on Monday, August 7. You would like to rent a car at the airport for the drive to the Many Glacier Hotel.
- You want to fly in and out of the airport closest to your home.

a. Start Word, open the File tab, click New, click Sample templates, and then select an appropriate letter template. Save the document as **WD A-Cummings Letter** to the drive and folder where you store your Data Files.

b. Replace the placeholders in the letterhead with your personal information. Include your name, address, phone number, and e-mail address. Delete any placeholders that do not apply. (*Hints*: Depending on the template you choose, the letterhead might be located at the top or on the side of the document. You can press [Enter] when typing in a horizontal placeholder to add an additional line of text. You can also change the format of text typed in a placeholder. If your e-mail address appears as a hyperlink, right-click the e-mail address and click Remove Hyperlink.)

c. Use the Pick the date content control to select the current date.

d. Replace the placeholders in the inside address. Be sure to include Mr. Cumming's title and the name of the organization. Make up a street address and zip code.

e. Type **Dear Mr. Cummings:** for the salutation.

f. Using the information listed previously, type the body of the letter:

- In the first paragraph, accept the invitation to speak.
- In the second paragraph, confirm the important conference details, confirm your lecture topic, and provide any relevant details.

Independent Challenge 3 (continued)

- In the third paragraph, state your travel preferences.
- Type a short final paragraph.

g. Type **Sincerely,** for the closing, then include your name in the signature block.

h. Adjust the formatting of the letter as necessary. For example, remove bold formatting or change the font color of text to a more appropriate color.

Advanced Challenge Exercise

ACE

- Zoom in on the title "Melting Glaciers, Changing Ecosystems", delete the quotation marks, then apply italics to the title.
- Select one word in the letter, such as an adjective, and replace it with another similar word to improve the meaning of the sentence.
- Correct your spelling and grammar errors, if any, by right-clicking any red- or green-underlined text and then choosing from the options on the shortcut menu.
- View the letter in Full Screen Reading view, then click the Close button to return to Print Layout view.

i. Proofread your letter, make corrections as needed, then save your changes.

j. Submit the letter to your instructor, close the document, then exit Word.

Real Life Independent Challenge

This Independent Challenge requires an Internet connection.

The computer keyboard has become as essential an office tool as the pencil. The more adept you become at touch typing—the fastest and most accurate way to type—the more comfortable you will be working with computers and the more saleable your office skills to a potential employer. The Internet is one source of information on touch typing, and many Web sites include free typing tests and online tutorials to help you practice and improve your typing skills. In this independent challenge, you will take an online typing test to check your typing skills. You will then research the fundamentals of touch typing and investigate some of the ergonomic factors important to becoming a productive keyboard typist.

a. Use your favorite search engine to search the Internet for information on typing. Use the keywords **typing** and **typing ergonomics** to conduct your search.

b. Review the Web sites you find. Choose a site that offers a free online typing test, take the test, then print the Web page showing the results of your typing test if requested to do so by your instructor.

c. Start Word and save a new blank document as **WD A-Touch Typing** to the drive and folder where you store your Data Files.

d. Type your name at the top of the document.

e. Type a brief report on the results of your research. Your report should answer the following questions:

- What are the URLs of the Web sites you visited to research touch typing and keyboard ergonomics? (*Hint*: A URL is a Web page's address. An example of a URL is www.course.com.)
- What are some benefits of using the touch typing method?
- Which keys should the fingers of the left and right hands rest on when using the touch typing method?
- What ergonomic factors are important to keep in mind while typing?

f. Save your changes to the document, preview and submit it to your instructor, then close the document and exit Word.

Visual Workshop

Create the cover letter shown in Figure A-20. Before beginning to type, click the No Spacing button in the Styles group on the Home tab. Add the bottom border to the letterhead after typing the letter. Save the document as **WD A-Lee Cover Letter** to the drive and folder where you store your Data Files, submit the letter to your instructor, then close the document and exit Word.

FIGURE A-20

Your Name

682 East 8th Avenue, Portland, ME 04105

Tel: 207-555-7283; Fax: 207-555-1445; E-mail: yourname@gmail.com

---

July 16, 2013

Ms. Ramona Lee
Lee Associates
657 Harbor Street
Suite 501
Portland, ME 04123

Dear Ms. Lee:

I read of the opening for a public information assistant in the July 13 edition of mainejobs.com, and I would like to be considered for the position. I am a recent graduate of Portland Community College (PCC), and I am interested in pursuing a career in public relations.

My interest in a public relations career springs from my publicly acknowledged writing and journalism abilities. For example, at PCC, I was a reporter for the student newspaper and frequently wrote press releases for campus and community events.

I have a wealth of experience using Microsoft Word in professional settings. Last summer, I worked as an office assistant for the architecture firm Coleman & Greenberg, where I used Word to create newsletters, brochures, and financial reports. During the school year, I also worked part-time in the PCC Office of Community Relations, where I used the Word mail merge feature to create form letters and mailing labels.

My enclosed resume details my skills and experience. I welcome the opportunity to discuss the position and my qualifications with you. I can be reached at 207-555-7283.

Sincerely,

Your Name

Enc.

UNIT
B
Word 2010

Editing Documents

Files You Will Need:

- WD B-1.docx
- WD B-2.docx
- WD B-3.docx
- WD B-4.docx
- WD B-5.docx
- WD B-6.docx
- WD B-7.docx

The sophisticated editing features in Word make it easy to revise and polish your documents. In this unit, you learn how to revise an existing file by opening it, copying and moving text, and then saving the document as a new file. You also learn how to perfect your documents using proofing tools and how to quickly prepare a document for distribution to the public. You have been asked to edit and finalize a press release for a QST promotional lecture series. The press release should provide information about the series so that newspapers, radio stations, and other media outlets can announce it to the public. QST press releases are disseminated by fax and by e-mail. Before distributing the file electronically to your lists of press contacts and local QST clients, you add several hyperlinks and then strip the file of private information.

OBJECTIVES

- Cut and paste text
- Copy and paste text
- Use the Office Clipboard
- Find and replace text
- Check spelling and grammar
- Research information
- Add hyperlinks
- Work with document properties

UNIT
B
Word 2010

Cutting and Pasting Text

The editing features in Word allow you to move text from one location to another in a document. Moving text is often called **cut and paste**. When you **cut** text, it is removed from the document and placed on the **Clipboard**, a temporary storage area for text and graphics that you cut or copy from a document. You can then paste, or insert, text that is stored on the Clipboard in the document at the location of the insertion point. You cut and paste text using the Cut and Paste buttons in the Clipboard group on the Home tab. You also can move selected text by dragging it to a new location using the mouse. This operation is called **drag and drop**. You open the press release that was drafted by a colleague, save it with a new filename, and then reorganize the information in the press release using the cut-and-paste and drag-and-drop methods.

STEPS

1. **Start Word, click the File tab, click Open, navigate to the drive and folder where you store your Data Files, click WD B-1.docx, then click Open**
   The document opens. Once you have opened a file, you can edit it and use the Save or the Save As command to save your changes. You use the **Save** command when you want to save the changes you make to a file, overwriting the file that is stored on a disk. You use the **Save As** command when you want to leave the original file intact and create a duplicate file with a different filename, file extension, or location.
2. **Click the File tab, click Save As, type WD B-Lecture PR in the File name text box, then click Save**
   You can now make changes to the press release file without affecting the original file.
3. **Replace Ron Dawson with your name, scroll down until the headline "Helen Moffit to Speak..." is at the top of your document window, then click the Show/Hide ¶ button in the Paragraph group on the Home tab to display formatting marks**
4. **Select Alaskan guide Gilbert Coonan, (including the comma and the space after it) in the third body paragraph, then click the Cut button in the Clipboard group**
   The text is removed from the document and placed on the Clipboard. Word uses two different clipboards: the **system Clipboard** (the Clipboard), which holds just one item, and the **Office Clipboard**, which holds up to 24 items. The last item you cut or copy is always added to both clipboards. You'll learn more about the Office Clipboard in a later lesson.
5. **Place the insertion point before African (but after the space) in the first line of the third paragraph, then click the Paste button in the Clipboard group**
   The text is pasted at the location of the insertion point, as shown in Figure B-1. The Paste Options button appears below text when you first paste it in a document. You'll learn more about the Paste Options button in the next lesson. For now, you can ignore it.
6. **Press and hold [Ctrl], click the sentence Ticket prices include lunch. in the fourth paragraph, then release [Ctrl]**
   The entire sentence is selected.
7. **Press and hold the mouse button over the selected text until the pointer changes to**
   The pointer's vertical line is the insertion point. You drag the pointer to position the insertion point where you want the text to be inserted when you release the mouse button.
8. **Drag the pointer's vertical line to the end of the fifth paragraph (between the period and the paragraph mark) as shown in Figure B-2, then release the mouse button**
   The selected text is moved to the location of the insertion point. It is convenient to move text using the drag-and-drop method when the locations of origin and destination are both visible on the screen. Text is not placed on the Clipboard when you drag and drop it.
9. **Deselect the text, then click the Save button on the Quick Access toolbar**

TROUBLE
If you make a mistake, click the Undo button on the Quick Access toolbar, then try again.

FIGURE B-1: Moved text with Paste Options button

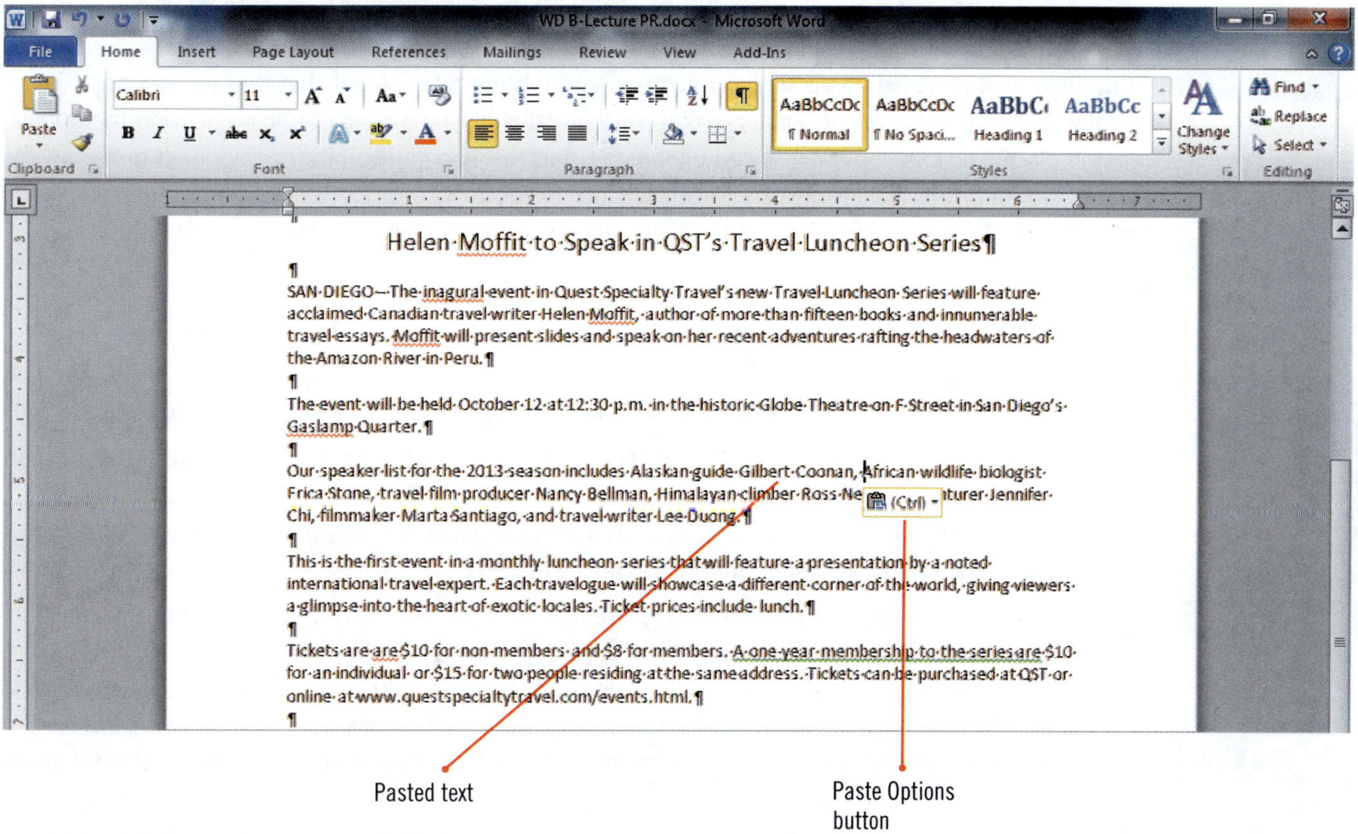

FIGURE B-2: Dragging and dropping text in a new location

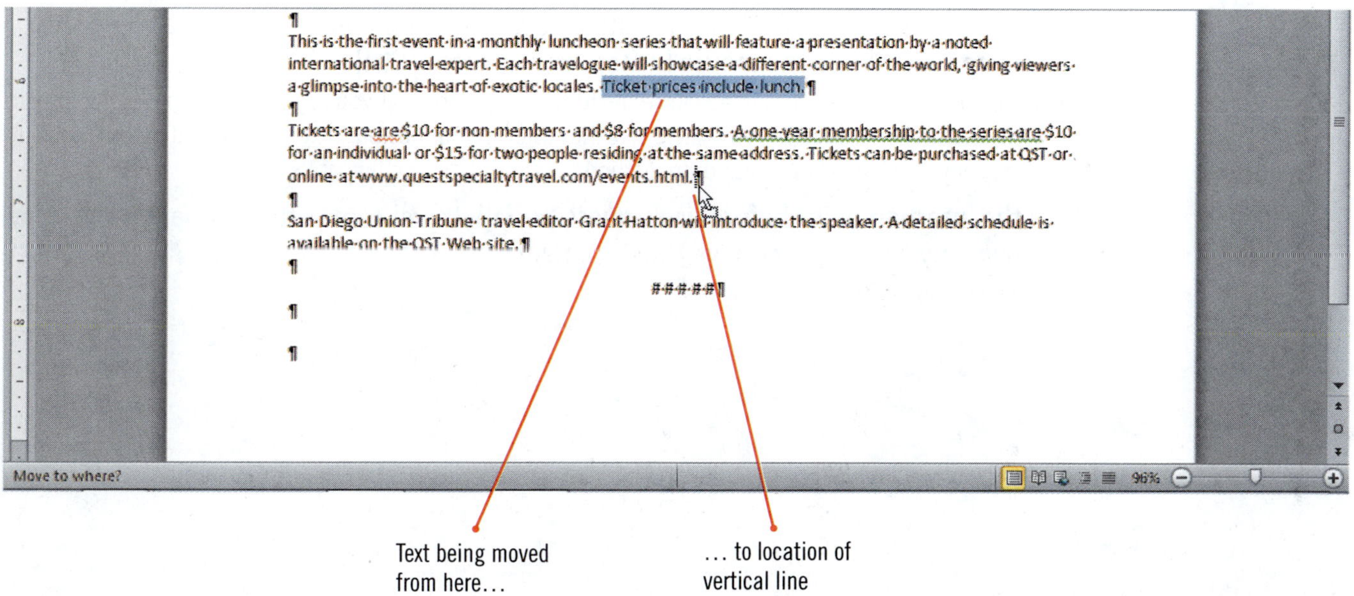

Using keyboard shortcuts

A **shortcut key** is a function key, such as [F1], or a combination of keys, such as [Ctrl][S], that you press to perform a command. For example, instead of using the Cut, Copy, and Paste commands on the Ribbon or the Mini toolbar, you can use the **keyboard shortcuts** [Ctrl][X] to cut text, [Ctrl][C] to copy text, and [Ctrl][V] to paste text. You can also press [Ctrl][S] to save changes to a document instead of clicking the Save button on the Quick Access toolbar or clicking Save on the File tab. Becoming skilled at using keyboard shortcuts can help you quickly accomplish many of the tasks you perform in Word. If a keyboard shortcut is available for a command, then it is listed in the ScreenTip for that command.

UNIT B

Word 2010

Copying and Pasting Text

Copying and pasting text is similar to cutting and pasting text, except that the text you **copy** is not removed from the document. Rather, a copy of the text is placed on the Clipboard, leaving the original text in place. You can copy text to the Clipboard using the Copy button in the Clipboard group on the Home tab, or you can copy text by pressing [Ctrl] as you drag the selected text from one location to another. You continue to edit the press release by copying text from one location to another.

STEPS

QUICK TIP
You can also cut or copy text by right-clicking the selected text, and then clicking the Cut or Copy command on the menu that opens.

QUICK TIP
If you don't like the result of a paste option, try another option or click the Undo button, and then paste the text again.

1. **Select Travel Luncheon in the headline, then click the Copy button in the Clipboard group**
   A copy of the selected text is placed on the Clipboard, leaving the original text you copied in place.
2. **Place the insertion point before season in the third paragraph, then click the Paste button in the Clipboard group**
   "Travel Luncheon" is inserted before "season," as shown in Figure B-3. Notice that the pasted text is formatted differently than the paragraph in which it was inserted.
3. **Click the Paste Options button, move the mouse over each button on the menu that opens to read its ScreenTip, then click the Keep Text Only (T) button**
   The formatting of "Travel Luncheon" is changed to match the rest of the paragraph. The buttons on the Paste Options menu allow you to change the formatting of pasted text. You can choose to keep the original formatting (Keep Source Formatting), match the destination formatting (Merge Formatting), or paste the text unformatted (Keep Text Only).
4. **Select www.questspecialtytravel.com in the fifth paragraph, press and hold [Ctrl], then press and hold the mouse button until the pointer changes to**
5. **Drag the pointer's vertical line to the end of the last paragraph, placing it between site and the period, release the mouse button, then release [Ctrl]**
   The text is copied to the last paragraph. Since the formatting of the text you copied is the same as the formatting of the destination paragraph, you can ignore the Paste Options button. Text is not copied to the Clipboard when you copy it using the drag-and-drop method.
6. **Place the insertion point before www.questspecialtytravel.com in the last paragraph, type at followed by a space, then save the document**
   Compare your document with Figure B-4.

Splitting the document window to copy and move items in a long document

If you want to copy or move items between parts of a long document, it can be useful to split the document window into two panes. This allows you to display the item you want to copy or move in one pane and the destination for the item in the other pane. To split a window, click the Split button in the Window group on the View tab, drag the horizontal split bar that appears to the location you want to split the window, and then click. Once the document window is split into two panes, you can drag the split bar to resize the panes and use the scroll bars in each pane to display different parts of the document. To copy or move an item from one pane to another, you can use the Cut, Copy, and Paste commands, or you can drag the item between the panes. When you are finished editing the document, double-click the split bar to restore the window to a single pane, or click the Remove Split button in the Window group on the View tab.

FIGURE B-3: Text pasted in document

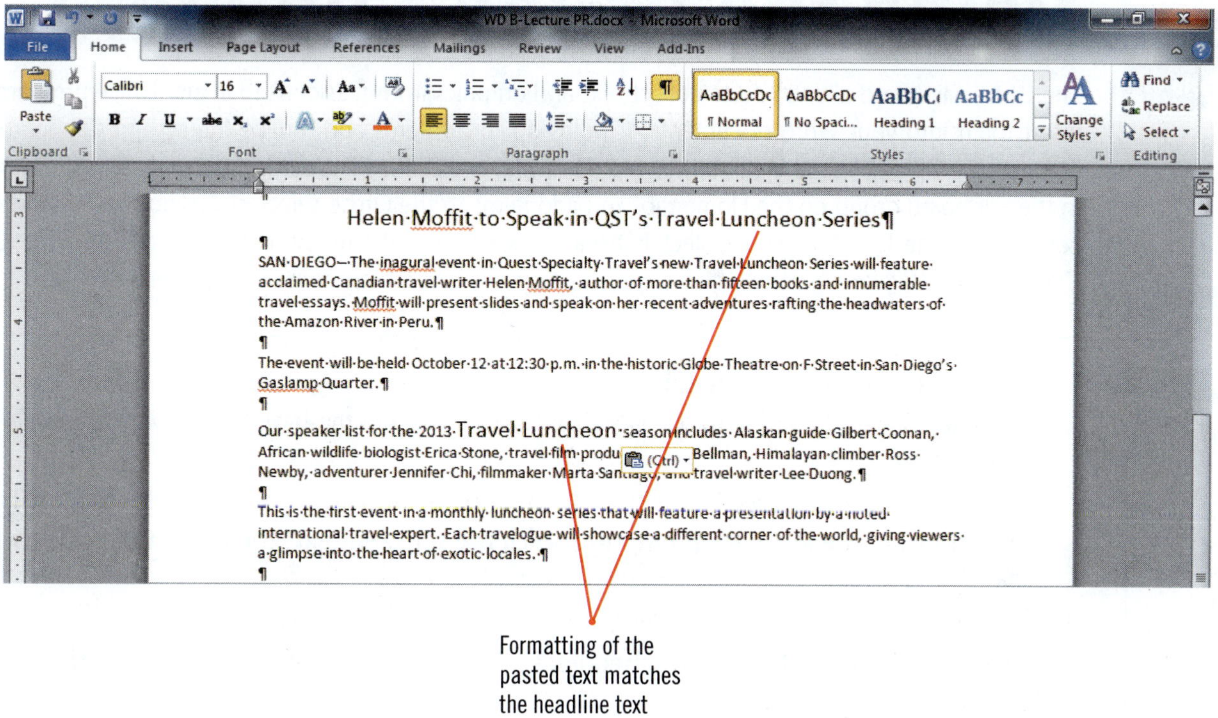

FIGURE B-4: Copied text in document

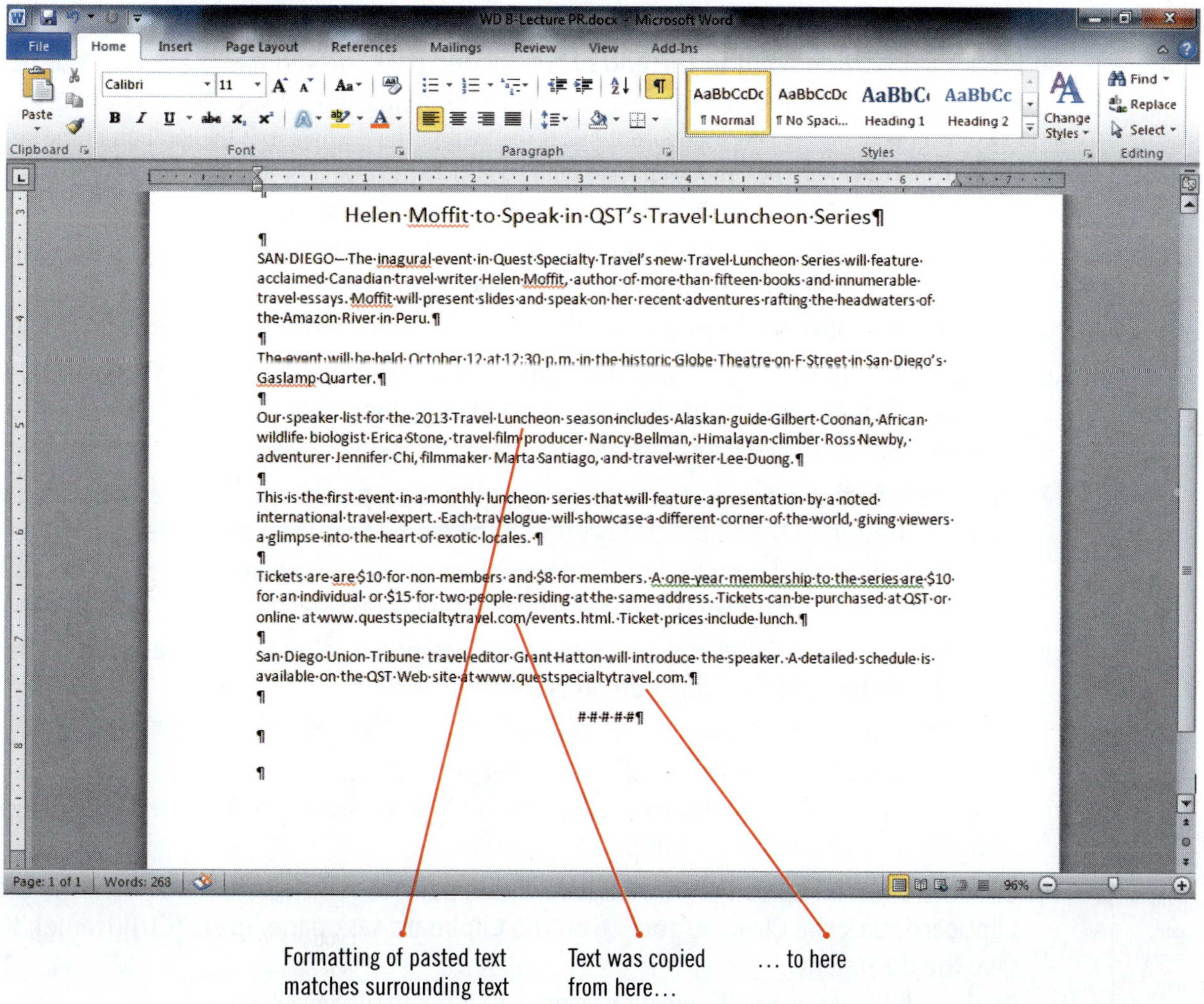

Word 2010

UNIT
B
Word 2010

Using the Office Clipboard

The Office Clipboard allows you to collect text and graphics from files created in any Office program and insert them into your Word documents. It holds up to 24 items and, unlike the system Clipboard, the items on the Office Clipboard can be viewed. To display the Office Clipboard, you simply click the launcher in the Clipboard group on the Home tab. You add items to the Office Clipboard using the Cut and Copy commands. The last item you collect is always added to both the system Clipboard and the Office Clipboard. You use the Office Clipboard to move several sentences in your press release.

STEPS

QUICK TIP
You can set the Office Clipboard to open automatically when you cut or copy two items consecutively by clicking Options in the Clipboard task pane, and then selecting Show Office Clipboard Automatically.

1. **Click the launcher in the Clipboard group**
   The Office Clipboard opens in the Clipboard task pane. It contains the Travel Luncheon item you copied in the last lesson.
2. **Select the sentence San Diego Union-Tribune travel editor ... (including the space after the period) in the last paragraph, right-click the selected text, then click Cut on the menu that opens**
   The sentence is cut to the Office Clipboard.
3. **Select the sentence A detailed schedule is... (including the ¶ mark), right-click the selected text, then click Cut**
   The Office Clipboard displays the items you cut or copied, as shown in Figure B-5. The icon next to each item indicates the items are from a Word document. The last item collected is displayed at the top of the Clipboard task pane. As new items are collected, the existing items move down the task pane.
4. **Place the insertion point at the end of the second paragraph (after "Quarter." but before the ¶ mark), then click the San Diego Union-Tribune... item on the Office Clipboard**
   Clicking an item on the Office Clipboard pastes the item in the document at the location of the insertion point. Items remain on the Office Clipboard until you delete them or close all open Office programs. Also, if you add a 25th item to the Office Clipboard, the first item you collected is deleted.
5. **Place the insertion point at the end of the third paragraph (after "Duong."), then click the A detailed schedule is... item on the Office Clipboard**
   The sentence is pasted into the document.
6. **Select the fourth paragraph, which begins with the sentence This is the first event... (including the ¶ mark), right-click the selected text, then click Cut**
   The paragraph is cut to the Office Clipboard.
7. **Place the insertion point at the beginning of the third paragraph (before "Our..."), click the Paste button in the Clipboard group on the Home tab, then press [Backspace]**
   The sentences from the "This is the first..." paragraph are pasted at the beginning of the "Our speaker list..." paragraph. You can paste the last item collected using either the Paste command or the Office Clipboard.
8. **Place the insertion point at the end of the third paragraph (after "www.questspecialtytravel.com." and before the ¶ mark), then press [Delete] twice**
   Two ¶ symbols and the corresponding blank lines between the third and fourth paragraphs are deleted.
9. **Click the Show/Hide ¶ button ¶ in the Paragraph group**
   Compare your press release with Figure B-6. Note that many Word users prefer to work with formatting marks on at all times. Experiment to see which method you prefer.

QUICK TIP
To delete an individual item from the Office Clipboard, click the list arrow next to the item, then click Delete.

10. **Click the Clear All button on the Clipboard task pane to remove the items from the Office Clipboard, click the Close button on the Clipboard task pane, press [Ctrl][Home], then save the document**
    Pressing [Ctrl][Home] moves the insertion point to the top of the document.

FIGURE B-5: Office Clipboard in Clipboard task pane

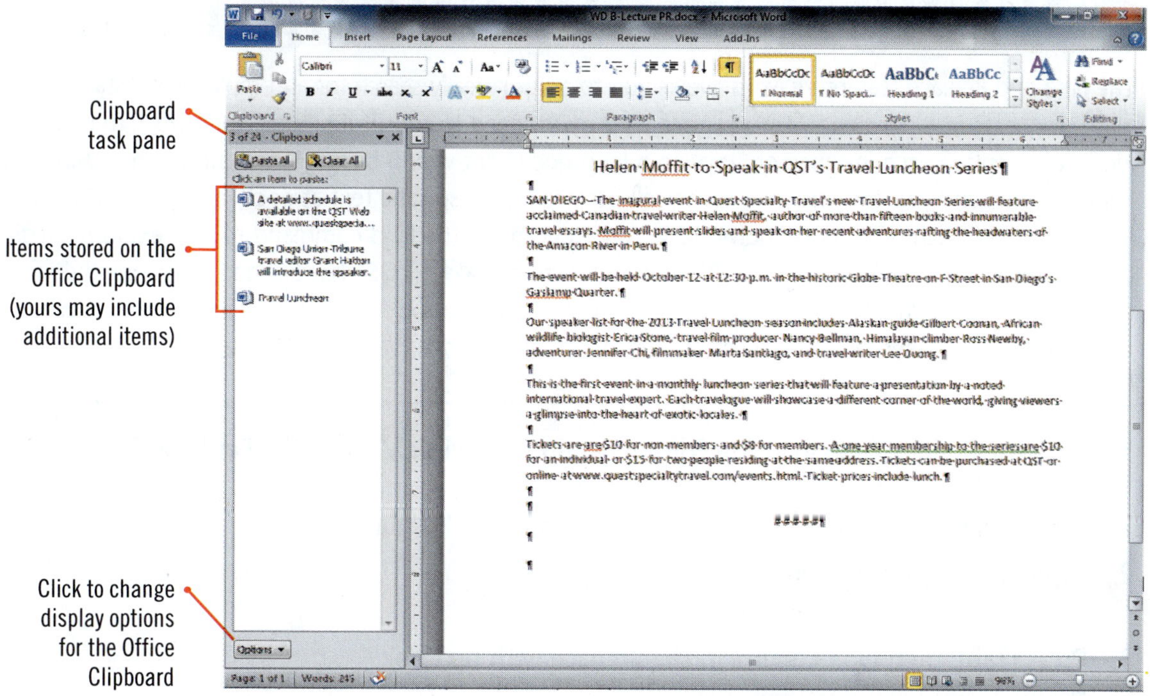

FIGURE B-6: Revised press release

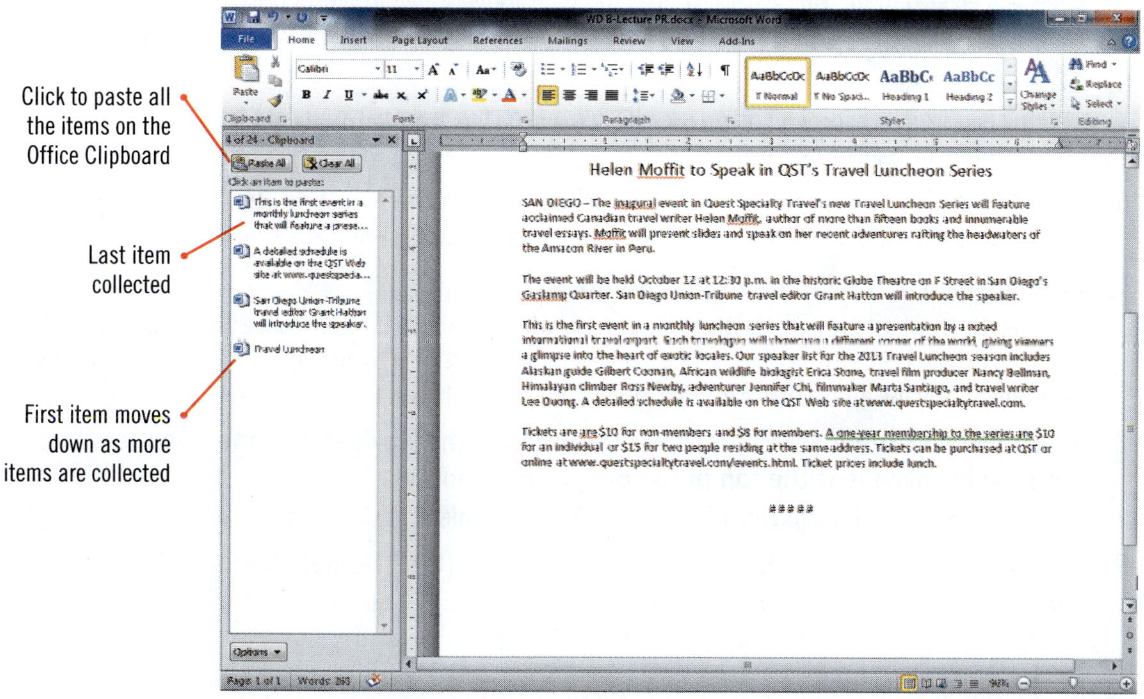

Copying and moving items between documents

You can also use the system and Office Clipboards to copy and move items between documents. To do this, open both documents and the Clipboard task pane in the program window. With multiple documents open, copy or cut an item from one document and then switch to the other document and paste the item. To switch between open documents, point to the Word icon on the taskbar, and then click the document you want to appear in the document window. You can also display more than one document at the same time by clicking the Arrange All button or the View Side by Side button in the Window group on the View tab.

Finding and Replacing Text

The Find and Replace feature in Word allows you to automatically search for and replace all instances of a word or phrase in a document. For example, you might need to substitute "tour" for "trip." To manually locate and replace each instance of "trip" in a long document would be very time-consuming. Using the Replace command you can find and replace all occurrences of specific text at once, or you can choose to find and review each occurrence individually. You also can use the Find command to locate and highlight every occurrence of a specific word or phrase in a document. QST has decided to change the name of the lecture series from "Travel Luncheon Series" to "Travel Lecture Series." You use the Replace command to search the document for all instances of "Luncheon" and replace them with "Lecture."

STEPS

TROUBLE

If any of the Search Options check boxes are selected in your Find and Replace dialog box, deselect them. If Format appears under the Find what or Replace with text box, click in the text box, then click the No Formatting button.

1. **Click the Replace button in the Editing group, then click More in the Find and Replace dialog box**

   The Find and Replace dialog box opens and expands, as shown in Figure B-7.

2. **Type Luncheon in the Find what text box**

   "Luncheon" is the text that will be replaced.

3. **Press [Tab], then type Lecture in the Replace with text box**

   "Lecture" is the text that will replace "Luncheon."

4. **Click the Match case check box in the Search Options section to select it**

   Selecting the Match case check box tells Word to find only exact matches for the uppercase and lowercase characters you entered in the Find what text box. You want to replace all instances of "Luncheon" in the proper name "Travel Luncheon Series." You do not want to replace "luncheon" when it refers to a lunchtime event.

QUICK TIP

To find, review, and replace each occurrence individually, click Find Next.

5. **Click Replace All**

   Clicking Replace All changes all occurrences of "Luncheon" to "Lecture" in the press release. A message box reports three replacements were made.

6. **Click OK to close the message box, then click Close in the Find and Replace dialog box**

   Word replaced "Luncheon" with "Lecture" in three locations, but did not replace "luncheon."

QUICK TIP

Alternately, you can also use the Find tab in the Find and Replace dialog box to find text in a document.

7. **Click the Find button in the Editing group**

   Clicking the Find button opens the Navigation pane, which is used to browse a longer document by headings, by pages, or by specific text or objects. The Find command allows you to quickly locate all instances of text in a document. You use it to verify that Word did not replace "luncheon."

8. **Type luncheon in the Search document text box in the Navigation pane, then scroll up until the headline is at the top of the document window**

   The word "luncheon" is highlighted and selected in the document, as shown in Figure B-8.

9. **Click the Close button in the Navigation pane, press [Ctrl][Home], then save the document**

   The highlighting is removed from the text when you close the Navigation pane.

FIGURE B-7: Find and Replace dialog box

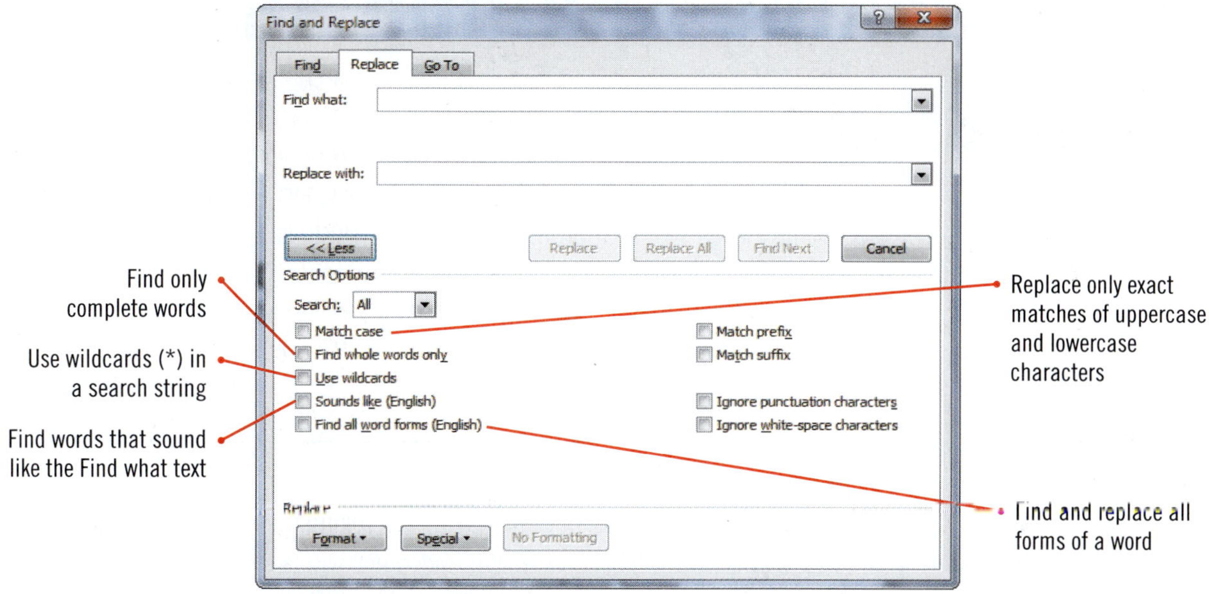

FIGURE B-8: Found text highlighted in document

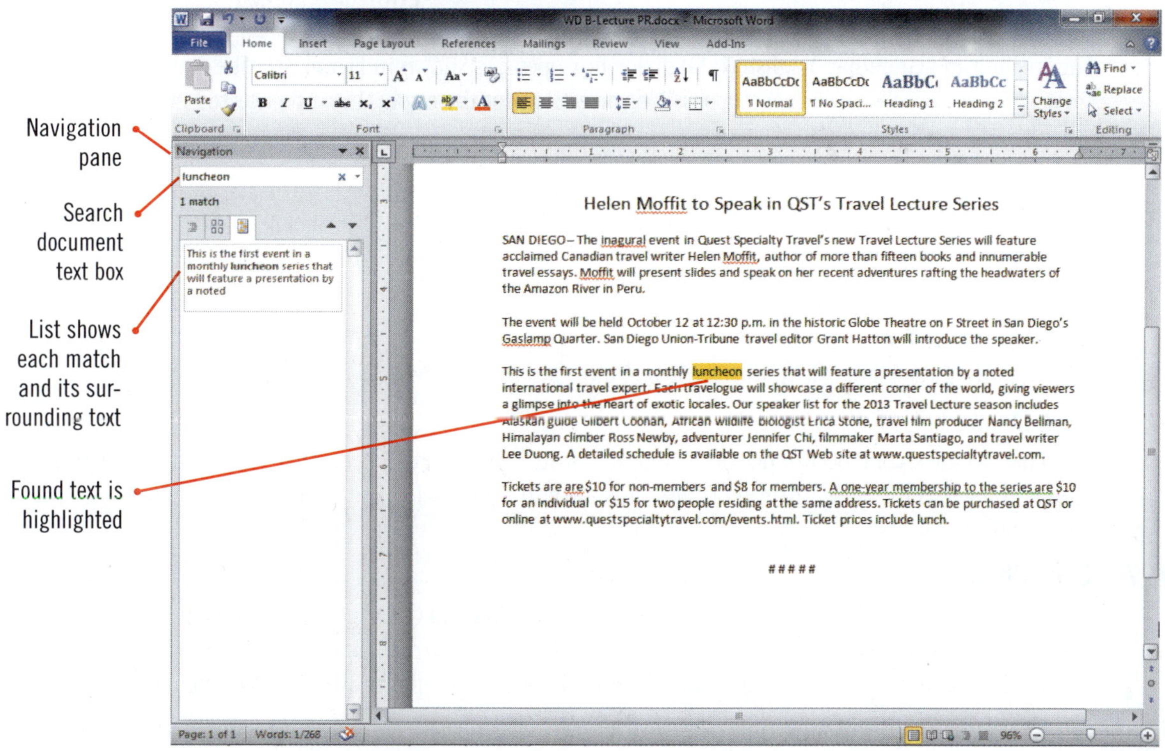

Navigating a document using the Go To command

Rather than scrolling to move to a different place in a longer document, you can use the Go To command to quickly move the insertion point to a specific location. To move to a specific page, section, line, table, graphic, or other item in a document, you use the Go To tab in the Find and Replace dialog box. To open the Find and Replace dialog box with the Go To tab active, click the Page number button on the status bar. On the Go To tab in the Find and Replace dialog box, select the type of item you want to find in the Go to what list box, enter the relevant information about that item, and then click Go To or Next to move the insertion point to the item.

UNIT B
Word 2010

Checking Spelling and Grammar

When you finish typing and revising a document, you can use the Spelling and Grammar command to search the document for misspelled words and grammar errors. The Spelling and Grammar checker flags possible mistakes, suggests correct spellings, and offers remedies for grammar errors such as subject–verb agreement, repeated words, and punctuation. You use the Spelling and Grammar checker to search your press release for errors. Before beginning the search, you set the Spelling and Grammar checker to ignore words, such as Moffit, that you know are spelled correctly.

STEPS

TROUBLE
If Word flags your name as misspelled, right-click it, then click Ignore All. If Moffit is not flagged as misspelled, skip to Step 3.

QUICK TIP
To change the language used by the Word proofing tools, click the Language button in the Language group on the Review tab, click Set Proofing Language, then click the language you prefer on the menu that opens.

TROUBLE
You might need to correct other spelling and grammar errors.

QUICK TIP
If Word does not offer a valid correction, correct the error yourself.

1. **Right-click Moffit in the headline**
   A menu that includes suggestions for correcting the spelling of "Moffit" opens. You can correct individual spelling and grammar errors by right-clicking text that is underlined with a red or green wavy line and selecting a correction. Although "Moffit" is not in the Word dictionary, it is spelled correctly in the document.
2. **Click Ignore All**
   Clicking Ignore All tells Word not to flag "Moffit" as misspelled.
3. **Press [Ctrl][Home], click the Review tab, then click the Spelling & Grammar button in the Proofing group**
   The Spelling and Grammar: English (U.S.) dialog box opens, as shown in Figure B-9. The dialog box identifies "inagural" as misspelled and suggests possible corrections for the error. The word selected in the Suggestions box is the correct spelling.
4. **Click Change**
   Word replaces the misspelled word with the correctly spelled word. Next, the dialog box identifies "Gaslamp" as a misspelled word and suggests the correction "Gas lamp." The proper name "Gaslamp Quarter" is spelled correctly in the document.
5. **Click Ignore Once**
   Word ignores the spelling. Next, the dialog box indicates that "are" is repeated in a sentence.
6. **Click Delete**
   Word deletes the second occurrence of the repeated word. Next, the dialog box flags a subject–verb agreement error and suggests using "is" instead of "are," as shown in Figure B-10. The phrase selected in the Suggestions box is correct.
7. **Click Change**
   Word replaces "are" with "is" in the sentence, and the Spelling and Grammar dialog box closes. Keep in mind that the Spelling and Grammar checker identifies many common errors, but you cannot rely on it to find and correct all spelling and grammar errors in your documents. Always proofread your documents carefully.
8. **Click OK to complete the spelling and grammar check, press [Ctrl][Home], then save the document**

FIGURE B-9: Spelling and Grammar: English (U.S.) dialog box

FIGURE B-10: Grammar error identified in Spelling and Grammar dialog box

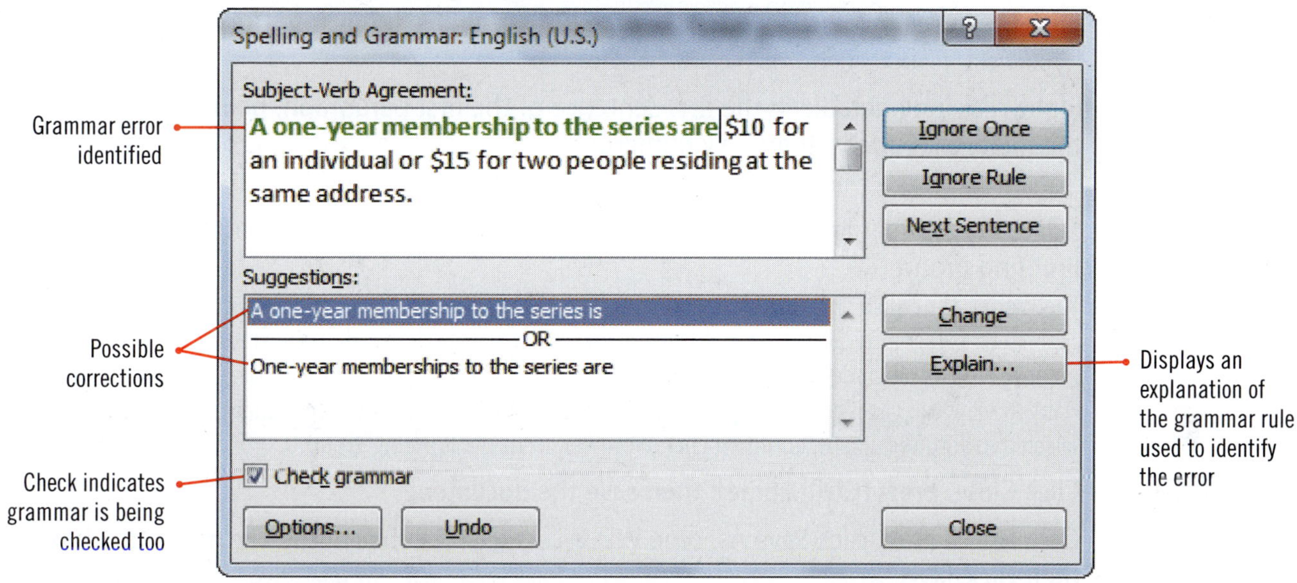

Inserting text with AutoCorrect

As you type, AutoCorrect automatically corrects many commonly misspelled words. By creating your own AutoCorrect entries, you can set Word to insert text that you type often, such as your name or contact information, or to correct words you misspell frequently. For example, you could create an AutoCorrect entry so that the name "Ronald T. Dawson" is automatically inserted whenever you type "rtd" followed by a space. You create AutoCorrect entries and customize other AutoCorrect and AutoFormat options using the AutoCorrect dialog box. To open the AutoCorrect dialog box, click the File tab, click Options, click Proofing in the Word Options dialog box that opens, and then click AutoCorrect Options. On the AutoCorrect tab in the AutoCorrect dialog box, type the text you want to be corrected automatically in the Replace text box (such as "rtd"), type the text you want to be inserted in its place automatically in the With text box (such as "Ronald T. Dawson"), and then click Add. The AutoCorrect entry is added to the list. Click OK to close the AutoCorrect dialog box, and then click OK to close the Word Options dialog box. Word inserts an AutoCorrect entry in a document when you press [Spacebar] or a punctuation mark after typing the text you want Word to correct. For example, Word inserts "Ronald T. Dawson" when you type "rtd" followed by a space.

If you want to remove an AutoCorrect entry you created, simply open the AutoCorrect dialog box, select the AutoCorrect entry you want to remove in the list, click Delete, click OK, and then click OK to close the Word Options dialog box.

UNIT
B
Word 2010

Researching Information

The Word Research feature allows you to quickly search reference sources and the World Wide Web for information related to a word or phrase. Among the reference sources available in the Research task pane is a Thesaurus, which you can use to look up synonyms for awkward or repetitive words. When you are working with an active Internet connection, the Research task pane also provides access to dictionary and translation sources, as well as to Web search engines such as Bing. After proofreading your document for errors, you decide the press release would read better if several adjectives were more descriptive. You use the Thesaurus to find synonyms.

STEPS

QUICK TIP
You can also click the Research button in the Proofing group to open the Research task pane.

1. **Scroll down until the headline is displayed at the top of your screen**
2. **Select noted in the first sentence of the third paragraph, then click the Thesaurus button in the Proofing group on the Review tab**
   The Research task pane opens, as shown in Figure B-11. "Noted" appears in the Search for text box, and possible synonyms for "noted" are listed under the Thesaurus: English (U.S.) heading in the task pane.

QUICK TIP
To look up synonyms for a different word, type the word in the Search for text box, then click the green Start searching button.

3. **Point to prominent in the list of synonyms**
   A box containing a list arrow appears around the word.
4. **Click the list arrow, click Insert on the menu that opens, then close the Research task pane**
   "Prominent" replaces "noted" in the press release.
5. **Right-click innumerable in the first sentence of the first paragraph, point to Synonyms on the menu that opens, then click numerous**
   "Numerous" replaces "innumerable" in the press release.
6. **Select the four paragraphs of body text, then click the Word Count button in the Proofing group**
   The Word Count dialog box opens, as shown in Figure B-12. The dialog box lists the number of pages, words, characters, paragraphs, and lines included in the selected text. Notice that the status bar also displays the number of words included in the selected text and the total number of words in the entire document. If you want to view the page, character, paragraph, and line count for the entire document, make sure nothing is selected in your document, and then click Word Count in the Proofing group.

QUICK TIP
To add or remove available reference sources, click Research options in the Research task pane.

7. **Click Close, press [Ctrl][Home], then save the document**
8. **Click the File tab, click Save As, type WD B-Lecture PR Public in the File name text box, then click Save**
   The WD B-Lecture PR file closes, and the WD B-Lecture PR Public file is displayed in the document window. You will modify this file to prepare it for electronic release to the public.

FIGURE B-11: Research task pane

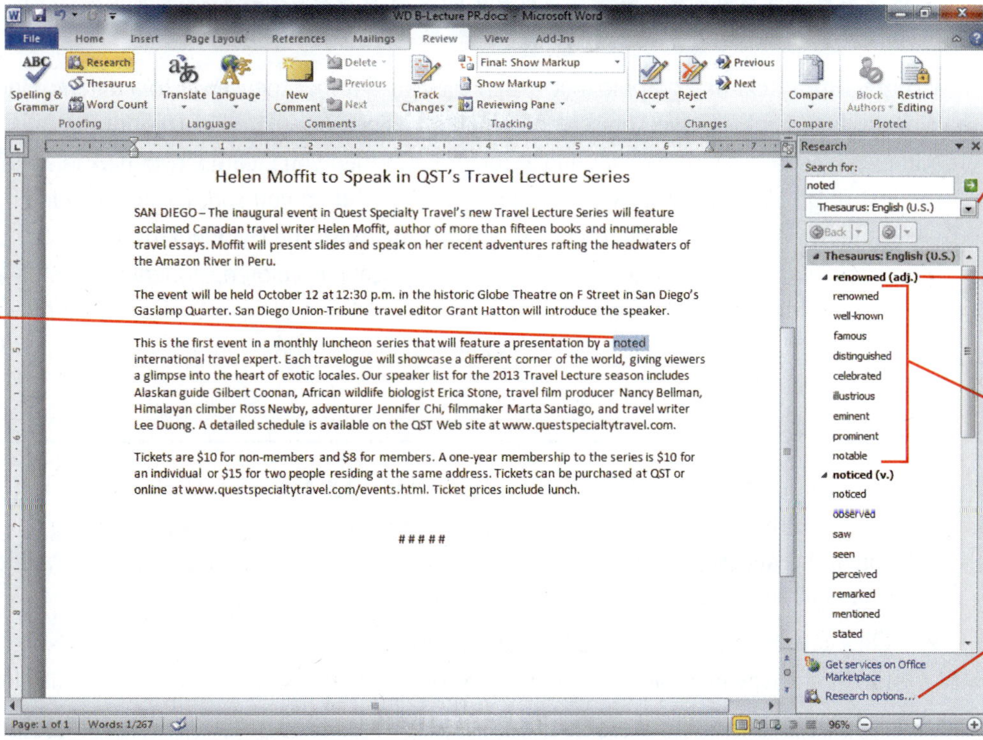

FIGURE B-12: Word Count dialog box

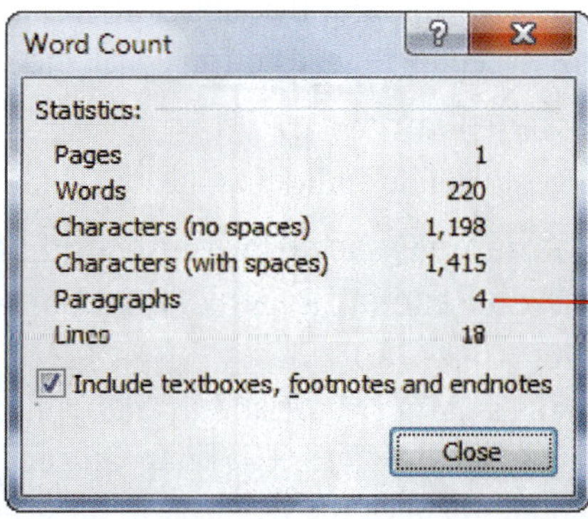

Publishing a blog directly from Word

A **blog**, which is short for weblog, is an informal journal that is created by an individual or a group and available to the public on the Internet. A blog usually conveys the ideas, comments, and opinions of the blogger and is written using a strong personal voice. The person who creates and maintains a blog, the **blogger**, typically updates the blog daily. If you have or want to start a blog, you can configure Word to link to your blog site so that you can write, format, and publish blog entries directly from Word.

To create a new blog post, click the File tab, click New, then double-click Blog post to open a predesigned blog post document that you can customize with your own text, formatting, and images. You can also publish an existing document as a blog post by opening the document, clicking the File tab, clicking Save & Send, and then clicking Publish as Blog Post. In either case, Word prompts you to log onto your personal blog account. To blog directly from Word, you must first obtain a blog account with a blog service provider. Resources, such as the Word Help system and online forums, provide detailed information on obtaining and registering your personal blog account with Word.

UNIT
B
Word 2010

Adding Hyperlinks

A **hyperlink** is text or a graphic that, when clicked, "jumps" the viewer to a different location or program. When a document is viewed on screen, hyperlinks allow readers to link (or jump) to a Web page, an e-mail address, a file, or a specific location in a document. When you create a hyperlink in a document, you select the text or graphic you want to use as a hyperlink and then you specify the location you want to jump to when the hyperlink is clicked. You create a hyperlink using the Hyperlink button in the Links group on the Insert tab. Text that is formatted as a hyperlink appears as colored, underlined text. Hundreds of people on your lists of press and client contacts will receive the press release by e-mail or Internet fax. To make it easier for these people to access additional information about the series, you add several hyperlinks to the press release.

STEPS

QUICK TIP
By default, Word automatically creates a hyperlink to an e-mail address or URL when you type the address or URL in a document.

1. **Select your name, click the Insert tab, then click the Hyperlink button in the Links group**
   The Insert Hyperlink dialog box opens, as shown in Figure B-13. You use this dialog box to specify the location of the Web page, file, e-mail address, or position in the current document you want to jump to when the hyperlink—in this case, your name—is clicked.
2. **Click E-mail Address in the Link to section**
   The Insert Hyperlink dialog box changes so you can create a hyperlink to your e-mail address.
3. **Type your e-mail address in the E-mail address text box, type Travel Lecture Series in the Subject text box, then click OK**
   As you type, Word automatically adds mailto: in front of your e-mail address. After you close the dialog box, the hyperlink text—your name—is formatted in blue and underlined.

QUICK TIP
To remove a hyperlink, right-click it, then click Remove Hyperlink. Removing a hyperlink removes the link, but the text remains.

4. **Press and hold [Ctrl], then click the your name hyperlink**
   An e-mail message addressed to you with the subject "Travel Lecture Series" opens in the default e-mail program. People can use this hyperlink to send you an e-mail message.
5. **Close the e-mail message window**
   The hyperlink text changes to purple, indicating the hyperlink has been followed.
6. **Scroll down, select Gaslamp Quarter in the second paragraph, click the Hyperlink button, click Existing File or Web Page in the Link to section, type www.gaslamp.org in the Address text box, then click OK**
   As you type the Web address, Word automatically adds "http://" in front of "www." The text "Gaslamp Quarter" is formatted as a hyperlink to the Gaslamp Quarter Association home page at www.gaslamp.org. When clicked, the hyperlink will open the Web page in the default browser window.
7. **Select detailed schedule in the last sentence of the third paragraph, click the Hyperlink button, type www.questspecialtytravel.com in the Address text box, then click OK**
   The text "detailed schedule" is formatted as a hyperlink to the QST Web site. If you point to a hyperlink in Word, the link to location appears in a ScreenTip. You can edit ScreenTip text to make it more descriptive.

QUICK TIP
You can also edit the hyperlink destination or the hyperlink text.

8. **Right-click Quarter in the Gaslamp Quarter hyperlink, click Edit Hyperlink, click ScreenTip in the Edit Hyperlink dialog box, type Map, parking, and other information about the Gaslamp Quarter in the ScreenTip text box, click OK, click OK, save your changes, then point to the Gaslamp Quarter hyperlink in the document**
   The ScreenTip you created appears above the Gaslamp Quarter hyperlink, as shown in Figure B-14.

TROUBLE
If you are not working with an active Internet connection, skip this step.

9. **Press [Ctrl], click the Gaslamp Quarter hyperlink, click the Word icon on the taskbar, press [Ctrl], click the detailed schedule hyperlink, verify that the links opened in separate tabs in your browser, close the tabs, then click the Word icon on the taskbar to return to the press release document in Word**
   Before distributing a document, it's important to test each hyperlink to verify it works as you intended.

FIGURE B-13: Insert Hyperlink dialog box

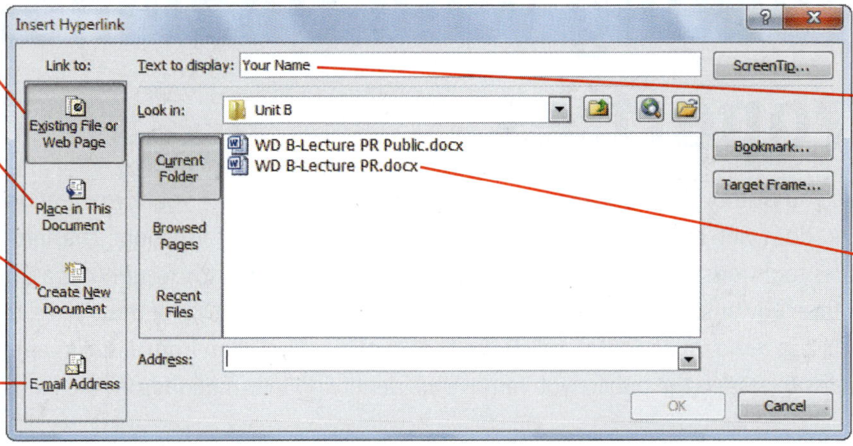

FIGURE B-14: Hyperlinks in the document

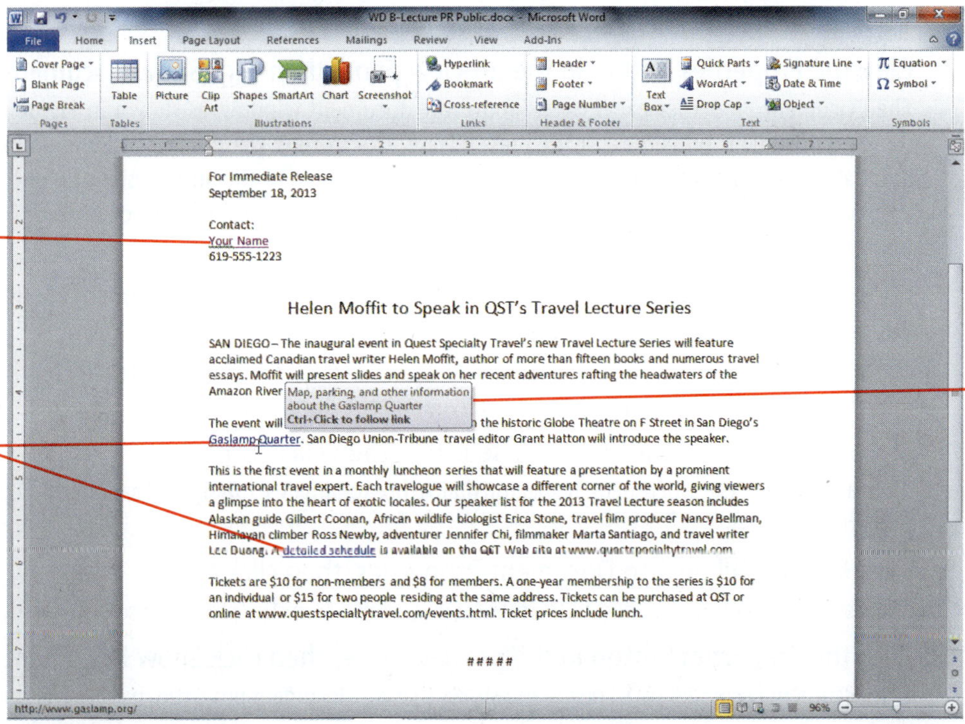

E-mailing and faxing documents directly from Word

Word includes several options for distributing and sharing documents over the Internet directly from within Word, including e-mailing and faxing documents. When you e-mail a document from within Word, the document is sent as an attachment to an e-mail message using your default e-mail program. To e-mail a file, open the file in Word, click the File tab, click Save & Send, and then select one of the options under Send Using E-mail on the Save & Send tab. You can choose to attach the document as a Word file, a .pdf file, or an .xps file, or to send it as an Internet fax. When you click an option, a message window opens that includes the filename of the current file as the message subject and the file as an attachment. Type the e-mail address(es) of the recipient(s) in the To and Cc text boxes, any message you want in the message window, and then click Send on the message window toolbar to send the message. The default e-mail program sends a copy of the document to each recipient. Note that faxing a document directly from Word requires registration with a third-party Internet fax service. Fax services generally charge a monthly or per page fee for sending and receiving faxes.

UNIT B
Word 2010

Working with Document Properties

Before you distribute a document electronically to people outside your organization, it's wise to make sure the file does not include embedded private or confidential information. The Info tab in Backstage view includes tools for stripping a document of sensitive information, for securing its authenticity, and for guarding it from unwanted changes once it is distributed to the public. One of these tools, the Document Inspector, detects and removes unwanted private or confidential information from a document. Before sending the press release to the public, you remove all identifying information from the file.

STEPS

QUICK TIP
To create or modify document properties for a file, type in the Document Properties panel text boxes.

1. **Press [Ctrl][Home], then click the File tab**
   Backstage view opens with the Info tab displayed. The Information pane, in the middle of the tab, includes options related to stripping the file of private information. See Table B-1. The preview pane, on the right side of the tab, displays basic information about the document. Notice that the file contains document properties. You might want to remove these before you distribute the press release to the public.
2. **Click the Properties button in the preview pane, then click Show Document Panel**
   The Document Properties panel opens above the document window, as shown in Figure B-15. It shows the standard document properties for the press release. **Document properties** are user-defined details about a file that describe its contents and origin, including the name of the author, the title of the document, and keywords that you can assign to help organize and search your files. You decide to remove this information from the file before you distribute it electronically.
3. **Click the File tab, click the Check for Issues button, then click Inspect Document, clicking Yes if prompted to save changes**
   The Document Inspector dialog box opens. You use this dialog box to indicate which private or identifying information you want to search for and remove from the document.
4. **Make sure all the check boxes are selected, then click Inspect**
   After a moment, the Document Inspector dialog box changes to indicate that the file contains document properties.

QUICK TIP
A document property, such as author name, might appear automatically in a content control in a document. Stripping a file of document properties does not remove this information from a content control.

5. **Click Remove All next to Document Properties, then click Close**
   The standard document property information is removed from the press release document.
6. **Click the Properties button in the preview pane, then click Show Document Panel**
   The Document Properties panel opens and shows that the document properties have been removed from the file.
7. **Click the Close button in the Document Properties panel, save the document, submit it to your instructor, close the file, then exit Word**
   The completed press release is shown in Figure B-16.

TABLE B-1: Options on the Info tab

option	use to
Protect Document	Mark a document as final so that it is read-only and cannot be edited; encrypt a document so that a password is required to open it; restrict what kinds of changes can be made to a document and by whom; and add a digital signature to a document to verify its integrity
Check for Issues	Detect and remove unwanted information from a document, including document properties and comments; check for content that people with disabilities might find difficult to read; and check the document for features that are not supported by previous versions of Microsoft Word
Manage versions	Browse through and delete draft versions of unsaved files

FIGURE B-15: Document Properties panel

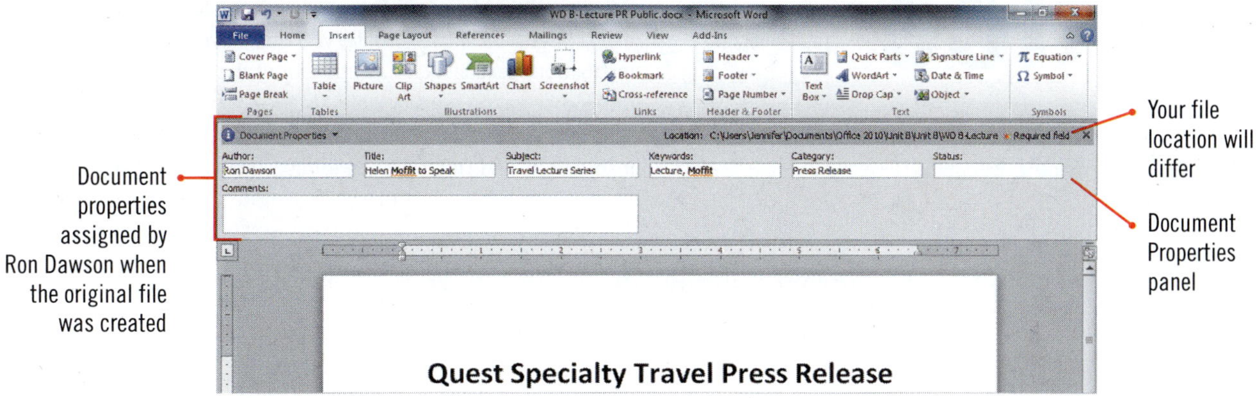

FIGURE B-16: Completed press release for electronic distribution

Quest Specialty Travel Press Release

340 West Market Street • San Diego, CA 92101 • Tel: 619-555-1223 • Fax: 619-555-0937 • www.questspecialty travel.com

For Immediate Release
September 18, 2013

Contact:
Your Name
619-555-1223

Helen Moffit to Speak in QST's Travel Lecture Series

SAN DIEGO – The inaugural event in Quest Specialty Travel's new Travel Lecture Series will feature acclaimed Canadian travel writer Helen Moffit, author of more than fifteen books and numerous travel essays. Moffit will present slides and speak on her recent adventures rafting the headwaters of the Amazon River in Peru.

The event will be held October 12 at 12:30 p.m. in the historic Globe Theatre on F Street in San Diego's Gaslamp Quarter. San Diego Union-Tribune travel editor Grant Hatton will introduce the speaker.

This is the first event in a monthly luncheon series that will feature a presentation by a prominent international travel expert. Each travelogue will showcase a different corner of the world, giving viewers a glimpse into the heart of exotic locales. Our speaker list for the 2013 Travel Lecture season includes Alaskan guide Gilbert Coonan, African wildlife biologist Erica Stone, travel film producer Nancy Bellman, Himalayan climber Ross Newby, adventurer Jennifer Chi, filmmaker Marta Santiago, and travel writer Lee Duong. A detailed schedule is available on the QST Web site at www.questspecialtytravel.com.

Tickets are $10 for non-members and $8 for members. A one-year membership to the series is $10 for an individual or $15 for two people residing at the same address. Tickets can be purchased at QST or online at www.questspecialtytravel.com/events.html. Ticket prices include lunch.

#####

Viewing and modifying advanced document properties

The Document Properties panel includes summary information about the document that you enter to suit your needs. To view more detailed document properties, including those entered automatically by Word when the document is created, click the Document Properties button in the Document Properties panel, and then click Advanced Properties to open the Properties dialog box. You can also click the Properties button on the Info tab and then click Advanced Properties to open the Properties dialog box. The General, Statistics, and Contents tabs of the Properties dialog box display information about the file that is automatically created and updated by Word. The General tab shows the file type, location, size, and date and time the file was created and last modified; the Statistics tab displays information about revisions to the document along with the number of pages, words, lines, paragraphs, and characters in the file; and the Contents tab shows the title of the document.

You can define other document properties using the Properties dialog box Summary and Custom tabs. The Summary tab shows information similar to the information shown in the Document Properties panel. The Custom tab allows you to create new document properties, such as client, project, or date completed. To create a custom property, select a property name in the Name list box on the Custom tab, use the Type list arrow to select the type of data you want for the property, type the identifying detail (such as a project name) in the Value text box, and then click Add. When you are finished viewing or modifying the document properties, click OK to close the Properties dialog box, then click the Close button on the Document Properties panel.

Practice

Concepts Review

For current SAM information, including versions and content details, visit SAM Central (http://www.cengage.com/samcentral). If you have a SAM user profile, you may have access to hands-on instruction, practice, and assessment of the skills covered in this unit. Since various versions of SAM are supported throughout the life of this text, check with your instructor for the correct instructions and URL/Web site for accessing assignments.

Label the elements of the Word program window shown in Figure B-17.

FIGURE B-17

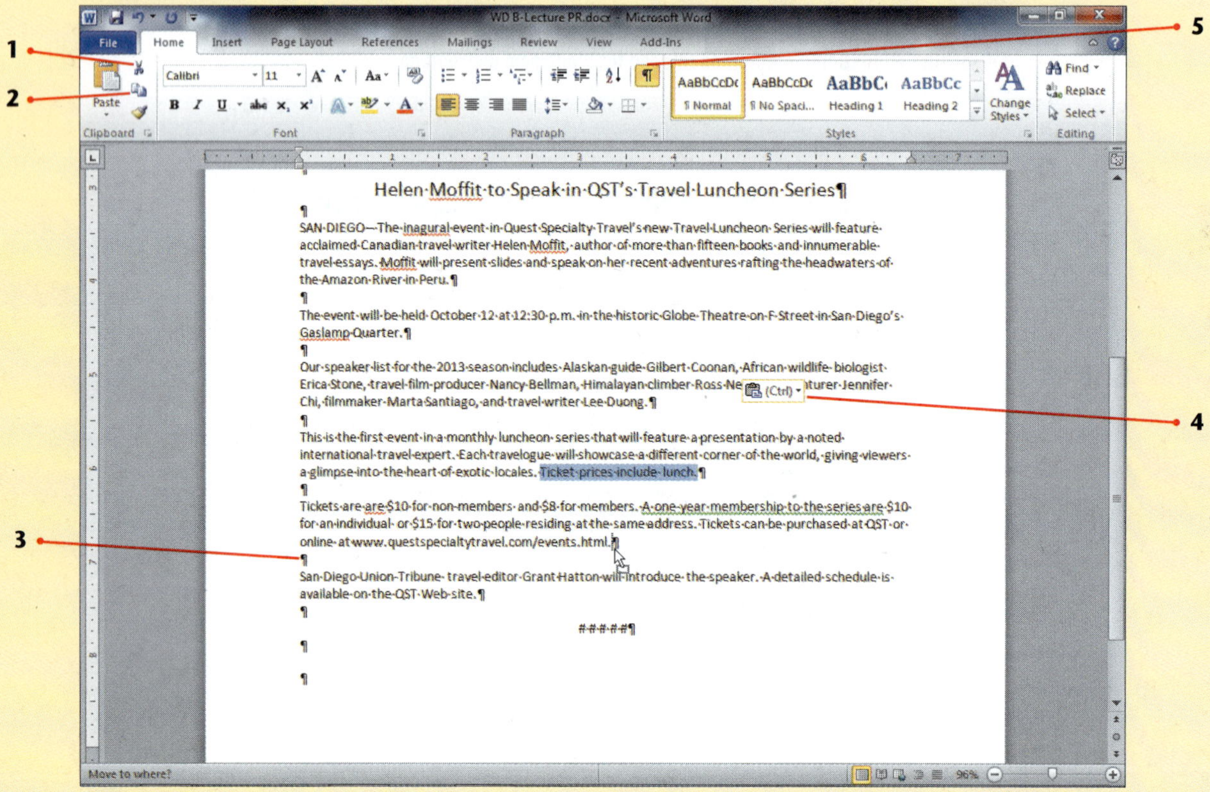

Match each term with the statement that best describes it.

6. **Paste**
7. **Shortcut key**
8. **System Clipboard**
9. **Document properties**
10. **Office Clipboard**
11. **Cut**
12. **Thesaurus**
13. **Hyperlink**
14. **Blog**

- **a.** Command used to insert text stored on the Clipboard into a document
- **b.** Temporary storage area for up to 24 items collected from Office files
- **c.** Temporary storage area for only the last item cut or copied from a document
- **d.** A function key or a combination of keys that perform a command when pressed
- **e.** Text or a graphic that jumps the reader to a different location or program when clicked
- **f.** An informal journal that is available to the public on the Internet
- **g.** User-defined details about a file that describe its contents and origin
- **h.** Feature used to suggest synonyms for words
- **i.** Command used to remove text from a document and place it on the Clipboard

Select the best answer from the list of choices.

15. Which of the following statements is *not* true?

- **a.** You can view the contents of the Office Clipboard.
- **b.** The Office Clipboard can hold more than one item.
- **c.** The last item cut or copied from a document is stored on the system Clipboard.
- **d.** When you move text by dragging it, a copy of the text you move is stored on the system Clipboard.

16. What is the keyboard shortcut for the Paste command?

- **a.** [Ctrl][P]
- **b.** [Ctrl][X]
- **c.** [Ctrl][V]
- **d.** [Ctrl][C]

17. Which command is used to display a document in two panes in the document window?

- **a.** Split
- **b.** New Window
- **c.** Arrange All
- **d.** Two Pages

18. To locate and select all instances of a word in a document, which command do you use?

- **a.** Find
- **b.** Search
- **c.** Highlight
- **d.** Replace

19. A hyperlink *cannot* be linked to which of the following?

- **a.** ScreenTip
- **b.** Document
- **c.** Web page
- **d.** E-mail address

20. Which of the following is an example of a document property?

- **a.** Permission
- **b.** URL
- **c.** Language
- **d.** Keyword

Word 2010

Skills Review

1. Cut and paste text.

- **a.** Start Word, click the File tab, then open the file WD B-2.docx from the drive and folder where you store your Data Files.
- **b.** Save the document with the filename **WD B-WAOS 2013 PR**.
- **c.** Select **Your Name** and replace it with your name.
- **d.** Display paragraph and other formatting marks in your document if they are not already displayed.
- **e.** Use the Cut and Paste buttons to switch the order of the two sentences in the fourth paragraph (which begins New group shows...).
- **f.** Use the drag-and-drop method to switch the order of the second and third paragraphs.
- **g.** Adjust the spacing if necessary so that there is one blank line between paragraphs, then save your changes.

2. Copy and paste text.

- **a.** Use the Copy and Paste buttons to copy **WAOS 2011** from the headline and paste it before the word **map** in the third paragraph.
- **b.** Change the formatting of the pasted text to match the formatting of the third paragraph, then insert a space between **2011** and **map** if necessary.
- **c.** Use the drag-and-drop method to copy **WAOS** from the third paragraph and paste it before the word **group** in the second sentence of the fourth paragraph, then save your changes.

3. Use the Office Clipboard.

- **a.** Use the launcher in the Clipboard group to open the Clipboard task pane.
- **b.** Scroll so that the first body paragraph is displayed at the top of the document window.
- **c.** Select the fifth paragraph (which begins Studio location maps...) and cut it to the Office Clipboard.
- **d.** Select the third paragraph (which begins Wilmington is easily accessible...) and cut it to the Office Clipboard.
- **e.** Use the Office Clipboard to paste the Studio location maps... item as the new fourth paragraph.
- **f.** Use the Office Clipboard to paste the Wilmington is easily accessible... item as the new fifth paragraph.
- **g.** Adjust the spacing if necessary so there is one blank line between each of the six body paragraphs.
- **h.** Turn off the display of formatting marks, clear and close the Office Clipboard, then save your changes.

Skills Review (continued)

4. Find and replace text.

  a. Using the Replace command, replace all instances of **2011** with **2013**.
  b. Replace all instances of **tenth** with **twelfth**.
  c. Replace all instances of the abbreviation **st** with **street**, taking care to replace whole words only when you perform the replace. (*Hint*: Deselect Match case if it is selected.)
  d. Use the Find tab in the Find and Replace dialog box to find all instances of **st** in the document and to make sure no errors occurred when you replaced st with street. (*Hint*: Deselect the Find whole words only check box.)
  e. Save your changes to the press release.

5. Check spelling and grammar and research information.

  a. Switch to the Review tab.
  b. Move the insertion point to the top of the document, then use the Spelling and Grammar command to search for and correct any spelling and grammar errors in the press release. (*Hint*: Riverwalk is not misspelled.)
  c. Use the Thesaurus to replace **thriving** in the second paragraph with a different suitable word.
  d. Check the word count of the press release.
  e. Proofread your press release, correct any errors, then save your changes.

6. Add hyperlinks.

  a. Save the document as **WD B-WAOS 2013 PR Public**, then switch to the Insert tab.
  b. Select your name, then open the Insert Hyperlink dialog box.
  c. Create a hyperlink to your e-mail address with the subject **WAOS 2013**.
  d. Test the your name hyperlink, then close the message window that opens. (*Hint*: Press [Ctrl], then click the hyperlink.)
  e. Select **NEA** in the last paragraph of the press release, then create a hyperlink to the Web page with the URL **www.nea.gov**.
  f. Right-click the NEA hyperlink, then edit the hyperlink ScreenTip to become **Information on the National Endowment for the Arts**.
  g. Point to the NEA hyperlink to view the new ScreenTip, then save your changes.
  h. If you are working with an active Internet connection, press [Ctrl], click the NEA hyperlink, view the NEA home page in the browser window, then close the browser window.

7. Work with document properties.

  a. Click the File tab, click the Properties button on the preview pane, then open the Document Properties panel to view the document properties for the press release.
  b. Click the File tab to return to Backstage view with the Info tab displayed, then use the Check for Issues command to run the Document Inspector.
  c. Remove the document property data, click the Home tab, close the Document Properties panel, then save your changes. The finished press release is shown in Figure B-18.
  d. Save the document, submit it to your instructor, close the file, then exit Word.

FIGURE B-18

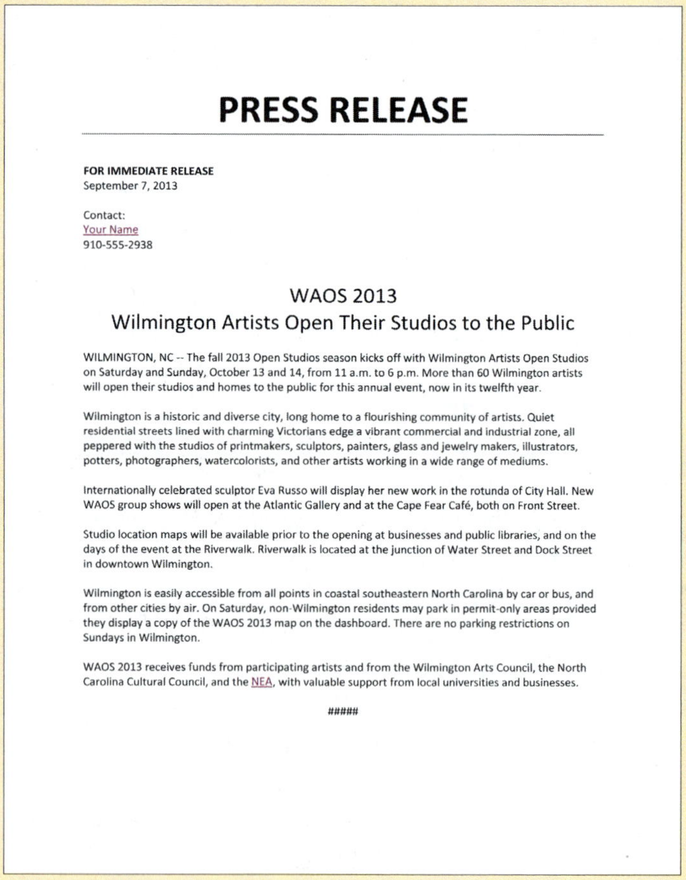

PRESS RELEASE

FOR IMMEDIATE RELEASE
September 7, 2013

Contact:
Your Name
910-555-2938

WAOS 2013
Wilmington Artists Open Their Studios to the Public

WILMINGTON, NC -- The fall 2013 Open Studios season kicks off with Wilmington Artists Open Studios on Saturday and Sunday, October 13 and 14, from 11 a.m. to 6 p.m. More than 60 Wilmington artists will open their studios and homes to the public for this annual event, now in its twelfth year.

Wilmington is a historic and diverse city, long home to a flourishing community of artists. Quiet residential streets lined with charming Victorians edge a vibrant commercial and industrial zone, all peppered with the studios of printmakers, sculptors, painters, glass and jewelry makers, illustrators, potters, photographers, watercolorists, and other artists working in a wide range of mediums.

Internationally celebrated sculptor Eva Russo will display her new work in the rotunda of City Hall. New WAOS group shows will open at the Atlantic Gallery and at the Cape Fear Café, both on Front Street.

Studio location maps will be available prior to the opening at businesses and public libraries, and on the days of the event at the Riverwalk. Riverwalk is located at the junction of Water Street and Dock Street in downtown Wilmington.

Wilmington is easily accessible from all points in coastal southeastern North Carolina by car or bus, and from other cities by air. On Saturday, non-Wilmington residents may park in permit-only areas provided they display a copy of the WAOS 2013 map on the dashboard. There are no parking restrictions on Sundays in Wilmington.

WAOS 2013 receives funds from participating artists and from the Wilmington Arts Council, the North Carolina Cultural Council, and the NEA, with valuable support from local universities and businesses.

#####

Independent Challenge 1

Because of your success in revitalizing a historic theatre in Wellington, New Zealand, you were hired as the director of The Canberra Lyric Theatre in Canberra, Australia, to breathe life into its theatre revitalization efforts. After a year on the job, you are launching your first major fund-raising drive. You'll create a fund-raising letter for the Lyric Theatre by modifying a letter you wrote for the theatre in Wellington.

If you have a SAM 2010 user profile, an autogradable SAM version of this assignment may be available at http://www.cengage.com/sam2010. Check with your instructor to confirm that this assignment is available in SAM. To use the SAM version of this assignment, log into the SAM 2010 Web site and download the instruction and start files.

a. Start Word, open the file WD B-3.docx from the drive and folder where you store your Data Files, then save it as **WD B-Lyric Fundraising Letter**.

b. Replace the theatre name and address, the date, the inside address, and the salutation with the text shown in Figure B-19.

c. Use the Replace command to replace all instances of **Wellington** with **Canberra**.

d. Use the Replace command to replace all instances of **Town Hall** with **Lyric**.

e. Use the Replace command to replace all instances of **New Zealanders** with **Australians**.

f. Use the Find command to locate the word **considerable**, then use the Thesaurus to replace the word with a synonym.

g. Move the fourth body paragraph so that it becomes the second body paragraph.

h. Create an AutoCorrect entry that inserts **Executive Director** whenever you type **exd**.

i. Replace Your Name with your name in the signature block, select Title, then type **exd** followed by a space.

j. Use the Spelling and Grammar command to check for and correct spelling and grammar errors.

k. Delete the AutoCorrect entry you created for exd. (*Hint*: Open the AutoCorrect dialog box, select the AutoCorrect entry you created, then click [Delete].)

FIGURE B-19

The Canberra Lyric Theatre

284 Constitution Avenue, Canberra ACT 2601, Australia

June 5, 2013

Mr. Andrew Davis
45 Robinson St.
O'Connor ACT 2602

Dear Mr. Davis:

Advanced Challenge Exercise

- Open the Document Properties panel, add your name as the author, change the title to **Canberra Lyric Theatre**, add the keyword **fund-raising**, then add the comment **Letter for the capital campaign**.
- Open the Properties dialog box, review the properties on the Summary tab, then review the paragraph, line, word, and character count on the Statistics tab.
- On the Custom tab, add a property named **Project** with the value **Capital Campaign**, then close the dialog box and the Document Properties panel.

l. Proofread the letter, correct any errors, save your changes, submit a copy to your instructor, close the document, then exit Word.

Independent Challenge 2

An advertisement for job openings in Denver caught your eye and you have decided to apply. The ad, shown in Figure B-20, was printed in last weekend's edition of your local newspaper. Instead of writing a cover letter from scratch, you revise a draft of a cover letter you wrote several years ago for a summer internship position.

a. Read the ad shown in Figure B-20 and decide which position to apply for. Choose the position that most closely matches your qualifications.

b. Start Word, open WD B-4.docx from the drive and folder where you store your Data Files, then save it as **WD B-Cover Letter**.

c. Replace the name, address, telephone number, and e-mail address in the letterhead with your own information.

d. Remove the hyperlink from the e-mail address.

e. Replace the date with today's date, then replace the inside address and the salutation with the information shown in Figure B-20.

f. Read the draft cover letter to get a feel for its contents.

g. Rework the text in the body of the letter to address your qualifications for the job you have chosen to apply for in the following ways:
- Delete the third paragraph.
- Adjust the first sentence of the first paragraph as follows: specify the job you are applying for, including the position code, and indicate where you saw the position advertised.
- Move the first sentence in the last paragraph, which briefly states your qualifications and interest in the position, to the end of the first paragraph, then rework the sentence to describe your current qualifications.
- Adjust the second paragraph as follows: describe your work experience and skills. Be sure to relate your experience and qualifications to the position requirements listed in the advertisement. Add a third paragraph if your qualifications are extensive.
- Adjust the final paragraph as follows: politely request an interview for the position and provide your phone number and e-mail address.

h. Include your name in the signature block.

i. When you are finished revising the letter, check it for spelling and grammar errors, and correct any mistakes. Make sure to remove any hyperlinks.

j. Save your changes to the letter, submit the file to your instructor, close the document, then exit Word.

FIGURE B-20

*Global*Dynamics

Career Opportunities in Denver

Global Dynamics, an established software development firm with offices in North America, Asia, and Europe, is seeking candidates for the following positions in its Denver facility:

Instructor
Responsible for delivering software training to our expanding Rocky Mountain customer base. Duties include delivering hands-on training, keeping up-to-date with product development, and working with the Director of Training to ensure the high quality of course materials. Successful candidate will have excellent presentation skills and be proficient in Microsoft PowerPoint and Microsoft Word. **Position B12C6**

Administrative Assistant
Proficiency with Microsoft Word a must! Administrative office duties include making travel arrangements, scheduling meetings, taking notes and publishing meeting minutes, handling correspondence, and ordering office supplies. Must have superb multitasking abilities, excellent communication, organizational, and interpersonal skills, and be comfortable working with e-mail and the Internet. **Position B16F5**

Copywriter
The ideal candidate will have marketing or advertising writing experience in a high tech environment, including collateral, newsletters, and direct mail. Experience writing for the Web, broadcast, and multimedia is a plus. Fluency with Microsoft Word required. **Position C13D4**

Positions offer salary, excellent benefits, moving expenses, and career growth opportunities.

Send resume and cover letter referencing position code to:

Thomas Finlay
Director of Recruiting
Global Dynamics
330 Fillmore Street
Denver, CO 80206

Independent Challenge 3

As administrative director of continuing education, you drafted a memo to instructors asking them to help you finalize the course schedule for next semester. Today, you'll examine the draft and make revisions before distributing it as an e-mail attachment.

a. Start Word, open the file WD B-5.docx from the drive and folder where you store your Data Files, then save it as **WD B-Business Courses Memo**.
b. Replace Your Name with your name in the From line, then scroll down until the first body paragraph is at the top of the screen.

Advanced Challenge Exercise

ACE

- Use the Split command on the View tab to split the window under the first body paragraph, then scroll until the last paragraph of the memo is displayed in the bottom pane.
- Use the Cut and Paste buttons to move the sentence **If you are planning to teach...** from the first body paragraph to become the first sentence in the last paragraph of the memo.
- Double-click the split bar to restore the window to a single pane.

c. Use the [Delete] key to merge the first two paragraphs into one paragraph.
d. Use the Office Clipboard to reorganize the list of twelve-week courses so that the courses are listed in alphabetical order, then clear and close the Office Clipboard.
e. Use the drag-and-drop method to reorganize the list of one-day seminars so that the seminars are listed in alphabetical order.
f. Select the phrase "Web site" in the first paragraph, then create a hyperlink to the URL **www.course.com** with the ScreenTip **Spring 2014 Business Courses**.
g. Select "e-mail me" in the last paragraph, then create a hyperlink to your e-mail address with the subject **Final Business Course Schedule**.
h. Use the Spelling and Grammar command to check for and correct spelling and grammar errors.
i. Use the Document Inspector to strip the document of document property information, ignore any other content that is flagged by the Document Inspector, then close the Document Inspector.
j. Proofread the memo, correct any errors, save your changes, submit a copy to your instructor, close the document, then exit Word.

Real Life Independent Challenge

This Independent Challenge requires an Internet connection.

Reference sources—dictionaries, thesauri, style and grammar guides, and guides to business etiquette and procedure—are essential for day-to-day use in the workplace. Much of this reference information is available on the World Wide Web. In this independent challenge, you will locate reference sources on the Web and use some of them to look up definitions, synonyms, and antonyms for words. Your goal is to familiarize yourself with online reference sources so you can use them later in your work.

a. Start Word, open the file WD B-6.docx from the drive and folder where you store your Data Files, then save it as **WD B-Web Reference Sources**. This document contains the questions you will answer about the Web reference sources you find. You will type your answers to the questions in the document.
b. Replace the placeholder text at the top of the Web Reference Sources document with your name and the date.
c. Use your favorite search engine to search the Web for grammar and style guides, dictionaries, and thesauri. Use the keywords **grammar**, **usage**, **dictionary**, **glossary**, and **thesaurus** to conduct your search.
d. Complete the Web Reference Sources document, then proofread it and correct any mistakes.
e. Save the document, submit a copy to your instructor, close the document, then exit Word.

Visual Workshop

Open WD B-7.docx from the drive and folder where you store your Data Files, then save the document as **WD B-Visa Letter**. Replace the placeholders for the date, letterhead, inside address, salutation, and closing with the information shown in Figure B-21, then use the Office Clipboard to reorganize the sentences to match Figure B-21. Correct spelling and grammar errors, remove the document property information from the file, then submit a copy to your instructor.

FIGURE B-21

Your Name

4637 Baker Street, Chicago, IL 60627; Tel: 630-555-2840

1/3/2013

Embassy of the People's Republic of China
2300 Connecticut Avenue NW
Washington, DC 20008-1724

Dear Sir or Madam:

I am applying for a long-stay tourist visa to China, valid for four years. I am scheduled to depart for Shanghai on March 13, 2013, returning to Chicago on September 8, 2013.

During my stay in China, I will be interviewing musicians and recording footage for a film I am making on contemporary Chinese music. I would like a multiple entry visa valid for four years so I can return to China after this trip to follow up on my initial research. I will be based in Shanghai, but I will be traveling frequently to record performances and to meet with musicians and producers.

Included with this letter are my completed visa application form, my passport, a passport photo, a copy of my return air ticket, and the visa fee. Please contact me if you need further information.

Sincerely,

Your Name

Enc: 5

UNIT

C

Word 2010

Formatting Text and Paragraphs

Files You Will Need:

WD C-1.docx

WD C-2.docx

WD C-3.docx

WD C-4.docx

WD C-5.docx

WD C-6.docx

Formatting can enhance the appearance of a document, create visual impact, and help illustrate a document's structure. The formatting of a document can also set a tone, allowing readers to know at a glance if the document is business-like, informal, or fun. In this unit you learn how to format text using fonts and a variety of paragraph-formatting effects, such as borders, shading, and bullets. You also learn how to illustrate a document with clip art. You have finished drafting the text for a two-page flyer advertising last minute specials for October tours. Now, you need to format the flyer so it is attractive and highlights the significant information.

OBJECTIVES

- Format with fonts
- Copy formats using the Format Painter
- Change line and paragraph spacing
- Align paragraphs
- Work with tabs
- Work with indents
- Add bullets and numbering
- Add borders and shading
- Insert clip art

UNIT C

Word 2010

Formatting with Fonts

Formatting text with fonts is a quick and powerful way to enhance the appearance of a document. A **font** is a complete set of characters with the same typeface or design. Arial, Times New Roman, Courier, Tahoma, and Calibri are some of the more common fonts, but there are hundreds of others, each with a specific design and feel. Another way to change the appearance of text is to increase or decrease its **font size**. Font size is measured in points. A **point** is 1/72 of an inch. You change the font and font size of the body text, title, and headings in the flyer. You select fonts and font sizes that enhance the sales tone of the document and help to structure the flyer visually for readers.

STEPS

QUICK TIP
There are two types of fonts: serif fonts have a small stroke, called a serif, at the ends of characters; sans serif fonts do not have a serif. Garamond is a serif font. Trebuchet MS is a sans serif font.

QUICK TIP
You can also type a font size in the Font Size text box.

QUICK TIP
To use a different set of theme colors, click the Page Layout tab, click the Theme Colors button in the Themes group, then select a different color set.

1. **Start Word, open the file WD C-1.docx from the drive and folder where you store your Data Files, then save it as WD C-Last Minute Deals**

   Notice that the name of the font used in the document, Calibri, is displayed in the Font list box in the Font group. The word "(Body)" in the Font list box indicates Calibri is the font used for body text in the current theme, the default theme. A **theme** is a related set of fonts, colors, styles, and effects that is applied to an entire document to give it a cohesive appearance. The font size, 11, appears in the Font Size list box in the Font group.

2. **Scroll the document to get a feel for its contents, press [Ctrl][Home], press [Ctrl][A] to select the entire document, then click the Font list arrow in the Font group**

   The Font list, which shows the fonts available on your computer, opens as shown in Figure C-1. The font names are formatted in the font. Font names can appear in more than one location on the font list.

3. **Drag the pointer slowly down the font names in the Font list, drag the scroll box to scroll down the Font list, then click Garamond**

   Dragging the pointer down the font list allows you to preview how the selected text will look in the highlighted font. Clicking a font name applies the font. The font of the flyer changes to Garamond.

4. **Click the Font Size list arrow in the Font group, drag the pointer slowly up and down the Font Size list, then click 12**

   Dragging the pointer over the font sizes allows you to preview how the selected text will look in the highlighted font size. Clicking 12 increases the font size of the selected text to 12 points.

5. **Select the title Quest Specialty Travel Last Minute Travel Deals, click the Font list arrow, scroll to and click Trebuchet MS, click the Font Size list arrow, click 22, then click the Bold button B in the Font group**

   The title is formatted in 22-point Trebuchet MS bold.

6. **Click the Font Color list arrow A in the Font group**

   A gallery of colors opens. It includes the set of theme colors in a range of tints and shades as well as a set of standard colors. You can point to a color in the gallery to preview it applied to the selected text.

7. **Click the Purple, Accent 4, Darker 25% color as shown in Figure C-2, then deselect the text**

   The color of the title text changes to purple. The active color on the Font Color button also changes to purple.

8. **Select the heading Rajasthan Desert Safari, then, using the Mini toolbar, click the Font list arrow, click Trebuchet MS, click the Font Size list arrow, click 14, click A, click B, then deselect the text**

   The heading is formatted in 14-point Trebuchet MS bold with a purple color. Notice that when you use the buttons on the Mini toolbar to format text, you cannot preview the formatting options in the document.

9. **Press [Ctrl][Home], then click the Save button on the Quick Access toolbar**

   Compare your document to Figure C-3.

FIGURE C-1: Font list

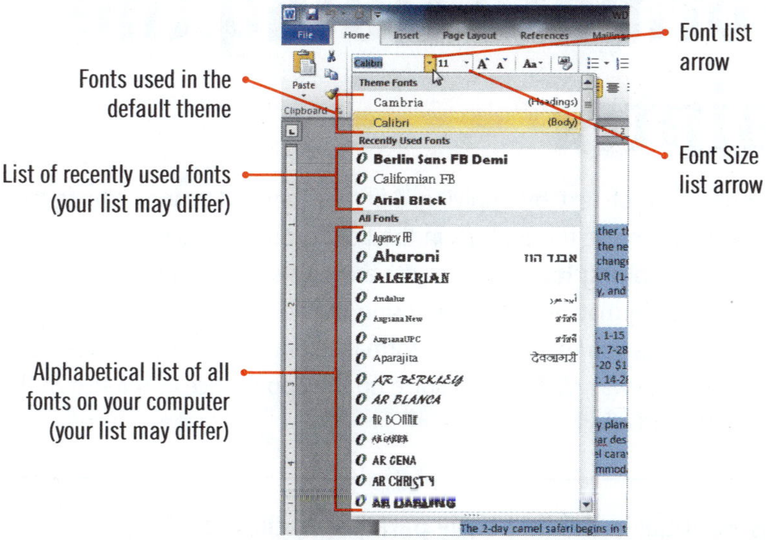

FIGURE C-2: Font Color Palette

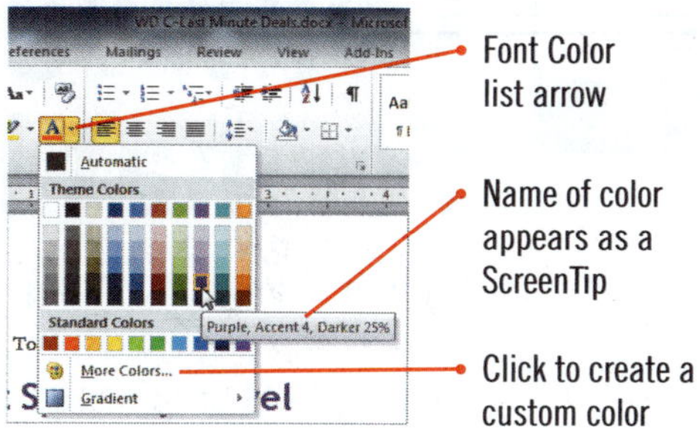

FIGURE C-3: Document formatted with fonts

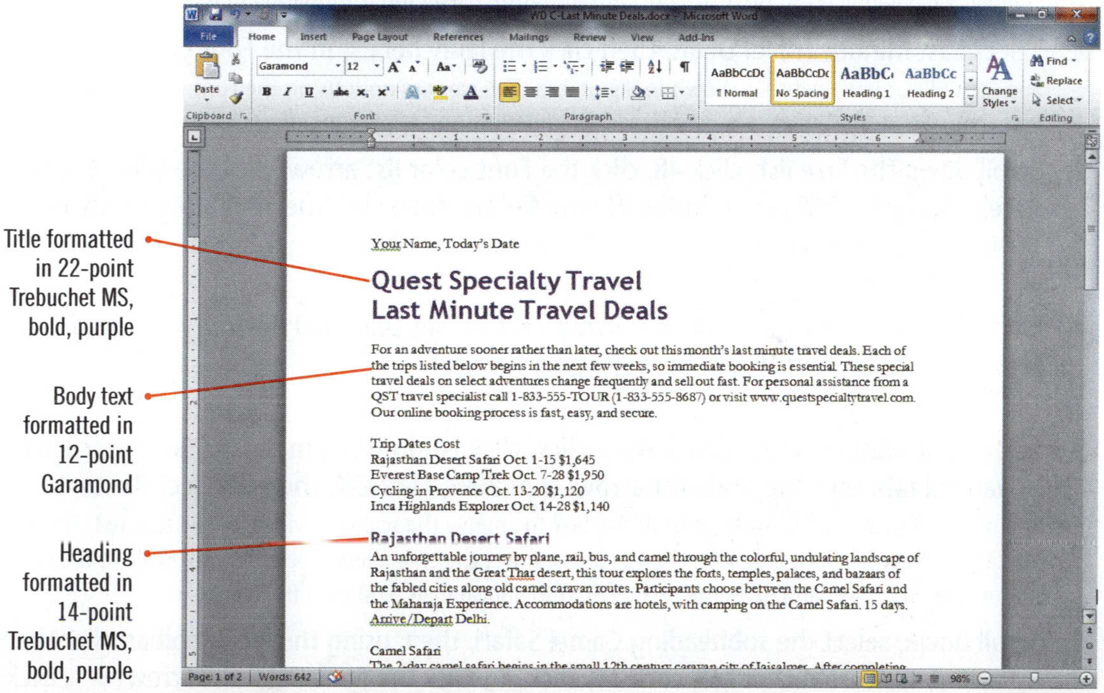

Adding a drop cap

A fun way to illustrate a document with fonts is to add a drop cap to a paragraph. A **drop cap** is a large initial capital letter, often used to set off the first paragraph of an article. To create a drop cap, place the insertion point in the paragraph you want to format, click the Insert tab, and then click the Drop Cap button in the Text group to open a menu of Drop cap options. Preview and select one of the options on the menu, or click Drop Cap Options to open the Drop Cap dialog box, shown in Figure C-4. In the Drop Cap dialog box, select the position, font, number of lines to drop, and the distance you want the drop cap to be from the paragraph text, and then click OK. The drop cap is added to the paragraph as a graphic object.

Once a drop cap is inserted in a paragraph, you can modify it by selecting it and then changing the settings in the Drop Cap dialog box. For even more interesting effects, you can enhance a drop cap with font color, font styles, or font effects. You can also fill the graphic object with shading or add a border around it. To enhance a drop cap, first select it, and then experiment with the formatting options available in the Font dialog box and in the Borders and Shading dialog box.

FIGURE C-4: Drop Cap dialog box

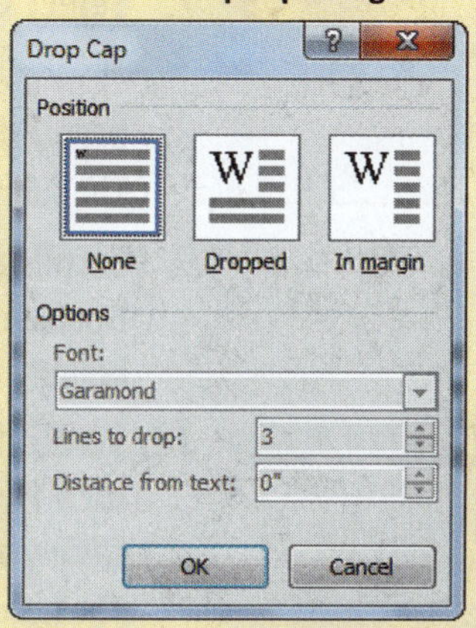

UNIT C

Word 2010

Copying Formats Using the Format Painter

You can dramatically change the appearance of text by applying different font styles, font effects, and character-spacing effects. For example, you can use the buttons in the Font group to make text darker by applying **bold** or to make text slanted by applying **italic**. When you are satisfied with the formatting of certain text, you can quickly apply the same formats to other text using the Format Painter. The **Format Painter** is a powerful Word feature that allows you to copy all the format settings applied to selected text to other text that you want to format the same way. You spice up the appearance of the text in the document by applying different font styles and effects.

STEPS

1. **Select immediate booking is essential in the first body paragraph, click the Bold button [B] on the Mini toolbar, select the entire paragraph, then click the Italic button [I]**
   "Immediate booking is essential" is bold, and the entire paragraph is formatted in italic.

QUICK TIP
To change the case of selected text from lowercase to uppercase—and visa versa—click the Change Case button in the Font group, and then select the case style you want to use.

2. **Select Last Minute Travel Deals, then click the launcher in the Font group**
   The Font dialog box opens, as shown in Figure C-5. You can use options on the Font tab to change the font, font style, size, and color of text, and to add an underline and apply font effects to text.
3. **Scroll down the Size list, click 48, click the Font color list arrow, click the Olive Green, Accent 3, Darker 25% color in the Theme Colors, then click the Text Effects button**
   The Format Text Effects dialog box opens. You use this dialog box to apply text effects, such as shadows, outlines, and reflections, to text.
4. **Click Shadow, click the Presets list arrow, click Offset Diagonal Bottom Right in the Outer section, click Close, click OK, then deselect the text**
   The text is larger, green, and has a shadow effect.
5. **Select Last Minute Travel Deals, right-click, click Font on the menu that opens, click the Advanced tab, click the Scale list arrow, click 80%, click OK, then deselect the text**
   You use the Advanced tab in the Font dialog box to change the scale, or width, of the selected characters, to alter the spacing between characters, or to raise or lower the characters. Decreasing the scale of the characters makes them narrower and gives the text a tall, thin appearance, as shown in Figure C-6.
6. **Scroll down, select the subheading Camel Safari, then, using the Mini toolbar, click the Font list arrow, click Trebuchet MS, click [B], click [I], click the Font Color list arrow, click the Olive Green, Accent 3, Darker 25% color in the Theme Colors, then deselect the text**
   The subheading is formatted in Trebuchet MS, bold, italic, and green.

TROUBLE
Move the pointer over the document text to see the pointer.

7. **Select Camel Safari, then click the Format Painter button in the Clipboard group**
   The pointer changes to .
8. **Scroll down, select Maharaja Experience with the pointer, then deselect the text**
   The subheading is formatted in Trebuchet MS, bold, italic, and green, as shown in Figure C-7.
9. **Scroll up as needed, select Rajasthan Desert Safari, then double-click**
   Double-clicking the Format Painter button allows the Format Painter to remain active until you turn it off. By keeping the Format Painter active, you can apply formatting to multiple items.

QUICK TIP
You can also press [Esc] to turn off the Format Painter.

10. **Scroll down, select the headings Everest Base Camp Trek, Cycling in Provence, and Inca Highlands Explorer with the pointer, click to turn off the Format Painter, then save your changes**
    The headings are formatted in 14-point Trebuchet MS bold with a purple font color.

FIGURE C-5: Font tab in Font dialog box

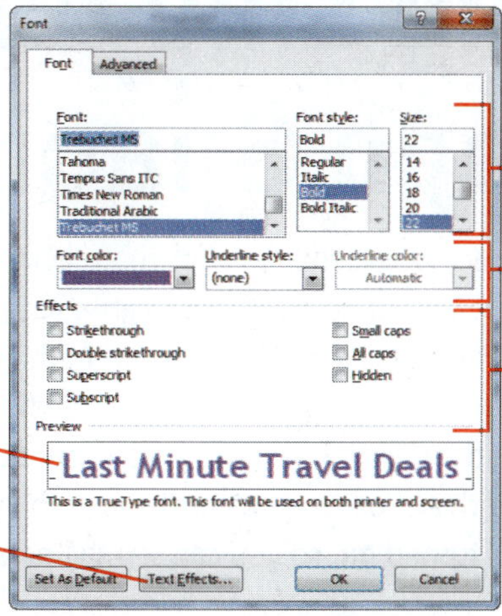

FIGURE C-6: Font and character spacing effects applied to text

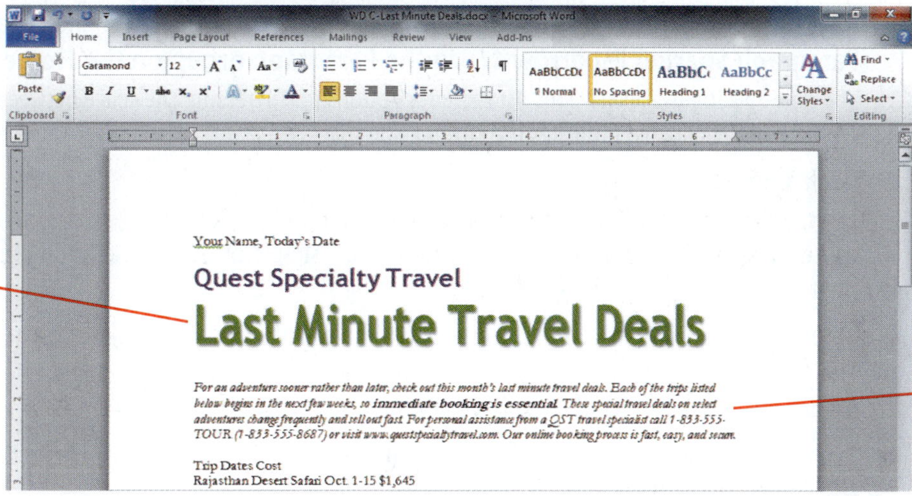

FIGURE C-7: Formats copied and applied using the Format Painter

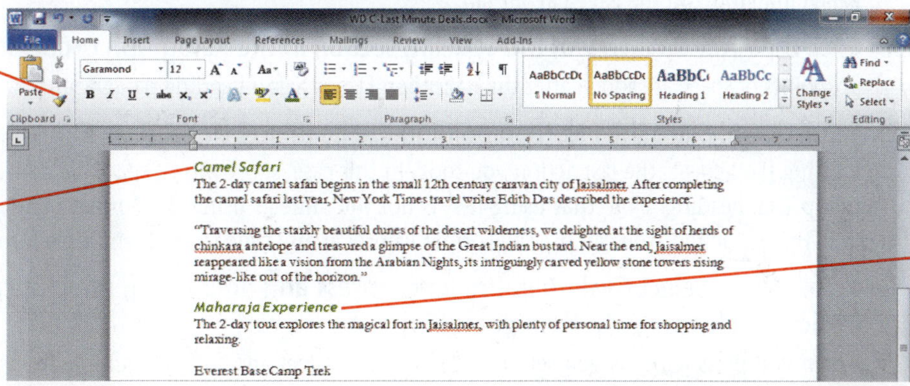

Underlining text

Another creative way to call attention to text and to jazz up the appearance of a document is to apply an underline style to words you want to highlight. The Underline list arrow in the Font group displays straight, dotted, wavy, dashed, and mixed underline styles, along with a gallery of colors to choose from. To apply an underline to text, simply select it, click the Underline list arrow, and then select an underline style from the list. For a wider variety of underline styles, click More Underlines in the list, and then select an underline style in the Font dialog box. You can change the color of an underline at any time by selecting the underlined text, clicking the Underline list arrow, pointing to Underline Color, and then choosing from the options in the color gallery. If you want to remove an underline from text, select the underlined text, and then click the Underline button.

Changing Line and Paragraph Spacing

Increasing the amount of space between lines adds more white space to a document and can make it easier to read. Adding space before and after paragraphs can also open up a document and improve its appearance. You use the Line and Paragraph Spacing list arrow in the Paragraph group on the Home tab to quickly change line spacing. To change paragraph spacing, you use the Spacing options in the Paragraph group on the Page Layout tab. Line and paragraph spacing are measured in points. You increase the line spacing of several paragraphs and add extra space under each heading to give the flyer a more open feel. You work with formatting marks turned on, so you can see the paragraph marks (¶).

STEPS

1. **Press [Ctrl][Home], click the Show/Hide ¶ button ¶ in the Paragraph group, place the insertion point in the italicized paragraph under the title, then click the Line and Paragraph Spacing list arrow in the Paragraph group on the Home tab**

   The Line Spacing list opens. This list includes options for increasing the space between lines. The check mark on the Line Spacing list indicates the current line spacing.

2. **Click 1.15**

   The space between the lines in the paragraph increases to 1.15 lines. Notice that you do not need to select an entire paragraph to change its paragraph formatting; simply place the insertion point in the paragraph you want to format.

> **QUICK TIP**
> Word recognizes any string of text that ends with a paragraph mark as a paragraph, including titles, headings, and single lines in a list.

3. **Select the five-line list that begins with "Trip Dates Cost", click , then click 1.5**

   The line spacing between the selected paragraphs changes to 1.5. To change the paragraph-formatting features of more than one paragraph, you must select the paragraphs.

4. **Scroll down, place the insertion point in the heading Rajasthan Desert Safari, then click the Page Layout tab**

   The paragraph spacing settings for the active paragraph are shown in the Before and After text boxes in the Paragraph group on the Page Layout tab.

> **QUICK TIP**
> You can also type a number in the Before and After text boxes.

5. **Click the After up arrow in the Spacing section in the Paragraph group so that 6 pt appears**

   Six points of space are added after the Rajasthan Desert Safari heading paragraph.

> **TROUBLE**
> If your [F4] key does not work, use the After up arrow to apply 6 pts of space to the headings listed in Steps 6 and 7, then continue with Step 8.

6. **Scroll down, place the insertion point in the heading Everest Base Camp Trek, then press [F4]**

   Pressing [F4] repeats the last action you took. In this case, six points of space are added after the Everest Base Camp Trek heading. Note that using [F4] is not the same as using the Format painter. Pressing [F4] repeats only the last action. You can use the Format Painter at any time to apply multiple format settings.

7. **Scroll down, select Cycling in Provence, press and hold [Ctrl], select Inca Highlands Explorer, release [Ctrl], then press [F4]**

   When you press [Ctrl] as you select items, you can select and format multiple items at once. Six points of space are added after each heading.

> **QUICK TIP**
> Adjusting the space between paragraphs is a more precise way to add white space to a document than inserting blank lines.

8. **Press [Ctrl][Home], place the insertion point in Last Minute Travel Deals, click the Before up arrow in the Spacing section in the Paragraph group twice so that 12 pt appears**

   The second line of the title has 12 points of space before it. Compare your document with Figure C-8.

9. **Click the Home tab, click ¶, then save your changes**

FIGURE C-8: Line and paragraph spacing applied to document

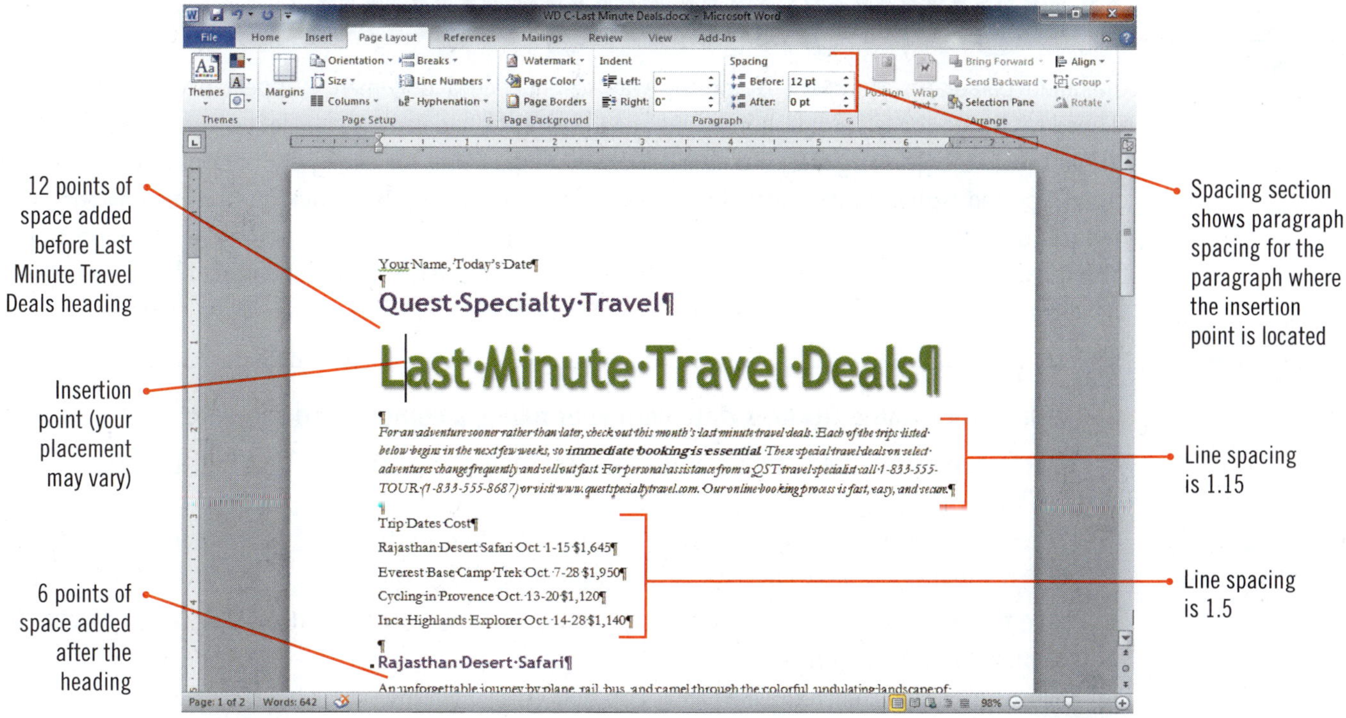

Word 2010

Formatting with Quick Styles

You can also apply multiple format settings to text in one step by applying a style. A **style** is a set of formats, such as font, font size, and paragraph alignment, that are named and stored together. Formatting a document with styles is a quick and easy way to give it a professional appearance. To make it even easier, Word includes sets of styles, called **Quick Styles**, that are designed to be used together in a document to make it attractive and readable. A Quick Style set includes styles for a title, several heading levels, body text, quotes, and lists. The styles in a Quick Style set use common fonts, colors, and formats so that using the styles together in a document gives the document a cohesive look.

To view the active set of Quick Styles, click the More button in the Styles group on the Home tab to expand the Quick Styles gallery, shown in Figure C-9. As you move the pointer over each style in the gallery, a preview of the style is applied to the selected text. To apply a style to the selected text, you simply click the style in the Quick Styles gallery. To remove a style from selected text, you click the Clear Formatting button in the Font group or in the Quick Styles gallery.

If you want to change the active set of Quick Styles to a Quick Style set with a different design, click the Change Styles button in the Styles group, point to Style Set, and then select the Quick Style set that best suits your document's content, tone, and audience. When you change the Quick Style set, a complete set of new fonts and colors is applied to the entire document. You can also change the color scheme or font used in the active Quick Style set by clicking the Change Styles button, pointing to Colors or to Fonts, and then selecting from the available color schemes or font options.

FIGURE C-9: Quick Styles gallery

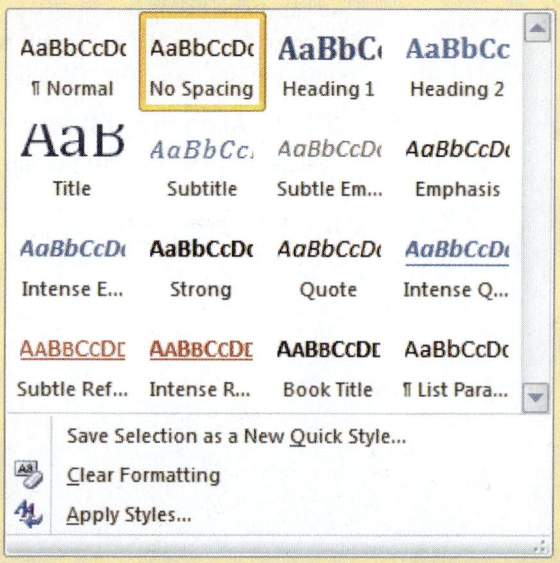

UNIT C

Word 2010

Aligning Paragraphs

Changing paragraph alignment is another way to enhance a document's appearance. Paragraphs are aligned relative to the left and right margins in a document. By default, text is **left-aligned**, which means it is flush with the left margin and has a ragged right edge. Using the alignment buttons in the Paragraph group, you can **right-align** a paragraph—make it flush with the right margin—or **center** a paragraph so that it is positioned evenly between the left and right margins. You can also **justify** a paragraph so that both the left and right edges of the paragraph are flush with the left and right margins. You change the alignment of several paragraphs at the beginning of the flyer to make it more visually interesting.

STEPS

TROUBLE

Click the View Ruler button at the top of the vertical scroll bar to display the rulers if they are not already displayed.

QUICK TIP

Click the Align Text Left button in the Paragraph group to left-align a paragraph.

1. **Replace Your Name, Today's Date with your name, a comma, and the date**
2. **Select your name, the comma, and the date, then click the Align Text Right button in the Paragraph group**

   The text is aligned with the right margin. In Page Layout view, the place where the white and shaded sections of the horizontal ruler meet shows the left and right margins.
3. **Place the insertion point between your name and the comma, press [Delete] to delete the comma, then press [Enter]**

   The new paragraph containing the date is also right-aligned. Pressing [Enter] in the middle of a paragraph creates a new paragraph with the same text and paragraph formatting as the original paragraph.
4. **Select the two-line title, then click the Center button in the Paragraph group**

   The two paragraphs that make up the title are centered between the left and right margins.
5. **Scroll down as needed, place the insertion point in the Rajasthan Desert Safari heading, then click**

   The Rajasthan Desert Safari heading is centered.
6. **Place the insertion point in the italicized paragraph under the title, then click the Justify button in the Paragraph group**

   The paragraph is aligned with both the left and right margins, as shown in Figure C-10. When you justify a paragraph, Word adjusts the spacing between words so that each line in the paragraph is flush with the left and the right margins.
7. **Place the insertion point in Rajasthan Desert Safari, then click the launcher in the Paragraph group**

   The Paragraph dialog box opens, as shown in Figure C-11. The Indents and Spacing tab shows the paragraph format settings for the paragraph where the insertion point is located. You can check or change paragraph format settings using this dialog box.
8. **Click the Alignment list arrow, click Left, click OK, then save your changes**

   The Rajasthan Desert Safari heading is left-aligned.

FIGURE C-10: Modified paragraph alignment

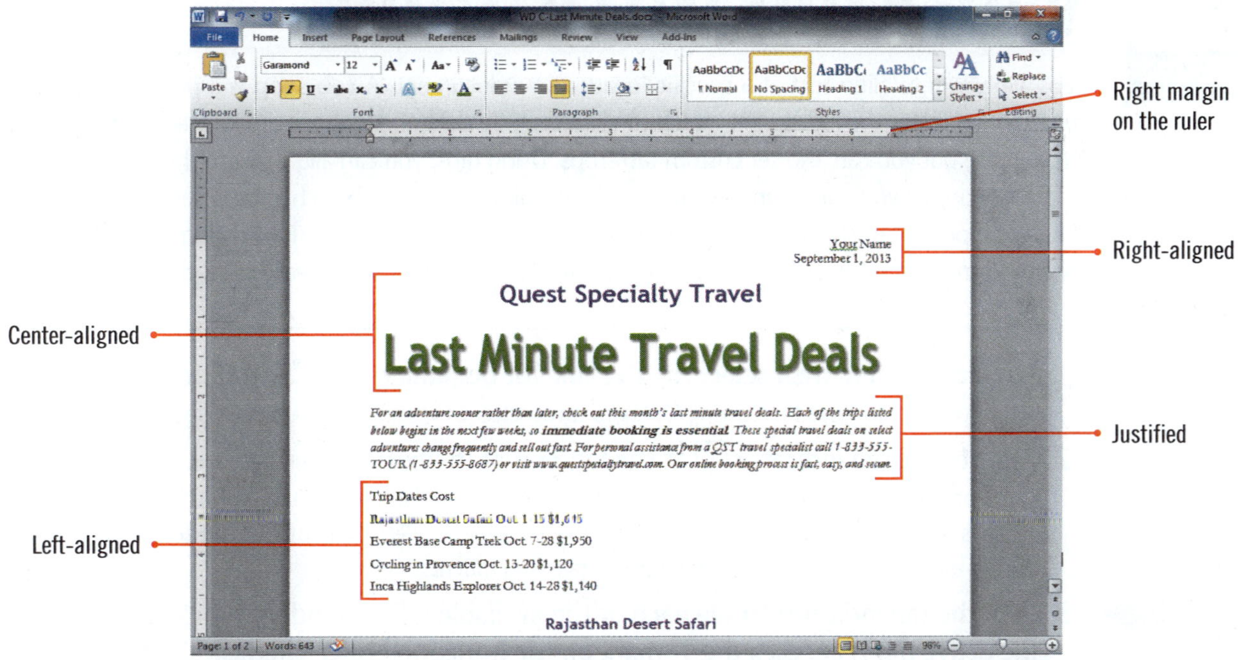

FIGURE C-11: Indents and Spacing tab in Paragraph dialog box

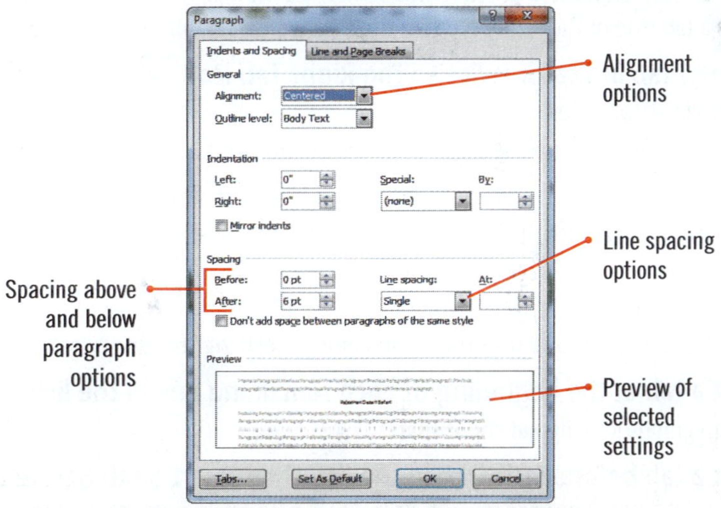

Formatting a document using themes

Changing the theme applied to a document is another powerful and efficient way to tailor a document's look and feel, particularly when a document is formatted with a Quick Style set. By default, all documents created in Word are formatted with the default Office theme—which uses Calibri as the font for the body text—but you can change the theme at any time to fit the content, tone, and purpose of a document. When you change the theme for a document, a complete set of new theme colors, fonts, and effects is applied to the whole document.

To preview how various themes look when applied to the current document, click the Themes button in the Themes group on the Page Layout tab, and then move the pointer over each theme in the gallery and notice how the document changes. When you click the theme you like, all document content that uses theme colors, all text that is formatted with a style, including default body text, and all table styles and graphic effects change to the colors, fonts, and effects used by the theme. In addition, the gallery of colors changes to display the set of theme colors, and the active Quick Style set changes to employ the theme colors and fonts. Note that changing the theme does not affect the formatting of text to which font formatting has already been applied, nor does it change any standard or custom colors used in the document.

If you want to tweak the document design further, you can modify it by applying a different set of theme colors, heading and body text fonts, or graphic effects. To do this, simply click the Theme Colors, Theme Fonts, or Theme Effects button in the Themes group, move the pointer over each option in the gallery to preview it in the document, and then click the option you like best.

UNIT
C
Word 2010

Working with Tabs

Tabs allow you to align text at a specific location in a document. A **tab stop** is a point on the horizontal ruler that indicates the location at which to align text. By default, tab stops are located every 1/2" from the left margin, but you can also set custom tab stops. Using tabs, you can align text to the left, right, or center of a tab stop, or you can align text at a decimal point or insert a bar character. Table C-1 describes the different types of tab stops. You set tabs using the horizontal ruler or the Tabs dialog box. You use tabs to format the summary information on last minute tour deals so it is easy to read.

STEPS

1. **Scroll as needed, then select the five-line list beginning with "Trip Dates Cost"**
   Before you set tab stops for existing text, you must select the paragraphs for which you want to set tabs.

2. **Point to the tab indicator at the left end of the horizontal ruler**
   The icon that appears in the tab indicator indicates the active type of tab; pointing to the tab indicator displays a ScreenTip with the name of the active tab type. By default, left tab is the active tab type. Clicking the tab indicator scrolls through the types of tabs and indents.

> **QUICK TIP**
> To remove a tab stop, drag it up or down off the ruler.

3. **Click the tab indicator to see each of the available tab and indent types, make Left Tab the active tab type, click the 1" mark on the horizontal ruler, then click the 3½" mark on the horizontal ruler**
   A left tab stop is inserted at the 1" mark and the 3½" on the horizontal ruler. Clicking the horizontal ruler inserts a tab stop of the active type for the selected paragraph or paragraphs.

4. **Click the tab indicator twice so the Right Tab icon is active, then click the 5" mark on the horizontal ruler**
   A right tab stop is inserted at the 5" mark on the horizontal ruler, as shown in Figure C-12.

5. **Place the insertion point before Trip in the first line in the list, press [Tab], place the insertion point before Dates, press [Tab], place the insertion point before Cost, then press [Tab]**
   Inserting a tab before "Trip" left-aligns the text at the 1" mark, inserting a tab before "Dates" left-aligns the text at the 3½" mark, and inserting a tab before "Cost" right-aligns "Cost" at the 5" mark.

6. **Insert a tab at the beginning of each remaining line in the list**
   The paragraphs left-align at the 1" mark.

> **QUICK TIP**
> Place the insertion point in a paragraph to see the tab stops for that paragraph on the horizontal ruler.

7. **Insert a tab before each Oct. in the list, then insert a tab before each $ in the list**
   The dates left-align at the 3½" mark. The prices right-align at the 5" mark.

8. **Select the five lines of tabbed text, drag the right tab stop to the 5½" mark on the horizontal ruler, then deselect the text**
   Dragging the tab stop moves it to a new location. The prices right-align at the 5½" mark.

> **QUICK TIP**
> Double-click a tab stop on the ruler to open the Tabs dialog box.

9. **Select the last four lines of tabbed text, click the launcher in the Paragraph group, then click the Tabs button at the bottom of the Paragraph dialog box**
   The Tabs dialog box opens, as shown in Figure C-13. You can use the Tabs dialog box to set tab stops, change the position or alignment of existing tab stops, clear tab stops, and apply tab leaders to tabs. **Tab leaders** are lines that appear in front of tabbed text.

10. **Click 3.5" in the Tab stop position list box, click the 2 option button in the Leader section, click Set, click 5.5" in the Tab stop position list box, click the 2 option button in the Leader section, click Set, click OK, deselect the text, then save your changes**
    A dotted tab leader is added before each 3.5" and 5.5" tab stop in the last four lines of tabbed text, as shown in Figure C-14.

FIGURE C-12: Left and right tab stops on the horizontal ruler

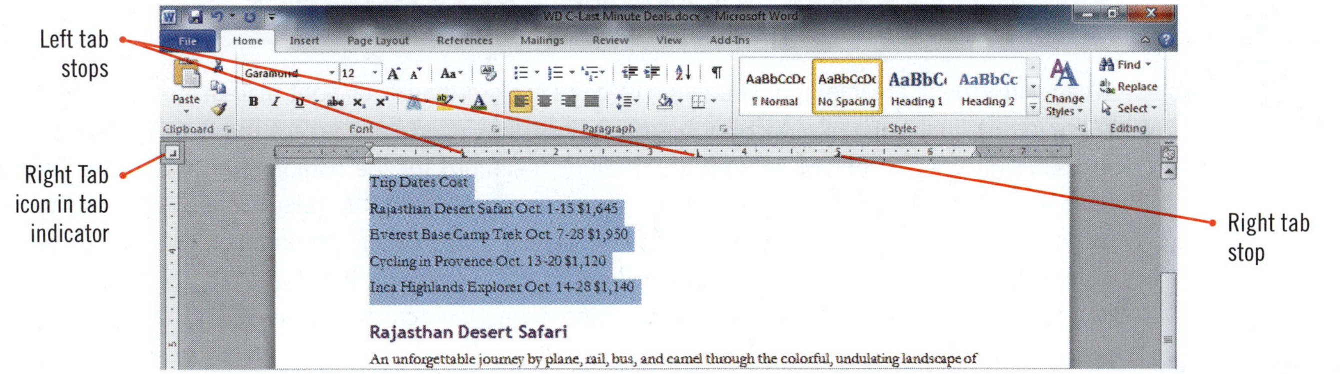

FIGURE C-13: Tabs dialog box

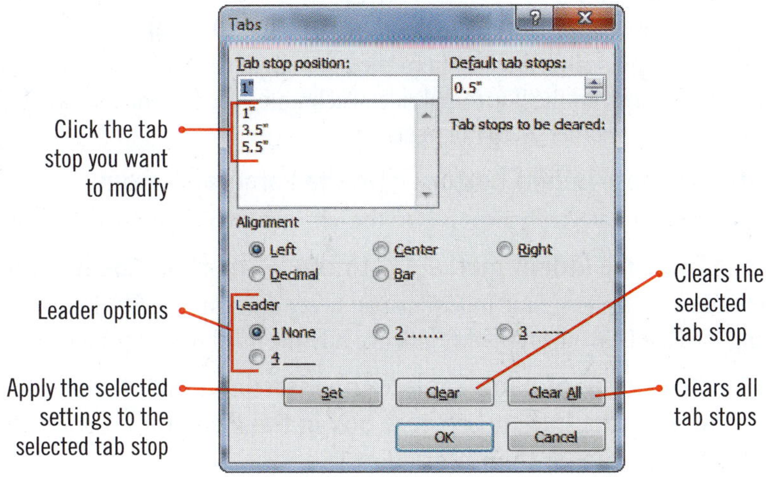

FIGURE C-14: Tab leaders

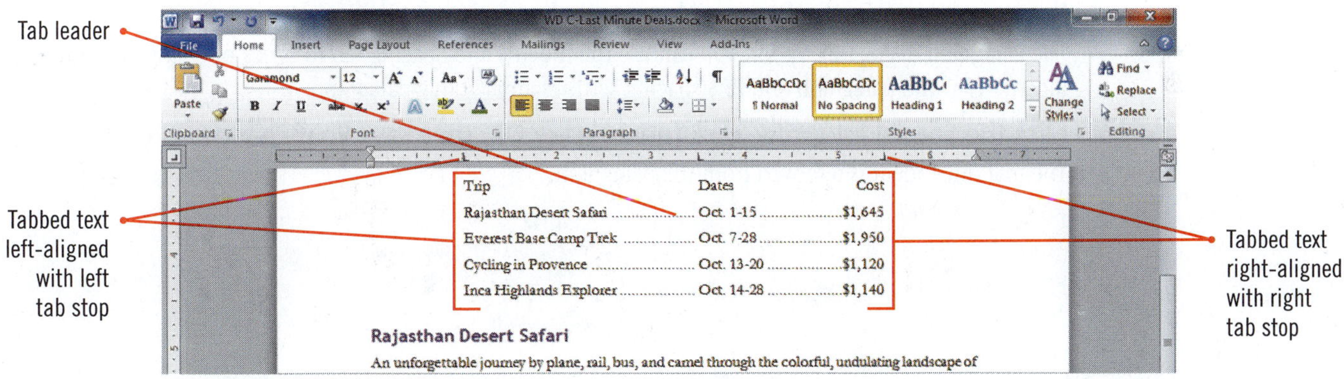

TABLE C-1: Types of tabs

tab	use to
Left tab	Set the start position of text so that text runs to the right of the tab stop as you type
Center tab	Set the center align position of text so that text stays centered on the tab stop as you type
Right tab	Set the right or end position of text so that text moves to the left of the tab stop as you type
Decimal tab	Set the position of the decimal point so that numbers align around the decimal point as you type
Bar tab	Insert a vertical bar at the tab position

UNIT C

Word 2010

Working with Indents

When you **indent** a paragraph, you move its edge in from the left or right margin. You can indent the entire left or right edge of a paragraph, just the first line, or all lines except the first line. The **indent markers** on the horizontal ruler indicate the indent settings for the paragraph in which the insertion point is located. Dragging an indent marker to a new location on the ruler is one way to change the indentation of a paragraph; changing the indent settings in the Paragraph group on the Page Layout tab is another; and using the indent buttons in the Paragraph group on the Home tab is a third. Table C-2 describes different types of indents and some of the methods for creating each. You indent several paragraphs in the flyer.

STEPS

QUICK TIP
Press [Tab] at the beginning of a paragraph to indent the first line ½".

1. **Press [Ctrl][Home], place the insertion point in the italicized paragraph under the title, then click the Increase Indent button in the Paragraph group on the Home tab**
   The entire paragraph is indented ½" from the left margin, as shown in Figure C-15. The indent marker also moves to the ½" mark on the horizontal ruler. Each time you click the Increase Indent button, the left edge of a paragraph moves another ½" to the right.

2. **Click the Decrease Indent button in the Paragraph group**
   The left edge of the paragraph moves ½" to the left, and the indent marker moves back to the left margin.

TROUBLE
Take care to drag only the First Line Indent marker. If you make a mistake, click the Undo button, then try again.

3. **Drag the First Line Indent marker to the ¼" mark on the horizontal ruler**
   Figure C-16 shows the First Line Indent marker being dragged. The first line of the paragraph is indented ¼". Dragging the First Line Indent marker indents only the first line of a paragraph.

4. **Scroll to the bottom of page 1, place the insertion point in the quotation, click the Page Layout tab, click the Indent Left text box in the Paragraph group, type .5, click the Indent Right text box, type .5, then press [Enter]**
   The left and right edges of the paragraph are indented ½" from the margins, as shown in Figure C-17.

5. **Press [Ctrl][Home], place the insertion point in the italicized paragraph, then click the launcher in the Paragraph group**
   The Paragraph dialog box opens. You can use the Indents and Spacing tab to check or change the alignment, indentation, and paragraph and line spacing settings applied to a paragraph.

6. **Click the Special list arrow, click (none), click OK, then save your changes**
   The first line indent is removed from the paragraph.

Clearing formatting

If you are unhappy with the way text is formatted, you can use the Clear Formatting command to return the text to the default format settings. The default format includes font and paragraph formatting: text is formatted in 11-point Calibri, and paragraphs are left-aligned with 1.15 point line spacing, 10 points of space below, and no indents. To clear formatting from text and return it to the default format, select the text you want to clear, and then click the Clear Formatting button in the Font group on the Home tab. If you prefer to return the text to the default font and remove all paragraph formatting, making the text 11-point Calibri, left-aligned, single spaced, with no paragraph spacing or indents, select the text and then simply click the No Spacing button in the Styles group on the Home tab.

FIGURE C-15: Indented paragraph

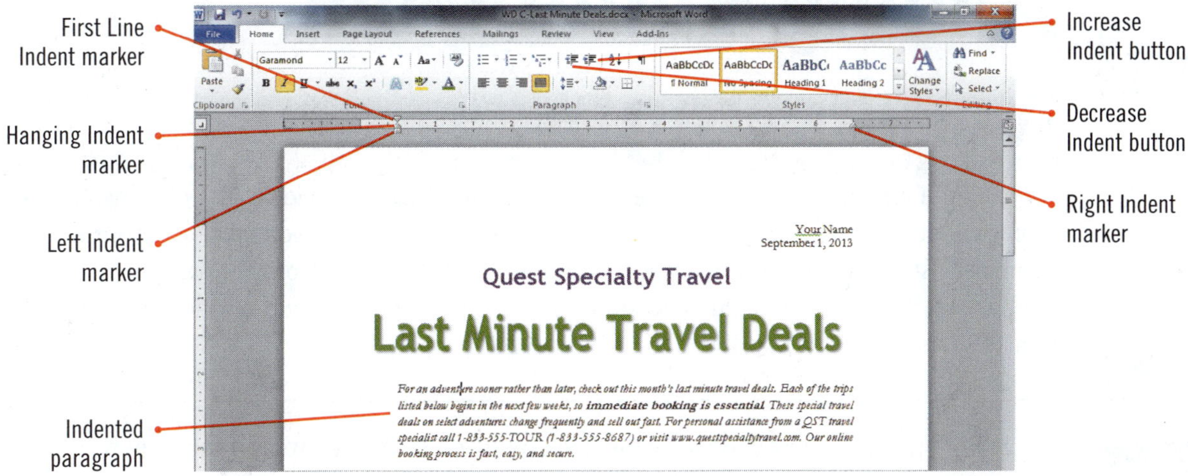

FIGURE C-16: Dragging the First Line Indent marker

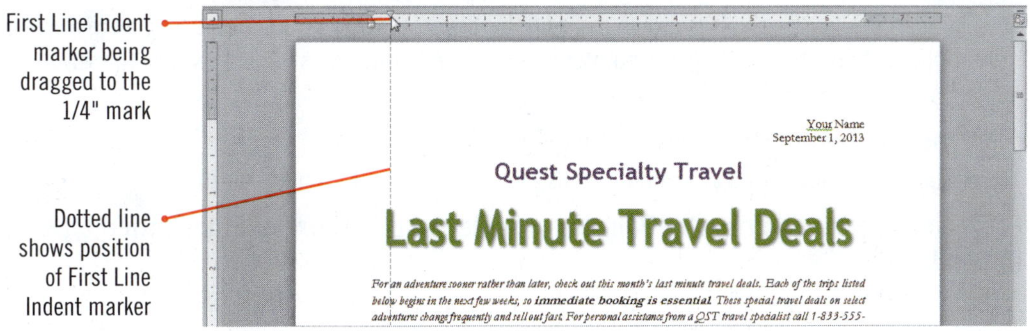

FIGURE C-17: Paragraph indented from the left and right

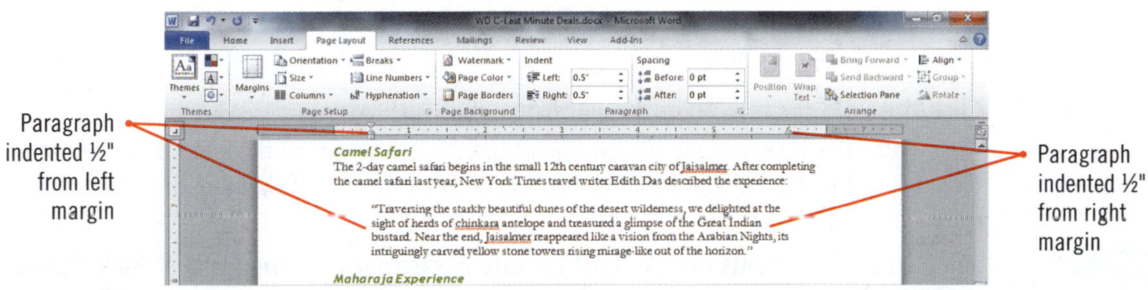

TABLE C-2: Types of indents

indent type: description	to create
Left indent: The left edge of a paragraph is moved in from the left margin	Drag the Left Indent marker on the ruler to the right to the position where you want the left edge of the paragraph to align
Right indent: The right edge of a paragraph is moved in from the right margin	Drag the Right Indent marker on the ruler to the left to the position where you want the right edge of the paragraph to align
First line indent: The first line of a paragraph is indented more than the subsequent lines	Drag the First Line Indent marker on the ruler to the right to the position where you want the first line of the paragraph to begin; or activate the First Line Indent marker in the tab indicator, and then click the ruler at the position where you want the first line of the paragraph to begin
Hanging indent: The subsequent lines of a paragraph are indented more than the first line	Drag the Hanging Indent marker on the ruler to the right to the position where you want the hanging indent to begin; or activate the Hanging Indent marker in the tab indicator, and then click the ruler at the position where you want the second and remaining lines of the paragraph to begin
Negative indent (or Outdent): The left edge of a paragraph is moved to the left of the left margin	Drag the Left Indent marker on the ruler to the left to the position where you want the negative indent to begin

UNIT C

Word 2010

Adding Bullets and Numbering

Formatting a list with bullets or numbering can help to organize the ideas in a document. A **bullet** is a character, often a small circle, that appears before the items in a list to add emphasis. Formatting a list as a numbered list helps illustrate sequences and priorities. You can quickly format a list with bullets or numbering by using the Bullets and Numbering buttons in the Paragraph group on the Home tab. You format the lists in your flyer with numbers and bullets.

STEPS

QUICK TIP
To change the style, font, number format, and alignment of the numbers in a list, right-click the list, point to Numbering, then click Define New Number Format.

QUICK TIP
To remove a bullet or number, select the paragraph(s), then click or .

QUICK TIP
To use a symbol or a picture for a bullet character, click Define New Bullet in the Bullet list, and then select from the options in the Define New Bullet dialog box.

1. **Scroll until the Everest Base Camp Trek heading is at the top of your screen**
2. **Select the three-line list of 3-day add-ons, click the Home tab, then click the Numbering list arrow in the Paragraph group**
   The Numbering Library opens, as shown in Figure C-18. You use this list to choose or change the numbering style applied to a list. You can drag the pointer over the numbering styles to preview how the selected text will look if the numbering style is applied.
3. **Click the numbering style shown in Figure C-18**
   The paragraphs are formatted as a numbered list.
4. **Place the insertion point after Pokhara — Valley of Lakes, press [Enter], then type Temples of Janakpur**
   Pressing [Enter] in the middle of the numbered list creates a new numbered paragraph and automatically renumbers the remainder of the list. Similarly, if you delete a paragraph from a numbered list, Word automatically renumbers the remaining paragraphs.
5. **Click 1 in the list**
   Clicking a number in a list selects all the numbers, as shown in Figure C-19.
6. **Click the Bold button in the Font group**
   The numbers are all formatted in bold. Notice that the formatting of the items in the list does not change when you change the formatting of the numbers. You can also use this technique to change the formatting of bullets in a bulleted list.
7. **Select the list of items under "Last minute participants in the Everest Base Camp trek…", then click the Bullets button in the Paragraph group**
   The four paragraphs are formatted as a bulleted list using the most recently used bullet style.
8. **Click a bullet in the list to select all the bullets, click the Bullets list arrow in the Paragraph group, click the check mark bullet style, click the document to deselect the text, then save your changes**
   The bullet character changes to a check mark, as shown in Figure C-20.

Creating multilevel lists

You can create lists with hierarchical structures by applying a multilevel list style to a list. To create a **multilevel list**, also called an outline, begin by applying a multilevel list style using the Multilevel List list arrow in the Paragraph group on the Home tab, then type your outline, pressing [Enter] after each item. To demote items to a lower level of importance in the outline, place the insertion point in the item, then click the Increase Indent button in the Paragraph group on the Home tab. Each time you indent a paragraph, the item is demoted to a lower level in the outline. Similarly, you can use the Decrease Indent button to promote an item to a higher level in the outline. You can also create a hierarchical structure in any bulleted or numbered list by using and to demote and promote items in the list. To change the multilevel list style applied to a list, select the list, click , and then select a new style.

FIGURE C-18: Numbering list

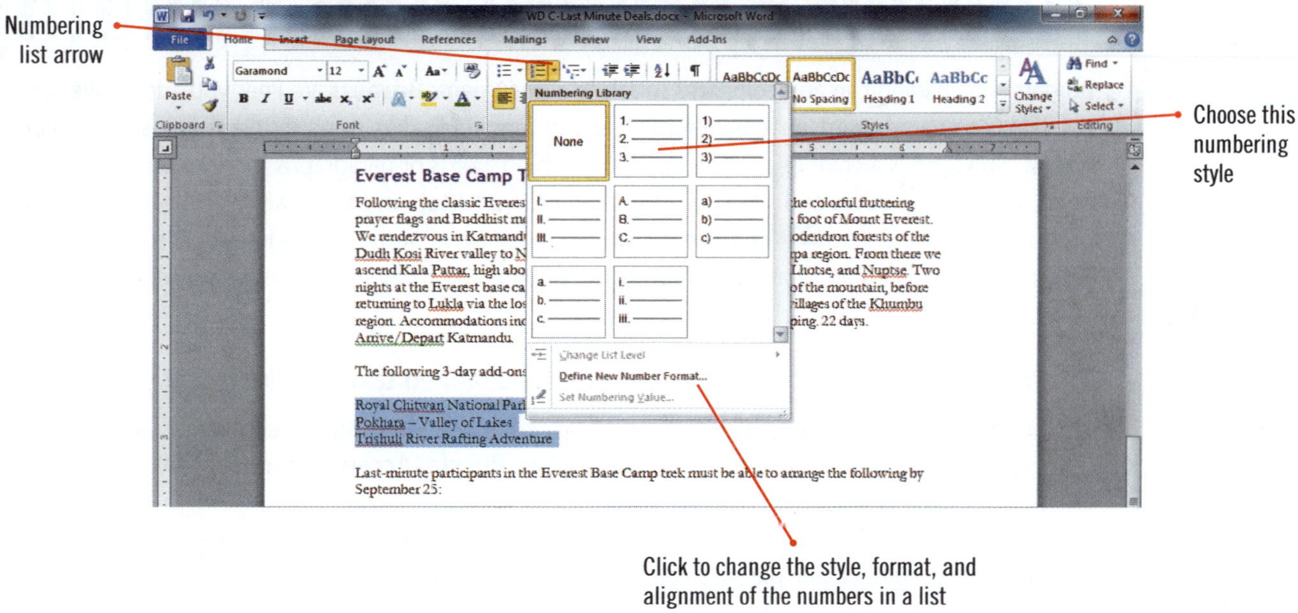

FIGURE C-19: Numbered list

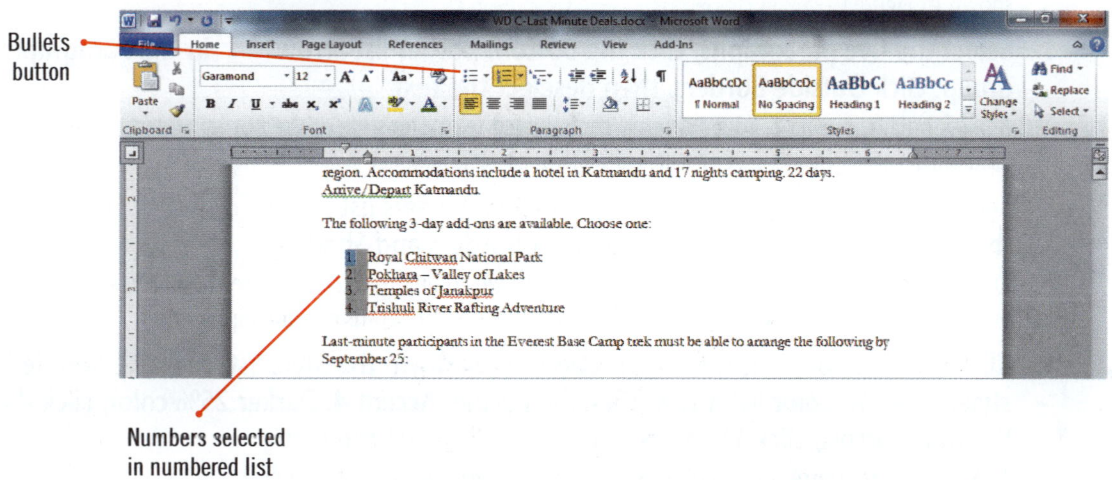

FIGURE C-20: Check mark bullets

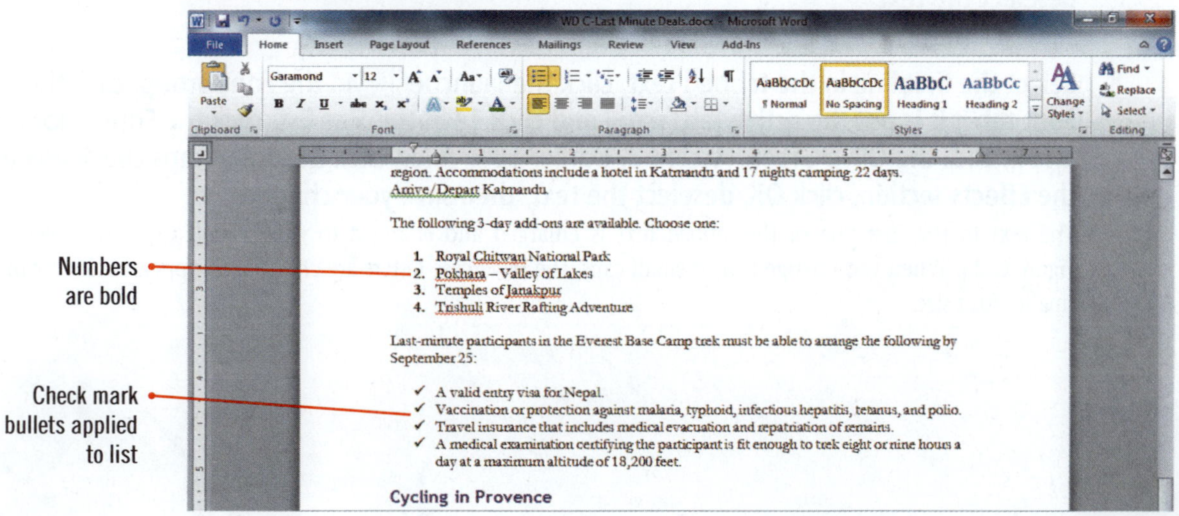

UNIT C
Word 2010

Adding Borders and Shading

Borders and shading can add color and splash to a document. **Borders** are lines you add above, below, to the side, or around words or paragraphs. You can format borders using different line styles, colors, and widths. **Shading** is a color or pattern you apply behind words or paragraphs to make them stand out on a page. You apply borders and shading using the Borders button and the Shading button in the Paragraph group on the Home tab. You enhance the tabbed text of the last minute tours schedule by adding shading to it. You also apply a border around the tabbed text to set it off from the rest of the document.

STEPS

1. **Press [Ctrl][Home], then scroll down until the tabbed text is at the top of your screen**
2. **Select the five paragraphs of tabbed text, click the Shading list arrow in the Paragraph group on the Home tab, click the Purple, Accent 4, Lighter 60% color, then deselect the text**

   Light purple shading is applied to the five paragraphs. Notice that the shading is applied to the entire width of the paragraphs, despite the tab settings.
3. **Select the five paragraphs, drag the Left Indent marker to the ¾" mark on the horizontal ruler, drag the Right Indent marker to the 5¾" mark, then deselect the text**

   The shading for the paragraphs is indented from the left and right, which makes it look more attractive, as shown in Figure C-21.
4. **Select the five paragraphs, click the Bottom Border list arrow in the Paragraph group, click Outside Borders, then deselect the text**

   A black outside border is added around the selected text. The style of the border added is the most recently used border style, in this case the default, a thin black line.
5. **Select the five paragraphs, click the Outside Borders list arrow, click No Border, click the No Border list arrow, then click Borders and Shading**

   The Borders and Shading dialog box opens, as shown in Figure C-22. You use the Borders tab to change the border style, color, and width, and to add boxes and lines to words or paragraphs.
6. **Click the Box box in the Setting section, scroll down the Style list, click the double-line style, click the Color list arrow, click the Purple, Accent 4, Darker 25% color, click the Width list arrow, click 1½ pt, click OK, then deselect the text**

   A 1½-point dark purple double-line border is added around the tabbed text.
7. **Select the five paragraphs, click the Bold button in the Font group, click the Font Color list arrow in the Font group, click the Purple, Accent 4, Darker 25% color, then deselect the text**

   The text changes to bold dark purple.
8. **Select the first line in the tabbed text, click the launcher in the Font group, click the Font tab if it is not the active tab, scroll and click 14 in the Size list, click the Font color list arrow, click the Olive Green, Accent 3, Darker 50% color, click the Small caps check box in the Effects section, click OK, deselect the text, then save your changes**

   The text in the first line of the tabbed text is enlarged and changed to green small caps, as shown in Figure C-23. When you change text to small caps, the lowercase letters are changed to uppercase letters in a smaller font size.

FIGURE C-21: Shading applied to the tabbed text

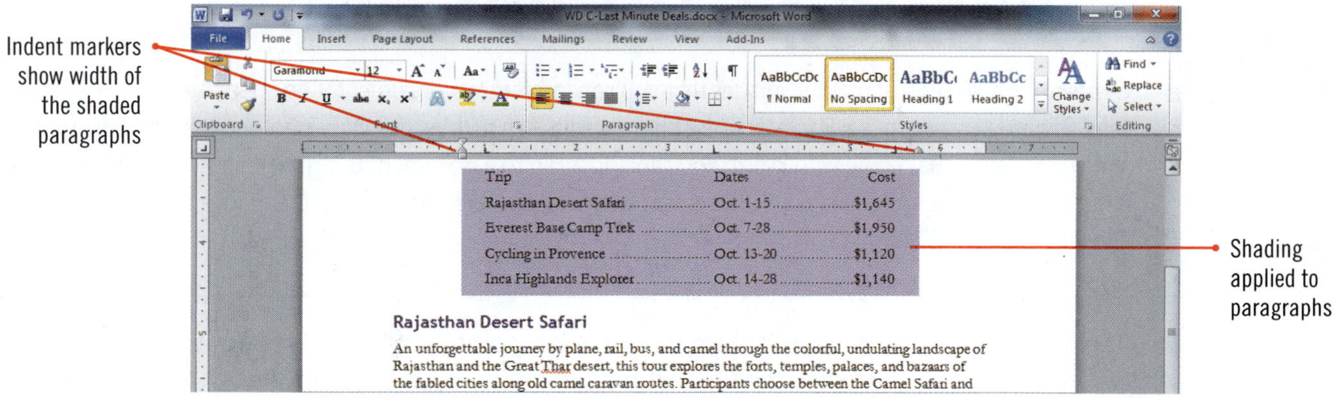

FIGURE C-22: Borders tab in Borders and Shading dialog box

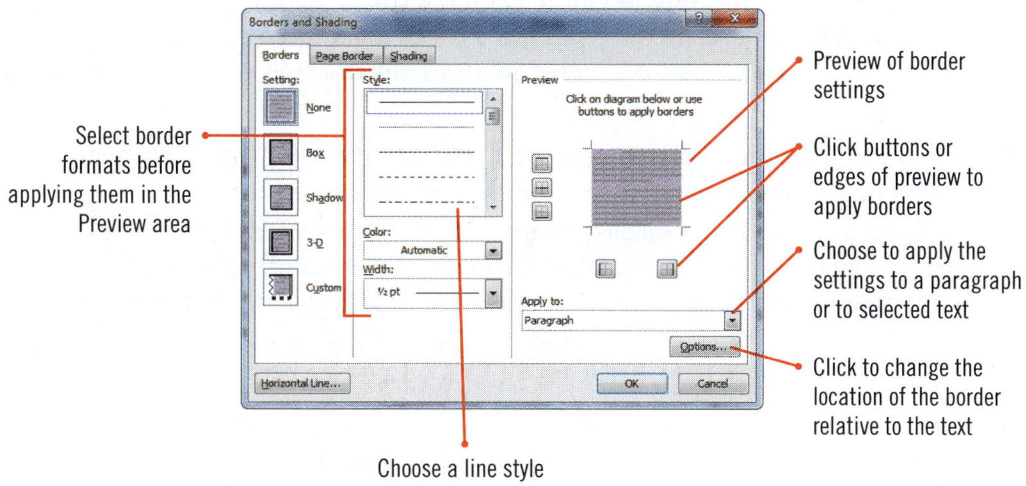

FIGURE C-23: Borders and shading applied to the document

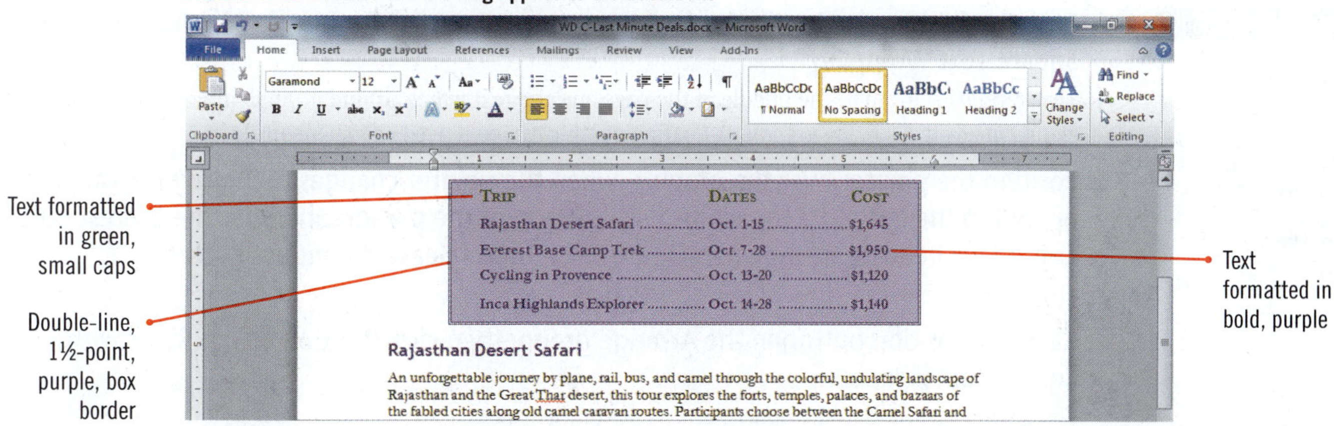

Highlighting text in a document

The Highlight tool allows you to mark and find important text in a document. **Highlighting** is transparent color that is applied to text using the Highlight pointer. To highlight text, click the Text Highlight Color list arrow in the Font group on the Home tab, select a color, then use the I-beam part of the pointer to select the text you want to highlight. Click to turn off the Highlight pointer. To remove highlighting, select the highlighted text, click, then click No Color. Highlighting prints, but it is used most effectively when a document is viewed on screen.

Inserting Clip Art

Clip art is a collection of graphic images that you can insert into a document. Clip art images are stored in the **Clip Organizer**, which is a library of the **clips**—media files such as graphics, photographs, sounds, movies, and animations—that come with Word. You can add a clip to a document using the Clip Art command on the Insert tab. Once you insert a clip art image, you can wrap text around it, resize it, enhance it, and move it to a different location. You illustrate the second page of the document with a clip art image.

STEPS

QUICK TIP
You must be working with an active Internet connection to complete this lesson.

1. **Scroll to the top of page 2, place the insertion point before Everest Base Camp Trek, click the Insert tab, then click the Clip Art button in the Illustrations group**
   The Clip Art task pane opens. You can use this task pane to search for clips related to a keyword.
2. **Select the text in the Search for text box if necessary, type Himalayas, make sure the Include Office.com content check box has a check mark, click the Results should be list arrow, make sure All media types has a check mark, then click Go**
   Clips that have the keyword "Himalayas" associated with them appear in the Clip Art task pane, as shown in Figure C-24.

TROUBLE
Select a different clip if the clip shown in Figure C-24 is not available to you. You can also search using the keyword "mountain."

3. **Point to the clip called out in Figure C-24, click the list arrow that appears next to the clip, click Insert on the menu, then close the Clip Art task pane**
   The clip is inserted at the location of the insertion point. When a graphic is selected, the active tab changes to the Picture Tools Format tab. This tab contains commands used to adjust, enhance, arrange, and size graphics. The white circles that appear on the square edges of the graphic are the **sizing handles**.
4. **Type 3.1 in the Shape Height text box in the Size group on the Picture Tools Format tab, then press [Enter]**
   The size of the graphic is reduced. When you decreased the height of the graphic, the width decreased proportionally. You can also resize a graphic proportionally by dragging a corner sizing handle. Now that the graphic is smaller, you can see that it was inserted at the location of the insertion point. Until you apply text wrapping to a graphic, it is part of the line of text in which it was inserted (an **inline graphic**). To move a graphic independently of text, you must make it a **floating graphic**.

QUICK TIP
To position a graphic using precise measurements, click the Position button, click More Layout Options, then adjust the settings on the Position tab in the Layout dialog box.

5. **Click the Position button in the Arrange group, then click Position in Middle Center with Square Text Wrapping**
   The graphic is moved to the middle of the page and the text wraps around it. Applying text wrapping to the graphic made it a floating graphic. A floating graphic can be moved anywhere on a page.
6. **Position the pointer over the graphic, when the pointer changes to drag the graphic up and to the left so its top aligns with the top of the paragraph under the Everest Base Camp Trek heading as shown in Figure C-25, then release the mouse button**
   The graphic is moved to the upper-left corner of the page.
7. **Click the Position button in the Arrange group, then click Position in Top Right with Square Text Wrapping**
   The graphic is moved to the upper-right corner of the page.
8. **Click the Picture Effects button in the Picture Styles group, point to Reflection, point to each reflection style to see a preview of the style applied to the graphic, then click Tight Reflection, touching**
   A reflection effect is applied to the graphic.

TROUBLE
If your document is longer than two pages, reduce the size of the clip art graphic by dragging the lower-left corner sizing handle up and to the right.

9. **Click the View tab, then click the Two Pages button**
   The completed document is shown in Figure C-26.
10. **Save your changes, submit the document to your instructor, then close the document and exit Word**

FIGURE C-24: Clip Art task pane

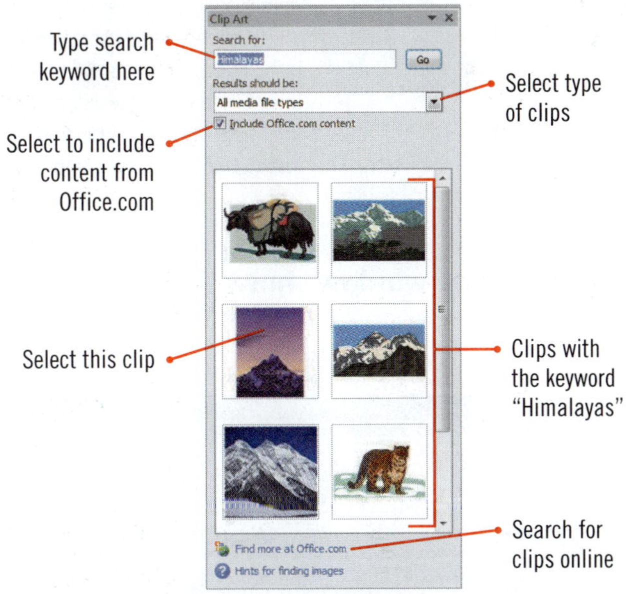

FIGURE C-25: Graphic being moved to a new location

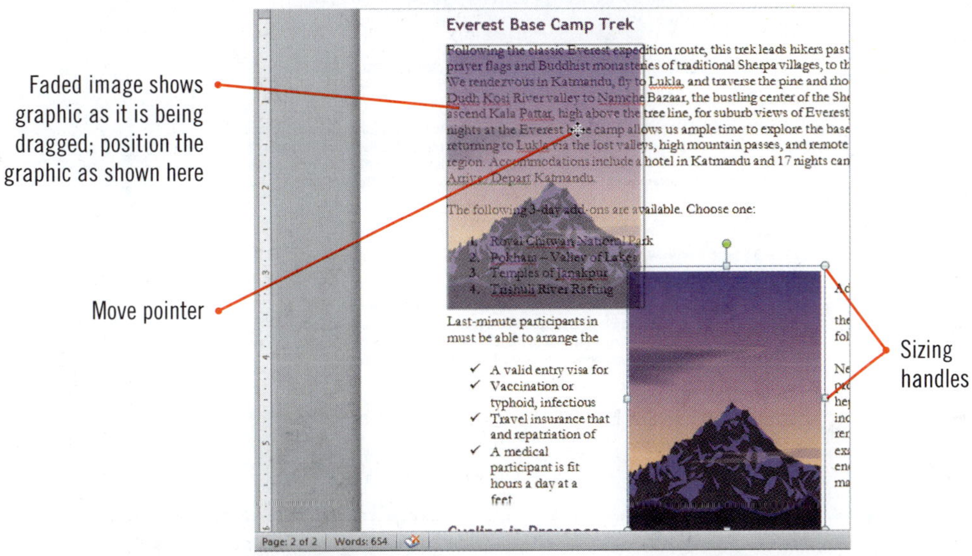

FIGURE C-26: Completed document

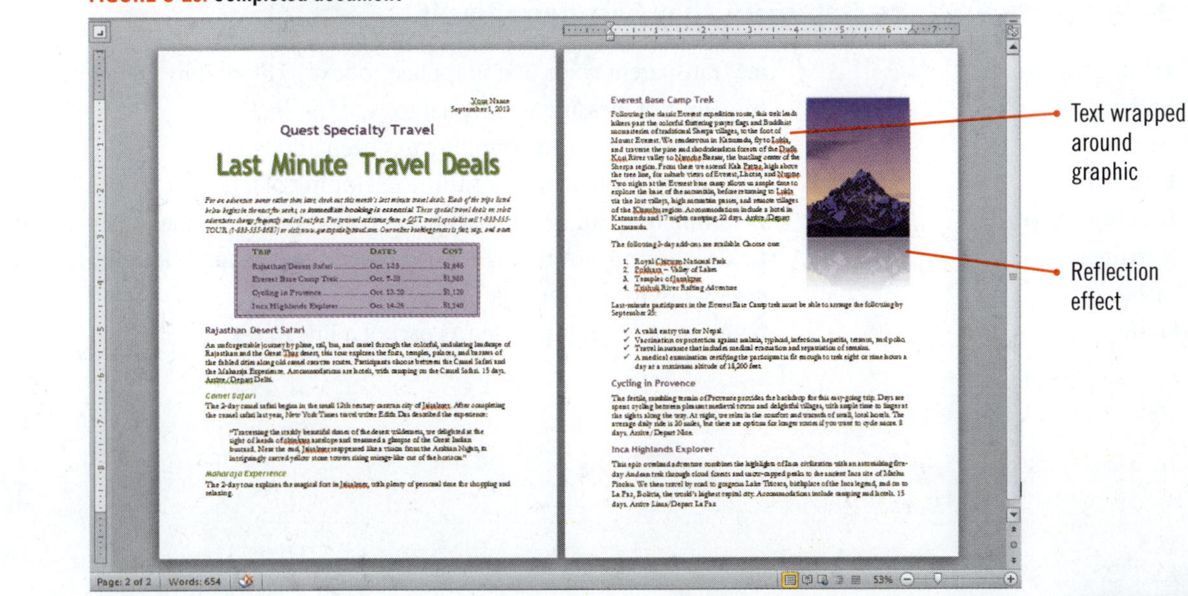

Practice

Concepts Review

For current SAM information, including versions and content details, visit SAM Central (http://www.cengage.com/samcentral). If you have a SAM user profile, you may have access to hands-on instruction, practice, and assessment of the skills covered in this unit. Since various versions of SAM are supported throughout the life of this text, check with your instructor for the correct instructions and URL/Web site for accessing assignments.

Label each element of the Word program window shown in Figure C-27.

FIGURE C-27

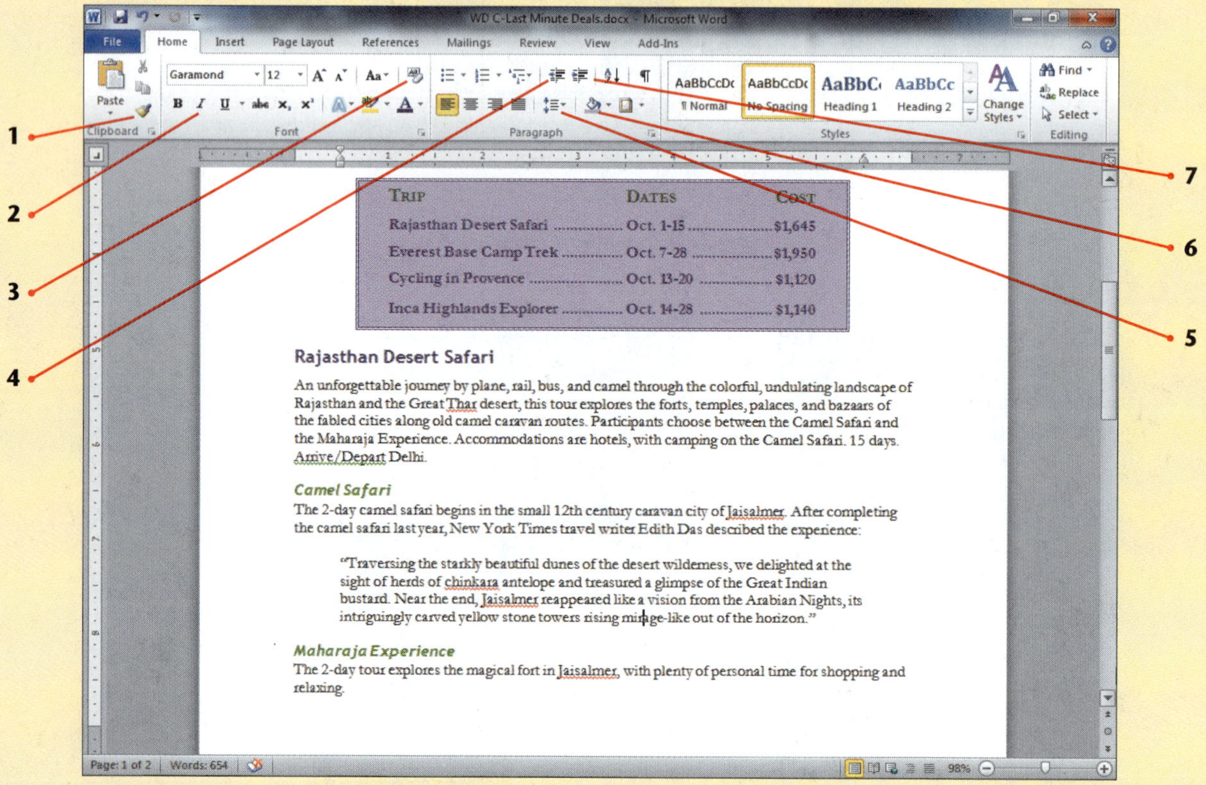

Match each term with the statement that best describes it.

8. Inline graphic
9. Shading
10. Point
11. Style
12. Floating graphic
13. Highlight
14. Bullet
15. Border

a. Transparent color that is applied to text to mark it in a document
b. A unit of measurement equal to 1/72 of an inch
c. An image that text wrapping has been applied to
d. A character that appears at the beginning of a paragraph to add emphasis
e. A line that can be applied above, below, or to the sides of a paragraph
f. Color or pattern that is applied behind text to make it look attractive
g. A set of format settings
h. An image that is inserted as part of a line of text

Select the best answer from the list of choices.

16. What is Calibri?

- **a.** A character format
- **b.** A style
- **c.** A font
- **d.** A text effect

17. Which type of indent results in subsequent lines of a paragraph being indented more than the first line?

- **a.** Right indent
- **b.** First line indent
- **c.** Negative indent
- **d.** Hanging indent

18. What is the most precise way to increase the amount of white space between two paragraphs?

- **a.** Indent the paragraphs
- **b.** Change the font size
- **c.** Change the before paragraph spacing for the second paragraph
- **d.** Change the line spacing of the paragraphs

19. Which button is used to align a paragraph with both the left and right margins?

- **a.** 
- **b.** 
- **c.** 
- **d.** 

20. Which dialog box is used to change the scale of characters?

- **a.** Tabs
- **b.** Font
- **c.** Paragraph
- **d.** Borders and Shading

Skills Review

1. Format with fonts.

- **a.** Start Word, open the file WD C-2.docx from the drive and folder where you store your Data Files, save it as **WD C-Arlington EDA Report**, then scroll through the document to get a feel for its contents.
- **b.** Press [Ctrl][A], then format the text in 12-point Californian FB. Choose a different serif font if Californian FB is not available to you.
- **c.** Press [Ctrl][Home], format the report title **Town of Arlington** in 28-point Berlin Sans FB Demi. Choose a different sans serif font if Berlin Sans FB Demi is not available to you.
- **d.** Change the font color of the report title to Red, Accent 2.
- **e.** Format the subtitle **Economic Development Authority Report Executive Summary** in 16-point Berlin Sans FB Demi, then press [Enter] before Executive in the subtitle.
- **f.** Format the heading **Mission Statement** in 14-point Berlin Sans FB Demi with the Red, Accent 2 font color.
- **g.** Press [Ctrl][Home], then save your changes to the report.

2. Copy formats using the Format Painter.

- **a.** Use the Format Painter to copy the format of the Mission Statement heading to the following headings: **Guiding Principles**, **Issues**, **Proposed Actions**.
- **b.** Show formatting marks, then format the paragraph under the Mission Statement heading in italic.
- **c.** Format **Years Population Growth**, the first line in the four-line list under the Issues heading, in bold, small caps, with Red, Accent 2, Darker 50% font color.
- **d.** Change the font color of the next two lines under Years Population Growth to Red, Accent 2, Darker 50%.
- **e.** Format the line **Source: Office of State Planning** in italic, then save your changes.

3. Change line and paragraph spacing.

- **a.** Change the line spacing of the three-line list under the first body paragraph to 1.5 lines.
- **b.** Add 6 points of space after the title Town of Arlington. Add 18 points of space before and 6 points of space after the Executive Summary line in the subtitle.
- **c.** Add 12 points of space after the Mission Statement heading, then add 12 points of space after each additional heading in the report (Guiding Principles, Issues, Proposed Actions).

Skills Review (continued)

- **d.** Add 6 points of space after each paragraph in the list under the Guiding Principles heading.
- **e.** Change the line spacing of the four-line list under the Issues heading that begins with Years Population Growth to 1.15.
- **f.** Add 6 points of space after each paragraph under the Proposed Actions heading.
- **g.** Press [Ctrl][Home], then save your changes to the report.

4. Align paragraphs.

- **a.** Press [Ctrl][A] to select the entire document, then justify all the paragraphs.
- **b.** Center the three-line report title.
- **c.** Press [Ctrl][End], type your name, press [Enter], type the current date, then right-align your name and the date.
- **d.** Save your changes to the report.

5. Work with tabs.

- **a.** Scroll up and select the four-line list of population information under the Issues heading.
- **b.** Set left tab stops at the 2" mark and the 3¾" mark.
- **c.** Insert a tab at the beginning of each line in the list.
- **d.** In the first line, insert a tab before Population. In the second line, insert a tab before 4.5%. In the third line, insert a tab before 53%.
- **e.** Select the first three lines, then drag the second tab stop to the 3" mark on the horizontal ruler.
- **f.** Press [Ctrl][Home], then save your changes to the report.

6. Work with indents.

- **a.** Indent the paragraph under the Mission Statement heading ½" from the left and ½" from the right.
- **b.** Indent the first line of the paragraph under the Guiding Principles heading ½".
- **c.** Indent the first line of the three body paragraphs under the Issues heading ½".
- **d.** Press [Ctrl][Home], then save your changes to the report.

7. Add bullets and numbering.

- **a.** Apply bullets to the three-line list under the first body paragraph. Change the bullet style to small black circles if that is not the current bullet symbol.
- **b.** Change the font color of the bullets to Red, Accent 2.
- **c.** Scroll down until the Guiding Principles heading is at the top of your screen.
- **d.** Format the six-paragraph list under Guiding Principles as a numbered list.
- **e.** Format the numbers in 14-point Berlin Sans FB Demi, then change the font color to Red, Accent 2.
- **f.** Scroll down until the Proposed Actions heading is at the top of your screen, then format the paragraphs under the heading as a bulleted list using check marks as the bullet style.
- **g.** Change the font color of the bullets to Red, Accent 2, press [Ctrl][Home], then save your changes to the report.

8. Add borders and shading.

- **a.** Add a 1-point Orange, Accent 6, Darker 25% border below the Mission Statement heading.
- **b.** Use the Format Painter or the F4 key to add the same border to the other headings in the report (Guiding Principles, Issues, Proposed Actions).
- **c.** Under the Issues heading, select the first three lines of tabbed text, which are formatted in red, then apply Orange, Accent 6, Lighter 40% shading to the paragraphs.
- **d.** Select the first three lines of tabbed text again if necessary, then add a 1½ -point Orange, Accent 6, Darker 25% single line box border around the paragraphs.
- **e.** Indent the shading and border around the paragraphs 1¾" from the left and 1¾" from the right.
- **f.** Turn off formatting marks, then save your changes.

9. Insert clip art.

- **a.** Press [Ctrl][Home], then open the Clip Art task pane.
- **b.** Search for clips related to the keyword **town**.

Skills Review (continued)

c. Insert the clip shown in Figure C-28, then close the Clip Art task pane. (*Note*: An active Internet connection is needed to select the clip shown in the figure. Select a different clip if this one is not available to you. It is best to select a clip that is similar in shape to the clip shown in Figure C-28.)

d. Select the graphic if necessary, then drag the upper-right sizing handle down and to the left so that the graphic is about 3" wide.

e. Use the Position command to position the clip art in the top left with square text wrapping.

f. Use the Shape Width text box in the Size group on the Format tab to change the width of the graphic to 2.2".

g. Apply an Offset Diagonal Bottom Right shadow style to the graphic.

h. Save your changes to the document, submit it to your instructor, close the file, and then exit Word.

FIGURE C-28

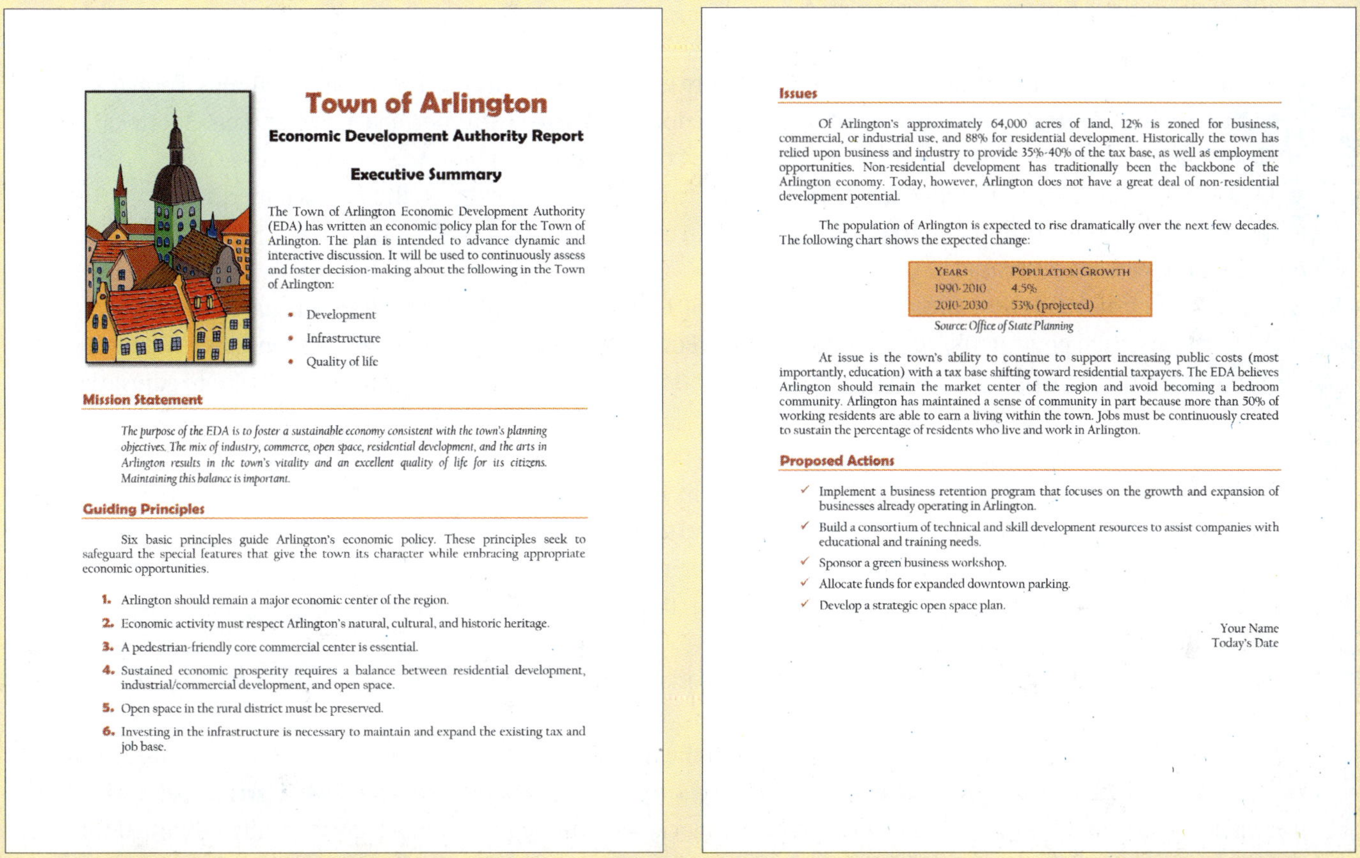

Town of Arlington

Economic Development Authority Report

Executive Summary

The Town of Arlington Economic Development Authority (EDA) has written an economic policy plan for the Town of Arlington. The plan is intended to advance dynamic and interactive discussion. It will be used to continuously assess and foster decision-making about the following in the Town of Arlington:

- Development
- Infrastructure
- Quality of life

Mission Statement

The purpose of the EDA is to foster a sustainable economy consistent with the town's planning objectives. The mix of industry, commerce, open space, residential development, and the arts in Arlington results in the town's vitality and an excellent quality of life for its citizens. Maintaining this balance is important.

Guiding Principles

Six basic principles guide Arlington's economic policy. These principles seek to safeguard the special features that give the town its character while embracing appropriate economic opportunities.

1. Arlington should remain a major economic center of the region.
2. Economic activity must respect Arlington's natural, cultural, and historic heritage.
3. A pedestrian-friendly core commercial center is essential.
4. Sustained economic prosperity requires a balance between residential development, industrial/commercial development, and open space.
5. Open space in the rural district must be preserved.
6. Investing in the infrastructure is necessary to maintain and expand the existing tax and job base.

Issues

Of Arlington's approximately 64,000 acres of land, 12% is zoned for business, commercial, or industrial use, and 88% for residential development. Historically the town has relied upon business and industry to provide 35%-40% of the tax base, as well as employment opportunities. Non-residential development has traditionally been the backbone of the Arlington economy. Today, however, Arlington does not have a great deal of non-residential development potential.

The population of Arlington is expected to rise dramatically over the next few decades. The following chart shows the expected change:

YEARS	POPULATION GROWTH
1990-2010	4.5%
2010-2030	53% (projected)

Source: Office of State Planning

At issue is the town's ability to continue to support increasing public costs (most importantly, education) with a tax base shifting toward residential taxpayers. The EDA believes Arlington should remain the market center of the region and avoid becoming a bedroom community. Arlington has maintained a sense of community in part because more than 50% of working residents are able to earn a living within the town. Jobs must be continuously created to sustain the percentage of residents who live and work in Arlington.

Proposed Actions

- ✓ Implement a business retention program that focuses on the growth and expansion of businesses already operating in Arlington.
- ✓ Build a consortium of technical and skill development resources to assist companies with educational and training needs.
- ✓ Sponsor a green business workshop.
- ✓ Allocate funds for expanded downtown parking.
- ✓ Develop a strategic open space plan.

Your Name
Today's Date

Independent Challenge 1

You are an estimator for GreenHome Construction in Springfield, Illinois. You have drafted an estimate for a home renovation job, and need to format it. It's important that your estimate have a clean, striking design, and reflect your company's professionalism.

If you have a SAM 2010 user profile, an autogradable SAM version of this assignment may be available at http://www.cengage.com/sam2010. Check with your instructor to confirm that this assignment is available in SAM. To use the SAM version of this assignment, log into the SAM 2010 Web site and download the instruction and start files.

a. Start Word, open the file WD C-3.docx from the drive and folder where you store your Data Files, save it as **WD C-GreenHome Construction**, then read the document to get a feel for its contents. Figure C-29 shows how you will format the letterhead.

FIGURE C-29

b. Select the entire document, change the style to No Spacing, then change the font to 12-point Times New Roman.

c. In the first line of the letterhead, format **Green Home** in 30-point Arial Black, then apply all caps. Format **Green** with the Olive Green, Accent 3, Darker 50% font color, format **Home** with the Olive Green, Accent 3 font color, then delete the space between the two words. Format **Construction** in 30-point Arial with an Olive Green, Accent 3, Darker 50% font color, then apply italic. (*Hint*: Type 30 in the Font Size text box, then press [Enter].)

d. Format the next line in 10-point Arial with an Olive Green, Accent 3, Darker 50% font color.

e. Center the two-line letterhead.

f. Add a 2¼-point dotted Olive Green, Accent 3, Darker 50% border below the address line paragraph.

g. With the insertion point in the address line, open the Borders and Shading dialog box, click Options to open the Border and Shading Options dialog box, change the Bottom setting to **5** points, then click OK twice to adjust the location of the border relative to the line of text.

h. Format the title **Proposal of Renovation** in 14-point Arial Black, then center the title.

i. Format the following headings (including the colons) in 11-point Arial Black: **Date**, **Work to be performed for and at**, **Scope of work**, **Payment schedule**, and **Agreement**.

j. Select the 14-line list under **Scope of work** that begins with **Demo of all...**, then change the paragraph spacing to add 4 points of space after each paragraph in the list. (*Hint*: Select 0 pt in the After text box, type 4, then press Enter.)

k. With the list selected, set a right tab stop at the 6¼" mark, insert tabs before every price in the list, then apply dotted line tab leaders.

l. Format the list as a numbered list, then apply bold to the numbers.

m. Apply bold to the two lines, **Total estimated job cost...** and **Approximate job time...** below the list.

n. Replace Your Name with your name in the signature block, select the signature block (Respectfully submitted through your name), set a left tab stop at the 3¼" mark, then indent the signature block using tabs.

o. Examine the document carefully for formatting errors, and make any necessary adjustments.

p. Save the document, submit it to your instructor, then close the file and exit Word.

Independent Challenge 2

Your employer, the Lange Center for Contemporary Arts in Halifax, Nova Scotia, is launching a membership drive. Your boss has written the text for a flyer advertising Lange membership, and asks you to format it so that it is eye catching and attractive.

FIGURE C-30

MEMBERSHIP DRIVE

2013

What we do for ARTISTS

Since 1982, the artist residency program at the Lange Center for Contemporary Arts has supported the work of more than 1500 artists from all over Canada and from 40 other nations. The residency awards include studio and living space, a monthly stipend to help artists with their expenses, and use of specialized equipment for all types of visual and performance art. Each artist gives a public lecture or performance at the Lange.

a. Open the file WD C-4.docx from the drive and folder where you store your Data Files, save it as **WD C-Membership Drive 2013**, then read the document. Figure C-30 shows how you will format the first several paragraphs of the flyer.

b. Select the entire document, change the style to No Spacing, then change the font to 11-point Arial Narrow.

c. Center the first line, **Membership Drive**, and apply shading to the paragraph. Choose a dark custom shading color of your choice for the shading color. (*Hint*: Click More Colors, then select a color from the Standard or Custom tab.) Format the text in 26-point Arial Narrow, bold, with a white font color. Expand the character spacing by 10 points. (*Hint*: Use the Advanced tab in the Font dialog box. Set the Spacing to Expanded, and then type **10** in the By text box.)

d. Format the second line, **2013**, in 36-point Arial Black. Expand the character spacing by 25 points, and change the character scale to 250%. Center the line.

e. Format each **What we do for...** heading in 12-point Arial, bold. Change the font color to the same custom color used for shading the title. (*Note*: The color now appears in the Recent Colors section of the Font Color gallery.) Add a single-line ½-point black border under each heading.

f. Format each subheading (**Gallery**, **Lectures**, **Library**, **All members...**, and **Membership Levels**) in 10-point Arial, bold. Add 3 points of spacing before each paragraph. (*Hint*: Select 0 in the Before text box, type 3, then press Enter.)

g. Indent each body paragraph ¼", except for the lines under the **What we do for YOU** heading.

h. Format the four lines under the **All members...** subheading as a bulleted list. Use a bullet symbol of your choice, and format the bullets in the custom font color.

i. Indent the five lines under the **Membership Levels** heading ¼". For these five lines, set left tab stops at the 1¼" mark and the 2" mark on the horizontal ruler. Insert tabs before the price and before the word All in each of the five lines.

j. Format the name of each membership level (**Artistic**, **Conceptual**, etc.) in 10-point Arial, bold, italic, with the custom font color.

k. Format the **For more information** heading in 14-point Arial, bold, with the custom font color, then center the heading.

l. Center the last two lines, replace Your Name with your name, then apply bold to your name.

Advanced Challenge Exercise

- Change the font color of **2013** to a dark gray, and add a shadow effect.
- Add a shadow effect to each **What we do for...** heading.
- Add a 3-point dotted black border above the **For more information** heading.

m. Examine the document carefully for formatting errors, and make any necessary adjustments.

n. Save the flyer, submit it to your instructor, then close the file and exit Word.

Independent Challenge 3

One of your responsibilities as program coordinator at Solstice Mountain Sports is to develop a program of winter outdoor learning and adventure workshops. You have drafted a memo to your boss to update her on your progress. You need to format the memo so it is professional looking and easy to read.

a. Start Word, open the file WD C-5.docx from the drive and folder where you store your Data Files, then save it as **WD C-Solstice Winter Memo**.

b. Select the heading **Solstice Mountain Sports Memorandum**, apply the Quick Style Title to it, then center the heading. (*Hint*: Open the Quick Style gallery, then click the Title style.)

c. In the memo header, replace Today's Date and Your Name with the current date and your name.

d. Select the four-line memo header, set a left tab stop at the ¾" mark, then insert tabs before the date, the recipient's name, your name, and the subject of the memo.

e. Apply the Quick Style Strong to **Date:**, **To:**, **From:**, and **Re:**.

f. Apply the Quick Style Heading 2 to the headings **Overview**, **Workshops**, **Accommodations**, **Fees**, and **Proposed winter programming**.

g. Under the Fees heading, apply the Quick Style Emphasis to the words **Workshop fees** and **Accommodations fees**.

h. Add a clip art graphic of a snowflake to the first page, wrap text around the graphic, then resize it and position it so it fits into the memo header below the title and aligns with the right margin.

i. On the second page of the document, format the list under the **Proposed winter programming** heading as a multilevel list. Figure C-31 shows the hierarchical structure of the outline. (*Hint*: Apply a multilevel list style, then use the Increase Indent and Decrease Indent buttons to change the level of importance of each item.)

j. Change the outline numbering style to the bullet numbering style shown in Figure C-31 if a different style is used in your outline.

k. Add a clip art graphic of a snowboarder or skier to page 2. Select a graphic that fits the tone of the document. Wrap text around the graphic, then resize it and position it so it aligns with the right margin.

FIGURE C-31

Proposed winter programming

- ❖ Skiing, Snowboarding, and Snowshoeing
  - ➢ Skiing and Snowboarding
    - ▪ Cross-country skiing
      - • Cross-country skiing for beginners
      - • Intermediate cross-country skiing
      - • Inn-to-inn ski touring
      - • Moonlight cross-country skiing
    - ▪ Telemarking
      - • Basic telemark skiing
      - • Introduction to backcountry skiing
      - • Exploring on skis
    - ▪ Snowboarding
      - • Backcountry snowboarding
  - ➢ Snowshoeing
    - ▪ Beginner
      - • Snowshoeing for beginners
      - • Snowshoeing and winter ecology
    - ▪ Intermediate and Advanced
      - • Intermediate snowshoeing
      - • Guided snowshoe trek
      - • Above tree line snowshoeing
- ❖ Winter Hiking, Camping, and Survival
  - ➢ Hiking
    - ▪ Beginner
      - • Long-distance hiking
      - • Winter summits
      - • Hiking for women
  - ➢ Winter camping and survival
    - ▪ Beginner
      - • Introduction to winter camping
      - • Basic winter mountain skills
      - • Building snow shelters
    - ▪ Intermediate
      - • Basic winter mountain skills II
      - • Ice climbing
      - • Avalanche awareness and rescue

Advanced Challenge Exercise

ACE

- Zoom out on the memo so that two pages are displayed in the document window, then, using the Change Styles button, change the style set to Modern.
- Using the Change Case button, change the title Solstice Mountain Sports Memorandum so that only the initial letter of each word is capitalized. Resize and reposition the clip art as needed so that it fits in the memo header and the title still fits on one line.
- Using the Themes button, change the theme applied to the document. Select a theme that works with the clip art graphics you chose.
- Using the Theme Fonts button, change the fonts to a font set of your choice. Choose fonts that allow the document to fit on two pages.
- Using the Theme Colors button, change the colors to a color palette of your choice.
- Apply different styles and adjust other formatting elements as necessary to make the memo attractive, eye catching, and readable. The finished memo should fit on two pages.

l. Save the document, submit it to your instructor, then close the file and exit Word.

Real Life Independent Challenge

The fonts you choose for a document can have a major effect on the document's tone. Not all fonts are appropriate for use in a business document, and some fonts, especially those with a definite theme, are appropriate only for specific purposes. In this Independent Challenge, you will use font formatting and other formatting features to design a letterhead and a fax coversheet for yourself or your business. The letterhead and coversheet should not only look professional and attract interest, but also say something about the character of your business or your personality. Figure C-32 shows an example of a business letterhead.

a. Start Word, and save a new blank document as **WD C-Personal Letterhead** to the drive and folder where you store your Data Files.

b. Type your name or the name of your business, your address, your phone number, your fax number, and your Web site or e-mail address.

c. Format your name or the name of your business in a font that expresses your personality or says something about the nature of your business. Use fonts, font colors, font effects, borders, shading, paragraph formatting, and other formatting features to design a letterhead that is appealing and professional.

d. Save your changes, submit the document to your instructor, then close the file.

e. Open a new blank document, and save it as **WD C-Personal Fax Coversheet**. Type FAX, your name or the name of your business, your address, your phone number, your fax number, and your Web site or e-mail address at the top of the document.

f. Type a fax header that includes the following: Date; To; From; Re; Number of pages, including cover sheet; and Comments.

g. Format the information in the fax coversheet using fonts, font effects, borders, shading, paragraph formatting, and other formatting features. Since a fax coversheet is designed to be faxed, all fonts and other formatting elements should be black.

h. Save your changes, submit the document to your instructor, close the file, then exit Word.

FIGURE C-32

Isabella Rodríguez Graphic Design

167 East 12th Street, 4th floor, New York, NY 10003 Tel: 212-555-9767 Fax: 212-555-2992 www.irodriguez.com

Visual Workshop

Open the file WD C-6.docx from the drive and folder where you store your Data Files. Create the menu shown in Figure C-33. (*Hints*: Find the clip art graphic using the keyword **diner**, then use the sizing handles to resize the graphic to be approximately 1.5" tall and 4.4" wide. Choose a different appropriate clip art graphic if the graphic shown in the figure is not available. Use Berlin Sans FB Demi and Calibri, or similar fonts, for the text. Change the font size of the café name to 28 points, the font size of Daily Specials to 18 points, the font size of the days to 14 points, and the font size of the descriptions to 12 points. Format the prices using tabs and leader lines. Use paragraph spacing to adjust the spacing between paragraphs so that all the text fits on one page. Make other adjustments as needed so your menu is similar to the one shown in Figure C-33.) Save the menu as **WD C-Nina's Trackside**, then submit a copy to your instructor.

FIGURE C-33

Nina's Trackside Café

Daily Specials

Monday

Chicken Cajun Bleu: Cajun chicken, chunky blue cheese, cucumbers, leaf lettuce, and tomato on our roasted garlic roll. $6.50

Tuesday

Clam Chowder: Classic New England thick, rich, clam chowder in our peasant French bread bowl. Served with a garden salad. $5.95

Wednesday

Veggie Chili: Hearty veggie chili with melted cheddar in our peasant French bread bowl. Topped with sour cream and scallions. $5.95

Thursday

French Dip: Lean roast beef topped with melted cheddar on our roasted garlic roll. Served with a side of au jus and red bliss mashed potatoes. $6.95

Friday

Turkey-Bacon Club: Double-decker roasted turkey, crisp bacon, leaf lettuce, tomato, and sun-dried tomato mayo on toasted triple seed. $6.50

Saturday

Greek Salad: Our large garden salad with Kalamata olives, feta cheese, and garlic vinaigrette. Served with an assortment of rolls. $5.95

Sunday

Hot Chicken and Gravy: Delicious chicken and savory gravy served on a thick slice of toasted honest white. Served with a garden salad. $6.95

Chef: Your Name

UNIT

D

Word 2010

Formatting Documents

Files You Will Need:

WD D-1.docx
WD D-2.docx
WD D-3.docx
WD D-4.docx
WD D-5.docx
WD D-6.docx
WD D-7.docx

The page-formatting features of Word allow you to lay out and design documents of all types, including reports, brochures, newsletters, and research documents. In this unit, you learn how to change the document margins, add page numbers, insert headers and footers, and format text in columns. You also learn how to work with the Word reference features to add footnotes, insert citations, and create a bibliography. You have written and formatted the text for an informational report for QST clients about staying healthy while traveling. You are now ready to format the pages. You plan to organize the text in columns, to illustrate the report with a table, and to add footnotes and a bibliography.

OBJECTIVES

- Set document margins
- Create sections and columns
- Insert page breaks
- Insert page numbers
- Add headers and footers
- Insert a table
- Add footnotes and endnotes
- Insert citations
- Manage sources and create a bibliography

UNIT
D
Word 2010

Setting Document Margins

Changing a document's margins is one way to change the appearance of a document and control the amount of text that fits on a page. The **margins** of a document are the blank areas between the edge of the text and the edge of the page. When you create a document in Word, the default margins are 1" at the top, bottom, left, and right sides of the page. You can adjust the size of a document's margins using the Margins command on the Page Layout tab or using the rulers. The report should be a four-page document when finished. You begin by reducing the size of the document margins so that more text fits on each page.

STEPS

TROUBLE
Click the View Ruler button at the top of the vertical scroll bar to display the rulers if they are not already displayed.

1. **Start Word, open the file WD D-1.docx from the drive and folder where you store your Data Files, then save it as WD D-Healthy Traveler**
   The report opens in Print Layout view.
2. **Scroll through the report to get a feel for its contents, then press [Ctrl][Home]**
   The report is currently five pages long. Notice that the status bar indicates the page where the insertion point is located and the total number of pages in the document.
3. **Click the Page Layout tab, then click the Margins button in the Page Setup group**
   The Margins menu opens. You can select predefined margin settings from this menu, or you can click Custom Margins to create different margin settings.
4. **Click Custom Margins**
   The Page Setup dialog box opens with the Margins tab displayed, as shown in Figure D-1. You can use the Margins tab to change the top, bottom, left, or right document margin, to change the orientation of the pages from portrait to landscape, and to alter other page layout settings. **Portrait orientation** means a page is taller than it is wide; **landscape orientation** means a page is wider than it is tall. This report uses portrait orientation. You can also use the Orientation button in the Page Setup group on the Page Layout tab to change the orientation of a document.
5. **Click the Top down arrow three times until 0.7" appears, then click the Bottom down arrow until 0.7" appears**
   The top and bottom margins of the report will be .7". Notice that the margins in the Preview section of the dialog box change as you adjust the margin settings.
6. **Press [Tab], type .7 in the Left text box, press [Tab], then type .7 in the Right text box**
   The left and right margins of the report will also be .7". You can change the margin settings by using the arrows or by typing a value in the appropriate text box.
7. **Click OK**
   The document margins change to .7", as shown in Figure D-2. The location of each margin (right, left, top, and bottom) is shown on the horizontal and vertical rulers at the intersection of the white and shaded areas. You can also change a margin setting by using the pointer to drag the intersection to a new location on the ruler.
8. **Click the View tab, then click the Two Pages button in the Zoom group**
   The first two pages of the document appear in the document window.
9. **Scroll down to view all five pages of the report, press [Ctrl][Home], click the Page Width button in the Zoom group, then save your changes**

QUICK TIP
You can also click the launcher in the Page Setup group to open the Page Setup dialog box.

QUICK TIP
The minimum allowable margin settings depend on your printer and the size of the paper you are using. Word displays a warning message if you set margins that are too narrow for your printer.

FIGURE D-1: Margins tab in Page Setup dialog box

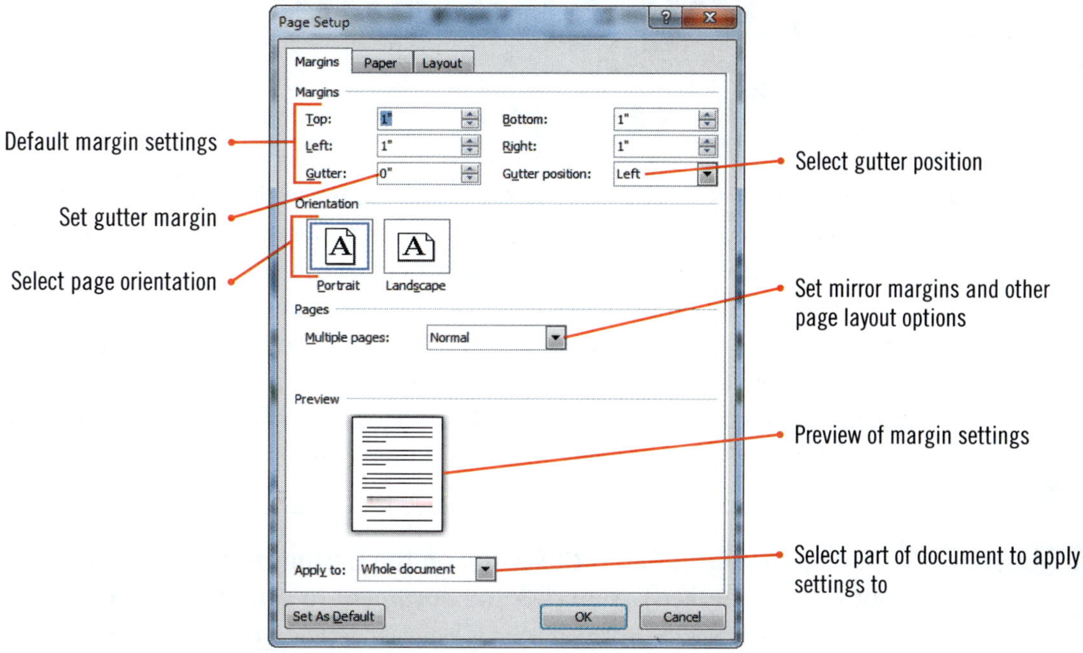

FIGURE D-2: Report with smaller margins

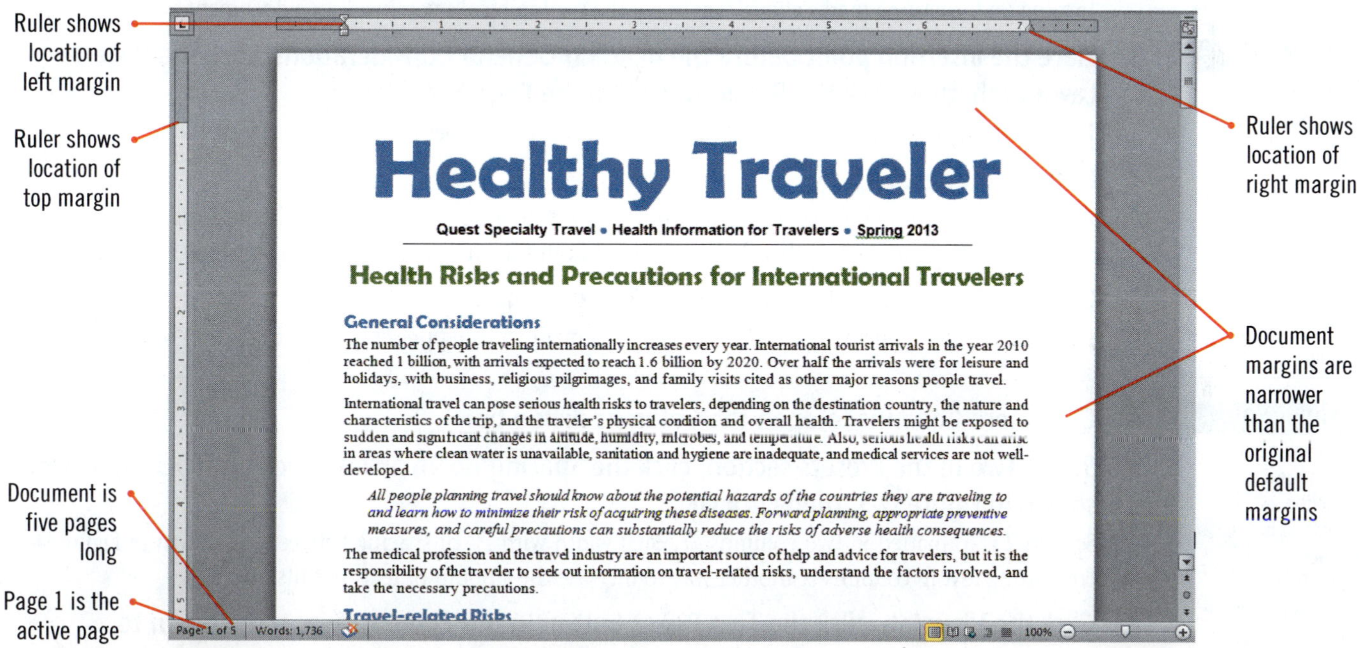

Changing orientation, margin settings, and paper size

By default, the documents you create in Word use an $8^1/_2" \times 11"$ paper size in portrait orientation with the default margin settings. You can change the orientation, margin settings, and paper size to common settings using the Orientation, Margins, and Size buttons in the Page Setup group on the Page Layout tab. You can also adjust these settings and others in the Page Setup dialog box. For example, to change the layout of multiple pages, use the Multiple pages list arrow on the Margins tab to create pages that use mirror margins, that include two pages per sheet of paper, or that are formatted using a book fold. **Mirror margins** are used in a document with facing pages, such as a magazine, where the margins on the left page of the document are a mirror image of the margins on the right page. Documents with mirror margins have inside and outside margins, rather than right and left margins. Another type of margin is a gutter margin, which is used in documents that are bound, such as books. A **gutter** adds extra space to the left, top, or inside margin to allow for the binding. Add a gutter to a document by adjusting the setting in the Gutter position text box on the Margins tab. To change the size of the paper used, use the Paper size list arrow on the Paper tab to select a standard paper size, or enter custom measurements in the Width and Height text boxes.

UNIT
D
Word 2010

Creating Sections and Columns

Dividing a document into sections allows you to format each section of the document with different page layout settings. A **section** is a portion of a document that is separated from the rest of the document by section breaks. **Section breaks** are formatting marks that you insert in a document to show the end of a section. Once you have divided a document into sections, you can format each section with different column, margin, page orientation, header and footer, and other page layout settings. By default, a document is formatted as a single section, but you can divide a document into as many sections as you like. You insert a section break to divide the document into two sections, and then format the text in the second section in two columns. First, you customize the status bar to display section information.

STEPS

1. **Right-click the status bar, click Section on the Customize Status Bar menu that opens (if it is not already checked), then click the document to close the menu**
   The status bar indicates the insertion point is located in section 1 of the document.

> **QUICK TIP**
> Use the Customize Status Bar menu to turn on and off the display of information in the status bar.

2. **Click the Home tab, then click the Show/Hide ¶ button ¶ in the Paragraph group**
   Turning on formatting marks allows you to see the section breaks you insert in a document.

3. **Place the insertion point before the heading General Considerations, click the Page Layout tab, then click the Breaks button in the Page Setup group**
   The Breaks menu opens. You use this menu to insert different types of section breaks. See Table D-1.

> **QUICK TIP**
> When you insert a section break at the beginning of a paragraph, Word inserts the break at the end of the previous paragraph. A section break stores the formatting information for the preceding section.

4. **Click Continuous**
   Word inserts a continuous section break, shown as a dotted double line, above the heading. The document now has two sections. Notice that the status bar indicates the insertion point is in section 2.

5. **Click the Columns button in the Page Setup group**
   The columns menu opens. You use this menu to format text using preset column formats or to create custom columns.

6. **Click More Columns to open the Columns dialog box**

> **QUICK TIP**
> When you delete a section break, you delete the section formatting of the text before the break. That text becomes part of the following section, and it assumes the formatting of that section.

7. **Select Two in the Presets section, click the Spacing down arrow twice until 0.3" appears as shown in Figure D-3, then click OK**
   Section 2 is formatted in two columns of equal width with .3" of spacing between, as shown in Figure D-4. Formatting text in columns is another way to increase the amount of text that fits on a page.

8. **Click the View tab, click the Two Pages button in the Zoom group, scroll down to examine all four pages of the document, press [Ctrl][Home], then save the document**
   The text in section 2—all the text below the continuous section break—is formatted in two columns. Text in columns flows automatically from the bottom of one column to the top of the next column.

TABLE D-1: Types of section breaks

section	function
Next page	Begins a new section and moves the text following the break to the top of the next page
Continuous	Begins a new section on the same page
Even page	Begins a new section and moves the text following the break to the top of the next even-numbered page
Odd page	Begins a new section and moves the text following the break to the top of the next odd-numbered page

FIGURE D-3: Columns dialog box

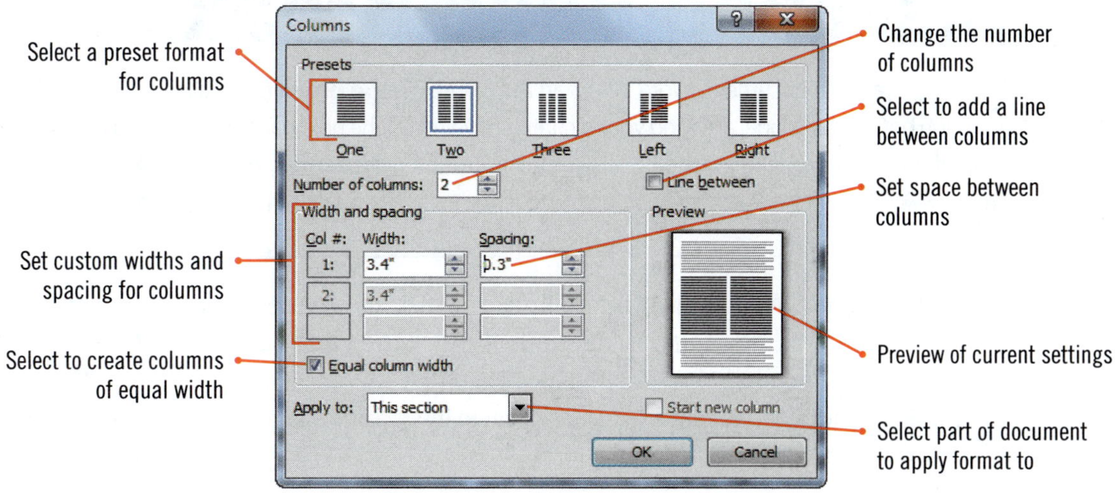

FIGURE D-4: Continuous section break and columns

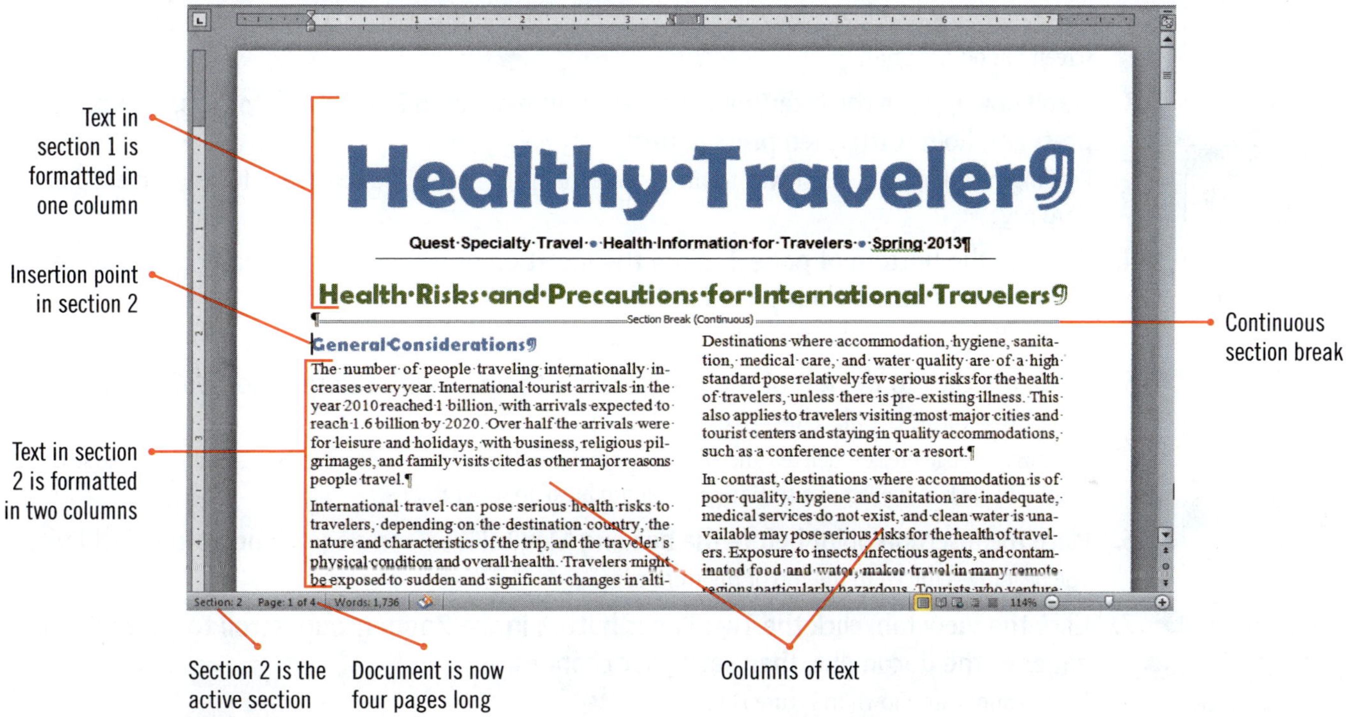

Word 2010

Changing page layout settings for a section

Dividing a document into sections allows you to vary the layout of a document. In addition to applying different column settings to sections, you can apply different margins, page orientation, paper size, vertical alignment, header and footer, page numbering, footnotes, endnotes, and other page layout settings. For example, if you are formatting a report that includes a table with many columns, you might want to change the table's page orientation to landscape so that it is easier to read. To do this, you would insert a section break before and after the table to create a section that contains only the table, and then you would change the page orientation of the section that contains the table to landscape. If the table does not fill the page, you could also change the vertical alignment of the table so that it is centered vertically on the page. To do this, use the Vertical alignment list arrow on the Layout tab of the Page Setup dialog box.

To check or change the page layout settings for an individual section, place the insertion point in the section, then open the Page Setup dialog box. Select any options you want to change, click the Apply to list arrow, click This section, then click OK. When you select This section in the Apply to list box, the settings are applied to the current section only. If you select Whole document in the Apply to list box, the settings are applied to all the sections in the document. Use the Apply to list arrow in the Columns dialog box or the Footnote and Endnote dialog box to change those settings for a section.

UNIT
D
Word 2010

Inserting Page Breaks

As you type text in a document, Word inserts an **automatic page break** (also called a soft page break) when you reach the bottom of a page, allowing you to continue typing on the next page. You can also force text onto the next page of a document by using the Breaks command to insert a **manual page break** (also called a hard page break). You insert manual page breaks where you know you want to begin each new page of the report.

STEPS

1. **Click the Page Width button, scroll to the bottom of page 1, place the insertion point before the heading Malaria: A Serious ..., click the Page Layout tab, then click the Breaks button in the Page Setup group**

   The Breaks menu opens. You also use this menu to insert page, column, and text-wrapping breaks. Table D-2 describes these types of breaks.

2. **Click Page**

   Word inserts a manual page break before "Malaria: A Serious Health Risk for Travelers" and moves all the text following the page break to the beginning of the next page, as shown in Figure D-5. The page break appears as a dotted line in Print Layout view when formatting marks are displayed. Page break marks are visible on the screen but do not print.

3. **Scroll down, place the insertion point before the heading Preventive Options... on page 2, press and hold [Ctrl], then press [Enter]**

   Pressing [Ctrl][Enter] is a fast way to insert a manual page break. The heading is forced to the top of the third page.

4. **Scroll to the bottom of page 3, place the insertion point before the heading Insurance for Travelers on page 3, then press [Ctrl][Enter]**

   The heading is forced to the top of the fourth page.

5. **Scroll up, click to the left of the page break on page 2 with the selection pointer to select the page break, then press [Delete]**

   The manual page break is deleted and the text from pages 2 and 3 flows together. You can also use the selection pointer to click to the left of a section or a column break to select it.

6. **Place the insertion point before the heading Medical Kit.... on page 2, then press [Ctrl][Enter]**

   The heading is forced to the top of the third page.

7. **Click the View tab, click the Two Pages button in the Zoom group, scroll to view all four pages of the document, then save your changes**

   Pages 3 and 4 are shown in Figure D-6.

QUICK TIP
To control the flow of text between columns, insert a column break to force the text after the break to the top of the next column.

QUICK TIP
You can also double-click a page break to select it, and then press [Delete] to delete it. You know the page break is selected when both the words and the paragraph mark at the end of the page break are selected.

QUICK TIP
You can balance columns of unequal length on a page by inserting a continuous section break at the end of the last column on the page.

Controlling automatic pagination

Another way to control the flow of text between pages (or between columns) is to apply pagination settings to specify where Word positions automatic page breaks. For example, you might want to make sure an article appears on the same page as its heading, or you might want to prevent a page from breaking in the middle of the last paragraph of a report. To manipulate automatic pagination, simply select the paragraphs(s) or line(s) you want to control, click the launcher in the Paragraph group on the Home or Page Layout tab, click the Line and Page Breaks tab in the Paragraph dialog box, select one or more of the following settings in the Pagination section, and then click OK. Pagination settings include the following:

- Keep with next setting—apply to any paragraph you want to appear together with the next paragraph on a single page in order to prevent the page from breaking between the paragraphs.
- Keep lines together setting—apply to selected paragraph or lines to prevent a page from breaking in the middle of a paragraph or between certain lines.
- Page break before setting—apply to specify that a selected paragraph follows an automatic page break.
- Widow/Orphan control setting—turned on by default in the Pagination section of the dialog box. This setting ensures that at least two lines of a paragraph appear at the top and bottom of every page. In other words, it prevents a page from beginning with just the last line of a paragraph (a **widow**), and prevents a page from ending with only the first line of a new paragraph (an **orphan**).

FIGURE D-5: Manual page break in document

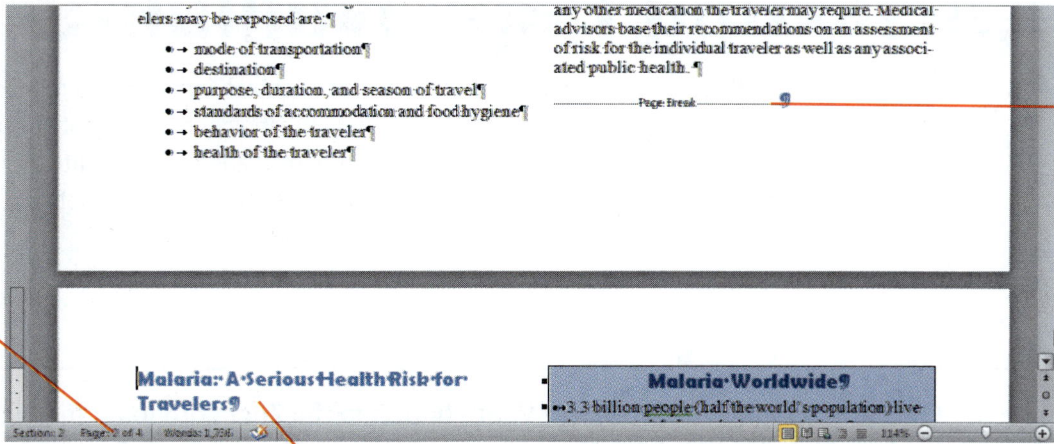

FIGURE D-6: Pages 3 and 4

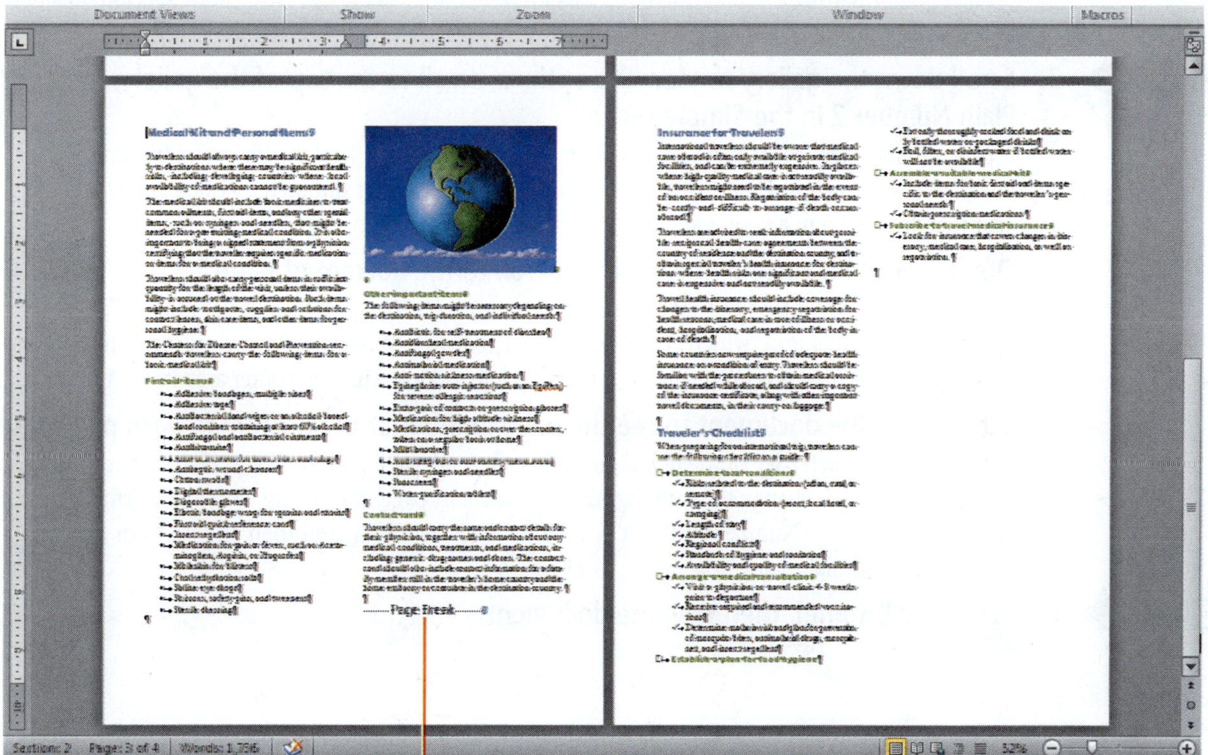

TABLE D-2: Types of breaks

break	function
Page	Forces the text following the break to begin at the top of the next page
Column	Forces the text following the break to begin at the top of the next column
Text Wrapping	Forces the text following the break to begin at the beginning of the next line

UNIT
D
Word 2010

Inserting Page Numbers

If you want to number the pages of a multiple-page document, you can insert a page number field to add a page number to each page. A **field** is a code that serves as a placeholder for data that changes in a document, such as a page number or the current date. When you use the Page Number button on the Insert tab to add page numbers to a document, you insert the page number field at the top, bottom, or side of any page, and Word automatically numbers all the pages in the document for you. You insert a page number field so that page numbers will appear centered between the margins at the bottom of each page in the document.

STEPS

QUICK TIP
Point to Current Position to insert a page number field at the location of the insertion point.

1. **Press [Ctrl][Home], click the Page Width button in the Zoom group on the View tab, click the Insert tab, then click the Page Number button in the Header & Footer group**

   The Page Number menu opens. You use this menu to select the position for the page numbers. If you choose to add a page number field to the top, bottom, or side of a document, a page number will appear on every page in the document. If you choose to insert it in the document at the location of the insertion point, the field will appear on that page only.

2. **Point to Bottom of Page**

   A gallery of formatting and alignment options for page numbers to be inserted at the bottom of a page opens, as shown in Figure D-7.

QUICK TIP
To change the location or formatting of page numbers, click the Page Number button, point to a page number location, then select a format from the gallery.

3. **Scroll down the gallery to view the options, scroll to the top of the gallery, then click Plain Number 2 in the Simple section**

   A page number field containing the number 1 is centered in the Footer area at the bottom of page 1 of the document, as shown in Figure D-8. The document text is gray, or dimmed, because the Footer area is open. Text that is inserted in a Footer area appears at the bottom of every page in a document.

4. **Double-click the document text, then scroll to the bottom of page 1**

   Double-clicking the document text closes the Footer area. The page number is now dimmed because it is located in the Footer area, which is no longer the active area. When the document is printed, the page numbers appear as normal text. You will learn more about working with the Footer area in the next lesson.

5. **Scroll down the document to see the page number at the bottom of each page**

   Word numbered each page of the report automatically, and each page number is centered at the bottom of the page. If you want to change the numbering format or start page numbering with a different number, you can simply click the Page Number button, click Format Page Numbers, and then choose from the options in the Page Number Format dialog box.

QUICK TIP
To remove page numbers from a document, click the Page Number button, then click Remove Page Numbers.

6. **Press [Ctrl][Home], then save the document**

Moving around in a long document

Rather than scrolling to move to a different place in a long document, you can use the Browse by Object feature to move the insertion point to a specific location quickly. Browse by Object allows you to browse to the next or previous page, section, line, table, graphic, or other item of the same type in a document. To do this, first click the Select Browse Object button below the vertical scroll bar to open a palette of object types. On this palette, click the button for the type of item you want to browse through, and then click the Next or Previous buttons to scroll through the items of that type in the document.

FIGURE D-7: Page Number gallery

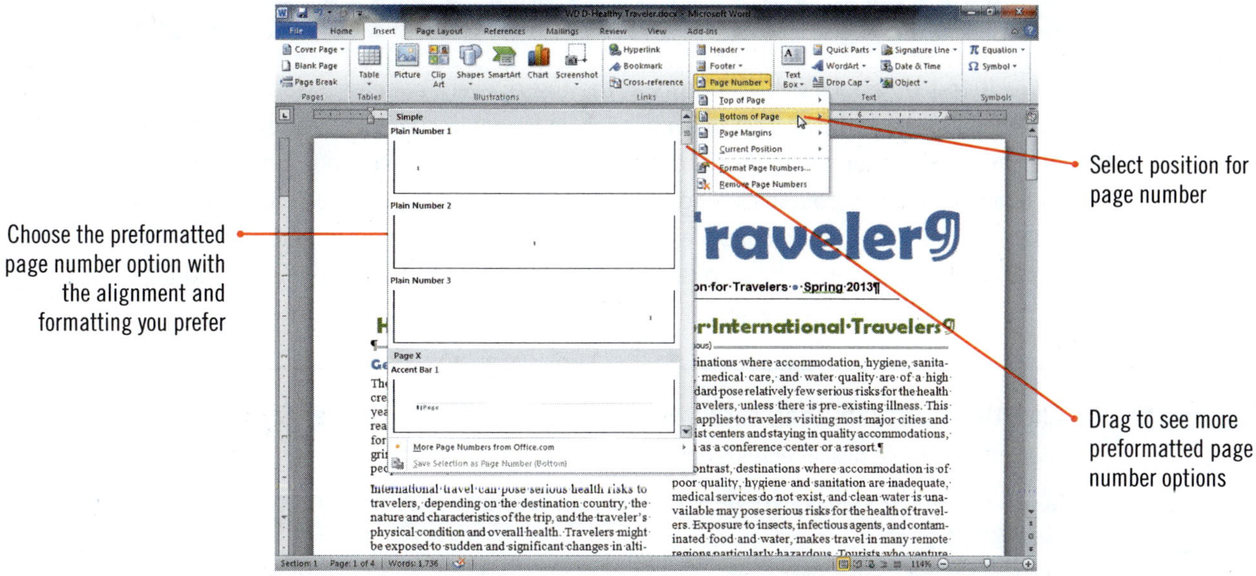

FIGURE D-8: Page number in document

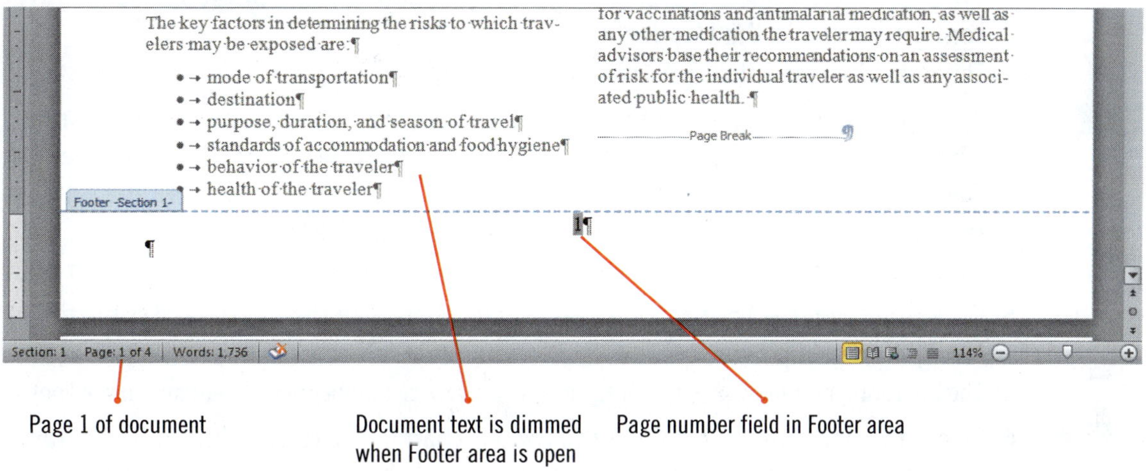

Inserting Quick Parts

The Word Quick Parts feature makes it easy to insert reusable pieces of content into a document quickly. The **Quick Parts** items you can insert include fields, such as for the current date or the total number of pages in a document; document property information, such as the author and title of a document; and building blocks, which are customized content that you create, format, and save for future use.

To insert a Quick Part into a document at the location of the insertion point, click the Quick Parts button in the Text group on the Insert tab (or, if headers and footers are open, click the Quick Parts button in the Insert group on the Header & Footer Tools Design tab), and then select the type of Quick Part you want to insert. To insert a field into a document, click Field on the Quick Parts menu that opens, click the name of the field you want to insert in the Field dialog box, and then click OK. Field information is updated automatically each time the document is opened or saved.

To insert a document property, point to Document Property on the Quick Parts menu, and then click the property you want to insert. The property is added to the document as a content control and contains the document property information you entered in the Document panel. If you did not assign a document property, the content control contains a placeholder, which you can replace with your own text. Once you replace the placeholder text—or edit the document property information that appears in the content control—this text replaces the document property information in the Document panel.

To insert a building block, click Building Blocks Organizer on the Quick Parts menu, select the building block you want, and then click Insert. You will learn more about working with building blocks in later lessons.

Adding Headers and Footers

A **header** is text or graphics that appears at the top of every page of a document. A **footer** is text or graphics that appears at the bottom of every page. In longer documents, headers and footers often contain the title of the publication or chapter, the name of the author, or a page number. You can add headers and footers to a document by double-clicking the top or bottom margin of a document to open the Header and Footer areas, and then inserting text and graphics into them. You can also use the Header or Footer command on the Insert tab to insert predesigned headers and footers that you can modify to include your information. You create a header that includes the name of the report.

STEPS

QUICK TIP
Unless you set different headers and footers for different sections, the information you insert in any Header or Footer area appears on every page in the document.

1. **Click the Insert tab, then click the Header button in the Header & Footer group**
   A gallery of built-in header designs opens.
2. **Scroll down the gallery to view the header designs, scroll to the top of the gallery, then click Blank**
   The Header and Footer areas open, and the document text is dimmed. When the document text is dimmed, it cannot be edited. The Header & Footer Tools Design tab also opens and is the active tab, as shown in Figure D-9. This tab is available whenever the Header and Footer areas are open.
3. **Type Healthy Traveler: Travel and Health Information from Quest Specialty Travel in the content control in the Header area**
   This text will appear at the top of every page in the document.

QUICK TIP
You can also use the Insert Alignment Tab button in the Position group to left-, center-, and right-align text in the Header and Footer areas.

4. **Select the header text, click the Home tab, click the Font list arrow in the Font group, click Berlin Sans FB Demi, click the Font Color list arrow, click Olive Green, Accent 3, Darker 25%, click the Center button in the Paragraph group, click the Bottom Border button, then click in the Header area to deselect the text**
   The text is formatted in olive green Berlin Sans FB Demi and centered in the Header area with a bottom border.
5. **Click the Header & Footer Tools Design tab, then click the Go to Footer button in the Navigation group**
   The insertion point moves to the Footer area, where a page number field is centered in the Footer area.

QUICK TIP
To change the distance between the header and footer and the edge of the page, change the Header from Top and Footer from Bottom settings in the Position group.

6. **Select the page number field in the footer, change the formatting to Berlin Sans FB Demi and Olive Green, Accent 3, Darker 25%, then click in the Footer area to deselect the text and field**
   The footer text is formatted in olive green Berlin Sans FB Demi.
7. **Click the Close Header and Footer button in the Close group, then scroll down until the bottom of page 1 and the top of page 2 appear in the document window**
   The Header and Footer areas close, and the header and footer text is dimmed, as shown in Figure D-10.
8. **Press [Ctrl][Home]**
   The report already includes the name of the document at the top of the first page, making the header information redundant. You can modify headers and footers so that the header and footer text does not appear on the first page of a document or a section.
9. **Position the pointer over the header text at the top of page 1, then double-click**
   The Header and Footer areas open. The Options group on the Header & Footer Tools Design tab includes options for creating a different header and footer for the first page of a document or a section, and for creating different headers and footers for odd- and even-numbered pages.

QUICK TIP
To remove headers or footers from a document, click the Header or Footer button, and then click Remove Header or Remove Footer.

10. **Click the Different First Page check box to select it, click the Close Header and Footer button, scroll to see the header and footer on pages 2, 3, and 4, then save the document**
    The header and footer text is removed from the Header and Footer areas on the first page.

FIGURE D-9: Header area

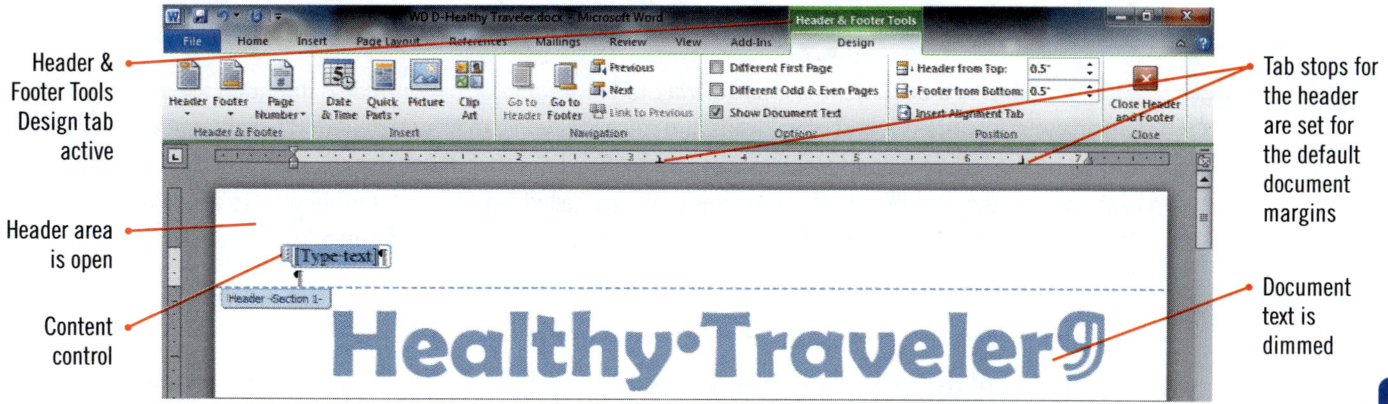

FIGURE D-10: Header and footer in document

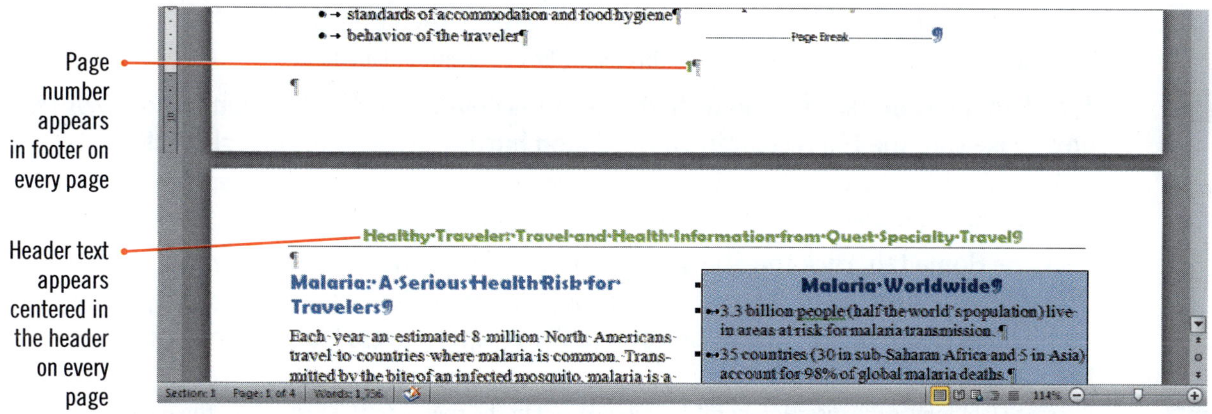

Adding a custom header or footer to the gallery

When you design a header that you want to use again in other documents, you can add it to the Header gallery by saving it as a building block. **Building blocks** are reusable pieces of formatted content or document parts, including headers and footers, page numbers, and text boxes, that are stored in galleries. Building blocks include predesigned content that comes with Word, as well as content that you create and save for future use. For example, you might create a custom header that contains your company name and logo and is formatted using the fonts, border, and colors you use in all company documents.

To add a custom header to the Header gallery, select all the text in the header, including the last paragraph mark, click the Header button, and then click Save Selection to Header Gallery. In the Create New Building Block dialog box that opens, type a unique name for the header in the Name text box, click the Gallery list arrow and select the appropriate gallery, verify that the Category is General, and then type a brief description of the new header design in the Description text box. This description appears in a ScreenTip when you point to the custom header in the gallery. When you are finished, click OK. The new header appears in the Header gallery under the General category.

To remove a custom header from the Header gallery, right-click it, click Organize and Delete, make sure the appropriate building block is selected in the Building Blocks Organizer that opens, click Delete, click Yes, and then click Close. You can follow the same process to add or remove a custom footer to the Footer gallery.

UNIT D
Word 2010

Inserting a Table

Adding a table to a document is a useful way to illustrate information that is intended for quick reference and analysis. A **table** is a grid of columns and rows that you can fill with text and graphics. A **cell** is the box formed by the intersection of a column and a row. The lines that divide the columns and rows of a table and help you see the grid-like structure of the table are called **borders**. A simple way to insert a table into a document is to use the Insert Table command on the Insert tab. You add a table to page 2 showing the preventive options for serious travel health diseases.

STEPS

1. **Scroll until the heading Preventive Options ... is at the top of your document window**
2. **Select the heading Preventive Options... and the two paragraph marks below it, click the Page Layout tab, click the Columns button in the Page Setup group, click One, click the heading to deselect the text, then scroll down to see the bottom half of page 2**
   A continuous section break is inserted before the heading and after the second paragraph mark, creating a new section, section 3, as shown in Figure D-11. The document now includes four sections, with the heading Preventive Options... in Section 3. Section 3 is formatted as a single column.
3. **Place the insertion point before the first paragraph mark below the heading, click the Insert tab, click the Table button in the Tables group, then click Insert Table**
   The Insert Table dialog box opens. You use this dialog box to create a blank table.
4. **Type 5 in the Number of columns text box, press [Tab], type 6 in the Number of rows text box, make sure the Fixed column width option button is selected, then click OK**
   A blank table with five columns and six rows is inserted in the document. The insertion point is in the upper-left cell of the table, and the Table Tools Design tab becomes the active tab.
5. **Click the Home tab, click the Show/Hide ¶ button ¶ in the Paragraph group, type Disease in the first cell in the first row, press [Tab], type Vaccine, press [Tab], type Prophylaxis Drug, press [Tab], type Eat and Drink Safely, press [Tab], type Avoid Insects, then press [Tab]**
   Pressing [Tab] moves the insertion point to the next cell in the row or to the first cell in the next row.
6. **Type Malaria, press [Tab][Tab], click the Bullets list arrow in the Paragraph group, click the check mark style, press [Tab][Tab], then click the Bullets button**
   The active bullet style changes to a check mark. A check mark is added to a cell when you click the Bullets button.
7. **Type the text shown in Figure D-12 in the table cells**
   Don't be concerned if the text wraps to the next line in a cell as you type because you will adjust the width of the columns later.
8. **Click the Table Tools Layout tab, click the AutoFit button in the Cell Size group, click AutoFit Contents, click the AutoFit button again, then click AutoFit Window**
   The width of the table columns is adjusted to fit the text and then the window.
9. **Click the Select button in the Table group, click Select Table, click the Align Center button in the Alignment group, click Disease in the table, click the Select button, click Select Column, click the Align Center Left button, then click in the table to deselect the column**
   The text in the table is centered in each cell, and then the text in the first column is left-aligned.
10. **Click the Table Tools Design tab, click the More button in the Table Styles group to expand the Table Styles gallery, click the Light List – Accent 3 style, then save your changes**
    The Light List - Accent 3 table style is applied to the table, as shown in Figure D-13. A **table style** includes format settings for the text, borders, and shading in a table.

QUICK TIP
To delete a table, click in the table, click the Table Tools Layout tab, click the Delete button in the Rows & Columns group, then click Delete Table.

QUICK TIP
You can also click in a cell to move the insertion point to it.

TROUBLE
If you pressed [Tab] after the last row, click the Undo button on the Quick Access toolbar to remove the blank row.

QUICK TIP
You can also format table text using the buttons on the Mini toolbar or the Home tab.

FIGURE D-11: New section

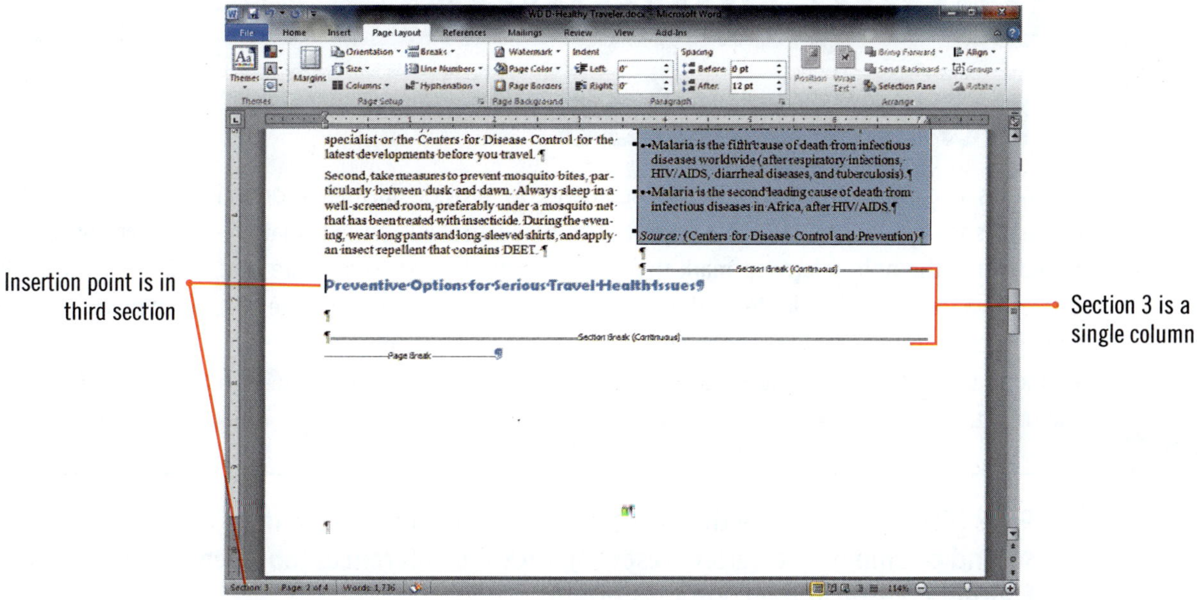

FIGURE D-12: Text in table

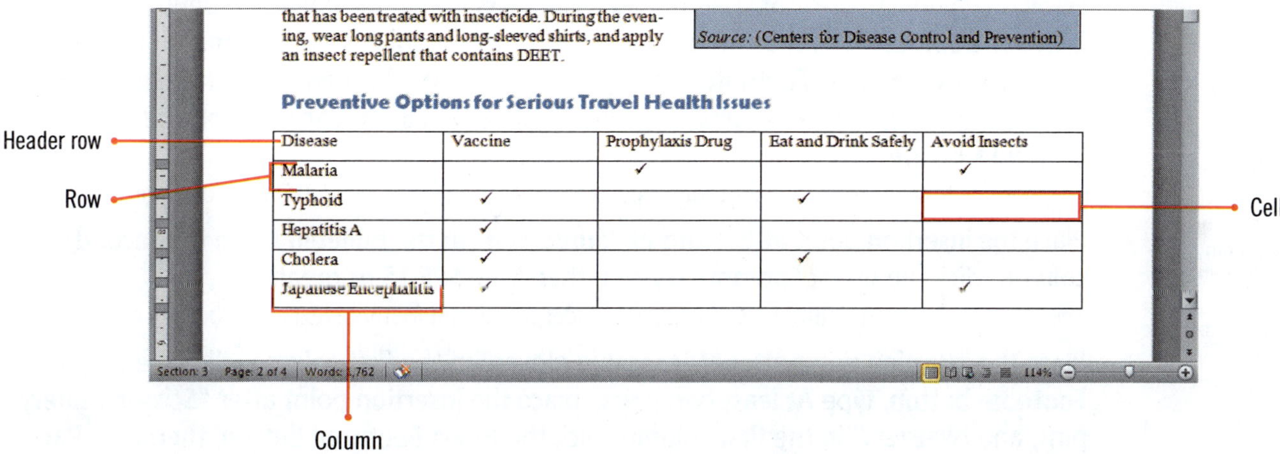

FIGURE D-13: Completed table

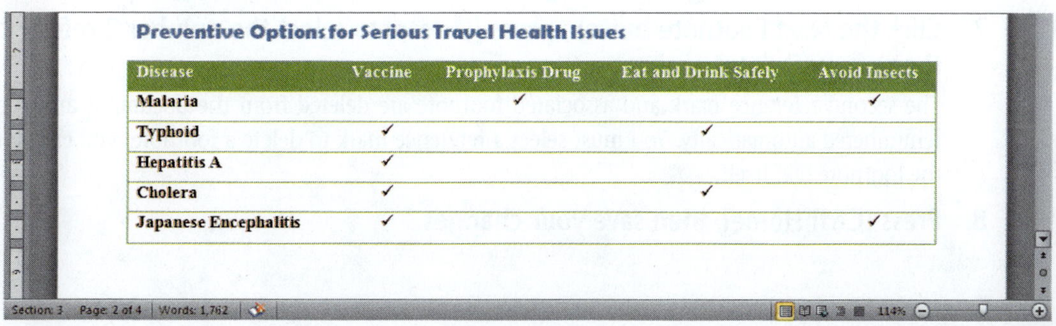

Word 2010

UNIT
D
Word 2010

Adding Footnotes and Endnotes

Footnotes and endnotes are used in documents to provide further information, explanatory text, or references for text in a document. A **footnote** or **endnote** is an explanatory note that consists of two linked parts: the note reference mark that appears next to text to indicate that additional information is offered in a footnote or endnote, and the corresponding footnote or endnote text. Word places footnotes at the end of each page and endnotes at the end of the document. You insert and manage footnotes and endnotes using the tools in the Footnotes group on the References tab. You add several footnotes to the report.

STEPS

TROUBLE
Scroll up as needed to see the note reference mark; then scroll down to see the footnote.

1. **Press [Ctrl][Home], place the insertion point at the end of the first body paragraph in the second column of text (after "resort."), click the References tab, then click the Insert Footnote button in the Footnotes group**
   A note reference mark, in this case a superscript 1, appears after "resort.", and the insertion point moves below a separator line at the bottom of the page. A note reference mark can be a number, a symbol, a character, or a combination of characters.
2. **Type Behavior is a critical factor, regardless of the quality of accommodations. For example, going outdoors in a malaria-endemic area could result in becoming infected with malaria.**
   The footnote text appears below the separator line at the bottom of page 1, as shown in Figure D-14.

QUICK TIP
To change the number format of the note reference mark or to use a symbol instead of a character, click the launcher in the Footnotes group, select from the options in the Footnote and Endnote dialog box, then click Apply.

3. **Scroll down until the bottom half of page 3 appears in the document window, place the insertion point at the end of "Medications taken on a regular basis at home" in the second column, click the Insert Footnote button, then type All medications should be stored in carry-on luggage, in their original containers with clear labels. Carry a duplicate supply in checked luggage.**
   The footnote text for the second footnote appears at the bottom of the second column on page 3.
4. **Place the insertion point at the end of "Sunscreen" in the bulleted list in the second column, click the Insert Footnote button, then type SPF 15 or greater.**
   The footnote text for the third footnote appears under the second footnote text at the bottom of page 3.
5. **Place the insertion point after "Disposable gloves" in the first column, click the Insert Footnote button, type At least two pairs., place the insertion point after "Scissors, safety pins, and tweezers" in the first column, click the Insert Footnote button, then type Pack these items in checked luggage.**
   Notice that when you inserted new footnotes between existing footnotes, Word automatically renumbered the footnotes. The new footnotes appear at the bottom of the first column on page 3, as shown in Figure D-15.
6. **Press [Ctrl][Home], then click the Next Footnote button in the Footnotes group**
   The insertion point moves to the first reference mark in the document.

QUICK TIP
To convert all footnotes to endnotes, click the launcher in the Footnotes group, click Convert, click OK, then click Close.

7. **Click the Next Footnote button, press [Delete] to select the number 2 reference mark, then press [Delete] again**
   The second reference mark and associated footnote are deleted from the document and the footnotes are renumbered automatically. You must select a reference mark to delete a footnote; you can not simply delete the footnote text itself.
8. **Press [Ctrl][Home], then save your changes**

FIGURE D-14: Footnote in the document

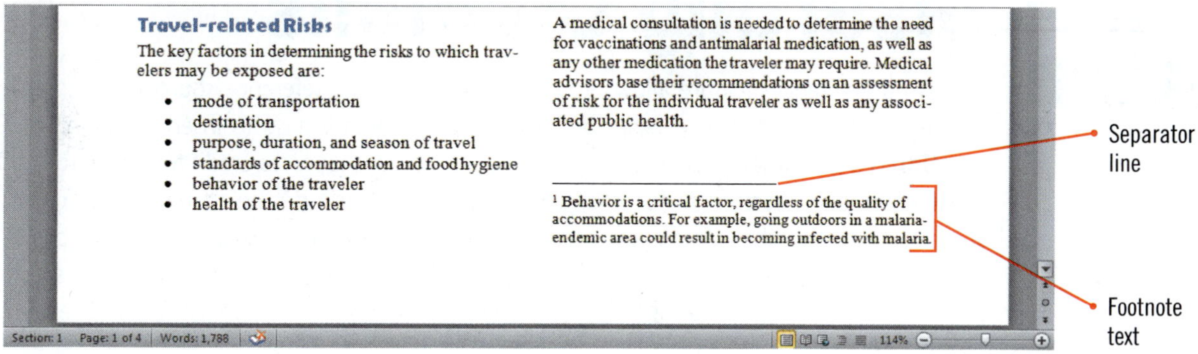

FIGURE D-15: Renumbered footnotes in the document

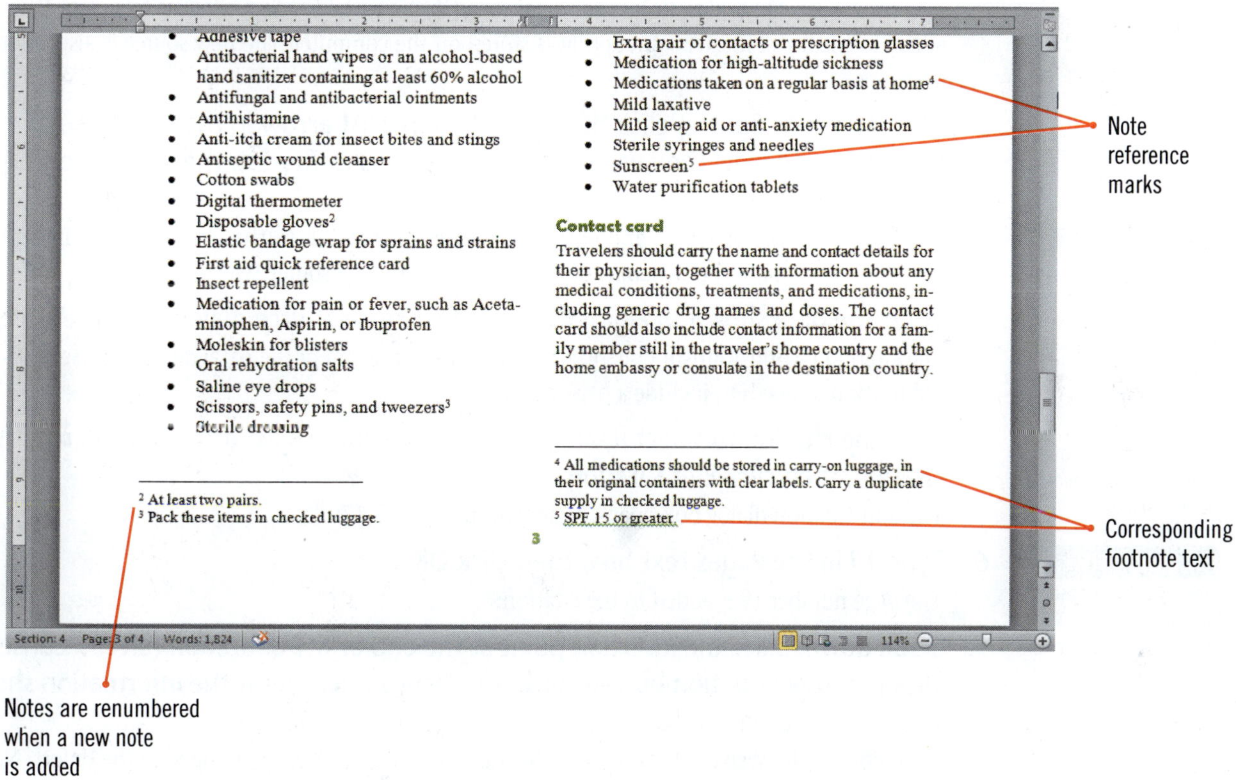

Word 2010

Inserting Citations

The Word References feature allows you to keep track of the reference sources you consult when writing research papers, reports, and other documents, and makes it easy to insert a citation in a document. A **citation** is a parenthetical reference in the document text that gives credit to the source for a quotation or other information used in a document. Citations usually include the name of the author and, for print sources, a page number. When you insert a citation you can use an existing source or create a new source. Each time you create a new source, the source information is saved on your computer so that it is available for use in any document. The report already includes two citations. You add several more citations to the report.

STEPS

1. **Place the insertion point after "people travel" but before the period at the end of the first paragraph in the first column of text, click the Style list arrow in the Citations & Bibliography group, then click MLA Sixth Edition**

   You will format the sources and citations in the report using the style recommended by the Modern Language Association (MLA).

> **QUICK TIP**
> When you create a new source for a document, it appears automatically in the bibliography when you generate it.

2. **Click the Insert Citation button in the Citations & Bibliography group**

   A list of the sources already used in the document opens. You can choose to cite one of these sources, create a new source, or add a placeholder for a source. When you add a new citation to a document, the source is added to the list of master sources that is stored on the computer. The new source is also associated with the document.

3. **Click Add New Source, click the Type of Source list arrow in the Create Source dialog box, scroll down to view the available source types, click Report, then click the Corporate Author check box**

   You select the type of source and enter the source information in the Create Source dialog box. The fields available in the dialog box change, depending on the type of source selected.

> **QUICK TIP**
> Only sources that you associate with a document stay with the document when you move it to another computer. The master list of sources remains on the computer where it was created.

4. **Enter the data shown in Figure D-16 in the Create Source dialog box, then click OK**

   The citation (World Tourism Organization) appears at the end of the paragraph. Because the source is a print publication, it needs to include a page number.

5. **Click the citation to select it, click the Citation Options list arrow on the right side of the citation, then click Edit Citation**

   The Edit Citation dialog box opens, as shown in Figure D-17.

> **QUICK TIP**
> You can also choose to add or remove the author, year, or title from a citation.

6. **Type 19 in the Pages text box, then click OK**

   The page number 19 is added to the citation.

7. **Scroll down, place the insertion point at the end of the quotation (after ...consequences.), click the Insert Citation button, click Add New Source, enter the information shown in Figure D-18, then click OK**

   A citation for the Web publication that the quotation was taken from is added to the report. No page number is used in this citation because the source is a Web site.

8. **Scroll to the bottom of page 2, click under the table, type Source:, italicize Source:, click after Source:, click the Insert Citation button, then click Johnson, Margaret in the list of sources**

   The citation (Johnson) appears under the table.

9. **Click the citation, click the Citation Options list arrow, click Edit Citation, type 55 in the Pages text box, click OK, then save your changes**

   The page number 55 is added to the citation.

FIGURE D-16: Adding a Report source

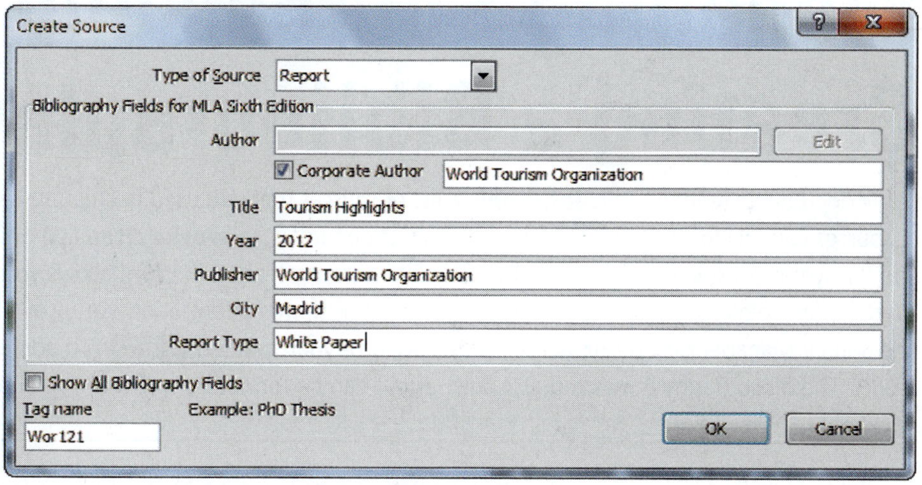

FIGURE D-17: Edit Citation dialog box

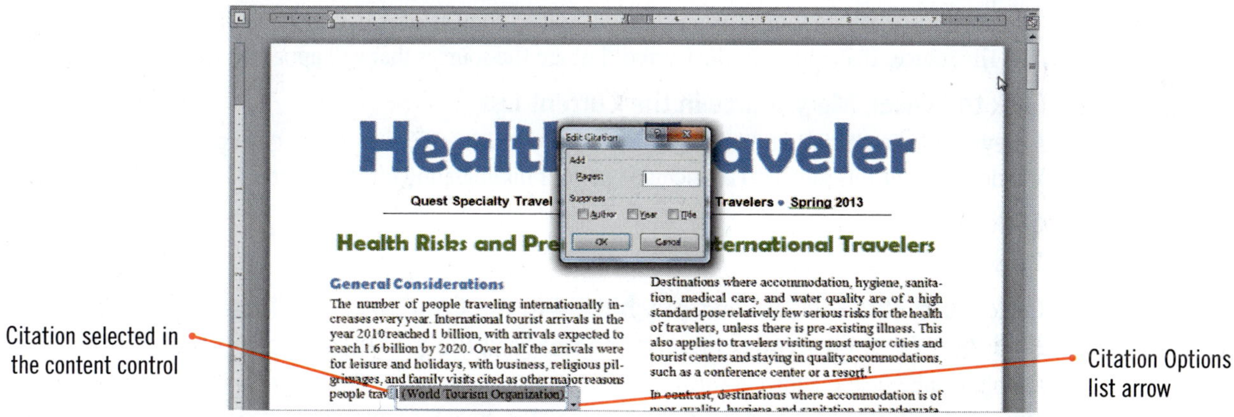

FIGURE D-18: Adding a Web publication source

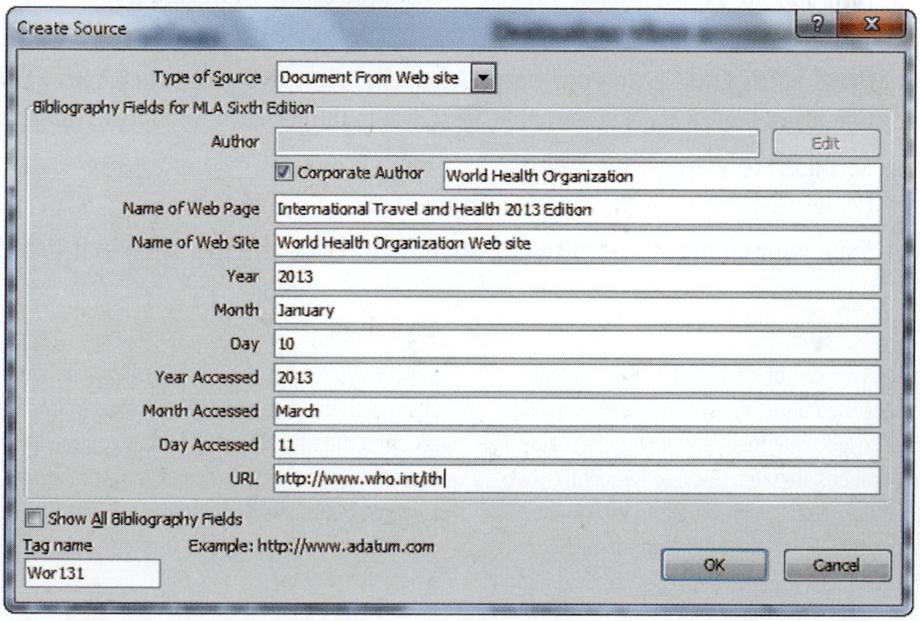

UNIT
D
Word 2010

Managing Sources and Creating a Bibliography

Many documents require a **bibliography**, a list of sources that you used in creating the document. The list of sources can include only the works cited in your document (a **works cited** list) or both the works cited and the works consulted (a bibliography). The Bibliography feature in Word allows you to generate a works cited list or a bibliography automatically based on the source information you provide for the document. The Source Manager dialog box helps you to organize your sources. You add a bibliography to the report. The bibliography is inserted as a field, and it can be formatted any way you choose.

STEPS

> **QUICK TIP**
> You must copy sources from the Master List to the Current List for the sources to be available when you open the document on another computer.

1. **Press [Ctrl][End] to move the insertion point to the end of the document, then click the Manage Sources button in the Citations & Bibliography group**
   The Source Manager dialog box opens, as shown in Figure D-19. The Master List shows the sources available on your computer. The Current List shows the sources available in the current document. A check mark next to a source indicates the source is cited in the document. You use the tools in the Source Manager dialog box to add, edit, and delete sources from the lists, and to copy sources between the Master List and the Current List. The sources that appear in the Current List are the sources that will appear in the bibliography.
2. **Click the Baker, Mary source in the Current List**
   A preview of the citation and bibliographical entry for the source in MLA style appears in the Preview box. You do not want this source to be included in your bibliography for the report.
3. **Click Delete**
   The source is removed from the Current List.
4. **Click Close, click the Bibliography button in the Citations & Bibliography group, click Bibliography, then scroll up to see the heading Bibliography at the top of the field**
   A Bibliography field is added at the location of the insertion point. The bibliography includes all the sources associated with the document, formatted in the MLA style for bibliographies. The text in the Bibliography field is formatted with the default styles. You want to format the text to match the rest of the report.

> **TROUBLE**
> Don't be concerned if the list of sources becomes gray when you select the heading Bibliography. This simply indicates the Bibliography field is active. Text that is selected is highlighted in blue.

5. **Select Bibliography; apply the following formats: Berlin Sans FB Demi, bold, and the Blue, Accent 1 font color; drag down the list of sources to select the entire list and change the font size to 11; then click outside the bibliography to deselect it**
   The format of the bibliography text now matches the rest of the report.
6. **Press [Ctrl][End], type your name, click the View tab, then click Two Pages**
   Completed pages 3 and 4 of the report are shown in the document window, as shown in Figure D-20.
7. **Scroll up to view pages 1 and 2**
   Completed pages 1 and 2 are shown in Figure D-21.
8. **Save your changes, submit your document, close the file, then exit Word**

Working with Web sources

Publications found on the Web can be challenging to document. Many Web sites can be accessed under multiple domains, and URLs change frequently or are so long that they cannot be typed easily. In addition, electronic publications are often updated frequently, making each visit to a Web site potentially unique. For these reasons, it's best to rely on the author, title, and publication information for a Web publication when citing it as a source in a research document. If possible, you can include a URL as supplementary information only, along with the date the Web site was last updated and the date you accessed the site. Whatever format you use for citing Web publications, it's important to be consistent throughout your document. Since Web sites are often removed, it's also a good idea to download or print any Web source you use so that it can be verified later.

FIGURE D-19: Source Manager dialog box

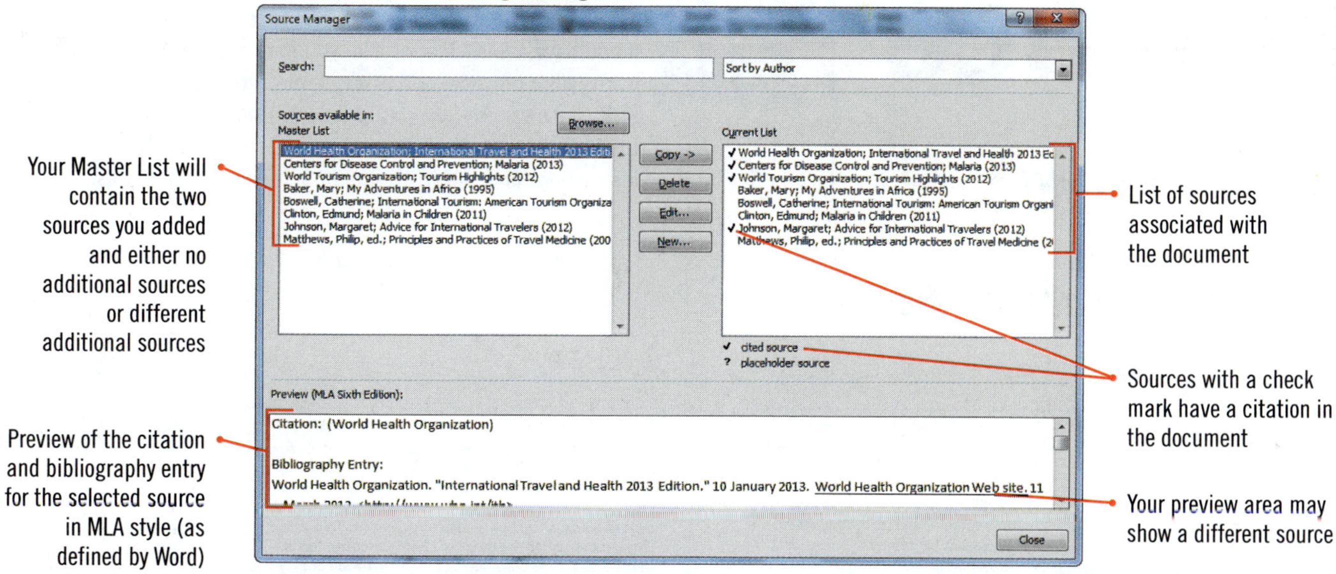

FIGURE D-20: Completed pages 3 and 4

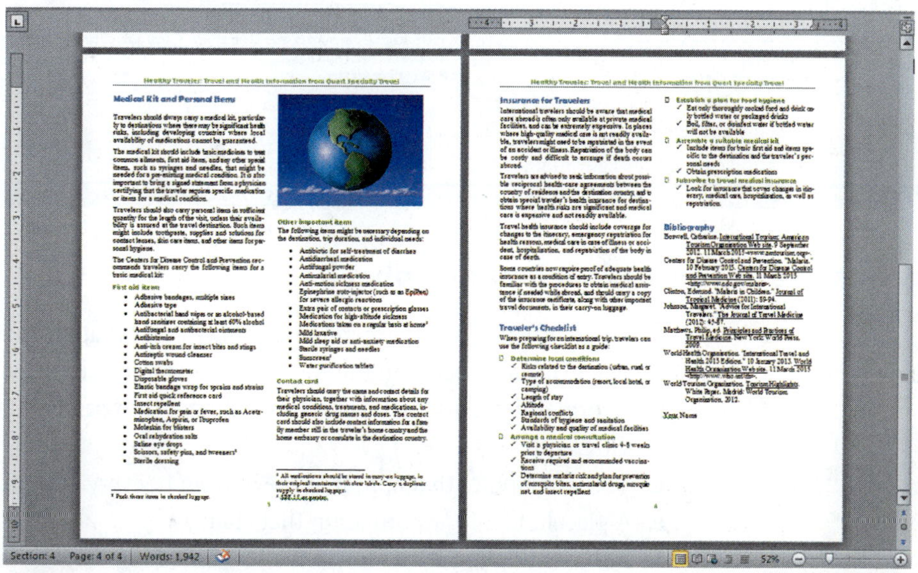

FIGURE D-21: Completed pages 1 and 2

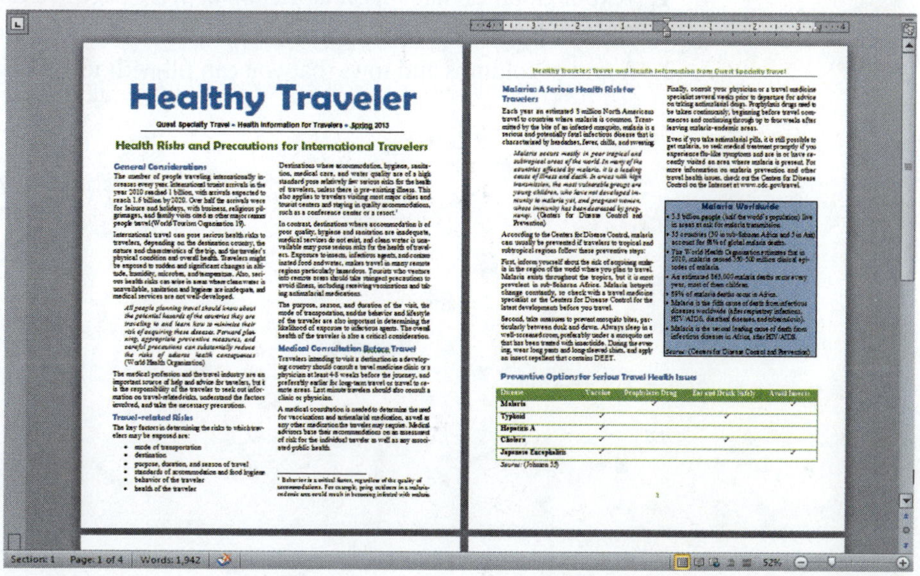

Practice

Concepts Review

For current SAM information, including versions and content details, visit SAM Central (http://www.cengage.com/samcentral). If you have a SAM user profile, you may have access to hands-on instruction, practice, and assessment of the skills covered in this unit. Since various versions of SAM are supported throughout the life of this text, check with your instructor for the correct instructions and URL/Web site for accessing assignments.

Label each element shown in Figure D-22.

FIGURE D-22

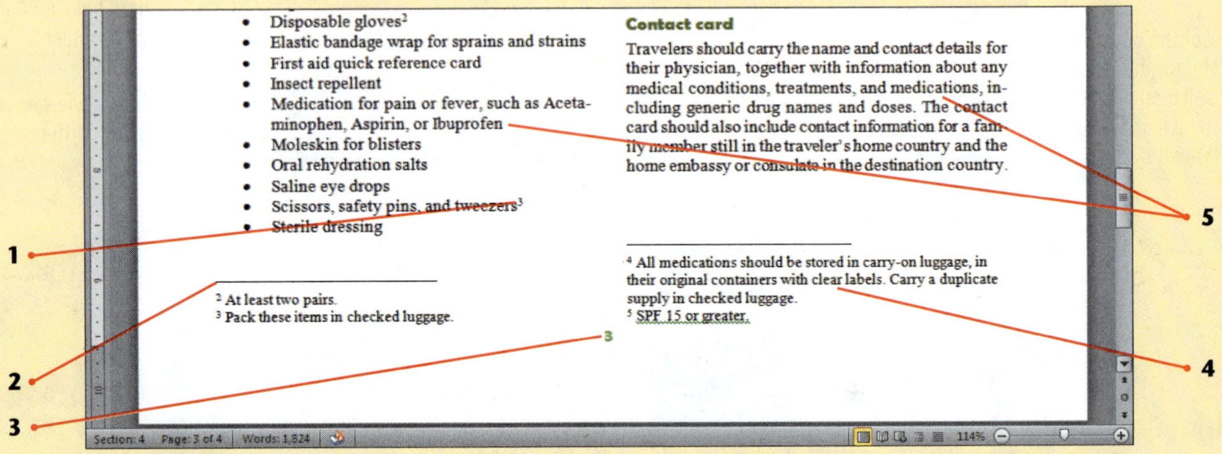

Match each term with the statement that best describes it.

6. **Table**
7. **Manual page break**
8. **Section break**
9. **Footer**
10. **Header**
11. **Citation**
12. **Field**
13. **Margin**
14. **Bibliography**

a. A parenthetical reference in the document text that gives credit to a source
b. The blank area between the edge of the text and the edge of the page
c. A formatting mark that divides a document into parts that can be formatted differently
d. Text or graphics that appear at the bottom of every page in a document
e. A placeholder for information that changes
f. A formatting mark that forces the text following the mark to begin at the top of the next page
g. Text or graphics that appear at the top of every page in a document
h. A list of the sources used to create a document
i. A grid of columns and rows that you can fill with text and graphics

Select the best answer from the list of choices.

15. Which type of break do you insert if you want to balance the columns in a section?

- **a.** Manual page break
- **b.** Text wrapping break
- **c.** Column break
- **d.** Continuous section break

16. Which type of break can you insert if you want to force text to begin on the next page?

- **a.** Text wrapping break
- **b.** Next page section break
- **c.** Automatic page break
- **d.** Continuous section break

17. Which of the following cannot be inserted using the Quick Parts command?

- **a.** Document property
- **b.** AutoText building block
- **c.** Page break
- **d.** Page number field

18. Which of the following do documents with mirror margins always have?

- **a.** Inside and outside margins
- **b.** Different first page headers and footers
- **c.** Gutters
- **d.** Landscape orientation

19. What name describes formatted pieces of content that are stored in galleries?

- **a.** Field
- **b.** Header
- **c.** Property
- **d.** Building Block

20. Which appears at the end of a document?

- **a.** Citation
- **b.** Endnote
- **c.** Footnote
- **d.** Page break

Skills Review

1. Set document margins.

- **a.** Start Word, open the file WD D-2.docx from the drive and folder where you store your Data Files, then save it as **WD D-Elmwood Fitness**.
- **b.** Change the top and bottom margin settings to Moderate: 1" top and bottom, and .75" left and right.
- **c.** Save your changes to the document.

2. Create sections and columns.

- **a.** Turn on the display of formatting marks, then customize the status bar to display sections if they are not displayed already.
- **b.** Insert a continuous section break before the **Welcome to the Elmwood Fitness Center** heading.
- **c.** Format the text in section 2 in two columns, then save your changes to the document.

3. Insert page breaks.

- **a.** Scroll to page 3, then insert a manual page break before the heading **Facilities and Services**.
- **b.** Scroll down and insert a manual page break before the heading **Membership**, then press [Ctrl][Home].
- **c.** On page 1, select the heading **Welcome to the Elmwood Fitness Center** and the paragraph mark below it, use the Columns button to format the selected text as one column, then center the heading on the page.
- **d.** Follow the direction in step c to format the heading **Facilities and Services** and the paragraph mark below it on page 3, and the heading **Membership** and the paragraph mark below it on page 4, as one column, with centered text, then save your changes to the document

4. Insert page numbers.

- **a.** Insert page numbers in the document at the bottom of the page. Select the Plain Number 2 page number style from the gallery.
- **b.** Close the Footer area, scroll through the document to view the page number on each page, then save your changes to the document.

5. Add headers and footers.

- **a.** Double-click the margin at the top of a page to open the Header and Footer areas.
- **b.** With the insertion point in the Header area, click the Quick Parts button in the Insert Group on the Header & Footer Tools Design tab, point to Document Property, then click Author.

Skills Review (continued)

c. Replace the text in the Author content control with your name, press [End] to move the insertion point out of the content control, then press [Spacebar]. (*Note*: If your name does not appear in the header, right-click the Author content control, click Remove Content Control, then type your name in the header.)

d. Click the Insert Alignment Tab button in the Position group, select the Right option button and keep the alignment relative to the margin, then click OK in the dialog box to move the insertion point to the right margin.

e. Use the Insert Date and Time command in the Insert group to insert the current date using a format of your choice as static text. (*Hint*: Be sure the Update Automatically check box is not checked.)

f. Apply italic to the text in the header.

g. Move the insertion point to the Footer area.

h. Double-click the page number to select it, then format the page number in bold and italic.

i. Move the insertion point to the header on page 1 if it is not already there, use the Header & Footer Tools Design tab to create a different header and footer for the first page of the document, type your name in the First Page Header area, then apply italic to your name.

j. Close headers and footers, scroll to view the header and footer on each page, then save your changes to the document.

6. Insert a table.

a. On page 4, double-click the word **Table** to select it at the end of the Membership Rates section, press [Delete], open the Insert Table dialog box, then create a table with two columns and five rows.

b. Apply the purple Light List - Accent 4 table style to the table.

c. Press [Tab] to leave the first cell in the header row blank, then type **Rate**.

d. Press [Tab], then type the following text in the table, pressing [Tab] to move from cell to cell.

Enrollment/Individual	**$100**
Enrollment/Couple	**$150**
Monthly membership/Individual	**$35**
Monthly membership/Couple	**$60**

e. With the insertion point in the table, right-click the table, use the AutoFit command to select the AutoFit to Contents option, and then select the AutoFit to Window option. (*Note*: In this case AutoFit to Window fits the table to the width of the column of text.)

f. Save your changes to the document.

7. Add footnotes and endnotes.

a. Press [Ctrl[Home], scroll down, place the insertion point at the end of the first body paragraph, insert a footnote, then type **People who are active live longer and feel better.**

b. Place the insertion point at the end of the first paragraph under the Benefits of Exercise heading, insert a footnote, then type **There are 1,440 minutes in every day. Schedule 30 of them for physical activity.**

c. Place the insertion point at the end of the first paragraph under the Tips for Staying Motivated heading, insert a footnote, type **Always consult your physician before beginning an exercise program.**, then save your changes.

8. Insert citations.

a. Place the insertion point at the end of the second paragraph under the Benefits of Exercise heading (after "down from 52% in 2010" but before the period), then change the style for citations and bibliography to MLA Sixth Edition.

b. Insert a citation, add a new source, enter the source information shown in the Create Source dialog box in Figure D-23, then click OK.

FIGURE D-23

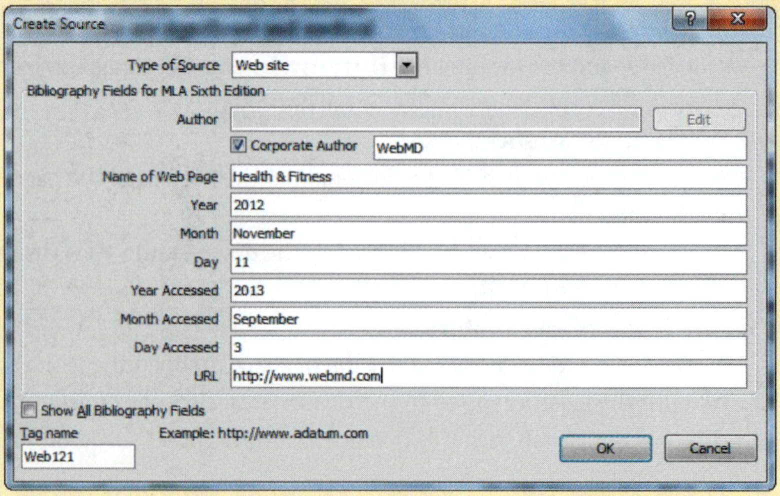

Skills Review (continued)

c. Place the insertion point at the end of the italicized quotation in the second column of text, insert a citation, then select Jason, Laura from the list of sources.

d. Edit the citation to include the page number **25**.

e. Scroll to page 2, place the insertion point at the end of the "Be a morning exerciser" paragraph but before the ending period, insert a citation for WebMD, then save your changes.

9. Manage sources and create a bibliography.

a. Press [Ctrl][End], then open the Source Manager dialog box.

b. Select the source Health, National Institute of in the Current List, click Edit, click the Corporate Author check box, edit the entry so it reads **National Institute of Health**, click OK, click Yes if prompted, then click Close.

c. Insert a bibliography.

d. Select Bibliography, then change the font to 14-point Tahoma with a black font color. Pages 1 and 4 of the formatted document are shown in Figure D-24.

e. Save your changes to the document, submit it to your instructor, then close the document and exit Word.

FIGURE D-24

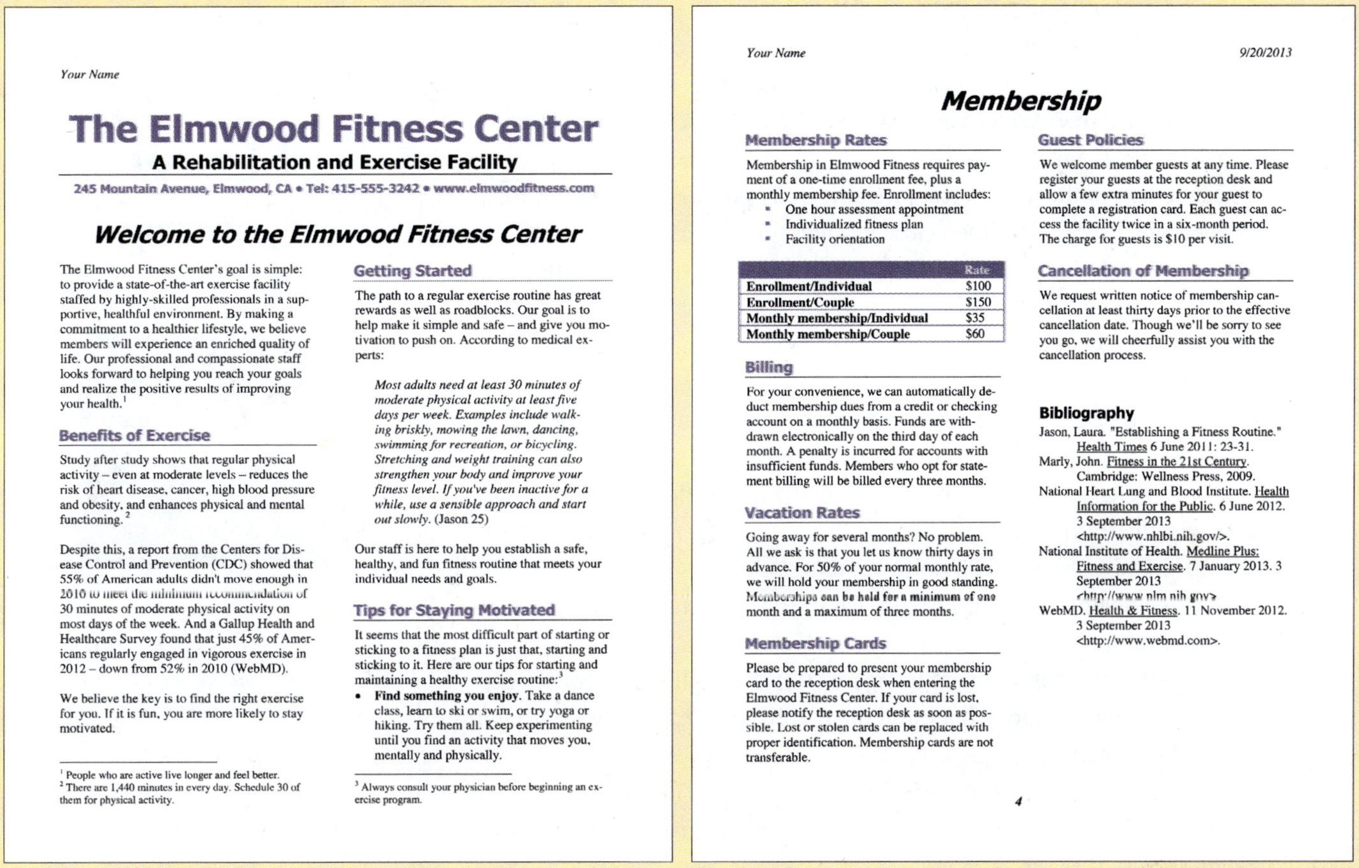

Your Name

The Elmwood Fitness Center

A Rehabilitation and Exercise Facility

245 Mountain Avenue, Elmwood, CA • Tel: 415-555-3242 • www.elmwoodfitness.com

Welcome to the Elmwood Fitness Center

The Elmwood Fitness Center's goal is simple: to provide a state-of-the-art exercise facility staffed by highly-skilled professionals in a supportive, healthful environment. By making a commitment to a healthier lifestyle, we believe members will experience an enriched quality of life. Our professional and compassionate staff looks forward to helping you reach your goals and realize the positive results of improving your health.[1]

Benefits of Exercise

Study after study shows that regular physical activity – even at moderate levels – reduces the risk of heart disease, cancer, high blood pressure and obesity, and enhances physical and mental functioning.[2]

Despite this, a report from the Centers for Disease Control and Prevention (CDC) showed that 55% of American adults didn't move enough in 2010 to meet the minimum recommendation of 30 minutes of moderate physical activity on most days of the week. And a Gallup Health and Healthcare Survey found that just 45% of Americans regularly engaged in vigorous exercise in 2012 – down from 52% in 2010 (WebMD).

We believe the key is to find the right exercise for you. If it is fun, you are more likely to stay motivated.

Getting Started

The path to a regular exercise routine has great rewards as well as roadblocks. Our goal is to help make it simple and safe – and give you motivation to push on. According to medical experts:

> *Most adults need at least 30 minutes of moderate physical activity at least five days per week. Examples include walking briskly, mowing the lawn, dancing, swimming for recreation, or bicycling. Stretching and weight training can also strengthen your body and improve your fitness level. If you've been inactive for a while, use a sensible approach and start out slowly.* (Jason 25)

Our staff is here to help you establish a safe, healthy, and fun fitness routine that meets your individual needs and goals.

Tips for Staying Motivated

It seems that the most difficult part of starting or sticking to a fitness plan is just that, starting and sticking to it. Here are our tips for starting and maintaining a healthy exercise routine:[3]

- **Find something you enjoy**. Take a dance class, learn to ski or swim, or try yoga or hiking. Try them all. Keep experimenting until you find an activity that moves you, mentally and physically.

[1] People who are active live longer and feel better.
[2] There are 1,440 minutes in every day. Schedule 30 of them for physical activity.
[3] Always consult your physician before beginning an exercise program.

Your Name *9/20/2013*

Membership

Membership Rates

Membership in Elmwood Fitness requires payment of a one-time enrollment fee, plus a monthly membership fee. Enrollment includes:

- One hour assessment appointment
- Individualized fitness plan
- Facility orientation

	Rate
Enrollment/Individual	$100
Enrollment/Couple	$150
Monthly membership/Individual	$35
Monthly membership/Couple	$60

Billing

For your convenience, we can automatically deduct membership dues from a credit or checking account on a monthly basis. Funds are withdrawn electronically on the third day of each month. A penalty is incurred for accounts with insufficient funds. Members who opt for statement billing will be billed every three months.

Vacation Rates

Going away for several months? No problem. All we ask is that you let us know thirty days in advance. For 50% of your normal monthly rate, we will hold your membership in good standing. Memberships can be held for a minimum of one month and a maximum of three months.

Membership Cards

Please be prepared to present your membership card to the reception desk when entering the Elmwood Fitness Center. If your card is lost, please notify the reception desk as soon as possible. Lost or stolen cards can be replaced with proper identification. Membership cards are not transferable.

Guest Policies

We welcome member guests at any time. Please register your guests at the reception desk and allow a few extra minutes for your guest to complete a registration card. Each guest can access the facility twice in a six-month period. The charge for guests is $10 per visit.

Cancellation of Membership

We request written notice of membership cancellation at least thirty days prior to the effective cancellation date. Though we'll be sorry to see you go, we will cheerfully assist you with the cancellation process.

Bibliography

Jason, Laura. "Establishing a Fitness Routine." Health Times 6 June 2011: 23-31.
Marly, John. Fitness in the 21st Century. Cambridge: Wellness Press, 2009.
National Heart Lung and Blood Institute. Health Information for the Public. 6 June 2012. 3 September 2013 <http://www.nhlbi.nih.gov/>.
National Institute of Health. Medline Plus: Fitness and Exercise. 7 January 2013. 3 September 2013 <http://www.nlm.nih.gov>
WebMD. Health & Fitness. 11 November 2012. 3 September 2013 <http://www.webmd.com>.

4

Word 2010

Independent Challenge 1

You are the owner of a small business called Harvest Catering. You have begun work on the text for a brochure advertising your business and are now ready to lay out the pages and prepare the final copy. The brochure will be printed on both sides of an 8½" × 11" sheet of paper, and folded in thirds.

SAM

If you have a SAM 2010 user profile, an autogradable SAM version of this assignment may be available at http://www.cengage.com/sam2010. Check with your instructor to confirm that this assignment is available in SAM. To use the SAM version of this assignment, log into the SAM 2010 Web site and download the instruction and start files.

a. Start Word, open the file WD D-3.docx from the drive and folder where you store your Data Files, then save it as **WD D-Harvest Catering**. Read the document to get a feel for its contents.

b. Change the page orientation to landscape, and change all four margins to .6".

c. Format the document in three columns of equal width.

d. Insert a next page section break before the heading **Catering Services**.

e. On page 1, insert column breaks before the headings **Sample Tuscan Banquet Menu** and **Sample Indian Banquet Menu**.

f. Change the column spacing in section 1 (which is the first page) to .4", add lines between the columns on the first page, then center the text in the columns.

g. Double-click the bottom margin to open the footer area, create a different header and footer for the first page, then type **Call for custom menus designed to your taste and budget.** in the First Page Footer -Section 1- area.

h. Center the text in the footer area, format it in 20-point Papyrus, bold, with a Red, Accent 2 font color, then close headers and footers.

i. On page 2, insert a column break before Your Name, then press [Enter] 22 times to move the contact information to the bottom of the second column.

j. Replace Your Name with your name, then center the contact information in the column.

k. Insert a column break at the bottom of the second column. Type the text shown in Figure D-25 in the third column, then apply the No Spacing style to the text. Refer to the figure as you follow the instructions for formatting the text in the third column.

l. Format Harvest Catering in 28-point Papyrus, bold.

m. Format the remaining text in 12-point Papyrus. Center the text in the third column.

n. Insert the clip art graphic shown in Figure D-25 or another appropriate clip art graphic. Do not wrap text around the graphic. (*Hint*: Use the search terms fruits and women.)

o. Resize the graphic and add or remove blank paragraphs in the third column of your brochure so that the spacing between elements roughly matches the spacing shown in Figure D-25.

FIGURE D-25

Advanced Challenge Exercise

- Insert a different appropriate clip art graphic at the bottom of the first column on page 2.
- Apply text wrapping to the graphic, then resize the graphic and position it so it enhances the design of the brochure.
- Apply a suitable picture style or picture effect to the graphic.

p. Save your changes, then submit a copy to your instructor. If possible, you can print the brochure with the two pages back to back so that the brochure can be folded in thirds.

q. Close the document and exit Word.

Independent Challenge 2

You work in the Campus Safety Department at Pacific State College. You have written the text for an informational flyer about parking regulations on campus, and now you need to format the flyer so it is attractive and readable.

a. Start Word, open the file WD D-4.docx from the drive and folder where you store your Data Files, then save it as **WD D-Parking FAQ**. Read the document to get a feel for its contents.
b. Change all four margins to .7".
c. Insert a continuous section break before **1. May I bring a car to school?** (*Hint*: Place the insertion point before May.)
d. Scroll down and insert a next page section break before **Sample Parking Permit**.
e. Format the text in section 2 in three columns of equal width with .3" of space between the columns.
f. Hyphenate the document using the automatic hyphenation feature. (*Hint*: Use the Hyphenation button in the Page Setup group on the Page Layout tab.)
g. Add a 3-point dotted-line bottom border to the blank paragraph under Pacific State College Department of Campus Safety. (*Hint*: Place the insertion point before the paragraph mark under Pacific State College...)
h. Open the Header area, and insert your name in the header. Right-align your name, and format it in 10-point Arial.
i. Add the following text to the footer, inserting symbols between words as indicated: **Parking and Shuttle Service Office • 54 Buckley Street • Pacific State College • 942-555-2227**. (*Hint*: Click the Symbol command in the Symbols group on the Insert tab to insert a symbol.)
j. Format the footer text in 9-point Arial Black, and center it in the footer. If necessary, adjust the font and font size so that the entire contact information fits on one line.
k. Apply a 3-point dotted-line border above the footer text. Make sure to apply the border to the paragraph.
l. Add a continuous section break at the end of section 2 to balance the columns in section 2.
m. Add the clip art graphic shown in Figure D-26 (or another appropriate clip art graphic) to the upper-right corner of the document, above the border. Make sure the graphic does not obscure the border. (*Hint*: Apply text wrapping to the graphic before positioning it.)
n. Place the insertion point on page 2 (which is section 4). Change the left and right margins in section 4 to 1". Also change the page orientation of section 4 to landscape.
o. Change the vertical alignment of section 4 to center. (*Hint*: Use the Vertical Alignment list arrow on the Layout tab in the Page Setup dialog box.)
p. Apply an appropriate table style to the table, such as the style shown in Figure D-27. (*Hint*: Check and uncheck the options in the Table Style Options group on the Table Tools Design tab to customize the style so it enhances the table data.)
q. Save your changes, submit your work, close the document, then exit Word.

FIGURE D-26

Frequently Asked Questions (FAQ)

Parking & Shuttle Service Office

Pacific State College Department of Campus Safety

FIGURE D-27

Sample Parking Permit

Pacific State College **Office of Parking and Shuttle Service** 2013-14 Student Parking Permit	
License number:	VA 498 359
Make:	Subaru
Model:	Forester
Year:	2004
Color:	Red
Permit Issue Date:	September 8, 2013
Permit Expiration Date:	June 4, 2014
Restrictions: ***Parking is permitted in the Pacific State College Greene Street lot 24 hours a day, 7 days a week. Shuttle service is available from the Greene Street lot to campus from 7 a.m. to 7 p.m. Monday through Friday. Parking is also permitted in any on-campus lot from 4:30 p.m. Friday to midnight Sunday.***	

Independent Challenge 3

A book publisher would like to publish an article you wrote on stormwater pollution in Australia as a chapter in a forthcoming book called *Environmental Issues for the New Millennium*. The publisher has requested that you format your article like a book chapter before submitting it for publication, and has provided you with a style sheet. According to the style sheet, the citations and bibliography should be formatted in Chicago style. You have already created the sources for the chapter, but you need to insert the citations.

a. Start Word, open the file WD D-5.docx from the drive and folder where you store your Data Files, then save it as **WD D-Chapter 7**.

b. Change the font of the entire document to 11-point High Tower Text. If this font is not available to you, select a different font suitable for the pages of a book. Change the alignment to justified.

c. Change the paper size to 6" × 9".

d. Create mirror margins. (*Hint*: Use the Multiple pages list arrow.) Change the top and bottom margins to .8", change the inside margin to .4", change the outside margin to .6", and create a .3" gutter to allow room for the book's binding.

e. Change the Zoom level to Page Width, open the Header and Footer areas, then apply the setting to create different headers and footers for odd- and even-numbered pages.

f. In the odd-page header, type **Chapter 7**, insert a symbol of your choice, then type **The Fairy Creek Catchment and Stormwater Pollution**.

g. Format the header text in 9-point High Tower Text italic, then right-align the text.

h. In the even-page header, type your name.

i. Format the header text in 9-point High Tower Text italic. The even-page header should be left-aligned.

j. Insert a left-aligned page number field in the even-page footer area, format it in 10-point High Tower Text, insert a right-aligned page number field in the odd-page footer area, then format it in 10-point High Tower Text.

k. Format the page numbers so that the first page of your chapter, which is Chapter 7 in the book, begins on page 101. (*Hint*: Select a page number field, click the Page Number button, then click Format Page Numbers.)

l. Go to the beginning of the document, press [Enter] 10 times, type **Chapter 7: The Fairy Creek Catchment and Stormwater Pollution**, press [Enter] twice, type your name, then press [Enter] twice.

m. Format the chapter title in 16-point Calibri bold, format your name in 14-point Calibri, then left-align the title text and your name.

n. Click the References tab, make sure the citations and bibliography style is set to Chicago Fifteenth Edition, place the insertion point at the end of the first body paragraph on page 1 but before the ending period, insert a citation for Alice Burke, et. al., then add the page number 40 to the citation, as shown in Figure D-28.

o. Add the citations listed in Table D-3 to the document using the sources already associated with the document.

FIGURE D-28

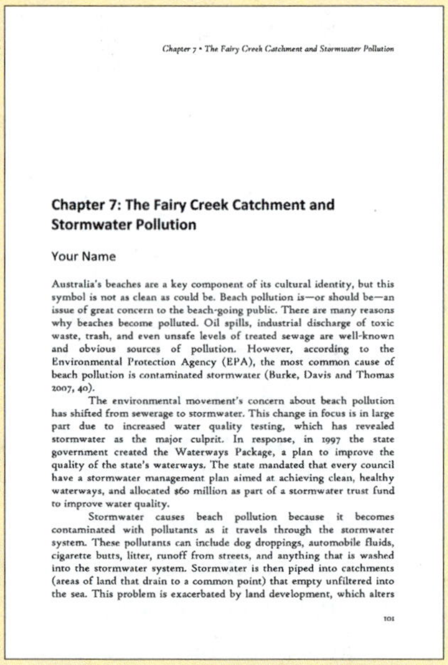
Chapter 7 • The Fairy Creek Catchment and Stormwater Pollution

Chapter 7: The Fairy Creek Catchment and Stormwater Pollution

Your Name

Australia's beaches are a key component of its cultural identity, but this symbol is not as clean as could be. Beach pollution is—or should be—an issue of great concern to the beach-going public. There are many reasons why beaches become polluted. Oil spills, industrial discharge of toxic waste, trash, and even unsafe levels of treated sewage are well-known and obvious sources of pollution. However, according to the Environmental Protection Agency (EPA), the most common cause of beach pollution is contaminated stormwater (Burke, Davis and Thomas 2007, 40).

The environmental movement's concern about beach pollution has shifted from sewerage to stormwater. This change in focus is in large part due to increased water quality testing, which has revealed stormwater as the major culprit. In response, in 1997 the state government created the Waterways Package, a plan to improve the quality of the state's waterways. The state mandated that every council have a stormwater management plan aimed at achieving clean, healthy waterways, and allocated $60 million as part of a stormwater trust fund to improve water quality.

Stormwater causes beach pollution because it becomes contaminated with pollutants as it travels through the stormwater system. These pollutants can include dog droppings, automobile fluids, cigarette butts, litter, runoff from streets, and anything that is washed into the stormwater system. Stormwater is then piped into catchments (areas of land that drain to a common point) that empty unfiltered into the sea. This problem is exacerbated by land development, which alters

101

TABLE D-3

page	location for citation	source	page number
2	End of the first complete paragraph (after ...WCSMP, but before the period)	City of Weston	3
3	End of the first complete paragraph (after ...pollution, but before the colon)	Jensen	135
4	End of second paragraph (after ...health effects, but before the period)	City of Weston	5
4	End of fourth bulleted list (after 1 month)	Seawatch	None
5	End of third paragraph (after ...problem arises, but before the period)	Burke, et. al.	55
6	End of first sentence (after ...stormwater system, but before the period)	City of Weston	7
6	End of first paragraph under Conclusion (after ...include, but before the colon)	Jensen	142

Independent Challenge 3 (continued)

p. Press [Ctrl][End], insert a Works Cited list, format the Works Cited heading in 11-point High Tower Text, black font color, bold, then format the list of works cited in High Tower Text.

Advanced Challenge Exercise

ACE

- Scroll to page 4 in the document, place the insertion point at the end of the paragraph above the Potential health effects... heading, press [Enter] twice, type **Table 1: Total annual pollutant loads per year in the Fairy Creek Catchment**, format the text as bold, then press [Enter] twice.
- Insert a table with four columns and four rows.
- Type the text shown in Figure D-29 in the table. Do not be concerned when the text wraps to the next line in a cell.

FIGURE D-29

Area	Nitrogen	Phosphorus	Suspended solids
Fairy Creek	9.3 tonnes	1.2 tonnes	756.4 tonnes
Durras Arm	6.2 tonnes	.9 tonnes	348.2 tonnes
Cabbage Tree Creek	9.8 tonnes	2.3 tonnes	485.7 tonnes

- Apply the Light List table style. Make sure the text in the header row is bold, then remove any bold formatting from the text in the remaining rows.
- Use AutoFit to make the table fit the contents, then use AutoFit to make the table fit the window.

q. Save your changes, submit your work, then close the document and exit Word.

Real Life Independent Challenge

One of the most common opportunities to use the page layout features of Word is when formatting a research paper. The format recommended by the *MLA Handbook for Writers of Research Papers*, a style guide that includes information on preparing, writing, and formatting research papers, is the standard format used by many schools, colleges, and universities. In this independent challenge, you will research the MLA guidelines for formatting a research paper and use the guidelines you find to format the pages of a sample research report.

a. Use your favorite search engine to search the Web for information on the MLA guidelines for formatting a research report. Use the keywords **MLA Style** and **research paper format** to conduct your search.

b. Look for information on the proper formatting for the following aspects of a research paper: paper size, margins, title page or first page of the report, line spacing, paragraph indentation, and page numbers. Also find information on proper formatting for citations and a works cited page. Print the information you find.

c. Start Word, open the file WD D-6.docx from the drive and folder where you store your Data Files, then save it as **WD D-Research Paper**. Using the information you learned, format this document as a research report.

d. Adjust the margins, set the line spacing, and add page numbers to the document in the format recommended by the MLA. Use **The Maori History of New Zealand** as the title for your sample report, use your name as the author name, and use the name of the course you are enrolled in currently as well as the instructor's name for that course. Make sure to format the title page exactly as the MLA style dictates.

e. Format the remaining text as the body of the research report. Indent the first line of each paragraph rather than use quadruple spacing between paragraphs.

f. Create three sources, insert three citations in the document—a book, a journal article, and a Web site—and create a works cited page, following MLA style. If necessary, edit the format of the citations and works cited page to conform to MLA format. (*Note*: For this practice document, you are allowed to make up sources. Never make up sources for real research papers.)

g. Save the document, submit a copy to your instructor, close the document, then exit Word.

Visual Workshop

Open the file WD D-7.docx from the drive and folder where you store your Data Files, then modify it to create the article shown in Figure D-30. (*Hint*: Change all four margins to .6". Add the footnotes as shown in the figure. To locate the flower clip art image, search using the keyword **wildflowers**, and be sure only the Photographs check box in the Results should be in list box in the Clip Art task pane has a check mark. Select a different clip if the clip shown in the figure is not available to you.) Save the document with the filename **WD D-Gardener's Corner**, then print a copy.

FIGURE D-30

GARDENER'S CORNER

Putting a Perennial Garden to Bed

By Your Name

A certain sense of peace descends when a perennial garden is put to bed for the season. The plants are safely tucked in against the elements, and the garden is ready to welcome the first signs of life. When the work is done, you can sit back and anticipate the bright blooms of spring. Many gardeners are uncertain about how to close a perennial garden. This week's column demystifies the process.

Clean up

Garden clean up can be a gradual process—plants will deteriorate at different rates, allowing you to do a little bit each week.

- Edge beds and borders and remove stakes, trellises, and other plant supports.
- Dig and divide irises, daylilies, and other early bloomers.
- Cut back plants when foliage starts to deteriorate, then rake all debris out of the garden and pull any weeds that remain.

Plant perennials

Fall is the perfect time to plant perennials.[1] The warm, sunny days and cool nights provide optimal conditions for new root growth, without the stress of summer heat.

- Dig deeply and enhance soil with organic matter.
- Use a good starter fertilizer to speed up new root growth and establish a healthy base.
- Untangle the roots of new plants before planting.
- Water deeply after planting as the weather dictates, and keep plants moist for several days after planting.

[1] Fall is also an excellent time to plant shrubs and trees.

Add compost

Organic matter is the key ingredient to healthy garden soil. Composting adds nutrients to the soil, helps the soil retain water and nutrients, and keeps the soil well aerated. If you take care of the soil, your plants will become strong and disease resistant.[2]

Before adding compost, use an iron rake to loosen the top few inches of soil. Spread a one to two inch layer of compost over the entire garden—the best compost is made up of yard waste and kitchen scraps—and then refrain from stepping on the area and compacting the soil.

Winter mulch

Winter protection for perennial beds can only help plants survive the winter. Winter mulch prevents the freezing and thawing cycles, which cause plants to heave and eventually die. Here's what works and what doesn't:

- Always apply mulch after the ground is frozen.
- Never apply generic hay because it contains billions of weed seeds. Also, whole leaves and bark mulch hold too much moisture.[3]
- Use a loose material to allow air filtration. Straw and salt marsh hay are excellent choices for mulch.
- Remove the winter mulch in the spring as soon as new growth begins.

[2] You can buy good compost, but it is easy and useful to make it at home. Composting kitchen scraps reduces household garbage by about one-third.

[3] If using leaves, use only stiff leaves such as Oak or Beech. Soft leaves, such as Maple, make it difficult for air and water to filtrate.

UNIT
A
Excel 2010

Getting Started with Excel 2010

Files You Will Need:

EX A-1.xlsx
EX A-2.xlsx
EX A-3.xlsx
EX A-4.xlsx
EX A-5.xlsx

In this unit, you will learn how spreadsheet software helps you analyze data and make business decisions, even if you aren't a math pro. You'll become familiar with the different elements of a spreadsheet and learn your way around the Excel program window. You will also work in an Excel worksheet and make simple calculations. You have been hired as an assistant at Quest Specialty Travel (QST), a company offering tours that immerse travelers in regional culture. You report to Grace Wong, the vice president of finance. As Grace's assistant, you create worksheets to analyze data from various divisions of the company, so you can help her make sound decisions on company expansion and investments.

OBJECTIVES

Understand spreadsheet software
Tour the Excel 2010 window
Understand formulas
Enter labels and values and use the Sum button
Edit cell entries
Enter and edit a simple formula
Switch worksheet views
Choose print options

UNIT A

Excel 2010

Understanding Spreadsheet Software

Microsoft Excel is the electronic spreadsheet program within the Microsoft Office suite. An **electronic spreadsheet** is an application you use to perform numeric calculations and to analyze and present numeric data. One advantage of spreadsheet programs over pencil and paper is that your calculations are updated automatically, so you can change entries without having to manually recalculate. Table A-1 shows some of the common business tasks people accomplish using Excel. In Excel, the electronic spreadsheet you work in is called a **worksheet**, and it is contained in a file called a **workbook**, which has the file extension .xlsx. At Quest Specialty Travel, you use Excel extensively to track finances and manage corporate data.

DETAILS

When you use Excel, you have the ability to:

- **Enter data quickly and accurately**

  With Excel, you can enter information faster and more accurately than with pencil and paper. Figure A-1 shows a payroll worksheet created using pencil and paper. Figure A-2 shows the same worksheet created using Excel. Equations were added to calculate the hours and pay. You can use Excel to recreate this information for each week by copying the worksheet's structure and the information that doesn't change from week to week, then entering unique data and formulas for each week. You can also quickly create charts and other elements to help visualize how the payroll is distributed.

- **Recalculate data easily**

  Fixing typing errors or updating data is easy in Excel. In the payroll example, if you receive updated hours for an employee, you just enter the new hours and Excel recalculates the pay.

- **Perform what-if analysis**

  The ability to change data and quickly view the recalculated results gives you the power to make informed business decisions. For instance, if you're considering raising the hourly rate for an entry-level tour guide from $12.50 to $15.00, you can enter the new value in the worksheet and immediately see the impact on the overall payroll as well as on the individual employee. Any time you use a worksheet to ask the question "What if?" you are performing **what-if analysis**. Excel also includes a Scenario Manager where you can name and save different what-if versions of your worksheet.

- **Change the appearance of information**

  Excel provides powerful features for making information visually appealing and easier to understand. You can format text and numbers in different fonts, colors, and styles to make it stand out.

- **Create charts**

  Excel makes it easy to create charts based on worksheet information. Charts are updated automatically in Excel whenever data changes. The worksheet in Figure A-2 includes a 3-D pie chart.

- **Share information**

  It's easy for everyone at QST to collaborate in Excel using the company intranet, the Internet, or a network storage device. For example, you can complete the weekly payroll that your boss, Grace Wong, started creating. You can also take advantage of collaboration tools such as shared workbooks, so that multiple people can edit a workbook simultaneously.

- **Build on previous work**

  Instead of creating a new worksheet for every project, it's easy to modify an existing Excel worksheet. When you are ready to create next week's payroll, you can open the file for last week's payroll, save it with a new filename, and modify the information as necessary. You can also use predesigned, formatted files called **templates** to create new worksheets quickly. Excel comes with many templates that you can customize.

FIGURE A-1: Traditional paper worksheet

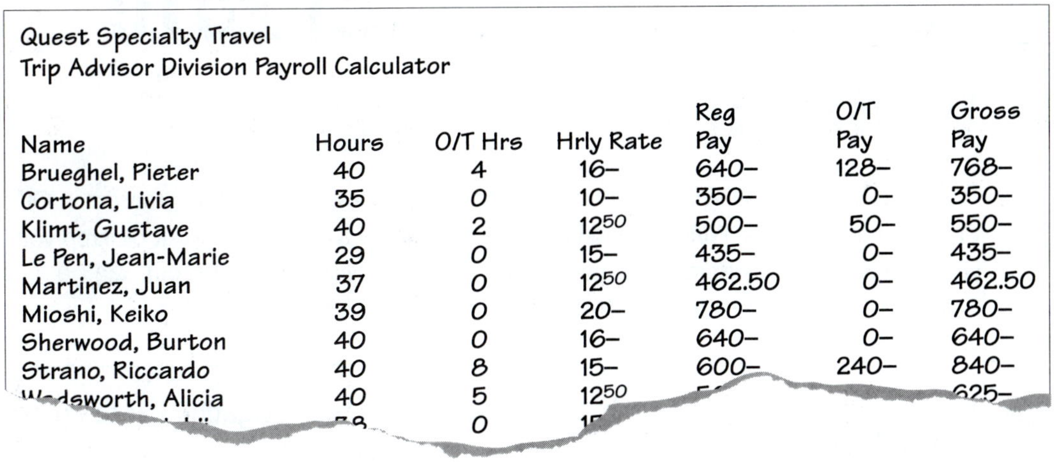

Quest Specialty Travel
Trip Advisor Division Payroll Calculator

Name	Hours	O/T Hrs	Hrly Rate	Reg Pay	O/T Pay	Gross Pay
Brueghel, Pieter	40	4	16–	640–	128–	768–
Cortona, Livia	35	0	10–	350–	0–	350–
Klimt, Gustave	40	2	12 50	500–	50–	550–
Le Pen, Jean-Marie	29	0	15–	435–	0–	435–
Martinez, Juan	37	0	12 50	462.50	0–	462.50
Mioshi, Keiko	39	0	20–	780–	0–	780–
Sherwood, Burton	40	0	16–	640–	0–	640–
Strano, Riccardo	40	8	15–	600–	240–	840–
Wadsworth, Alicia	40	5	12 50	[illegible]	[illegible]	625–
[illegible]	[illegible]	0	[illegible]			

FIGURE A-2: Excel worksheet

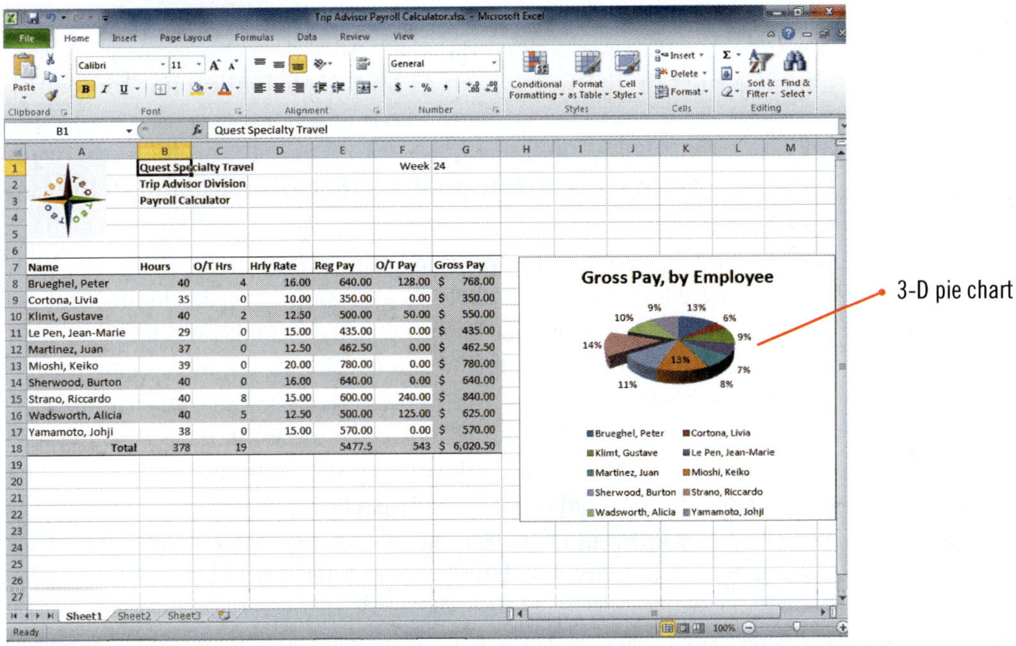

TABLE A-1: Business tasks you can accomplish using Excel

you can use spreadsheets to:	by:
Perform calculations	Adding formulas and functions to worksheet data; for example, adding a list of sales results or calculating a car payment
Represent values graphically	Creating charts based on worksheet data; for example, creating a chart that displays expenses
Generate reports	Creating workbooks that combine information from multiple worksheets, such as summarized sales information from multiple stores
Organize data	Sorting data in ascending or descending order; for example, alphabetizing a list of products or customer names, or prioritizing orders by date
Analyze data	Creating data summaries and short lists using PivotTables or AutoFilters; for example, making a list of the top 10 customers based on spending habits
Create what-if data scenarios	Using variable values to investigate and sample different outcomes, such as changing the interest rate or payment schedule on a loan

UNIT
A
Excel 2010

Touring the Excel 2010 Window

To start Excel, Microsoft Windows must be running. Similar to starting any program in Office, you can use the Start button on the Windows taskbar, or you may have a shortcut on your desktop you prefer to use. If you need additional assistance, ask your instructor or technical support person. You decide to start Excel and familiarize yourself with the worksheet window.

QUICK TIP
For more information on starting a program or opening and saving a file, see the unit "Getting Started with Microsoft Office 2010."

TROUBLE
If you don't see the extension .xlsx on the filenames in the Save As dialog box, don't worry; Windows can be set up to display or not to display the file extensions.

STEPS

1. **Start Excel, click the File tab, then click Open on the navigation bar to open the Open dialog box**

2. **In the Open dialog box, navigate to the drive and folder where you store your Data Files, click EX A-1.xlsx, then click Open**

   The file opens in the Excel window.

3. **Click the File tab, then click Save As on the navigation bar to open the Save As dialog box**

4. **In the Save As dialog box, navigate to the drive and folder where you store your Data Files if necessary, type EX A-Trip Advisor Payroll Calculator in the File name text box, then click Save**

   Using Figure A-3 as a guide, identify the following items:
   - The **Name box** displays the active cell address. "A1" appears in the Name box.
   - The **formula bar** allows you to enter or edit data in the worksheet.
   - The worksheet window contains a grid of columns and rows. Columns are labeled alphabetically and rows are labeled numerically. The worksheet window can contain a total of 1,048,576 rows and 16,384 columns. The intersection of a column and a row is called a **cell**. Cells can contain text, numbers, formulas, or a combination of all three. Every cell has its own unique location or **cell address**, which is identified by the coordinates of the intersecting column and row.
   - The **cell pointer** is a dark rectangle that outlines the cell you are working in. This cell is called the **active cell**. In Figure A-3, the cell pointer outlines cell A1, so A1 is the active cell. The column and row headings for the active cell are highlighted, making it easier to locate.
   - **Sheet tabs** below the worksheet grid let you switch from sheet to sheet in a workbook. By default, a workbook file contains three worksheets—but you can use just one, or have as many as 255, in a workbook. The Insert Worksheet button to the right of Sheet 3 allows you to add worksheets to a workbook. **Sheet tab scrolling buttons** let you navigate to additional sheet tabs when available.
   - You can use the **scroll bars** to move around in a worksheet that is too large to fit on the screen at once.
   - The **status bar** is located at the bottom of the Excel window. It provides a brief description of the active command or task in progress. The **mode indicator** in the lower-left corner of the status bar provides additional information about certain tasks.

5. **Click cell A4**

   Cell A4 becomes the active cell. To activate a different cell, you can click the cell or press the arrow keys on your keyboard to move to it.

6. **Click cell B5, press and hold the mouse button, drag ✚ to cell B14, then release the mouse button**

   You selected a group of cells and they are highlighted, as shown in Figure A-4. A selection of two or more cells such as B5:B14 is called a **range**; you select a range when you want to perform an action on a group of cells at once, such as moving them or formatting them. When you select a range, the status bar displays the average, count (or number of items selected), and sum of the selected cells as a quick reference.

FIGURE A-3: Open workbook

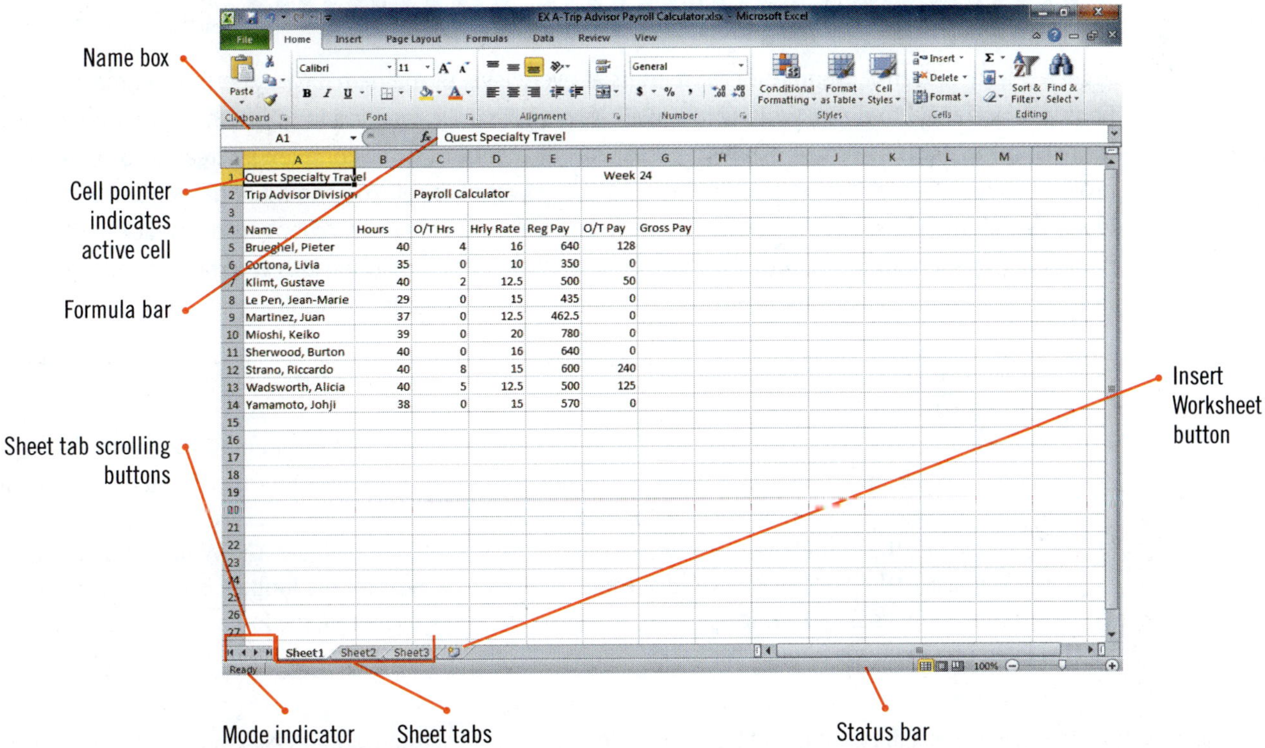

FIGURE A-4: Selected range

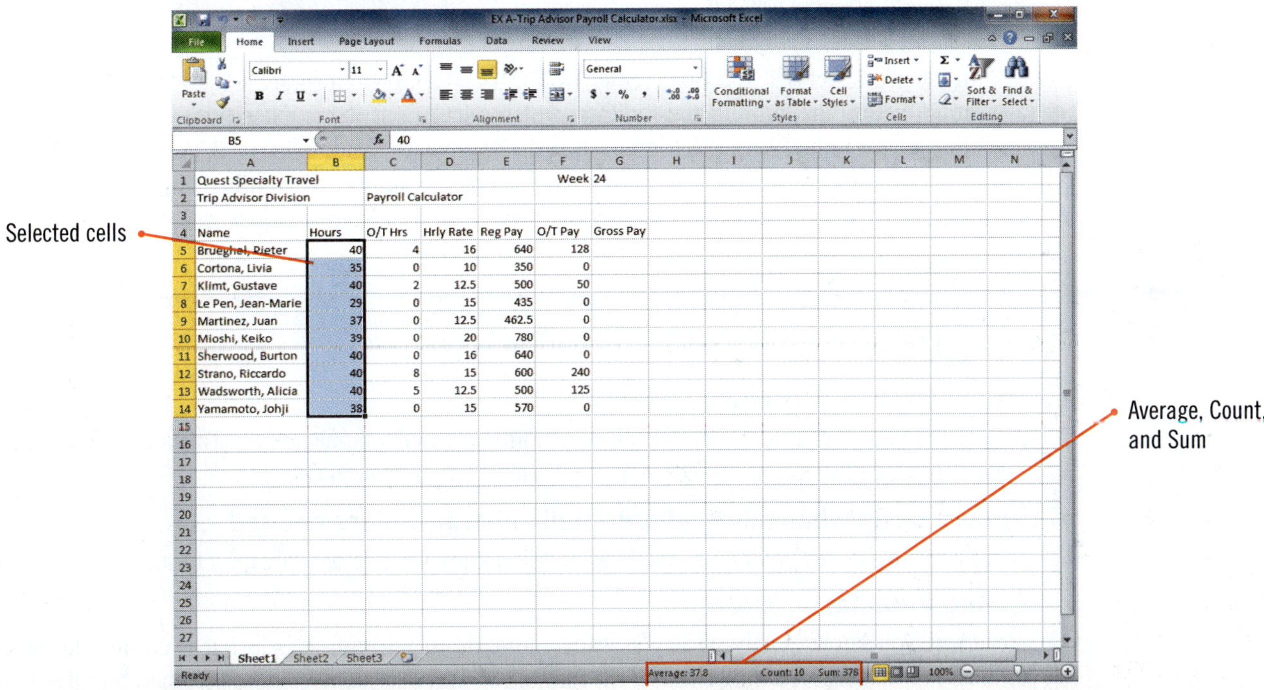

Windows Live and Microsoft Office Web Apps

All Office programs include the capability to incorporate feedback—called online collaboration—across the Internet or a company network. Using **cloud computing** (work done in a virtual environment), you can take advantage of Web programs called Microsoft Office Web Apps, which are simplified versions of the programs found in the Microsoft Office 2010 suite. Because these programs are online, they take up no computer disk space and are accessed using Windows Live SkyDrive, a free service from Microsoft. Using Windows Live SkyDrive, you and your colleagues can create and store documents in a "cloud" and make the documents available to whomever you grant access. To use Windows Live SkyDrive, you need a free Windows Live ID, which you obtain at the Windows Live Web site. You can find more information in the "Working with Windows Live and Office Web Apps" appendix.

Understanding Formulas

Excel is a truly powerful program because users at every level of mathematical expertise can make calculations with accuracy. To do so, you use formulas. A **formula** is an equation in a worksheet. You use formulas to make calculations as simple as adding a column of numbers, or as complex as creating profit-and-loss projections for a global corporation. To tap into the power of Excel, you should understand how formulas work. Managers at QST use the Trip Advisor Payroll Calculator workbook to keep track of employee hours prior to submitting them to the Payroll Department. You'll be using this workbook regularly, so you need to understand the formulas it contains and how Excel calculates the results.

STEPS

1. **Click cell E5**

   The active cell contains a formula, which appears on the formula bar. All Excel formulas begin with the equal sign (=). If you want a cell to show the result of adding 4 plus 2, the formula in the cell would look like this: =4+2. If you want a cell to show the result of multiplying two values in your worksheet, such as the values in cells B5 and D5, the formula would look like this: =B5*D5, as shown in Figure A-5. While you're entering a formula in a cell, the cell references and arithmetic operators appear on the formula bar. See Table A-2 for a list of commonly used arithmetic operators. When you're finished entering the formula, you can either click the Enter button on the formula bar or press [Enter].

2. **Click cell F5**

   An example of a more complex formula is the calculation of overtime pay. At QST, overtime pay is calculated at twice the regular hourly rate times the number of overtime hours. The formula used to calculate overtime pay for the employee in row 5 is:

   O/T Hrs times (2 times Hrly Rate)

   In the worksheet cell, you would enter: =C5*(2*D5), as shown in Figure A-6. The use of parentheses creates groups within the formula and indicates which calculations to complete first—an important consideration in complex formulas. In this formula, first the hourly rate is multiplied by 2, because that calculation is within the parentheses. Next, that value is multiplied by the number of overtime hours. Because overtime is calculated at twice the hourly rate, managers are aware that they need to closely watch this expense.

DETAILS

In creating calculations in Excel, it is important to:

- **Know where the formulas should be**

  An Excel formula is created in the cell where the formula's results should appear. This means that the formula calculating Gross Pay for the employee in row 5 will be entered in cell G5.

- **Know exactly what cells and arithmetic operations are needed**

  Don't guess; make sure you know exactly what cells are involved before creating a formula.

- **Create formulas with care**

  Make sure you know exactly what you want a formula to accomplish before it is created. An inaccurate formula may have far-reaching effects if the formula or its results are referenced by other formulas.

- **Use cell references rather than values**

  The beauty of Excel is that whenever you change a value in a cell, any formula containing a reference to that cell is automatically updated. For this reason, it's important that you use cell references in formulas, rather than actual values, whenever possible.

- **Determine what calculations will be needed**

  Sometimes it's difficult to predict what data will be needed within a worksheet, but you should try to anticipate what statistical information may be required. For example, if there are columns of numbers, chances are good that both column and row totals should be present.

FIGURE A-5: Viewing a formula

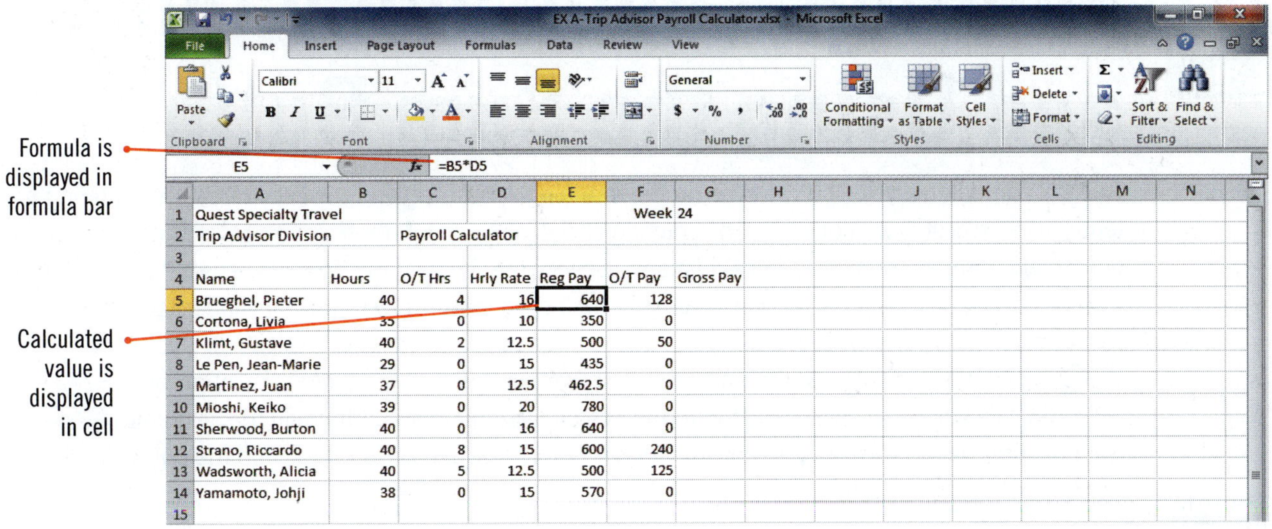

FIGURE A-6: Formula with multiple operators

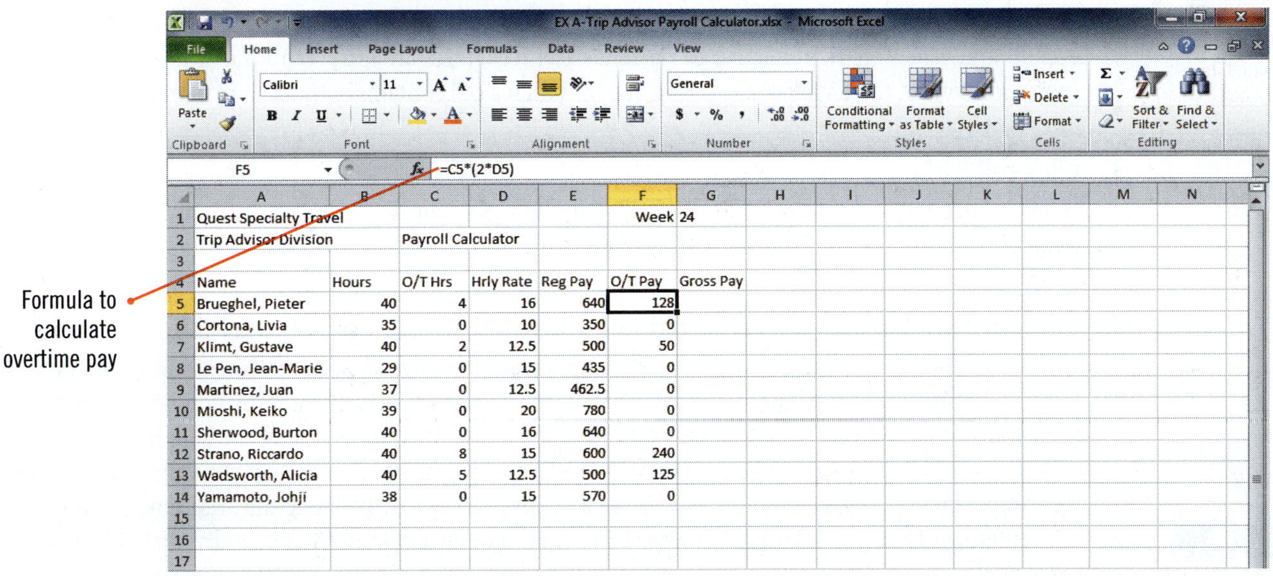

TABLE A-2: Excel arithmetic operators

operator	purpose	example
+	Addition	=A5+A7
-	Subtraction or negation	=A5-10
*	Multiplication	=A5*A7
/	Division	=A5/A7
%	Percent	=35%
^ (caret)	Exponent	=6^2 (same as 6^2)

UNIT A
Excel 2010

Entering Labels and Values and Using the Sum Button

To enter content in a cell, you can type on the formula bar or directly in the cell itself. When entering content in a worksheet, you should start by entering all the labels first. **Labels** are entries that contain text and numerical information not used in calculations, such as "2011 Sales" or "Travel Expenses." Labels help you identify data in worksheet rows and columns, making your worksheet easier to understand. **Values** are numbers, formulas, and functions that can be used in calculations. To enter a calculation, you type an equal sign (=) plus the formula for the calculation; some examples of an Excel calculation are "=2+2" and "=C5+C6." Functions are Excel's built-in formulas; you learn more about them in the next unit. You want to enter some information in the Trip Advisor Payroll Calculator workbook, and use a very simple function to total a range of cells.

STEPS

QUICK TIP
If you change your mind and want to cancel an entry in the formula bar, click the Cancel button on the formula bar.

QUICK TIP
You can create formulas in a cell even before you enter the values to be calculated; the results will be recalculated as soon as the data is entered.

QUICK TIP
You can also press [Tab] to complete a cell entry and move the cell pointer to the right.

1. **Click cell A15, then click in the formula bar**
   Notice that the **mode indicator** on the status bar now reads "Edit," indicating you are in Edit mode. You are in Edit mode any time you are entering or changing the contents of a cell.
2. **Type Totals, then click the Enter button on the formula bar**
   Clicking the Enter button accepts the entry. The new text is left-aligned in the cell. Labels are left-aligned by default, and values are right-aligned by default. Excel recognizes an entry as a value if it is a number or it begins with one of these symbols: +, -, =, @, #, or $. When a cell contains both text and numbers, Excel recognizes it as a label.
3. **Click cell B15**
   You want this cell to total the hours worked by all the trip advisors. You might think you need to create a formula that looks like this: =B5+B6+B7+B8+B9+B10+B11+B12+B13+B14. However, there's an easier way to achieve this result.
4. **Click the Sum button in the Editing group on the Home tab on the Ribbon**
   The SUM function is inserted in the cell, and a suggested range appears in parentheses, as shown in Figure A-7. A **function** is a built-in formula; it includes the **arguments** (the information necessary to calculate an answer) as well as cell references and other unique information. Clicking the Sum button sums the adjacent range (that is, the cells next to the active cell) above or to the left, though you can adjust the range if necessary by selecting a different range before accepting the cell entry. Using the SUM function is quicker than entering a formula, and using the range B5:B14 is more efficient than entering individual cell references.
5. **Click on the formula bar**
   Excel calculates the total contained in cells B5:B14 and displays the result, 378, in cell B15.The cell actually contains the formula =SUM(B5:B14), and the result is displayed.
6. **Click cell C13, type 6, then press [Enter]**
   The number 6 replaces the cell's contents, the cell pointer moves to cell C14, and the value in cell F13 changes.
7. **Click cell C18, type Average Gross Pay, then press [Enter]**
   The new label is entered in cell C18. The contents appear to spill into the empty cells to the right.
8. **Click cell B15, position the pointer on the lower-right corner of the cell (the fill handle) so that the pointer changes to +, drag the + to cell G15, then release the mouse button**
   Dragging the fill handle across a range of cells copies the contents of the first cell into the other cells in the range. In the range B15:F15, each filled cell now contains a function that sums the range of cells above, as shown in Figure A-8.
9. **Save your work**

FIGURE A-7: Creating a formula using the Sum button

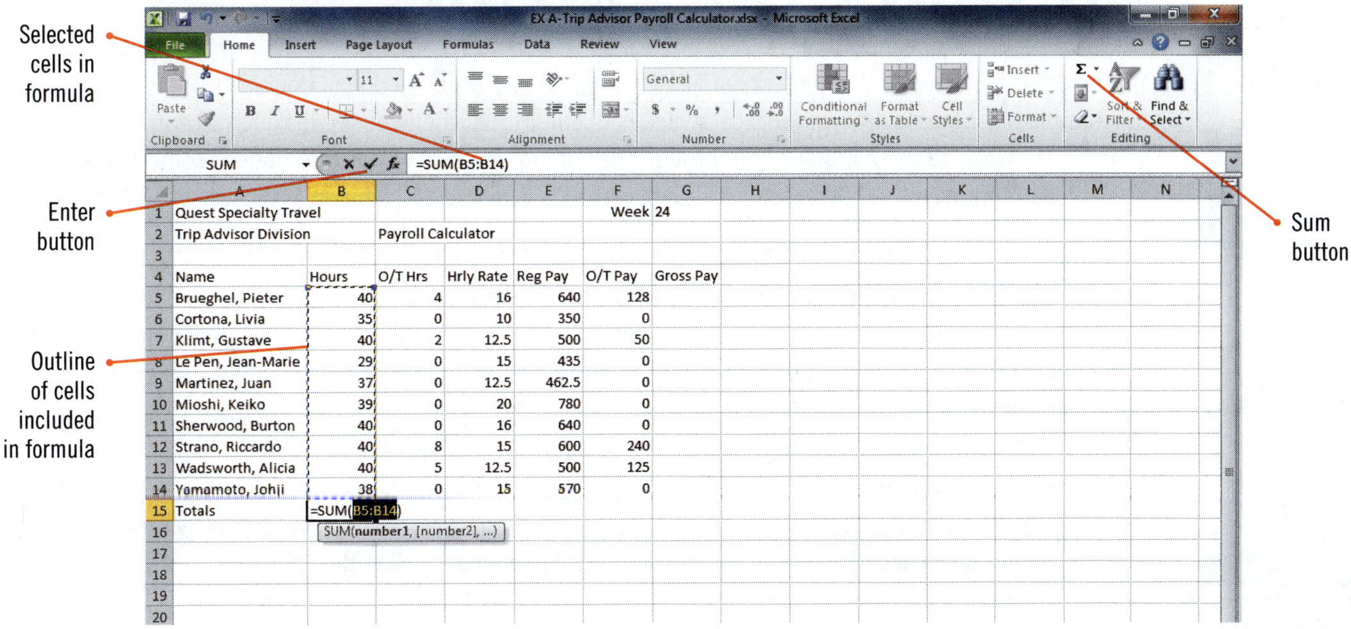

FIGURE A-8: Results of copied SUM functions

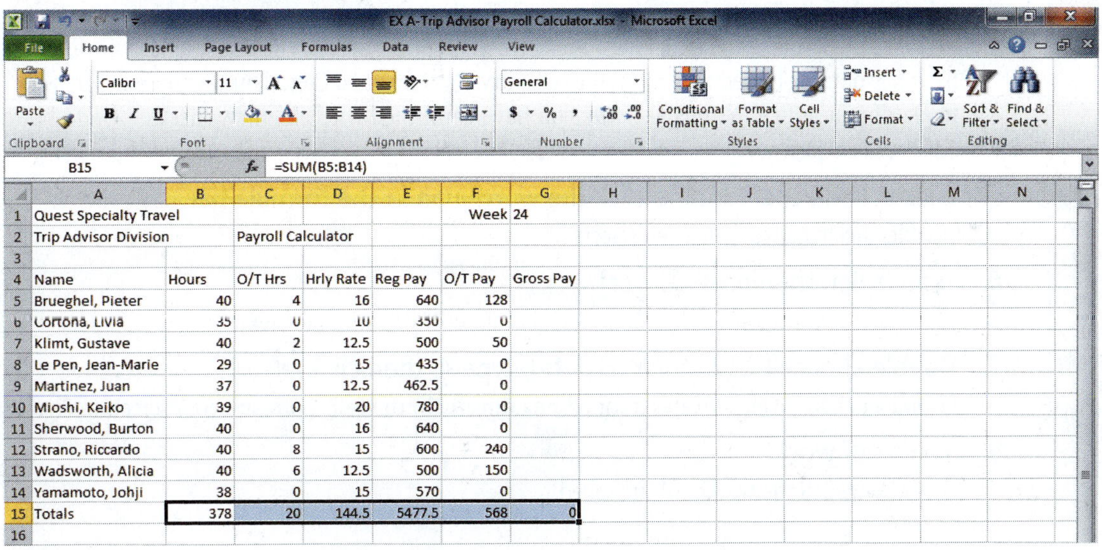

Navigating a worksheet

With over a million cells available in a worksheet, it is important to know how to move around in, or **navigate**, a worksheet. You can use the arrow keys on the keyboard [↑],[↓], [→], or [←] to move one cell at a time, or press [Page Up] or [Page Down] to move one screen at a time. To move one screen to the left press [Alt][Page Up]; to move one screen to the right press [Alt][Page Down]. You can also use the mouse pointer to click the desired cell. If the desired cell is not visible in the worksheet window, use the scroll bars or use the Go To command by clicking the Find & Select button in the Editing group on the Home tab on the Ribbon. To quickly jump to the first cell in a worksheet press [Ctrl][Home]; to jump to the last cell, press [Ctrl][End].

UNIT A
Excel 2010

Editing Cell Entries

You can change, or **edit**, the contents of an active cell at any time. To do so, double-click the cell, click in the formula bar, or just start typing. Excel switches to Edit mode when you are making cell entries. Different pointers, shown in Table A-3, guide you through the editing process. You noticed some errors in the worksheet and want to make corrections. The first error is in cell A5, which contains a misspelled name.

STEPS

1. **Click cell A5, then click to the right of P in the formula bar**
   As soon as you click in the formula bar, a blinking vertical line called the **insertion point** appears on the formula bar at the location where new text will be inserted. See Figure A-9. The mouse pointer changes to I when you point anywhere in the formula bar.
2. **Press [Delete], then click the Enter button ✓ on the formula bar**
   Clicking the Enter button accepts the edit, and the spelling of the employee's first name is corrected. You can also press [Enter] or [Tab] to accept an edit. Pressing [Enter] to accept an edit moves the cell pointer down one cell, and pressing [Tab] to accept an edit moves the cell pointer one cell to the right.
3. **Click cell B6, then press [F2]**
   Excel switches to Edit mode, and the insertion point blinks in the cell. Pressing [F2] activates the cell for editing directly in the cell instead of the formula bar. Whether you edit in the cell or the formula bar is simply a matter of preference; the results in the worksheet are the same.
4. **Press [Backspace], type 8, then press [Enter]**
   The value in the cell changes from 35 to 38, and cell B7 becomes the active cell. Did you notice that the calculations in cells B15 and E15 also changed? That's because those cells contain formulas that include cell B6 in their calculations. If you make a mistake when editing, you can click the Cancel button ✕ on the formula bar *before* pressing [Enter] to confirm the cell entry. The Enter and Cancel buttons appear only when you're in Edit mode. If you notice the mistake *after* you have confirmed the cell entry, click the Undo button on the Quick Access toolbar.
5. **Click cell A9, then double-click the word Juan in the formula bar**
   Double-clicking a word in a cell selects it.
6. **Type Javier, then press [Enter]**
   When text is selected, typing deletes it and replaces it with the new text.
7. **Double-click cell C12, press [Delete], type 4, then click ✓**
   Double-clicking a cell activates it for editing directly in the cell. Compare your screen to Figure A-10.
8. **Save your work**
   Your changes to the workbook are saved.

QUICK TIP
On some keyboards, you might need to press an [F Lock] key to enable the function keys.

QUICK TIP
The Undo button allows you to reverse up to 100 previous actions, one at a time.

QUICK TIP
You can use the keyboard to select all cell contents by clicking to the right of the cell contents in the cell or formula bar, pressing and holding [Shift], then pressing [Home].

Recovering unsaved changes to a workbook file

You can use Excel's AutoRecover feature to automatically save (Autosave) your work as often as you want. This means that if you suddenly lose power or if Excel closes unexpectedly while you're working, you can recover all or some of the changes you made since you saved it last. (Of course, this is no substitute for regularly saving your work: this is just added insurance.) To customize the AutoRecover settings, click the File tab, click Options, then click Save. AutoRecover lets you decide how often and into which location it should Autosave files. When you restart Excel after losing power, a Document Recovery pane opens and provides access to the saved and Autosaved versions of the files that were open when Excel closed. You can also click the File tab, click Recent on the navigation bar, then click Recover Unsaved Workbooks to open Autosaved workbooks using the Open dialog box.

FIGURE A-9: Worksheet in Edit mode

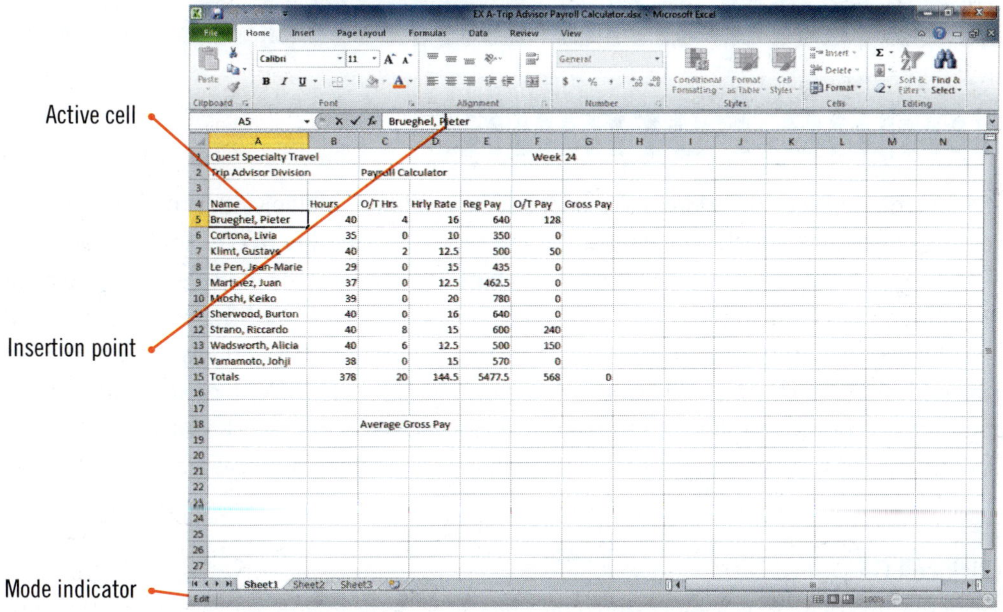

FIGURE A-10: Edited worksheet

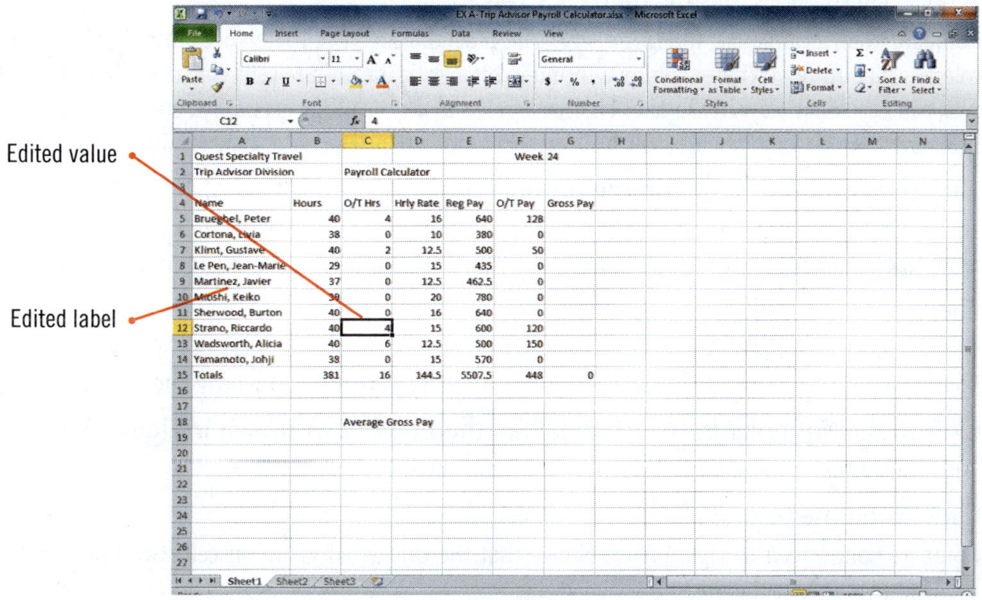

TABLE A-3: Common pointers in Excel

name	pointer	use to	visible over the
Normal		Select a cell or range; indicates Ready mode	Active worksheet
Fill handle		Copy cell contents to adjacent cells	Lower-right corner of the active cell or range
I-beam		Edit cell contents in active cell or formula bar	Active cell in Edit mode or over the formula bar
Move		Change the location of the selected cell(s)	Perimeter of the active cell(s)
Copy		Create a duplicate of the selected cell(s)	Perimeter of the active cell(s) when [Ctrl] is pressed
Column resize		Change the width of a column	Border between column heading indicators

UNIT
A
Excel 2010

Entering and Editing a Simple Formula

You use formulas in Excel to perform calculations such as adding, multiplying, and averaging. Formulas in an Excel worksheet start with the equal sign (=), also called the **formula prefix**, followed by cell addresses, range names, values, and calculation operators. **Calculation operators** indicate what type of calculation you want to perform on the cells, ranges, or values. They can include **arithmetic operators,** which perform mathematical calculations (see Table A-2 in the "Understanding Formulas" lesson); **comparison operators**, which compare values for the purpose of true/false results; **text concatenation operators**, which join strings of text in different cells; and **reference operators**, which enable you to use ranges in calculations. You want to create a formula in the worksheet that calculates gross pay for each employee.

STEPS

1. **Click cell G5**

   This is the first cell where you want to insert the formula. To calculate gross pay, you need to add regular pay and overtime pay. For employee Peter Brueghel, regular pay appears in cell E5 and overtime pay appears in cell F5.

2. **Type =, click cell E5, type +, then click cell F5**

   Compare your formula bar to Figure A-11. The blue and green cell references in cell G5 correspond to the colored cell outlines. When entering a formula, it's a good idea to use cell references instead of values whenever you can. That way, if you later change a value in a cell (if, for example, Peter's regular pay changes to 615), any formula that includes this information reflects accurate, up-to-date results.

3. **Click the Enter button ✓ on the formula bar**

   The result of the formula =E5+F5, 768, appears in cell G5. This same value appears in cell G15 because cell G15 contains a formula that totals the values in cells G5:G14, and there are no other values now.

4. **Click cell F5**

   The formula in this cell calculates overtime pay by multiplying overtime hours (C5) times twice the regular hourly rate (2*D5). You want to edit this formula to reflect a new overtime pay rate.

5. **Click to the right of 2 in the formula bar, then type .5 as shown in Figure A-12**

   The formula that calculates overtime pay has been edited.

6. **Click ✓ on the formula bar**

   Compare your screen to Figure A-13. Notice that the calculated values in cells G5, F15, and G15 have all changed to reflect your edits to cell F5.

7. **Save your work**

QUICK TIP

You can reference a cell in a formula either by typing the cell reference or clicking the cell in the worksheet; when you click a cell to add a reference, the Mode indicator changes to "Point."

Understanding named ranges

It can be difficult to remember the cell locations of critical information in a worksheet, but using cell names can make this task much easier. You can name a single cell or range of contiguous, or touching, cells. For example, you might name a cell that contains data on average gross pay "AVG_GP" instead of trying to remember the cell address C18. A named range must begin with a letter or an underscore. It cannot contain any spaces or be the same as a built-in name, such as a function or another object (such as a different named range) in the workbook. To name a range, select the cell(s) you want to name, click the Name box in the formula bar, type the name you want to use, then press [Enter]. You can also name a range by clicking the Formulas tab, then clicking the Define Name button in the Defined Names group. Type the new range name in the Name text box in the New Name dialog box, verify the selected range, then click OK. When you use a named range in a formula, the named range appears instead of the cell address. You can also create a named range using the contents of a cell already in the range. Select the range containing the text you want to use as a name, then click the Create from Selection button in the Defined Names group. The Create Names from Selection dialog box opens. Choose the location of the name you want to use, then click OK.

FIGURE A-11: Simple formula in a worksheet

Cell outline color corresponds to cell reference

Mode indicator changes to Point

Referenced cells are inserted in formula

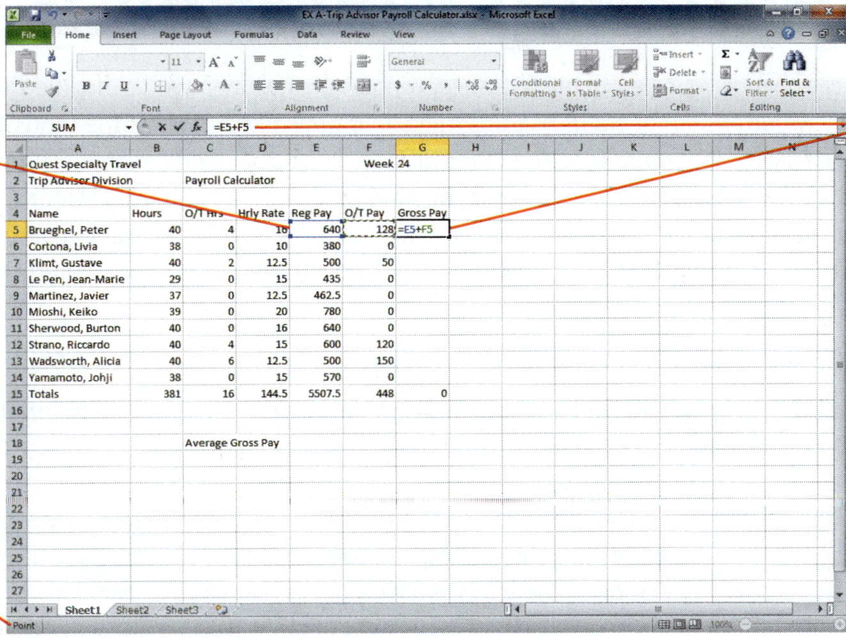

FIGURE A-12: Edited formula in a worksheet

Edited value in formula

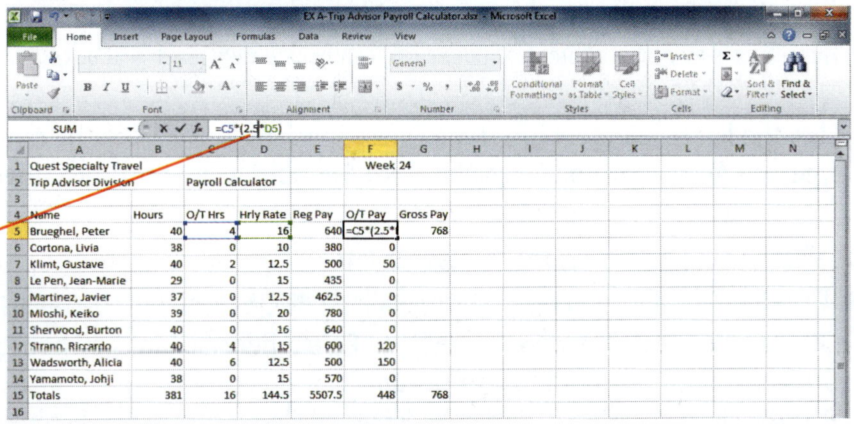

FIGURE A-13: Edited formula with changes

Edited formula results in changes to these other cells

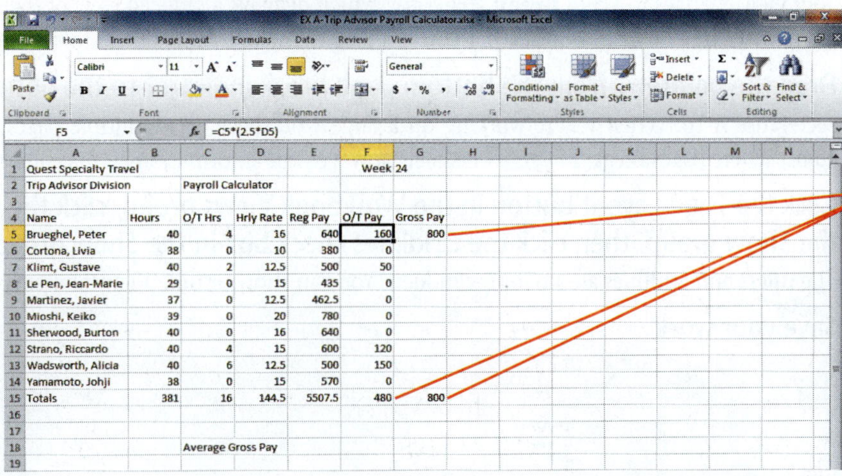

UNIT
A
Excel 2010

Switching Worksheet Views

You can change your view of the worksheet window at any time, using either the View tab on the Ribbon or the View buttons on the status bar. Changing your view does not affect the contents of a worksheet; it just makes it easier for you to focus on different tasks, such as entering content or preparing a worksheet for printing. The View tab includes a variety of viewing options, such as View buttons, zoom controls, and the ability to show or hide worksheet elements such as gridlines. The status bar offers fewer View options but can be more convenient to use. You want to make some final adjustments to your worksheet, including adding a header so the document looks more polished.

STEPS

QUICK TIP
Although a worksheet can contain more than a million rows and thousands of columns, the current document contains only as many pages as necessary for the current project.

1. **Click the View tab on the Ribbon, then click the Page Layout button in the Workbook Views group**

   The view switches from the default view, Normal, to Page Layout view. **Normal view** shows the worksheet without including certain details like headers and footers, or tools like rulers and a page number indicator; it's great for creating and editing a worksheet, but may not be detailed enough when you want to put the finishing touches on a document. **Page Layout view** provides a more accurate view of how a worksheet will look when printed, as shown in Figure A-14. The margins of the page are displayed, along with a text box for the header. A footer text box appears at the bottom of the page, but your screen may not be large enough to view it without scrolling. Above and to the left of the page are rulers. Part of an additional page appears to the right of this page, but it is dimmed, indicating that it does not contain any data. A page number indicator on the status bar tells you the current page and the total number of pages in this worksheet.

2. **Drag the pointer over the header *without clicking***

   The header is made up of three text boxes: left, center, and right. Each text box is highlighted blue as you pass over it with the pointer.

QUICK TIP
You can change header and footer information using the Header & Footer Tools Design tab that opens on the Ribbon when a header or footer is active. For example, you can insert the date by clicking the Current Date button in the Header & Footer Elements group, or insert the time by clicking the Current Time button.

3. **Click the left header text box, type Quest Specialty Travel, click the center header text box, type Trip Advisor Payroll Calculator, click the right header text box, then type Week 24**

   The new text appears in the text boxes, as shown in Figure A-15.

4. **Select the range A1:G2, then press [Delete]**

   The duplicate information you just entered in the header is deleted from cells in the worksheet.

5. **Click the View tab if necessary, click the Ruler check box in the Show group, then click the Gridlines check box in the Show group**

   The rulers and the gridlines are hidden. By default, gridlines in a worksheet do not print, so hiding them gives you a more accurate image of your final document.

6. **Click the Page Break Preview button on the status bar, then click OK in the Welcome to Page Break Preview dialog box, if necessary**

   Your view changes to **Page Break Preview**, which displays a reduced view of each page of your worksheet, along with page break indicators that you can drag to include more or less information on a page.

7. **Drag the pointer from the bottom page break indicator to the bottom of row 21**

   See Figure A-16. When you're working on a large worksheet with multiple pages, sometimes you need to adjust where pages break; in this worksheet, however, the information all fits comfortably on one page.

QUICK TIP
Once you view a worksheet in Page Break Preview, the page break indicators appear as dotted lines after you switch back to Normal view or Page Layout view.

8. **Click the Page Layout button in the Workbook Views group, click the Ruler check box in the Show group, then click the Gridlines check box in the Show group**

   The rulers and gridlines are no longer hidden. You can show or hide View tab items in any view.

9. **Save your work**

FIGURE A-14: Page Layout view

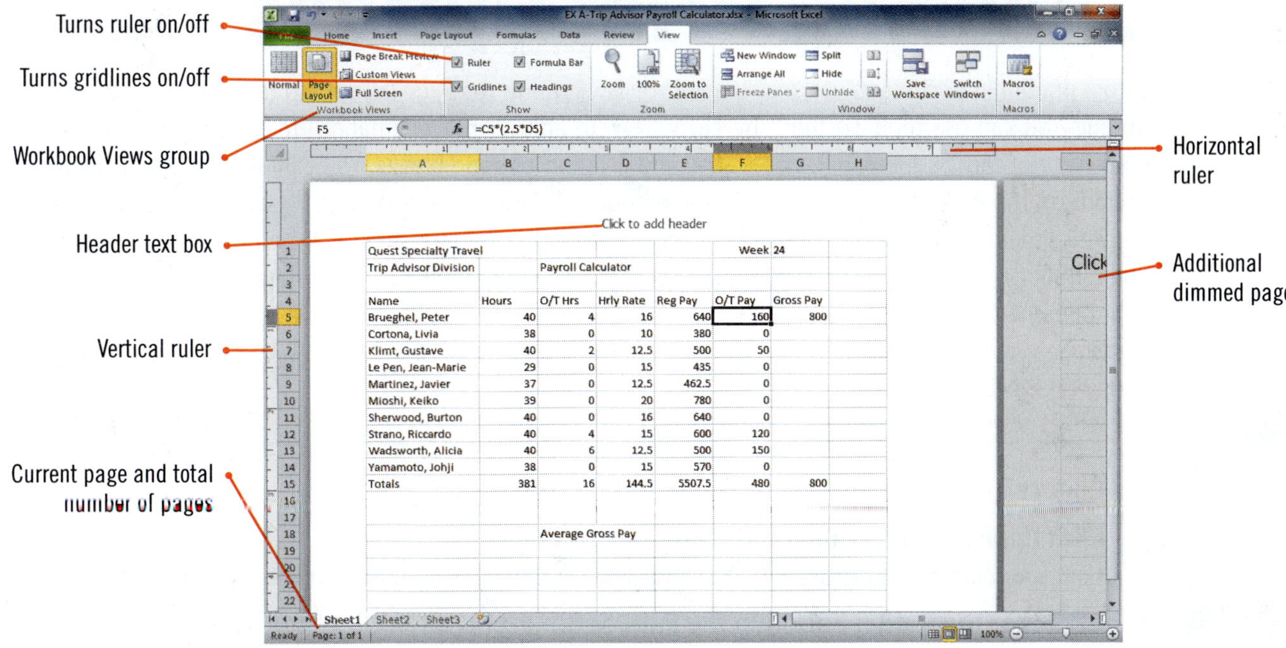

FIGURE A-15: Header text entered

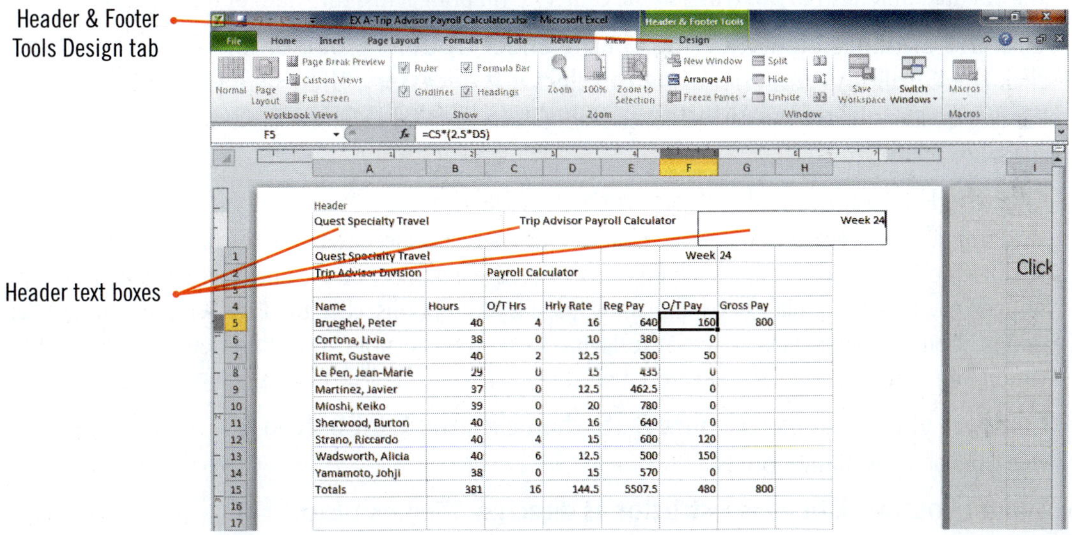

FIGURE A-16: Page Break Preview

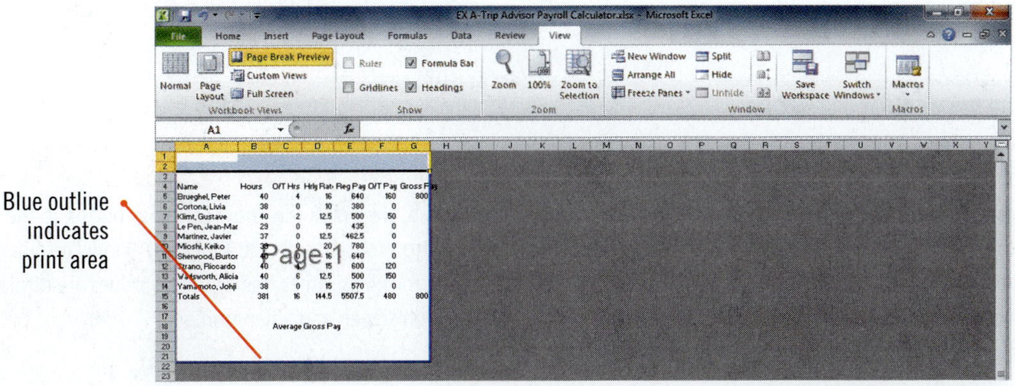

UNIT A
Excel 2010

Choosing Print Options

Before printing a document, you may want to review it using the Page Layout tab to fine-tune your printed output. You can use tools on the Page Layout tab to adjust print orientation (the direction in which the content prints across the page), paper size, and location of page breaks. You can also use the Scale to Fit options on the Page Layout tab to fit a large amount of data on a single page without making changes to individual margins, and to turn gridlines and column/row headings on and off. When you are ready to print, you can set print options such as the number of copies to print and the correct printer, and you can preview your document in Backstage view using the File tab. You can also adjust page layout settings from within Backstage view and immediately see the results in the document preview. You are ready to prepare your worksheet for printing.

STEPS

1. **Click cell A21, type your name, then press [Enter]**
2. **Click the Page Layout tab on the Ribbon**
   Compare your screen to Figure A-17. The dotted line indicates the default **print area**, the area to be printed.
3. **Click the Orientation button in the Page Setup group, then click Landscape**
   The paper orientation changes to **landscape**, so the contents will print across the length of the page instead of across the width.
4. **Click the Orientation button in the Page Setup group, then click Portrait**
   The orientation returns to **portrait**, so the contents will print across the width of the page.
5. **Click the Gridlines View check box in the Sheet Options group on the Page Layout tab, click the Gridlines Print check box to select it if necessary, then save your work**
   Printing gridlines makes the data easier to read, but the gridlines will not print unless the Gridlines Print check box is checked.
6. **Click the File tab, then click Print on the navigation bar**
   The Print tab in Backstage view displays a preview of your worksheet exactly as it will look when it is printed. To the left of the worksheet preview, you can also change a number of document settings and print options. To open the Page Setup dialog box and adjust page layout options, click the Page Setup link in the Settings section. Compare your preview screen to Figure A-18. You can print from this view by clicking the Print button, or return to the worksheet without printing by clicking the File tab again.
7. **Compare your settings to Figure A-18, then click the Print button**
   One copy of the worksheet prints.
8. **Submit your work to your instructor as directed, then exit Excel**

QUICK TIP
You can use the Zoom slider on the status bar at any time to enlarge your view of specific areas of your worksheet.

QUICK TIP
To change the active printer, click the current printer in the Printer section in Backstage view, then choose a different printer.

QUICK TIP
If the Quick Print button appears on the Quick Access Toolbar, you can print your worksheet using the default settings by clicking it.

Printing worksheet formulas

Sometimes you need to keep a record of all the formulas in a worksheet. You might want to do this to see exactly how you came up with a complex calculation, so you can explain it to others. To prepare a worksheet to show formulas rather than results when printed, open the workbook containing the formulas you want to print. Click the Formulas tab, then click the Show Formulas button in the Formula Auditing group to select it. When the Show Formulas button is selected, formulas rather than resulting values are displayed in the worksheet on screen and when printed.

FIGURE A-17: Worksheet with portrait orientation

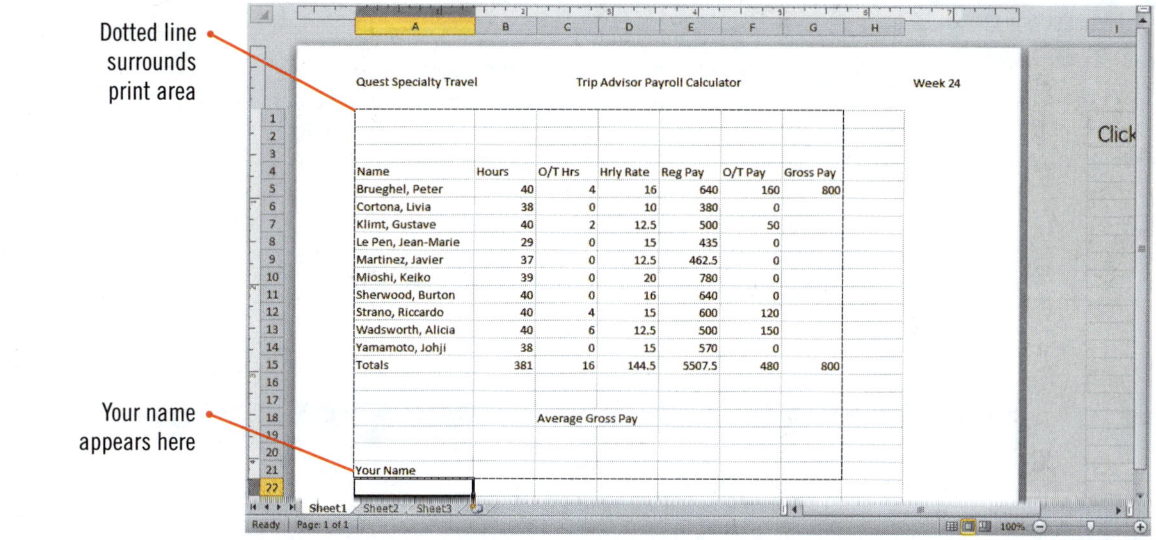

FIGURE A-18: Print tab in Backstage view

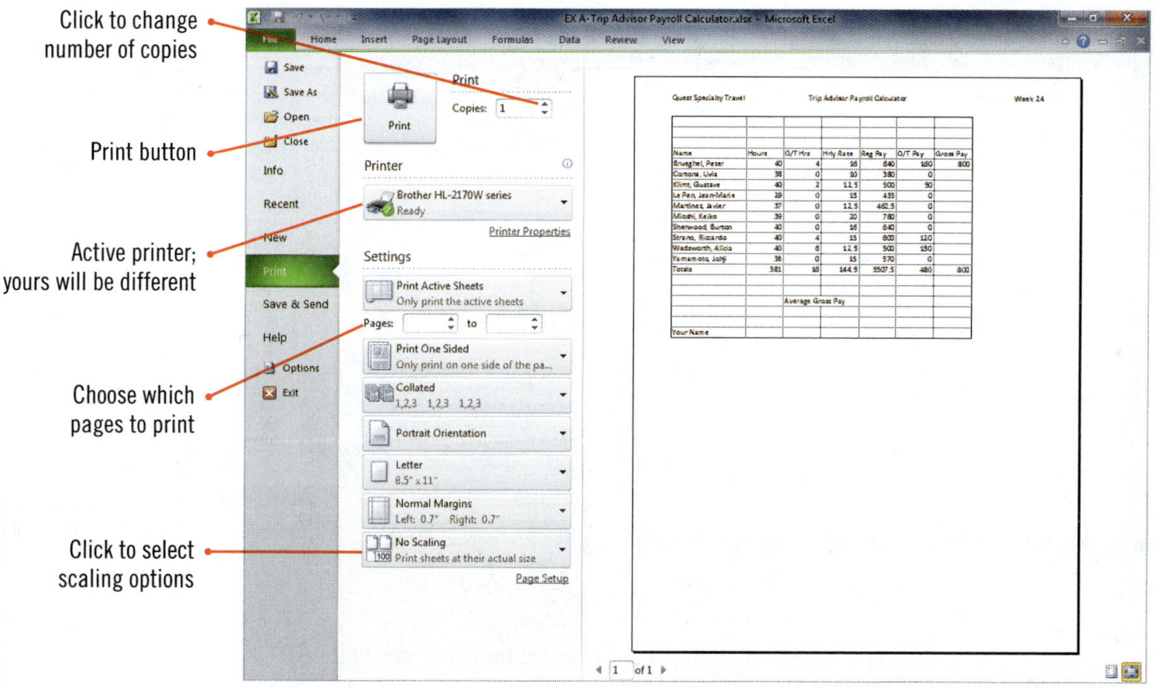

Scaling to fit

If you have a large amount of data that you want to fit to a single sheet of paper, but you don't want to spend a lot of time trying to adjust the margins and other settings, you have several options. You can easily print your work on a single sheet by clicking the No Scaling list arrow in the Settings section on the Print tab in Backstage view, then clicking Fit Sheet on One Page. Another method for fitting worksheet content onto one page is to click the Page Layout tab, then change the Width and Height settings in the Scale to Fit group each to 1 Page. You can also use the Fit to option in the Page Setup dialog box to fit a worksheet on one page. To open the Page Setup dialog box, click the dialog box launcher in the Scale to Fit group on the Page Layout tab, or click the Page Setup link on the Print tab in Backstage view. Make sure the Page tab is selected in the Page Setup dialog box, then click the Fit to option button.

Practice

Concepts Review

For current SAM information, including versions and content details, visit SAM Central (http://www.cengage.com/samcentral). If you have a SAM user profile, you may have access to hands-on instruction, practice, and assessment of the skills covered in this unit. Since various versions of SAM are supported throughout the life of this text, check with your instructor for the correct instructions and URL/Web site for accessing assignments.

Label the elements of the Excel worksheet window shown in Figure A-19.

FIGURE A-19

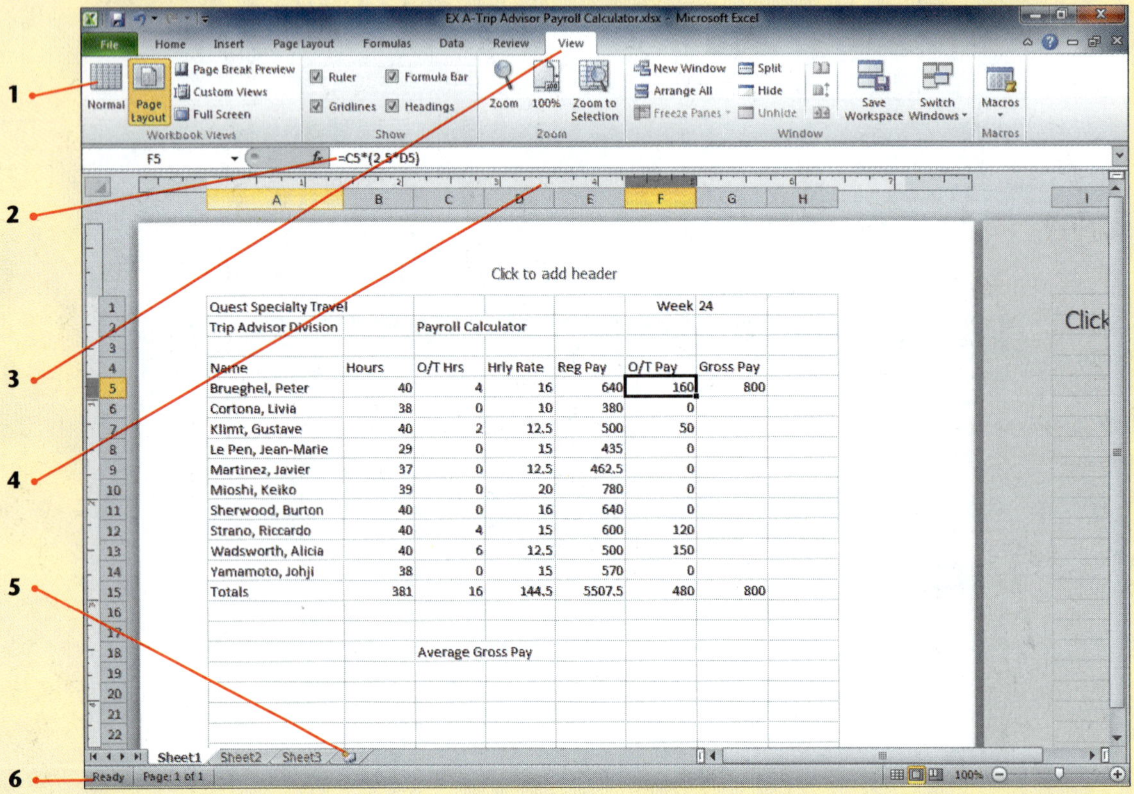

Match each term with the statement that best describes it.

7. **Formula prefix**
8. **Normal view**
9. **Name box**
10. **Cell**
11. **Orientation**
12. **Workbook**

- **a.** Default view in Excel
- **b.** Direction in which contents of page will print
- **c.** Equal sign preceding a formula
- **d.** File consisting of one or more worksheets
- **e.** Intersection of a column and a row
- **f.** Part of the Excel program window that displays the active cell address

Select the best answer from the list of choices.

13. The maximum number of worksheets you can include in a workbook is:

a. 3.
b. 250.
c. 255.
d. Unlimited.

14. Using a cell address in a formula is known as:

a. Formularizing.
b. Prefixing.
c. Cell referencing.
d. Cell mathematics.

15. Which feature could be used to print a very long worksheet on a single sheet of paper?

a. Show Formulas
b. Scale to fit
c. Page Break Preview
d. Named Ranges

16. A selection of multiple cells is called a:

a. Group.
b. Range.
c. Reference.
d. Package.

17. Which worksheet view shows how your worksheet will look when printed?

a. Page Layout
b. Data
c. Review
d. View

18. Which key can you press to switch to Edit mode?

a. [F1]
b. [F2]
c. [F4]
d. [F6]

19. Which view shows you a reduced view of each page of your worksheet?

a. Normal
b. Page Layout
c. Thumbnail
d. Page Break Preview

20. In which area can you see a preview of your worksheet?

a. Page Setup
b. Backstage view
c. Printer Setup
d. View tab

21. In which view can you see the header and footer areas of a worksheet?

a. Normal view
b. Page Layout view
c. Page Break Preview
d. Header/Footer view

Skills Review

1. Understand spreadsheet software.

a. What is the difference between a workbook and a worksheet?
b. Identify five common business uses for electronic spreadsheets.
c. What is what-if analysis?

2. Tour the Excel 2010 window.

a. Start Excel.
b. Open the file EX A-2.xlsx from the drive and folder where you store your Data Files, then save it as **EX A-Weather Statistics**.
c. Locate the formula bar, the Sheet tabs, the mode indicator, and the cell pointer.

3. Understand formulas.

a. What is the average high temperature of the listed cities? (*Hint*: Select the range B5:G5 and use the status bar.)
b. What formula would you create to calculate the difference in altitude between Denver and Phoenix? Enter your answer (as an equation) in cell D13.

4. Enter labels and values and use the Sum button.

a. Click cell H8, then use the Sum button to calculate the total snowfall.
b. Click cell H7, then use the Sum button to calculate the total rainfall.
c. Save your changes to the file.

Skills Review (continued)

5. **Edit cell entries.**
   a. Use [F2] to correct the spelling of SanteFe in cell G3 (the correct spelling is Santa Fe).
   b. Click cell A17, then type your name.
   c. Save your changes.
6. **Enter and edit a simple formula.**
   a. Change the value 41 in cell C8 to **52**.
   b. Change the value 37 in cell D6 to **35.4**.
   c. Select cell J4, then use the fill handle to copy the formula in cell J4 to cells J5:J8
   d. Save your changes.
7. **Switch worksheet views.**
   a. Click the View tab on the Ribbon, then switch to Page Layout view.
   b. Add the header **Average Annual Weather Statistics** to the center header text box.
   c. Add your name to the right header box.
   d. Delete the contents of cell A1.
   e. Delete the contents of cell A17.
   f. Save your changes.
8. **Choose print options.**
   a. Use the Page Layout tab to change the orientation to Portrait.
   b. Turn off gridlines by deselecting both the Gridlines View and Gridlines Print check boxes (if necessary) in the Sheet Options group.
   c. Scale the worksheet so all the information fits on one page. (*Hint*: Click the Width list arrow in the Scale to Fit group, click 1 page, click the Height list arrow in the Scale to Fit group, then click 1 page.) Compare your screen to Figure A-20.
   d. Preview the worksheet in Backstage view, then print the worksheet.
   e. Save your changes, submit your work to your instructor as directed, then close the workbook and exit Excel.

FIGURE A-20

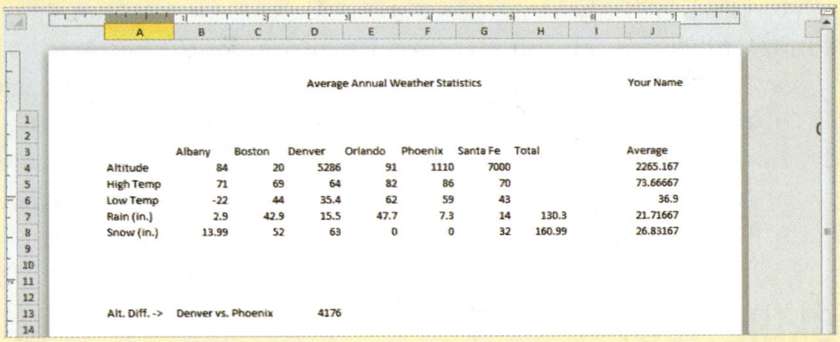

Independent Challenge 1

A local executive relocation company has hired you to help them make the transition to using Excel in their office. They would like to list their properties in a workbook. You've started a worksheet for this project that contains labels but no data.

If you have a SAM 2010 user profile, an autogradable SAM version of this assignment may be available at http://www.cengage.com/sam2010. Check with your instructor to confirm that this assignment is available in SAM. To use the SAM version of this assignment, log into the SAM 2010 Web site and download the instruction and start files.

a. Open the file EX A-3.xlsx from where you store your Data Files, then save it as **EX A-Property Listings**.
b. Enter the data shown in Table A-4 in columns A, C, D, and E (the property address information should spill into column B).

TABLE A-4

Property Address	Price	Bedrooms	Bathrooms
1507 Pinon Lane	475000	4	2.5
32 Zanzibar Way	325000	3	4
60 Pottery Lane	475500	2	2
902 Excelsior Drive	295000	4	3

Independent Challenge 1 (continued)

c. Use Page Layout view to create a header with the following components: the title **Property Listings** in the center and your name on the right.
d. Create formulas for totals in cells C6:E6.
e. Save your changes, then compare your worksheet to Figure A-21.
f. Submit your work to your instructor as directed.
g. Close the worksheet and exit Excel.

FIGURE A-21

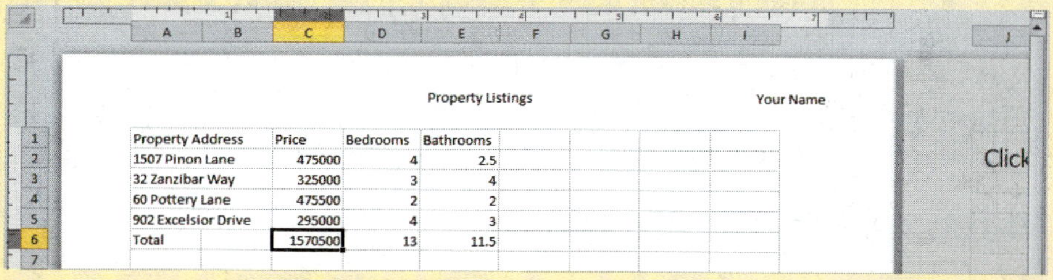

Independent Challenge 2

You are the General Manager for Prestige Import Motors, a small auto parts supplier. Although the company is just 5 years old, it is expanding rapidly, and you are continually looking for ways to save time. You recently began using Excel to manage and maintain data on inventory and sales, which has greatly helped you to track information accurately and efficiently.

a. Start Excel.
b. Save a new workbook as **EX A-Prestige Import Motors** in the drive and folder where you store your Data Files.
c. Switch to an appropriate view, then add a header that contains your name in the left header text box and the title **Prestige Import Motors** in the center header text box.
d. Using Figure A-22 as a guide, create labels for at least seven car manufacturers and sales for three months. Include other labels as appropriate. The car make should be in column A and the months should be in columns B, C, and D. A Total row should be beneath the data, and a Total column should be in column E.

FIGURE A-22

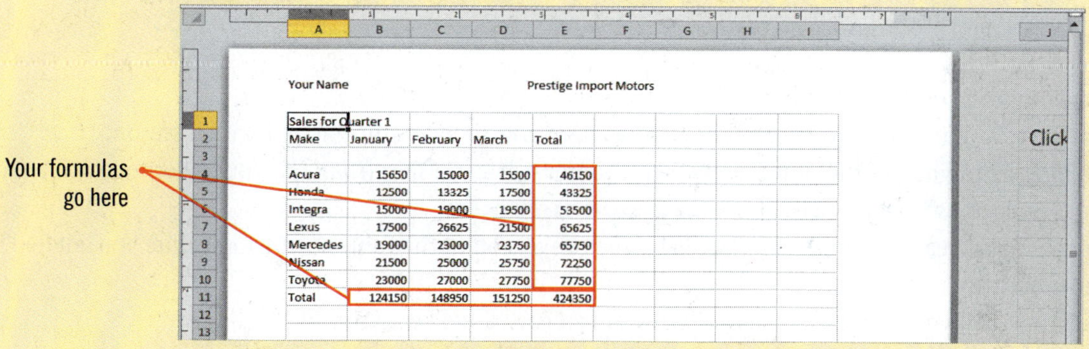

e. Enter values of your choice for the monthly sales for each make.
f. Add formulas in the Total column to calculate total quarterly sales for each make. Add formulas at the bottom of each column of values to calculate the total for that column. Remember that you can use the Sum button and the fill handle to save time.
g. Save your changes, preview the worksheet in Backstage view, then submit your work to your instructor as directed.

Excel 2010

Independent Challenge 2 (continued)

Advanced Challenge Exercise

- Create a label two rows beneath the data in column A that says **15% increase**.
- Create a formula in each of cells B13, C13, and D13 that calculates monthly sales plus a 15% increase.
- Display the formulas in the worksheet, then print a copy of the worksheet with formulas displayed.
- Save the workbook.

h. Close the workbook and exit Excel.

Independent Challenge 3

This Independent Challenge requires an Internet connection.

Your office is starting a branch in Paris, and you think it would be helpful to create a worksheet that can be used to convert Fahrenheit temperatures to Celsius, to help employees who are unfamiliar with this type of temperature measurement.

a. Start Excel, then save a blank workbook as **EX A-Temperature Conversions** in the drive and folder where you store your Data Files.

b. Create column headings using Figure A-23 as a guide. (*Hint*: You can widen column B by clicking cell B1, clicking the Format button in the Cells group on the Home tab, then clicking AutoFit Column Width.)

FIGURE A-23

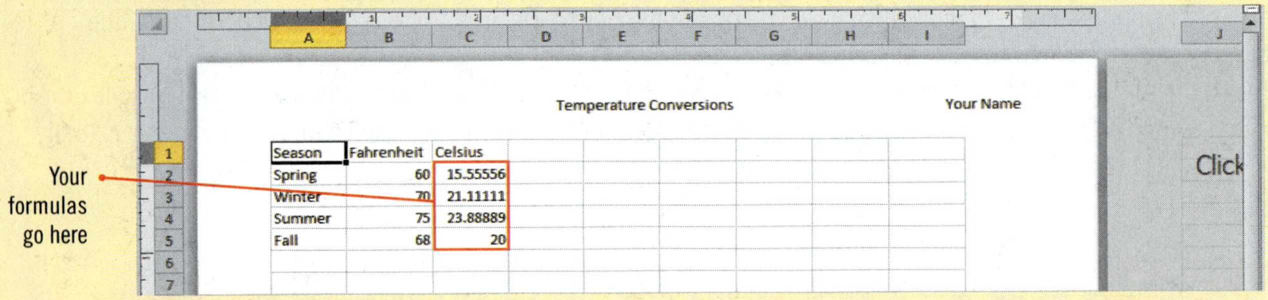

c. Create row labels for each of the seasons.

d. In the appropriate cells, enter what you determine to be a reasonable indoor temperature for each season.

e. Use your Web browser to find out the conversion rate for Fahrenheit to Celsius. (*Hint*: Use your favorite search engine to search on a term such as **temperature conversion formula**.)

f. In the appropriate cells, create a formula that calculates the conversion of the Fahrenheit temperature you entered into a Celsius temperature.

g. In Page Layout View, add your name and the title **Temperature Conversions** to the header.

h. Save your work, then submit your work to your instructor as directed.

i. Close the file, then exit Excel.

Real Life Independent Challenge

You've decided to finally get your life organized. You're going to organize your personal finances so you can begin saving money, and you're going to use Excel to keep track of your expenses.

a. Start Excel, open the file EX A-4.xlsx from the drive and folder where you store your Data Files, then save it as **EX A-Personal Checkbook**.

b. Type check numbers (using your choice of a starting number) in cells A5 through A9.

c. Create sample data for the date, item, and amount in cells B5 through D9.

d. Save your work.

Advanced Challenge Exercise

- Use Help to find out about creating a series of numbers.
- Delete the contents of cells A5:A9.
- Create a series of numbers in cells A5:A9.
- In cell C15, type a brief description of how you created the series.
- Save the workbook.

e. Create formulas in cells E5:E9 that calculate a running balance. (*Hint*: For the first check, the running balance equals the starting balance minus a check; for the following checks, the running balance equals the previous balance value minus each check value.)

f. Create a formula in cell D10 that totals the amount of the checks.

g. Enter your name in cell C12, then compare your screen to Figure A-24.

h. Save your changes to the file, submit your work to your instructor, then exit Excel.

FIGURE A-24

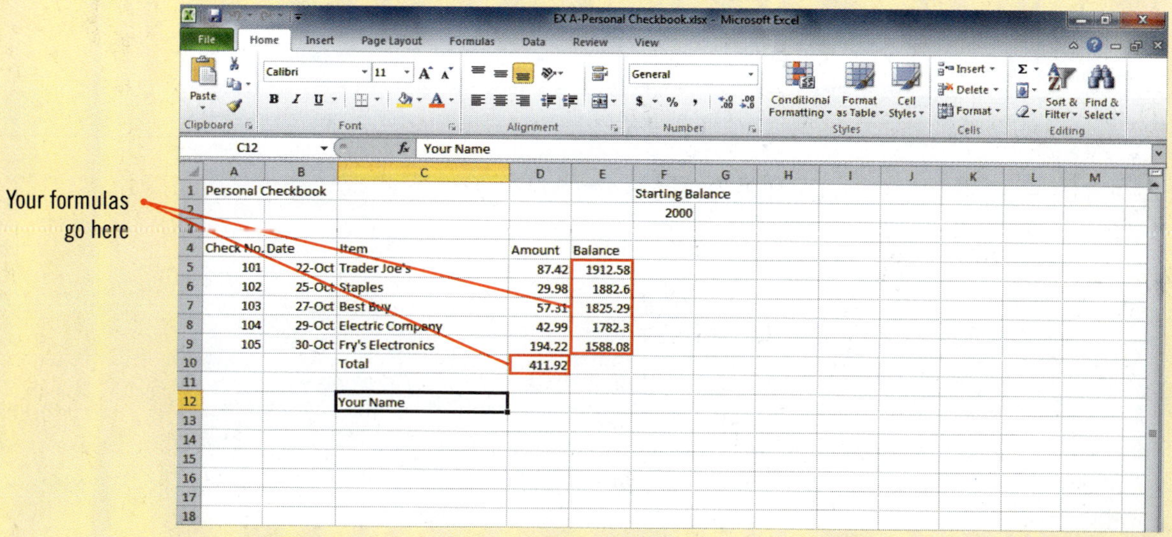

Visual Workshop

Open the file EX A-5.xlsx from the drive and folder where you store your Data Files, then save it as **EX A-Inventory Items**. Using the skills you learned in this unit, modify your worksheet so it matches Figure A-25. Enter formulas in cells D4 through D13 and in cells B14 and C14. Use the Sum button and fill handle to make entering your formulas easier. Add your name in the left header text box, then print one copy of the worksheet with the formulas displayed.

FIGURE A-25

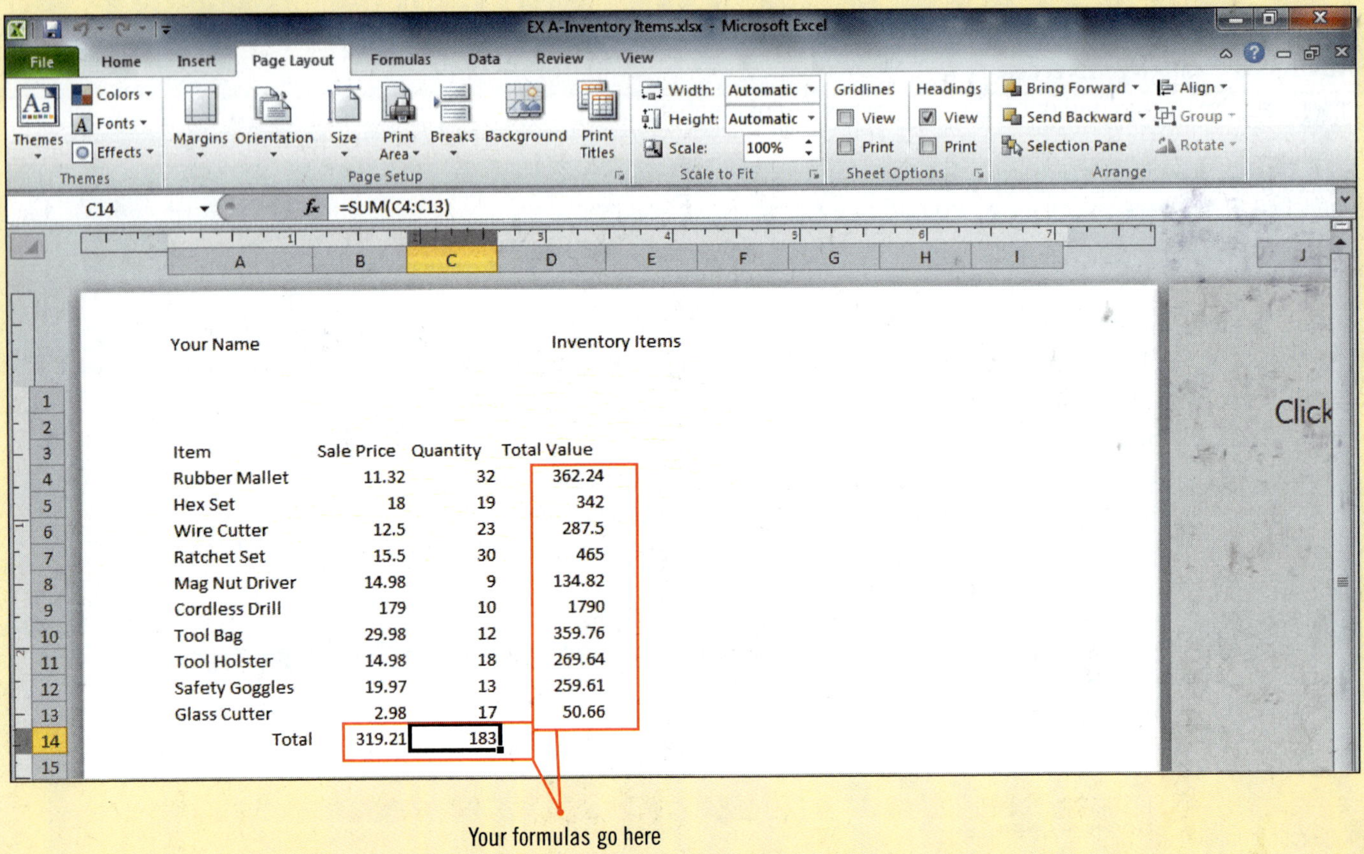

UNIT
B
Excel 2010

Working with Formulas and Functions

Files You Will Need:

EX B-1.xlsx
EX B-2.xlsx
EX B-3.xlsx
EX B-4.xlsx

Using your knowledge of Excel basics, you can develop your worksheets to include more complex formulas and functions. To work more efficiently, you can copy and move existing formulas into other cells instead of manually retyping the same information. When copying or moving, you can also control how cell references are handled so that your formulas always reference the intended cells. Grace Wong, vice president of finance at Quest Specialty Travel, needs to analyze tour expenses for the current year. She has asked you to prepare a worksheet that summarizes this expense data and includes some statistical analysis. She would also like you to perform some what-if analysis, to see what quarterly expenses would look like with various projected increases.

OBJECTIVES

- Create a complex formula
- Insert a function
- Type a function
- Copy and move cell entries
- Understand relative and absolute cell references
- Copy formulas with relative cell references
- Copy formulas with absolute cell references
- Round a value with a function

Creating a Complex Formula

A **complex formula** is one that uses more than one arithmetic operator. You might, for example, need to create a formula that uses addition and multiplication. In formulas containing more than one arithmetic operator, Excel uses the standard **order of precedence** rules to determine which operation to perform first. You can change the order of precedence in a formula by using parentheses around the part you want to calculate first. For example, the formula =4+2*5 equals 14, because the order of precedence dictates that multiplication is performed before addition. However, the formula =(4+2)*5 equals 30, because the parentheses cause 4+2 to be calculated first. You want to create a formula that calculates a 20% increase in tour expenses.

STEPS

1. **Start Excel, open the file EX B-1.xlsx from the drive and folder where you store your Data Files, then save it as EX B-Tour Expense Analysis**

QUICK TIP
When the mode indicator on the status bar says "Point," cells you click are added to the formula.

2. **Click cell B14, type =, click cell B12, then type +**
   In this first part of the formula, you are using a reference to the total expenses for Quarter 1.
3. **Click cell B12, then type *.2**
   The second part of this formula adds a 20% increase (B12*.2) to the original value of the cell (the total expenses for Quarter 1). Compare your worksheet to Figure B-1.
4. **Click the Enter button on the formula bar**
   The result, 41058.996, appears in cell B14.
5. **Press [Tab], type =, click cell C12, type +, click cell C12, type *.2, then click**
   The result, 41096.916, appears in cell C14.

QUICK TIP
You can also copy the formulas by selecting the range C14:E14, clicking the Fill button in the Editing group on the Home tab, then clicking Right.

6. **Drag the fill handle from cell C14 to cell E14**
   The calculated values appear in the selected range, as shown in Figure B-2. Dragging the fill handle on a cell copies the cell's contents or continues a series of data (such as Quarter 1, Quarter 2, etc.) into adjacent cells. This option is called **Auto Fill**.
7. **Save your work**

Reviewing the order of precedence

When you work with formulas that contain more than one operator, the order of precedence is very important because it affects the final value. If a formula contains two or more operators, such as 4+.55/4000*25, Excel performs the calculations in a particular sequence based on the following rules: Operations inside parentheses are calculated before any other operations. Reference operators (such as ranges) are calculated first. Exponents are calculated next, then any multiplication and division—progressing from left to right. Finally, addition and subtraction are calculated from left to right. In the example 4+.55/4000*25, Excel performs the arithmetic operations by first dividing 4000 into .55, then multiplying the result by 25, then adding 4. You can change the order of calculations by using parentheses. For example, in the formula (4+.55)/4000*25, Excel would first add 4 and .55, then divide that amount by 4000, then finally multiply by 25.

FIGURE B-1: Formula containing multiple arithmetic operators

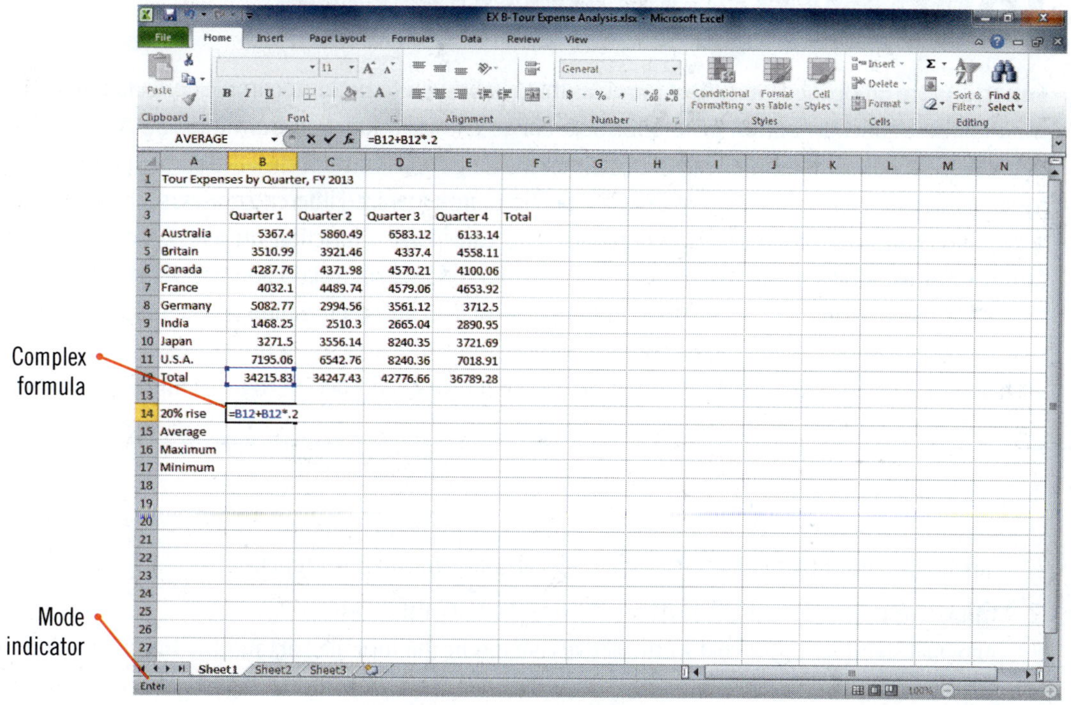

FIGURE B-2: Complex formulas in worksheet

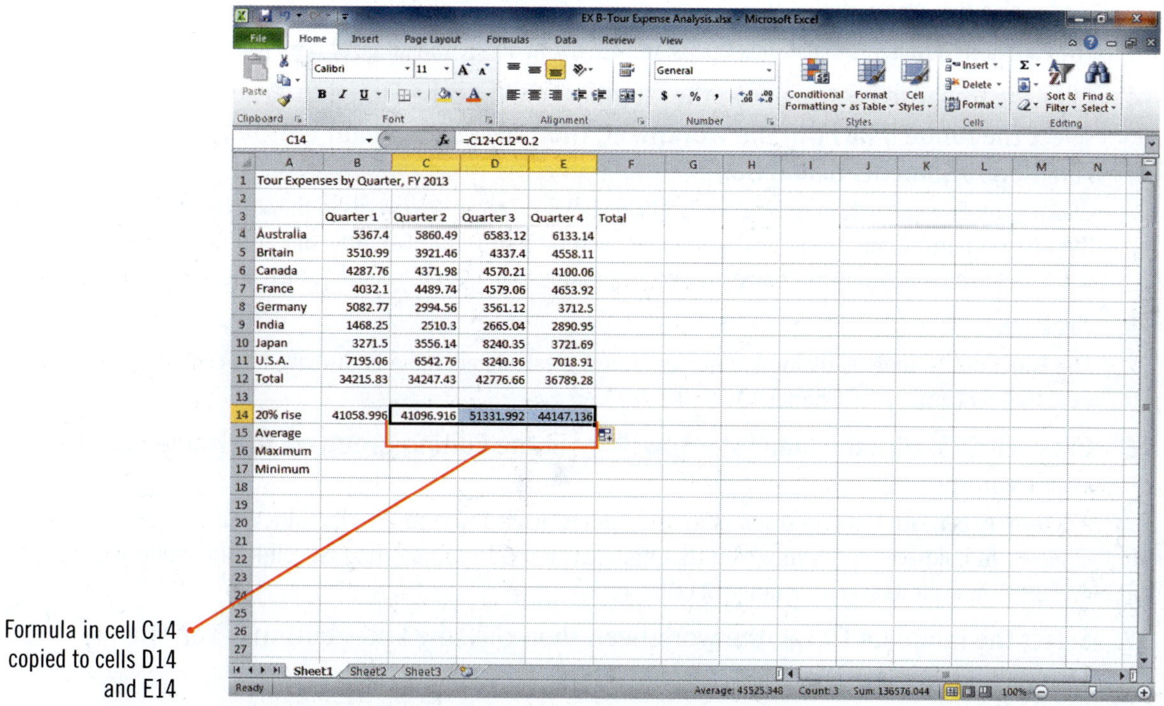

Excel 2010

UNIT
B
Excel 2010

Inserting a Function

Functions are predefined worksheet formulas that enable you to perform complex calculations easily. You can use the Insert Function button on the formula bar to choose a function from a dialog box. You can quickly insert the SUM function using the Sum button on the Ribbon, or you can click the Sum list arrow to enter other frequently used functions, such as AVERAGE. Functions are organized into categories, such as Financial, Date & Time, and Statistical, based on their purposes. You can insert a function on its own or as part of another formula. For example, you have used the SUM function on its own to add a range of cells. You could also use the SUM function within a formula that adds a range of cells and then multiplies the total by a decimal. If you use a function alone, it always begins with an equal sign (=) as the formula prefix. You need to calculate the average expenses for the first quarter of the year, and decide to use a function to do so.

STEPS

QUICK TIP
When using the Insert Function button or the Sum list arrow, it is not necessary to type the equal sign (=); Excel adds it as necessary.

QUICK TIP
To learn about a function, click it in the Select a function list. The arguments and format required for the function appear below the list.

QUICK TIP
When selecting a range, remember to select all the cells between and including the two references in the range.

1. **Click cell B15**
   This is the cell where you want to enter the calculation that averages expenses per country for the first quarter. You want to use the Insert Function dialog box to enter this function.
2. **Click the Insert Function button on the formula bar**
   An equal sign (=) is inserted in the active cell and in the formula bar, and the Insert Function dialog box opens, as shown in Figure B-3. In this dialog box, you specify the function you want to use by clicking it in the Select a function list. The Select a function list initially displays recently used functions. If you don't see the function you want, you can click the Or select a category list arrow to choose the desired category. If you're not sure which category to choose, you can type the function name or a description in the Search for a function field. The AVERAGE function is a statistical function, but you don't need to open the Statistical category because this function already appears in the Most Recently Used category.
3. **Click AVERAGE in the Select a function list if necessary, read the information that appears under the list, then click OK**
   The Function Arguments dialog box opens, in which you define the range of cells you want to average.
4. **Click the Collapse button in the Number1 field of the Function Arguments dialog box, select the range B4:B11 in the worksheet, then click the Expand button in the Function Arguments dialog box**
   Clicking the Collapse button minimizes the dialog box so you can select cells in the worksheet. When you click the Expand button, the dialog box is restored, as shown in Figure B-4. You can also begin dragging in the worksheet to automatically minimize the dialog box; after you select the desired range, the dialog box is restored.
5. **Click OK**
   The Function Arguments dialog box closes, and the calculated value is displayed in cell B15. The average expenses per country for Quarter 1 is 4276.97875.
6. **Click cell C15, click the Sum list arrow Σ in the Editing group on the Home tab, then click Average**
   A ScreenTip beneath cell C15 displays the arguments needed to complete the function. The text "number1" is shown in boldface type, telling you that the next step is to supply the first cell in the group you want to average. You want to average a range of cells.
7. **Select the range C4:C11 in the worksheet, then click the Enter button on the formula bar**
   The average expenses per country for the second quarter appears in cell C15.
8. **Drag the fill handle from cell C15 to cell E15**
   The formula in cell C15 is copied to the rest of the selected range, as shown in Figure B-5.
9. **Save your work**

FIGURE B-3: Insert Function dialog box

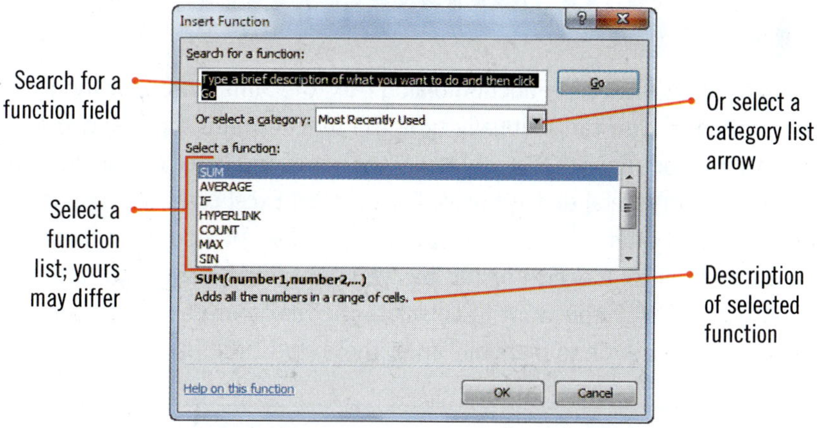

FIGURE B-4: Expanded Function Arguments dialog box

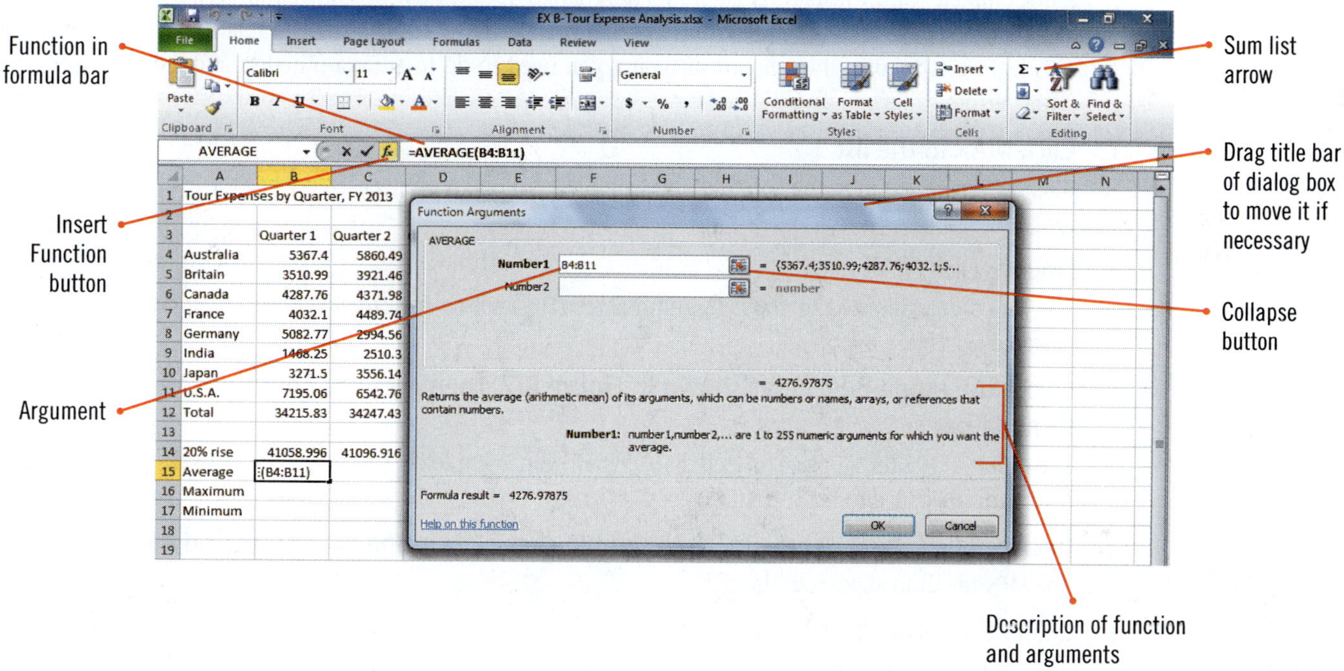

FIGURE B-5: Average functions used in worksheet

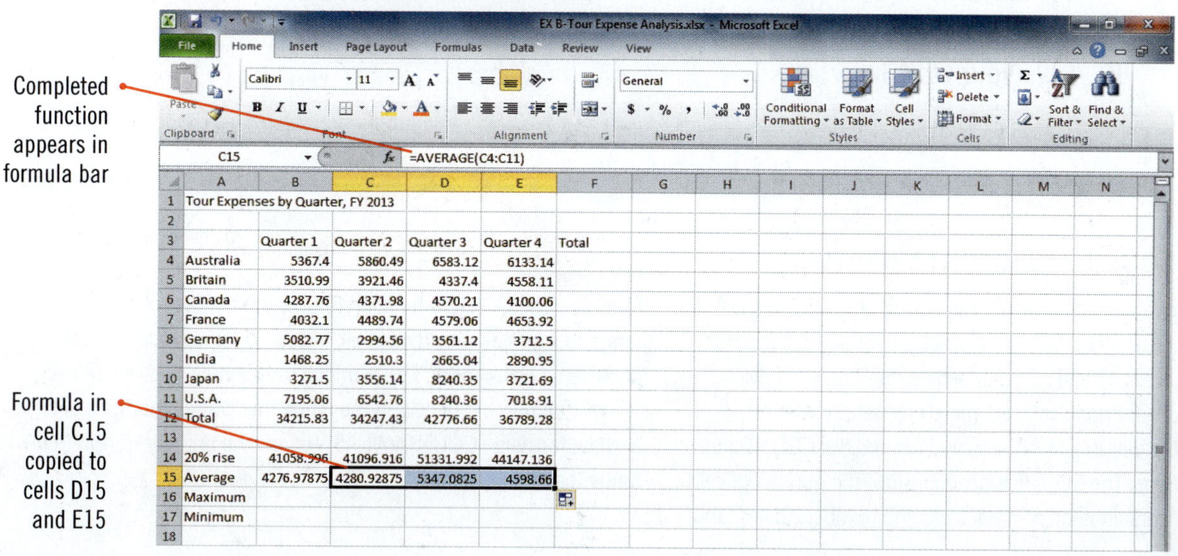

UNIT
B
Excel 2010

Typing a Function

In addition to using the Insert Function dialog box, the Sum button, or the Sum list arrow on the Ribbon to enter a function, you can manually type the function into a cell and then complete the arguments needed. This method requires that you know the name and initial characters of the function, but it can be faster than opening several dialog boxes. Experienced Excel users often prefer this method, but it is only an alternative, not better or more correct than any other method. Excel's Formula AutoComplete feature makes it easier to enter function names by typing, because it suggests functions depending on the first letters you type. You want to calculate the maximum and minimum quarterly expenses in your worksheet, and you decide to manually enter these statistical functions.

STEPS

1. **Click cell B16, type =, then type m**

   Because you are manually typing this function, it is necessary to begin with the equal sign (=). The Formula AutoComplete feature displays a list of function names beginning with "M" beneath cell B16. Once you type an equal sign in a cell, each letter you type acts as a trigger to activate the Formula AutoComplete feature. This feature minimizes the amount of typing you need to do to enter a function and reduces typing and syntax errors.

2. **Click MAX in the list**

   Clicking any function in the Formula AutoComplete list opens a ScreenTip next to the list that describes the function.

3. **Double-click MAX**

   The function is inserted in the cell, and a ScreenTip appears beneath the cell to help you complete the formula. See Figure B-6.

4. **Select the range B4:B11, as shown in Figure B-7, then click the Enter button ✓ on the formula bar**

   The result, 7195.06, appears in cell B16. When you completed the entry, the closing parenthesis was automatically added to the formula.

5. **Click cell B17, type =, type m, then double-click MIN in the list of function names**

   The MIN function appears in the cell.

6. **Select the range B4:B11, then press [Enter]**

   The result, 1468.25, appears in cell B17.

7. **Select the range B16:B17, then drag the fill handle from cell B17 to cell E17**

   The maximum and minimum values for all of the quarters appear in the selected range, as shown in Figure B-8.

8. **Save your work**

Using the COUNT and COUNTA functions

When you select a range, a count of cells in the range that are not blank appears in the status bar. For example, if you select the range A1:A5 and only cells A1 and A2 contain data, the status bar displays "Count: 2." To count nonblank cells more precisely, or to incorporate these calculations in a worksheet, you can use the COUNT and COUNTA functions. The COUNT function returns the number of cells in a range that contain numeric data, including numbers, dates, and formulas. The COUNTA function returns the number of cells in a range that contain any data at all, including numeric data, labels, and even a blank space. For example, the formula =COUNT(A1:A5) returns the number of cells in the range that contain numeric data, and the formula =COUNTA(A1:A5) returns the number of cells in the range that are not empty.

FIGURE B-6: MAX function in progress

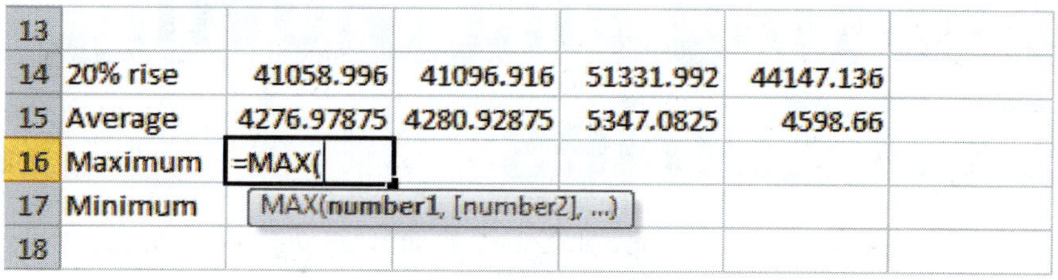

FIGURE B-7: Completing the MAX function

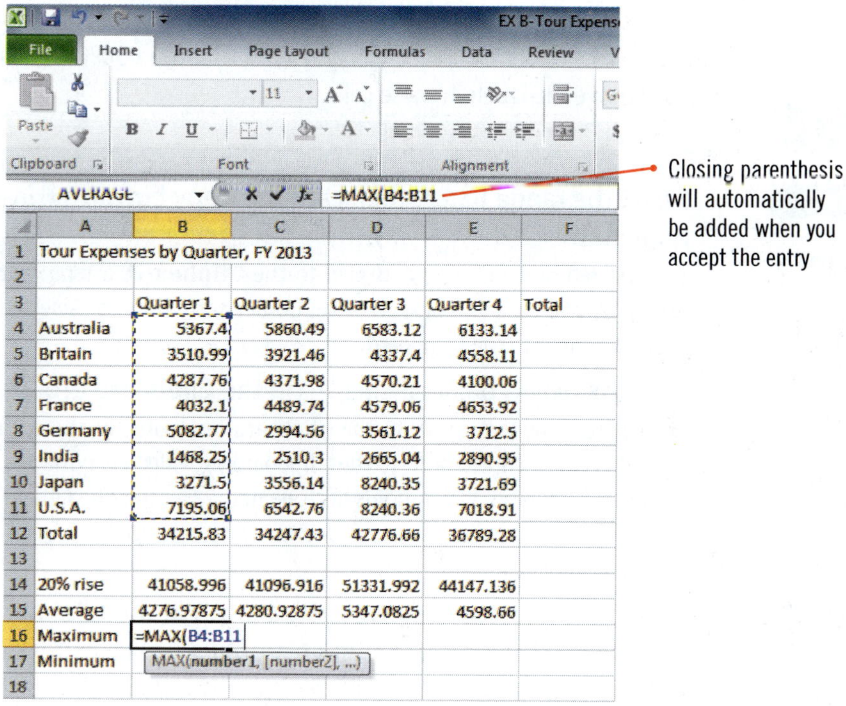

FIGURE B-8: Completed MAX and MIN functions

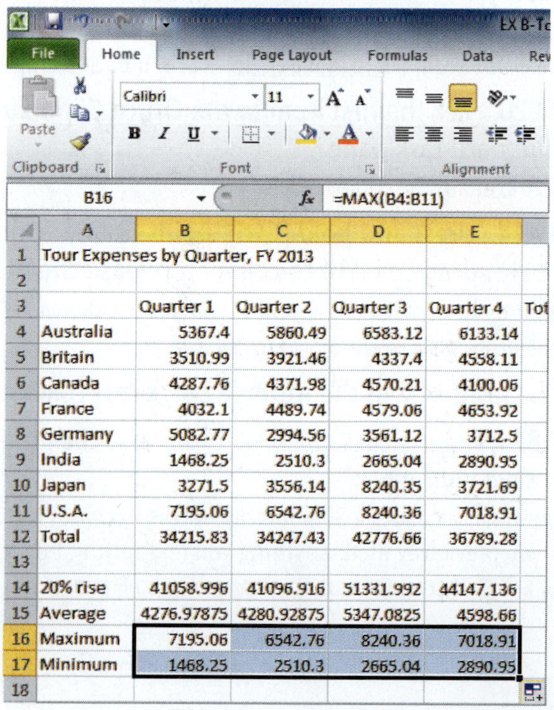

Excel 2010

UNIT B
Excel 2010

Copying and Moving Cell Entries

There are three ways you can copy or move cells and ranges (or the contents within them) from one location to another: the Cut, Copy, and Paste buttons on the Home tab on the Ribbon; the fill handle in the lower-right corner of the active cell or range; or the drag-and-drop feature. When you copy cells, the original data remains in the original location; when you cut or move cells, the original data is deleted from its original location. You can also cut, copy, and paste cells or ranges from one worksheet to another. In addition to the 20% rise in tour expenses, you also want to show a 30% rise. Rather than retype this information, you copy and move the labels in these cells.

STEPS

QUICK TIP
To cut or copy selected cell contents, activate the cell, then select the characters within the cell that you want to cut or copy.

QUICK TIP
Once the Office Clipboard contains 24 items, the oldest existing item is automatically deleted each time you add an item.

QUICK TIP
You can also close the Office Clipboard pane by clicking the dialog box launcher in the Clipboard group.

1. **Select the range B3:E3, then click the Copy button in the Clipboard group on the Home tab**
   The selected range (B3:E3) is copied to the **Clipboard**, a temporary Windows storage area that holds the selections you copy or cut. A moving border surrounds the selected range until you press [Esc] or copy an additional item to the Clipboard.
2. **Click the dialog box launcher in the Clipboard group**
   The Office Clipboard opens in the Clipboard task pane, as shown in Figure B-9. When you copy or cut an item, it is cut or copied both to the Clipboard provided by Windows and to the Office Clipboard. Unlike the Windows Clipboard, which holds just one item at a time, the Office Clipboard contains up to 24 of the most recently cut or copied items from any Office program. Your Clipboard task pane may contain more items than shown in the figure.
3. **Click cell B19, then click the Paste button in the Clipboard group**
   A copy of the contents of range B3:E3 is pasted into the range B19:E19. When pasting an item from the Office Clipboard or Clipboard into a worksheet, you only need to specify the upper-left cell of the range where you want to paste the selection. Notice that the information you copied remains in the original range B3:E3; if you had cut instead of copied, the information would have been deleted from its original location once it was pasted.
4. **Press [Delete]**
   The selected cells are empty. You have decided to paste the cells in a different row. You can repeatedly paste an item from the Office Clipboard as many times as you like, as long as the item remains in the Office Clipboard.
5. **Click cell B20, click the first item in the Office Clipboard, then click the Close button on the Clipboard task pane**
   Cells B20:E20 contain the copied labels.
6. **Click cell A14 , press and hold [Ctrl], point to any edge of the cell until the pointer changes to , drag cell A14 to cell A21, release the mouse button, then release [Ctrl]**
   The copy pointer continues to appear as you drag, as shown in Figure B-10. When you release the mouse button, the contents of cell A14 are copied to cell A21.
7. **Click to the right of 2 in the formula bar, press [Backspace], type 3, then press [Enter]**
8. **Click cell B21, type =, click cell B12, type *1.3, click the Enter button on the formula bar, then save your work**
   This new formula calculates a 30% increase of the expenses for Quarter 1, though using a different method from what you previously used. Anything you multiply by 1.3 returns an amount that is 130% of the original amount, or a 30% increase. Compare your screen to Figure B-11.

FIGURE B-9: Copied data in Office Clipboard

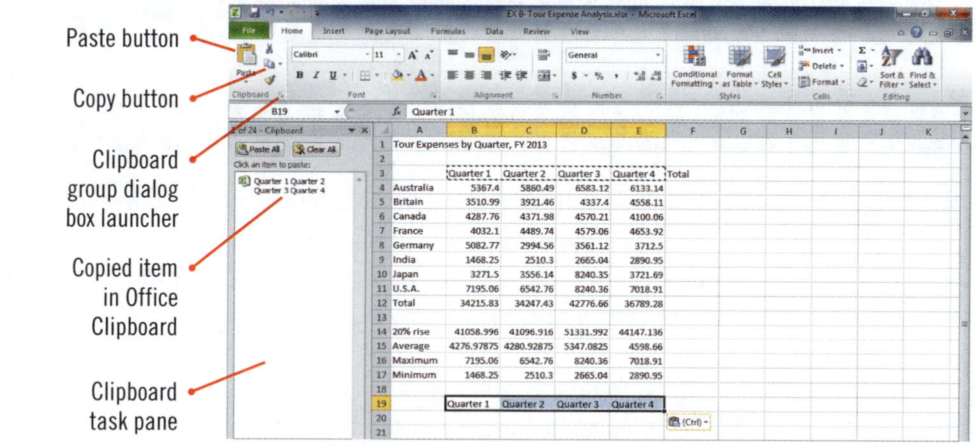

FIGURE B-10: Copying cell contents with drag-and-drop

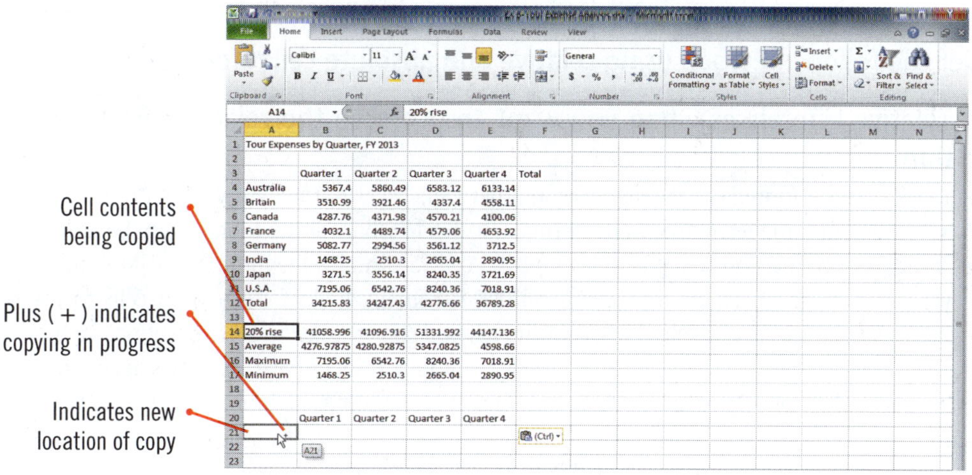

FIGURE B-11: Formula entered to calculate a 30% increase

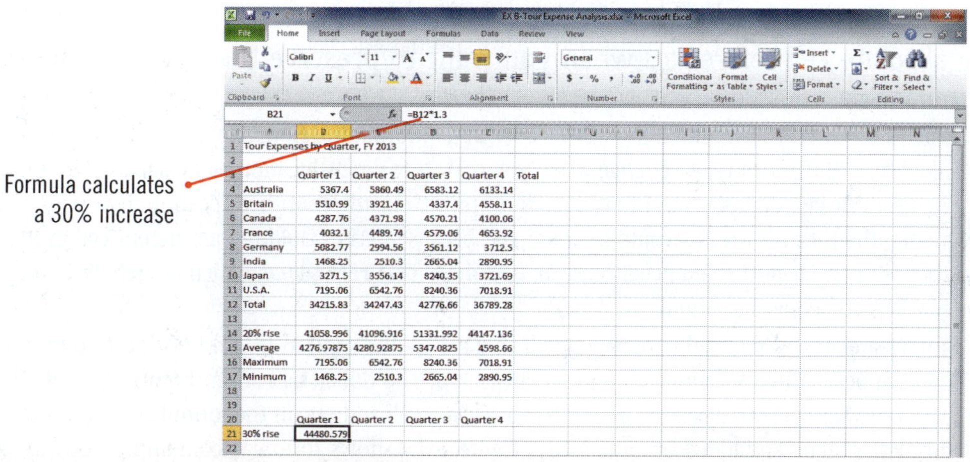

Inserting and deleting selected cells

As you add formulas to your workbook, you may need to insert or delete cells. When you do this, Excel automatically adjusts cell references to reflect their new locations. To insert cells, click the Insert list arrow in the Cells group on the Home tab, then click Insert Cells. The Insert dialog box opens, asking if you want to insert a cell and move the current active cell down or to the right of the new one. To delete one or more selected cells, click the Delete list arrow in the Cells group, click Delete Cells, and in the Delete dialog box, indicate which way you want to move the adjacent cells. When using this option, be careful not to disturb row or column alignment that may be necessary to maintain the accuracy of cell references in the worksheet. Click the Insert button or Delete button in the Cells group to insert or delete a single cell.

UNIT
B
Excel 2010

Understanding Relative and Absolute Cell References

As you work in Excel, you may want to reuse formulas in different parts of a worksheet to reduce the amount of data you have to retype. For example, you might want to include a what-if analysis in one part of a worksheet showing a set of sales projections if sales increase by 10%. To include another analysis in another part of the worksheet showing projections if sales increase by 50%, you can copy the formulas from one section to another and simply change the "1" to a "5". But when you copy formulas, it is important to make sure that they refer to the correct cells. To do this, you need to understand the difference between relative and absolute cell references. You plan to reuse formulas in different parts of your worksheets, so you want to understand relative and absolute cell references.

DETAILS

Consider the following when using relative and absolute cell references:

- **Use relative references when you want to preserve the relationship to the formula location**

  When you create a formula that references another cell, Excel normally does not "record" the exact cell address for the cell being referenced in the formula. Instead, it looks at the relationship that cell has to the cell containing the formula. For example, in Figure B-12, cell F5 contains the formula: =SUM(B5:E5). When Excel retrieves values to calculate the formula in cell F5, it actually looks for "the four cells to the left of the formula," which in this case is cells B5:E5. This way, if you copy the cell to a new location, such as cell F6, the results will reflect the new formula location, and will automatically retrieve the values in cells B6, C6, D6, and E6. These are **relative cell references**, because Excel is recording the input cells *in relation to* or *relative to* the formula cell.

  In most cases, you want to use relative cell references when copying or moving, so this is the Excel default. In Figure B-12, the formulas in F5:F12 and in B13:F13 contain relative cell references. They total the "four cells to the left of" or the "eight cells above" the formulas.

- **Use absolute cell references when you want to preserve the exact cell address in a formula**

  There are times when you want Excel to retrieve formula information from a specific cell, and you don't want the cell address in the formula to change when you copy it to a new location. For example, you might have a price in a specific cell that you want to use in all formulas, regardless of their location. If you use relative cell referencing, the formula results would be incorrect, because Excel would use a different cell every time you copy the formula. Therefore you need to use an **absolute cell reference**, which is a reference that does not change when you copy the formula.

  You create an absolute cell reference by placing a $ (dollar sign) in front of both the column letter and the row number of the cell address. You can either type the dollar sign when typing the cell address in a formula (for example, "=C12*B16"), or you can select a cell address on the formula bar and then press [F4] and the dollar signs are added automatically. Figure B-13 shows formulas containing both absolute and relative references. The formulas in cells B19 to E26 use absolute cell references to refer to a potential sales increase of 50%, shown in cell B16.

FIGURE B-12: Formulas containing relative references

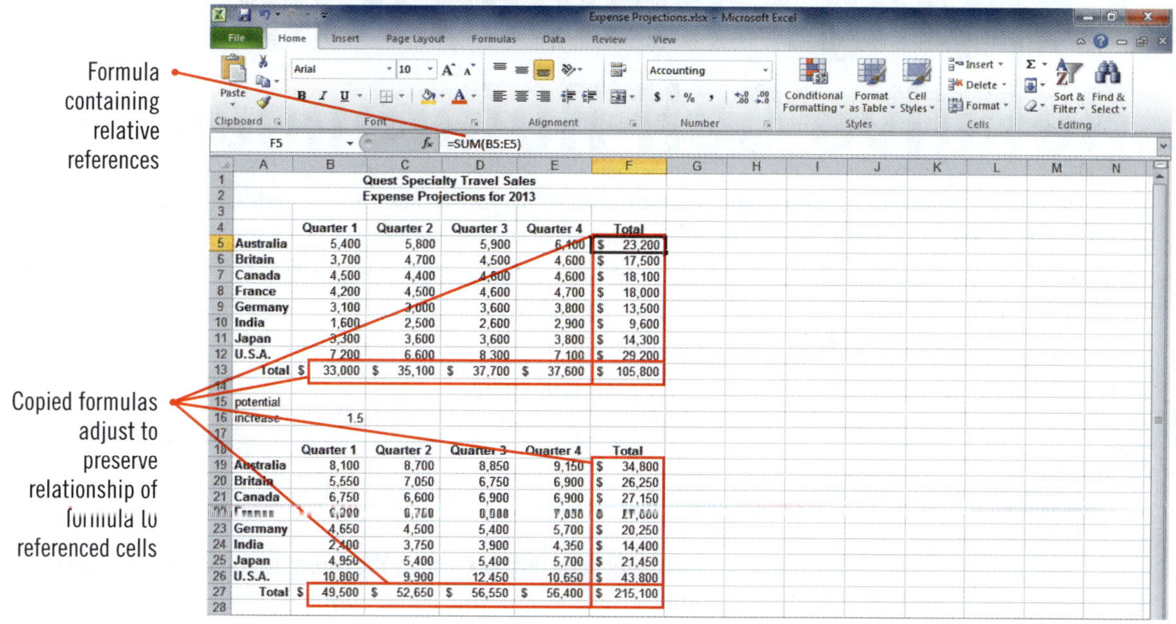

FIGURE B-13: Formulas containing absolute and relative references

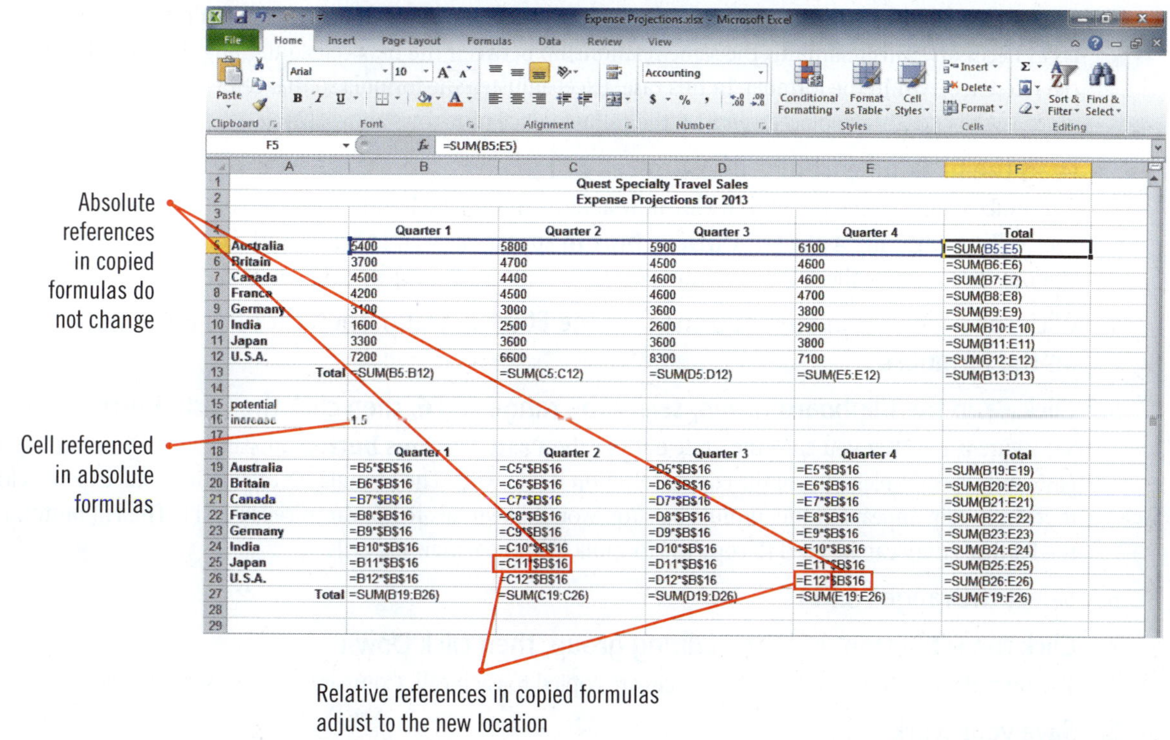

Using a mixed reference

Sometimes when you copy a formula, you want to change the row reference, but keep the column reference the same. This type of cell referencing combines elements of both absolute and relative referencing and is called a **mixed reference**. For example, when copied, a formula containing the mixed reference C$14 would change the column letter relative to its new location, but not the row number. In the mixed reference $C14, the column letter would not change, but the row number would be updated relative to its location. Like an absolute reference, a mixed reference can be created by pressing the [F4] function key with the cell reference selected. With each press of the [F4] key, you cycle through all the possible combinations of relative, absolute, and mixed references (C14, C$14, $C14, and C14).

Excel 2010

UNIT B
Excel 2010

Copying Formulas with Relative Cell References

Copying and moving a cell allows you to reuse a formula you've already created. Copying cells is usually faster than retyping the formulas in them and helps to prevent typing errors. If the cells you are copying contain relative cell references and you want to maintain the relative referencing, you don't need to make any changes to the cells before copying them. You want to copy the formula in cell B21, which calculates the 30% increase in quarterly expenses for quarter 1, to cells C21 through E21. You also want to create formulas to calculate total expenses for each tour country.

STEPS

1. **Click cell B21, if necessary, then click the Copy button in the Clipboard group on the Home tab**

   The formula for calculating the 30% expense increase during Quarter 1 is copied to the Clipboard. Notice that the formula =B12*1.3 appears in the formula bar, and a moving border surrounds the active cell.

2. **Click cell C21, then click the Paste button *(not the list arrow)* in the Clipboard group**

   The formula from cell B21 is copied into cell C21, where the new result of 44521.659 appears. Notice in the formula bar that the cell references have changed, so that cell C12 is referenced in the formula. This formula contains a relative cell reference, which tells Excel to substitute new cell references within the copied formulas as necessary. This maintains the same relationship between the new cell containing the formula and the cell references within the formula. In this case, Excel adjusted the formula so that cell C12—the cell reference nine rows above C21—replaced cell B12, the cell reference nine rows above B21.

3. **Drag the fill handle from cell C21 to cell E21**

   A formula similar to the one in cell C21 now appears in cells D21 and E21. After you use the fill handle to copy cell contents, the **Auto Fill Options button** appears, as seen in Figure B-14. You can use the Auto Fill Options button to fill the cells with only specific elements of the copied cell if you wish.

4. **Click cell F4, click the Sum button in the Editing group, then click the Enter button on the formula bar**

5. **Click in the Clipboard group, select the range F5:F6, then click the Paste button**

   See Figure B-15. After you click the Paste button, the **Paste Options button** appears, which you can use to paste only specific elements of the copied selection if you wish. The formula for calculating total expenses for tours in Britain appears in the formula bar. You would like totals to appear in cells F7:F11. The Fill button in the Editing group can be used to copy the formula into the remaining cells.

6. **Select the range F6:F11**

7. **Click the Fill button in the Editing group, then click Down**

   The formulas containing relative references are copied to each cell. Compare your worksheet to Figure B-16.

8. **Save your work**

QUICK TIP

To paste only specific components of a copied cell or range, click the Paste list arrow in the Clipboard group, then click Paste Special. You can selectively copy formulas, values, or other choices using options in the Paste Special dialog box.

Using Paste Preview

You can selectively copy formulas, values, or other choices using the Paste list arrow, and you can see how the pasted contents will look using the Paste Preview feature. When you click the Paste list arrow, a gallery of paste option icons opens. When you point to an icon, a preview of how the content will be pasted using that option is shown in the worksheet. Options include pasting values only, pasting values with number formatting, pasting formulas only, pasting formatting only, pasting transposed data so that column data appears in rows and row data appears in columns, and pasting with no borders (to remove any borders around pasted cells).

FIGURE B-14: Formula copied using the fill handle

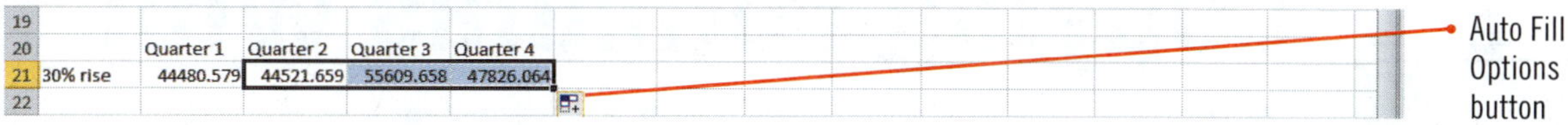

FIGURE B-15: Formulas pasted in the range F5:F6

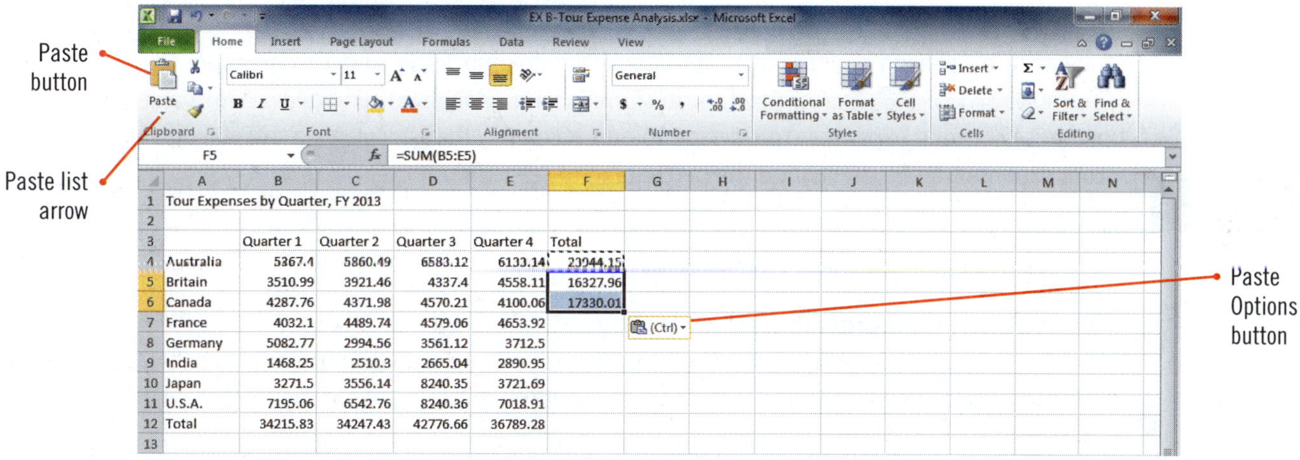

FIGURE B-16: Formula copied using Fill Down

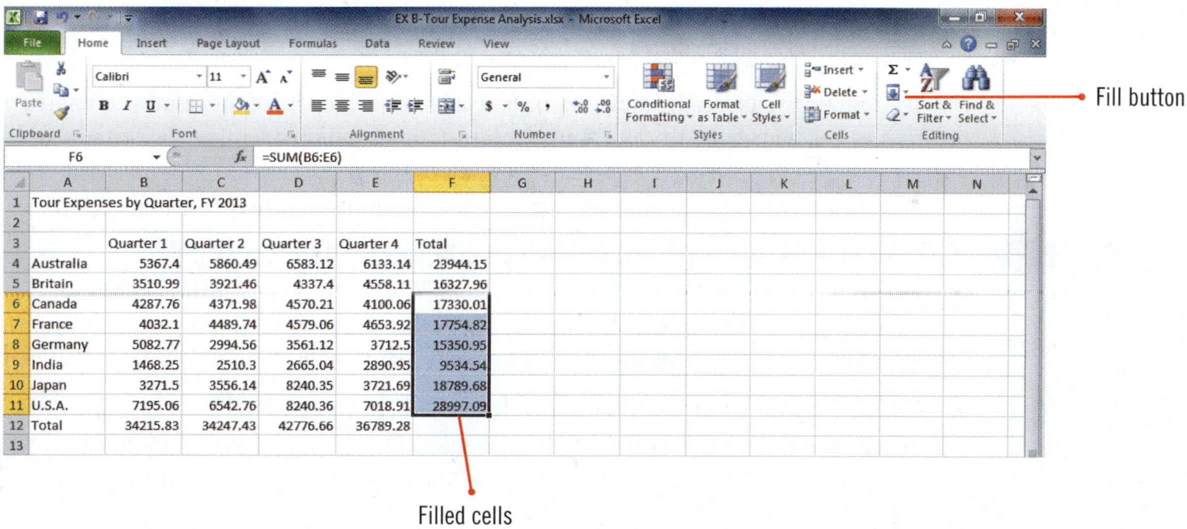

Using Auto Fill options

When you use the fill handle to copy cells, the Auto Fill Options button appears. Auto Fill options differ depending on what you are copying. If you had selected cells containing a series (such as "Monday" and "Tuesday") and then used the fill handle, you would see options for continuing the series (such as "Wednesday" and "Thursday") or for simply pasting the copied cells. Clicking the Auto Fill Options button opens a list that lets you choose from the following options: Copy Cells, Fill Series (if applicable), Fill Formatting Only, or Fill Without Formatting. Choosing Copy Cells means that the cell's contents and its formatting will be copied. The Fill Formatting Only option copies only the formatting attributes, but not cell contents. The Fill Without Formatting option copies the cell contents, but no formatting attributes. Copy Cells is the default option when using the fill handle to copy a cell, so if you want to copy the cell's contents and its formatting, you can ignore the Auto Fill Options button.

UNIT B
Excel 2010

Copying Formulas with Absolute Cell References

When copying formulas, you might want one or more cell references in the formula to remain unchanged in relation to the formula. In such an instance, you need to apply an absolute cell reference before copying the formula to preserve the specific cell address when the formula is copied. You create an absolute reference by placing a dollar sign ($) before the column letter and row number of the address (for example, A1). You need to do some what-if analysis to see how various percentage increases might affect total expenses. You decide to add a column that calculates a possible increase in the total tour expenses, and then change the percentage to see various potential results.

STEPS

1. **Click cell G1, type Change, then press [Enter]**
2. **Type 1.1, then press [Enter]**
   You store the increase factor that will be used in the what-if analysis in this cell (G2). The value 1.1 can be used to calculate a 10% increase: anything you multiply by 1.1 returns an amount that is 110% of the original amount.
3. **Click cell H3, type What if?, then press [Enter]**
4. **In cell H4, type =, click cell F4, type *, click cell G2, then click the Enter button ✓ on the formula bar**
   The result, 26338.57, appears in cell H4. This value represents the total annual expenses for Australia if there is a 10% increase. You want to perform a what-if analysis for all the tour countries.
5. **Drag the fill handle from cell H4 to cell H11**
   The resulting values in the range H5:H11 are all zeros, which is *not* the result you wanted. Because you used relative cell addressing in cell H4, the copied formula adjusted so that the formula in cell H5 is =F5*G3. Because there is no value in cell G3, the result is 0, an error. You need to use an absolute reference in the formula to keep the formula from adjusting itself. That way, it will always reference cell G2.
6. **Click cell H4, press [F2] to change to Edit mode, then press [F4]**
   When you press [F2], the range finder outlines the arguments of the equation in blue and green. The insertion point appears next to the G2 cell reference in cell H4. When you press [F4], dollar signs are inserted in the G2 cell reference, making it an absolute reference. See Figure B-17.
7. **Click ✓, then drag the fill handle from cell H4 to cell H11**
   Because the formula correctly contains an absolute cell reference, the correct values for a 10% increase appear in cells H4:H11. You now want to see what a 20% increase in expenses looks like.
8. **Click cell G2, type 1.2, then click ✓**
   The values in the range H4:H11 change to reflect the 20% increase. Compare your worksheet to Figure B-18.
9. **Save your work**

QUICK TIP
Before you copy or move a formula, always check to see if you need to use an absolute cell reference.

QUICK TIP
When changing a cell reference to an absolute reference, make sure the reference is selected or the insertion point is next to it in the cell before pressing [F4].

FIGURE B-17: Absolute reference created in formula

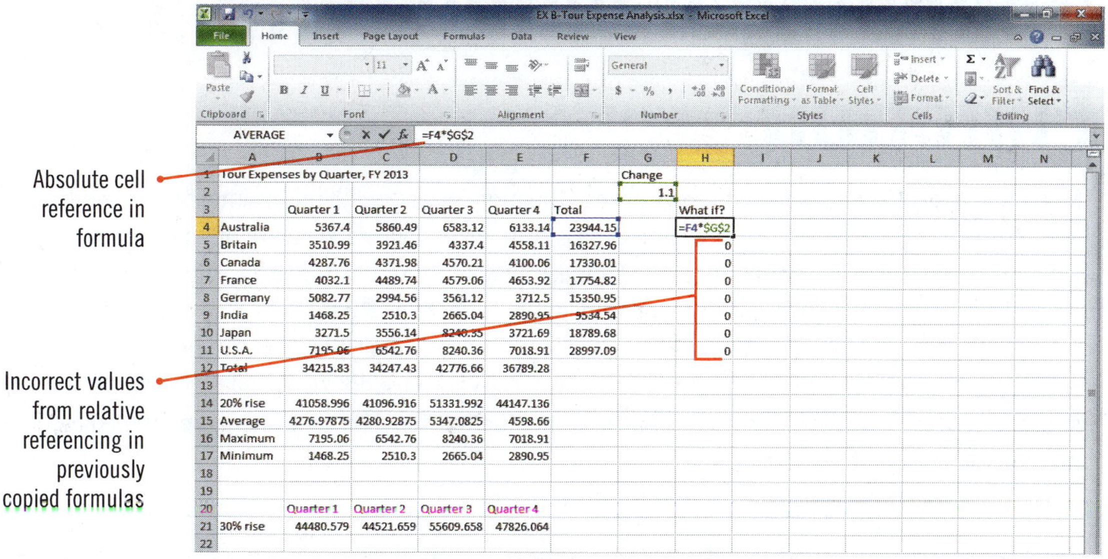

FIGURE B-18: What-if analysis with modified change factor

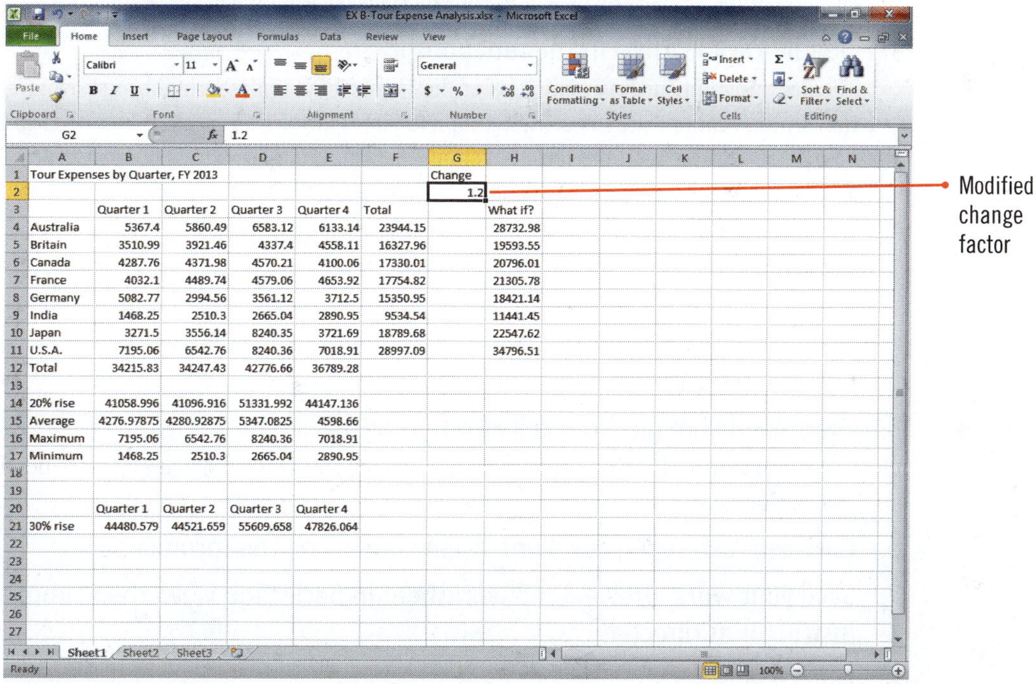

Using the fill handle for sequential text or values

Often, you need to fill cells with sequential text: months of the year, days of the week, years, or text plus a number (Quarter 1, Quarter 2,...). For example, you might want to create a worksheet that calculates data for every month of the year. Using the fill handle, you can quickly and easily create labels for the months of the year just by typing "January" in a cell. Drag the fill handle from the cell containing "January" until you have all the monthly labels you need. You can also easily fill cells with a date sequence by dragging the fill handle on a single cell containing a date. You can fill cells with a number sequence (such as 1, 2, 3,...) by dragging the fill handle on a selection of two or more cells that contain the sequence. To create a number sequence using the value in a single cell, press and hold [Ctrl] as you drag the fill handle of the cell. As you drag the fill handle, Excel automatically extends the existing sequence into the additional cells. (The content of the last filled cell appears in the ScreenTip.) To examine all the fill series options for the current selection, click the Fill button in the Editing group on the Home tab, then click Series to open the Series dialog box.

UNIT
B
Excel 2010

Rounding a Value with a Function

The more you explore features and tools in Excel, the more ways you'll find to simplify your work and convey information more efficiently. For example, cells containing financial data are often easier to read if they contain fewer decimal places than those that appear by default. You can round a value or formula result to a specific number of decimal places by using the ROUND function. In your worksheet, you'd like to round the cells showing the 20% rise in expenses to show fewer digits; after all, it's not important to show cents in the projections, only whole dollars. You want Excel to round the calculated value to the nearest integer. You decide to edit cell B14 so it includes the ROUND function, and then copy the edited formula into the other formulas in this row.

STEPS

QUICK TIP
In the Insert Function dialog box, the ROUND function is in the Math & Trig category.

TROUBLE
If you have too many or too few parentheses, the extraneous parenthesis is displayed in green, or a warning dialog box opens with a suggested solution to the error.

1. **Click cell B14, then click to the right of = in the formula bar**
   You want to position the function at the beginning of the formula, before any values or arguments.
2. **Type RO**
   Formula AutoComplete displays a list of functions beginning with RO beneath the formula bar.
3. **Double-click ROUND in the functions list**
   The new function and an opening parenthesis are added to the formula, as shown in Figure B-19. A few additional modifications are needed to complete your edit of the formula. You need to indicate the number of decimal places to which the function should round numbers and you also need to add a closing parenthesis around the set of arguments that comes after the ROUND function.
4. **Press [END], type ,0), then click the Enter button on the formula bar**
   The comma separates the arguments within the formula, and 0 indicates that you don't want any decimal places to appear in the calculated value. When you complete the edit, the parentheses at either end of the formula briefly become bold, indicating that the formula has the correct number of open and closed parentheses and is balanced.
5. **Drag the fill handle from cell B14 to cell E14**
   The formula in cell B14 is copied to the range C14:E14. All the values are rounded to display no decimal places. Compare your worksheet to Figure B-20.
6. **Click cell A25, type your name, then click on the formula bar**
7. **Save your work, preview the worksheet in Backstage view, then submit your work to your Instructor as directed**
8. **Exit Excel**

FIGURE B-19: ROUND function added to an existing formula

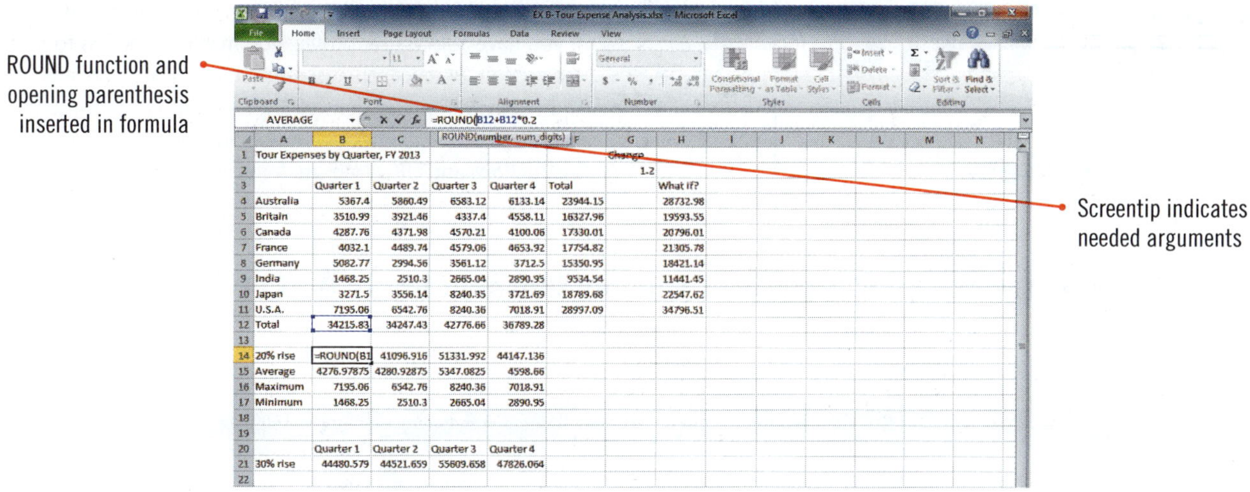

FIGURE B-20: Completed worksheet

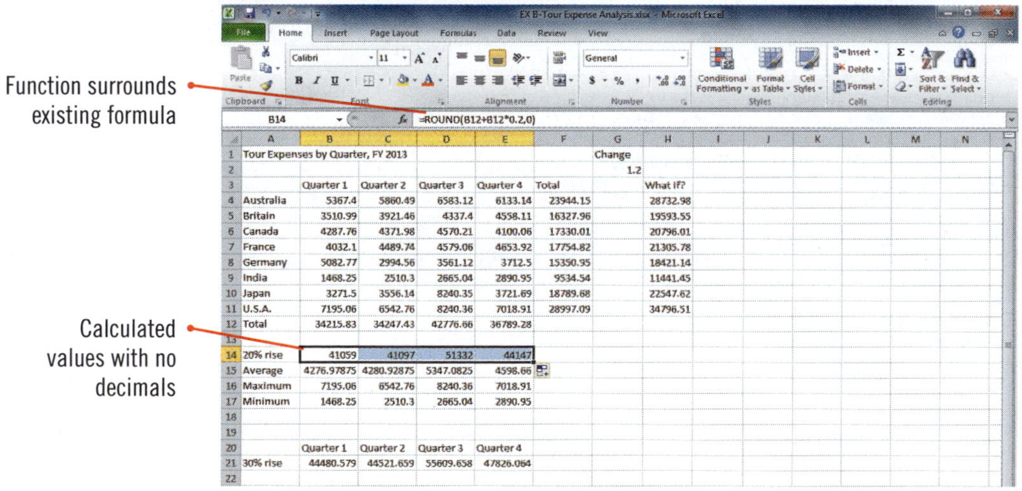

Creating a new workbook using a template

Excel **templates** are predesigned workbook files intended to save time when you create common documents such as balance sheets, budgets, or time cards. Templates contain labels, values, formulas, and formatting, so all you have to do is customize them with your own information. Excel comes with many templates, and you can also create your own or find additional templates on the Web. Unlike a typical workbook, which has the file extension .xlsx, a template has the extension .xltx. To create a workbook using a template, click the File tab, then click New on the navigation bar. The Available Templates pane in Backstage view lists templates installed on your computer and templates available through Office.com. The Blank Workbook template is selected by default and is used to create a blank workbook with no content or special formatting. A preview of the selected template appears to the right of the Available Templates pane. To select a template, click a category in the Available Templates pane, select the template you want in the category, then click Create (if you've selected an installed template) or Download (if you've selected an Office.com template). Figure B-21 shows a template selected in the Budgets category of Office.com templates. (Your list of templates may differ.) When you click Create or Download, a new workbook is created based on the template; when you save the new file in the default format, it has the regular .xlsx extension. To save a workbook of your own as a template, open the Save As dialog box, click the Save as type list arrow, then change the file type to Excel Template.

FIGURE B-21: Budget template selected in Backstage view

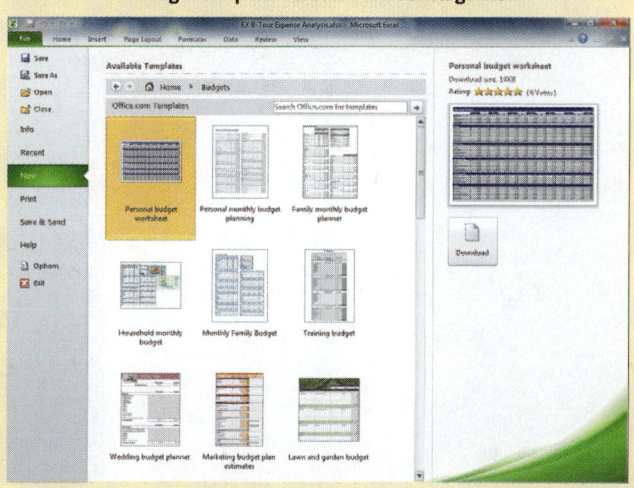

Practice

Concepts Review

For current SAM information, including versions and content details, visit SAM Central (http://www.cengage.com/samcentral). If you have a SAM user profile, you may have access to hands-on instruction, practice, and assessment of the skills covered in this unit. Since various versions of SAM are supported throughout the life of this text, check with your instructor for the correct instructions and URL/Web site for accessing assignments.

Label each element of the Excel worksheet window shown in Figure B-22.

FIGURE B-22

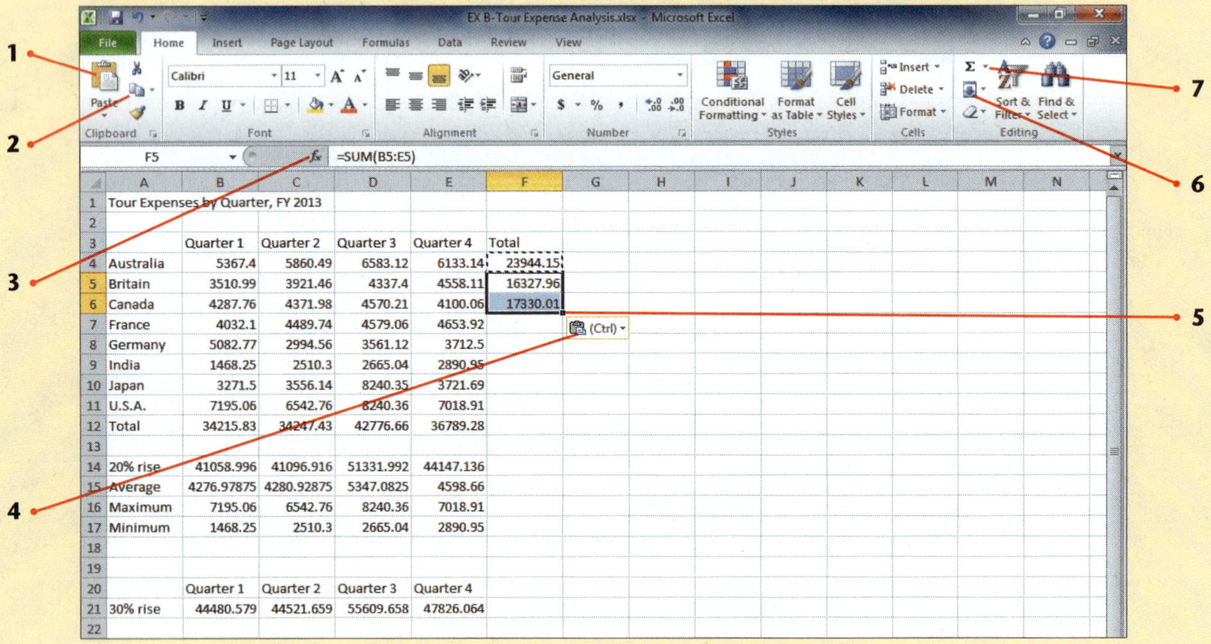

Match each term or button with the statement that best describes it.

8. Fill handle
9. Dialog box launcher
10. Drag-and-drop method
11. [Delete]
12. Formula AutoComplete

a. Clears the contents of selected cells
b. Item on the Ribbon that opens a dialog box or task pane
c. Lets you move or copy data from one cell to another without using the Clipboard
d. Displays an alphabetical list of functions from which you can choose
e. Lets you copy cell contents or continue a series of data into a range of selected cells

Select the best answer from the list of choices.

13. Which key do you press to copy while dragging and dropping selected cells?

- **a.** [Alt]
- **b.** [Ctrl]
- **c.** [F2]
- **d.** [Tab]

14. What type of cell reference is C$19?

- **a.** Relative
- **b.** Absolute
- **c.** Mixed
- **d.** Certain

15. What type of cell reference changes when it is copied?

- **a.** Circular
- **b.** Absolute
- **c.** Relative
- **d.** Specified

16. Which key do you press to convert a relative cell reference to an absolute cell reference?

- **a.** [F2]
- **b.** [F4]
- **c.** [F5]
- **d.** [F6]

17. You can use any of the following features to enter a function *except*:

- **a.** Insert Function button.
- **b.** Formula AutoComplete.
- **c.** Sum list arrow.
- **d.** Clipboard.

Skills Review

1. Create a complex formula.

- **a.** Open the file EX B-2.xlsx from the drive and folder where you store your Data Files, then save it as **EX B-Baking Supply Company Inventory**.
- **b.** In cell B11, create a complex formula that calculates a 30% decrease in the total number of cases of cake pans.
- **c.** Use the fill handle to copy this formula into cell C11 through cell E11.
- **d.** Save your work.

2. Insert a function.

- **a.** Use the Sum list arrow to create a formula in cell B13 that averages the number of cases of cake pans in each storage area.
- **b.** Use the Insert Function button to create a formula in cell B14 that calculates the maximum number of cases of cake pans in a storage area.
- **c.** Use the Sum list arrow to create a formula in cell B15 that calculates the minimum number of cases of cake pans in a storage area.
- **d.** Save your work.

3. Type a function.

- **a.** In cell C13, type a formula that includes a function to average the number of cases of pie pans in each storage area. (*Hint*: Use Formula AutoComplete to enter the function.)
- **b.** In cell C14, type a formula that includes a function to calculate the maximum number of cases of pie pans in a storage area.
- **c.** In cell C15, type a formula that includes a function to calculate the minimum number of cases of pie pans in a storage area.
- **d.** Save your work.

Skills Review (continued)

4. **Copy and move cell entries.**
   a. Select the range B3:F3.
   b. Copy the selection to the Clipboard.
   c. Open the Clipboard task pane, then paste the selection into cell B17.
   d. Close the Clipboard task pane, then select the range A4:A9.
   e. Use the drag-and-drop method to copy the selection to cell A18. (*Hint*: The results should fill the range A18:A23.)
   f. Save your work.
5. **Understand relative and absolute cell references.**
   a. Write a brief description of the difference between relative and absolute references.
   b. List at least three situations in which you think a business might use an absolute reference in its calculations. Examples can include calculations for different types of worksheets, such as time cards, invoices, and budgets.
6. **Copy formulas with relative cell references.**
   a. Calculate the total in cell F4.
   b. Use the Fill button to copy the formula in cell F4 down to cells F5:F8.
   c. Select the range C13:C15.
   d. Use the fill handle to copy these cells to the range D13:F15.
   e. Save your work.
7. **Copy formulas with absolute cell references.**
   a. In cell H1, enter the value **1.575**.
   b. In cell H4, create a formula that multiplies F4 and an absolute reference to cell H1.
   c. Use the fill handle to copy the formula in cell H4 to cells H5 and H6.
   d. Use the Copy and Paste buttons to copy the formula in cell H4 to cells H7 and H8.
   e. Change the amount in cell H1 to **2.3**.
   f. Save your work.
8. **Round a value with a function.**
   a. Click cell H4.
   b. Edit this formula to include the ROUND function showing zero decimal places.
   c. Use the fill handle to copy the formula in cell H4 to the range H5:H8.
   d. Enter your name in cell A25, then compare your work to Figure B-23.
   e. Save your work, preview the worksheet in Backstage view, then submit your work to your instructor as directed.
   f. Close the workbook, then exit Excel.

FIGURE B-23

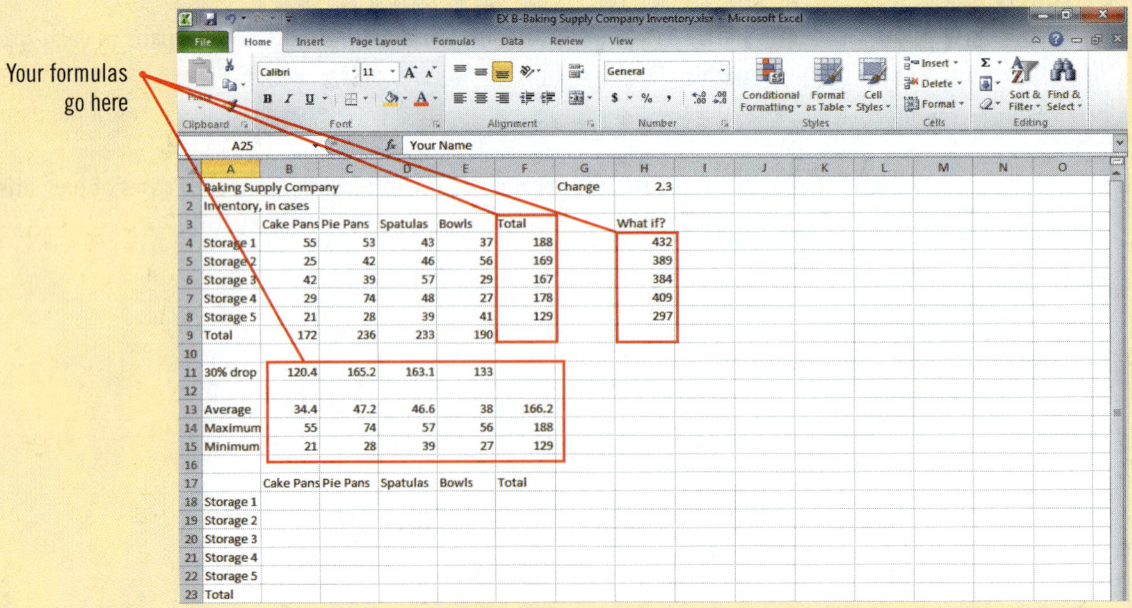

Independent Challenge 1

You are thinking of starting a small express oil change service center. Before you begin, you need to evaluate what you think your monthly expenses will be. You've started a workbook, but need to complete the entries and add formulas.

If you have a SAM 2010 user profile, an autogradable SAM version of this assignment may be available at http://www.cengage.com/sam2010. Check with your instructor to confirm that this assignment is available in SAM. To use the SAM version of this assignment, log into the SAM 2010 Web site and download the instruction and start files.

- **a.** Open the file EX B-3.xlsx from the drive and folder where you store your Data Files, then save it as **EX B-Express Oil Change Expenses**.
- **b.** Make up your own expense data, and enter it in cells B4:B10. (Monthly sales are already included in the worksheet.)
- **c.** Create a formula in cell C4 that calculates the annual rent.
- **d.** Copy the formula in cell C4 to the range C5:C10.
- **e.** Move the label in cell A15 to cell A14.
- **f.** Create formulas in cells B11 and C11 that total the monthly and annual expenses.
- **g.** Create a formula in cell C13 that calculates annual sales.
- **h.** Create a formula in cell B14 that determines whether you will make a profit or loss, then copy the formula into cell C14.
- **i.** Copy the labels in cells B3:C3 to cells E3:F3.
- **j.** Type **Projected Increase** in cell G1, then type **.2** in cell H2.
- **k.** Create a formula in cell E4 that calculates an increase in the monthly rent by the amount in cell H2. You will be copying this formula to other cells, so you'll need to use an absolute reference.
- **l.** Create a formula in cell F4 that calculates the increased annual rent expense based on the calculation in cell E4.
- **m.** Copy the formulas in cells E4:F4 into cells E5:F10 to calculate the remaining monthly and annual expenses.
- **n.** Create a formula in cell E11 that calculates the total monthly expenses, then copy that formula to cell F11.
- **o.** Copy the contents of cells B13:C13 into cells E13:F13.
- **p.** Create formulas in cells E14 and F14 that calculate profit/loss based on the projected increase in monthly and annual expenses.
- **q.** Change the projected increase to **.15**, then compare your work to the sample in Figure B-24.
- **r.** Enter your name in a cell in the worksheet.
- **s.** Save your work, preview the worksheet in Backstage view, submit your work to your instructor as directed, close the workbook, and exit Excel.

FIGURE B-24

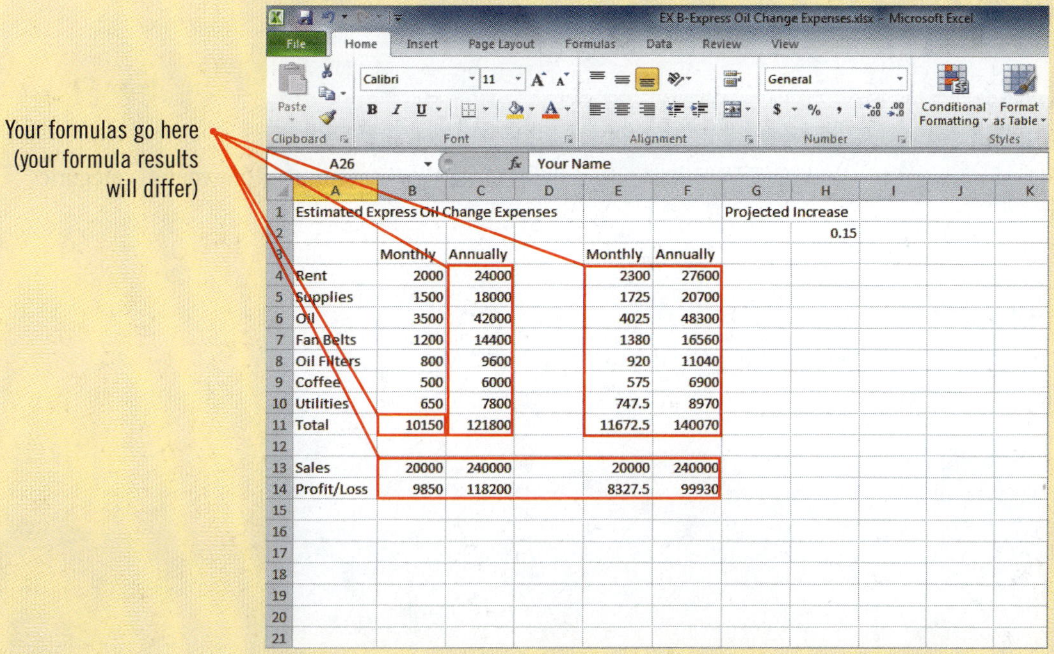

Excel 2010

Independent Challenge 2

The Dog Days Daycare Center is a small, growing pet care center that has hired you to organize its accounting records using Excel. The owners want you to track the company's expenses. Before you were hired, one of the bookkeepers began entering last year's expenses in a workbook, but the analysis was never completed.

- **a.** Start Excel, open the file EX B-4.xlsx from the drive and folder where you store your Data Files, then save it as **EX B-Dog Days Daycare Center Finances**. The worksheet includes labels for functions such as the average, maximum, and minimum amounts of each of the expenses in the worksheet.
- **b.** Think about what information would be important for the bookkeeping staff to know.
- **c.** Using the SUM function, create formulas for each expense in the Total column and each quarter in the Total row.
- **d.** Create formulas for each expense and each quarter in the Average, Maximum, and Minimum columns and rows using the method of your choice.
- **e.** Save your work, then compare your worksheet to the sample shown in Figure B-25.

FIGURE B-25

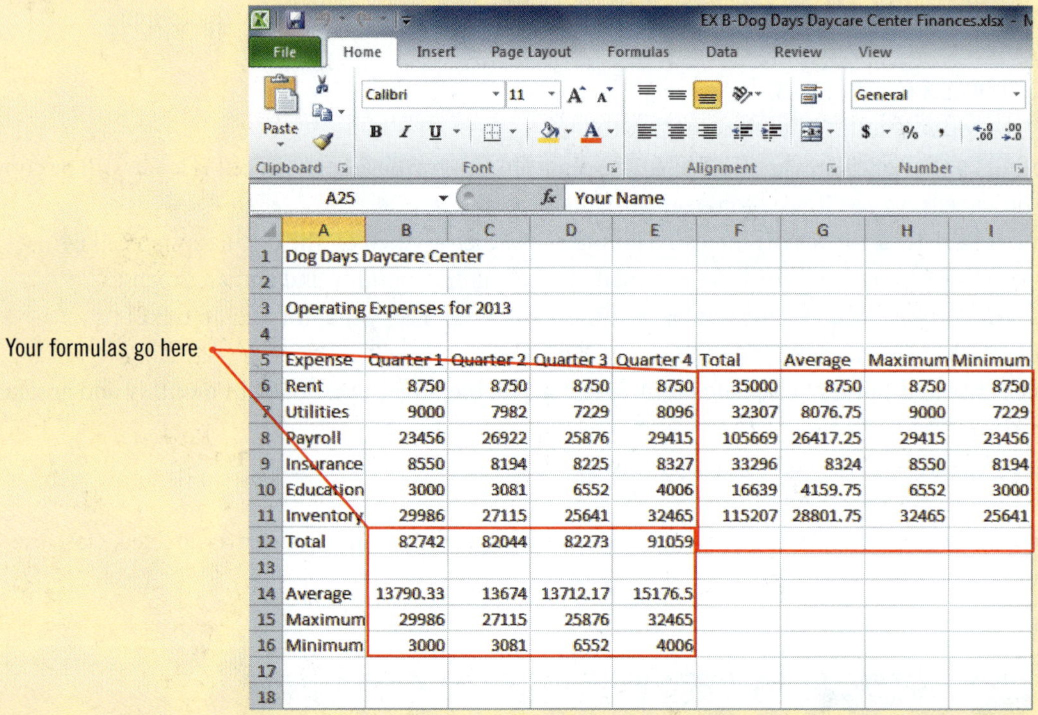

Advanced Challenge Exercise

- Create the label **Expense categories** in cell B19.
- In cell A19, create a formula using the COUNT function that determines the total number of expense categories listed per quarter.
- Save the workbook.

- **f.** Enter your name in cell A25.
- **g.** Preview the worksheet, then submit your work to your instructor as directed.
- **h.** Close the workbook and exit Excel.

Independent Challenge 3

As the accounting manager of a locally owned business, it is your responsibility to calculate accrued sales tax payments on a monthly basis and then submit the payments to the state government. You've decided to use an Excel workbook to make these calculations.

- **a.** Start Excel, then save a new, blank workbook to the drive and folder where you store your Data Files as **EX B-Sales Tax Calculations**.
- **b.** Decide on the layout for all columns and rows. The worksheet will contain data for six stores, which you can name by store number, neighborhood, or another method of your choice. For each store, you will calculate total sales tax based on the local sales tax rate. You'll also calculate total tax owed for all six stores.
- **c.** Make up sales data for all six stores.
- **d.** Enter the rate to be used to calculate the sales tax, using your own local rate.
- **e.** Create formulas to calculate the sales tax owed for each store. If you don't know the local tax rate, use **6.5%**.
- **f.** Create a formula to total all the owed sales tax, then compare your work to the sample shown in Figure B-26.

FIGURE B-26

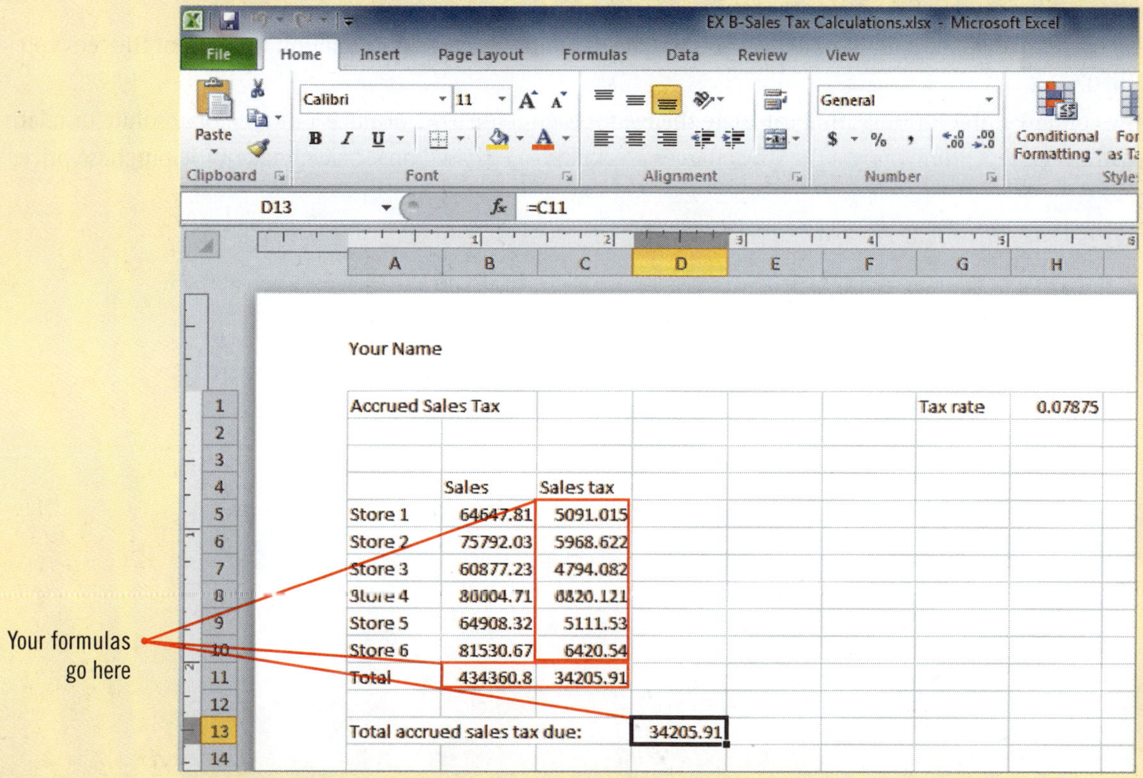

Advanced Challenge Exercise

- Use the ROUND function to eliminate any decimal places in the sales tax figures for each store and the total due.
- Save the workbook.

- **g.** Add your name to the header.
- **h.** Save your work, preview the worksheet, and submit your work to your instructor as directed.
- **i.** Close the workbook and exit Excel.

Real Life Independent Challenge

Since your recent promotion at work, you have started thinking about purchasing a home. As you begin the round of open houses and realtors' listings, you notice that there are many fees associated with buying a home. Some fees are based on a percentage of the purchase price, and others are a flat fee; overall, they seem to represent a substantial amount above the purchase prices you see listed. You've seen five houses so far that interest you; one is easily affordable, and the remaining four are all nice, but increasingly more expensive. Although you will be financing the home, the bottom line is still important to you, so you decide to create an Excel workbook to figure out the real cost of buying each one.

- **a.** Find out the typical cost or percentage rate of at least three fees that are usually charged when buying a home and taking out a mortgage. (*Hint*: If you have access to the Internet you can research the topic of home buying on the Web, or you can ask friends about standard rates or percentages for items such as title insurance, credit reports, and inspection fees.)
- **b.** Start Excel, then save a new, blank workbook to the drive and folder where you store your Data Files as **EX B-Home Purchase Costs**.
- **c.** Create labels and enter data for at least three homes. If you enter this information across the columns in your worksheet, you should have one column for each house, with the purchase price in the cell below each label. Be sure to enter a different purchase price for each house.
- **d.** Create labels for the Fees column and for an Amount or Rate column. Enter the information for each of the fees you have researched.
- **e.** In each house column, enter formulas that calculate the fee for each item. The formulas (and use of absolute or relative referencing) will vary depending on whether the charges are a flat fee or based on a percentage of the purchase price.

Real Life Independent Challenge (continued)

f. Total the fees for each house, then create formulas that add the total fees to the purchase price. A sample of what your workbook might look like is shown in Figure B-27.

g. Enter a title for the worksheet in the header.

h. Enter your name in the header, save your work, preview the worksheet, then submit your work to your instructor as directed.

i. Close the file and exit Excel.

FIGURE B-27

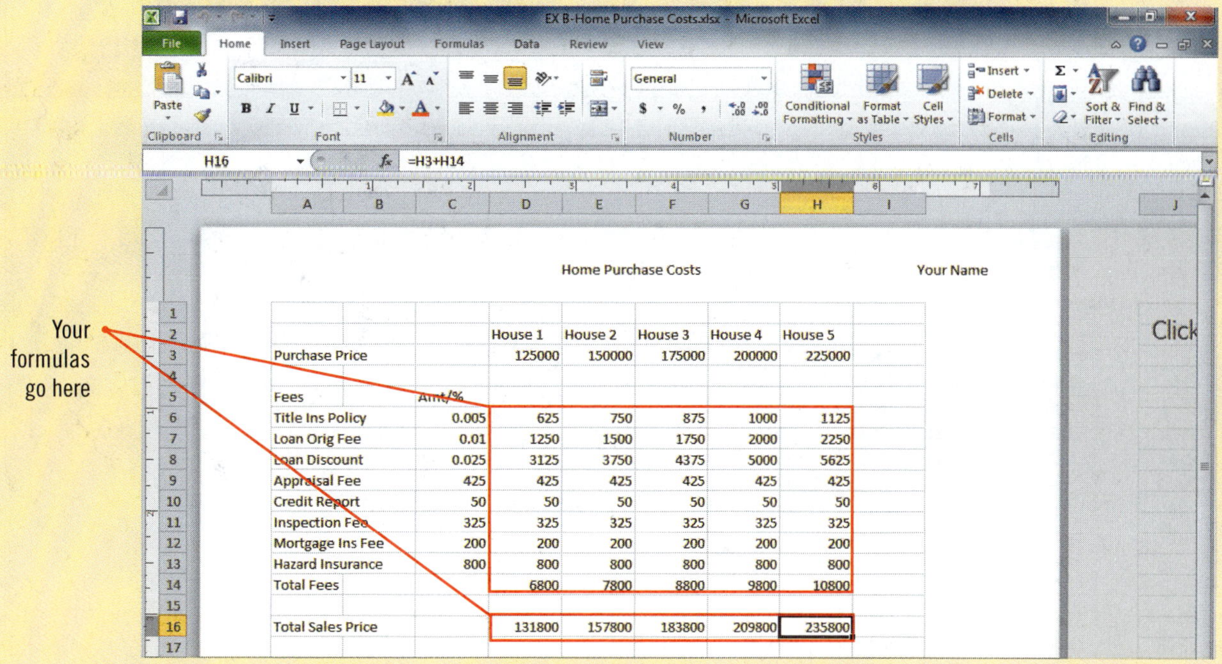

Visual Workshop

Create the worksheet shown in Figure B-28 using the skills you learned in this unit. Save the workbook as **EX B-Expense Analysis** to the drive and folder where you store your Data Files. Enter your name in the header as shown, hide the gridlines, preview the worksheet, and then submit your work to your instructor as directed.

FIGURE B-28

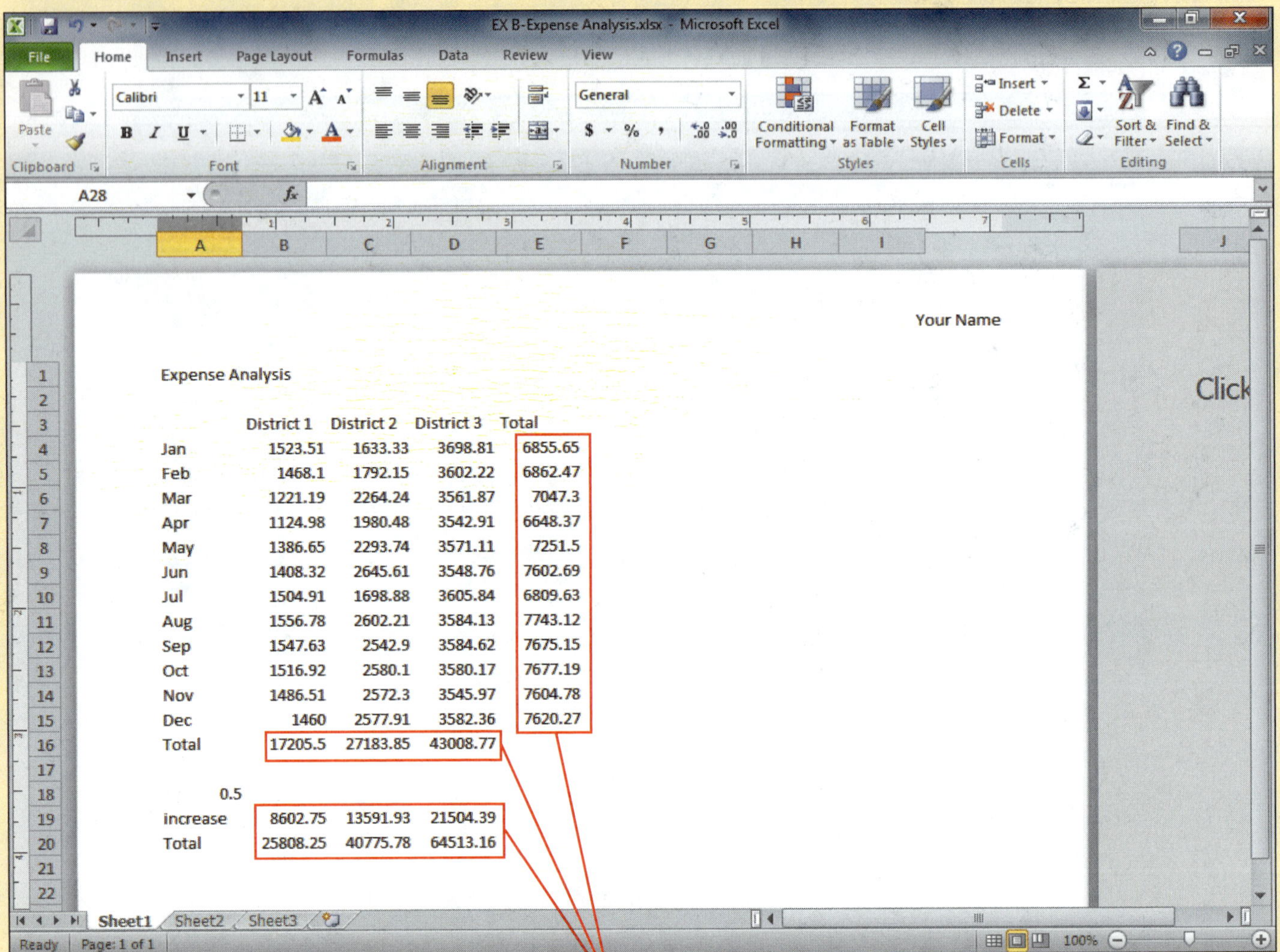

Expense Analysis				
	District 1	District 2	District 3	Total
Jan	1523.51	1633.33	3698.81	6855.65
Feb	1468.1	1792.15	3602.22	6862.47
Mar	1221.19	2264.24	3561.87	7047.3
Apr	1124.98	1980.48	3542.91	6648.37
May	1386.65	2293.74	3571.11	7251.5
Jun	1408.32	2645.61	3548.76	7602.69
Jul	1504.91	1698.88	3605.84	6809.63
Aug	1556.78	2602.21	3584.13	7743.12
Sep	1547.63	2542.9	3584.62	7675.15
Oct	1516.92	2580.1	3580.17	7677.19
Nov	1486.51	2572.3	3545.97	7604.78
Dec	1460	2577.91	3582.36	7620.27
Total	17205.5	27183.85	43008.77	
0.5				
increase	8602.75	13591.93	21504.39	
Total	25808.25	40775.78	64513.16	

Enter formulas and not values in these cells

UNIT C

Excel 2010

Formatting a Worksheet

Files You Will Need:

EX C-1.xlsx
EX C-2.xlsx
EX C-3.xlsx
EX C-4.xlsx
EX C-5.xlsx

You can use formatting features to make a worksheet more attractive or easier to read, and to emphasize key data. You can apply different formatting attributes such as colors, font styles, and font sizes to the cell contents; you can adjust column width and row height; and you can insert or delete columns and rows. You can also apply conditional formatting so that cells meeting certain conditions are formatted differently from other cells. This makes it easy to emphasize selected information, such as sales that exceed or fall below a certain threshold. The corporate marketing managers at QST have requested data from all QST locations for advertising expenses incurred during the first quarter of this year. Grace Wong has created a worksheet listing this information. She asks you to format the worksheet to make it easier to read and to call attention to important data.

OBJECTIVES

- Format values
- Change font and font size
- Change font styles and alignment
- Adjust column width
- Insert and delete rows and columns
- Apply colors, patterns, and borders
- Apply conditional formatting
- Rename and move a worksheet
- Check spelling

UNIT C
Excel 2010

Formatting Values

The **format** of a cell determines how the labels and values look—for example, whether the contents appear boldfaced, italicized, or with dollar signs and commas. Formatting changes only the appearance of a value or label; it does not alter the actual data in any way. To format a cell or range, first you select it, then you apply the formatting using the Ribbon, Mini toolbar, or a keyboard shortcut. You can apply formatting before or after you enter data in a cell or range. Grace has provided you with a worksheet that lists individual advertising expenses, and you're ready to improve its appearance and readability. You decide to start by formatting some of the values so they are displayed as currency, percentages, and dates.

STEPS

1. **Start Excel, open the file EX C-1.xlsx from the drive and folder where you store your Data Files, then save it as EX C-QST Advertising Expenses**

   This worksheet is difficult to interpret because all the information is crowded and looks the same. In some columns, the contents appear cut off because there is too much data to fit given the current column width. You decide not to widen the columns yet, because the other changes you plan to make might affect column width and row height. The first thing you want to do is format the data showing the cost of each ad.

> **QUICK TIP**
> You can use a different type of currency, such as Euros or British pounds, by clicking the Accounting Number Format list arrow, then clicking a different currency type.

2. **Select the range D4:D32, then click the Accounting Number Format button $ in the Number group on the Home tab**

   The default Accounting **number format** adds dollar signs and two decimal places to the data, as shown in Figure C-1. Formatting this data in Accounting format makes it clear that its values are monetary values. Excel automatically resizes the column to display the new formatting. The Accounting and Currency number formats are both used for monetary values, but the Accounting format aligns currency symbols and decimal points of numbers in a column.

> **QUICK TIP**
> Select any range of contiguous cells by clicking the upper-left cell of the range, pressing and holding [Shift], then clicking the lower-right cell of the range. Add a row to the selected range by continuing to hold down [Shift] and pressing ↓; add a column by pressing →.

3. **Select the range F4:H32, then click the Comma Style button in the Number group**

   The values in columns F, G, and H display the Comma Style format, which does not include a dollar sign but can be useful for some types of accounting data.

4. **Select the range J4:J32, click the Number Format list arrow, click Percentage, then click the Increase Decimal button in the Number group**

   The data in the % of Total column is now formatted with a percent sign (%) and three decimal places. The Number Format list arrow lets you choose from popular number formats and shows an example of what the selected cell or cells would look like in each format (when multiple cells are selected, the example is based on the first cell in the range). Each time you click the Increase Decimal button, you add one decimal place; clicking the button twice would add two decimal places.

5. **Click the Decrease Decimal button in the Number group twice**

   Two decimal places are removed from the percentage values in column J.

6. **Select the range B4:B31, then click the dialog box launcher in the Number group**

   The Format Cells dialog box opens with the Date category already selected on the Number tab.

7. **Select the first 14-Mar-01 format in the Type list box as shown in Figure C-2, then click OK**

   The dates in column B appear in the 14-Mar-01 format. The second 14-Mar-01 format in the list displays all days in two digits (it adds a leading zero if the day is only a single-digit number), while the one you chose displays single-digit days without a leading zero.

> **QUICK TIP**
> Make sure you examine formatted data to confirm that you have applied the appropriate formatting; for example, dates should not have a currency format, and monetary values should not have a date format.

8. **Select the range C4:C31, right-click the range, click Format Cells on the shortcut menu, click 14-Mar in the Type list box in the Format Cells dialog box, then click OK**

   Compare your worksheet to Figure C-3.

9. **Press [Ctrl][Home], then save your work**

FIGURE C-1: Accounting number format applied to range

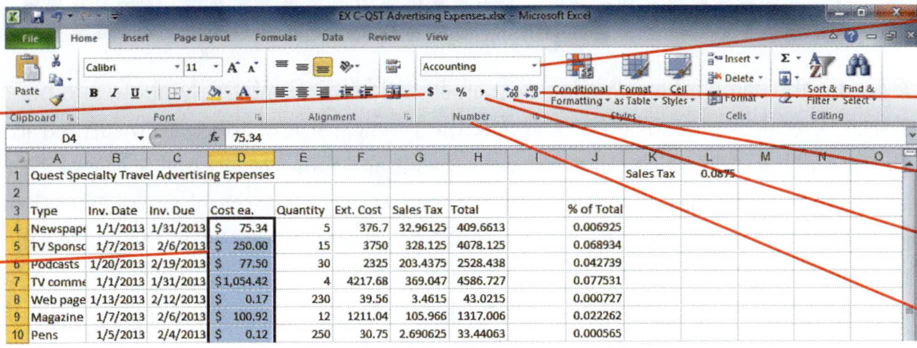

FIGURE C-2: Format Cells dialog box

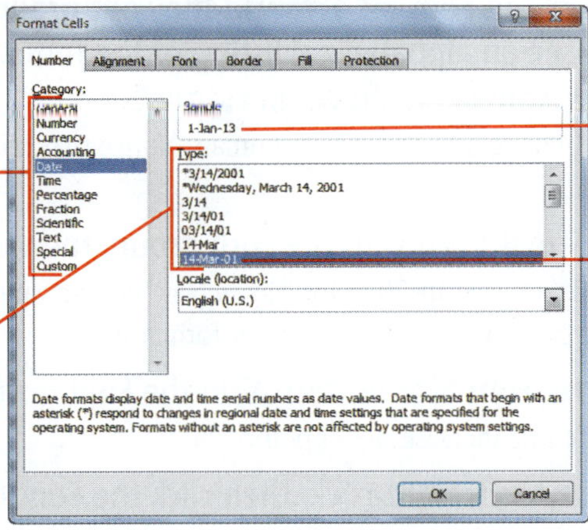

FIGURE C-3: Worksheet with formatted values

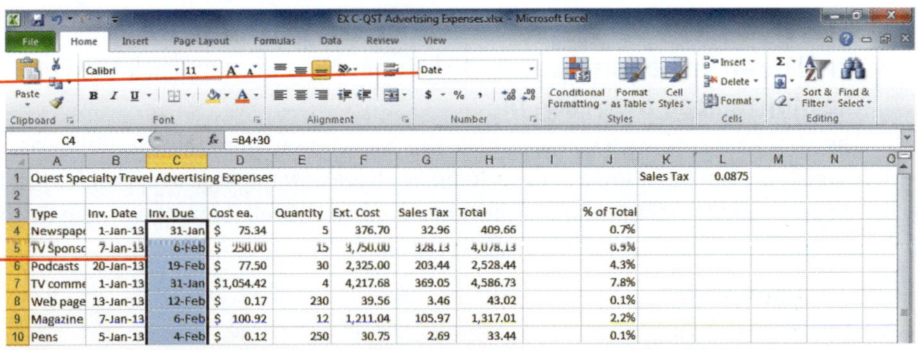

Formatting as a table

Excel includes 60 predefined **table styles** to make it easy to format selected worksheet cells as a table. You can apply table styles to any range of cells that you want to format quickly, or even to an entire worksheet, but they're especially useful for those ranges with labels in the left column and top row, and totals in the bottom row or right column. To apply a table style, select the data to be formatted or click anywhere within the intended range (Excel can automatically detect a range of cells filled with data), click the Format as Table button in the Styles group on the Home tab, then click a style in the gallery, as shown in Figure C-4. Table styles are organized in three categories: Light, Medium, and Dark. Once you click a style, Excel asks you to confirm the range selection, then applies the style. Once you have formatted a range as a table, you can use Live Preview to preview the table in other styles by pointing to any style in the Table Styles gallery.

FIGURE C-4: Table Styles gallery

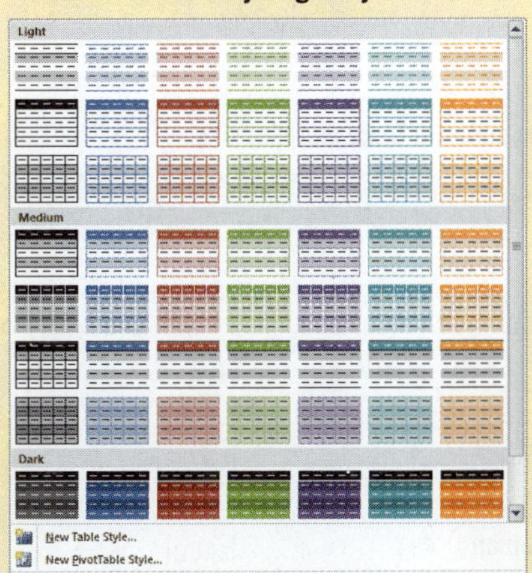

Changing Font and Font Size

A **font** is the name for a collection of characters (letters, numbers, symbols, and punctuation marks) with a similar, specific design. The **font size** is the physical size of the text, measured in units called points. A **point** is equal to 1/72 of an inch. The default font and font size in Excel is 11-point Calibri. Table C-1 shows several fonts in different font sizes. You can change the font and font size of any cell or range using the Font and Font Size list arrows. The Font and Font Size list arrows appear on the Home tab on the Ribbon and on the Mini toolbar, which opens when you right-click a cell or range. You want to change the font and font size of the labels and the worksheet title so that they stand out more from the data.

STEPS

QUICK TIP
To quickly move to a font in the Font list, type the first few characters of its name.

1. **Click cell A1, click the Font list arrow in the Font group on the Home tab, scroll down in the Font list to see an alphabetical listing of the fonts available on your computer, then click Times New Roman, as shown in Figure C-5**
   The font in cell A1 changes to Times New Roman. Notice that the font names on the list are displayed in the font they represent.

QUICK TIP
When you point to an option in the Font or Font Size list, Live Preview shows the selected cells with the option temporarily applied.

2. **Click the Font Size list arrow in the Font group, then click 20**
   The worksheet title appears in 20-point Times New Roman, and the Font and Font Size list boxes on the Home tab display the new font and font size information.
3. **Click the Increase Font Size button in the Font group twice**
   The font size of the title increases to 24 point.
4. **Select the range A3:J3, right-click, then click the Font list arrow in the Font group on the Mini toolbar**
   The Mini toolbar includes the most commonly used formatting tools, so it's great for making quick formatting changes.

QUICK TIP
You can format an entire row by clicking the row indicator button to select the row before formatting (or select an entire column by clicking the column indicator button before formatting).

5. **Scroll down in the Font list and click Times New Roman, click the Font Size list arrow on the Mini toolbar, then click 14**
   The Mini toolbar closes when you move the pointer away from the selection. Compare your worksheet to Figure C-6. Notice that some of the column labels are now too wide to appear fully in the column. Excel does not automatically adjust column widths to accommodate cell formatting; you have to adjust column widths manually. You'll learn to do this in a later lesson.
6. **Save your work**

TABLE C-1: Examples of fonts and font sizes

font	12 point	24 point
Calibri	Excel	Excel
Playbill	Excel	Excel
Comic Sans MS	Excel	Excel
Times New Roman	Excel	Excel

FIGURE C-5: Font list

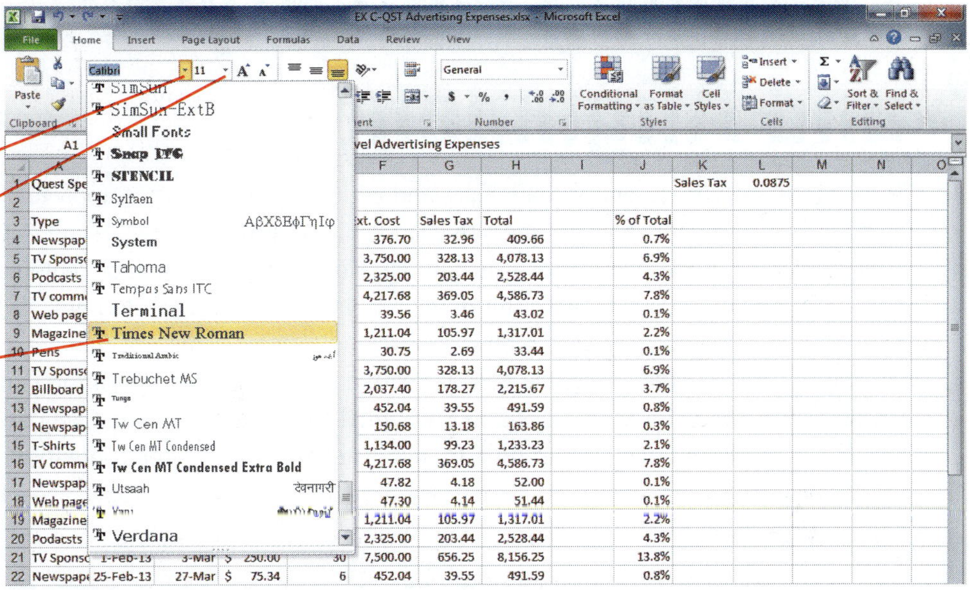

FIGURE C-6: Worksheet with formatted title and column labels

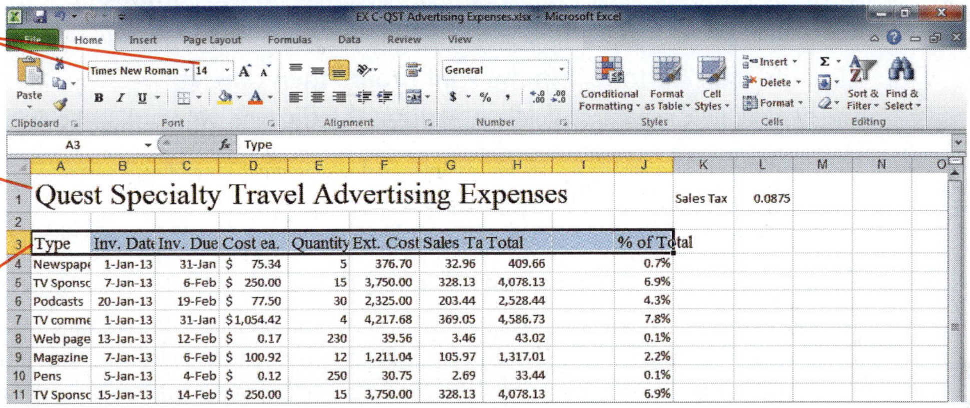

Excel 2010

Inserting and adjusting clip art and other images

You can illustrate your worksheets using clip art and other images. A **clip** is an individual media file, such as a graphic, sound, animation, or a movie. **Clip art** refers to images such as a corporate logo, a picture, or a photo. Microsoft Office comes with many clips available for your use. To add a clip to a worksheet, click the Clip Art button in the Illustrations group on the Insert tab. The Clip Art task pane opens. Here you can search for clips by typing one or more keywords (words related to your subject) in the Search for text box, then click Go. Clips that relate to your keywords appear in the Clip Art task pane, as shown in Figure C-7. (If you have a standard Office installation and an active Internet connection, click the Include Office.com content check box to see clips available through Office.com in addition to those on your computer.) When you click the image you want in the Clip Art task pane, the image is inserted at the location of the active cell. To add your own images to a worksheet, click the Insert tab on the Ribbon, then click the Picture button. Navigate to the file you want, then click Insert. To resize an image, drag any corner sizing handle. To move an image, point inside the clip until the pointer changes to ✥, then drag it to a new location.

FIGURE C-7: Results of Clip Art search

Changing Font Styles and Alignment

Font styles are formats such as bold, italic, and underlining that you can apply to affect the way text and numbers look in a worksheet. You can also change the **alignment** of labels and values in cells to position them in relation to the cells' edges—such as left-aligned, right-aligned, or centered. You can apply font styles and alignment options using the Home tab, the Format Cells dialog box, or the Mini toolbar. See Table C-2 for a description of common font style and alignment buttons that are available on the Home tab and the Mini toolbar. Once you have formatted a cell the way you want it, you can "paint" or copy the cell's formats into other cells by using the Format Painter button in the Clipboard group on the Home tab. This is similar to using copy and paste, but instead of copying cell contents, it copies only the cell's formatting. You want to further enhance the worksheet's appearance by adding bold and underline formatting and centering some of the labels.

STEPS

QUICK TIP
You can use the following keyboard shortcuts to format a selected cell or range: [Ctrl][B] to bold, [Ctrl][I] to italicize, and [Ctrl][U] to underline.

QUICK TIP
Overuse of any font style and random formatting can make a workbook difficult to read. Be consistent and add the same formatting to similar items throughout a worksheet or in related worksheets.

QUICK TIP
To clear all formatting from a selected range, click the Clear button in the Editing group on the Home tab, then click Clear Formats.

1. **Press [Ctrl][Home], then click the Bold button in the Font group on the Home tab**
   The title in cell A1 appears in bold.
2. **Click cell A3, then click the Underline button in the Font group**
   The column label is now underlined, though this may be difficult to see with the cell selected.
3. **Click the Italic button in the Font group, then click**
   The heading now appears in boldface, underlined, italic type. Notice that the Bold, Italic, and Underline buttons in the Font group are all selected.
4. **Click the Italic button to deselect it**
   The italic font style is removed from cell A3, but the bold and underline font styles remain.
5. **Click the Format Painter button in the Clipboard group, then select the range B3:J3**
   The formatting in cell A3 is copied to the rest of the column labels. To paint the formats on more than one selection, double-click the Format Painter button to keep it activated until you turn it off. You can turn off the Format Painter by pressing [Esc] or by clicking . You decide the title would look better if it were centered over the data columns.
6. **Select the range A1:H1, then click the Merge & Center button in the Alignment group**
   The Merge & Center button creates one cell out of the eight cells across the row, then centers the text in that newly created, merged cell. The title "Quest Specialty Travel Advertising Expenses" is centered across the eight columns you selected. To split a merged cell into its original components, select the merged cell, then click the Merge & Center button to deselect it. The merged and centered text might look awkward now, but you'll be changing the column widths shortly.
7. **Select the range A3:J3, right-click, then click the Center button on the Mini toolbar**
   Compare your screen to Figure C-8. Although they may be difficult to read, notice that all the headings are centered within their cells.
8. **Save your work**

FIGURE C-8: Worksheet with font styles and alignment applied

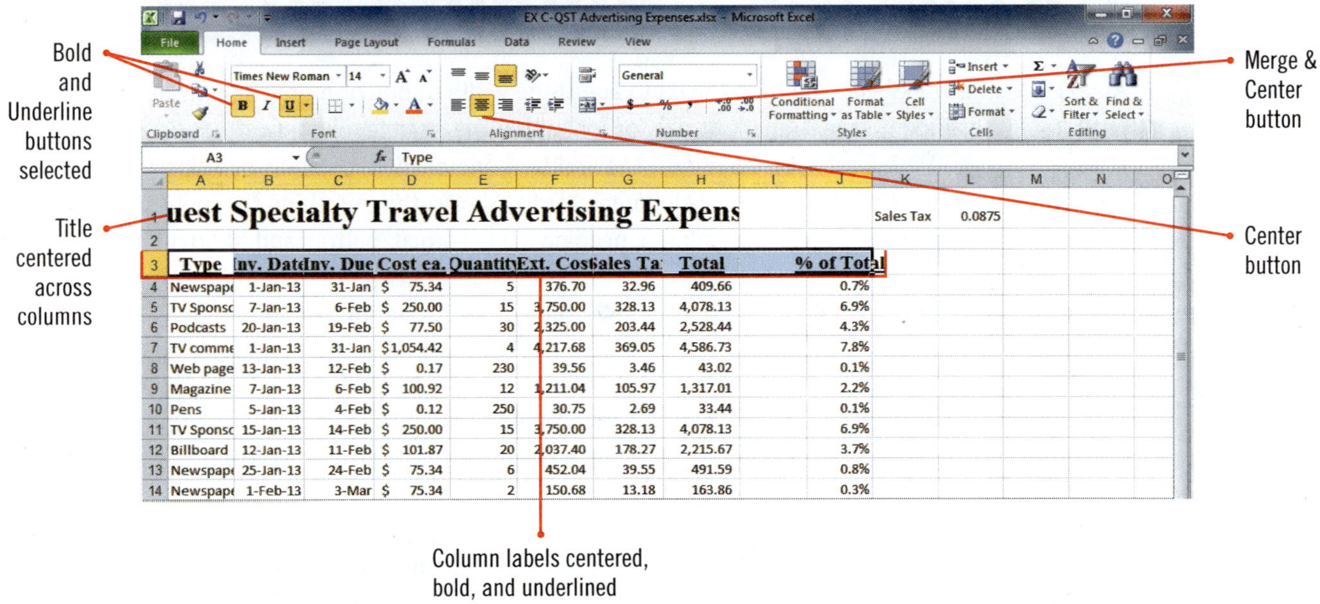

TABLE C-2: Common font style and alignment buttons

button	description	button	description
B	Bolds text		Aligns text at the left edge of the cell
I	Italicizes text		Centers text horizontally within the cell
U	Underlines text		Aligns text at the right edge of the cell
	Centers text across columns, and combines two or more selected, adjacent cells into one cell		

Rotating and indenting cell entries

In addition to applying fonts and font styles, you can rotate or indent data within a cell to further change its appearance. You can rotate text within a cell by altering its alignment. To change alignment, select the cells you want to modify, then click the dialog box launcher in the Alignment group to open the Alignment tab of the Format Cells dialog box. Click a position in the Orientation box or type a number in the Degrees text box to rotate text from its default horizontal orientation, then click OK. You can indent cell contents using the Increase Indent button in the Alignment group, which moves cell contents to the right one space, or the Decrease Indent button, which moves cell contents to the left one space.

Adjusting Column Width

As you format a worksheet, you might need to adjust the width of one or more columns to accommodate changes in the amount of text, the font size, or font style. The default column width is 8.43 characters, a little less than 1". With Excel, you can adjust the width of one or more columns by using the mouse, the Format button in the Cells group on the Home tab, or the shortcut menu. Using the mouse, you can drag or double-click the right edge of a column heading. The Format button and shortcut menu include commands for making more precise width adjustments. Table C-3 describes common column formatting commands. You have noticed that some of the labels in columns A through J don't fit in the cells. You want to adjust the widths of the columns so that the labels appear in their entirety.

STEPS

1. **Position the mouse pointer on the line between the column A and column B headings until it changes to ✛**

   See Figure C-9. The **column heading** is the box at the top of each column containing a letter. Before you can adjust column width using the mouse, you need to position the pointer on the right edge of the column heading for the column you want to adjust. The cell entry "TV commercials" is the widest in the column.

2. **Click and drag the ✛ to the right until the column displays the "TV commercials" cell entries fully (approximately 13.86 characters, 1.06", or 102 pixels)**

   As you change the column width, a ScreenTip is displayed listing the column width. In Normal view, the ScreenTip lists the width in characters and pixels; in Page Layout view, the ScreenTip lists the width in inches and pixels.

> **QUICK TIP**
> If "#######" appears after you adjust a column of values, the column is too narrow to display the values completely; increase the column width until the values appear.

3. **Position the pointer on the line between columns B and C until it changes to ✛, then double-click**

   Double-clicking the right edge of a column heading activates the **AutoFit** feature, which automatically resizes the column to accommodate the widest entry in the column. Column B automatically widens to fit the widest entry, which is the column label "Inv. Date".

4. **Use AutoFit to resize columns C, D, and J**

5. **Select the range E5:H5**

   You can change the width of multiple columns at once, by first selecting either the column headings or at least one cell in each column.

6. **Click the Format button in the Cells group, then click Column Width**

   The Column Width dialog box opens. Column width measurement is based on the number of characters that will fit in the column when formatted in the Normal font and font size (in this case, 11 pt Calibri).

> **QUICK TIP**
> If an entire column rather than a column cell is selected, you can change the width of the column by right-clicking the column heading, then clicking Column Width on the shortcut menu.

7. **Drag the dialog box by its title bar if its placement obscures your view of the worksheet, type 11 in the Column width text box, then click OK**

   The widths of columns E, F, G, and H change to reflect the new setting. See Figure C-10.

8. **Save your work**

TABLE C-3: Common column formatting commands

command	description	available using
Column Width	Sets the width to a specific number of characters	Format button; shortcut menu
AutoFit Column Width	Fits to the widest entry in a column	Format button; mouse
Hide & Unhide	Hides or displays hidden column(s)	Format button; shortcut menu
Default Width	Resets column to worksheet's default column width	Format button

FIGURE C-9: Preparing to change the column width

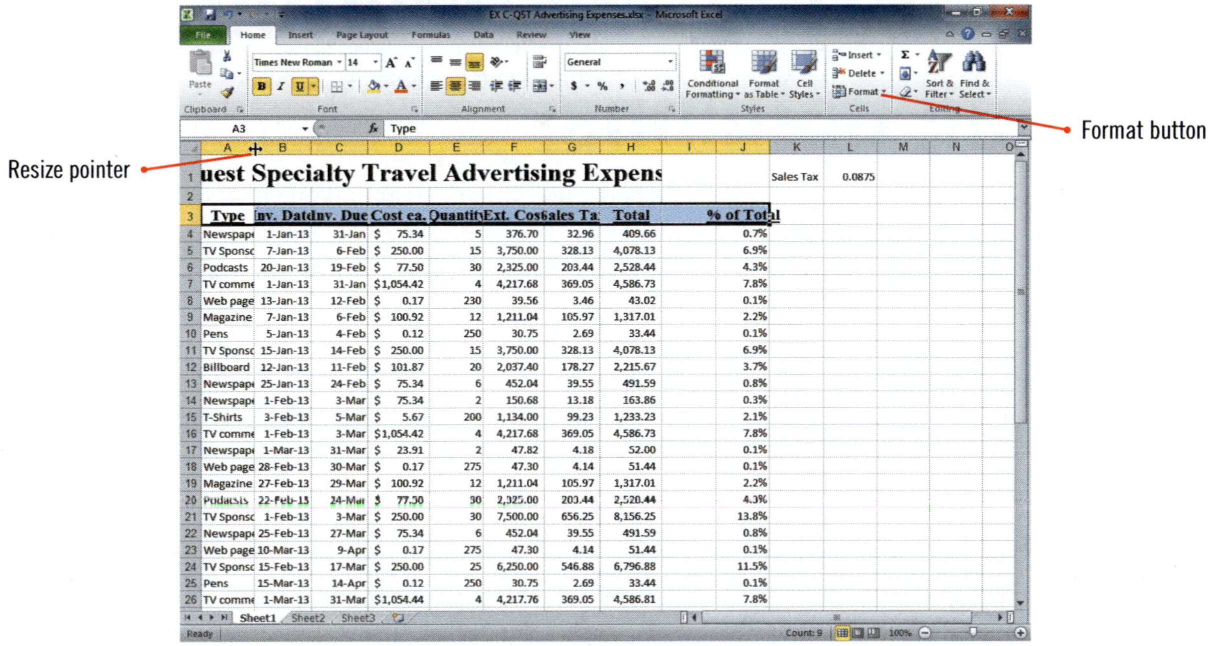

FIGURE C-10: Worksheet with column widths adjusted

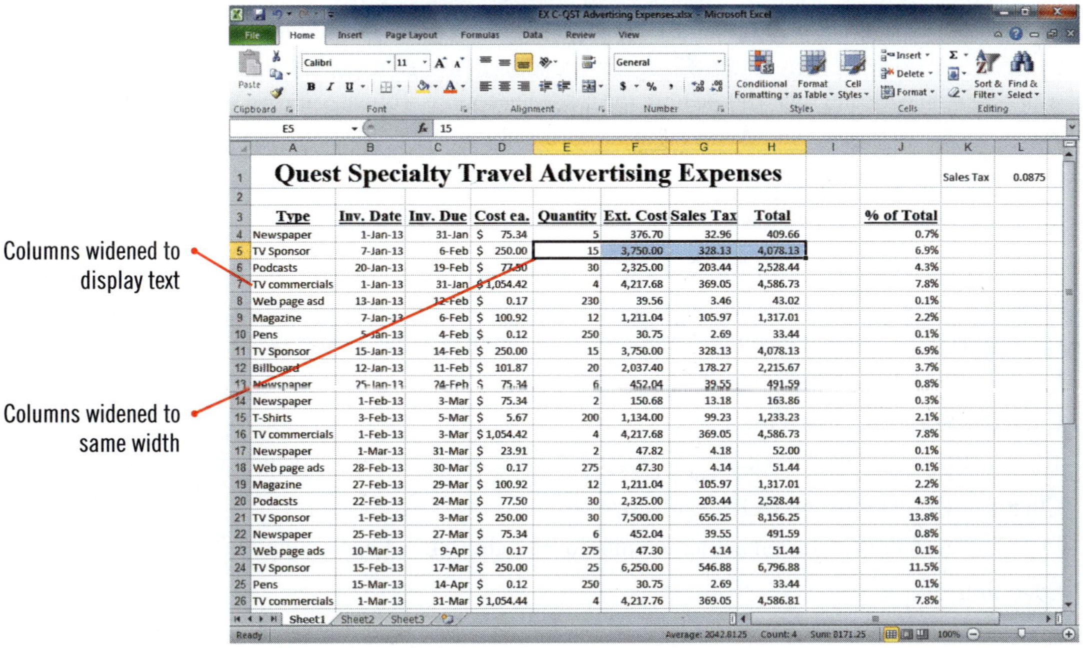

Changing row height

Changing row height is as easy as changing column width. Row height is calculated in points, the same units of measure used for fonts. The row height must exceed the size of the font you are using. Normally, you don't need to adjust row heights manually, because row heights adjust automatically to accommodate font size changes. If you format something in a row to be a larger point size, Excel adjusts the row to fit the largest point size in the row. However, you have just as many options for changing row height as you do column width. Using the mouse, you can place the ╪ pointer on the line dividing a row heading from the heading below, and then drag to the desired height; double-clicking the line AutoFits the row height where necessary. You can also select one or more rows, then use the Row Height command on the shortcut menu, or click the Format button on the Home tab and click the Row Height or AutoFit Row Height command.

UNIT C
Excel 2010

Inserting and Deleting Rows and Columns

As you modify a worksheet, you might find it necessary to insert or delete rows and columns to keep your worksheet current. For example, you might need to insert rows to accommodate new inventory products or remove a column of yearly totals that are no longer necessary. When you insert a new row, the row is inserted above the cell pointer and the contents of the worksheet shift down from the newly inserted row. When you insert a new column, the column is inserted to the left of the cell pointer and the contents of the worksheet shift to the right of the new column. To insert multiple rows, select the same number of row headings as you want to insert before using the Insert command. You want to improve the overall appearance of the worksheet by inserting a row between the last row of data and the totals. Also, you have learned that row 27 and column J need to be deleted from the worksheet.

STEPS

QUICK TIP
To insert a single row or column, right-click the row heading immediately below where you want the new row, or right-click the column heading to the right of where you want the new column, then click Insert on the shortcut menu.

1. **Right-click cell A32, then click Insert on the shortcut menu**
   The Insert dialog box opens. See Figure C-11. You can choose to insert a column or a row; insert a single cell and shift the cells in the active column to the right; or insert a single cell and shift the cells in the active row down. An additional row between the last row of data and the totals will visually separate the totals.
2. **Click the Entire row option button, then click OK**
   A blank row appears between the Billboard data and the totals, and the formula result in cell E33 has not changed. The Insert Options button appears beside cell A33. Pointing to the button displays a list arrow, which you can click and then choose from the following options: Format Same As Above (the default setting, already selected), Format Same As Below, or Clear Formatting.
3. **Click the row 27 heading**
   All of row 27 is selected, as shown in Figure C-12.

QUICK TIP
If you inadvertently click the Delete list arrow instead of the button itself, click Delete Sheet Rows in the menu that opens.

4. **Click the Delete button in the Cells group; *do not click the list arrow***
   Excel deletes row 27, and all rows below it shift up one row. You must use the Delete button or the Delete command on the shortcut menu to delete a row or column; pressing [Delete] on the keyboard removes only the *contents* of a selected row or column.
5. **Click the column J heading**
   The percentage information is calculated elsewhere and is no longer necessary in this worksheet.

QUICK TIP
After inserting or deleting rows or columns in a worksheet, be sure to proof formulas that contain relative cell references.

6. **Click the Delete button in the Cells group**
   Excel deletes column J. The remaining columns to the right shift left one column.
7. **Save your work**

Hiding and unhiding columns and rows

When you don't want data in a column or row to be visible, but you don't want to delete it, you can hide the column or row. To hide a selected column, click the Format button in the Cells group on the Home tab, point to Hide & Unhide, then click Hide Columns. A hidden column is indicated by a dark black vertical line in its original position. This black line disappears when you click elsewhere in the worksheet. You can display a hidden column by selecting the columns on either side of the hidden column, clicking the Format button in the Cells group, pointing to Hide & Unhide, and then clicking Unhide Columns. (To hide or unhide one or more rows, substitute Hide Rows and Unhide Rows for the Hide Columns and Unhide Columns commands.)

FIGURE C-11: Insert dialog box

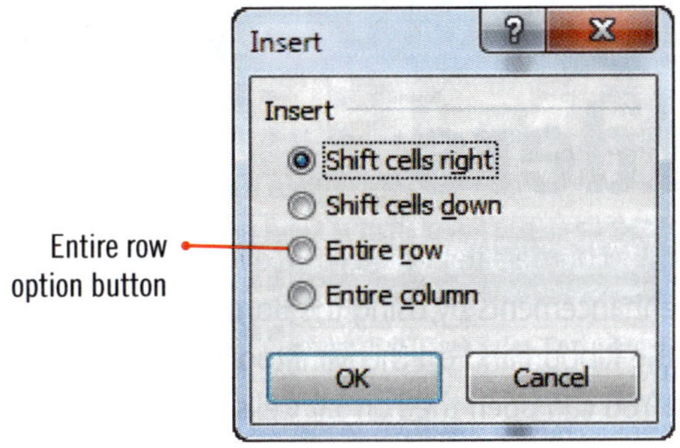

FIGURE C-12: Worksheet with row 27 selected

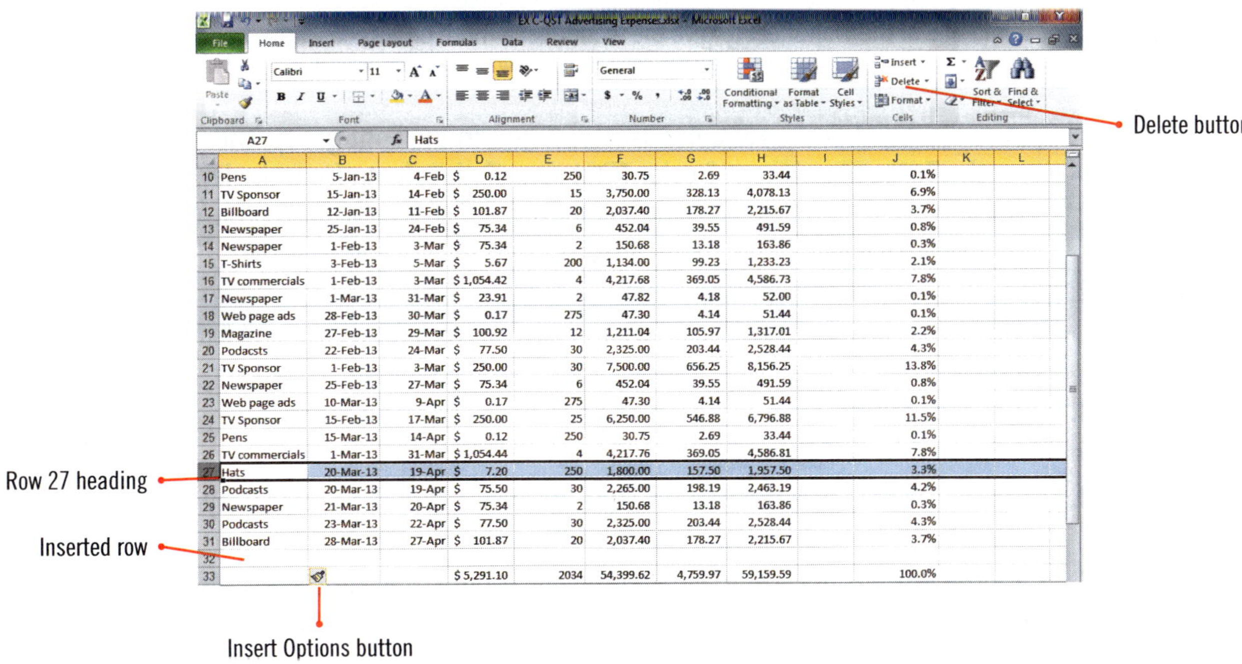

Adding and editing comments

Much of your work in Excel may be in collaboration with teammates with whom you share worksheets. You can share ideas with other worksheet users by adding comments within selected cells. To include a comment in a worksheet, click the cell where you want to place the comment, click the Review tab on the Ribbon, then click the New Comment button in the Comments group. You can type your comments in the resizable text box that opens containing the computer user's name. A small, red triangle appears in the upper-right corner of a cell containing a comment. If comments are not already displayed in a workbook, other users can point to the triangle to display the comment. To see all worksheet comments, as shown in Figure C-13, click the Show All Comments button in the Comments group. To edit a comment, click the cell containing the comment, then click the Edit Comment button in the Comments group. To delete a comment, click the cell containing the comment, then click the Delete button in the Comments group.

FIGURE C-13: Comments displayed in a worksheet

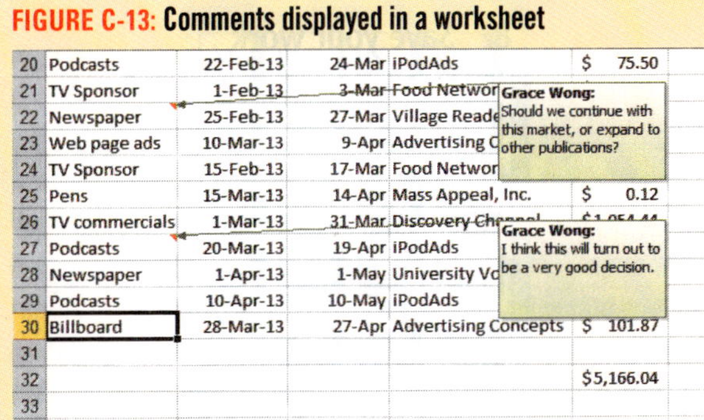

Practice

Concepts Review

For current SAM information, including versions and content details, visit SAM Central (http://www.cengage.com/samcentral). If you have a SAM user profile, you may have access to hands-on instruction, practice, and assessment of the skills covered in this unit. Since various versions of SAM are supported throughout the life of this text, check with your instructor for the correct instructions and URL/Web site for accessing assignments.

Label each element of the Excel worksheet window shown in Figure C-27.

FIGURE C-27

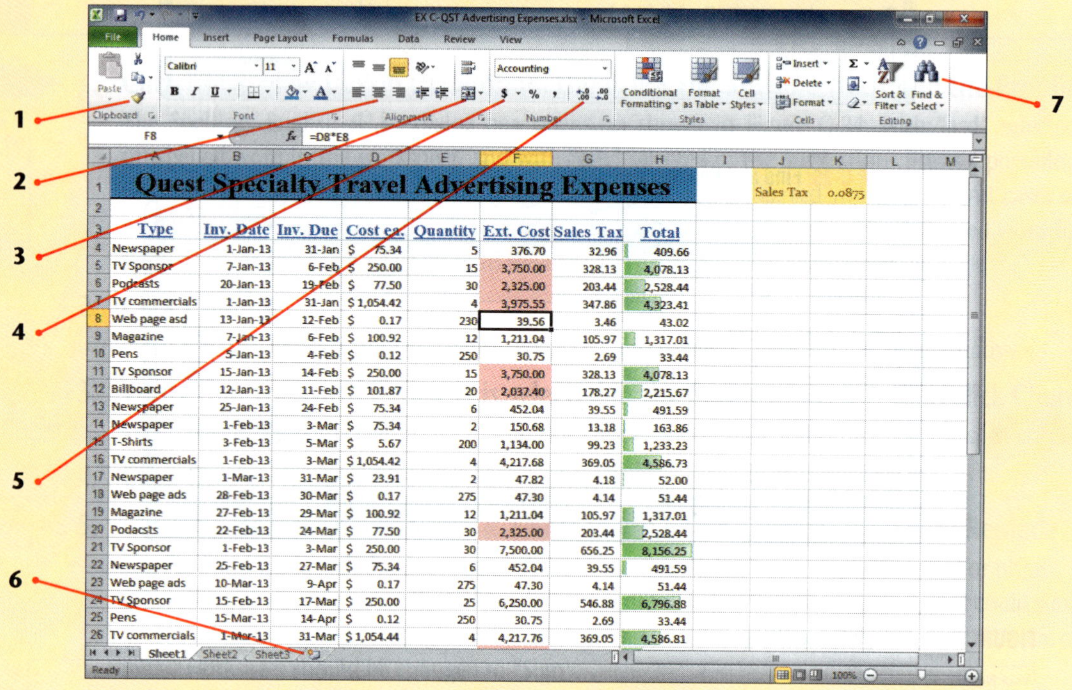

Match each command or button with the statement that best describes it.

8. Conditional formatting

9. 

10. Spelling button

11. [Ctrl][Home]

12. 

13. 

a. Centers cell contents over multiple cells

b. Adds dollar signs and two decimal places to selected data

c. Changes formatting of a cell that meets a certain rule

d. Displays background color options for a cell

e. Moves cell pointer to cell A1

f. Checks for apparent misspellings in a worksheet

Select the best answer from the list of choices.

14. Which of the following is an example of Accounting number format?

- **a.** 5555
- **b.** $5,555.55
- **c.** 55.55%
- **d.** 5,555.55

15. What feature is used to delete a conditional formatting rule?

- **a.** Rules Reminder
- **b.** Conditional Formatting Rules Manager
- **c.** Condition Manager
- **d.** Format Manager

16. Which button removes the italic font style from selected cells?

- **a.** 
- **b.** 
- **c.** 
- **d.** 

17. What is the name of the feature used to resize a column to accommodate its widest entry?

- **a.** AutoFormat
- **b.** AutoFit
- **c.** AutoResize
- **d.** AutoRefit

18. Which button increases the number of decimal places in selected cells?

- **a.** 
- **b.** 
- **c.** 
- **d.** 

19. Which button copies multiple formats from selected cells to other cells?

- **a.** 
- **b.** 
- **c.** 
- **d.** 

Skills Review

1. Format values.

- **a.** Start Excel, open the file EX C-2.xlsx from the drive and folder where you store your Data Files, then save it as **EX C-Life Insurance Premiums**.
- **b.** Enter a formula in cell B10 that totals the number of employees.
- **c.** Create a formula in cell C5 that calculates the monthly insurance premium for the accounting department. (*Hint*: Make sure you use the correct type of cell reference in the formula. To calculate the department's monthly premium, multiply the number of employees by the monthly premium in cell C14.)
- **d.** Copy the formula in cell C5 to the range C6:C10.
- **e.** Format the range C5:C10 using Accounting number format.
- **f.** Change the format of the range C6:C9 to the Comma Style.
- **g.** Reduce the number of decimals in cell B14 to 0 using a button in the Number group on the Home tab.
- **h.** Save your work.

2. Change font and font sizes.

- **a.** Select the range of cells containing the column labels (in row 4).
- **b.** Change the font of the selection to Times New Roman.
- **c.** Increase the font size of the selection to 12 points.
- **d.** Increase the font size of the label in cell A1 to 14 points.
- **e.** Save your changes.

3. Change font styles and alignment.

- **a.** Apply the bold and italic font styles to the worksheet title in cell A1.
- **b.** Use the Merge & Center button to center the Life Insurance Premiums label over columns A through C.
- **c.** Apply the italic font style to the Life Insurance Premiums label.
- **d.** Add the bold font style to the labels in row 4.
- **e.** Use the Format Painter to copy the format in cell A4 to the range A5:A10.
- **f.** Apply the format in cell C10 to cell B14.

Skills Review (continued)

- **g.** Change the alignment of cell A10 to Align Right using a button in the Alignment group.
- **h.** Select the range of cells containing the column labels, then center them.
- **i.** Remove the italic font style from the Life Insurance Premiums label, then increase the font size to 14.
- **j.** Move the Life Insurance Premiums label to cell A3, then add the bold and underline font styles.
- **k.** Save your changes.

4. Adjust column width.

- **a.** Resize column C to a width of 10.71 characters.
- **b.** Use the AutoFit feature to resize columns A and B.
- **c.** Clear the contents of cell A13 (do not delete the cell).
- **d.** Change the text in cell A14 to **Monthly Insurance Premium**, then change the width of the column to 25 characters.
- **e.** Save your changes.

5. Insert and delete rows and columns.

- **a.** Insert a new row between rows 5 and 6.
- **b.** Add a new department, **Charity**, in the newly inserted row. Enter **6** as the number of employees in the department.
- **c.** Copy the formula in cell C7 to C6.
- **d.** Add the following comment to cell A6: **New department**. Display the comment, then drag to move it out of the way, if necessary.
- **e.** Add a new column between the Department and Employees columns with the title **Family Coverage**, then resize the column using AutoFit.
- **f.** Delete the Legal row from the worksheet.
- **g.** Move the value in cell C14 to cell B14.
- **h.** Save your changes.

6. Apply colors, patterns, and borders.

- **a.** Add Outside Borders around the range A4:D10.
- **b.** Add a Bottom Double Border to cells C9 and D9 (above the calculated employee and premium totals).
- **c.** Apply the Aqua, Accent 5, Lighter 80% fill color to the labels in the Department column (do not include the Total label).
- **d.** Apply the Orange, Accent 6, Lighter 60% fill color to the range A4:D4.
- **e.** Change the color of the font in the range A4:D4 to Red, Accent 2, Darker 25%.
- **f.** Add a 12.5% Gray pattern style to cell A1.
- **g.** Format the range A14:B14 with a fill color of Dark Blue, Text 2, Lighter 40%, change the font color to White, Background 1, then apply the bold font style.
- **h.** Save your changes.

7. Apply conditional formatting.

- **a.** Select the range D5:D9, then create a conditional format that changes cell contents to green fill with dark green text if the value is between 150 and 275.
- **b.** Select the range C5:C9, then create a conditional format that changes cell contents to red text if the number of employees exceeds 10.
- **c.** Apply a blue gradient-filled data bar to the range C5:C9. (*Hint*: Click Blue Data Bar in the Gradient Fill section.)
- **d.** Use the Rules Manager to modify the conditional format in cells C5:C9 to display values greater than 10 in bold dark red text.
- **e.** Merge and center the title (cell A1) over columns A through D.
- **f.** Save your changes.

8. Rename and move a worksheet.

- **a.** Name the Sheet1 tab **Insurance Data**.
- **b.** Name the Sheet3 tab **Employee Data**.
- **c.** Change the Insurance Data tab color to Red, Accent 2, Lighter 40%.
- **d.** Change the Employee Data tab color to Aqua, Accent 5, Lighter 40%.
- **e.** Move the Employee Data sheet so it comes after (to the right of) the Insurance Data sheet.
- **f.** Make the Insurance Data sheet active, enter your name in cell A20, then save your work.

Skills Review (continued)

9. Check spelling.

a. Move the cell pointer to cell A1.

b. Use the Find & Select feature to replace the Accounting label in cell A5 with Accounting/Legal.

c. Check the spelling in the worksheet using the spell checker, and correct any spelling errors if necessary.

d. Save your changes, then compare your Insurance Data sheet to Figure C-28.

e. Preview the Insurance Data sheet in Backstage view, submit your work to your instructor as directed, then close the workbook and exit Excel.

FIGURE C-28

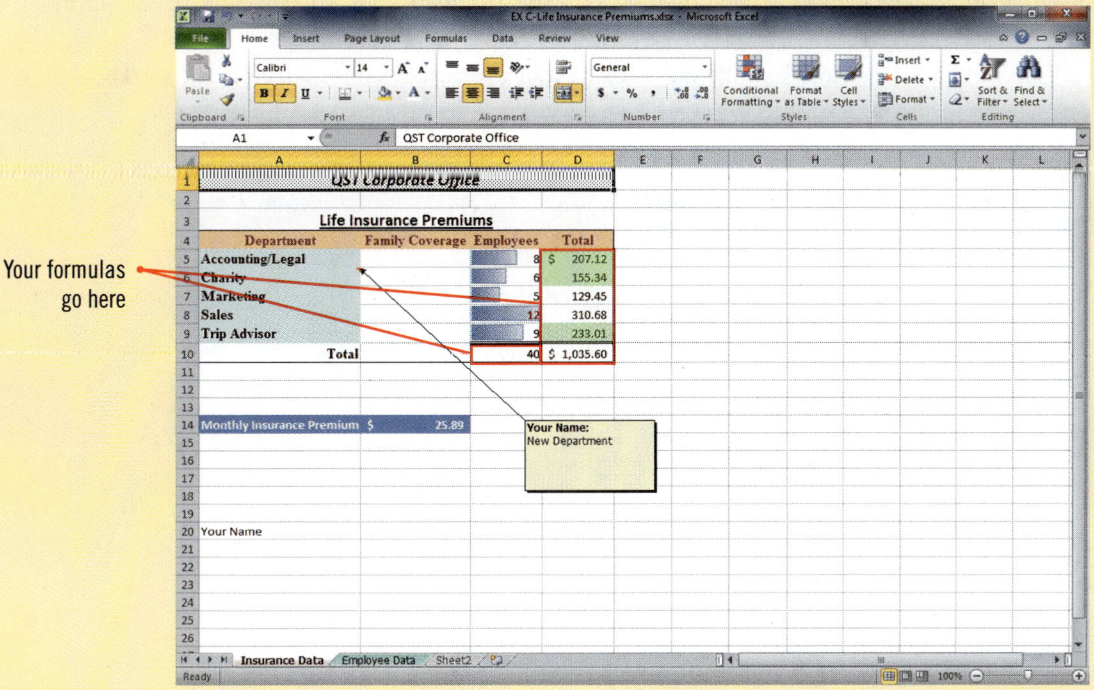

Independent Challenge 1

You run a freelance accounting business, and one of your newest clients is Pen & Paper, a small office supply store. Now that you've converted the store's accounting records to Excel, the manager would like you to work on an analysis of the inventory. Although more items will be added later, the worksheet has enough items for you to begin your modifications.

If you have a SAM 2010 user profile, an autogradable SAM version of this assignment may be available at http://www.cengage.com/sam2010. Check with your instructor to confirm that this assignment is available in SAM. To use the SAM version of this assignment, log into the SAM 2010 Web site and download the instruction and start files.

a. Start Excel, open the file EX C-3.xlsx from the drive and folder where you store your Data Files, then save it as **EX C-Pen & Paper Office Supply Inventory**.

b. Create a formula in cell E4 that calculates the value of the items in stock based on the price paid per item in cell B4. Format the cell in the Comma Style.

c. In cell F4, calculate the sale price of the items in stock using an absolute reference to the markup value shown in cell H1.

d. Copy the formulas created above into the range E5:F14; first convert any necessary cell references to absolute so that the formulas work correctly.

e. Apply bold to the column labels, and italicize the inventory items in column A.

f. Make sure all columns are wide enough to display the data and labels.

g. Format the values in the Sale Price column as Accounting number format with two decimal places.

h. Format the values in the Price Paid column as Comma Style with two decimal places.

Independent Challenge 1 (continued)

i. Add a row under #2 Pencils for **Digital cordless telephones**, price paid **53.45**, sold individually (**each**), with **23** on hand. Copy the appropriate formulas to cells E7:F7.

j. Verify that all the data in the worksheet is visible and formulas are correct. Adjust any items as needed, and check the spelling of the entire worksheet.

k. Use conditional formatting to apply yellow fill with dark yellow text to items with a quantity of less than 25 on hand.

l. Use an icon set of your choosing in the range D4:D15 to illustrate the relative differences between values in the range.

m. Add an outside border around the data in the Item column (do not include the Item column label).

n. Delete the row containing the Thumb tacks entry.

o. Enter your name in an empty cell below the data, then save the file. Compare your worksheet to the sample in Figure C-29.

p. Preview the worksheet in Backstage view, submit your work to your instructor as directed, close the workbook, then exit Excel.

FIGURE C-29

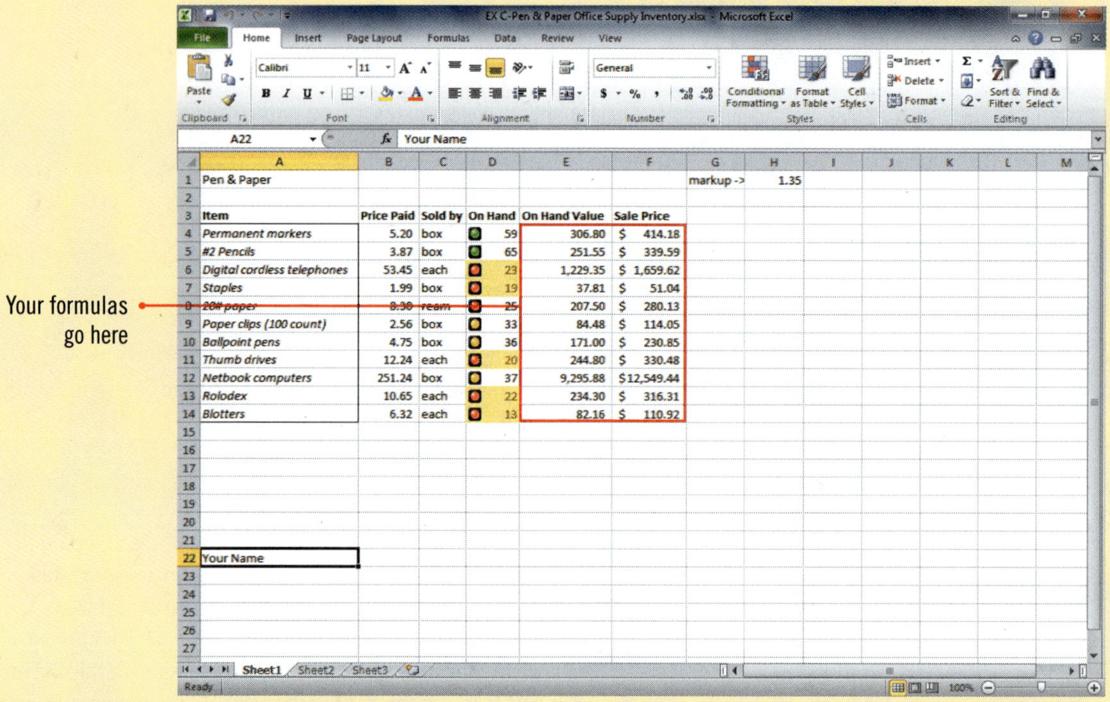

Independent Challenge 2

You volunteer several hours each week with the Assistance League of Boise, and you are in charge of maintaining the membership list. You're currently planning a mailing campaign to members in certain regions of the city. You also want to create renewal letters for members whose membership expires soon. You decide to format the list to enhance the appearance of the worksheet and make your upcoming tasks easier to plan.

a. Start Excel, open the file EX C-4.xlsx from the drive and folder where you store your Data Files, then save it as **EX C-Boise Assistance League**.

b. Remove any blank columns.

c. Create a conditional format in the Zip Code column so that entries greater than 83749 appear in light red fill with dark red text.

d. Make all columns wide enough to fit their data and labels.

e. Use formatting enhancements, such as fonts, font sizes, font styles, and fill colors, to make the worksheet more attractive.

f. Center the column labels.

Independent Challenge 2 (continued)

g. Use conditional formatting so that entries for Year of Membership Expiration that are between 2014 and 2017 appear in green fill with bold black text. (*Hint*: Create a custom format for cells that meet the condition.)

h. Adjust any items as necessary, then check the spelling.

i. Change the name of the Sheet1 tab to one that reflects the sheet's contents, then add a tab color of your choice.

j. Enter your name in an empty cell, then save your work.

k. Preview the worksheet in Backstage view, make any final changes you think necessary, then submit your work to your instructor as directed. Compare your work to the sample shown in Figure C-30.

l. Close the workbook, then exit Excel.

FIGURE C-30

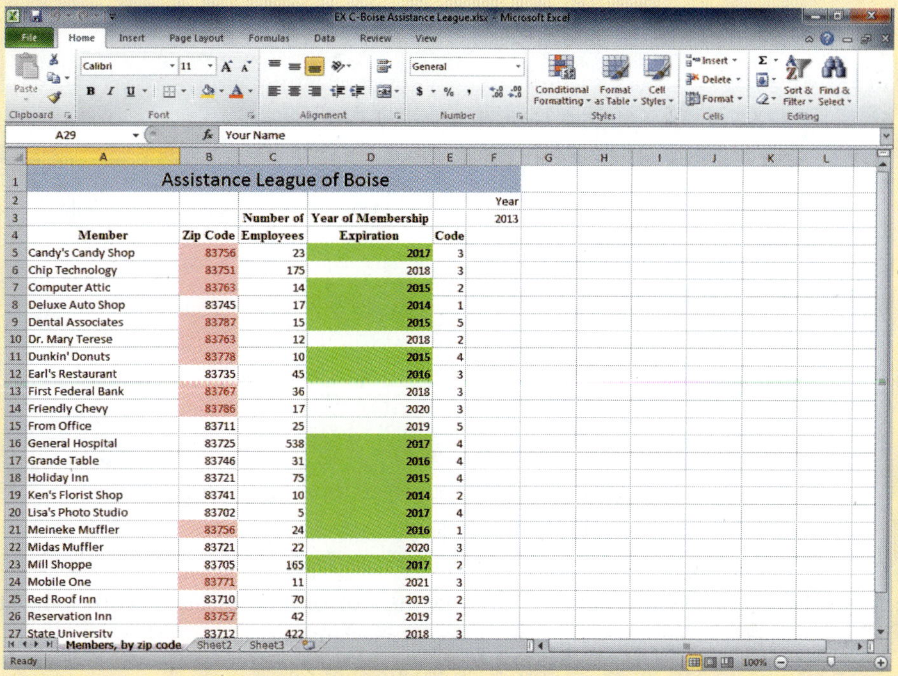

Independent Challenge 3

Prestige Press is a Boston-based publisher that manufactures children's books. As the finance manager for the company, one of your responsibilities is to analyze the monthly reports from the five district sales offices. Your boss, Joanne Bennington, has just asked you to prepare a quarterly sales report for an upcoming meeting. Because several top executives will be attending this meeting, Joanne reminds you that the report must look professional. In particular, she asks you to emphasize the company's surge in profits during the last month and to highlight the fact that the Northeastern district continues to outpace the other districts.

a. Plan a worksheet that shows the company's sales during the first quarter. Assume that all books are the same price. Make sure you include the following:

- The number of books sold (units sold) and the associated revenues (total sales) for each of the five district sales offices. The five sales districts are Northeastern, Midwestern, Southeastern, Southern, and Western.
- Calculations that show month-by-month totals for January, February, and March, and a 3-month cumulative total.
- Calculations that show each district's share of sales (percent of Total Sales).
- Labels that reflect the month-by-month data as well as the cumulative data.
- Formatting enhancements and data bars that emphasize the recent month's sales surge and the Northeastern district's sales leadership.

b. Ask yourself the following questions about the organization and formatting of the worksheet: What worksheet title and labels do you need, and where should they appear? How can you calculate the totals? What formulas can you copy to save time and keystrokes? Do any of these formulas need to use an absolute reference? How do you show dollar amounts? What information should be shown in bold? Do you need to use more than one font? Should you use more than one point size?

c. Start Excel, then save a new, blank workbook as **EX C-Prestige Press** to the drive and folder where you store your Data Files.

Excel 2010

Independent Challenge 3 (continued)

d. Build the worksheet with your own price and sales data. Enter the titles and labels first, then enter the numbers and formulas. You can use the information in Table C-4 to get started.

TABLE C-4

Prestige Press										
1st Quarter Sales Report										
		January		February		March		Total		
Office	Price	Units Sold	Sales	Units Sold	Sales	Units Sold	Sales	Units Sold	Sales	Total % of Sales
Northeastern										
Midwestern										
Southeastern										
Southern										
Western										

e. Add a row beneath the data containing the totals for each column.
f. Adjust the column widths as necessary.
g. Change the height of row 1 to 33 points.
h. Format labels and values to enhance the look of the worksheet, and change the font styles and alignment if necessary.
i. Resize columns and adjust the formatting as necessary.
j. Add data bars for the monthly Units Sold columns.
k. Add a column that calculates a 25% increase in total sales dollars. Use an absolute cell reference in this calculation. (*Hint*: Make sure the current formatting is applied to the new information.)

Advanced Challenge Exercise

ACE
- Delete the contents of cells J4:K4 if necessary, then merge and center cell I4 over column I:K.
- Insert a clip art image related to books in an appropriate location, adjusting its size and position as necessary.
- Save your work.

l. Enter your name in an empty cell.
m. Check the spelling in the workbook, change to a landscape orientation, save your work, then compare your work to Figure C-31.
n. Preview the worksheet in Backstage view, then submit your work to your instructor as directed.
o. Close the workbook file, then exit Excel.

FIGURE C-31

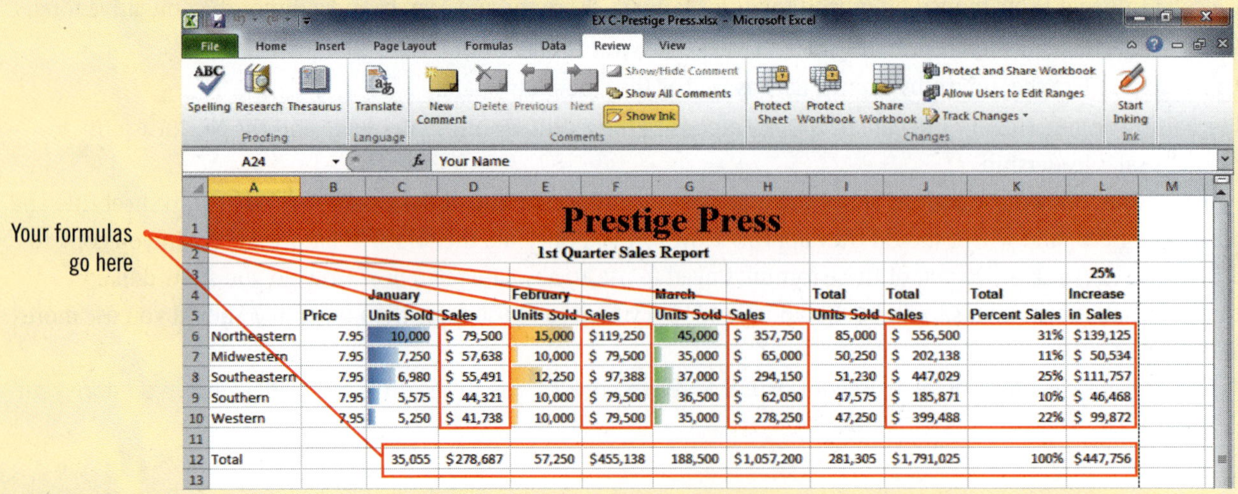

Real Life Independent Challenge

This project requires an Internet connection.

You are saving money to take an international trip you have always dreamed about. You plan to visit seven different countries over the course of 2 months, and you have budgeted an identical spending allowance in each country. You want to create a worksheet that calculates the amount of native currency you will have in each country based on the budgeted amount. You want the workbook to reflect the currency information for each country.

a. Start Excel, then save a new, blank workbook as **EX C-World Tour Budget** to the drive and folder where you store your Data Files.

b. Add a title at the top of the worksheet.

c. Think of seven countries you would like to visit, then enter column and row labels for your worksheet. (*Hint*: You may wish to include row labels for each country, plus column labels for the country, the $1 equivalent in native currency, the total amount of native currency you'll have in each country, and the name of each country's monetary unit.)

d. Decide how much money you want to bring to each country (for example, $1,000), and enter that in the worksheet.

e. Use your favorite search engine to find your own information sources on currency conversions for the countries you plan to visit.

f. Enter the cash equivalent to $1 in U.S. dollars for each country in your list.

g. Create an equation that calculates the amount of native currency you will have in each country, using an absolute cell reference in the formula.

h. Format the entries in the column containing the native currency $1 equivalent as Number number format with three decimal places, and format the column containing the total native currency budget with two decimal places, using the correct currency number format for each country. (*Hint*: Use the Number tab in the Format cells dialog box; choose the appropriate currency number format from the Symbol list.)

i. Create a conditional format that changes the font style and color of the calculated amount in the $1,000 US column to light red fill with dark red text if the amount exceeds **1000** units of the local currency.

j. Merge and center the worksheet title over the column headings.

k. Add any formatting you want to the column headings, and resize the columns as necessary.

l. Add a background color to the title.

Advanced Challenge Exercise

ACE

- Modify the conditional format in the $1,000 US column so that entries between 1500 and 3999 are displayed in red, boldface type; and entries above 4000 appear in blue, boldface type with a light red background.
- Delete all the unused sheets in the workbook.
- Save your work as **EX C-World Tour Budget ACE** to the drive and folder where you store your Data Files.
- If you have access to an e-mail account, e-mail this workbook to your instructor as an attachment.

m. Enter your name in the header of the worksheet.

n. Spell check the worksheet, save your changes, compare your work to Figure C-32, then preview the worksheet in Backstage view, and submit your work to your instructor as directed.

o. Close the workbook and exit Excel.

FIGURE C-32

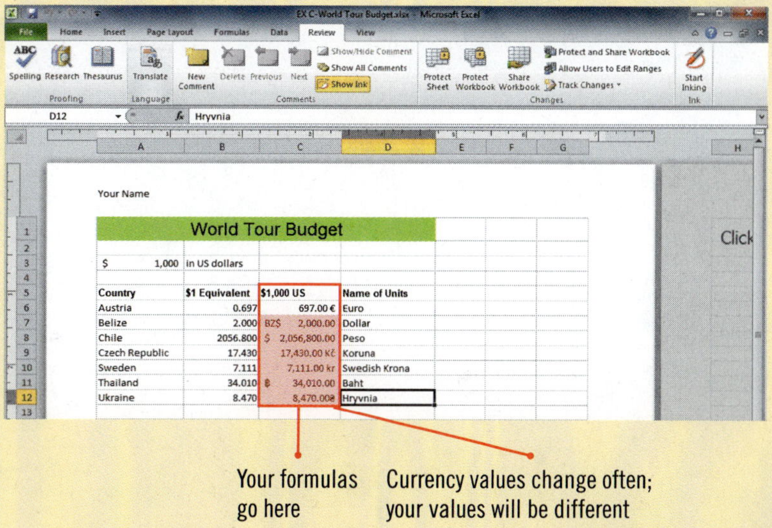

Visual Workshop

Open the file EX C-5.xlsx from the drive and folder where you store your Data Files, then save it as **EX C-Tip-Top Temps**. Use the skills you learned in this unit to format the worksheet so it looks like the one shown in Figure C-33. Create a conditional format in the Level column so that entries greater than 3 appear in red text. Create an additional conditional format in the Review Cycle column so that any value equal to 3 appears in green bold text. Replace the Accounting department label with **Legal**. (*Hint*: The only additional font used in this exercise is 16-point Times New Roman in row 1.) Enter your name in cell A25, check the spelling in the worksheet, save your changes, then submit your work to your instructor as directed.

FIGURE C-33

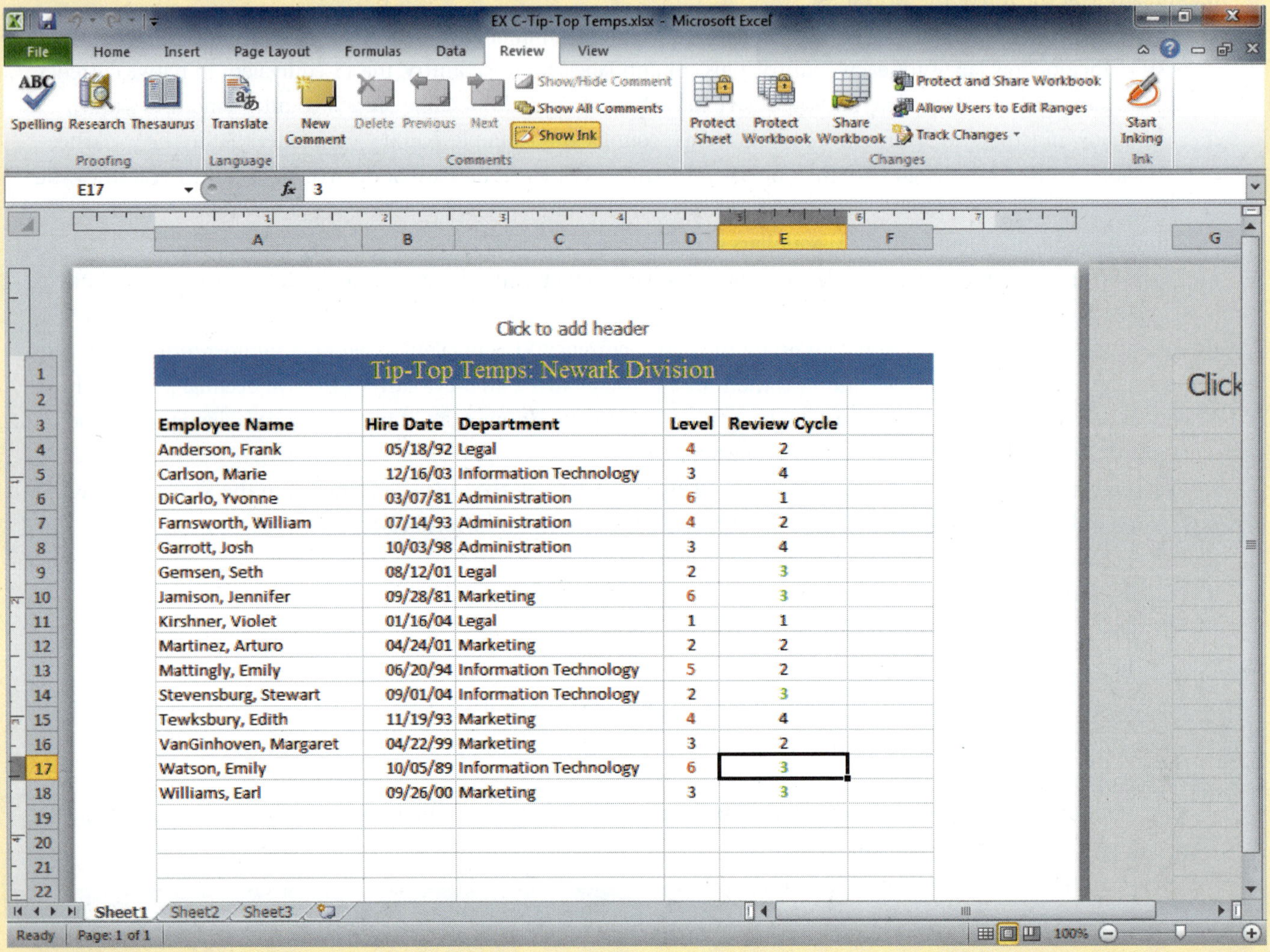

UNIT

D

Excel 2010

Working with Charts

Files You Will Need:

EX D-1.xlsx
EX D-2.xlsx
EX D-3.xlsx
EX D-4.xlsx
EX D-5.xlsx
EX D-6.xlsx

Worksheets provide an effective layout for calculating and organizing data, but the grid layout is not always the best format for presenting your work to others. To display information so it's easier to interpret, you can create a chart. **Charts**, sometimes called graphs, present information in a graphic format, making it easier to see patterns, trends, and relationships. In this unit, you learn how to create a chart, how to edit the chart and change the chart type, how to add text annotations and arrows, and how to preview and print the chart. At the upcoming annual meeting, Grace Wong wants to emphasize spending patterns at Quest Specialty Travel. She asks you to create a chart showing the trends in company expenses over the past four quarters.

OBJECTIVES

- Plan a chart
- Create a chart
- Move and resize a chart
- Change the chart design
- Change the chart layout
- Format a chart
- Annotate and draw on a chart
- Create a pie chart

UNIT
D
Excel 2010

Planning a Chart

Before creating a chart, you need to plan the information you want your chart to show and how you want it to look. Planning ahead helps you decide what type of chart to create and how to organize the data. Understanding the parts of a chart makes it easier to format and to change specific elements so that the chart best illustrates your data. In preparation for creating the chart for Grace's presentation, you identify your goals for the chart and plan its layout.

DETAILS

Use the following guidelines to plan the chart:

- **Determine the purpose of the chart, and identify the data relationships you want to communicate graphically**

  You want to create a chart that shows quarterly tour expenses for each country where Quest Specialty Travel provides tours. This worksheet data is shown in Figure D-1. You also want the chart to illustrate whether the quarterly expenses for each country increased or decreased from quarter to quarter.

- **Determine the results you want to see, and decide which chart type is most appropriate**

  Different chart types display data in distinctive ways. For example, a pie chart compares parts to the whole, so it's useful for showing what proportion of a budget amount was spent on tours in one country relative to what was spent on tours in other countries. A line chart, in contrast, is best for showing trends over time. To choose the best chart type for your data, you should first decide how you want your data displayed and interpreted. Table D-1 describes several different types of charts you can create in Excel and their corresponding buttons on the Insert tab on the Ribbon. Because you want to compare QST tour expenses in multiple countries over a period of four quarters, you decide to use a column chart.

- **Identify the worksheet data you want the chart to illustrate**

  Sometimes you use all the data in a worksheet to create a chart, while at other times you may need to select a range within the sheet. The worksheet from which you are creating your chart contains expense data for each of the past four quarters and the totals for the past year. You will need to use all the quarterly data contained in the worksheet except the quarterly totals.

- **Understand the elements of a chart**

  The chart shown in Figure D-2 contains basic elements of a chart. In the figure, QST tour countries are on the horizontal axis (also called the **x-axis**) and expense dollar amounts are on the vertical axis (also called the **y-axis**). The horizontal axis is also called the **category axis** because it often contains the names of data groups, such as locations, months, or years. The vertical axis is also called the **value axis** because it often contains numerical values that help you interpret the size of chart elements. (3-D charts also contain a **z-axis**, for comparing data across both categories and values.) The area inside the horizontal and vertical axes is the **plot area**. The **tick marks**, on the vertical axis, and **gridlines** (extending across the plot area) create a scale of measure for each value. Each value in a cell you select for your chart is a **data point**. In any chart, a **data marker** visually represents each data point, which in this case is a column. A collection of related data points is a **data series**. In this chart, there are four data series (Quarter 1, Quarter 2, Quarter 3, and Quarter 4). Each is made up of column data markers of a different color, so a **legend** is included to make it easy to identify them.

FIGURE D-1: Worksheet containing expense data

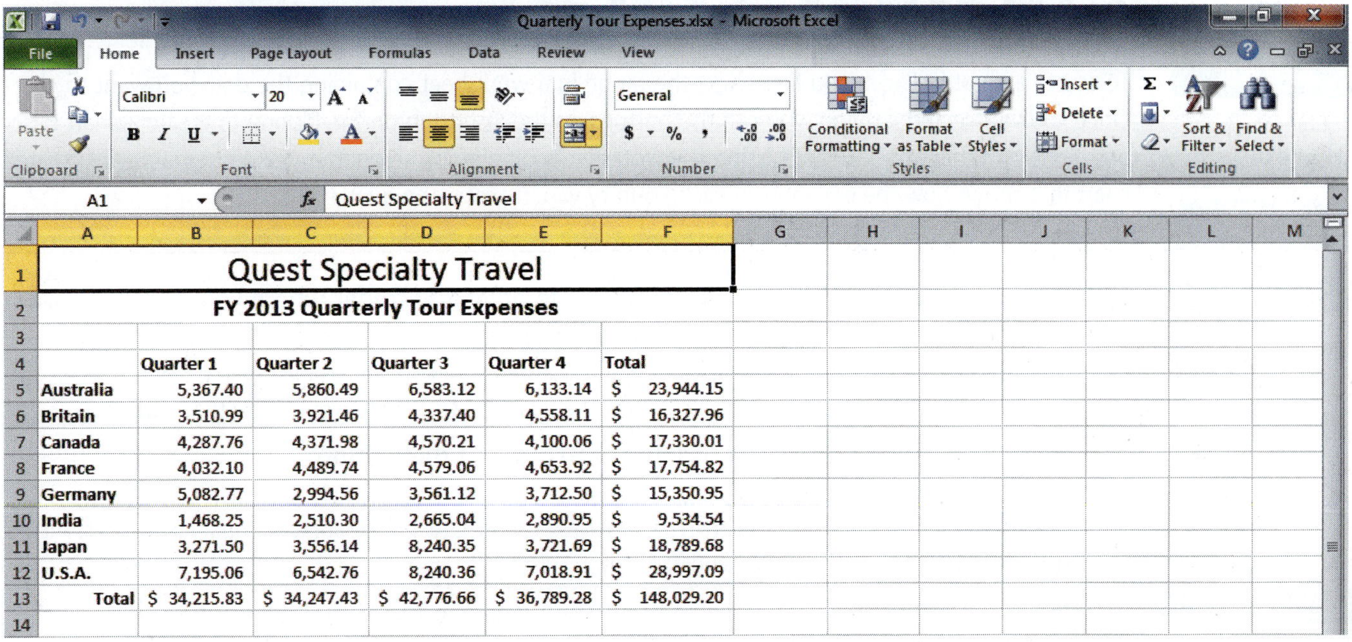

	A	B	C	D	E	F
1	Quest Specialty Travel					
2	FY 2013 Quarterly Tour Expenses					
3						
4		Quarter 1	Quarter 2	Quarter 3	Quarter 4	Total
5	Australia	5,367.40	5,860.49	6,583.12	6,133.14	$ 23,944.15
6	Britain	3,510.99	3,921.46	4,337.40	4,558.11	$ 16,327.96
7	Canada	4,287.76	4,371.98	4,570.21	4,100.06	$ 17,330.01
8	France	4,032.10	4,489.74	4,579.06	4,653.92	$ 17,754.82
9	Germany	5,082.77	2,994.56	3,561.12	3,712.50	$ 15,350.95
10	India	1,468.25	2,510.30	2,665.04	2,890.95	$ 9,534.54
11	Japan	3,271.50	3,556.14	8,240.35	3,721.69	$ 18,789.68
12	U.S.A.	7,195.06	6,542.76	8,240.36	7,018.91	$ 28,997.09
13	Total	$ 34,215.83	$ 34,247.43	$ 42,776.66	$ 36,789.28	$ 148,029.20
14						

FIGURE D-2: Chart elements

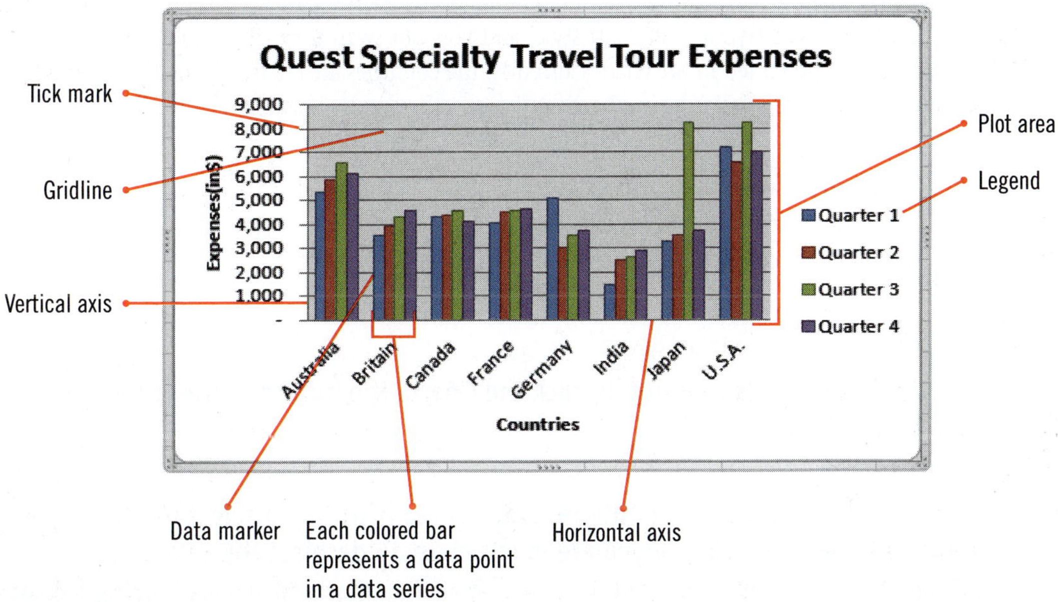

TABLE D-1: Common chart types

type	button	description
Column		Compares data using columns; the Excel default; sometimes referred to as a bar chart in other spreadsheet programs
Line		Compares trends over even time intervals; looks similar to an area chart, but does not emphasize total
Pie		Compares sizes of pieces as part of a whole; used for a single series of numbers
Bar		Compares data using horizontal bars; sometimes referred to as a horizontal bar chart in other spreadsheet programs
Area		Shows how individual volume changes over time in relation to total volume
Scatter		Compares trends over uneven time or measurement intervals; used in scientific and engineering disciplines for trend spotting and extrapolation

Creating a Chart

To create a chart in Excel, you first select the range in a worksheet containing the data you want to chart. Once you've selected a range, you can use buttons on the Insert tab on the Ribbon to create a chart based on the data in the range. Using the worksheet containing the quarterly expense data, you create a chart that shows how the expenses in each country varied across the quarters.

STEPS

QUICK TIP
When charting data for a particular time period, make sure all series are for the same time period.

1. **Start Excel, open the file EX D-1.xlsx from the drive and folder where you store your Data Files, then save it as EX D-Quarterly Tour Expenses**
   You want the chart to include the quarterly tour expenses values, as well as quarter and country labels. You don't include the Total column and row because the figures in these cells would skew the chart.
2. **Select the range A4:E12, then click the Insert tab on the Ribbon**
   The Insert tab contains groups for inserting various types of objects, including charts. The Charts group includes buttons for each major chart type, plus an Other Charts button for additional chart types, such as stock charts for charting stock market data.

QUICK TIP
To base a chart on data in nonadjacent ranges, press and hold [Ctrl] while selecting each range, then use the Insert tab to create the chart.

3. **Click the Column button in the Charts group, then click Clustered Column under 2-D Column in the Column chart gallery, as shown in Figure D-3**
   The chart is inserted in the center of the worksheet, and three contextual Chart Tools tabs appear on the Ribbon: Design, Layout, and Format. On the Design tab, which is currently in front, you can quickly change the chart type, chart layout, and chart style, and you can swap how the columns and rows of data in the worksheet are represented in the chart. Currently, the countries are charted along the horizontal x-axis, with the quarterly expense dollar amounts charted along the y-axis. This lets you easily compare the quarterly expenses for each country.
4. **Click the Switch Row/Column button in the Data group on the Chart Tools Design tab**
   The quarters are now charted along the x-axis. The expense amounts per country are charted along the y-axis, as indicated by the updated legend. See Figure D-4.
5. **Click the Undo button on the Quick Access toolbar**
   The chart returns to its original design.
6. **Click the Chart Tools Layout tab, click the Chart Title button in the Labels group, then click Above Chart**
   A title placeholder appears above the chart.

QUICK TIP
You can also triple-click to select the chart title text.

7. **Click anywhere in the Chart Title text box, press [Ctrl][A] to select the text, type Quarterly Tour Expenses, then click anywhere in the chart to deselect the title**
   Adding a title helps identify the chart. The border around the chart and the chart's **sizing handles**, the small series of dots at the corners and sides of the chart's border, indicate that the chart is selected. See Figure D-5. Your chart might be in a different location on the worksheet and may look slightly different; you will move and resize it in the next lesson. Any time a chart is selected, as it is now, a blue border surrounds the worksheet data range on which the chart is based, a purple border surrounds the cells containing the category axis labels, and a green border surrounds the cells containing the data series labels. This chart is known as an **embedded chart** because it is inserted directly in the current worksheet and doesn't exist in a separate file. Embedding a chart in the current sheet is the default selection when creating a chart, but you can also embed a chart on a different sheet in the workbook, or on a newly created chart sheet. A **chart sheet** is a sheet in a workbook that contains only a chart that is linked to the workbook data.
8. **Save your work**

FIGURE D-3: Column chart gallery

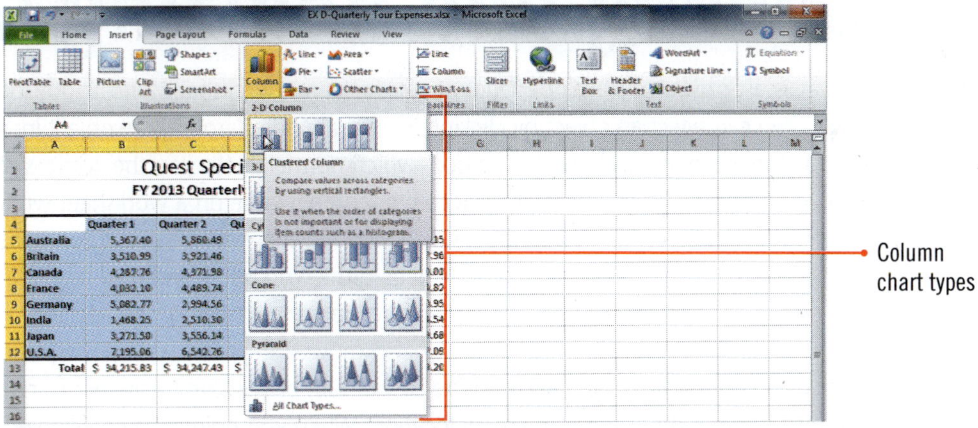

FIGURE D-4: Clustered Column chart with different presentation of data

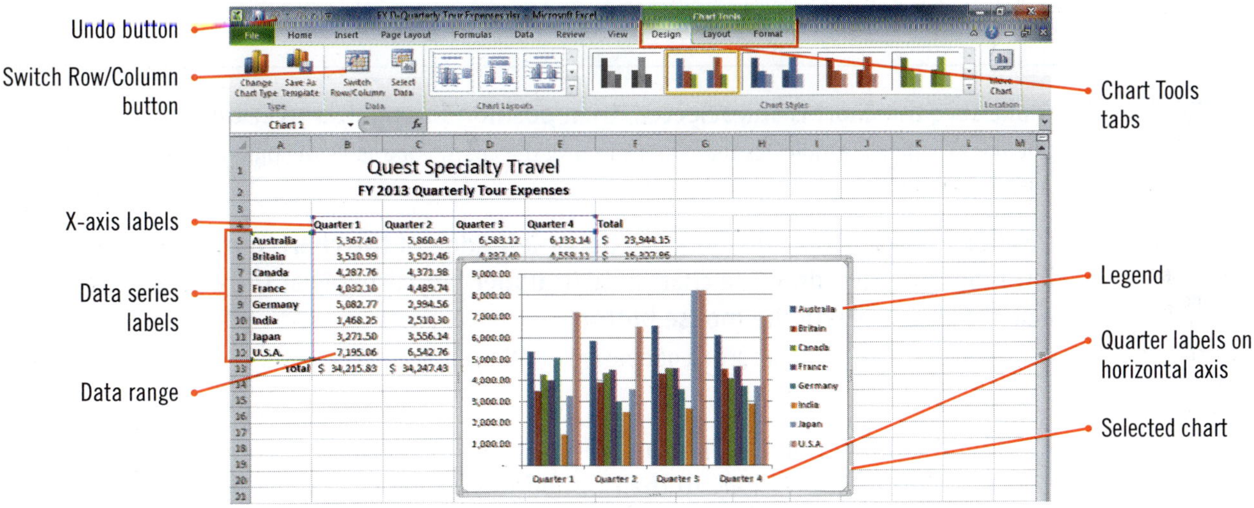

FIGURE D-5: Chart with rows and columns restored and title added

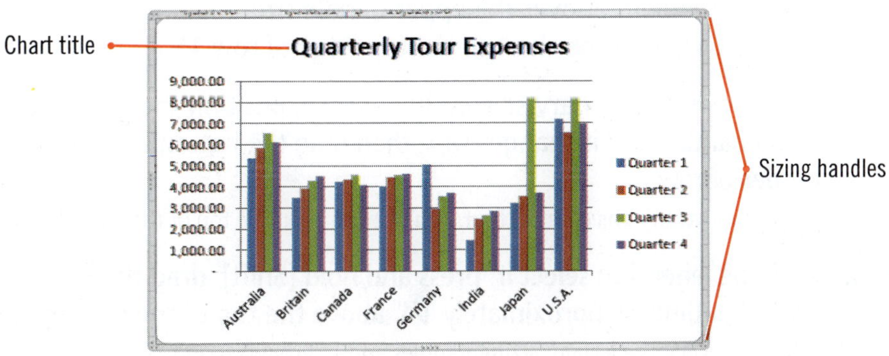

Creating sparklines

You can quickly create a miniature chart called a **sparkline** that serves as a visual indicator of data trends. To do this, select a range of data, click the Insert tab, then click the Line, Column, or Win/Loss button in the Sparklines group. In the Create Sparklines dialog box that opens, enter the cell in which you want the sparkline to appear, then click OK. Figure D-6 shows four sparklines created in four different cells. Any changes to data in the range are reflected in the sparkline. To delete a selected sparkline from a cell, click the Clear button in the Group group on the Sparkline Tools Design tab.

FIGURE D-6: Sparklines in cells

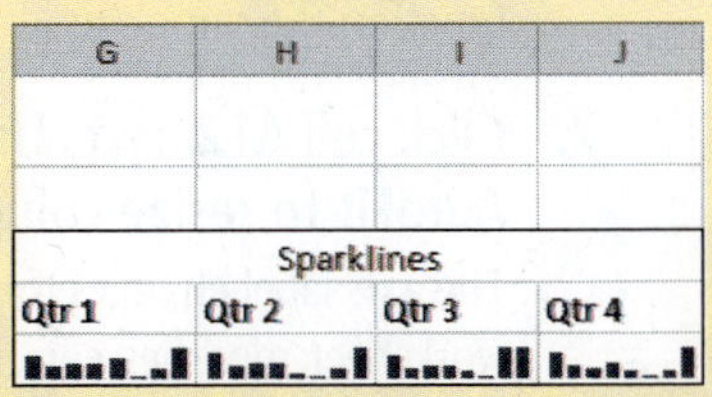

Excel 2010

UNIT
D
Excel 2010

Moving and Resizing a Chart

A chart is an **object**, or an independent element on a worksheet, and is not located in a specific cell or range. You can select an object by clicking it; sizing handles around the object indicate it is selected. (When a chart is selected in Excel, the Name box, which normally tells you the address of the active cell, tells you the chart number.) You can move a selected chart anywhere on a worksheet without affecting formulas or data in the worksheet. However, any data changed in the worksheet is automatically updated in the chart. You can even move a chart to a different sheet in the workbook, and it will still reflect the original data. You can resize a chart to improve its appearance by dragging its sizing handles. A chart contains chart objects, such as a title and legend, which you can also move and resize. You can reposition chart objects to predefined locations using commands on the Layout tab, or you can freely move any chart object by dragging it or by cutting and pasting it to a new location. When you point to a chart object, the name of the object appears as a ScreenTip. You want to resize the chart, position it below the worksheet data, and move the legend.

STEPS

QUICK TIP
To delete a selected chart, press [Delete].

TROUBLE
If you do not drag a blank area on the chart, you might inadvertently move a chart element instead of the whole chart; if this happens, undo the action and try again.

QUICK TIP
To resize a selected chart to an exact specification, click the Chart Tools Format tab, then enter the desired height and width in the Size group.

QUICK TIP
You can move a legend to the right, top, left, or bottom of a chart by clicking the Legend button in the Labels group on the Chart Tools Layout tab, then clicking a location option.

1. **Make sure the chart is still selected, then position the pointer over the chart**
   The pointer shape ✥ indicates that you can move the chart. For a table of commonly used object pointers, refer to Table D-2.

2. **Position ✥ on a blank area near the upper-left edge of the chart, press and hold the left mouse button, drag the chart until its upper-left corner is at the upper-left corner of cell A16, then release the mouse button**
   As you drag the chart, you can see an outline representing the chart's perimeter. The chart appears in the new location.

3. **Position the pointer on the right-middle sizing handle until it changes to ⇔, then drag the right border of the chart to the right edge of column G**
   The chart is widened. See Figure D-7.

4. **Position the pointer over the upper-middle sizing handle until it changes to ⇕, then drag the top border of the chart to the top edge of row 15**

5. **Scroll down if necessary so row 30 is visible, position the pointer over the lower-middle sizing handle until it changes to ⇕, then drag the bottom border of the chart to the bottom border of row 26**
   You can move any object on a chart. You want to align the top of the legend with the top of the plot area.

6. **Click the legend to select it, press and hold [Shift], drag the legend up using ✥ so the dotted outline is approximately 1/4" above the top of the plot area, then release [Shift]**
   When you click the legend, sizing handles appear around it and "Legend" appears as a ScreenTip when the pointer hovers over the object. As you drag, a dotted outline of the legend border appears. Pressing and holding the [Shift] key holds the horizontal position of the legend as you move it vertically. Although the sizing handles on objects within a chart look different from the sizing handles that surround a chart, they function the same way.

7. **Click cell A12, type United States, click the Enter button ✔ on the formula bar, use AutoFit to resize column A, then press [Ctrl][Home]**
   The axis label changes to reflect the updated cell contents, as shown in Figure D-8. Changing any data in the worksheet modifies corresponding text or values in the chart. Because the chart is no longer selected, the Chart Tools tabs no longer appear on the Ribbon.

8. **Save your work**

FIGURE D-7: Moved and resized chart

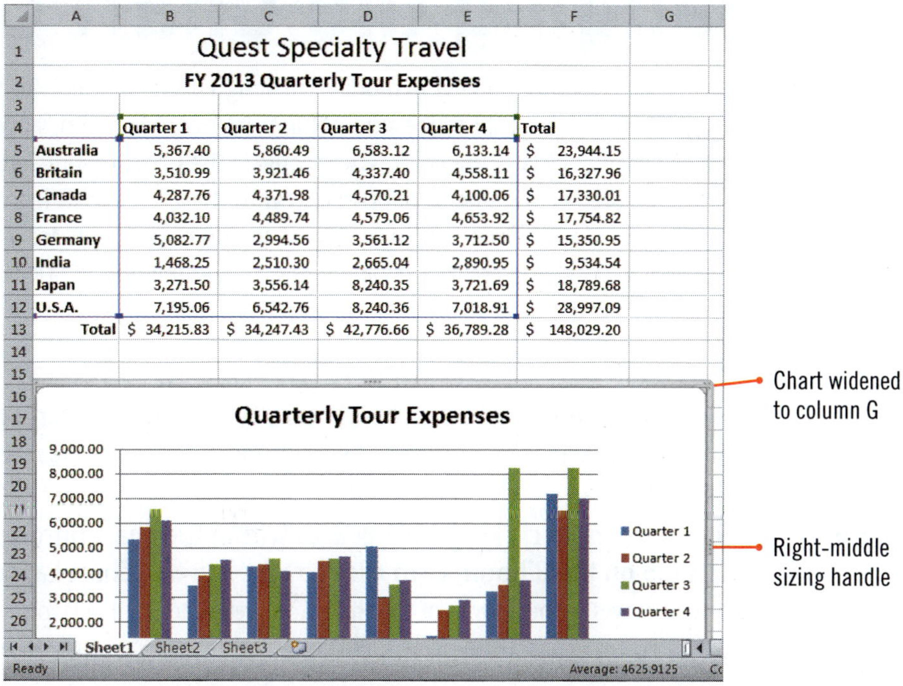

FIGURE D-8: Worksheet with modified legend and label

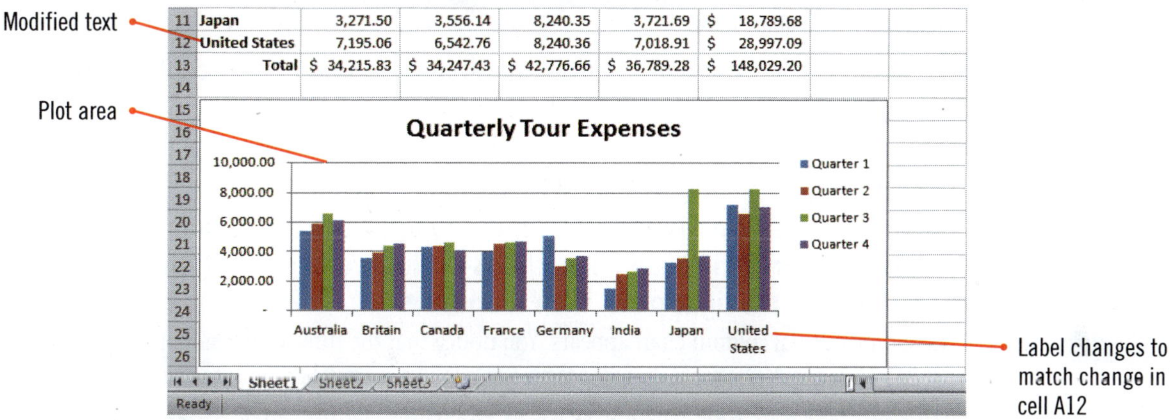

TABLE D-2: Common object pointers

name	pointer	use	name	pointer	use
Diagonal resizing	or	Change chart shape from corners	**I-beam**		Edit object text
Draw		Draw an object	**Move**		Move object
Horizontal resizing		Change object width	**Vertical resizing**		Change object height

Moving an embedded chart to a sheet

Suppose you have created an embedded chart that you decide would look better on a chart sheet or in a different worksheet. You can make this change without recreating the entire chart. To do so, first select the chart, click the Chart Tools Design tab, then click the Move Chart button in the Location group. The Move Chart dialog box opens. To move the chart to its own chart sheet, click the New sheet option button, type a name for the new sheet if desired, then click OK. If the chart is already on its own sheet, click the Object in option button, select the worksheet to where you want to move it, then click OK.

UNIT D

Excel 2010

Changing the Chart Design

Once you've created a chart, it's easy to modify the design using the Chart Tools Design tab. You can change the chart type, modify the data range and column/row configuration, apply a different chart style, and change the layout of objects in the chart. The layouts in the Chart Layouts group on the Chart Tools Design tab offer preconfigured arrangements of objects in your chart, such as its legend, title, or gridlines; choosing one of these layouts is an alternative to manually changing how objects are arranged in a chart. You look over your worksheet and realize the data for Japan and the United States in Quarter 3 is incorrect. After you correct this data, you want to see how the corrected data looks using different chart layouts and types.

STEPS

1. **Click cell D11, type 4568.92, press [Enter], type 6107.09, then press [Enter]**

   In the chart, the Quarter 3 data markers for Japan and the United States reflect the adjusted expense figures. See Figure D-9.

2. **Select the chart by clicking a blank area within the chart border, click the Chart Tools Design tab on the Ribbon, then click Layout 3 in the Chart Layouts group**

   The legend moves to the bottom of the chart. You prefer the original layout.

3. **Click the Undo button on the Quick Access toolbar, then click the Change Chart Type button in the Type group**

   The Change Chart Type dialog box opens, as shown in Figure D-10. The left pane of the dialog box lists the available categories, and the right pane shows the individual chart types. An orange border surrounds the currently selected chart type.

4. **Click Bar in the left pane of the Change Chart Type dialog box, confirm that the Clustered Bar chart type is selected in the right pane, then click OK**

   The column chart changes to a clustered bar chart. See Figure D-11. You look at the bar chart, then decide to see how the data looks in a three-dimensional column chart.

5. **Click the Change Chart Type button in the Type group, click Column in the left pane of the Change Chart Type dialog box, click 3-D Clustered Column (fourth from the left in the first row) in the right pane, then click OK**

   A three-dimensional column chart appears. You notice that the three-dimensional column format gives you a sense of volume, but it is more crowded than the two-dimensional column format.

6. **Click the Change Chart Type button in the Type group, click Clustered Column (first from the left in the first row) in the right pane of the Change Chart Type dialog box, then click OK**

7. **Click the Style 3 chart style in the Chart Styles group**

   The columns change to shades of blue. You prefer the previous chart style's color scheme.

8. **Click on the Quick Access toolbar, then save your work**

QUICK TIP

You can see more layout choices by clicking the More button in the Chart Layouts group.

QUICK TIP

If you plan to print a chart on a black-and-white printer, you may wish to apply a black-and-white chart style to your chart so you can see how the output will look as you work.

Creating a combination chart

A **combination chart** is two charts in one; a column chart with a line chart, for example. This type of chart (which cannot be used with all data) is helpful when charting dissimilar but related data. For example, you can create a combination chart based on home price and home size data, showing home prices in a column chart, and related home sizes in a line chart. In such a combination chart, a **secondary axis** (such as a vertical axis on the right side of the chart) would supply the scale for the home sizes. To create a combination chart, you can apply a chart type to a data series in an existing chart. Select the chart data series that you want plotted on a secondary axis, then click Format Selection in the Current Selection group on the Chart Tools Layout tab or Format tab to open the Format Data Series dialog box. In the dialog box, click Series Options if necessary, click the Secondary Axis option button under Plot Series On, then click Close. Click the Chart Tools Layout tab if necessary, click the Axes button in the Axes group, then click the type of secondary axis you want and where you want it to appear. To finish, click the Change Chart Type button in the Type group on the Design tab, then select a chart type for the data series.

FIGURE D-9: Worksheet with modified data

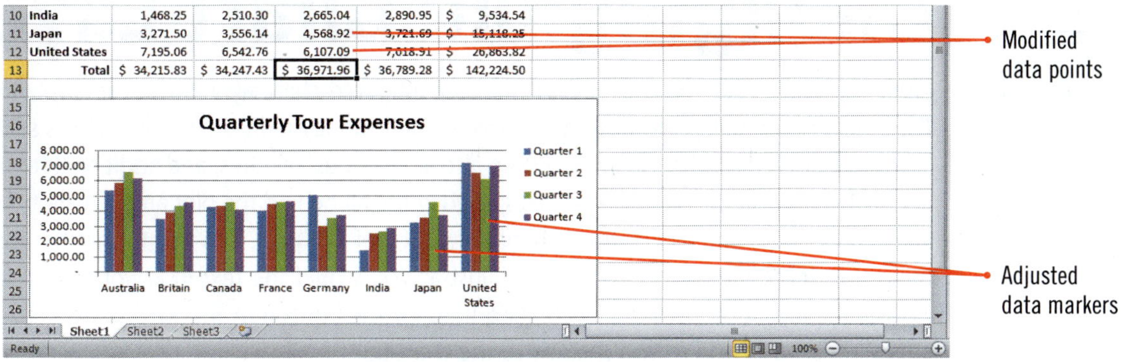

FIGURE D-10: Change Chart Type dialog box

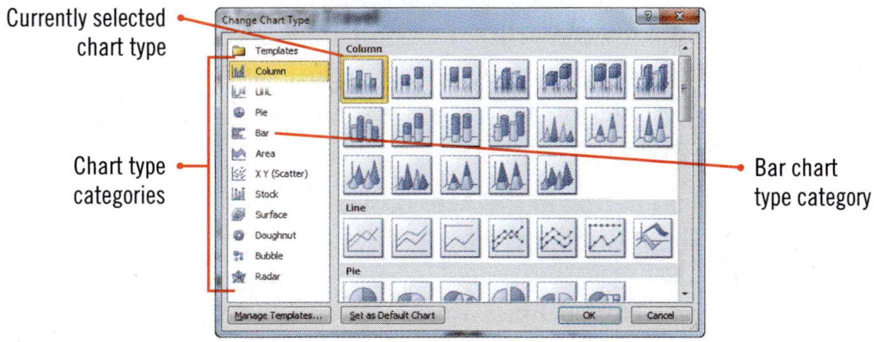

FIGURE D-11: Column chart changed to bar chart

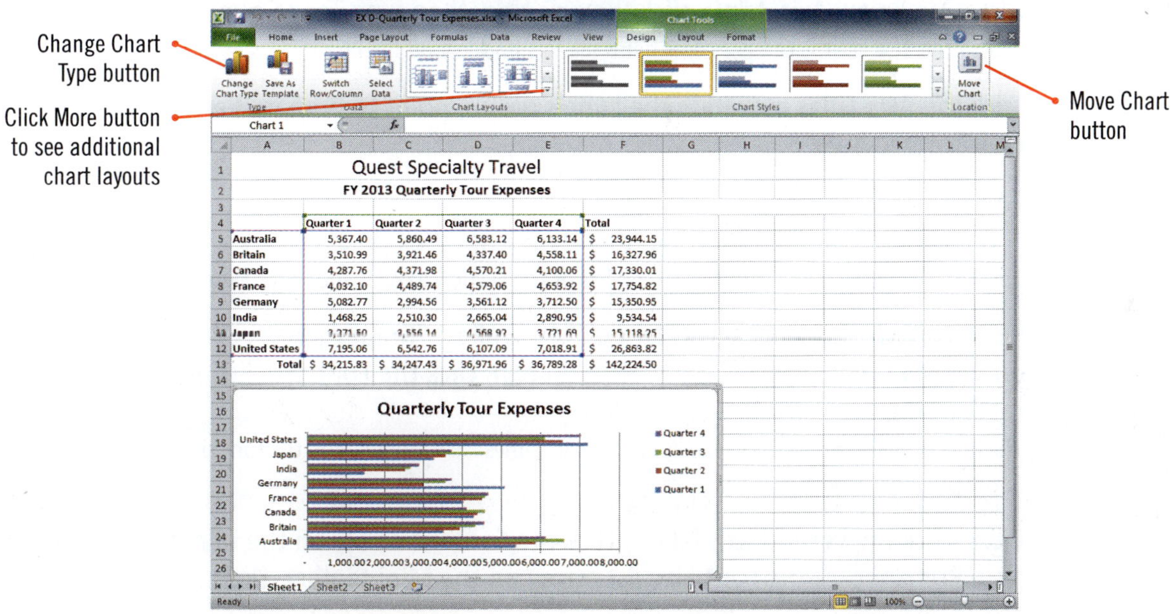

Working with a 3-D chart

Excel includes two kinds of 3-D chart types. In a true 3-D chart, a third axis, called the **z-axis**, lets you compare data points across both categories and values. The z-axis runs along the depth of the chart, so it appears to advance from the back of the chart. To create a true 3-D chart, look for chart types that begin with "3-D," such as 3-D Column. Charts that are formatted in 3-D, but are not true 3-D, contain only two axes but their graphics give the illusion of three-dimensionality. To create a chart that is only formatted in 3-D, look for chart types that end with "in 3-D." In any 3-D chart, data series can sometimes obscure other columns or bars in the same chart, but you can rotate the chart to obtain a better view. Right-click the chart, then click 3-D Rotation. The Format Chart Area dialog box opens with the 3-D Rotation category active. The 3-D Rotation options let you change the orientation and perspective of the chart area, plot area, walls, and floor. The 3-D Format category lets you apply three-dimensional effects to selected chart objects. (Not all 3-D Rotation and 3-D Format options are available on all charts.)

UNIT D Excel 2010

Changing the Chart Layout

While the Chart Tools Design tab contains preconfigured chart layouts you can apply to a chart, the Chart Tools Layout tab makes it easy to add, remove, and modify individual chart objects such as a chart title or legend. Using buttons on this tab, you can also add shapes, pictures, and additional text to a chart, add and modify labels, change the display of axes, modify the fill behind the plot area, create titles for the horizontal and vertical axes, and eliminate or change the look of gridlines. You can format the text in a chart object using the Home tab or the Mini toolbar, just as you would the text in a worksheet. You want to change the layout of the chart by creating titles for the horizontal and vertical axes. To improve the chart's appearance, you'll add a drop shadow to the chart title.

STEPS

1. **With the chart still selected, click the Chart Tools Layout tab on the Ribbon, click the Gridlines button in the Axes group, point to Primary Horizontal Gridlines, then click None**
   The gridlines that extend from the value axis tick marks across the chart's plot area are removed from the chart, as shown in Figure D-12.

2. **Click the Gridlines button in the Axes group, point to Primary Horizontal Gridlines, then click Major & Minor Gridlines**
   Both major and minor gridlines now appear in the chart. **Major gridlines** represent the values at the value axis tick marks, and **minor gridlines** represent the values between the tick marks.

3. **Click the Axis Titles button in the Labels group, point to Primary Horizontal Axis Title, click Title Below Axis, triple-click the axis title, then type Tour Countries**
   Descriptive text on the category axis helps readers understand the chart.

4. **Click the Axis Titles button in the Labels group, point to Primary Vertical Axis Title, then click Rotated Title**
   A placeholder for the vertical axis title is added to the left of the vertical axis.

5. **Triple-click the vertical axis title, then type Expenses (in $)**
   The text "Expenses (in $)" appears to the left of the vertical axis, as shown in Figure D-13.

6. **Right-click the horizontal axis labels ("Australia", "Britain", etc.), click the Font list arrow on the Mini toolbar, click Times New Roman, click the Font Size list arrow on the Mini toolbar, then click 8**
   The font of the horizontal axis labels changes to Times New Roman, and the font size decreases, making more of the plot area visible.

7. **Right-click the vertical axis labels, click the Font list arrow on the Mini toolbar, click Times New Roman, click the Font Size list arrow on the Mini toolbar, then click 8**

8. **Right-click the chart title ("Quarterly Tour Expenses"), click Format Chart Title on the shortcut menu, click Border Color in the left pane of the Format Chart Title dialog box, then click the Solid line option button in the right pane**
   A solid border will appear around the chart title with the default blue color.

9. **Click Shadow in the left pane of the Format Chart Title dialog box, click the Presets list arrow, click Offset Diagonal Bottom Right in the Outer group (first row, first from the left), click Close, then save your work**
   A blue border with a drop shadow surrounds the title. Compare your work to Figure D-14.

QUICK TIP
You can move any title to a new position by clicking one of its edges, then dragging it.

QUICK TIP
You can also edit text in a chart or axis title by positioning the pointer over the selected title until it changes to I, clicking the title, then editing the text.

QUICK TIP
You can also apply a border to a selected chart object by clicking the Shape Outline list arrow on the Chart Tools Format tab, and then selecting from the available options.

QUICK TIP
You can also apply a shadow to a selected chart object by clicking the Shape Effects button on the Chart Tools Layout tab, pointing to Shadow, and then clicking a shadow effect.

FIGURE D-12: Gridlines removed from chart

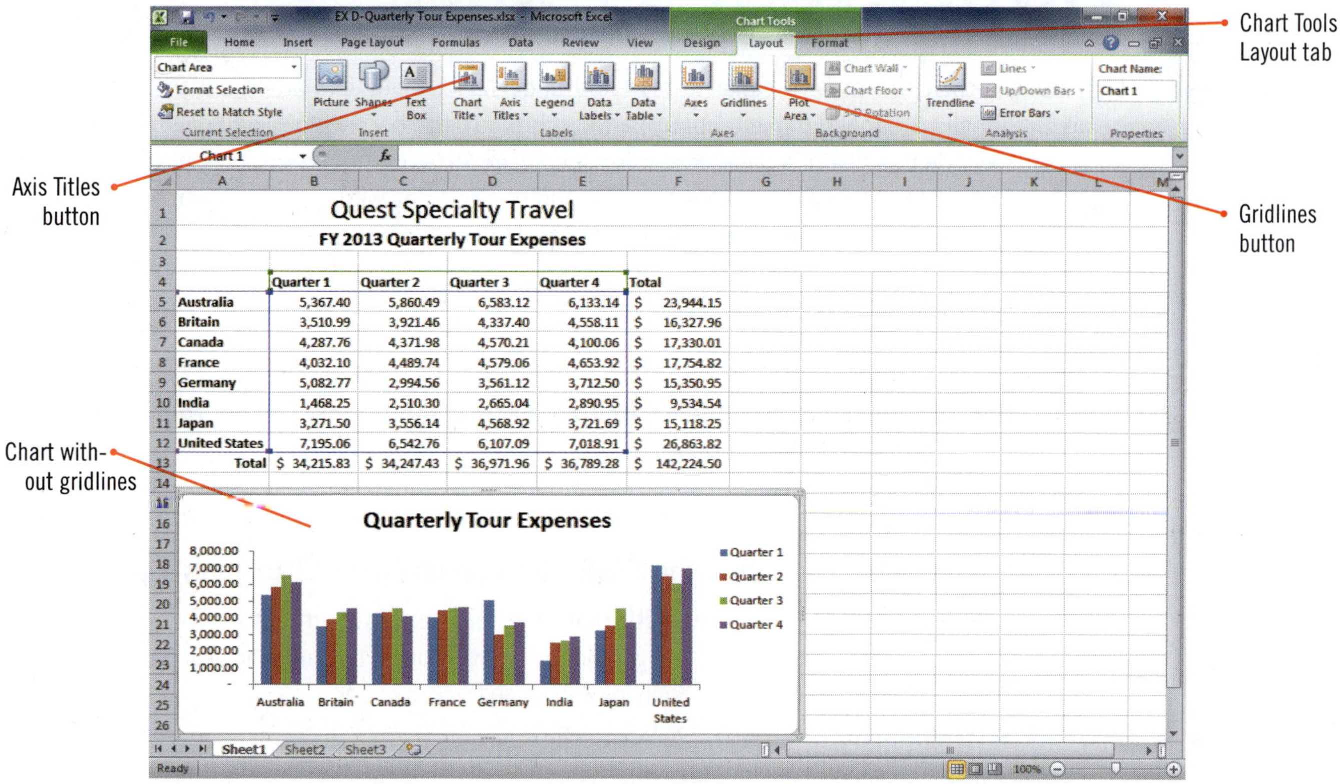

FIGURE D-13: Axis titles added to chart

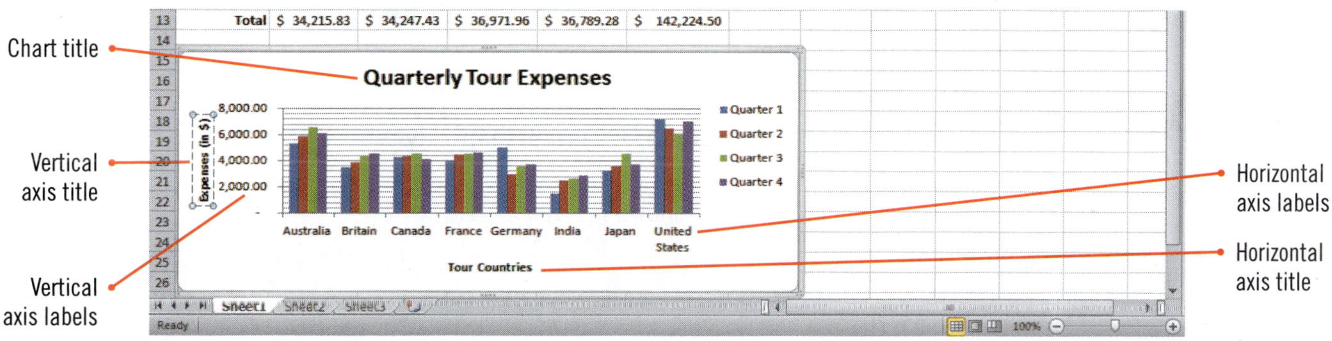

FIGURE D-14: Enhanced chart

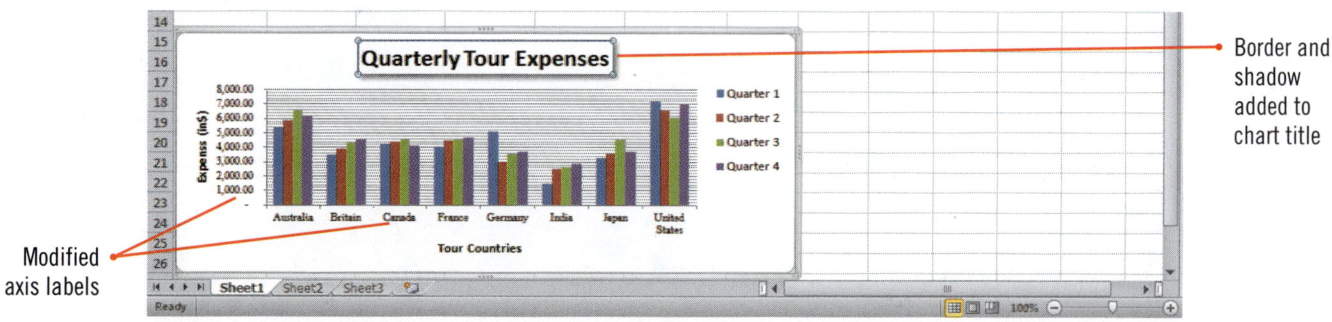

Adding data labels to a chart

There are times when your audience might benefit by seeing data labels on a chart. These labels appear next to the data markers in the chart and can indicate the series name, category name, and/or the value of one or more data points. Once your chart is selected, you can add this information to your chart by clicking the Data Labels button in the Labels group on the Chart Tools Layout tab, and then clicking a display option for the data labels. Once you have added the data labels, you can format them or delete individual data labels. To delete a data label, select it and then press [Delete].

Excel 2010

UNIT D Excel 2010

Formatting a Chart

Formatting a chart can make it easier to read and understand. Many formatting enhancements can be made using the Chart Tools Format tab. You can change the fill color for a specific data series, or you can apply a shape style to a title or a data series using the Shape Styles group. Shape styles make it possible to apply multiple formats, such as an outline, fill color, and text color, all with a single click. You can also apply different fill colors, outlines, and effects to chart objects using arrows and buttons in the Shape Styles group. You want to use a different color for one data series in the chart and apply a shape style to another to enhance the look of the chart.

STEPS

1. **With the chart selected, click the Chart Tools Format tab on the Ribbon, then click any column in the Quarter 4 data series**
   The Chart Tools Format tab opens, and handles appear on each column in the Quarter 4 data series, indicating that the entire series is selected.
2. **Click the Shape Fill list arrow in the Shape Styles group on the Chart Tools Format tab**
3. **Click Orange, Accent 6 (first row, 10th from the left) as shown in Figure D-15**
   All the columns for the series become orange, and the legend changes to match the new color. You can also change the color of selected objects by applying a shape style.
4. **Click any column in the Quarter 3 data series**
   Handles appear on each column in the Quarter 3 data series.
5. **Click the More button on the Shape Styles gallery, then hover the pointer over the Moderate Effect – Olive Green, Accent 3 shape style (fifth row, fourth from the left) in the gallery, as shown in Figure D-16**
   Live Preview shows the data series in the chart with the shape style applied.
6. **Click the Subtle Effect – Olive Green, Accent 3 shape style (fourth row, fourth from the left) in the gallery**
   The style for the data series changes, as shown in Figure D-17.
7. **Save your work**

QUICK TIP
To apply a WordArt style to a text object (such as the chart title), select the object, then click a style in the WordArt Styles group on the Chart Tools Format tab.

Changing alignment and angle in axis labels and titles

The buttons on the Chart Tools Layout tab provide a few options for positioning axis labels and titles, but you can customize their position and rotation to exact specifications using the Format Axis dialog box or Format Axis Title dialog box. With a chart selected, right-click the axis text you want to modify, then click Format Axis or Format Axis Title on the shortcut menu. In the dialog box that opens, click Alignment, then select the appropriate Text layout option. You can also create a custom angle by clicking the Custom angle up and down arrows. When you have made the desired changes, click Close.

FIGURE D-15: New shape fill applied to data series

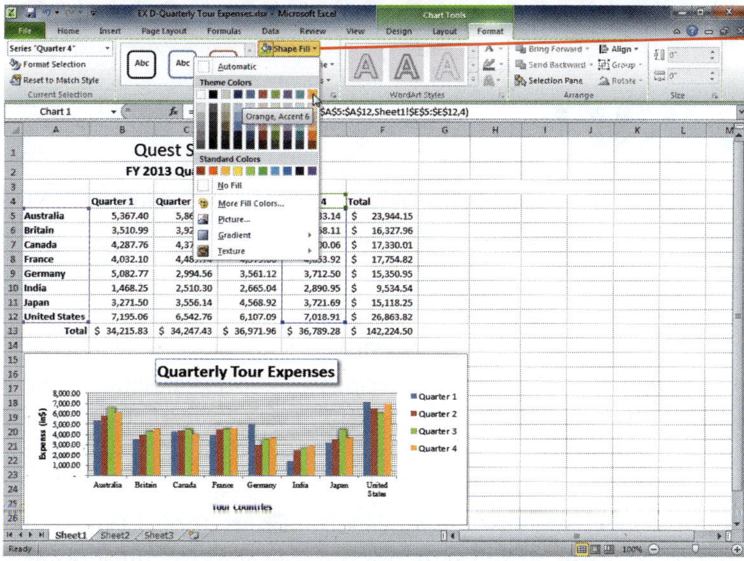

FIGURE D-16: Live Preview of new style applied to data series

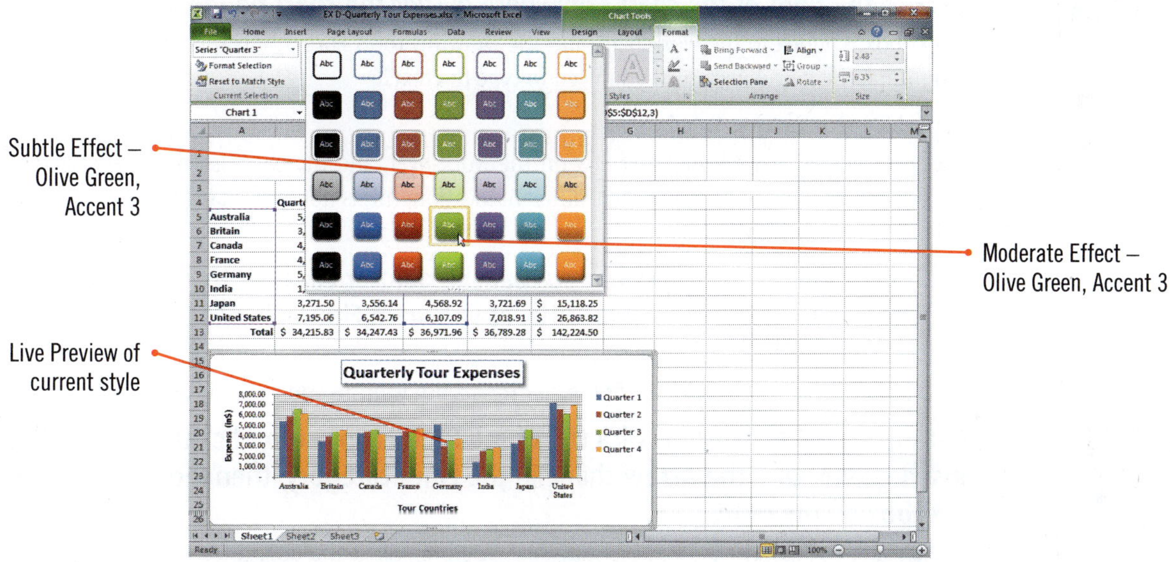

FIGURE D-17: Style of data series changed

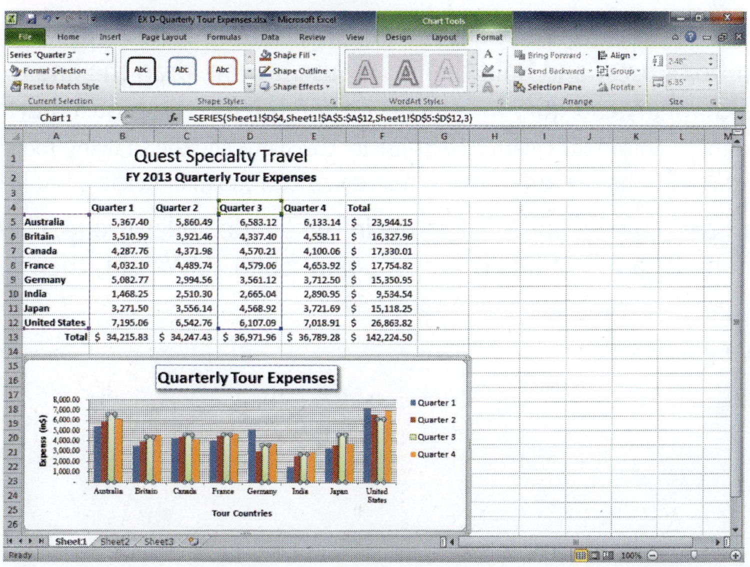

UNIT D

Excel 2010

Annotating and Drawing on a Chart

You can use text annotations and graphics to point out critical information in a chart. **Text annotations** are labels that further describe your data. You can also draw lines and arrows that point to the exact locations you want to emphasize. Shapes such as arrows and boxes can be added from the Illustrations group on the Insert tab or from the Insert group on the Chart Tools Layout group on the Ribbon. These groups are also used to insert pictures and clip art into worksheets and charts. You want to call attention to the Germany tour expense decrease, so you decide to add a text annotation and an arrow to this information in the chart.

STEPS

1. **Make sure the chart is selected, click the Chart Tools Layout tab, click the Text Box button in the Insert group, then move the pointer over the worksheet**
   The pointer changes to ↓, indicating that you will insert a text box where you next click.
2. **Click to the right of the chart (anywhere *outside* the chart boundary)**
   A text box is added to the worksheet, and the Drawing Tools Format tab appears on the Ribbon so that you can format the new object. First you need to type the text.
3. **Type Great improvement**
   The text appears in a selected text box on the worksheet, and the chart is no longer selected, as shown in Figure D-18. Your text box may be in a different location; this is not important, because you'll move the annotation in the next step.
4. **Point to an edge of the text box so that the pointer changes to ✥, drag the text box into the chart to the left of the chart title, as shown in Figure D-19, then release the mouse button**
   The text box is a text annotation for the chart. You also want to add a simple arrow shape in the chart.
5. **Click the chart to select it, click the Chart Tools Layout tab, click the Shapes button in the Insert group, click the Arrow shape in the Lines category, then move the pointer over the text box on the chart**
   The pointer changes to +, and the status bar displays "Click and drag to insert an AutoShape." When + is over the text box, red handles appear around the text in the text box. A red handle can act as an anchor for the arrow.
6. **Position + on the red handle to the right of the "t" in the word "improvement" (in the text box), press and hold the left mouse button, drag the line to the Quarter 2 column for the Germany category in the chart, then release the mouse button**
   An arrow points to the Quarter 2 expense for Germany, and the Drawing Tools Format tab displays options for working with the new arrow object. You can resize, format, or delete it just like any other object in a chart.
7. **Click the Shape Outline list arrow in the Shape Styles group, click the Automatic color, click the Shape Outline list arrow again, point to Weight, then click 1½ pt**
   Compare your finished chart to Figure D-20.
8. **Save your work**

QUICK TIP
You can also insert a text box by clicking the Text Box button in the Text group in the Insert tab, then clicking in the worksheet.

QUICK TIP
To annotate a chart using a callout, click the Shapes button in either the Illustrations group on the Insert tab or the Insert group on the Chart Tools Layout tab, then click a shape in the Callouts category of the Shapes gallery.

FIGURE D-18: Text box added

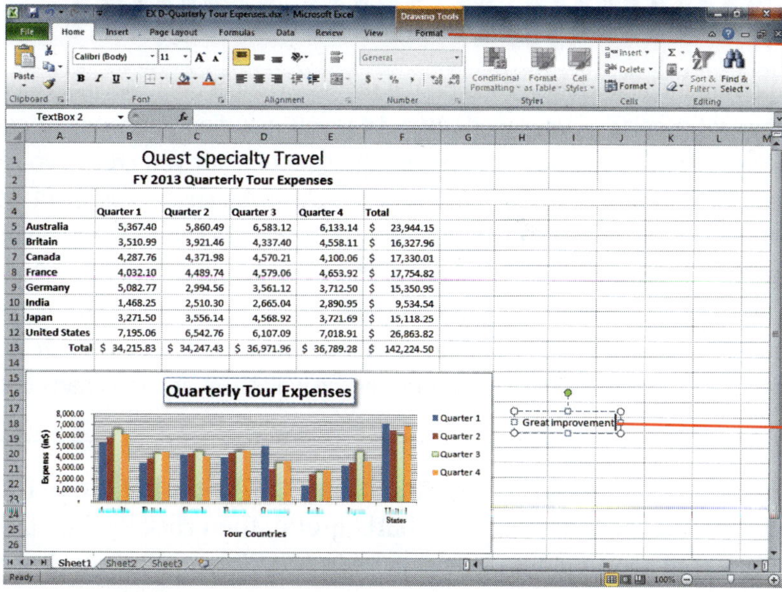

FIGURE D-19: Text annotation on the chart

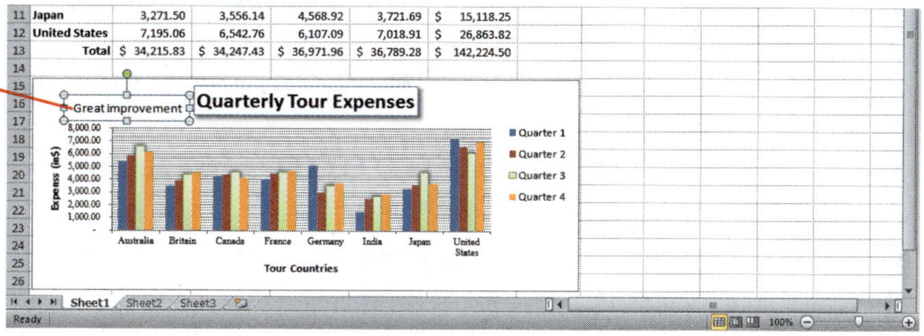

FIGURE D-20: Arrow shape added to chart

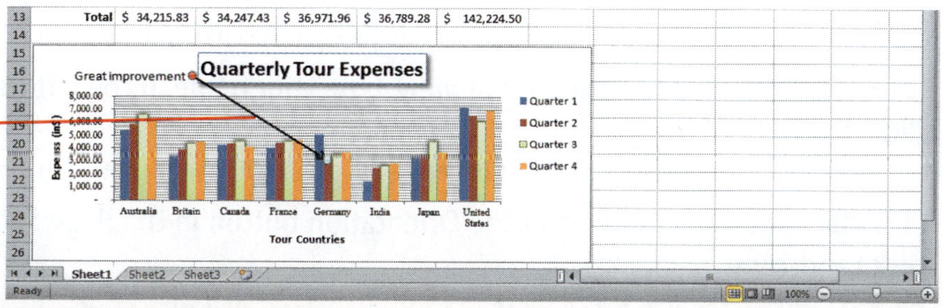

Adding SmartArt graphics

In addition to charts, annotations, and drawn objects, you can create a variety of diagrams using SmartArt graphics. **SmartArt graphics** are available in List, Process, Cycle, Hierarchy, Relationship, Matrix, and Pyramid categories. To insert SmartArt, click the SmartArt button in the Illustrations group on the Insert tab to open the Choose a SmartArt Graphic dialog box. Click a SmartArt category in the left pane, then click the layout for the graphic in the center pane. The right pane shows a sample of the selected SmartArt layout, as shown in Figure D-21. The SmartArt graphic appears in the worksheet as an embedded object with sizing handles. Click the Text Pane button on the SmartArt Tools Design tab to open a text pane next to the graphic; you can enter text into the graphic using the text pane or by typing directly in the shapes in the diagram.

FIGURE D-21: Choose a SmartArt Graphic dialog box

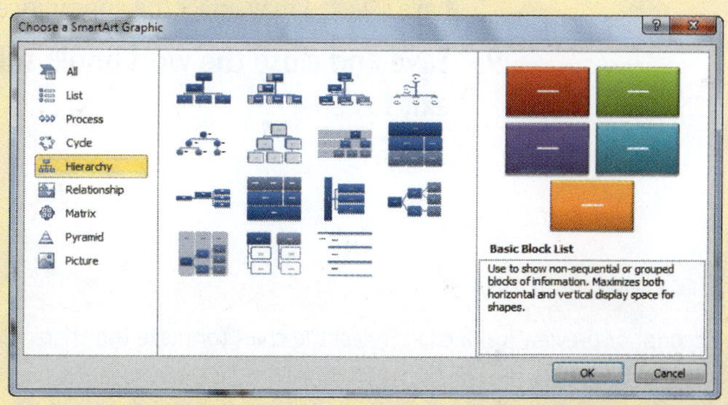

Excel 2010

UNIT
D
Excel 2010

Creating a Pie Chart

You can create multiple charts based on the same worksheet data. While a column chart may illustrate certain important aspects of your worksheet data, you may find you want to create an additional chart to emphasize a different point. Depending on the type of chart you create, you have additional options for calling attention to trends and patterns. For example, if you create a pie chart, you can emphasize one data point by **exploding**, or pulling that slice away from, the pie chart. When you're ready to print a chart, you can preview it just as you do a worksheet to check the output before committing it to paper. You can print a chart by itself or as part of the worksheet. At an upcoming meeting, Grace plans to discuss the total tour expenses and which countries need improvement. You want to create a pie chart she can use to illustrate total expenses. Finally, you want to fit the worksheet and the charts onto one worksheet page.

STEPS

QUICK TIP
The Exploded pie in 3-D button creates a pie chart in which all slices are exploded.

TROUBLE
If the Format Data Series command appears on the shortcut menu instead of Format Data Point, double-click the slice you want to explode to make sure it is selected by itself, then right-click it again.

1. **Select the range A5:A12, press and hold [Ctrl], select the range F5:F12, click the Insert tab, click the Pie button in the Charts group, then click Pie in 3-D in the Pie chart gallery**
   The new chart appears in the center of the worksheet. You can move the chart and quickly format it using a chart layout.
2. **Drag the chart so its upper-left corner is at the upper-left corner of cell G1, then click Layout 2 in the Chart Layouts group**
   The chart is repositioned on the page, and its layout changes so that a chart title is added and the legend appears just below the chart title.
3. **Select the chart title text, then type Total Expenses, by Country**
4. **Click the slice for the India data point, click it again so it is the only slice selected, right-click it, then click Format Data Point**
   The Format Data Point dialog box opens, as shown in Figure D-22.You can use the Point Explosion slider to control the distance a pie slice moves away from the pie, or you can type a value in the Point Explosion text box.
5. **Double-click 0 in the Point Explosion text box, type 40, then click Close**
   Compare your chart to Figure D-23. You decide to preview the chart and data before you print.
6. **Click cell A1, switch to Page Layout view, type your name in the left header text box, then click cell A1**
   You decide the chart and data would fit better on the page if they were printed in landscape orientation.
7. **Click the Page Layout tab, click the Orientation button in the Page Setup group, then click Landscape**
8. **Click the File tab, click Print on the navigation bar, click the No Scaling setting in the Settings section on the Print tab, then click Fit Sheet on One Page**
   The data and chart are positioned horizontally on a single page, as shown in Figure D-24. The printer you have selected may affect the appearance of your preview screen.
9. **Save and close the workbook, submit your work to your instructor as directed, then exit Excel**

Previewing a chart

To print or preview just a chart, select the chart (or make the chart sheet active), click the File tab, then click Print on the navigation bar. To reposition a chart by changing the page's margins, click the Show Margins button in the lower-right corner of the Print tab to display the margins in the preview. You can drag the margin lines to the exact settings you want; as the margins change, the size and placement of the chart on the page changes too.

FIGURE D-22: Format Data Point dialog box

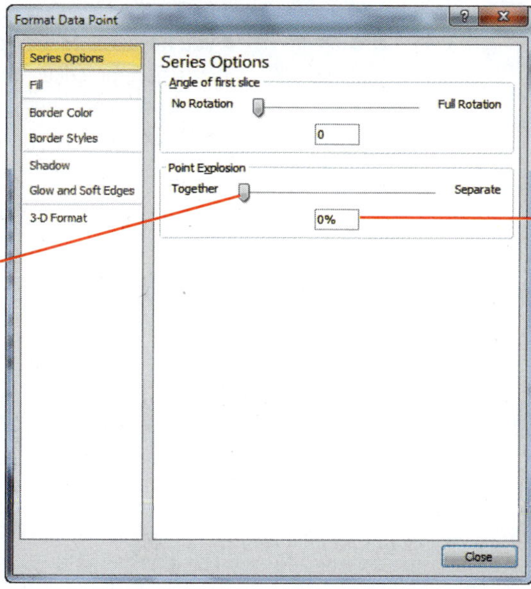

FIGURE D-23: Exploded pie slice

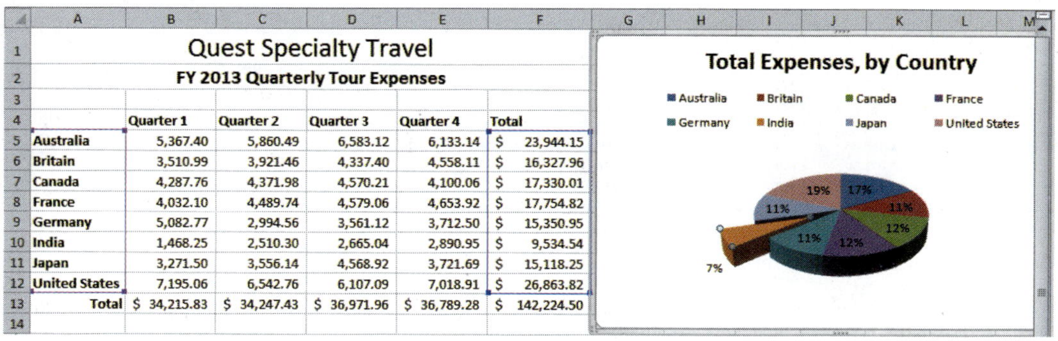

	Quarter 1	Quarter 2	Quarter 3	Quarter 4	Total
Australia	5,367.40	5,860.49	6,583.12	6,133.14	$ 23,944.15
Britain	3,510.99	3,921.46	4,337.40	4,558.11	$ 16,327.96
Canada	4,287.76	4,371.98	4,570.21	4,100.06	$ 17,330.01
France	4,032.10	4,489.74	4,579.06	4,653.92	$ 17,754.82
Germany	5,082.77	2,994.56	3,561.12	3,712.50	$ 15,350.95
India	1,468.25	2,510.30	2,665.04	2,890.95	$ 9,534.54
Japan	3,271.50	3,556.14	4,568.92	3,721.69	$ 15,118.25
United States	7,195.06	6,542.76	6,107.09	7,018.91	$ 26,863.82
Total	$ 34,215.83	$ 34,247.43	$ 36,971.96	$ 36,789.28	$ 142,224.50

FIGURE D-24: Preview of worksheet with charts in Backstage view

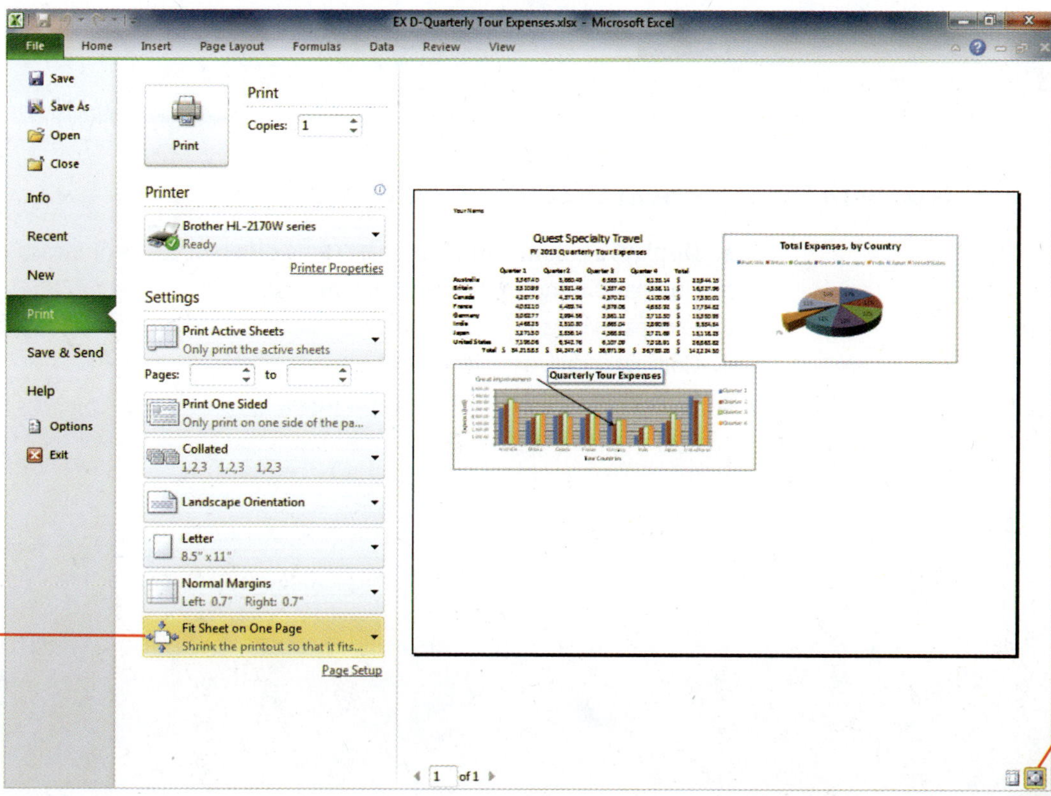

Practice

For current SAM information, including versions and content details, visit SAM Central (http://www.cengage.com/samcentral). If you have a SAM user profile, you may have access to hands-on instruction, practice, and assessment of the skills covered in this unit. Since various versions of SAM are supported throughout the life of this text, check with your instructor for the correct instructions and URL/Web site for accessing assignments.

Concepts Review

Label each element of the Excel chart shown in Figure D-25.

FIGURE D-25

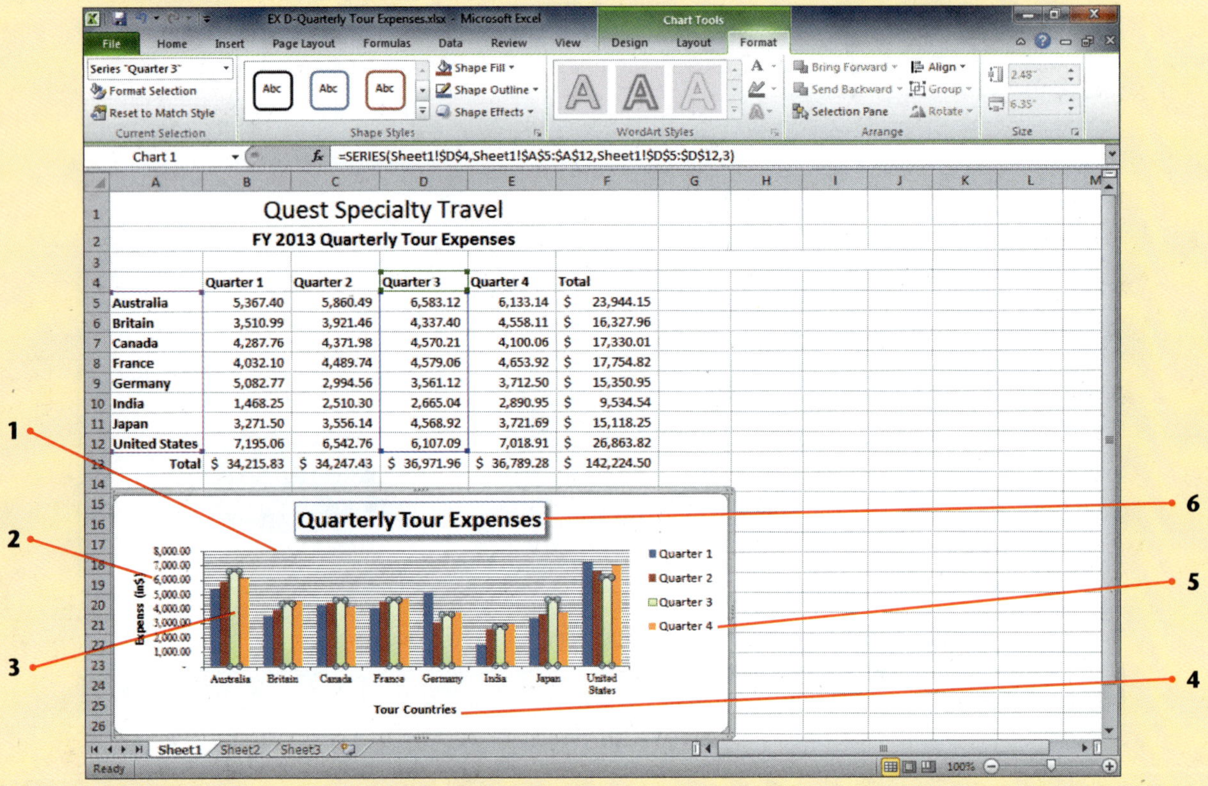

Match each chart type with the statement that best describes it.

7. **Column**
8. **Line**
9. **Combination**
10. **Pie**
11. **Area**

a. Displays a column and line chart using different scales of measurement
b. Compares trends over even time intervals
c. Compares data using columns
d. Compares data as parts of a whole
e. Shows how volume changes over time

Select the best answer from the list of choices.

12. Which pointer do you use to resize a chart?

- **a.** +
- **b.** I
- **c.** ↕
- **d.** ✥

13. The object in a chart that identifies the colors used for each data series is a(n):

- **a.** Data marker.
- **b.** Data point.
- **c.** Organizer.
- **d.** Legend.

14. Which tab appears only when a chart is selected?

- **a.** Insert
- **b.** Chart Tools Format
- **c.** Review
- **d.** Page Layout

15. How do you move an embedded chart to a chart sheet?

- **a.** Click a button on the Chart Tools Design tab.
- **b.** Drag the chart to the sheet tab.
- **c.** Delete the chart, switch to a different sheet, then create a new chart.
- **d.** Use the Copy and Paste buttons on the Ribbon.

16. Which tab on the Ribbon do you use to create a chart?

- **a.** Design
- **b.** Insert
- **c.** Page Layout
- **d.** Format

17. A collection of related data points in a chart is called a:

- **a.** Data series.
- **b.** Data tick.
- **c.** Cell address.
- **d.** Value title.

Skills Review

If you have a SAM 2010 user profile, an autogradable SAM version of this assignment may be available at http://www.cengage.com/sam2010. Check with your instructor to confirm that this assignment is available in SAM. To use the SAM version of this assignment, log into the SAM 2010 Web site and download the instruction and start files.

1. Plan a chart.

- **a.** Start Excel, open the Data File EX D-2.xlsx from the drive and folder where you store your Data Files, then save it as **EX D-Departmental Software Usage**.
- **b.** Describe the type of chart you would use to plot this data.
- **c.** What chart type would you use to compare the number of Excel users in each department?

2. Create a chart.

- **a.** In the worksheet, select the range containing all the data and headings.
- **b.** Click the Insert tab.
- **c.** Create a Clustered Column chart, then add the chart title **Software Usage, by Department** above the chart.
- **d.** Save your work.

Skills Review (continued)

3. **Move and resize a chart.**
   a. Make sure the chart is still selected.
   b. Move the chart beneath the worksheet data.
   c. Widen the chart so it extends to the right edge of column H.
   d. Use the Chart Tools Layout tab to move the legend below the charted data. (*Hint*: Click the Legend button, then click Show Legend at Bottom.)
   e. Resize the chart so its bottom edge is at the top of row 25.
   f. Save your work.
4. **Change the chart design.**
   a. Change the value in cell B3 to **15**. Observe the change in the chart.
   b. Select the chart.
   c. Use the Chart Layouts group on the Chart Tools Design tab to apply the Layout 7 layout to the chart, then undo the change.
   d. Use the Change Chart Type button on the Chart Tools Design tab to change the chart to a Clustered Bar chart.
   e. Change the chart to a 3-D Clustered Column chart, then change it back to a Clustered Column chart.
   f. Save your work.
5. **Change the chart layout.**
   a. Use the Chart Tools Layout tab to turn off the major horizontal gridlines in the chart.
   b. Change the font used in the horizontal and vertical axes labels to Times New Roman.
   c. Turn on the major gridlines for both the horizontal and vertical axes.
   d. Change the chart title's font to Times New Roman if necessary, with a font size of 20.
   e. Insert **Departments** as the horizontal axis title.
   f. Insert **Number of Users** as the vertical axis title.
   g. Change the font size of the horizontal and vertical axis titles to 10 and the font to Times New Roman, if necessary.
   h. Change "Personnel" in the worksheet column heading to **Human Resources**, then AutoFit column E.
   i. Change the font size of the legend to 14.
   j. Add a solid line border in the default color and an Offset Diagonal Bottom Right shadow to the chart title.
   k. Save your work.
6. **Format a chart.**
   a. Make sure the chart is selected, then select the Chart Tools Format tab, if necessary.
   b. Change the shape fill of the Excel data series to Dark Blue, Text 2.
   c. Change the shape style of the Excel data series to Subtle Effect Orange, Accent 6.
   d. Save your work.
7. **Annotate and draw on a chart.**
   a. Make sure the chart is selected, then create the text annotation **Needs more users**.
   b. Position the text annotation so the word "Needs" is just below the word "Software" in the chart title.
   c. Select the chart, then use the Chart Tools Layout tab to create a 1½ pt weight arrow that points from the bottom center of the text box to the Excel users in the Design department.
   d. Deselect the chart.
   e. Save your work.

Skills Review (continued)

8. Create a pie chart.

a. Select the range A1:F2, then create a Pie in 3-D chart.

b. Drag the 3-D pie chart beneath the existing chart.

c. Change the chart title to **Excel Users**.

d. Apply the Style 42 chart style to the chart.

e. Explode the Human Resources slice from the pie chart at **25%**.

f. In Page Layout view, enter your name in the left section of the worksheet header.

g. Preview the worksheet and charts in Backstage view, make sure all the contents fit on one page, then submit your work to your instructor as directed. When printed, the worksheet should look like Figure D-26.

h. Save your work, close the workbook, then exit Excel.

FIGURE D-26

Your Name

	Accounting	Marketing	Design	Human Resources	Purchasing
Excel	35	14	3	8	35
Word	15	35	17	15	10
PowerPoint	17	5	12	5	3
Access	20	25	8	10	15
Publisher	2	15	22	15	25

The position of your annotation may vary

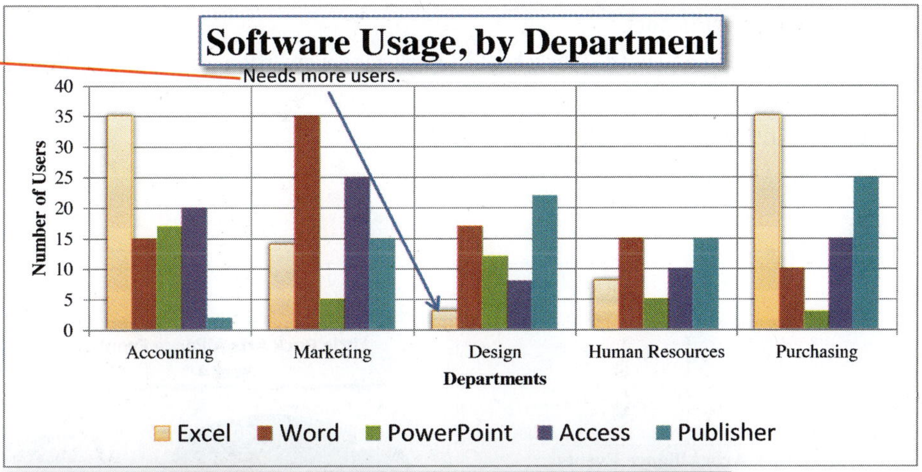

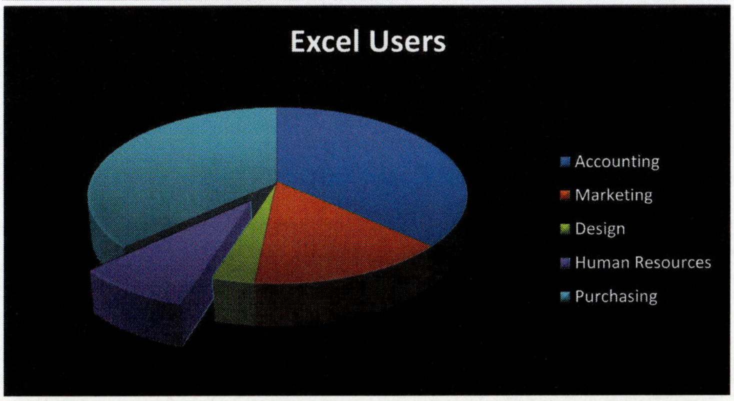

Independent Challenge 1

You are the operations manager for the Little Rock Arts Alliance in Arkansas. Each year the group applies to various state and federal agencies for matching funds. For this year's funding proposal, you need to create charts to document the number of productions in previous years.

a. Start Excel, open the file EX D-3.xlsx from the drive and folder where you store your Data Files, then save it as **EX D-Little Rock Arts Alliance**.

b. Take some time to plan your charts. Which type of chart or charts might best illustrate the information you need to display? What kind of chart enhancements do you want to use? Will a 3-D effect make your chart easier to understand?

c. Create a Clustered Column chart for the data.

d. Change at least one of the colors used in a data series.

e. Make the appropriate modifications to the chart to make it visually attractive and easier to read and understand. Include a legend to the right of the chart, and add chart titles and horizontal and vertical axis titles using the text shown in Table D-3.

TABLE D-3

title	text
Chart title	**Little Rock Arts Alliance Events**
Vertical axis title	**Number of Events**
Horizontal axis title	**Types of Events**

f. Create at least two additional charts for the same data to show how different chart types display the same data. Reposition each new chart so that all charts are visible in the worksheet. One of the additional charts should be a pie chart; the other is up to you.

g. Modify each new chart as necessary to improve its appearance and effectiveness. A sample worksheet containing three charts based on the worksheet data is shown in Figure D-27.

h. Enter your name in the worksheet header.

i. Save your work. Before printing, preview the worksheet in Backstage view, then adjust any settings as necessary so that all the worksheet data and charts print on a single page.

j. Submit your work to your instructor as directed.

k. Close the workbook, then exit Excel.

FIGURE D-27

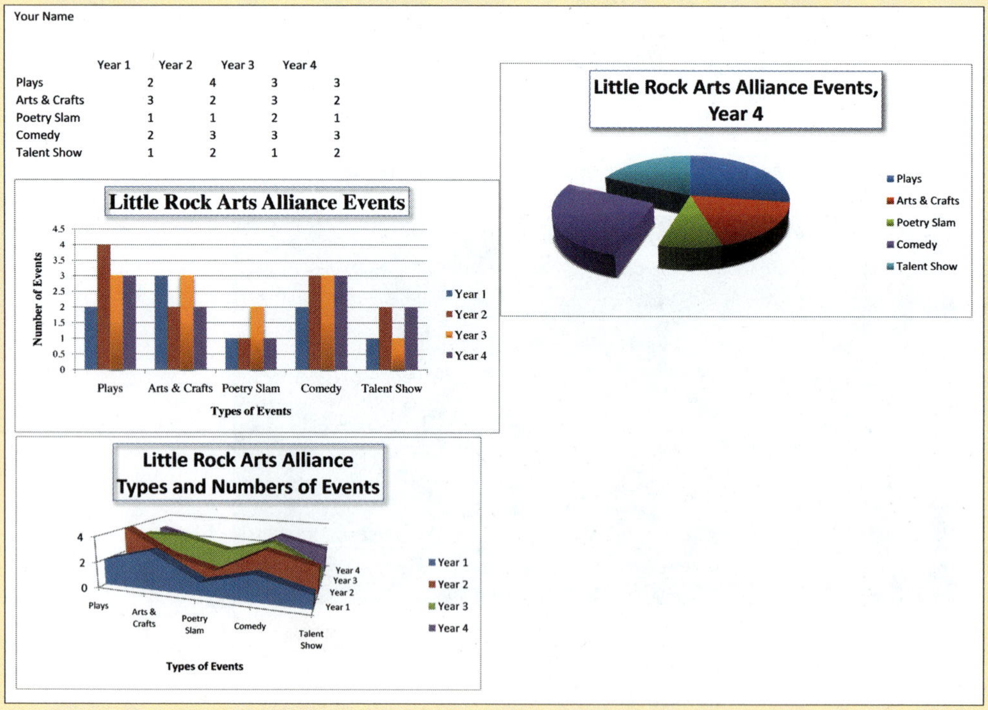

Independent Challenge 2

You work at Bark Bark Bark, a locally owned day spa for dogs. One of your responsibilities at the day spa is to manage the company's sales and expenses using Excel. Another is to convince the current staff that Excel can help them make daily operating decisions more easily and efficiently. To do this, you've decided to create charts using the previous year's operating expenses including rent, utilities, and payroll. The manager will use these charts at the next monthly meeting.

- **a.** Start Excel, open the Data File EX D-4.xlsx from the drive and folder where you store your Data Files, then save it as **EX D-Bark Bark Bark Doggie Day Spa Analysis**.
- **b.** Decide which data in the worksheet should be charted. What chart types are best suited for the information you need to show? What kinds of chart enhancements are necessary?
- **c.** Create a 3-D Clustered Column chart in the worksheet showing the expense data for all four quarters. (*Hint*: The expense categories should appear on the x-axis. Do not include the totals.)
- **d.** Change the vertical axis labels (Expenses data) so that no decimals are displayed. (*Hint*: Right-click the axis labels you want to modify, click Format Axis, click the Number category in the Format Axis dialog box, change the number of decimal places, then click Close.)
- **e.** Using the sales data, create two charts on this worksheet that compare the sales amounts. (*Hint*: Move each chart to a new location on the worksheet, then deselect it before creating the next one.)
- **f.** In one chart of the sales data, add data labels, then add chart titles as you see fit.
- **g.** Make any necessary formatting changes to make the charts look more attractive, then enter your name in a worksheet cell.
- **h.** Save your work.
- **i.** Preview each chart in Backstage view, and adjust any items as needed. Fit the worksheet to a single page, then submit your work to your instructor as directed. A sample of a printed worksheet is shown in Figure D-28.
- **j.** Close the workbook, then exit Excel.

FIGURE D-28

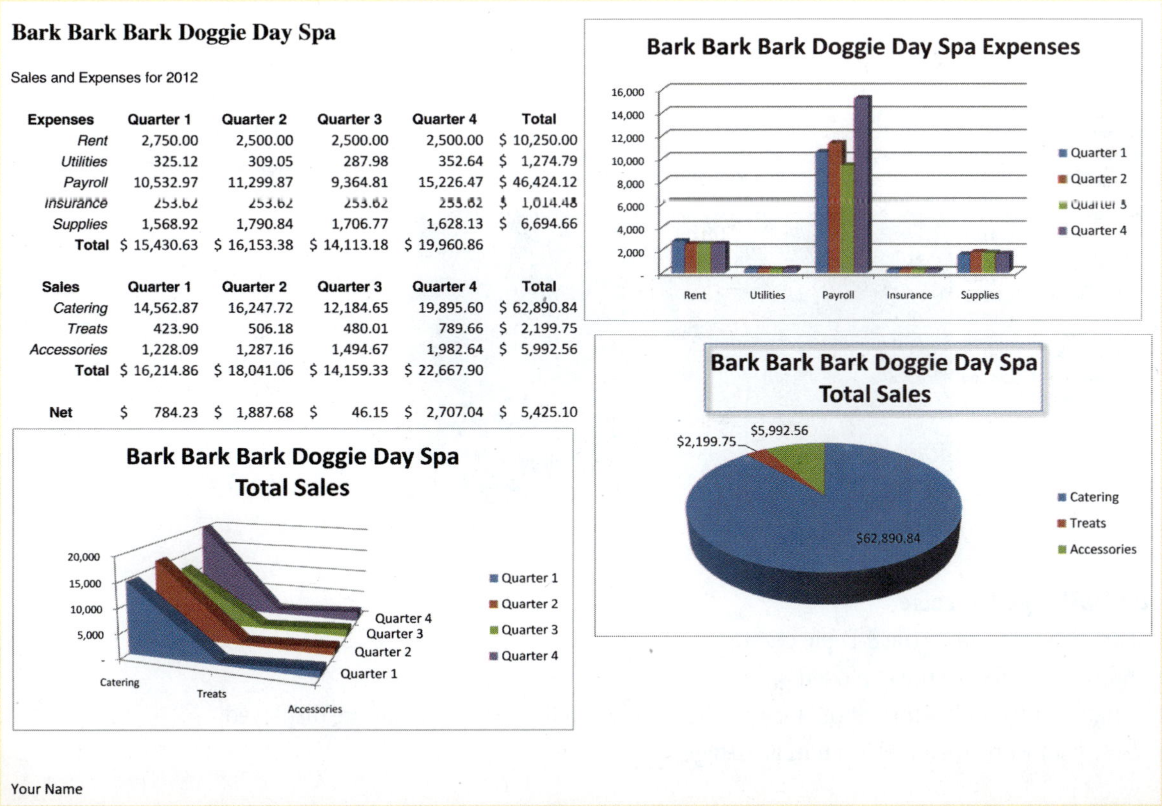

Expenses	Quarter 1	Quarter 2	Quarter 3	Quarter 4	Total
Rent	2,750.00	2,500.00	2,500.00	2,500.00	$ 10,250.00
Utilities	325.12	309.05	287.98	352.64	$ 1,274.79
Payroll	10,532.97	11,299.87	9,364.81	15,226.47	$ 46,424.12
Insurance	253.62	253.62	253.62	253.62	$ 1,014.48
Supplies	1,568.92	1,790.84	1,706.77	1,628.13	$ 6,694.66
Total	$ 15,430.63	$ 16,153.38	$ 14,113.18	$ 19,960.86	
Sales	**Quarter 1**	**Quarter 2**	**Quarter 3**	**Quarter 4**	**Total**
Catering	14,562.87	16,247.72	12,184.65	19,895.60	$ 62,890.84
Treats	423.90	506.18	480.01	789.66	$ 2,199.75
Accessories	1,228.09	1,287.16	1,494.67	1,982.64	$ 5,992.56
Total	$ 16,214.86	$ 18,041.06	$ 14,159.33	$ 22,667.90	
Net	$ 784.23	$ 1,887.68	$ 46.15	$ 2,707.04	$ 5,425.10

Independent Challenge 3

You are working as an account representative at a magazine called *Creativity*. You have been examining the expenses incurred recently. The CEO wants to examine expenses designed to increase circulation and has asked you to prepare charts that can be used in this evaluation. In particular, you want to see how dollar amounts compare among the different expenses, and you also want to see how expenses compare with each other proportional to the total budget.

- **a.** Start Excel, open the Data File EX D-5.xlsx from the drive and folder where you store your Data Files, then save it as **EX D-Creativity Magazine**.
- **b.** Identify three types of charts that seem best suited to illustrate the data in the range A16:B24. What kinds of chart enhancements are necessary?
- **c.** Create at least two different types of charts that show the distribution of circulation expenses. (*Hint*: Move each chart to a new location on the same worksheet.) One of the charts should be a 3-D pie chart.
- **d.** In at least one of the charts, add annotated text and arrows highlighting important data, such as the largest expense.
- **e.** Change the color of at least one data series in at least one of the charts.
- **f.** Add chart titles and category and value axis titles where appropriate. Format the titles with a font of your choice. Apply a shadow to the chart title in at least one chart.
- **g.** Add your name to a section of the header, then save your work.
- **h.** Preview the worksheet in Backstage view. Adjust any items as needed. Be sure the charts are all visible on one page. Compare your work to the sample in Figure D-29.

FIGURE D-29

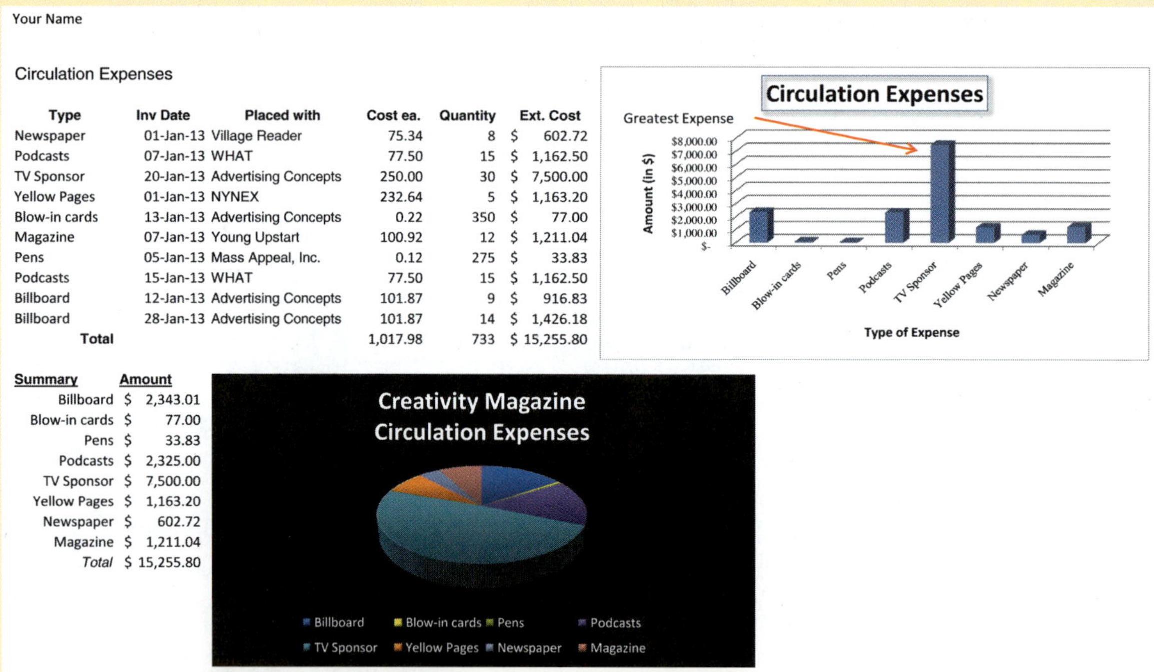
Your Name

Circulation Expenses

Type	Inv Date	Placed with	Cost ea.	Quantity	Ext. Cost
Newspaper	01-Jan-13	Village Reader	75.34	8	$ 602.72
Podcasts	07-Jan-13	WHAT	77.50	15	$ 1,162.50
TV Sponsor	20-Jan-13	Advertising Concepts	250.00	30	$ 7,500.00
Yellow Pages	01-Jan-13	NYNEX	232.64	5	$ 1,163.20
Blow-in cards	13-Jan-13	Advertising Concepts	0.22	350	$ 77.00
Magazine	07-Jan-13	Young Upstart	100.92	12	$ 1,211.04
Pens	05-Jan-13	Mass Appeal, Inc.	0.12	275	$ 33.83
Podcasts	15-Jan-13	WHAT	77.50	15	$ 1,162.50
Billboard	12-Jan-13	Advertising Concepts	101.87	9	$ 916.83
Billboard	28-Jan-13	Advertising Concepts	101.87	14	$ 1,426.18
Total			1,017.98	733	$ 15,255.80

Summary	Amount
Billboard	$ 2,343.01
Blow-in cards	$ 77.00
Pens	$ 33.83
Podcasts	$ 2,325.00
TV Sponsor	$ 7,500.00
Yellow Pages	$ 1,163.20
Newspaper	$ 602.72
Magazine	$ 1,211.04
Total	$ 15,255.80

Advanced Challenge Exercise

- Explode a slice from the 3-D pie chart.
- Add a data label to the exploded pie slice.
- Change the number format of labels in the non-pie chart so no decimals are displayed.
- Save your work, then preview it in Backstage view.

- **i.** Submit your work to your instructor as directed, close the workbook, then exit Excel.

Real Life Independent Challenge

This project requires an Internet connection.

A cash inheritance from a distant relative has finally been deposited in your bank account, and you have decided to purchase a home. You have a good idea where you'd like to live, and you decide to use the Web to find out more about houses that are currently available.

a. Start Excel, then save a new, blank workbook as **EX D-My Dream House** to the drive and folder where you save your Data Files.

b. Decide on where you would like to live, and use your favorite search engine to find information sources on homes for sale in that area. (*Hint*: Try using realtor.com or other realtor-sponsored sites.)

c. Determine a price range and features within the home. Find data for at least five homes that meet your location and price requirements, and enter them in the worksheet. See Table D-4 below for a suggested data layout.

TABLE D-4

suggested data layout					
Location					
Price range					
	House 1	House 2	House 3	House 4	House 5
Asking price					
Bedrooms					
Bathrooms					
Year built					
Size (in sq. ft.)					

d. Format the data so it looks attractive and professional.

e. Create any type of column chart using only the House and Asking Price data. Place it on the same worksheet as the data. Include a descriptive title.

f. Change the colors in the chart using the chart style of your choice.

g. Enter your name in a section of the header.

h. Save the workbook. Preview the worksheet in Backstage view and make adjustments if necessary to fit all of the information on one page. See Figure D-30 for an example of what your worksheet might look like.

i. Submit your work to your instructor as directed.

FIGURE D-30

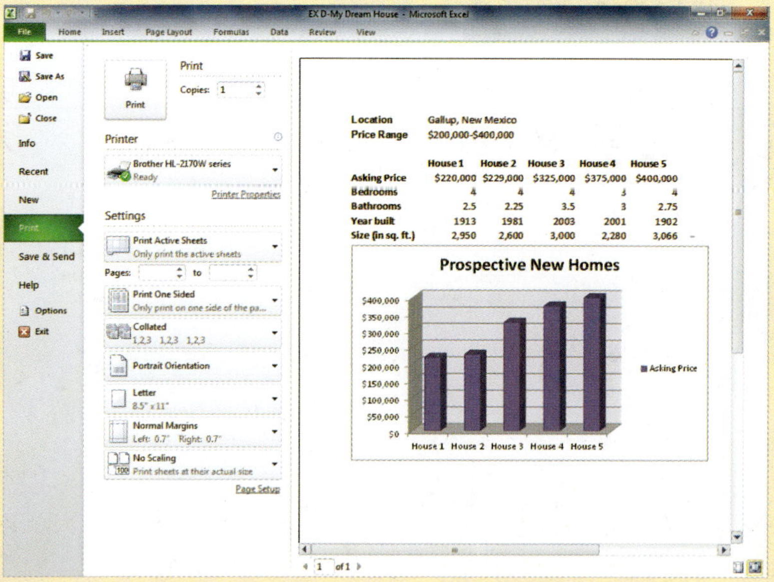

Advanced Challenge Exercise

- If necessary, change the chart type to a Clustered Column chart.
- Change the data used for the chart to include the size data in cells A9:F9.
- Create a combination chart that plots the asking price on one axis and the size of the home on the other axis. (*Hint*: Use Help to get tips on how to chart with a secondary axis.)

j. Close the workbook, then exit Excel.

Visual Workshop

Open the Data File EX D-6.xlsx from the drive and folder where you store your Data Files, then save it as **EX D-Projected Project Expenses**. Format the worksheet data so it looks like Figure D-31, then create and modify two charts to match the ones shown in the figure. You will need to make formatting, layout, and design changes once you create the charts. (*Hint*: The shadow used in the 3-D pie chart title is made using the Outer Offset Diagonal Top Right shadow.) Enter your name in the left text box of the header, then save and preview the worksheet. Submit your work to your instructor as directed, then close the workbook and exit Excel.

FIGURE D-31

Your Name

Projected Project Expenses

	Quarter 1	Quarter 2	Quarter 3	Quarter 4	Total
Project 1	1,725.00	1,835.00	1,935.00	2,400.00	7,895
Project 2	2,600.00	2,490.00	2,400.00	2,050.00	9,540
Project 3	2,750.00	2,930.00	3,190.00	3,400.00	12,270
Project 4	1,012.50	1,720.00	1,550.00	1,610.00	5,893
Project 5	2,190.00	2,060.00	6,400.00	2,700.00	13,350
Project 6	2,790.00	3,550.00	3,735.00	3,340.00	13,415
Total	13,068	14,585	19,210	15,500	

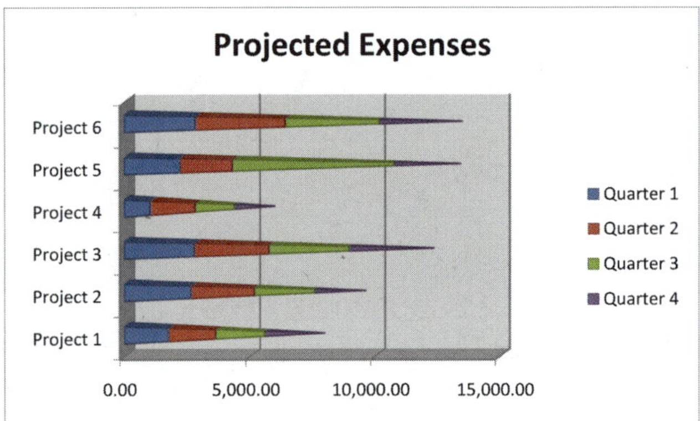

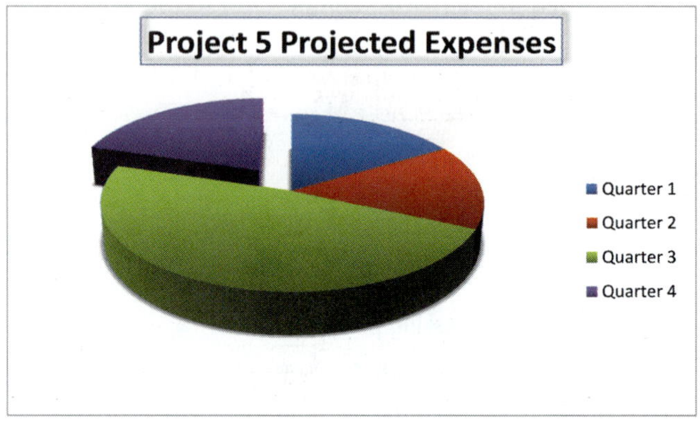

UNIT
A
Integration 2010

Integrating Word and Excel

Files You Will Need:

- INT A-1.xlsx
- INT A-2.docx
- INT A-3.xlsx
- INT A-4.docx
- INT A-5.xlsx
- INT A-6.docx
- INT A-7.xlsx
- INT A-8.docx
- INT A-9.docx
- INT A-10.xlsx
- INT A-11.xlsx
- INT A-12.docx
- INT A-13.xlsx
- INT A-14.docx
- INT A-15.xlsx
- INT A-16.docx

Now that you have experienced the power of Word and Excel, you'll learn how to use these two programs together. You can easily create sophisticated documents that incorporate data from both programs. For example, you can prepare a report in Word that contains a chart you created in Excel so that any changes you make to the chart in Excel also appear in the chart in the Word report. You can also copy words and numbers between Word and Excel, and you can insert a Word file into an Excel worksheet. You integrate data between programs to save time and effort so that you can work more efficiently. Instead of re-creating the same information in different programs, you create the information in one program and then reuse it in other programs. You are working as an assistant to Sheila Barton, the general manager of QST Sydney in Australia. Sheila has asked you to create a report in Word that includes information she created in Excel.

OBJECTIVES

- Integrate data between Word and Excel
- Copy data from Excel to Word
- Copy a chart from Excel to Word
- Create linked objects
- Embed a Word file in Excel

Integrating Data Between Word and Excel

Microsoft Office programs are designed to work together through a process called **integration**. When you integrate data from multiple Office programs, you work with both a source file and a destination file. The **source file** is the file from which the information is copied or used. The **destination file** is the file that receives the copied information. You can choose from three integration methods: pasting, linking, and embedding. As the operations assistant at QST Sydney, you often create documents such as reports and price lists that include data from both Word and Excel. You decide to review some of the ways in which you integrate data between the two programs.

DETAILS

You can integrate Word and Excel by:

- **Copying and pasting data from the Clipboard**
  You use the Copy and Paste commands to duplicate **objects** such as text selections, numbers (called values in Excel), and pictures from one program and place them into another program. When you copy and paste an object, changes that you make to the object in the source file do not appear in the destination file. The report shown in Figure A-1 was created in Word and includes two objects that were copied from Excel—the photograph that appears to the right of the document title and the shaded table under the document subtitle.

- **Linking data**
  Sometimes you want to connect the data that is included in two or more files. For example, suppose you copy the contents of a cell containing a formula from an Excel worksheet and paste it into a Word document. When you change the formula values in Excel, you want the corresponding values to change in the Word document. To create a **link** between data in two files, you select one of the link options that appears when you either click the Paste button list arrow or view options in the Paste Special dialog box. You use the term **linked object** to refer to the connected data. In the report shown in Figure A-1, the value 80% is a linked object. If this percentage changes in the Excel worksheet the linked percentage in the Word document also changes.

- **Copying and pasting charts**
  When you copy a chart from Excel and paste it into Word using the Paste command, Word automatically creates a link between the pasted chart and the original chart. In the report shown in Figure A-1, the column chart was copied from Excel and pasted into the Word document. When the chart values are updated in Excel, the same chart values are updated in the chart copied to Word. You can also copy a chart from the source file and then paste it into the destination file as an object that is not linked.

- **Embedding a Word file in Excel**
  You can **embed**, or place an unlinked copy of, the contents of a Word file into an Excel worksheet. You edit the embedded object by double-clicking it and using Word program tools to change text and formatting. This process changes the embedded copy of the Word object in Excel, but does not affect the original source document that you created in Word. Similarly, any changes to the source Word document are not reflected in the embedded copy in Excel. In the price list shown in Figure A-2, the text that describes the QST tours was inserted in Excel as an embedded Word file.

FIGURE A-1: Word report with objects copied from Excel

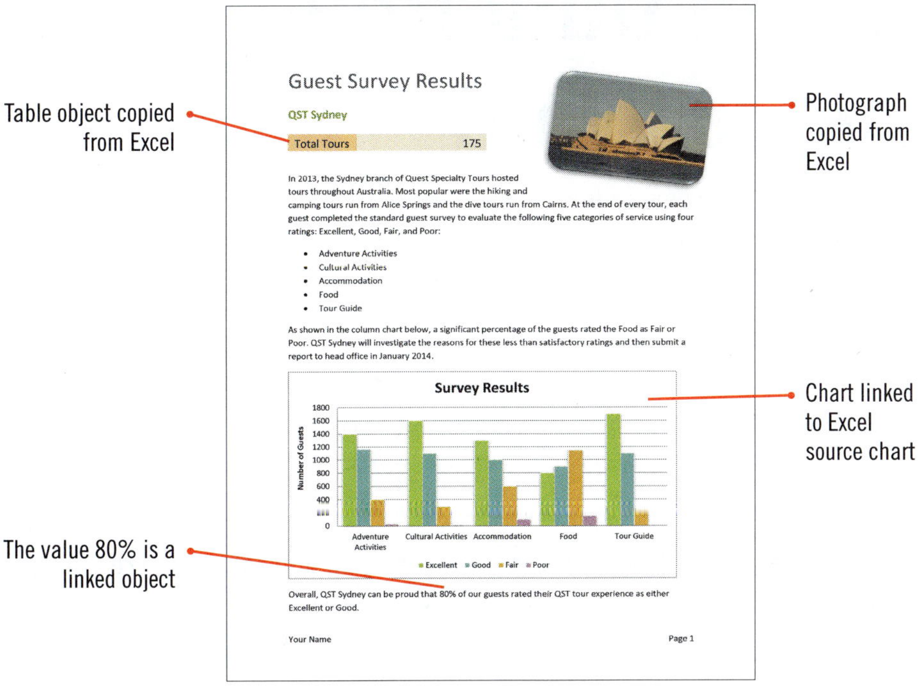

Guest Survey Results

QST Sydney

Total Tours	175

In 2013, the Sydney branch of Quest Specialty Tours hosted tours throughout Australia. Most popular were the hiking and camping tours run from Alice Springs and the dive tours run from Cairns. At the end of every tour, each guest completed the standard guest survey to evaluate the following five categories of service using four ratings: Excellent, Good, Fair, and Poor:

- Adventure Activities
- Cultural Activities
- Accommodation
- Food
- Tour Guide

As shown in the column chart below, a significant percentage of the guests rated the Food as Fair or Poor. QST Sydney will investigate the reasons for these less than satisfactory ratings and then submit a report to head office in January 2014.

Overall, QST Sydney can be proud that 80% of our guests rated their QST tour experience as either Excellent or Good.

Your Name Page 1

FIGURE A-2: Price list with embedded Word file

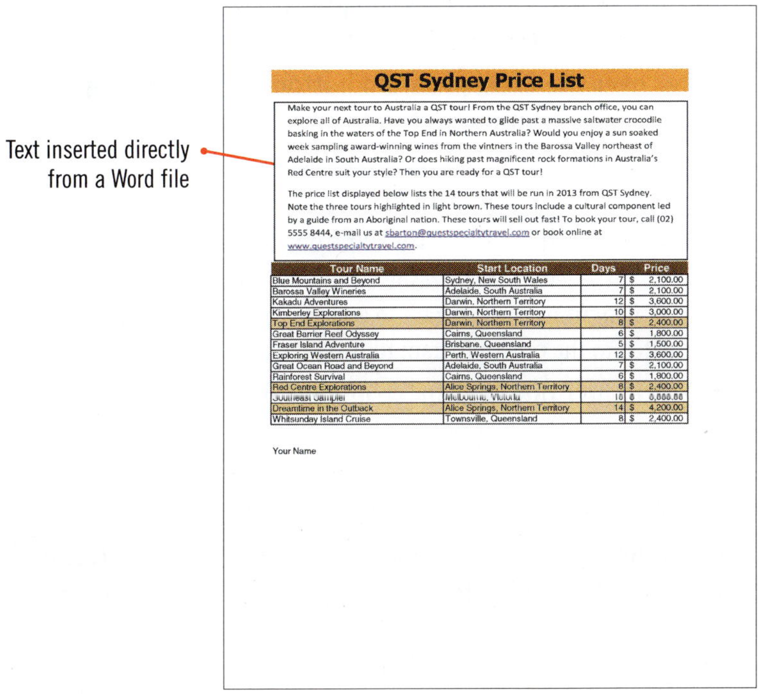

QST Sydney Price List

Make your next tour to Australia a QST tour! From the QST Sydney branch office, you can explore all of Australia. Have you always wanted to glide past a massive saltwater crocodile basking in the waters of the Top End in Northern Australia? Would you enjoy a sun soaked week sampling award-winning wines from the vintners in the Barossa Valley northeast of Adelaide in South Australia? Or does hiking past magnificent rock formations in Australia's Red Centre suit your style? Then you are ready for a QST tour!

The price list displayed below lists the 14 tours that will be run in 2013 from QST Sydney. Note the three tours highlighted in light brown. These tours include a cultural component led by a guide from an Aboriginal nation. These tours will sell out fast! To book your tour, call (02) 5555 8444, e-mail us at sbarton@questspecialtytravel.com or book online at www.questspecialtytravel.com.

Tour Name	Start Location	Days	Price
Blue Mountains and Beyond	Sydney, New South Wales	7	$ 2,100.00
Barossa Valley Wineries	Adelaide, South Australia	7	$ 2,100.00
Kakadu Adventures	Darwin, Northern Territory	12	$ 3,600.00
Kimberley Explorations	Darwin, Northern Territory	10	$ 3,000.00
Top End Explorations	Darwin, Northern Territory	8	$ 2,400.00
Great Barrier Reef Odyssey	Cairns, Queensland	6	$ 1,800.00
Fraser Island Adventure	Brisbane, Queensland	5	$ 1,500.00
Exploring Western Australia	Perth, Western Australia	12	$ 3,600.00
Great Ocean Road and Beyond	Adelaide, South Australia	7	$ 2,100.00
Rainforest Survival	Cairns, Queensland	6	$ 1,800.00
Red Centre Explorations	Alice Springs, Northern Territory	8	$ 2,400.00
Southeast Sampler	Melbourne, Victoria	[illegible]	[illegible]
Dreamtime in the Outback	Alice Springs, Northern Territory	14	$ 4,200.00
Whitsunday Island Cruise	Townsville, Queensland	8	$ 2,400.00

Your Name

Understanding object linking and embedding (OLE)

The term **object linking and embedding (OLE)** refers to the technology that Microsoft uses to let you integrate data between programs. You create an object in one program, and then you can choose to either link the object to or embed it in another program. The difference between linking and embedding relates to where the object is stored and how you update the object after you place it in a document. A linked object in a destination file is an image of an object contained in a source file, not a copy of it. Both objects share a single source, which means you make changes to an object only in the source file.

When you embed an object that you created in another program, you include a copy of the object in a destination file. To update the object, you double-click it in the destination file and then use the tools of the source program to make changes. You cannot edit the source object using the tools of the destination program.

UNIT
A
Integration 2010

Copying Data from Excel to Word

You use the Copy and Paste commands when you want to copy an item from one program to another program. The item might be a line of text, a value, or an object—such as a chart or a picture. The procedure is the same as the one you use to copy and paste an object from one location in a document to another location in the same document. By default, an object copied from one program to another program retains the formatting of the original object and is not linked to the original object. The exception occurs when you copy and paste a chart, which you will learn about in the next lesson. Sheila Barton, the general manager of QST Sydney, has summarized survey data in an Excel worksheet and created a report in Word to describe the survey results. She asks you to copy two objects from the Excel worksheet and paste them into the Word report.

STEPS

QUICK TIP
Throughout this unit, click Enable Editing on the Protected View bar near the top of your program window if prompted.

TROUBLE
If items already appear in the Clipboard task pane, click Clear All.

1. **Start Excel, open the file INT A-1.xlsx from the drive and folder where you store your Data Files, then save it as INT A-Sydney Survey Data**
   The values in the range B7:F10 represent the total number of responses in each of the four rating categories for the tours that QST operated out of the Sydney branch in 2013.
2. **Start Word, open the file INT A-2.docx from the drive and folder where you store your Data Files, then save it as INT A-Sydney Survey Report**
   The Word report contains text that describes the results of the survey.
3. **Move the mouse pointer over the Excel program button on the taskbar, as shown in Figure A-3, then click the Excel program button to switch to Excel**
   When you point to the Excel program button, a picture of the program and the file, along with the filename, appear.
4. **On the Home tab, click the launcher in the Clipboard group**
   The Clipboard task pane opens to the left of the worksheet window. You use the Clipboard when you want to copy and paste more than one item from one program to another program. You can "collect" up to 24 items to the Clipboard and then switch to the other program to paste them.
5. **Click the photograph, click the Copy button in the Clipboard group, select the range A4:C4, then click**
   Both items now appear on the Clipboard, as shown in Figure A-4. When you place multiple items on the Clipboard, newer items appear at the top of the list and older items move down.
6. **Click the Word program button on the taskbar, click the launcher in the Clipboard group, verify that the insertion point is to the left of the title, then click the photograph on the Clipboard**
   You pasted the photograph to the left of the document title.
7. **Click in the blank space below QST Sydney, click Total Tours 175 on the Clipboard, then click the Close button on the Clipboard task pane**
   You pasted the object as a table below the document subtitle. When you use the Copy and Paste commands, the default setting is for the copied object to retain the formatting applied to it in the source file.
8. **Right-click the photograph in the Word document, point to Wrap Text, click Square, then drag the photograph to the right of the title, as shown in Figure A-5**
9. **Click anywhere in the document to deselect the photograph, then save the document**

FIGURE A-3: Word and Excel on the taskbar

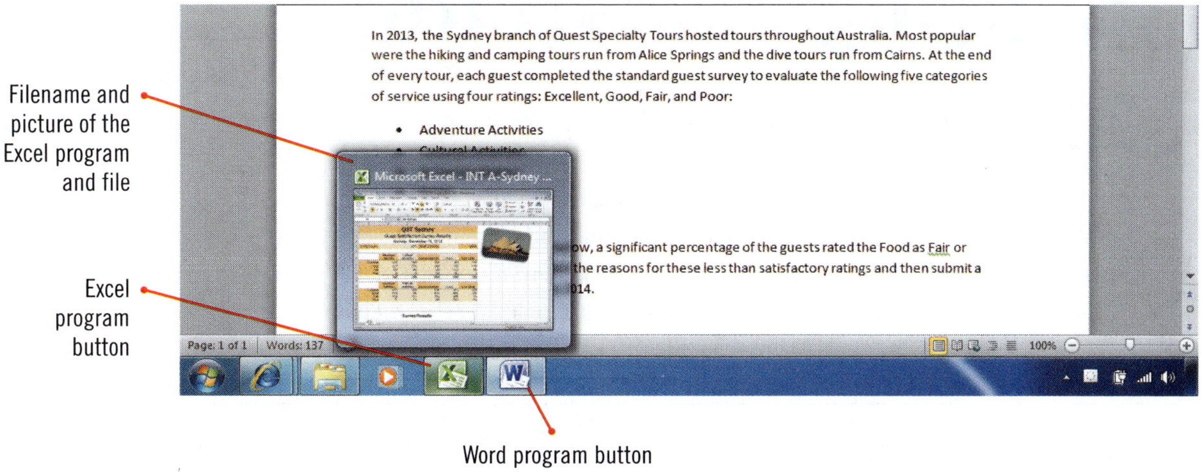

FIGURE A-4: Two items collected on the Clipboard

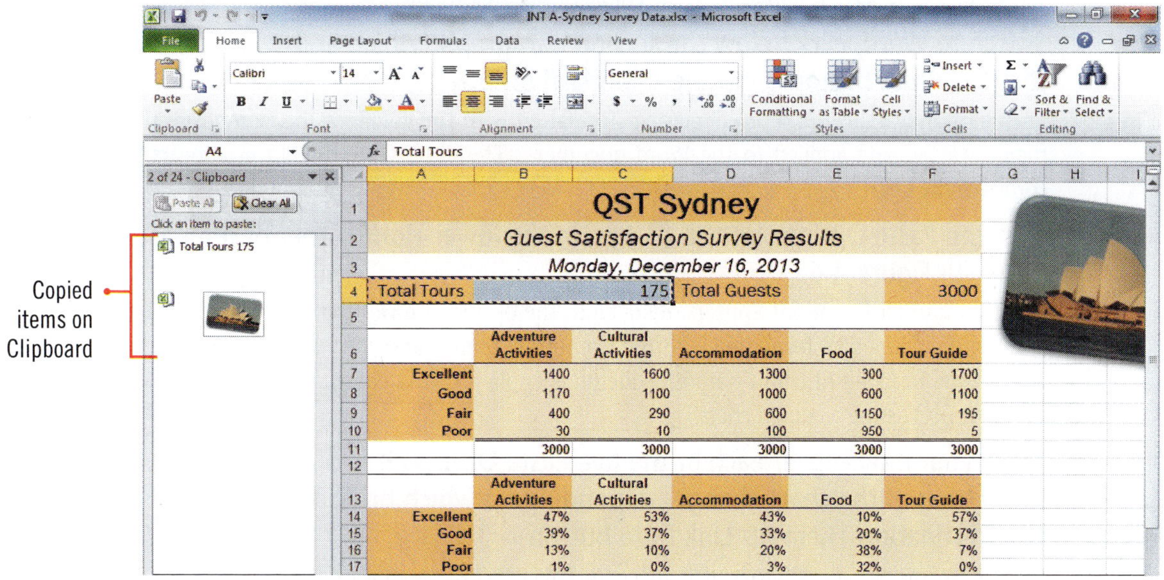

FIGURE A-5: Picture positioned in the Word report

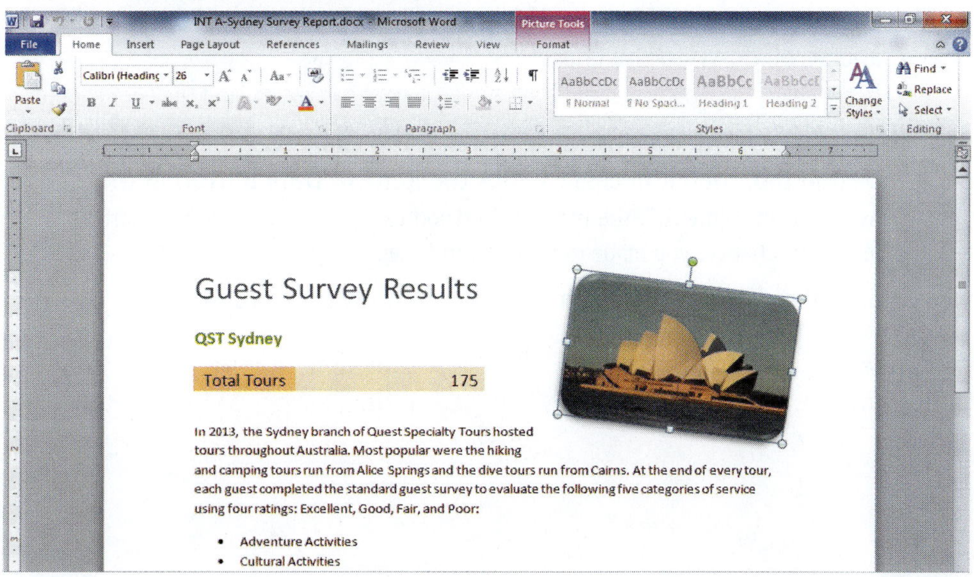

Integration 2010

Copying a Chart from Excel to Word

You use the Copy and Paste buttons to create a link between a chart in Excel and the same chart pasted into a document in Word. When you change the data in the source file, the linked data also changes in the destination file. You need to copy a column chart representing survey results from Excel and paste it into the Word report. By default, the copied chart will be linked to the chart in the Excel report. However, it will be formatted with the same theme applied to the destination document.

STEPS

1. **Click the Excel program button on the taskbar, then close the Clipboard task pane**
2. **Scroll down to view the column chart, click the chart to select it, then click the Copy button in the Clipboard group**

   The chart in Excel is formatted with the colors of the Trek theme.
3. **Switch to Word, click below the second paragraph (which ends with January 2014), then click the Paste button in the Clipboard group**

   The chart appears in the Word document formatted with the colors of the Composite theme, because this theme was already applied to the Word document. The Paste Options button appears in the lower-right corner of the chart.
4. **Click the Paste Options button (Ctrl) in the lower-right corner of the pasted chart, as shown in Figure A-6**

   A selection of paste options appears. By default, the option Use Destination Theme & Link Data is selected. The Word document is formatted with the Composite theme, and the Excel document is formatted with the Trek theme. As a result, the Composite theme is applied to the chart. Table A-1 describes the five options available for pasting a copied chart.
5. **Move your mouse over each of the five Paste Options buttons to view how the formatting of the chart changes depending on which button is selected, then click the Use Destination Theme & Link Data button**
6. **Switch to Excel, then note the position of the bars for the Food category in the column chart**

   At present, the Poor column is quite high compared to the Poor columns for the other categories.
7. **Scroll up, click cell E8, type 900, press [Enter], click cell E10, type 650, then press [Enter] and scroll down to the chart**

   In the chart, the Good column in the Food category has grown, and the Poor column has shrunk.
8. **Switch to Word, click the chart, then if the chart has not updated, click the Chart Tools Design tab, then if necessary click the Refresh Data button in the Data group**

   As shown in Figure A-7, the bars for the Food category in the column chart change in the linked chart to reflect the changes you made to the chart in Excel.
9. **Save the document, switch to Excel, then save the workbook**

FIGURE A-6: Paste Options

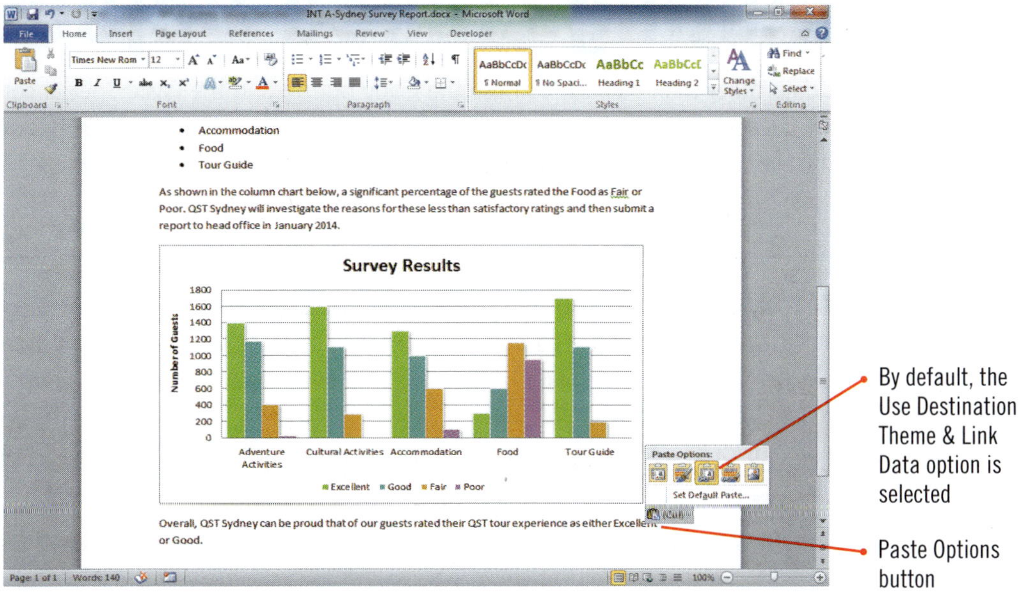

FIGURE A-7: Linked chart updated in Word

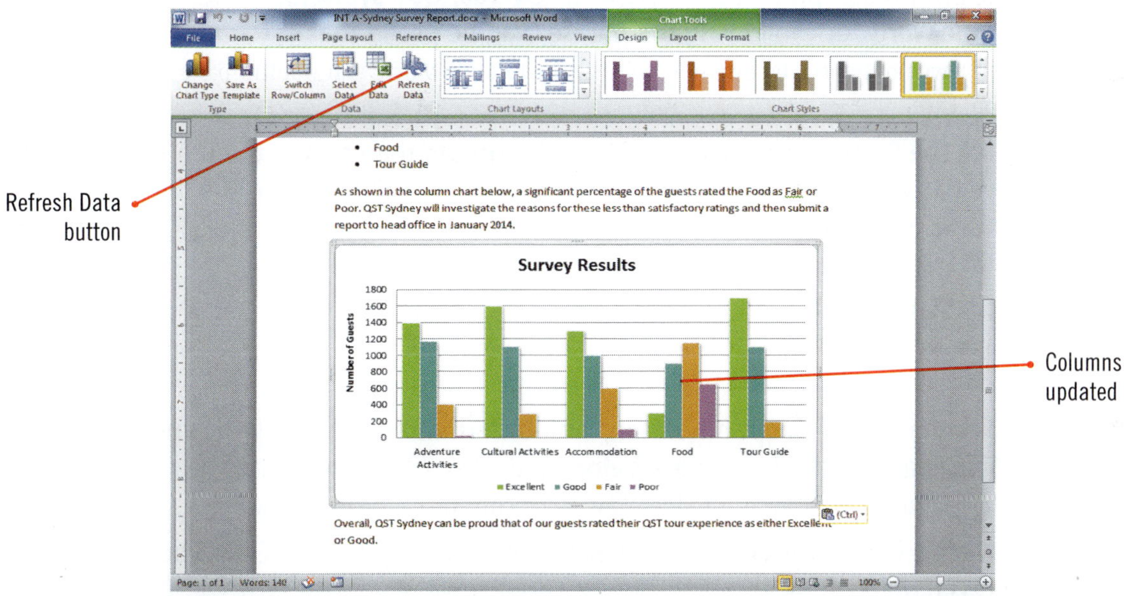

TABLE A-1: Paste options for charts

Paste Options button	button name	description
	Use Destination Theme & Embed Workbook	This button is selected by default when a chart is pasted into the destination document. The theme of the destination document is applied to the chart, and the chart is linked to the object in the source document.
	Keep Source Formatting & Embed Workbook	The pasted chart is not linked to the source document, and the pasted chart keeps the same formatting as the source document.
	Use Destination Theme & Link Data	The pasted chart is not linked to the source document, and the pasted chart assumes the formatting of the destination document.
	Keep Source Formatting & Link Data	The pasted chart is linked to the source document, so any changes made to the chart in the source document will be made to the copied chart in the Word document. In addition, the formatting of the source document is retained.
	Picture	The chart is pasted as a picture that cannot be modified, and uses the same formatting as the chart in the source document.

Creating Linked Objects

To link data other than a chart, you use the Copy button and the Paste Special command to create a link between the source file and the destination file. You need your report to include a value that represents the average tour ratings. You decide to link the report to the source file data so that you can update the data in both files when new information becomes available.

STEPS

1. **In Excel, click cell G14, type the formula =AVERAGE(B14:F14), press [Enter], click cell G14, then drag its fill handle to cell G17 to enter the remaining three percentages**
   The value 42% appears in cell G14. This value indicates that, on average, 42% of the responses were Excellent. Only 5% of the responses were Poor.
2. **Click cell F19, type Good/Excellent, press [Tab], type the formula =G14+G15 in cell G19, then press [Enter]**
   The value 77% appears in cell G19, indicating that 77% of guests rated their tour experience as Good or Excellent.
3. **Click cell G19, click the Copy button in the Clipboard group, switch to Word, scroll to the last paragraph (which starts with "Overall, QST Sydney..."), then click just to the left of the word "of", following the phrase "can be proud that"**
   You have positioned the insertion point at the location where you want to paste the contents of cell G19 from Excel.
4. **Click the Paste list arrow in the Clipboard group, then move your mouse over each of the five Paste Options to view how the pasted object will appear in the document**
   The two options that allow linking also insert a line break, so you look for additional paste options in the Paste Special dialog box.
5. **Click Paste Special**
   The Paste Special dialog box opens, as shown in Figure A-8. In this dialog box, you have more options for pasting the value and for controlling its appearance in the destination file.
6. **Click the Paste link option button, click Unformatted Text, click OK, then use the [Spacebar] to adjust the space before and after 77% as necessary**
   The percentage, 77%, appears in the Word document. You decide to test the link.
7. **Switch to Excel, click cell E7, type 800, press [Enter], click cell E10, type 150, then press [Enter]**
   The Good/Excellent rating in cell G18 is now 80%.
8. **Switch to Word; verify that 80% appears or, if it does not appear, right-click 77% and click Update Link**
   If the Update Link option is not available when you right click, you can update the links in the Edit Links dialog box as follows: Click the File tab, click Edit Links to Files in the lower-right corner of Backstage view, click the link to the worksheet object, click Update Now, then click OK. Click the Home tab to return to the document. The final document is shown in Figure A-9.
9. **Type your name where indicated in the Word footer, save the document, switch to Excel, type your name where indicated in cell A41, save the workbook, then submit your files to your instructor**

TROUBLE
If you print the Excel workbook, make sure you fit it on one page.

FIGURE A-8: Paste Special dialog box

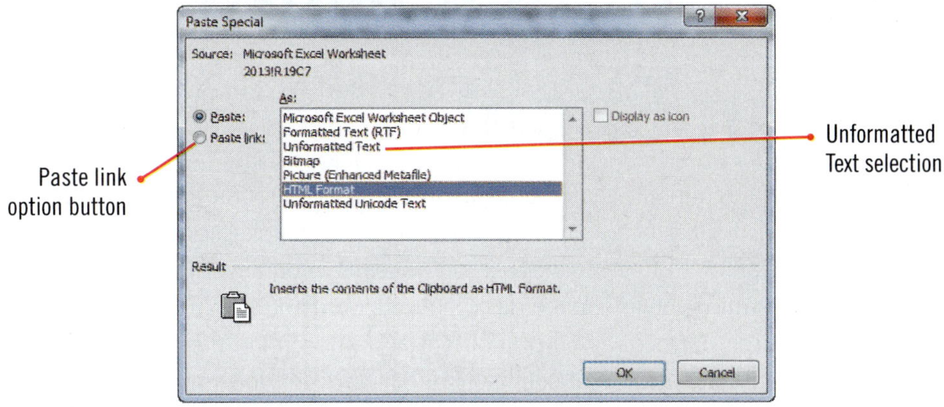

FIGURE A-9: Completed report

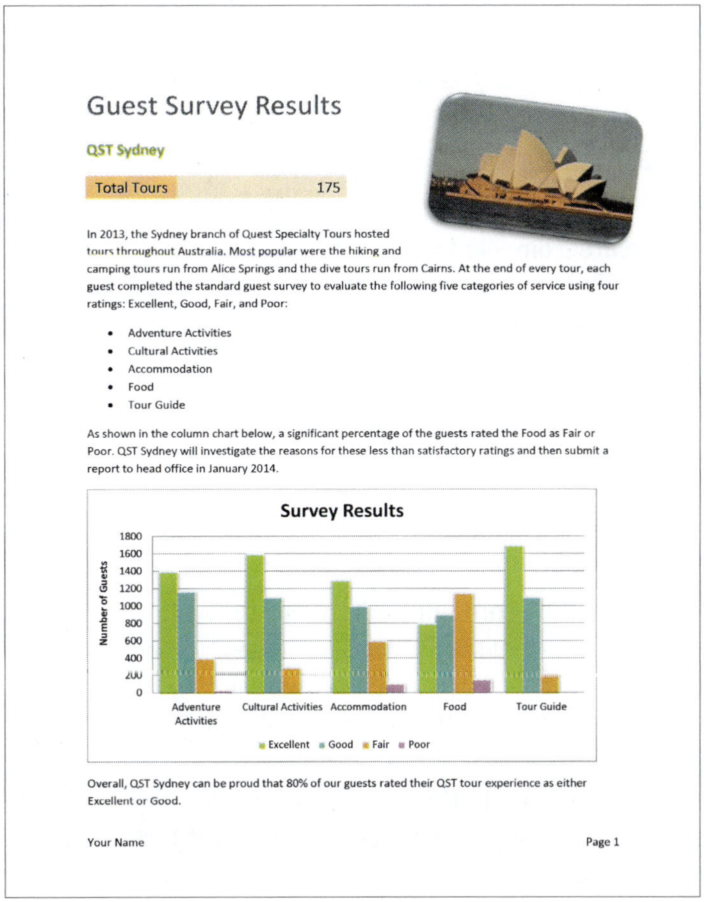

Opening linked files and reestablishing links to charts

When you open a Word file that contains links from an Excel file, a dialog box opens with a message telling you that the document contains links that may refer to other files. The message also asks if you want to update this document with the data from the linked file. Click Yes to update the document with data from the linked file. If you want to change information in both the Excel file and the Word file, you need to open the Excel workbook first, followed by the Word document.

If you make a change to a linked chart in the Excel file and then try to refresh the chart data in Word, you may receive an error message that tells you the linked Excel file cannot be found. To update the chart in Word, follow this procedure: Click the File tab, click Edit Links to Files in the lower-right corner of Backstage view, click the link you want to update, click Change Source, select the Excel file containing the linked data, click Open, click Update Now, click OK, then click the Home tab, and verify that the chart data is updated. You should only need to reestablish the link to the Excel file once and only if you need to update the Excel chart. For future updates, you should be able to simply refresh the data.

Embedding a Word File in Excel

You can embed an entire file that you create in one Office program into a document created in another Office program. You can then edit the embedded file by double-clicking it in the destination program to open the source program. You use the tools of the source program to make changes. Table A-2 summarizes the four ways in which you integrated data between Word and Excel in this unit. You have created a price list in Excel, but before you distribute it at an upcoming meeting at QST Sydney, you decide to include some explanatory text that you have stored in a Word document.

STEPS

1. **In Excel, open the file INT A-3.xlsx from the drive and folder where you store your Data Files, then save it as INT A-Sydney Price List; in Word, open the file INT A-4.docx from the drive and folder where you store your Data Files, save it as INT A-Sydney 2013 Tours, then close it**

2. **In Excel, click cell G3, click the Insert tab, then click the Object button in the Text group**
   The Object dialog box opens. Here you can choose to either create a new object or insert an object from a file.

3. **Click the Create from File tab, click Browse, navigate to where you stored the INT A-Sydney 2013 Tours file, double-click INT A-Sydney 2013 Tours, then click OK**
   The text from the Word document appears in a box that starts in cell G3. You can insert the Word object anywhere in the worksheet and then move it. When you insert an object from another program such as Word, you sometimes need to reposition the current worksheet contents to accommodate the inserted object.

4. **Select the range A4:D21, move the mouse pointer over any border of the selection to show the pointer, then drag the selection down to cell A18**

5. **Move the mouse pointer over the border of the box containing the Word text to show the pointer, then drag the selection to cell A3, as shown in Figure A-10**

6. **Double-click the box containing the Word text**
   Because the object is embedded, the Word Ribbon and tabs appear within the Excel window. As a result, you can use the tools from the source program (Word) to edit the text. The title bar shows "Microsoft Excel – Document in INT A-Sydney Price List.xlsx" because you are working within the destination file to edit the embedded object.

7. **Click the Select button in the Editing group, click Select All, click the launcher in the Paragraph group, select the contents of the Left text box in the Indentation section, type .2, press [Tab], type .2 in the Right text box, then click OK**

8. **Select 10 in the first line of paragraph 2, type 14, compare the edited object to Figure A-11, then click outside the object to return to Excel**
   The embedded object is updated in Excel. The text in the source file is not updated because the source file is not linked to the destination file.

9. **Type your name where indicated in cell A35, save and close the document, exit Word and Excel, then submit your files to your instructor**

FIGURE A-10: Embedded Word file positioned in Excel

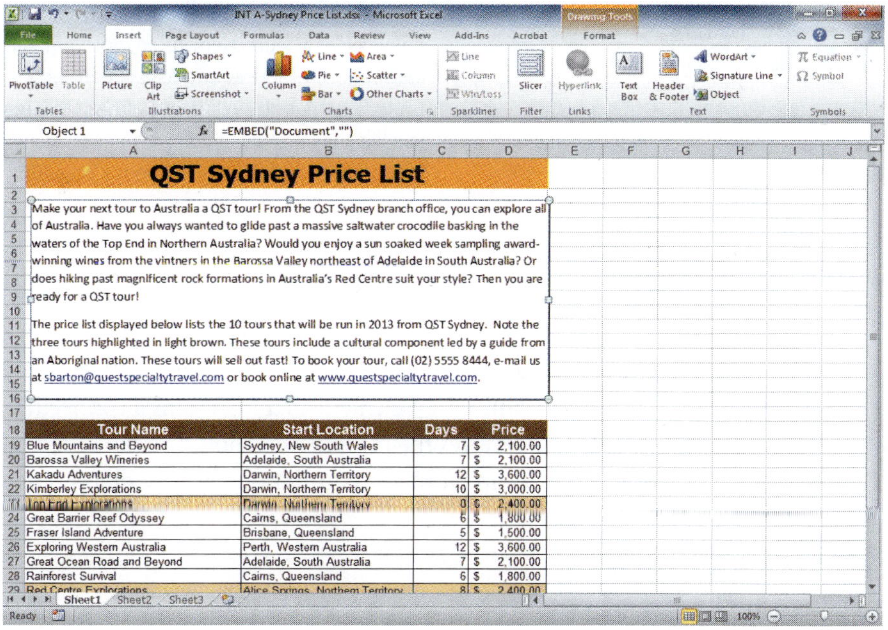

FIGURE A-11: Embedded object updated in Excel

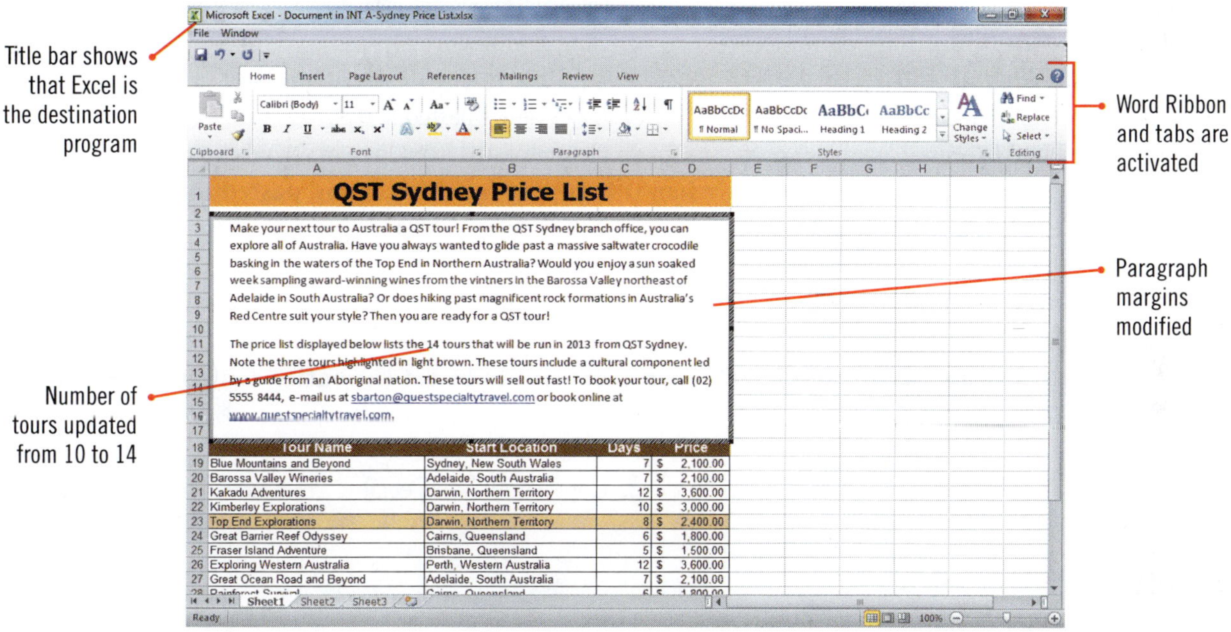

TABLE A-2: Unit A integration tasks

object	command	source program	destination program	result	connection	Page no.
Cells	Copy/Paste	Excel	Word	Object with Excel formatting	Pasted: no link	4
Chart	Copy/Paste	Excel	Word	Object with Word formatting	Linked	6
Cell	Copy/Paste Special/Paste link	Excel	Word	Formatting varies depending on formatting option chosen in the Paste Special dialog box	Linked	8
File	Insert/Object/ Create from File	Word	Excel	Text box containing the Word file: to update, double-click and use Word tools within the Excel destination file	Embedded: no link	10

Practice

Concepts Review

For current SAM information, including versions and content details, visit SAM Central (http://www.cengage.com/samcentral). If you have a SAM user profile, you may have access to hands-on instruction, practice, and assessment of the skills covered in this unit. Since various versions of SAM are supported throughout the life of this text, check with your instructor for the correct instructions and URL/Web site for accessing assignments.

Match each term with the statement that best describes it.

1. **Integration**
2. **Destination file**
3. **Paste Special**
4. **Source file**
5. **Linked object**

- **a.** The file containing information that is copied and often linked to a different file
- **b.** The ability to use information across multiple programs
- **c.** Within a document, an element that maintains a connection to a different file
- **d.** The file that receives the information copied from a different file
- **e.** Used to create and format a connection between objects copied from one file to another file

Select the best answer from the list of choices.

6. **Which of the following commands do you use when you do not need to maintain a link between an object from one file and its copy in another file?**
   - **a.** Copy and Insert
   - **b.** Copy and Paste Special
   - **c.** Insert File
   - **d.** Copy and Paste
7. **Which of the following objects is, by default, pasted as a link in the destination file?**
   - **a.** Excel chart pasted into Word
   - **b.** Word text pasted into Excel
   - **c.** Excel values pasted into Word
   - **d.** Picture pasted from Excel to Word
8. **By default, what theme is applied to a chart when it is copied from Excel and pasted into Word?**
   - **a.** The theme used in the source file (Excel)
   - **b.** The Word 2010 theme
   - **c.** The theme used in the destination file (Word)
   - **d.** No theme is applied
9. **Which of the following options do you select when you want to insert the entire contents of a Word file into Excel?**
   - **a.** Create File
   - **b.** Copy and Paste
   - **c.** Create from File
   - **d.** Copy and Paste Special

Skills Review

1. **Copy data from Excel to Word.**
   - **a.** Start Excel, open the file INT A-5.xlsx from the drive and folder where you store your Data Files, then save it as **INT A-Social Studies Data**.
   - **b.** Start Word, open the file INT A-6.docx from the drive and folder where you store your Data Files, then save it as **INT A-Social Studies Report**.
   - **c.** Switch to Excel, open the Clipboard, then click Clear All, if necessary.
   - **d.** Select cell A1, then copy the contents to the Clipboard.
   - **e.** Select the range A3:C7, then copy the contents to the Clipboard.
   - **f.** Switch to Word, open the Clipboard, paste the Social Studies object at the top of the document (at the current position of the insertion point), press [Enter] to add an additional blank line, then center the inserted text.
   - **g.** Paste the Subject Areas object on the line above paragraph 2 (which starts with "Students in the Santa Fe…"), then adjust the spacing if necessary so that one blank line appears above and below the pasted object.
   - **h.** Close the Clipboard, then save the document.

Skills Review (continued)

2. **Copy a chart from Excel to Word.**
   a. Switch to Excel, close the Clipboard, then copy the bar chart.
   b. Switch to Word, then paste the bar chart below the second paragraph of text (which ends with "and State scores").
   c. Switch to Excel, then note the position of the bars for History.
   d. Change the value in cell B4 to **85**, then switch to Word.
   e. Click the chart, refresh the data, if necessary, then save the document.
   f. Switch to Excel, then save the workbook.
3. **Create linked objects.**
   a. In Excel, enter **Difference** in cell D3, then enter the formula **=B4-C4** in cell D4.
   b. Use the Fill handle to copy the formula to the range D5:D7.
   c. Select the range A3:D7, copy it, switch to Word, then use the Paste Special command to paste the cells as a link below paragraph 3 (which ends with "state-wide"), using the Formatted Text (RTF) selection in the Paste Special dialog box.
   d. In Excel, copy cell D4, switch to Word, click to the left of "points" in the last paragraph, then use Paste Special to paste the cell as a link using the Unformatted Text option in the Paste Special dialog box.
   e. Ensure that there is a space before and after the pasted value.
   f. In Excel, change the value in cell B4 to **90**.
   g. In Word, refresh the chart if necessary, then verify that the district score for history is 90.
   h. Update the link in the table and the last paragraph so that 30 appears. If the Update Link option is not available when you right click, you can update the links in the Edit Links dialog box as follows: Click the File tab, click Edit Links to Files in the lower-right corner of Backstage view, click the link to the worksheet object, click Update Now, then click OK. Click the Home tab to return to the document.
   i. Enter your name where indicated in the footer in Word, preview the report in Backstage view, save and close the Word report, then submit your file to your instructor. The completed document is shown in Figure A-12.
   j. In Excel, enter your name in cell A30 where indicated, save and close the workbook, then submit the file to your instructor.
4. **Embed a Word file in Excel.**
   a. In Excel, open the file INT A-7.xlsx from the drive and folder where you store your Data Files, then save it as **INT A-New Mexico Art Workshops Revenue**.
   b. In Word, open the file INT A-8.docx from the drive and folder where you store your Data Files, save it as **INT A-New Mexico Art Workshops**, then close it.
   c. In Excel, in cell H5, insert the Word file INT A-New Mexico Art Workshops.docx as an embedded file.
   d. Select the range A8:F15, then move it to cell A19.
   e. Position the box containing the Word text so that its upper-left corner is in cell A3.
   f. Change $44.00 to $54.00 in paragraph 1, then change "Fun with Acrylics" to **Basic Pottery** in paragraph 2.
   g. Click outside the embedded object to return to Excel, compare your screen to Figure A-13, enter your name in cell A30, save and close the workbook, exit Word and Excel, then submit your file to your instructor.

FIGURE A-12

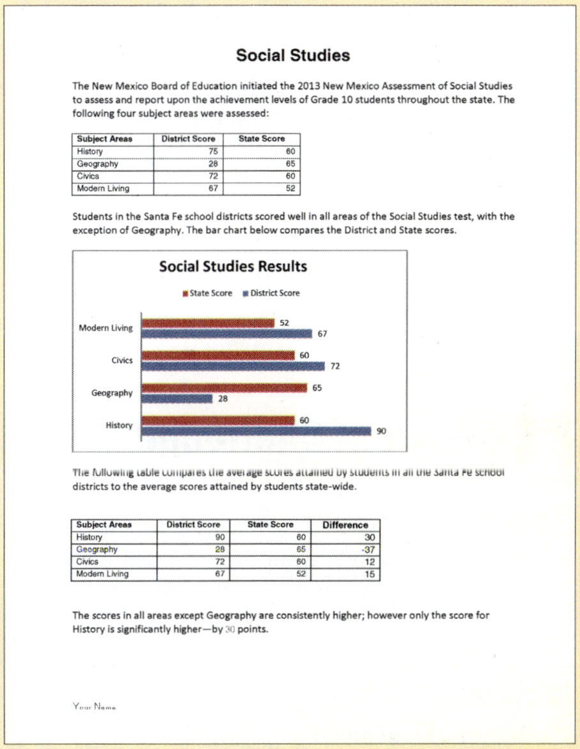
Social Studies

The New Mexico Board of Education initiated the 2013 New Mexico Assessment of Social Studies to assess and report upon the achievement levels of Grade 10 students throughout the state. The following four subject areas were assessed:

Subject Areas	District Score	State Score
History	75	60
Geography	28	65
Civics	72	60
Modern Living	67	52

Students in the Santa Fe school districts scored well in all areas of the Social Studies test, with the exception of Geography. The bar chart below compares the District and State scores.

The following table compares the average scores attained by students in all the Santa Fe school districts to the average scores attained by students state-wide.

Subject Areas	District Score	State Score	Difference
History	90	60	30
Geography	28	65	-37
Civics	72	60	12
Modern Living	67	52	15

The scores in all areas except Geography are consistently higher; however only the score for History is significantly higher—by 30 points.

Your Name

FIGURE A-13

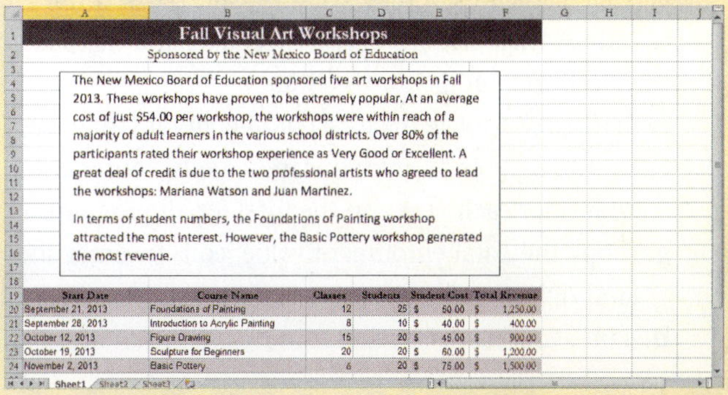
Fall Visual Art Workshops

Sponsored by the New Mexico Board of Education

The New Mexico Board of Education sponsored five art workshops in Fall 2013. These workshops have proven to be extremely popular. At an average cost of just $54.00 per workshop, the workshops were within reach of a majority of adult learners in the various school districts. Over 80% of the participants rated their workshop experience as Very Good or Excellent. A great deal of credit is due to the two professional artists who agreed to lead the workshops: Mariana Watson and Juan Martinez.

In terms of student numbers, the Foundations of Painting workshop attracted the most interest. However, the Basic Pottery workshop generated the most revenue.

Start Date	Course Name	Classes	Students	Student Cost	Total Revenue
September 21, 2013	Foundations of Painting	12	25	$ 50.00	$ 1,250.00
September 28, 2013	Introduction to Acrylic Painting	8	10	$ 40.00	$ 400.00
October 12, 2013	Figure Drawing	15	20	$ 45.00	$ 900.00
October 19, 2013	Sculpture for Beginners	20	20	$ 60.00	$ 1,200.00
November 2, 2013	Basic Pottery	6	20	$ 75.00	$ 1,500.00

Independent Challenge 1

As a member of the Bowen Island Arts Commission on Bowen Island, British Columbia, you are responsible for compiling the minutes of the commission's quarterly meetings. You have already written most of the text required for the minutes. Now you need to insert data from Excel that shows how much money was raised from various fund-raising activities.

- **a.** Start Word, open the file INT A-9.docx from the drive and folder where you store your Data Files, save it as **INT A-Bowen Island Arts Commission Minutes**, start Excel, open the file INT A-10.xlsx from the drive and folder where you store your Data Files, then save it as **INT A-Bowen Island Arts Commission Data**.
- **b.** In Excel, open the Clipboard, clear all items if necessary, then copy the photograph and cell A2.
- **c.** In Word, open the Clipboard and paste the photograph at the top of the Word document, then paste cell A2 below the document title.
- **d.** Change the text wrapping of the picture to Square, position the photograph to the right of the document title, then add a blank line above the pasted text.
- **e.** Copy the Fundraising Revenue chart from Excel, then paste it in the appropriate area in the Word document.
- **f.** In Excel, change the number of participants in the perennials sale to **700**; then in Word, refresh the data in the chart (the Perennials slice should be 56%).
- **g.** In Excel, copy the contents of cell E7, switch to Word, select XX in the bulleted list below the chart, then paste the value as a link using the Unformatted Text selection in the Paste Special dialog box.
- **h.** In Excel, click cell F9, then calculate the total funds raised by adding the contents of the range B7:F7.
- **i.** In cell B8, enter the formula **=B7/F9**, use [F4] to make cell F9 absolute, then copy the formula to the range C8:F8.
- **j.** Copy cell E8, switch to Word, select ZZ in the bulleted list below the chart, paste the value as a link using the Unformatted Text selection, then add a space after the pasted object if necessary.
- **k.** In Excel, change the number of participants in the perennials sale to **900**; then in Word, verify that the Perennials slice changes to 62% and that the links updated to $36,000 and 62%. If the links do not update automatically, right-click them and click Update Link. If the Update Link option is not available, click the File tab, click Edit Links to Files in the lower-right corner of Backstage view, click each of the links to update, click Update Now, then click OK. Click the Home tab to return to the document.
- **l.** Type your name in the Word footer, save and close the document, save and close the Excel workbook, then submit your files to your instructor.

Independent Challenge 2

You work at a summer camp in Maine that provides teens with training programs in leadership and communication skills. You have collected data about the camp enrollment from 2008 to 2013 in an Excel workbook. Now you need to prepare the workbook for distribution at an upcoming meeting with local businesspeople who are interested in sponsoring the camp. You want to include text in the workbook that you have stored in a Word document.

- **a.** Start Excel, open the file INT A-11.xlsx from the drive and folder where you store your Data Files, then save it as **INT A-Atlantic Shores Camp Report**.
- **b.** Start Word, open the file INT A-12.docx from the drive and folder where you store your Data Files, save it as **INT A-Atlantic Shores Camp Information**, then close it.
- **c.** In a blank area of the Excel worksheet, insert the Camp Information file as an embedded object.
- **d.** Adjust the positions of the Excel data and the box containing the Word text so that the Word text appears above the Excel data and below the title.
- **e.** In Excel, calculate the total enrollment for Leadership Training and Communication Skills programs in the appropriate cells.
- **f.** To the right of "Communication Skills," enter and format **Total**, then calculate the total enrollment for both programs for each year and the total for all programs from 2008 to 2013.
- **g.** Copy the Total enrollment value, edit the embedded Word document so that the text is indented by .3" from the left and right margins, then paste the correct total enrollment figure using the Text Only paste option.
- **h.** Enter your name in cell A22 in Excel, save and close the Excel workbook, exit Excel, then submit your file to your instructor.

Independent Challenge 3

You own Artistic Gardens, a landscaping business in Seattle, Washington. You have entered your projected income and expenses in Excel. Now you need to link objects to the company's sales summary in Word.

a. Start Excel, open the file INT A-13.xlsx from the drive and folder where you store your Data Files, then save it as **INT A-Artistic Gardens Sales Data**.
b. In cell B14, calculate the Cost of Sales by multiplying the Sales Amount by 60%. (*Hint*: In your formula, multiply the value in cell B6 times .6.) Copy the formula to the range C14:E14.
c. In cell B16, calculate the total profit or loss by subtracting the total expenses from the total income for the month, then copy the formula to the range C16:F16. You should see $42,960 in cell F16.
d. Save the workbook, start Word, open the file INT A-14.docx from the drive and folder where you store your Data Files, then save it as **INT A-Artistic Gardens Sales Report**.
e. Select EXPENSES in the paragraph under Projected Expenses, switch to Excel, then copy the value in cell F15 and paste it as a link and Formatted Text (RTF) in Word.
f. Use the same procedure to copy the INCOME and PROFIT amounts from Excel to the appropriate locations in the Word document. Make sure you paste the copied values as links in Formatted Text (RTF).
g. Copy the pie chart from Excel and paste it into the Word document below the first paragraph after Projected Expenses.
h. Click the pie chart to select it, then click the Center button in the Paragraph group on the Home tab.
i. In Excel, note the percentages in the pie chart, then increase the salaries expense for June to 15,000 and for July to 12,000.
j. Change the sales income for both April and May to 20,000. Note how the percentages change in the pie chart.
k. In Excel, open the Clipboard, then copy the heading in cell A1 and the picture to the Clipboard.
l. In Word, open the Clipboard; paste the heading at the top of the page and center it; then change the font to Calibri, the font size to 24 point, and the font color to Lime, Accent 1, Darker 50%, and apply Bold formatting.
m. Paste the picture below the Projected Income paragraph, then modify the text wrapping of the picture, and position it as shown in Figure A-14. Note that you may need to reduce the Zoom percentage to see the whole page and more easily position the picture. You might also need to reduce the size of the chart slightly so the picture fits on page 1.
n. Verify that the chart data has updated and refresh the data if necessary, then verify that the three links updated, or update them manually if required. Note that you may need to update the links in the Edit Links dialog box as follows: Click the File tab, click Edit Links to Files (lower-right corner of Backstage view), select each link and click Update Now, click OK, then click the Home tab to return to the document.
o. Add your name to the document footer, compare the completed sales report to Figure A-14, save and close the Word file, then submit your file to your instructor.
p. In Excel, enter your name in cell A40, save and close the workbook, then submit your file to your instructor.

FIGURE A-14

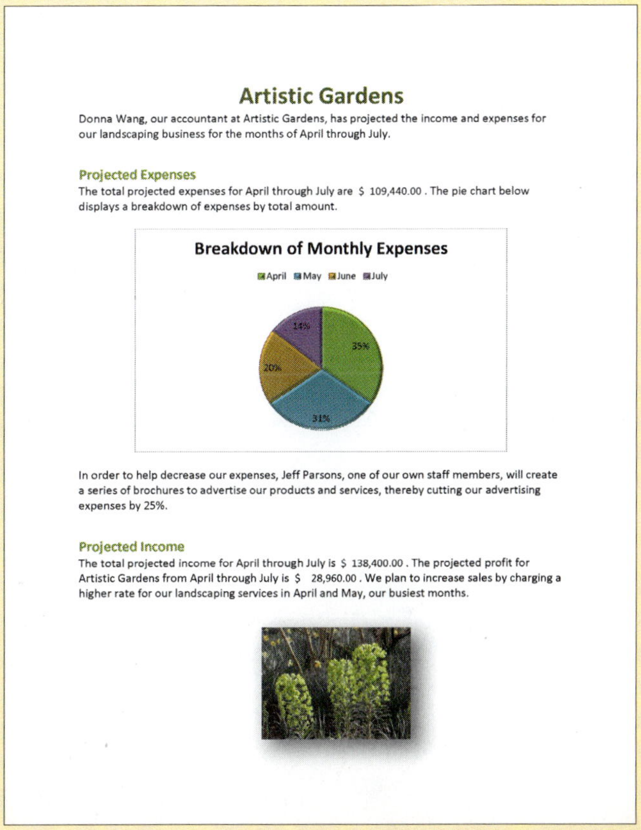

Artistic Gardens

Donna Wang, our accountant at Artistic Gardens, has projected the income and expenses for our landscaping business for the months of April through July.

Projected Expenses

The total projected expenses for April through July are $ 109,440.00 . The pie chart below displays a breakdown of expenses by total amount.

Breakdown of Monthly Expenses

April May June July

14% 35% 20% 31%

In order to help decrease our expenses, Jeff Parsons, one of our own staff members, will create a series of brochures to advertise our products and services, thereby cutting our advertising expenses by 25%.

Projected Income

The total projected income for April through July is $ 138,400.00 . The projected profit for Artistic Gardens from April through July is $ 28,960.00 . We plan to increase sales by charging a higher rate for our landscaping services in April and May, our busiest months.

Integration 2010

Visual Workshop

Using the Data Files INT A-15.xlsx and INT A-16.docx, create the price list shown in Figure A-15. Use formulas to calculate the prices for Two-Packs and Four-Packs. Save the workbook as **INT A-Campus Gourmet Price List** and save the Word document as **INT A-Campus Gourmet Information**. Embed the Word document into the Excel worksheet, position the inserted file and the price list in Excel as shown in Figure A-15, then format the embedded Word object as shown in Figure A-15. (*Hint*: The indentation on both sides of the text is .3, and the font size is 14 point.) Add your name to the Excel worksheet, save and close all files and programs, then submit your file to your instructor.

FIGURE A-15

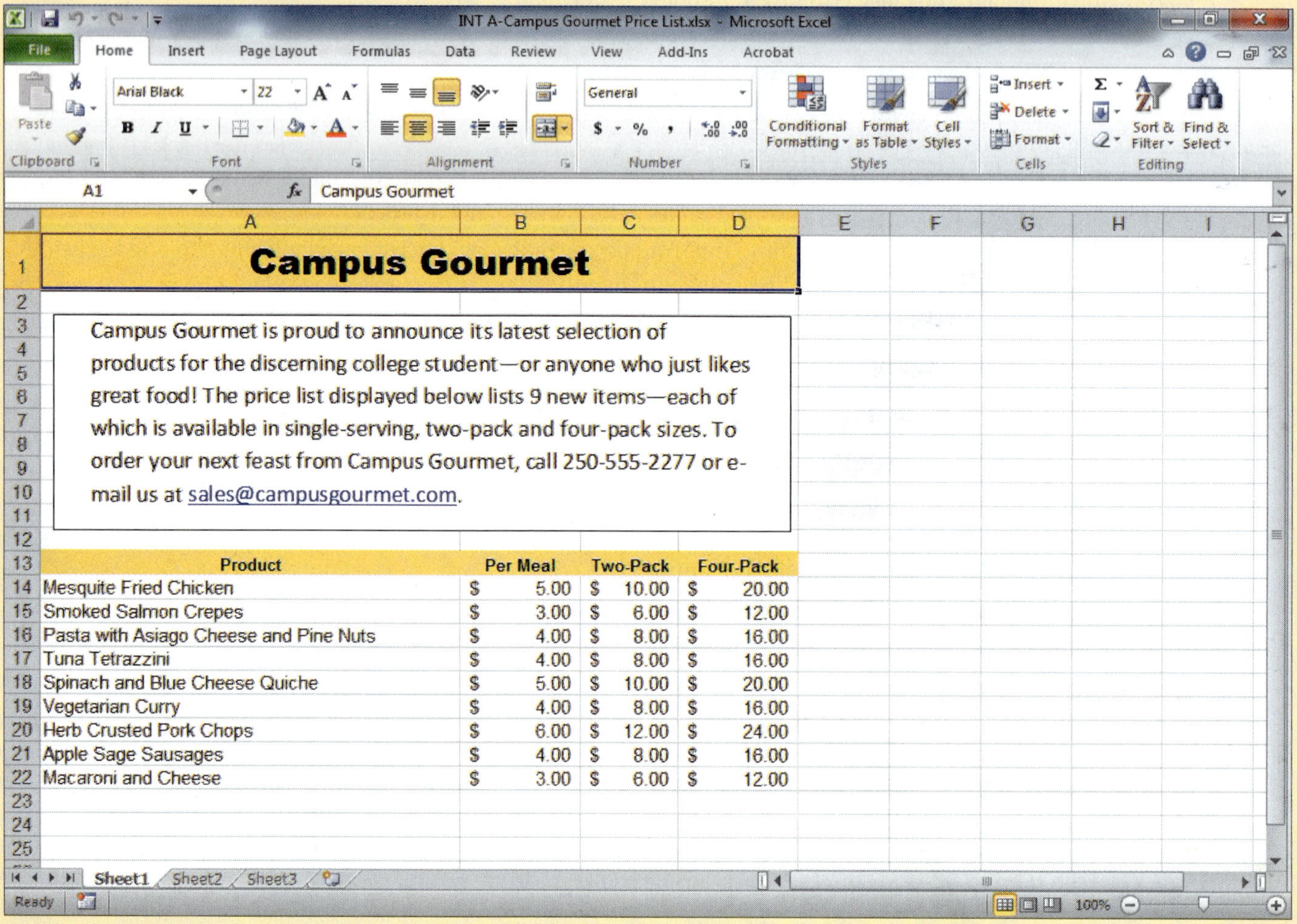

UNIT
A
Access 2010

Getting Started with Access 2010

Files You Will Need:

QuestTravel-A.accdb
RealEstate-A.accdb
Recycle-A.accdb
BusinessContacts-A.accdb
Basketball-A.accdb

In this unit, you will learn the purpose, advantages, and terminology of Microsoft Access 2010, the relational database program in the Microsoft Office 2010 suite of software. You will create and relate tables, the basic building blocks of an Access relational database. You'll also navigate, enter, update, preview, and print data. Samantha Hooper is the tour developer for United States group travel at Quest Specialty Travel (QST), a tour company that specializes in customized group travel packages. Samantha uses Access to store, maintain, and analyze customer and tour information.

OBJECTIVES

Understand relational databases
Explore a database
Create a database
Create a table
Create primary keys
Relate two tables
Enter data
Edit data

UNIT A

Access 2010

Understanding Relational Databases

Microsoft Access 2010 is relational database software that runs on the Windows operating system. You use **relational database software** to manage data that is organized into lists, such as information about customers, products, vendors, employees, projects, or sales. Many small companies track customer, inventory, and sales information in a spreadsheet program such as Microsoft Excel. Although Excel offers some list management features, Access provides many more tools and advantages for managing data. The advantages are mainly due to the "relational" nature of the lists that Access manages. Table A-1 compares the two programs. You and Samantha Hooper review the advantages of database software over spreadsheets for managing lists of information.

DETAILS

The advantages of using Access for database management include:

- **Duplicate data is minimized**

  Figures A-1 and A-2 compare how you might store sales data in a single Excel spreadsheet list versus three related Access tables. With Access, you do not have to reenter information such as a customer's name and address or tour name every time a sale is made, because lists can be linked, or "related," in relational database software.

- **Information is more accurate, reliable, and consistent because duplicate data is minimized**

  The relational nature of data stored in an Access database allows you to minimize duplicate data entry, which creates more accurate, reliable, and consistent information. For example, customer data in a Customers table is entered only once, not every time a customer makes a purchase.

- **Data entry is faster and easier using Access forms**

  Data entry forms (screen layouts) make data entry faster, easier, and more accurate than entering data in a spreadsheet.

- **Information can be viewed and sorted in many ways using Access queries, forms, and reports**

  In Access, you can save queries (questions about the data), data entry forms, and reports, allowing you to use them over and over without performing extra work to recreate a particular view of the data.

- **Information is more secure using Access passwords and security features**

  Access databases can be encrypted and password protected.

- **Several users can share and edit information at the same time**

  Unlike spreadsheets or word-processing documents, more than one person can enter, update, and analyze data in an Access database at the same time.

FIGURE A-1: Using a spreadsheet to organize sales data

	A	B	C	D	E	F	G	H	I
1	CustNo	FName	LName	SalesNo	SaleDate	TourName	TourStartDate	City	Cost
2	1	Gracita	Mayberry	13	11-Jul-12	Red Reef Scuba	07/24/2012	Islamadora	$1,500.00
3	2	Jacob	Alman	14	11-Jul-12	Red Reef Scuba	07/24/2012	Islamadora	$1,500.00
4	3	Julia	Bouchart	15	11-Jul-12	Red Reef Scuba	07/24/2012	Islamadora	$1,500.00
5	3	Julia	Bouchart	81	11-Jun-12	Piper-Heitman Wedding	06/17/2012	Captiva	$825.00
6	4	Kayla	Browning	5	01-Jun-12	American Heritage Tour	09/11/2012	Philadelphia	$1,200.00
7	4	Kayla	Browning	82	11-May-12	Red Reef Scuba	07/24/2012	Islamadora	$1,500.00
8	5	Samantha	Braven	16	11-Jul-12	Bright Lights Expo	12/19/2012	Branson	$200.00
9	5	Samantha	Braven	83	11-Jul-12	Red Reef Scuba	07/24/2012	Islamadora	$1,500.00
10	6	Kristen	Collins	1	30-Apr-12	Ames Ski Club	01/20/2013	Breckenridge	$850.00
11	6	Kristen	Collins	4	01-Jun-12	Yosemite National Park Great Cleanup	08/07/2012	Sacramento	$1,100.00
12	6	Kristen	Collins	8	07-Jul-12	Bright Lights Expo	12/19/2012	Branson	$200.00
13	6	Kristen	Collins	84	01-Jun-12	American Heritage Tour	09/11/2012	Philadelphia	$1,200.00

Customer information is duplicated each time that customer makes a purchase

Tour information is duplicated each time that tour is purchased

FIGURE A-2: Using a relational database to organize sales data

Customers table

Cust No	First	Last	Street	City	State	Zip	Phone
1	Gracita	Mayberry	222 Elm	Topeka	KS	66111	913-555-0000
2	Jacob	Alman	400 Oak	Lenexa	MO	60023	816-555-8877
3	Julia	Bouchart	111 Ash	Ames	IA	50010	515-555-3333

Sales table

Cust No	TourNo	Date	SalesNo
1	2	5/1/12	101
2	2	5/2/12	102
3	2	5/3/12	103

Tours table

TourNo	TourName	TourStartDate	City	Cost
1	Ames Ski Club	1/20/13	Breckenridge	$850
2	Red Reef Scuba	7/24/12	Islamadora	$1,500
3	American Heritage Tour	9/11/12	Philadelphia	$1,200

TABLE A-1: Comparing Excel to Access

feature	Excel	Access
Layout	Provides a natural tabular layout for easy data entry	Provides a natural tabular layout as well as the ability to create customized data entry screens called forms
Storage	Restricted to a file's limitations	Virtually unlimited when coupled with the ability to use Microsoft SQL Server to store data
Linked tables	Manages single lists of information—no relational database capabilities	Relates lists of information to reduce data redundancy and create a relational database
Reporting	Limited	Provides the ability to create an unlimited number of reports
Security	Limited to file security options such as marking the file "read-only" or protecting a range of cells	When used with SQL Server, provides extensive security down to the user and data level
Multiuser capabilities	Not allowed	Allows multiple users to simultaneously enter and update data
Data entry	Provides limited data entry screens	Provides the ability to create an unlimited number of data entry forms

Exploring a Database

You can start Access from the Start menu, from an Access shortcut icon, from a pinned program on the taskbar, or by double-clicking an Access database file on your computer. When you start the Access program from the Start menu, Access displays a window that allows you to open an existing database or create a new one from a template or as a blank database. Samantha Hooper has developed a database called QuestTravel-A, which contains tour information. She asks you to start Access and review this database.

STEPS

1. **Start Access from the Start menu**

   Access starts, as shown in Figure A-3. This window helps you open an existing database, create a new database from a template, or create a new blank database. At this point, if you click the Home, Create, External Data, or Database Tools tabs, no options would be available because Access is running, but no database is open.

> **TROUBLE**
> If a yellow Security Warning bar appears below the Ribbon, click Enable Content.

2. **Click the Open button, navigate to the drive and folder where you store your Data Files, click the QuestTravel-A.accdb database file, click Open, then click the Maximize button if the Access window is not already maximized**

   The QuestTravel-A.accdb database contains five tables of data named Customers, Sales, States, TourCategories, and Tours. It also contains four queries, two forms, and two reports. Each of these items (table, query, form, and report) is a different type of **object** in an Access database and is displayed in the **Navigation Pane**. The purpose of each object is defined in Table A-2. To learn about an Access database, you explore its objects.

> **TROUBLE**
> If the Navigation Pane is not open, click the Shutter Bar Open/Close button « to open it and view the database objects.

3. **In the Navigation Pane, double-click the Tours table to open it, then double-click the Customers table to open it**

   The Tours and Customers tables open to display the data they store. A **table** is the fundamental building block of a relational database because it stores all of the data.

4. **In the Navigation Pane, double-click the TourSales query to open it, double-click any occurrence of Heritage (as in American Heritage Tour), type Legacy, then click any other row**

   A **query** selects a subset of data from one or more tables. In this case, the TourSales query selects data from the Tours, Sales, and Customers tables. Editing data in one object changes it in every other object of the database, which demonstrates the power and productivity of a relational database.

5. **Double-click the TourEntryForm to open it, double-click Tour in "American Legacy Tour", type Rally, then click any name in the middle part of the window**

   An Access **form** is a data entry screen. Users prefer forms for data entry rather than tables and queries because the information can be presented in an easy-to-use layout.

6. **Double-click the TourSales report to open it**

   An Access **report** is a professional printout. A report is for printing purposes only, not data entry. As shown in Figure A-4, the edits made to the American Legacy Rally tour name have carried through to the report.

7. **Click the File tab, then click Exit**

   Exiting Access closes the database on which you are working. If you made any changes to the database that should be saved, Access would remind you to do so before closing. Changes to data, such as the edits you made to the American Legacy Rally tour, are automatically saved as you work.

FIGURE A-3: Opening Microsoft Access 2010 window

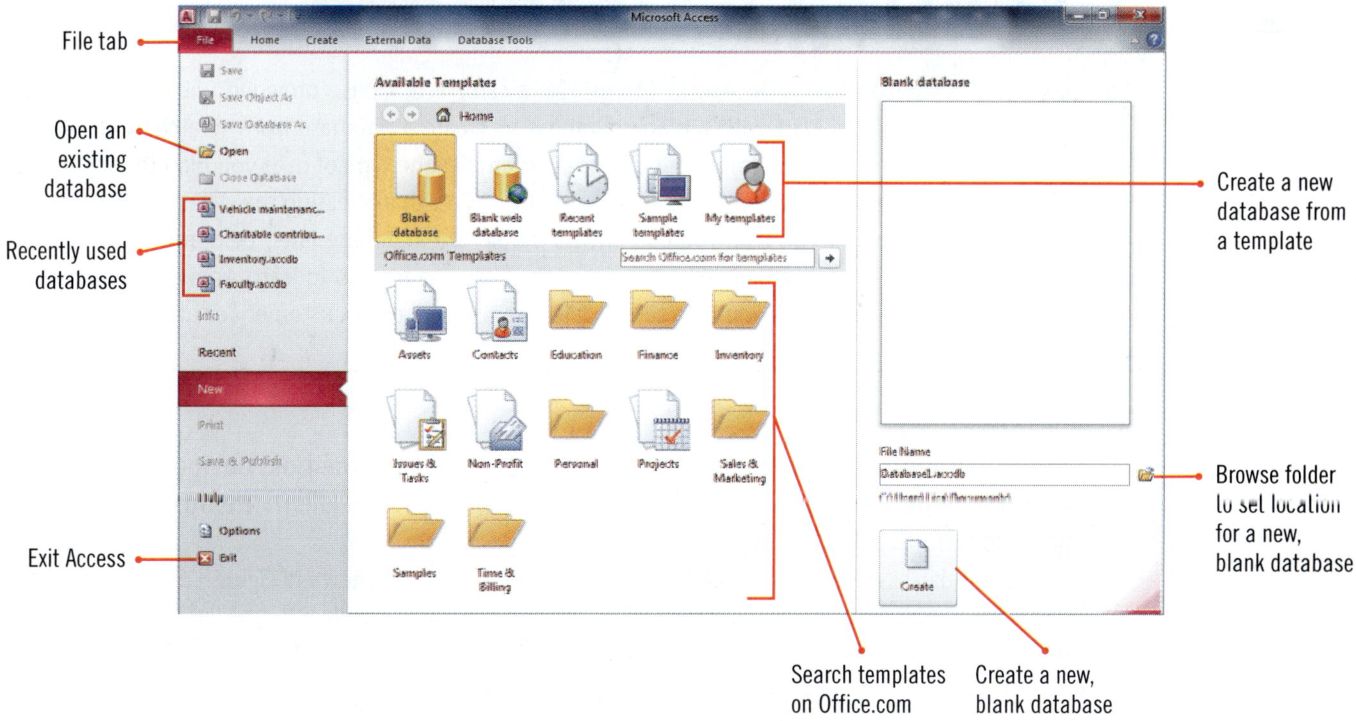

FIGURE A-4: Objects in the QuestTravel-A database

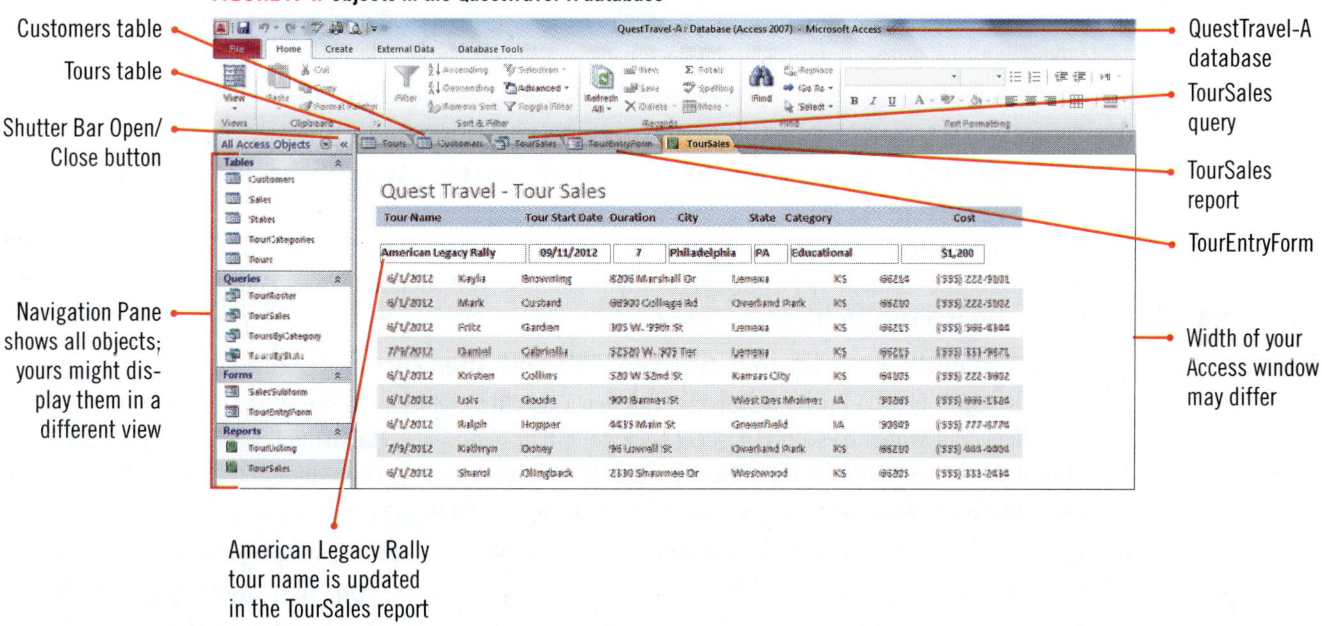

TABLE A-2: Access objects and their purpose

object	Navigation Pane icon	purpose
Table		Contains all of the raw data within the database in a spreadsheet-like view; tables are linked with a common field to create a relational database, which minimizes redundant data
Query		Allows you to select a subset of fields or records from one or more tables; queries are created when you have a question about the data
Form		Provides an easy-to-use data entry screen
Report		Provides a professional printout of data that can contain enhancements such as headers, footers, graphics, and calculations on groups of records

Creating a Database

You can create a database using an Access **template**, a sample database provided within the Microsoft Access program, or you can start with a blank database to create a database from scratch. Your decision depends on whether Access has a template that closely resembles the type of data you plan to manage. If it does, building your own database from a template might be faster than creating the database from scratch. Regardless of which method you use, you can always modify the database later, tailoring it to meet your specific needs. Samantha Hooper reasons that the best way for you to learn Access is to start a new database from scratch, so she asks you to create a database that will track customer communication.

STEPS

1. **Start Access**
2. **Click the Browse folder button to the right of the File Name box, navigate to the drive and folder where you store your Data Files, type Quest in the File name box, click OK, then click the Create button**

   A new, blank database file with a single table named Table1 is created as shown in Figure A-5. While you might be tempted to start entering data into the table, a better way to build a table is to first define the columns, or **fields**, of data that the table will store. **Table Design View** provides the most options for defining fields.
3. **Click the View button on the Fields tab to switch to Design View, type Customers as the table name, then click OK**

   The table name changes from Table1 to Customers, and you are positioned in Table Design View, a window you use to name and define the fields of a table. Access created a field named ID with an AutoNumber data type. The **data type** is a significant characteristic of a field because it determines what type of data the field can store, such as text, dates, or numbers. See Table A-3 for more information about data types.
4. **Type CustID to rename ID to CustID, press the [↓] to move to the first blank Field Name cell, type FirstName, press [↓], type LastName, press [↓], type Phone, press [↓], type Birthday, then press [↓]**

   Be sure to separate the first and last names so that you can easily sort, find, and filter on either part of the name later. The Birthday field will only contain dates, so you should change its data type from Text (the default data type) to Date/Time.
5. **Click Text in the Birthday row, click the list arrow, then click Date/Time**

   With these five fields properly defined for the new Customers table, as shown in Figure A-6, you're ready to enter data. You switch back to Datasheet View to enter or edit data. **Datasheet View** is a spreadsheet-like view of the data in a table. A **datasheet** is a grid that displays fields as columns and records as rows. The new **field names** you just defined are listed at the top of each column.
6. **Click the View button to switch to Datasheet View, click Yes when prompted to save the table, press [Tab] to move to the FirstName field, type your first name, press [Tab] to move to the LastName field, type your last name, press [Tab] to move to the Phone field, type 111-222-3333, press [Tab], type 1/32/80, and press [Tab]**

   Because 1/32/80 is not a valid date, Access does not allow you to make that entry and displays an error message as shown in Figure A-7. This shows that setting the best data type for each field before entering data helps prevent data entry errors.
7. **Edit the Birthday entry for the first record to 1/31/80, press [Tab], enter two more sample records containing reasonable data, right-click the Customers table tab, then click Close to close the Customers table**

TROUBLE

Tab through the CustID field rather than typing a value. The CustID value automatically increments to the next number.

FIGURE A-5: Creating a database with a new table

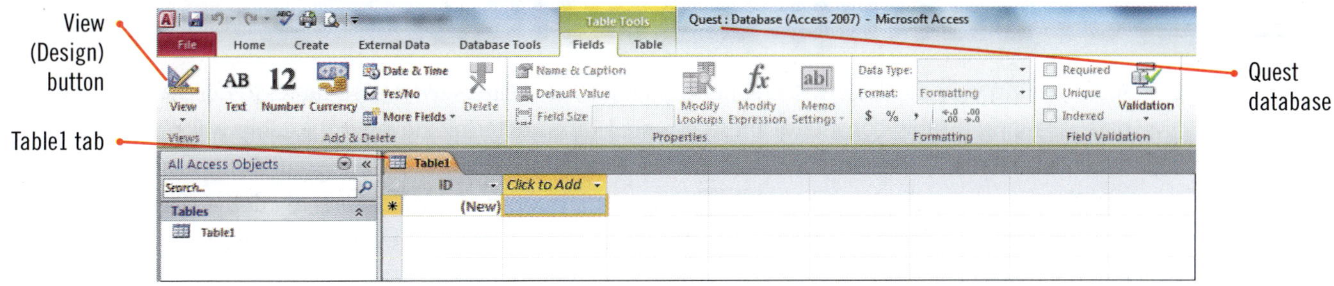

FIGURE A-6: Defining field names and data types for the Customers table in Table Design View

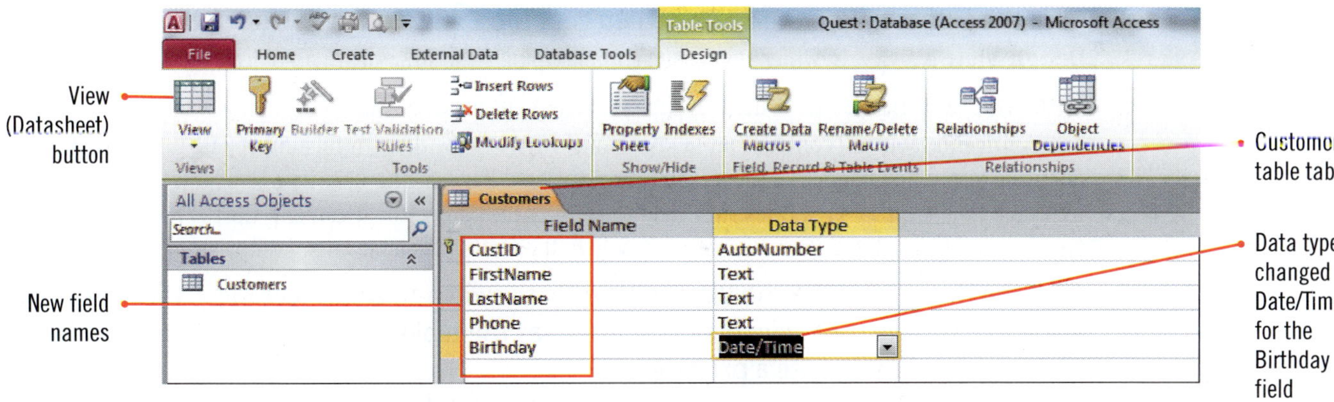

FIGURE A-7: Entering your first record in the Customers table

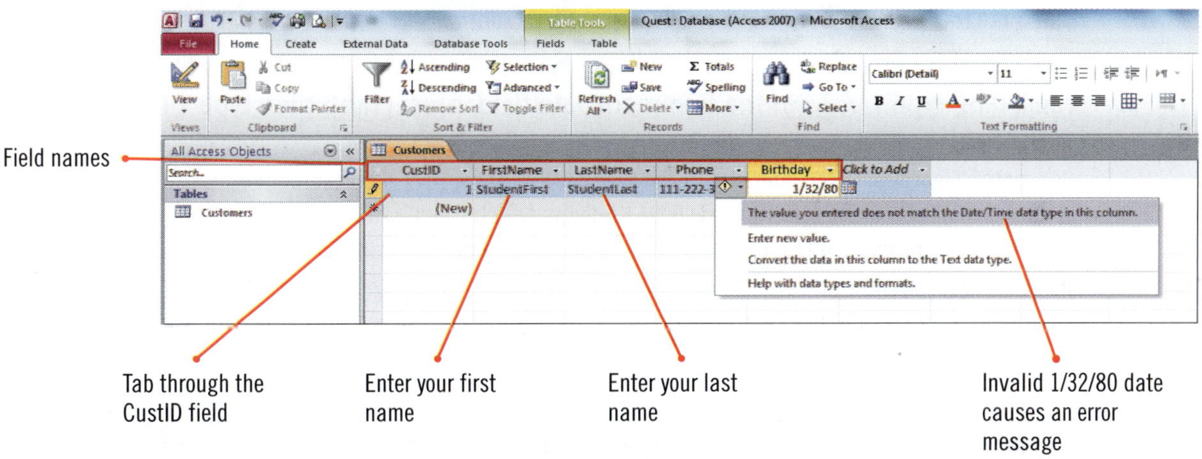

TABLE A-3: Data types

data type	description of data
Text	Text or numbers not used in calculations such as a name, zip code, or phone number
Memo	Lengthy text greater than 255 characters, such as comments or notes
Number	Numeric data that can be used in calculations, such as quantities
Date/Time	Dates and times
Currency	Monetary values
AutoNumber	Sequential integers controlled by Access
Yes/No	Only two values: Yes or No
Attachment	External files such as .jpg images, spreadsheets, and documents
Hyperlink	Web and e-mail addresses

UNIT A

Access 2010

Creating a Table

After creating your database and first table, you need to create new, related tables to build a relational database. Creating a table consists of these essential tasks: determining how the table will participate in the relational database, meaningful naming of each field in the table, selecting an appropriate data type for each field, and naming the table. Samantha Hooper asks you to create another table to store customer comments. The new table will be related to the Customers table so each customer's comments are linked to each customer.

STEPS

1. **Click the Create tab on the Ribbon, then click the Table Design button in the Tables group**
   Design View is a view in which you create and manipulate the structure of an object.
2. **Enter the field names and data types as shown in Figure A-8**
   The Comments table will contain four fields. CommentID is set with an AutoNumber data type so each record is automatically numbered by Access. The Comment field has a Memo data type so a large comment can be recorded. CommentDate is a Date/Time field to identify the date of the comment. CustID has a Number data type and will be used to link the Comments table to the Customers table later.
3. **Click the Home tab, click the View button to switch to Datasheet View, click Yes when prompted to save the table, type Comments as the table name, click OK, then click No when prompted to create a primary key**
   A **primary key field** contains unique data for each record. You'll identify a primary key field for the Comments table later. For now, you'll enter the first record in the Comments table in Datasheet View. A **record** is a row of data in a table. Refer to Table A-4 for a summary of important database terminology.
4. **Press [Tab] to move to the Comment field, type Interested in future tours to Australia, press [Tab], type 1/7/13 in the CommentDate field, press [Tab], then type 1 in the CustID field**
   As shown in Figure A-9, you entered 1 in the CustID field to connect this comment with the customer in the Customers table that has a CustID value of 1. Knowing which CustID value to enter for each comment is difficult. After you properly relate the tables (a task you have not yet performed), Access can make it easier to associate comments and customers.
5. **Right-click the Comments table tab, then click Close**

Creating a table in Datasheet View

In Access 2010, you can create a new table in Datasheet View using commands on the Fields tab of the Ribbon. You can also enter data in Datasheet View. Entering data in Datasheet View *before* finishing field design activities can introduce a wide variety of data entry errors, such as entering textual data in what should be defined as a Number or Date/Time field. If you design your tables using Table Design View, you avoid the temptation of entering data before you finish defining fields, which helps minimize many types of common data entry errors.

FIGURE A-8: Creating the Comments table

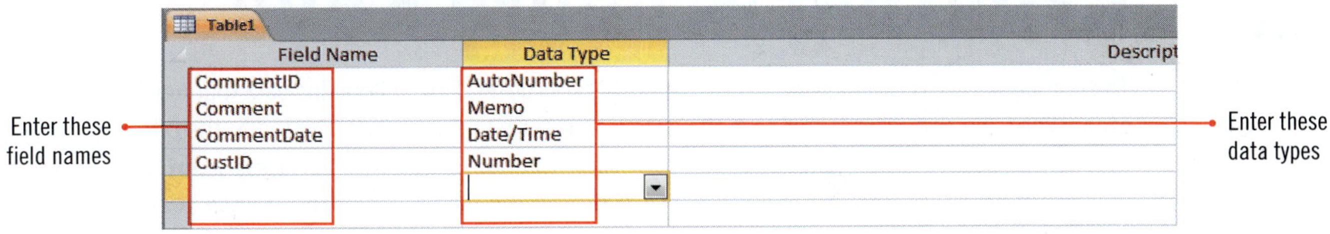

FIGURE A-9: Entering the first record in the Comments table

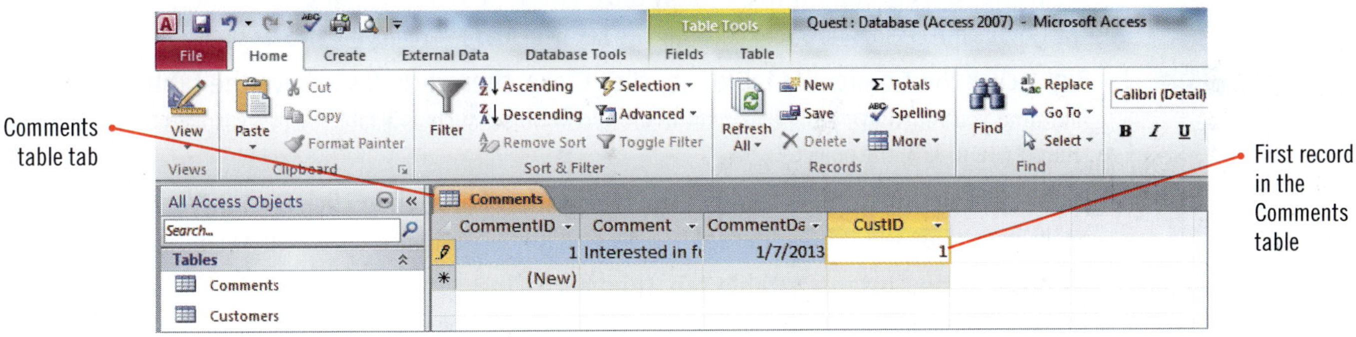

TABLE A-4: Important database terminology

term	description
Field	A specific piece or category of data such as a first name, last name, city, state, or phone number
Record	A group of related fields that describes a person, place, thing, or transaction such as a customer, location, product, or sale
Key field	A field that contains unique information for each record, such as a customer number for a customer
Table	A collection of records for a single subject such as Customers, Products, or Sales
Relational database	Multiple tables that are linked together to address a business process such as managing tours, sales, and customers at Quest Specialty Travel
Objects	The parts of an Access database that help you view, edit, manage, and analyze the data: **tables**, **queries**, **forms**, **reports**, **macros**, and **modules**

Creating Primary Keys

The primary key field of a table serves two important purposes. First, it contains data that uniquely identifies each record. No two records can have the exact same entry in the field designated as the primary key field. Secondly, the primary key field helps relate one table to another in a **one-to-many relationship**, where one record from one table is related to many records in the second table. For example, one record in the Customers table can be related to many records in the Comments table. (One customer can have many comments.) The primary key field is always on the "one" side of a one-to-many relationship between two tables. Samantha Hooper asks you to check that a primary key field has been appropriately identified for each table in the new Quest database.

STEPS

1. **Right-click the Comments table in the Navigation Pane, then click Design View**
   Table Design View for the Comments table opens. The field with the AutoNumber data type is generally the best candidate for the primary key field in a table because it automatically contains a unique number for each record.

TROUBLE
Make sure the Design tab is selected on the Ribbon.

2. **Click the CommentID field if it is not already selected, then click the Primary Key button in the Tools group on the Design tab**
   The CommentID field is now set as the primary key field for the Comments table as shown in Figure A-10.

QUICK TIP
You can also click the Save button on the Quick Access toolbar to save a table.

3. **Right-click the Comments table tab, click Close, then click Yes to save the table**
   Any time you must save design changes to an Access object such as a table, Access displays a dialog box to remind you to save the object.
4. **Right-click the Customers table in the Navigation Pane, then click Design View**
   Access has already set CustID as the primary key field for the Customers table as shown in Figure A-11.
5. **Right-click the Customers table tab, then click Close**
   You were not prompted to save the Customers table because you made no design changes. Now that you're sure that each table in the Quest database has an appropriate primary key field, you're ready to link the tables. The primary key field plays a critical role in this relationship.

FIGURE A-10: Creating a primary key field for the Comments table

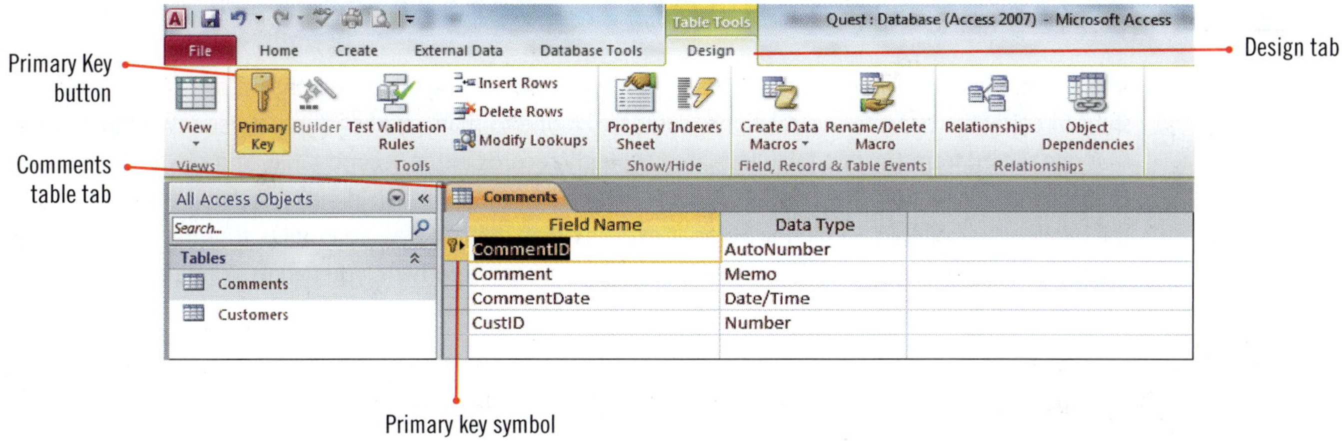

FIGURE A-11: Confirming the primary key field for the Customers table

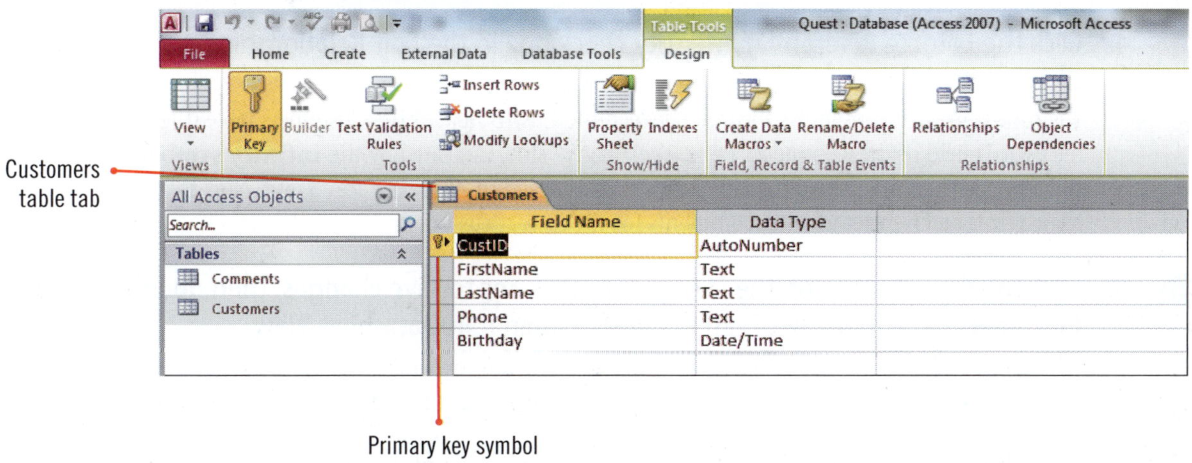

Learning about field properties

Properties are the characteristics that define the field. Two properties are required for every field: Field Name and Data Type. Many other properties, such as Field Size, Format, Caption, and Default Value, are defined in the Field Properties pane in the lower half of a table's Design View. As you add more property entries, you are generally restricting the amount or type of data that can be entered in the field, which increases data entry accuracy. For example, you might change the Field Size property for a State field to 2 to eliminate an incorrect entry such as FLL. Field properties change depending on the data type of the selected field. For example, date fields do not have a Field Size property because Access controls the size of fields with a Date/Time data type.

UNIT
A
Access 2010

Relating Two Tables

After you create tables and set primary key fields, you must link the tables together in one-to-many relationships to enjoy the benefits of a relational database. A one-to-many relationship between two tables means that one record from the first table is related to many records in the second table. You use a common field to make this connection. The common field is always the primary key field in the table on the "one" side of the relationship. Samantha Hooper explains that she has new comments to enter into the Quest database. To easily identify which customer is related to each comment, you define a one-to-many relationship between the Customers and Comments tables.

STEPS

1. **Click the Database Tools tab on the Ribbon, then click the Relationships button**

> **TROUBLE**
> If the Show Table dialog box doesn't appear, click the Show Table button on the Design tab.

2. **In the Show Table dialog box, double-click Customers, double-click Comments, then click Close**

   Each table is represented by a small **field list** window that displays the table's field names. A key symbol identifies the primary key field in each table. To relate the two tables in a one-to-many relationship, you connect them using the common field, which is always the primary key field on the "one" side of the relationship.

> **QUICK TIP**
> Drag a table's title bar to move the field list.

3. **Drag CustID in the Customers field list to the CustID field in the Comments field list**

   The Edit Relationships dialog box opens as shown in Figure A-12. **Referential integrity**, a set of Access rules that governs data entry, helps ensure data accuracy.

> **TROUBLE**
> If you need to delete an incorrect relationship, right-click a relationship line, then click Delete.

4. **Click the Enforce Referential Integrity check box in the Edit Relationships dialog box, then click Create**

   The **one-to-many line** shows the link between the CustID field of the Customers table (the "one" side) and the CustID field of the Comments table (the "many" side, indicated by the **infinity symbol**), as shown in Figure A-13. The linking field on the "many" side is called the **foreign key field**. Now that these tables are related, it is much easier to enter comments for the correct customer.

> **QUICK TIP**
> To print the Relationships window, click the Relationship Report button on the Design tab, then click Print.

5. **Click the Close button on the Design tab, click Yes to save changes, then double-click the Customers table in the Navigation Pane to open it in Datasheet View**

   When you relate two tables in a one-to-many relationship, expand buttons ⊞ appear to the left of each record in the table on the "one" side of the relationship. In this case, this is the Customers table.

6. **Click the expand button ⊞ to the left of the first record, then drag the ✛ pointer to widen the Comment field**

   A **subdatasheet** shows the related comment records for each customer. In other words, the subdatasheet shows the records on the "many" side of a one-to-many relationship. The expand button ⊞ also changed to the collapse button ⊟ for the first customer. Widening the Comment field allows you to see the entire entry in the Comments subdatasheet. Now the task of entering comments for the right customer is much more straightforward.

7. **Enter two more comments as shown in Figure A-14**

   Interestingly, the CustID field in the Comments table (the foreign key field) is not displayed in the subdatasheet. Behind the scenes, Access is entering the correct CustID value in the Comments table, which is the glue that ties each comment to the right customer.

8. **Close the Customers table, then click Yes if prompted to save changes**

FIGURE A-12: Edit Relationships dialog box

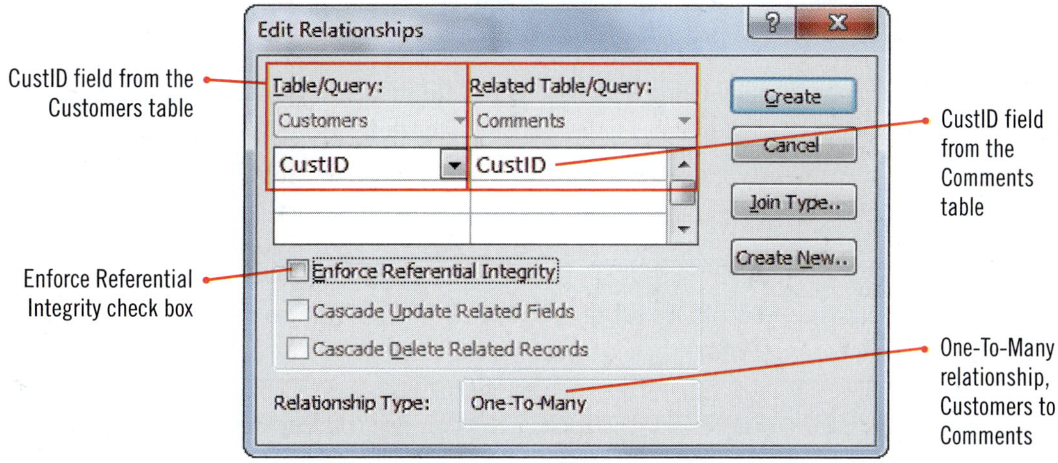

FIGURE A-13: Linking the Customers and Comments tables

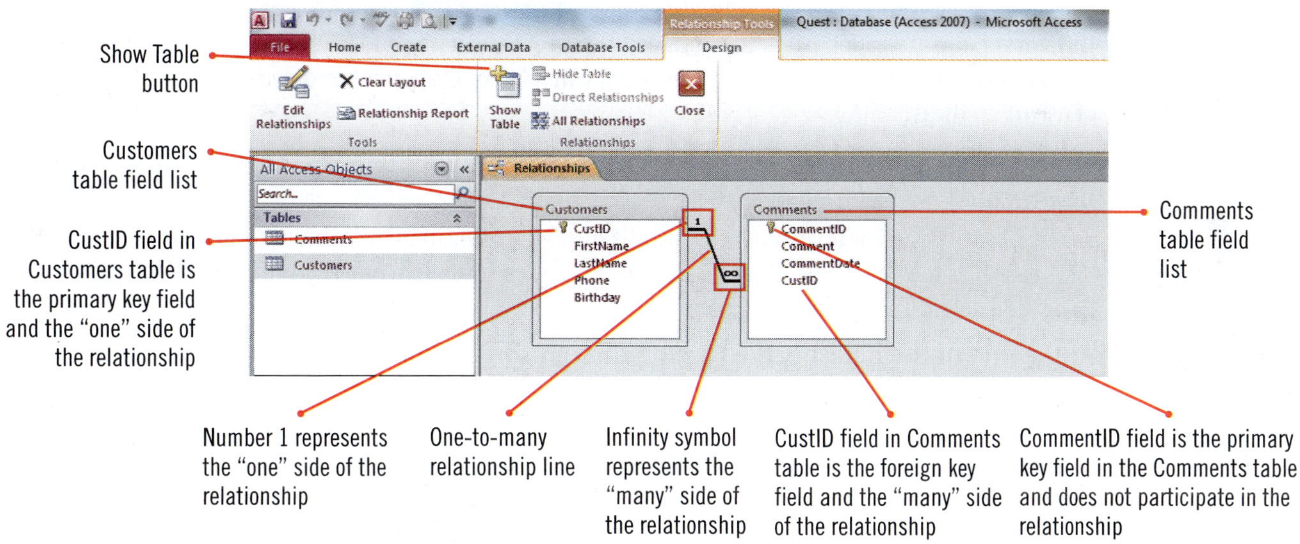

FIGURE A-14: Entering comments using the subdatasheet

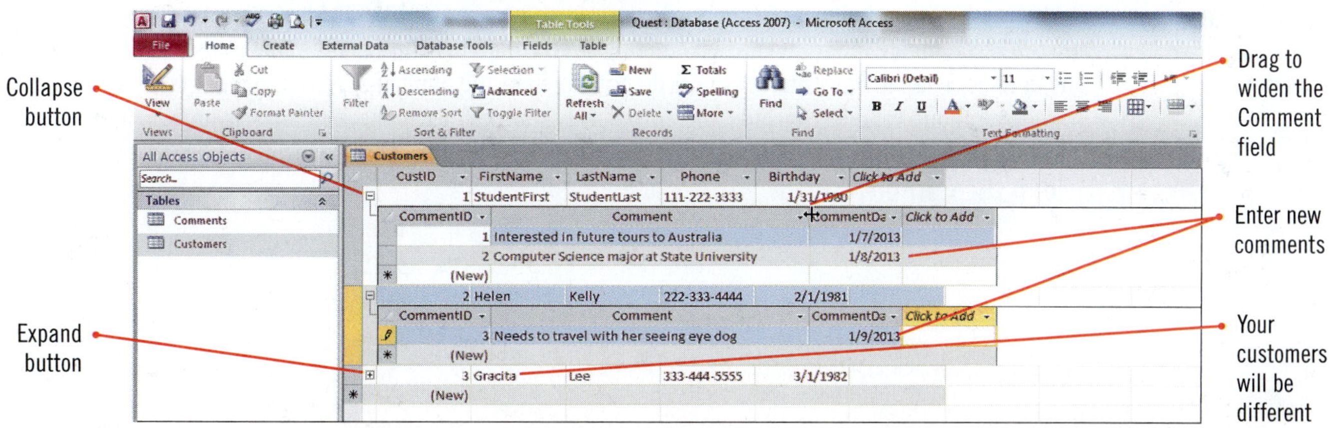

Enforcing referential integrity

Referential integrity is a set of rules that helps reduce invalid entries and orphan records. An **orphan record** is a record in the "many" table that doesn't have a matching entry in the linking field of the "one" table. With referential integrity enforced on a one-to-many relationship, you cannot enter a value in a foreign key field of the "many" table that does not have a match in the linking field of the "one" table. Referential integrity also prevents you from deleting a record in the "one" table if a matching entry exists in the foreign key field of the "many" table. You should enforce referential integrity on all one-to-many relationships if possible. If you are working with a database that already contains orphan records, you cannot enforce referential integrity on that relationship.

UNIT
A
Access 2010

Entering Data

Your skill in navigating and entering data is a key to your success with a relational database. You use either mouse or keystroke techniques to navigate the data in the table's datasheet. Even though you have already successfully entered some data, Samantha Hooper asks you to master this essential skill by entering several more customers in the Quest database.

STEPS

1. **Double-click the Customers table in the Navigation Pane to open it, press [Tab] three times, then press [Enter] three times**

   The Customers table reopens. The Comments subdatasheets are collapsed. Both the [Tab] and [Enter] keys move the focus to the next field. The **focus** refers to which data you would edit if you started typing. The record that has the focus is highlighted in light blue. The field name that has the focus is highlighted in light orange. When you navigate to the last field of the record, pressing [Tab] or [Enter] advances the focus to the first field of the next record. You can also use the Next record and Previous record **navigation buttons** on the navigation bar in the lower-left corner of the datasheet to navigate the records. The **Current record** text box on the navigation bar tells you the number of the current record as well as the total number of records in the datasheet.

2. **Click the FirstName field of the fourth record to position the insertion point to enter a new record**

   You can also use the New (blank) record button on the navigation bar to move to a new record. You enter new records at the end of the datasheet. You learn how to sort and reorder records later. A complete list of navigation keystrokes is shown in Table A-5.

QUICK TIP

Access databases are multiuser with one important limitation: two users cannot edit the same *record* at the same time. In that case, a message explains that the second user must wait until the first user moves to a different record.

3. **At the end of the datasheet, enter the three records shown in Figure A-15**

   The **edit record symbol** shown in Figure A-16 appears to the left of the record you are currently editing. When you move to a different record, Access saves the data. Therefore, Access never prompts you to save *data* because it performs that task automatically. Saving data automatically allows Access databases to be **multiuser** databases, which means that more than one person can enter and edit data in the same database at the same time.

   Your CustID values might differ from those in Figure A-16. Because the CustID field is an **AutoNumber** field, Access automatically enters the next consecutive number into the field as it creates the record. If you delete a record or are interrupted when entering a record, Access discards the value in the AutoNumber field and does not reuse it. AutoNumber values do not represent the number of records in your table. Instead, they provide a unique value per record, similar to check numbers. Each check number is unique, and does not represent the number of checks you have written.

Changing from Navigation mode to Edit mode

If you navigate to another area of the datasheet by clicking with the mouse pointer instead of pressing [Tab] or [Enter], you change from **Navigation mode** to Edit mode. In **Edit mode**, Access assumes that you are trying to make changes to the current field value, so keystrokes such as [Ctrl][End], [Ctrl][Home], [←], and [→] move the insertion point within the field. To return to Navigation mode, press [Tab] or [Enter] (thus moving the focus to the next field), or press [↑] or [↓] (thus moving the focus to a different record).

FIGURE A-15: Three records to add to the Customers table

CustID	FirstName	LastName	Phone	Birthday
[Tab]	Nicolas	McNeil	444-555-6666	4/1/1983
[Tab]	Toby	Stanton	555-666-7777	5/1/1984
[Tab]	Renada	Champ	666-777-8888	6/1/1985

FIGURE A-16: New records in the Customers table

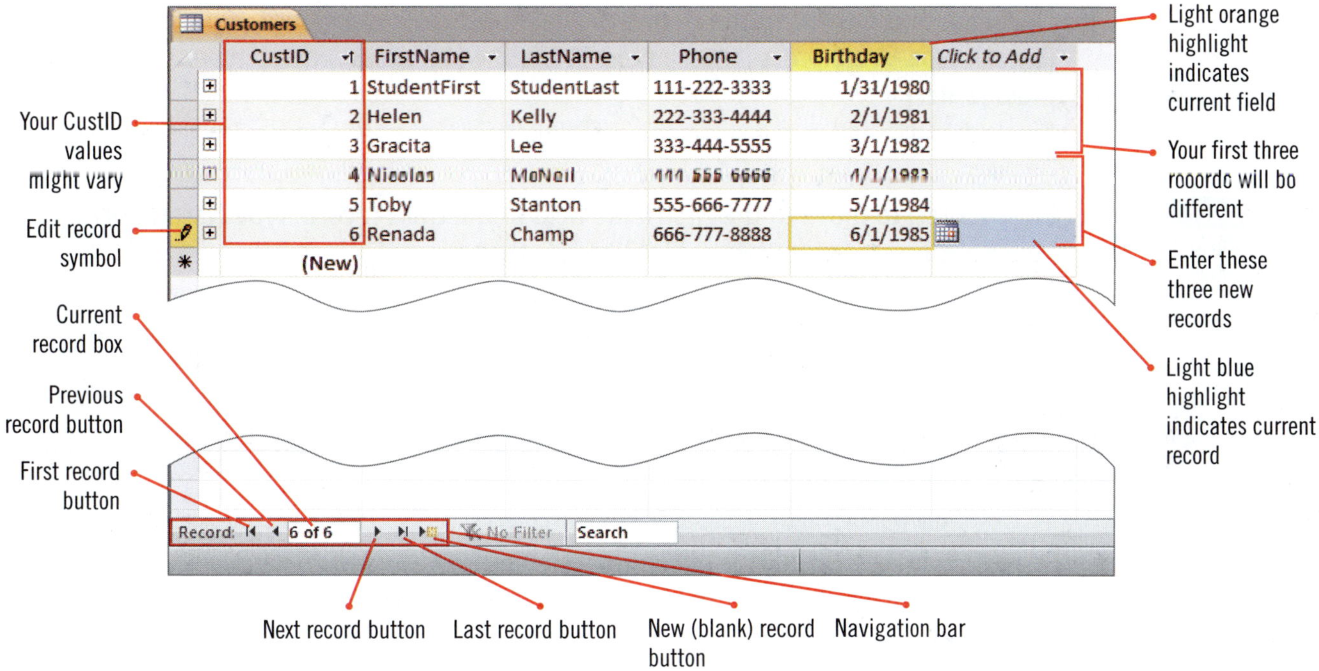

TABLE A-5: Navigation mode keyboard shortcuts

shortcut key	moves to the
[Tab], [Enter], or [→]	Next field of the current record
[Shift][Tab] or [←]	Previous field of the current record
[Home]	First field of the current record
[End]	Last field of the current record
[Ctrl][Home] or [F5]	First field of the first record
[Ctrl][End]	Last field of the last record
[↑]	Current field of the previous record
[↓]	Current field of the next record

Windows Live

Using **cloud computing** (work done in a virtual environment), you can take advantage of Windows Live SkyDrive, a free service from Microsoft. Using Windows Live SkyDrive, you and your colleagues can store files in a "cloud" and retrieve them anytime you are connected to the Internet. That way, you can access files containing data whenever you need them. To use Windows Live SkyDrive, you need a free Windows Live ID, which you obtain at the Windows Live Web site. You can find more information and projects in the "Working with Windows Live and Microsoft Office Web Apps" appendix.

UNIT
A
Access 2010

Editing Data

Updating information in a database is another critical data management task. To change the contents of an existing record, navigate to the field you want to change and type the new information. You can delete unwanted data by clicking the field and using [Backspace] or [Delete] to delete text to the left or right of the insertion point. Other data entry keystrokes are summarized in Table A-6. Samantha Hooper asks you to correct two records in the Customers table.

STEPS

1. **Double-click the name in the FirstName field of the second record, type Jesse, press [Enter], type Siren, press [Enter], type 111-222-4444, press [Enter], type 2/15/81, then press [Enter]**

   You changed the name, telephone number, and birthdate of the second customer. You'll also change the third customer.

2. **Press [Enter] to move to the FirstName field of the third record, type Naresh, press [Enter], type Kast, press [Enter], type 111-222-5555, then press [Esc]**

   Pressing [Esc] once removes the current field's editing changes, so the Phone value changes back to the previous entry. Pressing [Esc] twice removes all changes to the current record. When you move to another record, Access saves your edits, so you can no longer use [Esc] to remove editing changes to the current record. You can, however, click the Undo button on the Quick Access toolbar to undo changes to a previous record.

QUICK TIP
The ScreenTip for the Undo button displays the action you can undo.

3. **Retype 111-222-5555, press [Enter], click the Calendar icon, then click March 15, 1982 as shown in Figure A-17**

   When you are working in the Birthday field, which has a Date/Time data type, you can enter a date from the keyboard or use the **Calendar Picker**, a pop-up calendar to find and select a date.

4. **Click the record selector for the last record (the one for Renada Champ), click the Delete button in the Records group on the Home tab, then click Yes**

   A message warns that you cannot undo a record deletion. The Undo button is dimmed, indicating that you cannot use it. The Customers table now has five records, as shown in Figure A-18. Keep in mind that your CustID values might differ from those in the figure because they are controlled by Access.

5. **Click the File tab, click Print, click Print Preview to review the printout of the Customers table before printing, click the Print button, click OK, then click the Close Print Preview button**

6. **Click the File tab, click Exit to close the Quest.accdb database and Access 2010, then click Yes if prompted to save design changes to the Customers table**

Resizing and moving datasheet columns

You can resize the width of a field in a datasheet by dragging the **column separator**, the thin line that separates the field names to the left or right. The pointer changes to ↔ as you make the field wider or narrower. Release the mouse button when you have resized the field. To adjust the column width to accommodate the widest entry in the field, double-click the column separator. To move a column, click the field name to select the entire column, then drag the field name left or right.

FIGURE A-17: Editing customer records

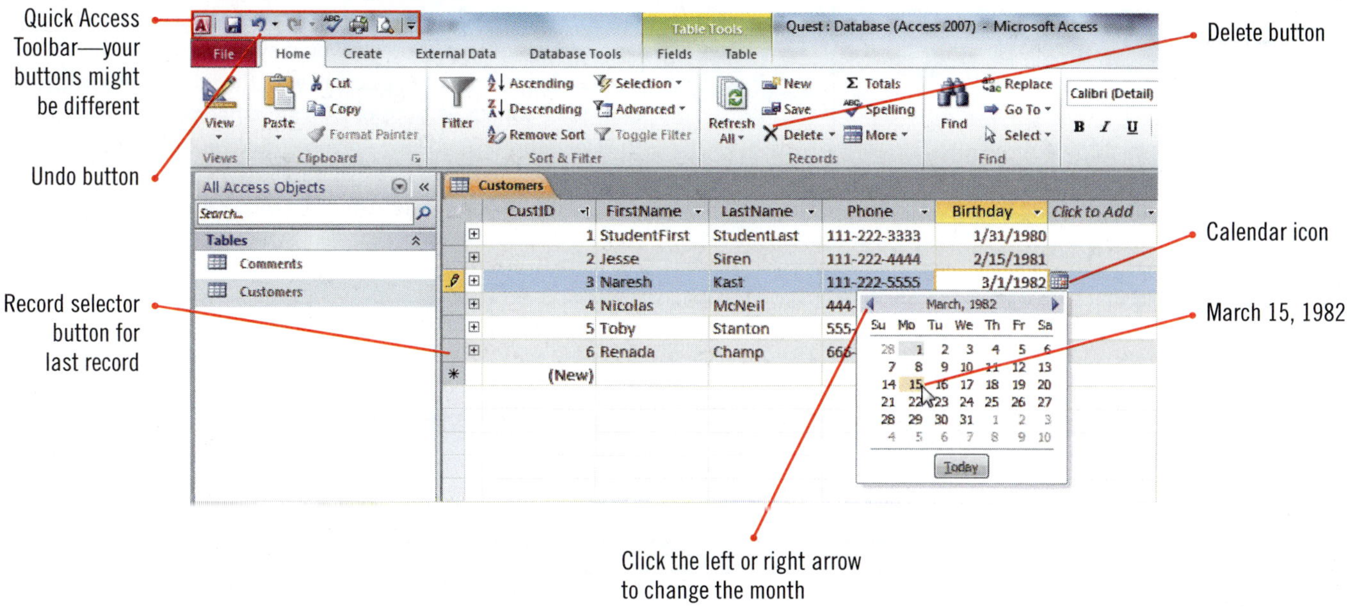

FIGURE A-18: Final Customers datasheet

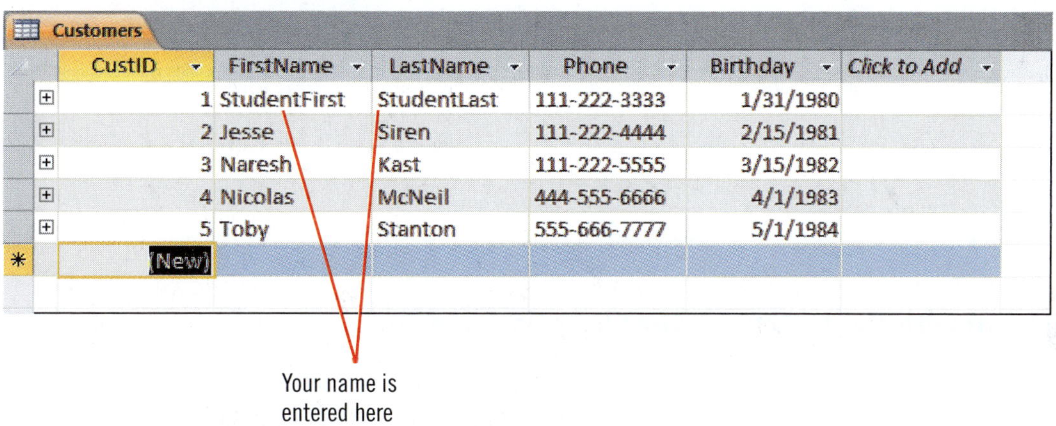

TABLE A-6: Edit mode keyboard shortcuts

editing keystroke	action
[Backspace]	Deletes one character to the left of the insertion point
[Delete]	Deletes one character to the right of the insertion point
[F2]	Switches between Edit and Navigation mode
[Esc]	Undoes the change to the current field
[Esc][Esc]	Undoes all changes to the current record
[F7]	Starts the spell-check feature
[Ctrl][']	Inserts the value from the same field in the previous record into the current field
[Ctrl][;]	Inserts the current date in a Date field

Practice

Concepts Review

For current SAM information, including versions and content details, visit SAM Central (http://www.cengage.com/samcentral). If you have a SAM user profile, you may have access to hands-on instruction, practice, and assessment of the skills covered in this unit. Since various versions of SAM are supported throughout the life of this text, check with your instructor for the correct instructions and URL/Web site for accessing assignments.

Label each element of the Access window shown in Figure A-19.

FIGURE A-19

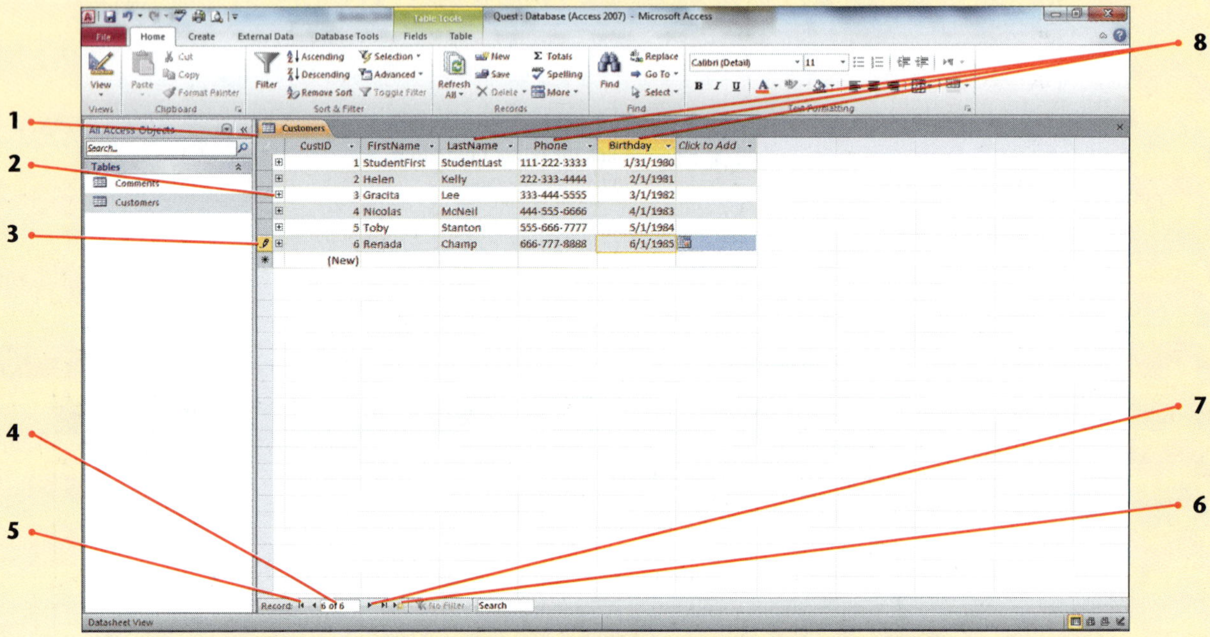

Match each term with the statement that best describes it.

9. Table
10. Query
11. Field
12. Record
13. Datasheet
14. Form
15. Report

a. A subset of data from one or more tables
b. A collection of records for a single subject, such as all the customer records
c. A professional printout of database information
d. A spreadsheet-like grid that displays fields as columns and records as rows
e. A group of related fields for one item, such as all of the information for one customer
f. A category of information in a table, such as a company name, city, or state
g. An easy-to-use data entry screen

Select the best answer from the list of choices.

16. Which of the following is *not* a typical benefit of relational databases?

a. More accurate data
b. Faster information retrieval
c. More common than spreadsheets
d. Minimized duplicate data entry

17. Which of the following is *not* an advantage of managing data with relational database software such as Access versus spreadsheet software such as Excel?

a. Allows multiple users to enter data simultaneously
b. Provides data entry forms
c. Reduces duplicate data entry
d. Uses a single table to store all data

18. The object that creates a professional printout of data that includes headers, footers, and graphics is the:

a. Query.
b. Report.
c. Table.
d. Form.

19. The object that contains all of the database data is the:

a. Report.
b. Page.
c. Form.
d. Table.

20. When you create a new database, which object is created first?

a. Query
b. Module
c. Table
d. Form

Skills Review

1. Understand relational databases.

a. Identify five advantages of managing database information in Access versus using a spreadsheet.
b. Create a sentence to explain how the terms *field, record, table,* and *relational database* relate to one another.

2. Explore a database.

a. Start Access.
b. Open the RealEstate-A.accdb database from the drive and folder where you store your Data Files. Enable content if a Security Warning message appears.
c. Open each of the three tables to study the data they contain. On a sheet of paper, complete Table A-7.
d. Double-click the ListingsByRealtor query in the Navigation Pane to open it. Change any occurrence of Gordon Matusek to your name. Move to another record to save your changes.
e. Double-click the RealtorsMainForm in the Navigation Pane to open it. Use the navigation buttons to navigate through the 11 realtors to observe each realtor's listings.
f. Double-click the RealtorListingReport in the Navigation Pane to open it. Scroll through the report to make sure your name is positioned correctly. The report is currently sorted in ascending order by realtor first names.
g. Close the RealEstate-A database, and then close Access 2010.

TABLE A-7

table name	number of records	number of fields

3. Create a database.

a. Start Access, use the Browse folder button to navigate to the drive and folder where you store your Data Files, type **RealEstateMarketing** as the File Name, click OK, and then click Create to create a new database named RealEstateMarketing.accdb.

Access 2010

Skills Review (continued)

b. Switch to Table Design View, name the table **Prospects**, then enter the following fields and data types:

field name	data type
ProspectID	**AutoNumber**
ProspectFirst	**Text**
ProspectLast	**Text**
Phone	**Text**
Email	**Hyperlink**
Street	**Text**
City	**Text**
State	**Text**
Zip	**Text**

c. Save the table, switch to Datasheet View, and enter two records using your name in the first record and your professor's name in the second. Tab through the ProspectID field, an AutoNumber field.

d. Enter **OK** (Oklahoma) as the value in the State field for both records. Use school or fictitious (rather than personal) data for all other field data, and be sure to fill out each record completely.

e. Widen each column in the Prospects table so that all data is visible, then save and close the Prospects table.

4. Create a table.

a. Click the Create tab on the Ribbon, click Table Design, then create a new table with the following two fields and data types:

field name	data type
StateAbbrev	**Text**
StateName	**Text**

b. Save the table with the name **States**. Click No when asked if you want Access to create the primary key field.

5. Create primary keys.

a. In Table Design View of the States table, set the StateAbbrev as the primary key field.

b. Save the States table and open it in Datasheet View.

c. Enter one state record, using **OK** for the StateAbbrev value and **Oklahoma** for the StateName value to match the State value of OK that you entered for both records in the Prospects table.

d. Close the States table.

6. Relate two tables.

a. From the Database Tools tab, open the Relationships window.

b. Add the States then the Prospects table to the Relationships window.

c. Drag the bottom edge of the Prospects table to expand the field list to display all of the fields.

d. Drag the StateAbbrev field from the States table to the State field of the Prospects table.

e. In the Edit Relationships dialog box, click the Enforce Referential Integrity check box, then click Create. Your Relationships window should look similar to Figure A-20. If you connect the wrong fields by mistake, right-click the line connecting the two fields, click Delete, then try again.

f. Close the Relationships window, and save changes when prompted.

FIGURE A-20

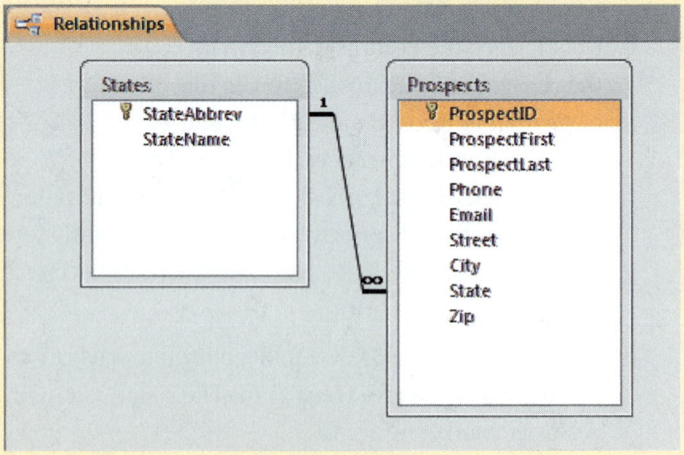

Skills Review (continued)

7. Enter data.

a. Open the States table and enter the following records:

StateAbbrev field	StateName field	StateAbbrev field	StateName field
CO	Colorado	NE	Nebraska
IA	Iowa	TX	Texas
KS	Kansas	WI	Wisconsin
MO	Missouri		

b. Add a few more state records using the correct two-character abbreviation for the state and the properly spelled state name.

c. Close and reopen the States table. Notice that Access sorts the records by the values in the primary key field, the StateAbbrev field.

8. Edit data.

a. Click the Expand button for the OK record to see the two related records from the Prospects table.

b. Enter two more prospects in the OK subdatasheet using any fictitious but realistic data as shown in Figure A-21. Notice that you are not required to enter a value for the State field, the foreign key field in the subdatasheet.

c. If required by your instructor, print the States datasheet and the Prospects datasheet.

d. Click the File tab, then click Exit to close all open objects as well as the RealEstateMarketing.accdb database and Access 2010. If prompted to save any design changes, click Yes.

FIGURE A-21

States

StateAbbrev	StateName	Click to Add
CO	Colorado	
IA	Iowa	
IL	Illinois	
IN	Indiana	
KS	Kansas	
MN	Minnesota	
MO	Missouri	
NE	Nebraska	
OH	Ohio	
OK	Oklahoma	

ProspectID	ProspectFirst	ProspectLast	Phone	Email	Street	City	Zip
1	StudentFirst	StudentLast	111-222-3333	student@state.edu	111 Elm	Fontanelle	50846
2	ProfessorFirst	ProfessorLast	222-333-4444	professor@state.edu	222 Oak	Bridgewater	50837
3	Samuel	Mitchell	333-444-5555	samuel@state.edu	333 Birch	Adair	50911
4	Andre	Andrews	444-555-6666	andre@state.edu	444 Cedar	Casey	50922
(New)							

StateAbbrev	StateName
TX	Texas
WI	Wisconsin

Independent Challenge 1

Review the following twelve examples of database tables:

- Telephone directory
- College course offerings
- Restaurant menu
- Cookbook
- Movie listing
- Islands of the Caribbean
- Encyclopedia
- Shopping catalog
- International product inventory
- Party guest list
- Members of the U.S. House of Representatives
- Ancient wonders of the world

In a Word document, complete the following tasks.

a. For each example, build a Word table with four to five columns. In the first row, identify four to five field names that you would expect to find in the table.

b. In the second and third rows of each table, enter two possible records. The first table, Telephone Directory, is completed in Figure A-22 as an example to follow.

FIGURE A-22

Table: Telephone Directory

FirstName	LastName	Street	Zip	Phone
Marco	Lopez	100 Main Street	88715	555-612-3312
Christopher	Stafford	253 Maple Lane	77824	555-612-1179

Access 2010

Independent Challenge 2

You are working with several civic groups to coordinate a community-wide cleanup effort. You have started a database called Recycle-A, which tracks the different clubs, their trash deposits, and the trash collection centers that are participating.

a. Start Access, then open the Recycle-A.accdb database from the drive and folder where you store your Data Files. Enable content if prompted.

b. Open each table's datasheet to study the number of fields and records per table. Notice that there are no expand buttons to the left of any records because relationships have not yet been established between these tables.

c. In a Word document, recreate and complete the table shown in Table A-8.

TABLE A-8

table name	number of fields	number of records

d. Close all table datasheets, then open the Relationships window and create the one-to-many relationships shown in Figure A-23. Click the Show Table button to add the field lists for each table to the Relationships window, and drag the title bars of the field lists to position them as shown in Figure A-23.

e. Be sure to enforce referential integrity on all relationships. If you create an incorrect relationship, right-click the line linking the fields, click Delete, and try again. Your final Relationships window should look like Figure A-23.

f. If required by your instructor, click the Relationship Report button on the Design tab, then click Print to print a copy of the Relationships for Recycle-A report. To close the report, right-click the Relationships for Recycle-A tab and click Close. Click No when prompted to save changes to the report.

FIGURE A-23

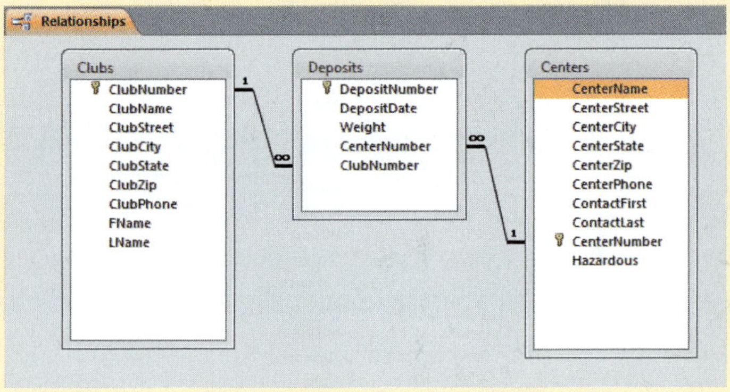

g. Save your changes to the Relationships window, if necessary, close the Recycle-A.accdb database, then exit Access 2010.

Independent Challenge 3

This Independent Challenge requires an Internet connection.

If you have a SAM 2010 user profile, an autogradable SAM version of this assignment may be available at http://www.cengage.com/sam2010. Check with your instructor to confirm that this assignment is available in SAM. To use the SAM version of this assignment, log into the SAM 2010 Web site and download the instruction and start files.

You are working for an advertising agency that provides advertising media for small and large businesses in the midwestern United States. You have started a database called BusinessContacts-A, which tracks your company's customers.

a. Start Access and open the BusinessContacts-A.accdb database from the drive and folder where you store your Data Files. Enable content if prompted.

b. Add a new record to the Customers table, using your own first and last names, $7,788.99 in the YTDSales field, and any reasonable entries for the rest of the fields.

c. Edit the Sprint Systems record (the first record). The Company name should be Embarq Corporation, and the Street value should be 2244 College St.

d. Delete the record for St Luke's Hospital (record 20), then close the Customers table.

e. Create a new table with two fields, State2 and StateName. Assign both fields a Text data type. The State2 field will contain the two-letter abbreviation for state names. The StateName field will contain the full state name.

f. Set the State2 field as the primary key field, then save the table as States.

Independent Challenge 3 (continued)

g. Enter at least three records into the States table, making sure that all of the states used in the Customers datasheet are entered in the States table. This includes *KS Kansas*, *MO Missouri*, and any other state you entered in Step b when you added a new record to the Customers table.

h. Close all open tables. Open the Relationships window, add both the States and Customers field lists to the window, then expand the size of the Customers field list so that all fields are visible.

i. Build a one-to-many relationship between the States and Customers tables by dragging the State2 field from the States table to the State field of the Customers table to create a one-to-many relationship between the two tables. Enforce referential integrity on the relationship. If you are unable to enforce referential integrity, it means that a value in the State field of the Customers table doesn't have a perfect match in the State2 field of the States table. Open both datasheets, making sure every state in the Customers table is also represented in the States table, close all datasheets, then reestablish the one-to-many relationship between the two tables with referential integrity.

j. Close the Relationships window and save your changes.

Advanced Challenge Exercise

- Use your favorite search engine to research the two-character abbreviations for the 13 provinces of Canada using the Web search criteria of **provinces of Canada postcodes**.
- Enter the 13 records into the States table, entering the two-character abbreviation in the State2 field and the province name in the StateName field. Note that all 13 entries are different from the 50 states in the United States. Close the States table.
- Right-click the States table in the Navigation Pane and click Rename. Enter **StatesProvinces** as the new table name.
- Reopen the Relationships window, click the Show Table button, double-click StatesProvinces, and click Close. The relationship between the StatesProvinces table and the Customers table has remained intact, but when you rename a table after establishing relationships, review the Relationships window to make sure all tables are visible.
- Click the Relationship Report button on the Design tab, then click Print to print the report.
- Right-click the Relationships for BusinessContacts-A tab, then click Close. Click Yes to save the report, then click OK to name the report Relationships for BusinessContacts-A.
- Close the Relationships window, saving changes as prompted.

k. Close the BusinessContacts-A.accdb database, and exit Access 2010.

Real Life Independent Challenge

This Independent Challenge requires an Internet connection.

Now that you've learned about Microsoft Access and relational databases, brainstorm how you might use an Access database in your daily life or career. Start by visiting the Microsoft Web site, and explore what's new about Access 2010.

a. Using your favorite search engine, look up the keywords *benefits of a relational database* or *benefits of Microsoft Access* to find articles that discuss the benefits of organizing data in a relational database.

b. Read several articles about the benefits of organizing data in a relational database such as Access, identifying three distinct benefits. Use a Word document to record those three benefits. Also, copy and paste the Web site address of the article you are referencing for each benefit you have identified.

c. In addition, as you read the articles that describe relational database benefits, list any terminology unfamiliar to you, identifying at least five new terms.

d. Using a search engine or a Web site that provides a computer glossary such as *www.whatis.com* or *www.webopedia.com*, look up the definition of the new terms, and enter both the term and the definition of the term in your document as well as the Web site address where your definition was found.

e. Finally, based on your research and growing understanding of Access 2010, list three ways you could use an Access database to organize, enhance, or support the activities and responsibilities of your daily life or career. Type your name at the top of the document, and submit it to your instructor as requested.

Visual Workshop

Open the Basketball-A.accdb database from the drive and folder where you store your Data Files, enable content if prompted, then open the Offense query datasheet, which lists offensive statistics by player by game. Modify any of the Kelsey Douglas records to contain your first and last names, then move to a new record, observing the power of a relational database to modify every occurrence of that name throughout the database. Close the Offense query, then open the Players table, shown in Figure A-24. Note that your name will be listed in alphabetical order based on the current sort field, PLast. Print the Players datasheet if requested by your instructor, then close the Players table, exit the Basketball-A.accdb database, and exit Access.

FIGURE A-24

Players

PFirst	PLast	Height	PlayerNo	GradYear	Position	HomeTown	HomeState	Lettered
Kristen	Czyenski	73	35	2015	F	Omaha	NE	☐
Denise	Franco	72	42	2016	F	Antigua	WI	☑
Sydney	Freesen	68	4	2014	G	Panora	IA	☐
Theresa	Grant	73	22	2013	F	McKinney	TX	☐
Megan	Hile	74	45	2015	F	Cumberland	IA	☑
Amy	Hodel	72	21	2014	F	Oakbrook	IL	☑
Ellyse	Howard	70	12	2016	G	Osseo	MN	☑
Jamie	Johnson	75	52	2016	F	Belleville	IL	☐
Sandy	Robins	65	23	2013	G	Anita	IA	☐
StudentFirst	StudentLast	69	5	2015	G	Linden	IA	☑
Ashley	Sydnes	75	30	2013	F	Salina	KS	☐
Morgan	Tyler	71	51	2014	G	Roseau	MN	☐
Abbey	Walker	76	32	2014	C	Fargo	ND	☐
*		0	0					

UNIT
B
Access 2010

Building and Using Queries

Files You Will Need:

QuestTravel-B.accdb
Recycle-B.accdb
Membership-B.accdb
Congress-B.accdb
Vet-B.accdb
Baseball-B.accdb

You build queries in an Access database to ask "questions" about data, such as which adventure tours are scheduled for July or what types of tours take place in Florida. Queries present the answer in a datasheet, which you can sort, filter, and format. Because queries are stored in the database, they can be used multiple times. Each time a query is opened, it displays a current view of the latest updates to the database. Samantha Hooper, tour developer for U.S. group travel at Quest Specialty Travel, has several questions about the customer and tour information in the Quest database. You'll develop queries to provide Samantha with up-to-date answers.

OBJECTIVES

Use the Query Wizard
Work with data in a query
Use Query Design View
Sort and find data
Filter data
Apply AND criteria
Apply OR criteria
Format a datasheet

UNIT
B
Access 2010

Using the Query Wizard

A **query** allows you to select a subset of fields and records from one or more tables and then present the selected data as a single datasheet. A major benefit of working with data through a query is that you can focus on only the information you need to answer your question, rather than navigating the fields and records from many large tables. You can enter, edit, and navigate data in a query datasheet just like a table datasheet. However, keep in mind that Access data is physically stored only in tables, even though you can view and edit it through other Access objects such as queries and forms. Because a query doesn't physically store the data, a query datasheet is sometimes called a **logical view** of the data. Technically, a query is a set of **SQL (Structured Query Language)** instructions, but because you can use Access query tools such as Query Design View, you are not required to know SQL to build or use Access queries. You use the Simple Query Wizard to build a query that displays a few fields from the Tours and Customers tables in one datasheet.

STEPS

1. **Start Access, open the QuestTravel-B.accdb database, enable content if prompted, then maximize the window**

   Access provides several tools to create a new query. One way is to use the **Simple Query Wizard**, which prompts you for information it needs to create a new query.

TROUBLE
If a Microsoft Access Security Notice dialog box opens, click the Open button.

2. **Click the Create tab on the Ribbon, click the Query Wizard button in the Queries group, then click OK to start the Simple Query Wizard**

   The first Simple Query Wizard dialog box opens, prompting you to select the fields you want to view in the new query.

3. **Click the Tables/Queries list arrow, click Table: Tours, double-click TourName, double-click City, double-click Category, then double-click Cost**

   So far, you've selected four fields from the Tours table to display basic tour information in this query. You also want to add the first and last name fields from the Customers table so you know which customers purchased each tour.

TROUBLE
Click the Remove Single Field button < if you need to remove a field from the Selected Fields list.

4. **Click the Tables/Queries list arrow, click Table: Customers, double-click FName, then double-click LName**

   You've selected four fields from the Tours table and two from the Customers table for your new query, as shown in Figure B-1.

5. **Click Next, click Next to select Detail, select Tours Query in the title text box, type TourCustomers as the name of the query, then click Finish**

   The TourCustomers datasheet opens, displaying four fields from the Tours table and two from the Customers table as shown in Figure B-2. The query can show which customers have purchased which tours because of the one-to-many table relationships established in the Relationships window.

FIGURE B-1: Selecting fields using the Simple Query Wizard

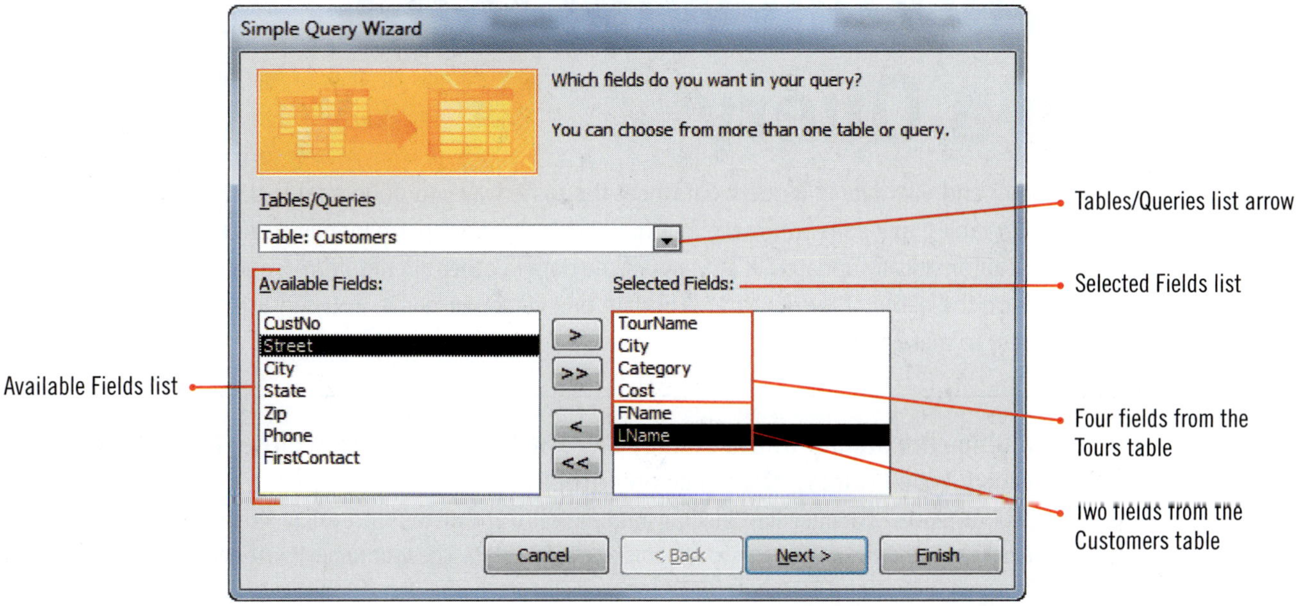

FIGURE B-2: TourCustomers datasheet

TourName	City	Category	Cost	FName	LName
Ames Ski Club	Breckenridge	Adventure	$850	Kristen	Collins
Stanley Bay Shelling	Captiva	Adventure	$750	Lisa	Wilson
Stanley Bay Shelling	Captiva	Adventure	$750	Kori	Yode
Yosemite National Park Great Cleanup	Sacramento	Service	$1,100	Kristen	Collins
American Heritage Tour	Philadelphia	Educational	$1,200	Kayla	Browning
American Heritage Tour	Philadelphia	Educational	$1,200	Mark	Custard
American Heritage Tour	Philadelphia	Educational	$1,200	Fritz	Garden
Bright Lights Expo	Branson	Site Seeing	$200	Kristen	Collins
Bright Lights Expo	Branson	Site Seeing	$200	Tom	Camel
Bright Lights Expo	Branson	Site Seeing	$200	Mark	Custard
Bright Lights Expo	Branson	Site Seeing	$200	Daniel	Cabriella
American Heritage Tour	Philadelphia	Educational	$1,200	Daniel	Cabriella
Red Reef Scuba	Islamadora	Adventure	$1,500	Gracita	Mayberry
Red Reef Scuba	Islamadora	Adventure	$1,500	Jacob	Alman
Red Reef Scuba	Islamadora	Adventure	$1,500	Julia	Bouchart
Bright Lights Expo	Branson	Site Seeing	$200	Samantha	Braven
Red Reef Scuba	Islamadora	Adventure	$1,500	Nancy	Diverman
Ames Ski Club	Breckenridge	Adventure	$850	Naresh	Hubert
Ames Ski Club	Breckenridge	Adventure	$850	Toby	Lang
Ames Ski Club	Breckenridge	Adventure	$850	Douglas	Margolis
Ames Ski Club	Breckenridge	Adventure	$850	Jenny	Nelson
Ames Ski Club	Breckenridge	Adventure	$850	Sharol	Olingback
Boy Scout Troop 274	Vail	Adventure	$1,900	Brad	Eahlie
Bridgewater Jaycees	Aspen	Adventure	$1,200	Nancy	Diverman
Bridgewater Jaycees	Aspen	Adventure	$1,200	Kathryn	Dotey

Access 2010

UNIT
B
Access 2010

Working with Data in a Query

You enter and edit data in a query datasheet the same way you do in a table datasheet. Because all data is stored in tables, any edits you make in a query datasheet are permanently stored in the underlying tables, and are automatically updated in all views of the data in other queries, forms, and reports. You want to change the name of two tours and update one customer name. You can use the TourCustomers query datasheet to make these edits.

STEPS

1. **Double-click Stanley in the Stanley Bay Shelling tour name in either the second or third record, type Princess, then click any other record**

   All occurrences of Stanley Bay Shelling automatically update to Princess Bay Shelling because this tour name value is stored only once in the Tours table (see Figure B-3). The tour name is selected from the Tours table and displayed in the TourCustomers query for each customer who purchased this tour.

2. **Double-click Cabriella in the LName field, type Dodds, then click any other record**

   All occurrences of Cabriella automatically update to Dodds because this last name value is stored only once in the Customers table. This name is selected from the Customers table and displayed in the TourCustomers query for each tour this customer purchased.

3. **Click the record selector button to the left of the first record, click the Home tab, click the Delete button in the Records group, then click Yes**

   You can delete records from a query datasheet the same way you delete them from a table datasheet. Notice that the navigation bar now indicates you have 79 records in the datasheet as shown in Figure B-4.

4. **Right-click the TourCustomers query tab, then click Close**

FIGURE B-3: Working with data in a query datasheet

TourName	City	Category	Cost	FName	LName
Ames Ski Club	Breckenridge	Adventure	$850	Kristen	Collins
Princess Bay Shelling	Captiva	Adventure	$750	Lisa	Wilson
Princess Bay Shelling	Captiva	Adventure	$750	Kori	Yode
Yosemite National Park Great Cleanu	Sacramento	Service	$1,100	Kristen	Collins
American Heritage Tour	Philadelphia	Educational	$1,200	Kayla	Browning
American Heritage Tour	Philadelphia	Educational	$1,200	Mark	Custard
American Heritage Tour	Philadelphia	Educational	$1,200	Fritz	Garden
Bright Lights Expo	Branson	Site Seeing	$200	Kristen	Collins
Bright Lights Expo	Branson	Site Seeing	$200	Tom	Camel
Bright Lights Expo	Branson	Site Seeing	$200	Mark	Custard
Bright Lights Expo	Branson	Site Seeing	$200	Daniel	Cabriella
American Heritage Tour	Philadelphia	Educational	$1,200	Daniel	Cabriella
Red Reef Scuba	Islamadora	Adventure	$1,500	Gracita	Mayberry

FIGURE B-4: Final TourCustomers datasheet

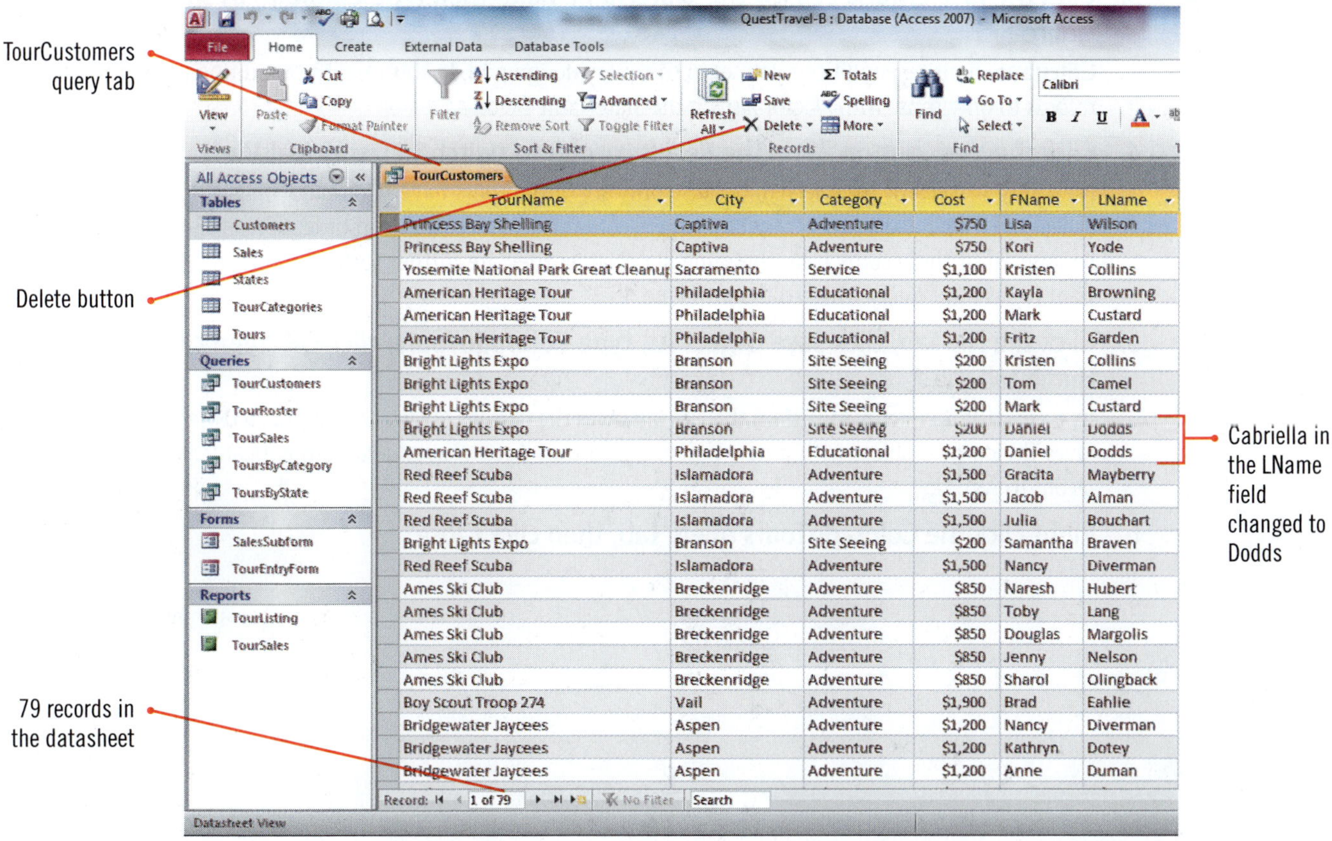

TourName	City	Category	Cost	FName	LName
Princess Bay Shelling	Captiva	Adventure	$750	Lisa	Wilson
Princess Bay Shelling	Captiva	Adventure	$750	Kori	Yode
Yosemite National Park Great Cleanu	Sacramento	Service	$1,100	Kristen	Collins
American Heritage Tour	Philadelphia	Educational	$1,200	Kayla	Browning
American Heritage Tour	Philadelphia	Educational	$1,200	Mark	Custard
American Heritage Tour	Philadelphia	Educational	$1,200	Fritz	Garden
Bright Lights Expo	Branson	Site Seeing	$200	Kristen	Collins
Bright Lights Expo	Branson	Site Seeing	$200	Tom	Camel
Bright Lights Expo	Branson	Site Seeing	$200	Mark	Custard
Bright Lights Expo	Branson	Site Seeing	$200	Daniel	Dodds
American Heritage Tour	Philadelphia	Educational	$1,200	Daniel	Dodds
Red Reef Scuba	Islamadora	Adventure	$1,500	Gracita	Mayberry
Red Reef Scuba	Islamadora	Adventure	$1,500	Jacob	Alman
Red Reef Scuba	Islamadora	Adventure	$1,500	Julia	Bouchart
Bright Lights Expo	Branson	Site Seeing	$200	Samantha	Braven
Red Reef Scuba	Islamadora	Adventure	$1,500	Nancy	Diverman
Ames Ski Club	Breckenridge	Adventure	$850	Naresh	Hubert
Ames Ski Club	Breckenridge	Adventure	$850	Toby	Lang
Ames Ski Club	Breckenridge	Adventure	$850	Douglas	Margolis
Ames Ski Club	Breckenridge	Adventure	$850	Jenny	Nelson
Ames Ski Club	Breckenridge	Adventure	$850	Sharol	Olingback
Boy Scout Troop 274	Vail	Adventure	$1,900	Brad	Eahlie
Bridgewater Jaycees	Aspen	Adventure	$1,200	Nancy	Diverman
Bridgewater Jaycees	Aspen	Adventure	$1,200	Kathryn	Dotey
Bridgewater Jaycees	Aspen	Adventure	$1,200	Anne	Duman

UNIT B
Access 2010

Using Query Design View

You use **Query Design View** to add, delete, or move the fields in an existing query, to specify sort orders, or to add **criteria** to limit the number of records shown in the resulting datasheet. You can also use Query Design View to create a new query from scratch. Query Design View presents the fields you can use for that query in small windows called field lists. If you use the fields of two or more related tables in the query, the relationship between two tables is displayed with a **join line** (also called a **link line**) identifying which fields are used to establish the relationship. Samantha Hooper asks you to print a list of Adventure tours in Colorado. You use Query Design View to modify the existing ToursByState query to meet her request.

STEPS

1. **Double-click the ToursByState query in the Navigation Pane to review the datasheet**
   The ToursByState query contains the StateName field from the States table, and the TourName, TourStartDate, and Cost fields from the Tours table.

2. **Click the View button in the Views group to switch to Query Design View**
   Query Design View displays the tables used in the query in the upper pane of the window. The link line shows that one record in the States table may be related to many records in the Tours table. The lower pane of the window, called the **query design grid** (or query grid for short) displays the field names, sort orders, and criteria used within the query.

> **QUICK TIP**
> Query criteria are not case sensitive, so Colorado equals COLORADO equals colorado.

3. **Click the first Criteria cell for the StateName field, then type Colorado as shown in Figure B-5**
   Criteria are limiting conditions you set in the query design grid. In this case, the condition limits the selected records to only those with "Colorado" in the StateName field.

4. **Click the View button in the Results group to switch to Datasheet View**
   Now only six records are selected, because only six of the tours have "Colorado" in the StateName field, as shown in Figure B-6. Remember that this query contains two ascending sort orders: StateName and TourName. Because all of the records have the same StateName, they are further sorted by the TourName values. You want to save this query with a different name.

5. **Click the File tab, click Save Object As, type ColoradoTours, click OK, then click the Home tab**
   In Access, the **Save command** on the File tab saves the current object, and the **Save Object As command** saves the current object with a new name. Recall that Access saves *data* automatically as you move from record to record.

6. **Right-click the ColoradoTours query tab, then click Close**

FIGURE B-5: ToursByState query in Design View

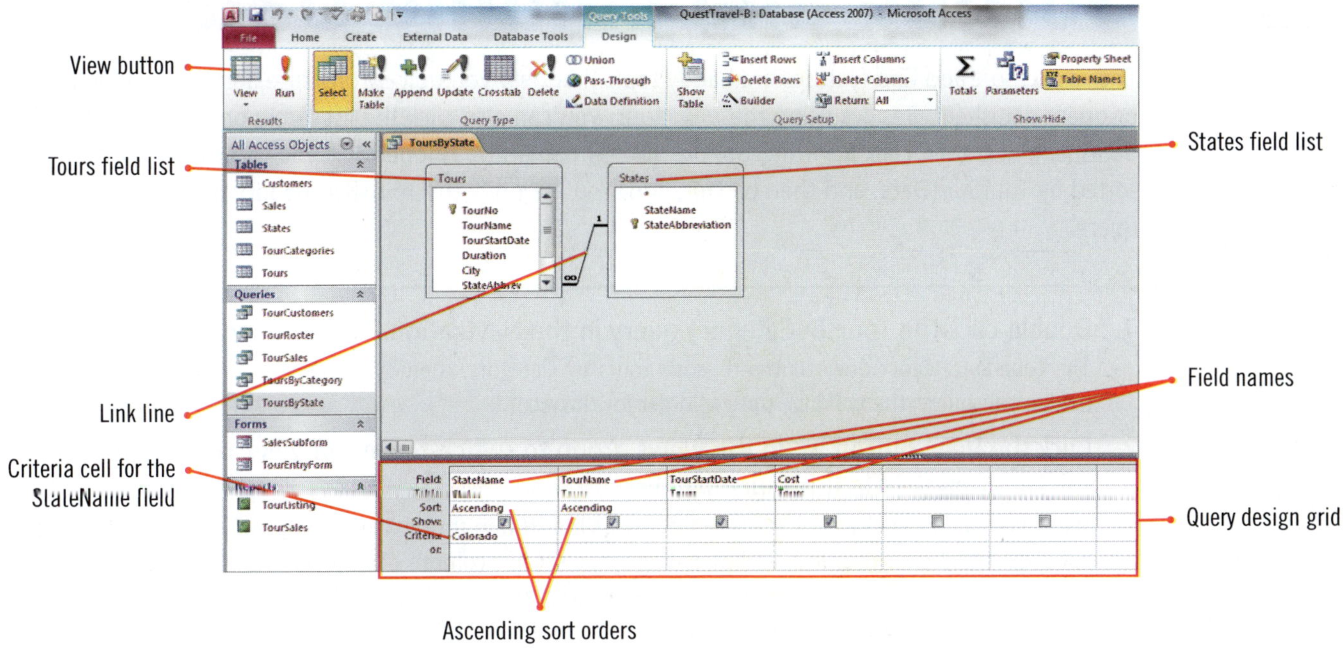

FIGURE B-6: ToursByState datasheet with Colorado criterion

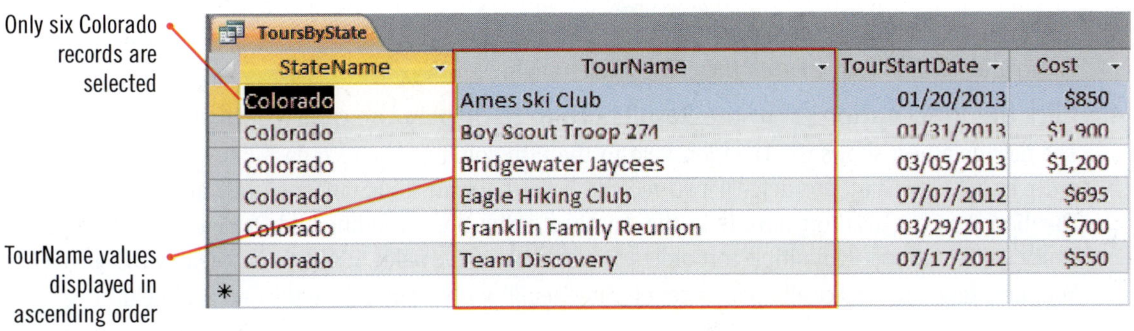

StateName	TourName	TourStartDate	Cost
Colorado	Ames Ski Club	01/20/2013	$850
Colorado	Boy Scout Troop 274	01/31/2013	$1,900
Colorado	Bridgewater Jaycees	03/05/2013	$1,200
Colorado	Eagle Hiking Club	07/07/2012	$695
Colorado	Franklin Family Reunion	03/29/2013	$700
Colorado	Team Discovery	07/17/2012	$550

Adding or deleting a table in a query

You might want to add a table's field list to the upper pane of Query Design View in order to select fields from that table for the query. To add a new table to Query Design View, click the Show Table button on the Design tab, then add the desired table(s). To delete an unneeded table from Query Design View, click its title bar, then press [Delete].

UNIT
B
Access 2010

Sorting and Finding Data

The Access sort and find features are handy tools that help you quickly organize and find data in a table or query datasheet. Besides using these buttons, you can also click the list arrow on the field name in a datasheet, and then click a sorting option. Samantha Hooper asks you to provide a list of tours sorted by TourStartDate, and then by Duration. You'll modify the ToursByCategory query to answer this query.

STEPS

1. **Double-click the ToursByCategory query in the Navigation Pane to open its datasheet**
   The ToursByCategory query currently sorts tours by Category, then by TourName. You'll add the Duration field to this query, then change the sort order for the records.

2. **Click the View button in the Views group to switch to Design View, then double-click the Duration field in the Tours field list**
   When you double-click a field in a field list, Access inserts it in the next available position in the query design grid. You can also select a field, and then drag it to a specific column of the query grid. To select a field in the query grid, you click its field selector. The **field selector** is the thin gray bar above each field in the query grid. If you want to delete a field from a query, click its field selector, then press [Delete]. Deleting a field from a query does not delete it from the underlying table; the field is only deleted from the query's logical view of the data.

   Currently, the ToursByCategory query is sorted by Category and then by TourName. Access evaluates sort specifications from left to right. You want to sort this query first by TourStartDate then by Duration.

3. **Click Ascending in the Category Sort cell, click the list arrow, click (not sorted), click Ascending in the TourName Sort cell, click the list arrow, click (not sorted), double-click the TourStartDate Sort cell to specify an Ascending sort, then double-click the Duration Sort cell to specify an Ascending sort**
   The records are now set to be sorted in ascending order, first by TourStartDate, then by the values in the Duration field, as shown in Figure B-7. Because sort orders always work left to right, you sometimes need to rearrange the fields before applying a sort order that uses more than one field. To move a field in the query design grid, click its field selector, then drag it left or right.

4. **Click the View button in the Results group to display the query datasheet**
   The new datasheet shows the Duration field in the fifth column. The records are now sorted in ascending order by the TourStartDate field. If two records have the same TourStartDate, they are further sorted by Duration. You can also sort directly in the datasheet using the Ascending and Descending buttons on the Home tab, but to specify multiple sort orders on nonconsecutive fields, it's best to use Query Design View. Your next task is to replace all occurrences of "Site Seeing" with "Cultural" in the Category field.

5. **Click the Find button on the Home tab, type Site Seeing in the Find What box, click the Replace tab, click in the Replace With box, then type Cultural**
   The Find and Replace dialog box is shown in Figure B-8.

TROUBLE
If your find-and-replace effort did not work correctly, click the Undo button and repeat Steps 5 and 6.

6. **Click the Replace All button in the Find and Replace dialog box, click Yes to continue, then click Cancel to close the Find and Replace dialog box**
   Access replaced all occurrences of "Site Seeing" with "Cultural" in the Category field, as shown in Figure B-9.

7. **Right-click the ToursByCategory query tab, click Close, then click Yes if prompted to save changes**

FIGURE B-7: Changing sort orders for the ToursByCategory query

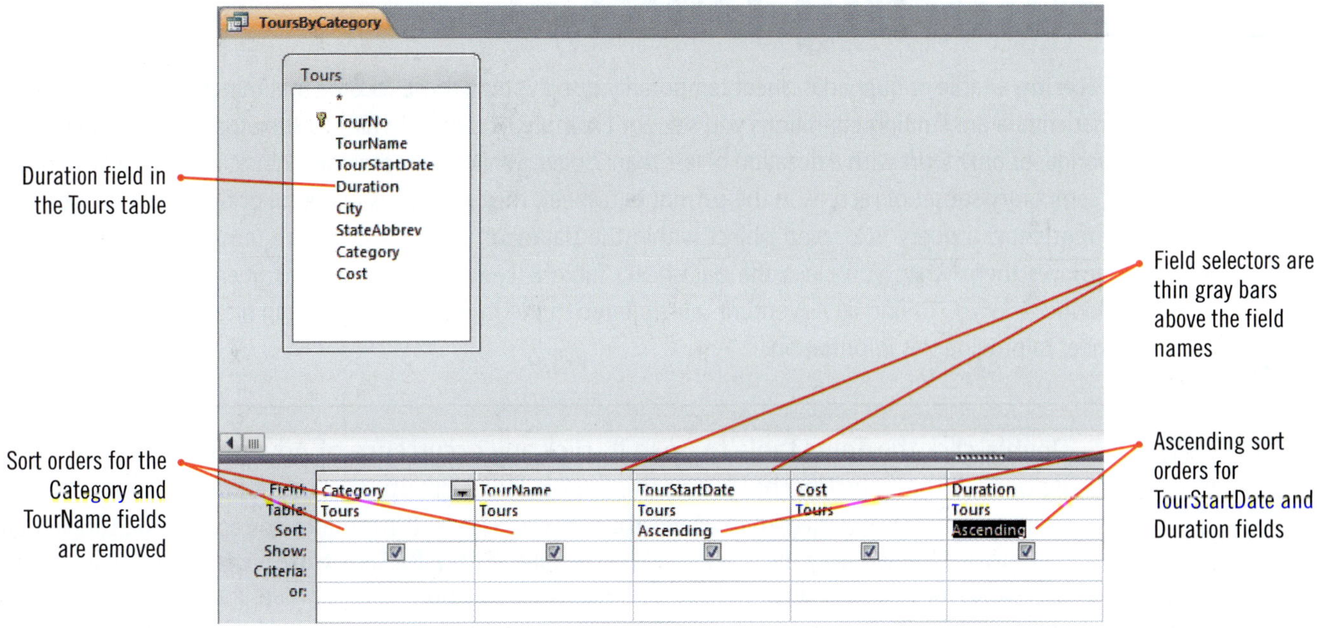

FIGURE B-8: Find and Replace dialog box

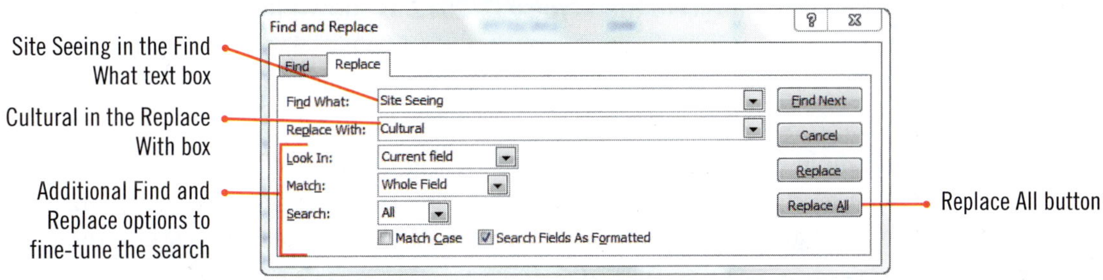

FIGURE B-9: Final ToursByCategory datasheet with new sort orders

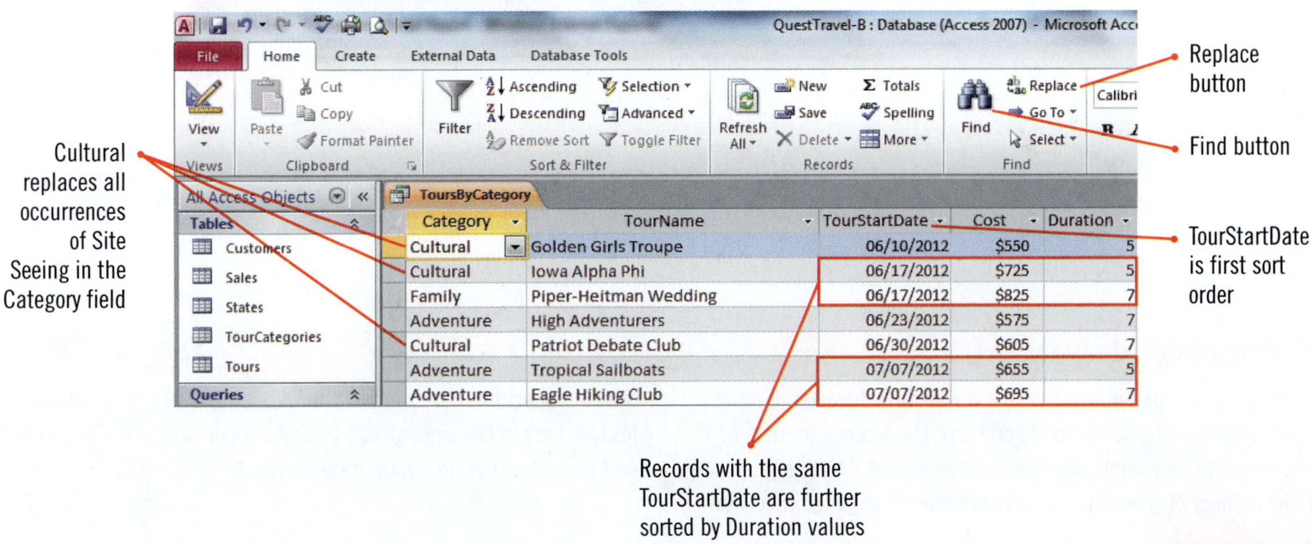

Filtering Data

Filtering a table or query datasheet temporarily displays only those records that match given criteria. Recall that criteria are limiting conditions you set. For example, you might want to show only tours in the state of Florida, or only tours with a duration of less than 7 days. While filters provide a quick and easy way to display a temporary subset of records in the current datasheet, they are not as powerful or flexible as queries. Most importantly, a query is a saved object within the database, whereas filters are temporary because Access removes them when you close the datasheet. Table B-1 compares filters and queries. Samantha Hooper asks you to find all Adventure tours offered in the month of July. You can filter the Tours table datasheet to provide this information.

STEPS

QUICK TIP
You can also apply a sort or filter by clicking the Sort and filter arrow to the right of the field name and choosing the sort order or filter values you want.

1. **Double-click the Tours table to open it, click any occurrence of Adventure in the Category field, click the Selection button in the Sort & Filter group, then click Equals "Adventure"**
   Eighteen records are selected, some of which are shown in Figure B-10. A filter icon appears to the right of the Category field. Filtering by the selected field value, called **Filter By Selection**, is a fast and easy way to filter the records for an exact match. To filter for comparative data (for example, where TourStartDate is *equal to* or *greater than* 7/1/2012), you must use the **Filter By Form** feature.
2. **Click the Advanced button in the Sort & Filter group, then click Filter By Form**
   The Filter by Form window opens. The previous Filter By Selection criterion, "Adventure" in the Category field, is still in the grid. Access distinguishes between text and numeric entries by placing "quotation marks" around text criteria.

QUICK TIP
If you need to clear previous criteria, click the Advanced button, then click Clear All Filters.

3. **Click the TourStartDate cell, then type 7/*/2012 as shown in Figure B-11**
   Filter by Form also allows you to apply two or more criteria at the same time. An asterisk (*) in the day position of the date criterion works as a wildcard, selecting any date in the month of July (the 7th month) in the year 2012.

QUICK TIP
Be sure to remove existing filters before applying a new filter, or the new filter will apply to the current subset of records instead of the entire datasheet.

4. **Click the Toggle Filter button in the Sort & Filter group**
   The datasheet selects nine records that match both filter criteria, as shown in Figure B-12. Note that filter icons appear next to the TourStartDate and Category field names as both fields are involved in the filter.
5. **Close the Tours datasheet, then click Yes when prompted to save the changes**
   Saving changes to the datasheet saves the last sort order and column width changes. Filters are not saved.

Using wildcard characters

To search for a pattern, you can use a **wildcard** character to represent any character in the condition entry. Use a question mark (?) to search for any single character, and an asterisk (*) to search for any number of characters. Wildcard characters are often used with the **Like operator**. For example, the criterion Like "12/*/13" would find all dates in December of 2013, and the criterion Like "F*" would find all entries that start with the letter F.

FIGURE B-10: Filtering the Tours table

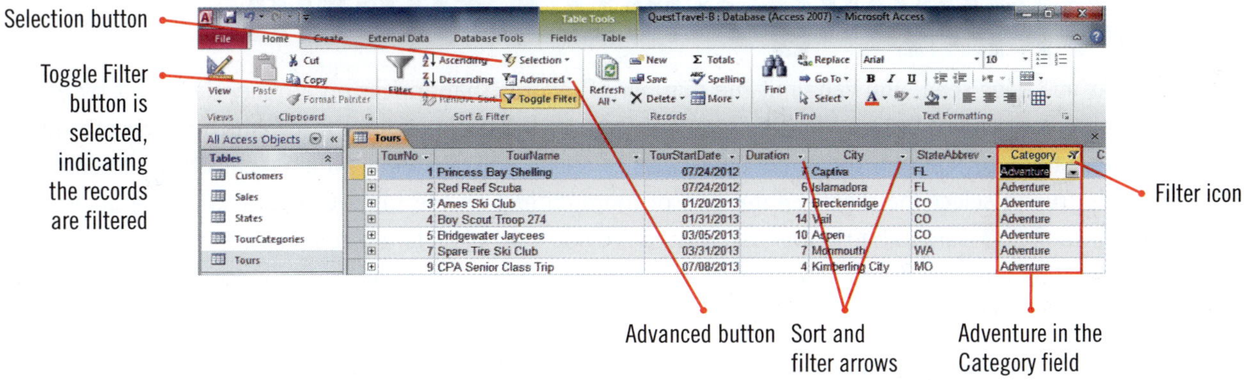

FIGURE B-11: Filtering by Form criteria

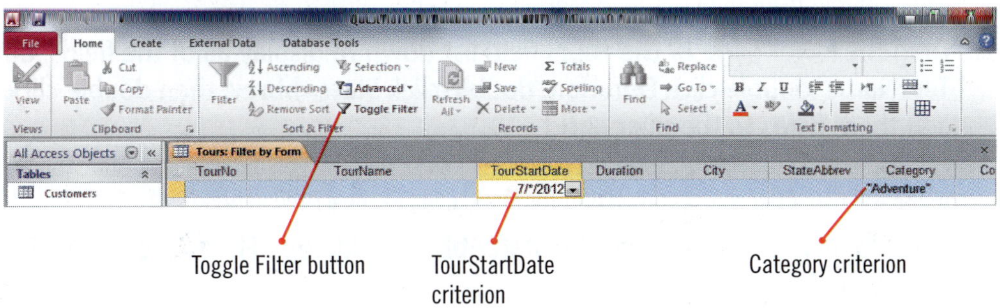

FIGURE B-12: Results of filtering by form

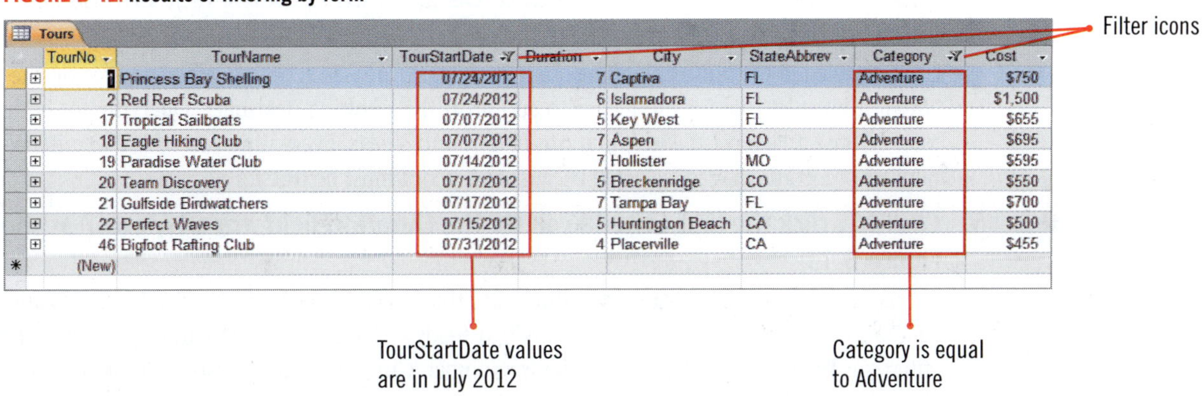

Access 2010

TABLE B-1: Filters vs. queries

characteristics	filters	queries
Are saved as an object in the database	No	Yes
Can be used to select a subset of records in a datasheet	Yes	Yes
Can be used to select a subset of fields in a datasheet	No	Yes
Resulting datasheet used to enter and edit data	Yes	Yes
Resulting datasheet used to sort, filter, and find records	Yes	Yes
Commonly used as the source of data for a form or report	No	Yes
Can calculate sums, averages, counts, and other types of summary statistics across records	No	Yes
Can be used to create calculated fields	No	Yes

UNIT
B
Access 2010

Applying AND Criteria

As you have seen, you can limit the number of records that appear on a query datasheet by entering criteria in Query Design View. Criteria are tests, or limiting conditions, for which the record must be true to be selected for the query datasheet. To create **AND criteria**, which means that all criteria must be true to select the record, enter two or more criteria on the same Criteria row of the query design grid. Samantha Hooper asks you to provide a list of all family tours in the state of Florida with a duration equal to or less than 7 days. Use Query Design View to create the query with AND criteria to meet her request.

STEPS

1. **Click the Create tab on the Ribbon, click the Query Design button in the Queries group, double-click Tours, then click Close in the Show Table dialog box**
   You want four fields from the Tours table in this query.
2. **Drag the lower edge of the Tours field list down to display all of the fields, double-click TourName, double-click Duration, double-click StateAbbrev, then double-click Category to add these fields to the query grid**
   First add criteria to select only those records in Florida. Because you are using the StateAbbrev field, you need to use the two-letter state abbreviation for Florida, FL, as the Criteria entry.
3. **Click the first Criteria cell for the StateAbbrev field, type FL, then click the View button to display the results**
   Querying for only those tours in the state of Florida selects 11 records. Next, you add criteria to select only those records in the Family category.
4. **Click the View button to switch to Design View, click the first Criteria cell for the Category field, type Family, then click**
   Criteria added to the same line of the query design grid are AND criteria. When entered on the same line, each criterion must be true for the record to appear in the resulting datasheet. Querying for both FL and Family tours selects three records with durations of 8, 7, and 3 days. Every time you add AND criteria, you *narrow* the number of records that are selected because the record must be true for *all* criteria.
5. **Click , click the first Criteria cell for the Duration field, then type <=7 as shown in Figure B-13**
   Access assists you with **criteria syntax**, rules that specify how to enter criteria. Access automatically adds "quotation marks" around text criteria in Text fields ("FL" and "Family") and pound signs (#) around date criteria in Date/Time fields. The criteria in Number, Currency, and Yes/No fields are not surrounded by any characters. See Table B-2 for more information about comparison operators such as > (greater than).
6. **Click to display the query datasheet**
   The third AND criterion further narrows the number of records selected to two, as shown in Figure B-14.
7. **Click the Save button on the Quick Access toolbar, type FamilyFL as the query name, click OK, then close the query**
   The query is saved with the new name, FamilyFL, as a new object in the QuestTravel-B database.

TROUBLE
If your datasheet doesn't match Figure B-14, return to Query Design View and compare your criteria to that of Figure B-13.

Searching for blank fields

Is Null and Is Not Null are two other types of common criteria. The **Is Null** criterion finds all records where no entry has been made in the field. **Is Not Null** finds all records where there is any entry in the field, even if the entry is 0. Primary key fields cannot have a null entry.

FIGURE B-13: Query Design View with AND criteria

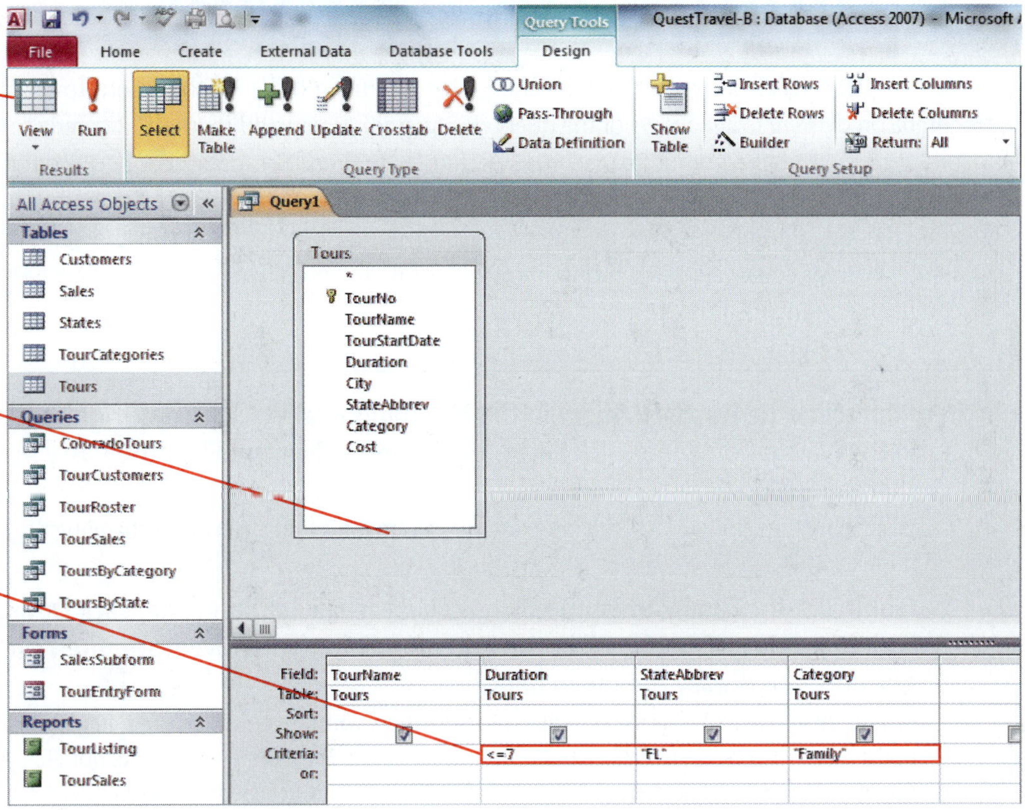

Click the View button to display the results of the query

Drag the bottom edge of the Tours field list down

AND criteria in one row to select Family tours in FL that are less than or equal to 7 days

FIGURE B-14: Final datasheet of FamilyFL query

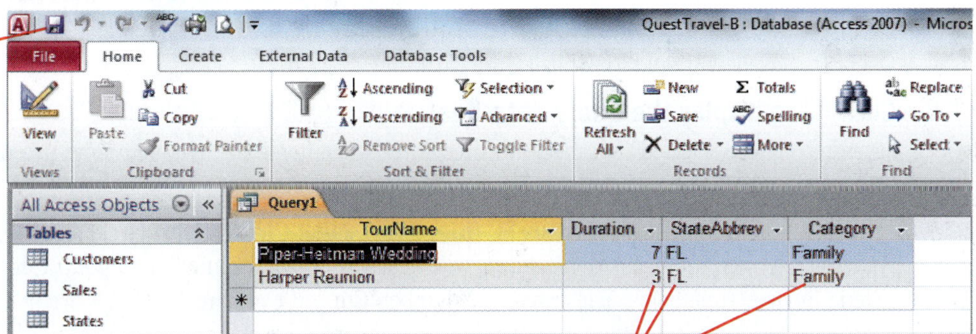

Save button

All three criteria are true for these two records: <=7 duration, FL, and Family

TABLE B-2: Comparison operators

operator	description	expression	meaning
>	Greater than	>500	Numbers greater than 500
>=	Greater than or equal to	>=500	Numbers greater than or equal to 500
<	Less than	<"Braveheart"	Names from A to Braveheart, but not Braveheart
<=	Less than or equal to	<="Bridgewater"	Names from A through Bridgewater, inclusive
<>	Not equal to	<>"Fontanelle"	Any name except for Fontanelle

UNIT
B
Access 2010

Applying OR Criteria

You use **OR criteria** when any one criterion must be true in order for the record to be selected. Enter OR criteria on *different* Criteria rows of the query design grid. As you add rows of OR criteria to the query design grid, you *increase* the number of records selected for the resulting datasheet because the record needs to match *only one* of the Criteria rows to be selected for the datasheet. Samantha Hooper asks you to add criteria to the previous query. She wants to include Adventure tours in the state of Florida that are shorter than or equal to 7 days in duration. To do this, you modify a copy of the FamilyFL query to use OR criteria to add the records.

STEPS

1. **Right-click the FamilyFL query in the Navigation Pane, click Copy, right-click a blank spot in the Navigation Pane, click Paste, type FamilyAdventureFL in the Paste As dialog box, then click OK**

   By copying the FamilyFL query before starting your modifications, you avoid changing the FamilyFL query by mistake.

2. **Right-click the FamilyAdventureFL query in the Navigation Pane, click Design View, click the second Criteria cell in the Category field, type Adventure, then click the View button to display the query datasheet**

   The query selected 20 records including all of the tours with Adventure in the Category field. Note that some of the Duration values are greater than 7 and some of the StateAbbrev values are not FL. Because each row of the query grid is evaluated separately, all Adventure tours are selected regardless of criteria in any other row. In other words, the criteria in one row have no effect on the criteria of other rows. To make sure that the Adventure tours are also in Florida and have a duration of less than or equal to 7 days, you need to modify the second row of the query grid (the "or" row) to specify that criteria.

3. **Click the View button, click the second Criteria cell in the Duration field, type <=7, click the second Criteria cell in the StateAbbrev field, then type FL**

   Query Design View should look like Figure B-15.

4. **Click to display the query datasheet**

   Seven records are selected that meet all three criteria as entered in row one *or* row two of the query grid, as shown in Figure B-16.

5. **Right-click the FamilyAdventureFL query tab, click Close, then click Yes to save and close the query datasheet**

QUICK TIP

The Datasheet, Design, and other view buttons are also located in the lower-right corner of the Access window.

FIGURE B-15: Query Design View with OR criteria

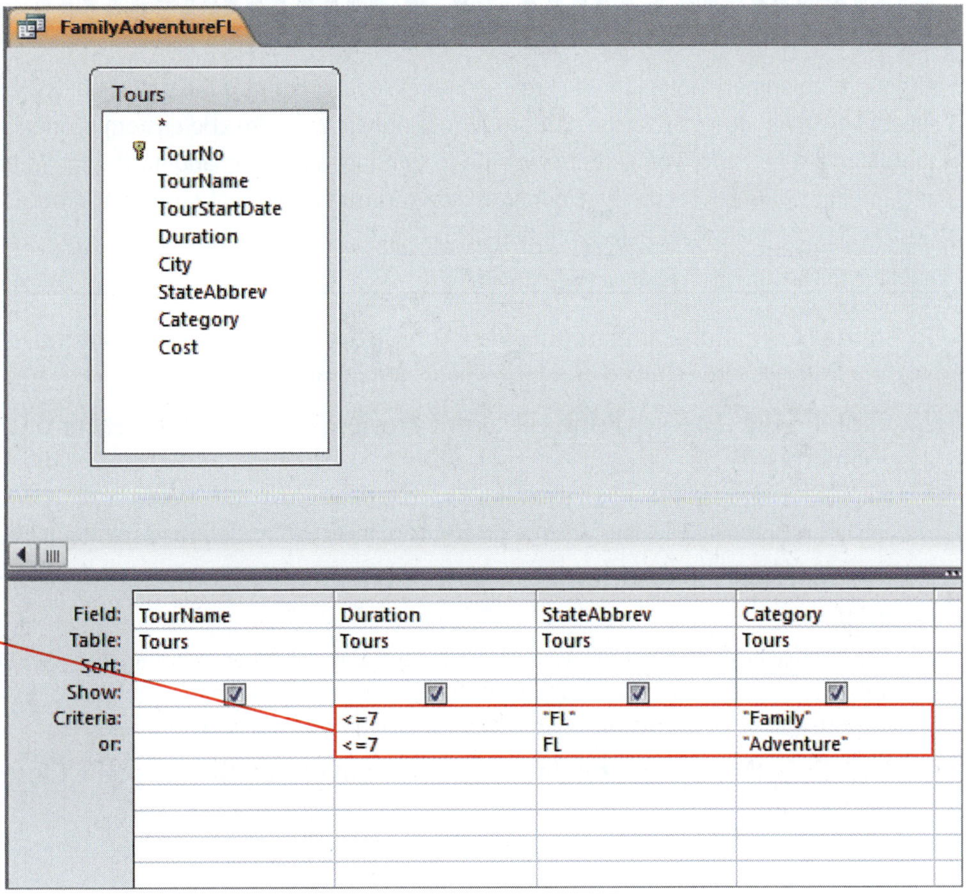

OR criteria in two rows to select both Family and Adventure tours in FL with a Duration less than or equal to 7 days

FIGURE B-16: Final datasheet of the FamilyAdventureFL query

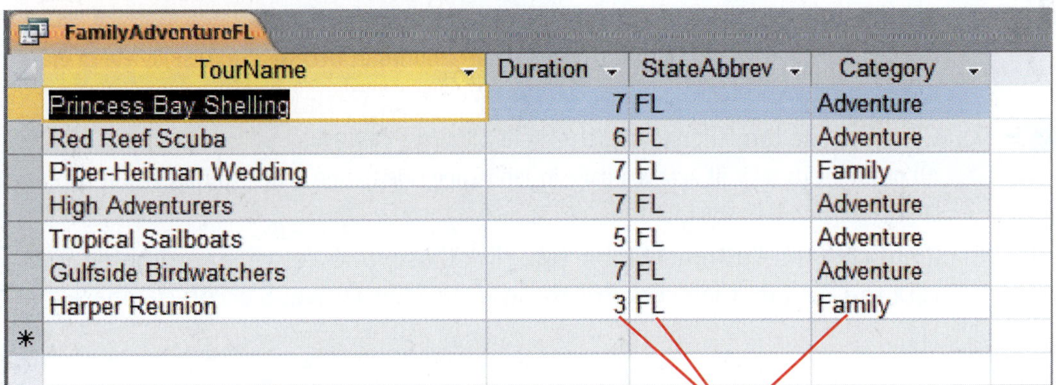

TourName	Duration	StateAbbrev	Category
Princess Bay Shelling	7	FL	Adventure
Red Reef Scuba	6	FL	Adventure
Piper-Heitman Wedding	7	FL	Family
High Adventurers	7	FL	Adventure
Tropical Sailboats	5	FL	Adventure
Gulfside Birdwatchers	7	FL	Adventure
Harper Reunion	3	FL	Family

All three criteria are true for either row:
<=7 duration, FL, and Family
or
<=7 duration, FL, and Adventure

UNIT
B
Access 2010

Formatting a Datasheet

Although the primary Access tool to create a professional printout is the report object, you can print a datasheet as well. Although a datasheet printout does not allow you to add custom headers, footers, images, or subtotals as reports do, you can apply some formatting, such as changing the font size, font face, colors, and gridlines. Samantha Hooper asked you to print a list of customers. You decide to format the Customers table datasheet before printing it for her.

STEPS

1. **In the Navigation Pane, double-click the Customers table to open it in Datasheet View**
   Before applying new formatting enhancements, you preview the default printout.
2. **Click the File tab, click Print, click Print Preview, then click the header of the printout to zoom in**
   The preview window displays the layout of the printout, as shown in Figure B-17. By default, the printout of a datasheet contains the object name and current date in the header. The page number is in the footer.
3. **Click the Next Page button in the navigation bar to move to the next page of the printout**
   The last two fields print on the second page because the first is not wide enough to accommodate them. You decide to switch the report to landscape orientation so that all of the fields print on one page, and then increase the size of the font before printing to make the text easier to read.
4. **Click the Landscape button in the Page Layout group, then click the Close Print Preview button**
   You return to Datasheet View where you can make font face, font size, font color, gridline color, and background color choices.
5. **Click the Font list arrow Calibri in the Text Formatting group, click Times New Roman, click the Font Size list arrow 11, then click 12**
   With the larger font size applied, you need to resize some columns to accommodate the widest entries.
6. **Use the ✛ pointer to double-click the field separator between the Street and City field names, then double-click the field separator between the Phone and FirstContact field names**
   Double-clicking the field separators widens the column as necessary to display every entry in that field, as shown in Figure B-18.
7. **Click the File tab, click Print, then click Print Preview**
   All of the fields now fit across a page in landscape orientation. The printout is still two pages, but with the larger font size, it is easier to read.
8. **Right-click the Customers table tab, click Close, click Yes when prompted to save changes, click the File tab, then click Exit to close the QuestTravel-B.accdb database and Access 2010**

QUICK TIP
If you need a printout of this datasheet, click the Print button on the Print Preview tab, then click OK.

FIGURE B-17: Preview of Customers datasheet

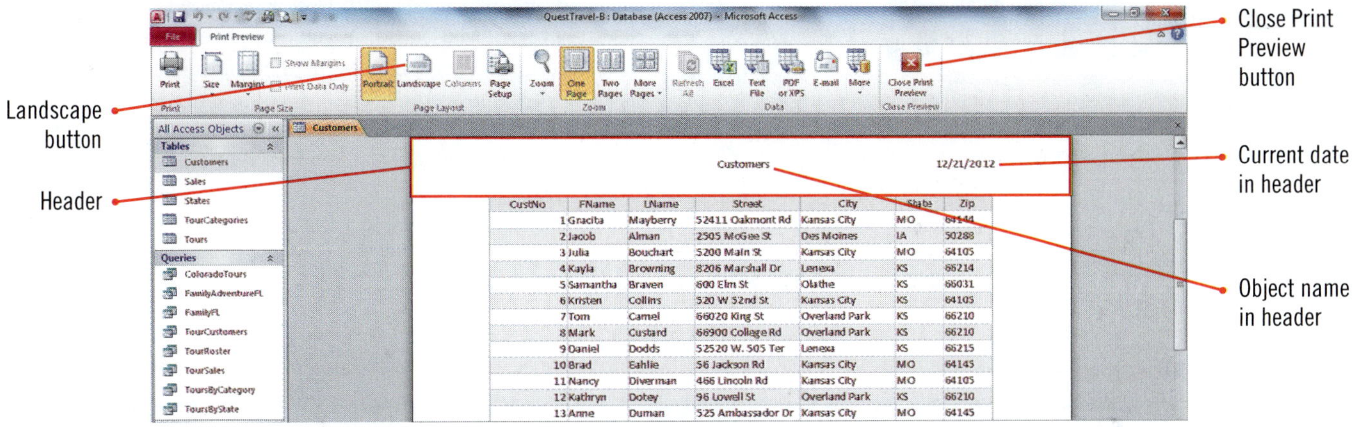

FIGURE B-18: Formatting the Customers datasheet

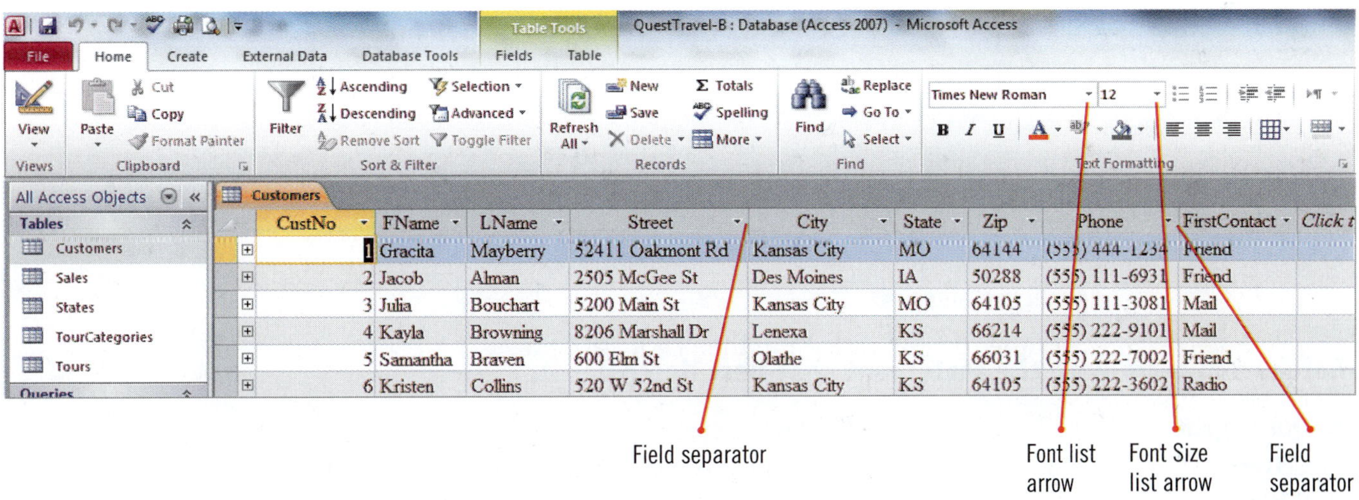

Practice

Concepts Review

For current SAM information, including versions and content details, visit SAM Central (http://www.cengage.com/samcentral). If you have a SAM user profile, you may have access to hands-on instruction, practice, and assessment of the skills covered in this unit. Since various versions of SAM are supported throughout the life of this text, check with your instructor for the correct instructions and URL/Web site for accessing assignments.

Label each element of the Access window shown in Figure B-19.

FIGURE B-19

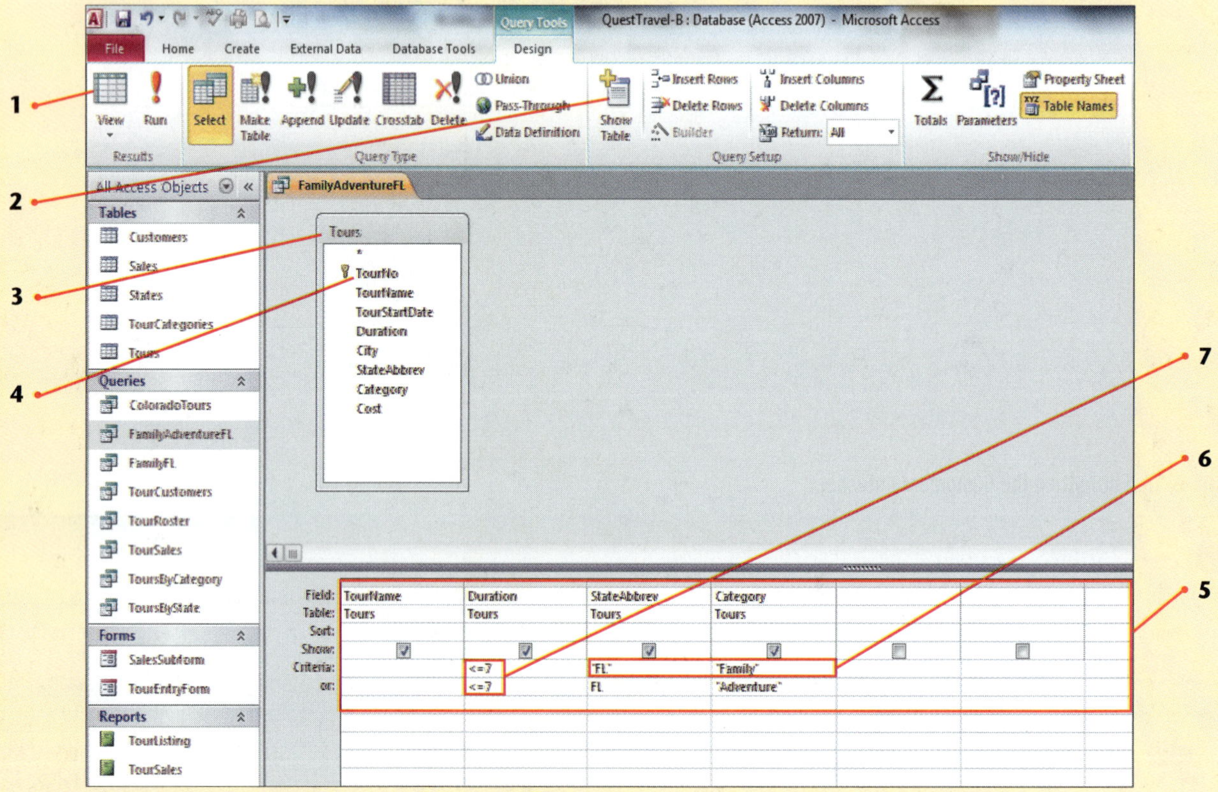

Match each term with the statement that best describes it.

8. Query grid
9. Criteria
10. Filter
11. Syntax
12. Field lists
13. Sorting
14. Wildcard
15. Is Null

a. Creates a temporary subset of records
b. Small windows that display field names
c. Rules that determine how criteria are entered
d. Limiting conditions used to restrict the number of records that are selected in a query
e. Used to search for a pattern of characters
f. Criterion that finds all records where no entry has been made in the field
g. The lower pane in Query Design View
h. Putting records in ascending or descending order based on the values of a field

Select the best answer from the list of choices.

16. AND criteria:

- **a.** Must all be true for the record to be selected.
- **b.** Determine sort orders.
- **c.** Determine fields selected for a query.
- **d.** Help set link lines between tables in a query.

17. SQL stands for which of the following?

- **a.** Standard Query Language
- **b.** Special Query Listing
- **c.** Structured Query Language
- **d.** Simple Query Listing

18. A query is sometimes called a logical view of data because:

- **a.** You can create queries with the Logical Query Wizard.
- **b.** Queries do not store data, they only display a view of data.
- **c.** Queries contain logical criteria.
- **d.** Query naming conventions are logical.

19. Which of the following describes OR criteria?

- **a.** Selecting a subset of fields and/or records to view as a datasheet from one or more tables
- **b.** Using two or more rows of the query grid to select only those records that meet given criteria
- **c.** Reorganizing the records in either ascending or descending order based on the contents of one or more fields
- **d.** Using multiple fields in the query design grid

20. Which of the following is *not* true about a query?

- **a.** A query can be used to create calculated fields.
- **b.** A query can be used to create summary statistics.
- **c.** A query can be used to enter and edit data.
- **d.** A query is the same thing as a filter.

Skills Review

1. Use the Query Wizard.

- **a.** Open the Recycle-B.accdb database from the drive and folder where you store your Data Files. Enable content if prompted.
- **b.** Create a new query using the Simple Query Wizard. Select the CenterName field from the Centers table, the DepositDate and Weight fields from the Deposits table, and the ClubName field from the Clubs table. Select Detail, and enter **CenterDeposits** as the name of the query.
- **c.** Open the query in Datasheet View, change any record with the Big Trash Can CenterName value to a center name that includes your last name.

2. Work with data in a query.

- **a.** Delete the first record.
- **b.** Change any occurrence of Lions in the ClubName field to **Lions of Okoboji**.
- **c.** Click any value in the DepositDate field, then click the Descending button in the Sort & Filter group on the Home tab to sort the records in descending order on the DepositDate field.
- **d.** Use the Calendar Picker to choose the date of **1/9/2013** for the first record.
- **e.** Save and close the CenterDeposits query.

3. Use Query Design View.

- **a.** Click the Create tab, click the Query Design button, double-click Clubs, double-click Deposits, and then click Close to add the Clubs and Deposits tables to Query Design View.
- **b.** Drag the bottom edge of the Clubs table down to display all of the field names.

Skills Review (continued)

c. Add the following fields from the Clubs table to the query design grid in the following order: FName, LName, ClubName. Add the following fields from the Deposits table in the following order: DepositNumber, DepositDate, Weight. View the results in Datasheet View observing the number of records that are selected.

d. In Design View, enter criteria to display only those records with a Weight value of **greater than or equal to 100**, then observe the number of records that are selected.

e. Save the query with the name **100PlusDeposits**, and close it.

4. Sort and find data.

a. Open the CenterDeposits query in Datasheet View to observe how the records are currently sorted (in descending order based on the DepositDate field).

b. In Query Design View, choose an ascending sort order for the CenterName and DepositDate fields. (*Note*: Queries that are created with the Query Wizard do not show the 1 and infinity symbols on the link lines between the tables. However, the one-to-many relationships between these tables are still intact.)

c. Display the query in Datasheet View noting how the records have been resorted.

d. Click any value in the ClubName field, then use the Find and Replace dialog box to find all occurrences of **Patriots**, and replace them with **Kansas City Patriots**.

5. Filter data.

a. Filter the CenterDeposits datasheet for only those records where the ClubName equals **Kansas City Patriots**.

b. Apply an advanced filter by form and use wildcard characters to further narrow the records so that only the deposits made in the year 2012 are selected.

c. If requested by your instructor, print the filtered CenterDeposits datasheet.

d. Save and close the CenterDeposits query.

6. Apply AND criteria.

a. Open the 100PlusDeposits query in Query Design View.

b. Modify the criteria to select all of the listings with a ClubName of **Ice Kings** and a Weight value of greater than or equal to 100.

c. In the results, edit Tara in any occurrence in the FName field to your initials.

d. If requested by your instructor, print the 100PlusDeposits query.

7. Apply OR criteria.

a. Open the 100PlusDeposits query in Query Design View.

b. Add criteria to include the records with **Jaycees** as the ClubName with a Weight value **greater than or equal to 100** to the existing selections so that both the Ice Kings and Jaycees large deposit records are selected.

c. Save the 100PlusDeposits query, then switch to Datasheet View.

8. Format a datasheet.

a. In the 100PlusDeposits datasheet, apply an Arial Narrow font and a 14-point font size.

b. Resize all columns so that all data and field names are visible. See Figure B-20.

c. Save the 100PlusDeposits query.

d. If requested by your instructor, print the datasheet.

e. Close the 100PlusDeposits query and the Recycle-B.accdb database, then exit Access 2010.

FIGURE B-20

100PlusDeposits

FName	LName	ClubName	DepositNumber	DepositDate	Weight
Francis	Weaver	Jaycees	25	8/21/2012	105
Francis	Weaver	Jaycees	59	3/7/2011	200
Francis	Weaver	Jaycees	63	4/23/2011	105
Francis	Weaver	Jaycees	75	7/9/2011	200
Francis	Weaver	Jaycees	82	1/31/2010	100
Francis	Weaver	Jaycees	99	3/6/2010	200
SI	Block	Ice Kings	6	2/23/2012	100
SI	Block	Ice Kings	42	1/31/2011	100
SI	Block	Ice Kings	46	2/14/2011	185
SI	Block	Ice Kings	50	2/19/2011	185
SI	Block	Ice Kings	60	3/8/2011	145
SI	Block	Ice Kings	61	4/20/2011	115
SI	Block	Ice Kings	67	5/2/2011	105
SI	Block	Ice Kings	86	2/14/2010	200
SI	Block	Ice Kings	94	2/27/2010	100
*			(New)		

Independent Challenge 1

You have built an Access database to track member-ship in a community service club. The database tracks member names and addresses as well as their status in the club, which moves from rank to rank as the members contribute increased hours of service to the community.

a. Start Access, open the Membership-B.accdb database from the drive and folder where you store your Data Files, enable content if prompted, then open the Activities, Members, and Zips tables to review their datasheets.

b. In the Zips table, click the expand button to the left of the 64131, Overland Park, KS, record to display the two members linked to that zip code. Click the expand button to the left of the Gabriel Hammer record to display the two activity records linked to Gabriel.

c. Close all three datasheets, click the Database Tools tab, then click the Relationships button. The Relationships window also shows you that one record in the Zips table is related to many records in the Members table through the common ZipCode field, and that one record in the Members table is related to many records in the Activities table through the common MemberNo field.

d. Close the Relationships window.

e. In Query Design View, build a query with the following fields: FirstName and LastName from the Members table, and ActivityDate and HoursWorked from the Activities table.

f. View the datasheet, observe the number of records selected, then return to Query Design View.

g. Add criteria to select only those records where the ActivityDate is in March of 2012. (*Hint*: Use a wildcard character in the day position of the date criterion.) Apply an ascending sort order to the LastName and ActivityDate fields, then view the datasheet.

h. Enter your name in the first record, widen all columns so that all data and field names are visible, and save the query with the name **March2012** as shown in Figure B-21.

i. If requested by your instructor, print the datasheet.

j. Close the March2012 query and the Membership-B.accdb database, then exit Access 2010.

FIGURE B-21

March2012

FirstName	LastName	ActivityDate	HoursWorked
StudentFirst	StudentLast	3/29/2012	4
Golga	Collins	3/31/2012	8
Martha	Duman	3/27/2012	4
Allie	Eahlie	3/29/2012	4
Jana	Eckert	3/29/2012	5
Quentin	Garden	3/29/2012	4
Quentin	Garden	3/30/2012	8
Loraine	Goode	3/29/2012	5
Gabriel	Hammer	3/29/2012	5
Jeremiah	Hopper	3/27/2012	4
Helen	Hubert	3/29/2012	5
Heidi	Kalvert	3/29/2012	4
Harvey	Mackintosh	3/30/2012	4
Jon	Maxim	3/30/2012	4
Micah	Mayberry	3/29/2012	4
Patch	Mullins	3/30/2012	8
Patch	Mullins	3/31/2012	8
Young	Nelson	3/30/2012	10
Mallory	Olson	3/31/2012	8
Su	Vogue	3/30/2012	8
Sherry	Walker	3/29/2012	4
Taney	Wilson	3/30/2012	8
*			

Independent Challenge 2

You work for a nonprofit agency that relies on grant money from the federal government. To keep in touch with elected members of Congress, you have developed an Access database with contact information for the House of Representatives. The director of the agency has asked you to create several state lists of representatives. You will use queries to extract this information.

If you have a SAM 2010 user profile, an autogradable SAM version of this assignment may be available at http://www.cengage.com/sam2010. Check with your instructor to confirm that this assignment is available in SAM. To use the SAM version of this assignment, log into the SAM 2010 Web site and download the instruction and start files.

a. Start Access, open the Congress-B.accdb database from the drive and folder where you store your Data Files, then enable content if prompted.

b. Open the Representatives and the States tables. Notice that one state is related to many representatives as evidenced by the expand buttons to the left of the records in the States tables.

Independent Challenge 2 (continued)

c. Close both datasheets, then using Query Design View, create a query with the StateAbbrev, StateName, and Capital fields from the States table (in that order) as well as the LName field from the Representatives table.

d. Sort the records in ascending order on the StateName field, then the LName field.

e. Add criteria to select the representatives from North Carolina or South Carolina. Use the StateAbbrev field to enter your criteria, using the two-character state abbreviations of NC and SC.

f. Save the query with the name **Carolinas**, view the results, then change the last name of Boehlert to your last name. Resize the columns as needed to view all the data and field names.

g. Print the datasheet if requested by your instructor, then save and close it.

h. Close the Congress-B.accdb database, then exit Access 2010.

Independent Challenge 3

You have built an Access database to track the veterinarians and clinics in your area.

a. Start Access, open the Vet-B.accdb database from the drive and folder where you store your Data Files, and enable content if prompted.

b. Open the Vets table and then the Clinics table to review the data in both datasheets.

c. Click the expand button next to the Veterinary Specialists record in the Clinics table, then add your name as a new record to the Vets subdatasheet.

d. Close both datasheets.

e. Using the Simple Query Wizard, select the VetLast and VetFirst fields from the Vets table, and select the ClinicName and Phone fields from the Clinics table. Title the query **ClinicListing**, then view the datasheet.

f. Find the single occurrence of Cooper in the VetLast field, and replace it with **Chen**.

g. Update any occurrence of Leawood Animal Clinic in the ClinicName field by changing Leawood to **Emergency**.

h. In Query Design View, add criteria to select only Emergency Animal Clinic or Veterinary Specialists in the ClinicName field, then view the results.

Advanced Challenge Exercise

- In Query Design View, move the ClinicName field to the first column, then add an ascending sort order on the ClinicName and VetLast fields.
- Display the ClinicListing query in Datasheet View, resize the fields as shown in Figure B-22, then print the datasheet if requested by your instructor.
- Return to Query Design View of the ClinicListing query. Notice the link line between the tables. This link line was created by the Simple Query Wizard.
- Save and close the ClinicListing query then open the Relationships window. Notice the link line between the tables. In a Word document, explain the difference in appearance and meaning of the link line between the Vets and Clinics tables in the Relationships window with that of Query Design View.

i. If you have not already done so, save and close the ClinicListing datasheet, then close the Vet-B.accdb database and exit Access 2010.

FIGURE B-22

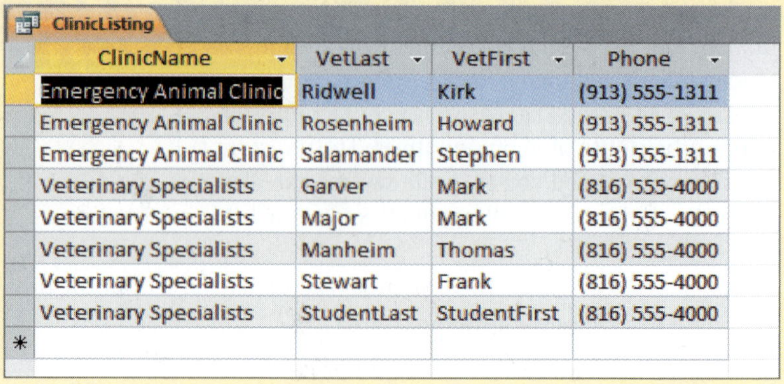

ClinicListing

ClinicName	VetLast	VetFirst	Phone
Emergency Animal Clinic	Ridwell	Kirk	(913) 555-1311
Emergency Animal Clinic	Rosenheim	Howard	(913) 555-1311
Emergency Animal Clinic	Salamander	Stephen	(913) 555-1311
Veterinary Specialists	Garver	Mark	(816) 555-4000
Veterinary Specialists	Major	Mark	(816) 555-4000
Veterinary Specialists	Manheim	Thomas	(816) 555-4000
Veterinary Specialists	Stewart	Frank	(816) 555-4000
Veterinary Specialists	StudentLast	StudentFirst	(816) 555-4000

Real Life Independent Challenge

An Access database is an excellent tool to help record and track job opportunities. For this exercise you'll create a database from scratch that you can use to enter, edit, and query data in pursuit of a new job or career.

a. Create a new database named **Jobs.accdb**.

b. Create a table named **Positions** with the following field names, data types, and descriptions:

field name	data type	description
PositionID	**AutoNumber**	**Primary key field**
Title	**Text**	**Title of position such as Accountant, Assistant Court Clerk, or Director of Finance**
CareerArea	**Text**	**Area of the career field such as Accounting, Information Systems, Retail, or Landscaping**
AnnualSalary	**Currency**	**Annual salary**
Desirability	**Number**	**Desirability rating of 1 = low to 5 = high to show how desirable the position is to you**
EmployerID	**Number**	**Foreign key field to the Employers table**

c. Create a table named **Employers** with the following field names, data types, and descriptions:

field name	data type	description
EmployerID	**AutoNumber**	**Primary key field**
CompanyName	**Text**	**Company name of the employer**
EmpStreet	**Text**	**Employer's street address**
EmpCity	**Text**	**Employer's city**
EmpState	**Text**	**Employer's state**
EmpZip	**Text**	**Employer's zip code**
EmpPhone	**Text**	**Employer's phone, including area code**

d. Be sure to set EmployerID as the primary key field in the Employers table and the PositionID as the primary key field in the Positions table.

e. Link the Employers and Positions table together in a one-to-many relationship using the common EmployerID field. One employer record will be linked to many position records. Be sure to enforce referential integrity.

f. Using any valid source of potential employer data, enter five records into the Employers table.

g. Using any valid source of job information, enter five records into the Positions table by using the subdatasheets from within the Employers datasheet. Because one employer may have many positions, all five of your Positions records may be linked to the same employer, you may have one position record per employer, or any other combination.

h. Build a query that selects CompanyName from the Employers table, and the Title, CareerArea, AnnualSalary, and Desirability fields from the Positions table. Sort the records in descending order based on Desirability. Save the query as **JobList**, and print it if requested by your instructor.

i. Close the JobList datasheet, then close the Jobs.accdb database and exit Access 2010.

Visual Workshop

Open the Baseball-B.accdb database from the drive and folder where you store your Data Files, and enable content if prompted. Create a query based on the Players and Teams tables as shown in Figure B-23. Criteria has been added to select only those records where the PlayerPosition field values are equal to 1 or 2 (representing pitchers and catchers). An ascending sort order has been added to the TeamName and PlayerPosition fields. Save the query with the name **PitchersAndCatchers**, then compare the results to Figure B-23, making changes as necessary. Change the name of Roy Campanella to your name before printing the datasheet if requested by your instructor. Close the query and the Baseball-B.accdb database, then exit Access 2010.

FIGURE B-23

PitchersAndCatchers

TeamName	PlayerLast	PlayerFirst	Position
Brooklyn Beetles	Campanella	Roy	1
Brooklyn Beetles	Young	Cycylie	2
Mayfair Monarchs	Durocher	Luis	1
Mayfair Monarchs	Mathewson	Carl	2
Rocky's Rockets	Spalding	Andrew	1
Rocky's Rockets	Koufax	Sanford	2
Snapping Turtles	Ford	Charles	1
Snapping Turtles	Perry	Greg	2

Using Forms

Files You Will Need:

- QuestTravel-C.accdb
- QuestLogo.bmp
- RealEstate-C.accdb
- ForSale.bmp
- QuestDives-C.accdb
- Membership-C.accdb
- PeoplePower.bmp
- Recycle-C.accdb
- JobSearch-C.accdb
- Baseball-C.accdb

Although you can enter and edit data on datasheets, most database designers develop and build forms as the primary method for users to interact with a database. In a datasheet, sometimes you have to scroll left or right to see all of the fields, which is inconvenient and time consuming. A form solves these problems by allowing you to organize the fields on the screen in any arrangement. A form also supports graphical elements such as pictures, buttons, and tabs, which make data entry faster and more accurate. In addition, forms provide a layer of database security and make the database much easier to use. Samantha Hooper, a tour developer at Quest Specialty Travel, asks you to create forms to make tour information easier to access, enter, and update.

OBJECTIVES

- Use the Form Wizard
- Create a split form
- Use Form Layout View
- Add fields to a form
- Modify form controls
- Create calculations
- Modify tab order
- Insert an image

UNIT
C
Access 2010

Using the Form Wizard

A **form** is an Access database object that allows you to arrange the fields of a record in any layout so you can enter, edit, and delete records. A form provides an easy-to-use data entry and navigation screen. Forms provide many productivity and security benefits for the **user**, who is primarily interested in entering, editing, and analyzing the data in the database. As the **database designer**, the person responsible for building and maintaining tables, queries, forms, and reports, you also need direct access to all database objects, and you use the Navigation Pane for this purpose. Not all users should be able to access all the objects in a database—imagine how disastrous it would be if someone accidentally deleted an entire table of data. You can add a layer of security to your database with well-designed forms. Samantha Hooper asks you to build a form to enter and maintain tour information.

STEPS

1. **Start Access, open the QuestTravel-C.accdb database from the drive and folder where you store your Data Files, then enable content if prompted**

   You can use many methods to create a new form, but the Form Wizard is a fast and popular tool to get started. The **Form Wizard** prompts you for information it needs to create a form, such as the fields, layout, and title for the form.

2. **Click the Create tab on the Ribbon, then click the Form Wizard button in the Forms group**

   The Form Wizard starts, prompting you to select the fields for this form. You want to create a form to enter and update data in the Tours table.

3. **Click the Tables/Queries list arrow, click Table: Tours, then click the Select All Fields button >>**

   You could now select fields from other tables, if necessary, but in this case, you have all of the fields you need.

4. **Click Next, click the Columnar option button, click Next, type Tours Entry Form as the title, then click Finish**

   The Tours Entry Form opens in **Form View**, as shown in Figure C-1. The three different form views are summarized in Table C-1. Each item on the form is called a **control**. Field names are shown as label controls in the first column of the form. A **label** displays fixed text that doesn't change as you navigate from record to record. Labels usually describe other controls on the form such as text boxes that show field values. A label control is also often used in headers or footers. Field values are displayed in text box and combo box controls in the second column of the form. A **text box** is the most common type of control used to display field values. You enter, edit, find, sort, and filter data by working with the data in a text box control. The Category field value is displayed in a combo box control. A **combo box** is a combination of two controls: a text box and a list. You click the arrow button on a combo box control to display a list of values, or you can edit data directly in the combo box itself.

> **QUICK TIP**
> Always click a value in a field to identify which field you want to sort or filter before clicking a sort or filter button.

5. **Click Princess Bay Shelling in the TourName text box, click the Ascending button in the Sort & Filter group, then click the Next record button in the navigation bar to move to the second record**

   The Ames Ski Club is the second record when the records are sorted in ascending order on the TourName field. Information about the current record number and total number of records appears in the navigation bar, just as it does in a datasheet.

6. **Edit Ames Ski Club to Story County Ski Club**

   Your screen should look like Figure C-2. Forms displayed in Form View are the primary tool used to enter, edit, and delete data in an Access database.

7. **Right-click the Tours Entry Form tab, then click Close**

   When a form is closed, Access automatically saves any edits made to the current record.

FIGURE C-1: Tours Entry Form in Form View

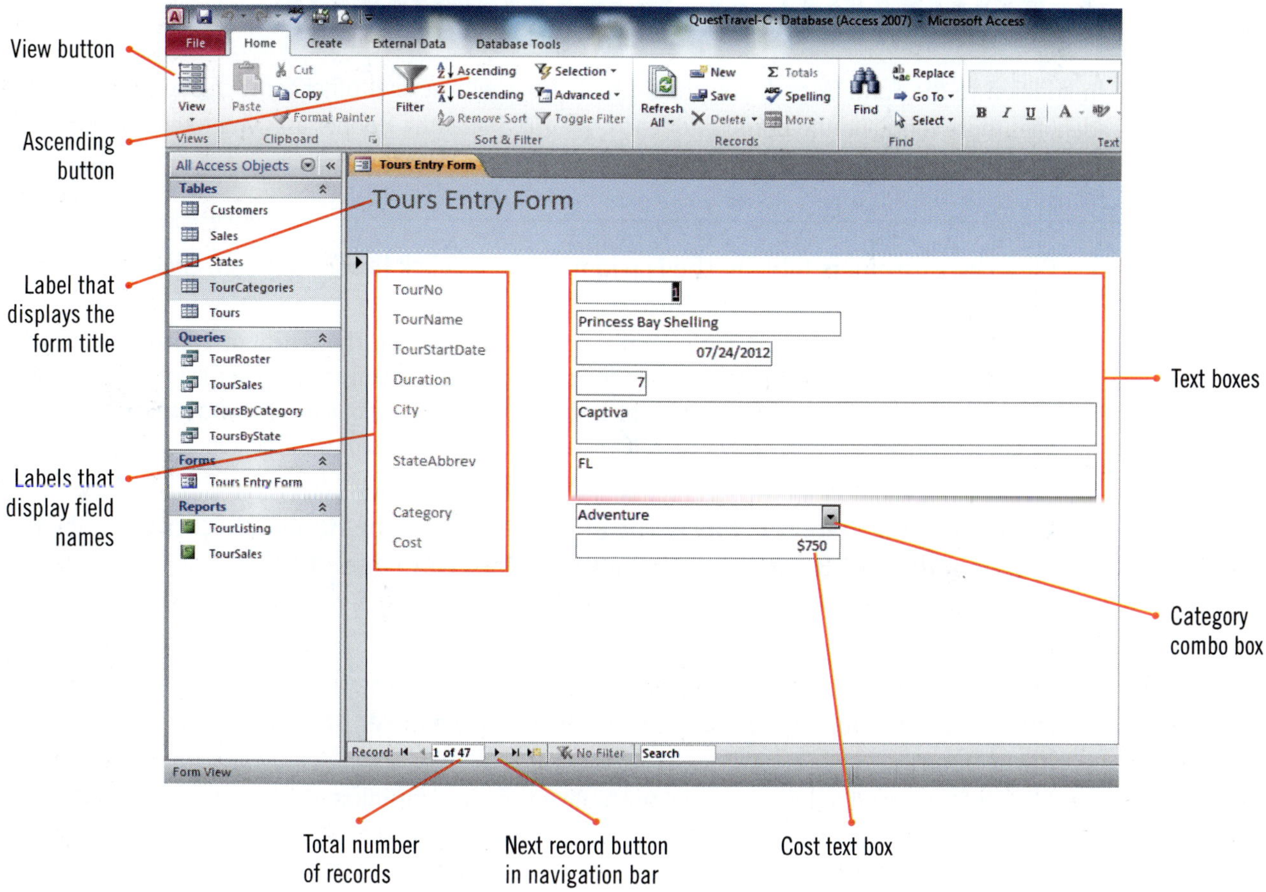

FIGURE C-2: Editing data in a text box

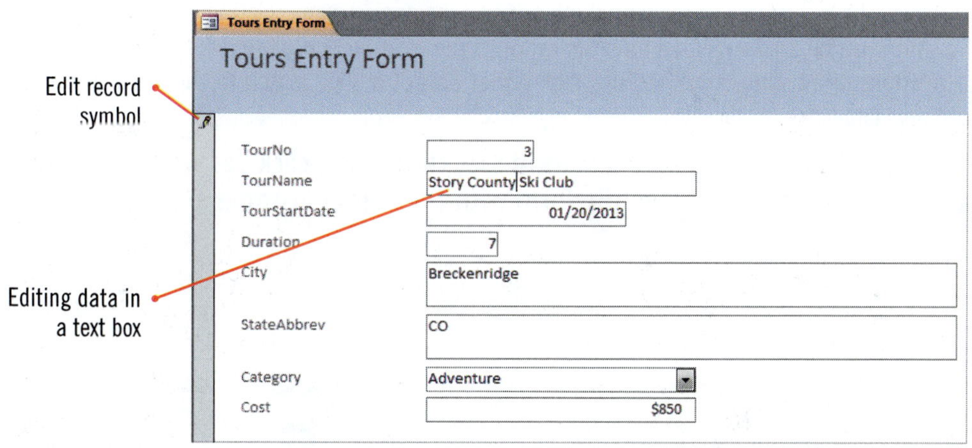

TABLE C-1: Form views

view	primary purpose
Form	To view, enter, edit, and delete data
Layout	To modify the size, position, or formatting of controls; shows data as you modify the form, making it the tool of choice when you want to change the appearance and usability of the form while viewing live data
Design	To modify the form header, detail, and footer section, or to access the complete range of controls and form properties; Design View does not display data

UNIT C

Access 2010

Creating a Split Form

In addition to the Form Wizard, you should be familiar with several other form creation tools. Table C-2 identifies those tools and the purpose for each. Samantha Hooper asks you to create another form to manage customer data. You'll work with the Split Form tool for this task.

STEPS

1. **Click the Customers table in the Navigation Pane, click the Create tab, click the More Forms button, then click Split Form**

   The Customers data appears in a split form as shown in Figure C-3. The benefit of a **split form** is that the upper pane allows you to display the fields of one record in any arrangement, and the lower pane maintains a datasheet view of the first few records, which you can navigate very quickly. The two panes of the split form are always synchronized. In other words, if you edit, sort, or filter records in the upper pane, the lower pane is automatically updated, and vice versa. The navigation bar shows that there are 37 total records.

2. **Click MO in the State text box in the upper pane, click the Home tab, click the Selection button in the Sort & Filter group, then click Does Not Equal "MO"**

   Twenty-six records are filtered where the State field is not equal to MO. You also need to change a value in the Jacob Alman record.

TROUBLE

Make sure you edit the record in the lower pane.

3. **In the lower pane, click Des Moines in the City field of the first record, edit the entry to read West Des Moines, click any other record in the lower pane, then click Jacob in the lower pane**

   Moving from record to record also automatically saves data, regardless of whether you are working in the upper or lower pane. Note that "West Des Moines" is the entry in the City field in both the upper and lower panes as shown in Figure C-4.

4. **Click the record selector for the Kristen Collins record in the lower pane, then click the Delete button in the Records group on the Home tab**

   A message appears indicating that you cannot delete this record because it contains related records in the Sales table. This is a benefit of referential integrity on the one-to-many relationships between the Customers, Sales, and Tours tables. Referential integrity prevents the creation of orphan records, records on the *many* side of a relationship (in this case, the Sales table), that do not have a match in the *one* side (in this case, the Customers table).

5. **Click OK, right-click the Customers form tab, click Close, click Yes when prompted to save changes, then click OK to save the form with the name Customers**

TABLE C-2: Form creation tools

tool	icon	creates a form:
Form		with one click based on the selected table or query
Form Design		from scratch with access to advanced design changes in Form Design View
Blank Form		with no controls starting in Form Layout View
Form Wizard		by answering a series of questions provided by the Form Wizard dialog boxes
Navigation		used to navigate or move between different areas of the database
More Forms		based on Multiple Items, Datasheet, Split Form, Modal Dialog, PivotChart, or PivotTable arrangements
Split Form		where the upper half displays data the fields of one record in any arrangement, and the lower half displays data as a datasheet

FIGURE C-3: Customers table in a split form

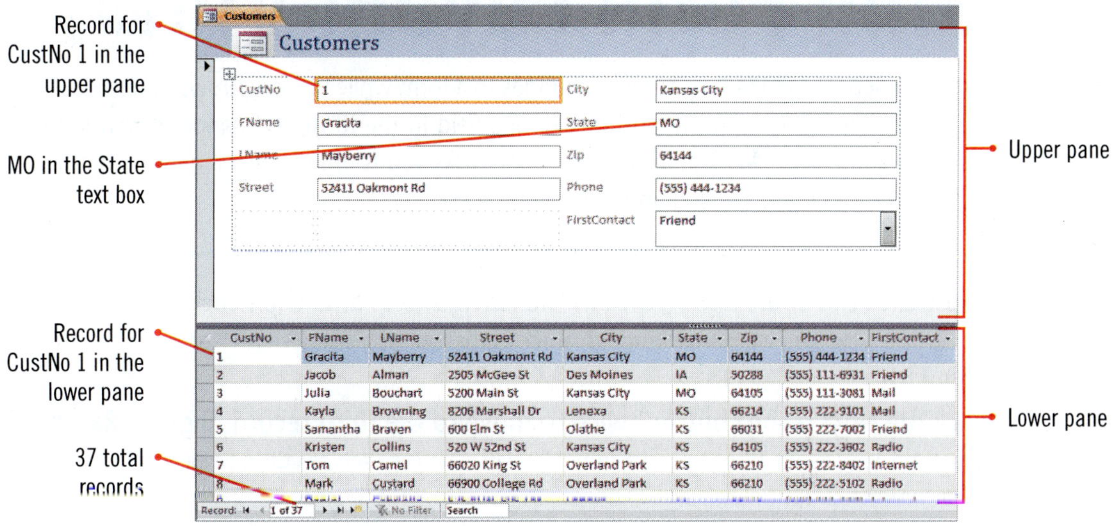

FIGURE C-4: Editing data in a split form

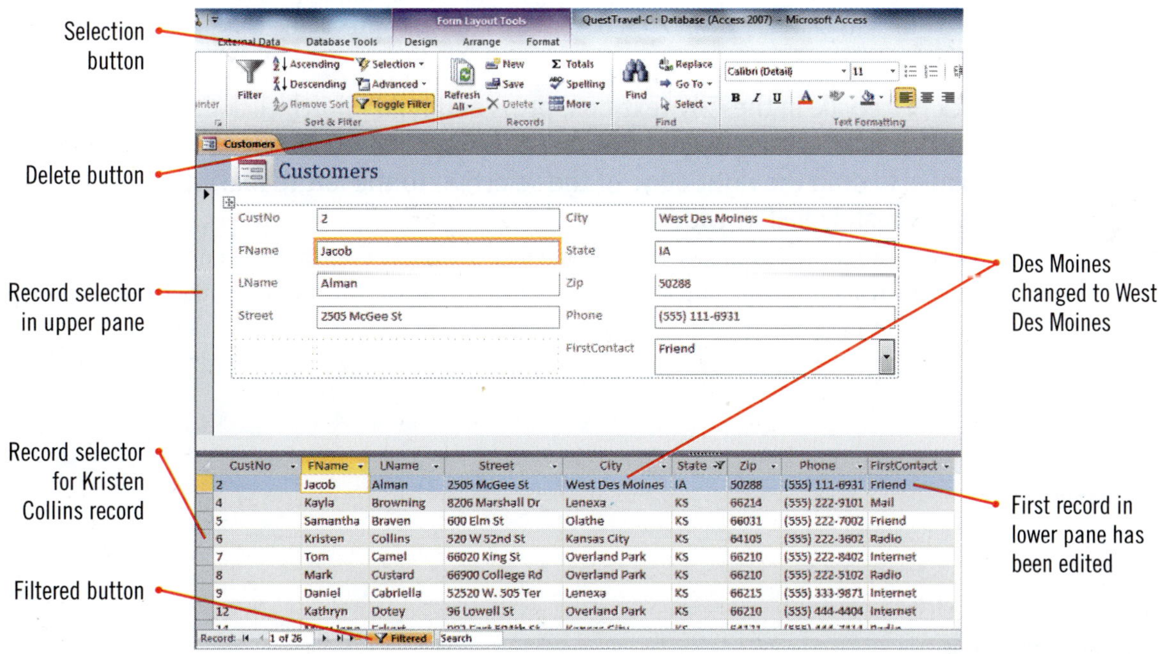

Using Form Layout View

Layout View lets you make some design changes to a form while you are browsing the data. For example, you can move and resize controls, add or delete a field in the form, or change formatting characteristics such as fonts and colors. Samantha Hooper asks you to make several design changes to the Tours Entry Form. You can make these changes in Layout View.

STEPS

1. **Right-click the Tours Entry Form in the Navigation Pane, then click Layout View**
   In Layout View, you can move through the records, but you cannot enter or edit the data as you can in Form View.

> **TROUBLE**
> If your third record is not Bigfoot Rafting Club, sort the records in ascending order on the TourName field.

2. **Click the Next record button twice to move to the third record, Bigfoot Rafting Club**
   You often use Layout View to make minor design changes such as editing labels and changing formatting characteristics.

3. **Click the TourNo label to select it, click between the words Tour and No, then press [Spacebar]**
   You also want to edit a few more labels.

> **TROUBLE**
> Be sure to modify the *labels in the left column* instead of the text boxes on the right.

4. **Continue editing the labels as shown in Figure C-5**
   You also want to change the text color of the first two labels, Tour No and Tour Name, to red to make them more visible.

5. **Click the Tour No label, click the Home tab, click the Font Color button, click the Tour Name label, then click**
   Often, you want to apply the same formatting enhancement to multiple controls. For example, you decide to narrow the City and State Abbrev text boxes. Select the text boxes at the same time to make the same change to both.

> **TROUBLE**
> Be sure to modify the *text boxes in the right column* instead of the labels on the left.

6. **Click Placerville in the City text box, press and hold [Shift], click CA in the State Abbrev text box to select the two text boxes at the same time, release [Shift], then use the ↔ pointer to drag the right edge of the selection to the left to make the text boxes approximately half as wide**
   Layout View for the Tours Entry Form should look like Figure C-6. Mouse pointers in Form Layout and Form Design View are very important as they indicate what happens when you drag the mouse. Mouse pointers are described in Table C-3.

TABLE C-3: Mouse pointer shapes

shape	when does this shape appear?	action
	When you point to any unselected control on the form (the default mouse pointer)	Single-clicking with this mouse pointer *selects* a control
	When you point to the upper-left corner or edge of a selected control in Form Design View or the middle of the control in Form Layout View	Dragging with this mouse pointer *moves* the selected control(s)
↕, ↔, ⤡, ⤢	When you point to any sizing handle (except the larger one in the upper-left corner in Form Design View)	Dragging with one of these mouse pointers *resizes* the control

FIGURE C-5: Using Layout View to modify form labels on the Tours Entry Form

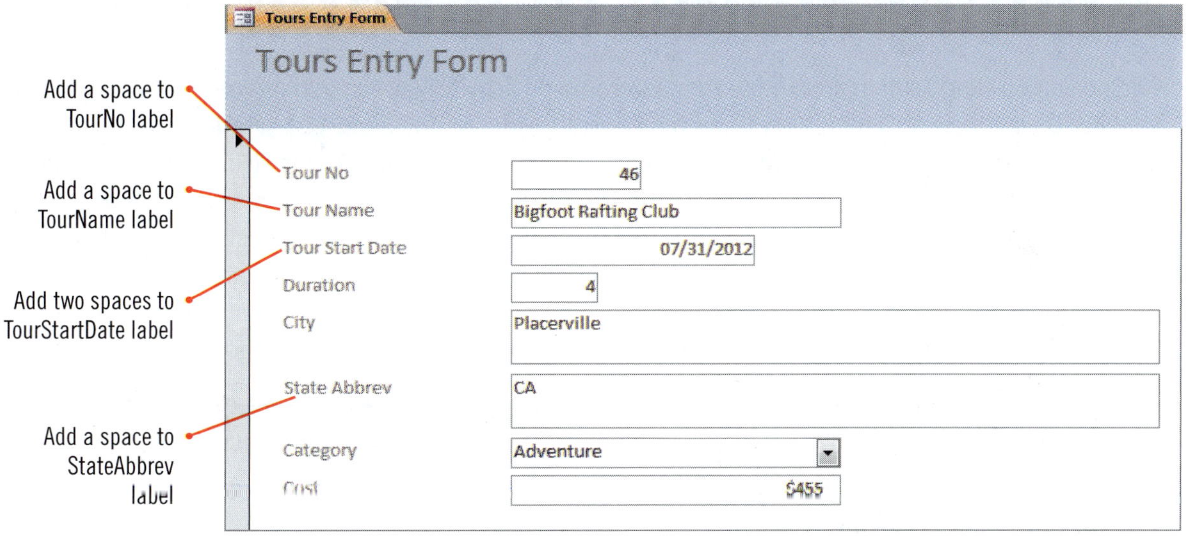

FIGURE C-6: Layout View for the Tours Entry Form

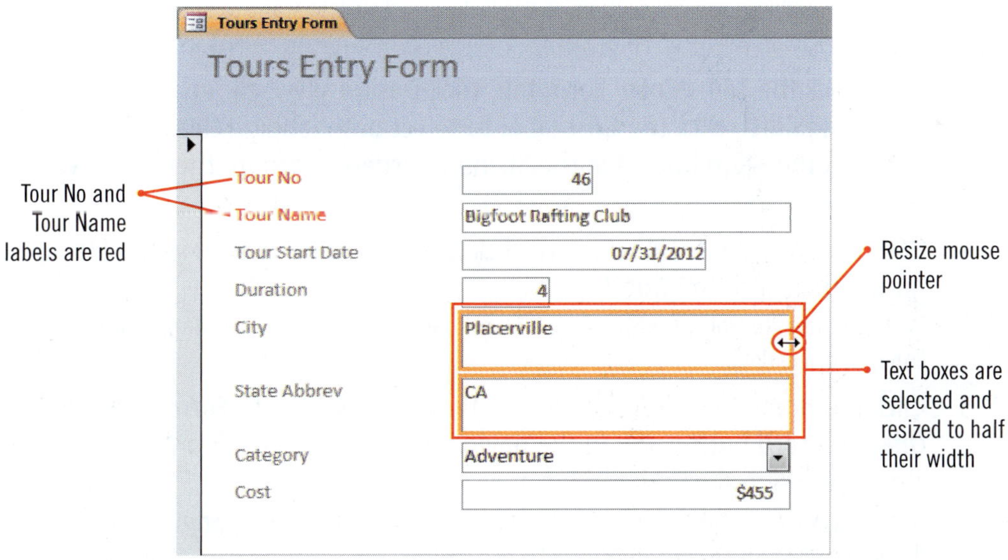

Access 2010

UNIT C
Access 2010

Adding Fields to a Form

Adding and deleting fields in an existing form is a common activity. You can add or delete fields in a form in either Layout View or Design View using the Field List window. The **Field List window** lists the database tables and the fields they contain. To add a field to the form, drag it from the Field List to the desired location on the form. To delete a field on a form, click the field to select it, then press the [Delete] key. Deleting a field from a form does not delete it from the underlying table nor does it have any effect on the data contained in the field. You can toggle the Field List on and off using the Add Existing Fields button on the Design tab. Samantha Hooper asks you to add the tour description from the TourCategories table to the Tours Entry Form. You can use Layout View and the Field List window to accomplish this goal.

STEPS

1. **Click the Design tab on the Ribbon, click the Add Existing Fields button in the Tools group, then click the Show all tables link in the Field List window if the Field List window does not look like Figure C-7**

   The Field List window opens in Layout View, as shown in Figure C-7. Notice that the Field List is divided into sections. The upper section shows the tables currently used by the form, the middle section shows related tables, and the lower section shows other tables. The expand/collapse button to the left of the table names allows you to expand (show) the fields within the table or collapse (hide) them. The Description field is in the TourCategories table in the middle section.

QUICK TIP
If you make a mistake, click the Undo button and try again.

2. **Click the expand button to the left of the TourCategories table, drag the Description field to the form, then use the pointer to drag the new Description combo box and label below the Cost controls**

   When you add a new field to a form, two controls are usually generated: a label and a text box. The label contains the field name and the text box displays the contents of the field. The TourCategories table moved from the middle to the top section of the Field List. You also want to align and size the new controls with others already on the form. Form Design View works best for alignment activities.

3. **Right-click the Tours Entry Form tab, click Design View, click the Description label, press and hold [Shift], click the Cost label to select both labels, release [Shift], click the Arrange tab, click the Align button in the Sizing & Ordering group, then click Left**

   Now resize the labels.

4. **With the two labels still selected, click the Size/Space button in the Sizing & Ordering group, then click To Widest**

   With the new controls in position, you want to enter a new record. You must switch to Form View to edit, enter, or delete data.

TROUBLE
Don't worry if your Tour No value doesn't match Figure C-8. It is an AutoNumber value, controlled by Access.

5. **Click the Home tab, click the View button to switch to Form View, click the New (blank) record button in the navigation bar, click the TourName text box, then enter a new record in the updated form, as shown in Figure C-8**

   Note that when you select a value in the Category combo box, the Description automatically updates. This is due to the one-to-many relationship between the TourCategories and Tours tables in the Relationships window.

FIGURE C-7: Field List in Form Layout View

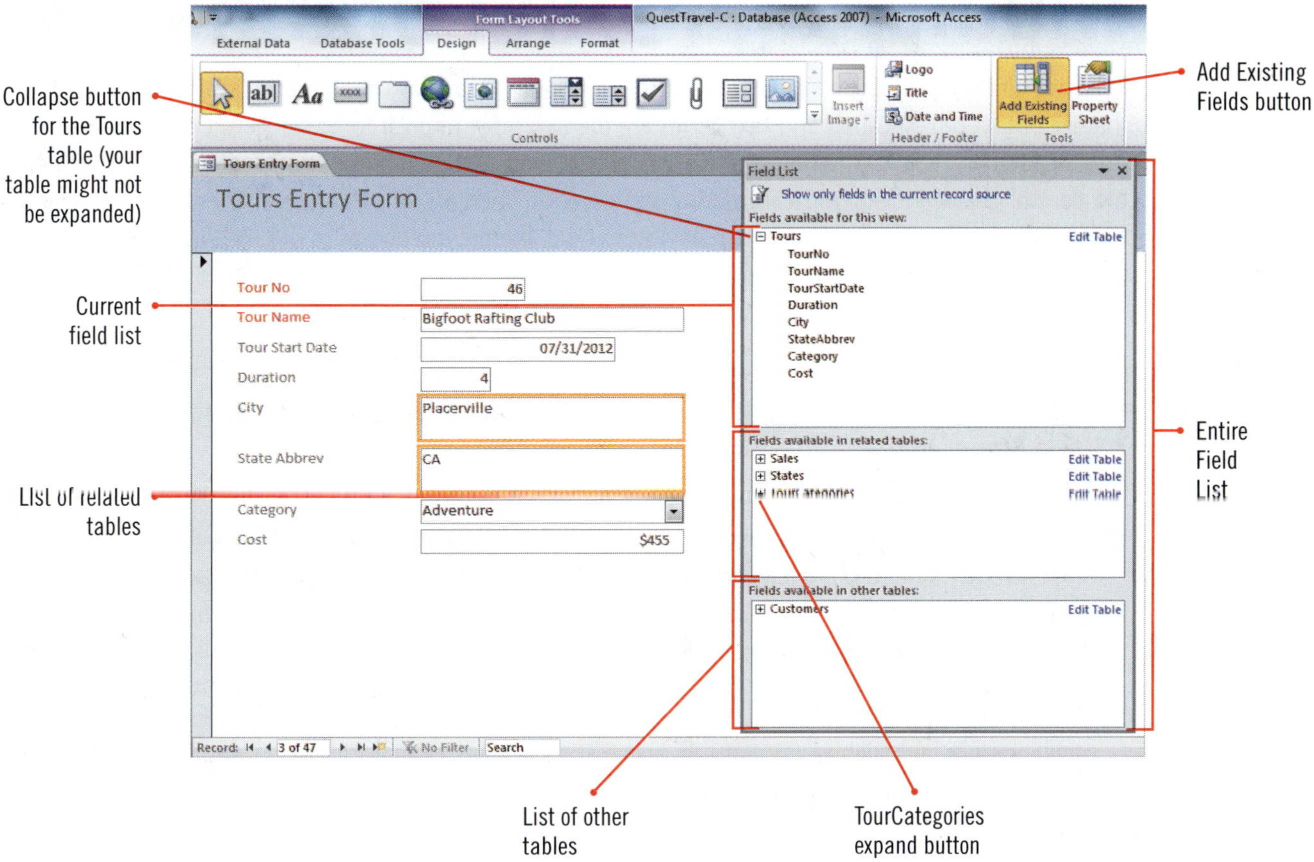

FIGURE C-8: Entering a record in the updated Tours Entry Form in Form View

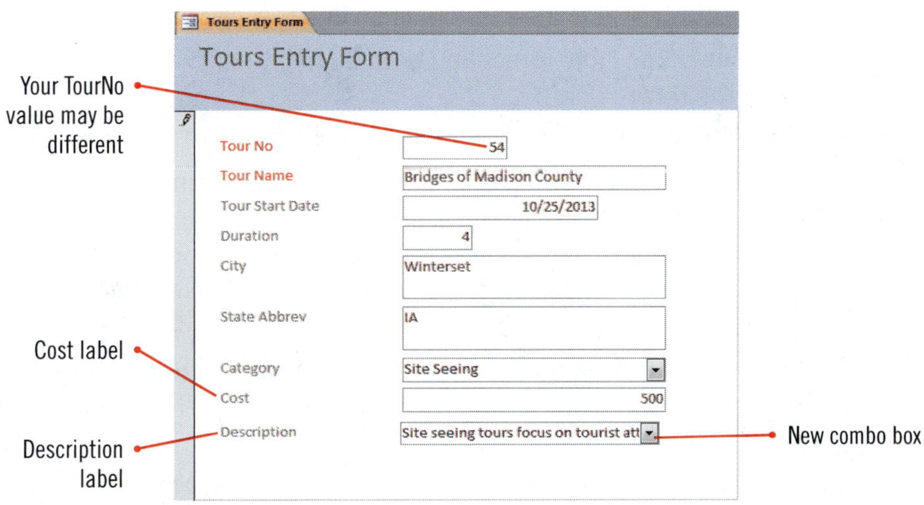

Bound versus unbound controls

Controls are either bound or unbound. **Bound controls** display values from a field such as text boxes and combo boxes. **Unbound controls** do not display data, but rather serve to describe data or enhance the appearance of the form. Labels are the most common type of unbound control, but other types include lines, images, tabs, and command buttons. Another way to distinguish bound from unbound controls is to observe the form as you move from record to record. Because bound controls display data, their contents change as you move through the records, displaying the entry in the field of the current record. Unbound controls such as labels and lines do not change as you move through the records in a form.

UNIT C

Access 2010

Modifying Form Controls

You have already made many modifications to form controls such as changing the font color of labels and the size of text boxes. Labels and text boxes are the two most popular form controls. Other common controls are listed in Table C-4. When you modify controls, you change their **properties** (characteristics). All of the control characteristics you can modify are stored in the control's **Property Sheet**. Because Quest offers more adventure tours than any other type of tour, you decide to use the Property Sheet of the Category field to modify the default value to be "Adventure." You also use the Property Sheet to make other control modifications to better size and align the controls.

STEPS

TROUBLE
Be sure to click the Tour No label on the left, not the TourNo text box on the right.

TROUBLE
You may need to click the Align Text Right button twice.

1. **Click the Layout View button on the Home tab, then click the Property Sheet button in the Tools group**

   The Property Sheet window opens, showing you all of the properties for the selected item.

2. **Click the Category combo box, click the Data tab in the Property Sheet window (if it is not already selected), click the Default Value box, type Adventure, then press [Enter]**

   The Property Sheet should look like Figure C-9. Access often helps you with the **syntax** (rules) of entering property values. In this case, Access added quotation marks around "Adventure" to indicate that the default entry is text. Properties are categorized in the Property Sheet with the Format, Data, Event, and Other tabs. The All tab is a complete list of all the control's properties. You can use the Property Sheet to make all control modifications, although you'll probably find that some changes are easier to make using the Ribbon. The Property Sheet changes as you modify a control using the Ribbon.

3. **Click the Format tab of the Property Sheet, click the Tour No label in the form to select it, click the Home tab on the Ribbon, then click the Align Text Right button in the Text Formatting group**

   Notice that the **Text Align property** in the Property Sheet is automatically updated from Left to Right even though you changed the property using the Ribbon instead of directly in the Property Sheet.

4. **Click the Tour Name label, press and hold [Shift], then click every other label in the first column on the form**

   With all the labels selected, you can modify their Text Align property at the same time.

5. **Click the Align Text Right button in the Text Formatting group**

   Don't be overwhelmed by the number of properties available for each control on the form or the number of ways to modify each property. Over time, you will learn about most of these properties. At this point, it's only important to know the purpose of the Property Sheet and understand that properties are modified in various ways.

6. **Click the Save button on the Quick Access toolbar, click the Form View button on the Design tab, click the New (blank) record button in the navigation bar, then enter the record shown in Figure C-10**

   For new records, "Adventure" is provided as the default value for the Category combo box, but you can change it by typing a new value or selecting one from the list. With the labels right-aligned, they are much closer to the data in the text boxes that they describe.

FIGURE C-9: Using the Property Sheet

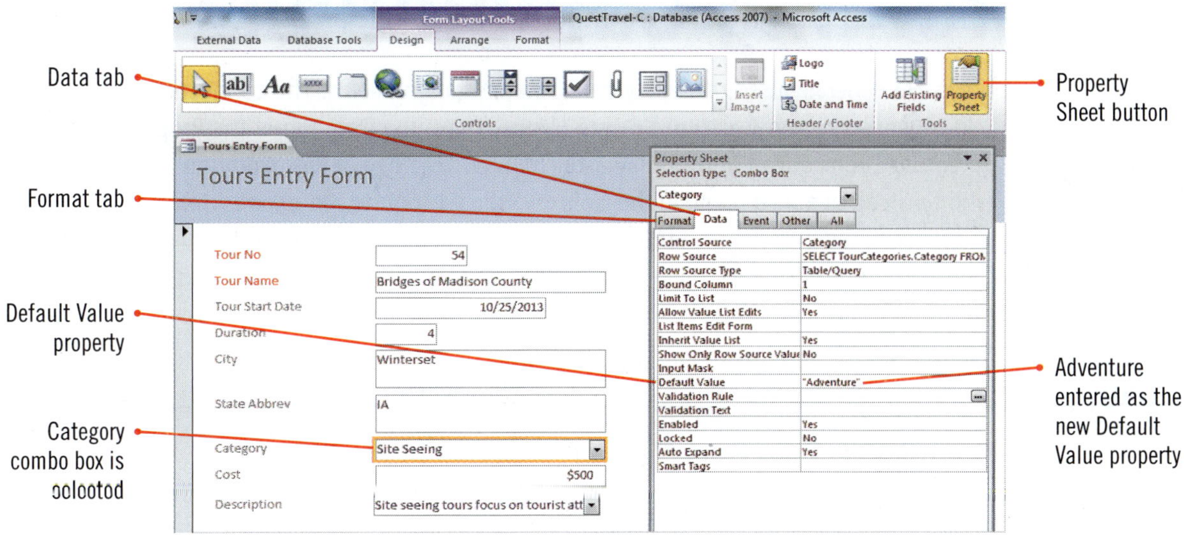

FIGURE C-10: Modified Tours Entry Form

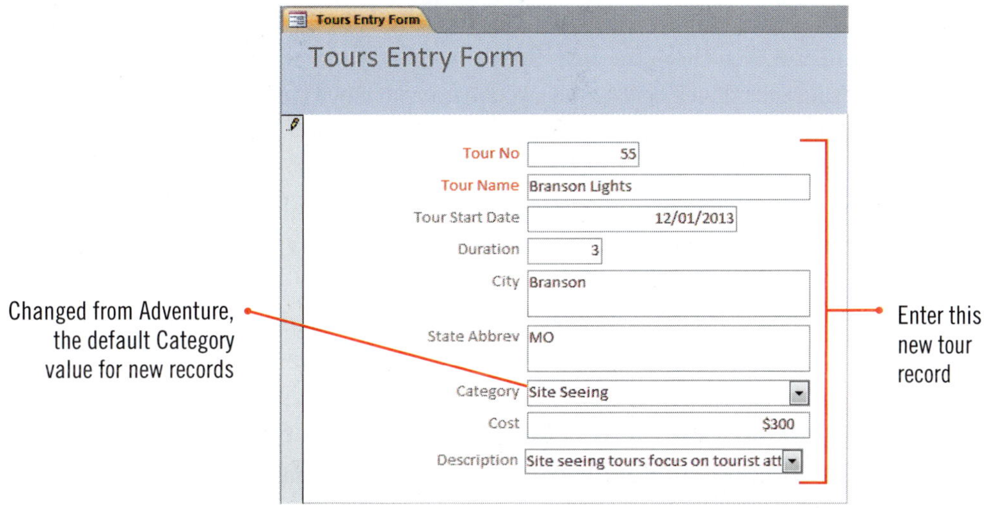

TABLE C-4: Common form controls

name	used to	bound	unbound
Label	Provide consistent descriptive text as you navigate from record to record; the label is the most common type of unbound control and can also be used as a hyperlink to another database object, external file, or Web page		x
Text box	Display, edit, or enter data for each record from an underlying record source; the text box is the most common type of bound control	x	
List box	Display a list of possible data entries	x	
Combo box	Display a list of possible data entries for a field, and provide a text box for an entry from the keyboard; combines the list box and text box controls	x	
Tab control	Create a three-dimensional aspect on a form		x
Check box	Display "yes" or "no" answers for a field; if the box is checked, it means "yes"	x	
Toggle button	Display "yes" or "no" answers for a field; if the button is pressed, it means "yes"	x	
Option button	Display a choice for a field	x	
Option group	Display and organize choices (usually presented as option buttons) for a field	x	
Line and Rectangle	Draw lines and rectangles on the form		x
Command button	Provide an easy way to initiate a command or run a macro		x

UNIT C

Access 2010

Creating Calculations

Text boxes are generally used to display data from underlying fields. The connection between the text box and field is defined by the **Control Source property** on the Data tab of the Property Sheet for that text box. A text box control can also display a calculation. To create a calculation in a text box, you enter an expression instead of a field name in the Control Source property. An **expression** is a combination of field names, operators (such as +, –, /, and *), and functions (such as Sum, Count, or Avg) that result in a single value. Sample expressions are shown in Table C-5. Samantha Hooper asks you to add a text box to the Tours Entry Form to calculate the tour end date. You can add a text box in Form Design View to accomplish this.

STEPS

1. **Right-click the Tours Entry Form tab, then click Design View**

   You want to add the tour end date calculation just below the Duration text box. First you'll resize the City and StateAbbrev fields.

2. **Click the City label, press and hold [Shift], click the City text box, click the StateAbbrev label, click the StateAbbrev text box to select the four controls together, release [Shift], click the Arrange tab, click the Size/Space button, then click To Shortest**

   With the City and StateAbbrev fields resized, you're ready to move them to make room for the new control to calculate the tour end date.

QUICK TIP

You can also press an arrow key to move a selected control.

3. **Click a blank spot on the form to deselect the four controls, click the StateAbbrev text box, use the pointer to move it down, click the City text box, then use the pointer to move it down**

   To add the calculation to determine the tour end date (the tour start date plus the duration), start by adding a new text box to the form between the Duration and City text boxes.

TROUBLE

If you position the new text box incorrectly, click Undo on the Quick Access toolbar and try again.

4. **Click the Design tab, click the Text Box button in the Controls group, then click between the Duration and City text boxes to insert the new text box**

   Adding a new text box automatically adds a new label to the left of the text box.

TROUBLE

The initial number in your label is based on previous work done to the form, so it might vary.

5. **Double-click the new Text22 label on the left, type Tour End Date, then press [Enter]**

   With the label updated to correctly identify the text box to the right, you're ready to enter the expression to calculate the tour end date.

6. **Click the new text box to select it, click the Data tab of the Property Sheet, click the Control Source property, type =[TourStartDate]+[Duration], then press [Enter] to update the form as shown in Figure C-11**

   All expressions entered in a control start with an equal sign (=). When referencing a field name within an expression, [square brackets]—(not parentheses) and not {curly braces}—surround the field name. In an expression, you must type the field name exactly as it was created in Table Design View, but you do not need to match the capitalization.

7. **Click the View button to switch to Form View, click the value in the Tour Name text box, click the Ascending button, select 7 in the Duration text box, type 5, then press [Enter]**

   Note that the tour end date, calculated by an expression, automatically changed to five days after the tour start date to reflect the new duration value. The updated Tours Entry Form with the tour date end calculation for the American Heritage Tour is shown in Figure C-12.

FIGURE C-11: Adding a text box to calculate a value

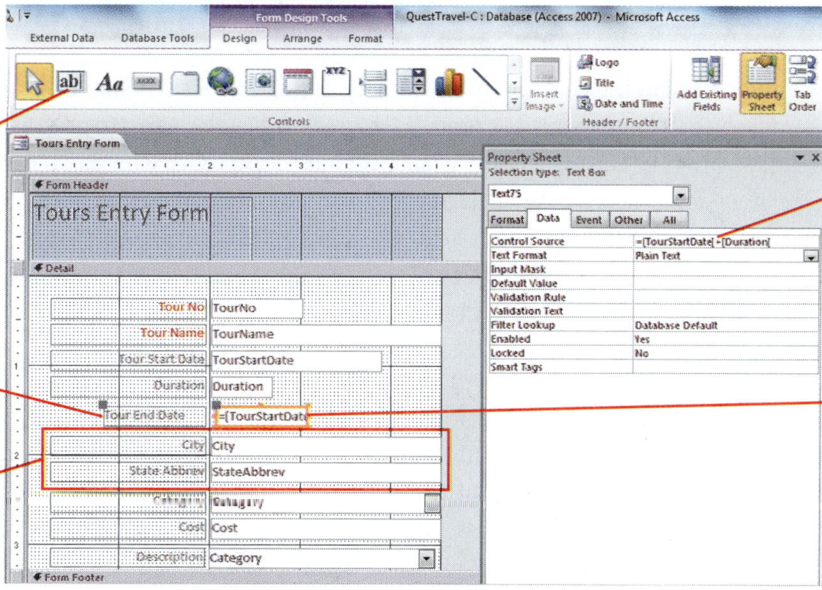

FIGURE C-12: Displaying the results of a calculation in Form View

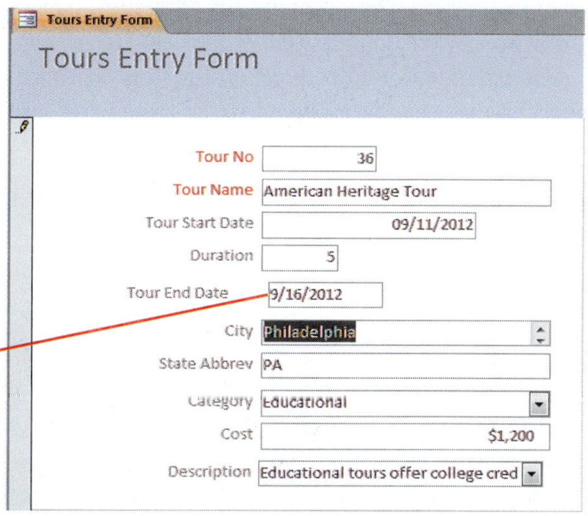

TABLE C-5: Sample expressions

sample expression	description
=Sum([Salary])	Uses the **Sum function** to add the values in the Salary field
=[Price] * 1.05	Multiplies the Price field by 1.05 (adds 5% to the Price field)
=[Subtotal] + [Shipping]	Adds the value of the Subtotal field to the value of the Shipping field
=Avg([Freight])	Uses the **Avg function** to display an average of the values in the Freight field
=Date()	Uses the **Date function** to display the current date in the form of mm-dd-yy
="Page " &[Page]	Displays the word Page, a space, and the result of the [Page] field, an Access field that contains the current page number
=[FirstName]& " " &[LastName]	Displays the value of the FirstName and LastName fields in one control, separated by a space
=Left([ProductNumber],2)	Uses the **Left function** to display the first two characters in the ProductNumber field

Modifying Tab Order

After positioning all of the controls on the form, you should check the tab order and tab stops. **Tab order** is the order the focus moves as you press [Tab] in Form View. A **tab stop** refers to whether a control can receive the focus in the first place. By default, the tab stop property for all text boxes and combo boxes is set to Yes, but some text boxes, such as those that contain expressions, will not be used for data entry. Therefore, the tab stop property for a text box that contains a calculation should be set to No. Unbound controls such as labels and lines do not have a tab stop property because they cannot be used to enter or edit data. You plan to check the tab order of the Tours Entry Form, then change tab stops and tab order as necessary.

STEPS

1. **Press [Tab] enough times to move through several records, watching the focus move through the bound controls of the form**

   Because the tour end date text box is a calculated field, you don't want it to receive the focus. To prevent the Tour End Date text box from receiving the focus, you set its tab stop property to No using its Property Sheet. You can work with the Property Sheet in either Layout or Design View.

QUICK TIP
You can also switch between views using the View buttons in the lower-right corner of the window.

2. **Right-click the Tours Entry Form tab, click Design View, click the Tour End Date text box, click the Other tab in the Property Sheet, double-click the Tab Stop property to toggle it from Yes to No, then change the Name property to TourEndDate as shown in Figure C-13**

   The Other tab of the Property Sheet contains the properties you need to change the tab stop and tab order. The **Tab Stop property** determines whether the field accepts focus, and the **Tab Index property** indicates the numeric tab order for all controls on the form that have the Tab Stop property set to Yes. The **Name property** on the Other tab is also important as it identifies the name of the control, which is used in other areas of the database. To review your tab stop changes, return to Form View.

QUICK TIP
In Form Design View, press [Ctrl][.] to switch to Form View. In Form View, press [Ctrl][,] to switch to Form Design View.

3. **Click the View button on the Design tab to switch to Form View, then press [Tab] nine times to move to the next record**

   Now that the tab stop has been removed from the TourEndDate text box, the tab order flows correctly from the top to the bottom of the form, but skips the calculated field. To review the tab order for the entire form in one dialog box, you must switch to Form Design View.

TROUBLE
If the order of your fields does not match those in Figure C-14, move a field by clicking the field selector and then dragging the field.

4. **Right-click the Tours Entry Form tab, click Design View, then click the Tab Order button in the Tools group to open the Tab Order dialog box as shown in Figure C-14**

   The Tab Order dialog box allows you to view and change the tab order by dragging fields up or down using the field selectors to the left of the field names. Moving fields up and down in this list also renumbers the Tab Index property for the controls in their respective Property Sheets.

5. **Click OK to close the Tab Order dialog box, click the Property Sheet button to toggle it off, then click the Save button on the Quick Access toolbar to save your work**

FIGURE C-13: Using the Property Sheet to set tab properties

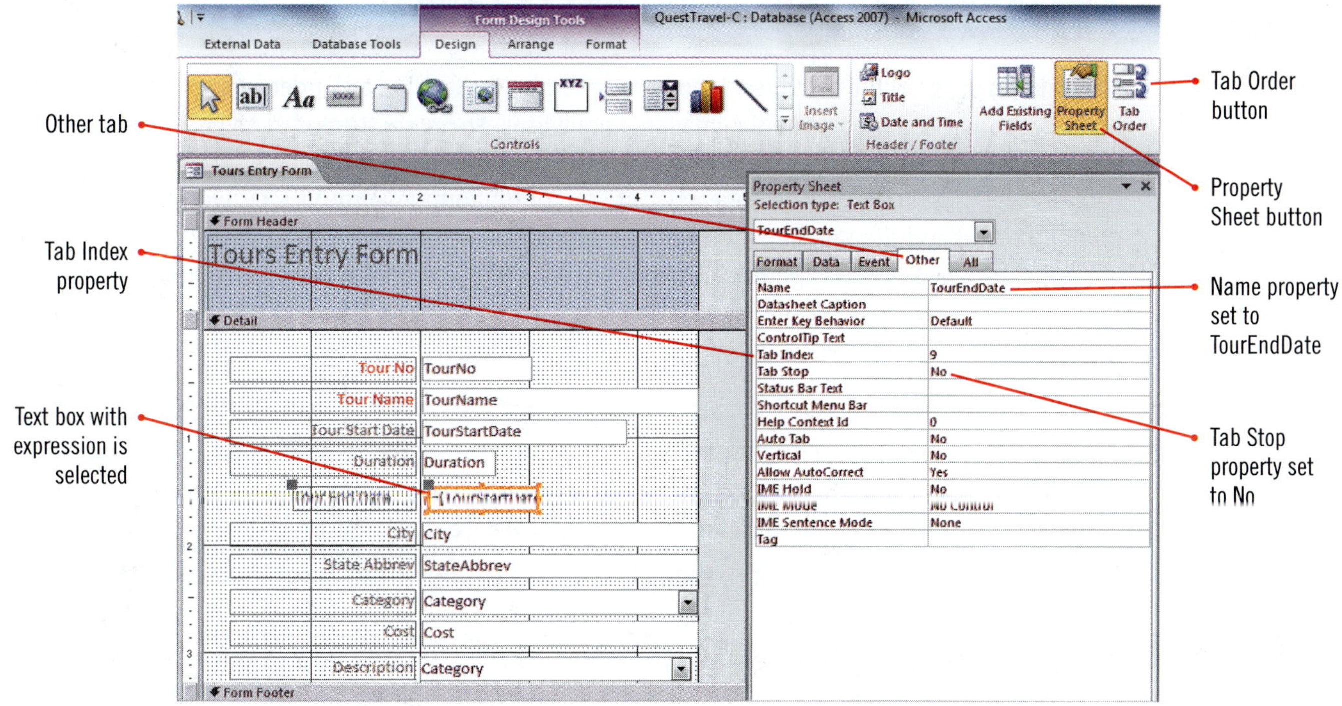

FIGURE C-14: Tab Order dialog box

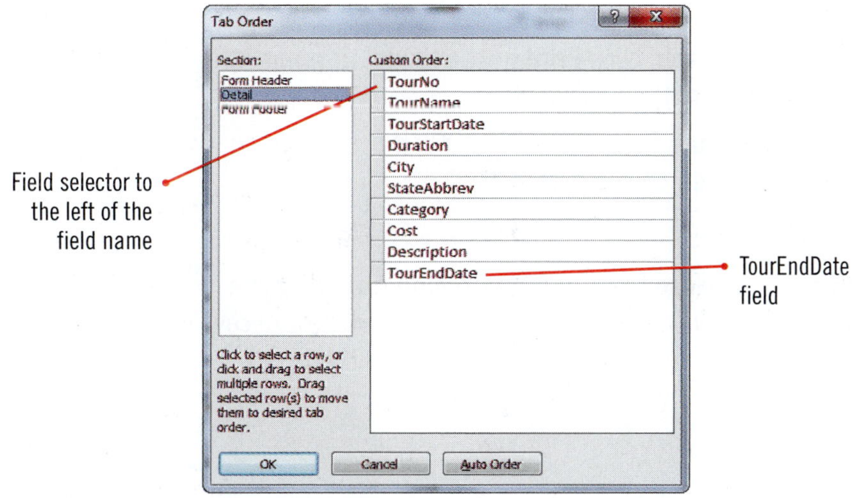

Access 2010

UNIT C

Access 2010

Inserting an Image

Graphic images, such as pictures, logos, or clip art, can add style and professionalism to a form. The form section in which you place the images is significant. **Form sections** determine where controls are displayed and printed; they are described in Table C-6. For example, if you add a company logo to the Form Header section, the image appears at the top of the form in Form View as well as at the top of a printout. If you add the same image to the Detail section, it prints next to each record in the printout because the Detail section is printed for every record. Samantha Hooper suggests that you add the Quest logo to the top of the Tours Entry Form. You can add the control in either Layout or Design View, but if you want to place it in the Form Header section, you have to work in Design View.

STEPS

1. **Click the Form Header section bar, click the Insert Image button in the Controls group, click Browse, then navigate to the drive and folder where you store your Data Files**

   The Insert Picture dialog box opens, prompting you for the location of the image.

2. **Double-click QuestLogo.bmp, then click the right side of the Form Header section**

   The QuestLogo image is added to the right side of the Form Header. You want to resize it to about 1.5" × 1.5".

3. **With the QuestLogo image still selected, use the pointer to drag the lower-right corner of the image up and to the left so that it is about 1.5" × 1.5", then drag the top edge of the Detail section up using the pointer as shown in Figure C-15**

   When an image or control is selected in Design View, you can use **sizing handles**, which are small squares at the corner of the selection box. Drag a handle to resize the image or control. With the form completed, you open it in Form View to observe the changes.

4. **Click the Save button on the Quick Access toolbar, then click the View button to switch to Form View**

   You decide to add one more record with your final Tours Entry Form.

5. **Enter the new record shown in Figure C-16, using your last name in the TourName field**

   Now print only this single new record.

6. **Click the File tab, click Print in the navigation bar, click Print, click the Selected Record(s) option button, then click OK**

7. **Close the Tours Entry Form, click Yes if prompted to save it, close the QuestTravel-C.accdb database, then exit Access 2010**

TROUBLE

The lower-right corner of the image touches the top edge of the Detail section. To resize the Quest logo, click it to select it.

TABLE C-6: Form sections

section	controls placed in this section print:
Form Header	Only once at the top of the first page of the printout
Detail	Once for every record
Form Footer	Only once at the end of the last page of the printout

FIGURE C-15: Adding an image to the Form Header section

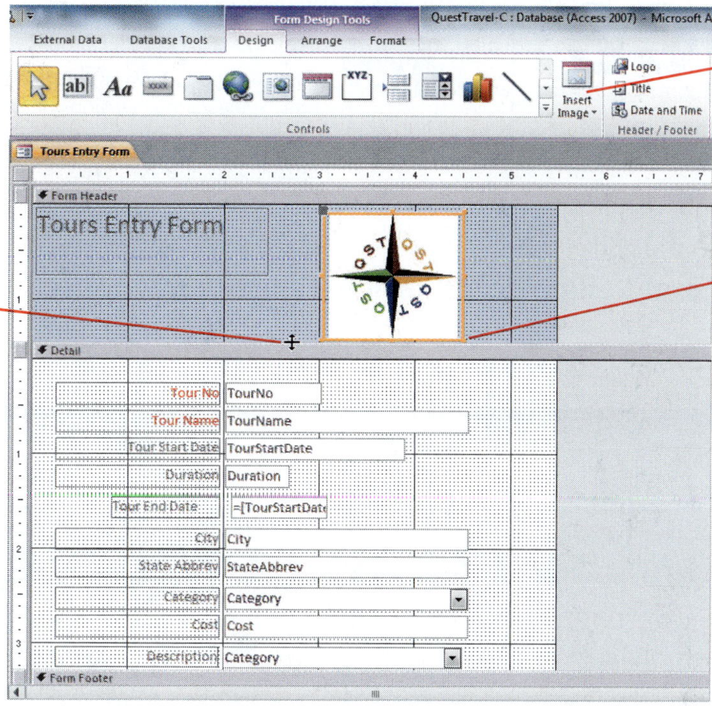

FIGURE C-16: Final Tours Entry Form with new record

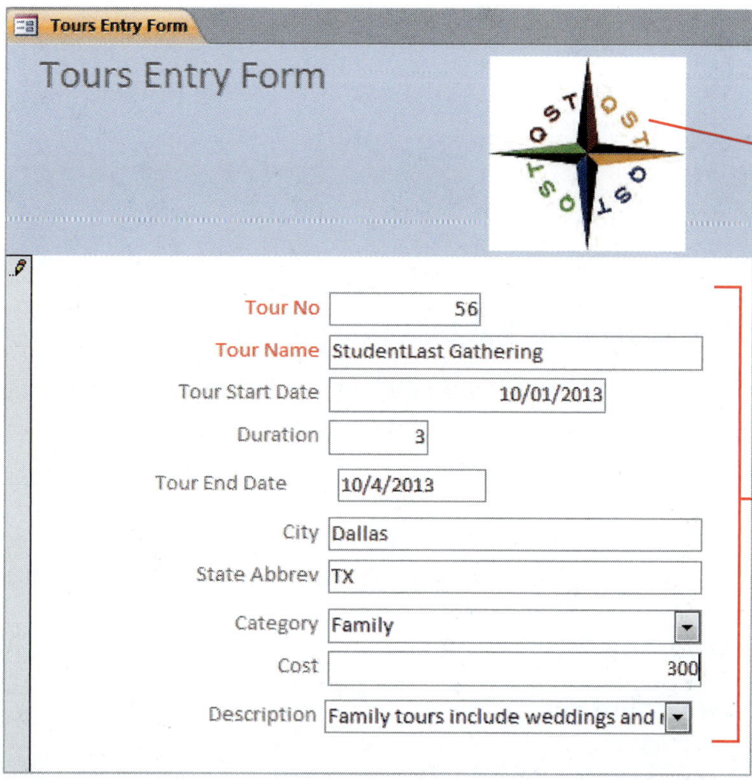

Practice

SAM

For current SAM information, including versions and content details, visit SAM Central (http://www.cengage.com/samcentral). If you have a SAM user profile, you may have access to hands-on instruction, practice, and assessment of the skills covered in this unit. Since various versions of SAM are supported throughout the life of this text, check with your instructor for the correct instructions and URL/Web site for accessing assignments.

Concepts Review

Label each element of Form Design View shown in Figure C-17.

FIGURE C-17

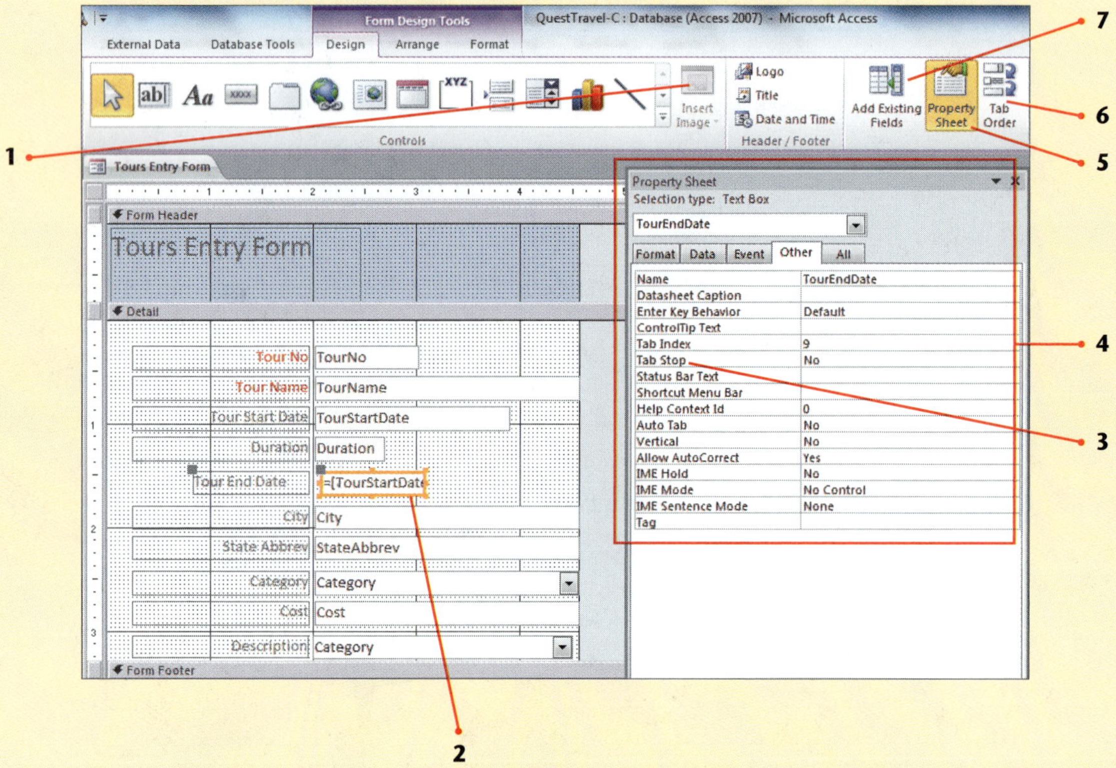

Match each term with the statement that best describes it.

8. **Bound control**
9. **Calculated control**
10. **Detail section**
11. **Database designer**
12. **Tab order**
13. **Form Footer section**

a. The way the focus moves from one bound control to the next in Form View
b. Created by entering an expression in a text box
c. Controls placed here print once for every record in the underlying record source
d. Used on a form to display data from a field
e. Controls placed here print only once at the end of the printout
f. Responsible for building and maintaining tables, queries, forms, and reports

Select the best answer from the list of choices.

14. Every element on a form is called a(n):

a. Control.
b. Item.
c. Tool.
d. Property.

15. Which of the following is probably *not* a graphic image?

a. Logo
b. Clip art
c. Calculation
d. Picture

16. The most common bound control is the:

- **a.** Label.
- **b.** Combo box.
- **c.** List box.
- **d.** Text box.

17. The most common unbound control is the:

- **a.** Command button.
- **b.** Label.
- **c.** Text box.
- **d.** Combo box.

18. Which form view *cannot* be used to view data?

- **a.** Layout
- **b.** Preview
- **c.** Design
- **d.** Datasheet

19. Which property helps you set tab order?

- **a.** Control Source
- **b.** Tab Index
- **c.** ControlTip
- **d.** Default

20. When you enter a calculation in a text box, the first character is a(n):

- **a.** Equal sign, =
- **b.** Left square bracket, [
- **c.** Left parenthesis, (
- **d.** Asterisk, *

Skills Review

1. Use the Form Wizard.

- **a.** Start Access and open the RealEstate-C.accdb database from the drive and folder where you store your Data Files. Enable content if prompted.
- **b.** Click the Create tab, then use the Form Wizard to create a form based on all of the fields in the Realtors table. Use a Columnar layout, and type **Realtor Entry Form** to title the form.
- **c.** Add a new record with your name. Note that the RealtorNo field is an AutoNumber field that is automatically incremented as you enter your first and last names. Enter your school's telephone number for the RPhone field value, and enter **4** as the AgencyNo field value.
- **d.** Save and close the Realtor Entry Form.

2. Create a split form.

- **a.** Click the Realtors table in the Navigation Pane, click the Create tab, click the More Forms button, then click Split Form.
- **b.** Switch to Form View, then navigate to the RealtorNo 11 (Rob Zacharias) record in either the upper or lower pane of the split form.
- **c.** Click the record selector in either the upper or lower pane for RealtorNo 11 (Rob Zacharias) and click the Delete button in the Records group to delete this realtor. Click Yes when prompted.
- **d.** Navigate to the RealtorNo 5 (Jane Ann Welch) record in either the upper or lower pane of the split form. Change Welch to **Rockaway**.
- **e.** Click the record selector in either the upper or lower pane for RealtorNo 5, Jane Ann Rockaway, and click the Delete button in the Records group. A message appears explaining why this record cannot be deleted. In a written document, explain the concept of an "orphan record" and how it applies to this situation. Click OK.
- **f.** Right-click the Realtors form tab, click Close, click Yes when prompted to save changes, and type **Realtors Split Form** as the name of the form.

3. Use Form Layout View.

- **a.** Open the Realtor Entry Form in Layout View.
- **b.** Modify the labels on the left to read: **Realtor Number**, **Realtor First Name**, **Realtor Last Name**, **Realtor Phone**, and **Agency Number**.
- **c.** Modify the text color of the labels to black.
- **d.** Resize the RFirst, RLast, and RPhone text boxes on the right to be the same width as the RealtorNo and AgencyNo text boxes.
- **e.** Save the Realtor Entry Form.

Skills Review (continued)

4. **Add fields to a form.**
   a. Open the Field List window, show all the tables, then expand the field list for the Agencies table.
   b. Drag the AgencyName field to the form, then move the AgencyName label and combo box to below the Agency Number controls.
   c. Modify the AgencyName label to read **Agency Name**.
   d. Modify the text color of the Agency Name label to black.
   e. Save the form and close the Field List window.
5. **Modify form controls.**
   a. In Layout View, use the Align Text Right button on the Home tab to right-align each of the labels in the left column.
   b. Switch to Form View, then use the Agency Name combo box to change the Agency Name to **Marvin and Pam Realtors** for Realtor Number 1.
   c. If the combo box is not wide enough to display the entire entry for Marvin and Pam Realtors, switch back to Layout View and widen the combo box as much as needed to display the entire entry in the combo box.
6. **Create calculations.**
   a. Switch to Form Design View, then add a text box below the Realtor Entry Form label in the Form Header section. Delete the extra label that is created when you add a new text box.
   b. Widen the text box to be almost as wide as the entire form, then enter the following expression into the text box, which will add the words **Information for** to the realtor's first name, a space, and then the realtor's last name. **="Information for "&[RFirst]&" "&[RLast]**
   c. Save the form, then view it in Form View. Be sure the new text box correctly displays spaces in the text. Return to Design View to edit the expression as needed.
   d. In Form View, change the Realtor Last Name in the first record from Matusek to **King**.
   e. Tab to the Realtor Phone text box, observing the automatic change to the expression in the Form Header section.
7. **Modify tab order.**
   a. Switch to Form Design View, then open the Property Sheet window.
   b. Select the new text box with the expression in the Form Header section, then change the Tab Stop property from Yes to No.
   c. Select the RealtorNo text box in the Detail section, then change the Tab Stop property from Yes to No. (AutoNumber fields cannot be edited, so they do not need to be in the tab order.)
   d. Close the Property Sheet.
   e. Save the form and view it in Form View. Tab through the form to make sure that the tab order is sequential. Use the Tab Order button on the Design tab in Form Design View to modify tab order, if necessary.
8. **Insert an image.**
   a. Switch to Design View, and click the Form Header section bar.
   b. Add the ForSale.bmp image to the right side of the Form Header, then resize the image to be about 1.5" × 1.5".
   c. Remove extra blank area in the Form Header section by dragging the top edge of the Detail section up as far as possible.
   d. Save the form, then switch to Form View. Move through the records, observing the calculated field from record to record to make sure it is calculating correctly.
   e. Find the record with your name as shown in Figure C-18, and then print only that record if requested by your instructor.
   f. Close the Realtor Entry Form, close the RealEstate-C.accdb database, then exit Access.

FIGURE C-18

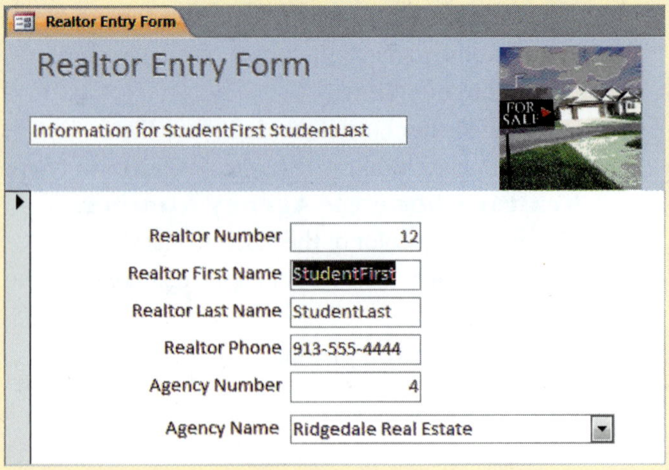

Independent Challenge 1

As the manager of the scuba divers branch of the Quest Specialty Travel tour company, you have developed a database to help manage scuba dives. In this exercise, you'll create a data entry form to manage the dive trips.

If you have a SAM 2010 user profile, an autogradable SAM version of this assignment may be available at http://www.cengage.com/sam2010. Check with your instructor to confirm that this assignment is available in SAM. To use the SAM version of this assignment, log into the SAM 2010 Web site and download the instruction and start files.

a. Start Access, then open the QuestDives-C.accdb database from the drive and folder where you store your Data Files. Enable content if prompted.

b. Using the Form Wizard, create a form that includes all the fields in the DiveTrips table and uses the Columnar layout, then type **Dive Trip Entry** as the title of the form.

c. Switch to Layout View, then delete the ID text box and label.

d. Using Form Design View, select all of the text boxes except the last one for TripReport, and resize them to the shortest size using the To Shortest option on the Size/Space button on the Arrange tab.

e. Using Form Design View, resize the Location, City, State/Province, Country, Lodging, and TripReport text boxes to be no wider than the Rating text box.

f. Using Form Design View and Form Layout View, move, edit, format, and align the labels and text boxes as shown in Figure C-19. Note that there are spaces between the words in the labels, the labels are right-aligned, and the text boxes are left-aligned. Use a Light Blue color for the labels and a Dark Blue for the text in the text boxes.

g. In Form View, enter the Trip Report record as shown in Figure C-19, using your own name instead of Enter Your Name.

h. Save the form, then print only the first record with your name, if requested by your instructor.

i. Close the Dive Trip Entry form, close the QuestDives-C.accdb database, then exit Access 2010.

FIGURE C-19

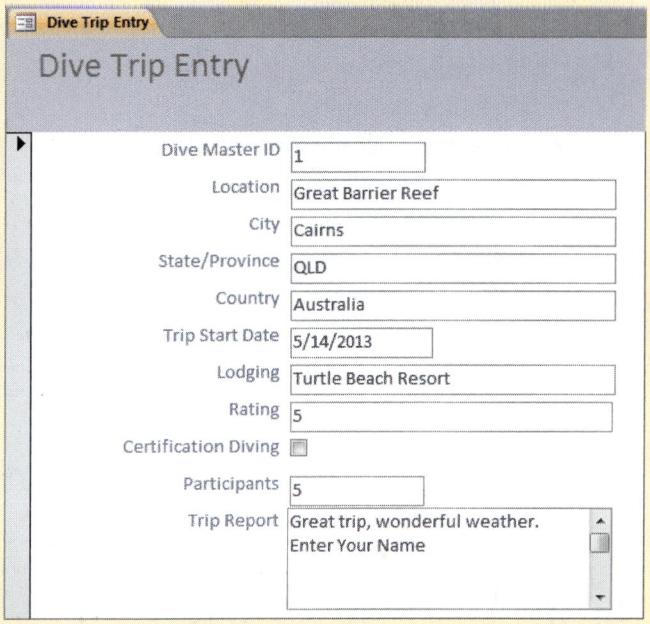

Independent Challenge 2

You have built an Access database to track membership in a community service club. The database tracks member names and addresses as well as their status in the club, which moves from rank to rank as the members contribute increased hours of service to the community.

a. Start Access, then open the Membership-C.accdb database from the drive and folder where you store your Data Files. Enable content if prompted.

b. Using the Form Wizard, create a form based on all of the fields of the Members table and only the DuesOwed field in the Status table.

c. View the data by Members, use a Columnar layout, then enter **Member Information** as the title of the form.

d. Enter a new record with your name and the school name, address, and phone number of your school. Give yourself a StatusNo entry of **1**. In the DuesPaid field, enter **75**. DuesOwed automatically displays 100 because that value is pulled from the Status table and is based on the entry in the StatusNo field, which links the Members table to the Status table.

e. In Layout View, add a text box to the form and move it below the DuesOwed text box.

f. Open the Property Sheet for the new text box, and in the Control Source property of the new text box, enter the expression that calculates the balance between DuesOwed and DuesPaid: **=[DuesOwed]-[DuesPaid]**.

g. Open the Property Sheet for the new label, and change the Caption property for the new label to **Balance**.

Independent Challenge 2 (continued)

h. Right-align all of the labels in the first column.

i. Set the Tab Stop property for the text box that contains the calculated Balance to **No**, then close the Property Sheet.

Advanced Challenge Exercise

- Switch to Form Design View, then drag the right edge of the form to the 7" mark on the horizontal ruler.
- Resize the last three text boxes that contain DuesPaid, DuesOwed, and the expression to calculate the Balance to be the same size as the new Balance text box, and right-align all data within the three text boxes.
- Open the Property Sheet for the text box that contains the expression, and change the Format property on the Format tab to Currency. Close the Property Sheet.
- Click a blank spot to the right of the text boxes, click the Insert Image button, browse for the PeoplePower.bmp image, then insert it to the right of the Company text box.
- Move and resize the controls as necessary to accommodate the picture, save the form, find the record with your name, and change the DuesPaid value to **85** as shown in Figure C-20.

FIGURE C-20

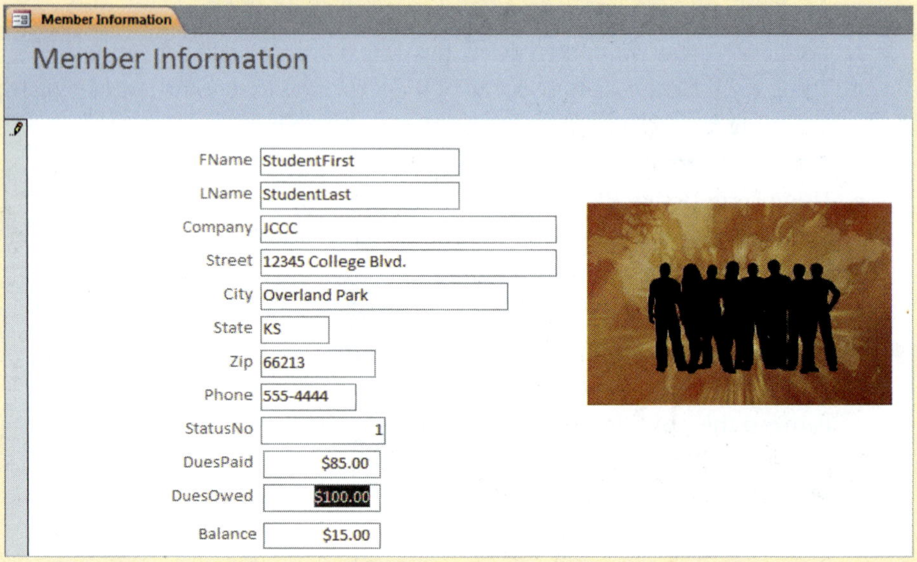

j. Print only the record with your name, if requested by your instructor.

k. Save and close the Member Information form, then close the Membership-C.accdb database and exit Access 2010.

Independent Challenge 3

You have built an Access database to organize the deposits at a recycling center. Various clubs regularly deposit recyclable material, which is measured in pounds when the deposits are made.

a. Open the Recycle-C.accdb database from the drive and folder where you store your Data Files. Enable content if prompted.

b. Using the Form Wizard, create a form based on all of the fields in the DepositList query. View the data by Deposits, use the Columnar layout, and title the form **Deposit Listing**.

c. Switch to Layout View, then make each label bold.

d. Switch to Form Design View and resize the CenterName and ClubName text boxes so they are the same height and width as the Weight text box.

e. Switch to Layout View and modify the DepositNumber and DepositDate labels so they read **Deposit Number** and **Deposit Date**. Modify the CenterName and ClubName labels so they read **Center Name** and **Club Name** as shown in Figure C-21.

FIGURE C-21

Independent Challenge 3 (continued)

f. Switch to Form View, find and change any entry of Jaycees in the ClubName field to your last name, then print a deposit record with your name if requested by your instructor.

Advanced Challenge Exercise

- Using Form View of the Deposit Listing form, filter for all records with your last name in the ClubName field.
- Using Form View of the Deposit Listing form, sort the filtered records in descending order on the DepositDate field.
- Preview, then print the first record of the filtered and sorted records, if requested by your instructor.

g. Save and close the Deposit Listing form, close the Recycle-C.accdb database, then exit Access.

Real Life Independent Challenge

One way you can use an Access database on your own is to record and track your job search efforts. In this exercise, you will develop a form to help you enter data into your job-tracking database.

a. Open the JobSearch-C.accdb database from the drive and folder where you store your Data Files. Enable content if prompted.

b. Click the Create tab, then use the Form Wizard to create a new form based on all the fields of both the Employers and Positions tables.

c. View the data by Employers, use a Datasheet layout, accept the default names for the form and subform, then open the form to view information.

d. Use Layout View and Design View to modify the form labels, text box positions, and sizes as shown in Figure C-22. Note that the columns within the subform have been resized to display all of the data in the subform.

e. Change the CompanyName of IBM in the first record to **Your Last Name's Software**, and if instructed to create a printout, print only that record.

f. Save and close the Employers form, close the JobSearch-C.accdb database, then exit Access.

FIGURE C-22

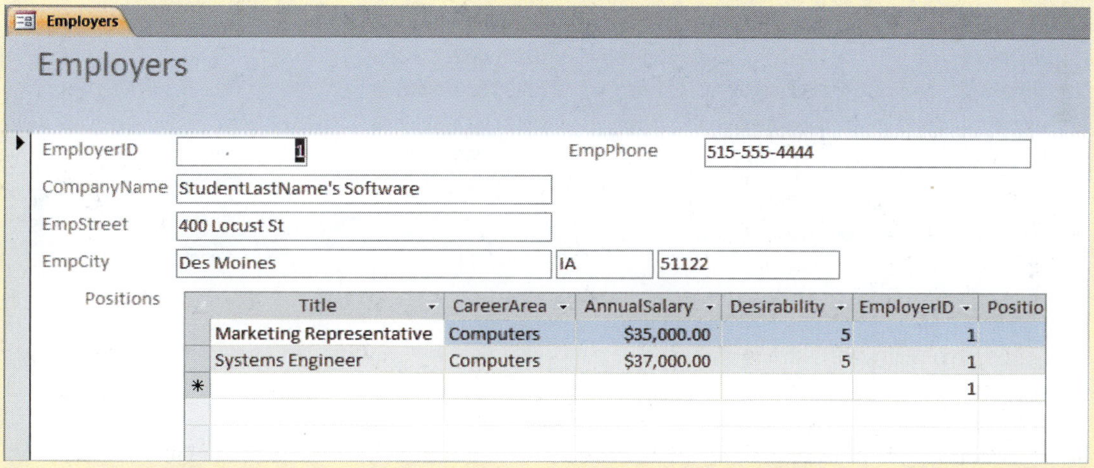

Visual Workshop

Open the Baseball-C.accdb database, enable content if prompted, then use the Split Form tool to create the form as shown in Figure C-23 based on the Players table. Resize the PlayerLast text box as shown. Modify the labels as shown. View the data in Form View, and sort the records in ascending order by last name. Change the name of Henry Aaron in the first record to **Your Name**, and if instructed to create a printout, print only that record. Save and close the Players form, close the Baseball-C.accdb database, then exit Access.

FIGURE C-23

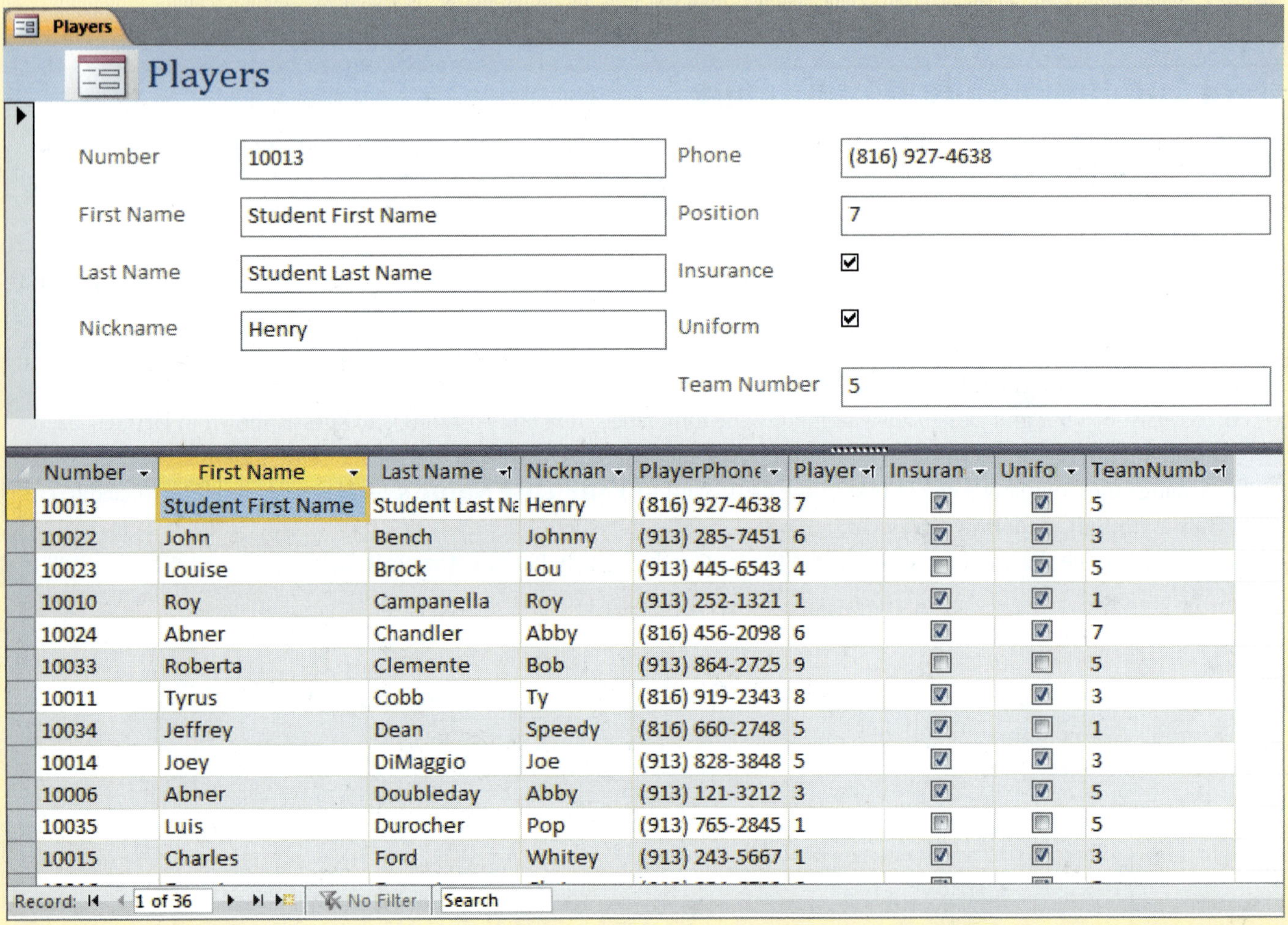

UNIT
D
Access 2010

Using Reports

Files You Will Need:

QuestTravel-D.accdb
RealEstate-D.accdb
Conventions-D.accdb
Membership-D.accdb
Recycle-D.accdb
JobSearch-D.accdb
Basketball-D.accdb

A **report** is an Access object used to create professional-looking printouts. Although you can print a datasheet or form, reports are the primary object you use to print database content because they provide the most formatting, layout, and summary options. For example, a report might include formatting embellishments such as multiple fonts and colors, extra graphical elements such as clip art and lines, and multiple headers and footers. Reports are also very powerful data analysis tools. A report can calculate subtotals, averages, counts, or other statistics for groups of records. Samantha Hooper, a tour developer at Quest Specialty Travel, asks you to produce some reports to help her share and analyze data.

OBJECTIVES

- Use the Report Wizard
- Use Report Layout View
- Review report sections
- Apply group and sort orders
- Add subtotals and counts
- Resize and align controls
- Format a report
- Create mailing labels

UNIT
D
Access 2010

Using the Report Wizard

You can create reports in Access by using the **Report Wizard**, a tool that asks questions to guide you through the initial development of the report, similar to the Form Wizard. Your responses to the Report Wizard determine the record source, style, and layout of the report. The **record source** is the table or query that defines the fields and records displayed on the report. The Report Wizard also helps you sort, group, and analyze the records. You use the Report Wizard to create a report to display the tours within each state.

STEPS

1. **Start Access, open the QuestTravel-D.accdb database, enable content if prompted, click the Create tab on the Ribbon, then click the Report Wizard button in the Reports group**

   The Report Wizard starts, prompting you to select the fields you want on the report. You can select fields from one or more tables or queries.

TROUBLE

If you select a field by mistake, click the unwanted field in the Selected Fields list, then click the Remove Field button <.

2. **Click the Tables/Queries list arrow, click Table: States, double-click the StateName field, click the Tables/Queries list arrow, click Table: Tours, click the Select All Fields button >>, click StateAbbrev in the Selected Fields list, then click the Remove Field button <**

   By selecting the StateName field from the States table, and all fields from the Tours table except the StateAbbrev field, you have all of the fields you need for the report as shown in Figure D-1. You selected the full state name stored in the States table instead of the two-letter state abbreviation used in the Tours table.

3. **Click Next, then click by States if it is not already selected**

   Choosing "by States" groups together the records for each state. In addition to record-grouping options, the Report Wizard later asks if you want to sort the records within each group. You can use the Report Wizard to specify up to four fields to sort in either ascending or descending order.

QUICK TIP

Click Back to review previous dialog boxes within a wizard.

4. **Click Next, click Next again to include no additional grouping levels, click the first sort list arrow, click TourStartDate, then click Next**

   The last questions in the Report Wizard deal with report appearance and creating a report title.

5. **Click the Stepped option button, click the Landscape option button, click Next, type Tours by State for the report title, then click Finish**

   The Tours by State report opens in **Print Preview**, which displays the report as it appears when printed, as shown in Figure D-2. The records are grouped by state, the first state being California, and then sorted in ascending order by the TourStartDate field within each state. Reports are **read-only** objects, meaning that they read and display data but cannot be used to change (write to) data. As you change data using tables, queries, or forms, reports constantly display those up-to-date edits just like all of the other Access objects.

6. **Scroll down to see the second grouping section on the report for the state of Colorado, then click the Next Page button ▶ in the navigation bar to see the second page of the report**

   Even in **landscape orientation** (11" wide by 8.5" tall as opposed to **portrait orientation**, which is 8.5" wide by 11" tall), the fields on the Tours by State report may not neatly fit on one sheet of paper. The labels in the column headings and the data in the columns need to be resized to improve the layout. Depending on your monitor, you might need to scroll to the right to display all the fields on this page.

FIGURE D-1: Selecting fields for a report using the Report Wizard

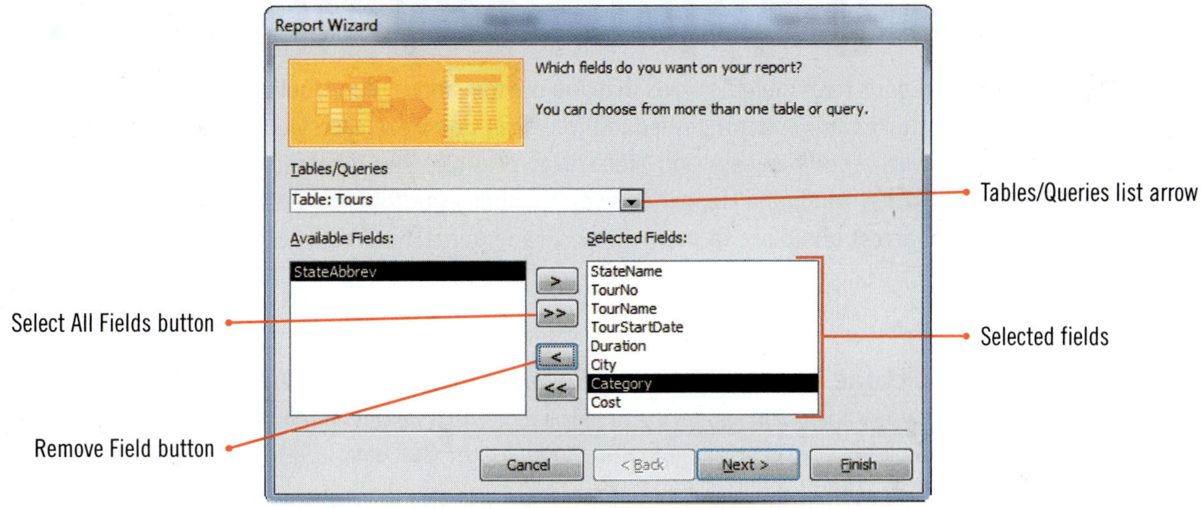

FIGURE D-2: Tours by State report in Print Preview

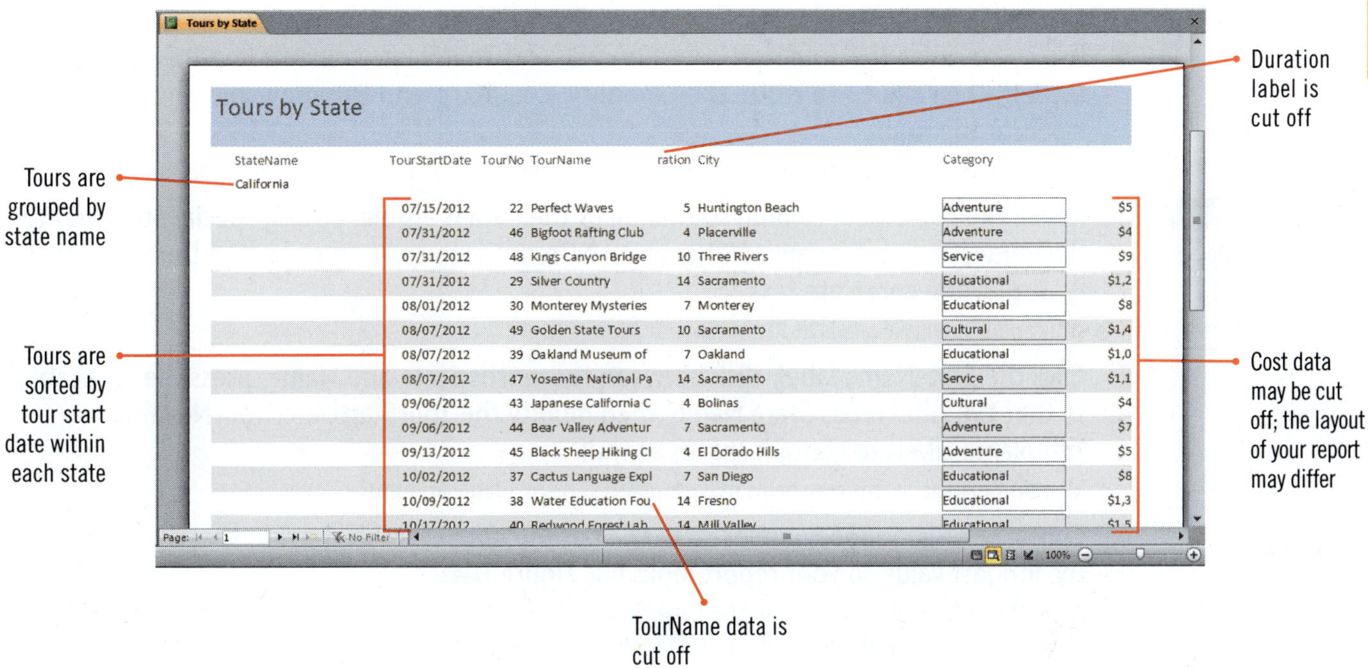

UNIT
D
Access 2010

Using Report Layout View

Like forms, reports have multiple views that you use for various report-building and report-viewing activities. While some tasks can be accomplished in more than one view, each view has a primary purpose to make your work with reports as easy and efficient as possible. The different report views are summarized in Table D-1. Samantha Hooper asks you to modify the Tours by State report so that all of the fields fit comfortably across one piece of paper in landscape orientation. You'll use Report Layout View to achieve this goal.

STEPS

1. **Right-click the Tours by State report tab, then click Layout View**
   Layout View opens and applies a grid to the report that helps you resize, move, and position controls. You decide to narrow the City column to make room for the Cost data.
2. **Click Sacramento (or any City value), then use the ↔ pointer to drag the right edge of the City column to the left to narrow it to about half of its current size as shown in Figure D-3**
   By narrowing the City column, you create extra space in the report.
3. **Click any value in the Cost column, use the pointer to drag the Cost values to the left of the Category column, click the Cost label, then use to move the Cost label to the left of the Category label**
   All the columns are now within the boundaries of a single piece of paper in landscape orientation. You also notice that centering some data would make it easier to read.
4. **Click any value in the TourNo column, click the Home tab, click the Center button in the Text Formatting group, click the TourNo label, then click again**
   The TourName column and Duration label could use a little more space.
5. **Use ↔ to resize the TourStartDate, TourNo, and TourName columns and their labels to the left, then use ↔ to resize the Category, Cost, City, and Duration columns and their labels to the right**
   Now the report has enough room to resize the TourName column and the Duration label.
6. **Resize the TourName column so that all of the data is visible, paying special attention to the longest value, Yosemite National Park Great Cleanup, then resize the Duration label to display the complete text**
   You can also rename labels in Report Layout View.
7. **Click the StateName label, click between the words State and Name, press the [Spacebar] so that the label reads State Name, then modify the TourStartDate, TourNo, and TourName labels to contain spaces as well**
   Modifying labels in this way helps make a report more readable and professional.
8. **Continue resizing the columns so that all of the data is visible, paying special attention to the longest value so your report looks like Figure D-4**
   All of the labels are positioned in the Page Header section so that they appear only once per page. The text box controls are positioned in the Detail section. Depending on your monitor, you might need to scroll to display all the columns in Report Layout View.

QUICK TIP
Resizing with ↔ instead of moving with maintains the vertical alignment of the controls.

QUICK TIP
Using the Undo button arrow, you can undo many actions in Layout View.

FIGURE D-3: Modifying the column width in Report Layout View

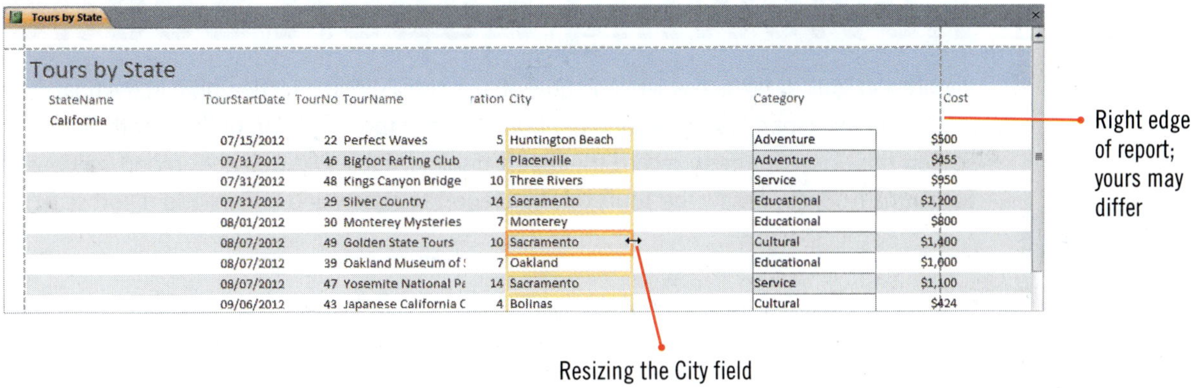

FIGURE D-4: Final Tours by State report in Report Layout View

Access 2010

TABLE D-1: Report views

view	primary purpose
Report View	To quickly review the report without page breaks
Print Preview	To review each page of an entire report as it will appear if printed
Layout View	To modify the size, position, or formatting of controls; shows live data as you modify the report, making it the tool of choice when you want to change the appearance and positioning of controls on a report while also reviewing live data
Design View	To work with report sections or to access the complete range of controls and report properties; Design View does not display data

UNIT
D
Access 2010

Reviewing Report Sections

Report **sections** determine where and how often controls in that section print in the final report. For example, controls in the Report Header section print only once at the beginning of the report, but controls in the Detail section print once for every record the report displays. Table D-2 describes report sections. You and Samantha Hooper preview the Tours by State report to review and understand report sections.

STEPS

TROUBLE
You may need to zoom in and out several times by clicking the report to position it where you want.

1. **Right-click the Tours by State tab, click Print Preview, click the First Page button in the navigation bar if you need to see the first page of the report, then click in the middle of the top edge of the report to zoom in to 100% if needed as shown in Figure D-5**

   The first page contains four sections: Report Header, Page Header, StateAbbreviation Header, and Detail section.

2. **Click the Next Page button on the navigation bar to move to the second page**

   The second page of the report may not contain data. The report may be too wide to fit on a single sheet of paper. You'll fix the report width in Report Design View.

QUICK TIP
Pointing to the error indicator displays a message about the error.

3. **Right-click the Tours by State tab, click Design View, scroll to the far right using the bottom horizontal scroll bar, drag the right edge of the report to the 11" mark on the horizontal ruler, point to the error indicator in the upper-left corner of the report, then drag the right edge of the report as far as you can to the left as shown in Figure D-6**

   In Report Design View, you can work with the report sections and make modifications to the report that you cannot make in other views, such as narrowing the width. Report Design View does not display any data, though. For your report to fit on one page in landscape orientation, you need to move all of the controls within the 10.5" mark on the horizontal **ruler** to allow for 0.25" left and right margins. The **error indicator** in the upper-left corner of the report indicates that the report is too wide to fit on one piece of paper.

4. **Drag the text box with the page expression in the Page Footer section to the left about 1", then drag the right edge of the report to the left so that the report is less than 10.5" wide**

   The error indicator automatically disappears now that the report fits within the margins of a single piece of paper. To review your modifications, show the report in Print Preview.

QUICK TIP
You can also use the View buttons in the lower-right corner of a report to switch views.

5. **Right-click the Tours by State tab, click Print Preview, click the report to zoom in and out to examine the page, then click twice on the navigation bar to navigate to the last page as shown in Figure D-7**

   The last page of the report, page 3, shows how the Page Header and Page Footer sections border all pages (except the first page where the Report Header is at the top of the page). It also shows how the Group Header, tied to the StateName field, prints once per state, and how the tours within each state are created by the Detail section. Previewing each page of the report also helps you confirm that no blank pages are created.

TABLE D-2: Report sections

section	where does this section print?
Report Header	At the top of the first page
Page Header	At the top of every page (but below the Report Header on the first page)
Group Header	Before every group of records
Detail	Once for every record
Group Footer	After every group of records
Page Footer	At the bottom of every page
Report Footer	At the end of the report

FIGURE D-5: Tours by State report in Report View

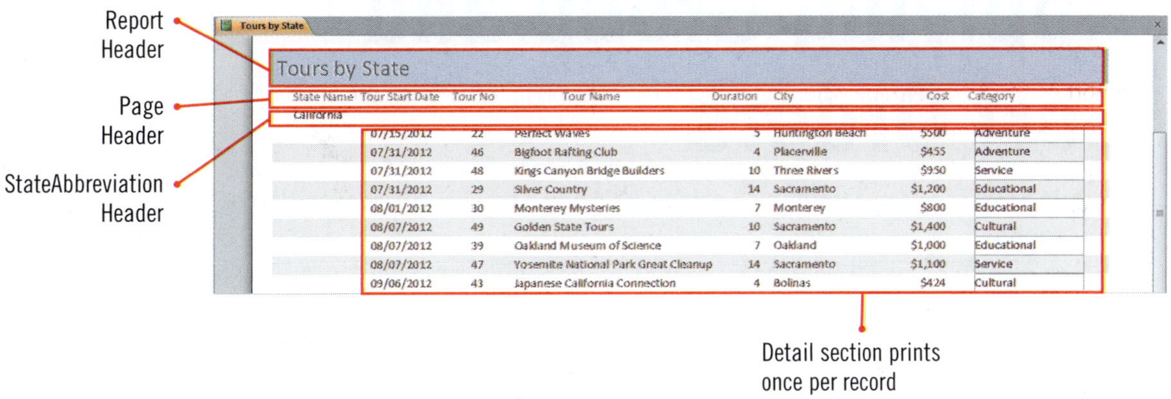

FIGURE D-6: Tours by State report in Design View

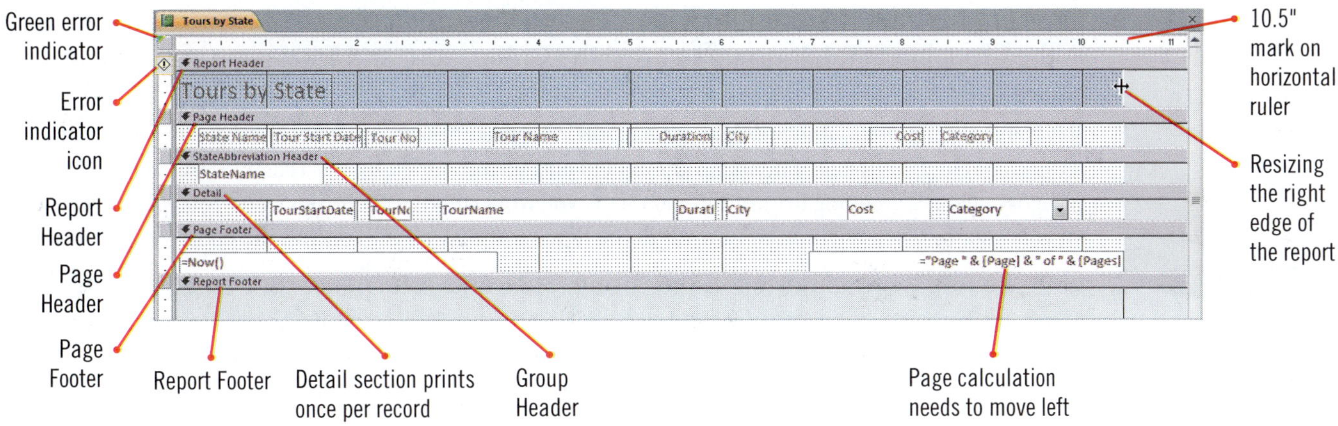

FIGURE D-7: Tours by State report in Print Preview

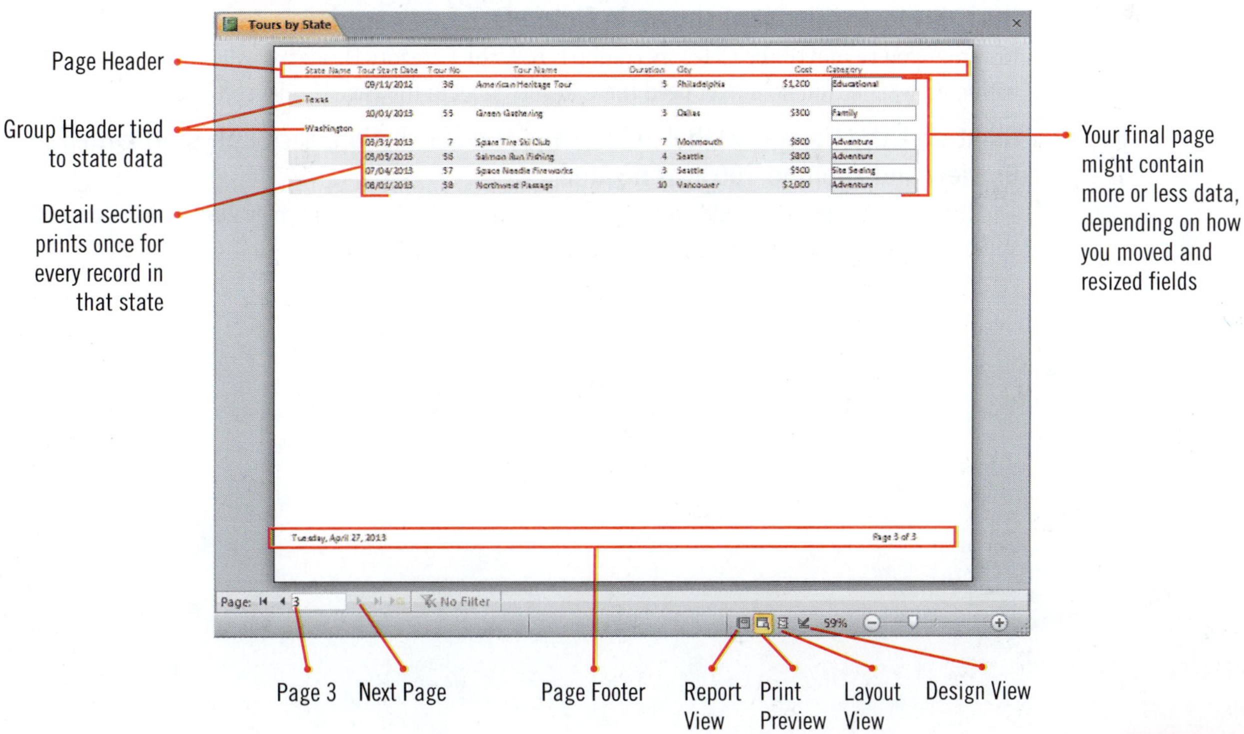

UNIT D

Access 2010

Applying Group and Sort Orders

Grouping means to sort records by a particular field *plus* provide a header and/or footer section before or after each group of sorted records. For example, if you group records by the StateName field, the Group Header is called the StateName Header and the Group Footer is called the StateName Footer. The StateName Header section appears once for each state in the report, immediately before the records in that state. The StateName Footer section also appears once for each state in the report, immediately after the records for that state. The records in the Tours by State report are currently grouped by the StateAbbreviation field. Samantha Hooper asks you to further group the records by the Category field (Adventure, Educational, and Family, for example) within each state.

STEPS

1. **Close Print Preview to return to Report Design View, then click the Group & Sort button in the Grouping & Totals group to open the Group, Sort, and Total pane as shown in Figure D-8**

   To change sorting or grouping options for a report, you need to work in Report Design View. Currently, the records are grouped by the StateAbbreviation field and further sorted by the TourStartDate field. To add the Category field as a grouping field within each state, you work with the Group, Sort, and Total pane. Depending on your monitor, you might need to scroll to the right to display all the controls in Report Design View.

QUICK TIP

The More Options button becomes the Less Options button when clicked.

2. **Click the Add a group button in the Group, Sort, and Total pane, click Category, click the Move up button so that Category is positioned between StateAbbreviation and TourStartDate, then click the More Options button to display the Category group options**

   A Category Header section is added to Report Design View just below the StateAbbreviation Header section. To print category information only once within each state, you move the Category control from the Detail section to the Category Header section.

TROUBLE

Use the Move up and Move down buttons as needed to make sure your Group, Sort, and Total pane looks exactly like Figure D-9.

3. **Right-click the Category combo box in the Detail section, click Cut on the shortcut menu, right-click the Category Header section, click Paste, then drag the Category combo box to the right to position it as shown in Figure D-9**

   Now that you've moved the Category combo box to the Category Header, it will print only once per category within each state. You no longer need the Category label in the Page Header section.

4. **Right-click the Category label in the Page Header section, click Cut, then switch to Print Preview and zoom to 100% as needed**

   The Tours by State report should look similar to Figure D-10. Notice that the values in the Category field now appear once per category, before the records in each category are listed.

FIGURE D-8: Group, Sort, and Total pane

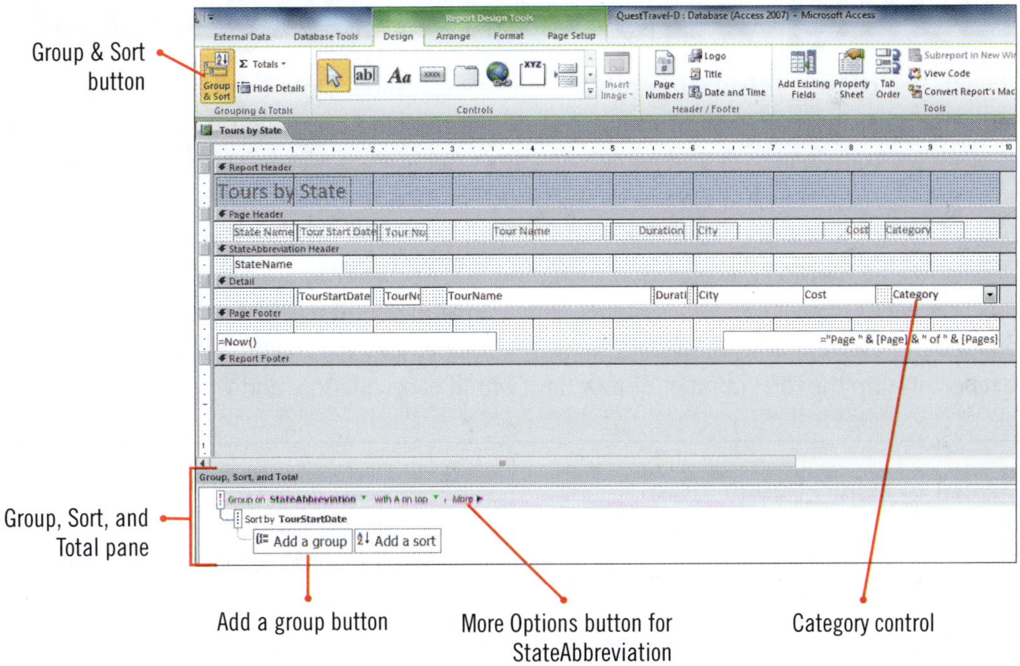

FIGURE D-9: Tours by State report with new Category Header section

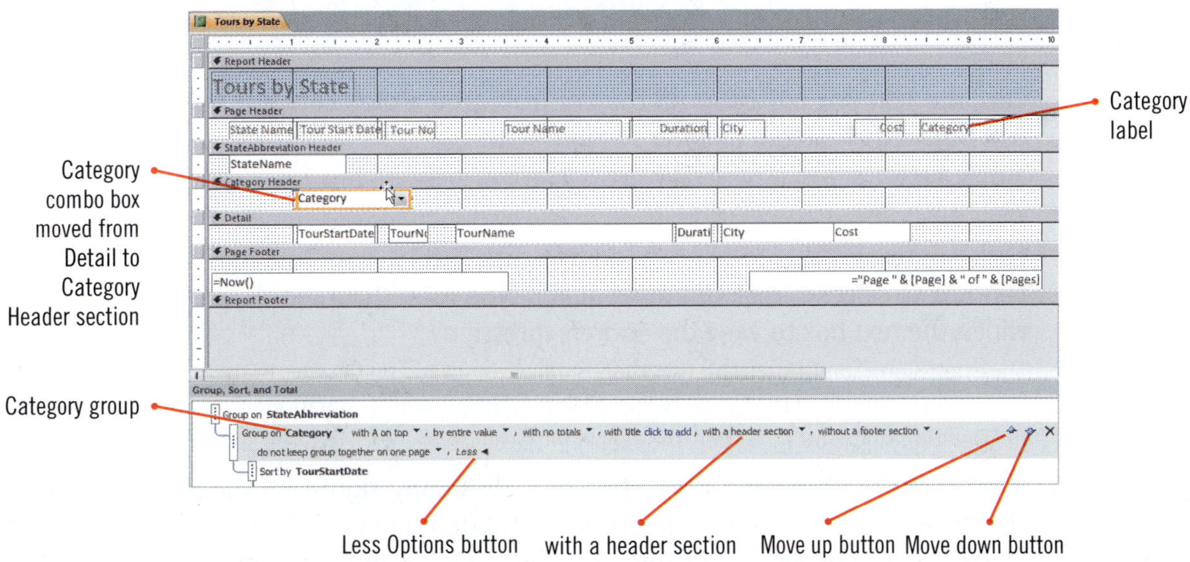

FIGURE D-10: Tours by State report grouped by state and category

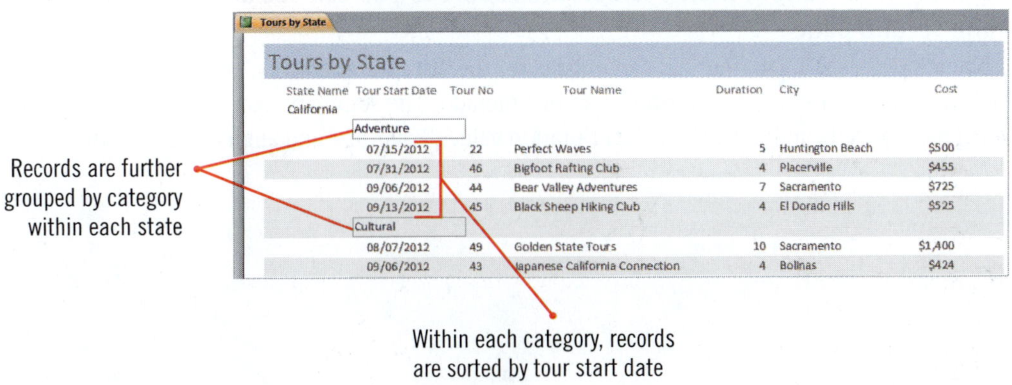

Access 2010

UNIT D

Access 2010

Adding Subtotals and Counts

In a report, you create a **calculation** by entering an expression into a text box. When a report is previewed or printed, the expression is evaluated and the resulting calculation is placed on the report. An **expression** is a combination of field names, operators (such as +, –, /, and *), and functions that result in a single value. A **function** is a built-in formula, such as Sum or Count, that helps you quickly create a calculation. Notice that every expression starts with an equal sign (=), and when it uses a function, the arguments for the function are placed in (parentheses). **Arguments** are the pieces of information that the function needs to create the final answer. When an argument is a field name, the field name must be surrounded by [square brackets]. Samantha Hooper asks you to add a calculation to the Tours by State report to sum the total number of tour days within each category and within each state.

STEPS

1. **Switch to Report Design View**

   A logical place to add subtotals for each group is immediately after the group in the Group Footer section. You need to use the Group, Sort, and Total pane to open the Group Footer sections for both the Category and StateAbbreviation fields.

TROUBLE

Click Category in the Group, Sort, and Total pane to display the grouping options.

2. **Click the More Options button for the StateAbbreviation field in the Group, Sort, and Total pane, click the without a footer section list arrow, click with a footer section, then do the same for the Category field as shown in Figure D-11**

   With the StateAbbreviation and Category Footer sections open, you're ready to add controls to calculate the total number of tour days within each category and state. You can use a text box control with an expression to make this calculation.

3. **Click the Text Box button in the Controls group, then click just below the Duration text box in the Category Footer section**

   Adding a new text box automatically adds a new label to its left. First, you modify the label to identify the information, then you modify the text box to contain the correct expression to sum the number of tour days.

TROUBLE

Depending on your activity in Report Design View, you may see a different number in the Text##: label.

4. **Click the Text19 label to select it, double-click Text19, type Total days:, click the Unbound text box to select it, click Unbound again, type =Sum([Duration]), press [Enter], then widen the text box to view the entire expression**

   The expression =Sum([Duration]) uses the Sum function to add up the days in the Duration field. Because the expression is entered in the Category Footer section, it will sum all Duration values for that category. To sum the Duration values for each state, the expression needs to be inserted in the StateAbbreviation Footer.

QUICK TIP

Pasting the expression in the Report Footer section would subtotal the duration values for the entire report.

5. **Right-click the =Sum([Duration]) text box, click Copy, right-click the StateAbbreviation Footer section, click Paste, then press [→] enough times to position the controls in the StateAbbreviation Footer section just below those in the Category Footer section as shown in Figure D-12**

   With the expression in the StateAbbreviation Footer section, you're ready to preview your work.

6. **Switch to Print Preview, then position the report so you can see all of the Colorado tours on the second page**

   As shown in Figure D-13, 43 tour days are totaled for the Adventure category, and 7 for the Family category, which is a total of 50 tour days for the state of Colorado. The summary data would look better if it were aligned more directly under the individual Duration values. You resize and align controls in the next lesson.

FIGURE D-11: Opening group footer sections

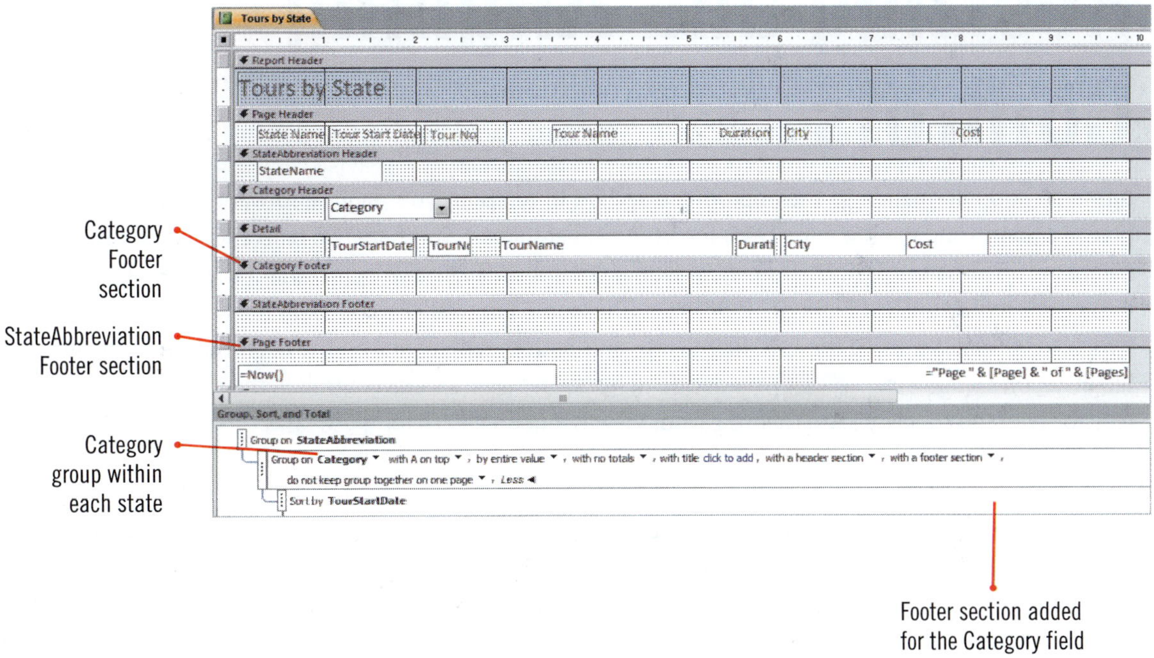

FIGURE D-12: Adding subtotals to group footer sections

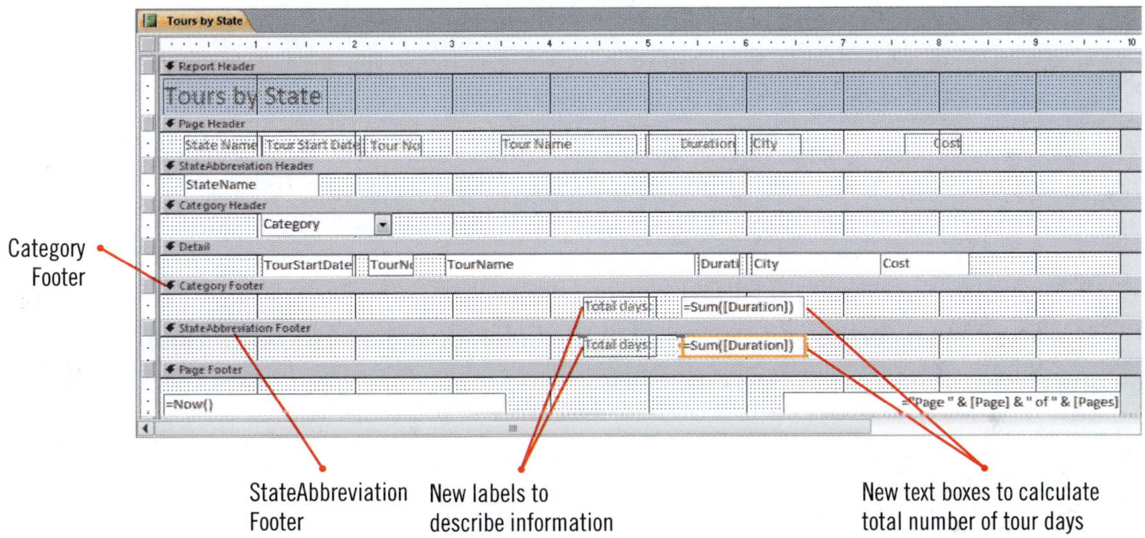

FIGURE D-13: Previewing the new group footer calculations

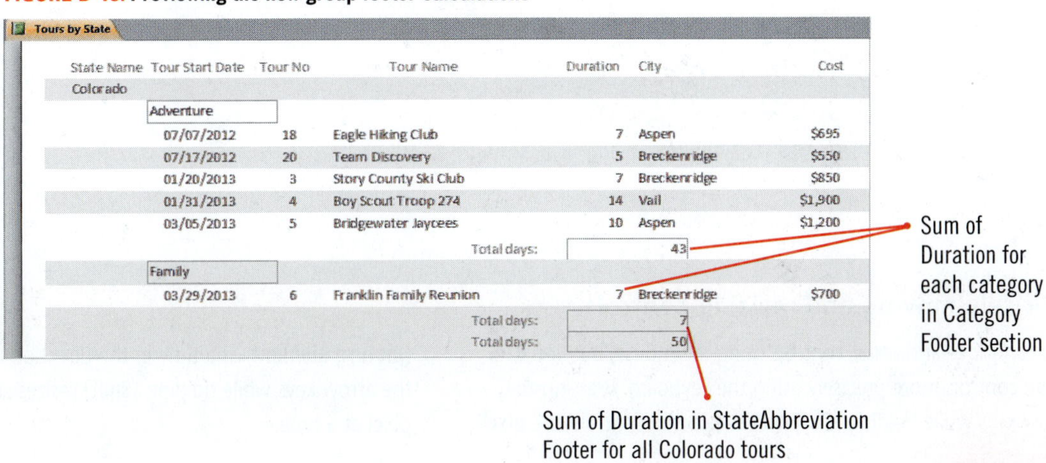

Access 2010

UNIT
D
Access 2010

Resizing and Aligning Controls

After you add information to the appropriate section of a report, you might also want to align the data in precise columns and rows to make the information easier to read. There are two different types of **alignment** commands. You can left-, right-, or center-align a control *within its own border* using the Align Text Left, Center, and Align Text Right buttons on the Home tab. You can also align the edges of controls *with respect to one another* using the Left, Right, Top, and Bottom commands on the Align button of the Arrange tab in Report Design View. You decide to resize and align several controls in the report to improve the readability of the Tours by State report. Layout View is a good choice for these tasks.

STEPS

1. **Switch to Layout View, then click the Group & Sort button to toggle off the Group, Sort, and Total pane**

   You decide to align the expressions that subtotal the number of tour days for each category within the Duration column.

2. **Click the Total days text box in the Category Footer, click the Home tab, click the Center button in the Text Formatting group, then use the ↔ pointer to resize the text box so that the data is aligned in the Duration column as shown in Figure D-14**

   With the calculation formatted as desired in the Category Footer, you can quickly apply those modifications to the calculation in the StateAbbreviation Footer as well.

3. **Scroll down the report far enough to find the StateAbbreviation Footer section, click the Total days text box in the StateAbbreviation Footer, click, then use the ↔ pointer to resize the text box so that it is the same width as the text box in the Category Footer section**

   With both expressions centered and aligned, they are easier to read on the report. For longer or more complex numbers, you can right-align the values so that they align on the decimal point.

4. **Scroll the report so you can see all of the Colorado tours as shown in Figure D-15**

   You can apply resize, alignment, or formatting commands to more than one control at a time. Table D-3 provides techniques for selecting more than one control at a time in Report Design View.

TROUBLE

If you make a mistake, click the Undo button on the Quick Access toolbar.

Precisely moving and resizing controls

You can move and resize controls using the mouse, but you can move controls more precisely using the keyboard. Pressing the arrow keys while holding [Ctrl] moves selected controls one **pixel** (**picture element**) at a time in the direction of the arrow. Pressing the arrow keys while holding [Shift] resizes selected controls one pixel at a time.

FIGURE D-14: Resizing controls in Layout View

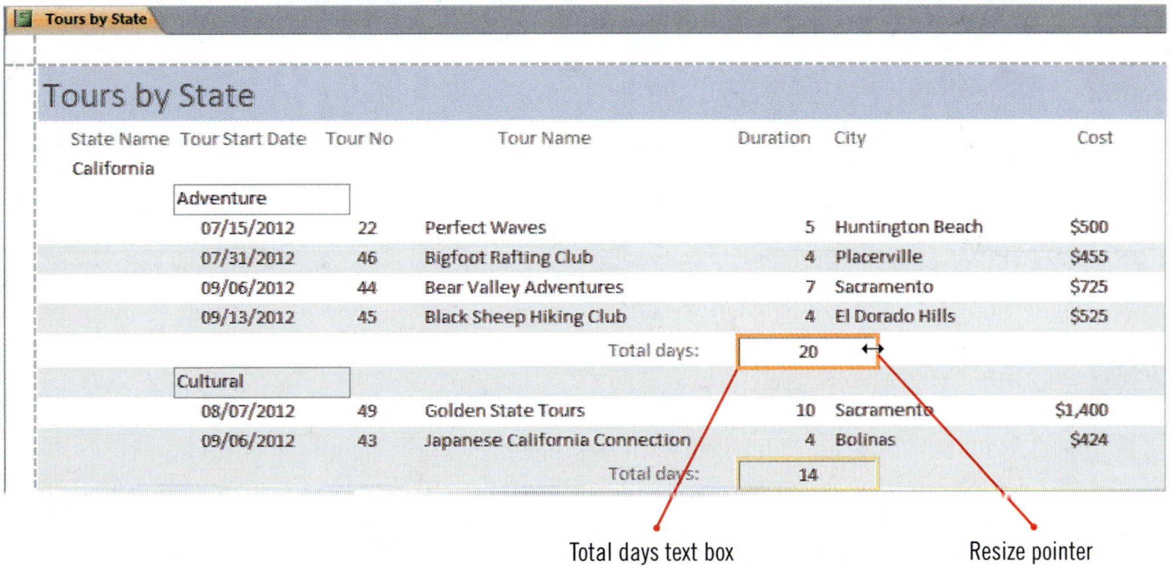

FIGURE D-15: Reviewing the widened and aligned controls

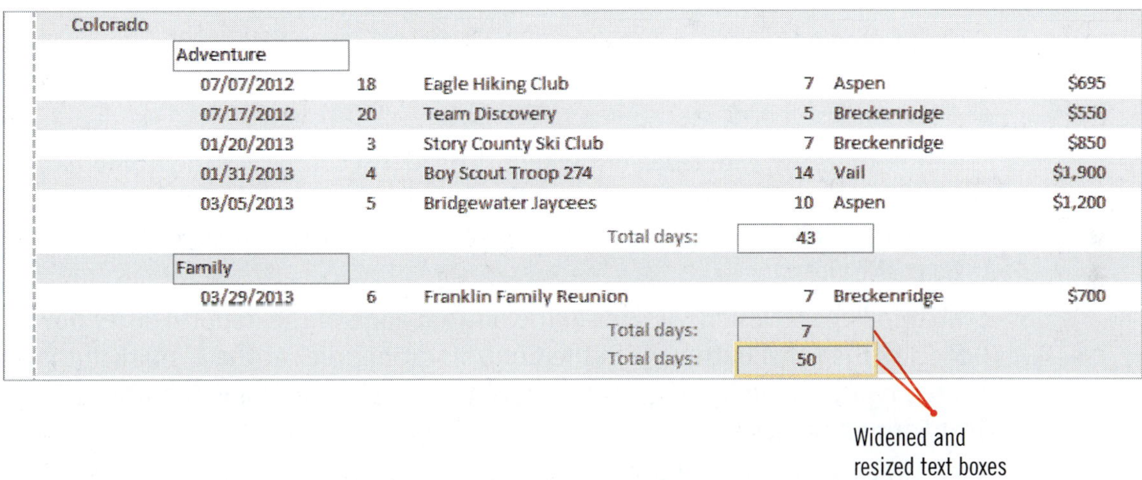

TABLE D-3: Selecting more than one control at a time in Report Design View

technique	description
Click, [Shift]+click	Click a control, then press and hold [Shift] while clicking other controls; each one is selected
Drag a selection box	Drag a selection box (an outline box you create by dragging the pointer in Report Design View); every control that is in or is touched by the edges of the box is selected
Click in the ruler	Click in either the horizontal or vertical ruler to select all controls that intersect the selection line
Drag in the ruler	Drag through either the horizontal or vertical ruler to select all controls that intersect the selection line as it is dragged through the ruler

UNIT
D
Access 2010

Formatting a Report

Formatting refers to enhancing the appearance of the information. Table D-4 lists several of the most popular formatting commands found on the Format tab when you are working in Report Design View. Although the Report Wizard automatically applies many formatting embellishments, you often want to improve the appearance of the report to fit your particular needs. When reviewing the Tours by State report with Samantha, you decide to change the background color of some of the report sections to make the data easier to read. Your first change will be to shade each StateAbbreviation Header and Footer section (rather than alternating sections, the format initially provided by the Report Wizard). To make changes to entire report sections, you must work in Report Design View.

STEPS

QUICK TIP
The quick keystroke for Undo is [Ctrl][Z]. The quick keystroke for Redo is [Ctrl][Y].

1. **Switch to Design View, click the StateAbbreviation Header section bar, click the Format tab, click the Alternate Row Color button arrow, click No Color, click the Shape Fill button, then click the Maroon 2 color square as shown in Figure D-16**
   Make a similar modification by applying a different fill color to the Category Header section.
2. **Click the Category Header section bar, click the Alternate Row Color button arrow, click No Color, click the Shape Fill button, click the Green 2 color square (just to the right of Maroon 2 in the Standard Colors section)**
   When you use the Alternate Row Color and Shape Fill buttons, you're actually modifying the **Back Color** and **Alternate Back Color** properties in the Property Sheet of the section or control you selected. Background shades can help differentiate parts of the report, but be careful with dark colors as they may print as solid black on some printers and fax machines.
3. **Switch to Layout View to review your modifications**
   The state and category sections are much clearer, but you decide to make one more modification to emphasize the report title.
4. **Click the Tours by State label in the Report Header section, click the Home tab, then click the Bold button in the Text Formatting group**
   The report in Layout View should look like Figure D-17. You also want to add a label to the Report Footer section to identify yourself.
5. **Switch to Report Design View, drag the bottom edge of the Report Footer down about 0.5", click the Label button in the Controls group, click at the 1" mark in the Report Footer, type Created by your name, press [Enter], click the Home tab, then click in the Text Formatting group**
6. **Save, preview, and print the Tours by State report if required, then close it**

FIGURE D-16: Formatting section backgrounds

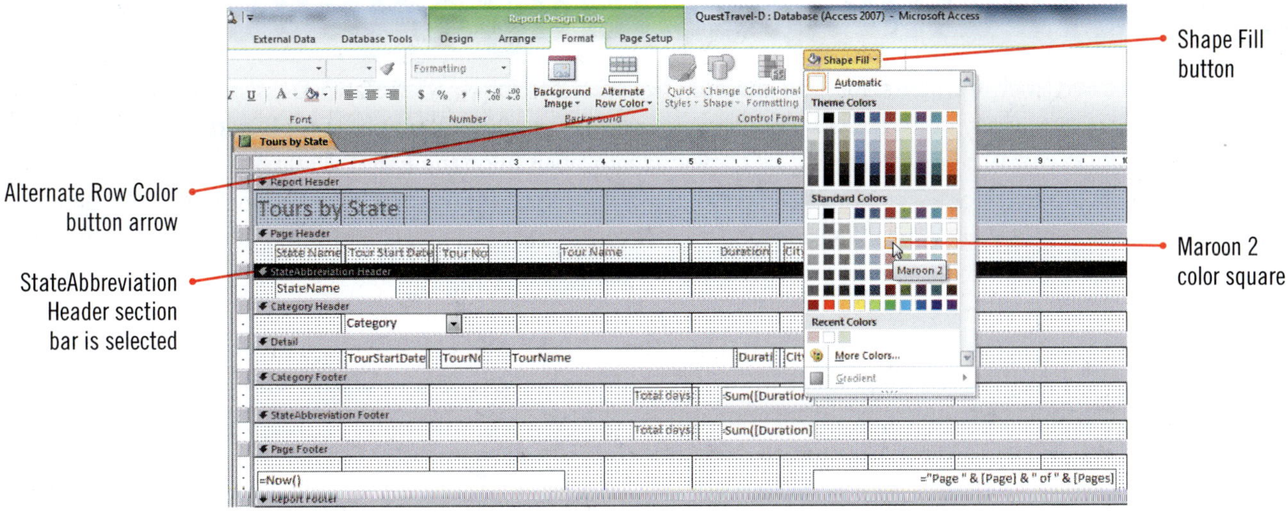

FIGURE D-17: Final formatted Tours by State report

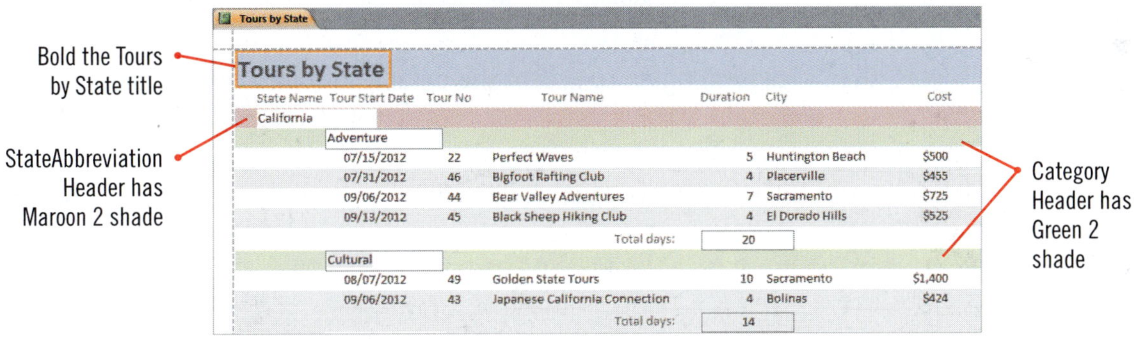

TABLE D-4: Useful formatting commands

button	button name	description
B	Bold	Toggles bold on or off for the selected control(s)
I	Italic	Toggles italics on or off for the selected control(s)
U	Underline	Toggles underline on or off for the selected control(s)
	Align Text Left	Left-aligns the selected control(s) within its own border
	Center	Centers the selected control(s) within its own border
	Align Text Right	Right-aligns the selected control(s) within its own border
Shape Fill	Shape Fill	Changes the background color of the selected control(s)
	Alternate Row Color	Changes the background color of alternate records in the selected section
A	Font Color	Changes the text color of the selected control(s)
Shape Outline	Shape Outline Line Thickness option Line Type option	Changes the border color of the selected control(s) Changes the border style of the selected control(s) Changes the special visual effect of the selected control(s)

UNIT
D
Access 2010

Creating Mailing Labels

Mailing labels are often created to apply to envelopes, postcards, or letters when assembling a mass mailing. They have many other business purposes too, such as using them on paper file folders or name tags. Any data in your Access database can be converted into labels using the **Label Wizard**, a special report wizard that precisely positions and sizes information for hundreds of standard business labels. Samantha Hooper asks you to create mailing labels for all of the addresses in the Customers table. You use the Label Wizard to handle this request.

STEPS

1. **Click the Customers table in the Navigation Pane, click the Create tab, then click the Labels button in the Reports group**
   The first Label Wizard dialog box opens. The Filter by manufacturer list box provides over 30 manufacturers of labels. Because Avery is the most common, it is the default choice. With the manufacturer selected, your next task is to choose the product number of the labels you will feed through the printer. The label list box is the best source for this information. In this case, you'll be using Avery 5160 labels, a common type of sheet labels used for mailings and other purposes.
2. **Scroll through the Product numbers, then click 5160 as shown in Figure D-18**
   Note that by selecting a product number, you also specify the dimensions of the label and number of columns.
3. **Click Next, then click Next again to accept the default font and color choices**
   The third question of the Label Wizard asks how you want to construct your label. You'll add the fields from the Customers table in a standard mailing format.
4. **Double-click FName, press [Spacebar], double-click LName, press [Enter], double-click Street, press [Enter], double-click City, type comma and press [Spacebar], double-click State, press [Spacebar], then double-click Zip**
   If your prototype label doesn't look exactly like Figure D-19, delete the fields and try again. Be careful to put a space between the FName and LName fields in the first row, a comma and a space between the City and State fields, and a space between the State and Zip fields.
5. **Click Next, double-click LName to select it as a sorting field, click Next, click Finish to accept the name Labels Customers for the new report, then click OK if prompted**
   A portion of the new report is shown in Figure D-20. It is generally a good idea to print the first page of the report on standard paper to make sure everything is aligned correctly before printing on labels.
6. **Click the Print button on the Print Preview tab, click the From box, type 1, click the To box, type 1, then click OK if a printout is desired**
7. **Close the Labels Customers report, close the QuestTravel-D.accdb database, then exit Access 2010**

QUICK TIP

To include your name on the printout, first change Jacob Alman's name to your own in the Customers table, then close and open the report again.

FIGURE D-18: Label Wizard dialog box

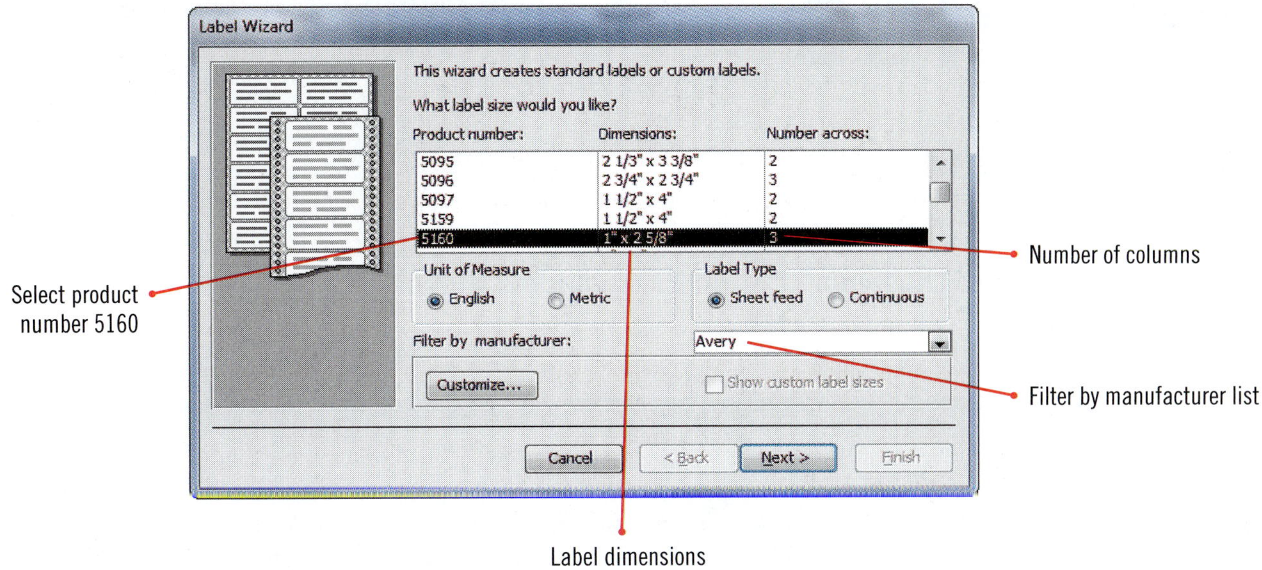

FIGURE D-19: Building a prototype label

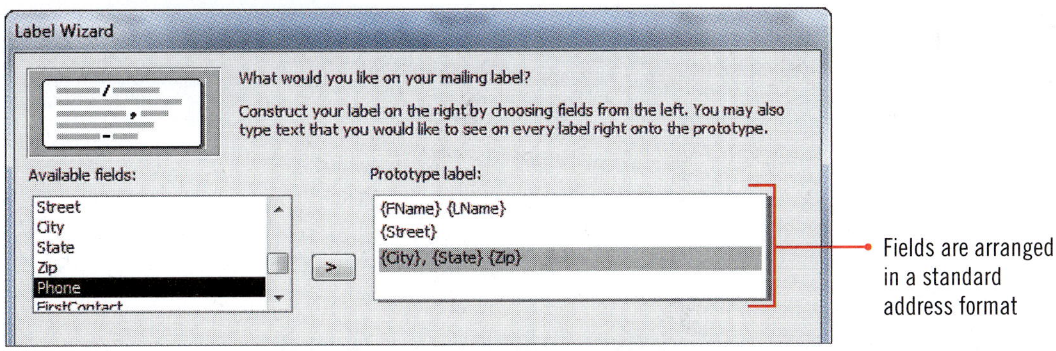

FIGURE D-20: Labels Customers report

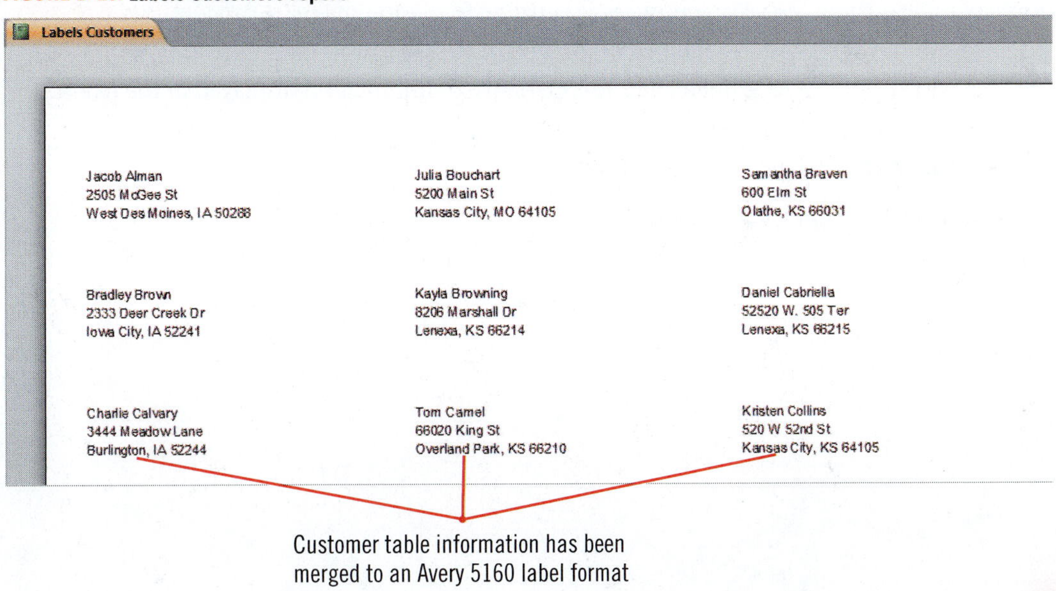

Access 2010

Practice

Concepts Review

For current SAM information, including versions and content details, visit SAM Central (http://www.cengage.com/samcentral). If you have a SAM user profile, you may have access to hands-on instruction, practice, and assessment of the skills covered in this unit. Since various versions of SAM are supported throughout the life of this text, check with your instructor for the correct instructions and URL/Web site for accessing assignments.

Label each element of the Report Design View window shown in Figure D-21.

FIGURE D-21

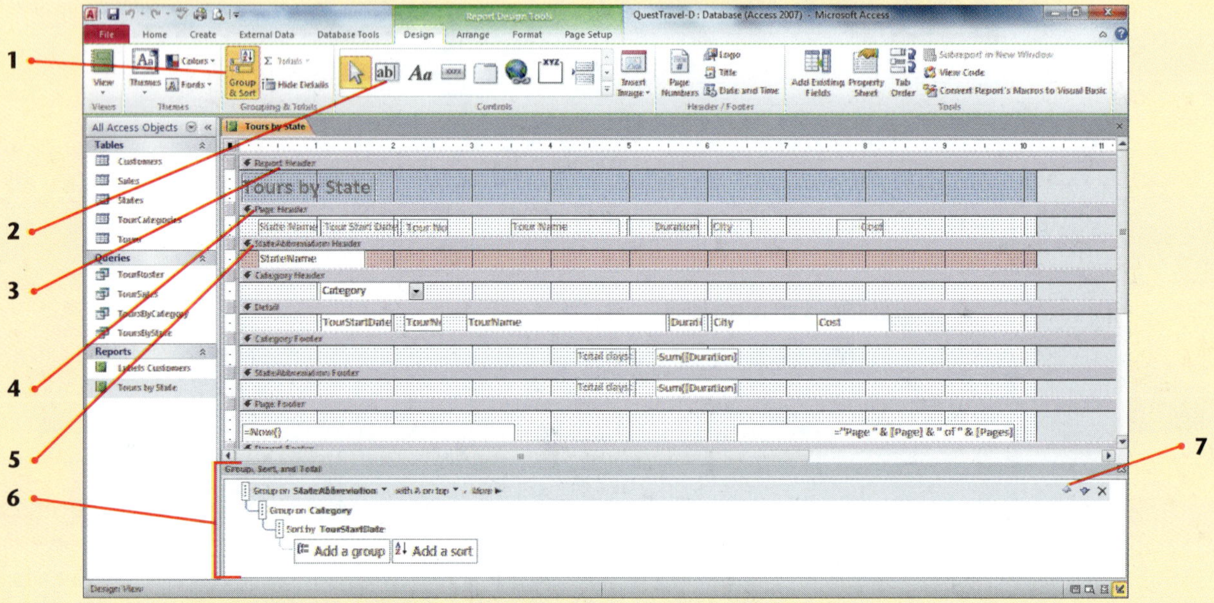

Match each term with the statement that best describes it.

8. Expression	**a.** Left, center, or right are common choices
9. Section	**b.** Prints once for every record
10. Detail section	**c.** Used to identify which fields and records are passed to the report
11. Record source	**d.** Sorting records *plus* providing a header or footer section
12. Formatting	**e.** Determines how controls are positioned on the report
13. Grouping	**f.** A combination of field names, operators, and functions that results in a single value
14. Alignment	**g.** Enhancing the appearance of information displayed in the report

Select the best answer from the list of choices.

15. Which of the following is *not* a valid report view?

a. Print Preview
b. Design View
c. Layout View
d. Section View

16. Which type of control is most commonly placed in the Detail section?

a. Image
b. Line
c. Label
d. Text box

17. A title for a report would most commonly be placed in which report section?

a. Report Header
b. Detail
c. Group Footer
d. Report Footer

18. A calculated expression that presents page numbering information would probably be placed in which report section?

a. Report Header
b. Group Footer
c. Detail
d. Page Footer

19. Which of the following expressions counts the number of records using the FirstName field?

a. =Count([FirstName])
b. =Count(FirstName)
c. =Count[FirstName]
d. =Count{FirstName}

20. To align the edges of several controls with each other, you use the alignment commands on the:

a. Formatting tab.
b. Print Preview tab.
c. Design tab.
d. Arrange tab.

Skills Review

1. Use the Report Wizard.

a. Start Access and open the RealEstate-D.accdb database from the drive and folder where you store your Data Files. Enable content if prompted.
b. Use the Report Wizard to create a report based on the RLast and RPhone fields from the Realtors table, and the Type, SqFt, BR, Bath, and Asking fields from the Listings table.
c. View the data by Realtors, do not add any more grouping levels, and sort the records in descending order by the Asking field.
d. Use a Stepped layout and a Landscape orientation. Title the report **Realtor Listings**.
e. Preview the first page of the new report. Notice whether any fields or field names need more space.

2. Use Report Layout View.

a. Switch to Layout View.
b. Narrow the RLast and RPhone columns enough so they are only as wide as necessary.
c. Modify the RLast label to read **Realtor**, the RPhone label to read **Phone**, the SqFt label to read **Square Feet**, the BR label to read **Bedrooms**, and the Bath label to read **Baths**.
d. Switch to Print Preview, and view each page of the report.

3. Review report sections.

a. Switch to Report Design View.
b. Drag the text box that contains the Page calculation in the lower-right corner of the Page Footer section to the left so that it is to the left of the 9" mark on the horizontal ruler.
c. Drag the right edge of the entire report to the left so it ends within the 10.5" mark on the horizontal ruler.

4. Apply group and sort orders.

a. Open the Group, Sort, and Total pane.
b. Add the Type field as a grouping field between the RealtorNo grouping field and Asking sort field.
c. Cut and paste the Type combo box from its current position in the Detail section to the Type Header section.
d. Move the Type combo box in the Type Header section so its left edge is at about the 1" mark on the horizontal ruler.
e. Delete the Type label in the Page Header section.
f. Switch to Layout View, and move the Asking column—the data and label—closer to the Square Feet column.
g. Select the Type text box, and right-align the information in the text box.

Skills Review (continued)

5. **Add subtotals and counts.**
   a. Switch to Report Design View, then open the RealtorNo Footer section.
   b. Add a text box control to the RealtorNo Footer section, just below the Asking text box in the Detail section. Change the label to read **Subtotal:**, and enter the expression **=Sum([Asking])** in the text box.
   c. Drag the bottom edge of the Report Footer down about 0.25" to add space to the Report Footer.
   d. Copy and paste the new expression in the RealtorNo Footer section to the Report Footer section. Position the controls as directly under the controls in the RealtorNo Footer section as possible.
   e. Modify the label in the Report Footer section to read **Grand Total:**.
   f. Preview the last page of the report to view both the new subtotals in the RealtorNo Footer section as well as in the Report Footer section.
6. **Resize and align controls.**
   a. Switch to Layout View, close the Group, Sort, and Total pane if it is open, and move to the last page of the report to view the Subtotal and Grand Total calculations.
   b. Right-align the text within the Subtotal and Grand Total labels. Move the labels so that their right edges are aligned.
   c. Move the labels and text boxes as needed so that the calculations are positioned directly under the Asking column. Also make sure that the right edges of text boxes that contain the calculations are aligned with the right edge of the Asking column. (*Hint*: If you want to precisely align the right edges of two controls, you need to switch to Report Design View, select both controls at the same time, click the Align button on the Arrange tab, and then click Right to right-align the right edges of the selected controls. Or you can use your mouse or arrow keys to move the right edges of the controls in Layout View.)
   d. Save the report.
7. **Format a report.**
   a. Switch to Report Design View, and change the Alternate Row Color of the Detail section to No Color.
   b. Change the Alternate Row Color of the Type Header section to No Color.
   c. Change the Alternate Row Color of the RealtorNo Header section to No Color, and change the Shape Fill color of the RealtorNo Header section to Green 2.
   d. Select the RLast text box in the RealtorNo Header section, and change the Shape Fill color to Green 2 to match the RealtorNo Header section. Apply the same Green 2 background color to the RPhone text box.
   e. Bold the title of the report, the **Realtor Listings** label in the Report Header.
   f. Double-click a sizing handle on the label in the Report Header to expand it to accommodate the entire label. Be sure to double-click a sizing handle of the label, not the label itself, which opens the Property Sheet.
   g. Change the font color of each label in the Page Header section to black.
   h. Save and preview the report in Report View. It should look like Figure D-22.
   i. In Report Design View, add a label to the left side of the Report Footer section with your name.
   j. Return to Print Preview, print the report if requested by your instructor, then close the Realtor Listings report.

FIGURE D-22

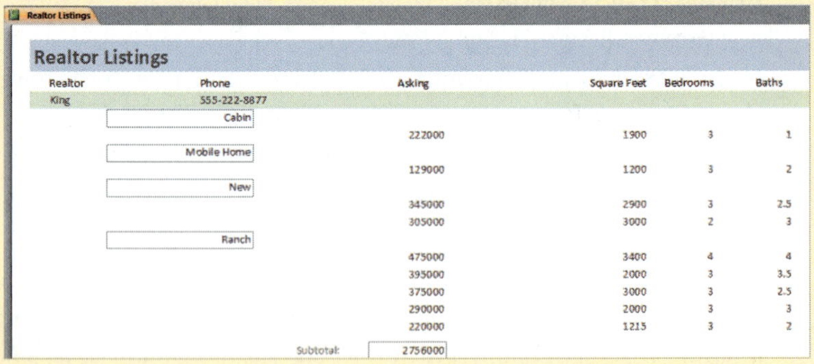

8. **Create mailing labels.**
   a. Click the Agencies table in the Navigation Pane, then start the Label Wizard.
   b. Choose Avery 5160 labels and the default text appearance choices.
   c. Build a prototype label with the AgencyName on the first line, Street on the second line, and City, State, and Zip on the third line with a comma and space between City and State, and a space between State and Zip.
   d. Sort by AgencyName, and name the report **Labels Agencies**.

Skills Review (continued)

e. Preview then close the report. Click OK if a warning dialog box appears regarding horizontal space.
f. If your instructor asks you to print the Labels Agencies report, open the Agencies table and change the name of Four Lakes Realtors to **YourLastName Realtors**. Close the Agencies table, reopen the Labels Agencies report, then print it.
g. Close the Labels Agencies report, close the RealEstate-D.accdb database, then exit Access 2010.

Independent Challenge 1

As the office manager of an international convention planning company, you have created a database to track convention, enrollment, and company data. Your goal is to create a report of up-to-date attendee enrollments.

If you have a SAM 2010 user profile, an autogradable SAM version of this assignment may be available at http://www.cengage.com/sam2010. Check with your instructor to confirm that this assignment is available in SAM. To use the SAM version of this assignment, log into the SAM 2010 Web site and download the instruction and start files.

a. Start Access, then open the Conventions-D.accdb database from the drive and folder where you store your Data Files. Enable content if prompted.
b. Use the Report Wizard to create a report with the AttendeeFirst and AttendeeLast fields from the Attendees table, the CompanyName field from the Companies table, and the ConventionName and CountryName from the Conventions table.
c. View your data by Conventions, do not add any more grouping levels, and sort in ascending order by CompanyName, then AttendeeLast.
d. Use the Block layout and Portrait orientation, then name the report **Convention Listing**.
e. In Layout View, change the labels in the Page Header section from ConventionName to **Convention**, CountryName to **Country**, CompanyName to **Company**, and AttendeeLast to **Attendee**. Delete the AttendeeFirst label.
f. Open the Group, Sort, and Total pane, then use the More Options button to open the CompanyName field's Group Header and Group Footer sections.
g. In Report Design View, expand the ConventionNo Header section about 0.5", then use Cut and Paste to move the ConventionName text box from the Detail section to the ConventionNo Header section. Left-align the ConventionName text box with the Convention label in the Page Header section. Drag the top edge of the CompanyName Header section up to close the extra space in the ConventionNo Header.
h. Expand the CompanyName Header section about 0.25". Drag the CompanyName text box to the bottom of the CompanyName Header section. Use Cut and Paste to move the CountryName text box from the Detail section to the ConventionNo Header section and position it directly above the CompanyName text box in the CompanyName Header section.
i. Delete the Country and CompanyName labels in the Page Header section.
j. In Layout View, scroll through the entire report and widen the ConventionName and CompanyName text boxes as necessary to show all of the data. Be careful, however, to not expand the report beyond the width of the portrait orientation of the report.
k. In Design View, expand the CompanyName Footer, and enter an expression in a new text box to count the values in the AttendeeLast field, **=Count([AttendeeLast])**. Position the new text box directly below the AttendeeLast text box.
l. Modify the new label in the Company Name Footer to read **Count:**. Format the text color of the label to black.
m. Change the color of the report title and the labels in the Page Header section to black. Preview the report. The subtotal count for the first convention should be 21.
n. If required to print the report, switch to Report Design View, add your name as a label to the Report Header section, then print the first page.
o. Save and close the Convention Listing report, close the Conventions-D.accdb database, then exit Access 2010.

Independent Challenge 2

You have built an Access database to track membership in a community service club. The database tracks member names and addresses as well as their status in the club, which moves from rank to rank as the members contribute increased hours of service to the community.

- **a.** Start Access and open the Membership-D.accdb database from the drive and folder where you store your Data Files. Enable content if prompted.
- **b.** Open the Members table, find and change the name of Traci Kalvert to your name, then close the Members table.
- **c.** Use the Report Wizard to create a report using the Status and DuesOwed fields from the Status table, and the FName, LName, and DuesPaid fields from the Members table.
- **d.** View the data by Status. Do not add any more grouping fields, and sort the records in ascending order by LName.
- **e.** Use a Stepped layout and Portrait orientation, title the report **Dues Report**, then preview the report.
- **f.** Switch to Report Design View, then use the Group, Sort, and Total pane to open the StatusNo Footer section.
- **g.** Add a text box to the StatusNo Footer section, just below the DuesPaid text box. Change the label to **Count:** and the expression in the text box to **=Count([DuesPaid])**.
- **h.** Expand the StatusNo Footer section as necessary, and add a second text box to the StatusNo Footer section, just below the first. Change the label to **Subtotal:** and the expression in the text box to **=Sum([DuesPaid])**.
- **i.** Move, resize, and align the controls in the StatusNo Footer section as needed so they are positioned directly under the DuesPaid text box in the Detail section.

Advanced Challenge Exercise

- Open the Property Sheet for the =Sum([DuesPaid]) text box. On the Format tab, set the Format property to Currency and the Decimal Places property to 2.
- Expand the StatusNo Footer section as necessary, and add a third text box to the StatusNo Footer section, just below the second. Change the label to **Balance:**.
- Change the text box expression to **=Count([LName])*[DuesOwed]–Sum([DuesPaid])**. This expression counts the number of values in the LName field, and multiplies it by the DuesOwed field. From that value, the sum of the DuesPaid field is subtracted. This calculates the balance between dues owed and dues paid.
- Open the Property Sheet for the text box with the balance calculation. On the Format tab, set the Format property to Currency and the Decimal Places property to 2.

- **j.** Align the right edges of the DuesPaid text box in the Detail section and all text boxes in the StatusNo Footer section.
- **k.** Save, then preview the Dues Report, print the first page of the Dues Report if requested by your instructor, then close it.
- **l.** Close the Membership-D.accdb database, then exit Access.

Independent Challenge 3

You have built an Access database to organize the deposits at a recycling center. Various clubs regularly deposit recyclable material, which is measured in pounds when the deposits are made.

- **a.** Start Access and open the Recycle-D.accdb database from the drive and folder where you store your Data Files. Enable content if prompted.
- **b.** Open the Centers table, change **Trash Can** to **YourLastName Recycling**, then close the table.
- **c.** Use the Report Wizard to create a report with the CenterName field from the Centers table, the Deposit Date and Weight from the Deposits table, and the ClubName field from the Clubs table.
- **d.** View the data by Centers, do not add any more grouping levels, and sort the records in ascending order by DepositDate.
- **e.** Use a Stepped layout and a Portrait orientation, then title the report **Deposit Listing**.
- **f.** In Layout View, center the Weight label and Weight data. Resize any other labels to display all of their text.
- **g.** Add spaces to the labels so that CenterName becomes **Center Name**, DepositDate becomes **Deposit Date**, and ClubName becomes **Club Name**.

Independent Challenge 3 (continued)

h. In Report Design View, open the Group, Sort, and Total pane and add a CenterNumber Footer section.
i. Add a text box to the CenterNumber Footer section just below the Weight text box with the expression **=Sum([Weight])**.
j. Rename the new label to be **Total Center Weight:** and move it to the left as needed so that it doesn't overlap the text box.
k. Resize and align the edges of the =Sum([Weight]) text box in the CenterNumber Footer section with the Weight text box in the Detail section. Center the data in the =Sum([Weight]) text box.
l. Expand the Report Footer section, then copy and paste the =Sum([Weight]) text box from the CenterNumber Footer section to the Report Footer section.
m. Move and align the controls in the Report Footer section with their counterparts in the CenterNumber Footer section.
n. Change the label in the Report Footer section to **Grand Total Weight:**.
o. Drag the top edges of every section bar up as far as possible to remove extra blank space in the report, then preview the last page of the report as shown in Figure D-23. Your spacing may be a bit different, but the Center subtotals and grand total should match.
p. Save and close the Deposit Listing report, close the Recycle-D.accdb database, then exit Access.

FIGURE D-23

4/23/2013	90	Boy Scouts #11
5/1/2013	105	Girl Scouts #11
6/4/2013	90	Lions
6/20/2013	85	Junior League
8/31/2013	50	Girl Scouts #11
10/2/2013	90	Lions
Total Center Weight:	2720	
Grand Total Weight:	9365	

Access 2010

Real Life Independent Challenge

One way you can use an Access database on your own is to record and track your job search efforts. In this exercise, you create a report to help read and analyze data into your job-tracking database.

a. Start Access and open the JobSearch-D.accdb database from the drive and folder where you store your Data Files. Enable content if prompted.
b. Open the Employers table, and enter five more records to identify five more potential employers.
c. Use subdatasheets in the Employers table to enter five more potential jobs. You may enter all five jobs for one employer, one job for five different employers, or any combination thereof. Be sure to check the spelling of all data entered.
d. Use the Report Wizard to create a report that lists all fields from the Employers table except for EmployerID, and all fields from the Positions table except for the Desirability, EmployerID, and PositionID fields.
e. View the data by Employers, do not add any more grouping levels, and do not add any sort orders.
f. Use a Block layout and a Landscape orientation, then title the report **Job Openings**.
g. In Layout View, revise the labels in the Page Header section from CompanyName to **Company**, EmpStreet to **Street**, EmpCity to **City**, EmpState to **State**, EmpZip to **Zip**, EmpPhone to **Phone**, CareerArea to **Area**, and AnnualSalary to **Salary**.
h. In Layout View, resize the columns so that all data fits on one landscape piece of paper.
i. In Report Design View, move the Page expression in the Page Footer section and the right edge of the report to the left, within the 10.5" mark on the horizontal ruler.
j. Preview and save the Job Openings report, then print it if requested by your instructor.
k. Close the Job Openings report, close the JobSearch-D.accdb database, then exit Access 2010.

Visual Workshop

Open the Basketball-D.accdb database from the drive and folder where you store your Data Files and enable content if prompted. Open the Players table, enter your own name instead of Kelsey Douglas, then close the table. Your goal is to create the report shown in Figure D-24. Use the Report Wizard, and select the PFirst, PLast, HomeTown, and HomeState fields from the Players table. Select the FieldGoals, 3Pointers, and FreeThrows fields from the Stats table. View the data by Players, do not add any more grouping levels, and do not add any more sorting levels. Use a Block layout and a Portrait orientation, then title the report **Scoring Report**. In Layout View, resize all of the columns so that they fit on a single piece of portrait paper, and change the labels in the Page Header section as shown. In Report Design View, move the page calculation in the Page Footer section within the margins of the report, and drag the right edge of the report to the left to eliminate blank pages. Open the PlayerNo Footer section and add text boxes with expressions to sum the FieldGoals, 3Pointers, and FreeThrow fields. Move, modify, and resize all controls as needed.

FIGURE D-24

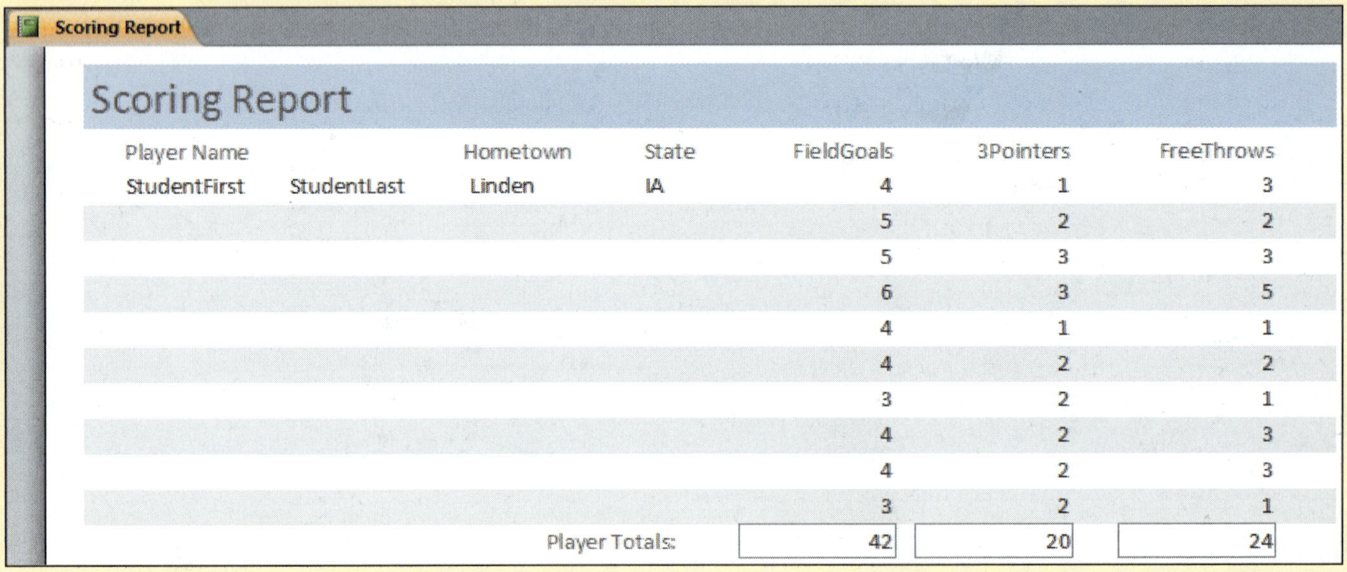

Scoring Report

Scoring Report

Player Name		Hometown	State	FieldGoals	3Pointers	FreeThrows
StudentFirst	StudentLast	Linden	IA	4	1	3
				5	2	2
				5	3	3
				6	3	5
				4	1	1
				4	2	2
				3	2	1
				4	2	3
				4	2	3
				3	2	1
			Player Totals:	42	20	24

UNIT
B
Integration 2010

Integrating Word, Excel, and Access

Files You Will Need:

- INT B-1.xlsx
- INT B-2.docx
- INT B-3.docx
- INT B-4.xlsx
- INT B-5.docx
- INT B-6.docx
- INT B-7.xlsx
- INT B-8.docx
- INT B-9.docx
- INT B-10.xlsx
- INT B-11.docx
- INT B-12.docx

As the administrator of a business, your typical to-do list might include creating sales charts, ordering new products, completing purchase orders, and producing proposals to obtain new contracts. You can use integration techniques in the Office suite to accomplish such diverse tasks quickly and easily. A good strategy is to build an Access database that contains customer and supplier names and addresses, inventory information, and sales records. You can then link data in the Access database to an Excel workbook and to a Word report. When you update information in the Access database, the linked information in the Excel and Word files also changes. Sheila Barton, general manager of the Sydney, Australia, branch of Quest Specialty Travel, often needs to compile reports that include data from files created in Word, Excel, and Access. She asks you to help her integrate the information from these data sources into one document.

OBJECTIVES

- Integrate data among Word, Excel, and Access
- Import an Excel worksheet into Access
- Copy a Word table to Access
- Link an Access table to Excel and Word
- Link an Access table to Word

Integrating Data Among Word, Excel, and Access

You can increase efficiency by integrating the information you create in Word, Excel, and Access so that it works together. For example, you can enter data into an Access database, make calculations using that data in Excel, and then create a report in Word that incorporates the Excel data and the Access table. You can also import data from an Excel spreadsheet into Access and copy a table created in Word into an Access table. Sheila Barton needs to create a database containing information about some of the tours that QST Sydney runs. She then needs to include this information in a report that she creates in Word. Before you create this report, you decide to review some of the ways in which information can be shared among Access, Excel, and Word.

DETAILS

You can integrate Word, Excel, and Access by:

- **Importing an Excel worksheet into Access**

  You can enter data directly into an Access database table, or you can import data from other sources such as an Excel workbook, another Access database, or even a text file. You use the Get External Data command in Access to import data from an outside source. Figure B-1 shows how data entered in an Excel file appears when imported into a new table in an Access database. During the import process, you can change the field names and the data types of selected fields.

- **Copying a Word table into Access**

  You can also create a table in Word that contains data you want to include in an Access database. To save time, you can copy the table from Word and paste it into a new Access table or into an existing Access table. By doing so, you save typing time and minimize errors.

- **Linking an Access table to Excel and Word**

  You link an Access table to Excel and then to Word when you want the data in all three applications to always remain current. First, you use the Copy and Paste Special commands to copy an Access table and paste it into Excel as a link. You can then make calculations using Excel tools that are not available in Access. Any changes you make to the data in Access are also reflected in the linked Excel copy. However, you cannot change the structure of the linked Access table in Excel. For example, you cannot delete any of the columns or rows that contain copied data. The data used in the Excel calculations is linked to the source file in Access. When the data in Access is changed, the results of the formulas in Excel also change.

  Once you have made calculations based on the data in Excel, you can then copy the data from Excel and paste it as a link into Word. When you change the data in Access, the data in both the Excel and the Word files also changes. Figure B-2 shows a Word document that contains two tables. The top table is linked to both Excel and Access. The table was copied from Access and pasted as a link into Excel, additional calculations were made in Excel, and then the table was copied to the Word report and pasted as a link.

- **Linking an Access table to Word**

  You can use the Copy and Paste Special commands to copy a table from Access and then paste it as a link into a Word document. You can then format the linked table attractively. In Figure B-2, the bottom table was copied from Access, pasted as a link in Word, and then reformatted.

FIGURE B-1: Excel data imported to an Access table

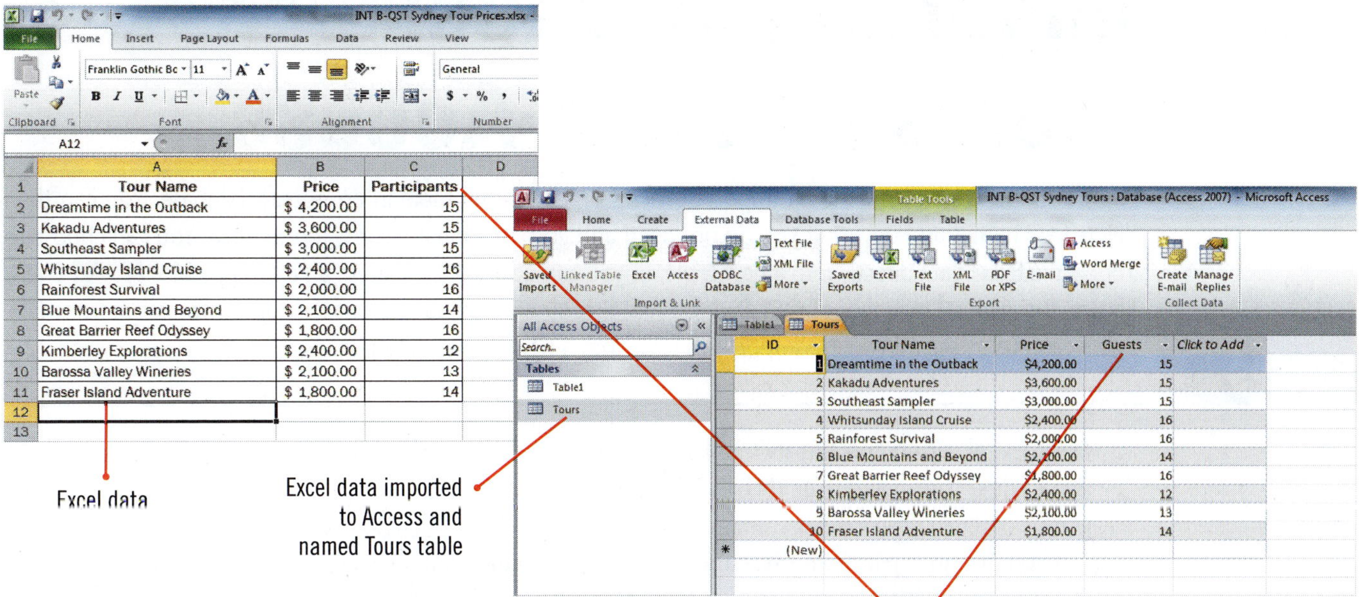

FIGURE B-2: Word report with links to Excel and Access

Quest Specialty Tours

Sydney Branch

Overview

QST Sydney runs tours throughout Australia, with home bases in Melbourne, Adelaide, Brisbane, Cairns, Townsville, Darwin, and Alice Springs. In 2013, QST Sydney offered fifteen separate tours. Most popular were adventure tours to the Outback from Alice Springs and to Kakadu National Park from Darwin. The top ten tours are listed below.

Tour Name	Start Location	Days	Price	Guests	Revenue
Dreamtime in the Outback	Alice Springs	12	$ 4,400.00	15	$ 66,000.00
Kakadu Adventures	Darwin	10	$ 3,600.00	15	$ 54,000.00
Southeast Sampler	Melbourne	10	$ 3,000.00	15	$ 45,000.00
Whitsunday Island Cruise	Townsville	8	$ 2,400.00	16	$ 38,400.00
Rainforest Survival	Cairns	10	$ 2,000.00	16	$ 32,000.00
Blue Mountains and Beyond	Sydney	8	$ 2,100.00	14	$ 29,400.00
Great Barrier Reef Odyssey	Cairns	6	$ 1,800.00	16	$ 28,800.00
Kimberley Explorations	Darwin	6	$ 2,400.00	12	$ 28,800.00
Barossa Valley Wineries	Adelaide	7	$ 2,100.00	13	$ 27,300.00
Fraser Island Adventure	Brisbane	5	$ 1,800.00	14	$ 25,200.00

Table linked to Excel and to Access

Tour Guides

The overwhelming success of the tours operated by QST Sydney is a direct result of the outstanding efforts of our team of dedicated, personable, and skilled guides. Shown below is a list of the guides who led our 2013 tours.

Guide ID	Last Name	First Name	Home Base	E-mail
1	Anstey	George	Cairns	gadams@qstsydney.com
2	Bartlett	Wendy	Darwin	wbartlett@qstsydney.com
3	Hart	Bruce	Sydney	bhart@qstsydney.com
4	Low	Dominique	Melbourne	dlow@qstsydney.com
5	Meredith	Patty	Adelaide	pmeredith@qstsydney.com
6	Watson	Robbie	Brisbane	rwatson@qstsydney.com
7	Wertz	Gary	Alice Springs	gwertz@qstsydney.com

Table copied from Access and pasted as a link

In every guest survey of every QST Sydney tour operated in 2013, the Tour Guides category received the highest rankings. In addition, the head office of Quest Specialty Travel has confirmed that these rankings exceed the rankings from all other guest surveys generated by all branch offices company-wide.

Your Name

Importing an Excel Worksheet into Access

You can minimize typing time by importing data directly into a table in an Access database. You can then delete field names and data that you do not need and add additional records to the table. You can choose to import the Excel data directly into a new table, or you can append the data to an existing table. Sheila Barton, the general manager of QST Sydney, has already entered data about the top 10 tours run from QST Sydney in 2013. She asks you to import this table into a new Access database.

STEPS

1. **Start Excel, open the file INT B-1.xlsx from the drive and folder where you store your Data Files, then save it as INT B-QST Sydney Tour Prices**

   Sheet 1 of the Excel workbook contains a list of the top 10 tours offered by QST Sydney in 2013. A workbook that you plan to export from Excel into Access should contain only the data that you want to appear in the Access table; you need to remove titles, subtitles, charts, and any other extraneous data.

2. **Move the mouse pointer to the left of row 1, click to select row 1, click the right mouse button, click Delete, then save and close the workbook**

3. **Start Access, click the File Name text box, type INT B-QST Sydney Tours, click the Browse button, navigate to the drive and folder where you store your Data Files, click OK, then click Create**

   A new database opens in Access.

> **TROUBLE**
> Be sure to click the Excel button in the Import & Link group, not the Export group.

4. **Click the External Data tab, click the Excel button in the Import & Link group, click Browse, then navigate to the drive and folder where you stored the INT B-QST Sydney Tour Prices file**

5. **Click INT B-QST Sydney Tour Prices, click the Access button on the taskbar, then click Open**

   In the Get External Data – Excel Spreadsheet dialog box shown in Figure B-3, you can choose from among three options. When you select the first or second option, any change you make to the data in the Excel source file will not be made to the data imported to Access. If you choose the third option, the imported Excel source file is linked to the data imported to Access. You want to import, rather than link, the data.

6. **Click OK to accept the default option and start the Import Spreadsheet Wizard, click Open if a security warning appears, click Next to accept Sheet1 as the location for the imported data, then verify that the First Row Contains Column Headings check box is selected**

   The column headings in the Excel spreadsheet become field names in the Access table. A preview of the Access table appears, with the column names shown in gray header boxes.

> **QUICK TIP**
> In this dialog box, you can also change the data types of imported data.

7. **Click Next, click the Participants column to select it, then type Guests as shown in Figure B-4**

   The field name changes in the Field Name text box and the table preview.

8. **Click Next, click Next to let Access set the primary key, type Tours as the table name, click Finish, then click Close**

   Access creates a new table called Tours. You can work with this table in the same way you work with any table you create in Access.

9. **Double-click Tours in the list of tables, widen the Tour Name column, then compare the table to Figure B-5**

   The imported Excel data now appears in a new Access table. You chose to import the data without links, so any changes you make to the Excel source data will not be reflected in the Access table.

FIGURE B-3: Options in the Get External Data dialog box

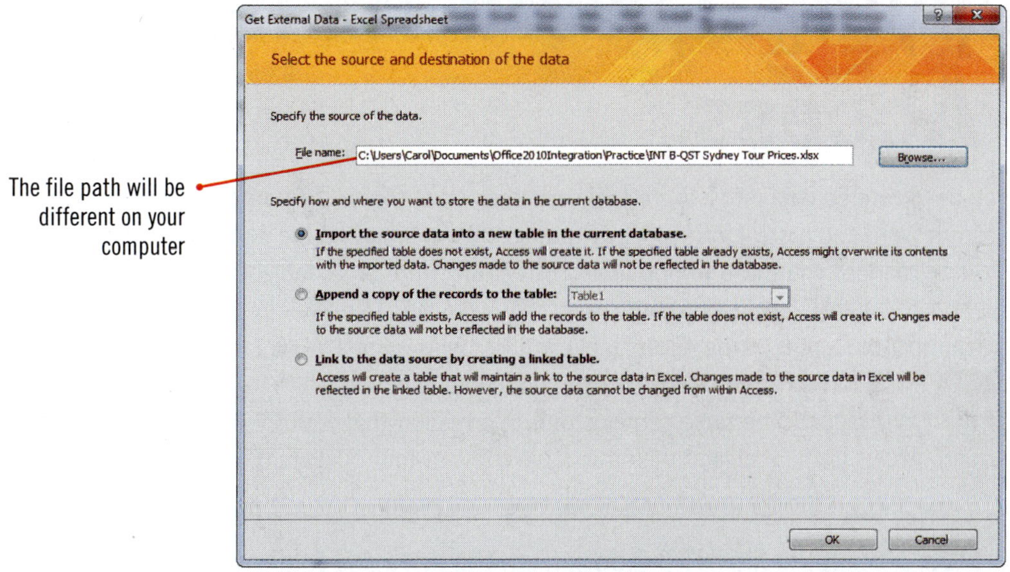

FIGURE B-4: Changing field names in an imported table

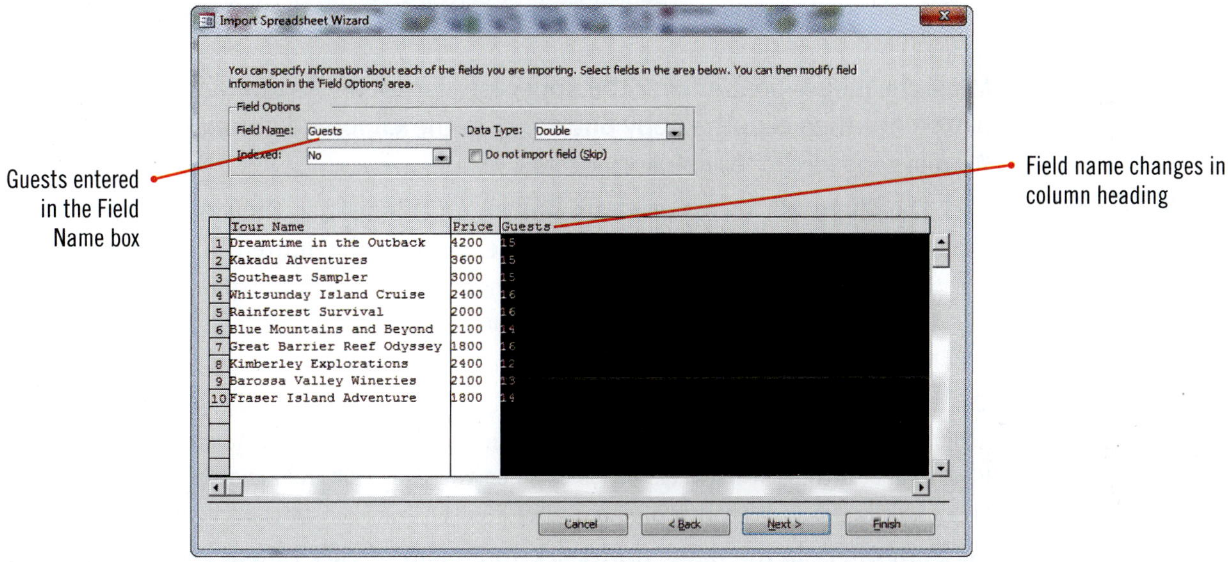

FIGURE B-5: Excel table imported to Access

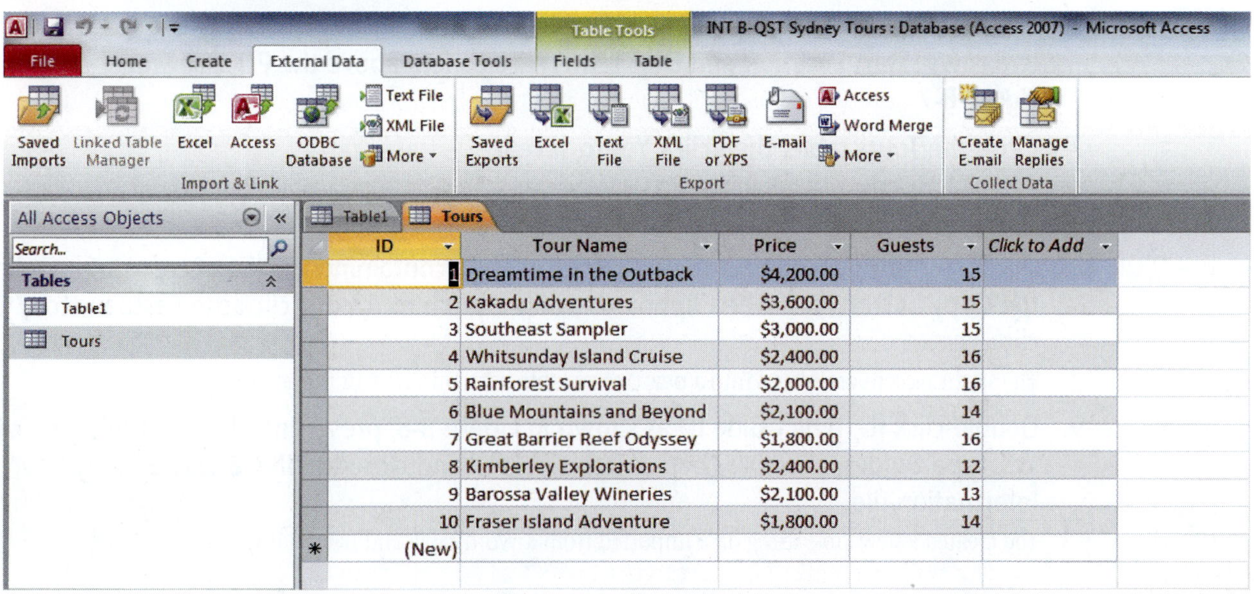

UNIT
B
Integration 2010

Copying a Word Table to Access

When you have entered data into a Word table and then want to make it part of a database, you can copy the table from Word and paste it into Access. The source Word table and the destination Access table are not linked, so any changes you make to one table do not affect the other table. If you want to paste a Word table into an Access table that already contains records, you need to make sure that the Word table contains the same number of records as the Access table. You can also paste a Word table into a new, blank Access table. Sheila has given you a Word document containing two tables that she wants you to incorporate into the Word report. One table contains tour information that was not included in the tour list you imported into Access from Excel, and the other table contains tour guide information.

STEPS

1. **Start Word, open the file INT B-2.docx from the drive and folder where you store your Data Files, then save it as INT B-QST Sydney Tour Information**

   The top table contains tour information, and the bottom table lists the tour guides who work from the QST Sydney office.

2. **Move the mouse pointer over the upper-left corner of the top table, click the table select button, then click the Copy button in the Clipboard group**

   You copied the selected table to the Clipboard.

3. **Click the Microsoft Access program button on the taskbar, then click Click to Add at the top of the blank column in the Tours table as shown in Figure B-6**

   The first blank column is selected. You want to insert the data from the Word table into the Tours database table. When you add data from a Word table to an existing table in Access, you need to make sure that the number of records is the same in both tables.

> **QUICK TIP**
> If you want to import additional records to an existing database, make sure that the imported Excel data contains the same number of fields (columns) as the database.

4. **Click Paste as Fields, then click Yes**

   Additional data for the 10 records is pasted into the Tours table in Access. You do not need the names of the tours to appear twice in the database table. When you copy data from another source and paste it into an Access table, you can delete fields and records in the same way you normally do in Access.

5. **Click anywhere in the table, right-click Tour Name1, click Delete Field, then click Yes**

   The table would be easier to read if the Start Location and Days fields appeared before the Price field.

6. **Click the Home tab, click the View button to switch to Design view, select the last two rows (Start Location and Days), then drag them above the Price row as shown in Figure B-7**

7. **Close the Tours table, then click Yes to save it**

   A blank table called Table1 appears in Datasheet view. You can copy a table directly from Word into a new blank table in Access.

8. **Switch to Word, scroll down and select the table containing the list of tour guides, click the Copy button in the Clipboard group, switch to Access, click the Paste button, then click Yes**

   The seven records are pasted into a new Access table.

9. **Double-click ID, type Guide ID as shown in Figure B-8, press [Enter], close the table, click Yes, type Guides, click OK, then switch to Word and close the INT B-QST Sydney Tour Information file**

   You created a new table using data imported from a Word table and named it Guides.

FIGURE B-6: Selecting the location for copied data

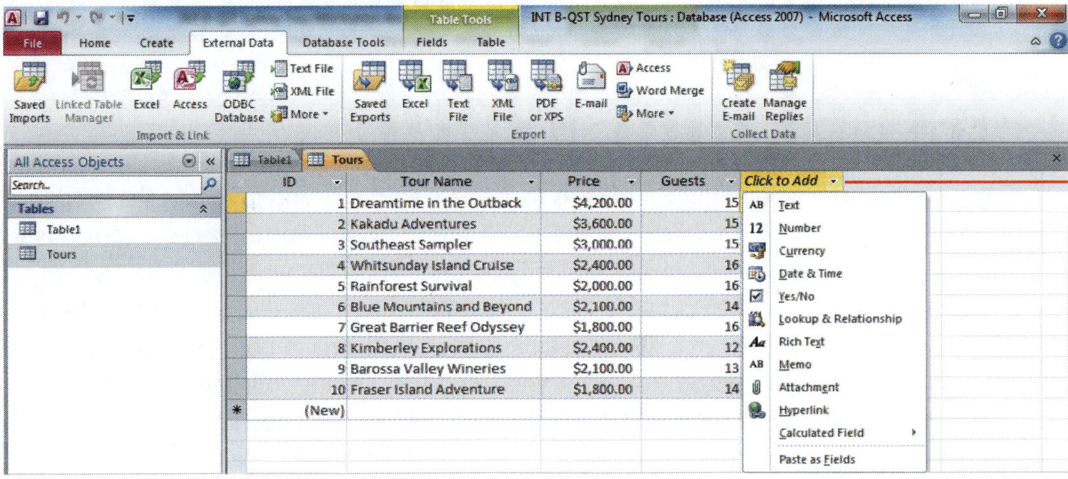

Click to Add selected

FIGURE B-7: Repositioning fields in Design view

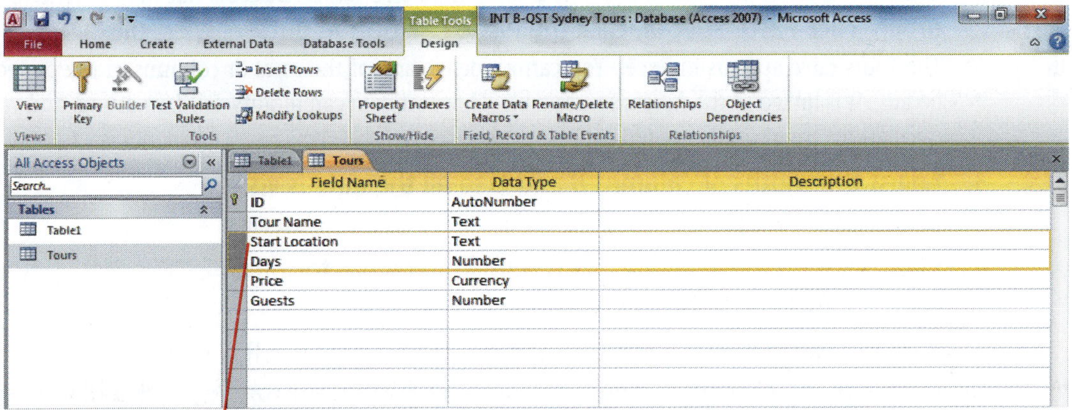

Start Location and Days moved above Price

FIGURE B-8: Renaming the ID field

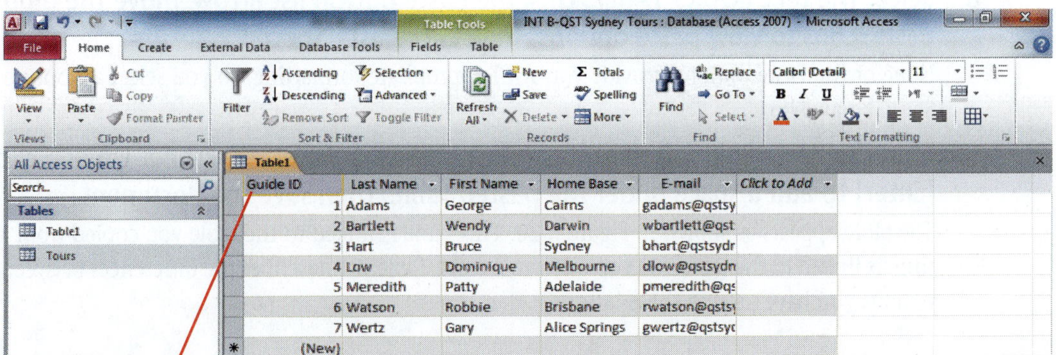

Guide ID entered

Linking an Access Table to Excel and Word

You can link data among three programs to increase efficiency and to reduce the need to enter the same data more than once. To do this, you can use the Copy and Paste Special commands to create a link between an Access database object and an Excel destination file, where you can perform calculations and create charts. You can then copy the Excel data, calculations, and charts to a Word document. When you change the data in the source Access database, the linked data in both Excel and Word update to reflect the new information. You want your report to include tour revenue information. You link the Access Tours table to an Excel worksheet, calculate the tour revenue using Excel tools, then link the calculation results to the tour report in Word. When you change the price of a tour in Access, the price will update in the table you copied to Excel and in the table you copied to Word.

STEPS

1. **In Access, click the Tours table in the list of tables if necessary, then click the Copy button in the Clipboard group**
2. **Create a new blank workbook in Excel, click the Paste button list arrow in the Clipboard group, click Paste Special, click the Paste link option button, then click OK**
   The Tours table appears in Excel. You cannot delete any of the rows or columns in the pasted data in Excel because it is linked to the Access source table. However, you can modify cell formatting, and you can perform calculations based on the pasted data.
3. **Adjust the widths of columns B and C so all the data is visible**
   In the copied table, you can make calculations based on the linked data.
4. **Click cell G1, type Revenue, press [Enter], type the formula =E2*F2, press [Enter], then copy the formula to the range G3:G11**
5. **With the range G2:G11 still selected, press and hold [Ctrl], select the range E2:E11, release [Ctrl], click the Accounting Number Format button $, click a blank cell, then save the workbook as INT B-QST Sydney Tour Revenue**
   The values in columns E and G are formatted in the Accounting format as shown in Figure B-9.
6. **Select the range B1:G11, then click the Copy button in the Clipboard group**
7. **Switch to Word, open the file INT B-3.docx from the drive and folder where you store your Data Files, then save it as INT B-QST Sydney Tour Report**
   The report contains information about the tours run from QST Sydney in 2013. Placeholders show where you will paste two tables.
8. **Select the text TOURS TABLE, click the Paste button list arrow, move the mouse over the paste icons to view paste options, then click Paste Special**
   None of the Paste options provide you with appropriate formatting, so you select an option from the Paste Special dialog box.
9. **Click the Paste link option button, click Microsoft Excel Worksheet Object, click OK, press [Enter] to add a space under the pasted table, then save the document**
   The table appears as shown in Figure B-10. This table is linked to the table you copied from Excel, which, in turn, is linked to the table you copied from Access. Table B-1 describes the differences between the three Paste options you have used in these lessons.

FIGURE B-9: Copied data formatted in Excel

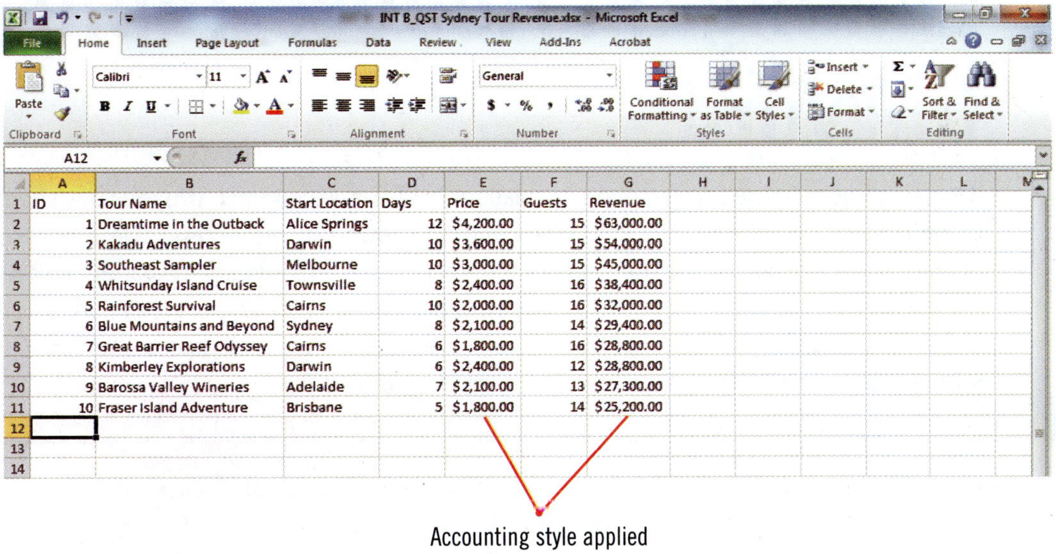

FIGURE B-10: Excel data pasted in Word

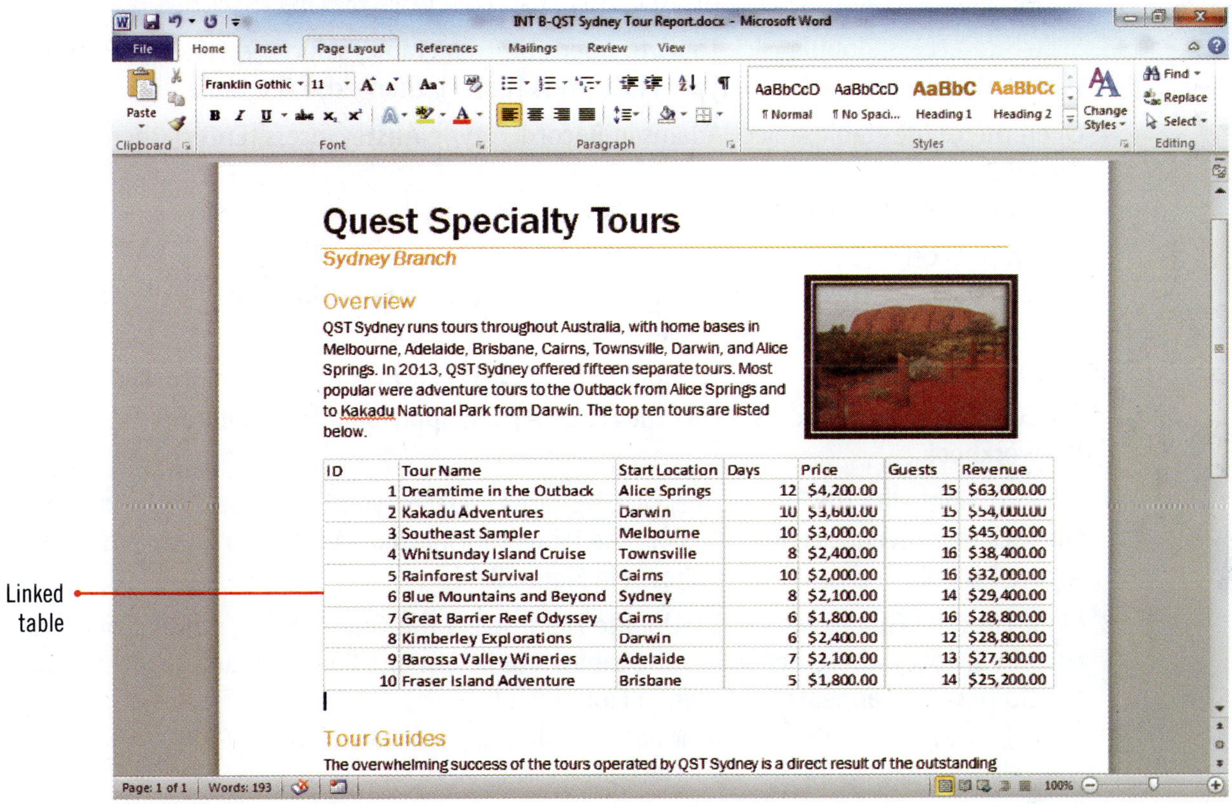

TABLE B-1

command	location	use to
Paste	Paste button in Word and Excel	Paste an object without creating a link; the exception is a chart—when you copy a chart from Excel and paste it into Word, the chart is, by default, linked to the source file in Excel
Paste Special	Paste button list shows Paste Special selection in Word and Excel	Paste an object when you want to create a link or you want to select from a variety of formatting options for the pasted object, whether linked or not
Paste Link	Paste button list shows Paste Link button in Excel	Paste an object such as a copied table from Access into Excel as a link

UNIT
B
Integration 2010

Linking an Access Table to Word

If you don't need to use Excel to make calculations based on Access data, you can copy an Access table and paste it directly into Word as a link. When you update the source Access table, the linked data is also updated in Word. You can also use Word tools to modify the formatting of the pasted table so that the table is attractive and communicates the data clearly. Table B-2 summarizes the integration tasks you performed in this unit. The Word report needs to contain a list of the tour guides. You copy the Guides table from Access and paste it into Word as a link, then test the links.

STEPS

1. **Switch to Access, click Guides in the list of tables to select it, click the Copy button in the Clipboard group, then switch to Word**
2. **Select the text GUIDES TABLE below paragraph 2, click the Paste button list arrow, click Paste Special, click the Paste link option button, click Formatted Text (RTF), then click OK**
   The Guides table is pasted as formatted text in Word. You decide to test the links you created.
3. **Switch to Access, double-click Tours to open the Tours table, select $4,200.00 in Record 1 (Dreamtime in the Outback), type 4400, press [Enter], then close the table**
4. **Open the Guides table, select Adams in Record 1, type Anstey, press [Enter], then close the table**
   When you modify data in Access, the data in the linked Excel and Word files also changes.
5. **Switch to Excel, then verify that the total revenue from the Outback tour is now $66,000.00; if the revenue did not update, click the Data tab in Excel, click Edit Links in the Connections group, click Update Values, then click Close**
6. **Select the range A1:G11, click the Home tab, click the Borders button list arrow in the Font group, click All Borders, select the range A1:G1, apply bold and centering, then save the workbook**
7. **In Word, right-click the Tours table, click Update Link, then verify that the Dreamtime in the Outback tour revenue is now $66,000, the table is formatted with border lines, and the text in row 1 is bold and centered as shown in Figure B-11**
8. **Right-click the Guides table, click Update Field, select the Guides table, double-click the column dividers where needed so the table data fits on one line, then adjust spacing so the Guides table appears as shown in Figure B-11**
   As shown in Figure B-11, the name of the first guide changes from George Adams to George Anstey, and the table columns are adjusted so that all the text is visible and easy to read.
9. **Type your name in the footer, save and close all files, then submit your files to your instructor**

QUICK TIP
You must always close the table in Access before you check if linked data has updated in Excel and Word.

TROUBLE
You may need to wait a few minutes for the data to update in Excel.

Opening linked files and enabling content

When you open files created in different applications, you need to open them in the order in which they were created. For example, if you wish to change the Word report and need to maintain links, open the Access database first, followed by the Excel workbook. After opening the file in Access, click Enable Content in response to the security warning. After opening the file in Excel, click Update in response to the message, then open the Word report. When you open the Word report, click Yes to update links. Broken links can occur when you move linked files to a different location — either to a new folder on your own computer or to another computer. When working with linked files, keep all the files together in one location.

FIGURE B-11: Completed Word report

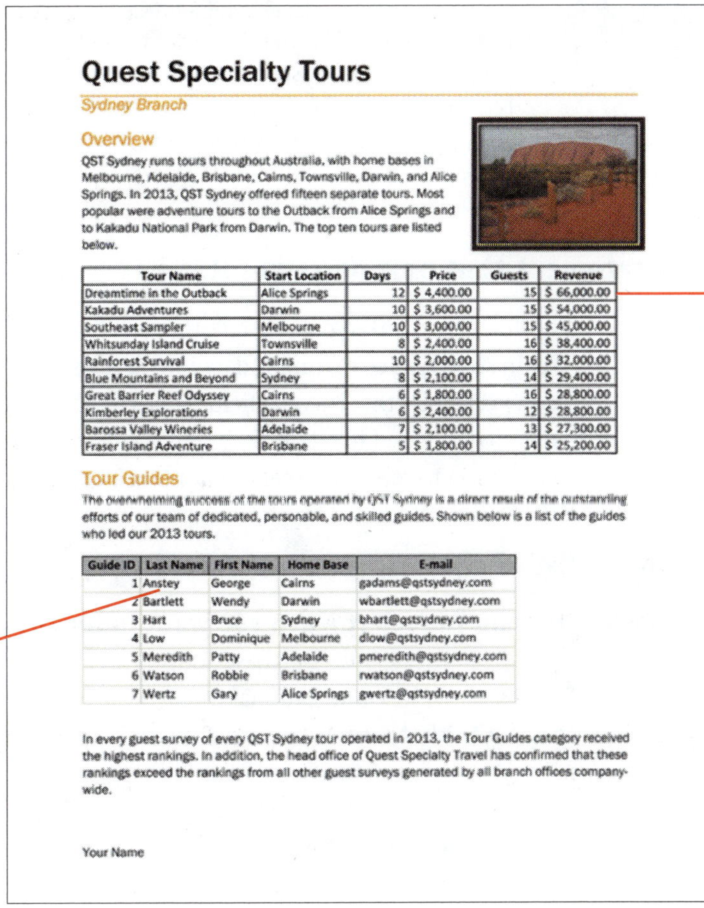

Quest Specialty Tours

Sydney Branch

Overview

QST Sydney runs tours throughout Australia, with home bases in Melbourne, Adelaide, Brisbane, Cairns, Townsville, Darwin, and Alice Springs. In 2013, QST Sydney offered fifteen separate tours. Most popular were adventure tours to the Outback from Alice Springs and to Kakadu National Park from Darwin. The top ten tours are listed below.

Tour Name	Start Location	Days	Price	Guests	Revenue
Dreamtime in the Outback	Alice Springs	12	$ 4,400.00	15	$ 66,000.00
Kakadu Adventures	Darwin	10	$ 3,600.00	15	$ 54,000.00
Southeast Sampler	Melbourne	10	$ 3,000.00	15	$ 45,000.00
Whitsunday Island Cruise	Townsville	8	$ 2,400.00	16	$ 38,400.00
Rainforest Survival	Cairns	10	$ 2,000.00	16	$ 32,000.00
Blue Mountains and Beyond	Sydney	8	$ 2,100.00	14	$ 29,400.00
Great Barrier Reef Odyssey	Cairns	6	$ 1,800.00	16	$ 28,800.00
Kimberley Explorations	Darwin	6	$ 2,400.00	12	$ 28,800.00
Barossa Valley Wineries	Adelaide	7	$ 2,100.00	13	$ 27,300.00
Fraser Island Adventure	Brisbane	5	$ 1,800.00	14	$ 25,200.00

Tour Guides

The overwhelming success of the tours operated by QST Sydney is a direct result of the outstanding efforts of our team of dedicated, personable, and skilled guides. Shown below is a list of the guides who led our 2013 tours.

Guide ID	Last Name	First Name	Home Base	E-mail
1	Anstey	George	Cairns	gadams@qstsydney.com
2	Bartlett	Wendy	Darwin	wbartlett@qstsydney.com
3	Hart	Bruce	Sydney	bhart@qstsydney.com
4	Low	Dominique	Melbourne	dlow@qstsydney.com
5	Meredith	Patty	Adelaide	pmeredith@qstsydney.com
6	Watson	Robbie	Brisbane	rwatson@qstsydney.com
7	Wertz	Gary	Alice Springs	gwertz@qstsydney.com

In every guest survey of every QST Sydney tour operated in 2013, the Tour Guides category received the highest rankings. In addition, the head office of Quest Specialty Travel has confirmed that these rankings exceed the rankings from all other guest surveys generated by all branch offices company-wide.

Your Name

Revenue updated to $66,000

Adams changed to Anstey

TABLE B-2: Unit B integration tasks

object	commands	source program(s)	destination program	result	connection	page no.
Excel file	External Data/ Excel	Excel	Access	Excel spreadsheet is imported into a new table in Access; the spreadsheet must contain only the rows and columns required for the Access table	None	20
Word table	Copy/Paste	Word	Access	Word table is pasted in a new or existing table in Access; if an existing table, the Word table should contain the same number of records as the Access table	None	22
Access table	Copy/Paste Special/ Paste Link	Access	Excel	Access table is pasted into Excel as a link; the linked data can be formatted in Excel and included in formulas but cannot be modified or deleted	Linked	24
Linked Access table in Excel	Copy/Paste Link in Excel Copy/Paste Special/Paste Link in Word	Access and Excel	Word	Access table is linked to Excel and then to Word; changes made in Access appear in Excel and Word	Linked	24
Access table	Copy/Paste Special/ Paste Link	Access	Word	Access table is pasted in Word and can be formatted using Word tools	Linked	26

Practice

For current SAM information, including versions and content details, visit SAM Central (http://www.cengage.com/samcentral). If you have a SAM user profile, you may have access to hands-on instruction, practice, and assessment of the skills covered in this unit. Since various versions of SAM are supported throughout the life of this text, check with your instructor for the correct instructions and URL/Web site for accessing assignments.

Concepts Review

Match each term with the statement that best describes it.

1. **Paste Link**
2. **Click to Add**
3. **Formatted Text (RTF)**
4. **Update**
5. **Column headings**

a. To change linked data in a destination file to match data in the source file
b. In Access, click to import data into an existing Access table
c. Excel labels that become field names in an Access table
d. Selection used to retain divisions of columns and rows in a pasted table
e. Option to select in Excel to maintain a connection with a pasted Access table

Select the best answer from the list of choices.

6. **In Access, which of the following tabs do you select when you want to import data into an Access table?**
   a. Insert
   b. Insert File
   c. Database Tools
   d. External Data
7. **Which command(s) do you use to copy a table from Access and paste it into Excel as a link?**
   a. Import
   b. Copy/Paste
   c. Copy/Paste Link
   d. Copy/Link
8. **Why would you copy a table from Access and paste it as a link in Excel?**
   a. To remove selected columns
   b. To change selected data
   c. To use pasted data in calculations
   d. To modify the number of records
9. **In Word, which option do you select to paste a copied table so that the structure of the table is maintained?**
   a. Unformatted Text
   b. HTML Text
   c. Formatted Text
   d. Formatted Text (RTF)

Skills Review

1. **Import an Excel worksheet into Access.**
   a. Start Excel, open the file INT B-4.xlsx from the drive and folder where you store your Data Files, then save it as **INT B-Grandview Gallery Image List**.
   b. Delete rows 1 and 2, then save and close the workbook.
   c. Start Access, then create a new database called **INT B-Grandview Gallery Inventory** in the location where you store your Data Files.
   d. In Access, import the file **INT B-Grandview Gallery Image List.xlsx** file from Excel as external data. Click Open in response to the security warning.
   e. In the Import Spreadsheet wizard, change the name of the Title field to **Image Title**, then name the new table **Images**.
   f. Close the wizard, open the Images table, then widen columns as necessary.
2. **Copy a Word table to Access.**
   a. Start Word, open the file INT B-5.docx from the drive and folder where you store your Data Files, then save it as **INT B-Grandview Gallery Information**.
   b. Select the top table (which contains the list of images), copy it, then switch to Access.
   c. Paste the table in the Images table, then delete the duplicate column.
   d. In Design view, move the Category and Artist fields above the Price field, then save and close the table.

Skills Review (continued)

- **e.** In Word, select the table containing the list of gift shop products, copy the table, then paste it as a new table in Access.
- **f.** Change the ID field to **Product ID**, then close the table and name it **Gift Shop Products**.
- **g.** In Word, close the Grandview Gallery Information file.

3. Link an Access table to Excel and Word.

- **a.** In Access, copy the Images table.
- **b.** Create a new Excel workbook, paste the Images table as a link from the Paste Special dialog box, save the workbook as **INT B-Grandview Gallery Inventory Data**, then adjust column widths where necessary.
- **c.** Enter **Total Value** in cell G1, adjust the column width, then in cell G2, enter a formula to multiply the Price by the Print Run.
- **d.** Copy the formula to the range G3:G16, then format the values in columns E and G in the Accounting format.
- **e.** Copy the range B1:G16, switch to Word, open the file INT B-6.docx from the drive and folder where you store your Data Files, then save it as **INT B-Grandview Gallery Report**.
- **f.** In the Word document, select POSTCARD LIST, then paste the copied data as a linked Microsoft Excel Worksheet Object, add a blank line above the Price List heading, then save the document.

4. Link an Access table to Word.

- **a.** In Access, copy the Gift Shop Products table, switch to Word, then select the PRICE LIST placeholder.
- **b.** Paste the copied table as a linked Formatted Text (RTF) object, then save the document.
- **c.** In Access, open the Images table, change the print run for Three Dancers (Record 7) to **100** units, then close the table.
- **d.** Open the Gift Shop Products table, change the title Green Horizons to **Blue Horizons**, then close the table.
- **e.** In Excel, verify that the total inventory value for Three Dancers has changed to $550. If the revenue did not update, click the Data tab in Excel, click Edit Links in the Connections group, click Update Values, then click Close.
- **f.** Select the range A1:G16, add border lines, select the range A1:G1, then apply bold and centering.
- **g.** In Word, update the link to the table that lists the postcard images (the top table), then click outside the table.
- **h.** Update the data in the Gift Shop Product table (the lower table), select the table, then double-click a column divider to set the column widths.
- **i.** Adjust spacing so the completed report appears as shown in Figure B-12, type your name where indicated in the footer, save and close all open files and programs, then submit your files to your instructor.

FIGURE B-12

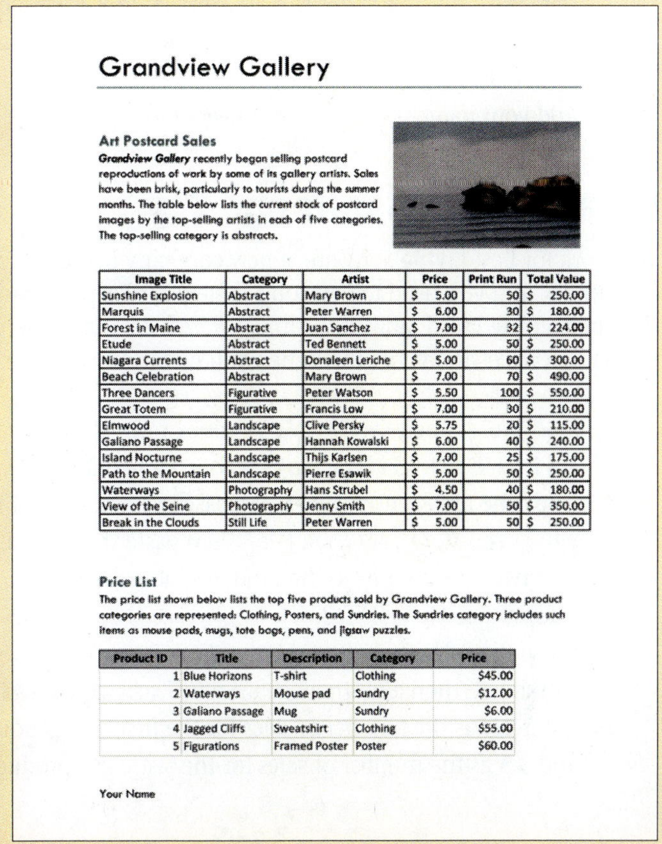

Grandview Gallery

Art Postcard Sales

Grandview Gallery recently began selling postcard reproductions of work by some of its gallery artists. Sales have been brisk, particularly to tourists during the summer months. The table below lists the current stock of postcard images by the top-selling artists in each of five categories. The top-selling category is abstracts.

Image Title	Category	Artist	Price	Print Run	Total Value
Sunshine Explosion	Abstract	Mary Brown	$ 5.00	50	$ 250.00
Marquis	Abstract	Peter Warren	$ 6.00	30	$ 180.00
Forest in Maine	Abstract	Juan Sanchez	$ 7.00	32	$ 224.00
Etude	Abstract	Ted Bennett	$ 5.00	50	$ 250.00
Niagara Currents	Abstract	Donaleen Leriche	$ 5.00	60	$ 300.00
Beach Celebration	Abstract	Mary Brown	$ 7.00	70	$ 490.00
Three Dancers	Figurative	Peter Watson	$ 5.50	100	$ 550.00
Great Totem	Figurative	Francis Low	$ 7.00	30	$ 210.00
Elmwood	Landscape	Clive Persky	$ 5.75	20	$ 115.00
Galiano Passage	Landscape	Hannah Kowalski	$ 6.00	40	$ 240.00
Island Nocturne	Landscape	Thijs Karlsen	$ 7.00	25	$ 175.00
Path to the Mountain	Landscape	Pierre Esawik	$ 5.00	50	$ 250.00
Waterways	Photography	Hans Strubel	$ 4.50	40	$ 180.00
View of the Seine	Photography	Jenny Smith	$ 7.00	50	$ 350.00
Break in the Clouds	Still Life	Peter Warren	$ 5.00	50	$ 250.00

Price List

The price list shown below lists the top five products sold by Grandview Gallery. Three product categories are represented: Clothing, Posters, and Sundries. The Sundries category includes such items as mouse pads, mugs, tote bags, pens, and jigsaw puzzles.

Product ID	Title	Description	Category	Price
1	Blue Horizons	T-shirt	Clothing	$45.00
2	Waterways	Mouse pad	Sundry	$12.00
3	Galiano Passage	Mug	Sundry	$6.00
4	Jagged Cliffs	Sweatshirt	Clothing	$55.00
5	Figurations	Framed Poster	Poster	$60.00

Your Name

Independent Challenge 1

Gold Computing provides computer consulting and repair services to computer users in Fort Lauderdale. You have been asked to build a database that the owner can use to keep track of contracts. The owner would also like you to create a report that analyzes sales trends.

- **a.** Start Excel, open the file INT B-7.xlsx from the drive and folder where you store your Data Files, then save it as **INT B-Gold Computing Sales Data**.
- **b.** Delete any rows and objects that cannot be imported into Access, then save and close the workbook.
- **c.** Create a database in Access called **INT B-Gold Computing**, and save it in the location where you store your Data Files.
- **d.** Import the Excel file INT B-Gold Computing Sales Data into the Access database; change the Type field name to **Category**, and name the new table **Contracts**.

Independent Challenge 1 (continued)

e. Start Word, open the file INT B-8.docx from the drive and folder where you store your Data Files, save it as **INT B-Gold Computing Technicians**, copy the table, close the document, then paste the table into the Contracts table in Access.

f. Delete the Date1, Client Name1, and Type columns from the pasted information, move the Technician field above the Category field, widen the columns if necessary, then close the table.

g. Copy the Contracts table, paste it as a linked file in a new Excel workbook, then adjust the column widths.

h. Format the data in column B with the Short Date style. (*Hint*: Select the range B2:B11, click the Number Format list arrow in the Number group, then click Short Date).

i. Calculate the total revenue from each contract based on an hourly rate of $75. (*Hint*: Add two new columns — one called "Rate" with "75" entered for each record and one called "Total" with the formula entered for each record.)

j. Format the values in columns G and H with the Accounting Number format, then save the Excel workbook as **INT B-Gold Computing Contract Fees**.

k. In Word, set up a new document and enter the text shown in Figure B-13, then save it as **INT B-Gold Computing Contracts**. Format the title in 20 point and the subtitle in 14 point.

FIGURE B-13

> **Gold Computing**
>
> **Spring 2013 Contracts**
>
> Gold Computing provides computer users with a one-stop shop for computer services for PCs and MACs. The table below lists the contracts filled by Gold Computing from January to March, 2013.

l. Copy cells B1 to H11 from Excel, paste them as a link using the Microsoft Excel Worksheet Object option in the Paste Special dialog box below the text paragraph in the INT B-Gold Computing Contracts document, then save the document.

m. In the Contracts table in Access, change the number of hours for the March 1 contract to 10, close the table, then verify that the March 1 revenue has changed from $375 to $750 in the Excel file. If the value does not update, click the Data tab, click Edit Links in the Connections group, click Update Values, then click Close.

n. Format the range A2:H11 with border lines, and bold and center column titles.

o. Update the worksheet object in the Word file, if necessary, then center the worksheet object.

p. Add your name below the worksheet object, save all files and close all programs, then submit your files to your instructor.

Independent Challenge 2

You work for Best Living Software, a new company based in Toronto, Ontario, that sells software online. The business is growing rapidly, and you need to develop a system for keeping track of inventory. You have a price list saved in a Word document. You transfer the Word table data into an Access database, then add some new records. You then perform some calculations on the data in Excel and verify that when you update data in the Access database, the data in Excel also changes.

a. Start Word, open the file INT B-9.docx from the drive and folder where you store your Data Files, then save it as **INT B-Best Living Software Price List**.

b. Copy the table, create a new database in Access called **INT B-Best Living Software** in the location where you store your Data Files, then paste the copied table into a new table named **Products**.

c. Add two new records to the Products table with the information in Table B-3.

d. Close the table, copy it and link it into a new Excel workbook, then add a new column in Excel called **Sales**.

e. Enter **10** as the number of sales for the first four products and **15** as the number of sales for the last eight products.

TABLE B-3

Product	Category	Price
Song Master	Entertainment	$29.95
Financial Freedom	Lifestyle	$34.95

Independent Challenge 2 (continued)

f. Add a new column called **Revenue**, calculate the total revenue for each product, then save the workbook as **INT B-Best Living Software Sales**. Format the Price and Revenue values with the Accounting Number format, then adjust column widths as necessary.

g. Note the current revenue amount for the Astrology Kit and the Amazing Brain Teasers.

h. In the Access Products table, change the price of the Amazing Brain Teasers to $40.95 and the price of the Astrology Kit to $35.95, then close the table.

i. In Excel, verify that the values have updated. If the value does not update, click the Data tab in Excel, click Edit Links in the Connections group, click Update Values, then click Close.

j. Bold and center the labels in row 1, insert a new row 1, enter **Best Living Software Sales**, center it across the range A1:F1, increase the font size to 18 points, apply bold formatting, then apply the fill color of your choice.

k. Type your name in cell A16, save and close all open files and programs, then submit your files to your instructor.

Independent Challenge 3

Blizzard Sports sells skis and snowboards from retail outlets at resorts in Washington, Oregon, and California. You need to create a report that analyzes the December sales posted by resort. First, you create a database for Blizzard Sports from data you copy from an Excel worksheet and a Word document, and then you create a report in Word that contains tables linked to the Access database.

a. Start Access, create a new database called **INT B-Blizzard Sports Inventory** in the location where you store your Data Files, then import the Excel file INT B-10.xlsx. In the Import Spreadsheet wizard, change the name of the Washington field to **Mount Baker**, the Oregon field to **Crystal Mountain**, and the California field to **Mammoth**.

b. Name the new table **Equipment**, then open the table and widen columns as necessary.

c. Close and save the Equipment table, copy it, paste it into a new Excel workbook as a link, adjust the widths of columns as necessary, then save the workbook as **INT B-Blizzard Sports Sales**.

d. Enter **Total** in cell G1, then, in the appropriate cell, enter a formula to add the values for Adventura Skis sales for the three locations. Copy and paste the formula to calculate the total sales for the remaining products.

e. Enter **Revenue** in cell H1, enter a formula to calculate total revenue for Adventura Skis sold in all three locations in the appropriate cell, then copy the formula to the appropriate cells for the rest of the products.

f. In cell H15, calculate the total revenue from all products.

g. Enter **Slipstream Sales** in cell B16, then in cell C16 enter the formula to add the total revenue from only the three Slipstream products.

h. Format all dollar amounts in the Accounting Number format, then save the workbook.

i. Copy the range B1:H14, start Word, open the file INT B-11.docx from the drive and folder where you store your Data Files, then save it as **INT B-Blizzard Sports December Sales**.

j. Replace the word SALES with the copied data as a linked object in the Microsoft Excel Worksheet Object format.

k. Drag the lower-left corner handle of the Excel worksheet object up and to the right until the entire worksheet object is visible, then add a blank line below the object.

l. In Excel, copy the value in cell H15, then paste it as a linked object into the appropriate area in Word using the Formatted Text (RTF) format from the Paste Special dialog box.

m. In Excel, copy the value in cell C16, then paste it as a linked object into the appropriate area in Word using the Formatted Text (RTF) format.

n. Verify that the total revenue is $2,011.940.00 and the total Slipstream sales are $1,258.800.00.

o. In Access, change the price of the Slipstream Snowboard XX to **$3,000**, then close the table.

p. Verify that the values are updated in Excel, then view the Word document. If the values are not updated, close the Word document, open it again, then answer Yes to update links. You should see total sales of $2,142,140.00 and Slipstream sales of $1,389,000.00.

q. Type your name where indicated in the report footer, save and close all open files and programs, then submit your files to your instructor.

Visual Workshop

Create a new database called **INT B-Greenwood Insurance**, then copy the table from the Word file INT B-12.docx into the database as a new table. Name the table **Staff Travel**. Copy the table, then paste it as linked data in a new Excel workbook. Add a new column called **Per Diem**, enter the per diem rate shown in Figure B-14, then calculate the total expenses for each staff person and the total expenses for the company. In the Access source table, change the number of days that Linda Watson was away to 14 and the number of days that Juan Inez was away to 12, then close the table. In Excel, verify that the appropriate values are updated, then as shown in Figure B-14, add and format a title and subtitle. (*Hint*: The font size of the title is 20 point, and the font size of the subtitle is 16 point.) Format data as shown in the figure. Save the workbook as **INT B-Greenwood Insurance Travel Expenses**. Include your name under the table, save and close all open files and programs, then submit your files to your instructor.

FIGURE B-14

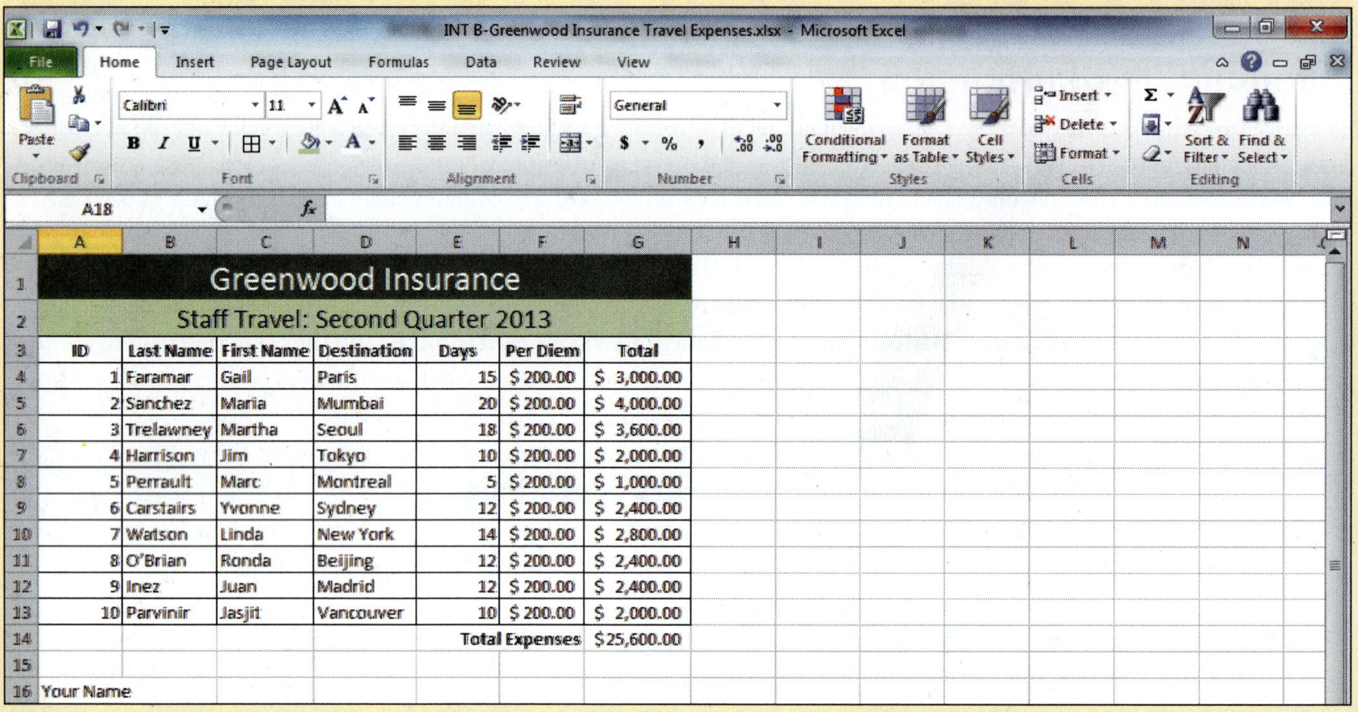

UNIT
A
PowerPoint 2010

Creating a Presentation in PowerPoint 2010

Files You Will Need:
No files needed.

Microsoft PowerPoint 2010 is a powerful computer software program that enables you to create visually dynamic presentations. With PowerPoint, you can create individual slides and display them as a slide show on your computer, a video projector, or over the Internet. Quest Specialty Travel (QST) is an adventure tour company dedicated to providing exclusive and unique cultural travel experiences for its clients. As a sales associate for QST, one of your responsibilities is to research new vacation tours throughout North America, including Canada and Alaska, that QST can sell over the Internet using the company Web site. You have just finished investigating Canadian train travel, and now you need to create a presentation using PowerPoint 2010 that describes the results of your research.

OBJECTIVES

- Define presentation software
- Plan an effective presentation
- Examine the PowerPoint window
- Enter slide text
- Add a new slide
- Apply a design theme
- Compare presentation views
- Print a PowerPoint presentation

UNIT
A
PowerPoint 2010

Defining Presentation Software

Presentation software is a computer program you use to organize and present information to others. Whether you are explaining a new product or moderating a meeting, presentation software can help you effectively communicate your ideas. You can use PowerPoint to create presentations, as well as speaker notes for the presenter and handouts for the audience. Table A-1 explains how your information can be presented using PowerPoint. You need to start work on the presentation you will use to present the new Canadian train tours. Because you are only somewhat familiar with PowerPoint, you get to work exploring its capabilities. Figure A-1 shows how a presentation looks printed as handouts. Figure A-2 shows how the same presentation might look printed as notes for a speaker.

DETAILS

You can easily complete the following tasks using PowerPoint:

- **Enter and edit text easily**
  Text editing and formatting commands in PowerPoint are organized by the task you are performing at the time, so you can enter, edit, and format text information simply and efficiently to produce the best results in the least amount of time.

- **Change the appearance of information**
  PowerPoint has many effects that can transform the way text, graphics, and slides appear. By exploring some of these capabilities, you discover how easy it is to change the appearance of your presentation.

- **Organize and arrange information**
  Once you start using PowerPoint, you won't have to spend much time making sure your information is correct and in the right order. With PowerPoint, you can quickly and easily rearrange and modify text, graphics, and slides in your presentation.

- **Incorporate information from other sources**
  Often, when you create presentations, you use information from a variety of sources. With PowerPoint, you can import text, photographs, numerical data, and facts from files created in programs such as Microsoft Word, Corel WordPerfect, Adobe Photoshop, Microsoft Excel, and Microsoft Access. You can also import graphic images from a variety of sources such as the Internet, other computers, a digital camera, or other graphics programs. Always be sure you have permission to use any work that you did not create yourself.

- **Present information in a variety of ways**
  With PowerPoint, you can present information using a variety of methods. For example, you can print handout pages or an outline of your presentation for audience members. You can display your presentation as an on-screen slide show using your computer, or if you are presenting to a large group, you can use a video projector and a large screen. If you want to reach an even wider audience, you can broadcast the presentation over the Internet so people anywhere in the world can use a Web browser to view your presentation.

- **Collaborate on a presentation with others**
  PowerPoint makes it easy to collaborate or share a presentation with colleagues and coworkers using the Internet. You can use your e-mail program to send a presentation as an attachment to a colleague for feedback. If you have a number of people that need to work together on a presentation, you can save the presentation to a shared workspace on the Internet so everyone in your group using a Web browser has access to the presentation.

FIGURE A-1: PowerPoint handout

FIGURE A-2: PowerPoint notes page

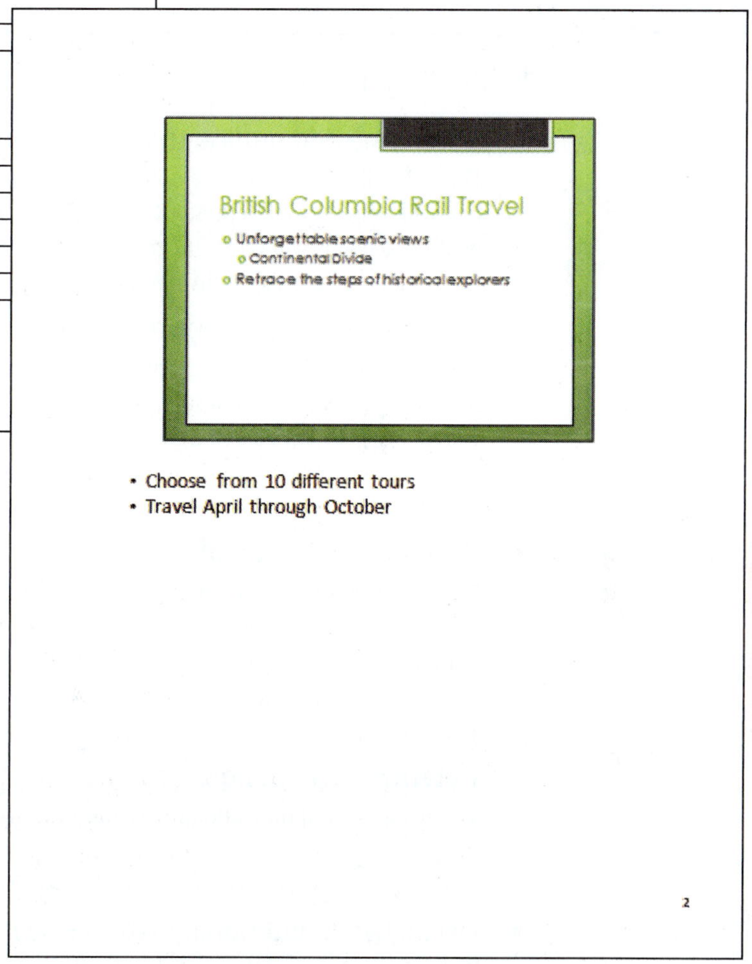

TABLE A-1: Presenting information using PowerPoint

method	description
On-screen presentations	Run a slide show from your computer or through a video projector to a large screen
Notes	Print a page with the image of a slide and notes about each slide for yourself or your audience
Audience handouts	Print handouts with one, two, three, four, six, or nine slides on a page
Broadcast a slide show	Broadcast a slide show to other viewers who watch using a Web browser
Outline pages	Print a text outline of your presentation to highlight the main points

Planning an Effective Presentation

Before you create a presentation, you need to have a general idea of the information you want to communicate. PowerPoint is a powerful and flexible program that gives you the ability to start a presentation simply by entering the text of your message. If you have a specific design or theme you want to use, you can start the presentation by working on the design. In most cases you'll probably enter the text of your presentation into PowerPoint first and then tailor the design to the message and audience. When preparing your presentation, you need to keep in mind not only who you are giving it to, but also where you are giving it. It is important to know what equipment you will need, such as a sound system, computer, or projector. Use the planning guidelines below to help plan an effective presentation. Figure A-3 illustrates a storyboard for a well-planned presentation.

DETAILS

In planning a presentation, it is important to:

- **Determine and outline the message you want to communicate**
  The more time you take developing the message and outline of your presentation, the better your presentation will be in the end. A presentation with a clear message that reads like a story and is illustrated with appropriate visual aids will have the greatest impact on your audience. Start the presentation by giving a general description of Canadian train travel and the types of tours offered by Quest Speciality Travel. See Figure A-3.

- **Identify your audience and delivery location**
  Audience and delivery location are major factors in the type of presentation you create. For example, a presentation you develop for a staff meeting that is held in a conference room would not necessarily need to be as sophisticated or detailed as a presentation that you develop for a large audience held in an auditorium. Room lighting, natural light, screen position, and room layout all affect how the audience responds to your presentation. This presentation will be delivered in a small auditorium to QST's management and sales team.

- **Determine the type of output**
  Output choices for a presentation include black-and-white or color handouts, on-screen slide show, or an online broadcast. Consider the time demands and computer equipment availability as you decide which output types to produce. Because you are speaking in a small auditorium to a large group and have access to a computer and projection equipment, you decide that an on-screen slide show is the best output choice for your presentation.

- **Determine the design**
  Visual appeal, graphics, and presentation design work to communicate your message. You can choose one of the professionally designed themes that come with PowerPoint, modify one of these themes, or create one of your own. You decide to choose one of PowerPoint's design themes to convey the new tour information.

- **Decide what additional materials will be useful in the presentation**
  You need to prepare not only the slides themselves but also supplementary materials, including speaker notes and handouts for the audience. You use speaker notes to help remember key details, and you pass out handouts for the audience to use as a reference during the presentation.

FIGURE A-3: Storyboard of the presentation

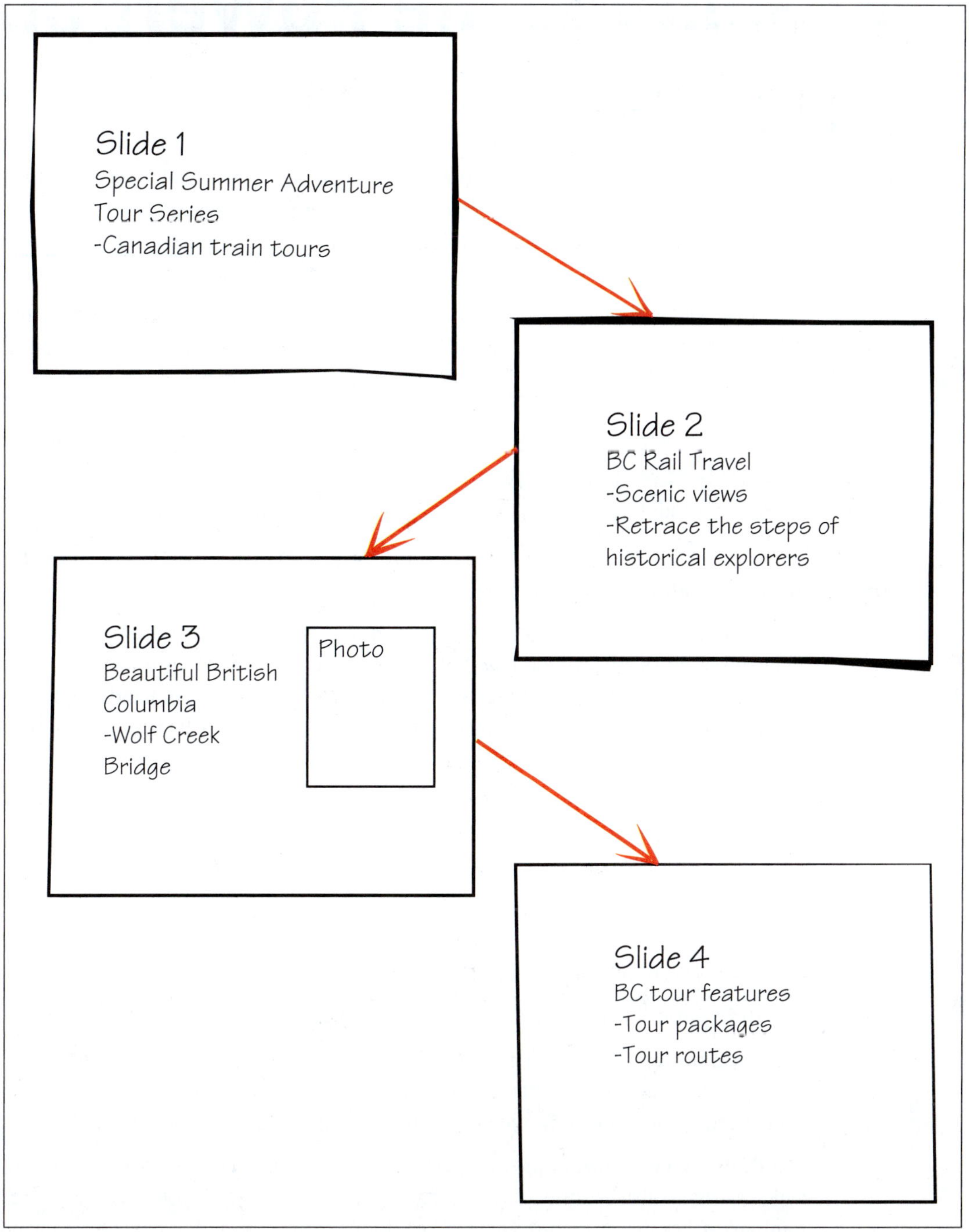

PowerPoint 2010

Understanding copyright

Intellectual property is any idea or creation of the human mind. Copyright law is a type of intellectual property law that protects works of authorship, including books, Web pages, computer games, music, artwork, and photographs. Copyright protects the expression of an idea, but not the underlying facts or concepts. In other words, the general subject matter is not protected, but how you express it *is*, such as when several people photograph the same sunset. Copyright attaches to any original work of authorship *as soon* as it is created, you do not have to register it with the Copyright Office or display the copyright symbol, ©.

Fair use is an exception to copyright and permits the public to use copyrighted material for certain purposes without obtaining prior consent from the owner. Determining whether fair use applies to a work depends on its purpose, the nature of the work, how much of the work you want to copy, and the effect on the work's value. Unauthorized use of protected work (such as downloading a photo or a song from the Web) is known as copyright infringement and can lead to legal action.

UNIT
A
PowerPoint 2010

Examining the PowerPoint Window

When you first start PowerPoint, a blank slide appears in the PowerPoint window. PowerPoint has different **views** that allow you to see your presentation in different forms. By default, the PowerPoint window opens in **Normal view**, which is the primary view that you use to write, edit, and design your presentation. Normal view is divided into three areas called **panes**: the pane on the left contains the Outline and Slides tabs, the large pane is the Slide pane, and the small pane below the Slide pane is the Notes pane. You move around in each pane using the scroll bars. The PowerPoint window and the specific parts of Normal view are described below.

STEPS

TROUBLE

If you have trouble finding Microsoft PowerPoint 2010 on the All Programs menu, check with your instructor or technical support person.

1. **Click the Start button on the taskbar, click All Programs, click Microsoft Office, then click Microsoft PowerPoint 2010**

   PowerPoint starts and the PowerPoint window opens, as shown in Figure A-4.

Using Figure A-4 as a guide, examine the elements of the PowerPoint window, then find and compare the elements described below:

- The **Ribbon** is a wide (toolbar-like) band that runs across the entire PowerPoint window that organizes all of PowerPoint's primary commands. Each set of primary commands is identified by a **tab**; for example, the Home tab is selected by default, as shown in Figure A-4. Commands are further arranged into **groups** on the Ribbon based on their function. So, for example, text formatting commands such as Bold, Underline, and Italic are located on the Home tab, in the Font group.
- The **Outline tab** displays the text of your presentation in the form of an outline, without showing graphics or other visual objects. Using this tab, it is easy to move text on or among slides by dragging text to reorder the information.
- The **Slides tab** displays the slides of your presentation as small images, called **thumbnails**. You can quickly navigate through the slides in your presentation by clicking the thumbnails on this tab. You can also add, delete, or rearrange slides using this tab.
- The **Slide pane** displays the current slide in your presentation.
- The **Notes pane** is used to type text that references a slide's content. You can print these notes and refer to them when you make a presentation or print them as handouts and give them to your audience. The Notes pane is not visible to the audience when you show a slide presentation in Slide Show view.
- The **Quick Access toolbar** provides access to common commands such as Save, Undo, and Redo. The Quick Access toolbar is always visible no matter which Ribbon tab you select. This toolbar is fully customizable. Click the Customize Quick Access Toolbar button to add or remove commands.
- The **View Shortcuts** icons on the status bar allow you to switch quickly between PowerPoint views.
- The **status bar**, located at the bottom of the PowerPoint window, shows messages about what you are doing and seeing in PowerPoint, including which slide you are viewing, and the design theme applied to the presentation. In addition, the status bar displays the Zoom slider controls, the Fit slide to current window button, and information on other functionality such as signatures and permissions.
- The **Zoom slider** is in the lower-right corner of the status bar, use to zoom the slide in and out quickly.

FIGURE A-4: PowerPoint window in Normal view

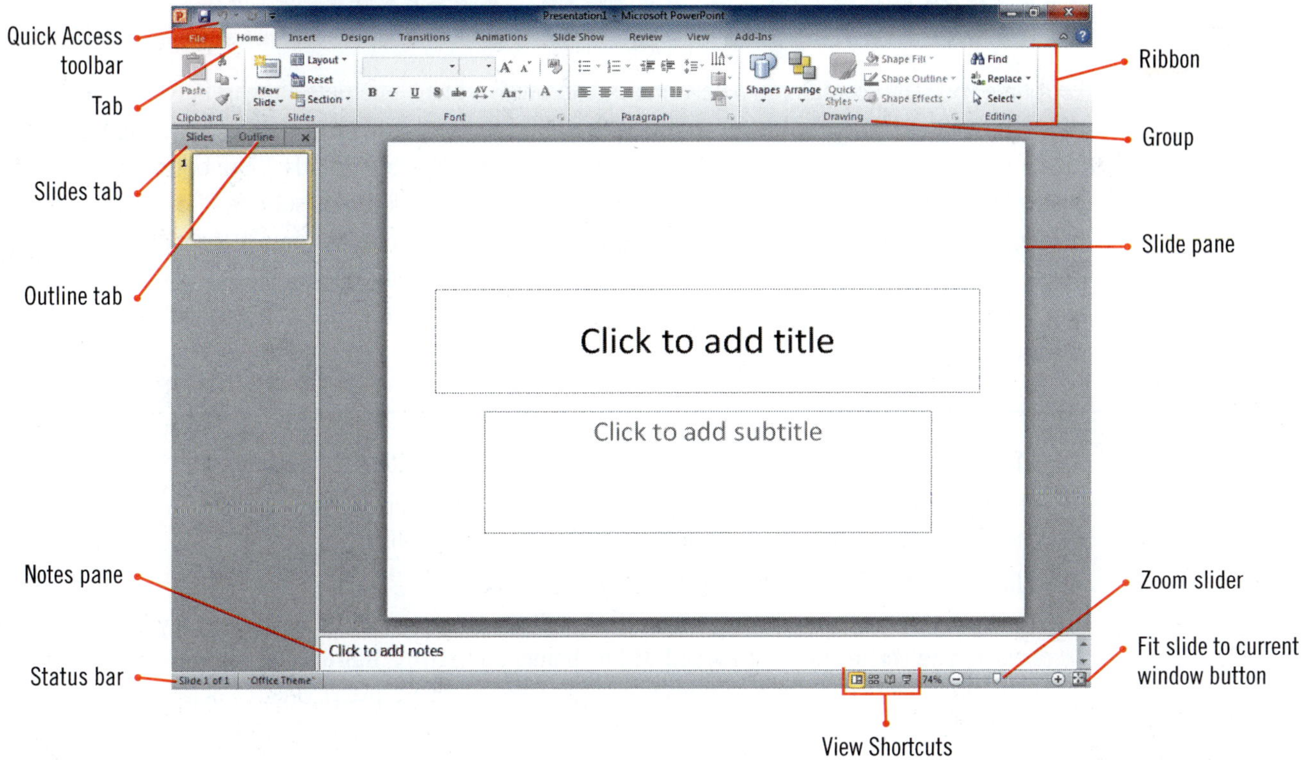

Viewing your presentation in grayscale or black and white

Viewing your presentation in grayscale (using shades of gray) or pure black and white is very useful when you are printing a presentation on a black-and-white printer and you want to make sure your presentation prints correctly. To see how your color presentation looks in grayscale or black and white, click the View tab, then click either the Grayscale or Black and White button in the Color/Grayscale group. Depending on which button you select, the Grayscale or the Black and White tab appears, and the Ribbon displays different settings that you can customize. If you don't like the way an individual object looks in black and white or grayscale, you can change its color. Click the object while still in Grayscale or Black and White view, then choose an option in the Change Selected Object group on the Ribbon.

UNIT
A
PowerPoint 2010

Entering Slide Text

Each time you start PowerPoint, a new presentation with a blank title slide appears in Normal view. The title slide has two **text placeholders**—boxes with dotted borders—where you enter text. The top text placeholder on the title slide is the **title placeholder**, labeled "Click to add title." The bottom text placeholder on the title slide is the **subtitle text placeholder**, labeled "Click to add subtitle." To enter text in a placeholder, click the placeholder and then type your text. After you enter text in a placeholder, the placeholder becomes a text object. An **object** is any item on a slide that can be modified. Objects are the building blocks that make up a presentation slide. Begin working on your presentation by entering text on the title slide.

STEPS

1. **Move the pointer over the title placeholder labeled Click to add title in the Slide pane**
   The pointer changes to I when you move the pointer over the placeholder. In PowerPoint, the pointer often changes shape, depending on the task you are trying to accomplish.
2. **Click the title placeholder in the Slide pane**
   The **insertion point**, a blinking vertical line, indicates where your text appears when you type in the placeholder. A **selection box** with a dashed line border and **sizing handles** appears around the placeholder, indicating that it is selected and ready to accept text. When a placeholder or object is selected, you can change its shape or size by dragging one of the sizing handles. See Figure A-5.
3. **Type Special Summer Adventure Tour Series**
   PowerPoint wraps and then center-aligns the title text within the title placeholder, which is now a text object. Notice that the text also appears on the slide thumbnail on the Slides tab.

TROUBLE
If you press a wrong key, press [Backspace] to erase the character.

4. **Click the subtitle text placeholder in the Slide pane**
   The subtitle text placeholder is ready to accept text.
5. **Type Canadian Train Tours, then press [Enter]**
   The insertion point moves to the next line in the text object.
6. **Type Quest Specialty Travel, press [Enter], type Adventure Tour Series, press [Enter], then type your name**
   Notice that the AutoFit Options button appears near the text object. The AutoFit Options button on your screen indicates that PowerPoint has automatically decreased the size of all the text in the text object so that it fits inside the text object.
7. **Click the AutoFit Options button, then click Stop Fitting Text to This Placeholder on the shortcut menu**
   The text in the text object changes back to its original size and no longer fits in the text object.
8. **In the subtitle text object, position I to the right of Series, drag left to select the entire line of text, press [Backspace], then click outside the text object in a blank area of the slide**
   The Adventure Tour Series line of text is deleted and the AutoFit Options button closes, as shown in Figure A-6. Clicking a blank area of the slide deselects all selected objects on the slide.
9. **Click the Save button on the Quick Access toolbar to open the Save As dialog box, then save the presentation as PPT A-QST in the drive and folder where you store your Data Files**
   Notice that PowerPoint automatically enters the title of the presentation as the filename in the Save As dialog box.

FIGURE A-5: Title text placeholder ready to accept text

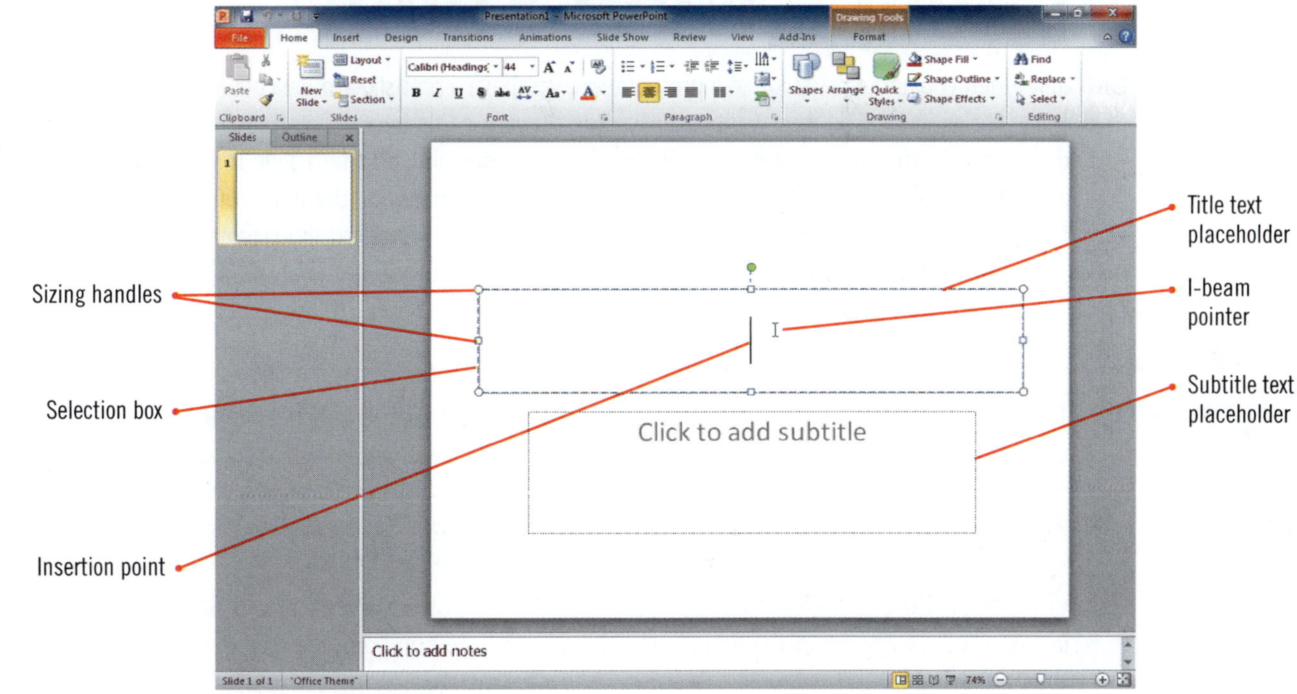

FIGURE A-6: Text on title slide

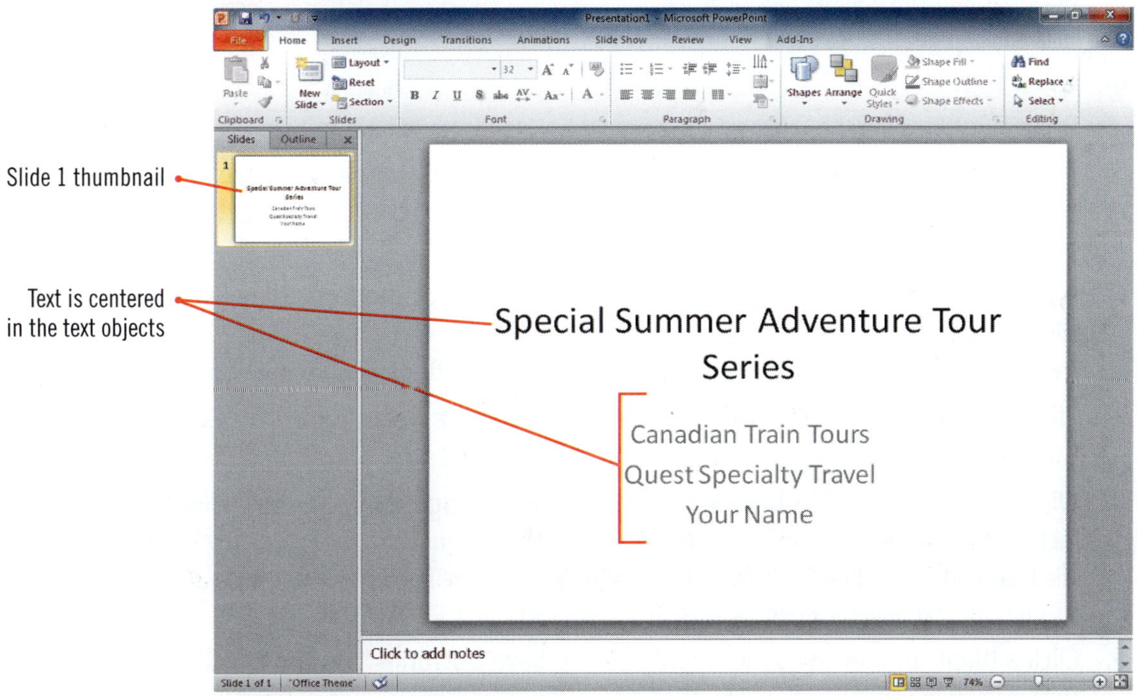

Saving fonts with your presentation

When you create a presentation, it uses the fonts that are installed on your computer. If you need to open the presentation on another computer, the fonts might look different if that computer has a different set of fonts. To preserve the look of your presentation on any computer, you can save, or embed, the fonts in your presentation. Click the File tab, then click the Options button. The PowerPoint Options dialog box opens. Click Save in the left pane, then click the Embed fonts in the file check box. Click the Embed all characters option button, then click OK to close the dialog box. Click Save on the Quick Access toolbar. Now the presentation looks the same on any computer that opens it. Using this option, however, significantly increases the size of your presentation, so only use it when necessary. You can freely embed any TrueType or OpenType font that comes with Windows. You can embed other TrueType fonts only if they have no license restrictions.

UNIT
A
PowerPoint 2010

Adding a New Slide

Ordinarily when you add a new slide to a presentation, you have a pretty good idea of what you want the slide to look like. For example, you may want to add a slide that has a title over bulleted text and a picture. To help you add a slide like this quickly and easily, PowerPoint provides nine standard slide layouts. A **slide layout** contains text and object placeholders that are arranged in a specific way on the slide. You have already worked with the Title Slide layout in the previous lesson. In the event that a standard slide layout does not meet your needs, you can modify an existing slide layout or create a new, custom slide layout. To continue developing the presentation, you create a slide that defines the new tour series.

STEPS

QUICK TIP
You can easily change the slide layout of the current slide by clicking the Layout button in the Slides group.

1. **Click the New Slide button in the Slides group on the Home tab on the Ribbon**
   A new blank slide (now the current slide) appears as the second slide in your presentation, as shown in Figure A-7. The new slide contains a title placeholder and a content placeholder. A **content placeholder** can be used to insert text or objects such as tables, charts, or pictures. Table A-2 describes the content placeholder icons. Notice that the status bar indicates Slide 2 of 2 and that the Slides tab now contains two slide thumbnails.
2. **Type British Columbia Rail Travel, then click the bottom content placeholder**
   The text you type appears in the title placeholder and the insertion point appears at the top of the bottom content placeholder.
3. **Type Unforgettable scenic views, then press [Enter]**
   The insertion point appears directly below the text when you press [Enter] and a new first-level bullet automatically appears.
4. **Press [Tab]**
   The new first-level bullet is indented and becomes a second-level bullet.

QUICK TIP
You can also press [Shift][Tab] to decrease the indent level.

5. **Type Continental Divide, press [Enter], then click the Decrease List Level button in the Paragraph group**
   The Decrease List Level button changes the second-level bullet into a first-level bullet.
6. **Type Retrace the steps of historical explorers, then click the New Slide list arrow in the Slides group**
   The Office Theme layout gallery opens. Each slide layout is identified by a descriptive name.
7. **Click the Content with Caption slide layout, then type Beautiful British Columbia**
   A new slide with three content placeholders appears as the third slide.
8. **Click the lower-left placeholder, type Wolf Creek Bridge, press [Enter], click the Increase List Level button, then type Established in 1857 by Fraser Ironworks**
   The Increase List Level button moves the insertion point to the right one level. Notice this text placeholder does not use text bullets to identify separate lines of text.
9. **Click a blank area of the slide, then click the Save button on the Quick Access toolbar**
   The Save button saves all of the changes to the file. Compare your screen with Figure A-8.

FIGURE A-7: New blank slide in Normal view

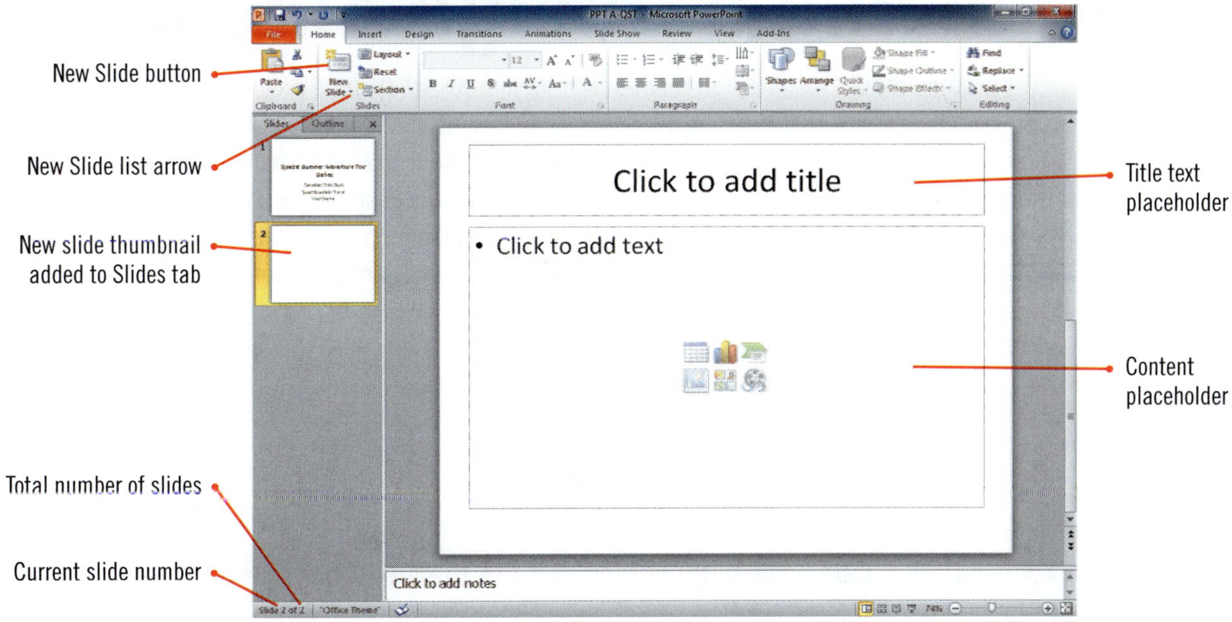

FIGURE A-8: New slide with Content with Caption slide layout

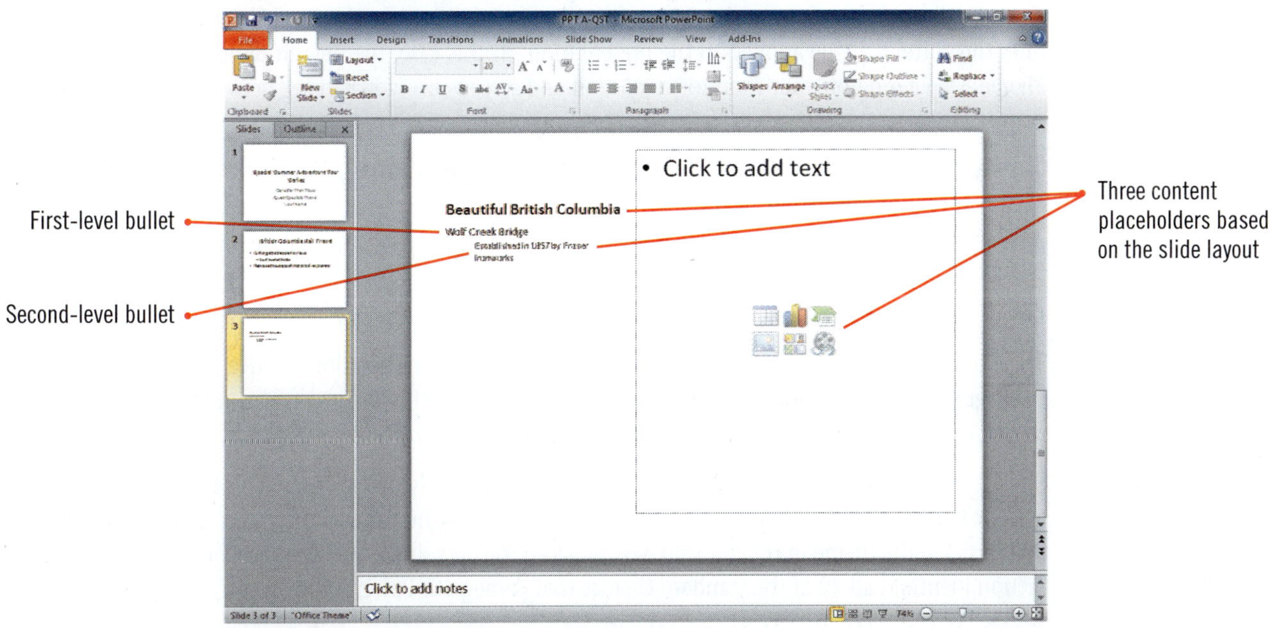

TABLE A-2: Content placeholder icons

click this icon	to insert a
	Table
	Graph chart
	SmartArt graphic
	Picture from a file
	Piece of clip art
	Video clip

UNIT A

PowerPoint 2010

Applying a Design Theme

PowerPoint provides a number of design themes to help you quickly create a professional and contemporary looking presentation. A design **theme** includes a set of 12 coordinated colors for fill, line, and shadow, called **theme colors**; a set of fonts for titles and other text, called **theme fonts**; and a set of effects for lines and fills, called **theme effects** to create a cohesive look. In most cases, you would apply one theme to an entire presentation; you can, however, apply multiple themes to the same presentation, or even a different theme on each presentation slide. You can use a design theme as is, or you can alter individual elements of the theme as needed. Unless you need to use a specific design theme, such as a company theme or product design theme, it is faster and easier to use one of the themes supplied with PowerPoint. If you design a custom theme, you can save it to use in the future. You decide to change the default design theme in the presentation to a new one.

STEPS

1. **Click the Slide 1 thumbnail on the Slides tab**

   Slide 1, the title slide, appears in the Slide pane.

2. **Click the Design tab on the Ribbon, then point to the Adjacency theme in the Themes group as shown in Figure A-9**

   The Design tab appears and a Live Preview of the Adjacency theme is displayed on the slide. A **Live Preview** allows you to see how your changes affect the slides before actually making the change. The Live Preview lasts about 1 minute and then your slide reverts back to its original state. The first (far left) theme thumbnail identifies the current theme applied to the presentation, in this case, the default design theme called the Office Theme. Depending on your monitor resolution and screen size, you can see between five and eleven design themes visible in the Themes group.

3. **Slowly move your pointer over the other design themes, then click the Themes group down scroll arrow once**

   A Live Preview of the theme appears on the slide each time you pass your pointer over the theme thumbnails, and a ScreenTip identifies the theme names.

4. **Move over the design themes, then click the Couture theme**

   The Couture design theme is applied to all the slides in the presentation. Notice the new slide background color, graphic elements, fonts, and text color. You decide that this theme isn't right for this presentation.

5. **Click the More button in the Themes group**

   The All Themes gallery window opens. At the top of the gallery window in the This Presentation section is the current theme applied to the presentation. Notice that just the Couture theme is listed here because when you changed the theme in the last step, you replaced the default theme with the Couture theme. The Built-In section identifies all 40 of the standard themes that come with PowerPoint.

6. **Right-click the Angles theme in the Built-In section, then click Apply to Selected Slides**

   The Angles theme is applied only to Slide 1. You like the Angles theme better and decide to apply it to all slides.

7. **Right-click the Angles theme in the Themes group, then click Apply to All Slides**

   The Angles theme is applied to all three slides. Preview the next slides in the presentation to see how it looks.

8. **Click the Next Slide button at the bottom of the vertical scroll bar**

   Compare your screen to Figure A-10.

9. **Click the Previous Slide button at the bottom of the vertical scroll bar, then save your changes**

QUICK TIP

One way to apply multiple themes to the same presentation is to click the Slide Sorter button on the status bar, select a slide or a group of slides, then click the theme.

FIGURE A-9: Slide showing a different design theme

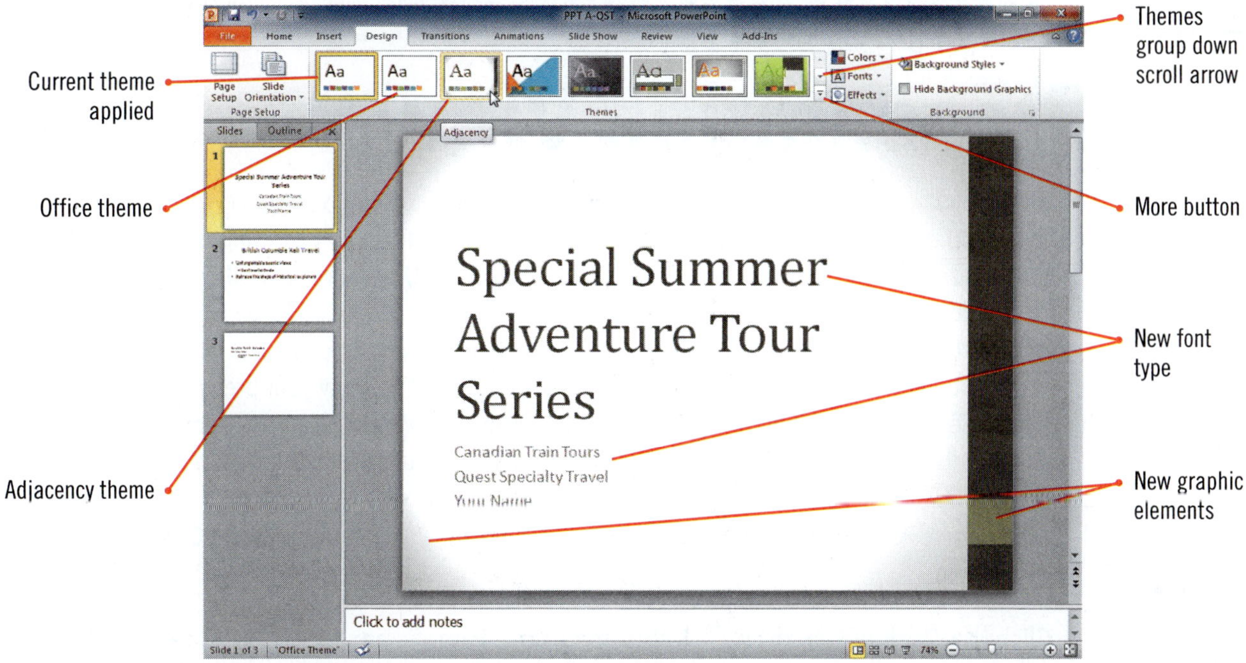

FIGURE A-10: Presentation with Angles theme applied

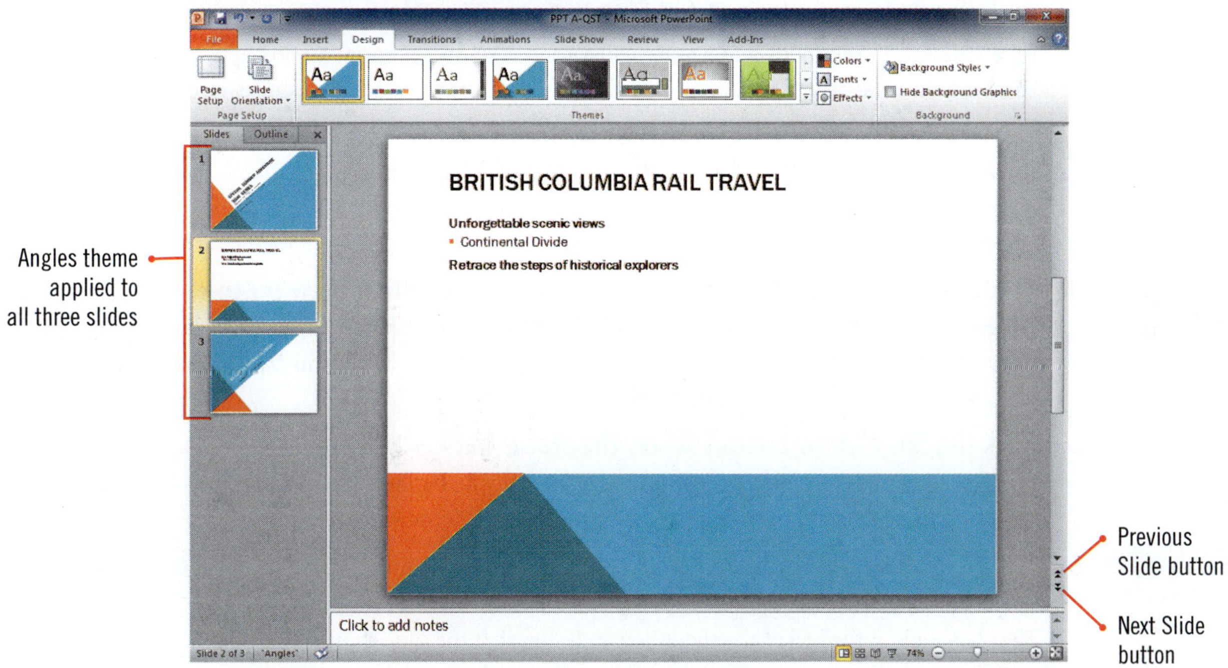

Customizing themes

You are not limited to using the standard themes PowerPoint provides; you can also modify a theme to create your own custom theme. For example, you might want to incorporate your school's or company's colors on the slide background of the presentation or be able to type using fonts your company uses for brand recognition. To modify an existing theme, you can change the color theme, font theme, or the effects theme and then save it for future use by clicking the More button in the Themes group, then clicking Save Current Theme. You also have the ability to create a new font theme or a new color theme from scratch by clicking the Theme Fonts button or the Theme Colors button and then clicking Create New Theme Fonts or Create New Theme Colors. You work in the Create New Theme Fonts or Create New Theme Colors dialog box to define the custom theme fonts or colors.

Comparing Presentation Views

PowerPoint has five primary views: Normal view, Slide Sorter view, Notes Page view, Slide Show view, and Reading view. Each PowerPoint view displays your presentation in a different way and is used for different purposes. Normal view is the primary editing view where you add text, graphics, and other elements to the slides. Slide Sorter view is primarily used to rearrange slides; however, you can also add slide effects and design themes in this view. You use Notes Page view to type notes that are important for each slide. Slide Show view displays your presentation over the whole computer screen and is designed to show your presentation to an audience. Similar to Slide Show view, Reading view is designed to view your presentation on a computer screen. To move easily among the main PowerPoint views, use the View Shortcuts buttons located on the Status bar next to the Zoom slider. Most PowerPoint views can be accessed using the View tab on the Ribbon. Table A-3 provides a brief description of the PowerPoint views. Examine each of the PowerPoint views, starting with Normal view.

STEPS

1. **Click the Outline tab, then click the small slide icon next to Slide 2 in the Outline tab**
   The text for Slide 2 is selected in the Outline tab, and Slide 2 appears in the Slide pane, as shown in Figure A-11. Notice that the status bar identifies the number of the slide you are viewing, the total number of slides in the presentation, and the name of the applied design theme.
2. **Click the Slides tab, then click the Slide 1 thumbnail**
   Slide 1 appears in the Slide pane. Thumbnails of the slides in your presentation appear again on the Slides tab. Since the Slides tab is by default narrower than the Outline tab, the Slide pane enlarges. The scroll box in the vertical scroll bar moves back up the scroll bar.
3. **Click the Slide Sorter button on the status bar**
   A thumbnail of each slide in the presentation appears in the window. You can examine the flow of your slides and drag any slide or group of slides to rearrange the order of the slides in the presentation.
4. **Double-click the Slide 1 thumbnail, then click the Reading View button on the status bar**
   The first slide fills the screen as shown in Figure A-12. Use Reading view to review your presentation or to show your presentation to someone directly on your computer. The status bar controls at the bottom of the window make it easy to move between slides in this view.
5. **Click the Slide Show button on the status bar**
   The first slide fills the entire screen now without the title bar and status bar. In this view, you can practice running through your slides as they would appear in a slide show.
6. **Click the left mouse button to advance through the slides one at a time until you see a black slide, then click once more to return to Normal view**
   The black slide at the end of the slide show indicates that the slide show is finished. At the end of a slide show you automatically return to the slide and PowerPoint view you were in before you ran the slide show, in this case Slide 1 in Normal view.
7. **Click the View tab on the Ribbon, then click the Notes Page button in the Presentation Views group**
   Notes Page view appears, showing a reduced image of the current slide above a large text placeholder. You can enter text in this placeholder and then print the notes page for your own use.
8. **Click the Normal button in the Presentation Views group**

QUICK TIP
You can also switch between views using the commands in the Presentation Views group on the View tab.

QUICK TIP
You can also press [Enter], [Spacebar], [Page Up], [Page Down], or the arrow keys to advance the slide show.

FIGURE A-11: Normal view with the outline tab displayed

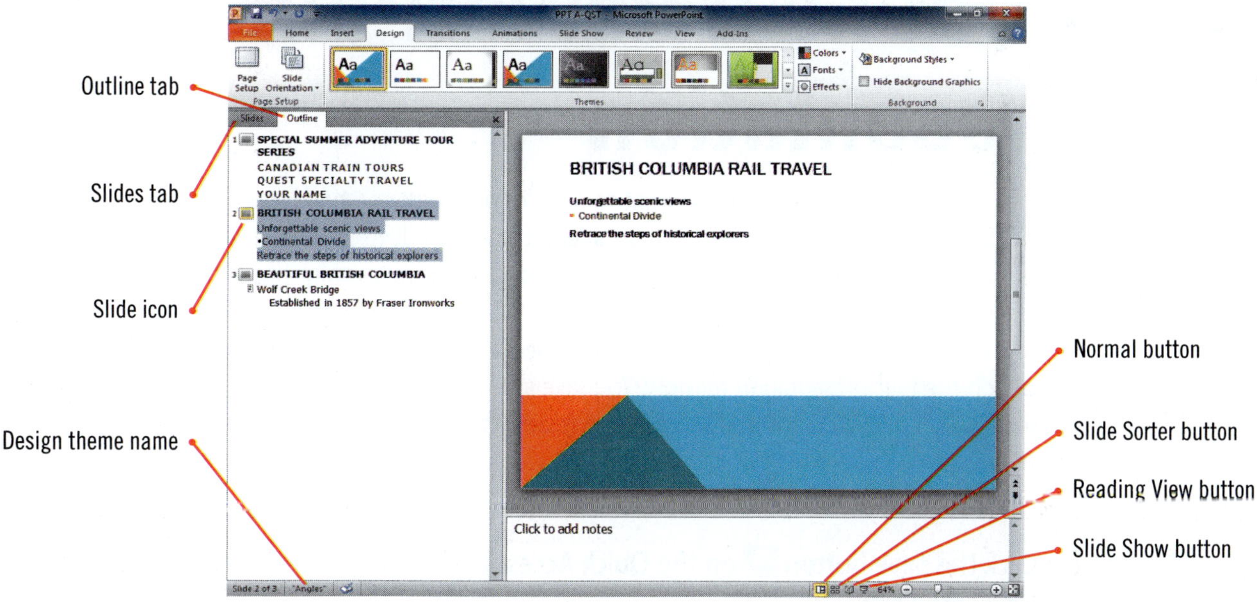

FIGURE A-12: Reading view

TABLE A-3: PowerPoint views

view name	button	button name	description
Normal		Normal	Displays the Outline and Slides tabs, the Slide pane, and the Notes pane at the same time; use this view to work on your presentation's content, layout, and notes concurrently
Slide Sorter		Slide Sorter	Displays thumbnails of all slides; use this view to rearrange and add special effects to your slides
Slide Show		Slide Show	Displays your presentation on the whole computer screen
Reading View		Reading View	Displays your presentation in a large window on your computer screen
Notes Page	(no View Shortcuts button)		Displays a reduced image of the current slide above a large text box where you can enter or view notes

UNIT
A
PowerPoint 2010

Printing a PowerPoint Presentation

You print your presentation when you want to review your work or when you have completed it and want a hard copy. Reviewing your presentation at different stages of development gives you a better perspective of the overall flow and feel of the presentation. You can also preview your presentation to see exactly how each slide looks before you print the presentation. When you are finished working on your presentation, even if it is not yet complete, you can close the presentation file and exit PowerPoint. You are done working on the tour presentation for now. You save and preview the presentation, then you print the slides and notes pages of the presentation so you can review them later. Before leaving for the day, you close the file and exit PowerPoint.

STEPS

QUICK TIP
To quickly print the presentation with the current Print options, add the Quick Print button to the Quick Access toolbar.

QUICK TIP
To print slides appropriate in size for overhead transparencies, click the Design tab, click the Page Setup button in the Page Setup group, click the Slides sized for list arrow, then click Overhead.

1. **Click the Save button on the Quick Access toolbar, click the File tab on the Ribbon, then click Print**

   The Print window opens as shown in Figure A-13. Notice the preview pane on the right side of the window that automatically displays the first slide of the presentation.

2. **Click the Next Page button at the bottom of the preview pane, then click again**

   Each slide in the presentation appears in the preview pane.

3. **Click the Print button**

   Each slide in the presentation prints.

4. **Click the File tab on the Ribbon, click Print, then click the Full Page Slides button in the Settings section**

   The Print Layout gallery opens. In this gallery you can specify what you want to print (slides, handouts, notes pages, or outline), as well as other print options. To save paper when you are reviewing your slides, you can print in handout format, which lets you print up to nine slides per page. The options you choose in the Print window remain there until you change them or close the presentation.

5. **Click 3 Slides, click the Color button in the Settings section, then click Pure Black and White**

   PowerPoint removes the color and displays the slides as thumbnails next to blank lines as shown in Figure A-14. Using the Handouts with three slides per page printing option is a great way to print your presentation when you want to provide a way for audience members to take notes. Printing pure black-and-white prints without any gray tones can save printer toner.

6. **Click the Print button**

   The presentation prints one page showing the all the slides of the presentation as thumbnails next to blank lines.

7. **Click the File tab on the Ribbon, then click Close**

   If you have made changes to your presentation, a Microsoft PowerPoint alert box opens asking you if you want to save changes you have made to your presentation file.

8. **Click Save, if necessary, to close the alert box**

   Your presentation closes.

9. **Click the File tab on the Ribbon, then click Exit**

   The PowerPoint program closes, and you return to the Windows desktop.

FIGURE A-13: Print window

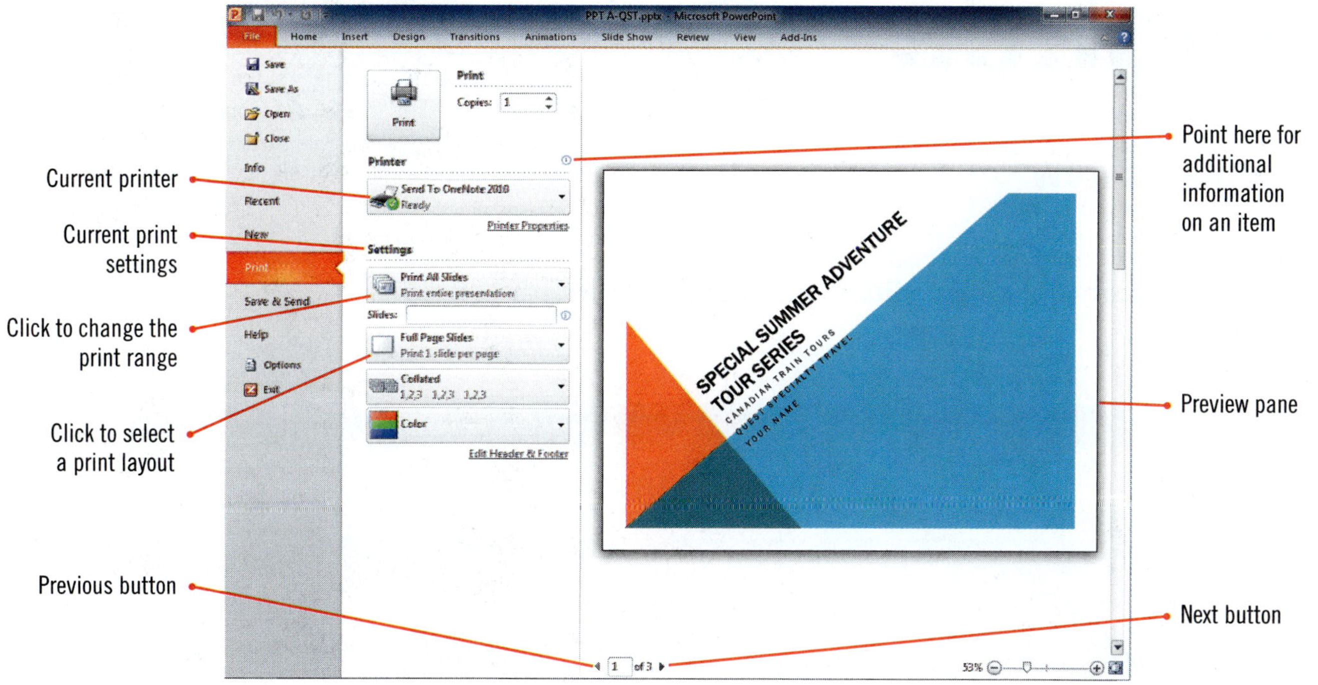

FIGURE A-14: Print window with changed settings

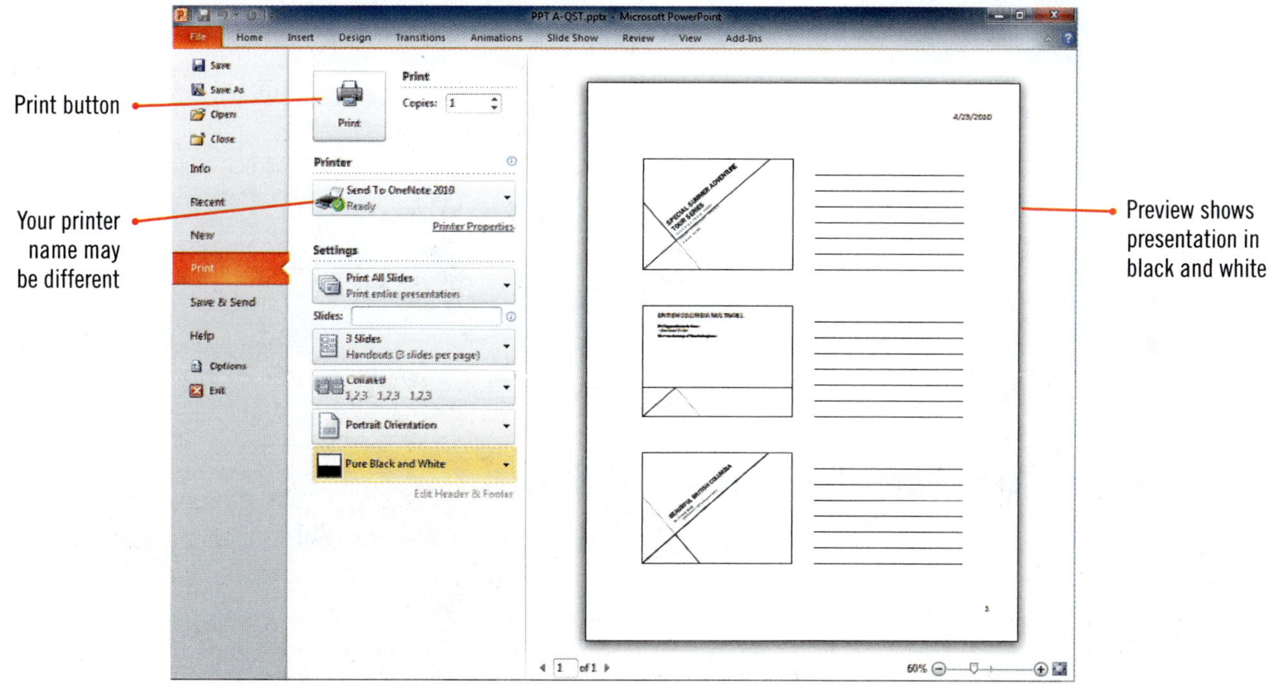

Windows Live and Microsoft Office Web Apps

All Office programs include the capability to incorporate feedback—called online collaboration—across the Internet or a company network. Using **cloud computing** (work done in a virtual environment), you can take advantage of Web programs called Microsoft Office Web Apps, which are simplified versions of the programs found in the Microsoft Office 2010 suite. Because these programs are online, they take up no computer disk space and are accessed using Windows Live SkyDrive, a free service from Microsoft. Using Windows Live SkyDrive, you and your colleagues can create and store documents in a "cloud" and make the documents available to whomever you grant access. To use Windows Live SkyDrive, you need a free Windows Live ID, which you obtain at the Windows Live Web site. You can find more information in the "Working with Windows Live and Microsoft Office Web Apps" appendix.

Practice

Concepts Review

For current SAM information, including versions and content details, visit SAM Central (http://www.cengage.com/samcentral). If you have a SAM user profile, you may have access to hands-on instruction, practice, and assessment of the skills covered in this unit. Since various versions of SAM are supported throughout the life of this text, check with your instructor for the correct instructions and URL/Web site for accessing assignments.

Label each element of the PowerPoint window shown in Figure A-15.

FIGURE A-15

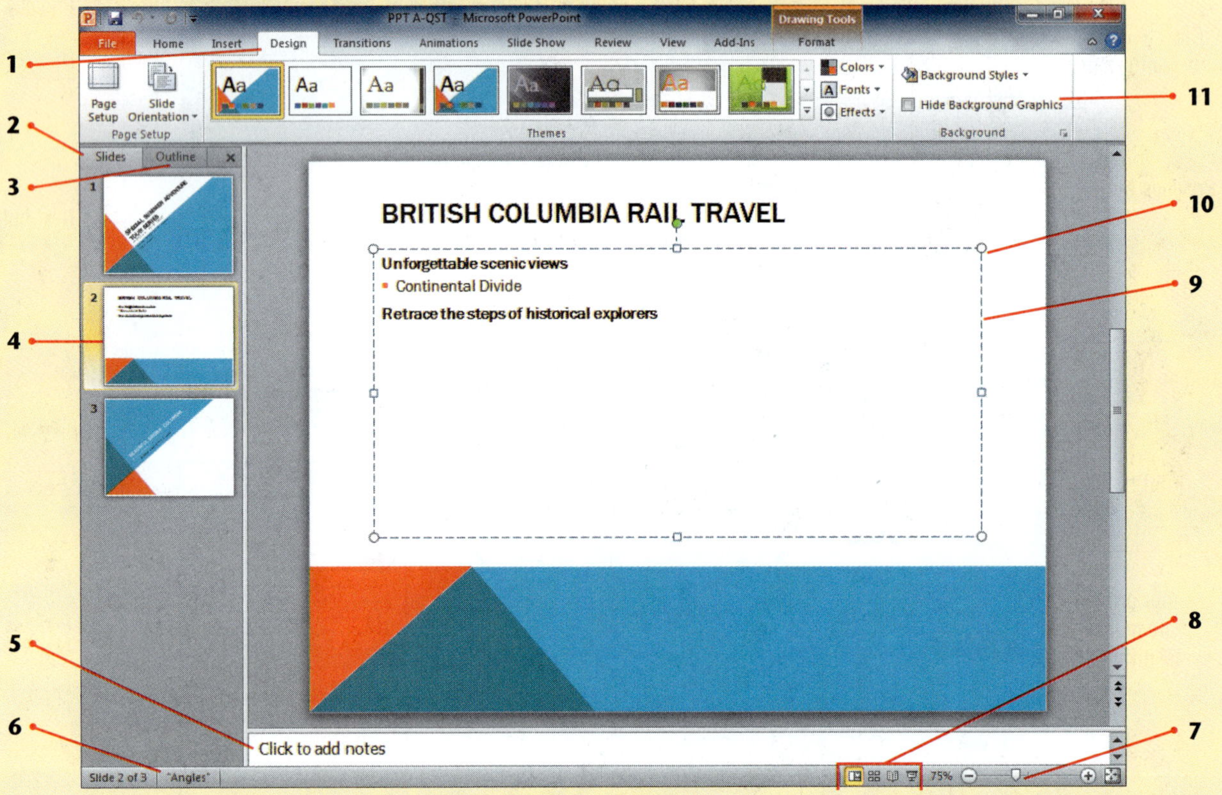

Match each term with the statement that best describes it.

12. Reading view
13. Notes pane
14. Slide Show view
15. Slide Layout
16. Ribbon
17. Zoom slider

a. A view that displays a presentation over an entire computer screen and that is used to show to an audience
b. Allows you to change the size of the slide in the window
c. A view that is used to review a presentation or to show someone a presentation directly on a computer screen
d. Arranges placeholders in a specific way on the slide
e. Used to type text that references slide content
f. Used to organize all of the commands in PowerPoint

Select the best answer from the list of choices.

18. Which statement about incorporating information is *not* correct?
- **a.** You can import text and numerical data into PowerPoint.
- **b.** You can open a PowerPoint presentation in another program to incorporate data.
- **c.** Images from Adobe Photoshop can be inserted into a presentation.
- **d.** Graphic images from a digital camera can be inserted into PowerPoint.

19. Finish the following sentence: "Copyright protects the expression of an idea,...":
- **a.** But not the underlying facts or concepts.
- **b.** Including all general subject matter.
- **c.** Only if you have it regestered with the Copyright Office.
- **d.** Under the Fair Use policy.

20. Which of the following is/are located on the status bar and allow you to quickly switch between views?
- **a.** Fit slide to current window button
- **b.** Switch view button
- **c.** Zoom Slider
- **d.** View Shortcuts

21. What is the blinking vertical line that appears when you type text called?
- **a.** Text handle
- **b.** Placeholder
- **c.** Text insertion line
- **d.** Insertion point

22. The view that fills the entire screen with each slide in the presentation without the title bar is called:
- **a.** Slide Show view.
- **b.** Fit to window view.
- **c.** Reading view.
- **d.** Normal view.

23. Other than the Slide pane, where else can you enter slide text?
- **a.** Reading pane
- **b.** Notes Page view
- **c.** Outline tab
- **d.** Slides tab

24. What does the slide layout do in a presentation?
- **a.** The slide layout puts all your slides in order.
- **b.** A slide layout automatically applies all the objects you can use on a slide.
- **c.** A slide layout defines how all the elements on a slide are arranged.
- **d.** The slide layout enables you to apply a template to the presentation.

25. Which of the following is not included in a design theme?
- **a.** Effects
- **b.** Pictures
- **c.** Colors
- **d.** Fonts

Skills Review

1. Examine the PowerPoint window.
- **a.** Start PowerPoint, if necessary.
- **b.** Identify as many elements of the PowerPoint window as you can without referring to the unit material.
- **c.** Be able to describe the purpose or function of each element.
- **d.** For any elements you cannot identify, refer to the unit.

2. Enter slide text.
- **a.** In the Slide pane in Normal view, enter the text **Alutiiq Indian Lands Protection Proposal** in the title placeholder. Refer to Figure A-16 as you complete the slide.
- **b.** In the subtitle text placeholder, enter **Karluk Lake on Kodiak Island**.

FIGURE A-16

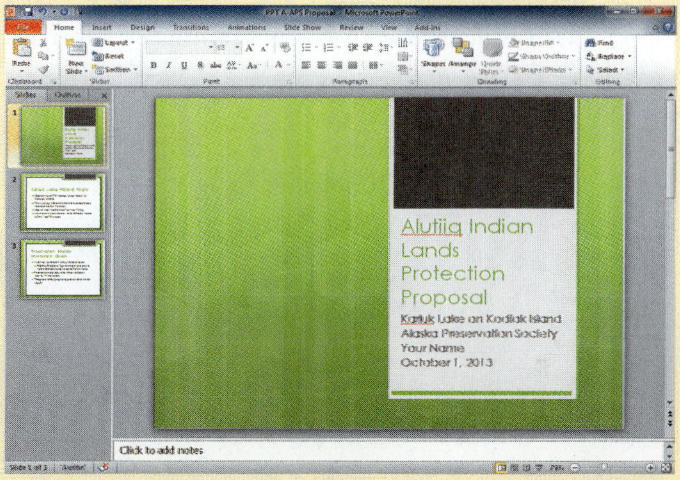

Skills Review (continued)

- **c.** On the next line of the placeholder, enter **Alaska Preservation Society**.
- **d.** On the next line of the placeholder, enter your name.
- **e.** On the next line of the placeholder, enter **October 1, 2013**. Let PowerPoint AutoFit the text in the text object.
- **f.** Deselect the text object.
- **g.** Save the presentation using the filename **PPT A-APS Proposal** to the drive and folder where you store your Data Files.

3. Add a new slide.

- **a.** Create a new slide.
- **b.** Using Figure A-17, enter text on the slide.
- **c.** Create another new slide.
- **d.** Using Figure A-18, enter text on the slide.
- **e.** Save your changes.

4. Apply a design theme.

- **a.** Click the Design tab.
- **b.** Click the Themes group More button, then point to all of the themes.
- **c.** Locate the Grid theme, then apply it to the selected slide.
- **d.** Move to Slide 1.
- **e.** Locate the Austin theme, then apply it to Slide 1.
- **f.** Apply the Austin theme to all of the slides in the presentation.
- **g.** Use the Next Slide button to move to Slide 3, then save your changes.

5. Compare presentation views.

- **a.** Click the View tab.
- **b.** Click the Slide Sorter button in the Presentation Views group.
- **c.** Click the Notes Page button in the Presentation Views group, then click the Previous Slide button twice.
- **d.** Click the Reading View button in the Presentation Views group, then click the Next button on the status bar.
- **e.** Click the Normal button on the status bar, then click the Slide Show button.
- **f.** Advance the slides until a black screen appears, then click to end the presentation.
- **g.** Save your changes.

6. Print a presentation.

- **a.** Print all the slides as handouts, 4 Slides Horizontal, in color.
- **b.** Print the presentation outline.
- **c.** Close the file, saving your changes.
- **d.** Exit PowerPoint.

FIGURE A-17

FIGURE A-18

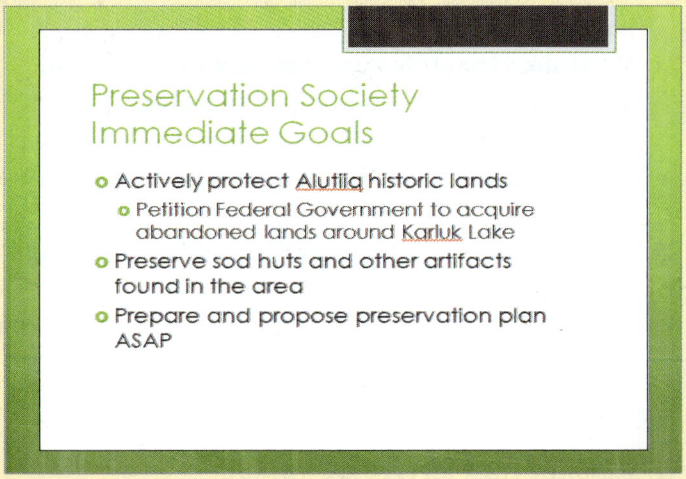

Independent Challenge 1

You work for BioCare Service Industries, a business that offers environmental hazard cleanup and project management. One of your jobs at the company is to go on new sales calls with your boss. Your boss has asked you to create a sales presentation that describes and compares the services BioCare Industries offers.

If you have a SAM 2010 user profile, an autogradable SAM version of this assignment may be available at http://www.cengage.com/sam2010. Check with your instructor to confirm that this assignment is available in SAM. To use the SAM version of this assignment, log into the SAM 2010 Web site and download the instruction and start files.

a. Start PowerPoint.
b. In the title placeholder on Slide 1, type **BioCare Service Industries**.
c. In the subtitle placeholder, type your name, press [Enter], then type today's date.
d. Apply the Thatch design theme to the presentation.
e. Save your presentation with the filename **PPT A-BioCare** to the drive and folder where you store your Data Files.
f. Use Figures A-19 and A-20 to add two more slides to your presentation. (*Hint*: Slide 2 uses the Comparison layout.)
g. Use the commands on the View tab to switch between all of PowerPoint's views.
h. Print the presentation using handouts, 3 Slides, in black and white.
i. Save and close the file, then exit PowerPoint.

FIGURE A-19

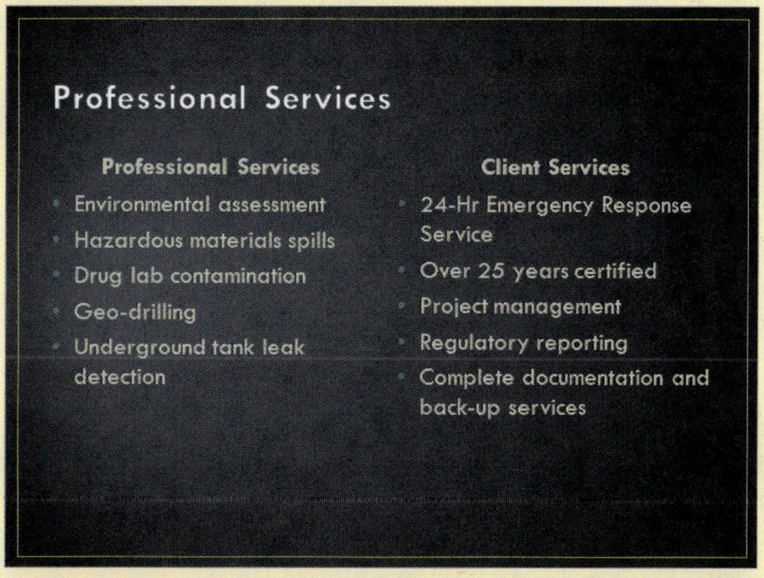

FIGURE A-20

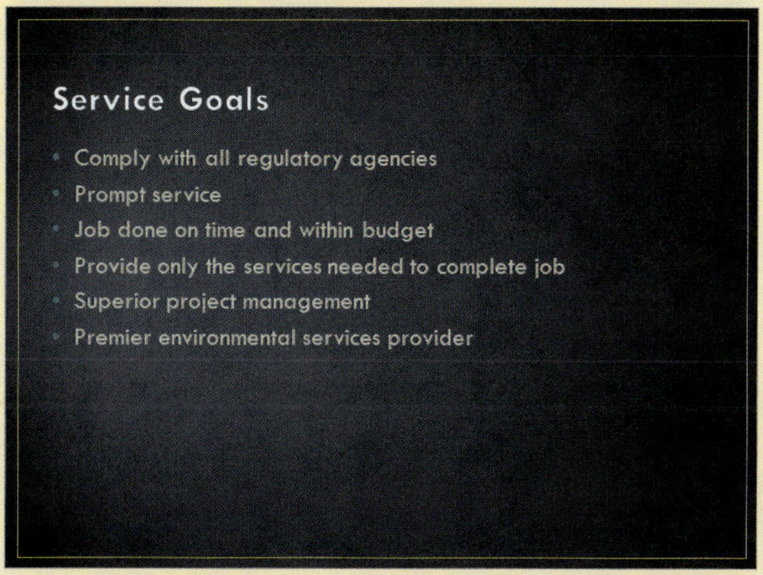

Independent Challenge 2

You have recently been promoted to sales manager at PowerCraft Sports, which manufactures personal aircraft, including different types of ultralite and composite airplanes. Part of your job is to present company sales figures at a yearly sales meeting. Use the following information as the basis for units sold nationally in your presentation: 283 Aircruiser, 105 Aero Twin, 89 UltraFlight, 73 Tomahawk V, and 47 Vision II. Assume that PowerCraft Sports has six sales regions throughout the country: Northwest, West, South, Midwest, Mid Atlantic, and Northeast. Also, assume overall sales rose 5% over last year, and gross sales reached $49 million. The presentation should have at least five slides.

a. Spend some time planning the slides of your presentation. What is the best way to show the information provided? What other information could you add that might be useful for this presentation?

b. Start PowerPoint.

c. Give the presentation an appropriate title on the title slide, and enter today's date and your name in the subtitle placeholder.

d. Add slides and enter appropriate slide text.

e. On the last slide of the presentation, include the following information:
PowerCraft Sports
PO Box 7373
Wrightsville, NC 19698-7373

f. Apply a design theme. A typical slide might look like the one shown in Figure A-21.

FIGURE A-21

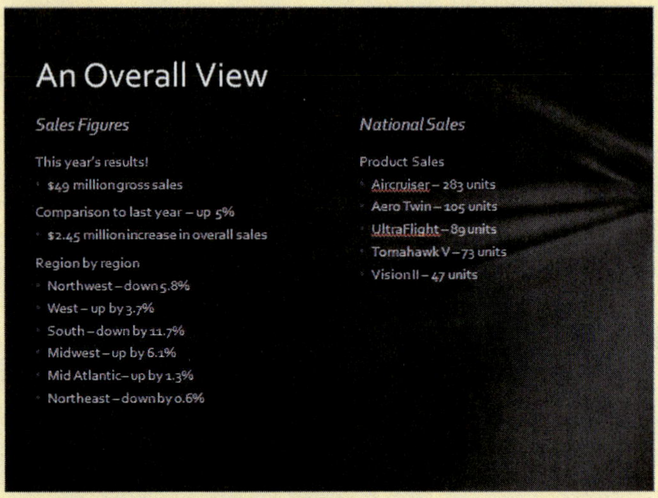

Advanced Challenge Exercise

- Open the Notes Page view.
- Add notes to three slides.
- Print the Notes Page view for the presentation.

g. Switch views. Run through the slide show at least once.

h. Save your presentation with the filename **PPT A-PowerCraft Sports** where you store your Data Files.

i. Close the presentation and exit PowerPoint.

Independent Challenge 3

You work for Baja Central, an emerging company that exports goods from Mexico. The company wants to expand its business globally. The Internet marketing director has asked you to plan and create a PowerPoint presentation that he will use to convey an expanded Internet service that will target Western countries. This new Internet service will allow customers to purchase all kinds of Mexican-made goods. Sample items for sale include silver and turquoise jewelry, hand crafts, folk art, terra cotta kitchenware, wood decorative items, and leather goods. Your presentation should contain product information and pricing. Use the Internet, if possible, to research information that will help you formulate your ideas. The presentation should have at least five slides.

a. Spend some time planning the slides of your presentation. What information would a consumer need to have to purchase items on this Web site?

b. Start PowerPoint.

c. Give the presentation an appropriate title on the title slide, and enter today's date and your name in the subtitle placeholder.

d. Add slides and enter appropriate slide text.

Independent Challenge 3 (continued)

e. On the last slide of the presentation, type the following information:
   Baja Central Ltd.
   Adolfo P Limon "T"
   Oaxaca, Oax
   ZC 98000
   Tel: 50-001-660-44
   info@bjacenltd.com
f. Apply a design theme. A typical slide might look like the one shown in Figure A-22.
g. Switch views. Run through the slide show at least once.
h. Save your presentation with the filename **PPT A-Baja** where you store your Data Files.
i. Close the presentation and exit PowerPoint.

FIGURE A-22

Real Life Independent Challenge

Every year your college holds a large fund-raising event to support a local charity. You are a member of the Student Council Advisory Board (SCAB), which is in charge of deciding which charity gets help. This year the board decided to support the city food bank by hosting a chili cook-off competition. The competition needs to include local and professional cooking teams from around the region. You have been chosen to present the charity proposal in a meeting of the College Events Council.

a. Spend some time planning the slides of your presentation. Assume the following: the competition is a 2-day event; event advertising will be city- and regionwide; local music groups will also be invited; there will be a kids section with events and games; the event will be held at the county fairgrounds. Use the Internet, if possible, to research information that will help you formulate your ideas.
b. Start PowerPoint.
c. Give the presentation an appropriate title on the title slide and enter your school's name, your name, and today's date in the subtitle placeholder.
d. Add slides and enter appropriate slide text. You must create at least three slides. Typical slides might look like the ones shown in Figure A-23 and Figure A-24.
e. View the presentation.
f. Save your presentation with the filename **PPT A-Chili Cookoff** where you store your Data Files.
g. Close the presentation and exit PowerPoint.

FIGURE A-23

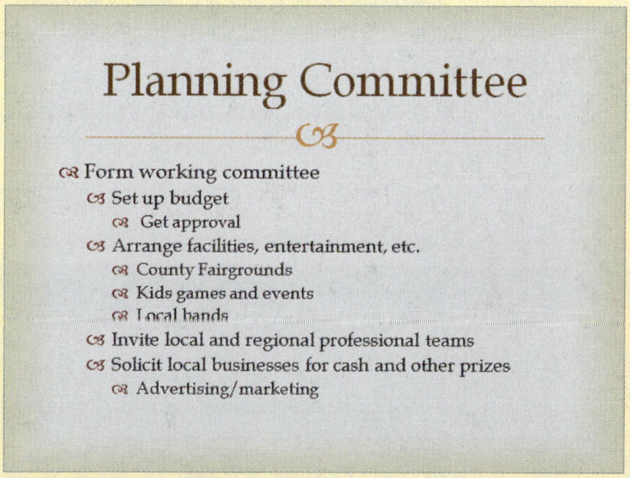

FIGURE A-24

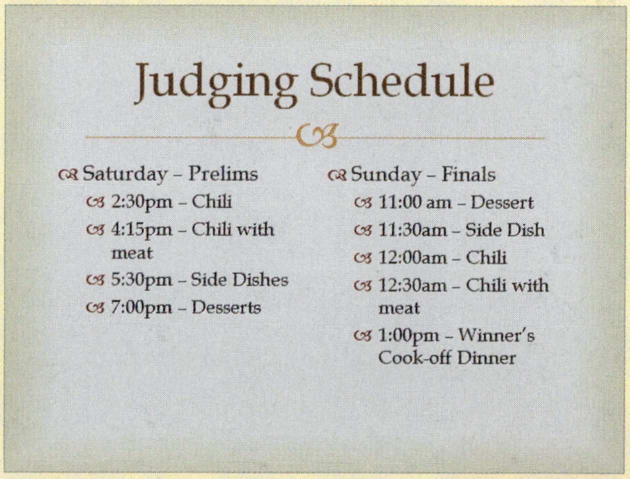

PowerPoint 2010

Visual Workshop

Create the presentation shown in Figures A-25 and A-26. Make sure you include your name on the title slide. Save the presentation as **PPT A-Landscape Industries** where you store your Data Files. Print the slides.

FIGURE A-25

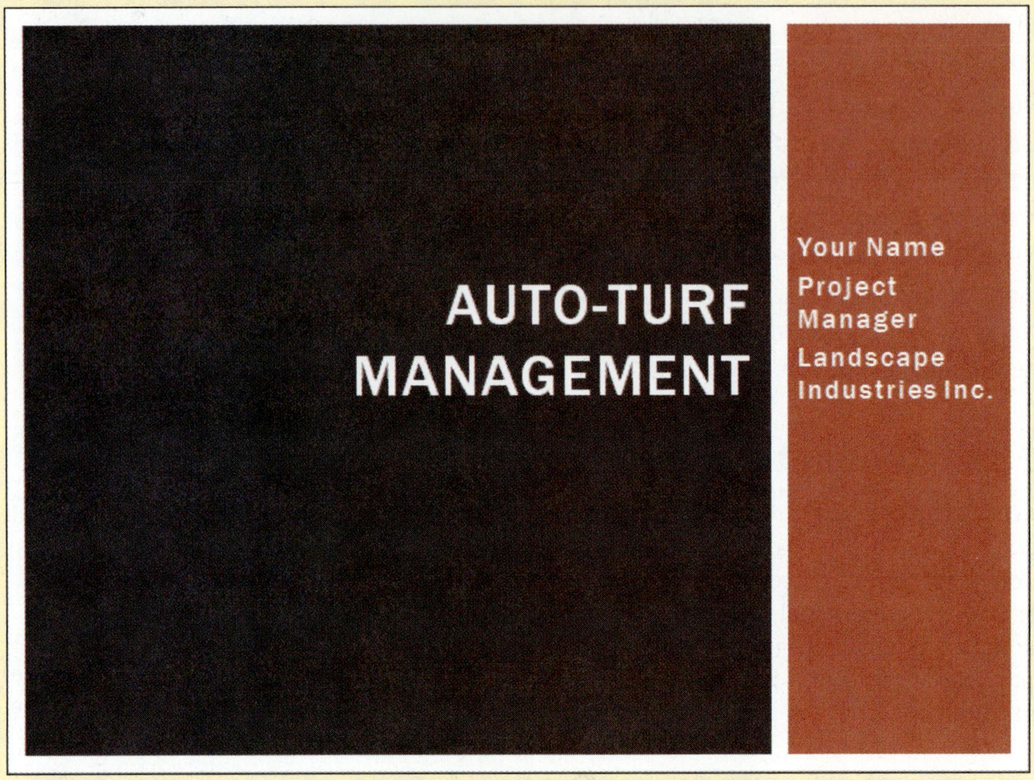

FIGURE A-26

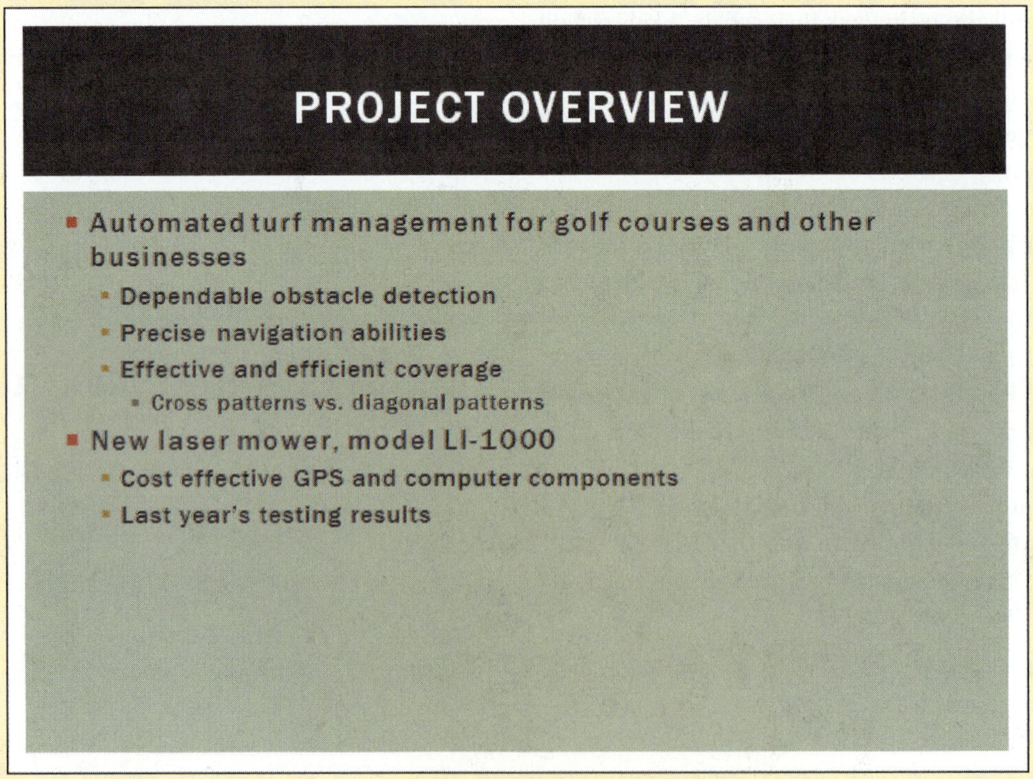

UNIT
B
PowerPoint 2010

Modifying a Presentation

Files You Will Need:
PPT B-1.pptx
PPT B-2.pptx
PPT B-3.pptx
PPT B-4.pptx
PPT B-5.pptx

In the previous unit you learned how to enter slide text, add a new slide, and apply a design theme. Now, you are ready to take the next step in creating professional-looking presentations by learning to format text and work with drawn objects. In this unit, you'll enter text in the Outline tab, format text, draw and modify objects, add slide footer information, and check the spelling in the presentation. You continue working on your Canadian Train tour presentation.

OBJECTIVES

- Enter text in the Outline tab
- Format text
- Convert text to SmartArt
- Insert and modify shapes
- Edit and duplicate shapes
- Align and group objects
- Add slide headers and footers
- Use proofing and language tools

Entering Text in the Outline Tab

You can enter presentation text by typing directly on the slide in the Slide pane, or, if you'd rather focus on the presentation text without worrying about the layout, you can enter text in the Outline tab. The outline is organized so that the headings, or slide titles, appear at the top of the outline. Beneath the title, each subpoint, or each line of bulleted text, appears as one or more indented lines under the title. Each indent in the outline creates another level of bulleted text on the slide. You switch to the Outline tab to enter text for two more slides for your presentation.

STEPS

QUICK TIP
To open a PowerPoint 97-2003 presentation in PowerPoint 2010, open the presentation, click the File tab, click the Convert button, name the presentation file in the Save As dialog box, then click Save.

1. **Start PowerPoint, open the presentation PPT B-1.pptx from the drive and folder where you store your Data Files, then save it as PPT B-QST.pptx**
   A presentation with the new name appears in the PowerPoint window.
2. **Click the Slide 2 thumbnail in the Slides tab, then click the Outline tab**
   The Outline tab enlarges to display the text that is on the slides. The slide icon and the text for Slide 2 are highlighted, indicating that it is selected.
3. **On the Home tab on the Ribbon, click the New Slide list arrow in the Slides group, then click Title and Content**
   A new slide, Slide 3, with the Title and Content layout appears as the current slide below Slide 2. A blinking insertion point appears next to the new slide in the Outline tab. Text that you enter next to a slide icon becomes the title for that slide.
4. **Type Canadian Rockies Tours, press [Enter], then press [Tab]**
   When you first press [Enter] you create a new slide, but because you want to enter bulleted text on Slide 3 you press [Tab] so that the text you type is entered as bullet text on Slide 3. See Figure B-1. Notice the text you type is in all uppercase letters because that is how the font is set in the design theme.
5. **Type British Columbia Railways Inc., press [Enter], type Based in Vancouver BC, then press [Enter]**
   Each time you press [Enter], the insertion point moves down one line.
6. **Press [Shift][Tab]**
   Because you are working in the Outline tab, a new slide, Slide 4, is created when you press [Shift][Tab].
7. **Type BC Railways Service Packages, press [Ctrl][Enter], type Royal Package, press [Enter], type Exclusve Package, make sure you misspell the word "Exclusve," press [Enter] type Deluxe Package, press [Enter], then type Classic Package**
   Pressing [Ctrl][Enter] while the cursor is in the title text object moves the cursor into the content placeholder.
8. **Position the pointer on the Slide 3 icon in the Outline tab**
   The pointer changes to ✥. Slide 3, Canadian Rockies Tours slide, is out of order.
9. **Drag the Slide 3 icon up until a horizontal indicator line appears above the Slide 2 icon, then release the mouse button**
   The third slide moves up and switches places with the second slide as shown in Figure B-2.
10. **Click the Slides tab, then save your work**
    The Outline tab closes and the Slides tab is now visible in the window.

QUICK TIP
Press [Ctrl][Enter] while the cursor is in the text object to create a new slide with the same layout as the previous slide.

FIGURE B-1: Outline tab showing new slide

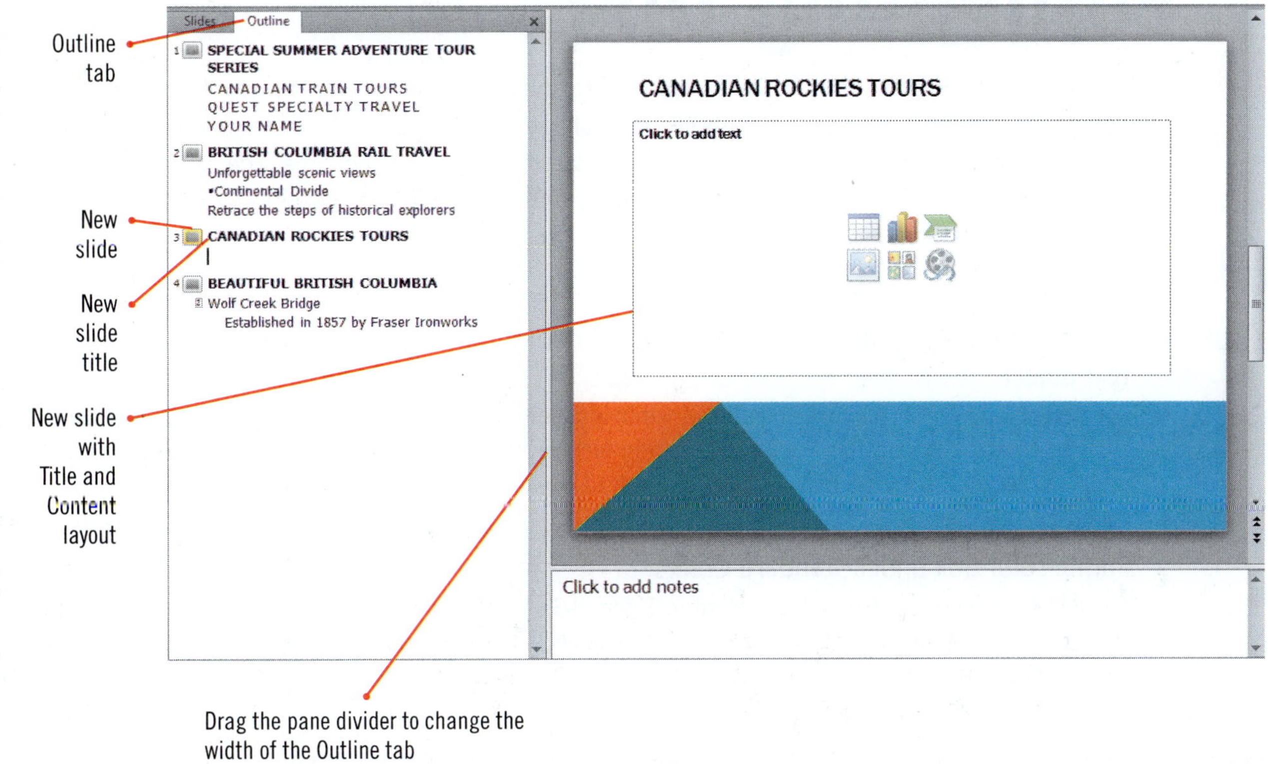

FIGURE B-2: Outline tab showing moved slide

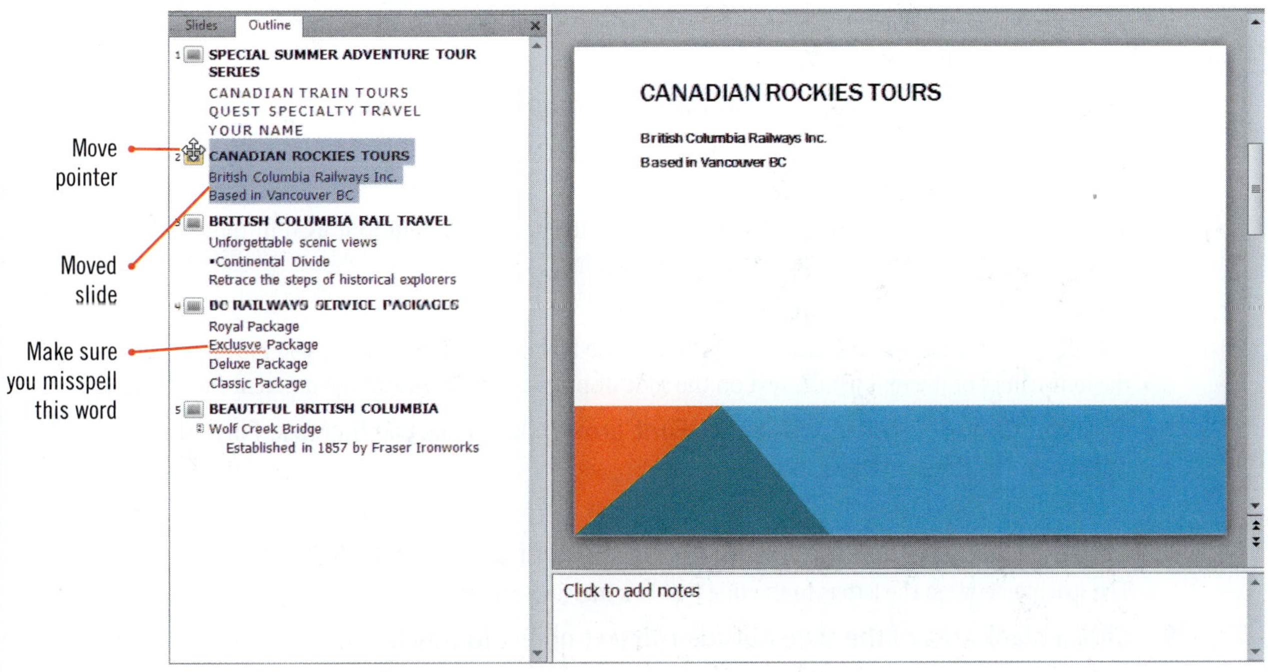

Setting permissions

In PowerPoint, you can set specific access permissions for people who review or edit your work, so you have better control over your content. For example, you may want to give a user permission to edit or change your presentation but not allow them to print it. You can also restrict a user by permitting them to view the presentation, without the ability to edit or print the presentation, or you can give the user full access or control of the presentation. To use this feature, you first have to have access to an Information Rights Management Service from Microsoft or another rights management company. Then, to set user access permissions, click the File tab, click Info, click the Protect Presentation button, point to Restrict Permission by People, then click an appropriate option.

UNIT
B
PowerPoint 2010

Formatting Text

Once you have entered and edited the text in your presentation, you can modify the way the text looks to emphasize your message. Important text should be highlighted in some way to distinguish it from other text or objects on the slide. For example, if you have two text objects on the same slide, you could draw attention to one text object by changing its color, font, or size. You decide to format the text on Slide 2 of the presentation.

STEPS

QUICK TIP
To show or hide the Mini toolbar, click the File tab on the Ribbon, then click Options.

1. **Click the Slide 2 thumbnail in the Slides tab, then double-click Canadian in the title text object**

   The word "Canadian" is selected, and a small semitransparent Mini toolbar appears above the text. The **Mini toolbar** contains basic text-formatting commands, such as bold and italic, and appears when you select text using the mouse. This toolbar makes it quick and easy to format text, especially when the Home tab is not open.

2. **Move the pointer over the Mini toolbar, click the Font Color list arrow, then click the Purple color box under Standard Colors**

   The text changes color to purple as shown in Figure B-3. As soon as you move the pointer over the Mini toolbar, the toolbar becomes clearly visible. When you click the Font Color list arrow, the Font Color gallery appears showing the Theme Colors and Standard Colors. Notice that the Font Color button on the Mini toolbar and the Font Color button in the Font group on the Home tab change color to reflect the new color choice.

QUICK TIP
To select an unselected text object, press [Shift], click the text object, then release [Shift].

3. **Move the pointer over the title text object border until the pointer changes to, then click the border**

   The entire title text object is selected, and changes you make now affect all of the text in the text object. When the whole text object is selected, you can change its size, shape, or other attributes. Changing the color of the text helps emphasize it.

4. **Click the Font Color button in the Font group**

   All of the text in the title text object changes to the purple color.

5. **Click the Font list arrow in the Font group**

   A list of available fonts opens with Franklin Gothic Medium, the current font used in the title text object, selected at the top of the list in the Theme Fonts section.

6. **Click Algerian in the All Fonts section**

   The Algerian font replaces the original font in the title text object. Notice that as you move the pointer over the font names in the font list the text on the slide displays a Live Preview of the different font choices.

7. **Click the Underline button in the Font group, then click the Increase Font Size button in the Font group**

   All of the text now displays an underline and increases in size to 32.

8. **Click the Character Spacing button in the Font group, then click Loose**

   The spacing between the letters in the title text box increases slightly. Compare your screen to Figure B-4.

9. **Click a blank area of the slide outside the text object to deselect it, then save your work**

FIGURE B-3: Selected word with Mini toolbar open

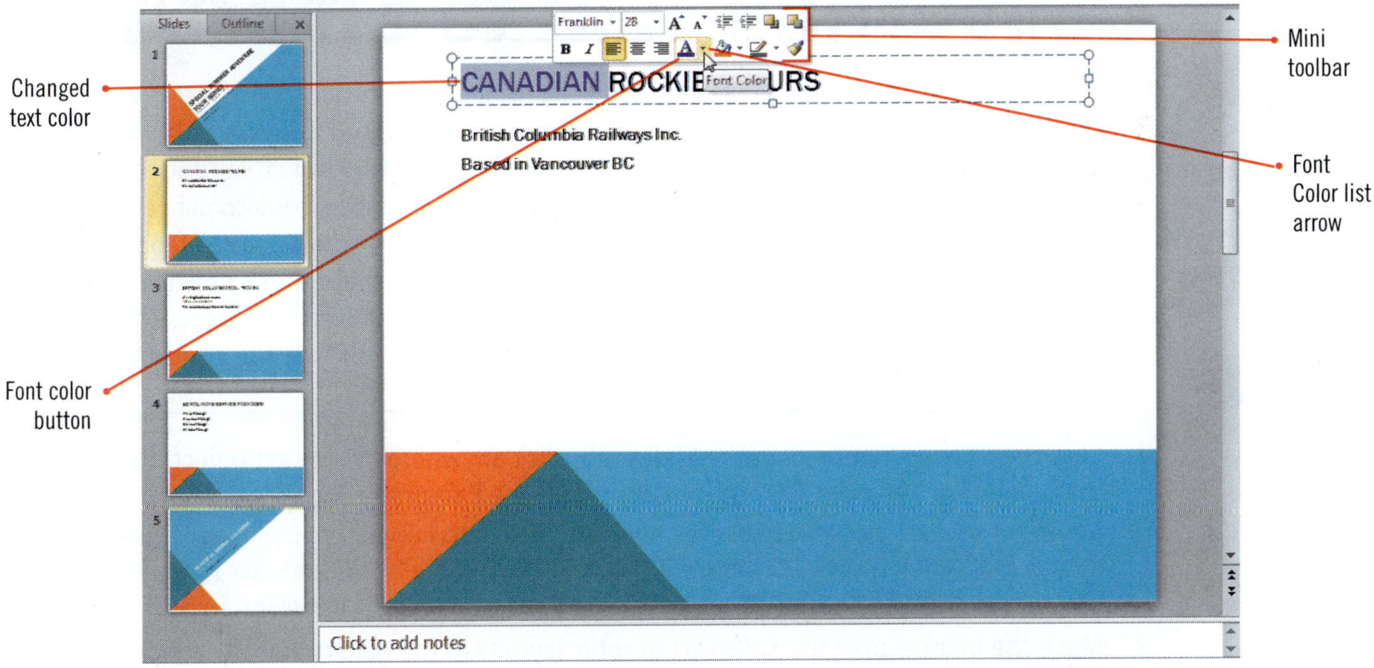

FIGURE B-4: Formatted text

Replacing text and fonts

As you review your presentation, you may decide to replace certain text or fonts throughout the entire presentation using the Replace command. Text can be a word, phrase, or sentence. To replace specific text, click the Home tab on the Ribbon, then click the Replace button in the Editing group. In the Replace dialog box, enter the text you want to replace then enter the text you want to use as its replacement. You can also use the Replace command to replace one font for another. Simply click the Replace button list arrow in the Editing group, then click Replace Fonts to open the Replace Font dialog box.

PowerPoint 2010

UNIT B

PowerPoint 2010

Converting Text to SmartArt

Sometimes when you are working with text it just doesn't capture your attention, no matter how you dress it up with color or other formatting attributes. The ability to convert text to a SmartArt graphic increases your ability to create dynamic-looking text. A **SmartArt** graphic is a professional-quality diagram that visually illustrates text. There are eight categories, or types, of SmartArt graphics that incorporate graphics to illustrate text differently. For example, you can show steps in a process or timeline, show proportional relationships, or show how parts relate to a whole. You can create a SmartArt graphic from scratch or create one by converting existing text you have entered on a slide with a few simple clicks of the mouse. You want the presentation to appear visually dynamic so you convert the text on Slide 4 to a SmartArt graphic.

STEPS

1. **Click the Slide 4 thumbnail in the Slides tab, click anywhere in the text object, then click the Convert to SmartArt Graphic button in the Paragraph group**

   A gallery of SmartArt graphic layouts opens. As with many features in PowerPoint, you can preview how your text will look prior to applying the SmartArt graphic layout by using PowerPoint's Live Preview feature. You can review each SmartArt graphic layout and see how it changes the appearance of text.

2. **Move the pointer over the SmartArt graphic layouts in the gallery**

   Notice how the text becomes part of the graphic and the color and font changes each time you move the pointer over a different graphic layout. SmartArt graphic names appear as ScreenTips.

3. **Click the Pyramid List layout in the SmartArt graphics gallery**

   A SmartArt graphic appears on the slide in place of the text object, and a new SmartArt Tools Design tab opens on the Ribbon as shown in Figure B-5. A SmartArt graphic consists of two parts: the SmartArt graphic itself and a Text pane where you type and edit text.

4. **Click each bullet point in the Text pane, then click the Text pane Close button**

   Notice that each time you select a bullet point in the text pane, a selection box appears around the text objects in the SmartArt graphic. The text pane closes.

5. **Click the More button in the Layouts group, click More Layouts, click the Basic Matrix layout in the Matrix section, then click OK**

   The SmartArt graphic changes to the new graphic layout. You can radically change how the SmartArt graphic looks by applying a SmartArt Style. A **SmartArt Style** is a preset combination of simple and 3-D formatting options that follows the presentation theme.

6. **Move the pointer slowly over the styles in the SmartArt Styles group, then click the More button in the SmartArt Styles group**

   A Live Preview of each style is displayed on the SmartArt graphic. The SmartArt styles are organized into sections; the top group offers suggestions for the best match for the document.

7. **Move the pointer over all the styles in the gallery, then click Intense Effect**

   Notice how the new Intense Effect style adds a bevel and top-left corner lighting to the text boxes.

8. **Click a blank area of the slide outside the SmartArt graphic object to deselect it, then save your work**

   Compare your screen to Figure B-6.

TROUBLE

If the text pane does not open as shown in Figure B-5, click the Text pane button in the Create Graphic group.

QUICK TIP

Text objects in the SmartArt graphic can be moved and edited like any other text object in PowerPoint.

QUICK TIP

Click the Convert button in the Reset group then click Convert to Text to revert the SmartArt graphic to a standard text object.

FIGURE B-5: Text converted to a SmartArt graphic

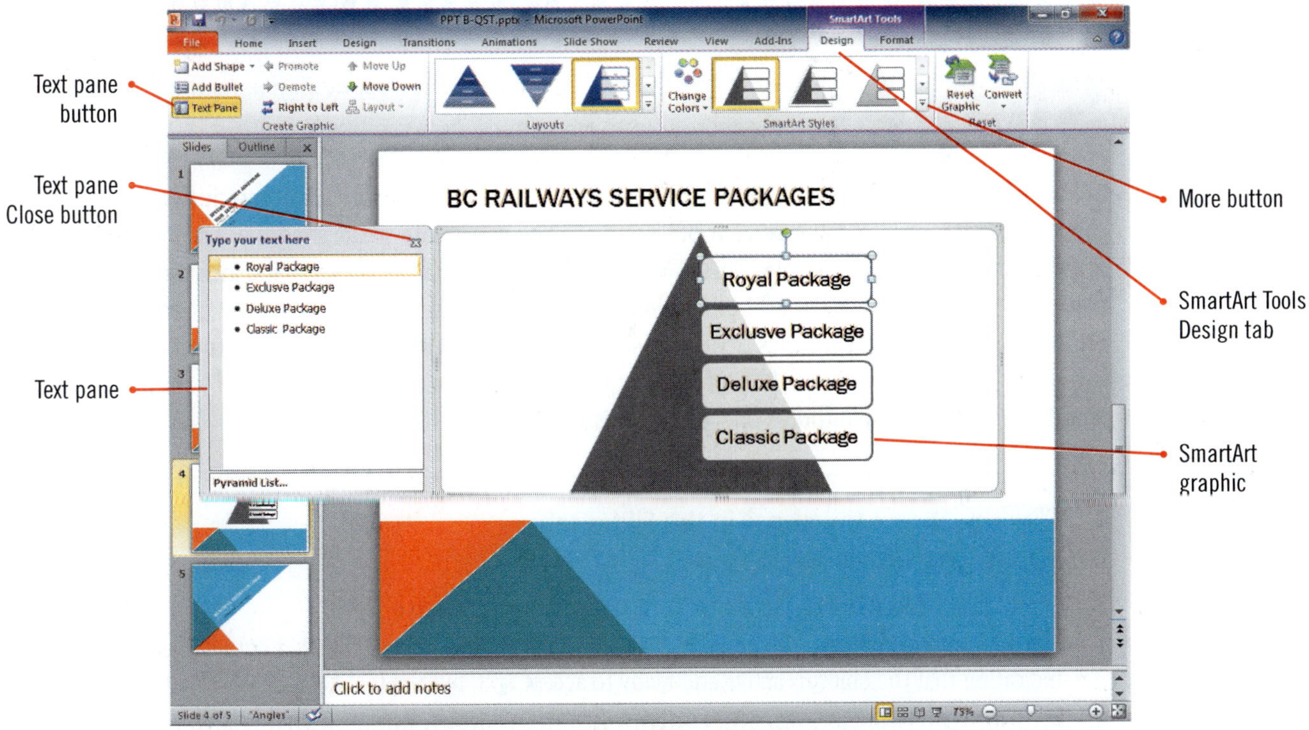

FIGURE B-6: Final SmartArt graphic

Choosing SmartArt graphics

When choosing a SmartArt graphic to use on your slide, remember that you want the SmartArt graphic to communicate the message of the text effectively; not every SmartArt graphic layout achieves that goal. You must consider the type of text you want to illustrate. For example, does the text show steps in a process, does it show a continual process, or does it show nonsequential information? The answer to this question will dictate the type of SmartArt graphic layout you should choose. Also, the amount of text you want to illustrate will have an effect on the SmartArt graphic layout you choose. Most of the time key points will be the text you use in a SmartArt graphic. Finally, some SmartArt graphic layouts are limited by the number of shapes that they can accommodate, so be sure to choose a graphic layout that can illustrate your text appropriately. Experiment with the SmartArt graphic layouts until you find the right one, and have fun in the process!

UNIT B
PowerPoint 2010

Inserting and Modifying Shapes

In PowerPoint you can insert many different types of shapes including lines, geometric figures, arrows, stars, callouts, and banners to enhance your presentation. You can create single shapes or combine several shapes together to make a more complex figure. You can modify many aspects of a shape including its fill color, line color, and line style, as well as add other effects like shadow and 3-D effects. Instead of changing individual attributes, you can apply a Quick Style to a shape. A **Quick Style** is a set of formatting options, including line style, fill color, and effects. You decide to draw some shapes on Slide 3 of your presentation that identify the different train routes offered by British Columbia Railways.

STEPS

1. **Click the Slide 3 thumbnail in the Slides tab**
   Slide 3 appears in the Slide pane.
2. **Press and hold [Shift], click the text object, then release [Shift]**
   The text object is selected. If you click a text object without pressing [Shift], a dotted selection box appears, indicating that the object is active and ready to accept text, but the text object itself is not selected.
3. **Position the pointer over the bottom-middle sizing handle, notice the pointer change to ↕, then drag the sizing handle up until the text object looks like Figure B-7**
   The text object decreases in size. When you position the pointer over a sizing handle, it changes to ↕. The pointer points in different directions depending on which sizing handle it is positioned over. When you drag a sizing handle, the pointer changes to +, and a faint gray outline appears, representing the size of the text object.
4. **Click the Shapes button in the Drawing group or click the More button in the Drawing group**
   A gallery of shapes organized by type opens. Notice that there is a section at the top of the gallery where all of the recently used shapes are placed. ScreenTips help you identify the shapes.
5. **Click the Snip Diagonal Corner Rectangle shape in the Rectangles section, position + in the blank area of the slide below the text object, drag down and to the right to create the shape, as shown in Figure B-8, then release the mouse button**
   A rectangle shape appears on the slide, filled with the default color. To change the style of the shape, apply a Quick Style from the Shape Styles group.
6. **Click the Drawing Tools Format tab, click the More button in the Shape Styles group, move the pointer over the styles in the gallery to review the effects on the shape, then click Subtle Effect — Olive Green, Accent 4**
   A light green Quick Style with coordinated gradient fill, line, and shadow color is applied to the shape.
7. **Click the Shape Outline button in the Shape Styles group, point to Weight, then move the pointer over the line weight options to review the effect on the shape**
   The outline line weight changes every time you move the pointer over a different effect.
8. **Click 2 ¼ pt, click in a blank area of the slide, then save your work**

QUICK TIP
If you press [Shift] as you drag to create a shape, the shape maintains even proportions.

TROUBLE
If your shape is not approximately the same size as the one shown in Figure B-8, drag one of the corner sizing handles to resize the object.

FIGURE B-7: Resized text object

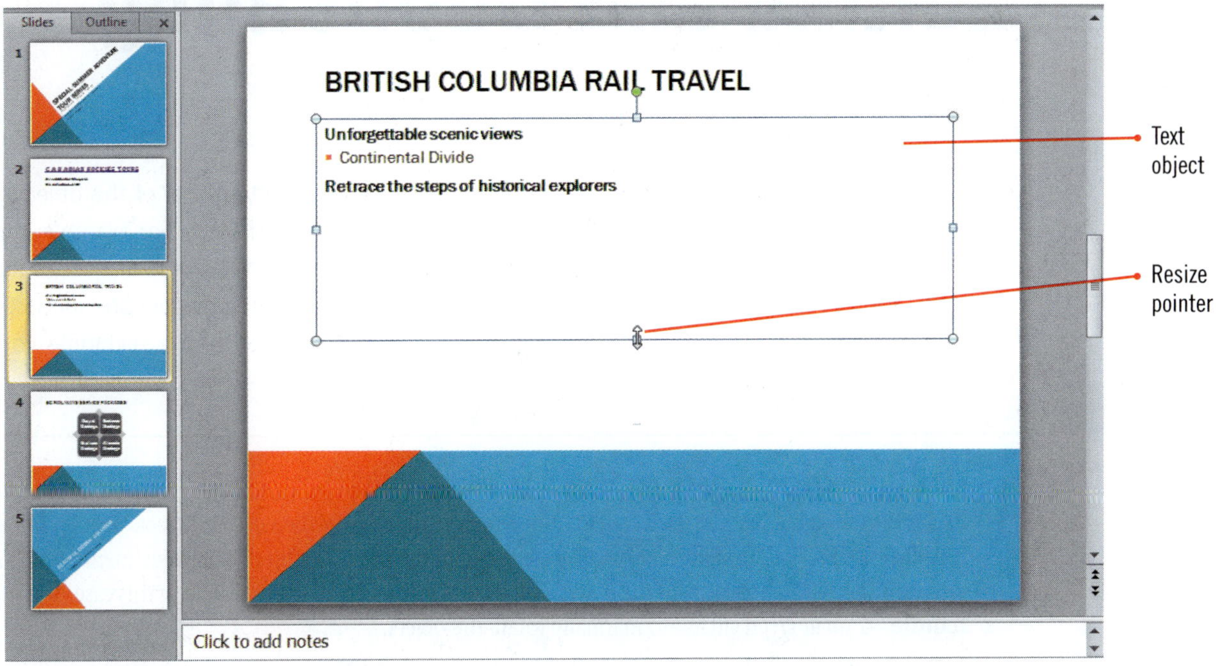

FIGURE B-8: Slide showing Snip Diagonal Corner Rectangle shape

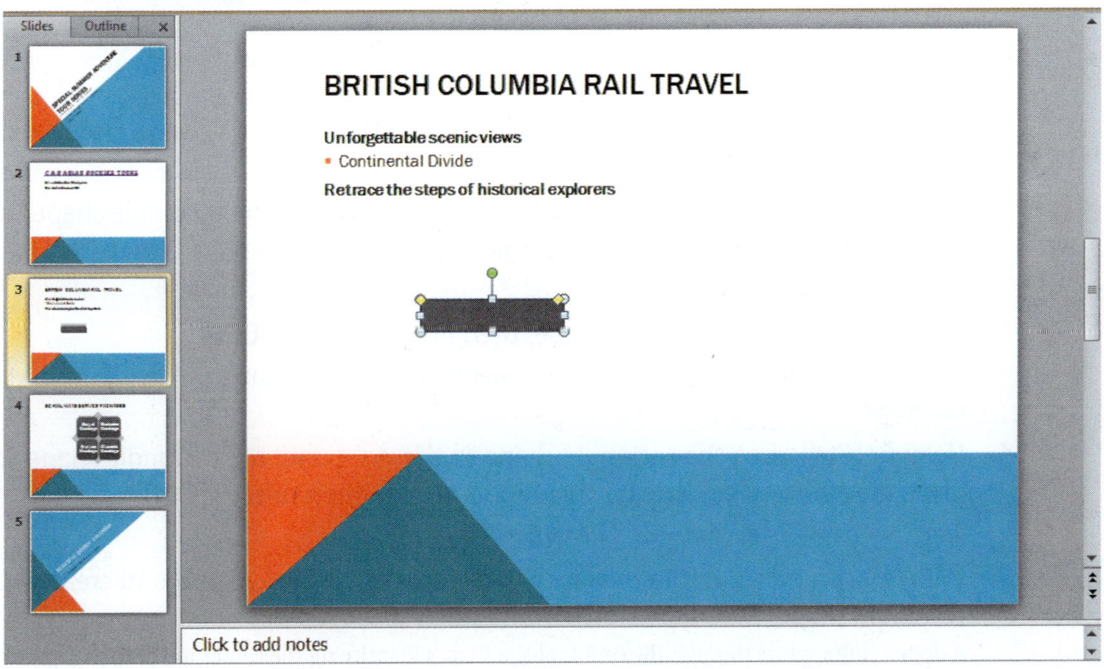

PowerPoint 2010

Changing the size and position of shapes

Usually when you resize a shape you can simply drag one of the sizing handles around the outside of the shape, but sometimes you may need to resize a shape more precisely. When you select a shape, the Drawing Tools Format tab appears on the Ribbon, offering you many different formatting options including some sizing commands located in the Size group. The Width and Height commands in the Size group allow you to change the width and height of a shape. You also have the option to open the Size and Position dialog box, which allows you to change the size of a shape, as well as the rotation, scale, and position of a shape on the slide.

UNIT B PowerPoint 2010

Editing and Duplicating Shapes

Once you have created a shape you still have the ability to refine the aspects of the object. PowerPoint allows you to adjust various aspects of shapes to help change the look of them. For example, if you create a shape with an arrowhead but the head of the arrow does not look quite like you want it to look, you can change it. You can also add text to most PowerPoint shapes, and you can move or copy shapes. You want three identical rectangles on Slide 3. You first change the shape of the rectangle you've already created, and then you make copies of it.

STEPS

1. **Click the rectangle shape on Slide 3 to select it**

   In addition to sizing handles, two other types of handles appear on the selected object. You use the **adjustment handle**—a small yellow diamond—to change the appearance of an object. The adjustment handle appears next to the most prominent feature of the object, like the diagonal sides of the rectangle in this case. You use the **rotate handle**—a small green circle—to manually rotate the object.

2. **Drag the left-middle sizing handle on the rectangle shape to the right approximately 1/4", then release the mouse button**

QUICK TIP
You can easily display or hide gridlines by clicking the Gridlines check box in the Show group on the View tab.

3. **Position the pointer over the middle of the selected rectangle shape so that it changes to, then drag the rectangle shape so that the rectangle aligns with the left edge of the text in the text object as shown in Figure B-9**

   A semitransparent copy of the shape appears as you move the rectangle shape to help you position it. PowerPoint uses gridlines to align objects; it forces objects to "snap" to the grid. To turn the snap-to-grid feature off while dragging objects, press and hold [Alt]. Make any needed adjustments to the rectangle shape position so it looks similar to Figure B-9.

TROUBLE
To make precise adjustments, press and hold [Alt], then drag the adjustment handle.

4. **Position the pointer over the right adjustment handle on the rectangle shape so that it changes to, then drag the adjustment handle all the way to the left**

   The rectangle shape appearance changes.

5. **Position over the rectangle shape, then press and hold [Ctrl]**

   The pointer changes to, indicating that PowerPoint makes a copy of the rectangle shape when you drag the mouse.

6. **Holding [Ctrl], drag the rectangle shape to the right until the rectangle shape copy is in a blank area of the slide, release the mouse button, then release [Ctrl]**

   An identical copy of the rectangle shape appears on the slide.

QUICK TIP
All shape objects use the dotted alignment line to help you align shapes to an object's top, bottom, or side.

7. **With the second rectangle shape still selected, repeat Steps 5 and 6 to create a third rectangle shape, then type Northern Route**

   A dotted line appears through the center of the shapes identifying the centerline of the shapes and helps you align the shapes. The text appears in the selected rectangle shape. The text is now part of the shape, so if you move or rotate the shape, the text moves with it. Compare your screen with Figure B-10.

8. **Click the middle rectangle shape, type Western Pass, click the left rectangle shape, type Explorer's Trail, then click in a blank area of the slide**

   Clicking a blank area of the slide deselects all objects that are selected.

9. **Save your work**

FIGURE B-9: Slide showing resized shape

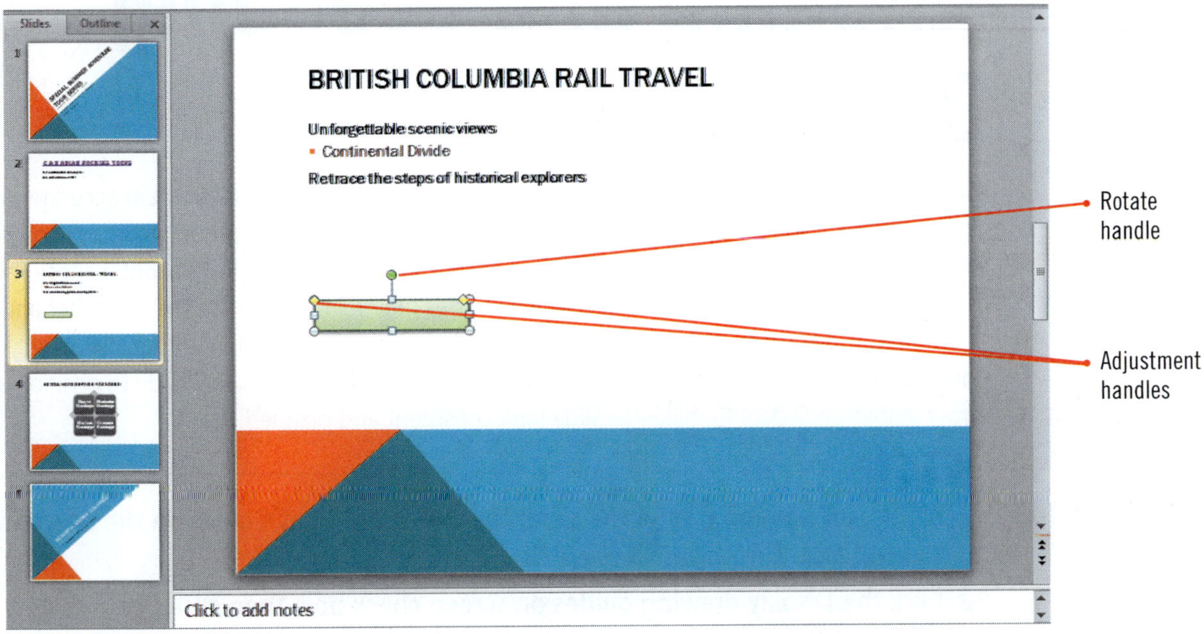

FIGURE B-10: Slide showing duplicated shapes

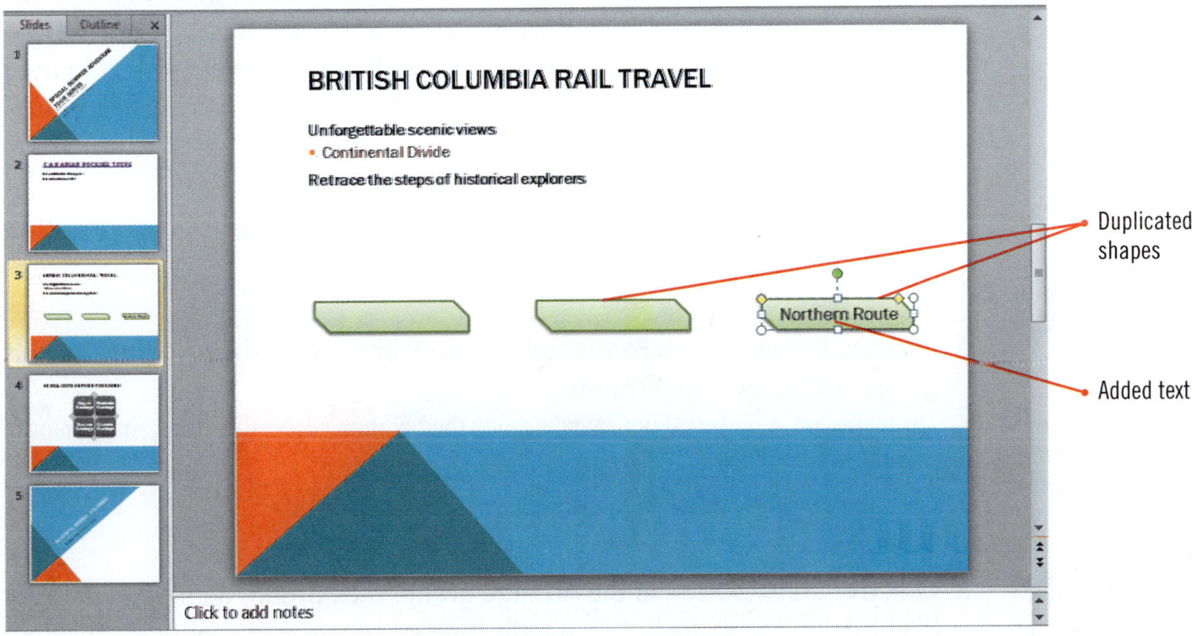

PowerPoint 2010

Understanding PowerPoint objects

Every object on a slide, whether it is a text object, a shape, a chart, a picture, or any other object, is stacked on the slide in the order it was created. So, for example, if you add three shapes to a slide, the first shape you create is on the bottom of the stack, and the last shape you create is on the top of the stack. Each object on a slide can be moved up or down in the stack depending on how you want the objects to look on the slide. To move an object to the front of the stack, select the object, then click the Bring Forward button in the Arrange group on the Drawing Tools Format tab. To move an object to the back of the stack, click the Send Backward button in the Arrange group on the Drawing Tools Format tab. You can also open the Selection and Visibility pane by clicking the Selection Pane button in the Arrange group to view and rearrange all of the objects on the slide.

UNIT
B
PowerPoint 2010

Aligning and Grouping Objects

After you are finished creating and modifying your objects, you can position them accurately on the slide to achieve the look you want. Using the Align commands in the Arrange group, you can align objects relative to each other by snapping them to a grid of evenly spaced vertical and horizontal lines. The Group command **groups** objects into one object, which secures their relative position to each other and makes it easy to edit and move them. The Distribute commands found with the Align commands evenly space objects horizontally or vertically relative to each other or the slide. You are ready to position and group the arrow shapes on Slide 3 to make the slide look consistent and planned.

STEPS

QUICK TIP
To add a new guide to the slide, press [Ctrl], then drag an existing guide. The original guide remains in place as you move the new guide. Drag a guide off the slide to delete it.

1. **Right-click a blank area of the slide, then click Grid and Guides on the shortcut menu**
   The Grid and Guides dialog box opens.
2. **Click the Display drawing guides on screen check box, then click OK**
   The PowerPoint guides appear as dotted lines on the slide and intersect at the center of the slide. They help you position a rectangle shape.
3. **Position over the horizontal guide in a blank area of the slide, press and hold the mouse button until the pointer changes to a measurement guide, then drag the guide down until the guide position box reads 1.25**
4. **Position over the Explorer's Trail rectangle shape (not over the text in the shape), then drag the shape so that the bottom edge of the shape touches the horizontal guide as shown in Figure B-11**
   The rectangle shape attaches or "snaps" to the horizontal guide.
5. **With the Explorer's Trail shape selected, press and hold [Shift], click the other two rectangle shapes, then release [Shift]**
   All three shapes are now selected.
6. **Click the Drawing Tools Format tab on the Ribbon, click the Align button in the Arrange group, then click Align Bottom**
   The shapes are now aligned horizontally along their bottom edges. The higher shapes move down and align with the bottom shape.
7. **Click the Align button, then click Distribute Horizontally**
   The shapes are now distributed equally between themselves.

QUICK TIP
Rulers can help you align objects. To display the rulers, position the pointer in a blank area of the slide, right-click, then click Ruler on the shortcut menu.

8. **Click the Group button in the Arrange group, click Group, then press [Left Arrow] or [Right Arrow] until the Rotate handle is on or very near the vertical grid line as shown in Figure B-12**
   The objects group to form one object without losing their individual attributes. Notice that the sizing handles and rotate handle now appear on the outer edge of the grouped object, not around each individual object.
9. **Drag the horizontal guide up until the guide position box reads 0.00, click the View tab on the Ribbon, then click the Guides check box in the Show group**
   The guides are no longer displayed on the slide
10. **Click a blank area of the slide, then save your work**

FIGURE B-11: Repositioned shape

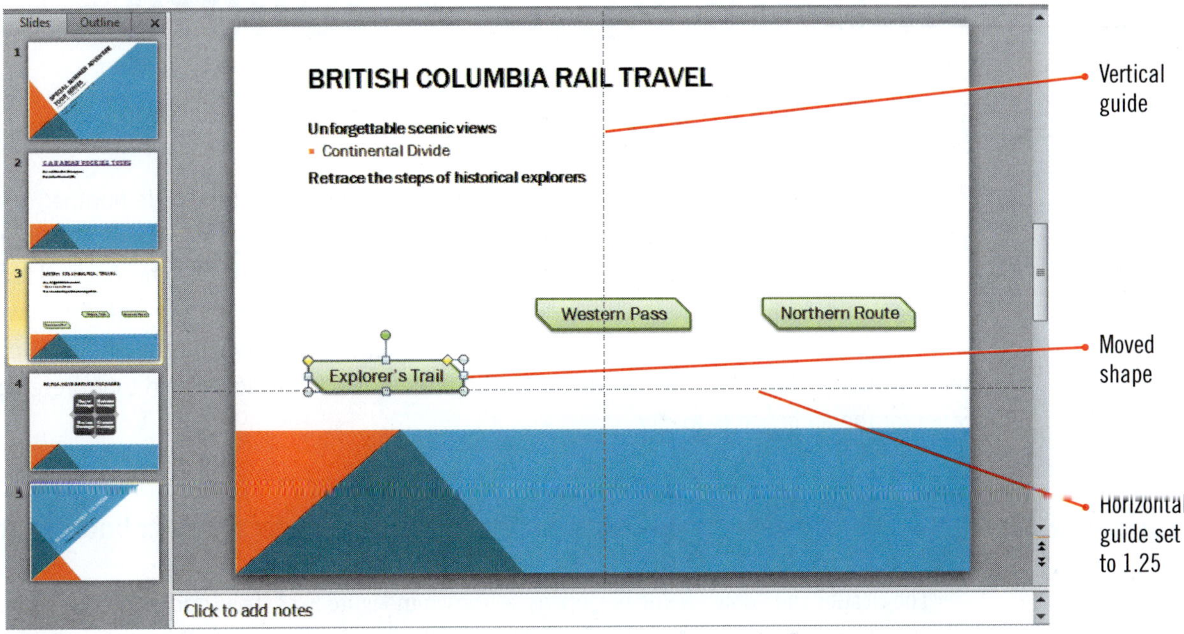

FIGURE B-12: Aligned and grouped shapes

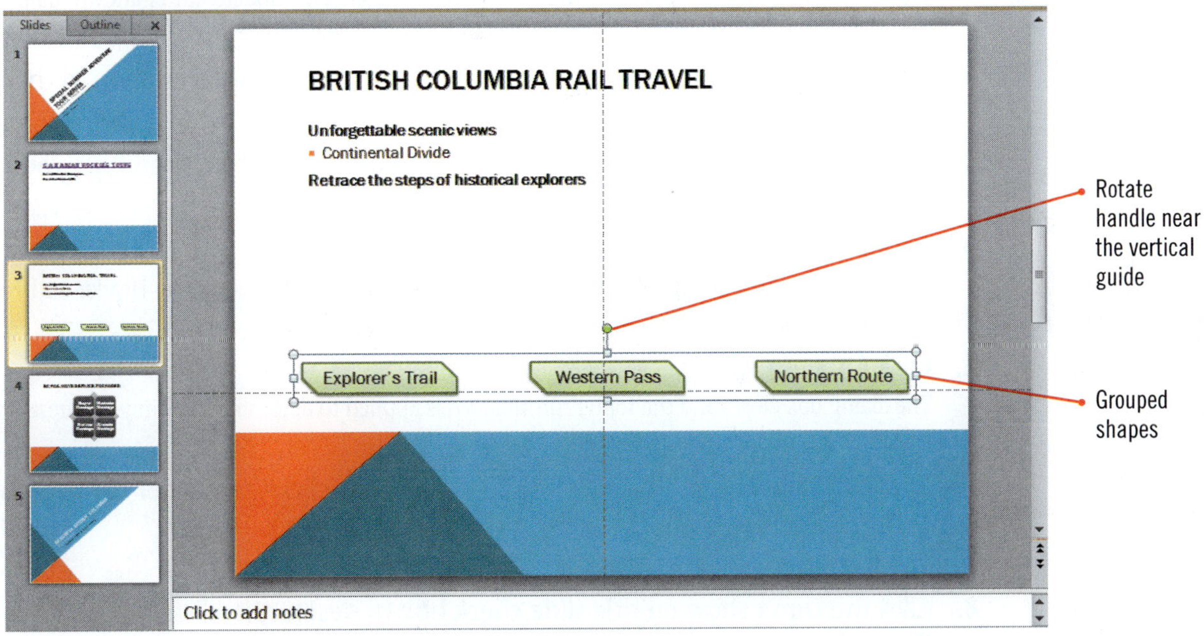

Distributing objects

There are two ways to **distribute** objects in PowerPoint: relative to each other and relative to the slide edge. If you choose to distribute objects relative to each other, PowerPoint evenly divides the empty space between all of the selected objects. When distributing objects in relation to the slide, PowerPoint evenly splits the empty space from slide edge to slide edge between the selected objects. To distribute objects relative to each other, click the Align button in the Arrange group on the Drawing Tools Format tab, then click Align Selected Objects. To distribute objects relative to the slide, click the Align button in the Arrange group on the Drawing Tools Format tab, then click Align to Slide.

Adding Slide Headers and Footers

Header and footer text, such as a company, school or product name, the slide number, and the date, can give your slides a polished look and make it easier for your audience to follow your presentation. On slides, you can add text to the footer; however, notes or handouts can include both header and footer text. Footer information that you apply to the slides of your presentation is visible in the PowerPoint views and when you print the slides. Notes and handouts header and footer text is visible when you print notes pages, handouts, and the outline. You add footer text to the slides of the Canadian train tour presentation to make it easier for the audience to follow.

STEPS

QUICK TIP
The placement of the footer text objects on the slide is dependent on the presentation theme.

1. **Click the Insert tab on the Ribbon, then click the Header & Footer button in the Text group**
   The Header and Footer dialog box opens, as shown in Figure B-13. The Header and Footer dialog box has two tabs: a Slide tab and a Notes and Handouts tab. The Slide tab is selected. There are three types of footer text, Date and time, Slide number, and Footer. The rectangles at the bottom of the Preview box identify the default position and status of the three types of footer text placeholders on the slides.
2. **Click the Date and time check box to select it**
   The date and time suboptions are now available to select. The Update automatically date and time option button is selected by default. This option updates the date and time every time you open or print the file.

QUICK TIP
If you want a specific date—such as the original date that the presentation was created—to appear every time you view or print the presentation, click the Fixed date option button, then type the date in the Fixed text box.

3. **Click the Update automatically list arrow, then click the eighth option in the list**
   The time is added to the date.
4. **Click the Slide number check box, click the Footer check box, then type your name**
   The Preview box now shows that all three footer placeholders are selected.
5. **Click the Don't show on title slide check box**
   Selecting this check box prevents the footer information you entered in the Header and Footer dialog box from appearing on the title slide.
6. **Click Apply to All**
   The dialog box closes and the footer information is applied to all of the slides in your presentation except the title slide. Compare your screen to Figure B-14.
7. **Click the Slide 1 thumbnail in the Slides tab, then click the Header & Footer button in the Text group**
   The Header and Footer dialog box opens again.
8. **Click the Don't show on title slide check box to deselect it, click the Footer check box, then select the text in the Footer text box**

TROUBLE
If you click Apply to All in Step 9, click the Undo button on the Quick Access toolbar and repeat Steps 7, 8, and 9.

9. **Type World's foremost traveling experience, click Apply, then save your work**
   Only the text in the Footer text box appears on the title slide. Clicking Apply applies the footer information to just the current slide.

FIGURE B-13: Header and Footer dialog box

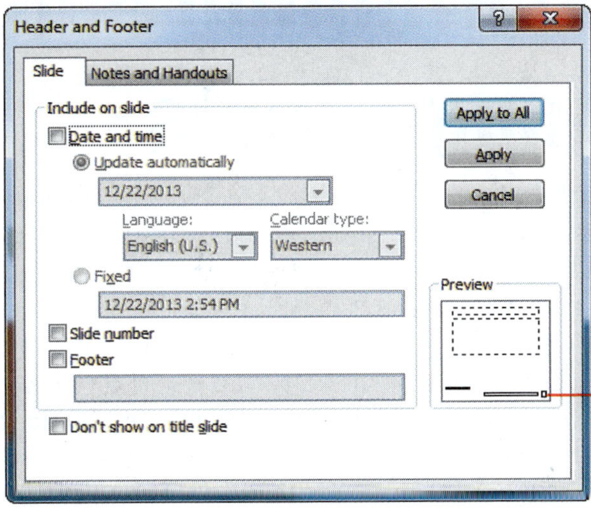

FIGURE B-14: Slide showing footer information

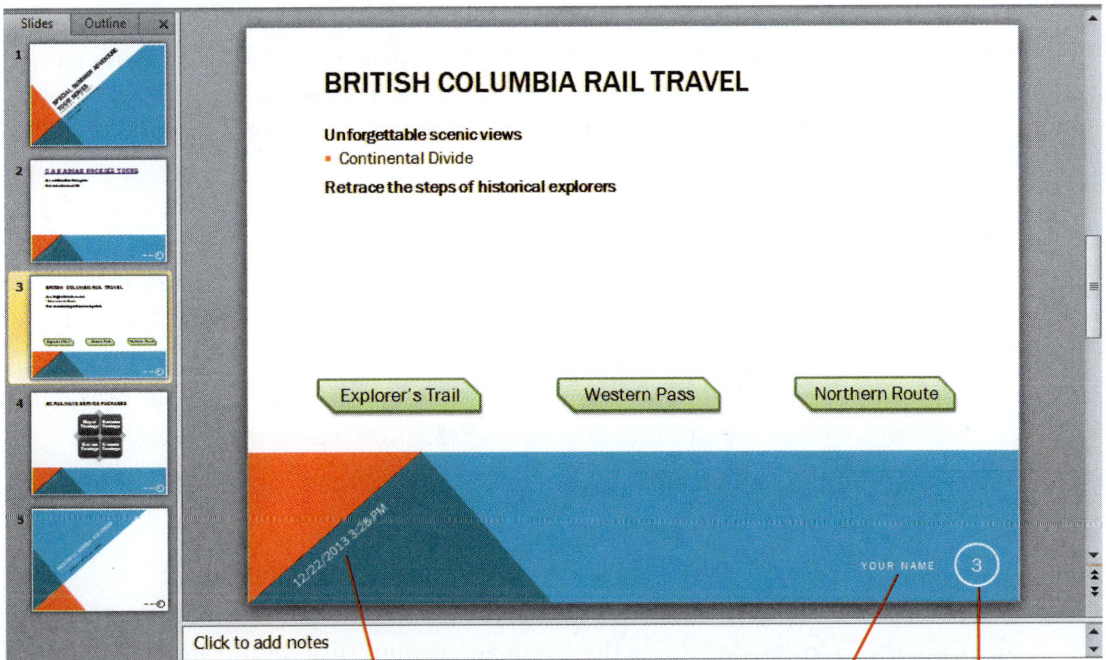

Entering and printing notes

You can add notes to your slides when there are certain facts you want to remember during a presentation or when there is information you want to hand out to your audience. Notes do not appear on the slides when you run a slide show. Use the Notes pane in Normal view or Notes Page view to enter notes for your slides. To enter text notes on a slide, click in the Notes pane, then type. If you want to insert graphics as notes, you must use Notes Page view. To open Notes Page view, click the View tab on the Ribbon, then click the Notes Page button in the Presentation Views group. You can print your notes by clicking the File tab to open Backstage view then clicking Print. Click the Full Page Slides list arrow in the Settings section (this button retains the last setting for what was printed previously so it might differ) to open the gallery, and then click Notes Pages. Once you verify your print settings, click the Print button. Notes pages can be a good handout to give your audience to use during the presentation. If you don't enter any notes in the Notes pane, and print the notes pages, the slides print as thumbnails with blank lines to the right of the thumbnails to hand write notes.

Using Proofing and Language Tools

As your work on the presentation file nears completion, you need to review and proofread your slides thoroughly for errors. You can use the spell-checking feature in PowerPoint to check for and correct spelling errors. This feature compares the spelling of all the words in your presentation against the words contained in PowerPoint's electronic dictionary. You still must proofread your presentation for punctuation, grammar, and word-usage errors because the spell checker recognizes only misspelled and unknown words, not misused words. For example, the spell checker would not identify the word "last" as an error, even if you had intended to type the word "cast." PowerPoint also includes language tools that translate words or phrases from your default language into another language using the Microsoft Translator. You're finished working on the presentation for now, so it's a good time to check spelling. You then experiment with language translation because the final presentation will be translated into French.

STEPS

TROUBLE
If your spell checker finds another word, such as your name on Slide 1, click Ignore All in the spelling dialog box.

1. **Click the Review tab on the Ribbon, then click the Spelling button in the Proofing group**
   PowerPoint begins to check the spelling in your presentation. When PowerPoint finds a misspelled word or a word it doesn't recognize, the Spelling dialog box opens, as shown in Figure B-15. In this case, PowerPoint identifies the misspelled word on Slide 4 and suggests you replace it with the correctly spelled word "Exclusive."
2. **Click Change**
   PowerPoint changes the misspelled word and then continues to check the rest of the presentation for errors. If PowerPoint finds any other words it does not recognize, either change or ignore them. When the spell checker finishes checking your presentation, the Spelling dialog box closes, and an alert box opens with a message that the spelling check is complete.

QUICK TIP
The spell checker does not check the text in inserted pictures or objects.

3. **Click OK, click the Slide 1 thumbnail in the Slides tab, then save your presentation**
   The alert box closes. Now you need to see how the language translation feature works.
4. **Click the Translate button in the Language group, then click Choose Translation Language**
   The Translation Language Options dialog box opens.
5. **Click the Translate to list arrow, click French (France), then click OK**
   The Translation Language Options dialog box closes.
6. **Click the Translate button in the Language group, click Mini Translator [French(France)], click anywhere in the footer text object, then select all of the text**
   The Microsoft Translator begins to analyze the selected text and a semitransparent Microsoft Translator box appears below the text.

QUICK TIP
To copy the translated text to a slide, click the Copy button at the bottom of the Microsoft Translator box, right-click the slide, then click a Paste option.

7. **Move the pointer over the Microsoft Translator box**
   A French translation of the text appears as shown in Figure B-16. The translation language setting remains in effect until you reset it.
8. **Click the Translate button in the Language group, click Choose Translation Language, click the Translate to list arrow, click Arabic, click OK, click the Translate button again, then click Mini Translator [Arabic]**
   The Mini Translator is turned off and the translation language is restored to the default setting.
9. **Submit your presentation to your instructor, then exit PowerPoint**

FIGURE B-15: Spelling dialog box

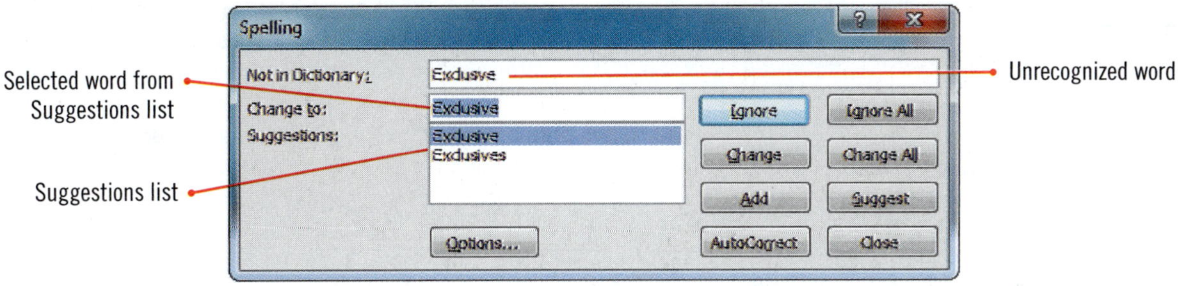

FIGURE B-16: Slide showing translated text

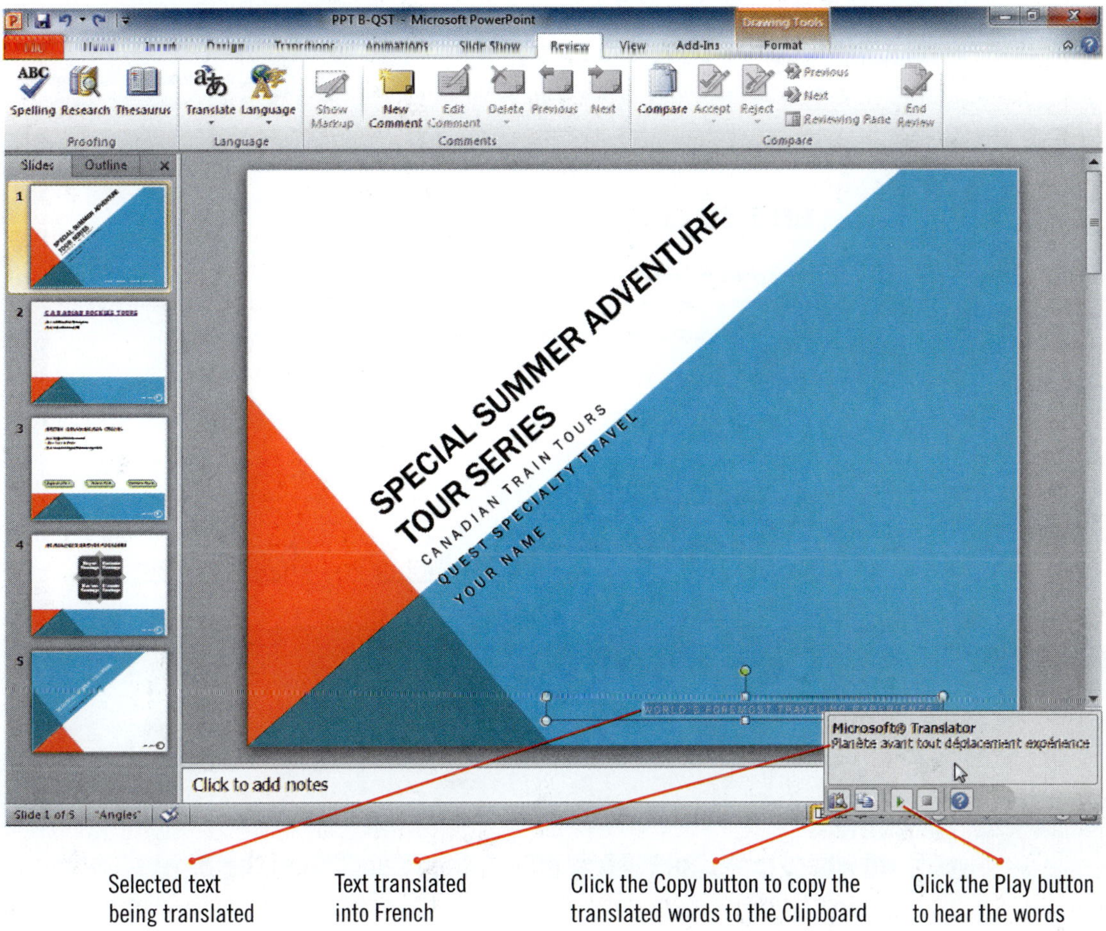

PowerPoint 2010

Checking spelling as you type

PowerPoint checks your spelling as you type. If you type a word that is not in the electronic dictionary, a wavy red line appears under it. To correct an error, right-click the misspelled word, then review the suggestions, which appear in the shortcut menu. You can select a suggestion, add the word you typed to your custom dictionary, or ignore it. To turn off automatic spell checking, click the File tab, then click Options to open the PowerPoint Options dialog box. Click the Proofing button, then click the Check spelling as you type check box to deselect it. To temporarily hide the wavy red lines, click the Hide spelling errors check box to select it. Contextual spelling in PowerPoint identifies common grammatically misused words, for example, if you type the word "their" and the correct word is "there," PowerPoint will identify the mistake and place a wavy blue line under the word. To turn contextual spelling on or off, click the Proofing button in the PowerPoint Options dialog box, then click the Use contextual spelling check box.

Practice

Concepts Review

For current SAM information, including versions and content details, visit SAM Central (http://www.cengage.com/samcentral). If you have a SAM user profile, you may have access to hands-on instruction, practice, and assessment of the skills covered in this unit. Since various versions of SAM are supported throughout the life of this text, check with your instructor for the correct instructions and URL/Web site for accessing assignments.

Label each element of the PowerPoint window shown in Figure B-17.

FIGURE B-17

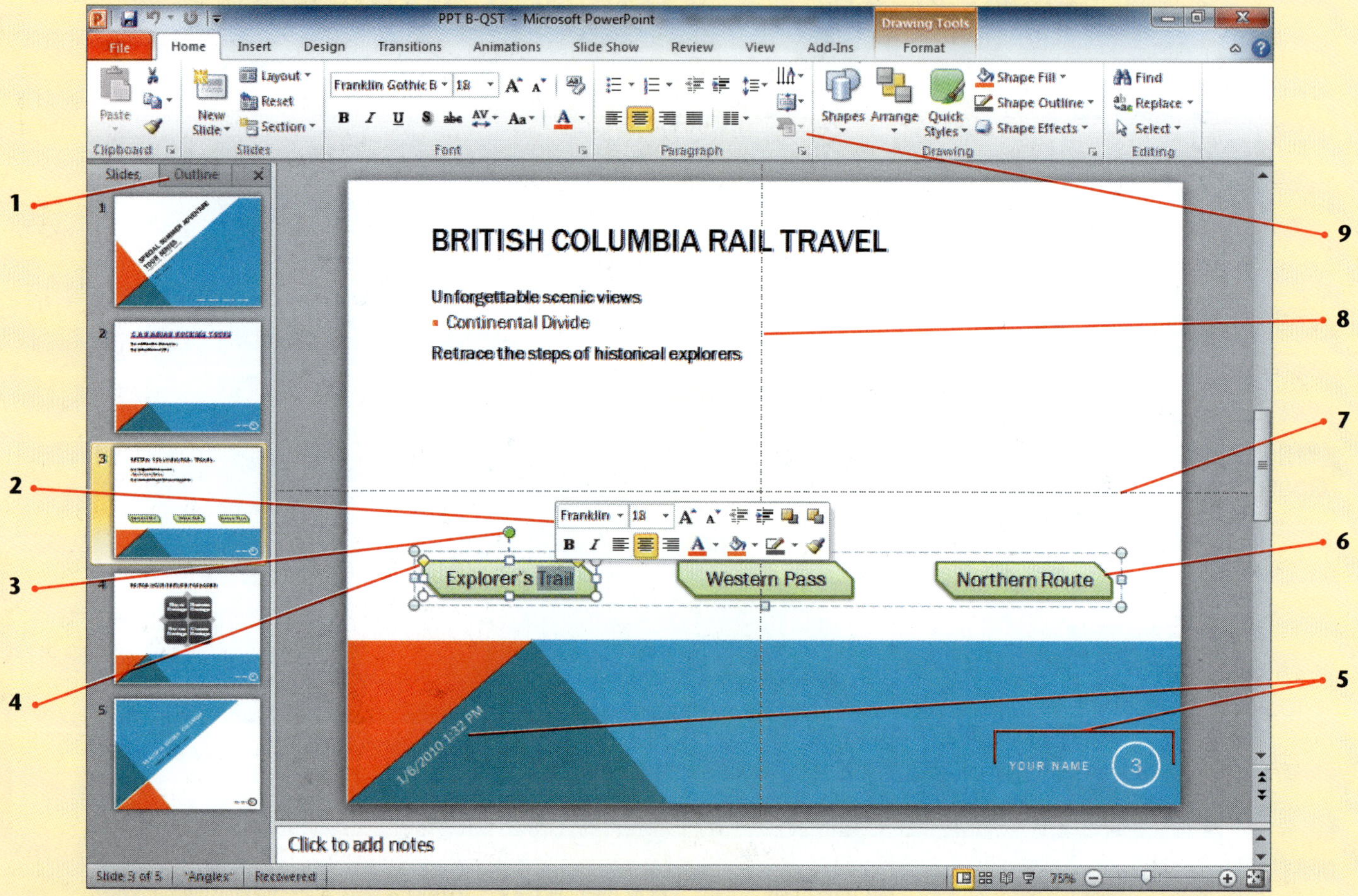

Match each term with the statement that best describes it.

10. Quick Style
11. Rotate handle
12. Distribute
13. Mini toolbar
14. SmartArt graphic
15. Group

a. Use to space objects evenly
b. A diagram that visually illustrates text
c. Use to manually turn an object
d. Combines multiple objects into one object
e. Use to format selected text
f. A preset combination of formatting options that you apply to an object

Select the best answer from the list of choices.

16. Which of the following statements is *not* true about the Outline tab?
- **a.** Each line of indented text creates a new slide title.
- **b.** You can enter text directly.
- **c.** It is organized using headings and subpoints.
- **d.** Headings are the same as slide titles.

17. What appears just above text when it is selected?
- **a.** QuickStyles
- **b.** Option button
- **c.** Mini toolbar
- **d.** AutoFit Options button

18. What does the adjustment handle do to a shape?
- **a.** Changes the appearance of a shape
- **b.** Changes the style of a shape
- **c.** Changes the size of a shape
- **d.** Changes the shape to another design

19. A professional-quality diagram that visually illustrates text best describes which of the following?
- **a.** A shape
- **b.** A SmartArt graphic
- **c.** A slide layout
- **d.** A QuickStyle object

20. Which of the following is not *true* about checking spelling in PowerPoint?
- **a.** The spell checker identifies unknown words as misspelled.
- **b.** Spelling is checked as you type.
- **c.** You can fix a misspelled word by right-clicking it and selecting a correct word.
- **d.** All misused words are automatically corrected.

21. What is *not* true about grouped objects?
- **a.** Grouped objects have one rotate handle.
- **b.** Sizing handles appear around the grouped object.
- **c.** Each object has individual sizing handles and a rotate handle.
- **d.** Grouped objects act as one object.

22. What do objects snap to when you move them?
- **a.** Slide edges
- **b.** Hidden grid
- **c.** Drawing lines
- **d.** Anchor points

Skills Review

1. Enter text in the Outline tab.
- **a.** Open the presentation PPT B-2.pptx from the drive and folder where you store your Data Files, then save it as **PPT B-PoolClean Pro**. The completed presentation is shown in Figure B-18.
- **b.** Create a new slide after Slide 2 with the Title and Content layout.
- **c.** Open the Outline tab, then type **Major Marketing Avenues**.
- **d.** Press [Enter], press [Tab], type **Online Forums**, press [Enter], type **Instant Messengers**, press [Enter], then type **Online Classifieds**.
- **e.** Move Slide 3 above Slide 2.
- **f.** Switch back to the Slides tab.
- **g.** Save your changes.

2. Format text.
- **a.** Go to Slide 1.
- **b.** Select the name **D.T. Wittenger**, then move the pointer over the Mini toolbar.
- **c.** Click the Font Color list arrow, then click Dark Blue, Text 2 under Theme Colors.

FIGURE B-18

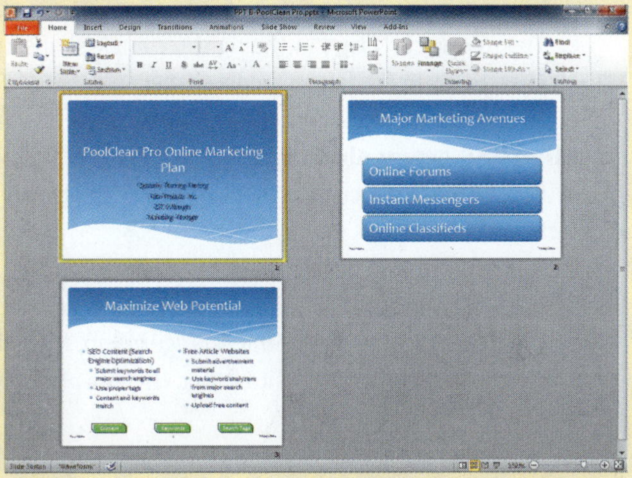

Skills Review (continued)

- **d.** Select the text object, then change all of the text to the color Dark Blue, Text 2.
- **e.** Click the Font Size list arrow, then click 24.
- **f.** Click the Italic button.
- **g.** Click the Character Spacing button, then click Tight.
- **h.** Save your changes.

3. Convert text to SmartArt.

- **a.** Click the text object on Slide 2.
- **b.** Click the Convert to SmartArt Graphic button, then apply the Vertical Block List graphic layout to the text object.
- **c.** Click the More button in the Layouts group, click More Layouts, click List in the Choose a SmartArt Graphic dialog box, then click Vertical Bullet List.
- **d.** Click the More button in the SmartArt Styles group, then apply the Intense Effect style to the graphic.
- **e.** Close the text pane if necessary, then click outside the SmartArt graphic in an empty part of the slide.
- **f.** Save your changes.

4. Insert and modify shapes.

- **a.** Go to Slide 3.
- **b.** Press [Shift], click both text objects, release [Shift], then drag the bottom-middle sizing handle up to decrease the size of the text objects.
- **c.** Click the Shapes button in the Drawing group, then insert the Round Diagonal Corner Rectangle shape from the Shapes gallery similar to the one in Figure B-19.
- **d.** On the Drawing Tools Format tab, click the More button in the Shape Styles group, then click Light 1 Outline, Colored Fill – Green, Accent 3.
- **e.** Click the Shape Effects button in the Shape Styles group, point to Shadow, then click Offset Diagonal Bottom Right.
- **f.** Click the Shape Outline button in the Shape Styles group, then click Black, Text 1, Lighter 25%.
- **g.** Click a blank area of the slide, then save your changes.

FIGURE B-19

5. Edit and duplicate shapes.

- **a.** Select the rectangle shape, then drag the left adjustment handle all the way to the right.
- **b.** Drag the rectangle shape so it lines up with the text in the left text object about ½ inch from the bottom of the slide.
- **c.** Click the Rotate button in the Arrange group, then click Flip Horizontal.
- **d.** Using [Ctrl] make two copies of the rectangle shape.
- **e.** Type **Search Tags** in the right rectangle shape, type **Keywords** in the middle rectangle shape, then type **Content** in the left rectangle shape.
- **f.** Click a blank area of the slide, then save your changes.

6. Align and group objects.

- **a.** Select the right rectangle shape, press [Shift], then move it to so it lines up with the right edge of the text in the right text object.
- **b.** Select all three rectangle shapes.
- **c.** Click the Drawing Tools Format tab if necessary, click the Align button, then click Align Bottom.
- **d.** Click the Align button in the Arrange group, then click Distribute Horizontally.
- **e.** Group all three rectangles together, then display the drawing guides on the screen.

Skills Review (continued)

f. Move the horizontal guide down until 3.17 appears, then press [Up Arrow] or press [Down Arrow] until the bottom of the rectangle shapes are on or near the horizontal guide. Compare your screen to Figure B-20.

g. Remove the drawing guides from your screen, then save your work.

FIGURE B-20

7. Add slide headers and footers.

a. Open the Header and Footer dialog box.

b. On the Slide tab, click the Date and time check box to select it, click the Fixed option button, then type today's date in the Fixed text box.

c. Add the slide number to the footer.

d. Type your name in the Footer text box.

e. Apply the footer to all of the slides except the title slide.

f. Open the Header and Footer dialog box again, then click the Notes and Handouts tab.

g. Type today's date in the Fixed text box.

h. Type the name of your class in the Header text box, then click the Page number check box.

i. Type your name in the Footer text box.

j. Apply the header and footer information to all the notes and handouts.

k. Save your changes.

8. Use proofing and language tools.

a. Check the spelling of the document, and change any misspelled words. Ignore any words that are correctly spelled but that the spell checker doesn't recognize. There is at least one misspelled word in the presentation.

b. Move to Slide 3, then set the Mini Translator language to Russian.

c. View the Russian translation of two or three individual words and a phrase on Slide 3.

d. Choose one other language (or as many as you want), translate words or phrases on the slide, reset the default language to Arabic, then turn off the Mini Translator.

e. Save your changes, submit your presentation to your instructor, close the presentation, then exit PowerPoint.

Independent Challenge 1

If you have a SAM 2010 user profile, an autogradable SAM version of this assignment may be available at http://www.cengage.com/sam2010. Check with your instructor to confirm that this assignment is available in SAM. To use the SAM version of this assignment, log into the SAM 2010 Web site and download the instruction and start files.

You are the Director of the Performing Arts Center in Council Bluffs, Iowa, and one of your many duties is to raise funds to cover operation costs. One of the primary ways you do this is by speaking to businesses, community clubs, and other organizations throughout the Council Bluffs region. Every year you speak to many organizations, where you give a short presentation detailing what the theater center plans to do for the coming season. You need to continue working on the presentation you started already.

a. Start PowerPoint, open the presentation PPT B-3.pptx from the drive and folder where you store your Data Files, and save it as **PPT B-Arts Center**.

b. Use the Outline tab to enter the following as bulleted text on the Commitment to Excellence slide:

Study
Diligence
Testing
Excellence

c. Apply the Technic design theme to the presentation.

d. Change the font color of each play name on Slide 3 to Gold, Accent 2, Lighter 40%.

e. Change the bulleted text on Slide 5 to the Vertical Accent List SmartArt graphic layout, then apply the Moderate Effect SmartArt Style.

Independent Challenge 1 (continued)

Advanced Challenge Exercise

- Open the Notes Page view.
- To at least two slides, add notes that relate to the slide content that you think would be important when giving this presentation.
- Save the presentation as **Arts Center ACE** to the drive and folder where you store your Data Files. When submitting the presentation to your instructor, submit the Notes Pages.

f. Check the spelling in the presentation (there is at least one spelling error), then view the presentation in Slide Show view.

g. Add your name as a footer on the notes and handouts, then save your changes.

h. Submit your presentation to your instructor, close your presentation, then exit PowerPoint.

Independent Challenge 2

You are a manager for Jess Hauser Investments Inc., a financial services company. You have been asked by your boss to develop a presentation outlining important details and aspects of the mortgage process to be used at a financial seminar.

a. Start PowerPoint, open the presentation PPT B-4.pptx from the drive and folder where you store your Data Files, and save it as **PPT B-Hauser**.

b. Apply the Hardcover design theme to the presentation.

c. On Slide 4 select the three shapes, Banks, Mortgage Bankers, and Private Investors, then using the Align command distribute them vertically and align them to their left edges.

d. On Slide 4 select the three shapes, Borrower, Mortgage Broker, and Mortgage Bankers, then using the Align command distribute them horizontally and align them to their bottom edges.

e. Select all of the shapes, then apply Intense Effect – Black, Dark 1 from the Shape Styles group, then move the shapes down as shown in Figure B-21.

f. Using the Arrow shape from the Shapes gallery, draw a 2 ¼-pt arrow between all of the shapes. (*Hint*: Draw one arrow shape, change the line weight to 2 ¼-pt using the Shape Outline button, then duplicate the shape.)

g. Create a sixth slide to end the presentation, then type the following information in the Outline tab:

Program Summary

    We will find the right loan for you

    You will be able to afford your loan

    You will save money with our loan

    No government interference

h. Check the spelling in the presentation, view the presentation in Slide Show view, then view the slides in Slide Sorter view.

i. Add the page number and your name as a footer on the notes and handouts, then save your changes.

j. Submit your presentation to your instructor, close your presentation, then exit PowerPoint.

FIGURE B-21

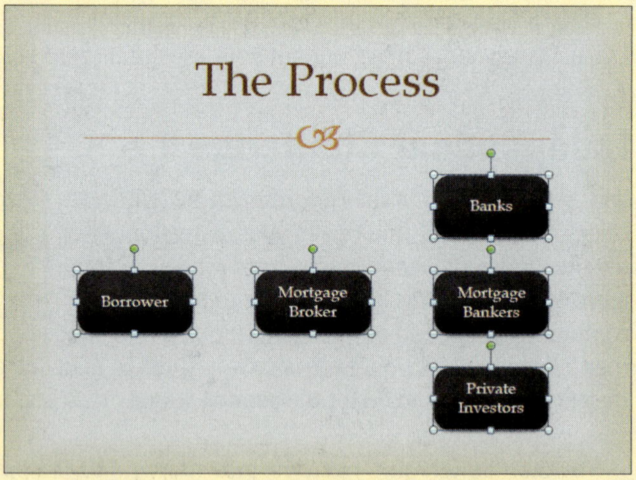

Independent Challenge 3

You are an independent distributor of natural foods in Spokane, Washington. Your business, Pacific Coast Natural Foods, has grown progressively since its inception 10 years ago, but sales have leveled off over the last 12 months. In an effort to stimulate growth, you decide to purchase Idaho Foods Inc., a natural food dealer in Idaho, which would allow your company to begin expanding into surrounding states. Use PowerPoint to develop a presentation that you can use to gain a financial backer for the acquisition. Create your own information for the presentation.

a. Start PowerPoint, create a new presentation, then apply the Thatch design theme to the presentation.
b. Type **A Plan for Growth** as the main title on the title slide, and **Pacific Coast Natural Foods** as the subtitle.
c. Save the presentation as **PPT B-Pacific Coast** to the drive and folder where you store your Data Files.
d. Add five more slides with the following titles: Slide 2-**Background**; Slide 3-**Current Situation**; Slide 4-**Acquisition Goals**; Slide 5-**Funding Required**; Slide 6-**Our Management Team**.
e. Enter appropriate text into the text placeholders of the slides. Use both the Slide pane and the Outline tab to enter text.
f. Convert text on one slide to a SmartArt graphic, then apply the SmartArt graphic style Inset Effect.

Advanced Challenge Exercise

- Click the Replace list arrow in the Editing group on the Home tab, then click Replace Fonts.
- Replace the Tw Cen MT font with the Eras Medium ITC font.
- Save the presentation as **PPT B-Pacific Coast ACE** to the drive and folder where you store your Data Files.

g. Check the spelling in the presentation, view the presentation as a slide show, then view the slides in Slide Sorter view.
h. Add the slide number and your name as a footer on the slides, then save your changes.
i. Submit your presentation to your instructor, close your presentation, then exit PowerPoint.

Real Life Independent Challenge

Your computer instructor at City Junior College has been asked by the department head to convert his Computer Basics 101 course into an accelerated course that both students and professional working people can take. Your instructor has asked you to help him create a presentation for the class that he can post on the Internet and use as a promotional tool at local businesses. Most of the raw information is already on the slides, you primarily need to jazz it up by adding a theme and some text formatting.

a. Start PowerPoint, open the presentation PPT B-5.pptx from drive and folder where you store your data files, and save it as **PPT B-Course 101**.
b. Add a new slide after the Course Facts slide with the same layout, type **Course Details** in the title text placeholder, then enter the following as bulleted text in the Outline tab:
Unix/Information Systems
Networking
Applied Methods
Technology Solutions
Software Design
Applications
c. Apply the Paper design theme to the presentation.
d. Select the title text object on Slide 1 (*Hint*: Press [Shift] to select the whole object), then change the text color to Yellow.
e. Change the font of the title text object to Century Gothic.
f. Click the subtitle text object, click the AutoFit Options button, then click Stop Fitting Text to This Placeholder.
g. Change the text on Slide 4 to a SmartArt graphic. Use an appropriate diagram type for a list.
h. Change the style of the SmartArt diagram using one of the SmartArt Styles, then view the presentation in Slide Show view.
i. Add the slide number and your name as a footer on the notes and handouts, then save your changes.
j Submit your presentation to your instructor, close your presentation, then exit PowerPoint.

Visual Workshop

Create the presentation shown in Figures B-22 and B-23. Add today's date as the date on the title slide. Save the presentation as **PPT B-Ag Trade** to the drive and folder where you store your Data Files. (*Hint*: The SmartArt style used for the SmartArt is a 3-D style.) Review your slides in Slide Show view, then add your name as a footer to the notes and handouts. Submit your presentation to your instructor, save your changes, close the presentation, then exit PowerPoint.

FIGURE B-22

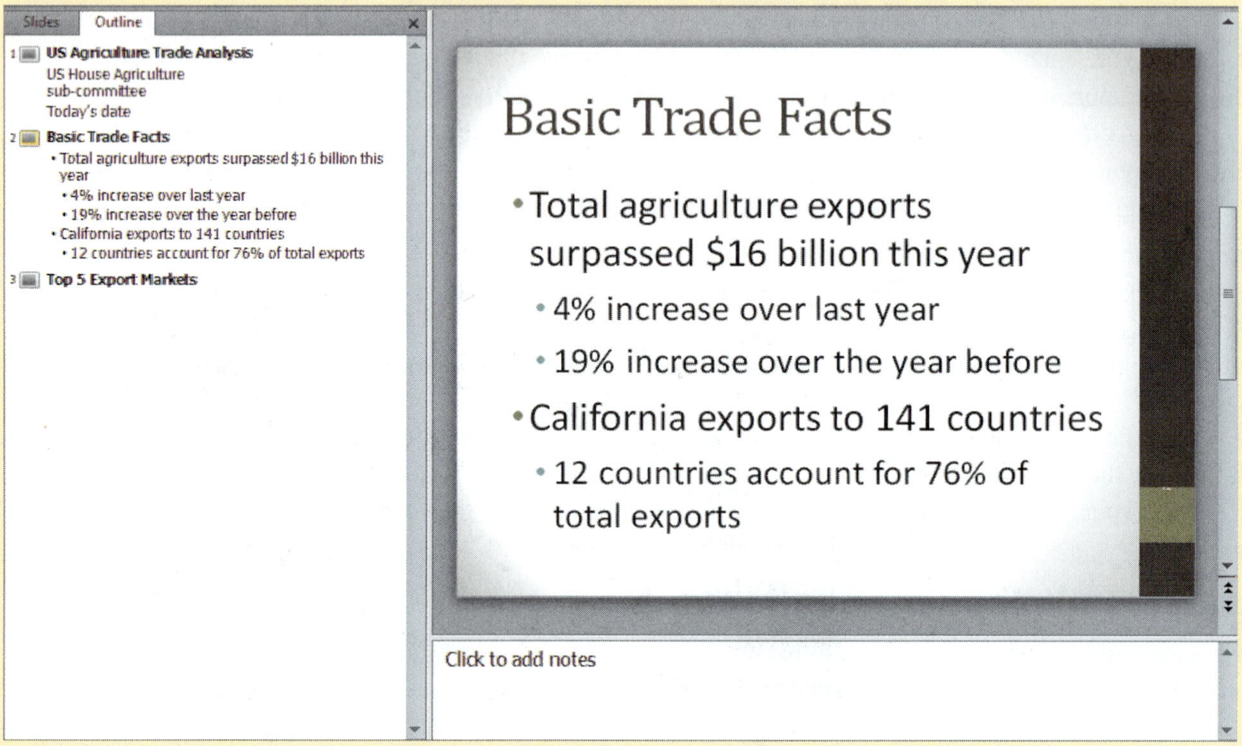

FIGURE B-23

Inserting Objects into a Presentation

Files You Will Need:

- PPT C-1.pptx
- PPT C-2.docx
- PPT C-3.jpg
- PPT C-4.pptx
- PPT C-5.docx
- PPT C-6.jpg
- PPT C-7.pptx
- PPT C-8.pptx
- PPT C-9.docx
- PPT C-10.pptx
- PPT C-11.docx
- PPT C-12.jpg
- PPT C-13.jpg
- PPT C-14.jpg
- PPT C-15.jpg

A good presenter will make use of visual elements, such as charts, graphics, and photographs, in conjunction with text to help communicate the presentation message. Visual elements keep the presentation interesting, illustrate concepts, and help the audience focus on what the presenter is saying. In this unit, you continue working on the presentation by inserting visual elements, including clip art, a photograph, and a chart, into the presentation. You format these objects using PowerPoint's powerful object-editing features.

OBJECTIVES

- Insert text from Microsoft Word
- Insert clip art
- Insert and style a picture
- Insert a text box
- Insert a chart
- Enter and edit chart data
- Insert a table
- Insert and format WordArt

UNIT
C
PowerPoint 2010

Inserting Text from Microsoft Word

It is easy to insert documents saved in Microsoft Word format (.docx), Rich Text Format (.rtf), plain text format (.txt), and HTML format (.htm) into a PowerPoint presentation. If you have an outline saved in a document file, you can import it into PowerPoint to create a new presentation or create additional slides in an existing presentation. When you import a document into a presentation, PowerPoint creates an outline structure based on the styles in the document. For example, a Heading 1 style in the Word document becomes a slide title and a Heading 2 style becomes the first level of text in a bulleted list. If you insert a plain text format document into a presentation, PowerPoint creates an outline based on the tabs at the beginning of the document's paragraphs. Paragraphs without tabs become slide titles and paragraphs with one tab indent become first-level text in bulleted lists. You have a Microsoft Word document with information about the different Canadian train routes that you want to insert into your presentation to create several new slides.

STEPS

1. **Start PowerPoint, open the presentation PPT C-1.pptx from the drive and folder where you store your Data Files, save it as PPT C-QST, click the Outline tab, then click the Slide 3 icon in the Outline tab**

   Slide 3 appears in the Slide pane. Clicking a slide icon in the Outline tab highlights the slide text indicating the slide is selected. Before you insert an outline into a presentation, you need to determine where you want the new slides to be placed. You want the text from the Word document inserted as new slides after Slide 3.

2. **Click the New Slide list arrow in the Slides group, then click Slides from Outline**

   The Insert Outline dialog box opens.

3. **Navigate to the drive and folder where you store your Data Files, click the Word document file PPT C-2.docx, then click Insert**

   Four new slides (4, 5, 6, and 7) are added to the presentation. See Figure C-1.

4. **Read the text for the new Slide 4 in the Slide pane, then review the text on slides 5, 6, and 7 in the Outline tab**

   Information on Slide 7 refers to an obsolete train route and is not needed for this presentation.

5. **Click the Slides tab, then right-click the Slide 7 thumbnail in the Slides tab**

   A shortcut menu opens displaying related, or contextual, commands that are currently available.

6. **Click Delete Slide on the shortcut menu**

   Slide 7 is deleted, and the next slide down becomes the new Slide 7 and appears in the Slide pane.

7. **Click the Slide 6 thumbnail in the Slides tab, then drag it above Slide 5**

   Slide 6 and Slide 5 change places. You want the text of the inserted outline to adopt the presentation theme.

8. **Click the Slide 4 thumbnail, then click the Reset button in the Slides group**

   Notice that the font type and formatting attributes of the slide text changes to reflect the current theme fonts for the presentation. The Reset button resets the slide placeholders to their default position, size, and text formatting based on the Angles presentation design theme.

9. **Click the Slide 5 thumbnail, press and hold [Shift], click the Slide 6 thumbnail, release [Shift], click the Reset button, then click the Save button on the Quick Access toolbar**

   Now all of the newly inserted slides have the same design theme as the rest of the presentation. Compare your screen to Figure C-2.

QUICK TIP

If your presentation has numerous slides, you can organize them into sections in the Slides tab. To create a section, click the slide in the Slides tab where you want the section to begin, click the Section button in the Slides group on the Home tab, then click Add Section.

FIGURE C-1: Outline tab showing imported text

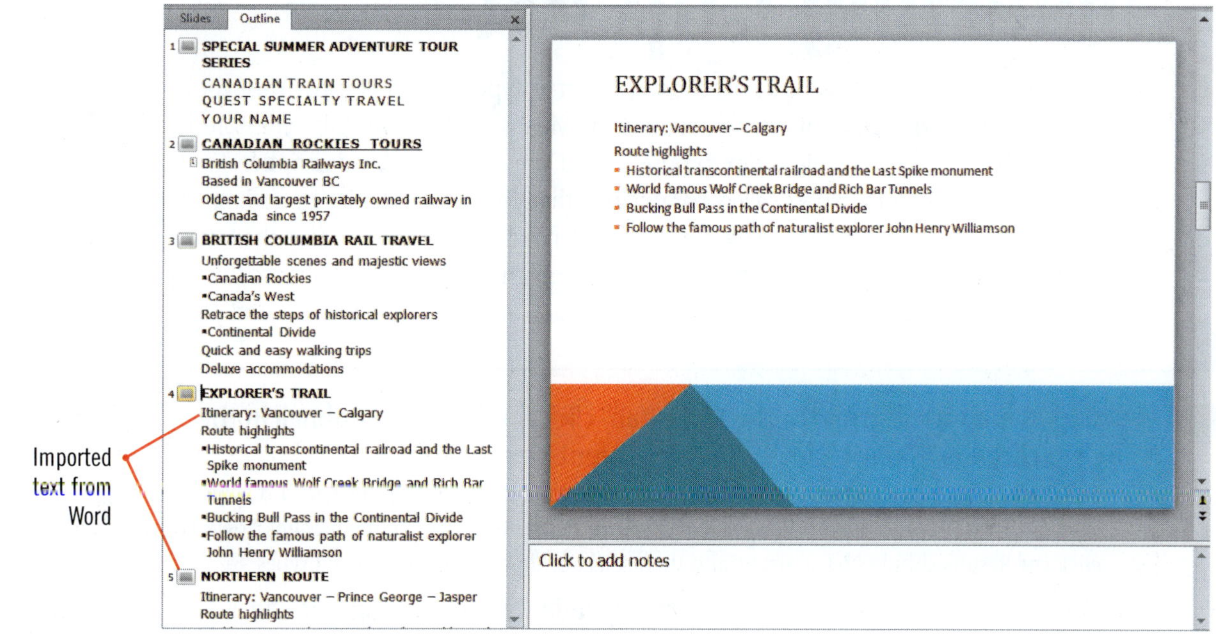

FIGURE C-2: Slide showing correct theme fonts

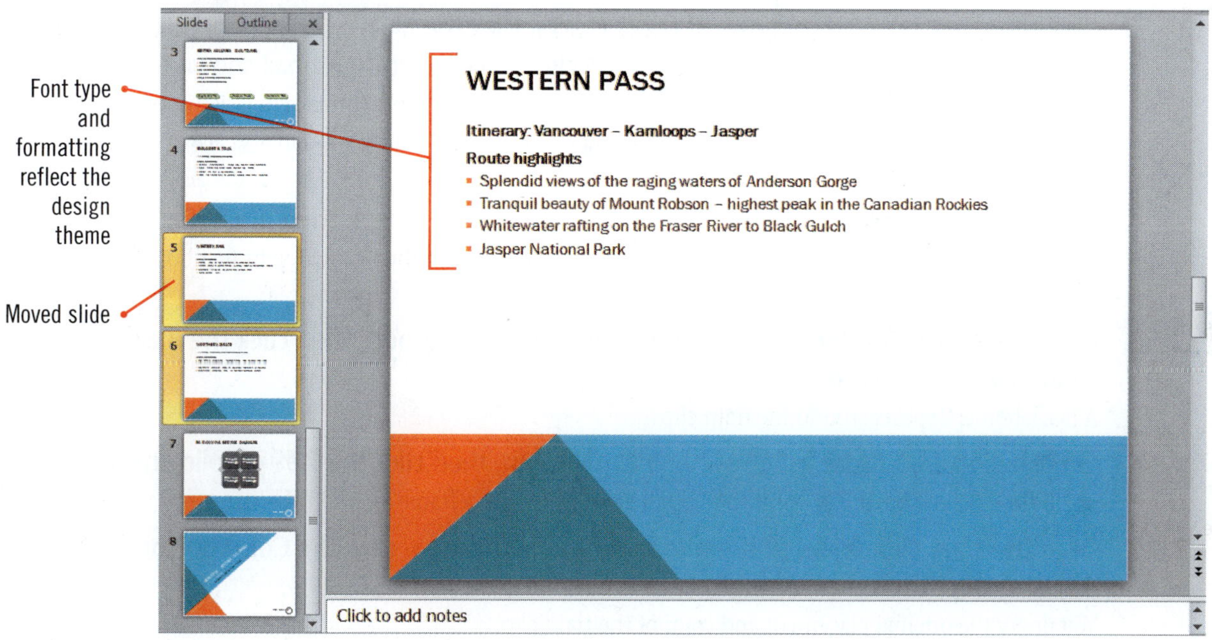

Inserting slides from other presentations

To insert slides from another presentation into the current presentation, click the New Slide list arrow in the Slides group, then click Reuse Slides. The Reuse Slides task pane opens on the right side of the window. Click the Browse button, click Browse File in the drop down list, locate the presentation you want to use, then click Open. Click each slide you want to place in the current presentation. The new slides automatically take on the theme of the current presentation, unless you check the Keep source formatting check box. You can also copy slides from one presentation to another. Open both presentations, change the view of each presentation to Slide Sorter view or use the Arrange All command to see both presentations, select the desired slides, then copy and paste them (or use drag and drop) into the desired presentation.

UNIT C

PowerPoint 2010

Inserting Clip Art

In PowerPoint you have access to a collection of assorted types of media clips. The types of clips include illustrations, called **clip art**, photographs, animations, videos, and sounds. Clips are stored in the Microsoft **Clip Organizer**, a separate file index program, and are identified by descriptive keywords. The Clip Organizer is organized into folders called **collections** that you can customize by adding, moving, or deleting clips. Clip art and other media clips are available from many sources, including the Microsoft Office Web site and commercially available collections that you can purchase. To enhance the QST presentation, you add a clip from the Clip Organizer to one of the slides, and then adjust its size and placement.

STEPS

QUICK TIP

You can insert clip art anywhere on a slide by clicking the ClipArt button in the Images group on the Insert tab.

1. **Click the up scroll arrow in the Slides tab, click the Slide 2 thumbnail in the Slides tab, then click the Clip Art icon in the Content placeholder**

   The Clip Art task pane opens. At the top of the task pane in the Search for text box, you enter a descriptive keyword to search for clips. If you want to limit or define the types of media clips PowerPoint searches for, click the Results should be list arrow, and then select or deselect specific media types.

2. **Verify that there is a check mark in the Include Office.com content check box, select any text in the Search for text box, type locomotive, then click the Results should be list arrow**

   You are only interested in finding clip art images that are located in the Illustrations category. Searching in only the categories you are interested in significantly reduces the number of media clips PowerPoint needs to search through to produce your results.

TROUBLE

If you don't see the clip shown in Figure C-3, select another one.

3. **Click the check boxes to remove all check marks, click the Illustrations check box, click the Go button, click the down scroll arrow, then click the clip art thumbnail shown in Figure C-3**

   The train clip appears in the content placeholder, and the Picture Tools Format tab is active on the Ribbon. Although you can change a clip's size by dragging a corner sizing handle, you can also **scale** it to change its size proportionally by a specific percentage or size.

4. **Select 2 in the Shape Width text box in the Size group, type 4, then press [Enter]**

   The train clip proportionally doubles in size. Notice the number in the Shape Height text box changes from 1.47 to 2.94.

5. **Click the Picture Border list arrow in the Picture Styles group, then click the Black, Text 1 color box in the top row**

   A black border appears around the train clip.

6. **Click the Picture Border list arrow, point to Weight, then click the 2 ¼ pt solid line style**

   The train clip now has a 2 ¼-point solid border, which creates a frame around the clip.

7. **Drag the train clip object to the middle of the blank area, click the Color button in the Adjust group, then click Orange, Accent color 2 Dark**

   You prefer the original placement and color of the train clip.

QUICK TIP

Click the Reset Picture button in the Adjust group to discard all the formatting changes.

8. **Click the Undo button list arrow on the Quick Access toolbar, click Move Object, click a blank area of the slide, then save your changes**

   Notice that by using the Undo button list arrow, you can undo multiple actions in one step, in this case the Recolor Picture and the Move Object commands.

9. **Click the Results should be list arrow in the Clip Art task pane, click the All media types check box, click Go, then click the task pane Close button**

   Now the next time you search for a clip, PowerPoint will search through all media types. Compare the slide on your screen to the slide shown in Figure C-4.

FIGURE C-3: Screen showing Clip Art task pane

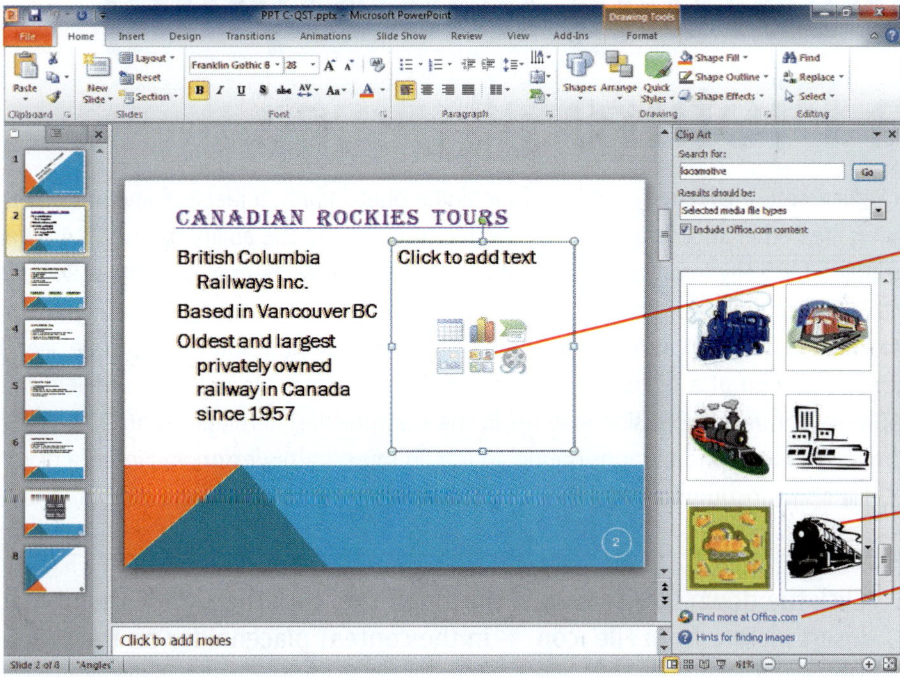

FIGURE C-4: Slide with formatted train clip

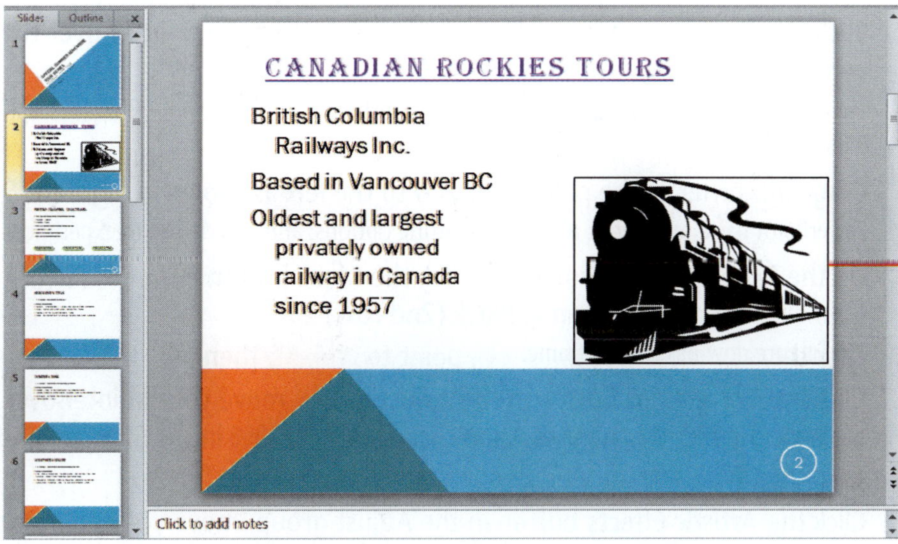

PowerPoint 2010

Finding more clips online

If you can't find exactly what you want using the Clip Art task pane, you can easily find and download clips from the Office.com Web site. To get clips online, click the Find more at Office.com hyperlink at the bottom of the Clip Art task pane. If your computer is connected to the Internet, this will start your Web browser and automatically connect you to the Office.com Web site. You can search the site by keyword or browse by category type. Each clip you download is automatically inserted into the Clip Organizer and appears in the Clip Art task pane.

UNIT C

PowerPoint 2010

Inserting and Styling a Picture

In PowerPoint, a **picture** is defined as a digital photograph, a piece of line art or clip art, or other artwork that is created in another program. PowerPoint gives you the ability to insert 14 different types of pictures including JPEG File Interchange Format and BMP Windows Bitmap files into a PowerPoint presentation. As with all objects in PowerPoint, you can format and style inserted pictures to help them fit the theme of your presentation. You can also hide a portion of the picture you don't want to be seen by **cropping** it. The cropped portion of a picture remains a part of the picture file unless you delete the cropped portion by applying picture compression settings in the Compression Settings dialog box. Using your digital camera, you took photographs during your train tours. In this lesson you insert a picture that you saved as a JPG file on your computer, and then you crop and style it to best fit the slide.

STEPS

QUICK TIP
You can also insert a picture by clicking the Picture button in the Images group on the Insert tab.

1. **Click the down scroll arrow in the Slides tab, click the Slide 8 thumbnail, then click the Insert Picture from File icon in the content placeholder on the slide**
   The Insert Picture dialog box opens displaying the pictures available in the default Pictures library.
2. **Navigate to the drive and folder where you store your Data Files, select the picture file PPT C-3.jpg, then click Insert**
   The picture appears in the content placeholder on the slide, and the Picture Tools Format tab opens on the Ribbon. The picture would look better if you cropped some of the window reflection images off the right edge.

QUICK TIP
Click the Crop button list arrow to take advantage of other crop options including cropping to a shape from the Shapes gallery and cropping to a common photo size or aspect ratio.

3. **Click the Crop button in the Size group, then place the pointer over the lower-right corner cropping handle of the picture**
   The pointer changes to ⌟. When the Crop button is active, cropping handles appear next to the sizing handles.
4. **Drag the corner of the picture up and to the left as shown in Figure C-5, then press [Esc]**
   PowerPoint has a number of picture formatting options, and you decide to experiment with some of them.
5. **On the Picture Tools Format tab, click the More button in the Picture Styles group, then click Compound Frame, Black (2nd row)**
   The picture now has a black frame.
6. **Click the Corrections button in the Adjust group, move your pointer over the thumbnails to see how the picture changes, then click Sharpen: 50% in the Sharpen and Soften section**
   The picture clarity is better.
7. **Click the Artistic Effects button in the Adjust group, move your pointer over the thumbnails to see how the picture changes, then click a blank area of the slide**
   The artistic effects are all interesting but none of them will work well for this picture. You decide to compress the picture to delete the cropped areas and make the file smaller.

QUICK TIP
If you want to apply an effect from the Artistic Effects gallery to a compressed picture, compress the picture first to maintain the best picture quality possible.

8. **Click the Compress Pictures button in the Adjust group, make sure the Use document resolution option button is checked, then click OK**
   The cropped portions of the picture are deleted and the picture is compressed.
9. **Drag the lower-right sizing handle down so the right side of the picture increases in size and aligns with the right side of the slide number, click a blank area on the slide, then save your changes**
   Compare your screen to Figure C-6.

FIGURE C-5: Using the cropping pointer to crop a picture

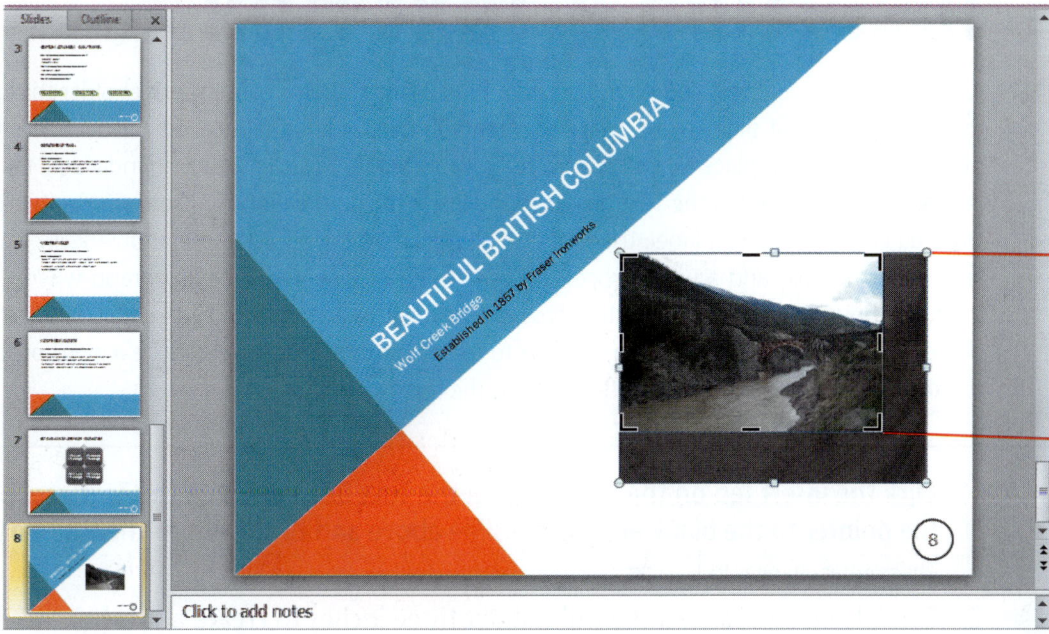

FIGURE C-6: Cropped and styled picture

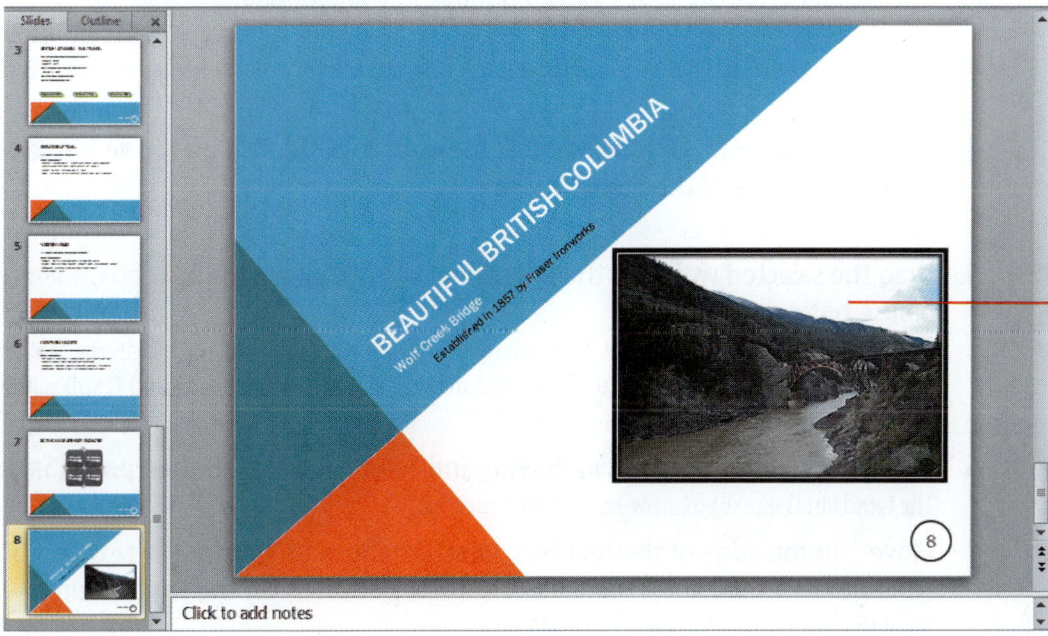

PowerPoint 2010

Things to know about picture compression

It's important to know that when you compress a picture you change the amount of detail in the picture, so it might look different than it did before the compression. Compressing a picture changes the amount of color used in the picture with no loss of quality. By default, all inserted pictures in PowerPoint are automatically compressed using the settings in the PowerPoint Options dialog box. To locate the compression settings, click the File tab, click Options, then click Advanced in the left pane. In the Image Size and Quality section, you can change picture compression settings or stop the automatic compression of pictures.

UNIT C
PowerPoint 2010

Inserting a Text Box

As you've already learned, you enter text on a slide using a title or content placeholder that is arranged on the slide based on a slide layout. Every so often you need additional text on a slide where the traditional placeholder does not place text effectively for your message. You can create an individual text box by clicking the Text Box button in the Text group on the Insert tab on the Ribbon. There are two types of text boxes that you can create: a text label, used for a small phrase where text doesn't automatically wrap to the next line inside the box; and a word-processing box, used for a sentence or paragraph where the text wraps inside the boundaries of the box. Either type of text box can be formatted and edited just like any other text object. You decide to add a text box to the picture on Slide 8. You create a word-processing box on the slide, enter text, edit text, and then format the text.

STEPS

1. **Click the Insert tab on the Ribbon, click the Text Box button in the Text group, then move the pointer to the blank area of the slide above and to the left of the title text**

   The pointer changes to ↓.

2. **Drag down and toward the right about three inches to create a text box**

   When you begin dragging, an outline of the text box appears, indicating how large a text box you are drawing. After you release the mouse button, an insertion point appears inside the text box, in this case a word-processing box, indicating that you can enter text. The font and font style appear in the Font group on the Ribbon.

3. **Type On day 2 of the tour east of Kamloops 20 kilometers**

   Notice that the text box increases in size as your text wraps to a second line inside the text box. Your screen should look similar to Figure C-7. After entering the text you realize the sentence could be clearer if written differently.

4. **Drag I over the phrase 20 kilometers to select it, position the pointer on top of the selected phrase, then press and hold the mouse button**

   The pointer changes to the drag pointer.

5. **Drag the selected words to the left of the word "east" in the text box, then release the mouse button**

   A light blue insertion line appears as you drag, indicating where PowerPoint places the text when you release the mouse button. The phrase "20 kilometers" moves before the word "east" and is still selected. Now fix the word spacing.

6. **Click between the words "kilometers" and "east" in the text, then press [Spacebar]**

   The words in the text box now have proper spacing.

7. **Move I to the edge of the text box, which changes to the move pointer, click the text box border (changes to a solid line), then click the Italic button *I* in the Font group**

   All of the text in the text box is italicized.

8. **Drag the right-middle sizing handle of the text box to the right until all the text fits on two lines, position the move pointer over the text box edge, then drag it above the picture**

   Your screen should look similar to Figure C-8.

9. **Click the Reading View button on the status bar, review the slide, press [Esc], then save your changes**

QUICK TIP

To create a text label, click the Text Box button, position the pointer where you want to place the text, click once, then enter your text.

QUICK TIP

You can also move text between text objects on a slide and in the Outline tab using this drag-and-drop method.

FIGURE C-7: New text object

FIGURE C-8: Formatted text object

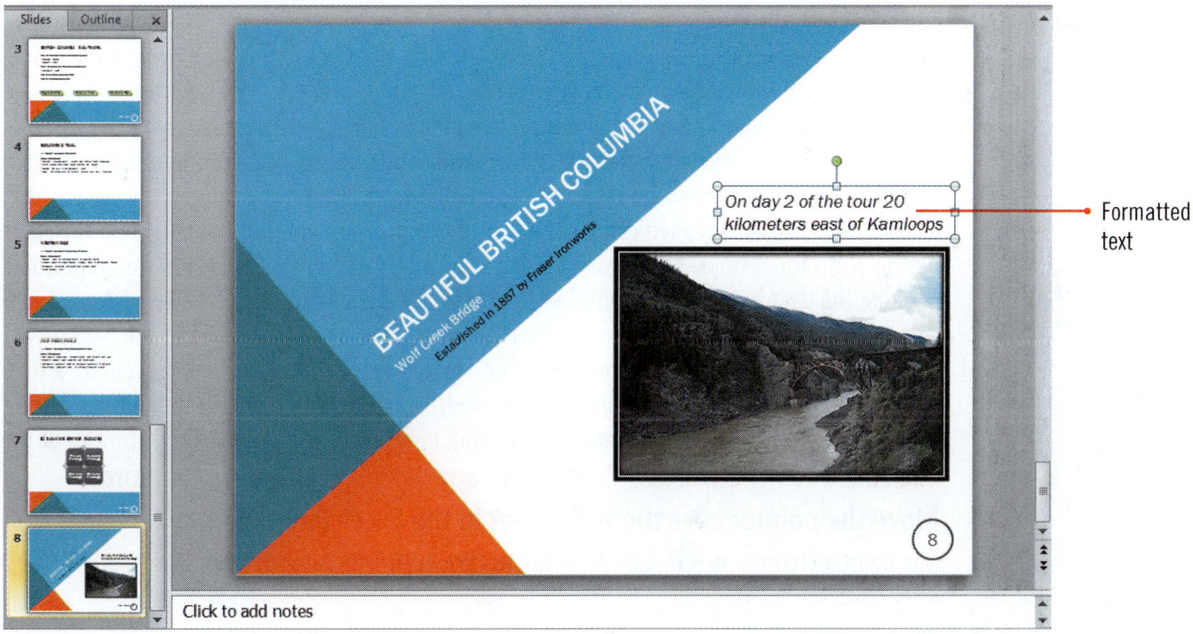

PowerPoint 2010

Sending a presentation using e-mail

You can send a copy of a presentation over the Internet to a reviewer to edit and add comments. You can use Microsoft Outlook to send your presentation. Although your e-mail program allows you to attach files, you can send a presentation using Outlook from within PowerPoint. Click the File tab, click Save & Send, click Send Using E-mail in the center pane, then click Send as Attachment. Outlook opens and automatically creates an e-mail with a copy of the presentation attached to it. You can also attach and send a PDF copy or an XPS copy of the presentation using your e-mail program. Both of these file formats preserve document formatting, enable file sharing, and can be viewed online and printed.

Inserting a Chart

Frequently, the best way to communicate numerical information is with a visual aid such as a chart. If you have Microsoft Excel installed on your computer, PowerPoint uses Excel to create charts. If you don't have Excel installed, a charting program called **Microsoft Graph** opens that you can use to create charts for your slides. A **chart** is the graphical representation of numerical data. Every chart has a corresponding **worksheet** that contains the numerical data displayed by the chart. When you insert a chart object into PowerPoint, you are actually embedding it. An **embedded object** is one that is a part of your presentation (just like any other object you insert into PowerPoint) except that an embedded object's data source can be opened, in this case Excel, for editing purposes. Changes you make to an embedded object in PowerPoint using PowerPoint's features do not affect the data source for the data. You insert a chart on a new slide.

STEPS

QUICK TIP
You can also add a chart to a slide by clicking the Insert Chart button in the Illustrations group on the Insert tab.

TROUBLE
If Excel is not installed on your computer, Microsoft Graph opens and your screen will look different.

1. **Click Slide 7 in the Slides tab, then press [Enter]**
   Pressing [Enter] adds a new blank slide to your presentation with the slide layout of the selected slide, in this case the Title and Content slide layout.
2. **Click the Title placeholder, then type Vacation Comparison Survey**
3. **Click the Insert Chart icon in the Content placeholder**
   The Insert Chart dialog box opens as shown in Figure C-9. Each chart type includes a number of 2-D and 3-D styles. The Column chart type, for example, includes 19 different 2-D and 3-D styles. The 2-D Clustered Column chart is the default chart style. For a brief explanation of chart types, refer to Table C-1.
4. **Click OK**
   Excel opens in a split window sharing the screen with the PowerPoint window as shown in Figure C-10. The PowerPoint window displays the clustered column chart, and the Excel window displays sample data in a worksheet. The Chart Tools Design tab on the Ribbon contains commands you use in PowerPoint to work with the chart. The worksheet consists of rows and columns. The intersection of a row and a column is called a **cell**. Cells are referred to by their row and column location; for example, the cell at the intersection of column A and row 1 is called cell A1. Cells in the first or left column contain **axis labels** that identify the data in a row for example, "Category 1" is an axis label. Cells in the first or top row appear in the **legend** and describe the data in the series. Cells below and to the right of the axis labels and legend names contain the data values that are represented in the chart. Each column and row of data in the worksheet is called a **data series**. Each data series has corresponding **data series markers** in the chart, which are graphical representations such as bars, columns, or pie wedges. The gray boxes with the numbers along the left side of the worksheet are **row headings**, and the gray boxes with the letters along the top of the worksheet are **column headings**.
5. **Move the pointer over the worksheet in the Excel window**
   The pointer changes to ✚. Cell A6 is the **active cell**, which means that it is selected. The active cell has a thick black border around it.
6. **Click cell C4**
   Cell C4 is now the active cell.
7. **Click the Excel Window Close button on the title bar**
   The Excel window closes, and the PowerPoint window fills the screen. The new chart on the slide displays the data from the Excel worksheet.
8. **Click in a blank area of the slide to deselect the chart, then save your changes**
   The Chart Tools Design tab is no longer active.

FIGURE C-9: Insert Chart dialog box

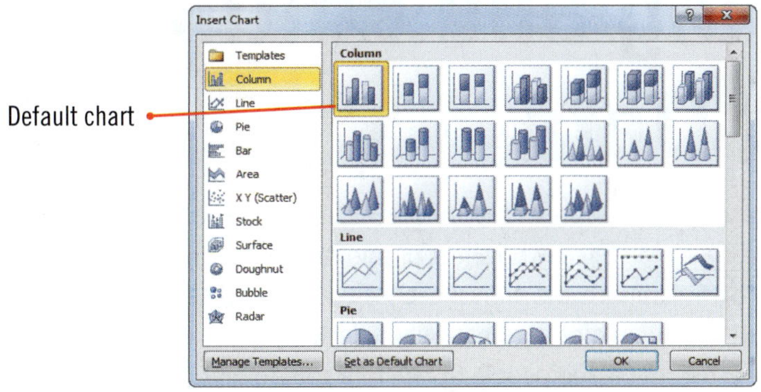

FIGURE C-10: The PowerPoint and Excel split windows

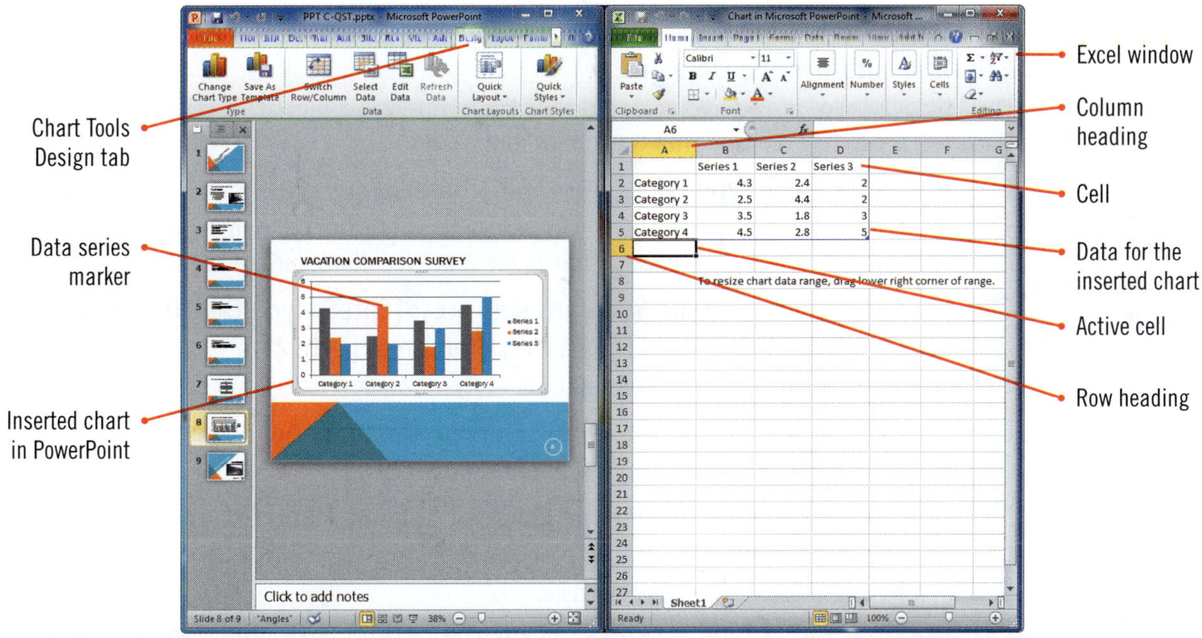

TABLE C-1: Chart types

chart type	icon looks like	use to
Column		Track values over time or across categories
Line		Track values over time
Pie		Compare individual values to the whole
Bar		Compare values in categories or over time
Area		Show contribution of each data series to the total over time
XY (Scatter)		Compare pairs of values
Stock		Show stock market information or scientific data
Surface		Show value trends across two dimensions
Doughnut		Compare individual values to the whole with multiple series
Bubble		Indicate relative size of data points
Radar		Show changes in values in relation to a center point

UNIT C
PowerPoint 2010

Entering and Editing Chart Data

After you insert a chart into your presentation, you need to replace the sample data with the correct information. If you have data in an Excel worksheet or another source, you can import it from Excel; otherwise, you can type your own data into the worksheet. As you enter data and make other changes in the Excel worksheet, the chart in PowerPoint automatically reflects the new changes. You enter and format survey data you collected that asked people to rate four categories of vacations with respect to three factors: price, safety, and culture.

STEPS

1. **Click the chart on Slide 8, click the Chart Tools Design tab on the Ribbon, then click the Edit Data button in the Data group**
   The chart is selected in PowerPoint, and the worksheet opens in a separate Excel window. The data in the worksheet needs to be replaced with the correct information.
2. **Click the Series 1 cell, type Price, press [Tab], type Safety, press [Tab], then type Culture**
   The Legend labels are entered. Pressing [Tab] in Excel moves the active cell from left to right one cell at a time in a row. Pressing [Enter] in the worksheet moves the active cell down one cell at a time in a column.
3. **Click the Category 1 cell, type Standard Rail, press [Enter], type Deluxe Rail, press [Enter], type Cruise, press [Enter], type Traditional, then press [Enter]**
   The axis labels are entered, and the chart in the PowerPoint window reflects all the changes.
4. **Enter the data shown in Figure C-11 to complete the worksheet, then press [Enter]**
   Column A needs to be wider to see all of the information in cell A2.
5. **Move over the column divider line between Column A and Column B, which changes to, then double-click**
   Column A widens so you can see all of the data.
6. **Click the Switch Row/Column button in the Data group in the PowerPoint window**
   The data charted on the x-axis switches and moves to the y-axis. The y-axis is also referred to as the vertical axis or **value axis**, and the x-axis is also referred to as the horizontal axis or **category axis**. Notice the legend now displays the row axis labels instead of the column axis labels. You have finished entering the data in the Excel worksheet.
7. **Click the Excel window Close button**
   Notice that the height of each column in the chart, as well as the values along the y-axis, adjust to reflect the numbers you typed. The column axis labels are now on the x-axis of the chart, and the row axis labels are listed in the legend.
8. **Click the More button in the Chart Styles group, then click Style 26 (4th row)**
   The new chart style gives the column data markers a three-dimensional look.
9. **Click a blank area on the slide, then save the presentation**
   Compare your chart to Figure C-12.

QUICK TIP
Click the chart in the PowerPoint window, then move your pointer over each bar in the chart to see the data source values.

QUICK TIP
You can also drag a column divider line to resize the column width to accommodate the widest entry.

FIGURE C-11: Worksheet showing chart data

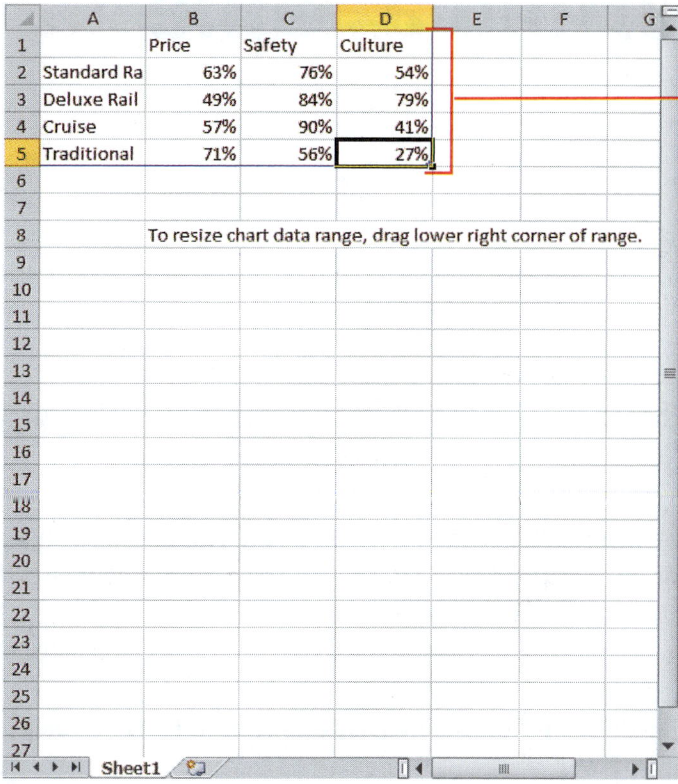

FIGURE C-12: Formatted chart

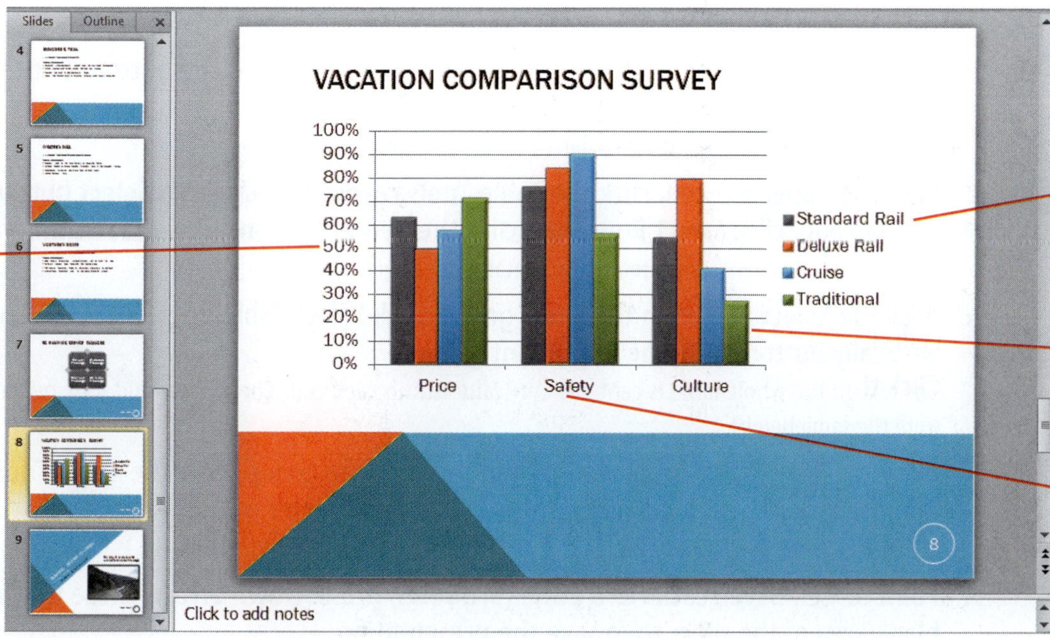

Switching rows and columns

If you have difficulty visualizing what the Switch Row/Column command does, think about what is represented in the chart. **Series in Rows** means that the data in the datasheet rows is plotted on the y-axis, and the row axis labels are shown on the x-axis. The column axis labels are shown in the legend. **Series in Columns** means that the data in the datasheet columns is plotted on the y-axis, and the row axis labels are shown in the legend. The column axis labels are plotted on the x-axis.

UNIT C
PowerPoint 2010

Inserting a Table

As you create your presentation, you may have some information that would look best organized in rows and columns. For example, if you wanted to compare the basic details of three different cruise tours side by side, a table is ideal for this type of information. Once you have created a table, two new tabs, the Table Tools Design tab and the Table Tools Layout tab, appear on the Ribbon. You can use the Design tab to apply color styles, change cell borders, and add cell effects. Using the Layout tab, you can add rows and columns to your table, adjust the size of cells, and align text in the cells. You decide that a table best illustrates the different services offered by the train tour company.

STEPS

QUICK TIP
You can also create a table by clicking the Table button in the Tables group on the Insert tab, then dragging over the table grid to create the size table you want.

QUICK TIP
Press [Tab] when the insertion point is in the last cell of a table to create a new row.

QUICK TIP
Change the height or width of any table cell by dragging its borders.

1. **Right-click Slide 7 in the Slides tab, click New Slide on the shortcut menu, click the title placeholder, then type Service Levels and Prices**
   A new slide with the Title and Content layout appears.
2. **Click the Insert Table icon, type 4 in the Number of columns text box, click the Number of rows text box, click the up arrow until 5 appears, then click OK**
   A formatted table with four columns and five rows appears on the slide, and the Table Tools Design tab opens on the Ribbon. The table has 20 cells. The insertion point is in the first cell of the table and is ready to accept text.
3. **Type Classic, press [Tab], type Deluxe, press [Tab], type Exclusive, press [Tab], type Royal, then press [Tab]**
   The text you typed appears in the top four cells of the table. Pressing [Tab] moves the insertion point to the next cell; pressing [Enter] moves the insertion point to the next line in the same cell.
4. **Enter the rest of the table information shown in Figure C-13**
   The table would look better if it were formatted differently.
5. **Click the More button in the Table Styles group, scroll to the bottom of the gallery, then click Medium Style 3 – Accent 2**
   The background and text color change to reflect the table style you applied.
6. **Click the upper-left cell, click the Table Tools Layout tab, click the Select button in the Table group, click Select Row, then click the Center button in the Alignment group**
   The text in the top row is centered horizontally in each cell.
7. **Click the Select button in the Table group, click Select Table, then click the Center Vertically button in the Alignment group**
   The text in the whole table is centered vertically within each cell. The table would look better if all the rows were the same height.
8. **Click the Distribute Rows button in the Cell Size group, click the Table Tools Design tab, then click the Effects button in the Table Styles group**
   The Table Effects gallery opens.
9. **Point to Cell Bevel, click Hard Edge (3rd row), press [Down arrow] three times, click a blank area of the slide, then save the presentation**
   The 3-D effect makes the cells of the table stand out. The table looks better nudged away from the slide title. Compare your screen with Figure C-14.

FIGURE C-13: Inserted table with data

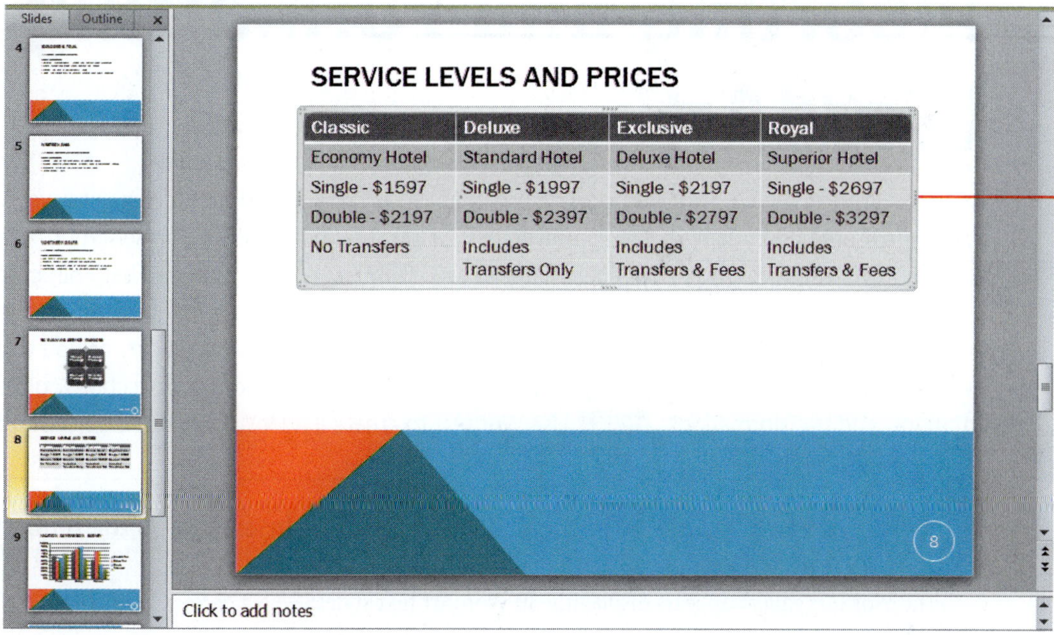

FIGURE C-14: Formatted table

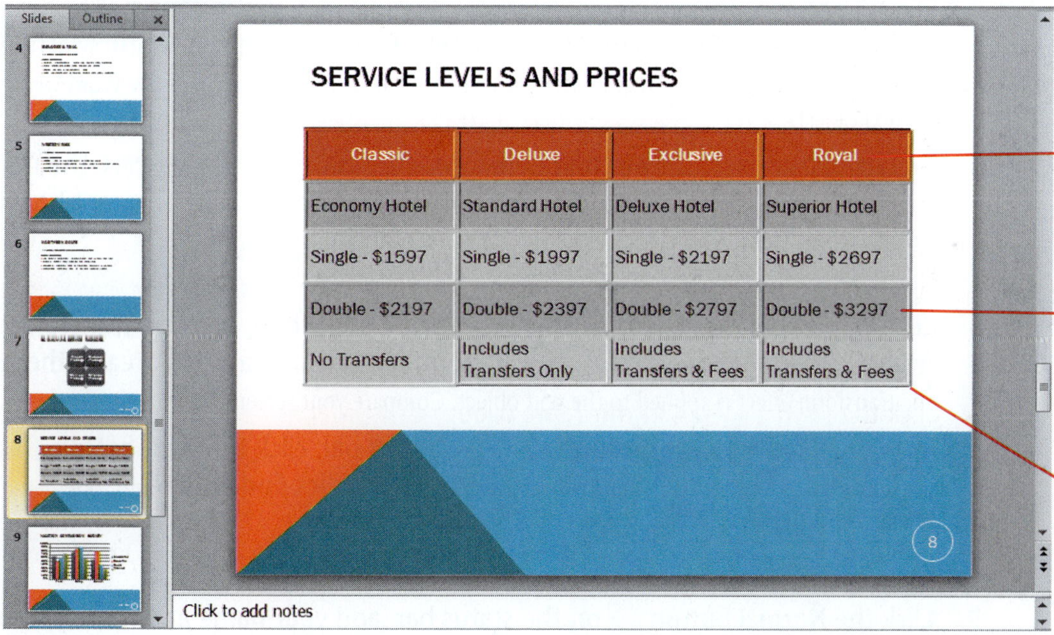

Drawing tables

Choose the slide where you want the table, click the Table button in the Tables group on the Insert tab, then click Draw Table. The pointer changes to ✎. Drag to define the boundaries of the table in the area of the slide where you want the table. A dotted outline appears as you draw. Next, you draw to create the rows and columns of your table. Click the Table Tools Design tab on the Ribbon, click the Draw Table button in the Draw Borders group, then draw lines for columns and rows. Be sure to draw within the boundary line of the table.

UNIT
C
PowerPoint 2010

Inserting and Formatting WordArt

As you work to create an interesting presentation, your goal should include making your slides visually appealing. Sometimes plain text can come across as dull and unexciting in a presentation. **WordArt** is a set of decorative text styles, or text effects, that you can apply to any text object to help direct the attention of your audience to a certain piece of information. You can use WordArt in two different ways: you can apply a WordArt text style to an existing text object that converts the text into WordArt, or you can create a new WordArt object. The WordArt text styles and effects include text shadows, reflections, glows, bevels, 3-D rotations, and transformations. Use WordArt to create a new WordArt text object on Slide 3.

STEPS

QUICK TIP
You can format any text with a WordArt style. Select the text, click the Drawing Tools Format tab on the Ribbon, then click a WordArt style option in the WordArt Styles group.

1. **Click the Slide 3 thumbnail in the Slides tab, click the Insert tab on the Ribbon, then click the WordArt button in the Text group**
   The WordArt gallery appears displaying 30 WordArt text styles.
2. **Click Fill – Ice Blue, Text 2, Outline – Background 2, (first style in the first row)**
   A text object appears in the middle of the slide displaying sample text with the WordArt style you just selected.
3. **Click the edge of the WordArt text object, then when the pointer changes to , drag the text object to the blank area of the slide**
4. **Click the More button in the WordArt Styles group, move your mouse over all of the WordArt styles in the gallery, then click Fill – Orange, Accent 2, Warm Matte Bevel**
   The WordArt Styles change the sample text in the WordArt text object. The new WordArt style is applied to the text object.
5. **Drag to select the text Your text here in the WordArt text object, click the Decrease Font Size button in the Mini toolbar until 40 appears in the Font Size text box, type Guaranteed best, press [Enter], then type vacation in Canada**
   The text is smaller and appears on two lines.
6. **Click the Text Effects button in the WordArt Styles group, point to Transform, click Triangle Down in the Warp section (first row), then click a blank area of the slide**
   The transform effect is applied to the text object. Compare your screen to Figure C-15.
7. **Click the Reading View button on the status bar, click the Next button until you reach Slide 10, click the Menu button , then click End Show**
8. **Click the Slide Sorter button on the status bar**
   Compare your screen with Figure C-16.
9. **Click the Normal button on the status bar, add your name as a footer to the notes and handouts, save your changes, submit your presentation to your instructor, then exit PowerPoint**

FIGURE C-15: WordArt inserted on slide

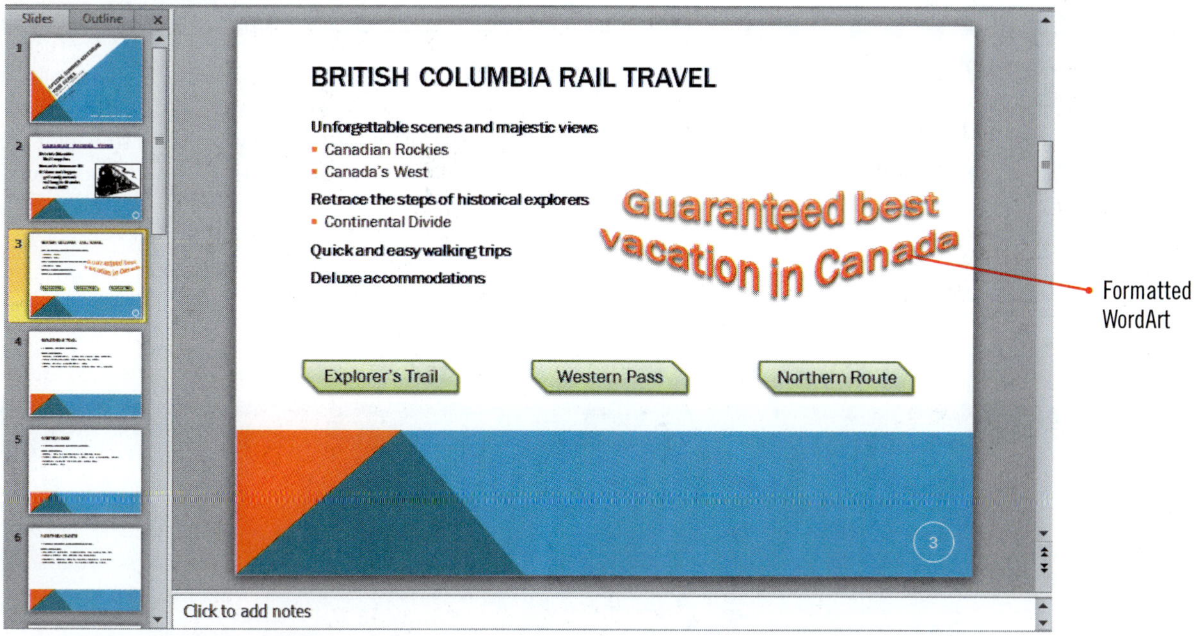

FIGURE C-16: Completed presentation in Slide Sorter view

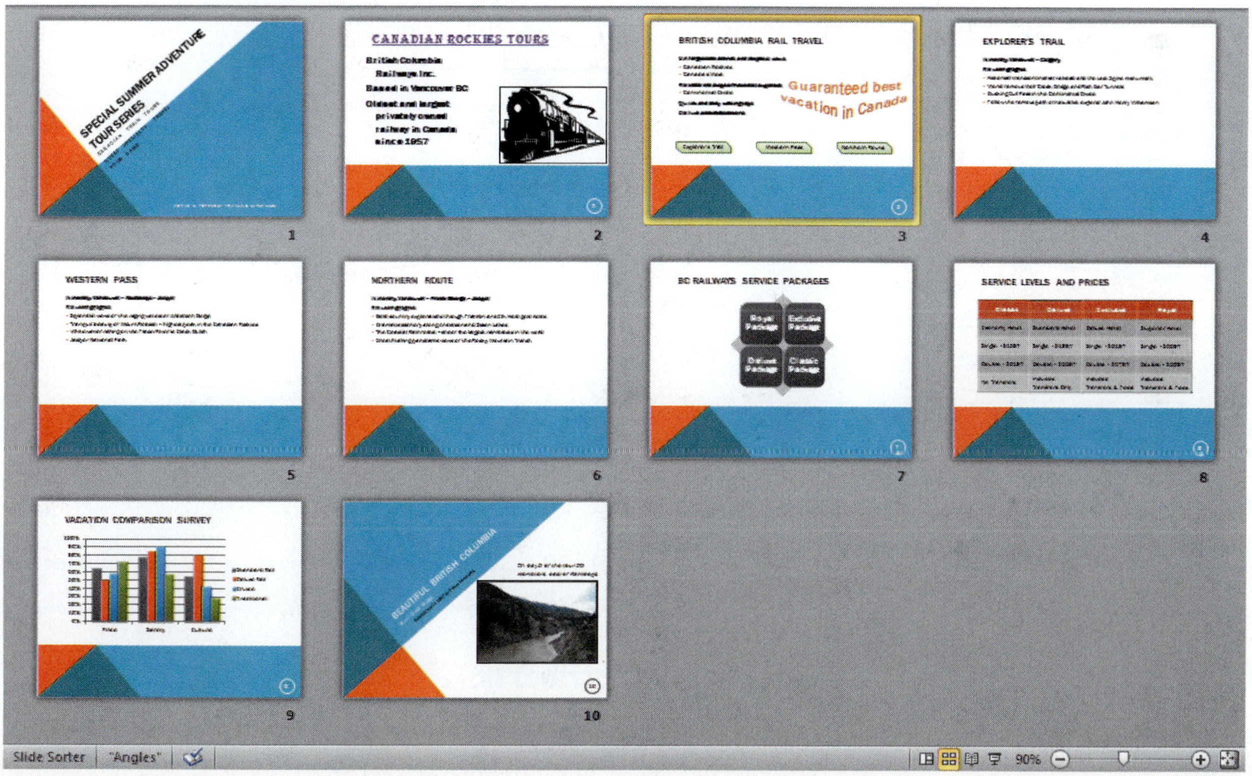

Saving a presentation as a video

You can save your PowerPoint presentation as a full-fidelity video, which incorporates all slide timings, transitions, animations, and narrations. The video can be distributed using a disc, the Web, or e-mail. Depending on how you want to display your video, you have three resolution settings from which to choose: Computer & HD Displays, Internet & DVD, and Portable Devices. The Large setting, Computer & HD Displays (960 × 720), is used for viewing on a computer monitor, projector, or other high definition displays. The Medium setting, Internet & DVD (640 × 480), is used for uploading to the Web or copying to a standard DVD. The Small setting, Portable Devices (320 × 240), is used on portable devices including portable media players such as Microsoft Zune. To save your presentation as a video, click the File tab, click Save & Send, click Create a Video, choose your settings, then click the Create Video button.

Practice

Concepts Review

For current SAM information, including versions and content details, visit SAM Central (http://www.cengage.com/samcentral). If you have a SAM user profile, you may have access to hands-on instruction, practice, and assessment of the skills covered in this unit. Since various versions of SAM are supported throughout the life of this text, check with your instructor for the correct instructions and URL/Web site for accessing assignments.

Label each element of the PowerPoint window shown in Figure C-17.

FIGURE C-17

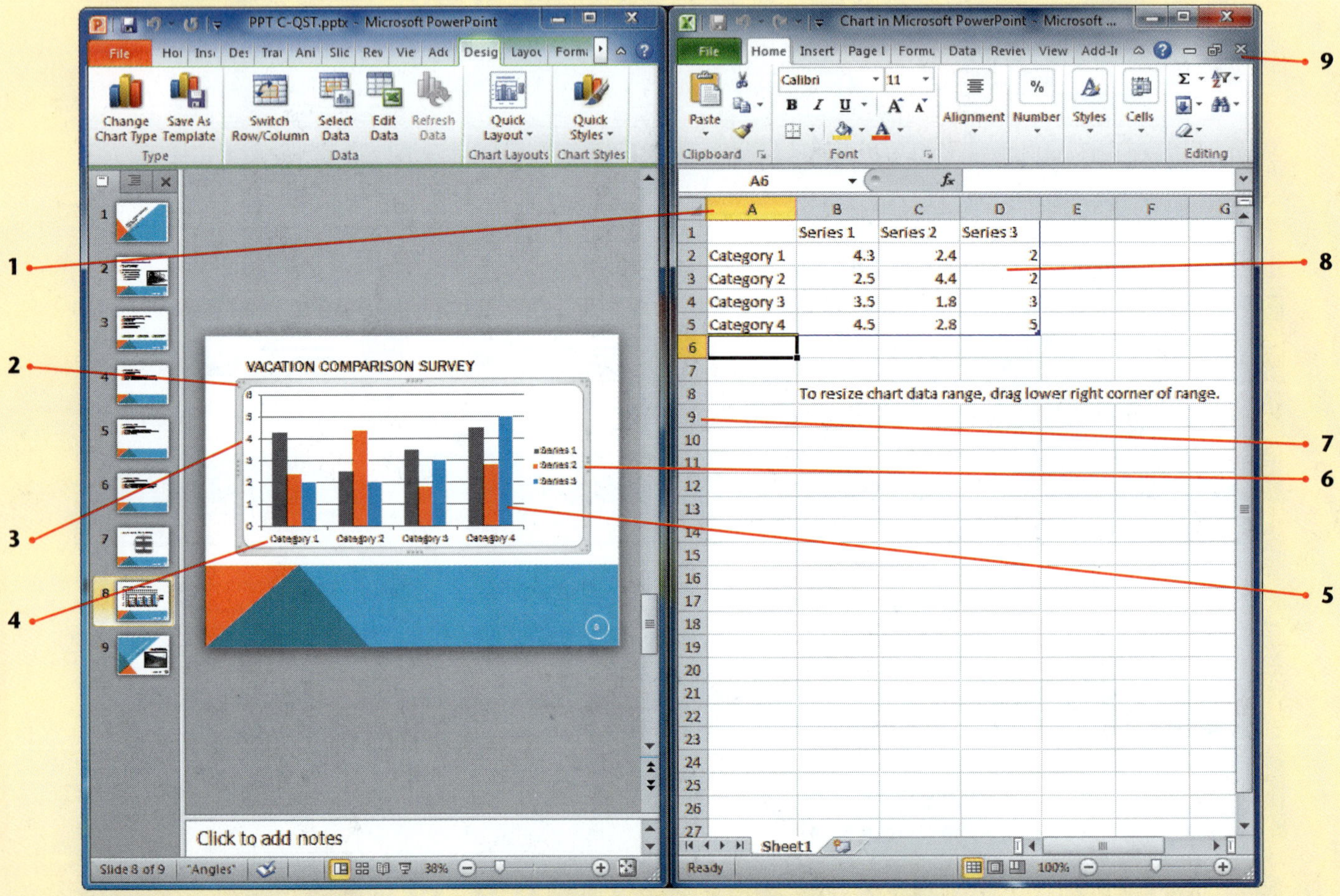

Match each term with the statement that best describes it.

10. Collection
11. Crop
12. Worksheet
13. Table
14. Template

a. Contains the numerical data displayed in a chart
b. The folder in the Clip Organizer that stores clip art
c. A presentation that is designed and formatted and usually comes with sample text
d. PowerPoint object that compares data in columns and rows
e. Hides a portion of a picture

Select the best answer from the list of choices.

15. What is the file index system that stores clip art, photographs, and movies called?
- **a.** Clip Art Index
- **b.** WordArt Gallery
- **c.** Microsoft Clip Organizer
- **d.** Office Media Collections

16. According to this unit, which media type is defined as line art or art work created in another program?
- **a.** Picture
- **b.** Clip art
- **c.** Video
- **d.** Animation

17. In PowerPoint, what is the graphical representation of data on a slide called?
- **a.** Table
- **b.** Worksheet
- **c.** Legend
- **d.** Chart

18. According to this unit, to compare data side by side, which of the following objects should you select?
- **a.** Table
- **b.** Chart
- **c.** Outline
- **d.** Grid

19. An object that has its own data source and becomes a part of your presentation after you insert it best describes which of the following?
- **a.** A Word outline
- **b.** An embedded object
- **c.** A WordArt object
- **d.** A table

20. A presentation designed and formatted with background elements, colors, and other graphic elements that you can use to create a new presentation is a ______________.
- **a.** template
- **b.** theme
- **c.** video
- **d.** gallery

21. Use ______________ to apply a set of decorative text styles or text effects to text.
- **a.** a template
- **b.** rich text format
- **c.** a collection
- **d.** WordArt

Skills Review

1. Insert text from Microsoft Word.

- **a.** Open the file PPT C-4.pptx from the drive and folder where you store your Data Files, then save it as **PPT C-Vista**. You will work to create the completed presentation as shown in Figure C-18.
- **b.** Click Slide 3 in the Slides tab, then use the Slides from Outline command to insert the file PPT C-5.docx from the drive and folder where you store your Data Files.
- **c.** In the Slides tab, drag Slide 5 above Slide 4.

FIGURE C-18

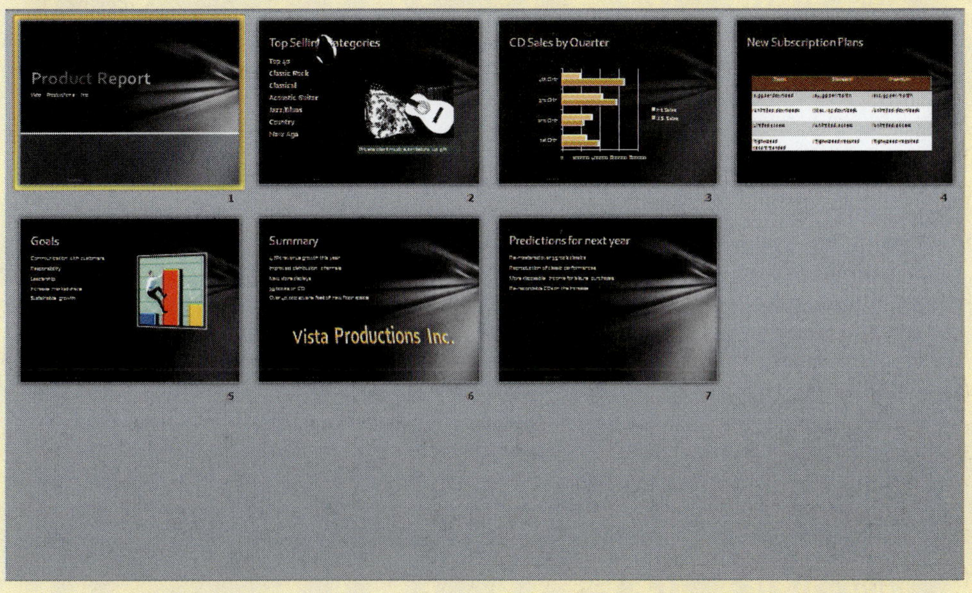

Skills Review (continued)

d. In the Slides tab, delete Slide 7, Expansion Potential.
e. Select Slides 4, 5, and 6 in the Slides tab, reset the slides to the default theme settings, then save your work.

2. Insert clip art.

a. Select Slide 4, then change the slide layout to the Two Content slide layout.
b. Press [Shift], click the text object, then change the font size to 18.
c. Click the clip art icon in the right content placeholder, search for clip art using the keywords **business goals**, insert the clip art shown in Figure C-18, then close the Clip Art task pane.
d. Click the Picture Border list arrow, change the color of the clip art border to White, Text 1.
e. Click the Picture Border list arrow, change the weight of the clip art border to 3 pt.
f. Click the Picture Effects button, point to 3-D Rotation, then click Perspective Left.
g. Drag the clip art so the top lines up with the top of the text object, then save your changes.

3. Insert and style a picture.

a. Select Slide 2, then insert the picture PPT C-6.jpg.
b. Completely crop the light blue section off the top of the picture, then crop the right side of the picture about 1/4 inch.
c. Drag the picture up so it is in the center of the blank area of the slide.
d. Click the Color button, then change the picture color to Black and White: 25%.
e. Save your changes.

4. Insert a text box.

a. On Slide 2, insert a text box below the picture.
b. Type **Private client submissions for music up 9%**.
c. Delete the word **for**, then drag the word **music** after the word **client**.
d. Select the text object, then click the More button in the Shape Styles group on the Drawing Tools Format tab.
e. Click Intense Effect – Green, Accent 6.
f. Center the text object under the picture.

5. Insert a chart.

a. Go to Slide 3, CD Sales by Quarter, click the Insert tab on the ribbon, click the Chart button in the Illustrations group, then insert a Clustered Bar chart.
b. Close Excel.

6. Enter and edit chart data.

a. Show the chart data.
b. Enter the data shown in Table C-2 into the worksheet.
c. Delete the data in each cell in Column D, then close Excel.
d. Change the chart style to Style 12 in the Chart Styles group.
e. Move the chart to the center of the blank area of the slide, then save your changes.

TABLE C-2

	U.S. Sales	Int. Sales
1st Qtr	390,957	263,902
2nd Qtr	229,840	325,854
3rd Qtr	585,063	435,927
4th Qtr	665,113	203,750

7. Insert a table.

a. Add a new slide after Slide 3 with the Title and Content layout.
b. Add the slide title **New Subscription Plans**.
c. Insert a table with three columns and five rows.
d. Enter the information shown in Table C-3, then change the table style to Medium Style 3 – Accent 3. (*Hint*: Use the Copy and Paste commands to enter duplicate information in the table.)
e. Center the text in the top row.
f. In the Table Tools Layout tab, distribute the table rows.
g. Move the table to the center of the blank area of the slide, then save your changes.

TABLE C-3

Basic	Standard	Premium
$.99 per download	$4.99 per month	$12.95 per month
Unlimited downloads	Max. 25 downloads	Unlimited downloads
Limited access	Unlimited access	Unlimited access
High-speed recommended	High-speed required	High-speed required

Skills Review (continued)

8. Insert and format WordArt.

- **a.** Go to Slide 6, then, insert a WordArt text object using the Fill – Brown, Accent 3, Outline – Text 2 style.
- **b.** Type **Vista Productions Inc.**, then apply the WordArt style Fill – Gold, Accent 2, Warm Matte Bevel.
- **c.** Apply the Inflate Top Transform effect (seventh row) to the text object, then move the text object to the middle of the blank area of the slide.
- **d.** View the presentation in Slide Show view, then check the spelling of the presentation.
- **e.** Add your name as a footer to all the slides, then save your changes.
- **f.** Submit your presentation to your instructor, close your presentation, and exit PowerPoint.

Independent Challenge 1

You are a financial management consultant for Goodrich & Young Investments LLP, located in Syracuse, New York. One of your responsibilities is to create standardized presentations on different financial investments for use on the company Web site. As part of the presentation for this meeting, you insert some clip art, add a text box, and insert a chart.

If you have a SAM 2010 user profile, an autogradable SAM version of this assignment may be available at http://www.cengage.com/sam2010. Check with your instructor to confirm that this assignment is available in SAM. To use the SAM version of this assignment, log into the SAM 2010 Web site and download the instruction and start files.

- **a.** Open the file PPT C-7.pptx from the drive and folder where you store your Data Files, then save it as **PPT C-Goodrich**.
- **b.** Add your name as the footer on all of the slides, then apply the Horizon Design Theme.
- **c.** Insert a clustered column chart on Slide 6, then enter the data in Table C-4 into the worksheet. Delete the unwanted placeholder data in the chart.
- **d.** Format the chart using Style 35, then move the chart down slightly away from the title text object.

TABLE C-4

	1 year	3 year	5 year	7 year
Bonds	2.2%	3.2%	3.9%	4.5%
Stocks	1.9%	2.2%	4.2%	3.6%
Mutual Funds	2.6%	4.0%	8.4%	6.4%

Advanced Challenge Exercise

ACE

- Click the Chart Tools Layout tab, click the Legend button, then click Show Legend at Top.
- Click the Chart Tools Format tab, then click the Chart Elements list arrow in the Current Selection group, then click Series "3 year."
- Click the Shape Fill list arrow in the Shape Styles group, then click Gold, Text 2, under Theme Colors.

- **e.** Insert clip art of a set of balance scales on Slide 2, then position and format as necessary. (*Hint*: Use the keyword **balance scales** to search for clips.)
- **f.** On Slide 3, use the Align command and Distribute command on the Drawing Tools Format tab in the Arrange group to align and distribute the objects so that the shapes are aligned on top and distributed horizontally.
- **g.** Check the spelling of the presentation, view the slide show, make any necessary changes, then save your work. See Figure C-19.
- **h.** Submit the presentation to your instructor, then close the presentation, and exit PowerPoint.

FIGURE C-19

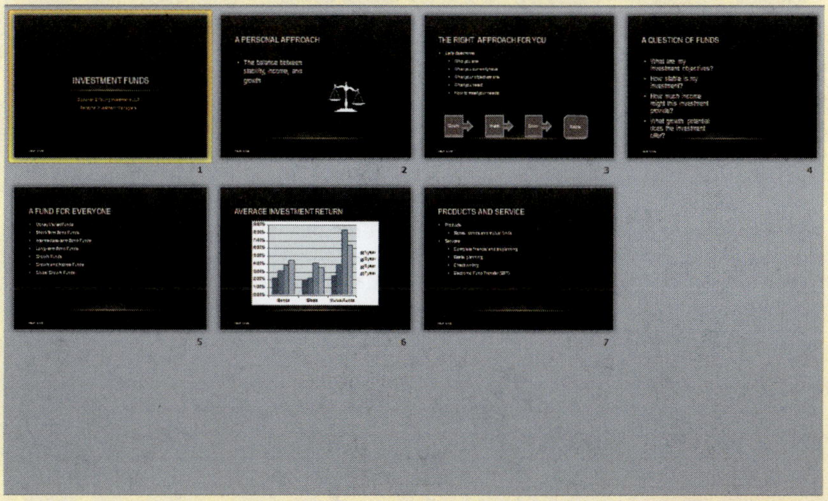

PowerPoint 2010

Independent Challenge 2

You work for Veil Home Systems, a company based in Michigan that provides integrated data, security, and voice command systems for homes. You have been asked to enhance a marketing presentation on a new product that the company is going to promote at a large trade fair in Las Vegas. You work on completing a presentation for the show. You insert some clip art, add a text box, and insert a chart.

a. Start PowerPoint, open the file PPT C-8.pptx from the drive and folder where you store your Data Files, and save it as **PPT C-Veil**.

b. Add your name and today's date to Slide 1 in the Subtitle text box.

c. Organize the objects on Slide 2 using the Align, Distribute, and Group commands. Add and format additional shapes to enhance the presentation.

d. On Slide 3, style the picture, recolor the picture, and use a picture effect.

e. Apply the Hardcover theme to the presentation.

f. Insert the Word document file PPT C-9.docx to create additional slides from an outline after Slide 2.

g. Select Slides 3 and 4, then reset the slides to their default settings.

h. Create a new slide after Slide 4, title the slide **Growth of Integrated Systems**, then insert a chart.

i. Enter the data in Table C-5, then format the chart using at least two formatting commands. Be able to name which formatting commands you applied to the chart.

TABLE C-5

	Last Yr.	Current Yr.	Next Yr.
Traditional	73	94	103
Integrated	15	36	55

j. Insert a text box on the Veil Home Systems slide (Slide 7). Create your own company contact and address information. Format the text box.

k. Check the spelling, then view the final slide show (refer to Figure C-20). Make any necessary changes.

l. Save the presentation, submit the presentation to your instructor, close the file, and exit PowerPoint.

FIGURE C-20

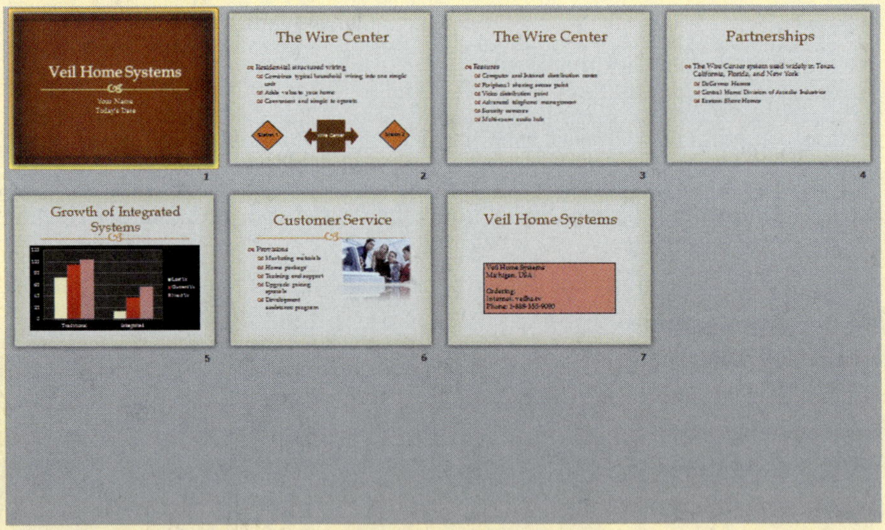

Independent Challenge 3

You work for LearnRight Inc. a company that produces instructional software to help people learn foreign languages. Once a year, LearnRight holds a meeting with their biggest client, the Department of State, to brief the government on new products and to receive feedback on existing products. Your boss has started a presentation and has asked you to look it over and add other elements to make it look better.

a. Start PowerPoint, open the file PPT C-10.pptx from the drive and folder where you store your Data Files, and save it as **PPT C-LearnRight**.

Independent Challenge 3 (continued)

b. Add an appropriate design theme to the presentation.

c. Insert the Word outline PPT C-11.docx after the Product Revisions slide, then reset Slides 5, 6, and 7 to the default settings.

d. Format the text so that the most important information is the most prominent.

e. Insert an appropriate table on a slide of your choice. Use your own information, or use text from a bulleted list on one of the slides.

f. Add at least two appropriate shapes that emphasize slide content. Format the objects using shape styles. If appropriate, use the Align, Distribute, and Group commands to organize your shapes.

Advanced Challenge Exercise (*Internet connection required*)

- Select a slide on which you want to add a clip art image. Open the Clip Art task pane, then click the Find more at Office.com link to go to the Office.com Web site.
- Download and insert an appropriate media clip from the Academic category. (*Hint*: Make sure you know the media clip's keywords; it will make searching for it in the Clip art task pane much easier.)
- Format the clip using Picture Tools Format tab.
- Be ready to explain how you formatted the clip.

g. Check the spelling and view the final slide show. Make any necessary changes.

h. Add your name as footer text on the notes and handouts, then save the presentation.

i. Submit your presentation to your instructor, close the file, then exit PowerPoint.

Real Life Independent Challenge

You are on the Foreign Exchange Commission at your college, and one of your responsibilities is to present information on past foreign student exchanges to different organizations on and off campus. You need to create a pictorial presentation that highlights a trip to a different country. Create a presentation using your own pictures or pictures given to you with permission by a friend.

Note: Three photographs (PPT C-12.jpg, PPT C-13.jpg, and PPT C-14.jpg) from Dijon, France, are provided to help you complete this Independent Challenge. You can use the provided photos if you have none of your own to use.

a. Start PowerPoint, create a new blank presentation, and save it as **PPT C-Exchange** to the drive and folder where you store your Data Files.

b. Locate and insert the pictures you want to use. Place one picture on each slide using the Content with Caption slide layout.

c. Add information about each picture in the text placeholder, and enter a slide title. If you use the pictures provided, research Dijon, France, using the Internet for relevant information to place on the slides (*Internet connection required*).

d. Apply an appropriate design theme, then apply an appropriate title and your name to the title slide.

e. Check the spelling, then view the final slide show (refer to Figure C-21).

f. Add a slide number and your class name as footer text to all of the slides, save your work, then submit your presentation to your instructor.

g. Close the file, and exit PowerPoint.

FIGURE C-21

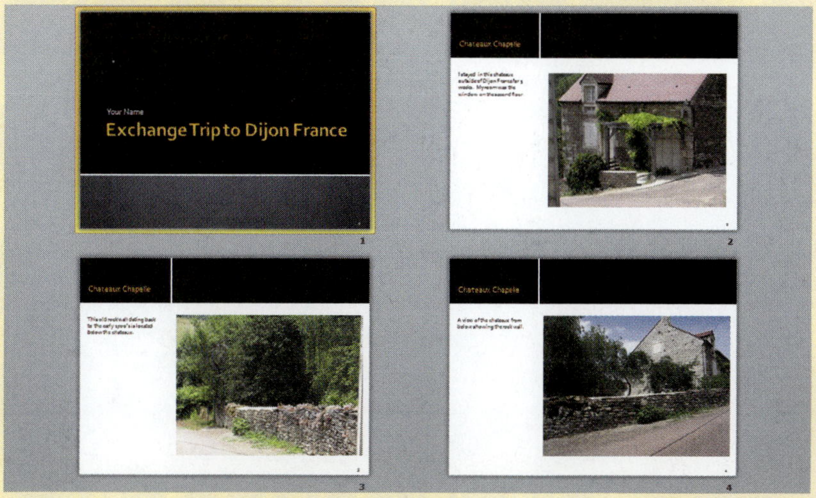

Visual Workshop

Create a one-slide presentation that looks like Figure C-22. The slide layout shown in Figure C-22 is a specific layout designed for pictures. Insert the picture file PPT C-15.jpg to complete this presentation. Add your name as footer text to the slide, save the presentation as **PPT C-Guide** to the drive and folder where you store your Data Files, check the spelling of the presentation, then submit your presentation to your instructor.

FIGURE C-22

UNIT D

PowerPoint 2010

Finishing a Presentation

Files You Will Need:

- PPT D-1.pptx
- PPT D-2.jpg
- PPT D-3.pptx
- PPT D-4.jpg
- PPT D-5.pptx
- PPT D-6.pptx
- PPT D-7.pptx

Though not required, having a consistent professional-looking theme throughout your presentation is best if you want to gain and retain your audience's interest in the subject you are presenting. PowerPoint helps you achieve a consistent look by providing ways to customize your slides' layout and background. Once you are finished working with the text and other objects of your presentation, you are ready to apply slide show effects, which determine the way the slides and objects on the slides appear in Slide Show view. You have reviewed the presentation and are pleased with the slides you created for the Quest Specialty Travel presentation. Now you are ready to finalize the look of the slides and add effects to make the presentation interesting to watch.

OBJECTIVES

- Modify masters
- Customize the background and theme
- Use slide show commands
- Set slide transitions and timings
- Animate objects
- Inspect a presentation
- Evaluate a presentation
- Create a template

Modifying Masters

Each presentation in PowerPoint has a set of **masters** that store information about the theme and slide layouts, including the position and size of text and content placeholders, fonts, slide background, color, and effects. There are three Master views: Slide Master view, Notes Master view, and Handout Master view. Changes made in Slide Master view are reflected on the slides in Normal view; changes made in Notes Master view are reflected in Notes Page view, and changes made in Handout Master view appear when you print your presentation using a handout printing option. The primary benefit to modifying a master is that you can make universal changes to your whole presentation instead of making individual repetitive changes to each of your slides. You want to add the QST company logo to every slide in your presentation, so you open your presentation and insert the logo to the slide master.

STEPS

1. **Start PowerPoint, open the presentation PPT D-1.pptx from the drive and folder where you store your Data Files, save the presentation as PPT D-QST, then click the View tab on the Ribbon**

   The title slide of the presentation appears.

2. **Click the Slide Master button in the Master Views group, scroll to the top of the slide thumbnail pane, then click the Angles Slide Master thumbnail (first thumbnail)**

   A new tab, the Slide Master tab, appears next to the Home tab on the Ribbon. The Slide Master view appears with the slide master displayed in the Slide pane as shown in Figure D-1. The slide master is the theme slide master (the Angles theme in this case). Each theme comes with its own associated slide masters. Each master text placeholder on the slide master identifies the font size, style, color, and position of text placeholders on the slides in Normal view. For example, the Master title placeholder positioned at the top of the slide uses a black, 28 pt, uppercase, Franklin Gothic Medium font. Slide titles use this font style and formatting. Design elements that you place on the slide master appear on every slide in the presentation. The slide layouts located below the slide master in the slide thumbnail pane follow the information on the slide master. All changes you make to the slide master, including font changes, are reflected in all of the slide layouts.

> **QUICK TIP**
> You can press and hold [Shift] and click the Normal button on the status bar to display the slide master.

3. **Point to the slide layouts in the slide thumbnail pane, then click the Two Content Layout thumbnail**

   As you point to each slide layout, a ScreenTip appears identifying each slide layout by name and lists if any slides in the presentation are using the layout. Slides 2, 5, 7, and 9 are using the Two Content Layout.

> **QUICK TIP**
> When working with slide layouts, you can right-click the thumbnail to open a shortcut list of commands.

4. **Click the Angles Slide Master thumbnail (first thumbnail), click the Insert tab on the Ribbon, then click the Picture button in the Images group**

   The Insert Picture dialog box opens.

5. **Select the picture file PPT D-2.jpg from the drive and folder where you store your Data Files, then click Insert**

   The QST graphic logo appears on the slide master and will appear on all slides in the presentation. The graphic is too large and needs to be repositioned on the slide.

6. **Click 1.61" in the Shape Width text box in the Size group, type 1, press [Enter], drag the graphic to the upper-left corner of the slide, then click a blank area of the slide**

   The graphic snaps into the corner of the slide.

7. **Click the Slide Master tab on the Ribbon, then click the Preserve button in the Edit Master group**

   Preserving the selected master assures that the Angles slide master remains with this presentation even if you eventually use another master. Compare your screen to Figure D-2.

8. **Click the Normal button on the status bar, then save your changes**

FIGURE D-1: Slide Master view

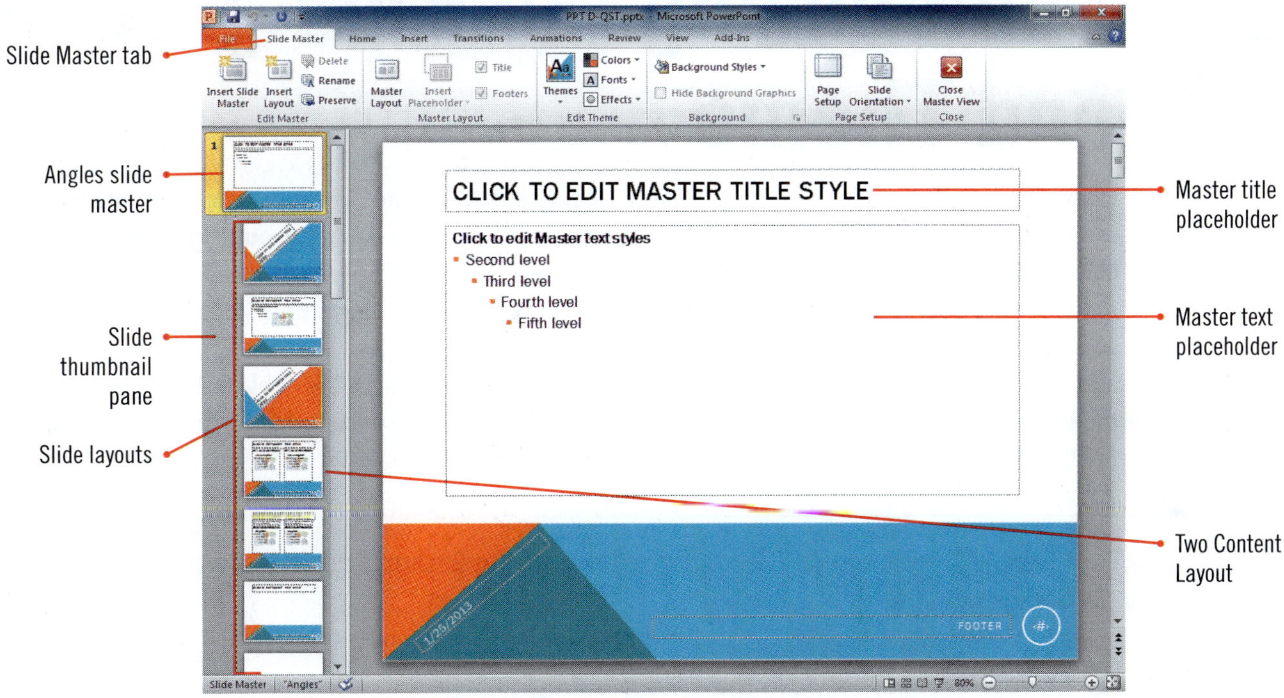

FIGURE D-2: Graphic added to slide master

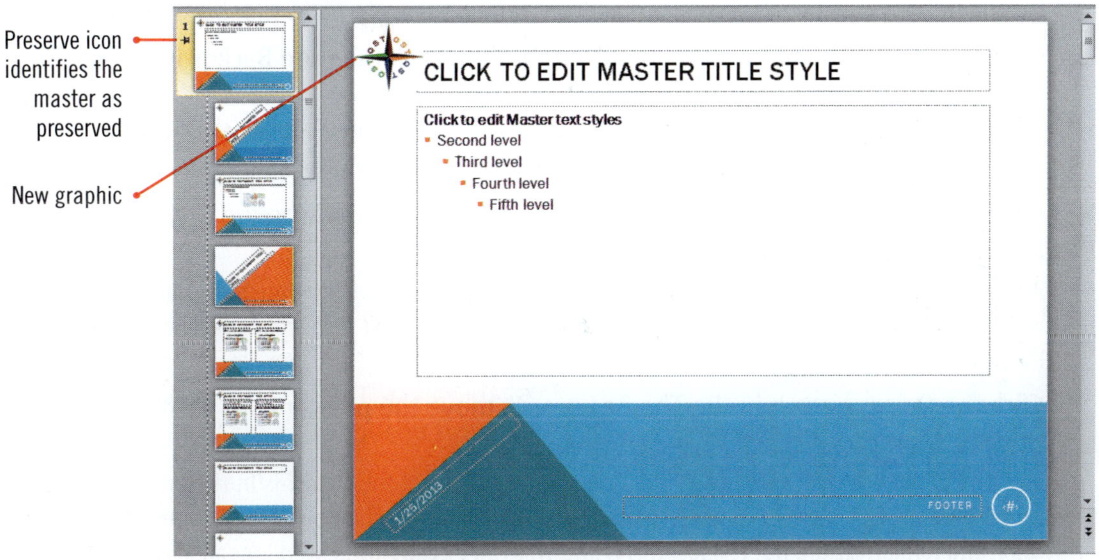

Create custom slide layouts

As you work with PowerPoint, you may find that you need to develop a customized slide layout. For example, you may need to create presentations for a client that has slides that display four pictures with a caption underneath each picture. To make everyone's job easier, you can create a custom slide layout that includes only the placeholders that you need. To create a custom slide layout, open Slide Master view, and then click the Insert Layout button in the Edit Master group. A new slide layout appears in the slide thumbnail pane. You can choose to add several different placeholders including Content, Text, Picture, Chart, Table, SmartArt, Media, and Clip Art. Click the Insert Placeholder list arrow in the Master Layout group, click the placeholder you want to add, drag + to create the placeholder, then position the placeholder on the slide. In Slide Master view, you can add or delete placeholders in any of the slide layouts. You can rename a custom slide layout by clicking the Rename button in the Edit Master group and entering a descriptive name to better identify the layout.

Customizing the Background and Theme

Every slide in a PowerPoint presentation has a **background**, the area behind the text and graphics. You modify the background to enhance the slides using images and color. A **background graphic** is an object placed on the slide master. You can quickly change the background appearance by applying a background style, which is a set of color variations derived from the theme colors. Theme colors determine the colors for all slide elements in your presentation, including slide background, text and lines, shadows, fills, accents, and hyperlinks. Every PowerPoint theme has its own set of theme colors. See Table D-1 for a description of the theme colors. The QST presentation needs some design enhancements. You decide to modify the background of the slides by changing the theme colors and fonts.

STEPS

1. **Click the Design tab on the Ribbon, then click the Background Styles button in the Background group**

   A gallery of background styles opens. Review the different backgrounds using Live Preview.

2. **Move over each style in the gallery, then click Style 2**

   Figure D-3 shows the new background on Slide 1 of the presentation and the other slides in the Slides tab. Even though you are working in Normal view, the new background style is applied to the slide master and slide layouts. The new background style does not appear over the whole slide, which indicates there are background items on the slide master preventing you from seeing the entire slide background.

3. **Click the Slide 2 thumbnail in the Slides tab, then click the Hide Background Graphics check box in the Background group**

   All of the background items (the QST graphic and colored shapes at the bottom of the slide) are hidden from view, and only the text objects, slide number, and train clip remain visible.

4. **Click the Hide Background Graphics check box, click the Background Styles button in the Background group, then click Style 1**

   All of the background items and the white background appear again. The white background color you started with actually looks the best. Theme colors that better match the QST logo would look better than the current theme colors.

5. **Click the Colors button in the Themes group, move the pointer over each of the built-in themes, then click Aspect**

   The new theme colors are applied to the slide master and all of the elements in the presentation including background items, tables, the SmartArt graphic on Slide 4, and the chart on Slide 11. Notice the title text font, color, and formatting did not change; this is known as an **exception**. Exceptions are changes that you make directly to text on the slide, which do not match the theme fonts on the slide master.

6. **Click the Slide 4 thumbnail in the Slides tab, click the Effects button in the Themes group, move the pointer over each of the built-in themes, then click Elemental**

   Notice how the new theme effects change the SmartArt graphic. Like the theme colors, the new theme effects are applied to the slide master and to all of the slides in the presentation.

7. **Click the Slide 5 thumbnail in the Slides tab, click the Fonts button in the Themes group, move the pointer over each of the built-in themes, click Composite, then save your work**

   The new theme fonts are applied to the presentation. Compare your screen to Figure D-4.

QUICK TIP

To apply a new background style to only selected slides, select the slides on the Slides tab or in Slide Sorter view, right-click the background style in the Background Styles gallery, then click Apply to Selected Slides.

QUICK TIP

To create custom theme colors, click the Colors button, then click Create New Theme Colors. You can also create custom theme fonts by clicking the Fonts button, then clicking Create New Theme Fonts.

FIGURE D-3: Slide with new background style applied

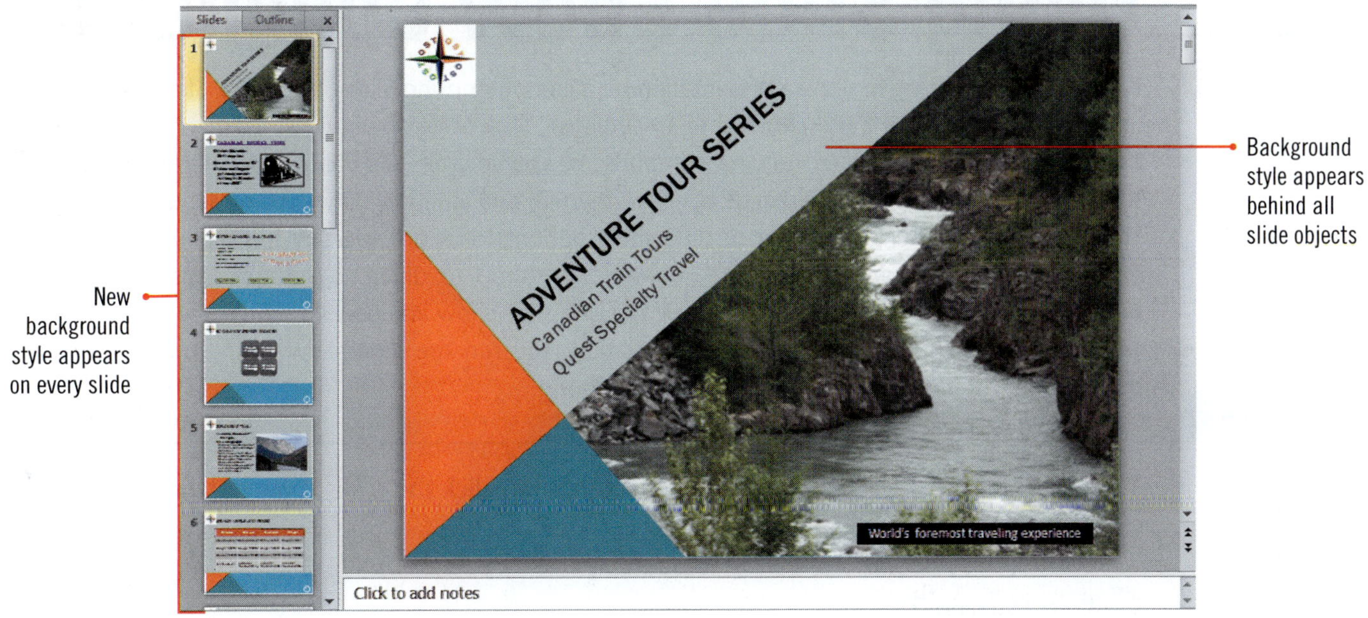

FIGURE D-4: Slide showing new theme colors and theme fonts

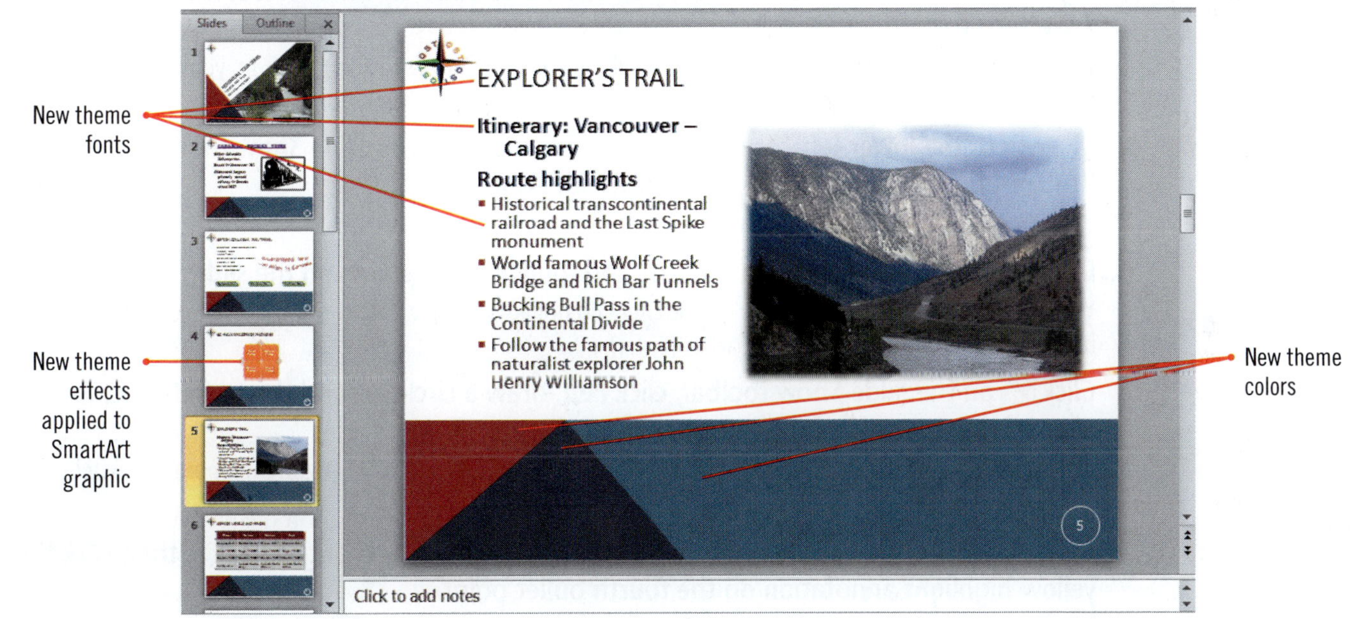

TABLE D-1: Theme colors

color element	description
Text/Background colors	Contrasting colors for typed characters and the slide background
Accent colors	There are six accent colors used for shapes, drawn lines, and text; the shadow color for text and objects and the fill and outline color for shapes are all accent colors; all of these colors contrast appropriately with background and text colors
Hyperlink color	Colors used for hyperlinks you insert
Followed Hyperlink color	Color used for hyperlinks after they have been clicked

UNIT D

PowerPoint 2010

Using Slide Show Commands

With PowerPoint, you can show a presentation on a computer using Slide Show view. Slide Show view is used primarily to deliver a presentation to an audience, either over the Internet using your computer or through a projector connected to your computer. As you've seen, Slide Show view fills your computer screen with the slides of the presentation, showing them one at a time. Once the presentation is in Slide Show view, you can use a number of slide show options to tailor the show to meet your needs. For example, you can draw, or **annotate**, on slides or jump to different slides in other parts of the presentation. You want to learn how to run a slide show and use the slide show options so you will be prepared when you give your presentation. You run the slide show of the presentation and practice using some of the custom slide show options.

STEPS

1. **Click the Slide 1 thumbnail in the Slides tab, then click the Slide Show button on the status bar**

   The first slide of the presentation fills the screen.

2. **Press [Spacebar]**

   Slide 2 appears on the screen. Pressing [Spacebar] or clicking the left mouse button is the easiest way to move through a slide show. See Table D-2 for other Slide Show view keyboard commands. You can also use the Slide Show shortcut menu for on-screen navigation during a slide show.

QUICK TIP

During a slide show you can also type the slide number, then press [Enter] to jump to a slide.

3. **Right-click anywhere on the screen, point to Go to Slide on the shortcut menu, then click 7 Western Pass**

   The slide show jumps to Slide 7. You can highlight or emphasize major points in your presentation by annotating the slide during a slide show using one of PowerPoint's annotation tools.

TROUBLE

The Slide Show toolbar buttons are semitransparent and blend in with the background color on the slide.

4. **Move to the lower-left corner of the screen to display the Slide Show toolbar, click the Pen Options menu button, then click Highlighter**

   The pointer changes to the highlighter pointer.

5. **Drag to highlight the text in the first and fourth bullet points on the slide**

   While the annotation tool is visible, mouse clicks do not advance the slide show; however, you can still move to the next slide by pressing [Spacebar] or [Enter].

6. **Click on the Slide Show toolbar, click Pen, draw a circle around the train tunnel in the picture, then press [Esc]**

   Pressing [Esc] or [Ctrl][A] while using an annotation pointer (pen pointer or highlighter pointer) switches the pointer back to . Compare your screen to Figure D-5.

7. **Click on the Slide Show toolbar, click Eraser, the pointer changes to , then click the yellow highlight annotation on the fourth bullet point**

   The annotation is erased.

8. **Press [Esc], click , then click Erase All Ink on Slide**

   The annotations on Slide 7 are erased. You also have the option of saving annotations you don't delete in Slide Show view when you quit the slide show. Saved annotations appear as drawn objects in Normal view.

QUICK TIP

To temporarily hide your slide during a slide show, right-click the screen, point to Screen, then click Black Screen or White Screen.

9. **Click the Slide Show menu button on the Slide Show toolbar, point to Go to Slide, then click 1 Adventure Tour Series on the menu**

   Slide 1 appears.

10. **Press [Enter] to advance through the slide show, then when you see a black slide, press [Spacebar]**

    The black slide indicates the end of the slide show, and you are returned to Slide 1 in Normal view.

FIGURE D-5: Slide 7 in Slide Show view showing annotations

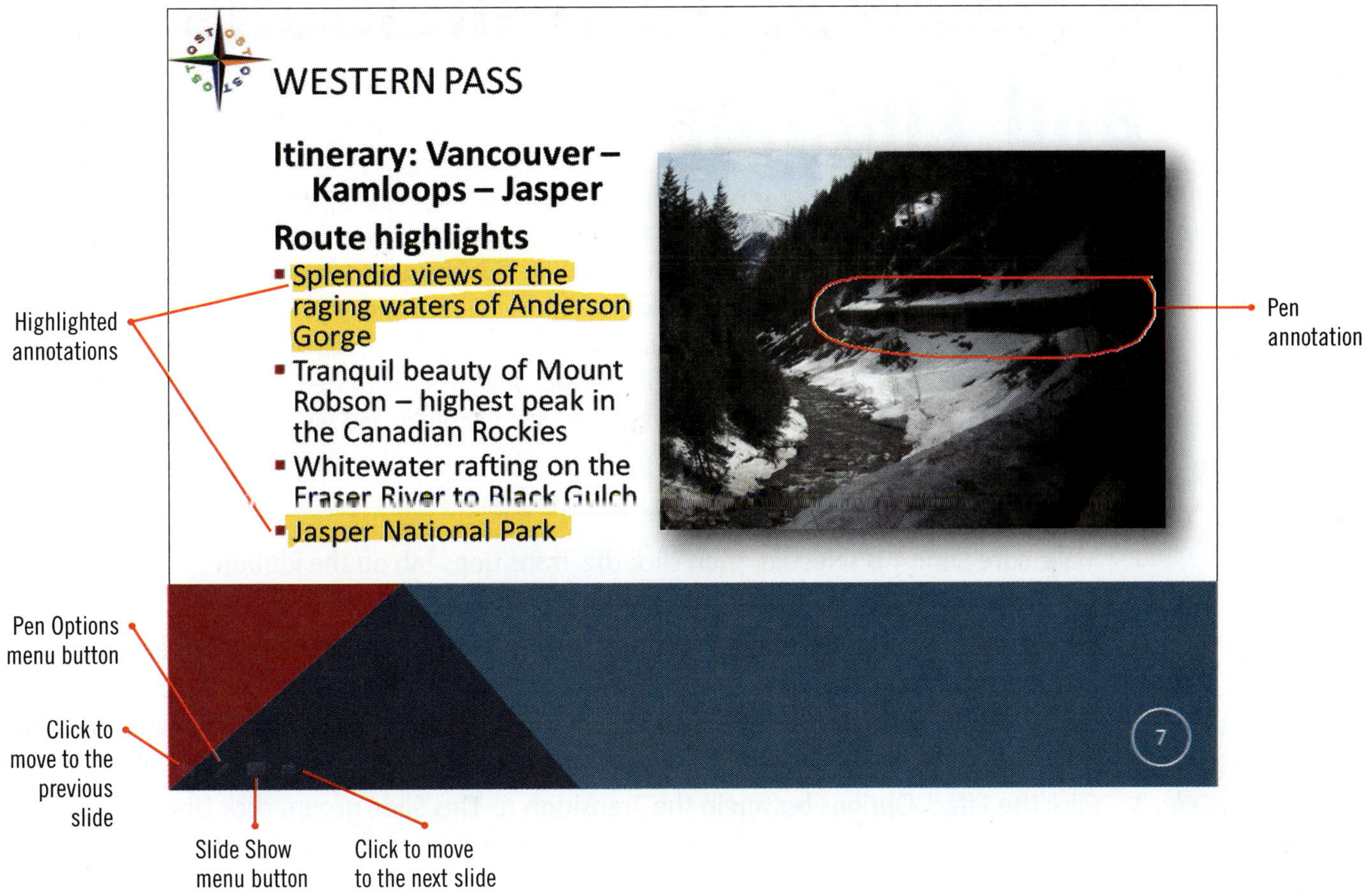

TABLE D-2: Basic slide show keyboard commands

keyboard commands	description
[Enter], [Spacebar], [PgDn], [N], [down arrow], or [right arrow]	Advances to the next slide
[E]	Erases the annotation drawing
[Home], [End]	Moves to the first or last slide in the slide show
[H]	Displays a hidden slide
[up arrow] or [PgUp]	Returns to the previous slide
[W]	Changes the screen to white; press again to return
[S]	Pauses the slide show; press again to continue
[B]	Changes the screen to black; press again to return
[Ctrl][M]	Shows or hides annotations on the slide
[Ctrl][A]	Changes pointer to 
[Esc]	Stops the slide show

UNIT D

PowerPoint 2010

Setting Slide Transitions and Timings

In a slide show, you can specify how each slide advances in and out of view, and for how long each slide appears on the screen. **Slide transitions** are the special visual and audio effects you apply to a slide that determine how it moves on and off the screen during the slide show. **Slide timing** refers to the amount of time a slide is visible on the screen. Typically, you only set slide timings if you want the presentation to automatically progress through the slides during a slide show. Setting the correct slide timing, in this case, is important because it determines how much time your audience has to view each slide. Each slide can have a different slide timing. You decide to set slide transitions and seven-second slide timings for all the slides.

STEPS

1. **Make sure Slide 1 is selected, then click the Transitions tab on the Ribbon**
   Transitions are organized by type into three groups.
2. **Click the More button in the Transition to This Slide group, then click Glitter in the Exciting section**
   The new slide transition plays on the slide, and a transition icon appears next to the slide thumbnail in the Slides tab as shown in Figure D-6. You can customize the slide transition by changing its direction and speed.
3. **Click the Effect Options button in the Transition to This Slide group, click Diamonds from Top, click the Duration down arrow in the Timing group until 2.00 appears, then click the Preview button in the Preview group**
   The Glitter slide transition now plays from the top of the slide for 2.00 seconds. You can apply this transition with the custom settings to all of the slides in the presentation.
4. **Click the Apply To All button in the Timing group, then click the Slide Sorter button on the status bar**
   All of the slides now have the customized Glitter transition applied to them as identified by the transition icons located below each slide. You also have the ability to determine how slides progress during a slide show—either manually by mouse click or automatically by slide timing.
5. **Click the On Mouse Click check box under Advance Slide in the Timing group to clear the check mark**
   This clears the option that manually advances slides during a slide show. You can set both manual and automatic slide timings within the same presentation, which is why you need to clear the manual option. Now you can set an automatic slide timing.
6. **Click the After up arrow until 00:07.00 appears in the text box, then click the Apply To All button**
   The timing between slides is 7 seconds as indicated by the time under each slide in Slide Sorter view. See Figure D-7. When you run the slide show, each slide will remain on the screen for 7 seconds. You can override a slide's timing and speed up the slide show by pressing [Spacebar], [Enter], or clicking the left mouse button.
7. **Click the Slide Show button on the status bar, then watch the slide show advance automatically**
8. **When you see the black slide at the end of the slide show, press [Spacebar], then save your changes**
   The slide show ends and returns to Slide Sorter view with Slide 1 selected.

QUICK TIP
You can add a sound that plays with the transition from the Sound list arrow in the Timing group.

QUICK TIP
Click the transition icon under any slide in Slide Sorter view to see its transition play.

FIGURE D-6: Applied slide transition

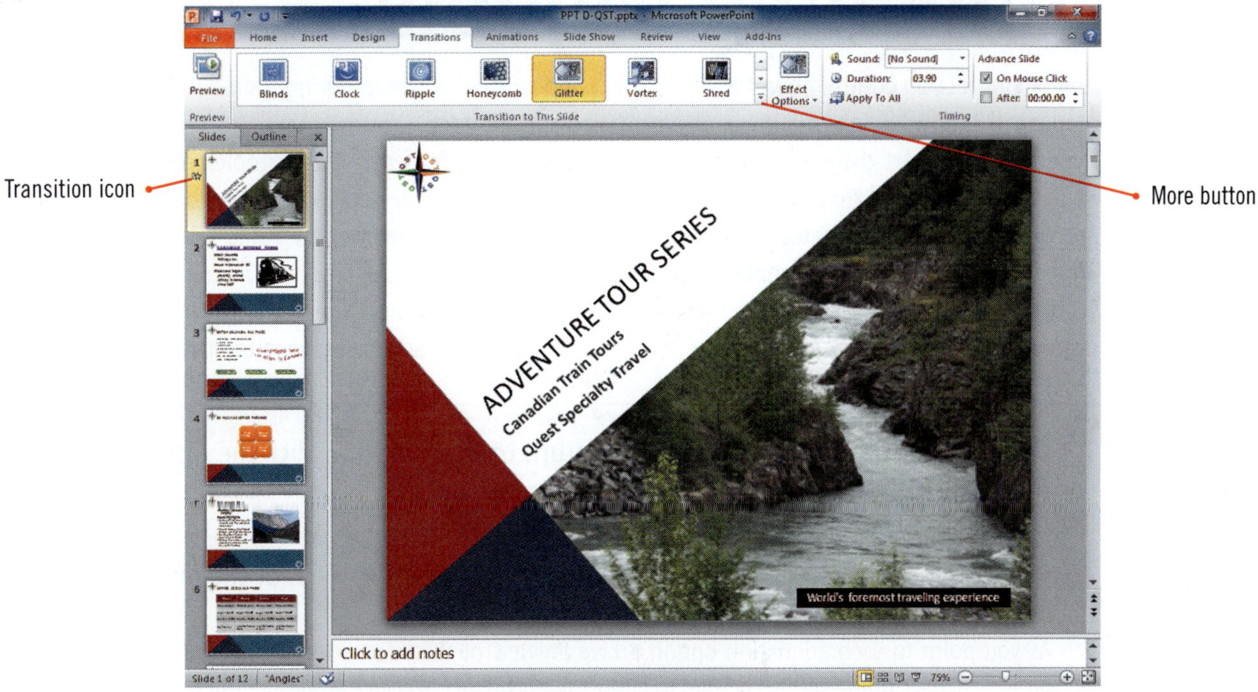

FIGURE D-7: Slide Sorter view showing applied transition and timing

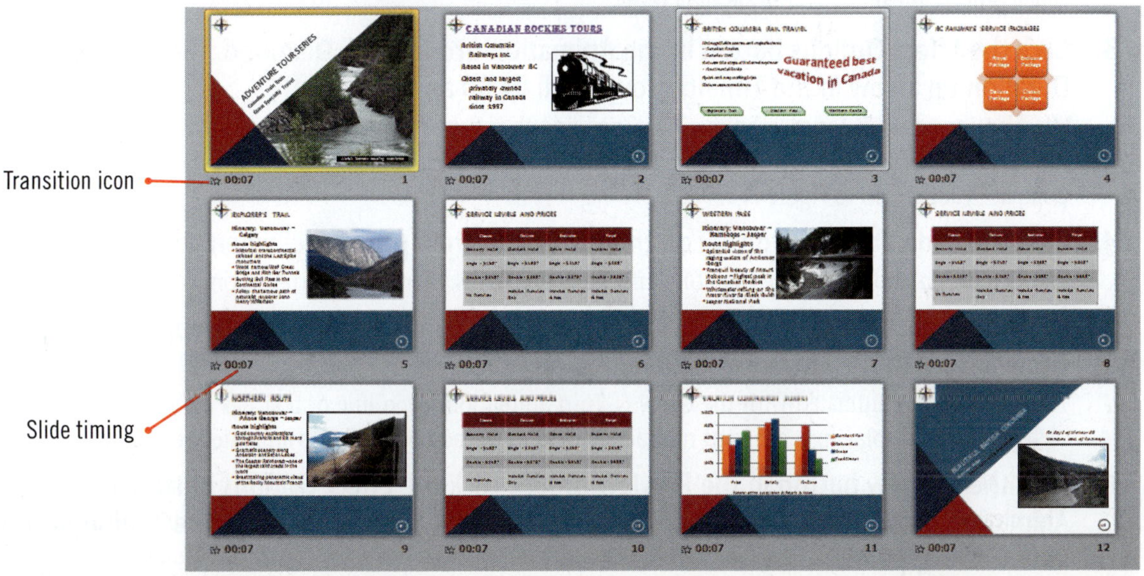

Rehearsing slide show timings

You can set different slide timings for each slide. For example, you can have the title slide appear for 20 seconds, the second slide for 1 minute, and so on. You can set timings by clicking the Rehearse Timings button in the Set Up group on the Slide Show tab. Slide Show view opens and the Recording toolbar shown in Figure D-8 opens. It contains buttons to pause between slides and to advance to the next slide. After opening the Recording toolbar, practice giving your presentation. PowerPoint keeps track of how long each slide appears and sets the timing accordingly. When you are finished rehearsing, PowerPoint displays the total recorded time for the presentation. The next time you run the slide show, you can use the timings you rehearsed.

FIGURE D-8: Recording toolbar

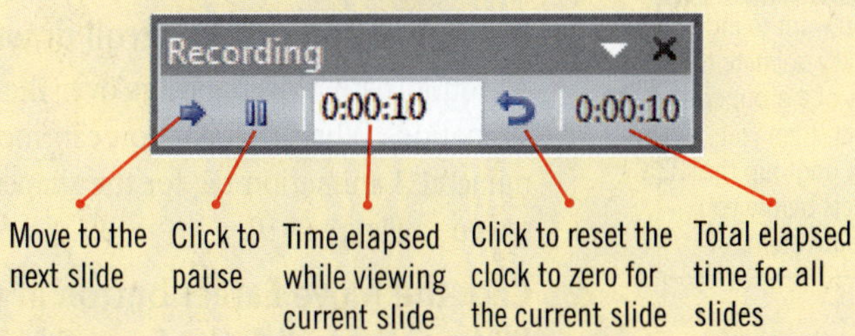

PowerPoint 2010

UNIT
D
PowerPoint 2010

Animating Objects

Animations let you control how objects and text appear on the screen during a slide show and allow you to manage the flow of information and emphasize specific facts. You can animate text, pictures, sounds, hyperlinks, SmartArt diagrams, charts, and individual chart elements. For example, you can apply a Fade animation to bulleted text so that each paragraph enters the slide separately from the others. Animations are organized into four categories, Entrance, Emphasis, Exit, and Motion Paths. The Entrance and Exit animations cause an object to enter or exit the slide with an effect. An Emphasis animation causes an object visible on the slide to have an effect and a Motion Path animation causes an object to move on a specified path on the slide. You animate the text and graphics of several slides in the presentation.

STEPS

1. **Double-click the Slide 1 thumbnail to return to Normal view, click the Animations tab on the Ribbon, then click the river picture**
   Text as well as other objects, like a picture, can be animated during a slide show.

QUICK TIP
There are additional animation options for each animation category located at the bottom of the animations gallery.

2. **Click the More button in the Animation group, point to each of the animation options in the gallery, then click Shape in the Entrance section**
   As you point to each animation option a Live Preview of the effect plays. Animations can be serious and business-like or humorous, so be sure to choose appropriate effects for your presentation. A small numeral 1, called an animation tag 1, appears at the top corner of the picture. **Animation tags** identify the order in which objects are animated during slide show.

3. **Click the Effect Options button in the Animation group, click Diamond, then click the Duration up arrow in the Timing group until 04.00 appears**
   Effect options change for each animation. Changing the shape of the animation to diamond complements the shape of the picture, and increasing the duration of the animation gives it a more dramatic effect. Compare your screen to Figure D-9.

4. **Click the Slide Show button on the status bar, then press [Esc] when you see Slide 3**
   The Shape animation, with the Diamond effect, which begins after the slide transition, is active on Slide 1.

5. **On Slide 3, click the bulleted list text object, click in the Animation group, then click Grow & Turn in the Entrance section**
   The text object is animated with the Grow & Turn animation. Each line of text has an animation tag with each paragraph displaying a different number. Accordingly, each paragraph is animated separately.

6. **Click the Preview button in the Preview group, click the Effect Options button in the Animation group, click All at Once, then click the Duration up arrow in the Timing group until 02.50 appears**
   Notice that the animation tags for each line of text in the text object now have the same numeral (1), indicating that each line of text animates at the same time.

QUICK TIP
If you want to individually animate the parts of a grouped object, then you must ungroup the objects before you animate them.

7. **Press [Shift], click the shapes object at the bottom of the slide, release [Shift], click in the Animation group, scroll down, then click Loops in the Motion Paths section**
   A motion path object appears over the shapes object and identifies the direction and shape, or path, of the animation. When needed, you can move, resize, and change the direction of the motion path. Notice the numeral 2 animation tag for the shapes object indicating it is animated *after* the text object. Compare your screen to Figure D-10.

8. **Click the Move Earlier button in the Timing group, click the Slide Show tab on the Ribbon, then click the From Beginning button in the Start Slide Show group**
   The slide show begins from Slide 1. The animations make the presentation more interesting to view.

9. **When you see the black slide, press [Spacebar], then save your changes**

FIGURE D-9: Slide showing animation applied to picture

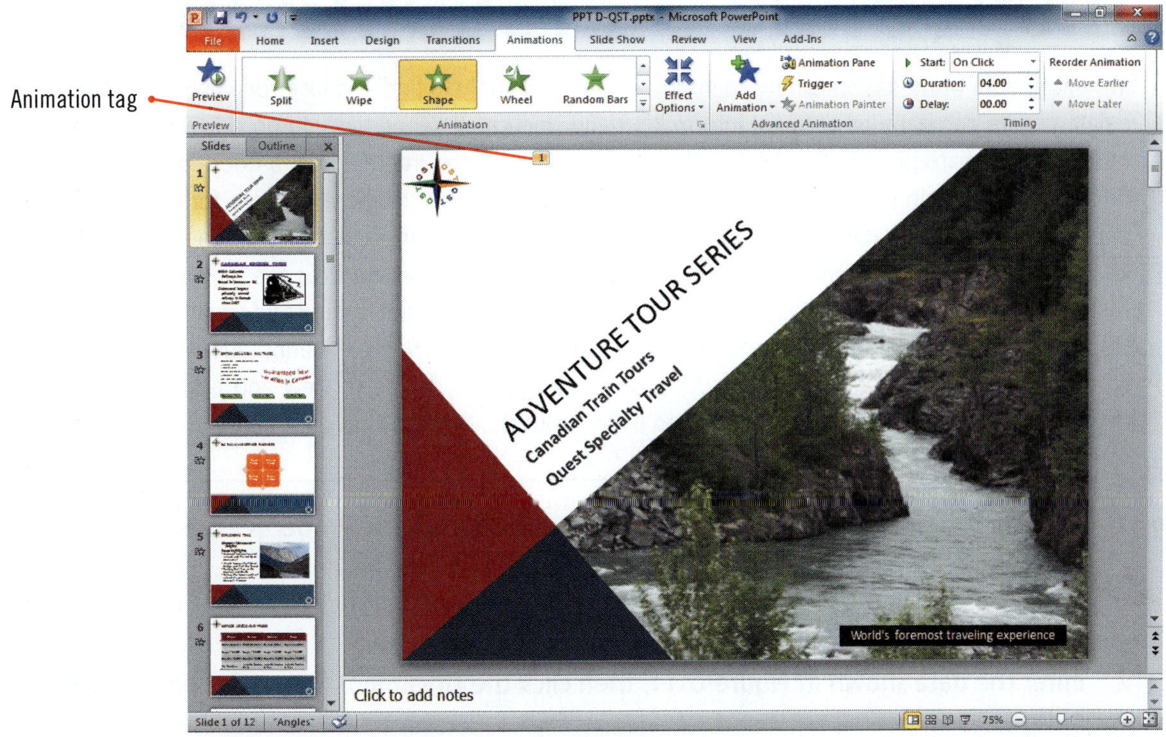

FIGURE D-10: Screen showing animated shapes object

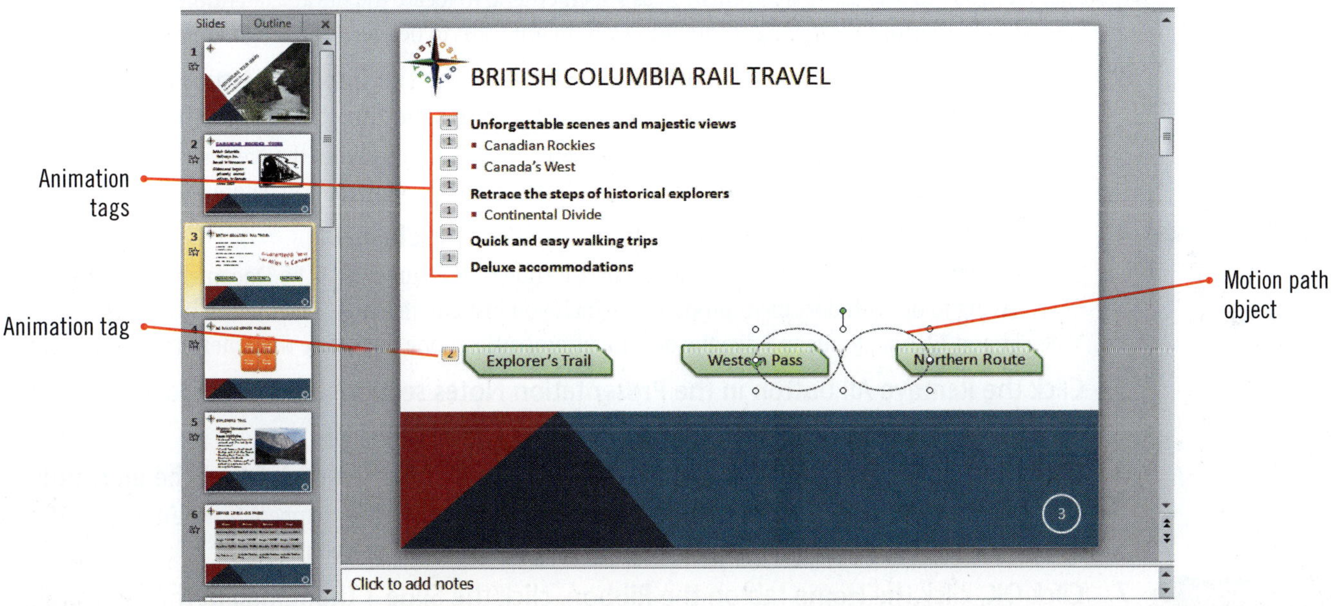

Presentation checklist

You should always rehearse your slide show. If possible, rehearse your presentation in the room and with the computer that you will use. Use the following checklist to prepare for the slide show:

- Is PowerPoint or PowerPoint Viewer installed on the computer?
- Is your presentation file on the hard drive of the computer you will be using? Try putting a shortcut for the file on the desktop. Do you have a backup copy of your presentation file on a removable storage device, like a flash drive?
- Is the projection device working correctly? Can the slides be seen from the back of the room?
- Do you know how to control **room lighting** so the audience can see both your slides and their handouts and notes? You may want to designate someone to control the lights if the controls are not close to you.
- Will the **computer** be situated so you can advance and annotate the slides yourself? If not, designate someone to advance them for you.
- Do you have enough copies of your **handouts**? Bring extras. Decide when to hand them out, or whether you prefer to have them waiting at the audience members' seats when they enter.

Inspecting a Presentation

Reviewing your presentation can be an important step, not only to find and fix errors, but also to locate and delete private company or personal information and document properties you do not want to share with others. If you share presentations with others, especially over the Internet, it is a good idea to inspect the presentation file using the Document Inspector. The **Document Inspector** looks for hidden data and personal information that is stored in the file itself or in the document properties. Document properties, also known as **metadata**, includes specific data about the presentation, such as the author's name, subject matter, title, who saved the file last, and when the file was created. Other types of information the Document Inspector can locate and remove include presentation notes, comments, ink annotations, invisible on-slide content, off-slide content, and custom XML data. You decide to view and add some document properties, inspect your presentation file, and learn about the Mark as Final command.

STEPS

QUICK TIP
Click the Properties button, then click Advanced Properties to open the Properties dialog box to see or change more document properties.

1. **Click the File tab on the Ribbon, with Info selected, click the Properties button in the right pane, then click Show Document Panel**
   The Document Properties pane opens showing the file location and the title of the presentation. Now enter some descriptive data for this presentation file.
2. **Enter the data shown in Figure D-11, then click the Document Properties pane Close button**
   This data provides detailed information about the presentation file that you can use to identify and organize your file. You can also use this information as search criteria to locate the file at a later time. You now use the Document Inspector to search for information you might want to delete in the presentation.
3. **Click the File tab on the Ribbon, with Info selected, click the Check for Issues button in the center pane, click Inspect Document, then click Yes to save the changes to the document**
   The Document Inspector dialog box opens. The Document Inspector searches the presentation file for six different types of information that you might want removed from the presentation before sharing it.

QUICK TIP
If you need to save a presentation to run in an earlier version of PowerPoint, check for unsupported features using the Check Compatibility feature.

4. **Make sure all of the check boxes are selected, then click Inspect**
   The presentation file is reviewed, and the results are shown in Figure D-12. The Document Inspector found items having to do with document properties, which you just entered, and presentation notes, which are on Slides 11 and 12. You decide to leave the document properties alone but delete the notes for all of the slides.
5. **Click the Remove All button in the Presentation Notes section, then click Close**
   All notes are removed from the Notes pane for the slides in the presentation.
6. **Click the Protect Presentation button, click Mark as Final, then click OK in the alert box**
   A message box opens. Be sure to read the message to understand what happens to the file and how to recognize a marked-as-final presentation. You decide to complete this procedure.

QUICK TIP
Presentations marked as final in PowerPoint 2010 are not read-only if they are opened in earlier versions of PowerPoint.

7. **Click OK, click the Home tab on the Ribbon, click the Slide 1 thumbnail in the Slides tab, then click anywhere in the title text object**
   Notice in Figure D-13 that the Ribbon is no longer displayed and an information alert box notes that the presentation is marked as final, making it a read-only file. A **read-only** file is one that can't be edited or modified in any way. Anyone who has received a read-only presentation can only edit the presentation by changing its marked-as-final status. You still want to work on the presentation, so you remove the marked-as-final status.
8. **Click the Edit Anyway button in the information alert box, then save your changes**
   The Ribbon and all commands are active again, and the file can now be modified.

FIGURE D-11: Properties pane

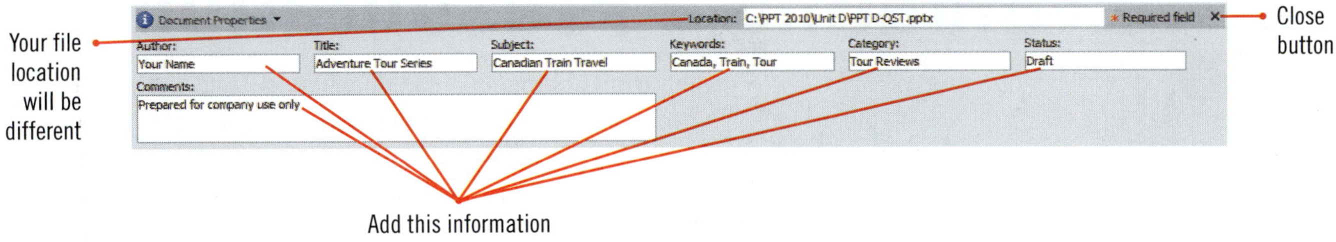

FIGURE D-12: Document Inspector dialog box

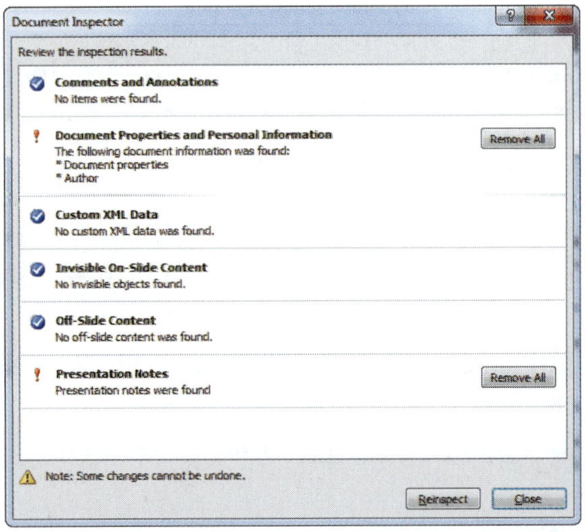

FIGURE D-13: Marked as final presentation

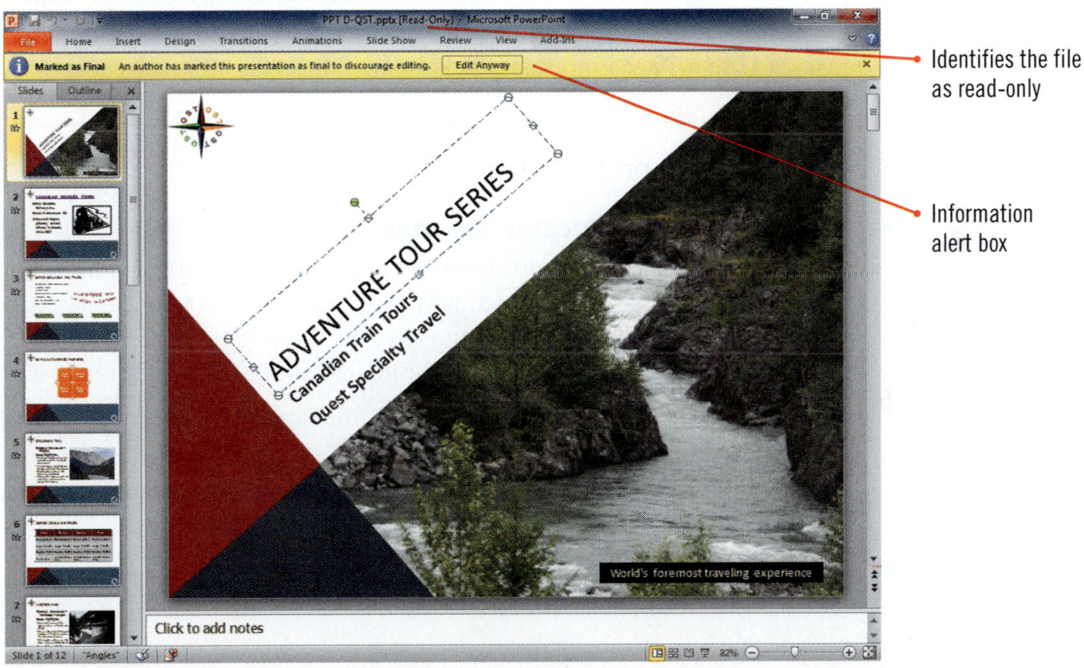

Digitally sign a presentation

What is a digital signature, and why would you want to use one in PowerPoint? A **digital signature** is similar to a hand-written signature in that it authenticates your document; however, a digital signature, unlike a hand-written signature, is created using computer cryptography and is not visible within the presentation itself. There are three primary reasons you would add a digital signature to a presentation: one, to authenticate the signer of the document; two, to assure that the content of the presentation has not been changed since it was signed; and three, to assure the origin of the signed document. To add a digital signature, click the File tab on the Ribbon, click the Protect Presentation button, click Add a Digital Signature, then follow the dialog boxes.

PowerPoint 2010

UNIT
D
PowerPoint 2010

Evaluating a Presentation

A well-designed and organized presentation requires thought and preparation. An effective presentation is focused and visually appealing—easy for the speaker to present and simple for the audience to understand. Visual elements can strongly influence the audience's attention and can influence the success of your presentation. See Table D-3 for general information on the impact a visual presentation has on an audience. You know your boss and other colleagues will critique your presentation, so you take the time to evaluate your presentation's organization and effectiveness.

STEPS

1. **Click the Reading View button on the status bar, then press [Spacebar] when the slide show finishes**
2. **Click the Slide 5 thumbnail in the Slides tab, click the Section button in the Slides group, then click Add Section**

   Two new sections appear in the Slides tab, the section you created, called the Untitled Section and a section for all the slides before the new section, called the Default Section. Sections help you organize your slides into logical groups.
3. **Right-click Untitled Section in the Slides tab, click Rename Section, type Tour Packages, then click Rename**
4. **Click the Slide Sorter view button on the status bar, save your work, then compare your screen to Figure D-14**
5. **Double-click Slide 1, add your name to the notes and handouts footer, evaluate your presentation according to the guidelines below, submit your presentation to your instructor, then close the presentation**

   Figure D-15 shows a poorly designed slide. Contrast this slide with guidelines below and your presentation.

QUICK TIP

You can also move, delete, collapse, and expand a section in the Slides tab or in Slide Sorter view.

DETAILS

When evaluating a presentation, it is important to:

- **Keep your message focused and your text concise**

  Don't put every point you plan to say on your slides. Keep the audience anticipating explanations to the key points in the presentation. Limit each slide to six words per line and six lines per slide. Use bulleted lists to help prioritize your points visually. Your presentation text should only provide highlights of your message. Supplement the information on your slides with further explanation and details during your presentation.

- **Keep the design simple, easy to read, and appropriate for the content**

  A design theme makes the presentation consistent. If you design your own layout, keep it simple and use design elements sparingly. Use similar design elements consistently throughout the presentation; otherwise, your audience may get confused.

- **Choose attractive colors that make the slide easy to read**

  Use contrasting colors for slide background and text to make the text readable. If you are giving an on-screen presentation, you can use almost any combination of colors that look good together.

- **Choose fonts and styles that are easy to read and emphasize important text**

  As a general rule, use no more than two fonts in a presentation and vary the font size, using nothing smaller than 24 points. Use bold and italic attributes selectively.

- **Use visuals to help communicate the message of your presentation**

  Commonly used visuals include clip art, photographs, charts, worksheets, tables, and videos. Whenever possible, replace text with a visual, but be careful not to overcrowd your slides. White space on your slides is okay!

FIGURE D-14: The final presentation in Slide Sorter view

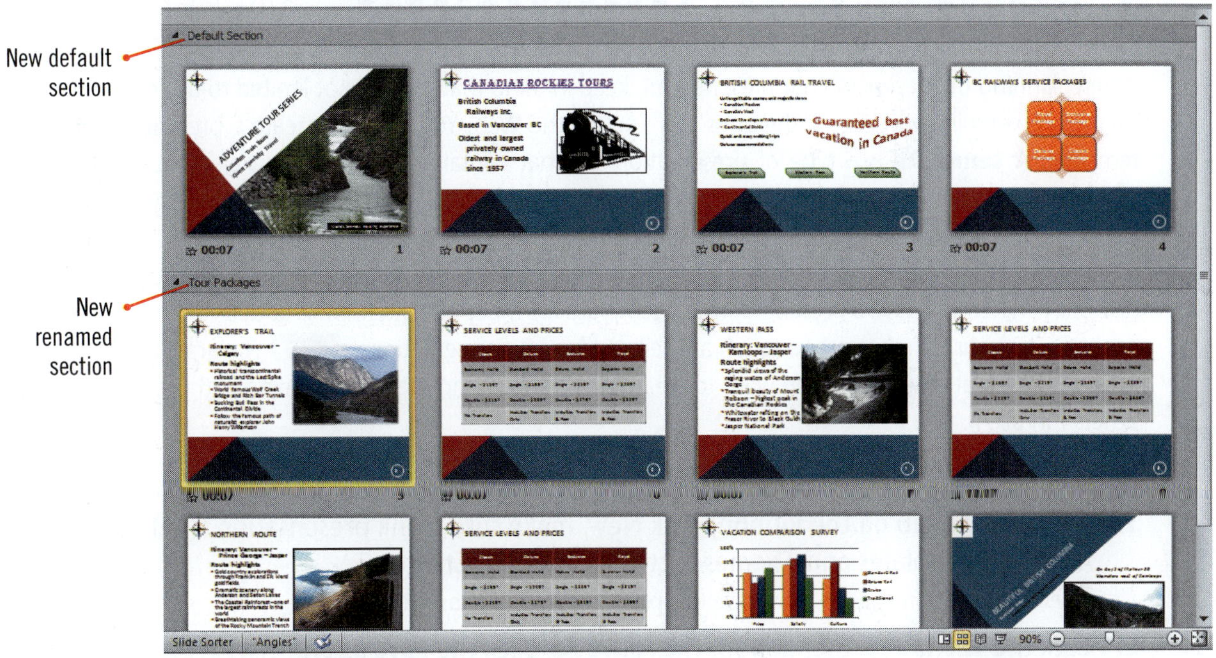

FIGURE D-15: A poorly designed slide

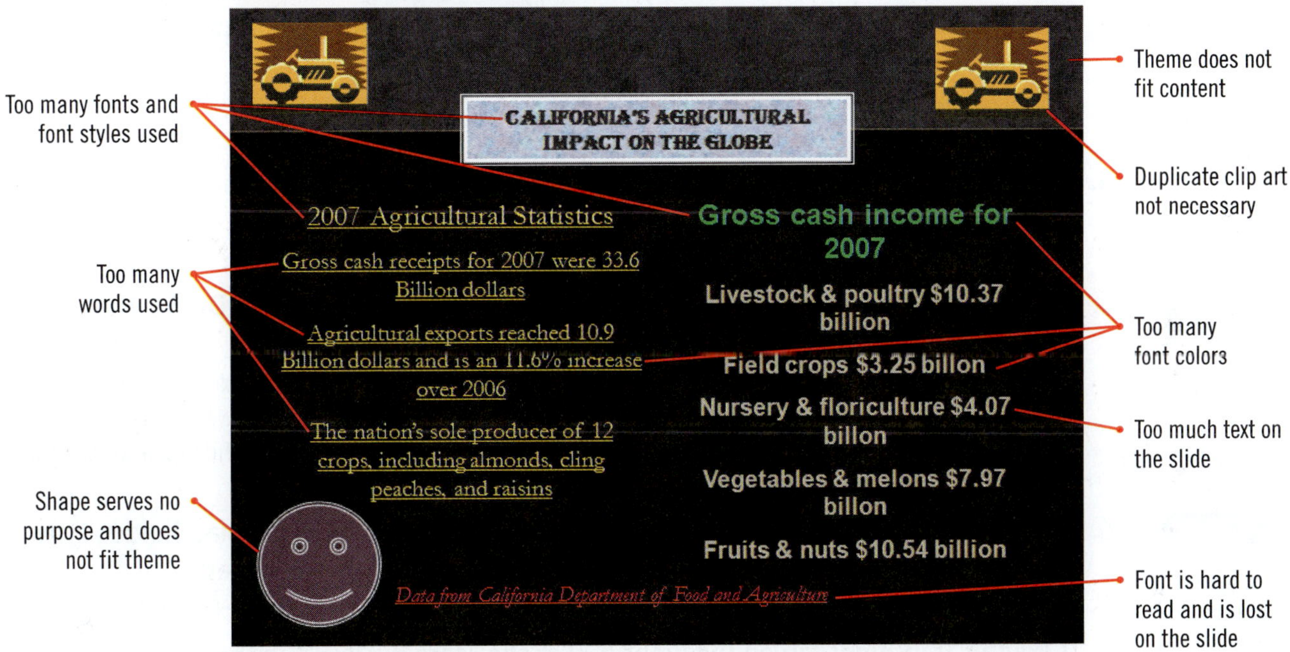

TABLE D-3: Audience impact from a visual presentation

impact	description
Visual reception	75% of all environmental stimuli is received through visual reception
Learning	55% of what an audience learns comes directly from visual messages
Retention	Combining visual messages with verbal messages can increase memory retention by as much as 50%
Presentation goals	You are twice as likely (67%) to achieve your communication objectives using a visual presentation
Meeting length	You are likely to decrease the average meeting length by 26.8% when you use a visual presentation

Source: Presenters Online, www.presentersonline.com

Creating a Template

When planning the design of your presentation, keep in mind that you are not limited to using the standard themes PowerPoint provides or the ones you find on the Web. You can also create a presentation using a template. A **template** is a type of presentation file that contains custom design elements on the slide master, background, slide layouts, and a theme, and can include graphics and content. You can create a new template from a blank presentation, or you can modify an existing PowerPoint presentation and save it as a template. If you modify an existing presentation, you can modify or delete any color, graphic, or font as necessary. When you save a presentation as a template file the .potx extension is added to the filename. You can then use your template presentation as the basis for new presentations. You are finished working on your presentation for now. You want to create a template using the design theme of this presentation so others can use it.

STEPS

1. **Click the File tab on the Ribbon, click New, make sure Blank presentation is selected in the Available Templates and Themes section, then click Create**
   A new presentation appears. Now save this presentation as a template.
2. **Click the File tab on the Ribbon, click Save As, click the Save as type list arrow, then click PowerPoint Template (*.potx)**
   Because this is a template, PowerPoint automatically opens the Templates folder on your hard drive.

> **QUICK TIP**
> Presentations saved to the Templates folder appear in the Recent templates folder. To locate this folder, click the File tab on the Ribbon, click New, then click Recent templates.

3. **Locate the drive and folder where you store your Data Files, click to select the default filename Presentation 1 in the File name text box, type PPT D-QST Template as shown in Figure D-16, then click Save**
   The presentation is saved as a PowerPoint template to the drive and folder where you store your Data Files, and the new template presentation appears in the PowerPoint window.
4. **Click the Design tab on the Ribbon, click the More button in the Themes group, then click Browse for Themes**
   The Choose Theme or Themed Document dialog box opens.
5. **Locate the drive and folder where you store your Data Files, click PPT D-QST, then click Apply**
   The design theme, including slide transitions and slide timings, from the presentation PPT D-QST is applied to the PPT D-QST Template presentation. All slide master elements, including slide layouts, colors, shapes, fonts, and background elements from the PPT D-QST presentation are applied over the existing design theme of the PPT D-QST Template presentation.

> **QUICK TIP**
> To quickly replace a word you have typed with a common synonym, right-click the word, then point to Synonyms on the shortcut menu.

6. **Click the title text placeholder, type QST Template, click the subtitle placeholder, type Standard Company Use Template – Your Name, then save your changes**
   You don't need to keep the slide transitions and slide timings that were applied from the PPT D-QST presentation.
7. **Click the Transitions tab on the Ribbon, click the More button in the Transition to This Slide group, click None, click the After check box in the Timing group, then click the Apply to All button in the Timing group**
   The slide transitions and slide timing are removed from the presentation.
8. **Click the View tab, click the Slide Sorter button in the Presentation Views group, then drag the Zoom Slider all the way to the right**
   Figure D-17 shows the final template presentation in Slide Sorter view.
9. **Double-click Slide 1, save your work, submit your presentation to your instructor, close the presentation, then exit PowerPoint**

FIGURE D-16: Save As dialog box

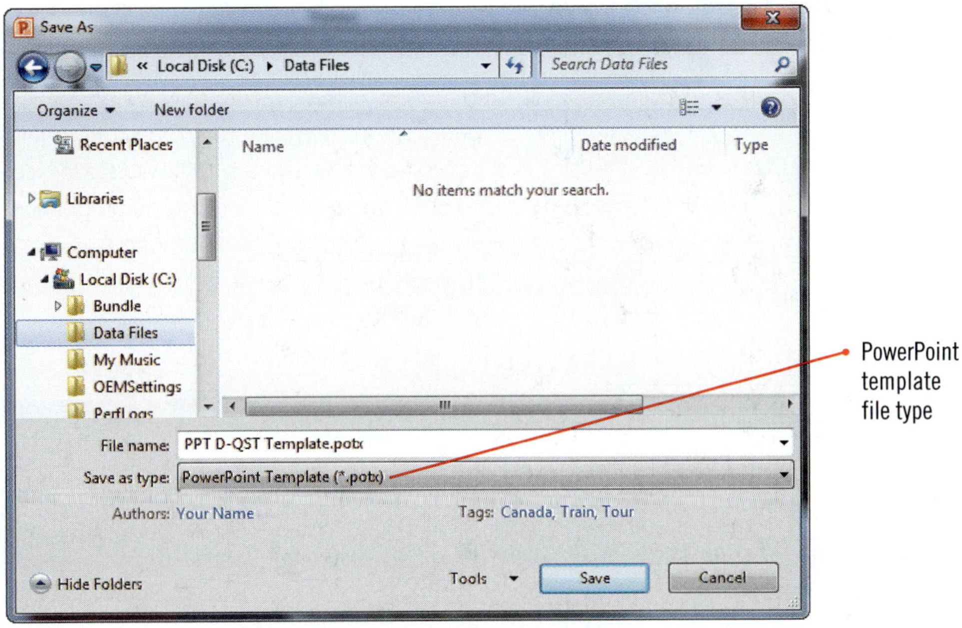

FIGURE D-17: Completed template presentation in Slide Sorter view

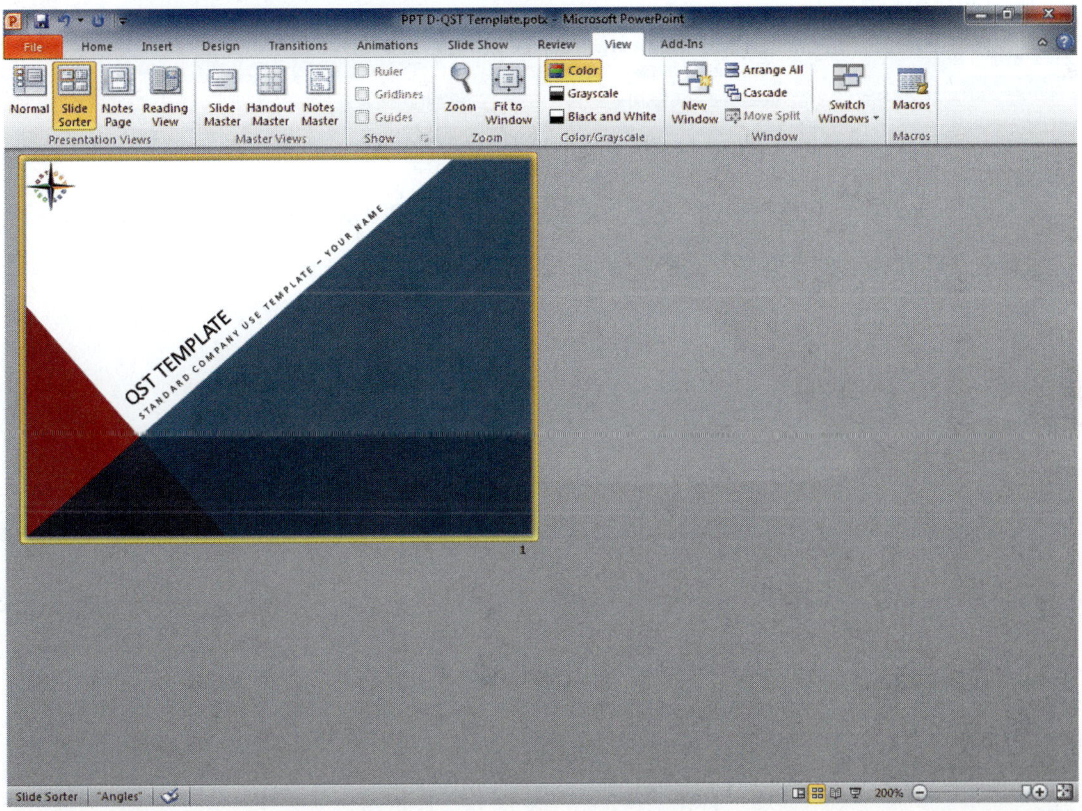

Using Paste Special

Paste Special is used to paste text or objects into PowerPoint using a specific file format. For example, you may want to paste some text as a picture or as plain text without formatting. Copy the text, then in PowerPoint click the Paste list arrow, click Paste Special, then select the appropriate file format option. You can also link an object or selected information from another program to PowerPoint using the Paste Special command. This technique is useful when you want to link part of an Excel worksheet or a chart from a workbook that contains both a worksheet and a chart. To link just the chart, open the Microsoft Excel worksheet, then copy the chart. Leaving Excel and the source file open, click the Paste list arrow, click Paste Special, click the Paste link option button, then click OK.

Practice

Concepts Review

For current SAM information, including versions and content details, visit SAM Central (http://www.cengage.com/samcentral). If you have a SAM user profile, you may have access to hands-on instruction, practice, and assessment of the skills covered in this unit. Since various versions of SAM are supported throughout the life of this text, check with your instructor for the correct instructions and URL/Web site for accessing assignments.

Label each element of the PowerPoint window shown in Figure D-18.

FIGURE D-18

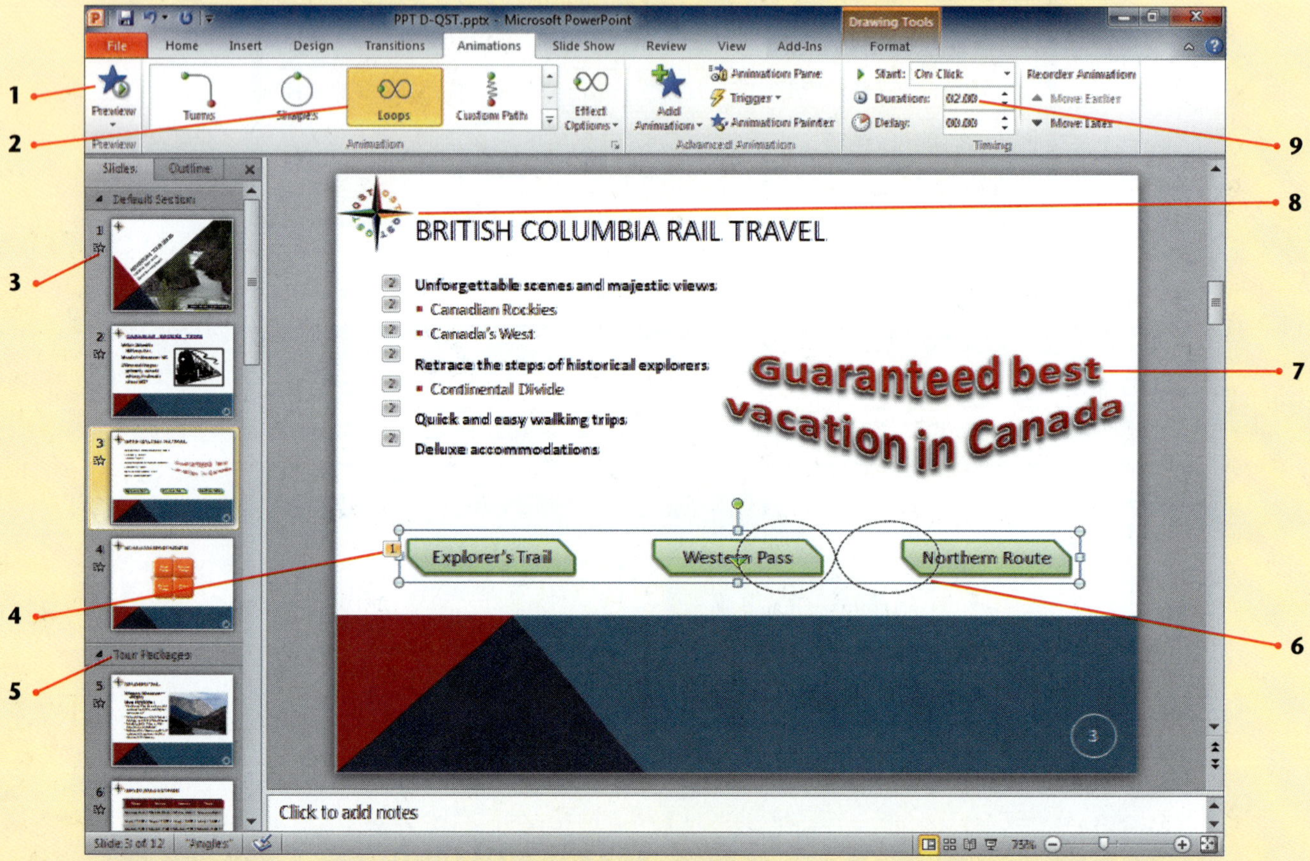

Match each term with the statement that best describes it.

10. Masters	**a.** Identifies the order in which objects are animated
11. Annotate	**b.** The area behind text and graphics
12. Metadata	**c.** Includes document properties such as the author's name
13. Animation tag	**d.** To draw on a slide during a slide show
14. Transitions	**e.** Slides that store theme and placeholder information
15. Background	**f.** Visual effects that determine how a slide moves in and out of view during a slide show

Select the best answer from the list of choices.

16. The effect that determines how a slide moves in and out of view during a slide show is called a(n):

a. Transition.
b. Timing.
c. Theme.
d. Animation.

17. An object placed on the slide master defines which of the following items?

a. Background graphic
b. Logo
c. Shape
d. Master placeholder

18. Which of the following statements about masters is *not* true?

a. Each slide layout in the presentation has a corresponding slide layout in Slide Master view.
b. The design theme is placed on the slide master.
c. Masters store information.
d. Changes made to the slide master are reflected in the handout and notes masters as well.

19. Which PowerPoint file *can't* be edited or modified?

a. Inspected file
b. File saved in another file format
c. Read-only file
d. Template file

20. The effect that controls how an object appears on the screen during a slide show is called a(n):

a. Transition.
b. Animation.
c. Path.
d. Template.

21. The Document Inspector looks for ______________ and personal information that is stored in the presentation file.

a. themes
b. hidden data
c. animation tags
d. video settings

22. According to the book, which standard should you follow to evaluate a presentation?

a. Replace visuals with text as often as possible.
b. Slides should include most of the information you wish to present.
c. Use many different design elements to keep your audience from getting bored.
d. The message should be outlined in a concise way.

Skills Review

1. Modify masters.

a. Open the presentation PPT D-3.pptx from the drive and folder where you store your Data Files, then save the presentation as **PPT D-New Product**.
b. Open Slide Master view using the View tab, then click the Origin Slide Master thumbnail.
c. Insert the picture PPT D-4.jpg, then resize the picture so it is 0.8" wide.
d. Drag the picture to the upper-right corner of the slide within the design frame of the slide, then deselect the picture.
e. Preserve the Origin master, switch to Normal view, then save your changes.

2. Customize the background and theme.

a. Switch to Slide 3, click the Design tab, then open the background styles gallery.
b. Change the background style to Style 5.
c. Open the Format Background dialog box.
d. Set the Transparency to 25%, apply the background to all of the slides, then close the dialog box.
e. Click the Colors button, then click Office. Click the Fonts button, then click Office Classic 2.
f. Save your changes.

3. Use slide show commands.

a. Begin the slide show on Slide 1, then proceed to Slide 4.
b. Use the Pen to circle the words **Early Adopters**, **Mass Adopters**, and **Late Adopters**.
c. Move to Slide 5, then use the Highlighter to highlight the words **Pricing**, **Look**, and **Fulfillment issues**.

Skills Review (continued)

- **d.** Right-click the slide and go to Slide 1, move to Slide 4, then erase all ink on the slide.
- **e.** Move to Slide 5, erase the ink on the slide, then change the pointer back to .
- **f.** Press [Home], advance through the slide show, don't save any ink annotations, then save your work.

4. Set slide transitions and timings.

- **a.** Go to Slide Sorter view, click the Slide 1 thumbnail, then apply the Vortex transition to the slide.
- **b.** Change the effect option to From Bottom, change the duration speed to 3.00, then apply to all the slides.
- **c.** Change the slide timing to 5 seconds, then apply to all of the slides.
- **d.** Switch to Normal view, view the slide show, then save your work.

5. Animate objects.

- **a.** Go to Slide 3, click the Animations tab, then select the E shape on the slide.
- **b.** Apply the Swivel effect to the object, click the Price arrow, apply the Float In effect, then preview the animations.
- **c.** On Slide 4 apply the Spin effect (Emphasis section) to the title text object.
- **d.** Select the six objects in the graphic, click the More button in the Animation group, click More Entrance Effects, then apply an animation of your choice from the Exciting group to the six selected objects in the graphic.
- **e.** Apply animation effects to objects on at least two more slides in the presentation.
- **f.** Edit the animations effects as needed, then save your changes.

6. Inspect a presentation.

- **a.** Open the Document Properties pane, type **Internet Product** in the Subject text box, then type **Review** in the Status text box.
- **b.** Close the Document Properties pane, then open the Document Inspector dialog box.
- **c.** Make sure the Off-Slide Content check box is selected, then inspect the presentation.
- **d.** Delete the off-slide content and the presentation notes, then close the dialog box. Save your changes.

7. Evaluate a presentation.

- **a.** Go to Slide 1, then run a slide show.
- **b.** Evaluate the presentation using the points described in the lesson as criteria, then submit a written evaluation to your instructor.
- **c.** Move Slide 6 below Slide 8.
- **d.** Check the spelling of the presentation, add the slide number and your name to the slide footer on all the slides, then save your changes.
- **e.** Switch to Slide Sorter view, then compare your presentation to Figure D-19.
- **f.** Submit your presentation to your instructor, then close the presentation.

FIGURE D-19

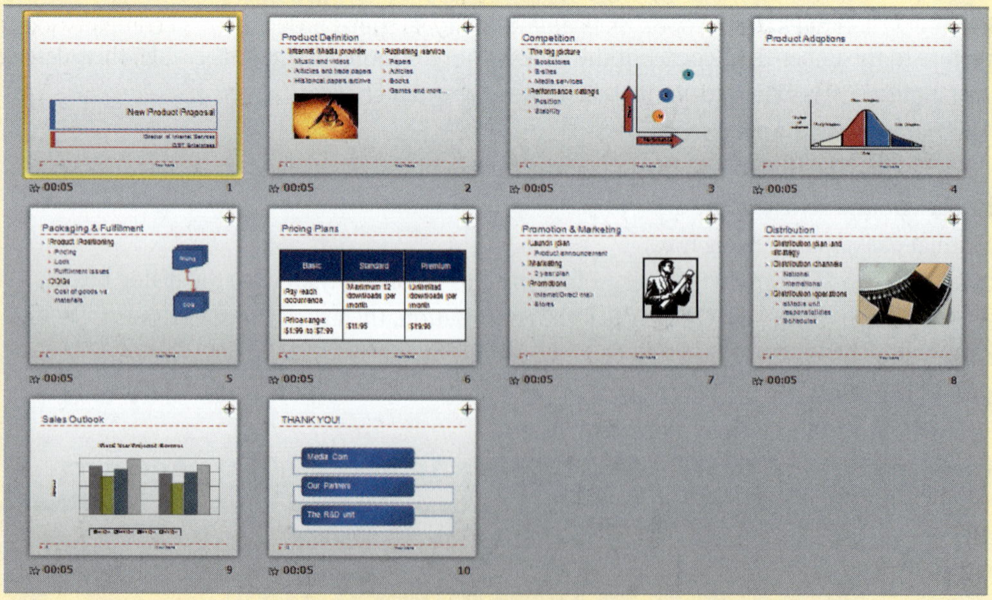

Skills Review (continued)

8. Create a template.

a. Create a new presentation, then save it as a PowerPoint template with the name **PPT D-Template** to the drive and folder where your Data Files are stored.

b. Click the More button in the Themes group, browse for themes, locate the drive and folder where you store your Data files, click PPT D-New Product, then click Apply.

c. Type **QST Template** in the title placeholder, then type your name in the subtitle placeholder.

d. Delete the slide transitions and animations, remove the slide timing, then select the On Mouse Click option in the Timing group.

e. Save your work, then submit your presentation to your instructor.

f. Close the presentation, then exit PowerPoint.

Independent Challenge 1

You are a travel consultant for Island Travel Services, located in Tampa, Florida. You have been working on a sales presentation that is going to be accessed by customers on the company Web site. You need to finish up what you have been working on by adding transitions, timings, and animation effects to the sales presentation.

If you have a SAM 2010 user profile, an autogradable SAM version of this assignment may be available at http://www.cengage.com/sam2010. Check with your instructor to confirm that this assignment is available in SAM. To use the SAM version of this assignment, log into the SAM 2010 Web site and download the instruction and start files.

a. Open the file PPT D-5.pptx from the drive and folder where you store your Data Files, and save the presentation as **PPT D-Island**.

b. Add the slide number and your name as the footer on all slides, except the title slide.

c. Apply the Float In animation to the title text on each slide.

d. Apply the Wipe animation to the bulleted text objects on each slide.

e. Apply the Shape animation to the table on Slide 8, then change the effect option to Box.

f. Apply the Shred slide transition, apply a 7-second slide timing, then apply to all of the slides.

g. Check the spelling of the presentation, then save your changes.

h. View the slide show, and evaluate your presentation. Make changes if necessary.

i. Submit your presentation to your instructor, close the presentation, then exit PowerPoint.

Independent Challenge 2

You are a development engineer at Extreme Sports, Inc., an international sports product design company located in Fargo, North Dakota. Extreme Sports designs and manufactures items such as bike helmets, bike racks, and kayak paddles, and markets these items primarily to countries in North America and Western Europe. You need to finish the work on a quarterly presentation that outlines the progress of the company's newest technologies by adding animations, customizing the background, and using the Document Inspector.

a. Open the file PPT D-6.pptx from the drive and folder where you store your Data Files, and save the presentation as **PPT D-Extreme**.

b. Apply an appropriate design theme, then apply a new slide background style. Make sure the new background style is appropriate for the design theme you have chosen.

c. Apply the Ripple slide transition to all slides, then animate the following objects: the text on Slide 2, the clip art object on Slide 3, the table on Slide 4, and the clip art on Slide 6. View the slide show to evaluate the effects you added and make adjustments as necessary.

d. Run the Document Inspector with all options selected, identify what items the Document Inspector finds, close the Document Inspector dialog box, then review the slides to find the items.

Independent Challenge 2 (continued)

- **e.** Add a slide at the end of the presentation that identifies the items the Document Inspector found.
- **f.** Run the Document Inspector again, and remove all items except the document properties.

Advanced Challenge Exercise

- Click the Rehearse Timings button on the Slide Sorter toolbar.
- Set slide timings for each slide in the presentation.
- Save new slide timings.

- **g.** Add your name as a footer to all slides, run the spell checker, save your work, then run a slide show to evaluate your presentation.
- **h.** Submit your presentation to your instructor, then close the presentation and exit PowerPoint.

Independent Challenge 3

You work for Young & Associates, a full-service investment and pension firm. Your boss wants you to create a presentation on small business pension plan options to be published on the company Web site. You have completed adding the information to the presentation, now you need to add a design theme, format some information, add some animation effects, and add slide timings.

- **a.** Open the file PPT D-7.pptx from the drive and folder where you store your Data Files, and save the presentation as **PPT D-IRAPlans**.
- **b.** Apply an appropriate design theme.
- **c.** Apply animation effects to the following objects: the shapes on Slide 3 and the text and clip art on Slide 5. View the slide show to evaluate the effects you added, and make adjustments as necessary.
- **d.** Convert the text on Slide 4 to a Basic Radial SmartArt graphic (Found in the Cycle category).
- **e.** Apply the Intense Effect style to the SmartArt graphic, then change the colors of the graphic to Colorful Range – Accent Colors 2 to 3.
- **f.** Switch to Slide 3, align the Sector and Quality arrow shapes to one another, then align the Allocation and Maturity arrow shapes to one another.
- **g.** Adjust the aligned arrow shapes so they are centered on the Buy/Sell oval shape, then apply a 15-second timing to Slides 3–7 and a 5-second timing to Slides 1 and 2.
- **h.** Add a section between Slide 5 and Slide 6, then rename the section **Plans**.
- **i.** Rename the Default section in the Slides tab to **Intro**.

Advanced Challenge Exercise

- Open Slide Master view, select the last slide layout, then click the Insert Layout button.
- Click the Insert Placeholder list arrow, click Table, then drag a placeholder in the blank area of the Slide Master layout. (*Hint*: Draw the table placeholder so it takes up most of the blank space in the layout.)
- Return to Normal view, apply the new Custom Layout to Slides 6 and 7. Adjust the placeholder in Slide Master view if necessary.

- **j.** Add your name as a footer to the slides, run the spell checker, save your work, then run a slide show to evaluate your presentation.
- **k.** Submit your presentation to your instructor, then close the presentation and exit PowerPoint.

Real Life Independent Challenge

You work for the operations supervisor at the Tennessee State University student union. Create a presentation that you can eventually publish to the college Web site that describes all of the services offered at the student union.

a. Plan and create the slide presentation that describes the services and events offered at the student union. To help create content, use the student union at your school or use the Internet to locate information on college student unions. The presentation should contain at least six slides.

b. Use an appropriate design theme.

c. Add clip art and photographs available in the Clip Organizer, then style and customize at least one photo.

d. Save the presentation as **PPT D-TSU** to the drive and folder where you store your Data Files. View the slide show, and evaluate the contents of your presentation. Make any necessary adjustments.

e. Add slide transitions, animation effects, and timings to the presentation. View the slide show again to evaluate the effects you added.

f. Add your name as a footer to the slides. Spell check the presentation, save, inspect, then submit your presentation to your instructor. An example of a finished presentation is shown in Figure D-20.

g. Create a template from this presentation using a new presentation, then save the presentation as **PPT D-TSU Template** to the drive and folder where you store your Data Files.

h. Type **TSU Template** in the title placeholder, type your name in the subtitle placeholder, delete transitions and animations, submit your presentation to your instructor, close the template presentation, then exit PowerPoint.

FIGURE D-20

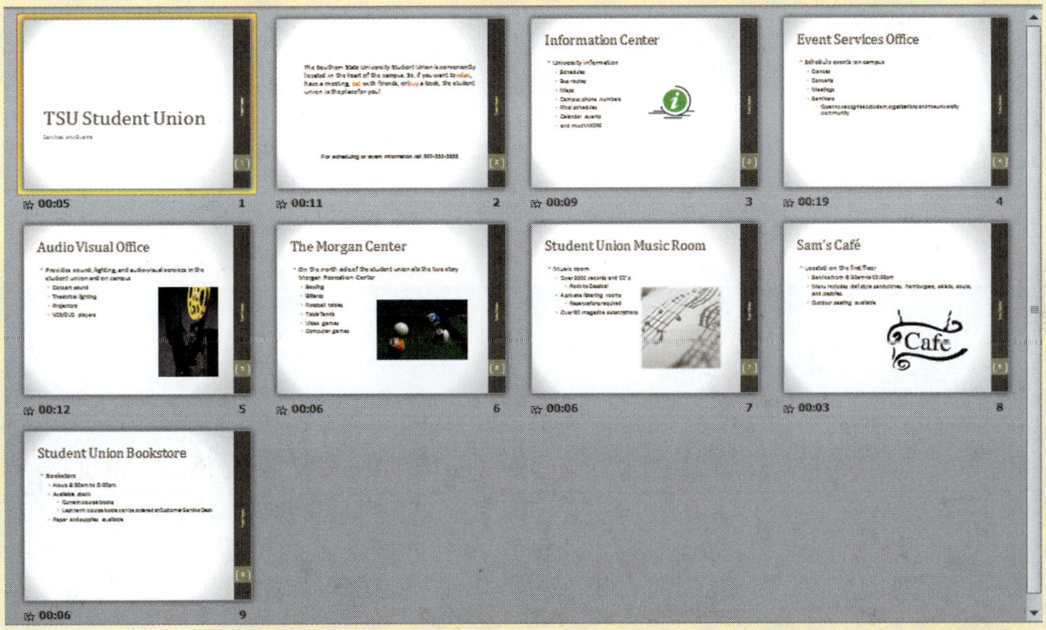

Visual Workshop

Create a new PowerPoint template (.potx) with the filename **PPT D-School Template** and save it to the drive and folder where you store your Data Files. Change the presentation to look like Figures D-21 and D-22. Figure D-22 shows a slide with a custom slide layout that you need to create. Submit your presentation to your instructor.

FIGURE D-21

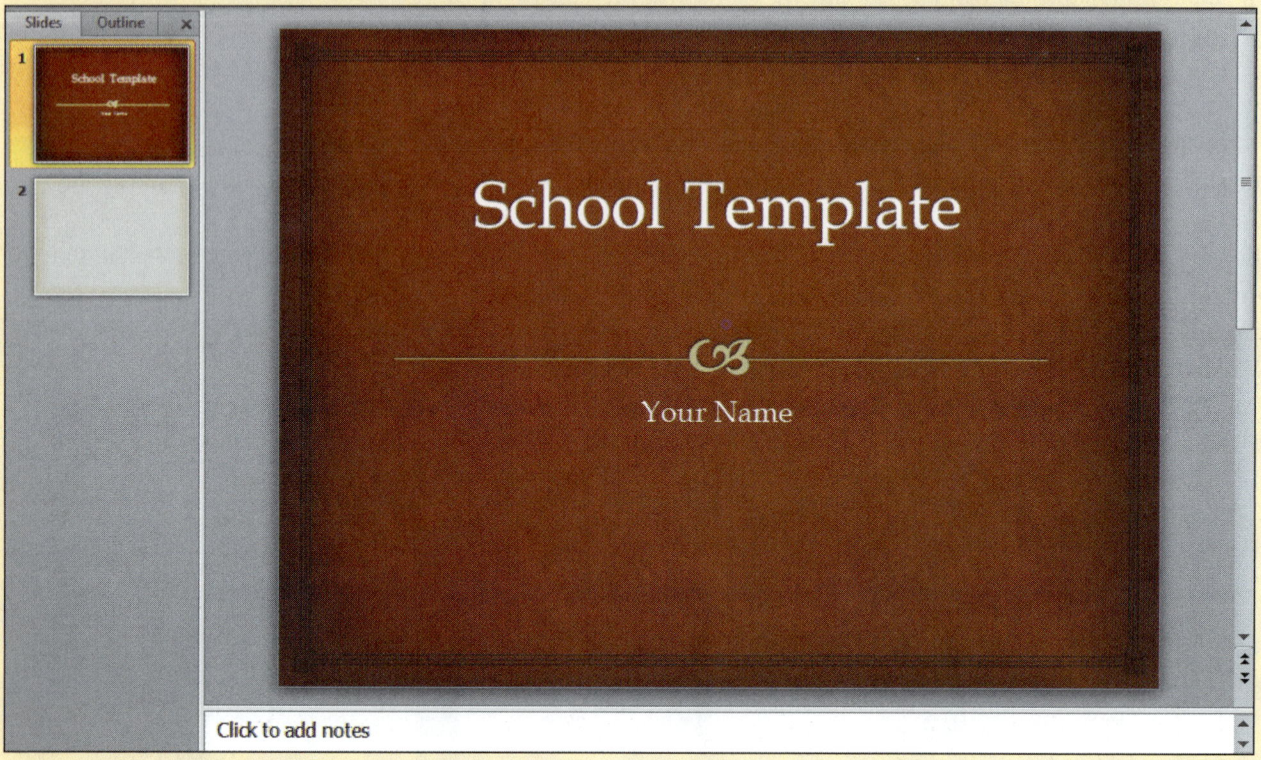

FIGURE D-22

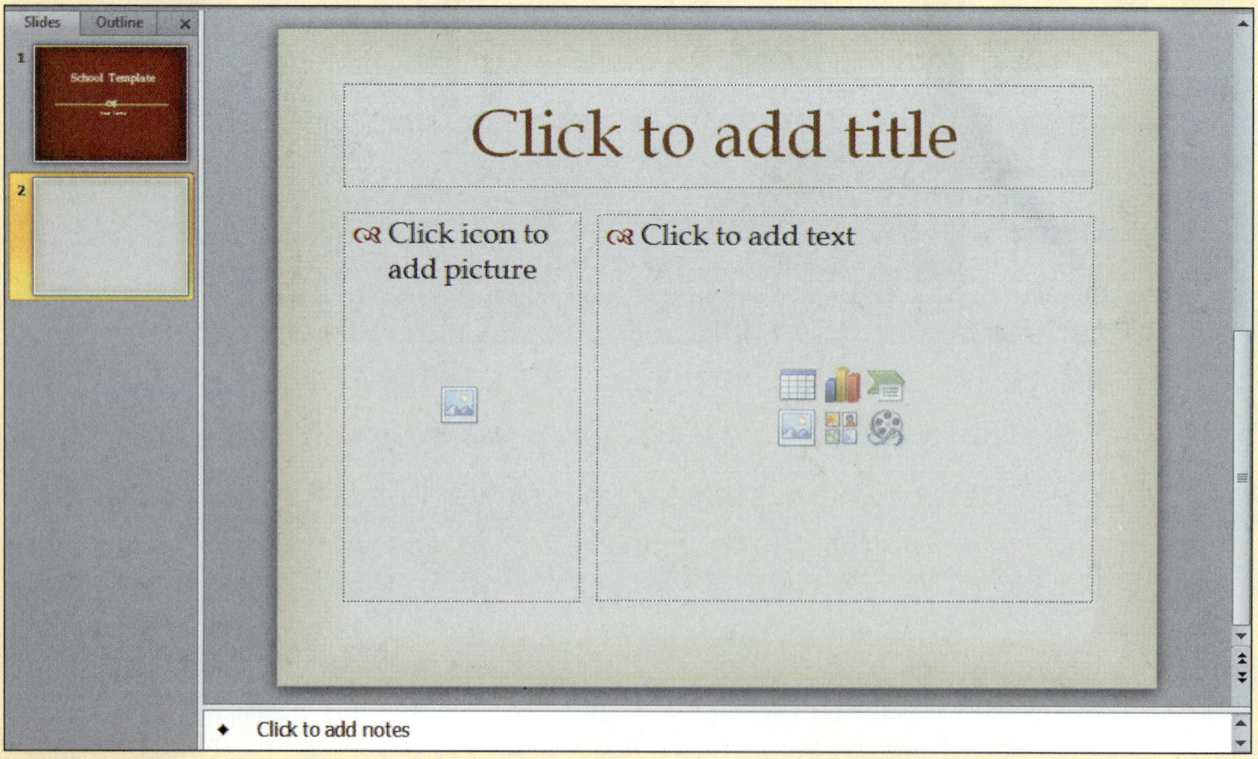

UNIT C

Integration 2010

Integrating Word, Excel, Access, and PowerPoint

Files You Will Need:

- INT C-1.docx
- INT C-2.accdb
- INT C-3.docx
- INT C-4.accdb
- INT C-5.docx
- INT C-6.accdb
- INT C-7.docx
- INT C-8.accdb
- INT C-9.accdb

You can integrate objects that you create in Word, Excel, and Access into PowerPoint presentations that cover a broad spectrum of company activities. For example, you might store information about your customers and products in an Access database, analyze financial information in an Excel workbook, and create sales literature in a Word document. You can combine and then communicate this information to others in the form of a PowerPoint presentation. By creating links between the PowerPoint presentation and the files in the source programs, you can also keep the presentation up to date and ready to go at a moment's notice. You are working as an assistant to Sheila Barton, the general manager of QST Sydney in Australia. Sheila has asked you to explore how you can use linking and embedding in PowerPoint, and then how to include objects from Word, Excel, and Access in a PowerPoint presentation.

OBJECTIVES

- Integrate data among Word, Excel, Access, and PowerPoint
- Import a Word outline into PowerPoint
- Embed an Excel worksheet in PowerPoint
- Link Access and Excel objects to PowerPoint
- Manage links

UNIT
C
Integration 2010

Integrating Data Among Word, Excel, Access, and PowerPoint

You can integrate information into a PowerPoint presentation using the linking and embedding techniques you learned with Word, Excel, and Access. As with those programs, you embed data created in other programs in PowerPoint when you want to be able to edit it from within the destination file. You use linking when you want the linked information in the destination file to update when you change the source file. In addition, you can import a Word outline into PowerPoint to automatically create slides without having to reenter information. The presentation in Figure C-1 includes information originally created in Word, Excel, and Access. Before you create the presentation, you review some of the ways you can integrate information among Word, Excel, Access, and PowerPoint.

DETAILS

You can integrate Word, Excel, Access, and PowerPoint by:

- **Importing a Word outline into PowerPoint**

  In the course of your work, you may create Word documents that contain information you also want to use in a PowerPoint presentation. Instead of retyping the information in PowerPoint, you can save time by importing the information directly from Word into PowerPoint. Figure C-1 shows how a Word outline appears before and after it is imported into a PowerPoint presentation. When you import an outline from Word to PowerPoint, you cannot create a link between the two files.

- **Embedding objects**

  Recall that when you embed an object, you do not create a link to the source file. However, you can use the source program tools to edit the embedded object within the destination file. An embedded object becomes a part of the PowerPoint file, which means that the file size of the PowerPoint presentation increases relative to the file size of the embedded object. For example, a large embedded object, such as a graphic, will increase the size of the PowerPoint presentation considerably. To embed an object in a PowerPoint presentation, you use the Object command in the Text group on the Insert tab. In Figure C-1, the table on Slide 3 is an embedded Excel worksheet object.

  To edit an embedded object, you double-click it. The source program starts, and the Ribbon and tabs of the source program appear inside the PowerPoint window.

- **Linking objects**

  When you link an object to a PowerPoint slide, a representation or picture of the object is placed on the slide instead of the actual object. This representation of the object is connected, or linked, to the original file. The object is still stored in the source file in the source program, unlike an embedded object, which is stored directly on the PowerPoint slide. Any change you make to a linked object's source file is reflected in the linked object. The pie chart shown on Slide 4 of the presentation in Figure C-1 is linked to values entered in an Excel worksheet, which is, in turn, linked to data entered in an Access database. The differences between embedding and linking are summarized in Figure C-2.

  You can open the source file and make changes to the linked object as long as you have access to the source program and to the source file. When you move files among machines or transmit files to other people, you need to ensure that recipients can access both the source programs and the linked files.

FIGURE C-1: PowerPoint presentation with integrated objects

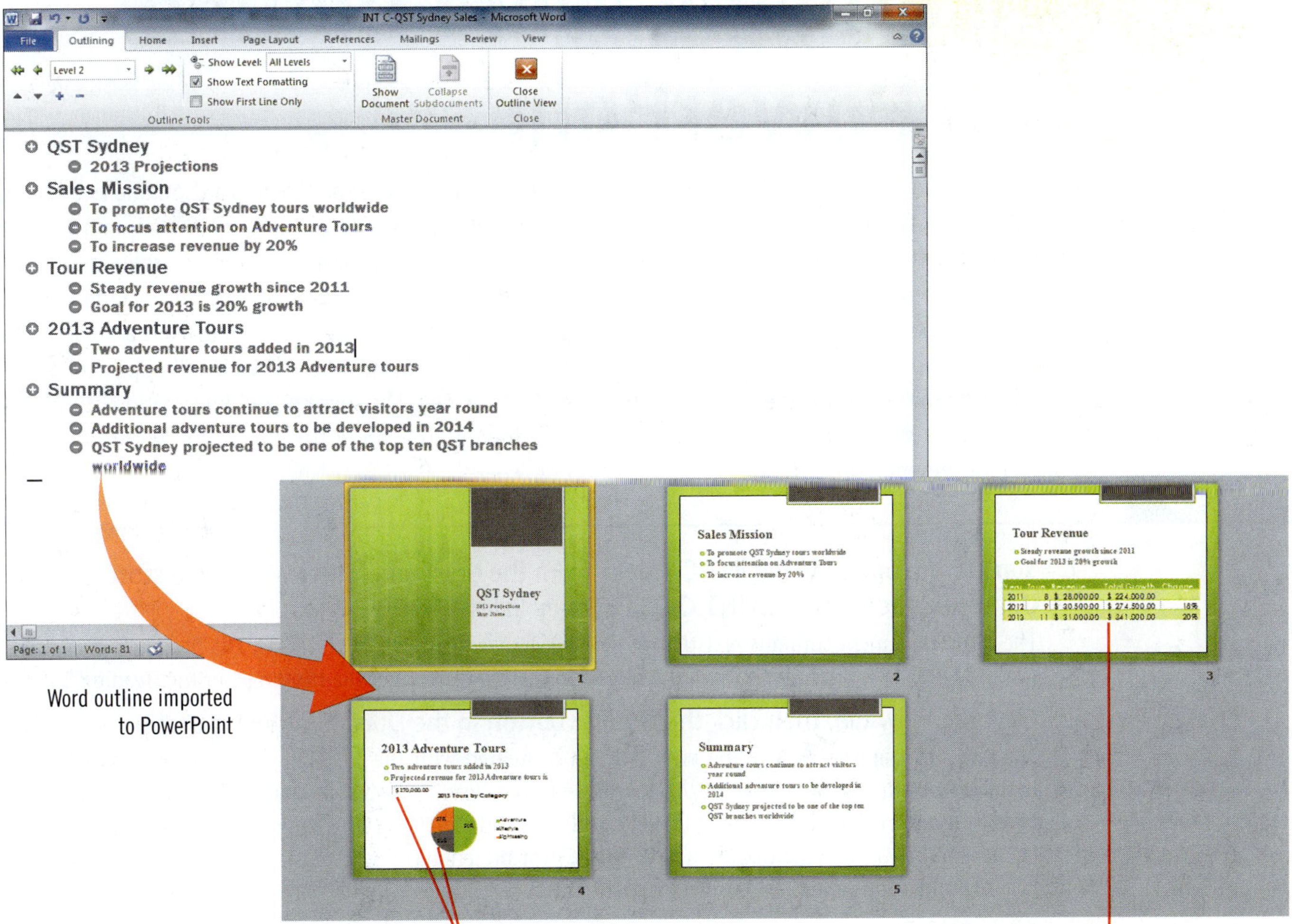

Word outline imported to PowerPoint

Chart and worksheet object linked to Excel and Access

Embedded Excel worksheet object is not linked

FIGURE C-2: Embedding vs. linking

When you would embed	When you would link
• You are the only user of an object, and you want the object to be a part of your presentation.	• You always want your object to include the latest information.
• You want to access the object in its source program, even if the source file is not available.	• The object's source file is shared on a network or where other users have access to the file and can change it.
• You want to update the object manually while working in PowerPoint.	• You want to keep the file size of the presentation small.

UNIT
C
Integration 2010

Importing a Word Outline into PowerPoint

Before you import a Word outline into PowerPoint, you should ensure that each Word outline heading is formatted with a heading style such as Heading 1, Heading 2, and so on. PowerPoint imports all text formatted with the Heading 1 style as a slide title and all text formatted with the Heading 2 style as a level 1 item in a bulleted list. Any block of text that is not formatted with a heading style is not included in the PowerPoint presentation. If you want the Word text to appear only in a text placeholder on a PowerPoint slide, you can copy a block of text from Word and paste it into PowerPoint, where it will appear in a text box. Sheila Barton, the general manager of QST Sydney, has summarized information about the 2013 tours in a Word document. She asks you to use the information in this document as the basis of a PowerPoint presentation.

STEPS

1. **Start Word, open the file INT C-1.docx from the drive and folder where you store your Data Files, then save it as INT C-QST Sydney Sales**

   The Word document contains text that projects QST tour sales for 2013. Each of the headings, except the subtitle "2013 Projections" following the title, is formatted with either the Heading 1 or the Heading 2 style.

2. **Click the View tab, then click the Outline button in the Document Views group**

   The document appears in Outline view. All text formatted with the Heading 1 style appears as a Level 1 heading in Outline view, and all text formatted with the Heading 2 style appears as a Level 2 heading. Each Level 1 heading will become a slide title in PowerPoint, and each Level 2 heading will become a bulleted item. Before you import a Word outline into a PowerPoint presentation, you must check to ensure that all the headings and subheadings are positioned at the correct levels.

3. **Click 2013 Projections, then click the Demote button in the Outline Tools group once**

   The text moves to the right one tab stop and changes from Subtitle text to a Level 2 heading. In PowerPoint, this text will appear as a bulleted item under the slide title "QST Sydney."

4. **Click Tour Revenue (the fourth bullet below the Sales Mission heading), click the Promote button in the Outline Tools group, click Two adventure tours added in 2013, then press [Tab]**

   > **QUICK TIP**
   > You can also use [Tab] and [Shift][Tab] to demote and promote headings in Outline view.

5. **Compare your Word outline to Figure C-3, then save and close the document**

6. **Start PowerPoint, create a blank presentation if necessary, then save it as INT C-QST Sydney Sales Presentation in the drive and folder where you store your Data Files**

7. **Click the New Slide list arrow in the Slides group, click Slides from Outline, navigate to the location where you stored INT C-QST Sydney Sales, then double-click INT C-QST Sydney Sales**

   The Slides tab and the status bar indicate that the presentation now contains six slides. Slide 1 is blank, and Slides 2 through 6 represent the Level 1 headings in the Word outline that are now slides in the PowerPoint presentation.

8. **Click Slide 1 on the Slides tab, press [Delete], click the Layout button in the Slides group, click Title Slide, click the Outline tab in the left pane, click after 2013 Projections on Slide 1, press [Enter], then type your name**

   You change the slide layout for the first slide so that the title of the presentation and your name appear in the middle of the slide.

9. **Click the Design tab, click the More button in the Themes group, click the Austin slide design, then save the presentation**

   The formatted presentation appears as shown in Figure C-4.

FIGURE C-3: Edited outline in Word Outline view

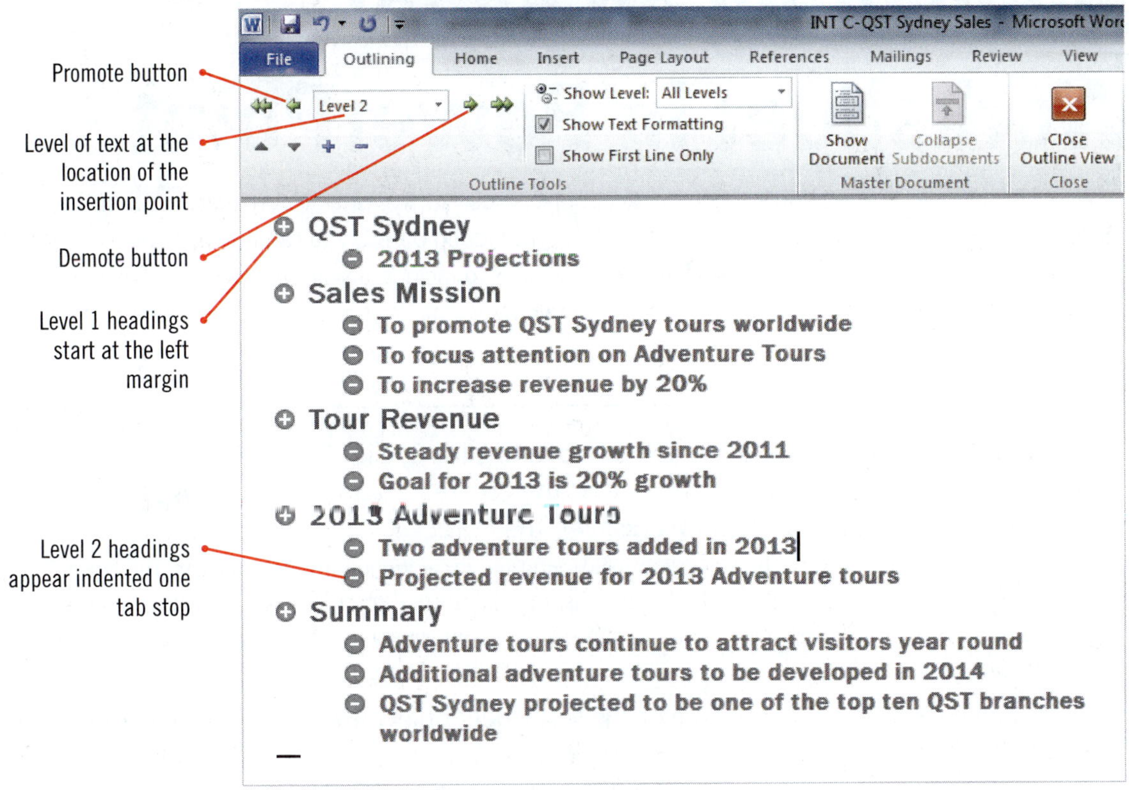

FIGURE C-4: Formatted presentation and Outline tab

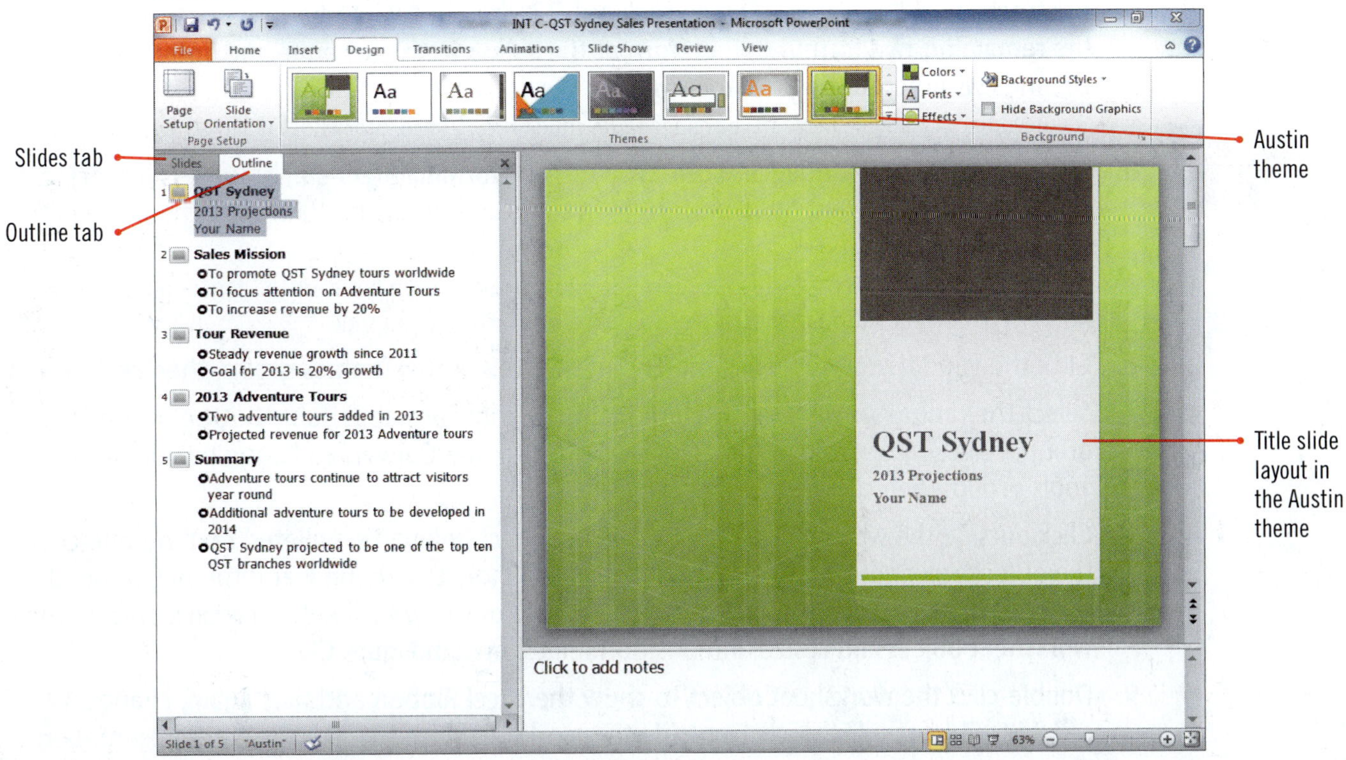

Embedding an Excel Worksheet in PowerPoint

You can use the Object command to embed Excel objects such as worksheets and charts into both Word and PowerPoint documents. When you double-click the embedded object, you can then use the tools of the source program to edit the object. You want Slide 3 to include a worksheet with calculations that you can update from within PowerPoint when you obtain new data. You create an Excel worksheet on the slide and then edit it using Excel tools.

STEPS

TROUBLE

When you drag to resize the embedded worksheet, you drag the handle slightly outside the desired size to accommodate the scroll bars. If your worksheet is not the right size, drag a corner or side resize handle as necessary.

TROUBLE

Press ↑, use the scroll bars, or press [Ctrl][Home] to move to the top of the embedded worksheet.

1. **Click Tour Revenue on the Outline tab to move to Slide 3, click the Insert tab, click the Object button in the Text group, verify that the Create new option button is selected, scroll to and click Microsoft Excel Worksheet, then click OK**

   An Excel worksheet appears on the PowerPoint slide, and the Excel Ribbon and tabs appear. The PowerPoint title bar and menu bar appear above the Excel tools, indicating that Excel is operating within PowerPoint. When you embed a worksheet object in a PowerPoint slide, you generally want to show only the cells that contain data.

2. **Drag the lower-right corner handle of the worksheet object up so that only columns A to F and rows 1 to 5 are visible, as shown in Figure C-5**

   You want to clearly see the data you need to enter into the worksheet object.

3. **Click the Select All button in the upper-left corner of the embedded worksheet to select all the worksheet cells, change the font size to 26 point, then click cell A1**

4. **Enter the labels and values in the range A1:D4 as shown in Figure C-6, click cell D2, enter the formula =B2*C2, press [Enter], click cell D2, drag its fill handle to cell D4 to enter the remaining two formulas, then format the values in the Revenue and Total Growth columns with Accounting number format**

   You need to calculate the percentage change in revenue from 2011 to 2012 and 2012 to 2013.

5. **Click cell E1, type Change, click cell E3, enter the formula =(D3-D2)/D3, press [Enter], click cell E3, click the Percent Style button in the Number group, then copy the formula to cell E4**

   The embedded worksheet uses the default Office 2010 theme, and you want the fonts and colors of the worksheet to use the Austin theme currently applied to the PowerPoint slide.

6. **Click the Page Layout tab, click the Themes button in the Themes group, then click Austin**

7. **Select the range A1:E4, click the Home tab, click the Format as Table button in the Styles group, select Table Style Medium 2, click OK, click the Convert to Range button in the Tools group, then click Yes**

8. **Click outside the worksheet object, drag the object below the bulleted text, double-click the object again, drag the middle-right sizing handle to column E and the bottom-middle sizing handle up to row 4 to remove blank areas of the worksheet, then click outside the worksheet object and resize and position it as shown in Figure C-7**

9. **Double-click the worksheet object to show the Excel Ribbon and tabs again, change 12 in cell B4 to 11, press [Tab], click outside the worksheet object, then save the presentation**

   The percentage growth for 2013 is now 20%.

FIGURE C-5: Resizing the worksheet object

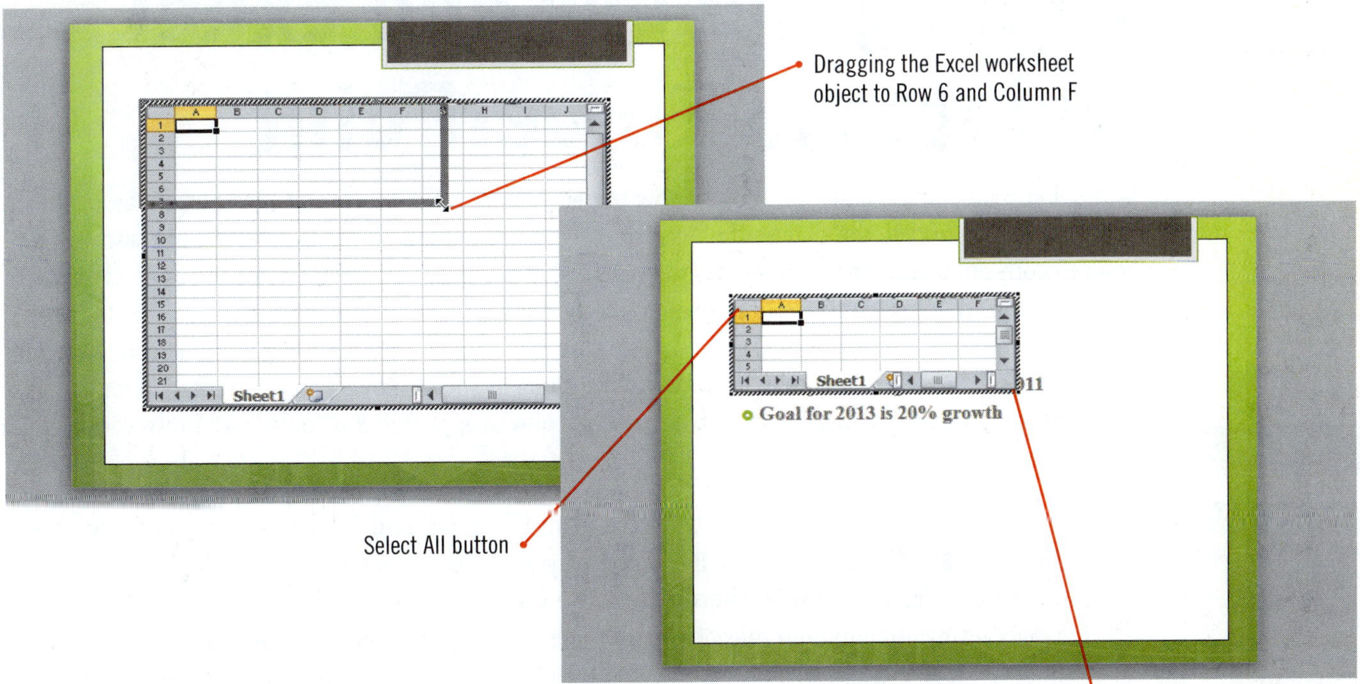

FIGURE C-6: Labels and values entered in the Excel worksheet object

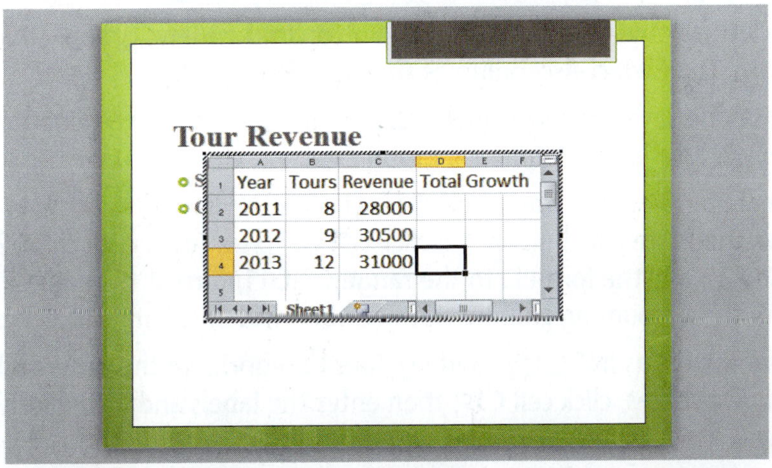

FIGURE C-7: Completed Excel worksheet object

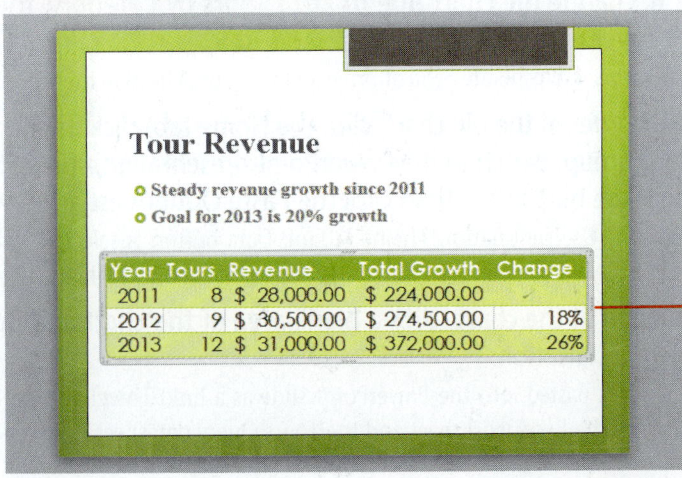

Worksheet object formatted, sized, and positioned

UNIT
C
Integration 2010

Linking Access and Excel Objects to PowerPoint

In the Unit B Integration unit, you learned how to copy a table from Access and then paste it as a link into Excel. When you update the data in the Access table, the linked data in the Excel workbook also updates. You can copy an Access table from Access to PowerPoint; however, you cannot paste the table as a link. To link data from an Access database to a PowerPoint presentation, you first need to copy the data to Excel as a link and then copy the data from Excel and paste it as a link into PowerPoint. You already have tour data stored in an Access database that you want to include in Sheila's PowerPoint presentation for her staff. You want any changes you make to the table in Access also to appear in the PowerPoint presentation.

STEPS

QUICK TIP
To save the database with a new name, click the File tab, point to Save Database As, navigate to the drive and folder where you store your Data Files, type the new filename, then click Save.

1. **Start Access, open the file INT C-2.accdb from the drive and folder where you store your Data Files, save the database as INT C-QST Sydney 2013 Tours, click Enable Content, double-click the Tours table, then review the Category field**
   The tours are divided into three categories: Adventure, Lifestyle, and Sightseeing. You need to sort the Tours table alphabetically by Category so that you can use the data in a chart you create in Excel. You need to create a query to sort the data. That way, the sorting is maintained when you copy the data to Excel.
2. **Close the Tours table, click the Create tab, click the Query Wizard button in the Queries group, click OK, click the Select All Fields button >> to add all the fields in the Tours table to the query, click Next, click Next, then click Finish**
3. **Click the Home tab, click the View button in the Views group, click the Category Sort list arrow, then select Ascending as shown in Figure C-8**
4. **Close and save the Tours query, click Tours Query in the Navigation Pane, then click the Copy button in the Clipboard group**
5. **Create a new blank workbook in Excel, click the Paste list arrow in the Clipboard group, click the Paste Link button, click cell G1, type Total, click cell G2, enter the formula =E2*F2, copy the formula to the range G3:G11, format the values in columns E and G with the Accounting Number format, then widen columns as necessary**
6. **Save the file as INT C-QST Sydney Tour Categories in the drive and folder where you store your Data Files, click cell C14, then enter the labels and formulas as shown in Figure C-9**

TROUBLE
You don't need to see the entire chart when you move it away from cells containing data.

7. **Select the range C14:E15, click the Insert tab, click the Pie button in the Charts group, click the top-left pie style, click the More button in the Chart Layouts group, select Layout 6, change the chart title to 2013 Tours by Category, then move the chart so that it doesn't cover cells containing data**
   Adventure tours will generate 50% of projected revenue, Lifestyle tours 23%, and Sightseeing tours 27%.
8. **Click the border of the pie chart, click the Home tab, click the Copy button in the Clipboard group, switch to the PowerPoint presentation, show Slide 4, click the Home tab, click the Paste button, then click the Paste Options list arrow as shown in Figure C-10**
   By default, the Use Destination Theme & Link Data button is selected, which means that the chart copied from Excel is linked by default to the source file but takes on the theme of the destination file.
9. **Click outside of the chart, click a blank area of the chart and drag it below the text, then save the presentation**
   The pie chart is pasted into the PowerPoint slide as a link. The chart you copied to the PowerPoint slide is linked to both the Excel worksheet and the Tours Query datasheet in Access.

FIGURE C-8: Sorting the Category field in Query Design view

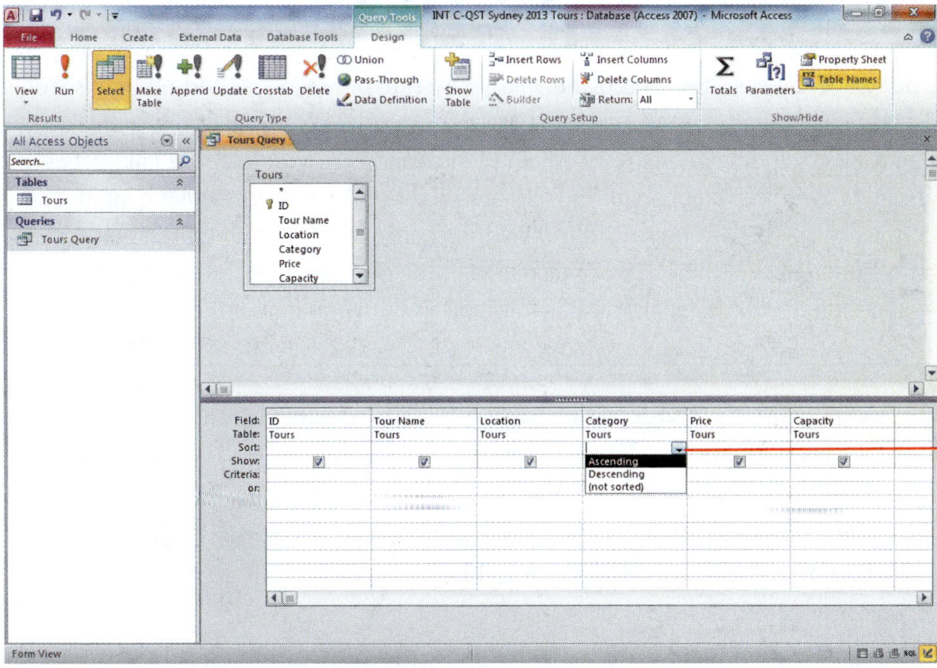

FIGURE C-9: Formulas to calculate total tours by Category

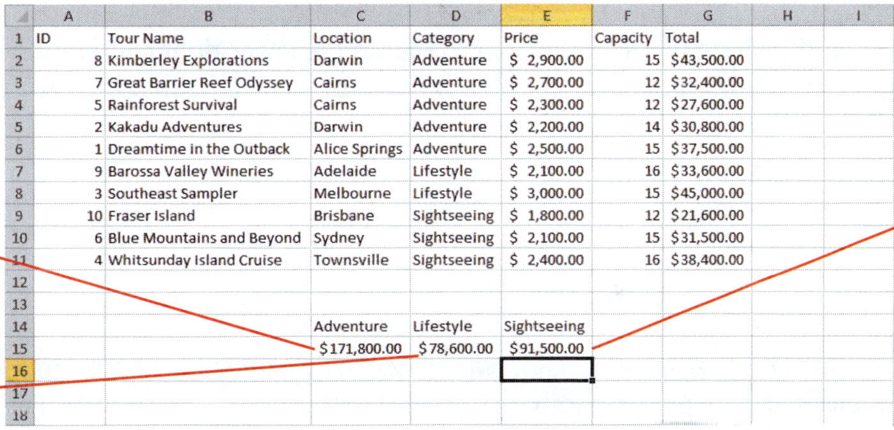

	A	B	C	D	E	F	G	H	I
1	ID	Tour Name	Location	Category	Price	Capacity	Total		
2	8	Kimberley Explorations	Darwin	Adventure	$ 2,900.00	15	$43,500.00		
3	7	Great Barrier Reef Odyssey	Cairns	Adventure	$ 2,700.00	12	$32,400.00		
4	5	Rainforest Survival	Cairns	Adventure	$ 2,300.00	12	$27,600.00		
5	2	Kakadu Adventures	Darwin	Adventure	$ 2,200.00	14	$30,800.00		
6	1	Dreamtime in the Outback	Alice Springs	Adventure	$ 2,500.00	15	$37,500.00		
7	9	Barossa Valley Wineries	Adelaide	Lifestyle	$ 2,100.00	16	$33,600.00		
8	3	Southeast Sampler	Melbourne	Lifestyle	$ 3,000.00	15	$45,000.00		
9	10	Fraser Island	Brisbane	Sightseeing	$ 1,800.00	12	$21,600.00		
10	6	Blue Mountains and Beyond	Sydney	Sightseeing	$ 2,100.00	15	$31,500.00		
11	4	Whitsunday Island Cruise	Townsville	Sightseeing	$ 2,400.00	16	$38,400.00		
12									
13									
14			Adventure	Lifestyle	Sightseeing				
15			$171,800.00	$78,600.00	$91,500.00				
16									
17									
18									

FIGURE C-10: Copying a chart to PowerPoint

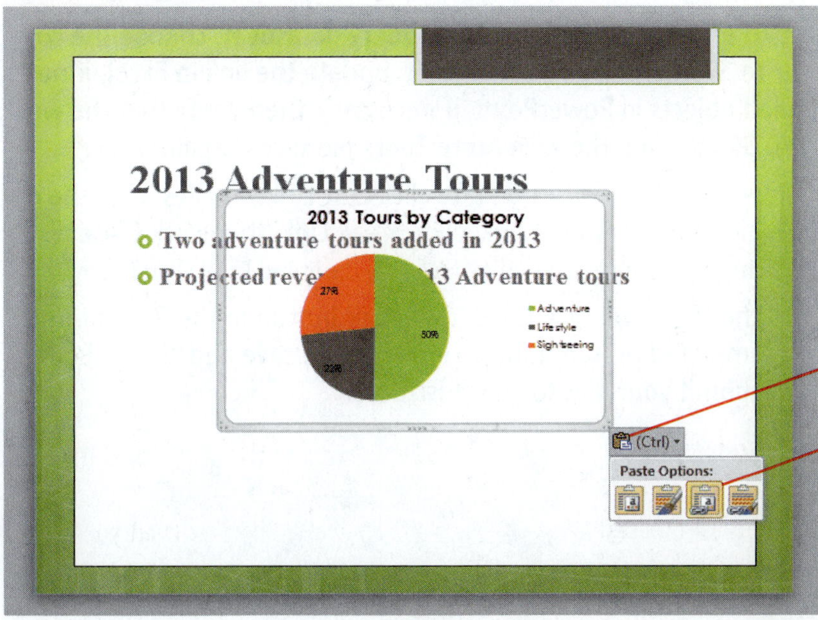

UNIT C

Integration 2010

Managing Links

You frequently need to manage the links you create between files and programs. You may need to update links manually, find the source of a link, or even break a link. You normally break a link when you need to send a file to another user. In PowerPoint, Word, and Excel, you manage links between files in the Edit Links dialog box, which you open from the File tab. Table C-1 summarizes all the integration tasks you performed in this unit. You want to modify the chart on Slide 4 of the presentation to reflect changing tour prices, then update the links you've created in the database, the spreadsheet, and the presentation. Finally, you decide to break the links so that you can send the presentation to the Marketing department.

STEPS

1. **Switch to Access, open the Tours Query datasheet, change the price of the Kimberley Explorations tour to $3,500, press [Enter], then close the Tours Query datasheet**

   When you change data in the Tours Query datasheet, the corresponding data in the Tours table also changes.

QUICK TIP

The linked values will update in Excel automatically if you wait a few minutes, but you speed up the updating process by updating the values manually in the Edit Links dialog box.

2. **Switch to Excel, click the File tab, then click Edit Links to Files in the lower-right corner of the screen, as shown in Figure C-11**

   The Edit Links dialog box opens.

3. **Click Update Values, click Close, click the Home tab, verify that Adventure tours now account for 52% of projected tour revenue, save the workbook, then switch to PowerPoint**

4. **Click the File tab, click Edit Links to Files in the lower-right corner of the dialog box, click Update Now, click Close, click the Home tab, then verify that the Adventure tours slice is now 52%**

5. **Right-click any pie chart label (for example, 52%), use the Mini toolbar to change the font size to 16 point, change the font size of the legend text to 16 point, then click outside the chart**

   When you insert an Excel chart into a PowerPoint presentation, you usually need to increase the font size of chart objects to make them easy to read.

QUICK TIP

A value you copy from Excel and paste into PowerPoint as a link is formatted as an object that you can move and resize the same as you would any object.

6. **Switch to Excel, copy cell C15, switch back to PowerPoint, click after tours in the second bulleted item, press [Spacebar], type is, click the Paste list arrow, click Paste Special, click the Paste link option button, click OK to paste the link as a Microsoft Excel Worksheet Object, then move the worksheet object under Projected and increase its size slightly**

7. **Switch to Access, open the Tours Query datasheet, change the cost of each Adventure tour to $2,500, close the datasheet, update the link in Excel, if necessary, update both copied objects in PowerPoint, if necessary, then verify that the worksheet object is now $170,000.00, and the Adventure Tours pie slice is again 50%**

8. **In PowerPoint, click the File tab, click Edit Links to Files, click the chart link, click Break Link, click the worksheet link, click Break Link, then click Close**

   Now when you change data in the Access file, the linked Excel chart in PowerPoint will not update.

9. **Click the View tab, click the Slide Sorter button in the Presentation Views group, compare the completed presentation to Figure C-12, save and close all open files and programs, then submit your files to your instructor**

FIGURE C-11: File tab

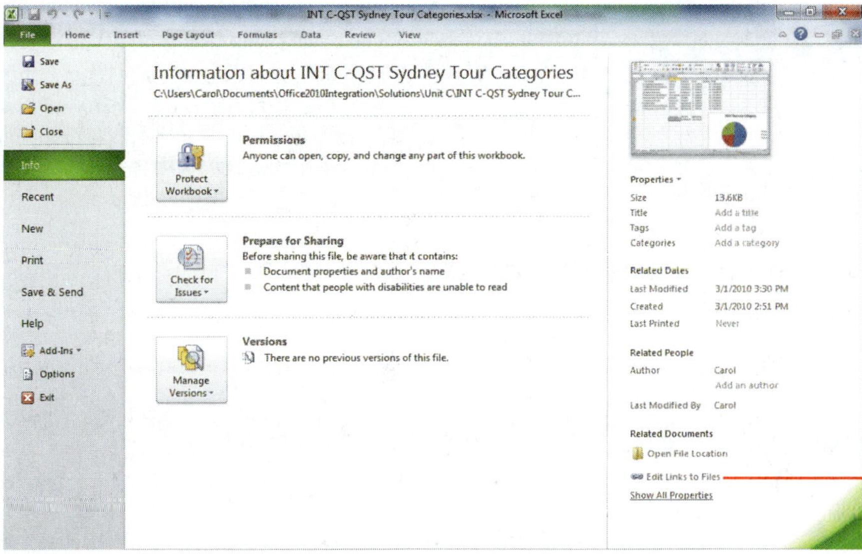

Edit Links to Files command

FIGURE C-12: Completed presentation in Slide Sorter view

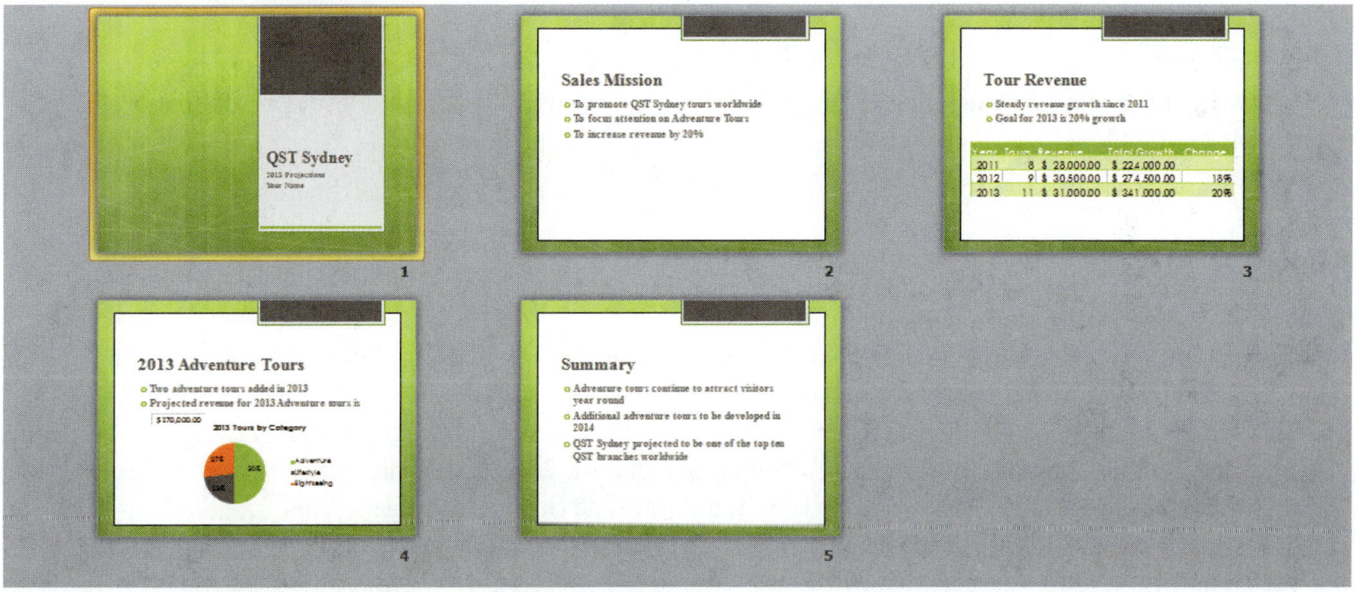

TABLE C-1: Unit C integration tasks

object	commands	source program(s)	destination program	result	connection	page no.
Word	In PowerPoint: New Slide/ Slides from Outline	Word	PowerPoint	Word outline inserted into PowerPoint; Level 1 headings are slide titles, and Level 2 headings are bulleted items	None	36
Excel worksheet	In PowerPoint: Insert/Object/ Create New	Excel	PowerPoint	Excel worksheet created in PowerPoint, then updated by double-clicking and using Excel tools	Embedded	38
Access query	Copy/Paste Link	Access	Excel	Access query is pasted into Excel as a link; linked data can only be formatted in Excel	Linked	40
Excel chart	Copy/Paste Link	Access/Excel	PowerPoint	Chart created from linked Access query is pasted into PowerPoint as a link; when Access data changes, Excel & PowerPoint data updates	Linked	40

Practice

For current SAM information, including versions and content details, visit SAM Central (http://www.cengage.com/samcentral). If you have a SAM user profile, you may have access to hands-on instruction, practice, and assessment of the skills covered in this unit. Since various versions of SAM are supported throughout the life of this text, check with your instructor for the correct instructions and URL/Web site for accessing assignments.

Concepts Review

Match each term with the statement that best describes it.

1. **Edit Links**
2. **Embedded object**
3. **Linked object**
4. **Destination program**
5. **Link**

a. Edit by making changes in the source file
b. The dialog box containing commands to manage connections between files
c. Contains embedded objects that can be edited using the tools of source programs
d. Increases the size of the destination file
e. The best way to share information when the file size should remain small

Select the best answer from the list of choices.

6. Which button's list arrow do you click to import a Word outline into PowerPoint?
   a. Import
   b. New Slide
   c. Object
   d. Office

7. In Word, which view do you work in to prepare text to import into a PowerPoint presentation?
   a. Draft
   b. Print
   c. Full Screen Reading
   d. Outline

Skills Review

1. Import a Word outline into PowerPoint.
   a. Start Word, open the file INT C-3.docx from the drive and folder where you store your Data Files, then save it as **INT C-Howe Sound Realty Outline**.
   b. Switch to Outline view, then demote the subheading West Vancouver, British Columbia to Level 2.
   c. Demote the three subheadings: Townhouses, Houses, and Estates to Level 3.
   d. Promote the subheading Property Values to Level 1, then save and close the document.
   e. Start a new presentation in PowerPoint, then save it as **INT C-Howe Sound Realty Presentation** in the drive and folder where you store your Data Files.
   f. Import the INT C-Howe Sound Realty Outline document into PowerPoint.
   g. Delete the blank Slide 1, apply the Title Slide layout to the new Slide 1, then add your name after the subtitle on Slide 1.
   h. Apply the Angles slide design, then save the presentation.

2. Embed an Excel worksheet in PowerPoint.
   a. Move to Slide 4, delete the blank text placeholder, then insert a Microsoft Excel Worksheet object.
   b. Resize the object so that only columns A to E and rows 1 to 6 are visible.
   c. Change the font size of all the cells to 28 point, enter labels and values as shown in Figure C-13, then adjust column widths.
   d. Enter a formula in cell D2 to multiply the number of homes by the average price for the first quarter, then copy the formula to the range D3:D5.

FIGURE C-13

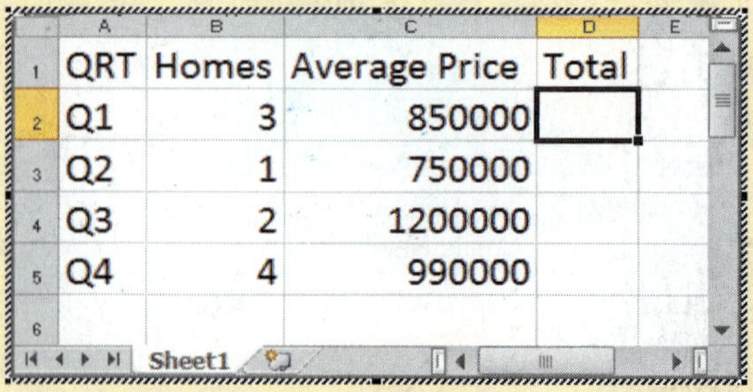

Skills Review (continued)

- **e.** Apply the Angles theme to the embedded workbook, apply the Table Style Medium 10 (one of the orange selections) table style, convert the table to a range, format the dollar values in columns C and D with the Accounting Number format, then widen columns if necessary.
- **f.** Resize the worksheet object so only the cells containing data are visible, position it below the slide title, then increase its size so that it fills the space attractively.
- **g.** In the worksheet object, change the number of homes sold in the third quarter to 5, then save the presentation.

3. Link Access and Excel objects to PowerPoint.

- **a.** Start Access, open the file INT C-4.accdb from the drive and folder where you store your Data Files, save it as **INT C-Howe Sound Realty Properties**, then enable the content.
- **b.** Create a query called **Properties Query** from the Properties table, containing all fields, that sorts the contents of the Category field in ascending order. *(Hint*: Remember to sort the Category field in Design view.)
- **c.** Close and save the query, copy it, create a new workbook in Excel, then paste the query datasheet as a link.
- **d.** Format the values in column F using the Accounting Number format, then widen columns as necessary.
- **e.** In the range B16:D17, enter labels and formulas to calculate the total value of all the houses in each of the three categories: Estate, House, and Townhouse, then save the workbook as **INT C-Howe Sound Realty Property Values**.
- **f.** Create a pie chart in the first 2D style from the range B16:D17, then apply Layout 1.
- **g.** Change the chart title to **Breakdown of Property Values**, copy the chart, then paste it on Slide 5 using the Use Destination Theme and Link Data option (the default).

4. Manage links.

- **a.** In the Access query, change the price of the Sentinel Hill estate to **$2,500,000**, then close the query.
- **b.** Switch to Excel, then update the link in the Edit Links dialog box if the value in cell E2 does not automatically update to 2500000. If the Edit Links to Files option does not appear in Backstage view, click the Data tab, then click Edit Links in the Connections group to open the Edit Links dialog box.
- **c.** Switch to PowerPoint, then update the link, if necessary, and verify that the Estate wedge is now 46%.
- **d.** Size and position the pie chart so it fills the blank area on the slide attractively, then change the font size of the labels in the pie chart to 14 pt. (*Hint*: The label for Townhouse may appear outside the pie wedge, which is acceptable.)
- **e.** In Excel, copy cell B17, then paste it as a linked worksheet object on Slide 5 in PowerPoint.
- **f.** Position the Excel object after "is" and resize it so its font size is comparable to the bullet text.
- **g.** In the Properties Query datasheet in Access, change the price of the Westmount Estate (the third record) to **$2,700,000**.
- **h.** Update the link in Excel, switch to PowerPoint, then update the links to the chart and the worksheet object.
- **i.** Break the links to the Excel chart and worksheet, view the presentation in Slide Sorter view, compare the presentation to Figure C-14, save and close all open files and programs, then submit your files to your instructor.

FIGURE C-14

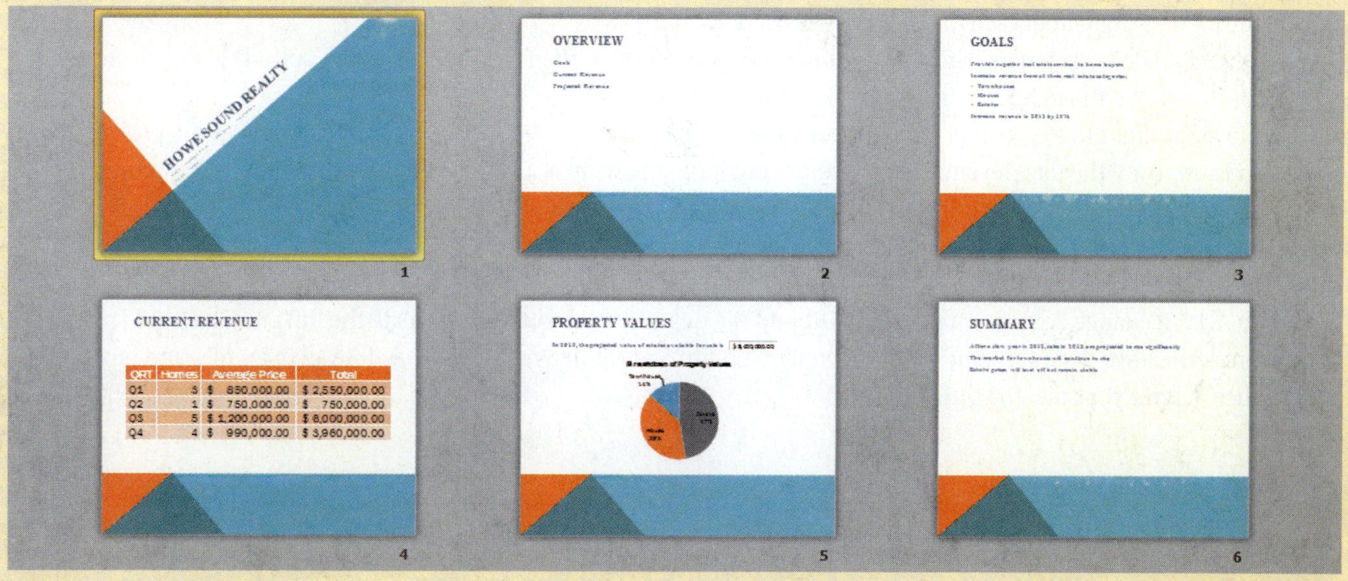

Independent Challenge 1

You work at Precious Pets, a boutique pet store that sells purebred puppies and dog accessories. You have collected data about recent sales in an Access database, and now you need to create a presentation in PowerPoint that contains links to the sales figures. You want to be able to update the links in PowerPoint, so you copy relevant data to an Excel worksheet. You also need to import some of the slides needed for the presentation from a Word outline.

a. In Word, open the file INT C-5.docx from the drive and folder where you store your Data Files, then save it as **INT C-Precious Pets Outline**.

b. In Outline view, demote the subtitle Dog Breed Information to Level 2, demote the list of the four breeds under the Promotions Level 1 heading to Level 3, then save and close the document.

c. Start a new presentation in PowerPoint, then save it as **INT C-Precious Pets Presentation** in the drive and folder where you store your Data Files.

d. Insert the Precious Pets Outline document into PowerPoint, delete Slide 1, add your name after the subtitle on Slide 1, then apply the Title Slide layout and the slide design of your choice.

e. On the new Slide 2 (Top Sellers), embed an Excel Worksheet object resized to column C and row 6 with a 22 pt font size and containing the information in Figure C-15.

f. Resize columns as necessary, calculate the total revenue in cell B5, then format the values with the Accounting Number format.

g. Apply the table style of your choice, convert the table to a range, apply the same theme as you applied to the presentation (the names of the themes in Excel are the same as the names of the designs in PowerPoint), bold and right-align Total, resize the worksheet object so only the cells containing labels or values are visible, then size and position the worksheet object attractively on the slide.

FIGURE C-15

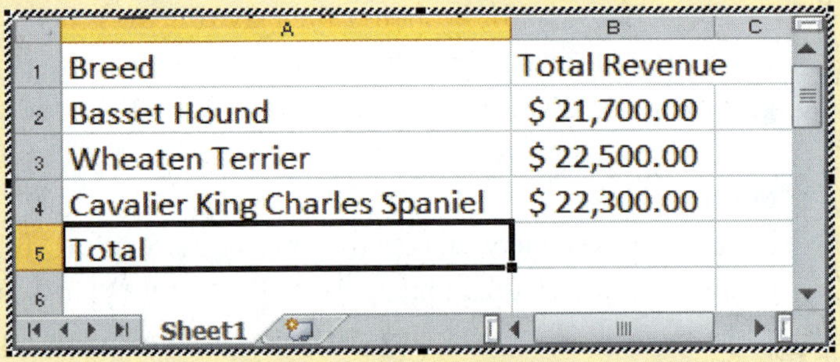

h. Start Access, open the file INT C-6.accdb from the drive and folder where you store your Data Files, then save the database as **INT C-Precious Pets Inventory** and enable content.

i. Add two new records to the Breeds table (records 16 and 17) as follows: a Poodle and a Great Dane. Describe each breed as Large, with sales of 5 dogs and a cost of $500.

j. Create a query called **Breeds Query** from the Breeds table, using all fields, that sorts the contents of the Size field in ascending order. Save and close the query, copy the query, paste it as a link into a new Excel workbook, then save the workbook as **INT C-Precious Pets Breed Information** in the drive and folder where you save your Data Files.

k. Calculate the total revenue for each breed in column F, then starting in cell D20, enter labels and formulas to calculate the total revenue from each of the three sizes of dogs.

l. Format all dollar amounts with the Accounting Number format, then use the data in the range D20:F21 to create a 2D pie chart entitled **Sales by Dog Size** using Layout 6.

m. Move the chart to the right of the data, copy the pie chart, then paste it on the appropriate slide in the presentation.

n. In Excel, copy the total revenue from Medium dogs, then paste it as a linked worksheet object in the appropriate location on the slide containing the chart.

o. Size and position the worksheet object attractively, then increase the font size of the chart labels and the legend labels so that they are easy to read.

p. In Access, change Boxer sale price to **$700** and the quantity sold to **6**, then update the links in Excel and PowerPoint.

q. Break the links in PowerPoint, view the presentation in Slide Sorter view, save and close all open files and programs, then submit your files to your instructor.

Independent Challenge 2

You are the Assistant Manager at a store in Sacramento, California, that sells camping, hiking, and mountaineering equipment. To assist your customers, you have created a database of trail information that they can access online. You have also decided to create a short PowerPoint presentation from information you have stored in Word. The presentation will include data from the database, an embedded worksheet, and a linked chart.

a. Start Word, open the file INT C-7.docx from the drive and folder where you store your Data Files, save it as **INT C-Sacramento Outdoor Shop Outline**, then, in Outline view, demote "All skill levels are accommodated" to Level 2 and promote "Distances" to Level 1.

b. Save and close the document, start a new PowerPoint presentation, save it as **INT C-Sacramento Outdoor Shop Presentation**, then import the INT C-Sacramento Outdoor Shop Outline document into the presentation.

c. Delete the blank Slide 1, apply the Title Slide layout to the new Slide 1, add your name as the subtitle on Slide 1, then apply the slide design of your choice.

d. On Slide 2, embed an Excel Worksheet object displaying four columns and six rows, apply a larger font size so the values are clearly visible, then enter the information shown in Table C-2 and adjust column widths.

e. Calculate the total sales in cell B5, then, in cell C2, enter the formula **=B2/B5** to calculate the average percentage of sales attributable to Backpacking/Hiking products. Widen columns as needed to view all the data.

f. Copy the formula to the other two product categories, then format values with the Accounting Number and Percent formats as necessary. Move the table down as necessary so you can see the bulleted text.

TABLE C-2

Category	Sales	Average
Backpacking/Hiking	36000	
Mountain Biking	23000	
Winter Sports	28000	
Total Sales		

g. In PowerPoint, delete XX in the bulleted item and replace it with the appropriate value from the worksheet.

h. Apply a theme that matches the presentation, apply the table style of your choice and convert the table to a range, right-align and bold Total Sales, resize and position the worksheet object attractively on the slide, then save the presentation.

i. Start Access, open the file INT C-8.accdb from the drive and folder where you store your Data Files, save the database as **INT C-Sacramento Outdoor Shop Trails Database**, then enable content.

j. Create a query called **California Trails Query** from all the fields in the California Trails table that sorts the contents of the Type field in ascending order.

k. Close and save the query, copy it, then paste it as a link into a new Excel workbook saved as **INT C-Sacramento Outdoor Shop Trails Information** in the drive and folder where you store your Data Files.

l. Starting in cell D15 of the worksheet, enter labels and formulas to calculate the total miles covered in each of the three trip types: Backpacking, Hiking, and Walking. (*Hint*: The formula for Backpacking is =SUM(E2:E5).)

m. Create a pie chart, using Layout 6, resize the labels and legend to 14 pt, and add a chart title: **Breakdown of Distances Covered by Trip**

n. Copy the pie chart, then paste it on the appropriate slide in the presentation and resize it to fit the space attractively.

o. Copy cell D16 in the source workbook, then paste it as a linked worksheet object so it replaces the YY placeholder. (*Hint*: Move "miles" to the right using the Spacebar and then size and position the worksheet object so that it fits.)

p. In the Access query, change the distance of the Pacific Crest Trail: Donner Pass to Squaw Valley trip to **16** miles and the Deadman Canyon Backpack Loop trip to **5** miles, then close the query.

q. Update links in Excel and PowerPoint, then close the Access database and save and close the Excel workbook.

r. In PowerPoint, break the links.

s. View the presentation, save and close all open files and programs, then submit your files to your instructor.

Visual Workshop

For a course on tourism in England, you have decided to create a presentation that focuses on popular hotels in various locations. The presentation will contain one slide displaying a pie chart showing the breakdown of hotel guests by location. In Access, open the file INT C-9.accdb from the drive and folder where you store your Data Files, then save the database as **INT C-England Hotels**. Create a query called **Locations** that includes all fields and that sorts the Hotels table in ascending order by Location. Copy the query and paste it as a link into Excel, then create the 3D pie chart similar to the one shown in Figure C-16 and copy it. Save the Excel workbook as **INT C-England Hotels Data**. As shown in the figure, create a one-slide PowerPoint presentation called **INT C-England Hotels Presentation**, apply the Title Only slide layout, then paste the pie chart onto the slide. Format the slide as shown, and insert clip art. (*Hint*: Use 18 pt text for the data labels, add the slide title, use the Grid design, and search clip art for Big Ben with the Include Office.com content check box selected if necessary.) Switch to Access, open the Locations query, change the number of guests who stayed at the Hotel Buckingham in London to 160, close the query, update the links in Excel and PowerPoint, then enter your name in the slide footer. Break the link to the PowerPoint presentation, save and close all open files and programs, then submit your files to your instructor.

FIGURE C-16

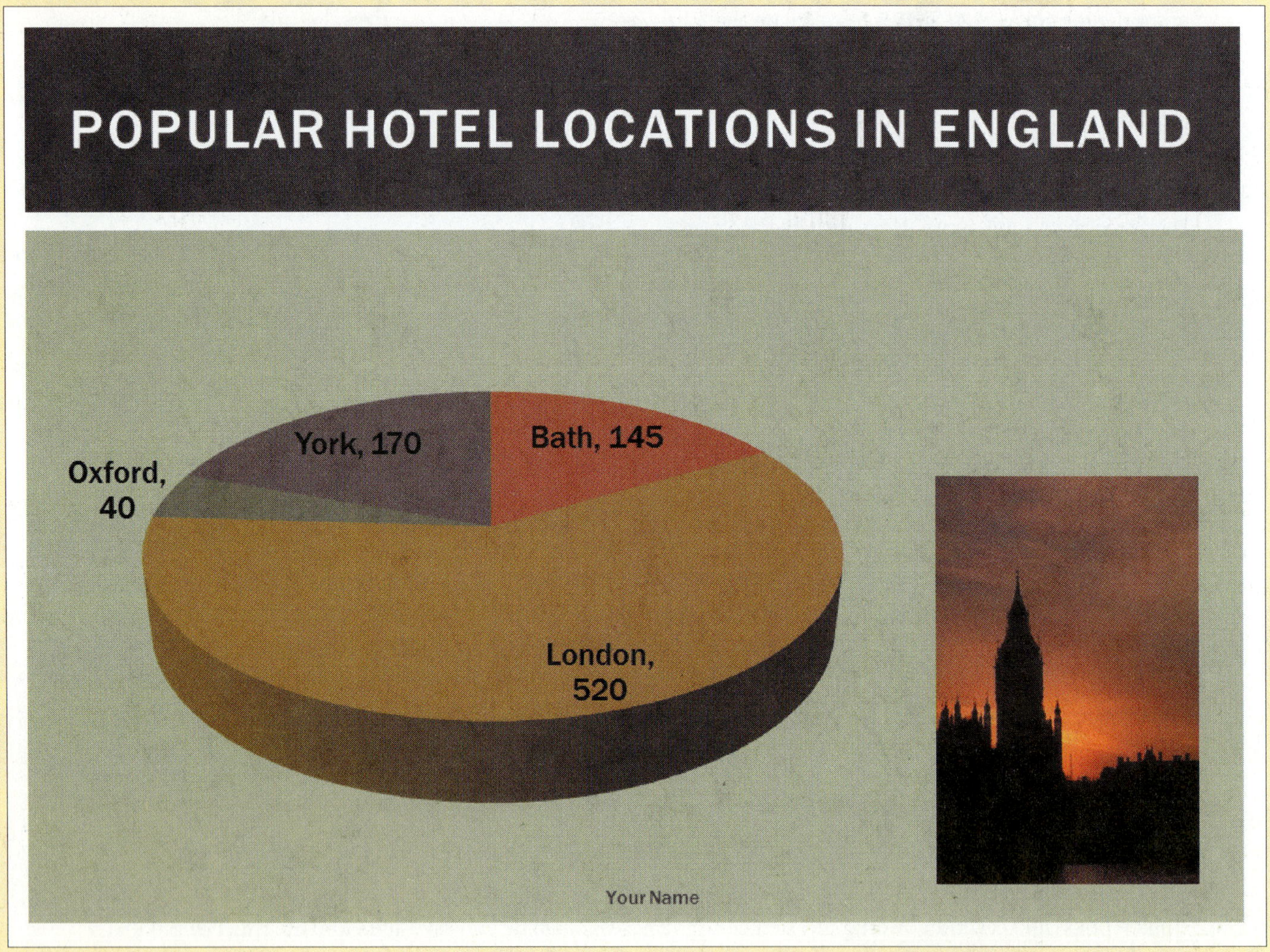

UNIT A
Outlook 2010

Getting Started with E-Mail

Files You Will Need:

Leave No Trace.docx
Bridge.jpg

E-mail is an essential communication tool for business and personal correspondence. You can use a desktop information management program like Microsoft Outlook 2010, an e-mail program, or any of several Web-based e-mail programs to send and receive e-mail. Once you learn the basic features of e-mail, you will be able to use Outlook or any other e-mail program to manage your e-mail. You are an assistant to Juan Ramirez, the personnel director at Quest Specialty Travel (QST). The company uses e-mail for much of its correspondence. Juan wants you to learn the basics of e-mail for your job.

OBJECTIVES

- Communicate with e-mail
- Compile an e-mail address book
- Create and send a message
- Manage e-mail folders
- Receive and reply to a message
- Forward a message
- Send a message with an attachment
- Employ good e-mail practices

UNIT
A
Outlook 2010

Communicating with E-Mail

Electronic mail (e-mail) is the technology that lets you send and receive written messages through the Internet. The messages sent using e-mail technology are known as **e-mail messages**, or **e-mail** for short. **E-mail software**, such as Microsoft Outlook, shown in Figure A-1, enables you to send and receive e-mail messages over a network, over an intranet, and over the Internet. A **computer network** is the hardware and software that enables two or more computers to share information and resources. An **intranet** is a computer network that connects computers in a local area only, such as computers in a company's office. The **Internet** is a network of connected computers and computer networks located around the world. Quest Specialty Travel employees use e-mail to communicate with each other and with clients around the world because it is fast, reliable, and easy.

DETAILS

E-mail enables you to:

QUICK TIP
E-mail uses store-and-forward technology. Messages are *stored* on a service provider's computer until a recipient logs on to a computer and requests his or her messages. At that time, the messages are *forwarded* to the recipient's computer.

- **Communicate conveniently and efficiently**
  E-mail is an effective way to correspond with coworkers or colleagues. E-mail can be sent from one person to another person or to a group of people anywhere in the world. You can send and receive messages directly from any computer with an Internet or network connection. You can also send and receive e-mail from wireless devices such as smartphones or handheld computers with e-mail capability. Unlike mail sent using the postal service, e-mail is delivered almost instantaneously. Unlike instant messaging recipients, e-mail recipients do not have to be at their computers at the same time that a message is sent in order to receive the message.

- **Send images, video, and documents as well as text information**
  Messages can be formatted so that they are easy to read and appear professional and attractive. Messages can include graphics in the body of the message to convey visual information. In addition, you can attach files to a message, such as a sound or video, photographs, graphics, spreadsheets, or word-processing documents.

- **Communicate with numerous people at once; never forget an address**
  You can create your own electronic address book that stores the names and e-mail addresses of people with whom you frequently communicate. You can send the same message to more than one person at one time. You can also create named groups of e-mail addresses and then send messages to that group of people by entering only the group name.

- **Ensure the delivery of information**
  With e-mail software, you have the option of receiving a delivery confirmation message when a recipient receives your e-mail. In addition, if you are away and unable to access e-mail because of a vacation or other plans, you can set up an automatic message that is delivered to senders so they are alerted to the fact that you might not receive your e-mail for a specified time period.

- **Correspond from a remote place**
  If you have an Internet connection and communications software, you can use your computer or handheld device to send and receive messages from any location. You sign up with an **ISP (Internet service provider)** to send and receive e-mail. If you are using a Web-based e-mail program, like those shown in Figures A-2 and A-3, you can access your e-mail from any computer that is connected to the Internet from anywhere in the world. You can connect to the Internet using a telephone line or use other, faster technologies, including satellite, DSL (digital subscriber line), cable, fiber optic, ISDN (Integrated Services Digital Network), T1, or T3.

- **Organize a record of your communications**
  You can organize the messages you send and receive in a way that best suits your working style. You can store e-mail messages in folders and refer to them again in the future. Organizing your saved messages lets you keep a record of communications to manage a project or business. You can also flag or categorize messages to give an instant visual cue that distinguishes messages that require immediate attention from those that can wait. You can download e-mail to your computer or keep it on the provider's Web server.

FIGURE A-1: Microsoft Outlook

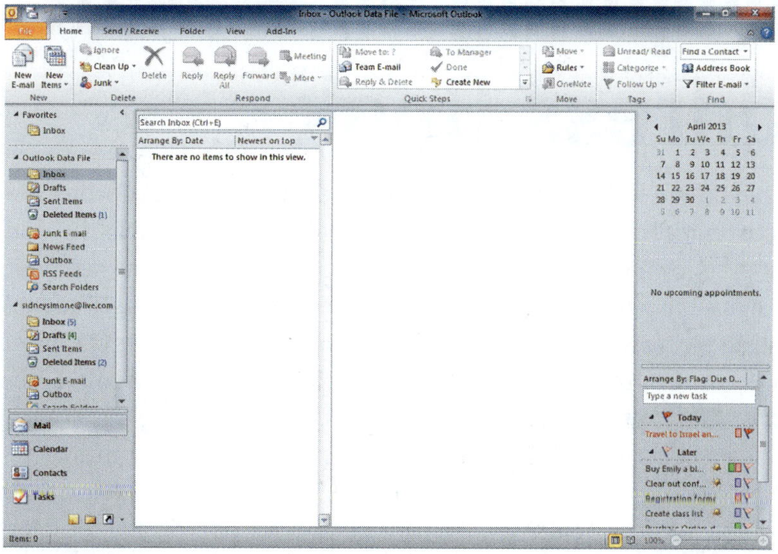

FIGURE A-2: Web-based e-mail: Gmail

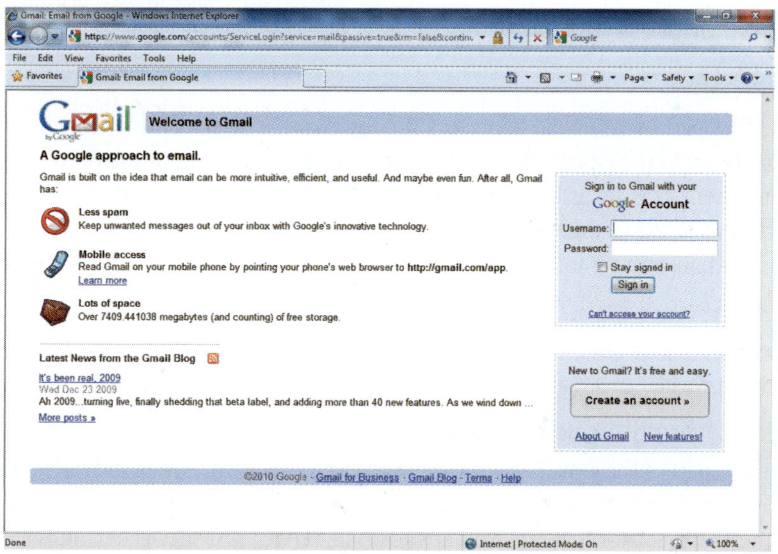

FIGURE A-3: Web-based e-mail: Hotmail

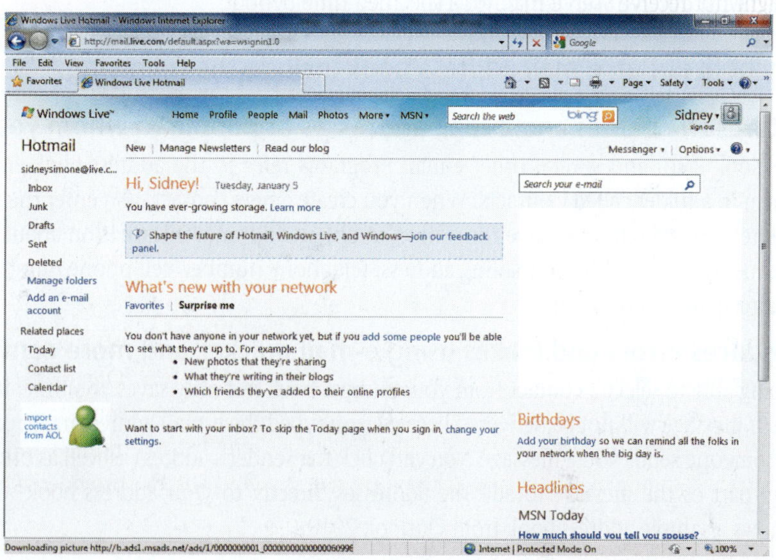

Compiling an E-Mail Address Book

E-mail can be sent from one person to another person or a group of people anywhere in the world. To send and receive e-mail over the Internet using an e-mail program, you must have an e-mail address. Each person has his or her own e-mail address and a password that lets him or her log in to an e-mail program and receive e-mail. To send an e-mail message, you need to know the e-mail address of the person to whom you are sending the message. Instead of having to remember the address of someone to whom you are sending an e-mail, you can select the name you want from an **address book**, a stored list of names and e-mail addresses. At Quest Specialty Travel, each employee is assigned an e-mail address. As the assistant to the personnel director in the Human Resources department, you maintain a list of all employee e-mail addresses in an electronic address book that you use to distribute information about company policies and events through e-mail. You review the parts of an e-mail address and the benefits of maintaining an e-mail address book.

DETAILS

An e-mail address has three parts:

- **Username**
  The first part of an e-mail address is the username. The **username** identifies the person who receives the e-mail sent to the e-mail address. At Quest Specialty Travel, as in many companies, universities, or organizations, usernames are assigned and are based on a specified format. At QST, a username is the first initial of the person's first name and his or her last name. In many e-mail systems, such as those used primarily for personal e-mail, you get to create your username, combining letters and numbers to create a unique username.
- **@ sign**
  The middle part of an e-mail address is the @ sign, called an "at sign." It separates the username from the service provider or e-mail provider name. Every e-mail address includes an @ sign.
- **Service provider or e-mail provider**
  The last part of the e-mail address is the service provider or e-mail provider. There are many different service providers. For example, the service provider might be the name of the company that a person works for or the name of the school that a person attends. The service provider generally is a company or organization that provides the connection to the Internet and provides e-mail. The service provider can also be the Web site name for a Web-based e-mail program. Table A-1 provides some examples of e-mail address formats that are used with different service providers.

QUICK TIP
A person can have more than one e-mail address.

The benefits of an e-mail address book include the following:

- **Stores the names and e-mail addresses of people to whom you send e-mail messages**
  Outlook 2010 and several other e-mail programs refer to the address book entries as "contacts" and place them in a folder called Contacts. When you create a new contact, you enter the person's full name and e-mail address. You might also have the option to enter additional information about that person, including his or her personal and business mailing address, telephone number, cell phone number, Web page, instant message address, and even a picture.
- **Reduces errors and makes using e-mail quicker and more convenient**
  Being able to select a contact from your address book not only saves you time; it also reduces the chance that your message will not be delivered because you typed the e-mail address incorrectly. In most e-mail programs, if someone sends you a message, you can click the sender's address as well as other recipients' addresses in the top part of the message to add the addresses directly to your address book without any errors. Figure A-4 shows a sample address book from Outlook 2010.

FIGURE A-4: Outlook 2010 address book with three contacts

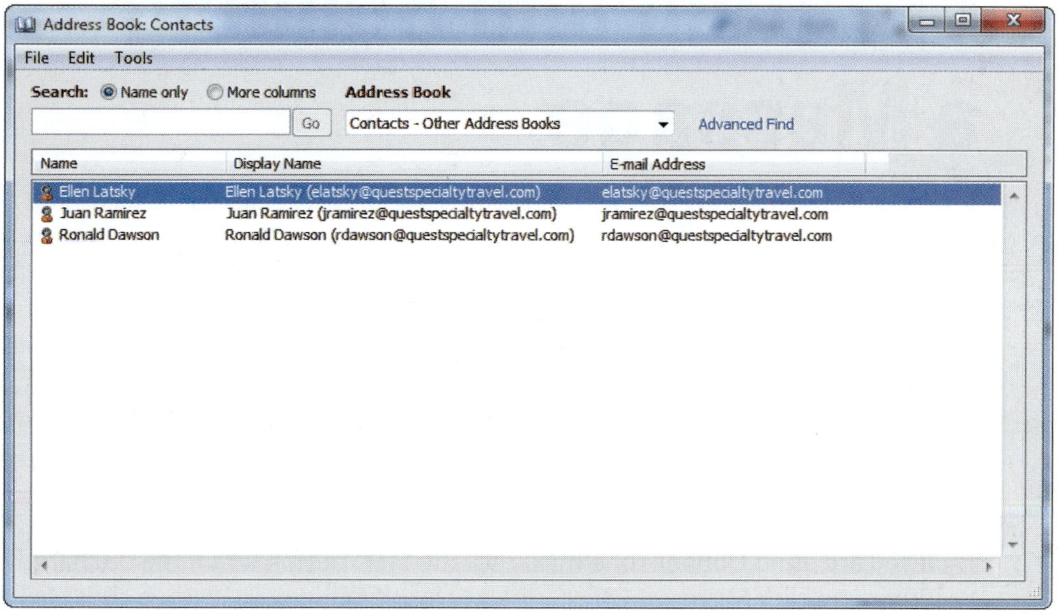

TABLE A-1: Examples of e-mail providers and addresses

e-mail sponsor	examples of service providers	description of e-mail services	where e-mail is stored	sample e-mail addresses
Corporate or company e-mail	Quest Specialty Travel	A company that provides e-mail for employees	Company server, or downloaded to user's computer	username@questspecialtytravel.com
Commercial provider: Cable TV, voice, and data communications companies	America Online, Comcast, Cablevision, EarthLink, Verizon	Also provide Web space and several e-mail addresses	ISP server, until downloaded to user's computer	username@aol.com username@comcast.net username@optimum.net username@earthlink.net username@verizon.net
Web-based e-mail	Hotmail (Microsoft), Gmail (Google), Yahoo! Mail (Yahoo!)	Web site that provides free e-mail addresses and service	On the Web site e-mail server	username@hotmail.com username@live.com username@gmail.com username@yahoo.com
Educational institution	Harvard University University of Delaware	Provide e-mail for faculty, staff, and students	On the university e-mail server	username@harvard.edu username@udel.edu

UNIT
A
Outlook 2010

Creating and Sending a Message

When you create an e-mail message, you must indicate to whom you are sending the message and specify any people who should receive a copy. You also need to enter a meaningful subject for the message to give its recipients an idea of its content. You write the text of your message in the **message body**. After you create the message, you send it. Outlook 2010 uses Microsoft Word as the default text editor in e-mail messages, which means that you have access to the same text-formatting features in Outlook that you use when you create Word documents. Most e-mail programs use a basic text editor that enables you to do such things as change the color of text, use different fonts, create a bulleted list, and check the spelling of your message. You write and send a message to several employees about an upcoming meeting.

STEPS

1. **If you are using Outlook for e-mail, click the Start button on the taskbar, click All Programs, click Microsoft Office, click Microsoft Outlook 2010, then click Mail if it is not already selected; if you are using Web-based e-mail, log into your e-mail account program**
   If you are using Outlook 2010 or another e-mail program, you can start the program and then create a message without connecting to the Internet. If your e-mail program is Web based, such as Hotmail or Gmail, you have to be connected to the Internet to create an e-mail message.

2. **Click the button or link that allows you to create new mail, such as the New E-mail button or the Compose Mail button**
   All e-mail programs provide a button or link to use to begin writing a new message. There are basic similarities in all programs, in that each new message window or page provides boxes or spaces to enter address information and message content, as shown in Figure A-5.

QUICK TIP
Use the e-mail address of a friend or associate to complete this lesson, or use your own e-mail address.

3. **Enter a valid e-mail address in the To text box as the address of the person to whom you are sending the message**
   You can send e-mail to more than one person at one time; just type each e-mail address in the To text box, and separate the addresses with a semicolon or comma (depending on what your e-mail program requires). You can also click the To button, or the Address Book button, to open the Select Names dialog box and select each e-mail address from the address book. If you click names or e-mail addresses in an address book, you are less likely to make an error as you enter addresses.

QUICK TIP
Bcc is available when you open the Select Names dialog box.

4. **Click the Cc text box, then type a friend's e-mail address as the e-mail address for a recipient who is to receive a courtesy copy**
   Cc stands for courtesy copy. **Courtesy copies** are typically sent to message recipients who need to be aware of the correspondence between the sender and the recipients. Bcc, or **blind courtesy copy**, is used when the sender does not want to reveal who he or she has sent courtesy copies to.

5. **Type Meeting August 20 in the Subject box as the subject for your message**
   The Subject text box should be a brief statement that indicates the purpose of your message. The subject becomes the title of the message.

6. **Type your message in the message window**
   Figure A-6 shows a completed message. Many e-mail programs provide a spell-checking program that alerts you of spelling errors in your message. Messages should be concise and polite. If you want to send a lengthy message, consider attaching a file to the message. (You will learn about attaching files later in this unit.)

QUICK TIP
Although you can write and read messages in Outlook and other programs when you are not online, you must be connected to the Internet to send or receive messages.

7. **Click the Send button to send your e-mail message**
   Once the message is sent, the message window or Web page closes. Most e-mail programs store a copy of the message in your Sent or Sent Items folder or give you the option to do so.

FIGURE A-5: New message window

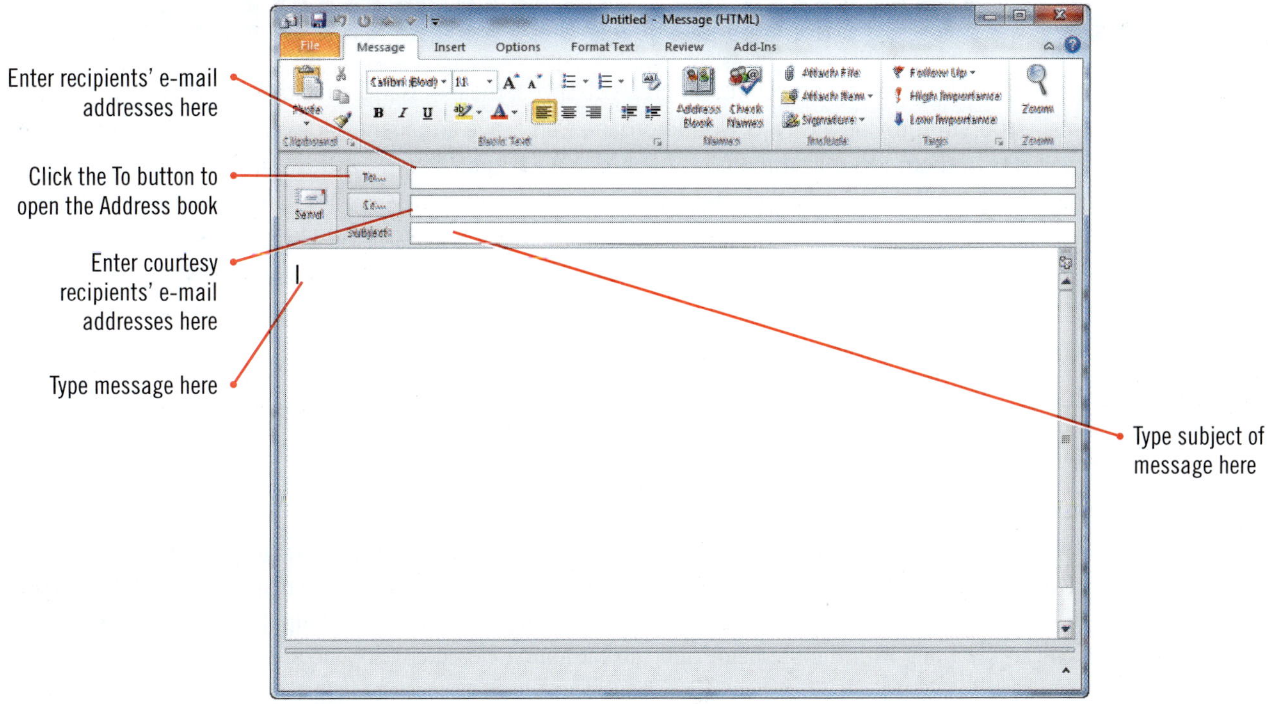

FIGURE A-6: A sample message

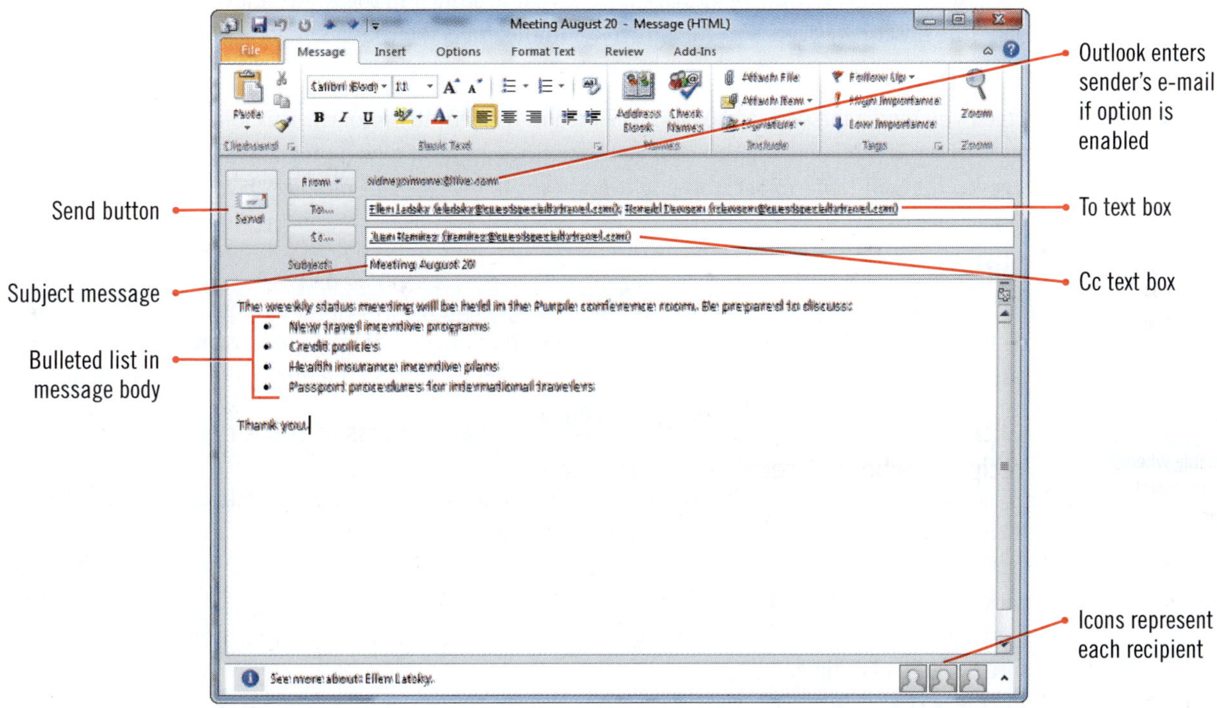

Understanding message headers

A **message header** contains the basic information about a message. It includes the sender's name and e-mail address, the names and e-mail addresses of recipients and Cc recipients, a date and time stamp, and the subject of the message. When e-mail travels through the e-mail system, the message header is the first information that you see when you retrieve your e-mail. Bcc recipients are not included in the message header. E-mail programs date- and time-stamp e-mail messages when they are received at the recipient's computer, using the current date and time.

UNIT
A
Outlook 2010

Managing E-Mail Folders

Just as you save files in folders on your computer, you save e-mail messages in folders in your e-mail program. All e-mail programs provide a way for you to organize and save e-mail messages. You save messages so that you can refer to them again in the future. Most e-mail programs come with several default folders. These include Inbox, Drafts, Sent Items, Outbox, Deleted Items, and Junk E-mail folders (or folders with similar names). See Figure A-7. In addition, most allow you to create and name additional folders. Once you save messages, you can sort them within folders to help you find the message you want. As an employee of the Human Resources department, you send and receive messages on several topics. You organize the e-mail so you can better track the messages you send and receive.

DETAILS

E-mail programs come with the following default folders:

- **Inbox**

  An Inbox is a mail folder that receives all incoming e-mail as it arrives. You know who sent the e-mail message because the username or e-mail address and subject line appear in the list of e-mail in your Inbox, as shown in Figure A-8. You will also know when the message came in because your computer puts a date on it, which you can see along with the username and subject line. A closed envelope icon means the message has not been read yet. Many e-mail systems allow you to preview the message before opening a message. You can organize e-mail by date, sender, subject, and other header data.

- **Drafts**

  If you want to finish writing a message later, save it to store it in the Drafts folder. Many programs automatically save unsent messages at regular intervals in the drafts folder as a safety measure.

- **Sent Items**

  When you send a message, a copy of it is stored in the Sent Items folder. This folder helps you track the messages that you send out. You can change the settings on most e-mail programs so that you do not save messages to the Sent Items folder. You might not want to save all sent messages because they take up computer storage space.

- **Outbox**

  The Outbox is a temporary storage folder for messages that have not yet been sent. If you are working offline or if you set your e-mail program so that messages do not get sent immediately after you click the Send button, the messages are placed in the Outbox. When you connect to the Internet or click the Send/Receive All Folders button, the messages in the Outbox are sent.

QUICK TIP
You should clear out the Sent Items and Deleted Items folders periodically to free up storage space on your computer.

- **Deleted Items or Trash**

  When you delete or erase a message from any folder, it is placed in the Deleted Items or Trash folder, rather than being immediately and permanently deleted. So if you delete a message accidentally, you can find it again. To empty the Deleted Items folder, right-click the folder or click a menu or toolbar button, and then click Empty Folder. Some programs have a special link to click in order to empty the folder. Some Web-based e-mail programs clear out the Trash folder if it gets too full or after messages have been in the folder for a specified period of time.

- **Junk E-Mail or Spam**

  Junk e-mail, or **spam**, is unwanted e-mail that arrives from unsolicited sources. Most junk e-mail is advertising or offensive messages. **Spamming** is the sending of identical or near-identical unsolicited messages to a large number of recipients. Many e-mail programs have filters that identify this type of e-mail and place it in a special folder. Then you can easily delete the e-mail you don't want. It is possible that a message that you do want might get caught by the spam filter. It is good practice to look at the headers in the Junk E-mail folder before deleting the messages stored there.

FIGURE A-7: Mail folders

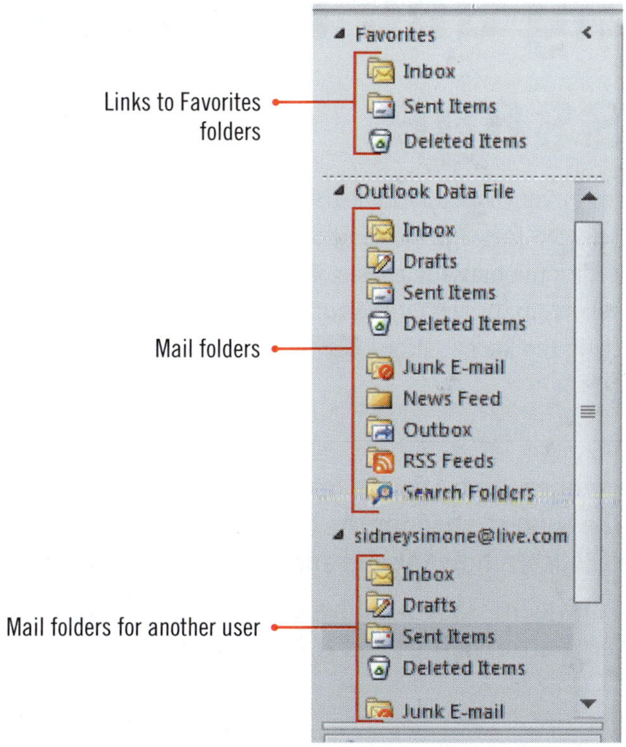

FIGURE A-8: Outlook Mail window

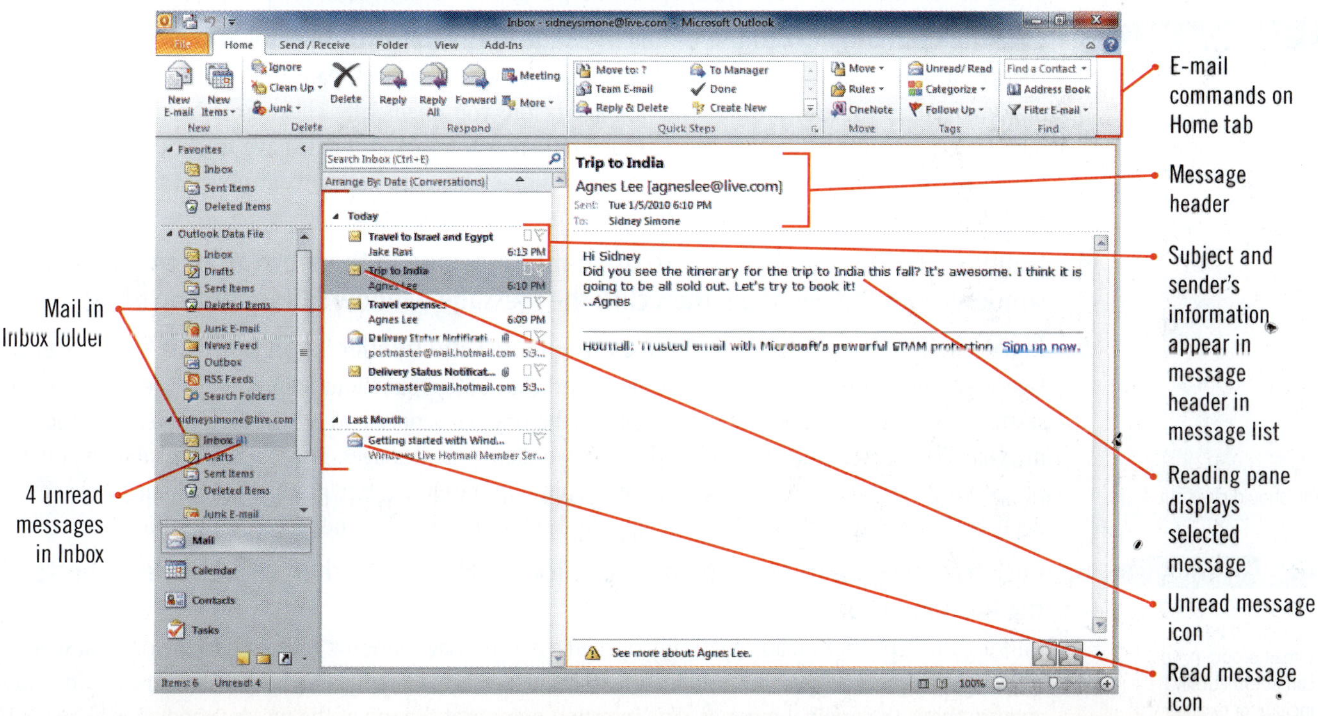

Sorting your mail

You would be surprised at how quickly your Inbox, Sent Items, and Deleted Items or Trash folders can fill up. How can you manage these? The best way is to create folders for specific projects or people that you know will be "high volume" for e-mail. For example, if you are working on a special project, create a folder for that project. Any e-mail that you receive or send about the project can be moved into that folder. Depending on your e-mail program, you can also categorize, flag, or label messages. You can sort e-mail by any message header, such as date, subject, flag or label, or sender to find an important message quickly. Once the project is completed, you can archive or delete that folder's e-mail. Check to see how much e-mail is accumulating in the Deleted Items or Trash folder. E-mail takes up storage space, and if you are running out of storage on your computer, your e-mail is a good place to start cleaning up the hard drive.

Receiving and Replying to a Message

To read a message that arrives in your Inbox, you first select it. Outlook and some other e-mail software programs let you preview a selected message in the Reading or Preview Pane. To open the message in its own window, you can double-click the message header. After reading a message, you can delete it, move it to another folder, flag it for follow-up, or keep it in your Inbox. You can also send a response back to the sender of the message by clicking the Reply button. You often reply to messages sent to you as you correspond with the staff at QST.

STEPS

1. **Open a new message window, enter your e-mail address in the To text box, type Learning how to use e-mail as the subject, then for the body of the message, type I am sending this message to myself to learn how to send and reply to messages.**

> **TROUBLE**
> You might have to check for mail several times before the e-mail message comes in.

2. **Click the Send button in the message window, click the Send/Receive tab, click the Send/Receive All Folders button in the Send & Receive group, then open the Inbox in the e-mail program**

   When you click the Send/Receive or Get Mail button, your e-mail program checks for any messages in the Outbox that need to be sent and delivers incoming messages to your Inbox. Many e-mail programs deliver e-mail to the Inbox at the time you sign in or log in with your username and password.

> **QUICK TIP**
> In many Web-based e-mail programs, you have to click the Get Mail button or link, and clicking an e-mail message opens the message.

3. **Click the Learning how to use e-mail message in the Inbox to select it and view the message**

   You can read the message header to identify the message by subject, date, and sender. If your e-mail has a preview feature, you can preview the message before you open it by clicking its header. In Outlook, the message appears in the Reading Pane in the Outlook window. You might have to click a link or button to display inserted graphics or video. Many programs hide images to protect your privacy, unless you configure the program's settings to accept images for each message in the Inbox.

4. **Double-click the Learning how to use e-mail message in the inbox to open it in a new window, read the message, then click the message window's Close button**

5. **Right-click the Learning how to use e-mail message header, then point to Quick Steps**

   Figure A-9 shows the Outlook shortcut menu and Quick Steps submenu. Reply lets you reply to the original sender. The Reply All option lets you reply to the original sender and all the Cc recipients of the original message. Bcc recipients are not included in Reply or Reply All messages. The Quick Steps submenu offers a list of customizable command sequences that also appear in the Quick Steps group on the Home tab. For example, Reply & Delete both replies to the message and deletes the original to help keep your Inbox clean.

> **QUICK TIP**
> Depending on how you set up your e-mail program, you can automatically include or exclude the text of the original sender's message in the message body along with the message header.

6. **Click the message to close the menus, click the Home tab, then click the Reply button in the Respond group**

   Clicking the Reply button automatically opened a new message window addressed to the original sender. The subject line is preceded by "RE:", indicating that the message is a reply. The header from the original message appears above the original message. The insertion point is at the top of the message body. See Figure A-10.

7. **Type This is my reply message. in the message body as the reply**

   It is helpful to include the original message in a reply to help the message recipient recall the topic.

8. **Click the Send button in the message window**

   The message is sent, and a copy of it is stored in your Sent Items folder. Most e-mail programs add a Replied to Message icon next to the original message in the Inbox, indicating that you have replied to the message. Often this is a small arrow pointing to the left.

9. **Close the original message if necessary to return to the Inbox**

FIGURE A-9: Message options

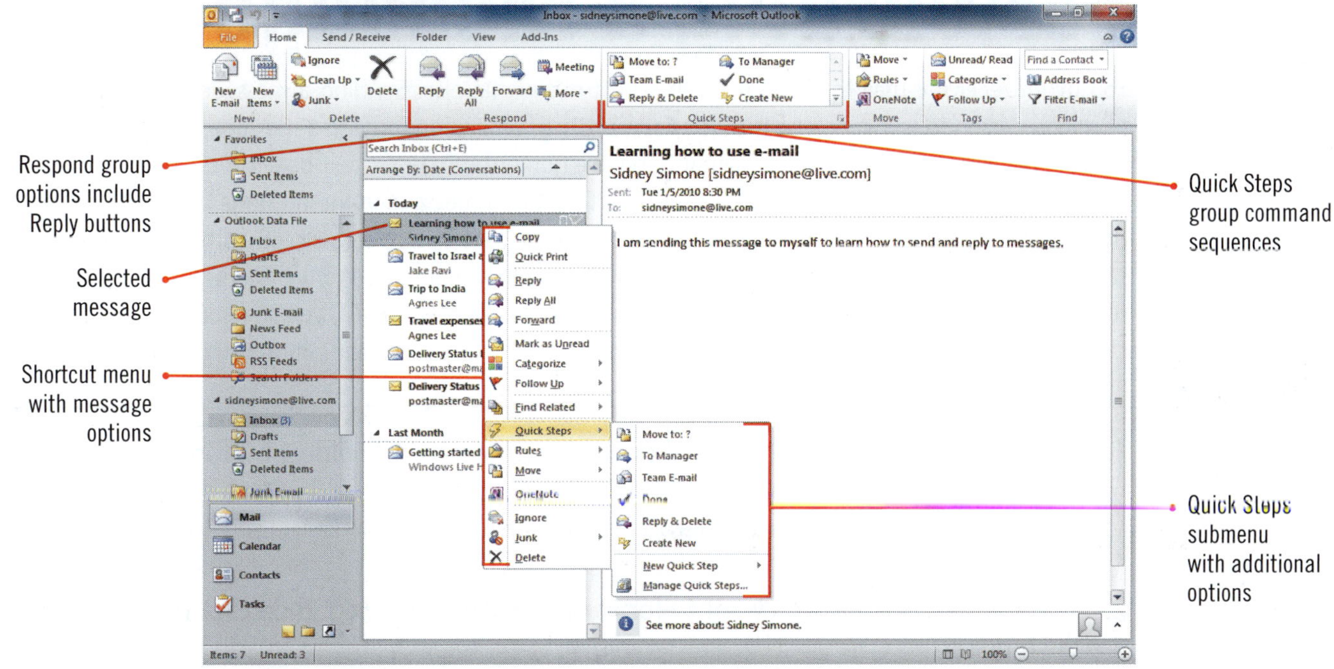

FIGURE A-10: Replying to a message

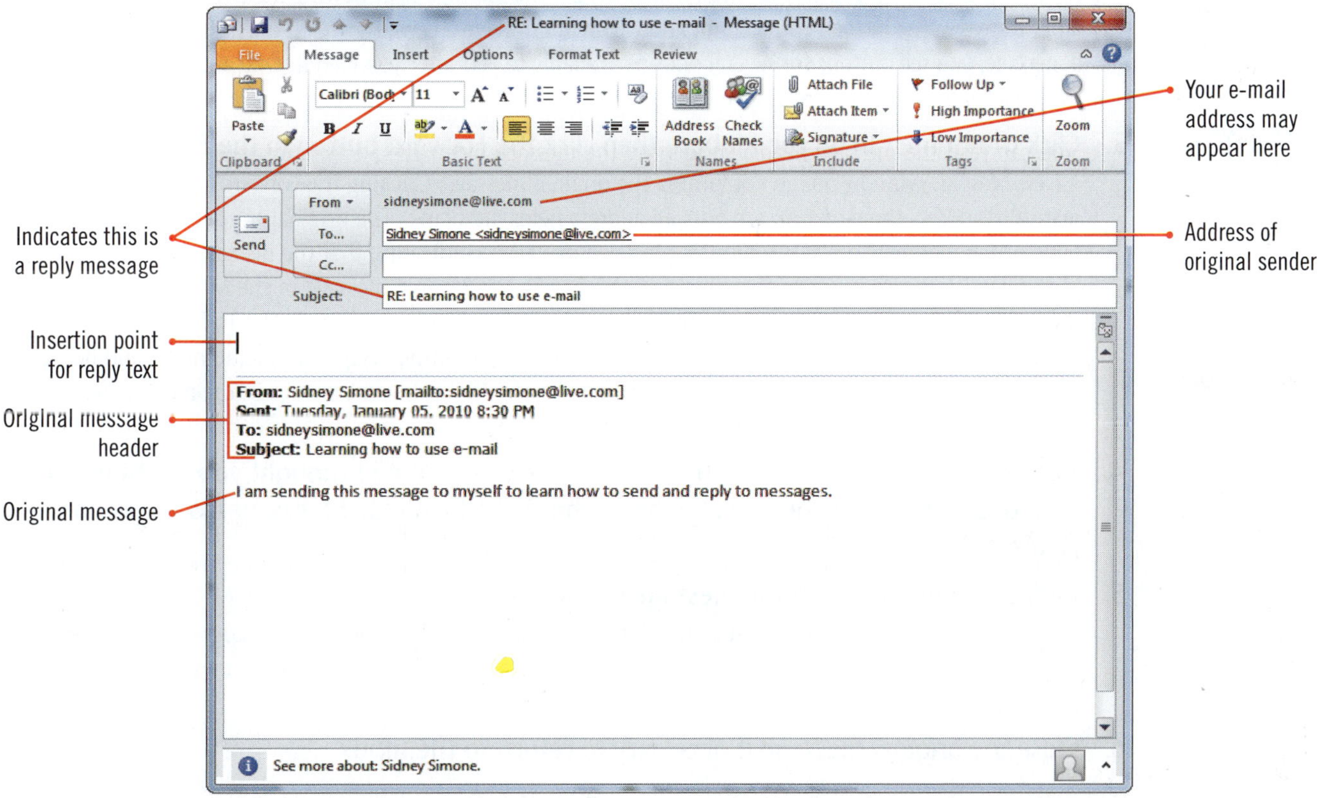

Setting up vacation responses

Most e-mail programs allow you to set up an automatic response or vacation message if you are not going to be able to get your e-mail for a specified period of time. This is a helpful way to let people know that you are not ignoring any e-mail they send, but rather that you are not reading your e-mail. When vacation mode is active, your e-mail program automatically sends out a reply when a message comes in. You determine the content of the reply message. A typical message might be "Thank you for your message. I am on vacation from July 1–July 10th and will respond to your message when I return." Most e-mail programs only send one automatic response to each sender each day or within a specified period of time.

Forwarding a Message

You might receive e-mail that you need to send to someone else. Sending a message you have received from one person to someone else is called **forwarding**. When you forward a message, you send it to people who have not already received it—that is, people not in the To or Cc text boxes of the original message. You can include an additional message about the forwarded message in the message body. The subject of the forwarded message stays the same, so you can organize it by subject with any other messages on the same topic, with the same subject heading. In most e-mail programs, you forward a message that you have received to another person by clicking the Forward button. At QST, you sometimes get e-mail from clients that you forward to the travel agents at their branch offices for their information.

STEPS

1. **Click the Send/Receive tab, then click the Send/Receive All Folders button or click the Get Mail or Check Mail button or link in your e-mail program**

   Your e-mail program checks for any messages in the Outbox that need to be sent and delivers any incoming messages to your Inbox.

2. **Select a message that you want to forward, if it is not selected, then click the message in the Inbox**

   You read the message header to identify the message. You can see the original recipients of the message by reviewing the header. You can see who, if anyone, got the message by reviewing the e-mail addresses in the To and Cc areas of the header. You will not know who might have received a Bcc on the message. When you view a message, you see buttons for several options available to you after you read it. One of the options is to click the Forward button to forward the message.

3. **Click the Home tab on the Ribbon, then click the Forward button in the Respond group**

   A New Message window opens, containing the original message. Clicking the Forward button does not automatically address the e-mail to anyone; all address fields are blank. The original message is included in the body of the message. The subject line is preceded by "FW:", indicating that the message is a forwarded one. Most e-mail software includes the message header from the original message in the Message window above the original message. The insertion point is at the top of the message window in the To field. You can address this message as you would any new e-mail. You can include multiple recipients, including Cc and Bcc recipients. If you want to provide a courtesy note explaining the forward, you can click in the message body above the original message header and type a brief note.

4. **Type a friend's e-mail address in the To text box, then type I thought you might like to read this message. in the message body above the forwarded message, as shown in Figure A-11**

5. **Click the Send button in the message window**

   The message is sent, and a copy of it is stored in your Sent Items folder. Most e-mail programs add a Forwarded Message icon next to the original message, indicating that you have forwarded the message. Often this is a small arrow pointing to the right.

6. **Close the original message if necessary to return to the Inbox**

QUICK TIP

To display the From e-mail address in a message window, click the Options tab, in the Show Fields group, then click From.

FIGURE A-11: Forwarding a message

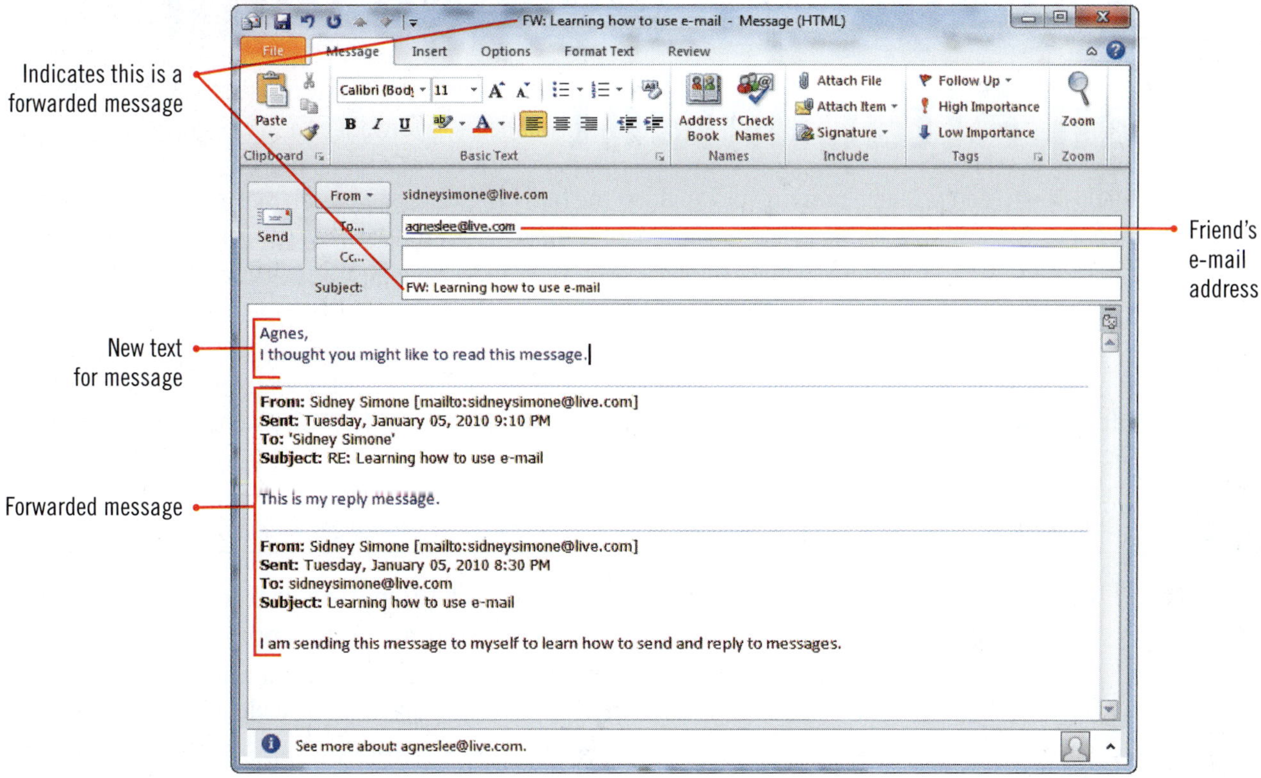

Outlook 2010

Flagging or labeling messages

Most e-mail programs provide a way to identify or categorize e-mail. If you use e-mail for business, school, or personal communication, you will find that you receive many e-mail messages. Some can be read and discarded. Others require additional attention or follow-up. Organizing your e-mail can help you keep up with the many messages you are likely to receive. If you are using Outlook, flags can assist you in your effort to manage your e-mail. If you click the flag icon next to the message, it is marked by default with a red Quick Flag. However, you can use flags of different shades of red to mark messages for different categories of follow-up. In Outlook, flags are available for Today, Tomorrow, This Week, Next Week, No Date, and Custom; the Today flag is the darkest shade of red, and the This Week and Next Week flags are the lightest. To apply a flag, click the flag in the message you want to flag. To select from a list of flag actions and specify a due date in the Custom dialog box, right-click a message, point to Follow Up, then click Add Reminder. Outlook also allows you to color code messages for categories. See Figure A-12. If you are using Web-based e-mail, you might have other options for categorizing, labelling, or flagging e-mail. For example, Gmail provides a way to assign a label to e-mail or to star e-mail for easy sorting or organizing.

FIGURE A-12: Flagging and categorizing messages

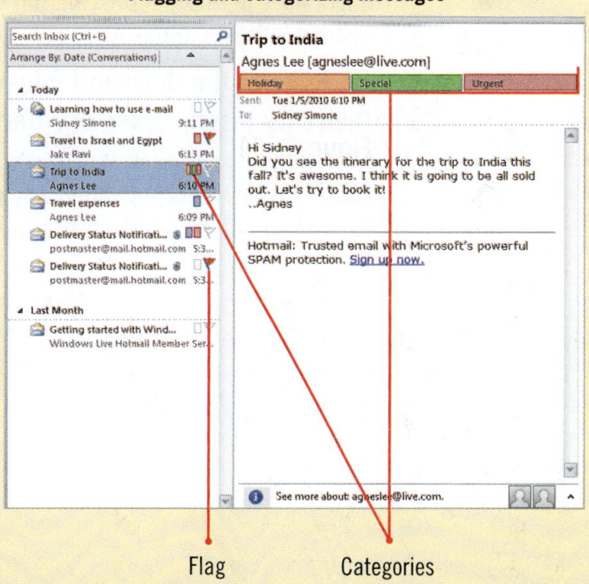

UNIT
A
Outlook 2010

Sending a Message with an Attachment

In addition to composing a message by typing in the Message window, you can **attach** a file to an e-mail message. For example, in an office environment, employees can attach Word or Excel documents to e-mail messages so that other employees can open them, make changes to them, and then return them to the original sender or forward them to others for review. You can attach any type of computer file to an e-mail message, including pictures, video, and audio. Keep in mind that to open an attachment created using a particular software program, the recipient of the attachment might need to have the appropriate software. You often send clients' trip photos to people in the office. You also have to send personnel documents to employees throughout the year. Attaching files is a common task in your job in the Human Resources department.

STEPS

QUICK TIP

Many e-mail programs will complete a previously used address once you start typing in the To box. You can click the address or press [Tab] to select the address to enter it into the To text box.

1. **Click the New E-mail button in the New group or click the button or link to open a new mail message window, then type your e-mail address in the To text box**

   You can send a message with an attachment to more than one person at one time; just enter each e-mail address in the To text box, separated by a semicolon or comma, just as you would an e-mail without an attachment. You can also click the Cc text box or Bcc text box, and then enter e-mail addresses for recipients who are to receive a Cc or Bcc.

2. **Type LNT Talking Points in the Subject box as the subject for the message, then in the message window, type Please review these Leave No Trace talking points for the National Parks presentation.**

3. **If you are using Outlook, click the Attach File button in the Include group on the Message tab**

   Most e-mail programs provide a way to attach files, either with an Attach link or with an Attach a File or Attach button. The name of the command or way to access the dialog box might differ slightly. Once the Insert File or Attach File dialog box opens, files appear in a dialog box as shown in Figures A-13 and A-14. You might have to click a Browse button to navigate to the file or files you want to attach. Often you can use the Thumbnails view in the dialog box to see what the files look like before you attach them to a message.

4. **Navigate to the drive and folder where you store your Data Files, click Leave No Trace.docx, then click Insert, Open, or Attach**

   Most programs will allow you to attach more than one file to a message. Some Internet service providers will limit message size or the number of attachments for one e-mail. Attachments such as movies might be too large for some e-mail systems to handle. Once attached, files appear in the Attached text box or another area of the message window. Often, an icon next to each filename indicates the type of file it is. The numbers in parentheses next to the filenames specify the size of each file. As a general rule, try to keep the total size of attachments below 1 MB. Also, consider the Internet connection speed of the recipient's computer. If a recipient does not have a fast Internet connection, a large file could take a long time to download.

5. **Send the message**

FIGURE A-13: Attaching a file in Outlook

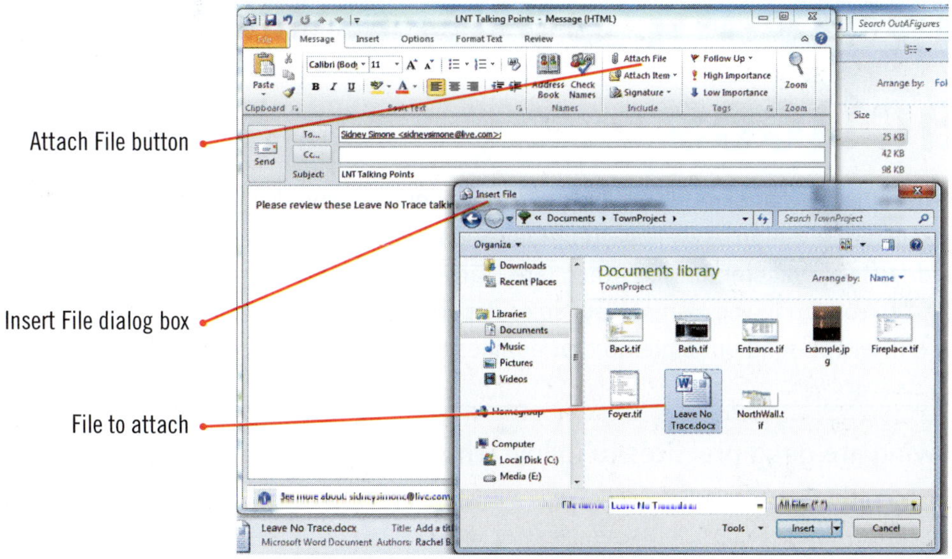

FIGURE A-14: Attaching a file using Hotmail

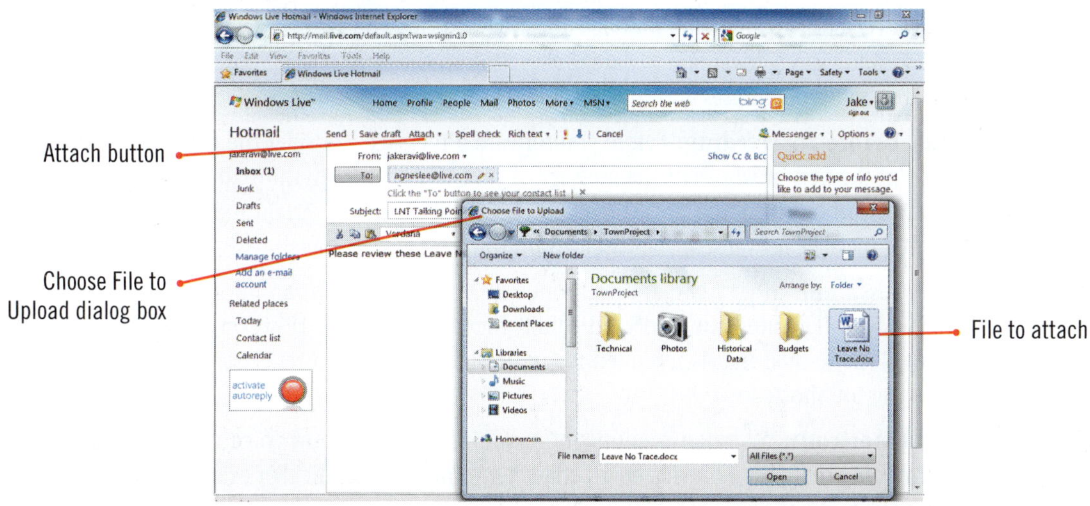

Reviewing options when sending messages

E-mail programs can have several options that affect how messages are delivered. To change these options in Outlook, click the Options tab in the Message window to view the Message Options, then click the launcher in the More Options group to open the Properties dialog box shown in Figure A-15. You can, for example, assign a level of importance and a level of sensitivity so that the reader can prioritize messages. You can also encrypt the message for privacy. If both the sender and recipient are using Outlook, you can add Voting buttons to your message for recipients to use in responding. In addition, when you want to know when a message has been received or read, you can select the Request a delivery receipt for this message check box or the Request a read receipt for this message check box. You can also specify a future date for delivering a message if the timing of the message is important. Lastly, if you want replies to your message to be sent to a different e-mail address than your own, you can click the "Have replies sent to" check box and then specify a new destination address for replies.

FIGURE A-15: Message options

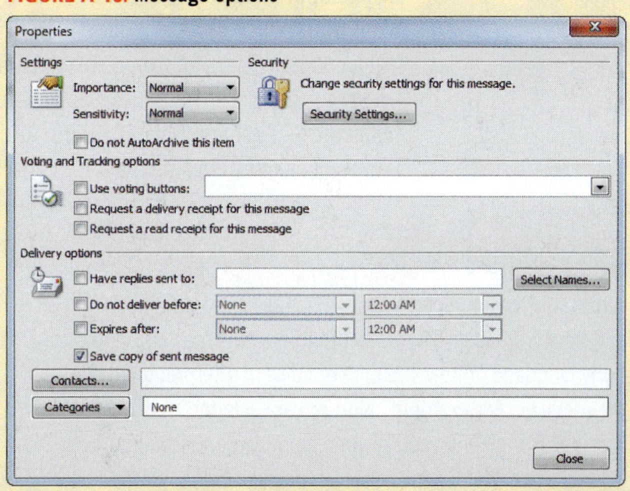

Employing Good E-Mail Practices

E-mail has become the standard for business correspondence. It has also become an accepted standard for personal communication as well as communication between students and teachers. Although it is an easy and fast way to communicate, there are many considerations to keep in mind before sending e-mail. Working in the Human Resources department, you are responsible for corporate policy relating to e-mail. You send out a memo that outlines the company policy for e-mail.

DETAILS

The following are good practices to follow when sending and receiving e-mail:

- **Be considerate:** Always be polite and use proper spelling and grammar in e-mail messages. Be sure to use the spelling checker as a last step before sending messages.

QUICK TIP

Consider using compression software to reduce the size of any attachment that exceeds the limit but must be sent.

- **Consider file size:** Unless you have consulted with the recipient and know that he or she can receive large file attachments, avoid sending any attachment that exceeds 1 MB.
- **Be safe:** Never open an e-mail message unless you know who sent it to you. Keep your spam filter, spyware software, and virus software up to date. Be sure to run the virus checker through all received e-mail. Keeping computers safe from viruses and spyware is very important.
- **Think before forwarding:** Before you forward a message, consider the contents of the message and the privacy of the person who sent the message. A joke, a story, or anything that is not personal usually can be forwarded without invading the sender's privacy. When you are certain the sender would not mind having his or her message forwarded, you can forward the message to others.
- **Be professional:** In very casual correspondence, you can present an informal message by using shortcuts like "LOL" for "laughing out loud" and "BRB!" for "be right back!" However, limit this technique to personal messages. Any e-mail that is intended for professional use or is a reflection on a professional organization should not use shortcuts.

QUICK TIP

The use of emoticons should also be limited to informal e-mail among close colleagues or friends, not professional correspondence.

- **Limit emoticons:** You can use emoticons in your text to show how you are feeling. You create an emoticon by combining more than one keyboard character to make a graphic. For example, type a colon and a closing parenthesis to make a smiley face ☺.
- **Maintain your account:** Outlook offers cleanup tools, as shown in Figure A-16. Most programs offer similar tools for maintaining your folders. When you are finished using an e-mail program, it is good practice to delete or archive e-mail messages that you no longer need. If working for a company, you should comply with corporate policy. For personal e-mail, you should periodically delete unneeded messages from the Sent Items folder to help manage storage on your computer. It is also good practice to empty the Trash folder. To delete a message, select it, then click the Delete button in the Delete group on the Home tab, or press [Delete]. To empty the Trash or Deleted Items folder, right-click the folder, then click Empty Folder, Empty Trash, or Empty Deleted Items folder. When you see a confirmation message, as shown in Figure A-17, click Yes.

Controlling your message

When you communicate with e-mail, take extra care in what you say and how you say it. The recipient of an e-mail message cannot see body language or hear the tone of voice to interpret the meaning of the message. For example, using all capital letters in the text of a message is the e-mail equivalent of shouting and is not appropriate. Carefully consider the content of a message before you send it, and don't send confidential or sensitive material. Remember, once you send a message, you might not be able to prevent it from being delivered. E-mail is not private; you cannot control who might read the message once it has been sent. Do not write anything in an e-mail that you would not write on a postcard that you send through the postal service. If your e-mail account is a company account, be sure you know the policy on whether or not your company permits the sending of personal messages. All messages you send through an employer's e-mail system legally belong to the company for which you work, so don't assume that your messages are private.

FIGURE A-16: Cleanup tools

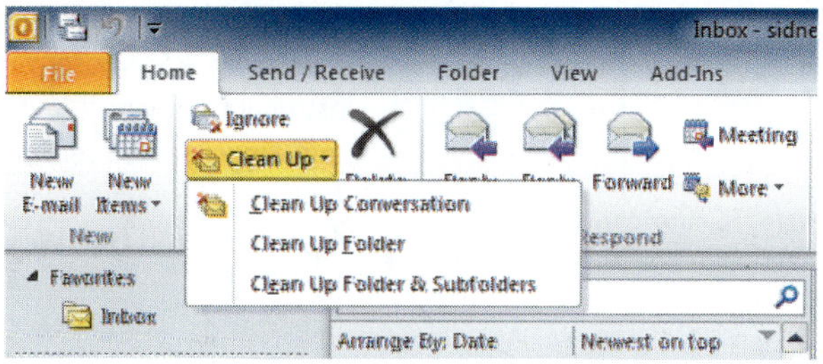

FIGURE A-17: Deleting items

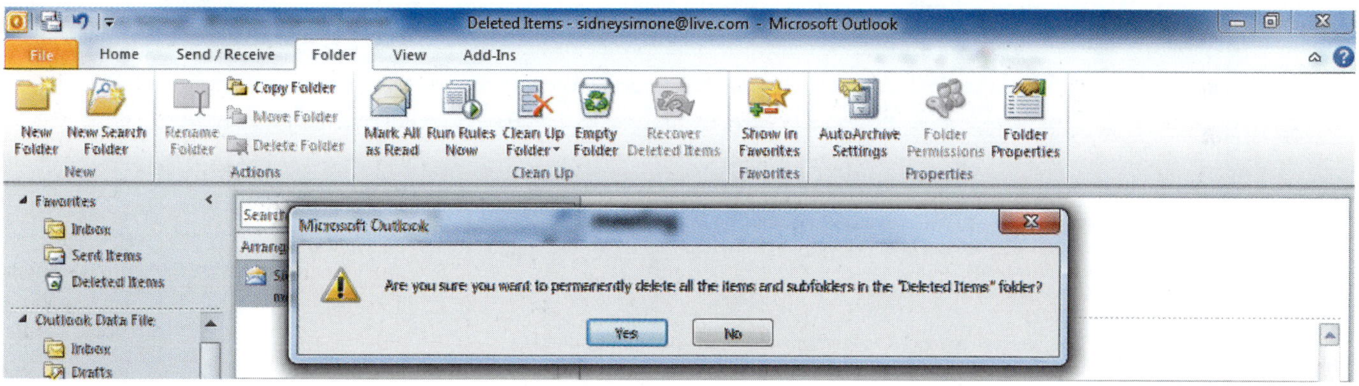

Creating distribution lists

When using an e-mail program to communicate with friends or coworkers, you might find that you need to send messages to the same group of people on a regular basis. If your address book contains many contacts, it can take time to scroll through all the names to select the ones you want, and you might forget to include someone in an important message. Fortunately, e-mail programs provide an easy way to group your contacts. You can create a **distribution list**, or a **contact group**, which is a collection of contacts to whom you want to send the same messages. Distribution lists, or contact groups, make it possible for you to send a message to the same group of e-mail addresses without having to select each contact in the group. For example, if you send messages reminding your Human Resources staff of a weekly meeting, you can create a distribution list called "HR-STAFF" that contains the names and e-mail addresses of your staff who must attend the meeting. When you want to send a message to everyone on the team, you simply select HR-STAFF from the address book, instead of selecting each person's name individually. Once you create a distribution list, you can add new members to it or delete members from it as necessary. If you change information about a contact that is part of a group or list, the list is automatically updated.

Practice

For current SAM information, including versions and content details, visit SAM Central (http://www.cengage.com/samcentral). If you have a SAM user profile, you may have access to hands-on instruction, practice, and assessment of the skills covered in this unit. Since various versions of SAM are supported throughout the life of this text, check with your instructor for the correct instructions and URL/Web site for accessing assignments.

Concepts Review

Label each element of the New Message window shown in Figure A-18.

FIGURE A-18

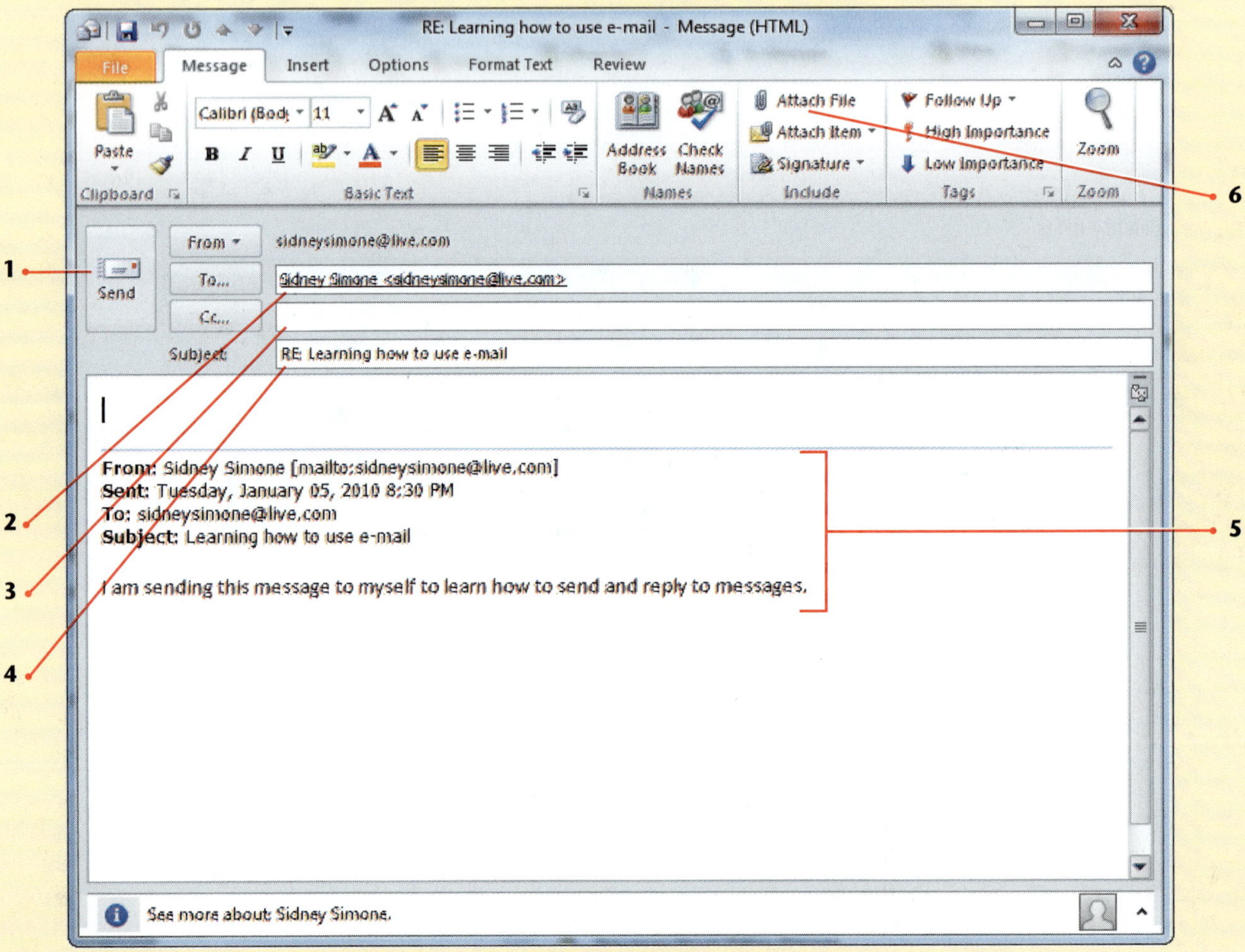

Match each term with the statement that best describes it.

7.	**sidneysimone@live.com**	**a.**	Stores names and e-mail addresses
8.	**FW**	**b.**	An e-mail address
9.	**Bcc**	**c.**	Stores all e-mail that you send out
10.	**Sent Items folder**	**d.**	Identifies a forwarded message
11.	**Inbox**	**e.**	Contains messages you have received
12.	**Address book**	**f.**	Hides e-mail address of recipient to all others

Select the best answer from the list of choices.

13. Any e-mail received as part of large unsolicited mailing is best placed automatically in the ____________.

a. Junk E-Mail or Spam folder
b. Deleted Items folder
c. Sent Items folder
d. Inbox

14. If you do not want the recipients of your message to see the others who got the same message, you should use the ____________ feature.

a. Cc
b. Bcc
c. Outbox
d. flag

15. Your e-mail ____________ can be files of any type, such as documents, spreadsheets, video, images, and sound files.

a. attachments
b. headers
c. drafts
d. first three lines of the message body

16. If you want people who send you an e-mail message to get a message from you even if you can't view or respond to their message right away, you should set up a(n) ____________.

a. voting and tracking option
b. vacation response
c. delivery option
d. importance setting

17. E-mail that you have finished writing but has not yet been sent is stored in the ____________.

a. Inbox
b. New Mail folder
c. Outbox
d. Sent Items folder

18. When you forward a selected message to another person, the e-mail addresses for the original recipients of the message ____________.

a. appear only in the To text box
b. do not appear in any text box
c. appear only in the Cc text box
d. appear in the To and the Cc text boxes

19. The ____________ feature helps you follow up and organize messages.

a. folders
b. flag
c. Bcc
d. FW

20. To ensure that you send the same message to the same group of multiple recipients, set up a(n) ____________.

a. address book
b. Quick Step
c. Draft folder
d. contact group or distribution list

Skills Review

1. Start Outlook or your e-mail program and view the Inbox.

a. Start Outlook or your e-mail program.
b. If necessary, select the mail part of the program.
c. Click the Send/Receive All Folders button or link to get new e-mail delivered to the Inbox, if necessary.
d. Open the Inbox to view any new messages.

2. Create and send a message.

a. Open a new message window.
b. Click the To text box, then type a friend's e-mail address.
c. Type your e-mail address in the Cc text box.
d. Type **Employee Discount Travel Program** as the subject of the message.
e. In the message body, type **Please be sure to process your travel invoices with the correct codes to get your discount.**
f. Send the message.

Skills Review (continued)

3. **Manage e-mail folders.**
   a. Review the mail folders in your e-mail program.
   b. Look for a Sent Items or Sent folder and see if the Employee Discount Travel Program message is in that folder.
   c. Open the Deleted Items or Trash folder. See if any e-mail is in that folder.
   d. Review the Spam or Junk E-Mail folder.
4. **Receive and reply to a message.**
   a. If necessary, click the Send/Receive All Folders button to deliver messages to your Inbox.
   b. Display the contents of the Inbox folder.
   c. Read the message from yourself.
   d. Click the Reply button.
   e. In the message body, type **Is there a list of codes in the handbook?**, then send the message.
5. **Forward a message.**
   a. Forward the message you received to another friend.
   b. In the top of the forwarded message body, type **This important message came to me from HR, be sure to read the entire message.** (Refer to Figure A-19.)
   c. Send the message.
   d. Close the original message.

FIGURE A-19

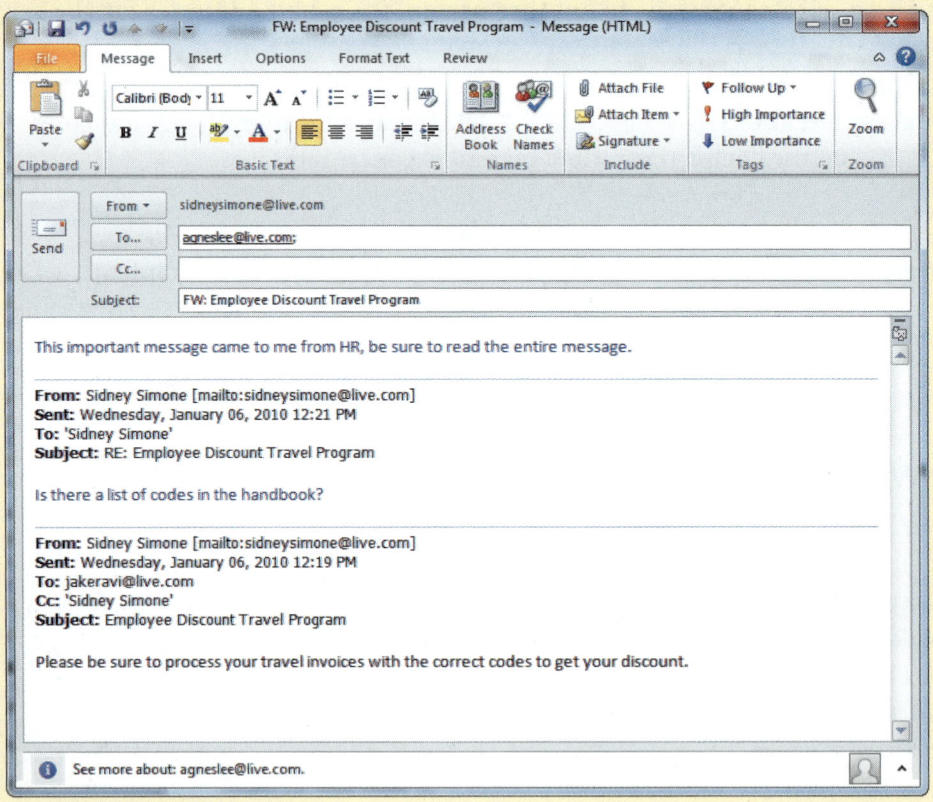

6. **Send a message with an attachment.**
   a. Create a new e-mail message.
   b. Enter your e-mail address as the message recipient.
   c. Enter a friend's e-mail address in the Cc text box.
   d. Enter **Travel photo** as the subject of the message.
   e. In the message body, type **Here is the photo from my trip to New York.**
   f. Click the Insert File, Attach File, or Attach button or link.
   g. Navigate to the drive and folder where you store your Data Files.

Skills Review (continued)

h. Select the file Bridge.jpg (see Figure A-20), then click Insert, Open, or Attach (depending on your program).
i. Send the message.

FIGURE A-20

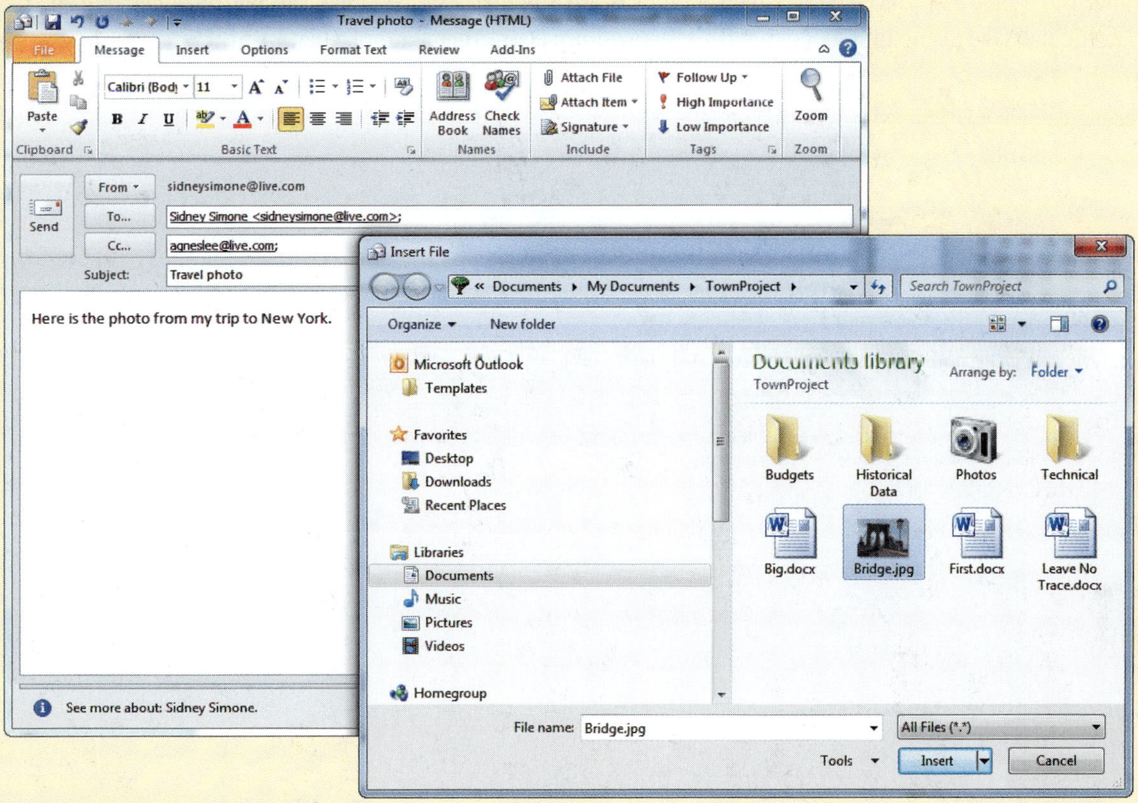

7. **Delete items.**
   a. Delete all of the messages received in this exercise from the Inbox folder.
   b. Delete all of the messages sent in this exercise from the Sent Items folder.
   c. Empty the Deleted Items folder.
   d. Exit the e-mail program.

Independent Challenge 1

You are a member of the zoning and development board in your town. You have been appointed to chair the committee to investigate a proposal for developing a two-acre section of town under the Green Acres Project. You decide to use e-mail to communicate with the other members of the committee as well as with the local newspaper, the town council, and the mayor.

a. Start Outlook or your e-mail program.
b. Open the address book and add yourself as well as three other new contacts to the address book. Use the names and e-mail addresses of classmates, teachers, or friends. (*Hint*: In Outlook, the Address Book button is in the Find group on the Home tab of the Mail window.)
c. Create a new message and address it to yourself, then use the Cc field to send this message to two of the new contacts.
d. Type **Green Acres Project** as the subject of the message.
e. In the message body, type **There will be a public hearing on Thursday at 8:00 p.m. We should prepare our presentation and contact the local newspaper to be sure they carry the story.**

Independent Challenge 1 (continued)

f. Press [Enter], then type your name. See Figure A-21.

g. Send the message, then click the Send/Receive All Folders button if necessary. Depending on the speed and type of Internet connection you are using, you might need to click the Send/Receive button again, after waiting a few moments, if you do not receive the e-mail in your Inbox the first time you click the Send/Receive button.

h. Open the message in the Inbox, flag it with a follow-up flag or other symbol, then print it.

FIGURE A-21

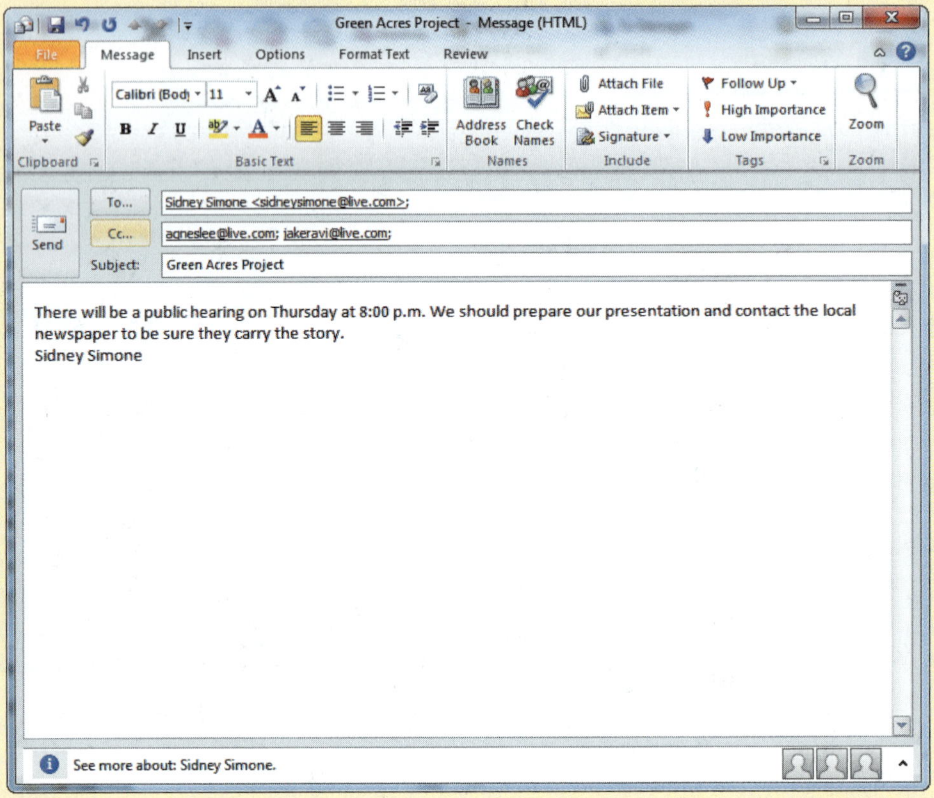

Advanced Challenge Exercise

- Forward the message to the person you did not include in the distribution list.
- In the message body, type **Forgot to include you in this mailing! Please read the message; hope you can be there.**
- Send the message.

i. Delete all of the messages related to this Independent Challenge from the Inbox folder.

j. Delete all of the messages related to this Independent Challenge from the Sent Items folder.

k. Delete the contacts that you added in this Independent Challenge from the address book.

l. Empty the Deleted Items folder.

m. Exit the e-mail program.

Independent Challenge 2

You are planning a study trip to India with a group from the university. You have to send e-mail messages with an attachment as you organize this trip.

a. Start Outlook or your e-mail program, then create a new message and address it to two contacts, such as friends, family members, or classmates.
b. Enter your e-mail address in the Cc text box.
c. Type **Trip to Mumbai** in the Subject text box.
d. Start your word processor and write a brief letter to your friends to encourage them to join you on the adventure. Conclude the document with a personal note about why you want to participate in a study program. Save the document file in the drive and folder where you store your Data Files, using a filename you will remember.
e. Type a short note in the message body of the e-mail to the recipients of the message, telling them that you thought they would like to join you on this trip and that you are looking forward to them joining you.
f. Attach the word-processing document to the message.
g. Send the message, then click the Send/Receive All Folders button. Depending on the speed and type of Internet connection you are using, you might need to click the Send/Receive button again, after waiting a few moments, if you do not receive a response e-mail the first time you click the Send/Receive button.
h. Print a copy of the message you receive in response.

Advanced Challenge Exercise

- Locate a picture or graphic image file on your computer that you want to send through e-mail.
- Right-click the picture, point to Send to, then click Mail recipient on the shortcut menu. (Alternatively, after right-clicking a picture, you might see these options: E-mail Picture or E-mail with [e-mail program]. These options will be different depending on your software and system.) Click OK if a dialog box opens asking if you want to make the picture smaller. Click Attach to attach the image to a new message window.
- When a new message window opens, enter your e-mail address in the To text box, then write a brief message in the body of the message. Add Bcc and Cc recipients. Set a priority level. Use Figure A-22 as a guide.
- Send the message, then read the message and view the picture when it arrives in your Inbox.

FIGURE A-22

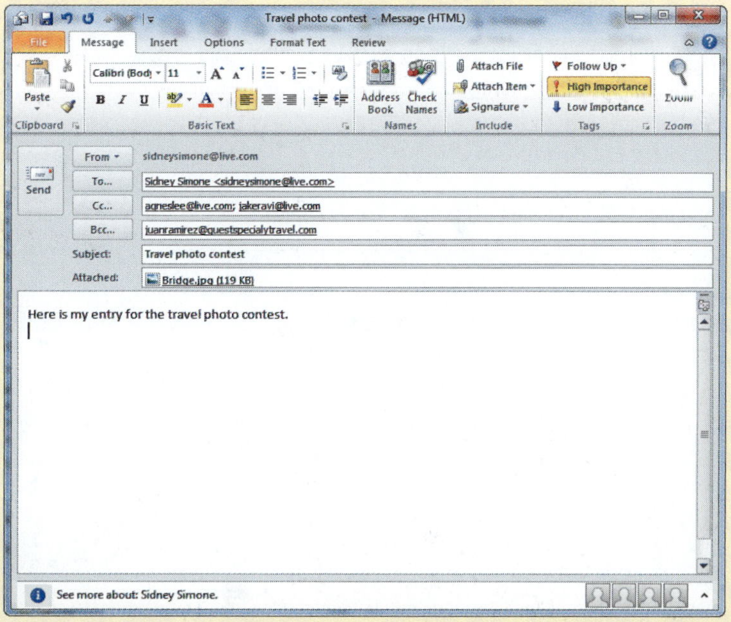

i. Delete all of the messages received for this Independent Challenge from your Inbox.
j. Delete all of the messages sent for this Independent Challenge from the Sent Items folder.
k. Empty the Deleted Items folder.
l. Exit Outlook.

Visual Workshop

Refer to the e-mail message in Figure A-23 to complete this Visual Workshop. Use your e-mail program to create and then send this message. Be sure to send the message to at least one recipient. Attach a file that you created on your computer. It can be a document, worksheet, image, or database file.

FIGURE A-23

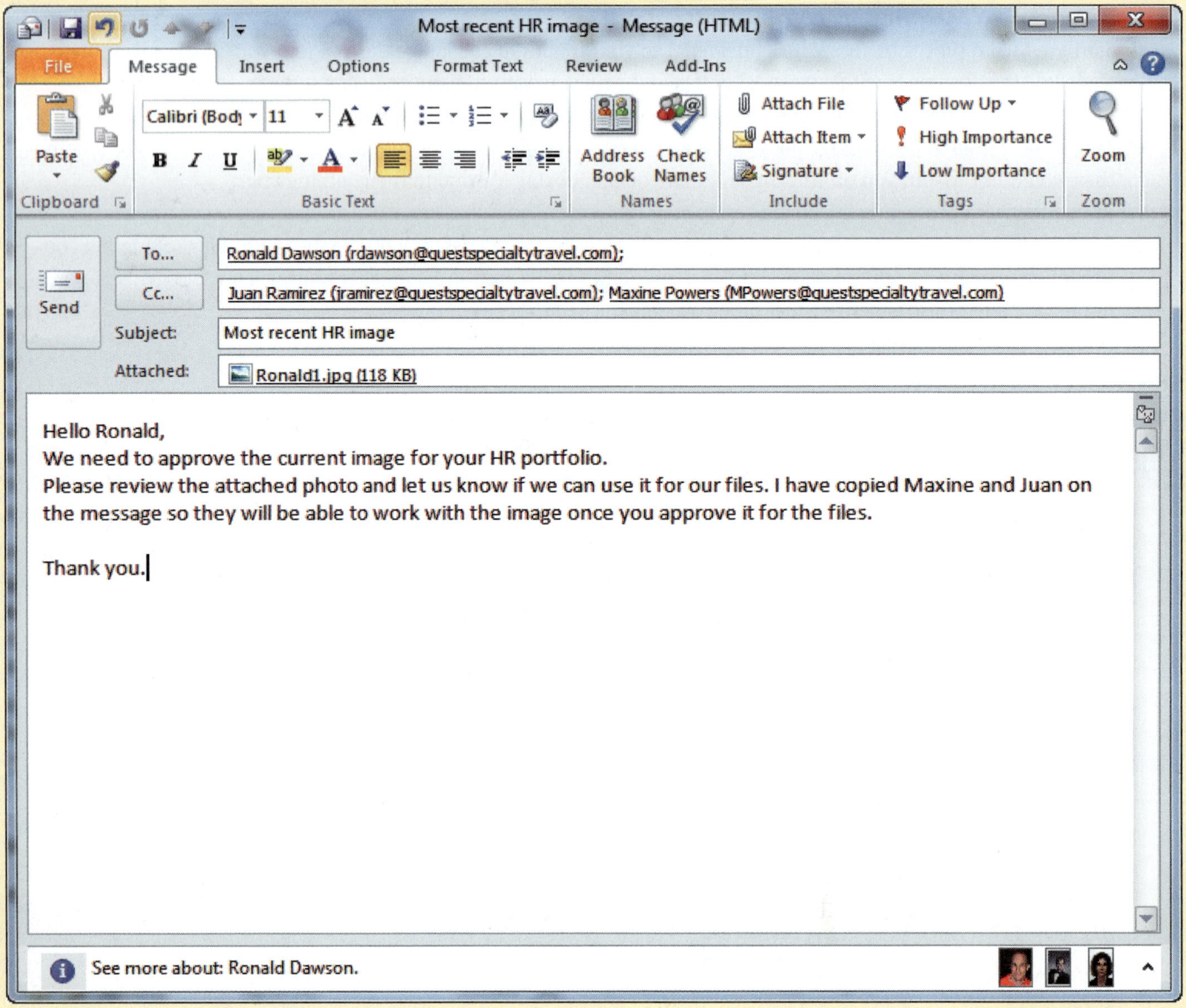

UNIT
B
Outlook 2010

Managing Information Using Outlook

Files You Will Need:
No files needed.

While Outlook lets you easily manage your e-mail, it can do a lot more. Outlook is a complete personal information and time management program you can use for all your business and personal information. Outlook integrates E-mail, Calendar, Contacts, Tasks, Notes, and Journal modules that let you manage your mail, appointments and activities, address book, to-do list, and notes all in one program. Now that you know how to send, receive, and manage your e-mail, you will learn how to use Outlook as a desktop information manager to help you organize your schedule, to-do list, communications, and associates.

OBJECTIVES

- Start Outlook
- Organize e-mail
- Add contacts
- Manage appointments
- Manage tasks
- Create notes
- Use the Journal
- Apply categories

UNIT
B
Outlook 2010

Starting Outlook

The Outlook screen is fully customizable to let you view your contacts, schedule, or mail with different levels of detail. You can change how the data is organized and sorted. The first time you start Outlook, you will be prompted to set up a personal **account** that identifies you as a user. If you want to use Outlook for e-mail, you must enter your e-mail address and password, the type of Internet service provider (ISP) you are using, and the incoming and outgoing mail server address for your ISP. You can set up more than one account in a single installation of Outlook. Each user has a username and password for his or her account. As the assistant to Juan Ramirez in the Human Resources department, you learn Outlook so you can use it for communication and scheduling. Refer to Figure B-1, which shows the Outlook Mail window, as you read about how to customize the window.

STEPS

TROUBLE
Because Outlook is fully customizable and depends on the accounts that have been set up, your screen will look different than the figures in this book. You might also see some differences in the menus.

1. **Click the Start button on the taskbar, point to All Programs, click Microsoft Office, then click Microsoft Outlook 2010 to start Outlook**

   Figure B-1 shows a typical Outlook window when you select Mail. The **Navigation Pane** lets you choose a module as well as specific areas within that module. In Figure B-1, the lower portion of the Navigation Pane shows that Mail is selected. You can click the Calendar, Contacts, or Tasks buttons to work with those Outlook modules. When Mail is selected, the upper part of the Navigation Pane shows the Folder List. The Inbox folder is where you get your new e-mail messages. The Reading Pane lets you read the selected e-mail message. The To-Do Bar includes the Date Navigator, appointments for the current week, and your upcoming tasks. The **People Pane** shows you any social media information available for the person sending the current message and included files, appointments, and notes related to that person.

2. **Click the View tab on the Ribbon, click the Navigation Pane button in the Layout group, click Normal, click the Reading Pane button, then click Right**

   The options on the View tab let you determine how the Navigation Pane, To-Do Bar, and Reading Pane appear in each of the Outlook modules. When you select Normal, the Navigation Pane appears on the left side of the screen. When you select Minimized, the Navigation Pane appears as a vertical bar along the left side of the Outlook window and shows only the module navigation and folder buttons.

QUICK TIP
If a To-Do Bar item does not have a check mark, click it once to select it.

3. **On the View tab, click the To-Do Bar button in the Layout group, then verify that there are check marks next to Normal, Date Navigator, Appointments, and Task List**

   The To-Do Bar, which appears on the right side of the window in Figure B-1, shows you what you need to do for the day. A calendar called the **Date Navigator** gives you an overview of the month. You can minimize the To-Do Bar so that it appears as a vertical bar on the right side of the window by clicking the Minimize the To-Do Bar button. You can also open the To-Do Bar Options dialog box, shown in Figure B-2, and adjust To-Do Bar display options. To open the To-Do Bar Options dialog box, click the To-Do Bar button in the Layout group, then click Options.

4. **Click the Home tab on the Ribbon, click the More button in the Quick Steps group, then click Manage Quick Steps**

   The Manage Quick Steps dialog box opens. See Figure B-3. Quick Steps are shortcuts that help you complete basic Outlook tasks with one click. You can set up Quick Steps for your own tasks or create your own Quick Steps based on other common e-mail tasks.

QUICK TIP
Drag the border between the Folder List and module buttons in the Navigation Pane to expand or shrink the list and minimize or maximize the buttons.

5. **Click Cancel to close the Manage Quick Steps dialog box**

6. **In the Navigation Pane, click Calendar, click Contacts, click Tasks, click the Notes button, click the Folder List button, then review the screen content after each view change**

   Mail, Calendar, Contacts, Tasks, Notes, and Journal are the modules in Outlook. The Journal module does not appear by default in the Outlook window. You will learn more about the Journal later in this unit. The Folder List shows you the available folders for storing your e-mail, calendar, contacts, and journal entries. You can open any of these modules by clicking the Navigation Pane. The Folder List in the Navigation Pane displays each folder under Personal Folders with Outlook items specific to your account.

FIGURE B-1: Opening screen in Outlook Mail

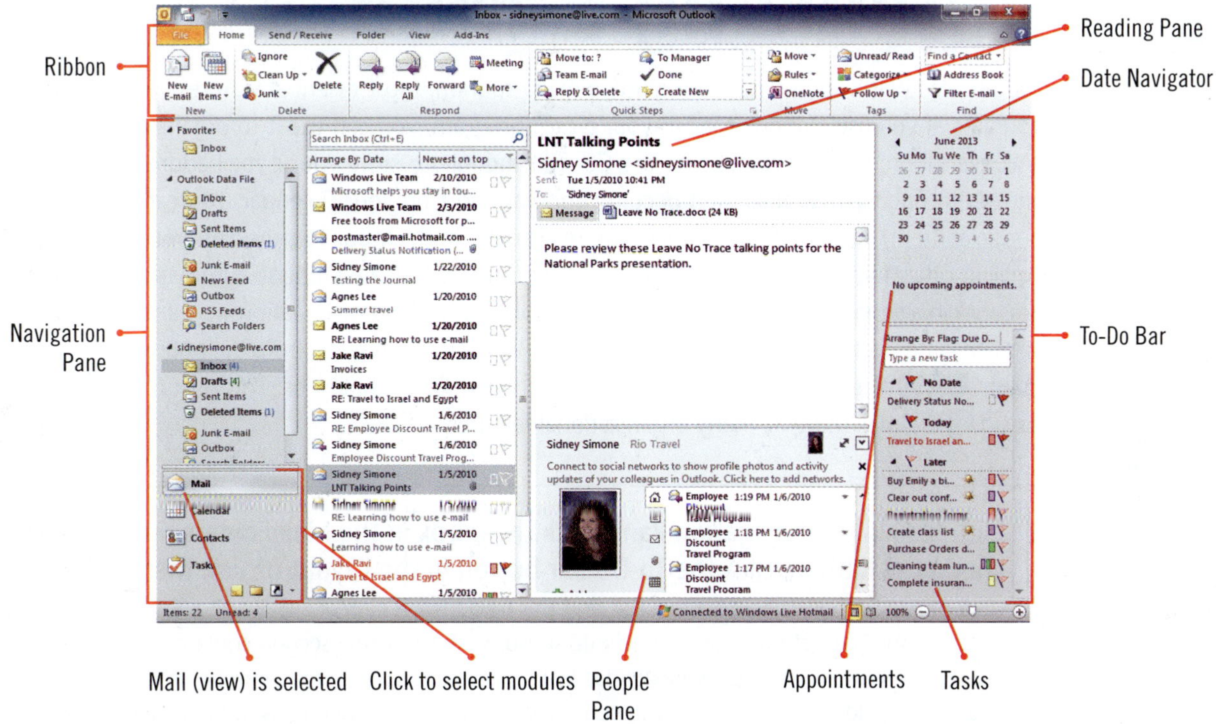

FIGURE B-2: To-Do Bar Options dialog box

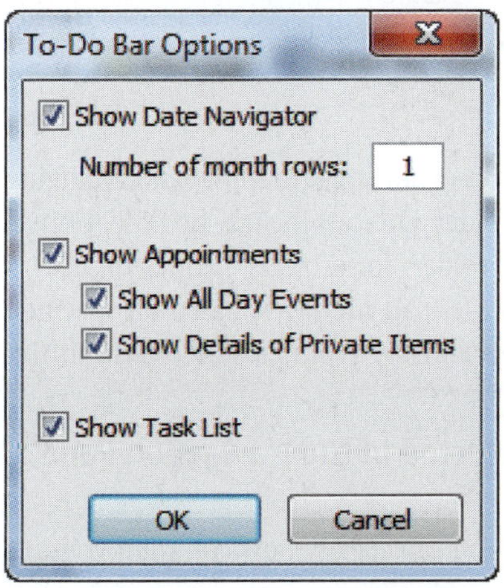

FIGURE B-3: Manage Quick Steps dialog box

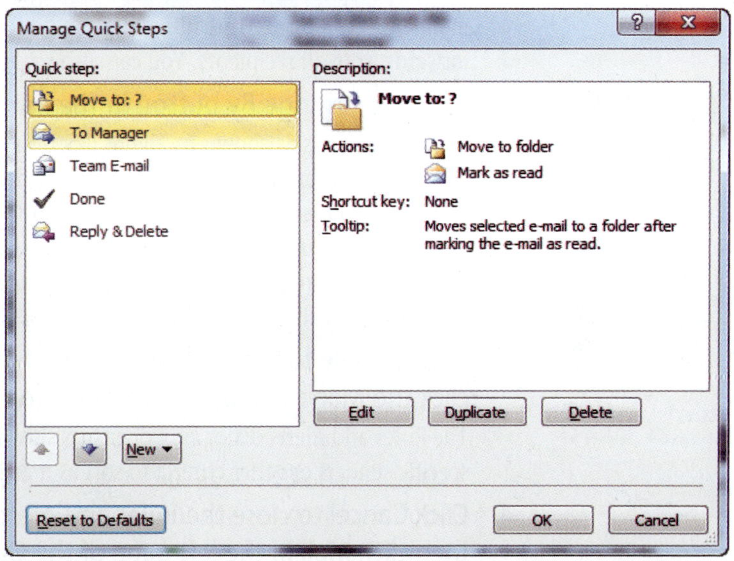

Explaining RSS

The Internet has many Web sites that provide an overwhelming amount and variety of information. News sites are updated hourly; some corporations deliver news about products daily; there are entertainment Web sites that provide information about films and shows weekly; and many organizations keep their sites current. To stay on top of all this changing information, you would have to visit each site each day—a seemingly impossible task. Fortunately, there are technologies on the Internet that can help you stay current in topics that interest you. **Really Simple Syndication (RSS)** is a format for "feeding" or "syndicating" news or any content from Web sites to your computer. Outlook provides a way to have this information come directly into an RSS Feeds folder. Click the Folder List button in the Navigation Pane to see the RSS Feeds folder. Access to RSS content is free, but you have to subscribe to a Web site that offers RSS feeds. RSS feeds provide subscribers with summaries that link to the full versions of the content. Once you see that you want to read more about the topic, you can click the link to view the article in the Reading Pane. You can organize the RSS feeds by creating folders for each topic or Web site that you subscribe to. The advantage to using RSS is that you may select different types of information from a variety of Web sites and view them all at the same time.

Organizing E-Mail

You can create and send e-mail using any e-mail program; most essential features are the same across the programs. If you use Outlook Mail as your e-mail program, you can use it to organize your e-mail, such as by conversation, view, or folder. Use the Contact module to store your e-mail addresses and get meeting requests through e-mail that then become appointments on your Calendar. You can search messages for specific content, dates, or senders. All new e-mail arrives in the Inbox folder unless you set up rules to deliver e-mail in other folders. A **rule** is an action you can create to have Outlook automatically handle particular messages in a certain way. By default, Outlook displays e-mail in Conversation view and **sorts**, or orders, the e-mail by date. To specify a different view, click the View tab, then select from the options in the Arrangement group. You will receive e-mail from clients and QST employees. You set up Outlook to view and manage the e-mail using its many organizational features.

STEPS

TROUBLE
If there are no messages in your Inbox, your screen will not display information in the center and right panes of the Mail window.

1. **Click Mail in the Navigation Pane, click the Inbox in the Mail Folders list, click the View tab on the Ribbon, click the To-Do Bar button in the Layout group, then click Off**

   Outlook Mail is now the active module, and the To-Do Bar is closed. See Figure B-4. You see a list of all Mail folders in the Navigation Pane, divided into sections. The Favorites section contains shortcuts to folders that you use most often. The folders are divided by user account. Each user account has a Mail Folders section with all available folders, including the Inbox, Drafts, Sent Items, Deleted Items, Junk E-mail, News Feed, Outbox, RSS Feeds, and Search folders. Icons in the Inbox help you identify mail that is read, unread, has been forwarded or replied to, or has threaded messages. A **threaded message** includes all e-mails that discuss a common subject. Message threading allows you to navigate through a group of messages, seeing all replies and forwards from all recipients. You can also set Follow-Up flags for messages.

QUICK TIP
Click the View Settings button in the Current View group on the View tab to open the dialog box and change filter settings.

2. **Click the Arrange By button in the Inbox**

   The menu opens as shown in Figure B-5. You see the many ways of sorting, grouping, and arranging e-mail messages. You can determine how you view the e-mail in any folder. Options include by Date, Conversation, Categories, Subject, Attachments, and Importance. Create mail folders for projects, people, or ideas. You can use Outlook to quickly **filter**, or show a specific group of your e-mail messages, based on specific criteria, such as who sent you a message. Search your messages for keywords by typing a search term in the Search Inbox box and clicking the Search button.

3. **Click the File tab on the Ribbon, verify that Info is selected in the Navigation Pane, then click the Manage Rules & Alerts button**

   The Rules and Alerts dialog box opens, as shown in Figure B-6. You can specify how you want your mail from specific senders or other criteria to sort as it arrives.

4. **Click Cancel to close the Rules and Alerts dialog box, click Options in the Navigation Pane, then click Mail in the left pane of the Outlook Options dialog box**

   The Mail options are shown in Figure B-7. You can set options for how messages are formatted and how mail looks and sounds when it arrives. Set how Outlook handles forwarding, replying to, sending, tracking, and formatting messages.

5. **Click Cancel, click the Home tab, then click the Junk button in the Delete group**

   By specifying safe senders and blocked senders, you can be sure that the e-mail you get is the e-mail you want to receive. You can add a person's e-mail address to your Safe Senders list. If e-mail comes in that you know is offensive add the source address to the Blocked Senders list.

QUICK TIP
The Inbox folder appears in both the Favorites list and the Mail Folders list. You can select the folder from either list.

6. **Click the Inbox for your account, click the View tab, click the Show as Conversations check box to select it, click All Folders, click the Change View button in the Current View group, click Single, click the Change View button, click Preview, click the Change View button, then click Compact**

   You can control how the Inbox appears by using the View options.

FIGURE B-4: Viewing Inbox arranged by date

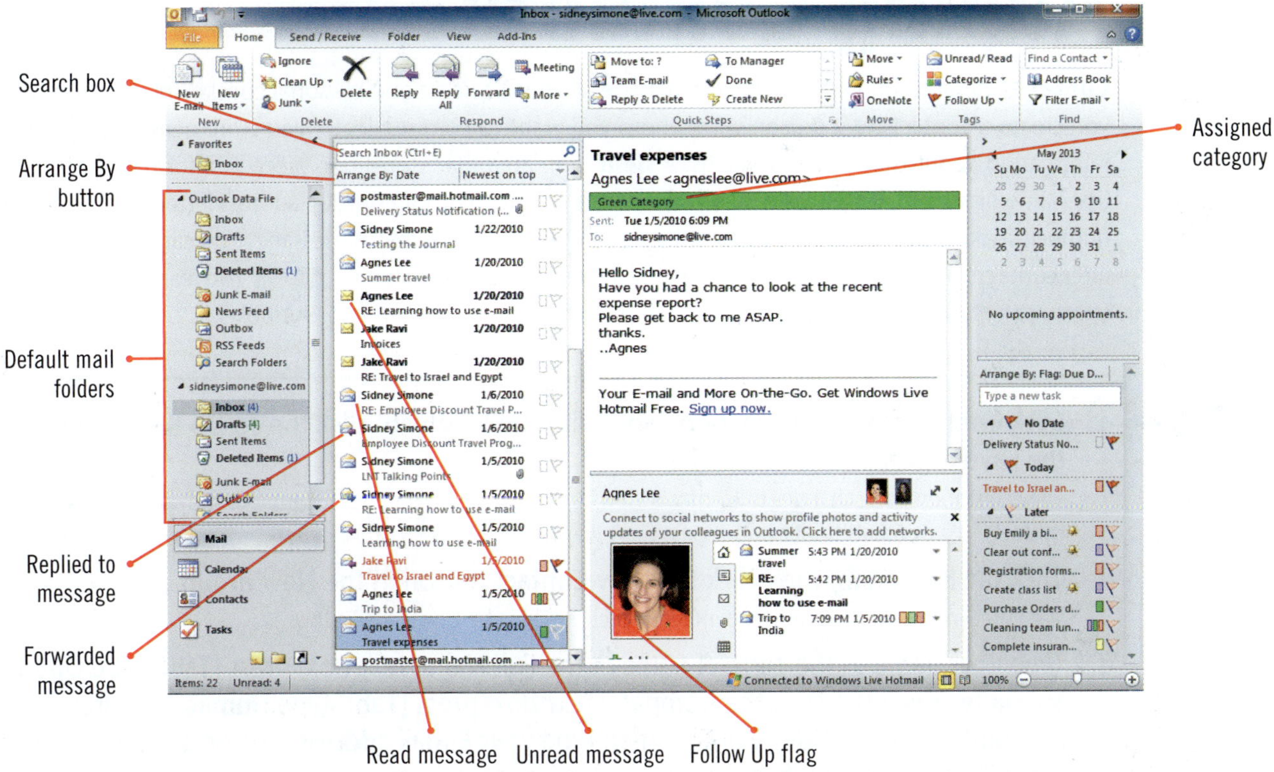

FIGURE B-5: Arrange By options

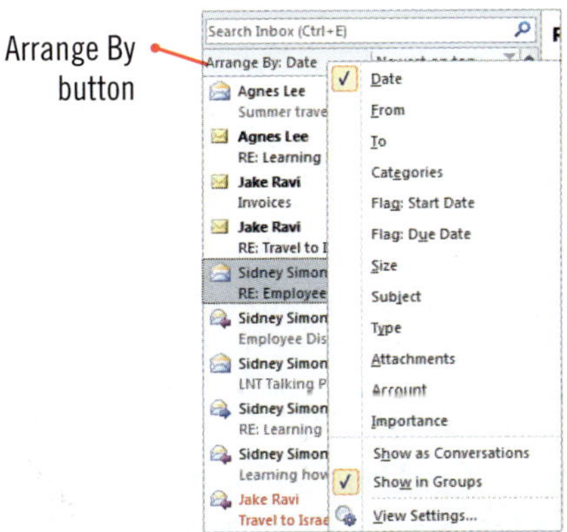

FIGURE B-6: Rules and Alerts dialog box

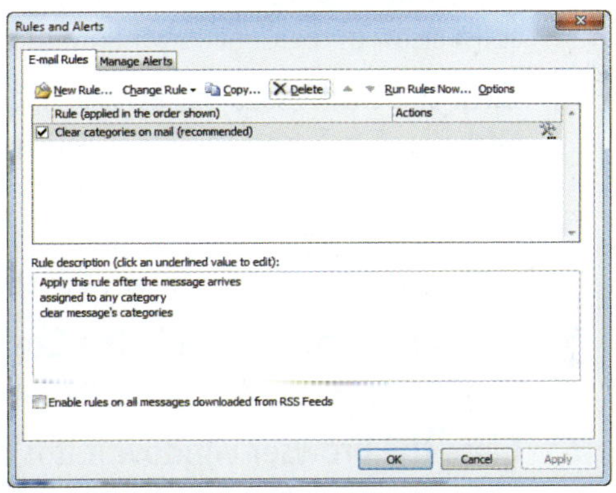

FIGURE B-7: Outlook Mail options

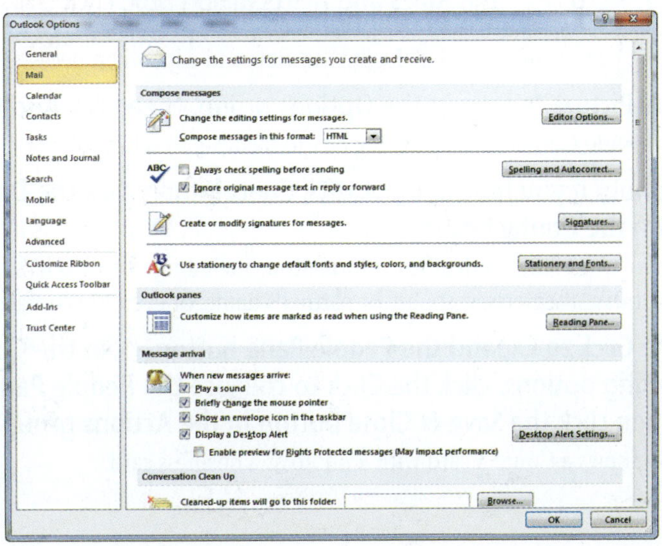

Adding Contacts

Contacts in Microsoft Outlook let you manage all your business and personal contact information. When you create a contact for a person with whom you want to communicate, you store general and detailed information about that person in fields. A **field** is an area that stores one piece of information, such as a first name or an e-mail address. Once you create a contact, you can quickly address letters, locate a phone number, make a call, send a meeting request, assign a task, or e-mail a message. You can sort, group, and filter contacts by any field. You can also easily share contacts with others. You learn about Contacts so you can store all the contact information for employees and clients in Outlook.

STEPS

QUICK TIP
Click the Normal or Cards Only buttons on the status bar to change the view. Use the Zoom slider to increase or decrease the size and number of cards that fit on a screen.

1. **Click Contacts in the Navigation Pane, click the View tab, click the To-Do Bar button in the Layout group, then click Off**

   The Navigation Pane changes to Contacts view, and the To-Do Bar closes. Figure B-8 shows several completed contacts in a Contacts folder in Business Card view.

2. **Click the Home tab, then click the New Contact button in the New group**

   You enter information for a new contact in each field in the Contact window.

3. **Type your name as the contact name in the Full Name text box, press [Tab], type Quest Specialty Travel (QST) in the Company text box, press [Tab], type Human Resources Assistant in the Job title text box, then type your E-mail address, Business, Home, and Mobile telephone numbers in the appropriate text boxes**

   If you do not enter a first and last name in the Full Name text box, the Check Full Name dialog box opens so you can enter the full name for the contact. Determine how Outlook files each contact by clicking the File as list arrow in the Contact window, then click by first name, last name, company, or job title.

TROUBLE
If the Location Information dialog box opens, enter your local area code, click OK, then click OK in the Phone and Modem dialog box.

4. **Click the Addresses list arrow, click Business if necessary, click the This is the mailing address check box to select it if necessary, then type your address in the Address text box**

   You can store up to three addresses in the Address text box. Choose Business, Home, or Other from the Addresses list, then type the address in the Address text box. If Outlook can't identify an address component that you type in the Address text box, the Check Address dialog box opens for you to verify the component.

5. **Click the MapIt button in the Contact card**

   If your computer is connected to the Internet, a browser window opens and shows the location on a map.

6. **Close the browser window if it is open, click the Business Card button in the Options group to open the Edit Business Card dialog box, click Full Name, Company, Job Title, Business Phone, and Business Address in the Fields list to view the information for each field in the Edit window on the right, then click Cancel**

   You use the Edit Business Card dialog box to view and edit, when necessary, contact information.

7. **Click the Picture button in the Options group, then click Add Picture**

   You use the Add Contact Picture dialog box to navigate to select the photo, and then click Open.

QUICK TIP
When you create a new Outlook item, such as a task, appointment, or note, you can link it to the contact or contacts to which it relates.

8. **Add a photo if you have one, or click Cancel, then click the Details button in the Show group on the Contact card**

   You can enter a contact's detailed information, including the contact's department, profession, assistant's name, birthday, anniversary, spouse or partner's name, or even the contact's nickname.

9. **Click the Click to Expand the People Pane button in the Contact card, view the Social Networking options, click the Click to collapse the People Pane button in the People Pane, then click the Save & Close button in the Actions group**

   Figure B-9 shows a Contact card with a photo as a business card.

FIGURE B-8: Contacts

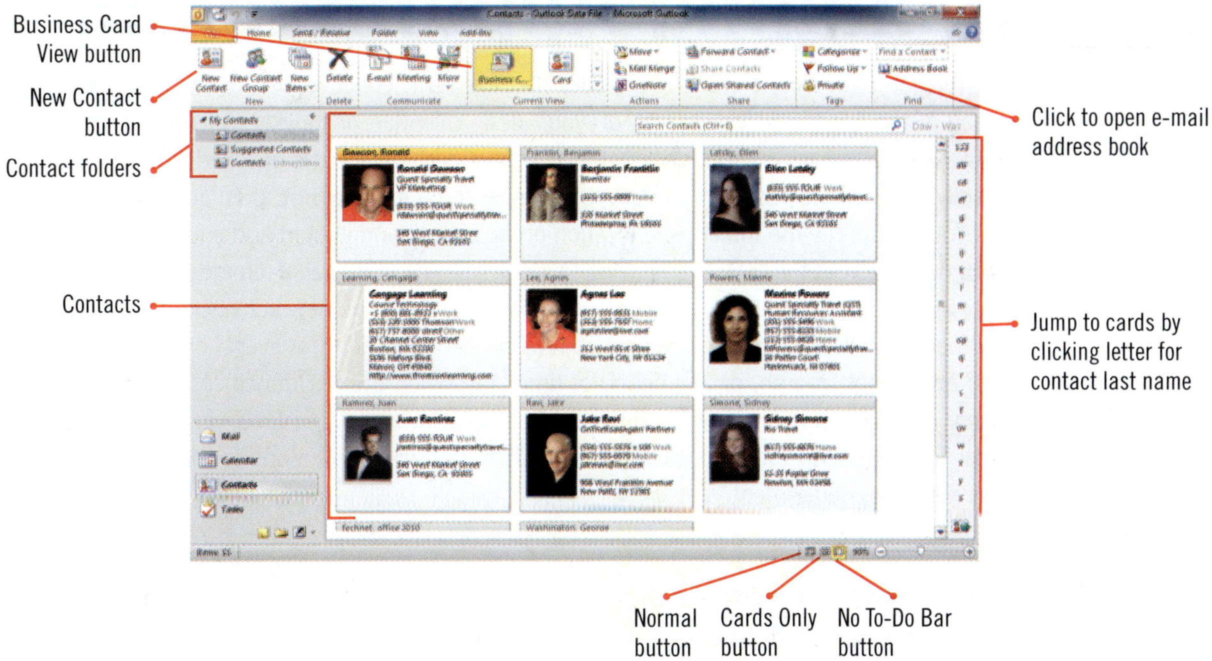

FIGURE B-9: Completed new Contact card

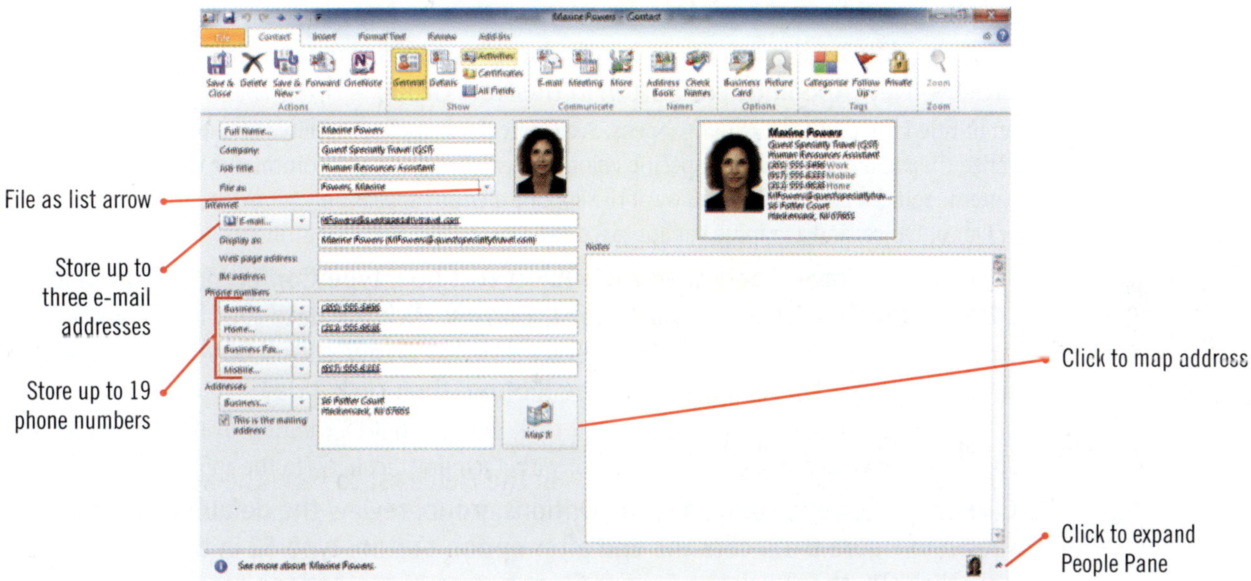

Creating a Contact Group

You can create a subset of your Contacts folder by creating a Contact Group. Contact Groups work in the same way as distribution lists. A **Contact Group** is a subset of the people in your Contacts folder, grouped together by e-mail addresses. You can create a Contact Group based on any criteria, such as all contacts that live in New York City, all contacts that are clients, all contacts that work for a specific company, or even a combination of such criteria. Once the Contact Group is created, you can send a message, task request, or meeting request to everyone in the group with a single click. To create a Contact Group from the Contacts module, click the Home tab, then click the New Contact Group button in the New group. In the Contact Group window that opens, enter a descriptive name for the group in the Name box. Click the Add Members button in the Members group to select Members from Outlook Contacts or from the address book. You can also add new e-mail contacts. Click the Save & Close button when you are done adding members.

UNIT
B
Outlook 2010

Managing Appointments

The **Calendar** in Microsoft Outlook provides a convenient, effective way to manage your appointments. Calendar is the electronic equivalent of your desk calendar or pocket calendar. Calendar defines an **appointment** as an activity that does not involve inviting other people or scheduling resources; a **meeting** as an activity you invite people to or reserve resources for; and an **event** as an activity that lasts 24 hours or longer. You can specify the subject and location of the activity and its start and end times. You can also ensure that you do not forget the activity by having Outlook sound and display a reminder for you before the start of the activity. When you create an activity, Outlook notifies you if the new activity conflicts with, or is adjacent to, another scheduled activity. You can set up recurring appointments or events by specifying the recurrence, such as every week, month, or any period of time, and when the recurrence ends. People in your group or company can each have their own calendars. To help with managing time, you can view more than one calendar side by side in the Outlook window. You will use Outlook to manage the schedule for the Human Resources department

STEPS

TROUBLE
If more than one calendar is open, remove the check marks to close all but your calendar.

1. **Click Calendar in the Navigation Pane, click the Week button in the Arrange group, then click the the Month button in the Arrange group**
   The calendar, as shown in Figure B-10 in Week view, can be viewed either by day, work week, week, or month. The To-Do Bar, if open, shows the current month in the Date Navigator; if the To-Do Bar is closed, the Date Navigator appears in the Navigation Pane. You can use the Date Navigator in the To-Do Bar or Navigation Pane to quickly view specific dates. Dates with appointments or events appear in bold in the Date Navigator. Tasks for each day appear below the calendar so you can see what tasks are due on each day.
2. **Click any date next week in your calendar, click the Home tab if it is not selected, then click the New Appointment button in the New Group**
   An untitled Appointment window opens. See Figure B-11. You can specify the subject and location and categorize the appointment with a specific color. You enter recurring appointments once, then set a recurrence pattern. You can choose how you want the appointment to appear on your calendar, as Free, Tentative, Busy, or Out of Office, and a graphic bar appears on the left side of the appointment.

QUICK TIP
To quickly enter an appointment, click the time slot in the calendar, then type the information.

3. **Type Review Travel Agendas in the Subject text box, type Conference Room A in the Location text box, click the Start time list arrow, click the date that is one week from the date you clicked in Step 2, click the Start time list arrow, click 9:00 AM, click the Reminder list arrow in the Options group on the Ribbon, then click 1 day**
   If this were a one-time meeting, you could click the Save & Close button in the Actions group and the appointment would be set. Reminders appear with a reminder icon in the appointment.
4. **Click the Recurrence button in the Options group, review the default recurrence options shown in Figure B-12, click the End after option button, type 52 in the occurrences text box, click OK, then click the Save & Close button in the Actions group**
   The Appointment window closes. This is a recurring event that will display on your calendar each week for 52 weeks. Recurring events or appointments appear with the icon.
5. **Click anywhere in the calendar, click the Home tab, click the Day button in the Arrange group, click the Work Week button, click the Week button, then click the Forward button in the calendar three times**
   You can view the calendar by day, week, or month. In all calendar views, click the Time Scale button in the Arrangement group on the View tab to change the level of detail of the days shown.

QUICK TIP
When viewing the calendar, if you click a meeting or appointment, the details appear in the Reading Pane.

6. **On the Home tab, in the Go To group, click the Today button to return to today's date**
7. **In the New group, click the New Meeting button, in the Show group click the Scheduling button, then click the Untitled Meeting Close button on the title bar**
   The calendar can check the availability of all the invitees and resources for the meetings you want to set up.

FIGURE B-10: Calendar for a week

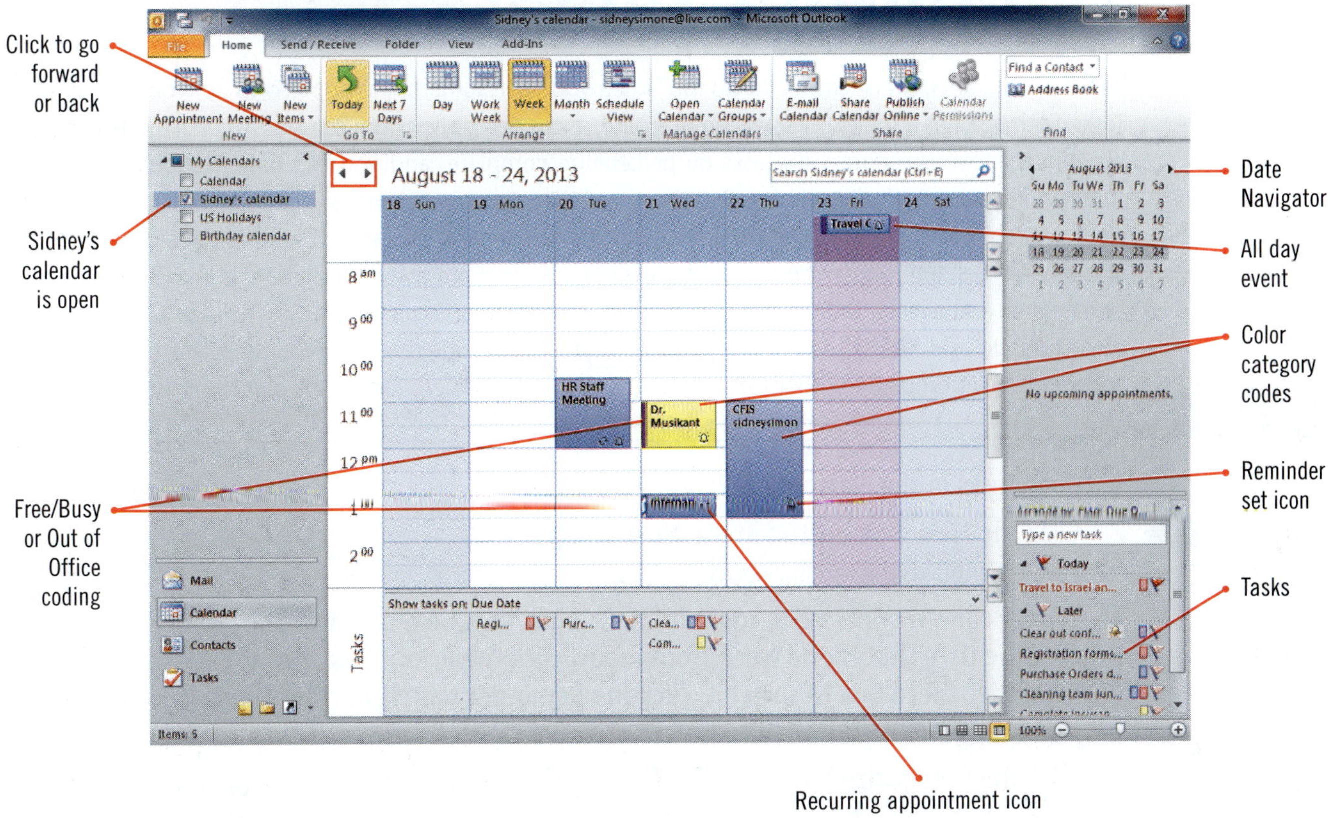

FIGURE B-11: New Appointment window

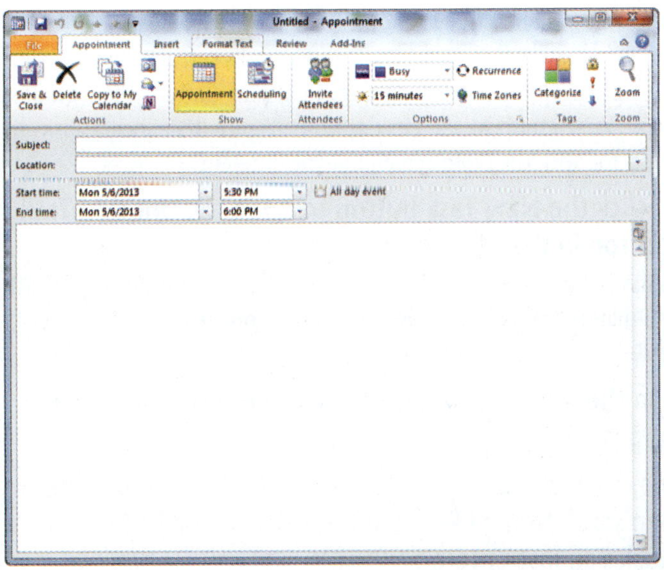

FIGURE B-12: Appointment Recurrence dialog box

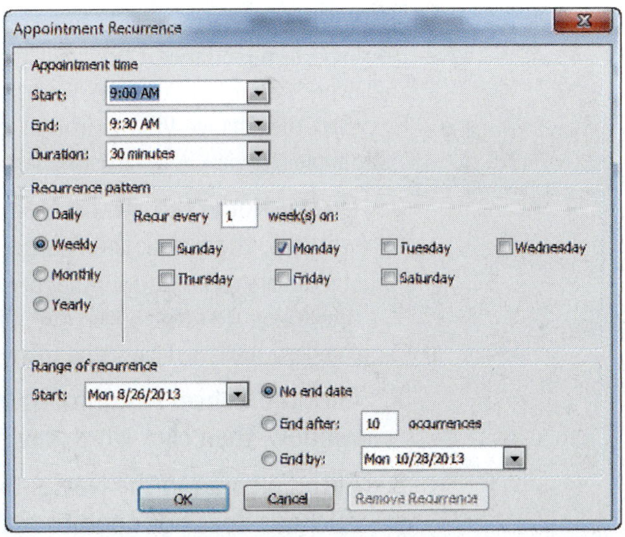

Sending electronic business cards

You can send contact information over the Internet easily with Outlook. If you know someone has Outlook, you can send a contact business card. In Contacts view, click the contact you want to send, then, on the Home tab, click the Forward Contact button in the Share group. You can choose to send the card as a business card or an Outlook contact, and you can forward the card as a text message. If you send it as a business card, you will send the contact as a .vcf electronic file to someone via e-mail.

Managing Tasks

Tasks in Outlook is an electronic to-do list. When you have something you need to do, you can enter it in Tasks. Each task has a subject, a start and due date, and a description. You can also assign a priority to a task. You can mark your progress on tasks by percentage complete, and you can have Outlook create status summary reports in e-mail messages and then send the summary to anyone on a task update list. Tasks can also have reminders. When you are in an Outlook module other than Tasks, your tasks appear at the bottom of the To-Do Bar, if it is open. You can also view the tasks that are due on each date in the Calendar. Similar to meetings and events, tasks can recur. You can also assign a flag and category to each task to help you organize your tasks. A week from tomorrow, the main conference room at the office is being painted, and you have to prepare the room. You enter the task in Outlook to keep track of it.

STEPS

1. **Click Tasks in the Navigation Pane**

2. **Click the New Task button in the New group**
   The new untitled Task window opens.

> **QUICK TIP**
> You can also quickly enter a task by typing in the Type a new task box at the top of the To-Do List.

3. **Type Clear out conference room in the Subject text box, click the Start date list arrow, click the date that is one week from today, click the Priority list arrow, click High, click the Reminder check box to select it, click the Reminder date list arrow, then click the date that is one week from yesterday**

4. **Click the Categorize button in the Tags group, click Purple Category (or the category that is purple, if it has a different name), click No in the Rename Category dialog box if necessary, click the Follow Up button in the Tags group, then click Next Week**
   The completed task looks like Figure B-13.

5. **Click the Save & Close button in the Actions group**
   You can arrange your tasks in several different ways, such as by Date, Category, Start Date, Due Date, Folder, Type, or Importance. Click a column header in the task list to change sort order. Tasks can also be viewed in many ways by clicking the View tab and using the options in the Arrangement and Current View groups. Click the Change View button in the Current View group to see view options. Figure B-14 shows Tasks in Simple List view. A few existing tasks appear in the window (your screen may be different).

6. **On the Home tab, in the New group click the New Task button to open the Untitled Task window, then click the Assign Task button in the Manage Task group**
   You can assign tasks to another person and have Outlook automatically update you on the status of the task completion. To assign a task, you fill in the e-mail address of the person to whom you are assigning the task, complete the task details, and then click Send.

7. **Click the Cancel Assignment button in the Manage Task group, close the Untitled Task window, then click No to saving changes**

8. **Click Calendar in the Navigation Pane, click the Today button in the Go To group if the calendar does not open to today, then scroll to next week in the calendar or Date Navigator or until you see the new task you just entered**
   To coordinate your tasks and your appointments, the task list from Tasks is displayed in the Tasks section below the calendar. The task you just created should appear under the calendar for next week. You can specify how tasks are organized in the To-Do Bar.

> **TROUBLE**
> If the To-Do Bar is not open, click the View tab, click the To-Do Bar button in the Layout group, then click Normal.

9. **Click the Arrange By button above the tasks in the To-Do Bar, then click Start Date**
   To schedule time to complete a task, drag a task from the To-Do Bar to a time block in the Calendar. Any changes you make to a task are reflected in both the To-Do Bar in Calendar and the task list in Tasks.

FIGURE B-13: Task information entered

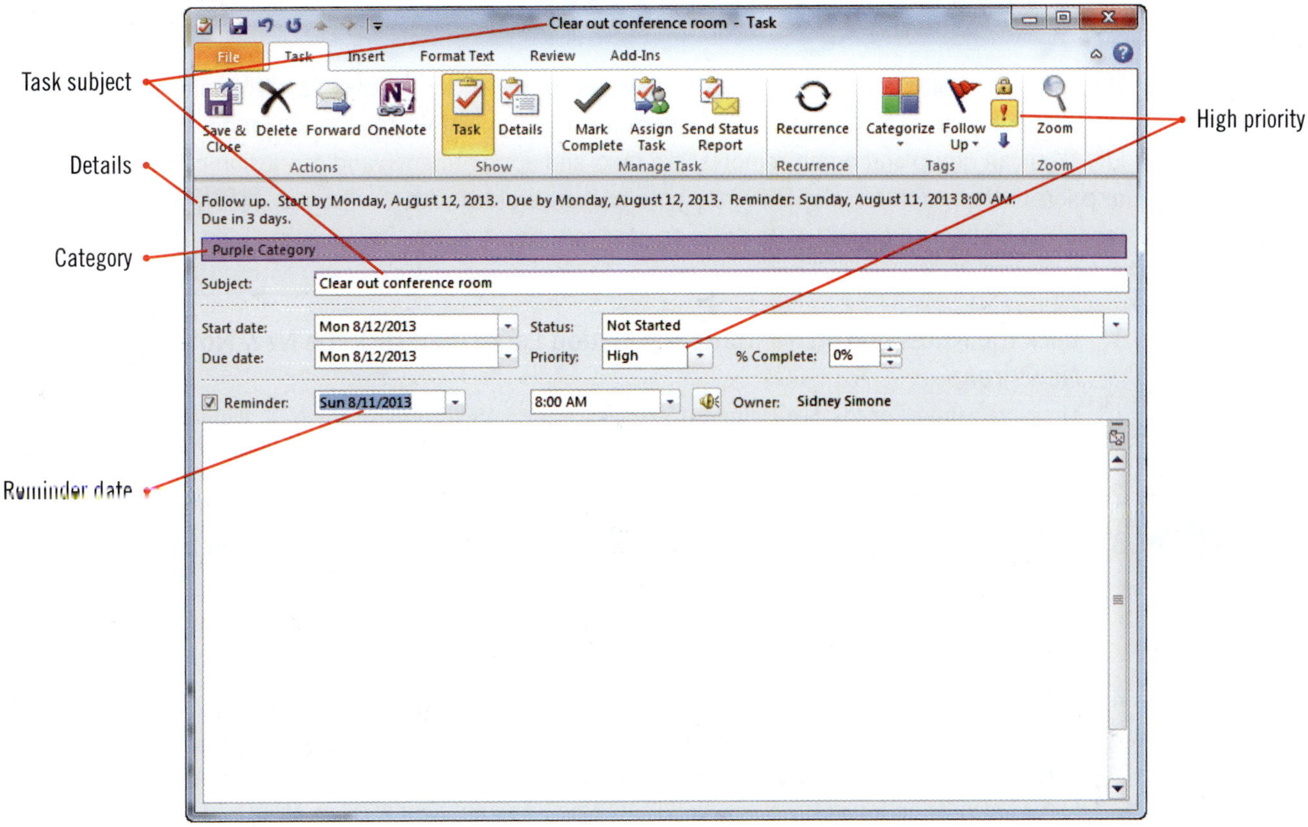

FIGURE B-14: Tasks in Simple List view

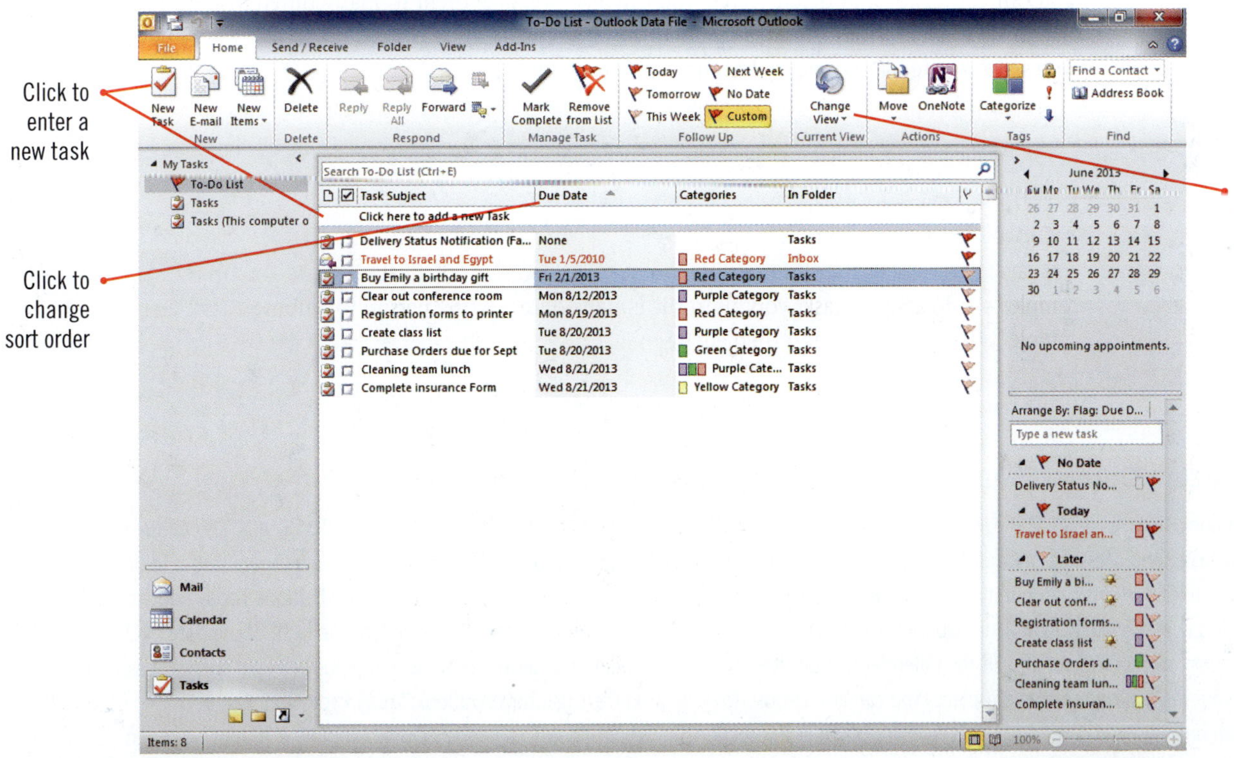

Outlook 2010

UNIT
B
Outlook 2010

Creating Notes

Notes in Microsoft Outlook is the electronic version of the sticky notes or Post-It™ notes you buy at your local stationery store. Notes created in Outlook are a convenient way to quickly jot down a reminder or an idea. You can group and organize notes, like tasks and appointments, and can assign categories, contacts, or colors to them. You can also forward a note to share an idea with a colleague. You use the Notes module in Outlook to quickly write down an idea concerning a new employee at Quest Specialty Travel.

STEPS

1. **Click the Notes button in the Navigation Pane, then click the New Note button in the New group**

   The Note window opens. See Figure B-15. You type the note directly in the Note window. The note should begin with a meaningful phrase so that the Notes list displays a clear descriptive title for it.

2. **Type Maxine Powers-File new health forms with insurance company**

3. **Click the Note icon in the upper-left corner of the Note window to open a menu, then point to Categorize**

   See Figure B-16. You can color code each note, assign a contact to the note, and forward or print the note. Notes are date- and time-stamped at the time they are created.

4. **Click Purple Category (or the name of the purple category, if necessary)**

   The Navigation Pane provides many options for viewing the notes in order to organize them the way you want. If you want to turn a note into an appointment or meeting, you drag the note from the Notes window to the Calendar button in the Navigation Pane. A new Appointment window opens with the details from the note filled in the appropriate fields. If you drag the note to the Tasks button in the Navigation Pane, a new task window opens and you can specify a due date and other details.

5. **Close the note**

   You can copy, move, or delete notes. You can also organize them in many different ways to best meet your needs. Right-click the Notes area to open the shortcut menu with options in a Notes window with several notes. Each note has a category assignment. See Figure B-17.

QUICK TIP

If a note is covering an area of the window you want to view, click the title bar of the note and drag it to a new location.

QUICK TIP

To quickly copy a note, drag the note while you press [Ctrl].

Customizing Outlook Today

When Outlook Today is open, you can see what is happening in the Calendar, Tasks, and Messages modules for the day. To open Outlook Today, click the Shortcuts button in the Navigation Pane, then click Outlook Today in the Navigation Pane. Outlook Today shows your appointments over a range of time in the Calendar section. It also displays your tasks in one convenient place. You can also choose to show from one to seven days of appointments in the Calendar section, and you can sort your tasks in Outlook Today by Importance, Due Date, Creation Time, or Start Date and in ascending or descending order. If you use Outlook for e-mail, Outlook Today displays how many messages are in your Inbox, Drafts, RSS Feeds, and Outbox folders. You can also add or delete folders from the Messages folder list. To customize Outlook Today, view the Outlook Today page, click the Customize Outlook Today link to the right of the date in Outlook Today, and set the options to fit your personal style and work habits. In the Customize Outlook Today Pane, you can decide to go directly to Outlook Today when Outlook opens, if it does not open automatically. Pick a different visual appearance for Outlook Today from an available list. Click the Save Changes link in the Customize Outlook Today Pane to save any changes you make.

FIGURE B-15: Create a new note

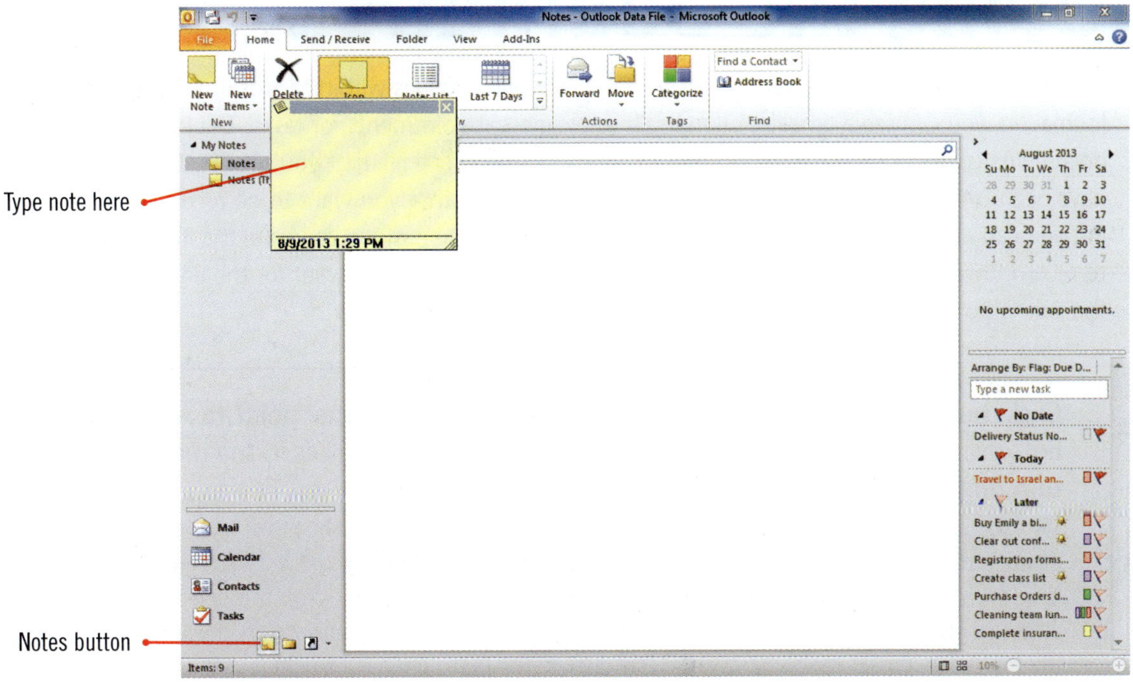

FIGURE B-16: Notes menu with Category options

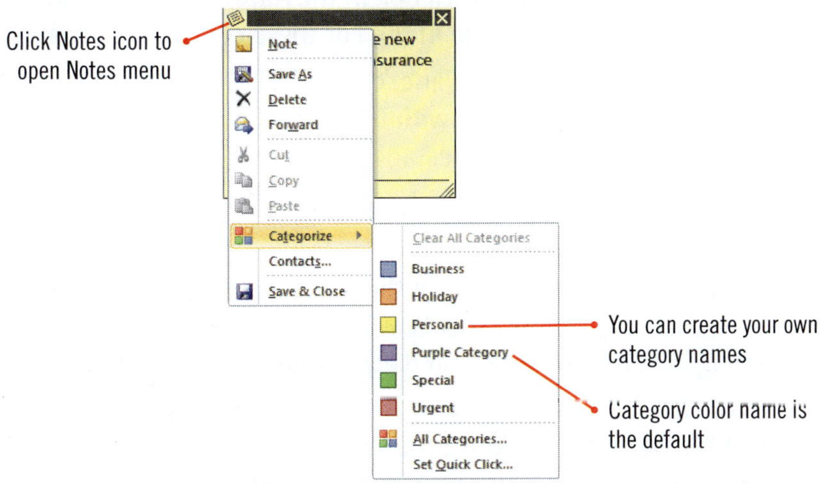

FIGURE B-17: Notes in Icon view

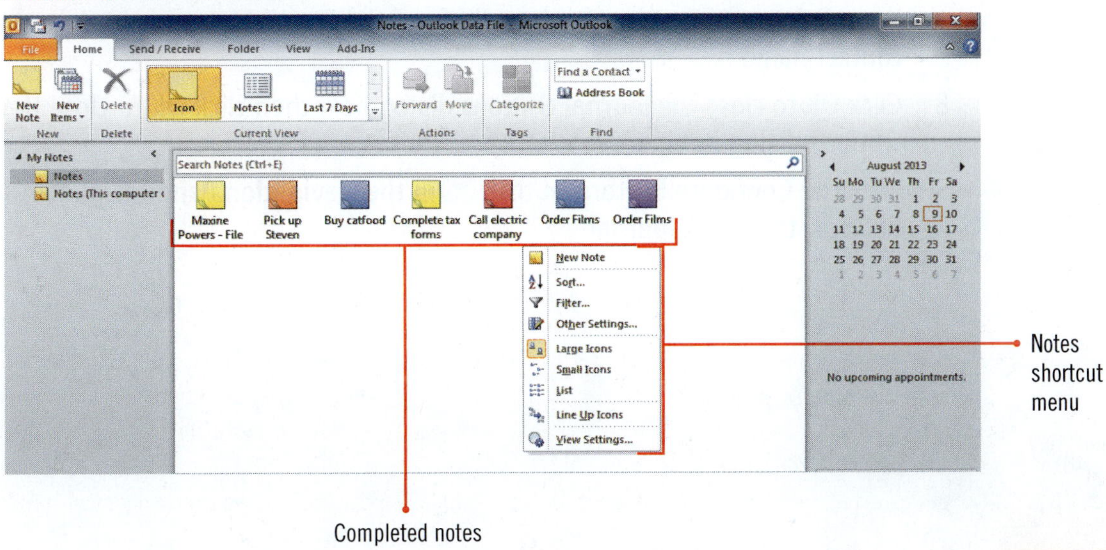

UNIT
B
Outlook 2010

Using the Journal

The **Journal** in Outlook is a way to provide a trail of your activities within Microsoft Office. If you turn the Journal on, you can see a timeline of any calls, messages, appointments, or tasks. The Journal also tracks all documents, spreadsheets, databases, presentations, or any Office file that you specify. The Journal may not have been on when you created a spreadsheet or document that you want to be recorded in the Journal. But you can add it to the Journal. Use Windows Explorer or the desktop to locate the file or item you want to record, then drag the item to the Journal and select the options you want for the entry. You use the Journal to help assign documents to contacts.

STEPS

1. **Click the Configure buttons button in the Navigation Pane, point to Add or Remove Buttons, click Journal, click the Journal button, then click Yes in the message box to turn on the Journal**

   To turn on the Journal, you specify the Journal options, such as which items to track, in the Journal Options dialog box, shown in Figure B-18. The Journal is displayed as a timeline on your screen. Any activities that have been specified to be tracked appear for each day as icons. You can scroll through the Journal to get an overview of your activities. You can sort or group the activities in the Journal. If you want to recall an event, the Journal is a great tool; you can see any documents that may have been created on a specific day. The Journal folder contains shortcuts to the activities that have been recorded.

QUICK TIP
You can remove, add, or change Journal options at any time by working in the Journal Options dialog box.

2. **Click the E-mail Message check box in the Automatically record these items box, click the check box next to your name in the For these contacts list, then click OK**

QUICK TIP
Make sure your e-mail address is listed in your contact information in Contacts so that it will be tracked in the Journal.

3. **Click Mail in the Navigation Pane, click the New E-Mail button in the New group, then send yourself a test message with the subject Testing the Journal and the body of the message I am sending this message to test the Journal.**

4. **Click the Journal button on the Naviation Pane, and view the Journal entry, as shown in Figure B-19**

5. **Click the Journal Entry button in the New group, then click the Entry type list arrow**

   A new Journal Entry window opens. You can create journal entries for activities such as phone calls or tasks using this dialog box. There are many different journal entries you can manually add to your journal.

QUICK TIP
E-mail is also tracked within Outlook contacts when the Journal is on.

6. **Click the Entry type list arrow to close the list, then in the Journal Entry window, click the Delete button in the Actions group**

   To turn off the Journal, you have to clear the Journal Options dialog box.

7. **Click the File tab, click Options, click the Notes and Journal tab, click Journal Options, then click to remove the check marks from the E-mail Message check box and from your contact name**

8. **Click OK to close the Journal Options dialog box, then click OK to close the Outlook Options dialog box**

9. **Click the Configure Buttons button in the Navigation Pane, point to Add or Remove Buttons, then click Journal**

FIGURE B-18: Journal Options dialog box

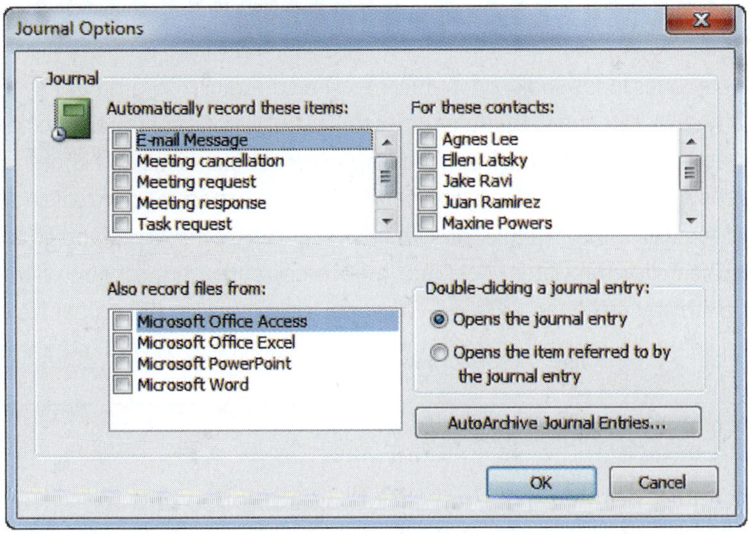

FIGURE B-19: The Journal

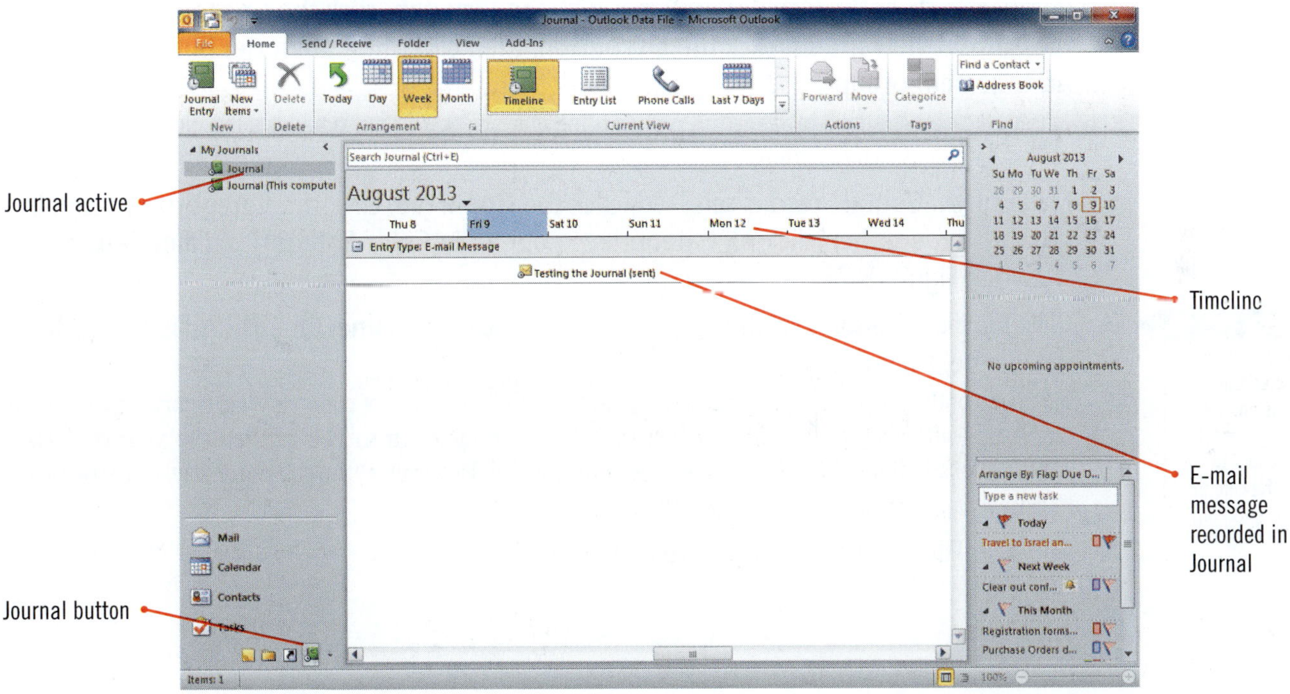

UNIT
B
Outlook 2010

Applying Categories

You use categories in Outlook to tag items so you can track and organize them by specific criteria. Outlook comes with color categories that are set by default. You can rename the colors as needed. For example, red can be urgent, blue can be business, and green can be personal. By assigning color categories to contacts, tasks, appointments, notes, or any item in Outlook, you can quickly review all items assigned to a specific category by reviewing the color. You can filter or sort by category. If you change your Contacts view to List view and then click the Categories button in the Arrangement section of the View tab, you can see your contacts clearly by category. QST wants to use color to help organize information about its contacts and staff. Eventually, you will set up a system to assign colors to contacts and staff based on region.

STEPS

1. **Click Contacts in the Navigation Pane**
2. **Click your Contact card, then click the Categorize button in the Tags group**
   Outlook comes with six predefined color categories: Purple, Orange, Blue, Green, Red, and Yellow.
3. **Click Purple Category (or the name of the purple category, if its name has been changed)**
   Your Contact card is now assigned the color purple. If you open the card, or if you view contacts as a list, you can see the color bar. You can assign more than one category to a contact.
4. **Click Calendar in the Navigation Pane, click the Forward button ▶ to scroll to next week, click the Review Travel Agendas appointment, click the Categorize button in the Tags group, then click Purple Category (or the category's name)**
   The appointment is also assigned the color purple.
5. **Click Contacts in the Navigation Pane, click the View tab, click the Change View button in the Current view group, click the List button, then click the Categories button in the Arrangement group**
   The contacts are grouped by category, as shown in Figure B-20. You can rename categories to be meaningful while retaining the color coding.
6. **Make sure a Contact card is selected, click the Home tab, click the Categorize button in the Tags group, then click All Categories to open the Color Categories dialog box, as shown in Figure B-21**
7. **Click Purple Category (or the category's name), click Rename, type HR Assistant as the new name, then click OK**
   The name of the purple category changes to "HR Assistant" in the list of contacts by category. As you work on other applications at your computer, you can leave Outlook open so you can refer to your contacts, be reminded of appointments, and track entries in the Journal. However, at the end of the day, it is good practice to close all applications and shut down the computer.
8. **Click the File tab, then click Exit to exit Outlook**

QUICK TIP
If you are working on a shared computer, such as in a lab setting, repeat Steps 6 and 7 to change the category name back to Purple Category.

FIGURE B-20: Contacts grouped by category

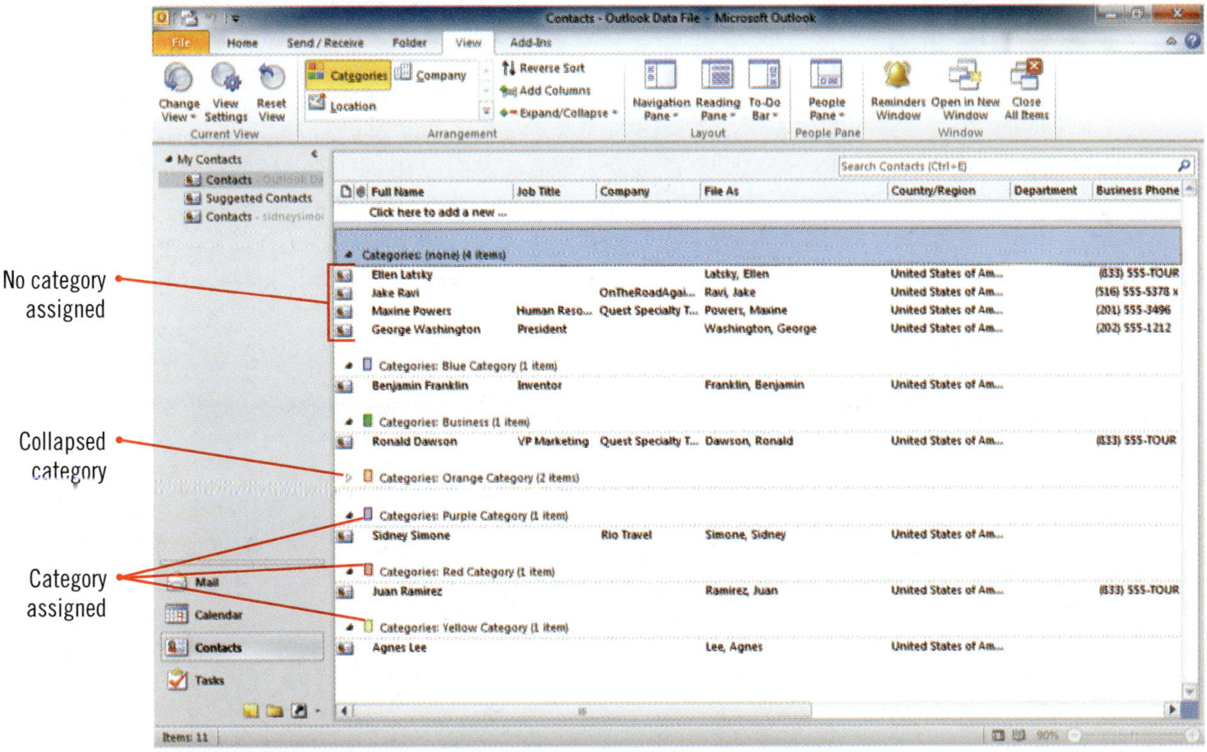

FIGURE B-21: Color Categories dialog box

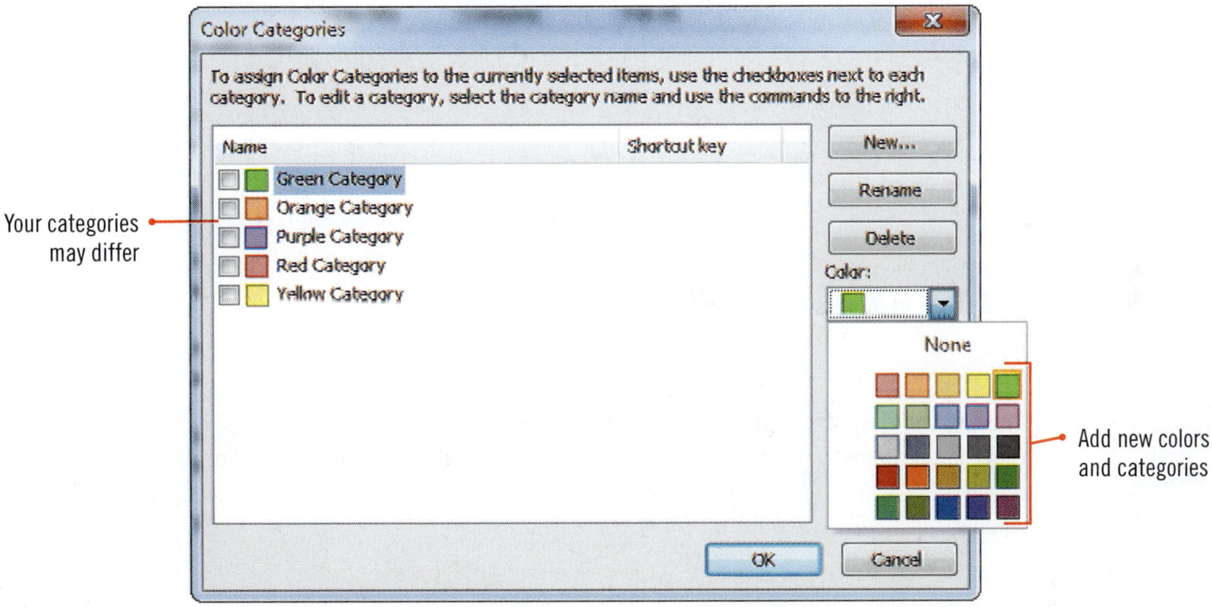

Coordinating calendars

Calendar can check the availability of all the people and resources for the meetings you want to set up.

Once you select a meeting time and location, you can send invitations in meeting requests by entering contact names in the To text box, then clicking the Send button. The meeting request arrives in the invitee's Inbox with buttons to Accept, Reject, or Request a change directly in the e-mail message. If an invitee accepts the invitation, a positive e-mail reply is sent back to you, and Outlook posts the meeting automatically to the invitee's calendar. If you share calendars through a network, you can click the Open a Shared Calendar link in the Navigation Pane to view the calendars of your colleagues. To send a copy of a time period in your calendar to someone through e-mail, click the Send a Calendar via E-mail link in the Navigation Pane, adjust the options in the Send a Calendar via E-mail dialog box, click OK, then address and send the e-mail.

Practice

Concepts Review

For current SAM information, including versions and content details, visit SAM Central (http://www.cengage.com/samcentral). If you have a SAM user profile, you may have access to hands-on instruction, practice, and assessment of the skills covered in this unit. Since various versions of SAM are supported throughout the life of this text, check with your instructor for the correct instructions and URL/Web site for accessing assignments.

Label each element of the Calendar window shown in Figure B-22.

FIGURE B-22

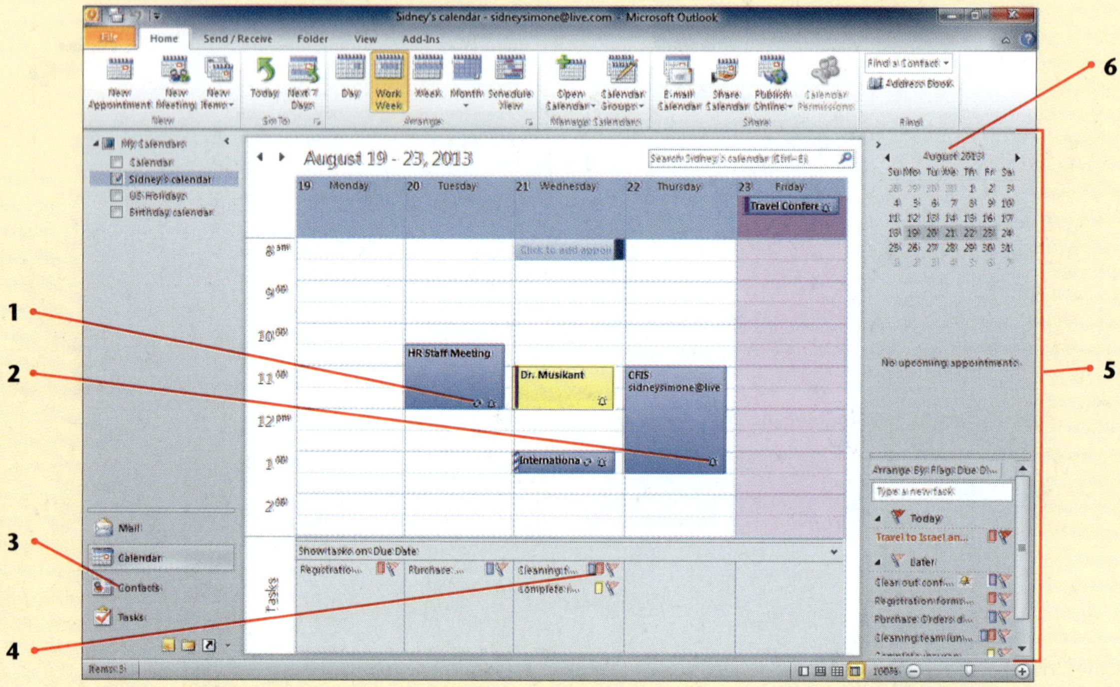

Match each term with the statement that best describes it.

7. **Notes**
8. **Tasks**
9. **E-mail**
10. **Calendar**
11. **Journal**

a. Manage a to-do list
b. Keep and track appointments
c. Send and receive messages
d. Track e-mail, documents, and activities
e. Jot down ideas or reminders

Select the best answer from the list of choices.

12. Which of the following is *not* available in Outlook?

- **a.** Mail
- **b.** Paint
- **c.** Calendar
- **d.** Notes

13. To color code your appointments, meetings, contacts, and events, use ______________.

- **a.** Flags
- **b.** Journal
- **c.** Categories
- **d.** Timeline

14. If you want to send an e-mail to the same 15 people every time, you should create and use a(n) ______________.

- **a.** Category
- **b.** Contact Group
- **c.** Address book
- **d.** Cluster

15. To see the Contact picture you added to a Contact card, use the ______________ view.

- **a.** Business Card
- **b.** Card
- **c.** List
- **d.** Graphic

16. The difference between an appointment and an event is that ______________.

- **a.** an event cannot recur
- **b.** an appointment lasts less than 12 hours
- **c.** an event lasts 24 hours or more
- **d.** you cannot categorize an event

17. Which of the following is *not* visible on the To-Do Bar?

- **a.** Date Navigator
- **b.** An appointment for today
- **c.** Tasks due today
- **d.** E-mail in the Inbox

18. If an appointment happens every Tuesday, you should set a ______________ when setting up the appointment.

- **a.** recurrence
- **b.** reminder
- **c.** category
- **d.** journal entry

19. When you enter an incomplete address that doesn't meet the field requirments in a new Contact card, Outlook ______________.

- **a.** maps the address to help you find it
- **b.** leaves the address as is
- **c.** closes the dialog box and cancels the contact
- **d.** opens the Check Address dialog box

20. When you enter an incomplete name that doesn't meet the field requirments in a new Contact card, Outlook ______________.

- **a.** opens the Check Full Name dialog box
- **b.** leaves the name as is
- **c.** closes the dialog box and cancels the contact
- **d.** offers a list of possible suggestions

Skills Review

1. Start Outlook.

- **a.** Start Outlook.
- **b.** Arrange the Outlook window so that the Navigation Pane is in Normal view with the folder list on the left side of the screen and the To-Do Bar on the right side.
- **c.** If there is any mail in the Inbox, click a message and view the message in the Reading Pane.
- **d.** Click each tab on the Ribbon and view the different command buttons.
- **e.** Click the Home tab on the Ribbon.

2. Organize e-mail.

- **a.** View the Inbox.
- **b.** View the e-mail in the Inbox by Sender, view the Inbox by Size, then view the e-mail in the Inbox by Date (Conversations), with the most recent on top. (*Hint*: Sender is From on the list.)
- **c.** If you have any messages in your Inbox, select the message, expand the People Pane, review the contents, then collapse the People Pane.

Skills Review (continued)

d. Open a New Message window and write an e-mail message to your instructor or a friend. Include an address in the Cc box, then type **Study group plans** as the subject of the message. As the body of the message, enter the message shown in Figure B-23.

e. Send the message.

f. Open the Sent Items folder, review the e-mail options, then return to the Inbox.

FIGURE B-23

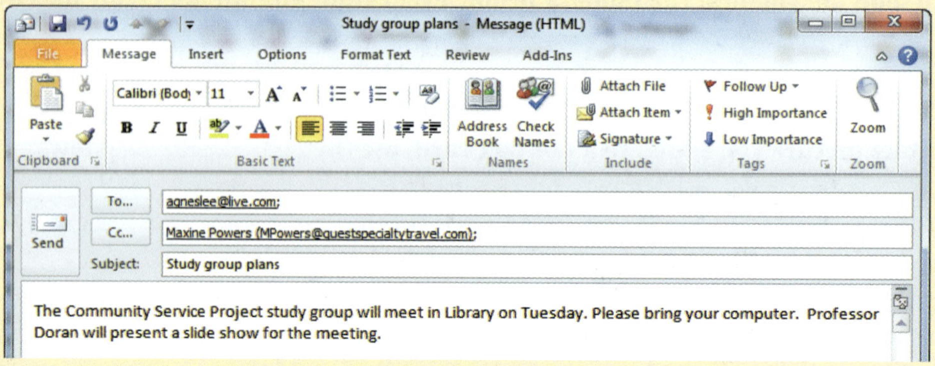

3. Add contacts.

a. Open Contacts.

b. Open a new untitled Contact window.

c. Create a new contact using the information in Figure B-24.

d. If you have a photo or any picture, add it to the Contact card.

e. If you are connected to the Internet, click the MapIt button and locate the address on a map.

f. Save and close the contact.

FIGURE B-24

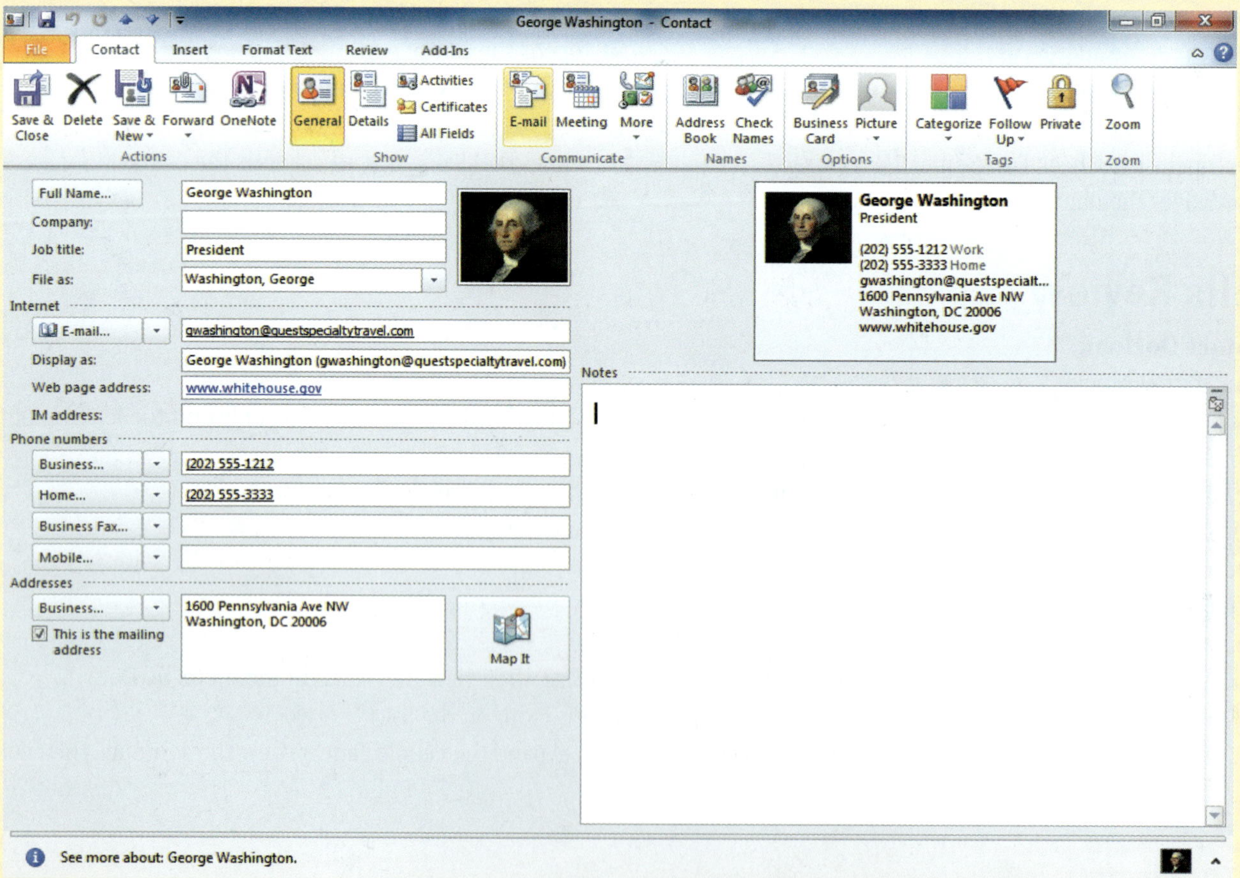

Skills Review (continued)

4. Manage appointments.

- **a.** Open Calendar.
- **b.** View the calendar by full week.
- **c.** View the calendar for today.
- **d.** Create a new appointment for next week for a two-and-a-half hour lunch meeting with Ruth, Maureen, and Janice at noon in the Stardust Diner. Set a reminder for four hours. See Figure B-25.
- **e.** Save and close the appointment.

FIGURE B-25

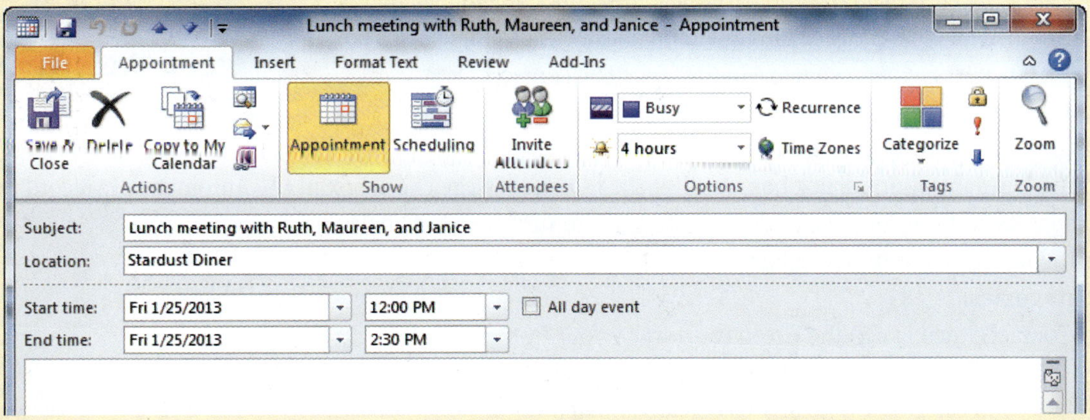

5. Manage tasks.

- **a.** Open Tasks.
- **b.** Create a new task that starts next month.
- **c.** The subject of the task is **Buy Emily a birthday gift**.
- **d.** Assign the task to the Red category.
- **e.** Set a reminder for early morning one week before the task is due. See Figure B-26.
- **f.** Save and close the task.
- **g.** View the task list in Simple List and Detailed List views.

FIGURE B-26

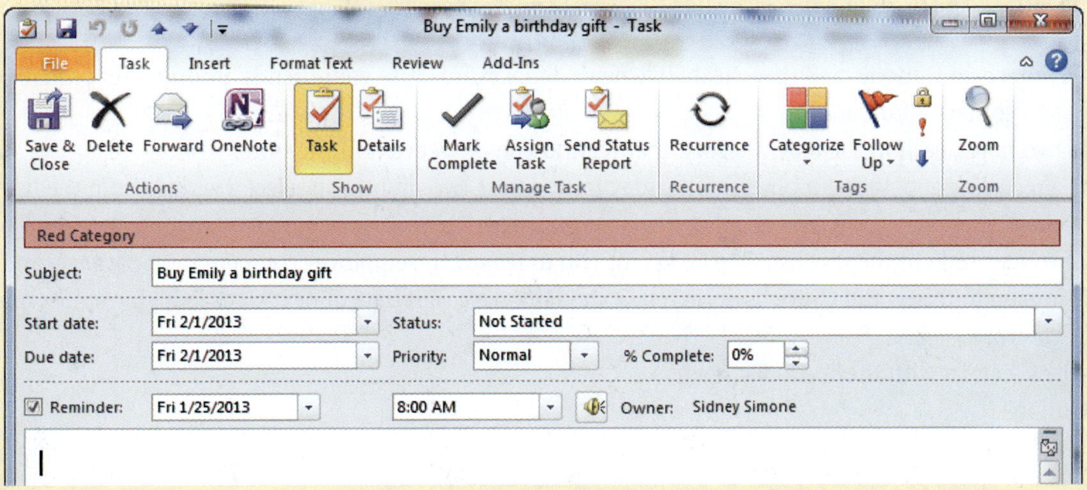

Skills Review (continued)

6. **Create notes.**
   a. Open Notes.
   b. Create a new note with the following text: **Call town hall about the new library hours.**
   c. Categorize the note in the Blue category. See Figure B-27.
   d. Close the note.

FIGURE B-27

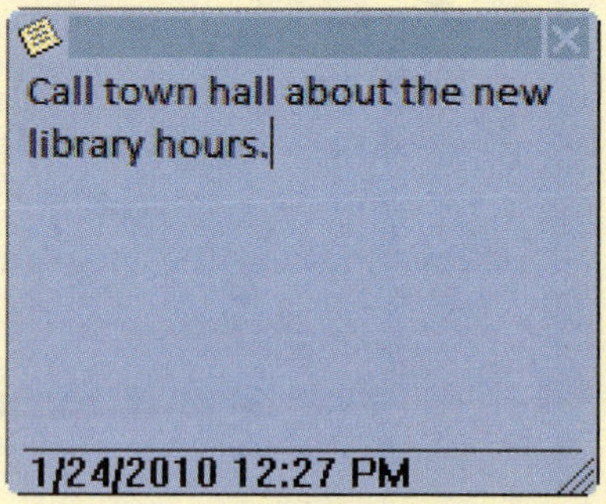

7. **Use the Journal.**
   a. Turn on the Journal.
   b. In the Journal Options dialog box, to have the Journal track your e-mail messages, click the E-mail Message check box in the Automatically record these items box and the check box next to your own name in the "For these contacts."
   c. Send yourself an e-mail message.
   d. Open the Journal to view the Journal entry.
   e. Open the Journal Options dialog box, deselect the E-mail Message check box in the Automatically record these items box, then deselect the check box next to your name to turn tracking off.
   f. Close the Journal Options dialog box.
8. **Apply categories.**
   a. Open Contacts, then assign the Green category to your Contact card.
   b. Assign a category to the lunch appointment that you created in Step 4.
   c. Assign a second category to the task you created in Step 5.
   d. View Contacts by category.
   e. View the tasks by category.
   f. Exit Outlook.

Independent Challenge 1

As manager of a local pet store, your job is to develop a contact list of all customers that come into the store. The list will be used to send direct mail for future promotions. You created a form for customers to complete so that you can gather their contact information. The information includes first and last name, mailing address, e-mail address, and at least one phone number. Each week, you select one customer from the list of new names to receive a small prize package. You need to create the contact list in Outlook and use Outlook to schedule the weekly prize giveaway.

a. Open Contacts in Outlook, and then create five new Contact cards. Use your friends' information or make up fictitious names and contact information.
b. Create two notes, each in the Blue category, that remind you of an event in the store.
c. Create a recurring appointment on each Thursday for the next two months to select a winner from the list of new names.
d. Enter two new tasks in the task list. One task is for you to review the employee compensation package, and the other task is for you to review the utility bills. Each task should have a start date of next week, a high priority, and be in the Yellow category.
e. View the Calendar with the To-Do Bar open.
f. Exit Outlook.

Independent Challenge 2

Outlook is an integrated information management system that stores information in folders specific to the type of information stored. Outlook stores e-mail in Mail folders, contacts in Contact folders, and so on. You can create new folders for specific types of information and view them in the folders list. You can also transfer one type of item to another, for example, you can drag a task to the Calendar to create an appointment. The integration of the different types of information is what makes Outlook so powerful. You are going to move items from one Outlook module to another to see how easily you can integrate information.

- **a.** Open Mail in Outlook, then drag an e-mail message from the Inbox to Tasks in the Navigation Pane to create a new task. In a word-processing document or on a piece of paper, explain what happens. What elements of the mail message are entered in which task fields?
- **b.** Drag an e-mail message from the Inbox to Notes in the Navigation Pane, then explain what happens.
- **c.** Open the Calendar, drag an existing appointment from the Calendar to Tasks in the Navigation Pane, then explain what happens.
- **d.** Drag the same appointment to Mail in the Navigation Pane.
- **e.** View the Contacts list in Business Card view. Drag a Contact card from the Contacts list to Calendar in the Navigation Pane, then explain what happens.

Advanced Challenge Exercise

ACE

- Open an existing contact, click the Categorize button, then click All Categories.
- Rename the Purple and Red categories to a name of your choice, close the Color Categories dialog box, then assign the contact to both categories.
- Click the Details button in the Show group on the Contact tab, then enter at least two details in the fields.
- Save and close the contact.

- **f.** View the Contacts list in Business Card view. Drag a Contact card from the Contacts list to Mail in the Navigation Pane, then explain what happens.
- **g.** Exit Outlook.

Visual Workshop

Start Outlook. First, create a new contact, as shown in Figure B-28, using any photo you want. Create an appointment as shown in Figure B-29, using a weekday in the next two weeks as the date for the appointment. Finally, using the same date as for the appointment, create a task, as shown in Figure B-30. Note that the dates in the figures will differ from those on your screen.

FIGURE B-28

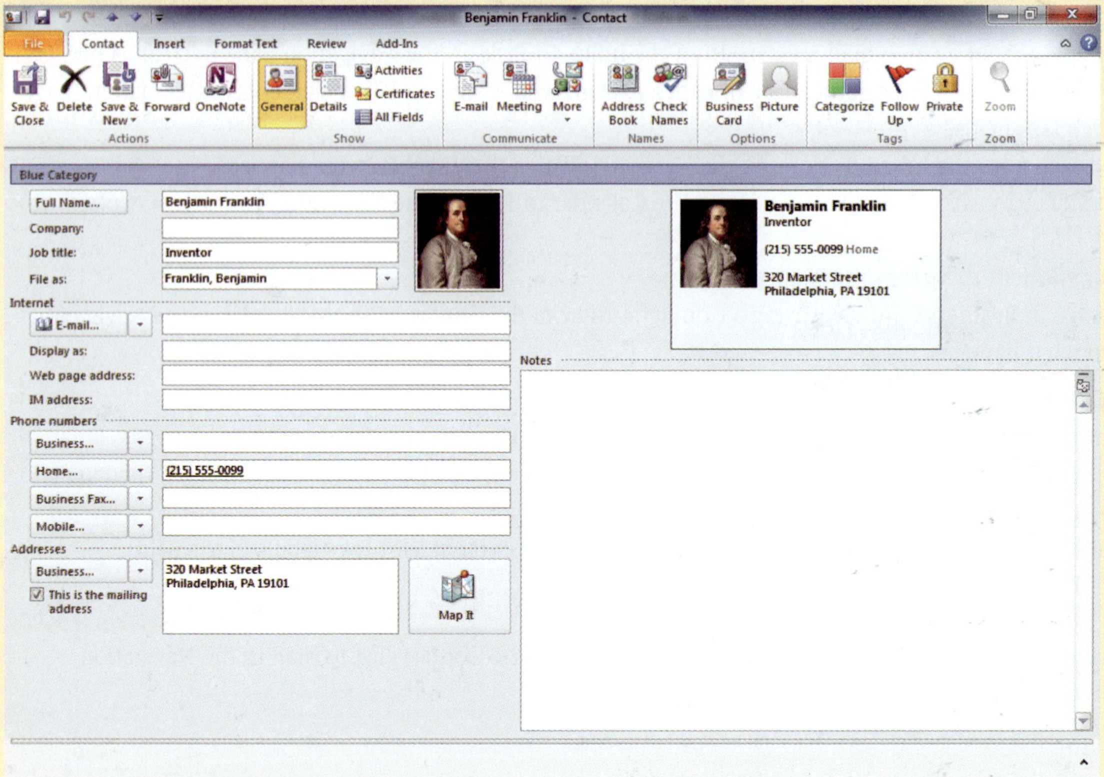

FIGURE B-29

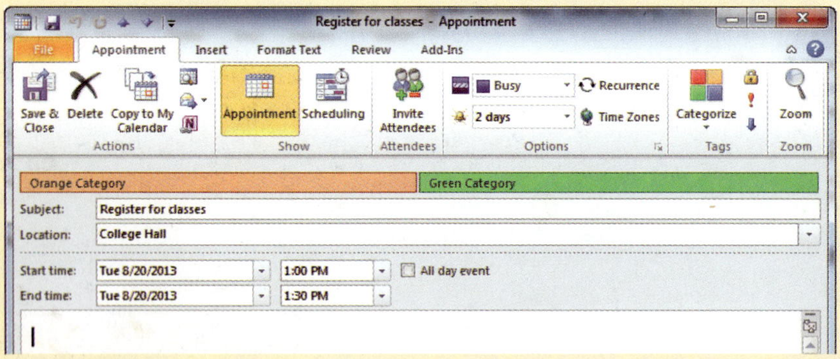

FIGURE B-30

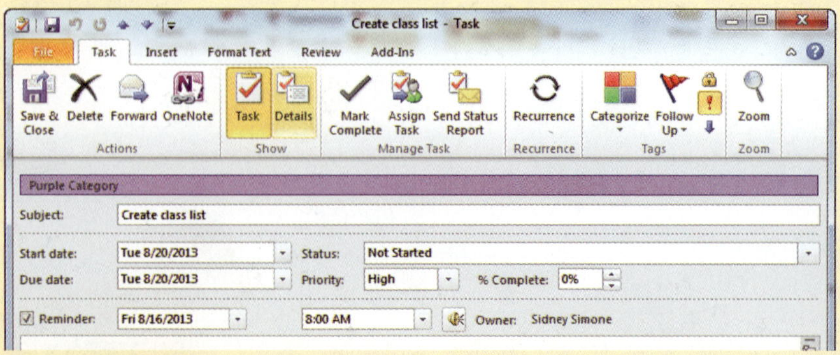

Appendix
Web Apps
Office 2010

Working with Windows Live and Office Web Apps

Files You Will Need:
WEB-1.pptx
WEB-2.xlsx

If the computer you are using has an active Internet connection, you can go to the Microsoft Windows Live Web site and access a wide variety of services and Web applications. For example, you can check your e-mail through Windows Live, network with your friends and coworkers, and use SkyDrive to store and share files. From SkyDrive, you can also use Office Web Apps to create and edit Word, PowerPoint, Excel, and OneNote files, even when you are using a computer that does not have Office 2010 installed. You work in the Vancouver branch of Quest Specialty Travel. Your supervisor, Mary Lou Jacobs, asks you to explore Windows Live and learn how she can use SkyDrive and Office Web Apps to work with her files online.

(*Note*: SkyDrive and Office Web Apps are dynamic Web pages, and might change over time, including the way they are organized and how commands are performed. The steps and figures in this appendix were accurate at the time this book was published.)

OBJECTIVES

- Explore how to work online from Windows Live
- Obtain a Windows Live ID and sign in to Windows Live
- Upload files to Windows Live
- Work with the PowerPoint Web App
- Create folders and organize files on SkyDrive
- Add people to your network and share files
- Work with the Excel Web App

Appendix
Web Apps
Office 2010

Exploring How to Work Online from Windows Live

You can use your Web browser to upload your files to Windows Live from any computer connected to the Internet. You can work on the files right in your Web browser using Office Web Apps and share your files with people in your Windows Live network. You review the concepts and services related to working online from Windows Live.

DETAILS

- **What is Windows Live?**
  Windows Live is a collection of services and Web applications that you can use to help you be more productive both personally and professionally. For example, you can use Windows Live to send and receive e-mail, to chat with friends via instant messaging, to share photos, to create a blog, and to store and edit files using SkyDrive. Table WEB-1 describes the services available on Windows Live. Windows Live is a free service that you sign up for. When you sign up, you receive a Windows Live ID, which you use to sign in to Windows Live. When you work with files on Windows Live, you are cloud computing.

- **What is Cloud Computing?**
  The term **cloud computing** refers to the process of working with files online in a Web browser. When you save files to SkyDrive on Windows Live, you are saving your files to an online location. SkyDrive is like having a personal hard drive in the cloud.

- **What is SkyDrive?**
  SkyDrive is an online storage and file sharing service. With a Windows Live account, you receive access to your own SkyDrive, which is your personal storage area on the Internet. On your SkyDrive, you are given space to store up to 25 GB of data online. Each file can be a maximum size of 50 MB. You can also use SkyDrive to access Office Web Apps, which you use to create and edit files created in Word, OneNote, PowerPoint, and Excel online in your Web browser.

- **Why use Windows Live and SkyDrive?**
  On Windows Live, you use SkyDrive to access additional storage for your files. You don't have to worry about backing up your files to a memory stick or other storage device that could be lost or damaged. Another advantage of storing your files on SkyDrive is that you can access your files from any computer that has an active Internet connection. Figure WEB-1 shows the SkyDrive Web page that appears when accessed from a Windows Live account. From SkyDrive, you can also access Office Web Apps.

- **What are Office Web Apps?**
  Office Web Apps are versions of Microsoft Word, Excel, PowerPoint, and OneNote that you can access online from your SkyDrive. An Office Web App does not include all of the features and functions included with the full Office version of its associated application. However, you can use the Office Web App from any computer that is connected to the Internet, even if Microsoft Office 2010 is not installed on that computer.

- **How do SkyDrive and Office Web Apps work together?**
  You can create a file in Office 2010 using Word, Excel, PowerPoint, or OneNote and then upload the file to your SkyDrive. You can then open the Office file saved to SkyDrive and edit it using your Web browser and the corresponding Office Web App. Figure WEB-2 shows a PowerPoint presentation open in the PowerPoint Web App. You can also use an Office Web App to create a new file, which is saved automatically to SkyDrive while you work. In addition, you can download a file created with an Office Web App and continue to work with the file in the full version of the corresponding Office application: Word, Excel, PowerPoint, or OneNote. Finally, you can create a SkyDrive network that consists of the people you want to be able to view your folders and files on your SkyDrive. You can give people permission to view and edit your files using any computer with an active Internet connection and a Web browser.

FIGURE WEB-1: SkyDrive on Windows Live

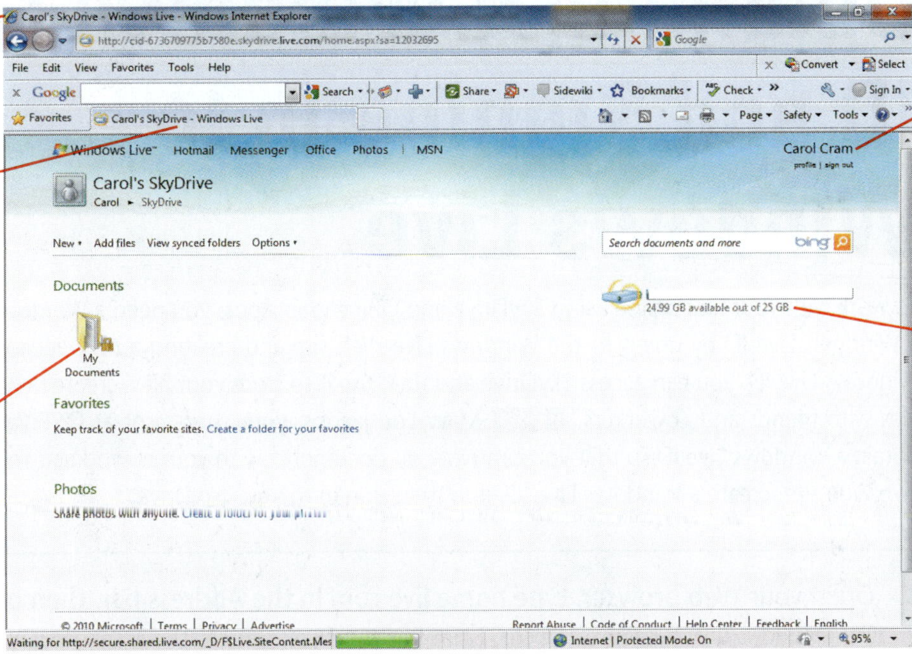

FIGURE WEB-2: PowerPoint presentation open in the PowerPoint Web App

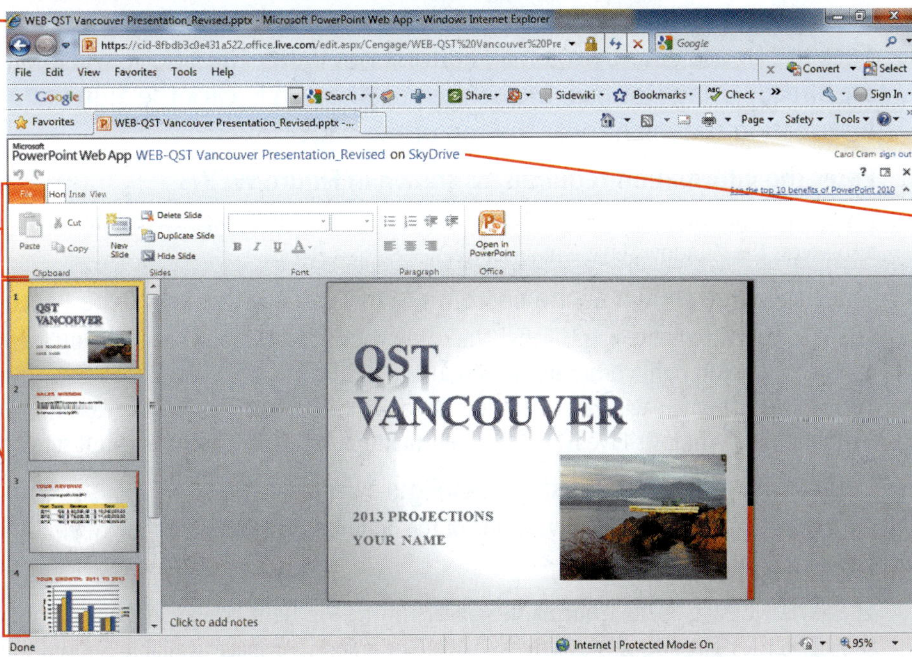

TABLE WEB-1: Services available via Windows Live

service	description
E-mail	Send and receive e-mail using a Hotmail account
Instant Messaging	Use Messenger to chat with friends, share photos, and play games
SkyDrive	Store files, work on files using Office Web Apps, and share files with people in your network
Photos	Upload and share photos with friends
People	Develop a network of friends and coworkers, then use the network to distribute information and stay in touch
Downloads	Access a variety of free programs available for download to a PC
Mobile Device	Access applications for a mobile device: text messaging, using Hotmail, networking, and sharing photos

Appendix
Web Apps
Office 2010

Obtaining a Windows Live ID and Signing In to Windows Live

To work with your files online using SkyDrive and Office Web Apps, you need a Windows Live ID. You obtain a Windows Live ID by going to the Windows Live Web site and creating a new account. Once you have a Windows Live ID, you can access SkyDrive and then use it to store your files, create new files, and share your files with friends and coworkers. Mary Lou Jacobs, your supervisor at QST Vancouver, asks you to obtain a Windows Live ID so that you can work on documents with your coworkers. You go to the Windows Live Web site, create a Windows Live ID, and then sign in to your SkyDrive.

STEPS

QUICK TIP
If you already have a Windows Live ID, go to the next lesson and sign in as directed using your account.

1. **Open your Web browser, type home.live.com in the Address bar, then press [Enter]**
   The Windows Live home page opens. From this page, you can create a Windows Live account and receive your Windows Live ID.
2. **Click the Sign up button** ***(Note: You may see a Sign up link instead of a button)***
   The Create your Windows Live ID page opens.
3. **Click the Or use your own e-mail address link under the Check availability button or if you are already using Hotmail, Messenger, or Xbox LIVE, click the Sign in now link in the Information statement near the top of the page**
4. **Enter the information required, as shown in Figure WEB-3**
   If you wish, you can sign up for a Windows Live e-mail address such as yourname@live.com so that you can also access the Windows Live e-mail services.

TROUBLE
The code can be difficult to read. If you receive an error message, enter the new code that appears.

5. **Enter the code shown at the bottom of your screen, then click the I accept button**
   The Windows Live home page opens. The name you entered when you signed up for your Windows Live ID appears in the top right corner of the window to indicate that you are signed in to Windows Live. From the Windows Live home page, you can access all the services and applications offered by Windows Live. See the Verifying your Windows Live ID box for information on finalizing your account set up.
6. **Point to Windows Live, as shown in Figure WEB-4**
   A list of options appears. SkyDrive is one of the options you can access directly from Windows Live.

TROUBLE
Click I accept if you are asked to review and accept the Windows Live Service Agreement and Privacy Statement.

7. **Click SkyDrive**
   The SkyDrive page opens. Your name appears in the top right corner, and the amount of space available is shown on the right side of the SkyDrive page. The amount of space available is monitored, as indicated by the gauge that fills with color as space is used. Using SkyDrive, you can add files to the existing folder and you can create new folders.
8. **Click sign out in the top right corner under your name, then exit the Web browser**
   You are signed out of your Windows Live account. You can sign in again directly from the Windows Live page in your browser or from within a file created with PowerPoint, Excel, Word, or OneNote.

FIGURE WEB-3: Creating a Windows Live ID

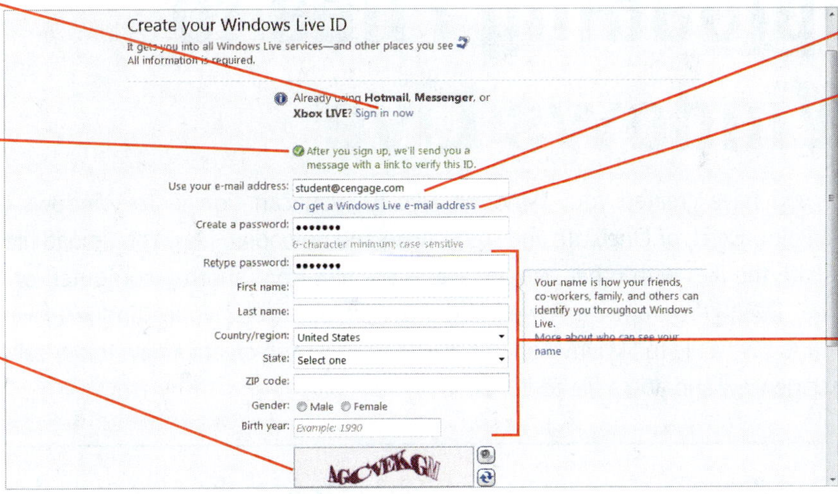

FIGURE WEB-4: Selecting SkyDrive

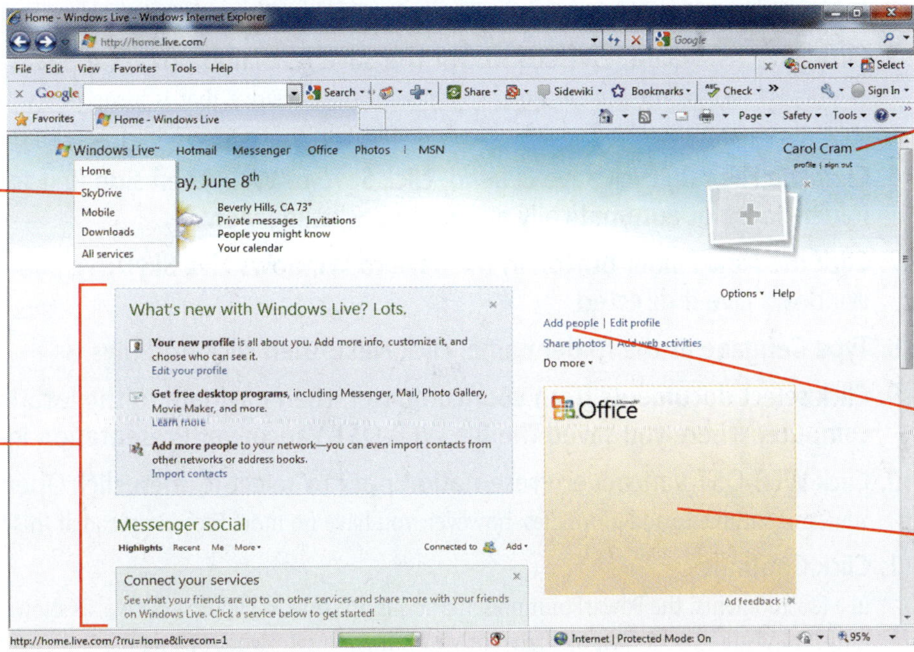

Verifying your Windows Live ID

As soon as you accept the Windows Live terms, an e-mail is sent to the e-mail address you supplied when you created your Windows Live ID. Open your e-mail program, and then open the e-mail from Microsoft with the Subject line: Confirm your e-mail address for Windows Live. Follow the simple, step-by-step instructions in the e-mail to confirm your Windows Live ID. When the confirmation is complete, you will be asked to sign in to Windows Live, using your e-mail address and password. Once signed in, you will see your Windows Live Account page.

Appendix
Web Apps
Office 2010

Uploading Files to Windows Live

Once you have created your Windows Live ID, you can sign in to Windows Live directly from Word, PowerPoint, Excel, or OneNote and start saving and uploading files. You upload files to your SkyDrive so you can share the files with other people, access the files from another computer, or use SkyDrive's additional storage. You open a PowerPoint presentation, access your Windows Live account from Backstage view, and save a file to SkyDrive on Windows Live. You also create a new folder called Cengage directly from Backstage view and add a file to it.

STEPS

QUICK TIP
Skip this step if the computer you are using signs you in automatically.

1. **Start PowerPoint, open the file WEB-1.pptx from the drive and folder where you store your Data Files, then save the file as WEB-QST Vancouver Presentation**
2. **Click the File tab, then click Save & Send**
   The Save & Send options available in PowerPoint are listed in Backstage view, as shown in Figure WEB-5.
3. **Click Save to Web**
4. **Click Sign In, type your e-mail address, press [Tab], type your password, then click OK**
   The My Documents folder on your SkyDrive appears in the Save to Windows Live SkyDrive information area.
5. **Click Save As, wait a few seconds for the Save As dialog box to appear, then click Save**
   The file is saved to the My Documents folder on the SkyDrive that is associated with your Windows Live account. You can also create a new folder and upload files directly to SkyDrive from your hard drive.
6. **Click the File tab, click Save & Send, click Save to Web, then sign in if the My Documents folder does not automatically appear in Backstage view**
7. **Click the New Folder button in the Save to Windows Live SkyDrive pane, then sign in to Windows Live if directed**
8. **Type Cengage as the folder name, click Next, then click Add files**
9. **Click select documents from your computer, then navigate to the location on your computer where you saved the file WEB-QST Vancouver Presentation in Step 1**
10. **Click WEB-QST Vancouver Presentation.pptx to select it, then click Open**
    You can continue to add more files; however, you have no more files to upload at this time.
11. **Click Continue**
    In a few moments, the PowerPoint presentation is uploaded to your SkyDrive, as shown in Figure WEB-6. You can simply store the file on SkyDrive or you can choose to work on the presentation using the PowerPoint Web App.
12. **Click the PowerPoint icon on your taskbar to return to PowerPoint, then close the presentation and exit PowerPoint**

FIGURE WEB-5: Save & Send options in Backstage view

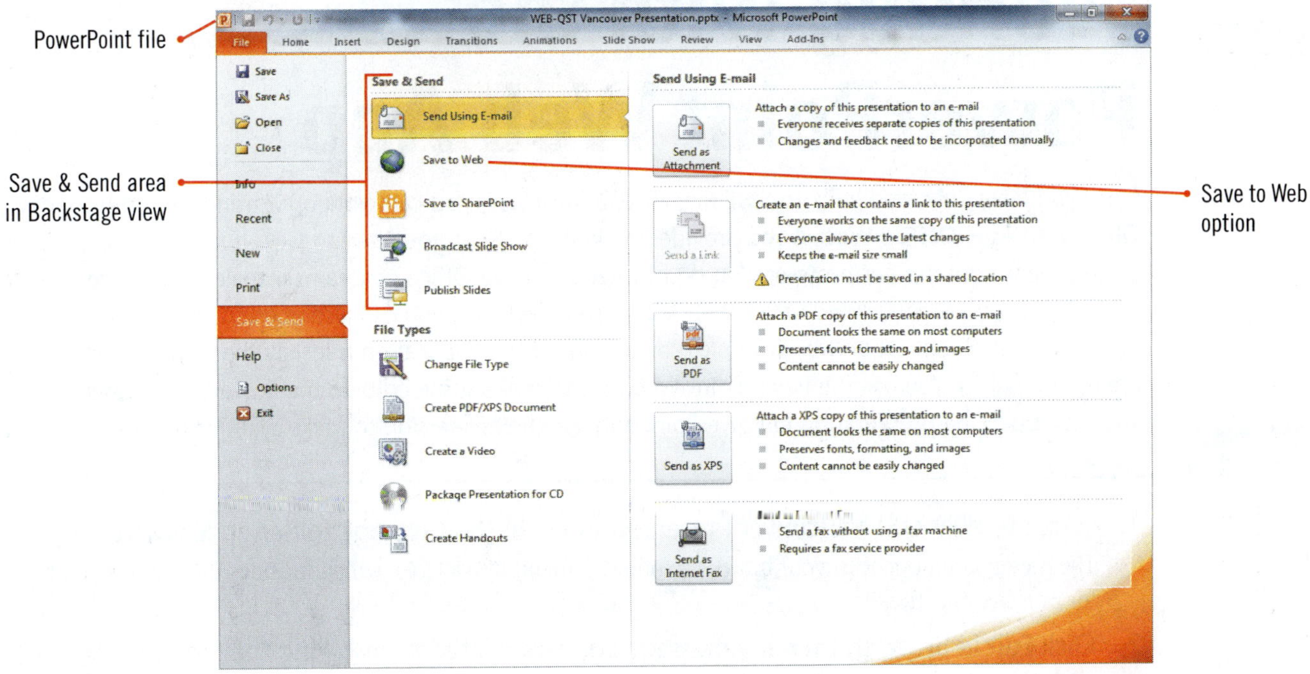

FIGURE WEB-6: File uploaded to the Cengage folder on Windows Live

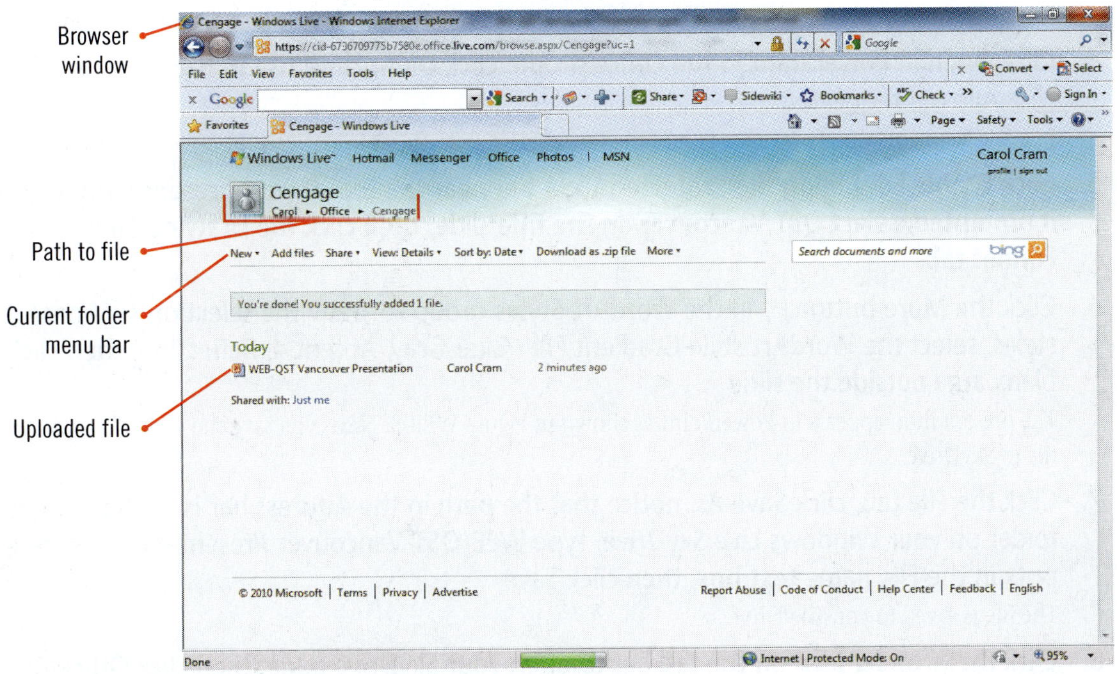

Working with the PowerPoint Web App

Once you have uploaded a file to SkyDrive on Windows Live, you can work on it using its corresponding Office Web App. **Office Web Apps** provide you with the tools you need to view documents online and to edit them right in your browser. You do not need to have Office programs installed on the computer you use to access SkyDrive and Office Web Apps. From SkyDrive, you can also open the document directly in the full Office application (for example, PowerPoint) if the application is installed on the computer you are using. You use the PowerPoint Web App to make some edits to the PowerPoint presentation. You then open the presentation in PowerPoint and use the full version to make additional edits.

STEPS

TROUBLE

Click the browser button on the taskbar, then click the Windows Live SkyDrive window to make it the active window.

QUICK TIP

The changes you make to the presentation are saved automatically on SkyDrive.

QUICK TIP

Use the ScreenTips to help you find the required WordArt style.

TROUBLE

The browser opens to the Cengage folder but the file is not visible. Follow Step 8 to open the Cengage folder and refresh thelist of files in the folder.

1. **Click the WEB-QST Vancouver Presentation file in the Cengage folder on SkyDrive**

   The presentation opens in your browser window. A menu is available, which includes the options you have for working with the file.

2. **Click Edit in Browser, then if a message appears related to installing the Sign-in Assistant, click the Close button to the far right of the message**

   In a few moments, the PowerPoint presentation opens in the PowerPoint Web App, as shown in Figure WEB-7. Table WEB-2 lists the commands you can perform using the PowerPoint Web App.

3. **Enter your name where indicated on Slide 1, click Slide 3 (New Tours) in the Slides pane, then click Delete Slide in the Slides group**

   The slide is removed from the presentation. You decide to open the file in the full version of PowerPoint on your computer so you can apply WordArt to the slide title. You work with the file in the full version of PowerPoint when you want to use functions, such as WordArt, that are not available on the PowerPoint Web App.

4. **Click Open in PowerPoint in the Office group, click OK in response to the message, then click Allow if requested**

   In a few moments, the revised version of the PowerPoint slide opens in PowerPoint on your computer.

5. **Click Enable Editing on the Protected View bar near the top of your presentation window if prompted, select QST Vancouver on the title slide, then click the Drawing Tools Format tab**

6. **Click the More button in the WordArt Styles group to show the selection of WordArt styles, select the WordArt style Gradient Fill - Blue-Gray, Accent 4, Reflection, then click a blank area outside the slide**

   The presentation appears in PowerPoint as shown in Figure WEB-8. Next, you save the revised version of the file to SkyDrive.

7. **Click the File tab, click Save As, notice that the path in the Address bar is to the Cengage folder on your Windows Live SkyDrive, type WEB-QST Vancouver Presentation_Revised.pptx in the File name text box, then click Save**

   The file is saved to your SkyDrive.

8. **Click the browser icon on the taskbar to open your SkyDrive page, then click Office next to your name in the SkyDrive path, view a list of recent documents, then click Cengage in the list to the left of the recent documents list to open the Cengage folder**

   Two PowerPoint files now appear in the Cengage folder.

9. **Exit the Web browser and close all tabs if prompted, then exit PowerPoint**

FIGURE WEB-7: Presentation opened in the PowerPoint Web App from Windows Live

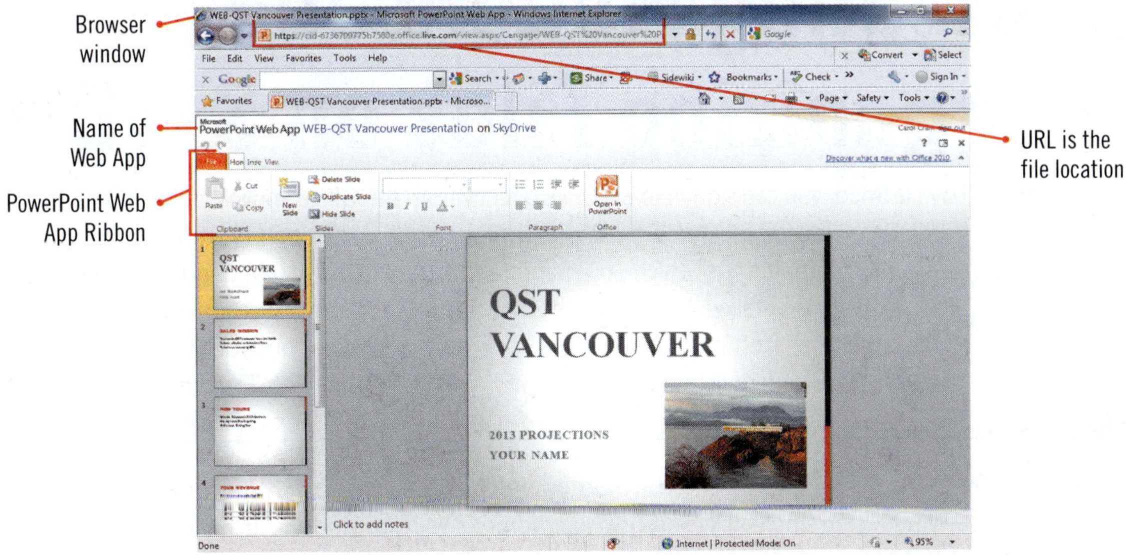

FIGURE WEB-8: Revised PowerPoint presentation

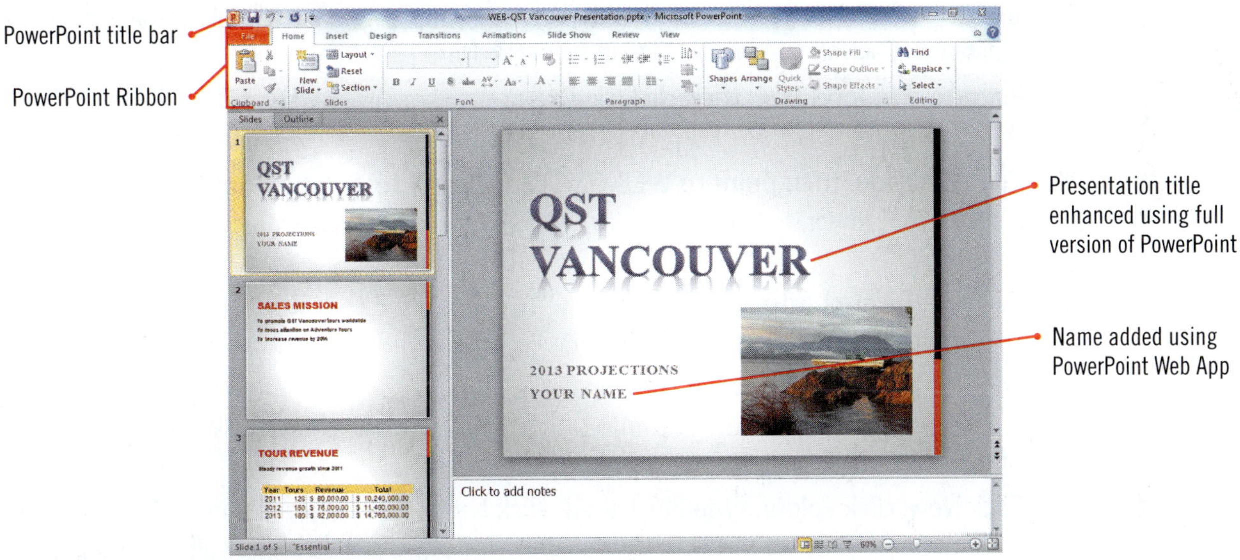

TABLE WEB-2: Commands on the PowerPoint Web App

tab	commands available
File	• Open in PowerPoint: select to open the file in PowerPoint on your computer • Where's the Save Button?: when you click this option, a message appears telling you that you do not need to save your presentation when you are working on it with PowerPoint Web App. The presentation is saved automatically as you work. • Print • Share • Properties • Give Feedback • Privacy • Terms of Use • Close
Home	• Clipboard group: Cut, Copy, Paste • Slides group: Add a New Slide, Delete a Slide, Duplicate a Slide, and Hide a Slide • Font group: Work with text: change the font, style, color, and size of selected text • Paragraph group: Work with paragraphs: add bullets and numbers, indent text, align text • Office group: Open the file in PowerPoint on your computer
Insert	• Insert a Picture • Insert a SmartArt diagram • Insert a link such as a link to another file on SkyDrive or to a Web page
View	• Editing view (the default) • Reading view • Slide Show view • Notes view

Creating Folders and Organizing Files on SkyDrive

As you have learned, you can sign in to SkyDrive directly from the Office applications PowerPoint, Excel, Word, and OneNote, or you can access SkyDrive directly through your Web browser. This option is useful when you are away from the computer on which you normally work or when you are using a computer that does not have Office applications installed. You can go to SkyDrive, create and organize folders, and then create or open files to work on with Office Web Apps. You access SkyDrive from your Web browser, create a new folder called Illustrated, and delete one of the PowerPoint files from the My Documents folder.

STEPS

TROUBLE
Go to Step 3 if you are already signed in.

TROUBLE
Type your Windows Live ID (your e-mail) and password, then click Sign in if prompted to do so.

1. **Open your Web browser, type home.live.com in the Address bar, then press [Enter]**
   The Windows Live home page opens. From here, you can sign in to your Windows Live account and then access SkyDrive.
2. **Sign into Windows Live as directed**
   You are signed in to your Windows Live page. From this page, you can take advantage of the many applications available on Windows Live, including SkyDrive.
3. **Point to Windows Live, then click SkyDrive**
   SkyDrive opens.
4. **Click Cengage, then point to WEB-QST Vancouver Presentation.pptx**
   A menu of options for working with the file, including a Delete button to the far right, appears to the right of the filename.
5. **Click the Delete button, then click OK**
   The file is removed from the Cengage folder on your SkyDrive. You still have a copy of the file on your computer.
6. **Point to Windows Live, then click SkyDrive**
   Your SkyDrive screen with the current selection of folders available on your SkyDrive opens, as shown in Figure WEB-9.
7. **Click New, click Folder, type Illustrated, click Next, click Office in the path under Add documents to Illustrated at the top of the window, then click View all in the list under Personal**
   You are returned to your list of folders, where you see the new Illustrated folder.
8. **Click Cengage, point to WEB-QST Vancouver Presentation_Revised.pptx, click More, click Move, then click the Illustrated folder**
9. **Click Move this file into Illustrated, as shown in Figure WEB-10**
   The file is moved to the Illustrated folder.

FIGURE WEB-9: Folders on your SkyDrive

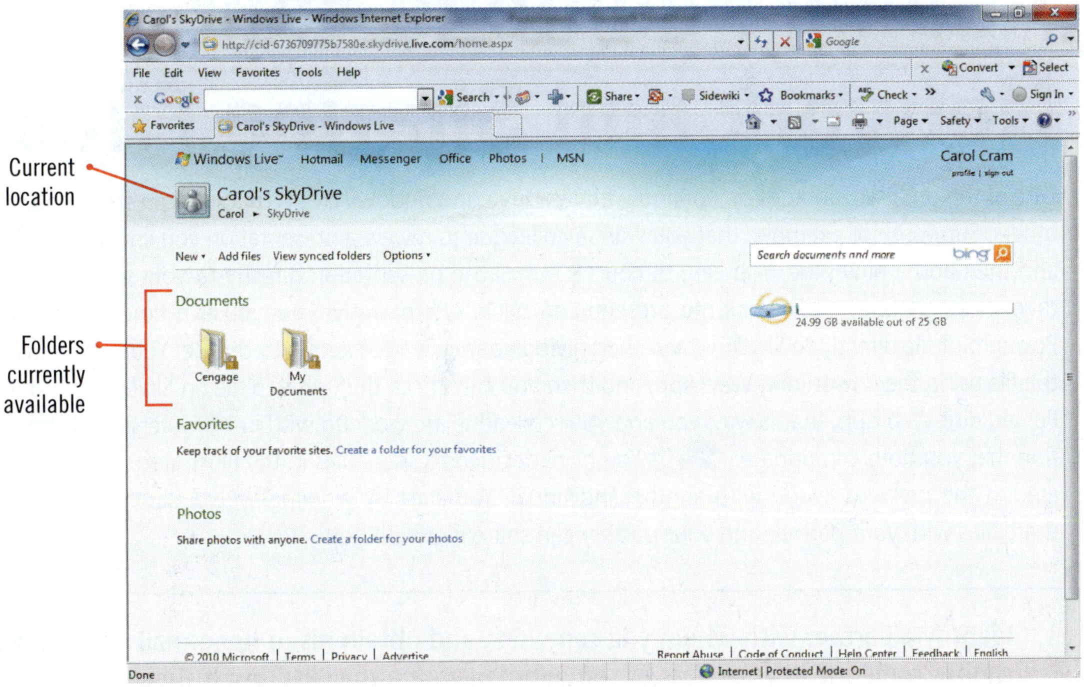

FIGURE WEB-10: Moving a file to the Illustrated folder

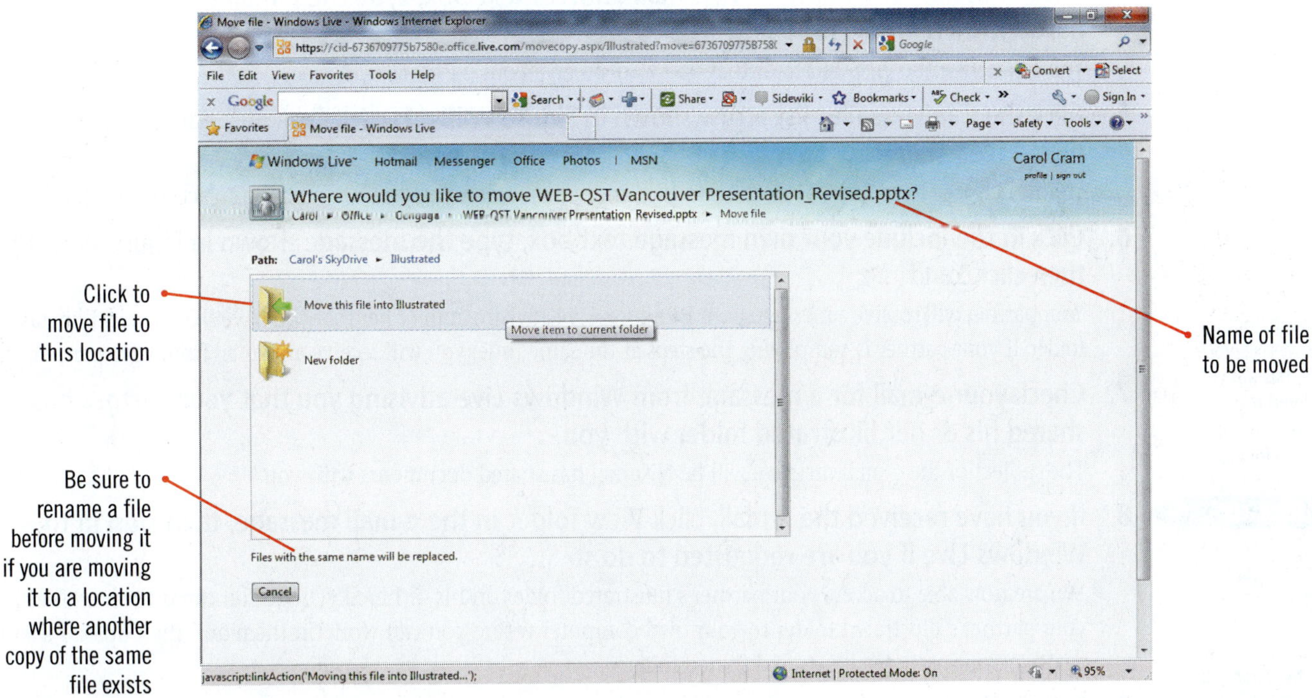

Adding People to Your Network and Sharing Files

One of the great advantages of working with SkyDrive on Windows Live is that you can share your files with others. Suppose, for example, that you want a colleague to review a presentation you created in PowerPoint and then add a new slide. You can, of course, e-mail the presentation directly to your colleague, who can then make changes and e-mail the presentation back. Alternatively, you can save time by uploading the PowerPoint file directly to SkyDrive and then giving your colleague access to the file. Your colleague can edit the file using the PowerPoint Web App, and then you can check the updated file on SkyDrive, also using the PowerPoint Web App. In this way, you and your colleague are working with just one version of the presentation that you both can update. You have decided to share files in the Illustrated folder that you created in the previous lesson with another individual. You start by working with a partner so that you can share files with your partner and your partner can share files with you.

STEPS

TROUBLE

If you cannot find a partner, read the steps so you understand how the process works.

1. **Identify a partner with whom you can work, and obtain his or her e-mail address; you can choose someone in your class or someone on your e-mail list, but it should be someone who will be completing these steps when you are**
2. **From the Illustrated folder, click Share**
3. **Click Edit permissions**

   The Edit permissions page opens. On this page, you can select the individual with whom you would like to share the contents of the Illustrated folder.
4. **Click in the Enter a name or an e-mail address text box, type the e-mail address of your partner, then press [Tab]**

   You can define the level of access that you want to give your partner.
5. **Click the Can view files list arrow shown in Figure WEB-11, click Can add, edit details, and delete files, then click Save**

   You can choose to send a notification to each individual when you grant permission to access your files.
6. **Click in the Include your own message text box, type the message shown in Figure WEB-12, then click Send**

   Your partner will receive a message from Windows Live advising him or her that you have shared your Illustrated folder. If your partner is completing the steps at the same time, you will receive an e-mail from your partner.

TROUBLE

If you do not receive a message from Windows Live, your partner has not yet completed the steps to share the Illustrated folder.

7. **Check your e-mail for a message from Windows Live advising you that your partner has shared his or her Illustrated folder with you**

   The subject of the e-mail message will be "[Name] has shared documents with you."

QUICK TIP

You will know you are on your partner's SkyDrive because you will see your partner's first name at the beginning of the SkyDrive path.

8. **If you have received the e-mail, click View folder in the e-mail message, then sign in to Windows Live if you are requested to do so**

   You are now able to access your partner's Illustrated folder on his or her SkyDrive. You can download files in your partner's Illustrated folder to your own computer where you can work on them and then upload them again to your partner's Illustrated shared folder.
9. **Exit the browser**

FIGURE WEB-11: Editing folder permissions

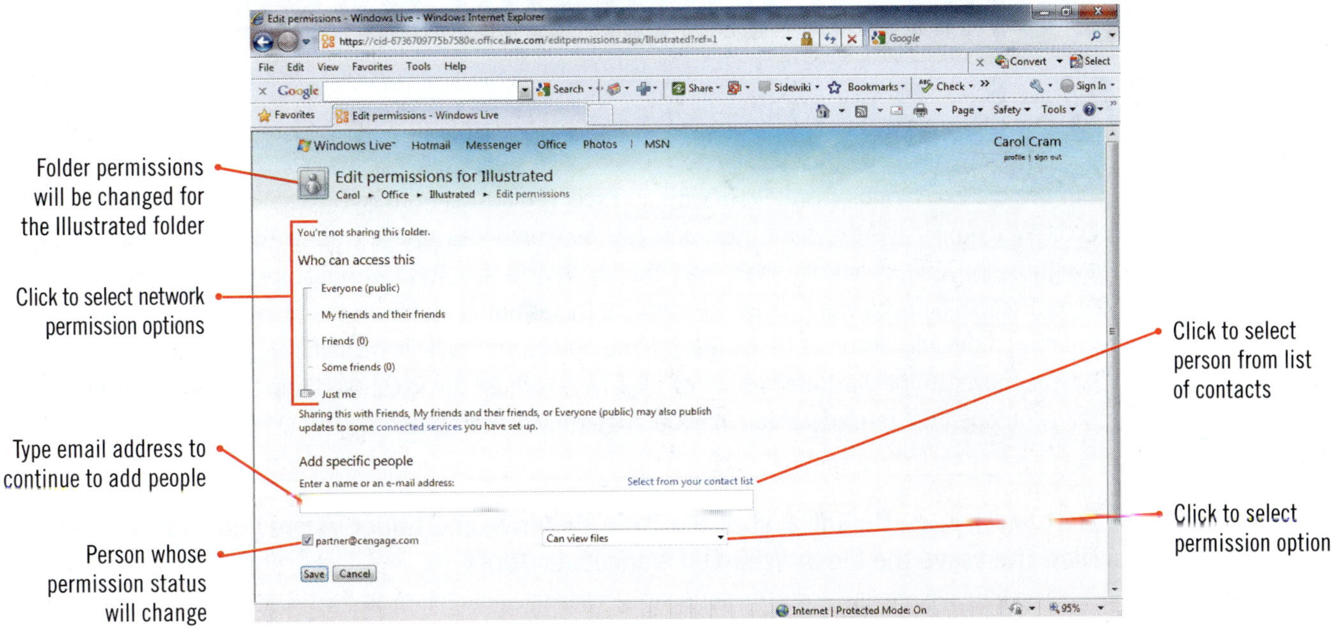

FIGURE WEB-12: Entering a message to notify a person that file sharing permission has been granted

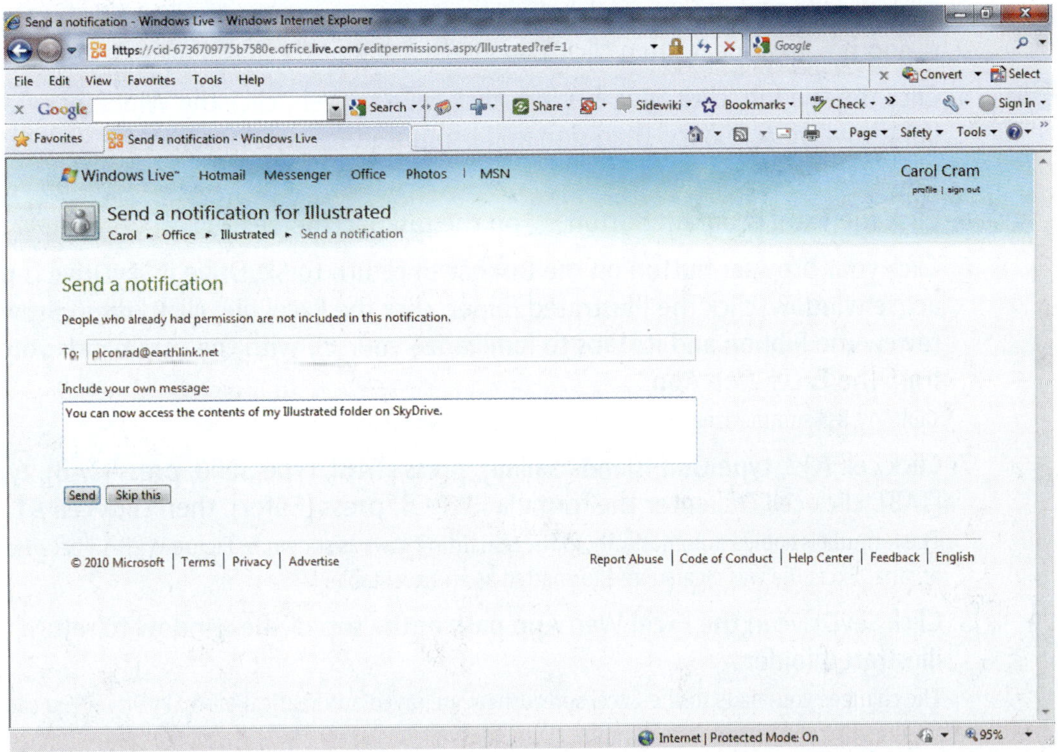

Sharing files on SkyDrive

When you share a folder with other people, the people with whom you share a folder can download the file to their computers and then make changes using the full version of the corresponding Office application. Once these changes are made, each individual can then upload the file to SkyDrive and into a folder shared with you and others. In this way, you can create a network of people with whom you share your files.

Working with the Excel Web App

You can use the Excel Web App to work with an Excel spreadsheet on SkyDrive. Workbooks opened using the Excel Web App have the same look and feel as workbooks opened using the full version of Excel. However, just like the PowerPoint Web App, the Excel Web App has fewer features available than the full version of Excel. When you want to use a command that is not available on the Excel Web App, you need to open the file in the full version of Excel. You upload an Excel file containing a list of the tours offered by QST Vancouver to the Illustrated folder on SkyDrive. You use the Excel Web App to make some changes, and then you open the revised version in Excel 2010 on your computer.

STEPS

TROUBLE

If prompted, sign in to your Windows Live account as directed.

QUICK TIP

Alternately, you can open your Web browser and go to Windows Live to sign in to SkyDrive.

1. **Start Excel, open the file WEB-2.xlsx from the drive and folder where you store your Data Files, then save the file as WEB-QST Vancouver Tours**

   The data in the Excel file is formatted using the Excel table function.

2. **Click the File tab, click Save & Send, then click Save to Web**

   In a few moments, you should see three folders to which you can save spreadsheets. My Documents and Cengage are personal folder that contains files that only you can access. Illustrated is a shared folder that contains files you can share with others in your network. The Illustrated folder is shared with your partner.

3. **Click the Illustrated folder, click the Save As button, wait a few seconds for the Save As dialog box to appear, then click Save**

4. **Click the File tab, click Save & Send, click Save to Web, click the Windows Live SkyDrive link above your folders, then sign in if prompted**

   Windows Live opens to your SkyDrive.

5. **Click the Excel program button on the taskbar, then exit Excel**

6. **Click your browser button on the taskbar to return to SkyDrive if SkyDrive is not the active window, click the Illustrated folder, click the Excel file, click Edit in Browser, then review the Ribbon and its tabs to familiarize yourself with the commands you can access from the Excel Web App**

   Table WEB-3 summarizes the commands that are available.

7. **Click cell A12, type Gulf Islands Sailing, press [TAB], type 3000, press [TAB], type 10, press [TAB], click cell D3, enter the formula =B3*C3, press [Enter], then click cell A1**

   The formula is copied automatically to the remaining rows as shown in Figure WEB-13 because the data in the original Excel file was created and formatted as an Excel table.

8. **Click SkyDrive in the Excel Web App path at the top of the window to return to the Illustrated folder**

   The changes you made to the Excel spreadsheet are saved automatically on SkyDrive. You can download the file directly to your computer from SkyDrive.

9. **Point to the Excel file, click More, click Download, click Save, navigate to the location where you save the files for this book, name the file WEB-QST Vancouver Tours_Updated, click Save, then click Close in the Download complete dialog box**

   The updated version of the spreadsheet is saved on your computer and on SkyDrive.

10. **Exit the Web browser**

FIGURE WEB-13: Updated table in the Excel Web App

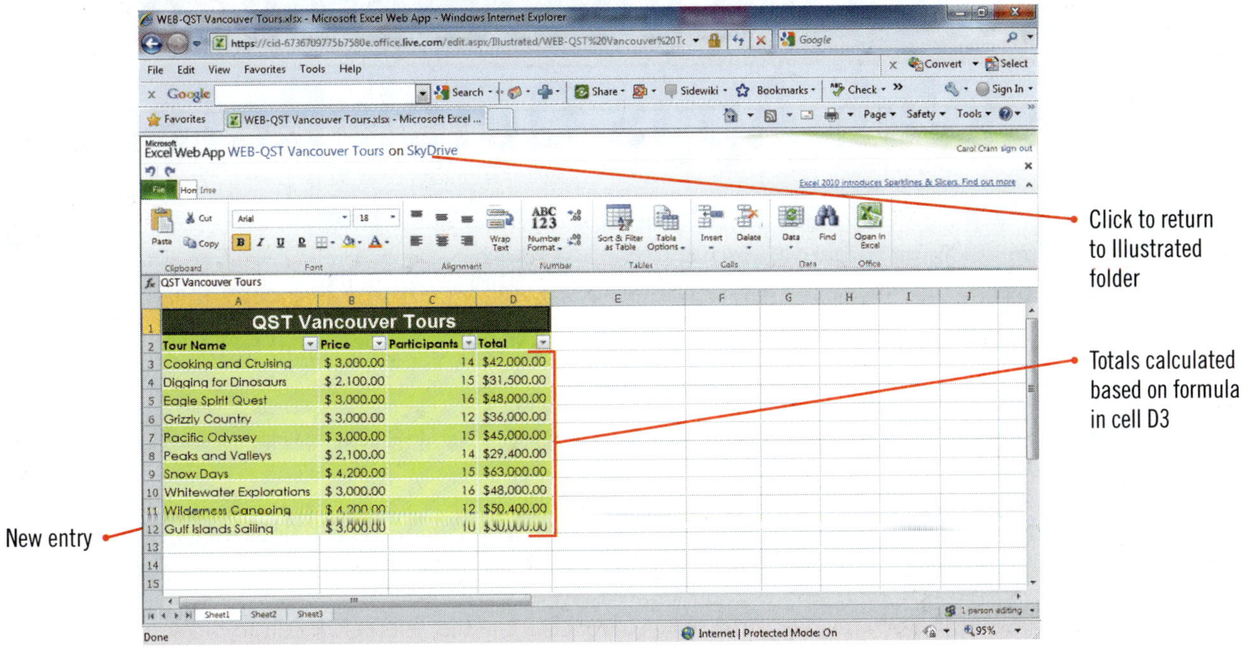

TABLE WEB-3: Commands on the Excel Web App

tab	commands available
File	• Open in Excel: select to open the file in Excel on your computer • Where's the Save Button?: when you click this option, a message appears telling you that you do not need to save your spreadsheet when you are working in it with Excel Web App; the spreadsheet is saved automatically as you work • Save As • Share • Download a Snapshot: a snapshot contains only the values and the formatting; you cannot modify a snapshot • Download a Copy: the file can be opened and edited in the full version of Excel • Give Feedback • Privacy Statement • Terms of Use • Close
Home	• Clipboard group: Cut, Copy, Paste • Font group: change the font, style, color, and size of selected labels and values, as well as border styles and fill colors • Alignment group: change vertical and horizontal alignment and turn on the Wrap Text feature • Number group: change the number format and increase or decrease decimal places • Tables: sort and filter data in a table and modify Table Options • Cells: insert and delete cells • Data: refresh data and find labels or values • Office: open the file in Excel on your computer
Insert	• Insert a Table • Insert a Hyperlink to a Web page

Exploring other Office Web Apps

Two other Office Web Apps are Word and OneNote. You can share files on SkyDrive directly from Word or from OneNote using the same method you used to share files from PowerPoint and Excel. After you upload a Word or OneNote file to SkyDrive, you can work with it in its corresponding Office Web App. To familiarize yourself with the commands available in an Office Web App, open the file and then review the commands on each tab on the Ribbon. If you want to perform a task that is not available in the Office Web App, open the file in the full version of the application.

In addition to working with uploaded files, you can create files from new on SkyDrive. Simply sign in to SkyDrive and open a folder. With a folder open, click New and then select the Web App you want to use to create the new file.

Windows Live and Microsoft Office Web Apps Quick Reference

To Do This	Go Here
Access Windows Live	From the Web browser, type **home.live.com**, then click Sign In
Access SkyDrive on Windows Live	From the Windows Live home page, point to Windows Live, then click SkyDrive
Save to Windows Live from Word, PowerPoint, or Excel	File tab | Save & Send | Save to Web | Select a folder | Save As
Create a New Folder from Backstage view	File tab | Save & Send | Save to Web | New Folder button
Edit a File with a Web App	From SkyDrive, click the file, then click Edit in Browser
Open a File in a desktop version of the application from a Web App: Word, Excel, PowerPoint	Click Open in [Application] in the Office group in each Office Web App
Share files on Windows Live	From SkyDrive, click the folder containing the files to share, click Share on the menu bar, click Edit permissions, enter the e-mail address of the person to share files with, click the Can view files list arrow, click Can add, edit details, and delete files, then click Save

Glossary

Absolute cell reference In a formula, a cell address that refers to a specific cell and does not change when you copy the formula; indicated by a dollar sign before the column letter and/or row number. *See also* Relative cell reference.

Accelerator An Internet Explorer feature that appears as a button when you highlight a word or phrase. Click the Accelerator button to link to services related to the selected text, such as mapping, translation, or searching.

Accessories Simple Windows programs that perform specific tasks, such as the Calculator accessory for performing calculations.

Account Log-on information including ISP, e-mail address and password for each person using Outlook; used to create folders in Outlook for contacts, e-mail and schedules. *See also* User account.

Active The currently available document, program, or object; on the taskbar, when more than one program is open, the button for the active program appears slightly lighter.

Active cell A selected cell in an Excel worksheet.

Active tab In the browser window, the tab in front when you view one or more Web pages, with each page open on a separate tab.

Active window The window you are currently using; if multiple windows are open, the window with the darker title bar.

Address A sequence of drive and folder names that describes a folder's or file's location in the file hierarchy; the highest hierarchy level is on the left, with lower hierarchy levels separated by the ▶ symbol to its right.

Address bar In a window, the white area just below the title bar that shows the file hierarchy, or address of the files that appear in the file list below it; the address appears as a series of links (separated by the ▶ symbol) you can click to navigate to other locations on your computer.

Address book A stored list of names and e-mail addresses that you can access through an e-mail program such as Outlook to address messages.

Adjustment handle A small yellow diamond that changes the appearance of an object's most prominent feature.

Adware Software installed with another program that generates advertising revenue for the program's creator by displaying targeted ads to the program's user.

Aero A Windows 7 viewing option that shows windows as translucent objects and features subtle animations; only available on a computer that has enough memory to support Aero and on which a Windows Aero theme has been selected.

Aero Flip 3D A Windows 7 feature that lets you preview all open folders and documents without using the taskbar and that displays open windows in a stack if you press [Ctrl][⊞][Tab]; only available if using a Windows Aero theme.

Aero Peek A Windows 7 feature that lets you point to a taskbar icon representing an open program and see a thumbnail (small version) of the open file; only visible if the computer uses a Windows Aero theme.

Align To place objects' edges or centers on the same plane.

Alignment (Excel) The placement of cell contents in relation to a cell's edges; for example, left-aligned, centered, or right-aligned. (Word) The position of text in a document relative to the margins.

Alignment command In Access, command used in Layout or Design View for a form or report to either left-, center-, or right-align a value within its control, or to align the top, bottom, right, or left edge of the control with respect to other controls.

Alternate Back Color property A property that determines the alternating background color of the selected section in a form or report.

American Standard Code for Information Interchange *See* ASCII.

Analog signal A continuous wave signal (sound wave) that can traverse ordinary phone lines.

AND criteria Criteria placed in the same row of the query design grid. All criteria on the same row must be true for a record to appear on the resulting datasheet.

Animation tag Identifies the order an object is animated on a slide during a slide show.

Annotate A freehand drawing on the screen made by using the pen or highlighter tool. You can annotate only in Slide Show view.

Anti-spyware software Software that detects and removes spyware.

Antivirus software Software that searches executable files for the sequences of characters that may cause harm and disinfects the files by erasing or disabling those commands. *Also called* virus protection software.

Application software Software that enables you to perform specific computer tasks, such as document production, spreadsheet calculations, database management, and presentation preparation.

Appointment In the Calendar in Outlook, an activity that does not involve inviting other people or scheduling resources.

Architecture The design and construction of a computer; *also called* configuration.

Argument Information that a function uses to create the final answer. Multiple arguments are separated by commas. All of the arguments for a function are surrounded by a single set of parentheses.

Arithmetic operators In a formula, symbols that perform mathematical calculations, such as addition (+), subtraction (–), multiplication (*), division (/), or exponentiation (^).

ASCII (American Standard Code for Information Interchange) The number system that personal computers use to represent character data.

Attachment A file, such as a picture, audio clip, video clip, document, worksheet, or presentation, that is sent in addition to the e-mail message composed by typing in the Message window.

AutoComplete A feature that automatically suggests text to insert.

AutoCorrect A feature that automatically detects and corrects typing errors, minor spelling errors, capitalization, and inserts certain typographical symbols as you type.

AutoFill Feature activated by dragging the fill handle; copies a cell's contents or continues a series of entries into adjacent cells.

AutoFill Options button Button that appears after using the fill handle to copy cell contents; enables you to choose to fill cells with specific elements (such as formatting) of the copied cell if desired.

AutoFit A feature that automatically adjusts the width of a column or the height of a row to accommodate its widest or tallest entry.

Automatic page break A page break that is inserted automatically at the bottom of a page.

AutoNumber A field data type in which Access enters a sequential integer for each record added into the datasheet. Numbers cannot be reused even if the record is deleted.

Avg function Built-in Access function used to calculate the average of the values in a given field.

Axis label Text in the first row and column of a worksheet that identifies data.

Back Color property A property that determines the background color of the selected control or section in a form or report.

Background The area behind the text and graphics on a slide.

Background graphic An object placed on the slide master.

Backstage view View available in all Microsoft Office programs that allows you to perform many common tasks, such as opening and saving a file, printing and previewing a document, and protecting a document before sharing it with others.

Backup A duplicate copy of a file that is stored in another location.

Backward-compatible Software feature that enables documents saved in an older version of a program to be opened in a newer version of the program.

BD-R A Blu-ray disc on which you can record data once.

BD-RE A Blu-ray disc on which you can record data as on a BD-R, and then delete or re-record data on it as needed.

Bibliography A list of sources that you consulted or cited while creating a document.

Binary digit (bit) The representation of data as a 1 or 0.

BIOS Stands for basic input/output system, the set of instructions stored in ROM that the computer uses to check its components to ensure they are working and to activate the software that provides the basic functionality of the computer when you turn on the computer.

Bit *See* Binary digit.

Bits per second (bps) The unit of measurement for the speed of data transmission.

Blind courtesy copy (BCC) In e-mail, a way to send a message to a recipient who needs to be aware of the correspondence between the sender and the recipients, but is not the primary recipient of the message, and is used when the sender does not want to reveal who has received courtesy copies.

Blog An informal journal that is created by an individual or a group and available to the public on the Internet; short for Web log.

Blogger The person who creates and maintains a blog.

Bluetooth A wireless technology standard that allows electronic devices to use short range radio waves to communicate with one another or connect to the Internet; the radio waves can be transmitted around corners and through walls.

Blu-ray A disc used for storing high-definition video that stores 25 GB of data per layer.

Bold Formatting applied to text to make it thicker and darker.

Boot process The set of events that occurs between the moment you turn on the computer and the moment you can begin to use the computer.

Boot up The act of turning on the computer.

Border A line that can be added above, below, or to the sides of a paragraph, text, or table cell; a line that divides the columns and rows of a table. Also refers to a window's edge; drag to resize the window.

Bound control A control used in either a form or report to display data from the underlying field; used to edit and enter new data in a form.

Bps *See* Bits per second.

Broadband connection A high-speed connection to the Internet.

Browser A software program that lets you open and display Web pages. *Also called* a Web browser.

Browser window The specific area on the screen where the current Web page appears.

Building block In Office programs, a reusable piece of formatted content or document part that is stored in a gallery.

Built-in graphics card *See* Graphics processor.

Bullet A small graphic symbol used to identify an item in a list.

Byte A series of eight bits.

Cable Plastic-enclosed wires that attach a peripheral device to a computer port.

Cache memory Special high-speed memory chips on the motherboard or CPU that store frequently accessed and recently accessed data and commands; *also called* RAM cache *or* CPU cache.

Calculation A new value that is created by entering an expression in a text box on a form or report.

Calculation operators Symbols in a formula that indicate what type of calculation to perform on the cells, ranges, or values.

Calendar In Microsoft Outlook, provides a convenient way to manage your appointments and events.

Calendar Picker A pop-up calendar from which you can choose dates for a date field.

Canvas In the Paint accessory program, the area in the center of the program window that you use to create drawings.

Card A removable circuit board that is inserted into a slot in the motherboard to expand the capabilities of the motherboard.

Case sensitive Describes a program's ability to differentiate between uppercase and lowercase letters; usually used to describe how an operating system evaluates passwords that users type to gain entry to user accounts.

Categories In Outlook, a feature used to tag items so you can track and organize them by specific criteria.

Category axis The horizontal axis in a chart, usually containing the names of data categories; in a 2-dimensional chart, also known as the x-axis.

CD (compact disc) An optical storage device that can store 700 MB of data.

CD-R (compact disc recordable) A CD that on which you can record data with a laser that changes the reflectivity of a dye layer on the blank disk, creating dark spots on the disk's surface that represent the data; once the data is recorded, you cannot erase or modify it.

CD-ROM (compact disc read-only memory) A CD that contains software or music when you purchase it, but you cannot record additional data on it.

CD-RW (compact disc rewritable) A CD on which you can record data as on a CD-R, and then delete or re-record data on it as needed.

Cell The intersection of a column and row in a worksheet, datasheet, or table.

Cell address The location of a cell, expressed by cell coordinates; for example, the cell address of the cell in column A, row 1 is A1.

Cell pointer The dark rectangle that outlines the active cell.

Cell styles Predesigned combinations of formats based on themes that can be applied to selected cells to enhance the look of a worksheet.

Center Alignment in which an item is centered between the margins.

Central processing unit (CPU) *See* Microprocessor.

Channel The medium, such as telephone or coaxial cable, over which a message is sent in data communications.

Character spacing Formatting that changes the width or scale of characters, expands or condenses the amount of space between characters, raises or lowers characters relative to the line of text, and adjusts kerning (the space between standard combinations of letters).

Characters per second (cps) The unit of measurement for the speed of dot matrix printers.

Chart Pictorial representation of worksheet data that makes it easier to see patterns, trends, and relationship. Types include 2-D and 3-D column, bar, pie, area, and line charts. *Also called* graph.

Chart sheet A separate sheet in a workbook that contains only a chart, which is linked to the workbook data.

Check box A box that turns an option on when checked or off when unchecked.

Chip An integrated circuit embedded in semiconductor material.

Circuit A path along which an electric current travels.

Circuit board A rigid piece of insulating material with circuits on it that control specific functions.

Citation A parenthetical reference in the document text that gives credit to the source for a quotation or other information used in a document.

Click To quickly press and release the left button on the pointing device; *also called* single-click.

Click and Type A feature that allows you to automatically apply the necessary paragraph formatting to a table, graphic, or text when you insert the item in a blank area of a document in Print Layout or Web Layout view.

Click and Type pointer A pointer used to move the insertion point and automatically apply the paragraph formatting necessary to insert text at that location in the document.

Client A computer networked to and dependent on a server.

Client/server network A network with a server and computers dependent on the server.

Clip A media file, such as a graphic, photograph, sound, movie, or animation, that can be inserted into a document.

Clip art A collection of graphic images that can be inserted into documents, presentations, Web pages, spreadsheets, and other Office files.

Clip Organizer A library of art, pictures, sounds, video clips, and animations that all Office applications share.

Clipboard A temporary storage area for text, images, or other objects that are cut or copied from any file and are available for pasting. *See also* Office Clipboard and System Clipboard.

Clock speed The pulse of the processor measured in megahertz or gigahertz.

Close button In a Windows title bar, the rightmost button; closes the open window, program, and/or document.

Cloud computing When data, applications, and resources are stored on servers accessed over the Internet or a company's internal network rather than on users' computers.

CMOS *See* Complementary metal oxide semiconductor memory.

Collections The folders in the Clip Organizer where are the clip art is stored.

Column break A break that forces text following the break to begin at the top of the next column.

Column heading The gray box that appears above each column in a worksheet; identifies the column letter, such as A, B, etc.

Column separator The thin line that separates column or field names to the left or right.

Combination chart Two charts in one, such as a column chart combined with a line chart, that together chart related but dissimilar data.

Combo box A bound control used to display a list of possible entries for a field in which you can also type an entry from the keyboard. It is a "combination" of the list box and text box controls.

Command An instruction to perform a task, such as opening a file or emptying the Recycle Bin.

Command bar An area of the Internet Explorer window above an open Web page that provides buttons for many options, such as printing Web pages, adding Favorites, and searching for information on the Internet.

Command button A button you click to issue instructions to modify program objects.

Commercial provider A company that typically provides electronic services such cable, TV, voice, e-mail, and data communications, as well as Web space, such as America Online.

Compact disc *See* CD.

Compact disc read-only memory *See* CD-ROM.

Compact disc recordable *See* CD-R.

Compact disc rewritable *See* CD-RW.

Comparison operators In a formula, symbols that compare values for the purpose of true/false results.

Compatibility The ability of different programs to work together and exchange data.

Complementary metal oxide semiconductor (CMOS) memory A chip installed on the motherboard powered by a battery whose content changes every time you add or remove hardware on your computer system and that is activated during the boot process so it can identify where essential software is stored. *Also called* semipermanent memory.

Complex formula A formula that uses more than one arithmetic operator.

Computer An electronic device that accepts input, processes data, displays output, and stores data for retrieval later.

Computer network The hardware and software that makes it possible for two or more computers to share information and resources.

Computer system A computer, its peripheral devices, and software.

Conditional formatting A type of cell formatting that changes based on the cell's value or the outcome of a formula.

Configuration *See* Architecture.

Contact Group A named subset of the people in your Outlook Contacts folder, grouped together by e-mail addresses.

Contacts In Microsoft Outlook, enables you to manage all your business and personal contact information.

Content control An interactive object that is embedded in a document you create from a template and that expedites your ability to customize the document with your own information.

Content placeholder A placeholder that is used to enter text or objects such as, clip art, charts, or pictures.

Contextual tab Tab on the Ribbon that appears when needed to complete a specific task; for example, if you select a graphic, the Picture Tools Format tab appears.

Control Any element on a form or report such as a label, text box, line, or combo box. Controls can be bound, unbound, or calculated.

Control Source property A property of a bound control in a form or report that determines the field to which the control is connected.

Controller card A card that plugs into a slot on the motherboard and connects to a port to provide an electrical connection to a peripheral device. *Also called* expansion card *or* interface card.

Copy To duplicate a file, folder, or other object that you want to store in another location.

Copy and paste To move text or graphics using the Copy and Paste commands.

Copy-and-paste operation The feature in document production software that allows you to duplicate selected words and objects somewhere else in the document.

Courtesy copy (CC) In e-mail, a way to send a message to a recipient who needs to be aware of the correspondence between the sender and the recipients, but is not the primary recipient of the message.

Cps *See* Characters per second.

CPU *See* Microprocessor.

CPU cache *See* Cache memory.

Criteria Entries (rules and limiting conditions) that determine which records are displayed when finding or filtering records in a datasheet or form, or when building a query.

Criteria syntax Rules by which criteria need to be entered. For example, text criteria syntax requires that the criteria are surrounded by quotation marks (" "). Date criteria are surrounded by pound signs (#).

Crop To hide part of an object, such as clip art using the Cropping tool or to delete a part of a picture.

Current record The record that has the focus or is being edited.

Cut To remove an item from a document and place it on the Clipboard.

Cut and paste To move text or graphics using the Cut and Paste commands.

Cut-and-paste operation The feature in document production software that allow you to delete words and objects from one place in a document and place them somewhere else.

D

Data The words, numbers, figures, sounds, and graphics that describe people, events, things, and ideas.

Data bus The path between the microprocessor, RAM, and the peripherals along which communication travels.

Data communications The transmission of data from one computer to another or to a peripheral device via a channel using a protocol.

Data file A file created by a user, usually with software, such as a report that you write with a word processing program.

Data marker A graphical representation of a data point, such as a bar or column.

Data point Individual piece of data plotted in a chart.

Data series The selected range in a worksheet whose related data points Excel converts into a chart.

Data series marker A graphical representation of a data series, such as a bar or column.

Data type A required property for each field that defines the type of data that can be entered in each field. Valid data types include AutoNumber, Text, Number, Currency, Date/Time, and Memo.

Database A collection of information stored on one or more computers organized in a uniform format of records and fields.

Database designer The person responsible for building and maintaining tables, queries, forms, and reports.

Database management software Software you use to collect and manage data.

Datasheet A spreadsheet-like grid that displays fields as columns and records as rows.

Datasheet View A view that lists the records of the object in a datasheet. Tables, queries, and most form objects have a Datasheet View.

Date function Built-in Access function used to display the current date on a form or report; enter the Date function as Date().

Date Navigator A monthly calendar in the To-Do Bar that gives you an overview of the month.

Default In a program window or dialog box, a value that is already set by the program; you can change the default to any valid value.

Delete To permanently remove an item from a document.

Deleted Items folder The folder that stores items when you delete or erase a message from any mail folder, rather than being immediately, permanently deleted. *Also called* trash folder.

Design View A view in which the structure of the object can be manipulated. Every Access object (table, query, form, report, macro, and module) has a Design View.

Desktop A shaded or picture background that appears to fill the screen after a computer starts up; usually contains icons, which are small images that represent items on your computer and allow you to interact with the computer.

Desktop background The shaded area behind your desktop objects; can show colors, designs, or photographs, which you can customize.

Desktop computer A personal computer designed to sit compactly on a desk.

Destination file In integration, the file that receives the copied information. A Word file that contains an Excel file is the destination file.

Details pane A pane located at the bottom of a window that displays information about the selected disk, drive, folder, or file.

Device A hardware component that is part of your computer system, such as a disk drive or a pointing device.

Device driver System software that handles the transmission protocol between a computer and its peripheral devices. *Also called* driver.

Dialog box A window with controls that lets you tell Windows how you want to complete a program command.

Dialog box launcher An icon available in many groups on the Ribbon that you can click to open a dialog box or task pane, offering an alternative way to choose commands. *Also called* launcher.

Digital certificate Verifies the identity of a person or indicates the security of a Web site.

Digital signal A stop-start signal that your computer outputs.

Digital signature A way to authenticate a presentation file using computer cryptography. A digital signature is not visible in a presentation.

Digital subscriber line *See* DSL.

Distribute To evenly divide the space horizontally or vertically between objects relative to each other or the slide edges.

Distribution list A collection of contacts to whom you want to send the same messages; makes it possible for you to send a message to the same group without having to select each contact in the group. *See also* Contact Group.

DNS server A computer responsible for directing Internet traffic.

Document The electronic file you create using Word.

Document Inspector A PowerPoint feature that examines a presentation for hidden data or personal information.

Document production software Software, such as word processing software, desktop publishing software, e-mail editors, and Web authoring software, that assists you in writing and formatting documents, including changing the font and checking the spelling.

Document properties Details about a file, such as author name or the date the file was created, that are used to describe, organize, and search for files.

Document window The portion of a program window in which you create the document; displays all or part of an open document.

Documents folder The folder on your hard drive used to store most of the files you create or receive from others; might contain subfolders to organize the files into smaller groups.

Domain name The Web site's name, such as "cengage" in www.cengage.com.

Dot matrix printer A printer that transfers ink to paper by striking a ribbon with pins.

Dot pitch (dp) The distance between pixels on a monitor.

Double-click To quickly press and release (or click) the left button on the pointing device twice.

Dp *See* Dot pitch.

Draft view A view that shows a document without margins, headers and footers, or graphics.

Drafts folder Stores unfinished e-mail messages that you can finish writing at a later time. Many programs automatically save unsent messages at regular intervals in the drafts folder as a safety measure.

Drag To point to an object, press and hold the left button on the pointing device, move the object to a new location, and then release the left button.

Drag and drop To use a pointing device to move or copy a file or folder to a new location.

Drive A physical location on your computer where you can store files.

Drive name A name for a drive that consists of a letter followed by a colon, such as C: for the hard disk drive.

Driver *See* Device driver.

Drop cap A large dropped initial capital letter that is often used to set off the first paragraph of an article.

DSL (digital subscriber line) A high-speed connection over phone lines.

Dual-core processor A CPU that has two processors on the chip.

DVD An optical storage device that can store up to 15.9 GB of data; was originally an acronym for *digital video disc* and later *digital versatile disc*.

DVD+R, DVD-R A DVD on which you can record data once.

DVD+RW, DVD-RW A DVD on which you can record data as on a DVD-R, and then delete or re-record data on it as needed.

DVI (digital video interface) port A port that digitally transmits video.

Edit To make a change to the contents of a file or an active cell.

Edit mode The mode in which Access assumes you are trying to edit a particular field, so keystrokes such as [Ctrl][End], [Ctrl][Home], [↑], and [↓] move the insertion point within the field.

Edit record symbol A pencil-like symbol that appears in the record selector box to the left of the record that is currently being edited in either a datasheet or a form.

Electronic mail (e-mail) The technology that makes it possible for you to send and receive messages through the Internet.

Electronic spreadsheet A computer program used to perform calculations and analyze and present numeric data.

E-mail An electronic message sent from one user's computer to another.

E-mail message A message sent using e-mail technology.

E-mail software Enables you to send and receive e-mail messages over a network, within an intranet, and through the Internet.

Embed To place an object such as a text selection, value, or picture created in a source file into a destination file. An embedded object is edited by opening it in the destination file and then using the tools of the source file to make changes. These changes appear only in the embedded object in the destination file.

Embedded chart A chart displayed as an object in a worksheet.

Embedded object An object that is created in one application and inserted to another. Embedded objects remain connected to the original program file in which they were created for editing.

Emoticon A symbol created by combining keyboard characters; used to communicate feelings in e-mails.

Endnote Text that provides additional information or acknowledges sources for text in a document and that appears at the end of a document.

Ergonomic Designed to fit the natural placement of the body to reduce the risk of repetitive-motion injuries.

Error indicator An icon that automatically appears in Design View to indicate some type of error. For example, a green error indicator appears in the upper left corner of a text box in Form Design View if the text box Control Source property is set to a field name that doesn't exist.

Ethernet port A port used to connect computers in a LAN or sometimes directly to the Internet; it allows for high-speed data transmission.

Event In the Calendar in Outlook, an activity that lasts 24 hours or longer.

Exception A change you make directly to text on the slide, which does not match the theme fonts on the slide master.

Executable file A file that contains the instructions that tell a computer how to perform a specific task, such as the files that are used during the boot process.

Expansion card *See* Controller card.

Expansion port The interface between a cable and a controller card. *Also called* port.

Expansion slot An electrical connector on the motherboard into which a card is plugged. *Also called* slot.

Exploding Visually pulling a slice of a pie chart away from the whole pie chart in order to add emphasis to the pie slice.

Expression A combination of values, functions, and operators that calculates to a single value. Access expressions start with an equal sign and are placed in a text box in either Form Design View or Report Design View.

Favorites Bar A convenient place to store links to Web pages that you use often. Add a link to the Favorites Bar by dragging the Internet Explorer icon that precedes the URL in the Address bar to the Links bar.

Favorites Center Stores and organizes the links to the Web pages that you want to revisit often. To open the Favorites Center, click the Favorites button on the Command bar.

Feeds Your subscriptions to Web site updates and news.

Field (Access and Excel) In a table, a field corresponds to a column of data, a specific piece or category of data such as a first name, last name, city, state, or phone number. (Outlook) In an Outlook contact, an area that stores one piece of information, such as a first name or an e-mail address. (Word) A code that serves as a placeholder for data that changes in a document, such as a page number.

Field list A list of the available fields in the table or query that the field list represents.

Field name The name given to each field in a table.

Field selector The button to the left of a field in Table Design View that indicates which field is currently selected. Also the thin gray bar above each field in the query grid.

File An electronic collection of stored data that has a unique name, distinguishing it from other files, such as a letter, video, or program.

File extension A three- or four-letter sequence, preceded by a period, at the end of a filename that identifies the file as a particular type of document; documents in the Rich Text Format have the file extension .rtf.

File hierarchy The tree-like structure of folders and files on your computer.

File list In Windows Explorer, the right section of the window; shows the contents of the folder selected in the Navigation pane on the left.

File management The ability to organize folders and files on your computer.

File properties Details that Windows stores about a file, such as the date it was created or modified.

File tab Provides access to Backstage view and the Word Options dialog box.

Filename A unique, descriptive name for a file that identifies the file's content.

Filter To temporarily display only those records that match given criteria.

Filter By Form A way to filter data that allows two or more criteria to be specified at the same time.

Filter By Selection A way to filter records for an exact match.

Firewall Hardware or software that prevents other computers on the Internet from accessing a computer or prevents a program on a computer from accessing the Internet.

FireWire A standard for transferring information between digital devices developed by Apple Computer company and the Institute of Electrical and Electronics Engineers (IEEE); was standardized as IEEE 1394 interface.

First line indent A type of indent in which the first line of a paragraph is indented more than the subsequent lines.

Flag In many e-mail programs such as Microsoft Outlook, a method of coding the messages by assigning different colored flags to messages to categorize them or indicate their level of importance for followup.

Flash drive *See* USB flash storage device.

Flash memory Memory that is similar to ROM except that it can be written to more than once; *also called* solid state storage.

Flash memory card A small, portable card encased in hard plastic to which data can be written and rewritten.

Flat panel monitor A lightweight monitor that takes up very little room on the desktop and uses LCD technology to create the image on the screen.

Floating graphic A graphic to which text wrapping has been applied, making the graphic independent of text and able to be moved anywhere on a page.

Focus The property that indicates which field would be edited if you were to start typing.

Folder An electronic container that helps you organize your computer files, like a cardboard folder on your desk; it can contain subfolders for organizing files into smaller groups.

Folder name A unique, descriptive name for a folder that helps identify the folder's contents.

Font The typeface or design of a set of characters (letters, numbers, symbols, and punctuation marks).

Font effect Font formatting that applies a special effect to text, such as small caps or superscript.

Font size The size of characters, measured in points (pts).

Font style Format such as bold, italic, and underlining that can be applied to change the way characters look in a document, worksheet or chart.

Footer Information, such as text, a page number, or a graphic, that appears at the bottom of every page in a document or a section.

Footnote Text that provides additional information or acknowledges sources for text in a document and that appears at the bottom of the page on which the note reference mark appears.

Foreign key field In a one-to-many relationship between two tables, the foreign key field is the field in the "many" table that links the table to the primary key field in the "one" table.

Form An Access object that provides an easy-to-use data entry screen that generally shows only one record at a time.

Form View View of a form object that displays data from the underlying recordset and allows you to enter and update data.

Form Wizard An Access wizard that helps you create a form.

Format The appearance of a cell and its contents, including font, font styles, font color, fill color, borders, and shading. *See also* Number format.

Format Painter A feature used to copy the format settings applied to the selected text to other text you want to format the same way.

Formatting Enhancing the appearance of the information through font, size, and color changes.

Formatting marks Nonprinting characters that appear on screen to indicate the ends of paragraphs, tabs, and other formatting elements.

Formula A set of instructions used to perform one or more numeric calculations, such as adding, multiplying, or averaging, on values or cells.

Formula bar The area above the worksheet grid where you enter or edit data in the active cell.

Formula prefix An arithmetic symbol, such as the equal sign (=), used to start a formula.

Forwarding Sending an e-mail message you have received to someone else.

Full Screen Reading view A view that shows only the document text on screen, making it easier to read and annotate.

Function A special, predefined formula that provides a shortcut for a commonly used or complex calculation, such as SUM (for calculating a sum) or FV (for calculating the future value of an investment).

Gadget An optional program you can display on your desktop that presents helpful or entertaining information, such as a clock, current news headlines, a calendar, a picture album, or a weather report.

Gallery A visual collection of choices you can browse through to make a selection. Often available with Live Preview.

GB *See* Gigabyte.

GHz *See* Gigahertz.

Gigabyte (GB) 1,073,741,824 bytes, or about one billion bytes.

Gigahertz (GHz) One billion cycles per second.

Graphic image *See* Image.

Graphical user interface (GUI) A computer environment in which the user manipulates graphics, icons, and dialog boxes to execute commands.

Graphics card A card installed on the motherboard that controls the signals the computer sends to the monitor. *Also called* video display adapter *or* video card.

Graphics display A monitor that is capable of displaying graphics by dividing the screen into a matrix of pixels.

Graphics processor A processor that controls the signals the computer sends to the monitor. *Also called* built-in graphics card.

Graphics software Software that allows you to create illustrations, diagrams, graphs, and charts.

Gridlines Evenly spaced horizontal and/or vertical lines used in a worksheet or chart to make it easier to read.

Group (n.) In a Microsoft program window's Ribbon, a section containing related command buttons.

Group (v.) To combine multiple objects into one object.

Grouping To sort records in a particular order, plus provide a section before and after each group of records.

GUI *See* Graphical user interface.

Gutter Extra space left for a binding at the top, left, or inside margin of a document.

Hand-held computer A small computer designed to fit in the palm of your hand and that generally has fewer capabilities than personal computers.

Hanging indent A type of indent in which the second and subsequent lines of a paragraph are indented more than the first.

Hard copy A printed copy of computer output.

Hard disk A magnetic storage device that contains several magnetic oxide-covered metal platters that are usually sealed in a case inside the computer. *Also called* hard disk drive.

Hard page break *See* Manual page break.

Hardware The physical components of a computer.

HDMI (high-definition multimedia interface) port A port that digitally transmits video and audio.

Header Information, such as text, a page number, or a graphic, that appears at the top of every page in a document or a section.

Highlighted Describes the changed appearance of an item or other object, usually a change in its color, background color, and/or border; often used for an object on which you will perform an action, such as a desktop icon.

Highlighting Transparent color that can be applied to text to call attention to it.

Home page The first Web page that opens every time you start Internet Explorer; also applies to the main page that opens when you first go to a Web site.

Homegroup A named group of Windows 7 computers that can share information, including libraries and printers.

Horizontal ruler A ruler that appears at the top of the document window in Print Layout, Draft, and Web Layout view.

Horizontal scroll bar *See* Scroll bar.

Hyperlink Text or a graphic that opens a file, Web page, or other item when clicked. *Also called* link.

I-beam pointer The pointer used to move the insertion point and select text.

Icon A small image, usually on the desktop, which represents items on your computer, such as the Recycle Bin; you can rearrange, add, and delete desktop icons.

IEEE 1394 interface *See* FireWire.

Image A nontextual piece of information such as a picture, piece of clip art, drawn object, or graph. Because images are graphical (and not numbers or letters), they are sometimes referred to as graphical images.

Inactive window An open window you are not currently using; if multiple windows are open, the window(s) with the dimmed title bar.

Inbox A mail folder that stores all incoming mail.

Indent The space between the edge of a line of text or a paragraph and the margin.

Indent marker A marker on the horizontal ruler that shows the indent settings for the active paragraph.

Infinity symbol The symbol that indicates the "many" side of a one-to-many relationship.

Information management software Software that keeps track of schedules, appointments, contacts, and "to-do" lists.

Infrared technology A wireless technology in which devices communicate with one another using infrared light waves; the devices must be positioned so that the infrared ports are pointed directly at one another.

Inkjet printer A printer that sprays ink onto paper and produces output whose quality is comparable to that of a laser printer.

Inline graphic A graphic that is part of a line of text.

InPrivate Browsing Feature in Internet Explorer that lets you view Web sites without the browser storing data about your browsing session.

InPrivate Filtering Feature in Internet Explorer that helps prevent Web site or third-party developers from collecting information about the sites you visit.

Input The data or instructions you type into the computer.

Input and output (I/O) The flow of data from the microprocessor to memory to peripherals and back again.

Input device An instrument, such as a keyboard or a mouse, that you use to enter data and issue commands to the computer.

Insertion point A blinking vertical line that appears when you click in the formula bar, a document, a field or a placeholder indicates where new text will be inserted.

Integrate To incorporate a document and parts of a document created in one program into another program; for example, to incorporate an Excel chart into a PowerPoint slide, or an Access table into a Word document.

Integration Term used to describe the process of integrating objects between programs. *See also* Integrate.

Interface The look and feel of a program; for example, the appearance of commands and the way they are organized in the program window.

Interface card *See* Controller card.

Internet A network of connected computers and computer networks located around the world.

Internet Explorer A popular browser that is part of the Microsoft Windows operating system.

Internet Service Provider (ISP) A company that maintains Internet computers and telecommunications equipment in order to provide Internet access to businesses, organizations, and individuals.

Intranet A computer network that connects computers in a local area only, such as computers in a company's office.

I/O *See* Input and output.

Is Not Null A criterion that finds all records in which any entry has been made in the field.

Is Null A criterion that finds all records in which no entry has been made in the field.

Italic Formatting applied to text to make the characters slant to the right.

Join line The line identifying which fields establish the relationship between two related tables.

Journal In Outlook, provides a trail of your activities within Microsoft Office by tracking all documents, spreadsheets, databases, presentations, or any Office file that you specify. When turned on, you can see a timeline of any calls, messages, appointments, or tasks.

Junk e-mail Unwanted mail that arrives from unsolicited sources. *Also called* spam.

Justify Alignment in which an item is flush with both the left and right margins.

K *See* Kilobyte.

KB *See* Kilobyte.

Keyboard The most frequently used input device; consists of three major parts: the main keyboard, the keypads, and the function keys.

Keyboard shortcut A combination of keys or a function key that can be pressed to perform a command.

Keyword A descriptive word or phrase you enter to obtain a list of results that include that word or phrase.

Kilobyte (KB or **K)** 1,024 bytes, or approximately one thousand bytes.

Label (Access) An unbound control that displays text to describe and clarify other information on a form or report. (Outlook) In some e-mail programs, the ability to assign an indicator to an e-mail message to help sort or organize your e-mail messages. (Excel) Descriptive text or other information that identifies data in rows, columns, or charts, but is not included in calculations.

Label Wizard A report wizard that precisely positions and sizes information to print on a vast number of standard business label specifications.

LAN *See* Local area network.

Landscape Page orientation in which the contents of a page span the length of a page rather than its width, making the page wider than it is tall.

Landscape orientation A way to print or view a page that is 11 inches wide by 8.5 inches tall.

Laptop computer *See* Notebook computer.

Laser printer A printer that produces high-quality output quickly and efficiently by transferring a temporary laser image onto paper with toner.

Launch To open or start a program on your computer.

Launcher *See* Dialog box launcher.

Layout view An Access view that lets you make some design changes to a form or report while you are browsing the data.

LCD (liquid crystal display) A display technology that creates images by manipulating light within a layer of liquid crystal.

LED (light emitting diode) monitor A flat-panel monitor that uses LEDs to provide backlight.

Left function An Access function that returns a specified number of characters, starting with the left side of a value in a Text field.

Left indent A type of indent in which the left edge of a paragraph is moved in from the left margin.

Left-align Alignment in which the item is flush with the left margin.

Legend In a chart, information that identifies how data is represented by colors or patterns.

Library A window that shows files and folders stored in different storage locations; default libraries in Windows 7 include the Documents, Music, Pictures, and Videos libraries.

Like operator An operator used in a query to find values in a field that match the pattern you specify.

Line spacing The amount of space between lines of text.

Link (Internet) Words, phrases, or graphics that you click, to connect to and view other Web pages when you view Web pages with a browser. Can also open graphics or text files or play sound or video files. *Also called* hyperlinks. (Integration) A connection created between a source file and a destination file. When an object created in a source file is inserted into or copied to a destination file, any changes made to the object in the source file also appear in the object contained in the destination file.

Link line The line identifying which fields establish the relationship between two related tables.

Linked object An object such as a text selection, value, or picture that is contained in a destination file and linked to a source file. When a change is made to the linked object in the source file, the change also occurs in the linked object in the destination file.

Liquid crystal display *See* LCD.

List box A box that displays a list of options from which you can choose (you may need to scroll and adjust your view to see additional options in the list).

Live Preview A feature that lets you point to a choice in a gallery or palette and see the results in the document without actually clicking the choice.

Local area network (LAN) A network in which the computers and peripheral devices are located relatively close to each other, generally in the same building, and are usually connected with cables.

Log in To select a user account name when a computer starts up, giving access to that user's files. *Also called* log on.

Log off To close all windows, programs, and documents, then display the Welcome screen. *Also called* log out.

Logical view The datasheet of a query is sometimes called a logical view of the data because it is not a copy of the data, but rather, a selected view of data from the underlying tables.

Macro An Access object that stores a collection of keystrokes or commands such as those for printing several reports in a row or providing a toolbar when a form opens.

Magnetic storage media An object that stores data as magnetized particles on a surface.

Mainframe computer A computer used by larger business and government agencies that provides centralized storage, processing, and management for large amounts of data.

Major gridlines In a chart, the gridlines that represent the values at the tick marks on the value axis.

Malware A broad term that describes any program that is intended to cause harm or convey information to others without the owner's permission.

Manual page break A page break inserted to force the text following the break to begin at the top of the next page.

MapIt An Outlook feature on a Contact card that lets you view a contact's address on a map.

Margin The blank area between the edge of the text and the edge of a page.

Masters One of three views that stores information about the presentation theme, fonts, placeholders, and other background objects. The three views are Slide Master view, Handout Master view, and Notes Master view.

Maximize button On the right side of a window's title bar, the center button of three buttons; use to expand a window so that it fills the entire screen. In a maximized screen, this button turns into a Restore Down button.

Maximized window A window that fills the desktop.

MB *See* Megabyte.

Meeting In the Calendar in Outlook, an activity you invite people to or reserve resources for.

Megabyte (MB) 1,048,576 bytes, or about one million bytes.

Megahertz (MHz) One million cycles per second.

Memory A set of storage locations on the main circuit board that store instructions and data.

Memory capacity The amount of data that the device can handle at any given time. *Also called* storage capacity.

Menu A list of related commands.

Menu bar A horizontal bar in a window that displays menu names, or categories of related commands, providing access to most of the program's features through a series of menus.

Message body In an e-mail message, where you write the text of your message.

Message header Contains the basic information about a message including the sender's name and e-mail address, the names and e-mail addresses of recipients and CC recipients, a date and time stamp, and the subject of the message.

Metadata Another name for document properties that includes the author name, the document subject, the document title, and other personal information.

MHz *See* Megahertz.

Microprocessor A silicon chip, located on the motherboard, that is responsible for executing instructions to process data; *also called* processor *or* central processing unit (CPU).

Microsoft Answers A Microsoft Web site that lets you search forums, Microsoft Help files, and demonstration videos.

Microsoft Graph A program that creates a chart to graphically depict numerical information when you don't have access to Microsoft Excel.

Microsoft Office Word Help button A button used to access the Word Help system.

Microsoft Windows 7 An operating system.

Mini toolbar A small toolbar that appears next to selected text that contains basic text formatting commands.

Minimize button On the right side of a window's title bar, the leftmost button of three buttons; use to reduce a window so that it only appears as an icon on the taskbar.

Minimized window A window that is visible only as an icon on the taskbar.

Mininotebook computer *See* Subnotebook computer.

Minor gridlines In a chart, the gridlines that represent the values between the tick marks on the value axis.

Mirror margins Margins used in documents with facing pages, where the inside and outside margins are mirror images of each other.

Mixed reference Cell reference that combines both absolute and relative cell addressing.

Mode indicator An area on the left end of the status bar that indicates the program's status. For example, when you are changing the contents of a cell, the word 'Edit' appears in the mode indicator.

Modem Stands for *mo*dulator-*dem*odulator; a device that converts the digital signals from your computer into analog signals that can traverse ordinary phone lines, and then converts analog signals back into digital signals at the receiving computer.

Module An Access object that stores Visual Basic programming code that extends the functions of automated Access processes.

Monitor The TV-like peripheral device that displays the output from the computer.

Motherboard The main circuit board of the computer on which processing tasks occur.

Mouse A pointing device that has a rolling ball or electronic sensor on its underside and two or more buttons for clicking commands; you control the movement of the pointer by moving the entire mouse around on your desk.

Mouse pointer A small arrow or other symbol on the screen that you move by manipulating the pointing device; *also called* a pointer.

Move To change the location of a file, folder, or other object by physically placing it in another location.

MP3 player A hand-held computer that is used primarily to play and store music, but that can also be used to play digital movies or television shows, allow you to listen to FM radio stations, and access the Internet and e-mail.

Multilevel list A list with a hierarchical structure; an outline.

Multimedia authoring software Software that allows you to record digital sound files, video files, and animations that can be included in presentations and other documents.

Multiuser A characteristic that means more than one person can enter and edit data in the same Access database at the same time.

Name box Box to the left of the formula bar that shows the cell reference or name of the active cell.

Name property A property that uniquely identifies each object and control on a form or report.

Navigate (Excel) To move around in a worksheet; for example, you can use the arrow keys on the keyboard to navigate from cell to cell, or press [Page Up] or [Page Down] to move a screen at a time. (Windows) To move around in your computer's folder and file hierarchy.

Navigate downward To move to a lower level in your computer's folder and file hierarchy.

Navigate upward To move to a higher level in your computer's folder and file hierarchy.

Navigation buttons Buttons in the lower-left corner of a datasheet or form that allow you to quickly navigate between the records in the underlying object as well as add a new record.

Navigation mode A mode in which Access assumes that you are trying to move between the fields and records of the datasheet (rather than edit a specific field's contents), so keystrokes such as [Ctrl][Home] and [Ctrl][End] move you to the first and last field of the datasheet.

Navigation Pane (Access) A pane in the Access program window that provides a way to move between objects (tables, queries, forms, reports, macros, and modules) in the database. (Windows) A pane on the left side of a window that contains links to folders and libraries on your computer; click an item in the Navigation pane to display its contents in the file list or click the or symbols to display or hide subfolders in the Navigation pane. (Outlook) In Normal view, it is typically on the left side of the screen, showing you the folder list in addition to the navigation shortcuts.

Negative indent A type of indent in which the left edge of a paragraph is moved to the left of the left margin. *Also called* outdent.

Netbook A type of subnotebook computer that is primarily designed to allow users to access the Internet and check e-mail. *See also* Slate computer.

Network Two or more computers that share data and resources and which are connected to each other and to peripheral devices.

Network interface card (NIC) The card in a computer on a network that creates a communications channel between the computer and the network.

Network software Software that establishes the communications protocols that will be observed on the network and controls the "traffic flow" as data travels throughout the network.

NIC *See* Network interface card.

Node Any device connected to a network.

Nonvolatile memory *See* Read-only memory.

Normal view (Excel) Default worksheet view that shows the worksheet without features such as headers and footers; ideal for creating and editing a worksheet, but may not be detailed enough when formatting a document. (PowerPoint) The primary view that you use to write, edit, and design your presentation. Normal view is divided into three areas: Slides or Outline tab, Slide pane, and Notes pane.

Note reference mark A mark (such as a letter or a number) that appears next to text to indicate that additional information is offered in a footnote or endnote.

Notebook computer A small, lightweight computer designed for portability. *Also called* laptop computer.

Notes In Outlook, the electronic version of the sticky notes or Post-It™ notes you buy at your local stationery store; a convenient way to quickly jot down a reminder or an idea.

Notes Page view A presentation view that displays a reduced image of the current slide above a large text box where you can type notes.

Notes pane The area in Normal view that shows speaker notes for the current slide; also in Notes Page view, the area below the slide image that contains speaker notes.

Notification area An area on the right side of the Windows 7 taskbar that displays the current time as well as icons representing programs; displays pop-up messages when a program on your computer needs your attention.

Number format A format applied to values to express numeric concepts, such as currency, date, and percentage.

Object (Access) A table, query, form, report, macro, or module in a database. (PowerPoint) An item you place or draw on a slide that can be modified. Examples of objects include drawn lines and shapes, text, clip art, and imported pictures. (Excel) Independent element on a worksheet (such as a chart or graphic) that is not located in a specific cell or range; can be moved and resized and displays handles when selected.

Object Linking and Embedding (OLE) The term used to refer to the technology Microsoft uses to allow the integration of data between programs. The difference between linking and embedding relates to where the object is stored and how the object is updated after placement in a document. A linked object in a destination file is an image of an object contained in a source file. Both objects share a single source, which means the object is updated only in the source file.

Office Clipboard A temporary storage area shared by all Office programs that can be used to cut, copy, and paste multiple items within and between Office programs. The Office Clipboard can hold up to 24 items collected from any Office program. *See also* System Clipboard.

Office Web App Versions of the Microsoft Office applications with limited functionality that are available online from Windows Live SkyDrive. Users can view documents online and then edit them in the browser using a selection of functions. Office Web Apps are available for Word, PowerPoint, Excel, and One Note.

OLE *See* Object linking and embedding.

One-to-many line The line that appears in the Relationships window and shows which field is duplicated between two tables to serve as the linking field. The one-to-many line displays a "1" next to the field that serves as the "one" side of the relationship and displays an infinity symbol next to the field that serves as the "many" side of the relationship when referential integrity is specified for the relationship. *Also called* the one-to-many join line.

One-to-many relationship The relationship between two tables in an Access database in which a common field links the tables together. The linking field is called the primary key field in the "one" table of the relationship and the foreign key field in the "many" table of the relationship.

Online collaboration The ability to incorporate feedback or share information across the Internet or a company network or intranet.

Open To use one of the methods for opening a document to retrieve it and display it in the document window.

Operating environment An operating system that provides a graphical user interface, such as Microsoft Windows and the MAC OS.

Operating system A program that manages the complete operation of your computer and lets you interact with it; allocates system resources, manages storage space, maintains security, detects equipment failure, and controls basic input and output.

Optical storage device A polycarbonate disk coated with a reflective metal on which data is recorded using laser technology as a trail of tiny pits or dark spots in the surface of the disk; the data that these pits or spots represent can then be "read" with a beam of laser light.

Option button A small circle in a dialog box that you click to select only one of two or more related options.

OR criteria Criteria placed on different rows of the query design grid. A record will appear in the resulting datasheet if it is true for any single row.

Order of precedence Rules that determine the order in which operations are performed within a formula containing more than one arithmetic operator.

Orphan The first line of a paragraph when it appears alone at the bottom of a page.

Orphan record A record in the "many" table of a one-to-many relationship that doesn't have a matching entry in the linking field of the "one" table.

Outbox A temporary storage folder for e-mail messages that have not yet been sent.

Outdent *See* Negative indent.

Outline tab The section in Normal view that displays your presentation text in the form of an outline, without graphics.

Outline view A view that shows the headings of a document organized as an outline.

Outlook Today Shows your day at a glance, like an electronic version of a daily planner book. When it is open, you can see what is happening in the Calendar, Tasks, and Messages for the day.

Output The result of the computer processing input.

Output device A device, such as a monitor or printer, that displays output.

Page Break Preview A worksheet view that displays a reduced view of each page in your worksheet, along with page break indicators that you can drag to include more or less information on a page.

Page Layout View Provides an accurate view of how a worksheet will look when printed, including headers and footers.

Pages per minute (ppm) The unit of measurement for the speed of laser and inkjet printers.

PAN *See* Personal area network.

Pane A section of the PowerPoint window, such as the Slide or Notes pane.

Paragraph spacing The amount of space between paragraphs.

Password A special sequence of numbers and letters, known only to selected users, that users can create to control who can access the files in their user account area; helps keep users' computer information secure.

Paste To insert items stored on the Clipboard into a document.

Paste Options button Button that appears onscreen after pasting content; enables you to choose to paste only specific elements of the copied selection, such as the formatting or values, if desired.

Path The sequence of folders that describes a file location in the file hierarchy; appears in the Address bar of Windows Explorer and the Open and Save dialog boxes.

PC *See* Personal computer.

Peer-to-peer network A network in which all the computers essentially are equal, and programs and data are distributed among them.

Peripheral device The components of a computer that accomplish its input, output, and storage functions.

Permanent memory *See* Read-only memory.

Personal account In Outlook, identifies you as a user with information such as your e-mail address and password, the type of Internet service provider (ISP) you are using, and the incoming and outgoing mail server address for your ISP.

Personal area network (PAN) A network in which two or more devices communicate directly with each other.

Personal computer (PC) A computer typically used by a single user in the home or office for general computing tasks such as word processing, working with photographs or graphics, e-mail, and Internet access.

Pharm To break into a DNS server and redirect any attempts to access a particular Web site to a spoofed site.

Phishing An illicit activity used by hackers to trick computer users into revealing personal or financial information through an e-mail message or Web site.

Photo editing software Software that allows you to manipulate digital photos.

Picture A digital photograph, piece of line art, or clip art that is created in another program and is inserted into PowerPoint.

Pixel (picture element) One of the small dots in a matrix into which a graphics display is divided. One pixel is the measurement of one picture element on the screen.

Plot area In a chart, the area inside the horizontal and vertical axes.

Point (n.) A unit of measure used for font size and row height. One point is equal to 1/72nd of an inch.

Point (v.) To position the tip of the mouse pointer over an object, option, or item.

Pointer A small arrow or other symbol on the screen controlled by a pointing device. *See also* Mouse pointer.

Pointing device A device that lets you interact with your computer by controlling the movement of the mouse pointer on your computer screen; examples include a mouse, trackball, touchpad, pointing stick, on-screen touch pointer, or tablet.

Pointing device action A movement you execute with your computer's pointing device to communicate with the computer; the five pointing device actions are point, click, double-click, drag, and right-click.

Pointing stick A small, eraser-like device embedded among the typing keys on a notebook computer that you push up, left, right, or down to move the pointer; buttons for clicking commands are located in front of the spacebar.

Pop-up Window that opens on your screen as you visit Web sites, generally to advertise products you may or may not want.

Port *See* Expansion port.

Portrait Page orientation in which the contents of a page span the width of a page, so the page is taller than it is wide.

Portrait orientation A way to print or view a page that is 8.5 inches wide by 11 inches tall.

Power button 1) The physical button on your computer that turns your computer on. 2) The Start menu button or button on the right side of the Welcome screen that let you shut down or restart your computer. Click the button arrow to log off your user account, switch to another user, or hibernate the computer to put your computer to sleep so that your computer appears off and uses very little power.

PowerPoint Viewer A special application designed to run a PowerPoint slide show on any compatible computer that does not have PowerPoint installed.

PowerPoint window A window that contains the running PowerPoint application. The PowerPoint window includes the Ribbon, the panes, and Presentation window.

ppm *See* Pages per minute.

Presentation software Software that allows you to display or project graphics and other information before a group, print them for quick reference, or transmit them to remote computers.

Preview pane A pane on the right side of a window that shows the actual contents of a selected file without opening a program; might not work for some types of files.

Previewing Prior to printing, seeing onscreen exactly how the printed document will look.

Primary key field A field that contains unique information for each record. A primary key field cannot contain a null entry.

Print area The portion of a worksheet that will be printed; can be defined by selecting a range and then using the Print Area button on the Page Layout tab.

Print Layout view A view that shows a document as it will look on a printed page.

Print Preview An Access view that shows you how a report or other object will print on a sheet of paper.

Printer The peripheral computer component that produces a hard copy of the text or graphics processed by the computer.

Process To modify data in a computer.

Processor *See* Microprocessor.

Program A set of instructions written for a computer, such as an operating system program or an application program; *also called* an application.

Program tab A single tab on the Ribbon specific to a particular view, such as Print Preview.

Program window The window that opens after you start a program, showing you the tools you need to use the program and any open program documents.

Programming language Software used to write computer instructions.

Properties (Windows) Characteristics or settings of a file, folder, or other item, such as its size or the date it was created. (Access) A characteristic that further defines a field (if field properties), control (if control properties), section (if section properties), or object (if object properties).

Property sheet A window that displays an exhaustive list of properties for the chosen control, section, or object within the Form Design View or Report Design View.

Protocol The set of rules that establishes the orderly transfer of data between the sender and the receiver in data communications.

PS/2 port A port through which a keyboard or a mouse is connected.

Quad-core processor A CPU with four processors on the chip.

Query An Access object that provides a spreadsheet-like view of the data, similar to that in tables. It may provide the user with a subset of fields and/or records from one or more tables. Queries are created when the user has a "question" about the data in the database.

Query design grid The bottom pane of the Query Design View window in which you specify the fields, sort order, and limiting criteria for the query.

Query Design View The window in which you develop queries by specifying the fields, sort order, and limiting criteria that determine which fields and records are displayed in the resulting datasheet.

Quick Access toolbar A small toolbar on the left side of a Microsoft application program window's title bar, containing icons that you click to quickly perform common actions, such as saving a file.

Quick Part A reusable piece of content that can be inserted into a document, including a field, document property, or a preformatted building block.

Quick style A set of styles that are designed to be used together in a document. Determines how fonts, colors, and effects of the theme are combined and which color, font, and effect is dominant. A quick style can be applied to shapes or text.

RAM (random access memory) The storage location that is part of every computer. It consists of chips on cards plugged into the motherboard that temporarily store open programs and documents information while a computer is on. *Also called* volatile memory *or* temporary memory.

RAM cache *See* Cache memory.

Random access memory *See* RAM.

Range A selection of two or more cells, such as B5:B14.

Reading view A view you use to review your presentation or present a slide show to someone on a computer monitor.

Read-only Describes a file that can't be edited or modified.

Read-only memory *See* RAM.

Really Simple Syndication (RSS) A format for feeding or syndicating news or any content from Web sites to your computer.

Receiver The computer or peripheral at the message's destination in data communications.

Record A collection of data items in a database.

Record Source property In a form or report, the property that determines which table or query object contains the fields and records that the form or report will display. It is the most important property of the form or report object. A bound control on a form or report has Control Source property. In this case, the Control Source property identifies the field to which the control is bound.

Recycle Bin A desktop object that stores folders and files you delete from your hard drive(s) and that enables you to restore them.

Reference operators In a formula, symbols that enable you to use ranges in calculations.

Referential integrity A set of Access rules that govern data entry and help ensure data accuracy.

Relational database software Software such as Access that is used to manage data organized in a relational database.

Relative cell reference In a formula, a cell address that refers to a cell's location in relation to the cell containing the formula and that automatically changes to reflect the new location when the formula is copied or moved; default type of referencing used in Excel worksheets. *See also* Absolute cell referencing.

Removable storage Storage media that you can easily transfer from one computer to another, such as DVDs, CDs, or USB flash drives.

Report An Access object that creates a professional printout of data that may contain such enhancements as headers, footers, and calculations on groups of records.

Report View An Access view that maximizes the amount of data you can see on the screen.

Report Wizard An Access wizard that helps you create a report.

Resolution The number of pixels that a monitor displays.

Restore Down button On the right side of a maximized window's title bar, the center of three buttons; use to reduce a window to its last non-maximized size.

Ribbon In many Microsoft application program windows, a horizontal strip near the top of the window that contains tabs (pages) of command buttons, organized into groups, that you click to interact with the program.

Right indent A type of indent in which the right edge of a paragraph is moved in from the right margin.

Right-align Alignment in which an item is flush with the right margin.

Right-click To press and release the right button on the pointing device; use to display a shortcut menu with commands you issue by left-clicking them.

ROM *See* Read-only memory.

Rotate handle A green circular handle at the top of a selected object that you can drag to rotate the selected object.

Router A device that controls traffic between network components and usually has a built-in firewall.

Row heading The gray box containing the row number to the left of the row in a worksheet.

Rule In Outlook, enables you to organize your mail, by setting parameters for incoming mail. For example, you can specify that all mail from a certain person goes into the folder for a specific project.

Ruler A vertical or horizontal guide that both appear in Form and Report Design View to help you position controls.

Sans serif font A font (such as Calibri) whose characters do not include serifs, which are small strokes at the ends of letters.

Save To store a file permanently on a disk or to overwrite the copy of a file that is stored on a disk with the changes made to the file.

Save As Command used to save a file for the first time or to create a new file with a different filename, leaving the original file intact.

Save command A command on the File tab or Quick Access toolbar that saves the current object.

Save Object As command A command on the File tab that saves the current object with a new name.

Scale To change the size of a graphic to a specific percentage of its original size.

Scanner A device that transfers the content on a piece of paper into memory; you place a piece of paper on the glass, a beam of light moves across the glass, similar to a photocopier, and stores the image or words on the piece of paper as digital information.

Screen capture An electronic snapshot of your screen, as if you took a picture of it with a camera, which you can paste into a document.

Screen size The diagonal measurement from one corner of the screen to the other.

ScreenTip A label that appears when you position the mouse pointer over an object; identifies the name of the button or feature, briefly describes its function, conveys any keyboard shortcut for the command, and includes a link to associated help topics, if any.

Scroll To use the scroll bars or the arrow keys to display different parts of a document in the document window.

Scroll arrow A button at each end of a scroll bar for adjusting your view in a window in small increments in that direction.

Scroll bar The bar on the right edge (vertical scroll bar) or bottom edge (horizontal scroll bar) of the document window that is used to display different parts of the document in the document window.

Scroll box A box in a scroll bar that you can drag to display a different part of a window; indicates your relative position within the Web page.

Scroll wheel A wheel on a mouse that you roll to scroll the page on the screen.

SDRAM *See* Synchronous dynamic RAM.

Search bar A feature in Internet Explorer that helps you search for Web sites about a particular topic. Enter a keyword or words in the Search box, then click the Search button to activate the search.

Search box A feature in Internet Explorer Search bar that helps you search for information by typing in a keyword then searching the Web using the selected search provider.

Search criteria Descriptive text that helps Windows identify the program, folder, file, or Web site you want to locate.

Search engine A special Web site that searches the Internet for Web sites based on words or phrases that you enter.

Secondary axis In a combination chart, an additional axis that supplies the scale for one of the chart types used.

Section (Access) A location of a form or report that contains controls. The section in which a control is placed determines where and how often the control prints. (Word) A portion of a document that is separated from the rest of the document by section breaks.

Section break A formatting mark inserted to divide a document into sections.

Security The steps a computer owner takes to prevent unauthorized use of or damage to the computer.

Select To change the appearance of an item by clicking, double-clicking, or dragging across it, to indicate that you want to perform an action on it.

Select pointer The mouse pointer shape that looks like a white arrow oriented toward the upper-left corner of the screen.

Selection box A dashed border that appears around a text object or placeholder, indicating that it is ready to accept text.

Semipermanent memory *See* Complementary metal oxide semiconductor memory.

Sender The computer that originates the message in data communications.

Sent Items folder When you send an e-mail message, a copy of the message is stored in this folder to help you track the messages you send out.

Series in Columns The data in the datasheet columns is plotted on the y-axis, and the row axis labels are shown in the legend. The column axis labels are plotted on the x-axis.

Series in Rows The data in the datasheet rows is plotted on the y-axis, and the row axis labels are shown on the x-axis.

Serif font A font (such as Times New Roman) whose characters include serifs, which are small strokes at the ends of letters.

Server A computer on a network that acts as the central storage location for programs and provides mass storage for most of the data used on the network.

Service provider The organization or company that provides e-mail or Internet access. *See also* Internet Service Provider.

Shading A background color or pattern that can be applied to text, tables, or graphics.

Sheet tab scrolling buttons Allow you to navigate to additional sheet tabs when available; located to the left of the sheet tabs.

Sheet tabs Identify the sheets in a workbook and let you switch between sheets; located below the worksheet grid.

Shortcut An icon that acts as a link to a program, file, folder, or device that you use frequently.

Shortcut key *See* Keyboard shortcut.

Shortcut menu A menu of context-appropriate commands for an object that opens when you right-click that object.

Shut down To turn off your computer.

Simple Query Wizard A wizard that prompts you for information it needs to create a new query.

Single-click *See* Click.

Single-core processor A CPU with one processor on the chip.

Sizing handles The small circles and squares that appear around a selected object, such as a graphic, chart, or control. Dragging a sizing handle resizes the object.

SkyDrive An online storage and file sharing service. Access to SkyDrive is through a Windows Live account. Up to 25 GB of data can be stored in a personal SkyDrive, with each file a maximum size of 50 MB.

Slate computer A thin computer primarily used to read electronic books, view video, and access the Internet, and that does not have an external keyboard or a mouse; instead users touch the screen or use a stylus to accomplish tasks.

Slide layout Determines how all of the elements on a slide are arranged, including text and content placeholders.

Slide pane The section of Normal view that contains the current slide.

Slide Show view A view that shows a presentation as an electronic slide show; each slide fills the screen.

Slide Sorter view A view that displays a thumbnail of all slides in the order in which they appear in your presentation; used to rearrange slides and slide transitions.

Slide timing The amount of time a slide is visible on the screen during a slide show.

Slide transition The special effect that moves one slide off the screen and the next slide on the screen during a slide show. Each slide can have its own transition effect.

Slider A shape you drag to select a setting, such as the slider on the View menu that you drag to select a view.

Slides tab The section in Normal View that displays the slides of your presentation as small thumbnails.

Slot *See* Expansion slot.

SmartArt A professional quality graphic diagram that visually illustrates text.

SmartArt graphics Predesigned diagram types for the following types of data: List, Process, Cycle, Hierarchy, Relationship, Matrix, and Pyramid.

SmartArt Style A pre-set combination of formatting options that follows the design theme that you can apply to a SmartArt graphic.

Smartphone A handheld computer used to make and receive phone calls, maintain an address book, electronic appointment book, calculator, and notepad, send e-mail, connect to the Internet, play music, take photos or video, and perform some of the same functions as a PC, such as word processing.

SmartScreen Filter A feature in Internet Explorer 8 that helps detect phishing Web sites.

Soft page break *See* Automatic page break.

Software The intangible components of a computer system, particularly the programs that the computer needs to perform a specific task.

Solid state storage *See* Flash memory.

Sort Change the order of, such as the order of files or folders in a window based on criteria such as date, file size, or alphabetical by filename.

Source The file from which data is copied or linked into another file.

Source file In integration, the file from which the information is copied or used. An Excel file that is inserted into a file that contains a Word report is the source file.

Spam Unwanted mail that arrives from unsolicited sources. *Also called* junk e-mail.

Spamming The sending of identical or near-identical unsolicited messages to a large number of recipients. Many e-mail programs have filters that identify this mail and place it in a special folder.

Sparkline A quick, simple chart located within a cell that serves as a visual indicator of data trends.

Specifications The technical details about a hardware component.

Spell check The feature in document production software that helps you avoid typographical and grammatical errors.

Spin box A text box with up and down arrows; you can type a setting in the text box or click the arrows to increase or decrease the setting.

Split form A form split into two panes; the upper pane allows you to display the fields of one record in any arrangement, and the lower pane maintains a datasheet view of the first few records.

Spoof To create a Web site that looks exactly like another legitimate site on the Web but steals the information people enter.

Spreadsheet software Software that helps you analyze numerical data.

Spyware Software that track a computer user's Internet usage and sends this data back to the company or person that created it, usually without the computer user's permission or knowledge.

SQL (Structured Query Language) A language that provides a standardized way to request information from a relational database system.

Standalone computer A personal computer that is not connected to a network.

Start button The round button on the left side of the Windows 7 taskbar; click it to start programs, to find and open windows that show you the contents of your computer, to get help, to end your Windows session, and to turn off your computer.

Status bar A horizontal bar at the bottom of a program window that displays simple helpful information and tips. In Internet Explorer 8 window, it displays information about your connection progress; in Excel, it displays a brief description of the task in progress; in PowerPoint, it displays the current slide number or the current theme; in Word, it displays the current page number and other information.

Status indicator Located towards the right side of the status bar, an animated green bar that lets you know the progress of a new Web page while the Web page loads.

Storage capacity *See* Memory capacity.

Store-and-forward technology Messages are *stored* on a service provider's computer until a recipient logs on to a computer and requests his or her messages. At that time, the messages are *forwarded* to the recipient's computer.

Strong password A string of at least eight characters of upper and lowercase letters and numbers.

Style A named collection of character and paragraph formats that are stored together and can be applied to text to format it quickly.

Subdatasheet A datasheet that is nested within another datasheet to show related records; the subdatasheet shows the records on the "many" side of a one-to-many relationship.

Subfolder A folder within another folder for organizing sets of related files into smaller groups.

Subnotebook computers Notebook computers that are smaller and lighter than ordinary notebooks. *Also called* ultraportable computer *and* mini notebook.

Subscript A font effect in which text is formatted in a smaller font size and placed below the line of text.

Subtitle text placeholder A box on the title slide reserved for subpoint text.

Suite A group of programs that are bundled together and share a similar interface, making it easy to transfer skills and program content among them.

Sum function A mathematical function that totals values in a field.

Supercomputer The largest and fastest type of computer used by large corporations and government agencies for processing a tremendous volume of data.

Superscript A font effect in which text is formatted in a smaller font size and placed above the line of text.

Switch User To lock your user account and display the Welcome screen so another user can log on.

Symbol A special character that can be inserted into a document using the Symbol command.

Synchronous dynamic RAM (SDRAM) RAM that is synchronized with the CPU to allow faster access to its contents.

Syntax Rules that govern how to enter property values and other information.

System Clipboard A clipboard that stores only the last item cut or copied from a document. *See also* Clipboard and Office Clipboard.

System resource Any part of the computer system, including memory, storage devices, and the microprocessor, that can be used by a computer program.

System software A collection of programs and data that helps the computer carry out its basic operating tasks.

Tab A page in an application program's Ribbon, or in a dialog box, that contains a group of related settings.

Tab Index property A form property that indicates the numeric tab order for all controls on the form that have the Tab Stop property set to Yes.

Tab leader A line that appears in front of tabbed text.

Tab order The sequence in which the controls on the form receive the focus when the user presses [Tab] or [Enter] in Form view.

Tab stop (Word) A location on the horizontal ruler that indicates where to align text. (Access) Refers to whether you can tab into a control when entering or editing data; in other words, whether the control can receive the focus.

Tab stop property A form property that determines whether a field accepts focus.

Tabbed browsing Allows you to open more than one Web page at a time in a browser window. Click the tab for a Web page to display that Web page in front.

Table (Access) A collection of records for a single subject, such as all of the customer records; the fundamental building block of a relational database because it stores all of the data. (Excel) An organized collection of rows and columns of similarly structured data on a worksheet.

Table Design View A view of a table that provides the most options for defining fields.

Table style A named set of table format settings that can be applied to a table to format it all at once.

Tablet PC A computer designed for portability that includes the capability of recognizing ordinary handwriting on the screen.

Task pane A separate pane that contains sets of menus, lists, options, and hyperlinks such as the Custom Animation task pane that are used to customize objects.

Taskbar The horizontal bar at the bottom of the Windows 7 desktop; displays the Start button, the Notification area, and icons representing programs, folders, and/or files.

Tasks In Outlook, the electronic to-do list, whereby each task has a subject, a start and end date, priority, and a description.

TB *See* Terabyte.

Telecommunications The transmission of data over a comparatively long distance using a phone line.

Template A formatted document or sample file that contains placeholder text you can replace with your own text.

Temporary memory *See* Random access memory.

Terabyte (TB) 1,024 GB, or approximately one trillion bytes.

Text Align property A control property that determines the alignment of text within the control.

Text annotations Labels added to a chart to draw attention to or describe a particular area.

Text box (Windows) A box in which you type text, such as the Search programs and files text box on the Start menu. (Office) An area in a dialog box where you type text. (Access) The most common type of control used to display field values.

Text concatenation operators In a formula, symbols used to join strings of text in different cells.

Text effect Formatting that applies a visual effect to text, such as a shadow, glow, outline, or reflection.

Text label A text box you create using the Text Box button, where the text does not automatically wrap inside the box. Text box text does not appear in the Outline tab.

Text placeholder A box with a dotted border and text that you replace with your own text.

Theme A related set of fonts, colors, styles, and effects that is applied to an entire document in any Office program to give it a cohesive appearance.

Theme colors The set of twelve coordinated colors that make up a theme; a color scheme assigns colors for text, lines, fills, accents, hyperlinks, and background.

Theme effects The set of effects for lines and fills.

Theme fonts The set of fonts for titles and other text.

Threaded message Includes all e-mails that discuss a common subject. Message threading allows you to navigate through a group of messages, seeing all replies and forwards from all recipients

Thumbnail A small image of a slide. Thumbnails are visible on the Slides tab and in Slide Sorter view.

Tick marks Notations of a scale of measure on a chart axis.

Title The first line or heading on a slide.

Title bar Bar at the top of every program window that displays the document and program name. In Internet Explorer, usually contains the name of the Web page currently displayed in the Web browser's active tab window.

Title placeholder A box on a slide reserved for the title of a presentation or slide.

Title slide The first slide in a presentation.

Toggle button A button that turns a feature on and off.

Toner A powdery substance used by laser printers to transfer a laser image onto paper.

Toolbar In an application program, a set of buttons you can click to issue program commands.

Top-level domain The letters that follow the domain name in a Web page address that tell you the type of site you are visiting, for example .edu for universities or .gov for government Web sites.

Touch pad A touch-sensitive device on a laptop computer that you drag your finger over to control the pointer; buttons for clicking commands are located in front of the touch pad.

Touch pointer A pointer on the screen for performing pointing operations with a finger if touch input is available on your computer.

Touchscreen A display that shows you output and allows you to touch it with your finger or a stylus to input commands.

Trackball A pointing device with a rolling ball on the top side and buttons for clicking commands; you control the movement of the pointer by moving the ball.

Translucency The transparency feature of Windows Aero that enables you to locate content by seeing through one window to the next window.

Trash folder *See* Deleted Items folder.

U

Ultraportable computer *See* Subnotebook computer.

Unbound A group of controls that do not display data.

Unbound control A control that does not change from record to record and exists only to clarify or enhance the appearance of the form, using elements such as labels, lines, and clip art.

Uniform Resource Locator (URL) A Web page's address; appears in the Address box on the Address bar after you open (or load) the page.

Universal Serial Bus port *See* USB port.

URL An address on the Web.

USB connector A small, rectangular plug attached to a peripheral device and that you connect to a USB port.

USB drive *See* USB flash drive.

USB flash drive A removable storage device for folders and files that you plug into a USB port on your computer; makes it easy to transport folders and files to other computers. *Also called* pen drive, flash drive, jump drive, keychain drive, or thumb drive.

USB flash storage device *See* USB flash drive.

USB (Universal Serial Bus) port A high-speed port to which you can connect a device with a USB connector to have the computer recognize the device and allow you to use it immediately.

User The person primarily interested in entering, editing, and analyzing the data in the database.

User account A special area in a computer's operating system where users can store their own files.

User interface A collective term for all the ways you interact with a software program.

Username The first part of an e-mail address that identifies the person who receives the mail that is sent to this e-mail address.

Utility A type of system software that augments the operating system by taking over some of its responsibility for allocating hardware resources.

Vacation response An automatically generated e-mail you can have sent in response to received e-mails when you are away; most e-mail programs allow you to create a vacation response.

Value axis In a chart, the axis that contains numerical values; in a 2-dimensional chart, also known as the y-axis.

Values Numbers, formulas, and functions used in calculations.

Vertical alignment The position of text in a document relative to the top and bottom margins.

Vertical ruler A ruler that appears on the left side of the document window in Print Layout view.

Vertical scroll bar Appears along the right side of a page window if the page is longer than the window's viewable area; allows you to move the current Web page up or down in the browser window.

VGA (video graphics array) port A port that transmits analog video.

Video card *See* Graphics card.

Video display adapter *See* Graphics card.

Video editing software Software that allows you to edit video by clipping it, adding captions or a soundtrack, or rearranging clips.

View A way of displaying a document in the document window; each view provides features useful for editing and formatting different types of documents.

View buttons Buttons on the status bar that are used to change document views.

View Shortcuts The buttons at the bottom of the PowerPoint window that you click to switch among views.

Virtual memory Space on the computer's storage devices that simulates additional RAM.

Virus A harmful program that instructs a computer to perform destructive activities, such as erasing a disk drive; variants are called worms and Trojan horses.

Virus protection software *See* Antivirus software.

Volatile memory *See* Random access memory.

WAN *See* Wide area network.

Web The part of the Internet that contains interconnected Web pages. *Also called* the World Wide Web *or* WWW.

Web browser A software program that lets you open and display Web pages. *Also called* a browser.

Web Layout view A view that shows a document as it will look when viewed with a Web browser.

Web pages Electronic documents that can contain text, graphics, sound, and video.

Web site A group of Web pages focused on a particular subject.

Web site creation and management software Software that allows you to create and manage Web sites and to see what the Web pages will look like as you create them.

Web-based e-mail Web site that provides free e-mail addresses and service.

Welcome screens An initial startup screen that displays icons for each user account on the computer.

What-if analysis A decision-making tool in which data is changed and formulas are recalculated, in order to predict various possible outcomes.

Wide area network (WAN) A network that connects one or more LAN.

Widow The last line of a paragraph when it is carried over to the top of the following page, separate from the rest of the paragraph.

Wi-Fi *See* Wireless fidelity.

Wildcard A special character used in criteria to find, filter, and query data. The asterisk (*) stands for any group of characters. For example, the criteria I* in a State field criterion cell would find all records where the state entry was IA, ID, IL, IN, or Iowa. The question mark (?) wildcard stands for only one character.

WiMAX (Worldwide Interoperability for Microwave Access) A standard of wireless communication defined by the IEEE that allows computers to communicate wirelessly over many miles; signals are transmitted from WiMAX towers to a WiMAX receiver in a device.

Window A rectangular-shaped work area that displays a program or a collection of files, folders, and Windows tools.

Windows Aero *See* Aero.

Windows Explorer An accessory program that displays windows, allowing you to navigate your computer's file hierarchy and interact with your computer's contents.

Windows Live A collection of services and Web applications that people can access through a login. Windows Live services include access to e-mail and instant messaging, storage of files on SkyDrive, sharing and storage of photos, networking with people, downloading software, and interfacing with a mobile device.

Windows Remote Assistance A Windows Help feature that lets you connect with another computer so that user can operate your computer using an Internet connection.

Windows Search The Windows feature that lets you look for files and folders on your computer storage devices; to search, type text in the Search text box in the title bar of any open window, or click the Office button and type text in the Search programs and files text box.

Wireless fidelity The term created by the nonprofit Wi-Fi Alliance to describe networks connected using a standard radio frequency established by the Institute of Electrical and Electronics Engineers (IEEE); frequently referred to as *Wi-Fi*.

Wireless local area network (WLAN) A LAN connected using high frequency radio waves rather than cables.

WLAN *See* Wireless local area network.

Word processing box A text box you create using the Text Box button, where the text automatically wraps inside the box.

Word processing program A software program that includes tools for entering, editing, and formatting text and graphics.

Word program window The window that contains the Word program elements, including the document window, Quick Access toolbar, Ribbon, and status bar.

Word size The amount of data that is processed by a microprocessor at one time.

WordArt A set of decorative styles or text effects that is applied to text.

Word-wrap A feature that automatically moves the insertion point to the next line as you type.

Workbook A collection of related worksheets contained within a single file.

Works cited A list of sources that you cited while creating a document.

Worksheet A single sheet within a workbook file; also, the entire area within an electronic spreadsheet that contains a grid of columns and rows.

Worksheet window Area of the program window that displays part of the current worksheet; the worksheet window displays only a small fraction of the worksheet, which can contain a total of 1,048,576 rows and 16,384 columns.

Workstation A computer that is connected to a network.

World Wide Web (Web) A huge database of information that is stored on network servers in places that allow public access.

Worldwide Interoperability for Microwave Access *See* WiMAX.

X-axis The horizontal axis in a chart; because it often shows data categories, such as months or locations; *also called* category axis.

XML Acronym that stands for eXtensible Markup Language, which is a language used to structure, store, and send information.

XML format New file format for Word documents beginning with Word 2007.

Y-axis The vertical axis in a chart; because it often shows numerical values, *also called* value axis.

Z-axis The third axis in a 3-D chart, lets you compare data points across both categories and values.

Zoom level button A button on the status bar that is used to change the zoom level of the document in the document window.

Zoom slider An adjustment on the status bar that is used to enlarge or decrease the display size of the document in the document window.

Zooming in A feature that makes a document appear larger but shows less of it on screen at once; does not affect actual document size.

Zooming out A feature that shows more of a document on screen at once but at a reduced size; does not affect actual document size.

Index

KEY TO PAGE NUMBER ABBREVIATIONS

Access	AC
Essential Computer Concepts	ECC
Excel	EX
Integration	INT
Internet	IE
Office A	OFF
Outlook	OUT
PowerPoint	PPT
Web Apps	WEB
Windows 7	WIN
Word	WD

C

D

E

F

G

H

I

J

K

L

M

N

O

P

T

U

V